(4)

ECONOMICS EXPLAINED

A Coursebook in A Level Economics

Peter Maunder

Senior Lecturer in Economics,
Loughborough University
Joint Chief Examiner for A Level, London Board

Danny Myers

Head of Economics and Sociology Department
New College (16-19), Swindon

Nancy Wall

Head of Economics Department
Beacon School, Crowborough

Roger LeRoy Miller

Centre for Policy Studies and Department of Economics
Clemson University

COLLINS EDUCATIONAL

©P. Maunder, D. Myers, N. Wall, R. L. Miller

First published 1987, reprinted 1987

ISBN 000 327397 0

Printed by Butler and Tanner, Frome and London
Published by Collins Educational, 8 Grafton Street,
London W1X 3LA, United Kingdom.

Important Notice

In the 'Exam Preparation and Practice' sections,
some questions have been changed since *Economics Explained* was first published. This is of
particular importance to those few centres
who are using a combination of texts from the
first and subsequent impressions. The new
questions and their answers have been identified with a dagger (†).

PREFACE

We are grateful to Roger Leroy Miller and his publishers for
allowing us to adapt his excellent textbook *Economics Today* for
the UK market. Our intention was to retain the visual
appeal of *Economics Today* while rewriting, adapting and
extending the contents so they are appropriate for students
studying for A level examinations. We believe that the
resulting text really *explains* the nature of economics.

We received helpful advice from several teachers and
lecturers who keenly supported the project at the outset.
Particular thanks are due to David Whitehead, Peter Chap-
man, Leslie Potts, Andrew Leake and Bill Green. We are also
grateful to Joan Lawrence for her detailed comments on the
final typescript.

For her unflagging enthusiasm for the project we owe
much to Jayne Potter and also to Kate Harris in co-
ordinating our efforts once the projects got underway. We
wish to acknowledge the input of other participants at
Collins Educational in the production of this book and in
particular Karen Dolby our desk editor. Our manuscript
received the benefit of a critical scrutiny from Conan
Nicholas and we feel the final product has been thoughtfully
designed by John Fitzmaurice to present the book in the best
possible manner for our readers. To Su Spencer we owe
much for transforming successive drafts from three hands
into a superbly presented typescript. The typing over many
evenings meant that yet another household was affected in
the production of this book. But we hope that all spouses and
families now feel that the publication of *Economics Explained*
justifies the earlier preoccupations of all participants.

Peter Maunder
Danny Myers
Nancy Wall

Contents

Part D
Factor Markets

Part E
Economic Policies and Issues

Acknowledgments

The authors and publishers wish to acknowledge the following photograph sources: BBC Hulton Picture Library pp. 22, 32, 217; Chris Davies, NETWORK p. 158.

The authors and publishers are grateful to the following Boards for permission to reproduce Multiple Choice Questions (MCQs) and Related Essay Questions (REQs) from past examination papers:

The Associated Examining Board
Chapter 1: MCQs 3 (June 86), 5 (June 87), 6 (June 82); REQs 1 (June 82), 2 (Nov. 82), 3 (June 85). *Chapter 2:* MCQ 2 (Nov. 83). *Chapter 4:* REQ 3 (Nov. 83). *Chapter 5:* MCQs 5 (June 84), 7 (Nov. 83). *Chapter 7:* MCQ 4 (June 87); REQ 3 (June 85). *Chapter 8:* MCQ 1 (June 87); REQs 1 (June 82), 2 (June 83). *Chapter 9:* MCQs 1 (June 87), 2 (Nov. 83), 3 (June 86), 4 (June 83), 5 (Nov. 83), 6 (June 83). *Chapter 10:* MCQs 3 (June 84), 4 (June 84), 5 (June 84); REQs 1 (June 84), 2 (June 83), 5 (Nov. 84). *Chapter 11:* MCQ 3 (June 84); REQ 3 (June 82). *Chapter 13:* MCQs 2 (June 83), 3 (June 83). *Chapter 15:* MCQ 1 (June 85); REQ 2 (June 84). *Chapter 16:* MCQ 3 (Nov. 82); REQ 2 (June 84). *Chapter 17:* MCQs 5 (Nov. 82), 6 (Nov. 82). *Chapter 18:* REQ 1 (Nov. 82). *Chapter 19:* MCQ 3 (June 83); REQ 3 (June 84). *Chapter 20:* MCQ 5 (Nov. 85); REQ 1 (Nov. 84). *Chapter 21:* MCQ 6 (June 86). *Chapter 22:* MCQ 5 (June 82). *Chapter 23:* MCQ 7 (June 82). *Chapter 24:* MCQs 2 (June 82), 3 (Nov. 82). *Chapter 25:* MCQs 2 (June 87), 3 (June 85); REQs 2 (June 82), 4 (June 83), 5 (June 85), 6 (June 85). *Chapter 26:* MCQs 1 (Nov. 82), 2 (June 87), 6 (June 85). *Chapter 27:* REQs 1 (June 83), 2 (June 84). *Chapter 28:* MCQs 1 (June 85), 3 (June 82); REQ 4 (June 84). *Chapter 29:* MCQ 5 (Nov. 86); REQ 1 (June 82). *Chapter 33:* MCQs 1 (June 86), 2 (June 86); REQ 1 (June 82). *Chapter 34:* MCQs 2 (Nov. 86), 4 (Nov. 85); REQ 2 (Nov. 85).

Joint Matriculation Board
Chapter 4: REQs 5 (June 84), 7 (June 86). *Chapter 7:* REQ 5 (June 80). *Chapter 9:* REQ 4 (June 86). *Chapter 10:* REQ 6 (June 81). *Chapter 11:* REQ 4 (June 83). *Chapter 22:* REQ 2 (June 80). *Chapter 26:* REQs 4 (June 85), 6 (June 86), 7 (June 86). *Chapter 28:* REQ 5 (June 86). *Chapter 29:* REQ 3 (June 83). *Chapter 31:* REQ 6 (June 86). *Chapter 33:* REQs 4 (June 81), 5 (June 82, Special Paper). *Chapter 34:* REQ 7 (June 86). *Chapter 35:* REQ 4 (June 86).

Northern Ireland GCE Examinations Board
Chapter 7: REQ 1 (June 84). *Chapter 13:* REQ 2 (June 84). *Chapter 34:* REQ 6 (June 84).

Oxford and Cambridge Schools Examination Board
Chapter 2: REQ (July 84). *Chapter 9:* REQ 2 (July 80). *Chapter 13:* REQ 5 (June 83). *Chapter 17:* REQ 4 (June 85). *Chapter 19:* REQ 2 (June 81). *Chapter 20:* REQs 2 (June 80), 3 (June 81). *Chapter 22:* REQ 3 (June 81). *Chapter 27:* REQ 5 (July 84). *Chapter 31:* REQ 4 (June 85). *Chapter 34:* REQ 3 (July 82).

Southern Universities Joint Board
Chapter 12: REQ 1 (June 79). *Chapter 15:* REQ 1 (June 83). *Chapter 20:* REQ 4 (June 85). *Chapter 31:* REQ 5 (June 84).

University of Cambridge Local Examinations Syndicate
Chapter 11: REQ 1 (Nov. 84). *Chapter 12:* REQ 2 (Nov. 84). *Chapter 17:* REQs 2 (June 85), 5 (June 85). *Chapter 26:* REQ 2 (June 85). *Chapter 27:* REQs 2 (June 81), 3 (June 82). *Chapter 28:* REQ 4 (June 82). *Chapter 30:* REQs 1 (June 85), 2 (June 85).

University of London School Examinations Board
Chapter 1: MCQs 2 (Jan. 83), 5 (Jan. 86). *Chapter 2:* MCQ 1 (Jan. 83). *Chapter 3:* REQ 1 (June 81). *Chapter 4:* REQs 2 (June 87), 4 (June 85, Special Paper), 6 (June 86, Special Paper). *Chapter 5:* MCQs 1 (June 84), 2 (June 84), 3 (Jan. 84), 6 (Jan. 87). *Chapter 6:* REQ (June 85). *Chapter 7:* MCQs 1 (Jan. 87), 2 (Jan. 87), 3 (June 86), 5 (June 83), 6 (Jan. 84). *Chapter 8:* MCQs 3 (Jan. 84), 4 (Jan. 83); REQs 3 (June 86), 4 (Jan. 86), 5 (June 85, Special Paper). *Chapter 9:* REQ 3 (June 85). *Chapter 10:* MCQ 8 (Jan. 85). *Chapter 11:* MCQs 1 (Jan. 83), 2 (June 83); REQs 2 (Jan. 85), 5 (June 85). *Chapter 12:* MCQs 2 (June 86), 5 (June 87). *Chapter 13:* MCQ 5 (Jan. 84); REQs 1 (June 85), 4 (Jan. 86). *Chapter 15:* MCQ 3 (June 85); REQs 3 (June 85), 4 (Jan. 84). *Chapter 16:* MCQ 4 (June 86); REQ 1 (Jan. 85). *Chapter 17:* MCQs 1 (June 85), 2 (June 85), 3 (June 86), 4 (Jan. 86); REQ 1 (Jan. 85). *Chapter 18:* MCQ 1 (Jan. 85); REQs 3 (Jan. 85), 4 (Jan. 79). *Chapter 19:* MCQ 2 (June 84); REQ 1 (Jan. 84). *Chapter 20:* MCQ 4 (June 86). *Chapter 21:* MCQs 1 (Jan. 86), 2 (June 85), 3 (Jan. 86), 4 (June 85), 5 (June 83); REQs 1 (June 84) , 2 (June 82). *Chapter 22:* REQ 1 (Jan. 83). *Chapter 23:* MCQs 1 (June 86), 2 (Jan. 87), 3 (Jan. 87), 4 (June 84), 5 (June 84), 6 (Jan. 86); REQs 1 (June 83), 2 (June 84). *Chapter 24:* MCQs 1 (Jan. 87), 4 (Jan. 84), 5 (Jan. 84); REQs 1 (Jan. 84), 2 (June 84), 3 (June 85), 4 (Jan. 83), 5 (June 82). *Chapter 25:* MCQs 1 (June 87), 4 (June 81), 5 (Jan. 84), 6 (June 87), 7 (June 87), 8 (June 87), 9 (Jan. 86), 10 (Jan. 85); REQs 1 (Jan. 86), 3 (June 85), 8 (June 86, Special Paper). *Chapter 26:* MCQs 3 (June 81), 4 (June 86), 5 (June 85); REQ 3 (Jan. 85). *Chapter 27:* MCQs 1 (Jan. 86), 2 (June 86), 3 (June 81). *Chapter 28:* MCQs 4 (June 81), 5 (June 85); REQ 3 (Jan. 85). *Chapter 30:* REQs 2 (June 83), 7 (June 86, Special Paper). *Chapter 31:* MCQs 1 (June 81), 2 (Jan. 86), 4 (Jan. 87), 5 (Jan. 86), 6 (June 87); REQ 3 (Jan. 85). *Chapter 33:* MCQ 3 (June 81); REQ 3 (June 83, Special Paper). *Chapter 34:* MCQ 1 (Jan. 87); REQ 1 (June 85). *Chapter 35:* REQs 2 (June 76, Special Paper), 3 (June 82).

University of Oxford Delegacy of Local Examinations (OLE)
Chapter 4: REQ 1 (June 84). *Chapter 4:* REQ 4 (June 81). *Chapter 9:* MCQ 1 (June 80). *Chapter 10:* REQ 3 (June 84). *Chapter 13:* REQ 3 (June 84). *Chapter 14:* REQ 1 (June 86). *Chapter 16:* REQ 4 (June 85). *Chapter 26:* REQ 1 (June 85). *Chapter 27:* REQ 6 (June 85). *Chapter 28:* REQ 1 (June 85). *Chapter 29:* REQs 2 (June 84, Special Paper), 4 (June 85, Special Paper). *Chapter 30:* REQ 6 (June 86).

Welsh Joint Education Committee
Chapter 10: REQ 4 (June 80). *Chapter 16:* REQ 3 (June 85). *Chapter 17:* REQ 3 (June 85). *Chapter 26:* REQ 5 (June 85).

The following questions are reproduced by permission from A. Baker (ed.), *Multiple Choice Questions in Advanced Level Economics*, Cambridge University Press, 1981: *Chapter 1:* MCQ 1. *Chapter 3:* MCQ 1. *Chapter 8:* MCQs 5, 6. *Chapter 10:* MCQs 1, 2. *Chapter 13:* MCQ 6. *Chapter 15:* MCQs 2, 4. *Chapter 16:* MCQs 1, 2. *Chapter 19:* MCQ 4. *Chapter 20:* MCQs 1, 2, 3. *Chapter 22:* MCQs 1, 2, 3. *Chapter 29:* MCQ 3.

MCQs 3 and 4 in Chapter 18 are reproduced by permission from Maile and Jenkins, *A Textbook of Questions and Answers in A Level Economics*, Bell and Hyman, 1983. MCQs 1–5 in Chapter 6 are reproduced by permission from T. Wilson, *Test Bank to R. Miller, Economics Today*, 3rd edn, Harper and Row, 1979.

Every effort has been made to contact copyright holders, but in some cases this has been impossible. The publishers would be grateful to hear from anyone who has not yet given us permission to reproduce material.

How to Use this Book Effectively

This book has been designed around six key features to help you build towards exam success. These are outlined below as a guide to guarantee your effective use of this new and distinctive book.

Firstly, each chapter has brief summaries every few pages to help you identify and remember the main concepts that have been surveyed. These are numbered and called ▶ **Key Points**.

These key points are also picked up in the second feature of the book, namely ▶ **Key Points to Review**. Each chapter begins with a list of these, to encourage you to refer back to the relevant sections already covered. This highlights the integrated nature of the subject matter.

▶ Thirdly, each chapter is also preceded by a list of **Questions for Preview**. These are designed to encourage you to scan forwards through the chapter to get the flavour of it before embarking on a serious study of that chapter's content. These questions could be used as homework or for discussion.

Fourthly, each time a new technical term or phrase is introduced it is identified in bold type. These and other essential terms are then gathered at the back with brief ▶ definitions to form a **Dictionary of Economics** to help you come to terms with your new subject and its peculiar language. Some important concepts require detailed definitions in the text. These are identified in blue type.

▶ Next, as you move towards the close of each chapter you will notice two further important features. Chapters conclude with at least one **Case Study** and some have even more. These have been selected to help you to apply what you have learnt; to appreciate economics in action; to become familiar with the related literature (therefore note the sources) and also to prepare you for the stimulus question that most of you will experience in your A level exam in a year or two from now.

▶ Finally, each chapter closes with an **Exam Preparation and Practice** section. This contains a battery of questions selected from past papers of the UK exam boards. The number of multiple-choice and essay questions that follow each chapter will vary according to the nature of the topic. Examiners have a tendency to explore different topics via different exam strategies. Consequently some chapters have half a dozen multiple-choice questions and others half a dozen essays. There are also constructive introductory exercises which we have included to set your thoughts on the right tracks.

The Answers to the multiple-choice questions and introductory exercises are gathered at the back. Essay questions are a 'free response' (as some exam boards describe them) so it would unfortunately be impossible to standardize the answers.

You may find you want, or need, to have access to additional up-to-date information on the UK economy. For this purpose you will find the *Collins Economics Brief Series* helpful. Each book in the series focuses on an important empirical area of the A level syllabus. These Briefs are regularly updated to take account of the latest developments, trends and statistics.

You may find your Economics course hard work at times but we are sure that once you have mastered the principles you will find it a fascinating and enjoyable subject.

Part A

Introductory Microeconomics

1 What Economics is all about

Questions for Preview

1 The United Kingdom is one of the most developed nations in the world. Do its inhabitants face the problem of scarcity?

2 Fresh air and clean water can often be consumed in the United Kingdom free of charge. Does this mean that these 'goods' are free or costless to society?

3 Why does the scarcity problem force people to consider opportunity costs?

4 What is the difference between positive and normative economics?

The reason that we face economic problems individually and as a nation is that none of us can have all that we want – we live in a world of *scarcity*. Economic problems face you, me, your friends, the nation, and the world. It is impossible to avoid these problems personally or as a nation. They involve choosing a career and where to live, what price to pay for a house, how to solve the problems of unemployment and rising prices, plus thousands of other decisions.

This book is about economics and economic problem-solving. Consequently, it relates to you as an individual who must decide how to earn income and how to spend it. It relates to you as an individual who must vote for political candidates who decide how much of your income to tax and how to spend tax revenues. Finally, it relates to your country and how much it buys from and sells to the rest of the world. We study economics because the economic system that we have helps to determine our political, social, religious, and personal environment.

Scarcity – the Bane of Civilization

Would you like to be able to study more and also to have more time to relax and drink coffee with your friends? Would you like to own an expensive home computer as well as enjoy a skiing holiday? Would you like to have more clothes but not give up any spending on records and video tapes? Your answer to all of these questions is highly likely to be a resounding, *yes*.

But why can't we have more of everything? It is because individually and collectively we face a constraint called scarcity. **Scarcity** is the most basic concept in all of economics. Scarcity means that we do not and cannot have enough income or wealth to satisfy our every desire. Note that we are not referring to any *measurable* standard of wants; rather, we are referring to the way people want, need, or desire *relative* to what is available at any moment. If the world were such that everyone could have as much of everything as desired, without sacrifice, then economics would no longer exist as a meaningful intellectual or practical pursuit. But there is scarcity. And we have not just recently moved into the 'age of scarcity', as many people seem to believe. Scarcity has always been with us and will be with us as long as we cannot get everything we want at a zero or free price, that is one where there is no charge.

It is important to distinguish scarcity from poverty. Scarcity occurs among poor people and among rich people. It applies to everyone because there will never be enough of everything that people want to go round at a zero or free price. And, because there are limits on people's time, even the richest person on earth will still have unfulfilled wants.

Resources (or Factors of Production) are Scarce

The scarcity concept just described arises from the existence of scarce resources. Resources can be defined as the inputs used in the production of those things that we desire. When resources are productive, they are typically called *factors of production*. Indeed, some economists use the terms resources and factors of production synonymously. The total quantity, or stock, of resources that an economy has determines what that economy can produce. Every economy has, in varying degrees of quantities, vast amounts of different resources, or factors of production. Factors of production can be classified in many ways. One common scheme of classification includes natural, human, and manufactured resources.

NATURAL RESOURCES = LAND AND MINERAL DEPOSITS

Basically, **land** with its inherent mineral deposits is the natural resource we think of most often. Some land can grow very large amounts of crops without any addition of fertilizer; other land is incapable of growing anything in its natural state. Today, some economists contend that natural resources are often the least important factors of production in an economy. They believe that what is more important is the transformation of existing natural resources into what is truly usable by man, and that transformation requires the other types of resources – labour and capital. This point becomes understandable if we do not simply think of land as the only natural resource. The resources of the oceans and polar ice-caps are attracting increasing interest. Thus natural resources include water, climate, and vegetation in a global context.

HUMAN RESOURCES = LABOUR

In order to produce the things we desire, a human resource must be used. That human resource consists of the productive contributions of **labour** made by individuals who work – for example, coal-miners, ballet-dancers, and professional soccer players. The contribution of labour to the production process can be increased. Whenever potential labourers obtain schooling and training and whenever actual labourers obtain new skills, labour's contribution to productive output will increase. When there is such an improvement to human resources we say that human capital has been improved.

MANUFACTURED RESOURCES = CAPITAL

When labour is applied to land to grow wheat, for example, something else is used. Usually it is a plough or a tractor. That is to say, land and labour are combined with manufactured resources in order to produce the things that we desire. These manufactured resources are called **capital**, which consists of machines, buildings, and tools. Additionally, capital consists of improvements to natural resources, such as irrigation channels.

ANOTHER HUMAN RESOURCE = ENTREPRENEURSHIP

There is, in effect, a fourth type of input used in production. It is a special type of human resource; it consists of entrepreneurial ability, or **entrepreneurship**. Entrepreneurship is associated with the found-

ing of new businesses, or the introduction of new products and new techniques. But it means more than that: it encompasses taking risks (possibly losing large sums of wealth on new ventures), inventing new methods of making existing goods, and generally experimenting with any type of new thinking that could lead to a monetary benefit.

Without entrepreneurship, virtually no business organizations could operate. Clearly, entrepreneurship as a human resource is scarce: not everyone is willing to take risks or has the ability to undertake successful business decision-making.

We see the classification of resources in Figure 1.1.

Figure 1.1

Resource Classification. We can arbitrarily classify resources or factors of production into those that are natural, human, and manufactured. We have denoted specific names within those three classifications.

Natural Resources	Human Resources	Manufactured Resources
Land	Labour and entrepreneurship	Capital

Scarce resources produce what are called **economic goods** – the subject of our study throughout this book.

ECONOMIC GOODS

Any good (or service) produced from scarce resources is also scarce and is called an economic good. Because economic goods are scarce, we constantly face decisions about how best to use them. After all, the desired quantity of an economic good, by definition, exceeds the amount that is directly available from nature at a zero or free price.

However, not all goods are economic; some are free.

FREE GOODS

There are, of course, some things that are free. We call them **free goods**, as opposed to economic goods. Not many are left. Economics textbooks used to call air a free good, but that is really no longer true, because in many of the world's cities pollution makes air unpleasant to breathe. In many mountain areas, clean air is still a free good (once you are there); you can have as much as you want at a zero or free price, and so can anybody else who bothers to hike up to where you are. There is no scarcity involved. Who is interested in free goods, then? Certainly not most economists. Perhaps physicists, hydrologists, biologists, and chemists are interested in free air and water, but the economist steps in only when the problem of scarcity arises and people become concerned about how to use the scarce resource. We have seen throughout our history that as population and production increase, many 'free' goods become 'economic' goods, such as land for mining, water and air for industrial uses, and water for hydroelectric power. To the population of native American Indians, tobacco leaves were a free good before the time of Sir Walter Raleigh. The Indians could have all that they wanted. Later, however, tobacco leaves became (and remain) an economic good.

Choice

Scarcity forces us to choose. You have to choose whether to carry on at school or to go to work. If you take a job then you have given up taking unemployment pay. You have to choose between going out on a date or studying. Government policy-makers have to choose between using more resources in the production of military goods or using more resources in the production of, say, educational services. In fact, the concept of choice forms the basis of our formal definition of **economics**:

Economics is the social science studying human behaviour, and, in particular, the way in which individuals and societies choose among the alternative uses of scarce resources to satisfy wants.

As we see throughout our study of economics, the choices we make affect not only how we live today, but how we will live in the future. Moreover, the choices that we can make are constrained not only by scarcity, but also by political, legal, traditional, and moral forces. In other words, there are numerous non-economic forces that determine and mould our decision-making processes. In this text, however, we will concentrate on how economic forces affect our choices. We are not, though, denying that the others are important too.

Unlimited Wants

As pointed out earlier, scarcity exists because there are not enough resources to satisfy our wants. And economics is a science studying how individuals make choices about the use of resources in order to satisfy wants. Does that mean that economists are only interested in how people make choices about what kind of car to buy, how many clothes to purchase, and whether to add a swimming-pool to their house? The answer is certainly, *no*. Of course, wants include material goods, such as houses, cars, stereos, clothes, and computers. But wants also include desires for more love, affection, power, prestige, justice, fairness, equity, charity, friendship, improved health, and peace in the world. Clearly, then, economics is not the study of the 'baser material desires' of men and women. The wants that individuals wish to satisfy are, indeed, unlimited and encompass virtually anything that at least someone believes is 'good' or 'preferred'.

Wants versus Needs

Wants are not the same thing as needs. Indeed, from the economists's point of view, the term 'need' is objectively *un*definable. When someone says, 'I need some new clothes', there is no way of knowing whether that person is simply stating a wish or a want, or a 'need' in the commonly accepted sense of the word indicating 'absolute necessity'. If the individual making the statement were dying of over-exposure in a northern country during the winter, we might argue, indeed, that the person *did* need new clothes perhaps, or at least some more warm clothes. Typically, however, the term 'need' is used in a very casual manner in most conversations. What people mean, usually, is that they want or desire something that they do not

---

Key Points 1.1

▶ **Scarcity exists because we cannot have all that we want from nature without sacrifice.**

▶ **We use scarce resources, such as land, capital, and entrepreneurship, to produce economic goods.**

▶ **Economic goods are those that are desired but are not directly obtainable from nature to the extent demanded or desired.**

▶ **Scarcity requires us to choose, and economics is the study of how we make those choices.**

▶ **Wants are unlimited; they include all material wants plus all non-material wants, such as love, affection, power, and prestige.**

▶ **The concept of need is objectively difficult to define for every person; consequently, we simply consider that individual's wants are unlimited. In a world of scarcity, satisfaction of one want necessarily means the non-satisfaction of one or more other possible wants.**

currently have. That is quite a different statement from one indicating an absolute, life-or-death need for some item. Even when we discuss so-called 'basic' needs – such as food – there is no fixed, absolute minimum. Some individuals in some countries can survive on 50 per cent fewer calories than other individuals 'need' in order to survive in other countries. As it turns out, one person's need may be considered a folly by another person.

Analytically, it is best to consider the reality of scarcity: every individual has competing 'needs' or wants but cannot satisfy all of them given limited resources. Therefore, a choice must be made. When that choice is made, something that is also desired has to be forgone. In other words, in a world of scarcity, every want that ends up being satisfied results in some other want, or wants, remaining unsatisfied. Also, new wants may arise as a result of some wants being satisfied.

Choice and Opportunity Costs

Choosing one thing requires giving up something else. When you sit down to read this book, you are making a choice. You have chosen not to do at least a thousand other things with your time. You could have read another book or you could have watched television. You could have slept, or you could have listened to the cassette player. Thus, the time scarcity that you face requires you to choose between reading this book and doing something that is presumably less valuable. In other words, there is a cost associated with spending time reading these words. Economists call it **opportunity cost**.

Let us assume that of all the other things you could have done instead of reading this book, the thing you *most* wanted to do, but did not do, was to watch television. If that is the case, then watching television is the opportunity cost of reading this book. Opportunity cost is defined as the highest valued alternative that had to be sacrificed for the option that was chosen. Opportunity cost is a powerful concept that allows us to place a value on the resources that are used to produce something.

The Trade-offs Facing You

Whatever you do, you are trading off one use of a resource for one or more alternative uses. The value of these **trade-offs** is represented by the opportunity cost just discussed. We can examine the opportunity cost of reading this book. Let us assume that you have a maximum of 4 hours per week to spend studying just two topics – economics and geography (or whatever other subject is relevant to you). The more you study economics, the higher will be your expected grade; the more you study geography, the higher will be your expected grade in that subject. There is a trade-off, then, between spending one more hour reading this book and spending that hour studying geography.

This can be more clearly brought out in a graph* that shows the trade-off involved.

Graphical Analysis

In Figure 1.2, we have put the expected grade in geography on the vertical axis and the expected grade in economics on the horizontal axis. In this simplified world, if you spend all your time on economics, you will get a B in the course, but you will fail geography. On the other hand, if you spend all your time on geography you will get a B in that subject and you will fail economics. The trade-off is a special case: one to one. A one-to-one trade-off means that in this case the opportunity cost of receiving one grade higher in economics (for example, improving from a D to a C) is one grade lower in geography (falling from a D to an E in our example).

Production Possibilities Curve

The diagram in Figure 1.2 illustrates the relationship between the possible results that can be produced in each of two activities, depending on how much time you choose to put into each activity. Economists call this kind of diagram a **production possibilities curve**.†

If you consider that what you are producing is a grade when you study economics and geography then Figure 1.2 can be related to the production possibilities that you face. The line that goes from B on one axis to the B on the other therefore becomes a production possibilities curve. *It is defined as all possible combinations of the maximum amount of any two goods or services that can be produced from a fixed amount of resources.* In the example, your time for studying was limited to 4 hours per week. The two possible outputs were grades in geography and grades in economics. The particular production possibilities curve presented in Figure 1.2 is a graphic representation of the opportunity cost of studying one more hour in one subject. It is a *straight-line production possibilities curve*, which is a special case. (The more general case will be discussed next.) If the student decides to be at point x in Figure 1.2, then 2 hours of study time will be spent on geography and 2 hours will be spent on economics. The expected grade in each course will be a D. If the student is more interested in getting a C in economics, then he or she will go to point y on the production possibilities curve, spending only 1 hour on geography but 3 hours on economics. The expected grade in geography will then drop from a D to an E. Note that these trade-offs

---

*Readers needing a refresher on graphical techniques should now read the Appendix to this chapter.
†Other terms used for production possibilities curves are: production possibilities frontier, production possibilities boundary, production possibility curve and transformation curve. We use the word possibilities rather than possibility to emphasize the multiplicity of combinations of output exemplified in this diagram.

Figure 1.2

Production Possibilities Curve for Grades in Geography and Economics. On the vertical axis, we measure the expected grade in geography; on the horizontal axis, the expected grade in economics. We assume that there are only 4 hours total time that can be spent per week on studying. If all 4 hours are spent on economics, a B is received in economics and an F in geography. If all 4 hours are spent on geography, a B is received in that subject and an F in economics. There is a one-to-one trade-off. If the student is at point *x*, equal time (2 hours a week) is spent on both courses and equal grades of D will be received. If a higher grade in economics is desired, the student may go to point *y* where 1 hour is spent on geography and 3 hours on economics and receive a C in economics, but an E in geography.

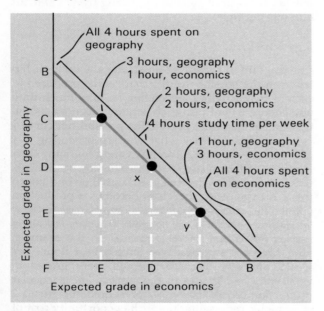

between expected grades in geography and economics are given holding constant total study time as well as all other factors that may influence the student's ability to learn. Quite clearly, if the student wished to spend more total time studying, then it would be possible to have higher grades in both economics and geography! However, then we would no longer be on the specific production possibilities curve illustrated in Figure 1.2. We would have to draw a new curve in order to show the greater total study time and a

different set of possible trade-offs. A grades might then be possible!

Society's Choices

The straight-line production possibilities curve presented in Figure 1.2 can be generalized to demonstrate the related concepts of scarcity, choice, and trade-offs facing an entire nation. You may have already heard the phrase, 'guns or butter'. Implicit in that phrase is that at any point in time a nation can either have more military goods (guns) or civilian goods (butter). Let us restrict our example to the production of military goods and civilians goods. We assume that these are the only two classes of goods that can be produced in the economy. In Figure 1.3(a), there are the hypothetical numerical trade-offs, expressed in terms of units of military goods produced per year. If no civilian goods are produced, all resources will be used in the production of military goods, of which 5000 units will be produced per year. On the other hand, if no military goods are produced, all resources will be used to produce 6000 units of civilian goods per year. In between, there are various combinations that are possible. These combinations are plotted as points A, B, C, D, C, F, and G in Figure 1.3(b). If these points are connected with a smooth curve, society's production possibilities curve is shown, and it demonstrates the trade-off between the production of military and civilian goods. These trade-offs occur *on* the production possibilities curve.

Assumptions Underlying the Production Possibilities Curve

There are a number of assumptions underlying this particular production possibilities curve. The first one relates to the fact that we are referring to the output possible on a *yearly* basis. In other words, we have specified a time-period over which the production takes place.

Second, we are assuming that resources are *fixed* over this time period. To understand fully what is meant by a fixed amount of resources, consider that there are (a) factors that influence labour hours available for work and (b) factors that influence *productivity*, or the output per unit of input.

Key Points 1.2

► **Any use of a resource involves an opportunity cost because an alternative use, by necessity, was sacrificed.**

► **We look only at the highest valued alternative to determine opportunity cost.**

► **The graphic representation of trade-offs that must be made is displayed in a production possibilities curve.**

Figure 1.3

Society's Trade-off between Military Goods and Civilian Goods. The production of military goods is measured in units per year. The production of civilian goods is measured in units per year also. We look at seven combinations from *A* to *G*. The first one, *A*, involves the production of no civilian goods, which allows us – using all of our resources – to produce 5000 units of military goods. At the other extreme, combination *G*, society produces no military goods and can therefore use its productive resources to produce 6000 units of civilian goods per year. These combinations are given in panel (a). The combinations *A* to *G* are plotted on the graph in panel (b). Connecting the points *A* to *G* with a smooth line gives society's production possibilities curve for military goods and civilian goods. Point *R* lies outside the production possibilities curve and is therefore unattainable at the point in time for which the graph is given; point *S* lies inside the production possibilities curve and therefore represents an inefficient use of available resources.

Panel (a)

Combination	Military goods (units per year)	Civilian goods (units per year)
A	5000	0
B	4800	1000
C	4500	2000
D	4000	3000
E	3300	4000
F	2250	5000
G	0	6000

Panel (b)

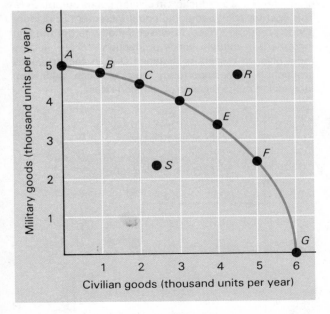

FACTORS INFLUENCING LABOUR HOURS AVAILABLE FOR WORK

We must recognize that the number of labour hours will depend on the state of human resources in society. What determines how much labour can be available?

Hours available for work are determined by the following:

1. The size of population, its age structure, and dependants (children, retired persons)
2. The resulting potential size of the labour force
3. The percentage of available individuals who then choose to work
4. Custom and tradition (for example, women working).

FACTORS INFLUENCING PRODUCTIVITY

There are a number of factors influencing how productive our society can be and if you recall our discussion of the inputs used in production then we can list the following:

1. Quantity and quality of natural resources
2. Quantity and quality of capital
3. Health, education, motivation, and skill levels of the labour force
4. Research and development.

We are assuming that at the present time our society is using all its human, natural, and manufactured resources to maximum effect *given the state of knowledge* about how to make military goods and civilian goods. If the state of technology does not change, then our society cannot make more productive use of its resources. Thus we assume when drawing a production possibilities curve that no earth-shaking invention that could reduce significantly the cost of producing either military or civilian goods in our example is possible in the present time-period. We are further assuming that the size of the labour force remains the same during this time-period, that the health, motivation, and skill levels remain the same, and so on. If any one of the factors influencing labour hours or productivity changes, then the production possibilities curve will shift. Any improvement in technology (productivity) will move the entire curve outwards to the right, as in Figure 1.4(a). Any significant reduction in the labour force, all other things held constant, will shift the entire production possibilities curve inwards to the left, as in Figure 1.4(b).

The third and final assumption that we are making when we draw the production possibilities curve is that we are making efficient use of all available resources. (The concept of efficiency will be examined more closely in Chapter 6.) Society cannot for the moment be more productive with the present quantity and quality of its resources.

BEING OFF THE PRODUCTION POSSIBILITIES CURVE

Point *R* lies outside the production possibilities curve in Figure 1.3(b). Any point outside the curve is impossible to achieve during the present time-period. By definition, the possibilities curve relates to a specific unit of time. Additionally, the production possibilities curve is drawn for a given resource base. Under these

Figure 1.4

Shifting Production Possibilities Curve. In panel (a), we see that improved productivity will shift the entire production possibilities curve outwards over time. In panel (b), a reduced amount of labour available to the economy will shift the entire production possibilities curve inwards over time.

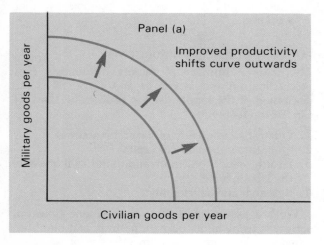

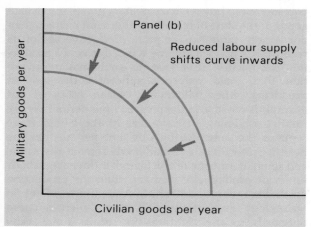

two constraints, the production possibilities curve therefore indicates, by definition, the maximum quantity of one good available, given some quantity of the other. Point *R*, lying outside the production possibilities curve, occurs because we live in a world of scarcity. Look at point *S* in Figure 1.3(b). It is inside the curve, which means that society's resources are not being fully utilized. This could be due to unemployment.

Why the Production Possibilities Curve is Bowed Outward

In the example in Figure 1.2, the trade-off between a grade in geography and a grade in economics was one to one. The trade-off ratio was fixed. That is to say, the production possibilities curve is a straight line, which, as we pointed out before, is a special case. Figure 1.3 is the more general case, showing a bowed production possibilities curve. The opportunity cost of obtaining

more and more units of military goods rises. That is to say, each additional unit costs society more in forgone alternatives than the previously produced unit. We can see this more clearly in Figure 1.5. Each increment in military output is the same, but look at what we have to *give up* in civilian goods when we go from the next to last unit of military output to the last unit where the entire economy is producing just military goods. The opportunity cost is very large relative to what an equivalent increase in military goods costs society when we start with none being produced at all. Figure 1.5 illustrates the law of **increasing relative costs**. As society takes more and more resources and applies them to the production of any specific item, the opportunity cost for each additional unit produced increases at an increasing rate.

Why are we faced with the law of increasing relative costs? Why is the production possibilities curve bowed outwards? The answers to these questions are basic, and are related to the fact that some resources are better suited for the production of some things than they are for other things. In other words, many economic resources are not as a rule easily adaptable to alternative uses. Start in a world with a production of no military goods, only civilian goods. At first, we might find some sophisticated engineers working on

Figure 1.5

The Law of Increasing Costs. Consider equal increments in military goods production, as measured on the vertical axis. Thus, all of the vertical arrows – *H–I, J–K, L–M, N–O*, and *P–Q* – are of equal length. What is the cost to society of obtaining the first such increment in military goods production? It is a reduction in civilian goods output, *G–H*. This cost for each additional equal increment in military goods production rises, however. Finally, to get the last increment in military goods production – *P–Q* – society must give up the entire distance *O–P* in civilian goods production. The opportunity cost of each additional increase in military goods production rises.

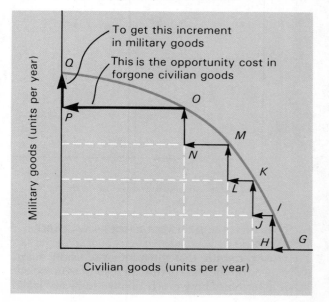

Key Points 1.3

► Trade-offs are represented graphically by a production possibilities curve showing the maximum output combinations obtainable over a 1-year period from a given set of resources.

► Points outside the production possibilities curve are unattainable; points inside represent an inefficient use or underutilization of available resources.

► Since many resources are better suited for certain productive tasks than for others, society's production possibilities curve is bowed outwards reflecting the law of increasing relative cost.

---

computerized watering and fertilizing systems, for example, who could be easily transferred to the production of military goods. The job that these people would be doing while producing military goods might be relatively similar to the one they were doing when they were used in producing civilian goods. Their productivity might be approximately the same as it was prior to the move.

Eventually, however, when we attempt to transfer manual labourers used to harvesting potatoes to the production of military goods, we will find that their talents will be relatively ill-suited to such tasks. We might have to use fifty manual labourers to obtain the same increment in military goods output that we got when we hired one sophisticated engineer for the first units of military goods. Thus the opportunity cost of an additional unit of military goods will be higher when we use resources that are ill-suited to the task. That cost – of using poorly suited resources – increases as we attempt to produce more and more military goods and less and less civilian goods.

As a rule of thumb, the more highly specialized resources are, the more bowed society's production possibilities curve will be. At the other extreme, if all resources were equally suitable for all production purposes, then the curves in Figures 1.3, 1.4, and 1.5 would have simply approached a straight line, as in Figure 1.2.

Economics as a Science

Economics is a social science that makes use of the same kinds of methods as other sciences, such as biology, physics, and chemistry. Like these other sciences, economics uses models, or theories. Economic models and theories are simplified representations of the real world that we use to help us to understand, explain, and predict economic phenomena in the real world.

For many centuries, most people thought that the world was flat. Using this model, they predicted that if one sailed to the edge of the world, one would fall off into space. Columbus, however, applied a new model. His **model**, or **theory**, postulated that the world was round. He predicted that one could round the world without falling off an edge, because there were no edges. He tested his model, or theory, by sailing and sailing and sailing. He did not fall off any edges, and thereby refuted the flat-earth model empirically.

Economic models, or theories, are no different from those presented in other sciences. They may take on various forms such as verbal statements, numerical tables, graphs, mathematical equations. For the most part, the models that we present in this text consist of verbal statements and graphs.

Models and Realism

At the outset, it must be emphasized that no model in *any* science, and therefore no economic model, is complete in the sense that it captures every detail and interrelationship that exists. Indeed, a model, by definition, is an abstraction from reality. It may be conceptually impossible to construct a perfectly realistic model. For example, in physics we cannot account for every atom and its position and certainly not for every molecule and subparticle. Not only is such a model impossibly expensive to build, but it would also be impossible to work with. No model of the solar system, for example, could possibly take into account *all* aspects of the entire solar system.

The nature of scientific model building is such that the model should capture only the *essential* relationships that are sufficient to analyse the particular problem or answer the particular question with which we are concerned.

Let us return to our production possibility curve concerning you as a student. We looked at the trade-offs concerning your use of scarce time in studying geography and economics. As a model it illustrated the principle of opportunity cost. But you may have thought that various factors were left out of account in this model so let us now recognize these.

Your performance in either geography or economics was assumed to improve by exactly one grade for every hour of study. There was, it seems, no particular difficulty in using one hour to raise the standard of your assessed performance. Now you may say that you would find more difficulty in improving your performance in economics than in geography: in other words another 2 or even 3 hours would be necessary to move from a C grade to a B grade and not just one! For some of your fellow students still more hours than this might be needed, but for yet others less than a full hour might be sufficient to achieve a similar result. But on reflection did not our discussion of the production of military and civilian goods recognize the possibility of a production possibility curve that was not a straight line? Figure 1.3 was drawn as a curve not as a line: we could now redraw a curve rather than a line in Figure 1.2. Our model of study of geography and economics can also easily incorporate the principle of increasing relative cost!

If you reread carefully you will note we assumed that not only was the amount of study time held constant but also 'all other factors that may influence the student's ability to learn'. Thus it was implicitly assumed that it is as effective to study during a hot summer afternoon as during a cold winter evening. Or that it makes no difference whether you are studying alone in your own room or in a public library. What particular book you are reading in the hour of study also makes no difference at all. Now you may well wonder whether, in the light of these and other influences on the student's learning situation, our model is not too simplistic.

What we have just recognized is that there are indeed many factors which would influence a student's performance in a subject. But in our model we are assuming that we are *holding all other things constant*. In our model we are showing the relationship between

the amount of time devoted to a subject and the assessed performance resulting from the amount of study. In Figure 1.6 we show this relationship.

Of course, there are other influencing variables, but they are not explicitly shown on any graph that has only two variables, such as study time and grade performance. In other words, the relationships shown on our graphs, by their very nature, cannot explicitly include all of the other relationships that are involved in determining the grades of students. We say, therefore, that when we draw a graph showing the relationship between two variables, we are holding all other things constant. The graph shown in Figure 1.6 is therefore holding constant, or fixed, the time of year, place of study, student motivation, and all other influences on the learning situation. This is sometimes referred to as the **ceteris paribus assumption**, where the words 'ceteris paribus' mean 'other things constant'. There is a way to show the effect of changes in 'other things' that are not explicitly depicted in two-dimensional graphs. When some other determining variable changes, it will affect the *position* of the line, or curve, representing the relationship between the two variables on the curve. For example, consider Figure 1.6 showing the relationship between study time and study grade. If the place where one studies affects *grade performance*, and there is a change in study location, that entire line will move somewhere else in the graph when this variable is recognized as a relevant factor in the learning situation.

In sum, then, an economic model cannot be faulted as unrealistic merely because it does not represent every detail of the real world. That same model may be very realistic in terms of elucidating the *central* issue at hand or forces at work. Every theory is an abstraction of reality.

Assumptions

Every model, or theory, must be based on a set of assumptions. Assumptions define the set of circumstances in which our model is most likely to be applicable. When scientists predicted that sailing-ships would fall off the edge of the earth, they used the assumption that the earth was flat. Columbus did not accept the implications of such a model. He tested the predictions of his own model, which was based on the assumption that the world was round. He sailed and did not fall off any 'edge'. The empirical test of his own model refuted the flat-earth model. Indirectly, then, it was a test of the assumption of that model that the earth was flat.

Models in physics and chemistry contain numerous assumptions. In physics, for instance, there is a model that uses a 'perfect gas'. A perfect gas is one whose molecules are so far apart that you can ignore any interaction between them, except when they collide. Of course, no gas in the real world behaves like a perfect gas. None the less, the model that is based on this assumption of a perfect gas is well known and

---

Figure 1.6
The Relationship between Study Time and Performance in Economics.

grade obtained in economics depends on the amount of time devoted to the study of the subject. The relationship is a direct one and assumes there is no influence on the learning situation other than the amount of time devoted to the study of economics.

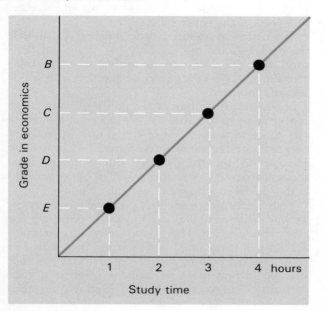

accepted. It is called Boyle's Law. The assumption of the model is unrealistic as are the physicists' models that assume a frictionless world. We still accept these assumptions and the resulting models, provided that they *work* well. Now, you ask, what does 'work well' mean?

Deciding on the Usefulness of a Model

We generally do not attempt to determine the usefulness of a model or how 'good' it is merely by evaluating how realistic its assumptions are. Rather, we consider that a model is 'good' if it yields usable predictions and implications for the real world. In other words, can we predict what will happen in the world around us with the model? Are there implications in the model of how things will happen in our world?

Once we have determined that the model does predict real-world phenomena, then the scientific approach to analysis of the world around us requires that we consider evidence. Evidence is used to test the usefulness of a model. This is why we call economics an empirical science – empirical meaning that real evidence (data) is looked at to see whether we are right.

Consider two competing models that concern ourselves with the following imaginary situation. Suppose that every time that I leave some money on a table in the sixth-form room, it disappears. The first model is based on several assumptions, including that of self-interest – making oneself as well-off as possible. This model predicts that if it does not take too much effort to take possession of the money (which can then be spent), individuals will engage in this clearly worthwhile activity. The competing model may seem strange. It uses a theory of 'coin fascination'. Money has a fascination as an object that causes people's hands to pick it up! A testable (that is, refutable) implication of the first model is that money will disappear faster the greater the number of the coins left.

The implication of the 'coin fascination' model, on the other hand, is that no matter what the number of the coins is, they will disappear equally fast. We can run an experiment now to test the predictive capacity of these two models. On some days we randomly leave two 50-pence coins on a table at different time-intervals. Then we keep increasing the possible take, next leaving ten of these coins at a time, then twenty such coins, then twenty 50-pence coins. If we observe that more individuals hang around the sixth-form room as the pile of coins increases, we have an observed fact that does not refute the implication or prediction of the first model. It does, however, refute the second model, which would predict that the number of students who hang around will be the same no matter how large the pile of coins. In this case, because the number of 50-pence coins does not determine the fascination for them, we would then choosen the first model and reject the second.

Models of Behaviour, not Thought Processes

Take special note of the fact that economists' models do not relate to the way people *think*. Rather, they relate to the way people *act*, to what they do in life with their limited resources. Models tend to generalize human behaviour. In no way does the economist attempt to predict how people will think about a particular topic, such as the high price of oil products, accelerated inflation, higher taxes, or the like. Rather, the task at hand is to predict how people will act, which may be quite different from what they say they will do (much to the consternation of opinion pollsters and market researchers).

Microeconomics versus Macroeconomics

Economics is typically divided into two types of analysis: microeconomics and macroeconomics. Consider the definitions of the two terms.

Microeconomics is the study of individual decision-making by both individuals and firms.

Macroeconomics is the study of economy-wide phenomena resulting from group decision-making in entire markets. As such, it deals with the economy as a whole.

The best way to understand the distinction between microeconomics and macroeconomics is to consider some examples. Microeconomic analysis would tackle the effects of changes in the price of petrol relative to other energy sources. It would be involved in the examination of the effects of new taxes on a specific product or industry. If price controls were reinstituted in the United Kingdom, how individual firms and consumers would react to such price controls would be in the realm of microeconomics. The raising of wages by an effective union strike would be analysed, using the tools of microeconomics.

On the other hand, questions relating to the rate of inflation, the amount of national unemployment, the growth in production in the whole economy, and numerous other economy-wide subjects fall into the realm of macroeconomic analysis. In other words, macroeconomics deals with, so-called *aggregates* or totals, such as total output in an economy. It is a study, therefore, of aggregate behaviour rather than individual behaviour.

You should be aware, however, of the blending together of microeconomics and macroeconomics in modern economic theory. Modern economists are increasingly using microeconomic analysis – the study of decision-making by individuals and by firms – as the basis of macroeconomic analysis. They do this because, even though in macroeconomic analysis aggregates are being examined, those aggregates are made up of individuals and firms. Consider an example: some economists believe that reducing income tax rates will lead to greater total output. Why? Because, using microeconomic analysis, they predict that individuals will respond to lower income tax rates by working longer, taking fewer holidays, and taking on second jobs. The task is then to establish whether empirical evidence supports these predictions.

Positive versus Normative Economics – What is versus What ought to be

Economics is a social science; it uses *positive* analysis. This is a scientific term that relates to the value-free nature of the inquiry; no subjective or 'gut' feelings enter into the analysis. Positive analysis relates to basic statements, such as *if A, then B*. For example, if the price of petrol goes up relative to all other prices, then the amount of it that people will buy will fall. That is a positive economic statement. It is a statement of *what is*. It is not a statement of anyone's value-judgement, or subjective feelings. 'Hard' sciences, such as physics and chemistry, are considered to be virtually value-free. After all, how can someone's values enter into a theory of molecular behaviour? But economists face a different problem. They deal with the behaviour of individuals, not molecules. Thus, it is more difficult to stick to what we consider to be value-free or **positive economics** without reference to our feelings.

When our values come into the analysis, we enter the realm of **normative economics**, or normative analysis, which is defined as analysis containing whether explicity or implicitly, someone's values. A positive economic statement is: 'If the price of books goes up, people will buy less'. If we add to that analysis the statement 'and therefore we *should* not allow the price to go up', we have entered the realm of normative economics; we have expressed a personal opinion or value-judgement. In fact, any time you see the word *should*, you will know that values are entering into the discussion.

The world of value-judgements is the world in which individuals' preferences are at issue. Each of us has a desire for different things: we have different values. When we express a value-judgement, we are simply saying what we prefer, like, or desire. Since individual values are quite diverse, we expect – and indeed observe – people expressing widely varying value-judgements about how the world should or ought to be.

Using Positive Economics in Normative Analysis

Even though this economics textbook, along with virtually all others, contains mostly positive economic analyses, such analyses can be used when one passes into the realm of policy-making in which values enter. Suppose, for example, that you desire to raise the income of employed teenagers. That is a normative judgement (that is, a value-judgement) that you have made and in which you believe. Assume that you are a policy-maker with many options available to you such as specifying minimum wage-levels. Here is where positive analysis can come to your aid.

Suppose that you construct a model of the teenage labour market. Your examination of real-world evidence tells you that in the past raising the minimum wage has not led to higher incomes for employed teenagers.

In fact you find out that it can even cause increased unemployment among teenagers. Even though your normative goal is to help unemployed teenagers, you may use positive economic analysis to decide that you must seek an alternative policy to raising the minimum wage. Hence, positive economics can be used as the basis for deciding on the appropriate policies to carry out one's goals or the goals of the nation.

A Warning

It is easy to define positive economics. It is quite another matter to catch all unlabelled normative statements in a textbook like this one, even though an author goes over the manuscript many times before it is printed. Therefore, do not get the impression that a textbook author will be able to keep his or her values out of the book. They will slip through. In fact, the choice itself of which topics to include in an introduc-

---

Key Points 1.4

▶ Models, or theories, can be represented by verbal statements, numerical tables, graphs, or mathematical equations.

▶ A model, or theory, uses assumptions and is by nature a simplification of the real world.

▶ Models in economics relate to behaviour rather than individuals' thought processes.

▶ Positive economics indicates what *is*, whereas normative economics tells us what *ought* to be.

tory textbook involves normative economics. There is no value-free or objective way to decide which ones to use in a textbook. The author's 'gut feelings' ultimately make a difference when choices have to be made. From your own personal standpoint, what you might hope to do is to be able to recognize *when* you are engaging in normative as opposed to positive economic analysis. Reading this text should equip you for that task.

CASE STUDY

Is it Possible to Have More Guns and More Butter Simultaneously?

When the United States was involved in a war in Vietnam, the late President Johnson made a speech in which he assured the American public that the United States would not sacrifice butter for guns. In other words, there could be more guns for the war *and* also more domestic social programmes. Is that possible? There are, in fact, only two ways in which President Johnson could have been correct, and then only in a very loose way.

Question
What are the two situations which might have justified President Johnson's claim? (Use Figures 1.3–1.5 to help your answer.)

Exam Preparation and Practice

INTRODUCTORY EXERCISES

1. Construct four separate models to predict the probability that a person will die within the next 5 years. Include only one determining factor in each of your models.

2. The following sets of numbers represent a set of hypothetical production possibilities for a nation in 1986.

Butter	Guns
4	0
3	1.6
2	2.4
1	2.8
0	3.0

Plot these points on a piece of graph paper. Does the law of increasing relative costs seem to hold? Why? On the same graph, now plot and draw the production possibilities curve that will represent 10 per cent economic growth.

MULTIPLE CHOICE QUESTIONS

1. The diagram below shows the production possibilities available to a closed economy without foreign trade.

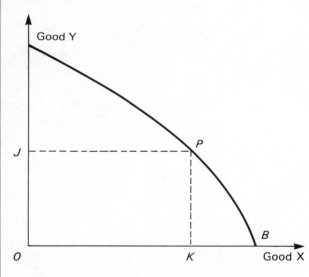

If the economy produces *OK* of good X then it forgoes

A *OJ* of good Y
B *OA* of good Y
C *AJ* of good Y
D *KB* of good X for *OA* of good Y
E *KB* of good X for *AJ* of good Y

†2. The opportunity cost to society of constructing a motorway would be the

A money spent on the road
B goods and services that could otherwise have been produced had the road not been constructed
C the cost of government borrowing to finance the construction of the road
D increased taxation needed to pay the cost of the new road
E goods and services that could otherwise have been produced by the labour employed in constructing the road, had the road not been constructed

†3. In the following diagram, XY represents an economy's production possibility curve. Which point (**A, B, C** or **D**) would indicate that the country could increase its standard of living without incurring an opportunity cost?

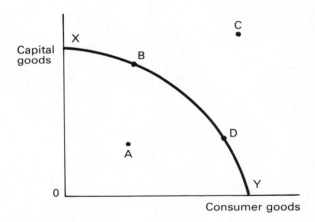

4. Assume you bought a bicycle for £100, but never use it. A similar bicycle would now cost £120 new, but yours would fetch only £40 second-hand. The present opportunity cost of owning the bicycle is

A £20
B £40
C £60
D £100
E £120

†5. A farmer can feed any combination of animals within the following range:

Pigs		Cows
84	and	12
75	and	15

Given the options available to him, what is the opportunity cost to the farmer of rearing one cow?

A 1 pig
B 3 pigs
C 5 pigs
D 7 pigs
E 9 pigs

One or more of the options given in Question 6 may be correct. Select your answer by means of the code set out in line grid:

A	B	C	D
1,2,3	**1,2**	**2,3**	**1**
all	only	only	only
correct	correct	correct	correct

6. A normative statement in economics

1 is one that it is possible to refute by an appeal to the facts
2 typically contains the words 'ought' or 'should'
3 depends on value-judgements

RELATED ESSAY QUESTIONS

1. Define opportunity cost, and explain the importance of the concept.
2. Explain what is meant by a production possibility curve and discuss the circumstances in which such a curve would change its position.
3. Explain what is meant by

(a) microeconomics and macroeconomics
(b) positive economics and normative economics.

Discuss the relevance of each concept to the problem of scarcity and choice.

Appendix A:
Reading and Working with Graphs

'A picture is worth a thousand words...' And so is a graph! It is often easier to communicate an idea by using a picture than to read or listen to a lengthy description. A graph performs much the same function as a picture. A graph is a visual representation of the relationship between two or more variables. In this Appendix, we shall stick to just two variables – an **independent variable**, which can change in value freely, and a **dependent variable**, which changes in value according to changes in the value of the independent variable.

Before we present the 'picture', that is, a graph, let us return to the 'thousand words', that is, a table. A table is a 'list' of values showing the relationship between two variables. Any table can be converted into a graph, which is a visual representation of that list.

Graphs Represent Relationships

Two variables can be related in different ways, some simple, others more complex, for example, a person's weight and height are often related. If we measured the height and weight of thousands of people, we would surely find that taller people tend to weigh more than shorter people. That is, we would discover that there is a **direct relationship** between height and weight. By direct relationship we simply mean that an *increase* in one variable is usually associated with an *increase* in the related variable. This can easily be seen in panel (a) of Figure 1.A1.

Let us look at another simple way two variables can

be related: much evidence indicates that as price rises for a specific commodity, the amount purchased decreases – there is an **inverse relationship** between the variable's 'price per unit' and 'quantity purchased'. A table listing the data for this relationship would indicate that for higher and higher prices, smaller and smaller quantities would be purchased. We see this relationship in panel (b) of Figure 1.A1.

Now for a slightly complicated relationship between two variables: beginning with the average person's first job, earnings increase each year up to a certain age, then beyond that age, earnings decline each year. This is not a surprising economic research finding. Most people are more energetic and productive in the early and middle years of life. In this example, the two variables – earnings and age – would yield a more complex pattern. At earlier ages, these variables are directly related – earnings increase as age increases – and at later ages these variables are inversely related – earnings decline as age increases. We have also implied the concept of *maximum* – that is, there is an age at which annual earnings are at a maximum over the lifetime of annual earnings. We see all this in panel (c) of Figure 1.A1.

Note that an inverse relationship between two variables shows up on a graph as a line or curve that slopes downwards, that is, from left to right. (You may as well get used to the idea that economists call a straight line on a graph, a curve, even though it may not 'curve' at all. Much of economists' data turns out to be curves, so they refer to everything represented graphically as curves, even straight lines.)

Figure 1.A1

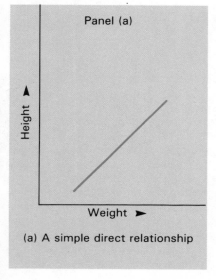

(a) A simple direct relationship

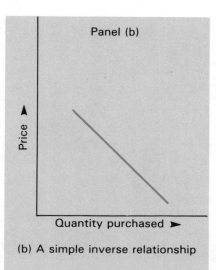

(b) A simple inverse relationship

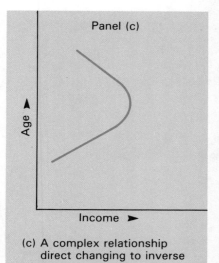

(c) A complex relationship direct changing to inverse

The Slope of a Linear Line (A Linear Curve)

An important property of a curve represented on a graph is its **slope**. Consider the table and its corresponding graph shown in Figure 1.A2. The table and graph represent the quantities of suits per week that a seller is willing to offer at different prices.

Figure 1.A2

Price	Quantity of Suits Offered per Week	Point on graph	
£100	400	A	(400, 100)
80	320	B	(320, 80)
60	240	C	(240, 60)
40	160	D	(160, 40)
20	80	E	(80, 20)

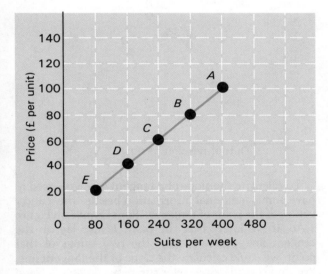

The slope of a line is defined as the change in the y values, divided by the corresponding change in the x values, as we move along the line. In Figure 1.A2, let us move from point E to point D. As we do so, we note that the change in the y values, which is the change in price, is since we have moved from a price of £20 to £40 per suit. As we move from E to D, the change in the x values is therefore:

$$\frac{20}{80} = +\tfrac{1}{4}$$

It may be helpful for you to think of slope as 'rise' (movement in the vertical direction) over a 'run' (movement in the horizontal direction). We show this abstractly in Figure 1.A3. The slope is measured by the amount of rise divided by the amount of run. In the example in Figure 1.A3, and of course 1.A2, the amount of rise is positive and so is the amount of run. That is because it is a direct relationship. We show an inverse relationship in Figure 1.A4. The slope is still

equal to the rise divided by the run, but in this case, the rise is negative because the curve is sloping downward. That means that the slope will have to be negative, and that means that we are dealilng with an inverse relationship.

Now let us calculate the slope for a different part of the curve back in Figure 1.A2. We will find the slope as we move from point B to point A. Again, we note that slope, or rise/run, from B to A equals:

$$\frac{20}{80} = +\tfrac{1}{4}$$

Figure 1.A3

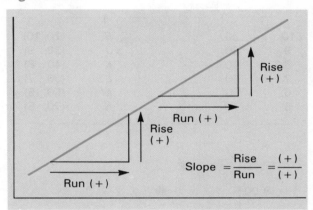

Figure 1.A4

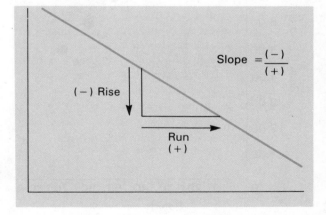

A specific property of a straight line is that its slope is the same between any two points; or, a slope is constant at any point on a straight line on a graph.

We conclude that for our example in Fig. 1.A2, the relationship between the price of a suit and the quantity of suits willingly offered per week is 'linear', which simply means straight line, and our calculations indicate a constant slope. Moreover, we calculate a direct relationship between these two variables, which turns out to be an upward-sloping (from left to right) curve, that is, straight line. Upward-sloping curves have positive slopes – in this case, it is $+\tfrac{1}{4}$.

We know that an inverse relationship between two variables shows up as a downward-sloping curve –

'rise' over 'run' will be a negative slope because the 'rise' is really a fall, as shown in the graph. When we see a negative slope, we know that increases in one variable are associated with decreases in the other. Therefore, we refer to downward-sloping curves as negative slopes. Can you verify that the slope of the graph representing the relationship between T-shirt prices and the quantity of T-shirts purchased per week in Figure 1.A5 is –¹⁄₁₀?

Figure 1.A5

Price	T-shirts purchased per Week	Point on graph	
£10	20	R	(20, 10)
9	30	J	(30, 9)
8	40	K	(40, 8)
7	50	L	(50, 7)
6	60	M	(60, 6)
5	70	N	(70, 5)

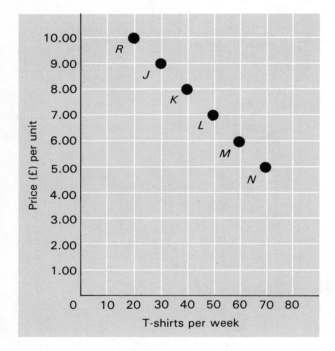

Slopes of Non-Linear Curves

The graph presented in Figure 1.A6 indicates a non-linear (which simply means not a straight-line) relationship between two variables, total yearly profits and output per year. Inspection of this graph indicates that, at first, increases in output lead to increases in total profits; that is, total profits rise as output increases. But beyond some output level, further increases in output cause decreases in total profits.

Since this curve is non-linear (it obviously is not a straight line), should we expect a constant slope when we compute changes in y divided by corresponding

changes in x in moving from one point to another? A quick inspection, even without specific numbers, should lead us to conclude that the slopes of lines joining different points in this curve, such as between A and B and C, or C and D, are *not* the same. In fact, the slope of the line between any two points on this curve will usually be different from the slope of the line between any two other points.

Instead of using a line between two points to discuss slope, mathematicians and economists prefer to discuss the slope at a particular point, rather than the slope between points. The slope at a point on the curve, such as point B in the graph in Figure 1.A6, is the slope of the line *tangent* to that point. A tangent line is a straight line that touches a curve at only one point.

Figure 1.A6

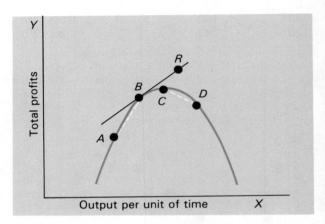

To calculate the slope of a tangent line, you need to have some additional information besides the x and y values of the point of tangency. For example, in Figure 1.A6, if we knew that the point R also lay on the tangent line, and we knew the two values of that point, we could calculate the slope of the tangent line. We could calculate rise over run between points B and R, and the result would be the slope of the line tangent to the one point B on the curve.

From now on, we will refer to the slope of the line tangent to a curve at a point as a slope at that point. Furthermore, you should realize that every point on a non-linear curve will have a different tangent line.

Graphs and the Real World

So far, we have talked about plotting relationships between two economic variables. Throughout much of this text, most of the graphs shown will be hypothetical in nature. But economists do quite often examine actual (empirical) relationships between the two economic variables in order to confirm theories about how the world works. (Actually, one never confirms a theory; one simply attempts to reject it by submitting it to real-world evidence.) Consequently, economists gather one of two types of real-world data:

time-series data and **cross-section data**. Time-series data involve obtaining information on the value of economic variables over time. For example, an economist might collect information on average family income and average family expenditures each year over a 25-year period. These data can then be plotted on a graph to show the relationship, over time, of family income and family expenditures. Alternatively, cross-section data could be gathered at a point in time. Different families with different incomes and their resulting expenditure levels would be used as the observations. A similar graph would show the relationship between family income and family expenditures at a point in time.

Scatter Diagrams

Of course, the economists who make these real-world measurements about economic variables do not usually get nice, neat curves like the ones we draw in our hypothetical examples. Rather, economists typically obtain observations that are scattered 'all over the place', and from these they try to derive trends. To illustrate, say that an economist has collected data on family income and expenditure, as above. Using these data, the economist has plotted the observations on a graph, shown in Figure 1.A7(a). Such a graph is known as a **scatter diagram**, for obvious reasons. Looking at this graph, it is easy to see that a pattern exists. While the relationship is not perfect, it does appear that when income rises, expenditure rise; and when income falls, expenditures fall. There are techniques that can be used to 'fit' a curve which best summarizes all the points in the scatter diagram. Such a curve would be analogous to the nice, neat lines of the hypothetical graphs we have shown so far and the ones we will show throughout the text. It would not perfectly describe the *actual relationship between the two economic variables* (here, family income and expenditure),

Figure 1.A7(a)
A Scatter Diagram of Observations on family income and family expenditures

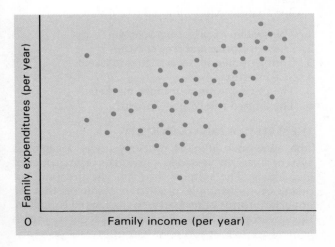

Figure 1.A7(b)
A Random Scatter Pattern

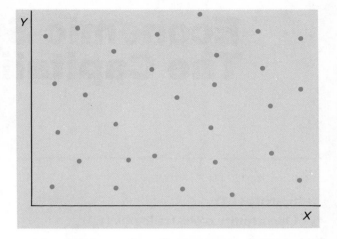

but it can come close. Of course, when economists fit lines to scatter diagrams, they have to report how well the lines fit, and there are statistics that do just that.

Now consider the scatter diagram in Figure 1.A7(b). Can a line be fitted to best describe these observations? No. Any line would do just as well as any other, which means that no line will do. When an economist gets results such as these, he or she reports that 'no relationship appears to exist'.

How to Lie with Graphs – What to Watch Out For

Irrespective of the type of data collected, there are numerous pitfalls in the collection, interpretation, and use of such data in graphical analysis. In other words, it is easy to 'lie with graphs'. Consider obtaining information on family income and expenditures at a point in time. Since it is impossible to collect data on all families in the United Kingdom, a sample must be taken. What if the sample is unrepresentative? Then the resulting plotted graphical relationship between family income and expenditures may be quite wrong. Also, the collection of the data could be done improperly – numbers transcribed incorrectly, some families left out, and so on. That means that the researcher must constantly be on the look-out for improper measurement before he or she 'believes' in the resulting plotted graphical relationship.

Consider the time-series example just discussed. What if the time-series data on average family income and expenditure starts during the Great Depression of the 1930s and includes the years 1939–45? The resulting plotted relationship may not be indicative of the average relationship during peacetime and when the UK was not suffering from a serious fall in the state of business activity. The choice of years covered, therefore, can seriously bias a plotted graphical relationship.

2 Economic Systems: The Capitalist Economy

Key Points to Review

▶ Scarcity (1.1)

▶ Opportunity costs, trade-offs (1.2)

▶ Production possibilities curve (1.3)

Questions for Preview

1 Capitalist economies are associated with great economic freedoms with regard to ownership and use of private property. Why does all this freedom not lead to chaos and anarchy? What gives *direction* and *regulation* to a capitalist economy?

2 Money economies are more advanced than barter economies. Why?

3 A trade-off exists between present consumption and future consumption. Why?

Economic Systems

We characterize an **economic system** as all the institutional means through which national resources are used to satisfy human wants. By **institutions**, we mean principally the laws of the nation, but also the habits, ethics, and customs of its society. From the outset, you should be aware that all economic systems are artificial in the sense that the institutions in an economy are exactly what human beings have made them. In this chapter we define capitalism as one economic system and examine how it faces up to the fundamental problems facing any society.

An Analysis of Capitalist Ideology

Capitalism is a type of economic system that is typically characterized by limited involvement of government in the economy, coupled with individual ownership of the means of production. We might further add that in a capitalist system individuals can pursue their own self-interest without many constraints. The capitalist system is thus one where decisions are decentralized.

Analysing the Institutions and Assumptions of Capitalist Ideology

Capitalist ideology is based on a set of fundamental assumptions. These assumptions are not, of course, accepted by all, but they must be understood in order to understand what capitalist ideology is all about. The institutions of capitalist ideology are, in many senses, abstract but play an important role in determining the way in which individuals can act in a pure capitalist system.

Our analysis will be limited to a discussion of:

1. The system of private property
2. Free enterprise and free choice
3. Competition and unrestricted markets
4. Self-interest
5. The pricing system in those markets
6. The limited role of government.

THE SYSTEM OF PRIVATE PROPERTY

The ownership of most property under a capitalist system is usually vested in individuals or in groups of individuals. The state is thus not the predominant owner of, for example, productive resources that are important forms of property. In the United Kingdom, the government does own certain property, but in general we live within a system of private property.

Private property is controlled and enforced through the legal framework of laws, courts, and policy. Under capitalism, individuals have their *property rights* protected; individuals are usually free to use their private property as they choose, so long as they do not infringe on the legal property rights of others.

FREE ENTERPRISE AND FREE CHOICE

Another attribute of a capitalist system is free enterprise, which is merely an extension of the concept of property rights. **Free enterprise** exists when private individuals are allowed to obtain resources, to organize those resources, and to sell the resulting product in any way the person chooses. In other words, there are no artificial obstacles or restrictions that a government or other producers can put up to block a business person's choice in the matter of purchasing inputs and selling outputs.

Additionally, all members of the economy are free to choose to do whatever they wish. Workers will be free to enter any line of work for which they are qualified and consumers can buy the desired basket of goods and services that they feel is most appropriate for them. The ultimate voter in the capitalist system is the consumer, who votes with pounds and decides which product 'candidates' will survive; that is, there is **consumer sovereignty** in that the ultimate purchaser of products and services determines what, in fact, is produced.

COMPETITION AND UNRESTRICTED MARKETS

Competition is rivalry among sellers who wish to attract customers and rivalry among buyers to obtain desired goods. In general, competition exists among buyers and sellers of all resources who wish to obtain the best terms possible when they transact their business.

Competition requires, at a minimum, two things:

(a) A relatively large number of independently acting sellers and buyers, and

(b) The freedom of sellers and buyers to enter or leave a particular industry.

(a) **Many participants**. The presence of a large number of buyers and sellers means that power is diffuse, that no one buyer or one seller can noticeably influence the price that a particular product fetches in the market-place.

Basically, economic competition – rivalry among buyers and sellers – imposes limits on the self-interest of buyers and sellers. Competition, then, is the regulating force in capitalism.

(b) **Easy entry and exit**. Another thing that makes competition a regulatory force is the ability of individuals to enter an industry that is profitable. Furthermore, those who feel that they could earn more profits in another industry must have the legal ability to leave the industry they are in now. We say, then, that there are weak *barriers to entry and exit* from industries so that competition can prevail throughout.

SELF-INTEREST AND THE INVISIBLE HAND

In 1776, Adam Smith, the author of *The Wealth of Nations*, described a system in which government had a limited role and individuals pursued their own self-interest. Smith reasoned that, in so doing, individuals will be guided as if by an invisible hand to achieve maximum social welfare for the nation. In his own words:

[An individual] generally, indeed, neither intends to promote the public interest, nor knows how much he is promoting it... he intends only his own gain, and he is in this, as in many other cases, led by an invisible hand to promote an end which was no part of his intention. Nor is it always the worse for the society that it was no part of it. By pursuing his own interest he frequently promotes that of the society more effectually than when he really intends to promote it.*

What does self-interest entail? For the entrepreneur it normally means maximizing profits or minimizing losses. For the consumer, it means maximizing the amount of satisfaction possible from spending a given amount of income. From the worker's point of view, it means obtaining the highest level of income possible for a given amount of work. For the owner of a resource, it means obtaining the highest price possible when that resource is sold, or the greatest rent if it is rented.

Capitalism, therefore, presumes self-interest as the fundamental way that people operate in the system. Self-interest is the guiding light in capitalism.

THE PRICING SYSTEM

Capitalism is a **market economy** defined as one in which buyers and sellers express their opinions through how much they are willing to pay for or how much they demand of goods and services. A market economy is also called **a price system**. In a price system, or market economy, prices are used to *signal* the *value* of individual resources. Prices are the guide-posts to which resource owners, entrepreneurs, and consumers refer when they make their choices as they attempt to improve their lives. In other words, the **market economic system** is the organizing force in our economy. When we refer to **organization**, we mean the co-ordination of individuals, often doing different things, in the furtherance of a common end. This process of co-ordinating economic activity can be considered as being mechanical or machine-like in its mode of working. Hence we can also refer to the market system as using the mechanism of prices to effect changes in resource use. How does the **price mechanism** achieve this?

Resources tend to flow where they yield the highest rate of return, or highest profit. Prices generate the signals for resource movements, they provide information cheaply and quickly, and they affect incentives.

---

*A. Smith *Wealth of Nations* (1776), Bk. IV, Ch. 11, Everyman Edn (1964), p. 400.

ADAM SMITH
SCOTTISH ECONOMIST (1723–90)

Of Markets and Men

'I have never known much good done by those who affected to trade for the public good', Adam Smith once remarked. If he put little stock in good intentions, Smith did invest heavily in demonstrating that selfish intentions could lead to public good. In *The Theory of Moral Sentiments* (1759), his first book, Smith tried to show how altruism could come out of self-interest. In his second and more famous book, Smith attempted to reveal how the self-interest of private individuals could be transformed by the sleight of an invisible hand (the unfettered market) into social harmony and public benefit, producing the wealth of the nation in the best of all possible ways. The result of this effort was *An Inquiry into the Nature and Causes of the Wealth of Nations* (1776), perhaps the most influential economics treatise ever written, one that has set the tone for capitalist ideology for the past two centuries.

As the title indicates, Smith attempted to examine the sources of the wealth of nations. He proposed that first on the list of such sources

was the division of labour [discussed in Chapter 6]. Smith's pin-factory example of the dramatic increases in productivity possible through the division of labour has made its mark on virtually every textbook written on the subject since then. He went on to point out that the division of labour does not occur because individuals possess an overall perception of its ultimate benefit to society. Rather, the division of labour occurs simply because it is in each individual's self-interest to specialize and to exchange: 'The natural effort of

every individual to better his own condition, when suffered to exert itself with freedom and security, is so powerful a principle, that it is alone, and without any assistance ... capable of carrying on the society to wealth and prosperity.'

In addition to Smith's famous 'invisible hand' theme, referred to above, the theme of individual economic freedom also was quite strong in the *Wealth of Nations*. He believed that any governmental attempt to guide or to regulate the actions of individuals in the economic market-place would end up doing more harm than good. Smith was especially harsh on legally protected monopolies.

Smith's critics of today contend that his model may have fit the United Kingdom at the time he wrote his treatise, but it does not fit industrialized Western countries today – where the state plays a large role and large corporations have replaced the shopkeepers. None the less, for many, the *Wealth of Nations* remains a *laissez-faire* Bible, and Smith remains a central figure in the development of economic thought.

THE LIMITED ROLE OF GOVERNMENT

Even in an 'idealized' capitalistic system there is still a role for government, for someone has to define and enforce private property rights. The government protects the rights of individuals and entrepreneurs to keep private property private and to keep the control of that property vested with the owners. Even Adam Smith, the so-called father of free enterprise, described in detail the role of government in a purely capitalist system. He suggested the need for government in providing national defence and in eliminating monopolies that would restrain trade. Smith further suggested that the functions of government within a capitalist system might include issuing money, prescribing standards of weights and measures, raising funds by taxation and assorted other means for public works, and settling disputes judicially. Government is thus essential to the existence of even a purely capitalist system but operates in a restrained way. The words **laissez-faire** referred to in the biography of Adam Smith indicate that the business community should be left alone by government.

Finally – A Definition of Capitalism

We are now in a position formally to define in more detail what we mean by **capitalism**:

Capitalism is an economic system in which individuals privately own productive resources and possess the right to use these resources in whatever manner they choose, subject to certain (minimal) legal restrictions.

Notice here that we use the words *productive resources*, rather than capital. This takes into account not only machines and land, but also labour services.

Fundamental Problems Facing Any Society

The previous chapter explained the significance of economic goods. We now turn to the three major questions concerning the production and distribution of such goods. These questions are simply put.

> ## Key Points 2.1
>
> ► An idealized capitalist system works within the institution of private property that is controlled and enforced through the legal framework of laws, courts, and police.
>
> ► Further, such a system is one of free enterprise, where producers freely choose the resources they use in the products they produce. Consumers have freedom of choice also, as do workers and owners of resources in general.
>
> ► Individuals and producers express their desires through the market system, where prices are signals about the relative scarcities of different goods, services, and resources.
>
> ► The role of government is a limited one.

1. What goods are to be produced?
2. How should these goods be produced?
3. For whom should these goods be produced?

These three questions have varying 'answers' depending on the nature of the economic system. We must thus now examine how the capitalist economic system faces up to these three questions.

What? How? For Whom? – in Pure Capitalism

In pure capitalism, **consumers** ultimately determine what will be produced by their spending – their voting in the market-place – what they are willing to spend their income on. As far as producers are concerned their motivation as to what goods are produced is determined by the search for profit. Only those goods that can be produced profitably will be produced.

Since resources can substitute for one another in the production process, the pure capitalist economy must decide *how* to produce a commodity once society votes for it. Producers will be forced (by the discipline of the market-place) to combine resources in the cheapest way for a particular standard of quality. The cheapest way will depend on relative resource prices. Those firms that combine resources in the most efficient manner will earn the highest profits and force losses on their competitors. Competitors will be driven out of business or forced to combine resources in the same way as the profit-makers.

What and *how* questions are concerned with production. The *for whom* question is concerned with the

distribution of goods after they are produced. How is the pie divided? In pure capitalism, production and distribution are closely linked, because in the production of goods incomes are automatically generated. People get paid according to their productivity; that is, a person's income reflects the value that society places on that person's resources. Since income largely determines one's share of the output 'pie' in pure capitalism, what people get out of the economic system is based on what they put into it. Any exception to this situation – for example the welfare provided to those persons in society such as the handicapped and elderly who are not capable of contributing to the productive process – arises only if that society, through its government chooses to make it so.

The Use of Money

Figure 2.1 demonstrates the flow of resources and the flow of goods and services within a capitalist system. It is called the **circular flow** model. This model of a monetary economy makes it necessary to explain why we use money.

In a capitalist economic system, money is used as a *medium of exchange*. In other words, we have one standard good that everyone knows everyone else is willing to accept in exchange for all other goods and services. Money also serves many other functions that are described in later chapters.

Using money as a medium of exchange facilitates specialization and exchange among people. In fact, it is necessary that there be a convenient means of exchanging goods and services in order for us to be able to specialize. Consider the alternative to using

> ## Key Points 2.2
>
> ► Any economic system must answer the questions: (1) *what* will be produced? (2) *how* will it be produced? and (3) *for whom* will it be produced?

Figure 2.1
The Circular Flow – A Monetary Economy. In this simplified model there are only households and businesses (or firms). Money is used as the medium of exchange. Households sell the services of land, labour, capital, and entrepreneurship that they own to firms. Firms, in turn, pay households rent, wages, interest, and profits. Firms also sell goods and services to households for which the firms receive payment in the form of consumer expenditures of money income.

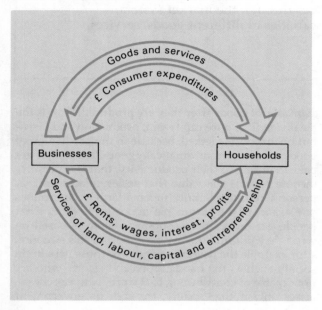

is that it must be generally acceptable by sellers in exchanges. Whatever fits this definition can be called money.

Our willingness to accept paper money, metal money, or any other type of money allows each person and each region to specialize in production despite a non-coincidence of wants.

The Circular Flow of Income

With money being used as a medium of exchange, households sell economic resources to businesses, and in return they are paid money income in the form of wages, interest, rents, and profits. They receive wages for their labour services, interest for the capital services that they provide, rents for the land that they own, and profits for their entrepreneurial abilities. (These money incomes are examined in detail later.) This is shown in the bottom loops in Figure 2.1. Firms, on the other hand, sell finished goods and services to households, for which, in exchange, they are paid money. This is shown in the top loop in Figure 2.1.

The circular flow diagram does offer us a context within which to understand how the three basic questions are faced up to in the capitalist model.

What?

1. What goods? *Households 'vote' with money for goods and services desired.*

How?

2. How? *Competitive forces exert pressures on firms to produce goods and services as efficiently as possible. Competition regulates profits which are the driving force for firms.*

For Whom?

3. For whom? *Goods and services are obtained by those with money available.*

Each of these three 'answers' in the pure capitalist model raise many fascinating issues. Is it really true that households possess consumer sovereignty or are they persuaded to buy goods and services that they do not really want as a result of successful advertising by firms? Does the capitalist model really contain such

money – **barter** – where we exchange goods for goods, or services for goods, or services for services.

Bartering has been around a long time. However, it requires a double coincidence of wants between two individuals or businesses.

Suppose that you make frying-pans and I make shoes. I decide I want a frying-pan. If you, at the same time, want shoes, then we can probably make a barter exchange. Suppose, though, that you want a couple of new hats. I must go and find someone who wants some shoes in exchange for some hats. When I finally get the hats, then perhaps I can exchange them for your frying-pans.

The time involved in this process is tremendous compared to the facility with which exchange takes place when money is used. Money is thus one of the most important inventions of man. It has existed in many forms, such as shells, pieces of metal, cigarettes, and more recently, paper money. The essential characteristic that it must have in order to facilitate exchange

---

> *Key Points 2.3*
>
> ▶ **Money is any generally accepted medium of exchange. It facilitates exchange and thereby allows for increased specialization.**

strong competitive pressures to which firms are responsive? How fair is such a system when some households have more money than others? These questions raise some normative questions which we cannot ignore. Before considering these we can note some value-free or positive observations of the circular flow model.

Limitations in Simple Circular Flow Models

Of course, the model of the monetary economy given in Figure 2.1 is an extreme simplification of the workings of capitalism. For example, it has the following shortcomings:

1. Nothing is said about transactions or exchanges that occur within the business sector and within the household sector. The whole distribution chain between manufacturers of intermediate parts is ignored, as is the chain of events that goes from manufacturer to wholesaler to retailer. For example, the model ignores the many steps it takes for a motor car to get to market. It ignores the selling of car tyres and other components to the car assembly firms. The latter sell vehicles to car distributors and retailers before consumers make their decisions on the purchase of a car.
2. The model makes no mention of the economic role of government which does, of course, tax and spend, as well as regulate. In a purely capitalist world, we would have a self-regulated economy in which the government's role would be minor anyway. In a more complete model of our actual economy the role of government cannot be ignored.
3. The model assumes our monetary economy is one that has no dealings with any other economic system. There is no international trade or any other transactions such as tourism. It is a **closed economy** which is clearly not a picture of a real-life capitalist economic system or **open economy**.
4. Nothing is said about how resources and products come into existence and at what prices they are sold. That is the job of supply and demand analysis and also requires an explanation of our pricing system, which is explained in a later chapter.

You should also note that there is nothing shown in the model relating to what happens to that part of money income of households which is not spent on goods but in fact saved. Neither is it suggested how firms create and expand their production systems so as to be able to offer goods for sale to consumers. Thus we need to comment on this further limitation on our simple model. This involves us in extending our consideration of the scarcity problem in the first chapter. We need to explain that there are in fact differences in the goods that are produced and that this has important implications over time for the growth rate of the economic system.

Scarcity Revisited

In Chapter 1 it was emphasized that productive resources are limited. Thus, we must make choices about how we use them. We have to decide how much of which goods we will produce with our resources. For our purposes here, there will be only two choices: those goods that we consume directly, called **consumer goods** – food, clothes, cars – and those that we consume indirectly, called **capital goods** – machines and equipment. Everyone acts as a consumer in using consumer goods. On the other hand, capital goods, such as lathes, factories, and engines are used to make the consumer goods to which we just referred.

WHY WE MAKE CAPITAL GOODS

Why would we be willing to use productive resources to make things – capital goods – that we cannot consume directly? One of the reasons we use productive resources to make capital goods is that the latter enable us to produce larger quantities of consumer goods or to produce them more cheaply than we otherwise could. Before fish are produced for the market, fishing-boats and nets are first produced. Now imagine, for example, how expensive it would be to obtain fish for market without using these capital goods. Getting fish with one's hands is not an easy task. The price per fish would be very high if capital were not used.

FORGOING CURRENT CONSUMPTION

Whenever we use productive resources to make capital goods, we are implicitly forgoing current consumption. We are waiting for some time in the future to consume the fruits that will be reaped from the use of capital goods. Indeed, if we were to produce only consumer goods now and no capital goods, then our capacity to produce consumer goods in the future would suffer. Here we see a trade-off situation, one which lends itself to the sort of graphical analysis that we developed in Chapter 1.

THE TRADE-OFF BETWEEN CONSUMPTION GOODS AND CAPITAL GOODS

In order to have more consumer goods in the future, we must accept fewer consumer goods today. With the resources that we do not use to produce consumer goods for today, we invest in capital goods that will produce more consumer goods for us later. The trade-off is depicted in Figure 2.2. On the left-hand diagram of panel (a), you can see this trade-off depicted as a production possibilities curve between capital goods and consumption goods. If we decide to use all our resources to produce goods and services for consumption today, we can produce £2 million worth per year, which is represented as point B. In this extreme case, using all out productive resources for only consumption goods leads to no future growth.

Figure 2.2
Capital Goods and Growth

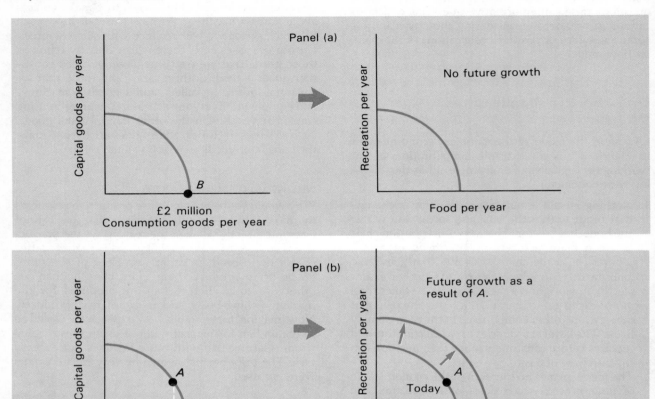

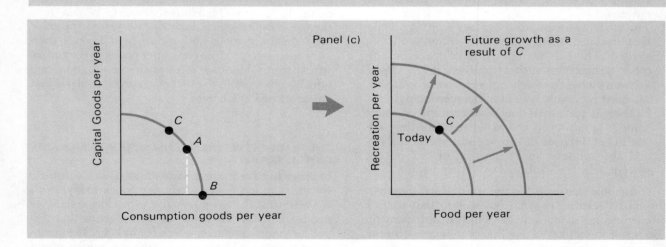

Now assume, however, that we are willing to give up, say, £200 000 worth of consumption today. We will be at point A in the left-hand diagram of panel (b). This will allow the economy to grow. We will have more future consumption because we invested in more capital goods today. In the right-hand diagram of panel (b), we see two goods represented – food and recreation. The production possibilities curve will

move outwards if we collectively decide to restrict consumption each year and invest in capital goods – that is, if we agree to be at point A.

In panel (c), we show the result of our willingness to forgo quite a bit more current consumption. We move to point C, where we have many fewer consumer goods today, but produce a lot more capital goods. This leads to more future growth in this simplified model,

---

Key Points 2.4

▶ Consumer goods are used directly by consumers.

▶ Capital goods are the means by which consumer goods are produced and are not directly used by consumers.

▶ The use of capital requires using productive resources to produce capital goods that in turn will later produce consumer goods.

▶ A trade-off is involved between current consumption and capital goods, or alternatively, between current consumption and future consumption, because the more we invest in capital goods today, the greater the amount of consumer goods we can produce in the future.

---

and thus the production possibilities curve in the right-hand side of panel (c) shifts outwards more than it did in the right-hand side of panel (b).

In other words, the more we give up today, the more we can have tomorrow.

In the light of the above the issue is thus as follows: will a capitalist system based on self-interest prefer the present rather than the future? Could a more centralized economic system secure a faster rate of economic growth than the capitalist system? How might this be? It is because consumer preferences are regulated in a command economy. So it is easier to effect a sacrifice of current consumption in favour of the production of capital goods. This bias in favour of capital goods may ultimately mean more consumption goods but not till quite some time in the future. It is this trade-off that we will consider in the next chapter, which looks at the command economy.

CASE STUDY

'All Change in Toy Town'

Once upon a time – and not so long ago – Britain had an efficient industry. Technically it was the wonder of the world; it exported its products to the ends of the earth in ever-increasing quantities, even to countries which prided themselves on producing the goods themselves. The firms involved were a happy mixture of old-established and world-renowned names, new native entrepreneurs, and refugees from Europe giving Britain the benefit of their inherited knowledge. All was for the best in the best of all possible worlds; and since the industry was toys, the world itself had a fantasy ring about it.

From Germany, the traditional home of quality toy-makers had come the Ullmanns and the Katzes of Mettoy, and the Ehrmanns of Airfix; the traditional English values

were worthily represented by the Lines Bros, whose own Triang tricycles had recently been reinforced when they took Meccano and Hornby Dublo under their capacious wing. Among new native entrepreneurs were the men of Lesney, with their die-cast revolution.

But this Christmas they are no longer happy; they are contemplating the cost of a tidal wave. For a few years ago the Americans came.

Now everyone knows that, in theory, there are enormous benefits from US investment. It sharpens competition, so the theory goes, it increases the range of goods available, it wakes up sleepy local manufacturers, it provides a good general tonic, leading, in the long run, to the profitable survival of the fittest,

both among the invaders and the native entrepreneurs. For all I know this is actually true in other industries (though the native British car makers) were pretty dozy for the 40 years after General Motors and Ford arrived here). But in toys the coming of the Americans, especially the all-conquering Mattel Corporation, has been an unmitigated disaster all round.

Pre-Mattel the toy industry had an atmosphere all its own. There was a genuine pride in the workmanship involved in the Corgis, the Matchbox toys, the Airfix kits, and a real desire to give proper value for money.

The Americans changed all that. They wanted to make toys into a fashion-conscious industry; to do so involved the latest marketing techniques, starting with a hard

continued overleaf

sell through TV of your Cindys, your Hot Wheels, your dreadful, dreadful Action Men. To maintain the momentum you pushed the wretched retailers to fit in with the marketing techniques used in other countries and in other industries: stocks to be taken on regularly, paid for early, displayed to a rigid formula. Out went the lengthy credit usual in the trade; out went all recognition that these shops would only sell at Christmas, so could not pay much until afterwards.

These techniques worked – for a time. The trade had, after all, been rather sloppy; manufacturers had allowed too much credit, produced too many varieties. They had shrunk from selling on TV. They were angry but they had to respond in kind to the Americans. And, worst of all, they had to listen to outsiders telling them how good it was for them to have their sleepy old industry woken up by a fresh transatlantic breeze. Their pleas – that their way had been profitable, that they were the envy of the world, selling mechanical toys to the Germans, cheap precision toys to the Japanese, and hordes of everything to the Americans –

went unheard. From being everyone's favourite industry, and the stock market's darlings, they fell from grace to become yet another seemingly shaky corner of our national industrial fabric. No one, not even the invaders themselves, made much money.

The most famous name of all, Lines Bros, actually went broke; the lame duck fell to the nursery floor with a prolonged clatter and the greedy children hovered round grabbing bits of it to add to their own collection. Others, the Lesneys and the Mettoys, barely staggered through the crisis. Elsewhere there were great regroupings, and outsiders, financiers like John Bentley, moved in, boys barely old enough to have put away their toy trains, too young even to remember the *Meccano Magazine*.

Ironically, the worst victim of this state of chaos is probably the invader which started the rout. Mattel, faced with a consumer revolt at home against its hard-sell approach and reporting losses for the first time after decades of fast growth, is cutting back, moving in this country into smaller premises and not advertising quite so

furiously. With a sigh of relief, other companies are following suit.

The American tide seems to be receding – none of the American companies has yet picked up any of the Lines companies for instance. But the Americans leave behind a sadder and a wiser industry, nursing its bruises, contemplating its shrunken numbers of products, its narrower profit margins; its new, irksome cost controls, with their restriction on developing hundreds of new products. What they do *not* leave behind is an industry aware that it has had good done to it by an invigorating outside influence.

Source: Nicholas Faith, 'How the Americans Took the Fun out of Toys', *Sunday Times*, 12 Dec. 1971.

Questions
1. In what ways does the above article illustrate the operation of a free enterprise system?
2. The article makes no reference to government intervention in the toy industry. Does this surprise you?
3. What are your impressions about the nature of competition between toy manufacturers at the present time?

Exam Preparation and Practice

INTRODUCTORY EXERCISES

1. List the main characteristics of a capitalist economy.

2. Some critics believe and have attacked consumer sovereignty as non-existent in economies like that of the USA and the UK. List the possible reasons that consumer sovereignty might not exist.

MUTIPLE CHOICE QUESTIONS

1. The following question is based on the production possibility curve illustrated below.

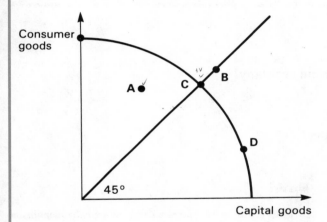

Which of the points (**A, B, C** or **D**) would be *most* likely to lead to the fastest rate of economic growth in the next time-period?

2. In most modern societies the price mechanism plays some part in the distribution of resources. This means that

   A prices are always held stable

   ✓**B** rising prices of some goods encourage production of them, so diverting resources to them, and vice versa

   C prices are entirely determined by the cost of production

   D the price system could not work in societies that did not use some universally recognized form of money

   E prices are bound to rise

†3. Which of the following statements is *untrue* about the operation of a wholly capitalist economy?

   A the price mechanism allocates resources

   B households freely decide how to spend on goods and services

   ✓**C** there is government intervention in price determination

   D consumer sovereignty exists

   E all decisions are assumed to be made in a rational manner

4. The term 'consumer sovereignty' means that in a capitalist economy

   A consumers have a great deal more economic power than do producing firms simply because they are so much greater in number

   B each consumer knows what is good for him or her and they are all fully aware of available consumption possibilities

   C each consumer is like a medieval monarch being able to ensure that he or she gets what they want through being able to purchase an unlimited quantity of a good at the prevailing market price

   ✓**D** consumers are responsible for determining the nature of economic activity as determined by their demands, as backed by money, on manufacturers and producers

5. The essence of a market economy is that

   A fruit and vegetables are commonly sold in open markets in many large towns

   B manufacturers sell a restricted variety of goods

   C the costs incurred by manufacturers in advertising their goods is not generally considered to be too high

   ✓**D** resource allocation is effected by a set of signals which link buyers and sellers

RELATED ESSAY QUESTION

How does a market economy decide what to produce, how to produce, and for whom to produce?

3 Economic Systems: The Command Economy

Key Points to Review

▶ Capitalism (2.1)
▶ What, how, for whom to produce? (2.2)

▶ The trade-off between consumption goods and capital goods (2.4)

Questions for Preview

1 What are the characteristics of a socialist command economy?

2 What is Marxian economics?

3 What problems face socialist command economies?

Capitalism is not the only theoretical model of an economic system that exists. The polar extreme alternative to 'pure' capitalism, from a theoretical point of view, is an economic system of a command economy.

Command Economy

The central issues in a **command economy** again relate to who should have the property rights to all non-labour productive resources, who should make decisions about the use of these goods, and how income should be distributed once it is created. We can once more consider how the three fundamental questions facing any society are resolved in a command economy in direct contrast to the market economy.

What? How? For Whom? – in a Command Economy

What?

1. What goods? *In the command economy the decentralized decision-making process is replaced by the collective preferences of the central planners.*

How?

2. How? *The central planners decide on not only quantities of output but also appropriate methods of production. They have to co-ordinate all aspects of productive activity through an organized system of resource allocation.*

For Whom?

3. For whom? *The forces that determine the relative rewards people get from producing are set by the central planners not by the market. Thus market forces are not given full expression to determine wage-rates.*

The Political Dimension

Too often the command economy is seen as synonymous with a socialist or communist system. This is quite wrong as a right-wing dictatorship could also operate a command economy. It is thus misleading to attach a political label to the two contrasting types of economic system. Concern about political control, i.e. how democratic is a society, is, strictly speaking, a separate issue from that of economic control. A socialist system could be a democratic society when the key government officials making decisions about the use of resources are elected in genuine elections, i.e. where there is a choice of candidates facing electors. A socialist system could also come under the political control of a dictator just as in a capitalist system.

Having confronted the political dimension in our discussion we now briefly distinguish between **socialism** and **communism**.

Socialism

In a 'pure' socialist system the state owns the major non-labour productive resources – land and capital goods. Individuals can own consumer goods and consumer durables, but they are not allowed to own factories, machines, and other things that are used to produce what society wants. Second, people are induced to produce by wage differentials. However, taxation of large incomes to redistribute income may reduce some of the incentives to produce as much. Third, the state determines people's wage-rates and who should be paid what in government-owned and –operated factories. Fourth, individuals are allowed to enter only certain areas of activity. They cannot, for example, freely set up their own factories. They cannot become entrepreneurs or capitalists, for the state has this function and controls all enterprises.

Communism

With 'pure' communism all resources are, in principle, owned in common. What then about the role of the state? Here we turn to Karl Marx (1818–83) who perhaps more than anyone else in the history of economic thought is responsible for the development of the communist movement.

Marx envisaged the fall of capitalism leading to the rise of socialism and eventually to the world of ideal communism. Marx foresaw a final state where the relations of production and distribution would be: 'From each according to his ability, to each according to his needs.' In fact, in the ideal communist world that Marx predicted would eventually emerge, there would be little or no need for government. Everything would take care of itself, for man's basic human nature would have been changed because the relations of

production and distribution would no longer create class conflict and alienation would not occur.

Having now made this summary explanation of socialism and communism we must not lose sight of the important point made earlier. Neither socialism nor communism are theoretically necessary features of a command economy. None the less it is true that in practice socialism is the main political system under which most command economies are administered. This being so we need briefly to examine the case for socialism put forward by critics of the market economy.

Marxian Economics

What was it about the market economy to which Marx objected? Basically he saw a conflict existing between the capitalist class and those they employed as labourers. The capitalists were regarded as exploiting their workers and also possessing considerable market and political power. Marx rejected the notion that the capitalists meekly responded to the wishes of consumers. In their long-term struggle to survive the capitalists were seen by Marx as trying to cut the costs of production by mechanizing production, i.e. reducing employment. Rising unemployment would eventually provoke the development of class consciousness among workers and the capitalist order be overthrown.

The Marxian critique of the market economy is, inevitably, the subject of continuing debate. The revolutionary ideology he offered makes him the subject of much study by social scientists. What can we offer here in a brief but carefully couched response to his picture of capitalism as a historically limited form of economic system?

A first comment is that Marx was essentially a critic of capitalism rather than an architect of the ideal communist world that he thought would ultimately emerge. Because of this he is open to criticism concerning how such an economy should actually be organized. In particular the immense problems facing the central planners in a socialist command economy were played down. The central planners have to make

---

Key Points 3.1

▶ We can simplify the different types of economic systems by looking at them in terms of decentralization. Pure market capitalism would be on one end of the scale, pure command socialism on the other.

▶ The key attributes of socialism are: (1) The government owns the major productive resources. (2) People are induced to produce by wage differentials, but taxation is often used to redistribute income, thereby reducing some incentive to produce. (3) The rewards for producing are usually set by the state rather than the market. (4) Individuals can enter only certain areas of activity and cannot, for example, freely set up their own factories.

KARL MARX
GERMAN ECONOMIST (1818–1883)

Ghost of Western Economics

Marx was more than an economist. He was a revolutionary who was instrumental in developing the communist movement, a sociologist, and a historian. He marshalled all these talents for his analysis of capitalism and the ways in which this economic system affected social life. According to Marx (and his frequent collaborator Friedrich Engels), history is the struggle for power of competing classes based on their material interests in the production process. Unlike most economists since the time of Adam Smith, Marx saw capitalism as a specific and historically limited form of social organization. The internal dynamics of capitalism, he argued, would eventually create conditions ripe for its overthrow by the working class and the institution of a new form of social organization based on collective ownership.

Marx was a prolific writer, but the culminating work of his career is undoubtedly *Das Kapital*, the first volume of which appeared in 1867. In this gigantic text, Marx set out to do nothing less, he said, than 'to lay bare the economic law of motion of modern society'. Like Adam Smith and David Ricardo, Marx adhered to

the labour theory of value – the theory that the value of commodities ultimately depends on the human labour time expended in their production. But to explain how profits could be generated in a society built on equivalent exchanges of commodities and money, Marx added a new concept – *surplus value*. Under capitalism, labour power is treated as a commodity like any other; workers are paid according to the cost of their reproduction and maintenance. But workers in fact can produce an equivalent to their subsistence in only part of a working day. The difference between the labour time workers spend producing for a capitalist and the labour

time equivalent to the wages they actually receive Marx called *surplus value*. Here, he argued, was a scientific index of exploitation.

But it was, Marx argued, the workers who would get the last laugh. Capitalists, faced with competition, are continually driven to expand and mechanize production, thus eliminating some labour costs. But since labour is the ultimate source of value, capitalists, in effect, are cutting their own throats. Over the long term, Marx argued, the rate of profit would fall, while at the same time more and more people would be left without jobs. Through a combination of economic crises of increasing severity and the development of class consciousness among workers, capitalism would finally collapse.

The capitalist economic system appeared to break down partially in the 1930s depression, but Marx had not considered the possibility of Keynesian intervention by the state. Furthermore, the rate of profit has not fallen in the way he expected. But if the Marxian vision of capitalist breakdown has not taken place, Marx's analysis of the workings of capitalism contains many insights, some of which have only begun to be appreciated in the non-communist nations.

decisions concerning production targets and ensure that the necessary inputs be available in the right place and at the right time to make meeting such targets actually possible. This requires an effective organizational structure or bureaucracy to exist. As regards the labour input the socialist economy requires some sort of incentive (moral or by way of threat) to exist for people to become fully involved in the economic process. Critics of the socialist economy have thus doubted whether a mixture of patriotic exhortation and brute fear are an effective substitute for the self-interest motivation on which the capitalist system is based.

As in the case of capitalism the extreme form of central planning is a stylized description that has no counterpart in the real world. Even the USSR does not correspond to a pure command economy because in

recent years there has been a greater use of market prices and profitability to allocate resources. None the less if we look at the experience of central planning in the USSR it should give us some evidence on how a basically socialist economy has performed.

The Growth of the Soviet Economy after 1917

The most influential disciple of Marxist ideology has been Vladimir Ilyich Lenin. His Bolsheviks came to power in Russia in 1917 soon after the overthrow of the Russian monarchy. Lenin did not immediately get rid of all capitalist institutions in Russia. His New Economic Policy (NEP) allowed small industry and trade to be privately owned. In the agricultural sector, forced requisitions were eliminated – the peasants no longer had to give away any products to the government or the army. The market was once again used. Peasant farmers found it profitable to sow fallow land in order to sell the crops. Only heavy industry, transportation, foreign trade, and banking remained in government hands. In retrospect, the NEP was a success. By 1928, industry and agricultural production surpassed pre-revolutionary war levels. In 1924, however, Lenin had died; Stalin his successor decided to take the 'several steps forward' that Lenin had promised.

Stalin did not like the inability of central authorities to control the direction of the economy, which was the result of Lenin's having allowed so much of the economy to revert to private hands. Stalin felt that there were certain industries that should be treated favourably in order to get the economy growing rapidly. Thus, a course of economic development *in advance* was plotted in **five-year plans**. These plans were called five-year plans because they plotted a course of economic activity for the following five years. Special industries were picked for growth, which was to be 'financed' by obtaining more agricultural produce to feed urban industrial workers. In order to obtain more agricultural products, collectivization was to be the key. Between 1928 and 1932, over 15 million peasant households were formed into over 200 000 collective farms. On the collectives, land and livestock were owned in common – that is, they were not private property. Land was also worked in common, since no one person owned it, and a system of wage-payments to collective farmers was introduced. Communist Party control over the peasant was strengthened.

Agricultural collectivization was not an overwhelming success. Peasants slaughtered and then ate, sold, or traded much of their livestock rather than turn it over to the collectives. At the end of the first five-year plan, the number of livestock had fallen by half. Grain output also fell, perhaps because of the reduced incentive to produce but partly because of the problems of instituting collectives at the onset. None the less, at the point of a gun more agricultural products flowed from the country to the city, and that was in fact the major objective of the first five-year plan. Clearly, since agricultural output had fallen, with more going to the city, much less was left for the peasants.

Capital Goods and Growth

In Chapter 2 we showed that there was a trade-off between current consumption and future consumption. If you turn back to Figure 2.2 you will see how we showed with the use of the production possibility curve that the more we invest in capital goods the more likely it is that the economy will grow so as to allow greater consumption by households in the future. The Russian economy after 1928 illustrates this trade-off. There was a marked increase in the proportion of resources devoted to the production of capital goods. Whereas in 1928 investment accounted for about 15 per cent of all output, by 1937 it had doubled. Under the first five-year plan there was a massive development of heavy industry and the output of the coal, steel, and electricity industries increased very rapidly. If one realizes that at that time well over 80 per cent of the Russian population was rural-based, then one can appreciate the massive emphasis placed on rapid industrialization. The second and third five-year plans continued the emphasis on capital goods and since too the Russian leadership developed an enthusiasm for defence expenditure there was a reduced share of resources left available for production of consumption goods. It was indeed machinery and guns rather than butter. Any hope by the Russian peasant of more consumption tomorrow was counteracted by conscious actions by the state to lower current consumption standards. The preference for capital equipment and military goods meant that for many Russians a major improvement in the material standard of living was denied them. The Russian economy indeed grew impressively between 1928 and 1937 but decisions on the quantity, quality, and variety of goods for private consumption were not made by consumers but by the central planners. Thus there is a problem in appraising the 'success' of the Russian approach to development in the inter-war period.

We have looked back to the inter-war period in Russia to consider the decision of the central planners concerning the question *what goods are to be produced?* Our next question, you will recall, was *how are these to be produced?* This makes it necessary to explain what 'the planners' means.

The Soviet Economy Today

Figure 3.1 shows central planning for industry in the Soviet Union. At the top is the Presidium, which is the administrative body of the Soviet government. The Presidium delegates authority to the Council of Ministers, which establishes broad goals for the economy – such as what proportion of available resources should be devoted to consumer goods, what percentage to producer goods, what percentage to military goods. Once these goals have been established, the State Planning Commission (Gosplan) must then decide how the goals are to be achieved. The Gosplan generates production targets for each particular industry and also decides where the output of each industry will go. Next, the planners in each of the fifteen republics within the Soviet Union apply the Gosplan's decisions to their jurisdiction.

These plans are then forwarded to regional planning councils, who assign production targets and allocate resources to specific industries. The final level in this planning hierarchy are the plant managers. They can affect planning by asking the regional

Figure 3.1
Central Planning for Industry in the Soviet Union

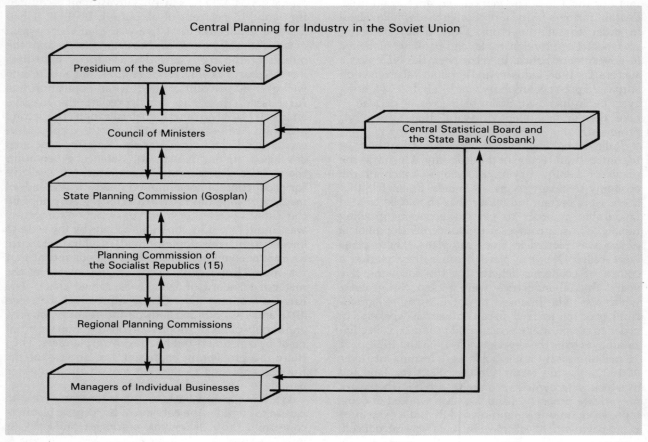

Central Planning for Industry in the Soviet Union

councils for lower or higher production quotas and by demanding greater resources.

This complex planning system does have some checks and balances. Each level is responsible to, and supervised by, the level above it. Gosplan is also the official government banking system so it can verify all receipts and expenditures and discover fraud and corruption.

The central statistical board evaluates businesses in terms of their abilities to meet quotas and reports its findings to the Council of Ministers. Communist Party officials oversee the operation of actual factories. Union officials represent management (the government), not the workers. These unions encourage workers and businesses to meet their quotas and to handle the numerous welfare programmes for workers.

The problem of incentives in a socialist economy has already been mentioned. Soviet experience shows that there are numerous problems in setting quotas for plant managers. Forcing plant managers to meet quotas sometimes contributes to the poor quality of the goals produced. Quotas are typically measured in the number of units produced, or by weight or volume – not by quality. Pressure to meet quotas has also encouraged the rise of a black economy which involves

illegal transactions – such as bartering for supplies among plant managers, buying supplies on the black market, and bribing government officials to reduce quotas or change allocations.

Some students of the Soviet system argue that quotas have kept managers from experimenting with new production techniques for fear of not meeting their quotas. This presumed unwillingness to develop and use technology could in principle have caused the Soviet economy to fall further behind Western nations in its ability to produce. Some experts have claimed that the Soviet Union is many years behind in production techniques in many vital industries.

There is a relatively small but important part of the Russian economy that is not illegal, but it is not part of the centralized command economy. It involves the legal production of crops and the maintenance of livestock on small, 'private' plots of land. The plots are not actually private, but the individuals who are allowed to use them can more or less sell their output in a free market. These farms are usually less than an acre in size. The people cultivating them are typically moonlighting from their farming or factory jobs. Estimates of the total amount of 'private' plots range from 1 to 3 per cent of all Soviet farm land. Estimates of the output of these private plots range from a low

---

Key Points 3.2

▶ In Russia after 1928 there was less production of goods to satisfy consumer wants. More production went into capital formation.

▶ Heavy industry grew rapidly. Collectivization of agriculture resulted in lower food production.

▶ In any command economy, there are problems of co-ordination among different sectors. Millions of planning decisions must be made, and they are all interrelated. The Russian planning system is thus not surprisingly complex.

---

of 20 to a high of 33 per cent of the total value of agricultural output. In other words, the productivity per acre on these plots has been estimated at about forty times that of the collectively farmed acreage.

In addition to agriculture, there is a legal 'second'

economy in some services. For example, Soviet doctors who, by definition, work for the state are allowed to treat patients at home for a fee. The government sets the fee and taxes it heavily thus curbing this use of time by state doctors.

CASE STUDY

Checkmate and Win a Dacha

Anatoly Karpov, the chess star, has a car telephone in his chauffeur-driven limousine.

All members of the élite in the sporting world, the arts, and above all in the Kremlin bureaucracy enjoy carefully graded privileges to which the ordinary Soviet worker can never hope to aspire. Karpov's car telephone puts him in the superstar bracket, but even middle-ranking officials and celebrities can expect to get a Moscow flat larger than the usual cramped allocation of five or six square metres per person (the official figure is nine metres minimum), a place at the head of the long waiting-list for a car, as well as access to top health care and to the best schools and colleges.

They also get a government-provided country home, or *dacha*. All Russians love to retreat to a *dacha* in the beautiful countryside around Moscow, but the definition of a *dacha* can range from a dilapidated garden shed for the lower orders to a magnificent mansion screened by discreet birch

trees and security fences for the cultural and political élite.

Karpov, who is judged to have earned his privileged status by conquering the world of chess, is building an £80,000 *dacha* outside the city, and has an Audi 100 for his personal use as well as his official car. One prominent musician recently acquired a palatial country house which formerly belonged to a KGB general and which, like other élite *dachas*, is set in a closed area rarely penetrated by either foreigners or ordinary Russians.

The extraordinary aspect of all this to a Western mind is that working-class Muscovites fighting their way on to crammed buses or standing in long queues in the snow for scarce foodstuffs do not seem to resent this hidden privilege in the least. They are aware that those who govern them, from the President downwards, have access to special shops and even Western goods.

The official Marxist-Leninist ideology, hammered home every

day in the press and media, professes egalitarianism and social justice. Yet most Russians seem to accept fatalistically that abuse of power and humiliation by officialdom are inevitable, possibly because this has been so since Tsarist times.

The Tsar's ministers used to drive their carriages at speed down the middle of the city's avenues, scattering the *hoi polloi* to right and left, much as today's Kremlin Zils thunder down the middle lane pushing mere mortals to either side.

Although there is no overt resentment of official privilege, condemnation of the abuse of such privilege does occasionally surface in the Soviet press and at party meetings. The late Yuri Andropov's stern drive against official abuses won him widespread popular approval, and the late Konstantin Chernenko continued to attack corruption, noting that it caused 'profound anger' among the masses.

One female lathe-operator from

continued overleaf

Rostov-on-Don recently wrote to *Komsomolskaya Pravda* to complain that her monthly wage of 200 roubles (£200) had little purchasing power.

'I understand that our society cannot yet afford for everyone to dress well and fashionably', she wrote. 'But the point is that those who deserve them should receive the most benefits, and by that I mean the workers.'

There is little sign, however, of privilege being reduced – if anything the reverse. When, at the local Soviet elections, officials and their well-dressed wives turned up to vote in chauffeur-driven Chaikas, there was not a murmur of protest from the proletariat trudging through the ice and snow to the ballot-box.

The newest development, which again has aroused some public protest but is likely to go ahead anyway with full Kremlin approval, is the establishment of a series of luxury clothing stores for those with spare roubles, regardless of rank or status.

The new shops are to be for those who find the ordinary Soviet stores too drab.

It seems doubtful whether Lenin or Marx would have approved.

Source: R. Owen, 'Letter from Moscow: Lives of Luxury in the Land of Marx', *The Times*, 2 Apr. 1985.

Questions

1. In what ways does the above article suggest that life in Russia differs from the socialist model?
2. Are the departures from an egalitarian system (a) inevitable and (b) desirable?

CASE STUDY

Does the Man in the Russian Ministry Know Best?

The Soviet Union's new economic experiment, on which hangs hopes of a better economic performance, has been extended from the beginning of this year to 2 300 enterprises, responsible for 12 per cent of total industrial production, according to a senior Soviet official.

The experiment, first applied to five ministries at the beginning of 1984, gives the managers of individual enterprises greater responsibility for budgets, labour, wages, production, and contract fulfilment.

Among the aims of the reform is to link higher productivity and efficiency to increased wages. Managers will pay more attention to demand and there will be greater accountability for poor quality goods. Decentralized management is to be combined with more centralized planning at the very top. Individual ministries will lose some of their old authority, which they are resisting very strongly.

'Expanding the rights of enterprises means granting them some of the functions in planning and economic activity which were formerly the prerogative of senior officials of the ministry concerned,' said daily newspaper *Izvestia* recently. 'But ministry officials have been slow to relinquish petty tutelage of enterprises.'

Source: P. Cockburn, 'Soviet Union Extends Economic Experiment', *Financial Times*, 15 Feb. 1985.

Questions

1. How are the 2 300 enterprises supposed to perform better than previously?
2. Why is such an experiment in Russia necessarily difficult to introduce?

Exam Preparation and Practice

INTRODUCTORY EXERCISE

Suppose you are an economic planner and you have been told by your country's political leaders that they want to increase car production by 10 per cent over the previous year. What other industries will be affected by this decision? *tyre, steel, glass, leather*

MULTIPLE CHOICE QUESTIONS

1. Which one of the following statements is necessarily true of any centrally planned economy?

  A It cannot overcome the problem of economic scarcity, because it cannot use increases in the money supply to finance government expenditure.

  B It cannot overcome the problem of economic scarcity, because it will come up against the constraint of factor limitation. ✓

  C It can overcome the problem of economic scarcity by deciding what is to be produced, thus relieving the consumer of the problem of choice.

  D It can overcome the problem of economic scarcity by income redistribution from rich to poor. ✗

  E It can overcome the problem of scarcity by regulating the price mechanism. ✗

2. Which of the following statements is necessarily incorrect as a feature of a fully centrally planned economy?

  A Resources are directed by the price mechanism. ✓

  B Workers do not earn equal wages.

  C The profit motive is severely constrained.

  D There is a bureaucratic structure to take decisions about how the economy is organized.

One or more of the options given in Questions 3, 4, 5, and 6 may be correct. Select your answer by means of the code set out in the grid:

A	B	C	D
1,2,3 all correct	**1,2** only correct	**2,3** only correct	**1** only correct

3. A command economy is a term to describe an economic system which is
  1. state regulated   *B*
  2. decentralized
  3. motivated by self-interest

4. It would be incorrect to suggest that after the Russian Revolution
  1. the Russian economy was totally controlled by the state
  2. the Russian economy grew very slowly
  3. some elements of a market economy were reintroduced

5. In Russia collectivization of agriculture after 1928
  1. resulted in a rapid rise in agricultural output
  2. led to food shortages in rural areas
  3. was a policy favoured by Stalin

6. The Russian economy after 1928 illustrates the fact that
  1. there is a trade-off between current consumption and future consumption
  2. the central planners preferred capital equipment to consumer goods
  3. a complex planning system can experience major difficulties in operation

RELATED ESSAY QUESTIONS

1. Compare and contrast the principal economic characteristics of a free market with those of a planned economy.

2. 'A centrally planned economy has both advantages and disadvantages compared with a free market economy.' Discuss.

4 Economic Systems: The Mixed Economy

Key Points to Review

▶ Capitalism (2.1)

▶ Socialism (3.1)

Questions for Preview

1 How can economic systems be classified?

2 How do privately owned firms in the UK mixed economy differ from those of the pure capitalist type?

3 Why is the extent of state intervention in Western economies not easy to measure?

The two previous chapters have discussed two model economic systems – capitalism and the socialist command economy. In practice most countries around the world have an economic system neither purely capitalist nor purely of the socialist command type. They have a **mixed economic system** – that is a mixture of private decision-making and central organization. Private enterprise responding to market forces operates to a greater or lesser extent with some measure of state control and economic planning. In this chapter we show how the private sector and the state relate in some of the real world's mixed economic systems. We focus on the UK economy but include case material relating to China.

Looking at the Spectrum of Systems

One possible way of comparing several economic systems in the world is to look at them according to

how decentralized their decision-making processes are. In other words, to what degree do individuals make the decisions about what to produce, how to produce it, how much to produce, and for how much to sell it? In Figure 4.1 we have put on the extreme right-hand side of the scale pure free market capitalism, where all economic decisions are made by individuals without government intervention. On the extreme left-hand side of the scale, we have put pure command socialism, where economic decisions are made by some central authority such as a group of government planners or even a dictator. Somewhere in between would be the mixed economic systems such as those existing in the United States, France, the USSR, and the United Kingdom. Very broadly speaking the closer we go to a pure capitalist system, the less political centralization there is, and vice versa.

Albania is a country whose system is extremely centralized and relatively close to pure command socialism. On the other extreme is Hong Kong, which is virtually totally decentralized and relatively close to

---

Key Points 4.1

▶ In reality all economies are mixed economies or mixed systems since private markets, self-interest, state allocation of resources, income redistribution, and altruism exist to some degree in all societies.

Figure 4.1

Economic Systems: The Scale of Decentralization. On the extreme right-hand side of the diagram we find pure market capitalism, and on the extreme left-hand side is pure command socialism. Albania is a country whose system is extremely centralized and relatively close to pure command socialism. On the other extreme is Hong Kong, which is virtually totally decentralized and relatively close to pure market capitalism. In between are the mixed economies of the world, with varying degrees of government intervention and centralization, represented by their closeness to the left-hand side of the diagram.

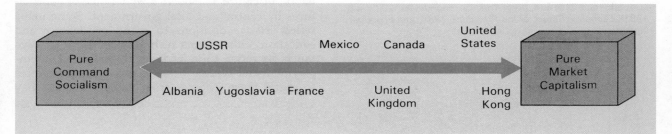

pure market capitalism. In between are the mixed economies of the world, with varying degrees of government intervention and centralization, represented by their closeness to the left-hand side of the diagram. You will note Figure 4.1 has no scale. This highlights the very real problem of actually measuring the absolute differences between the countries shown of their overall public/private sector mixture.

The United States

If we had to place the US economic system somewhere within the spectrum of economic systems ranging from pure capitalism to pure command socialism it would have to be put closer to the former system than the latter. But it has tended through the years towards

Figure 4.2

Government Spending in the US. Here we show government *purchases* at all levels – federal, state, and local – of goods and services expressed as a percentage of total national output, or gross national product. (See dictionary for these items.) The biggest jumps occurred during the First World War and the Second World War; although, proportionally, government spending fell dramatically after the Second World War, it did not remain at previous peacetime levels for long.
Source: Economic Report of the President and Economic Indicators.

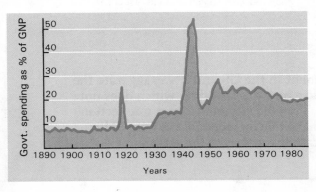

one in which the government plays an ever more influential role. The role of government in the US economic system has expanded greatly, especially since World War II. When we speak of government in the US – federal, state, and local – we are referring to the collective total of all individuals who, in one way or another, are paid out of tax revenue and who regulate private transactions. This regulatory activity means that apart from the cost of employing persons in the service of the US government there is cost of providing appropriate tools and equipment for them to go about their work. The business of government is thus costly. Figure 4.2 shows the growth in government spending in the US as a percentage of the gross national product in the period since 1890.

Not only does government directly control an important share of the US economy, but it has entered into many aspects of hitherto private economic dealings. For example, it has stepped in to help out (subsidize) certain industries, e.g. loan guarantees to Lockheed and Chrysler, or to tax others, e.g. a windfall profits tax on oil companies. As another example, the US government has put many restrictions on the working of the agricultural sector. Additionally, through its many departments and agencies, the government controls numerous aspects of energy, transportation, communication, and commerce in general. In the last several decades, the government has increased its welfare programmes – tax dollars are redistributed to those who are deemed 'needy'. Education has become primarily a government activity but the desirability of state intervention in medical care continues to be a politically contentious issue. The business of modern government in the US is thus complex and much debated. Furthermore, the extent of government involvement in the economy is not simply revealed by the size of government spending as shown in Figure 4.2. Apart from hiring staff and purchasing equipment the US government is also engaged in making **transfer payments**. Part of government tax revenues are used to make payments to some citizens in the form of cash and other welfare benefits. If these transfer payments are now included

Figure 4.3

Government Spending in the US (including Transfers) as a Percentage of Gross National Product. Taking account of all government outlays, including transfer payments, shows an increasing trend for government outlays as a percentage of GNP.

Source: Derived from *Facts and Figures on Government Finance,* 20th edn. and 21st edn. (New York Tax Foundation, 1979 and 1981); *Economic Report of the President, 1984;* and *Economic Indicators.*

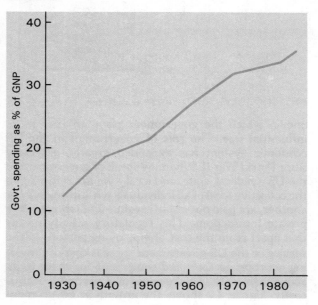

as part of all government spending we then find there is an upward trend in the proportion of GNP accounted for by all aspects of government.

Figure 4.3 shows how total government expenditures in the US have accounted for a growing share of all spending on goods and services.

The United Kingdom

Broadly speaking there has been a similar growth in the scale of government activity in most other developed economies as in the US economy during the past fifty years. The extent of this influence of the state would seem to be based on whatever is the size of the **public sector**. As we have shown in the case of the US the public sector can be defined as the part of the

economy that falls within the domain of central (or federal) government plus local (or provincial) government.

Figure 4.4 shows the size of public expenditure in the UK for 1983–4. However, we must treat these figures with great caution in viewing them as a measure of the influence of the state. Careful examination of Figure 4.4 shows a wide range of expenditures by central and local government. Some items reflect *collective* decisions to spend on defence and education. Other items such as social security leave much discretion to individuals. Recipients of unemployment and sickness benefits are, within limits, able to spend these incomes from government as they

Figure 4.4

Public Expenditure in the UK (Financial Year 1984-5)

	£bn
Social security	38.1
Defence	17.2
Health and personal social services	15.8
Education and science	14.0
Trade and industry, energy and employment	7.8
Scotland	7.0
Home Office	5.0
Transport	4.6
Northern Ireland	4.0
Other environmental services	4.0
Housing	3.2
Overseas aid and other services	2.7
Other departments	2.7
Wales	2.6
Agriculture, fisheries, food and forestry	2.1
Arts and libraries	0.7
Adjustments	
Special sales of assets	−2.1
Total	**129.6**

Source: Economic Progress Report, No. 182, Jan. 1986, p. 7.

Notes
1. The sales of assets refers to the privatization of publicly owned assets (see Chapter 29).
2. In addition to the total shown the UK government also incurred spending on debt interest of £15.6bn.

Key Points 4.2

▶ Public expenditure by all forms of government in the US and UK exaggerate the influence of the state because the total figure includes spending which does not involve any claims on economic resources. Transfer payments from one section of society to another by government should not be included in a list of public expenditure programmes intended to indicate the extent of the state's interference in a pure market economy.

wish. Thus Figure 4.4 cannot be used as an unambiguous measure of 'the state's influence' and by implication, of the weakening of individual freedom of choice. The important point, which is not a subjective matter, is that when governments redistribute money from one section of society to another in the form of *transfer payments*, they do not add to the sum of expenditures which involve collective decision-making. In other words public expenditure includes both some spending which involves a claim on economic resources available and also other spending which involves

government acting as a giant redistribution agency. In this latter case resources are *not* diverted from the private sector in favour of the state. This matter is considered further in Chapter 10.

We see that in 1984–5 social security accounted for the largest single element in government expenditure. Over £13 billion was spent by government in each of three other areas of expenditure – defence, health, and education. In Figure 4.5 we show the UK government's spending plans for the financial year 1985–6. It reveals clearly the significance of the state in effecting transfer payments. The sum involved in 1985–6 was expected to be well in excess of the total cost of wages and salaries for those working in the public sector. Having just touched on the cost to government of those in its employ we should establish what are the numbers of men and women obtaining employment in the public sector. With roughly 24 million in employment in 1984 the UK had some 6.8 million within the public sector. Just under one-third of these were engaged in market activity, the rest in the production of services such as the Army where market prices played little or no role in resource allocation. Figure 4.6 which shows employment by sector in 1984 makes clear that local authorities employed more people than did central government.

Figure 4.5

Planned Public Spending for 1985-6: Where, Who, and What (percentages)

This three-dimensional diagram shows planned spending by spending authority, programme, and economic category. Central government is the major spending authority and social security accounts for the biggest single programme of spending. The significance of transfer payments as a category of spending is evident being greater than the labour costs of those involved in central and local government.

Source: Economic Progress Report, No. 174, Jan. 1985, p 8.

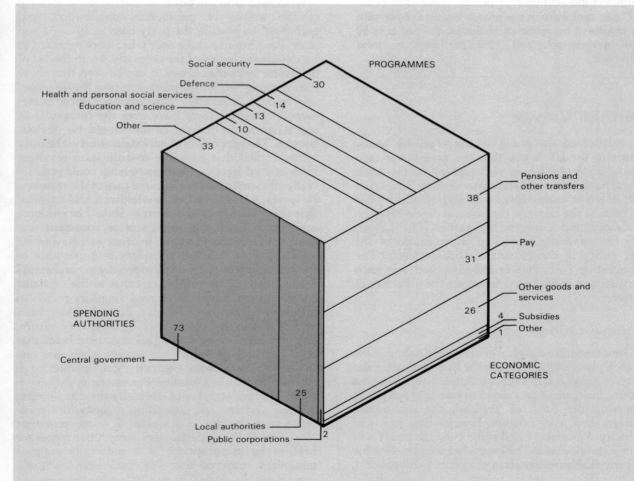

	Numbers employed at mid-year (000s)		Changes in numbers employed mid-year (000s) 1978 to 1984	Percentage change
	1978	*1984*		
Total employed labour force	24 999	23 979	−1 020	− 4.1
Private sector	17 668	17 149	− 519	− 2.9
Public sector	7 331	6 830	− 501	− 6.8
Public corporations	2 061	1 611	− 450	−21.8
General government	5 270	5 219	− 51	− 1.0
Central government	2 338	2 335	− 3	− 0.1
HM Forces	318	326	+ 8	+ 2.5
National Health Service	1 120	1 223	+ 103	+ 9.2
Other	900	786	− 114	−12.7
Local authorities	2 932	2 884	− 48	− 1.6
Education	1 512	1 430	− 82	− 5.4
Social services	334	368	+ 34	+10.2
Police	170	187	+ 17	+10.0
Other	916	899	− 17	− 1.9

Source: Department of Employment

Figure 4.6
United Kingdom Employed Labour Force: by Sector. In mid-1984 of the 24 million employed labour force in the UK, 71 per cent were in the private sector, 6.7 per cent were employed by public corporations, 9.7 per cent by central government, and 12.9 per cent by local government.

Political Views

The balance of the public sector – private sector mixture in the UK is one that has varied over time because of the differing philosophies of the main political parties towards state intervention. The desirability of less or more public ownership of industry has long been at the heart of the political divide between the Labour and Conservative parties. The Labour Party has generally aspired to an extension of the public sector in the pursuit of socialist ideals. The Conservative Party has broadly opposed any such extension and indeed tried to reduce the influence of the state.

Nationalization

The fundamental extension of the public sector in the UK took place within the space of five years after the end of World War II in 1945. Mr Attlee's newly elected Labour government proceeded to take into full public ownership the Bank of England, the coal-mines, railways, steel, civil aviation, broadcasting, gas, and electricity. Waterways and some road transport also became state-owned. The overwhelming reasons for this remarkable interventionist activity were political. The party's commitment to managing the capitalist

system and to injecting a socialist philosophy was paramount. Clause Four of the Labour Party's constitution called (and still does) for 'the public ownership of the means of production, distribution, and exchange'. In practice the party both in 1945–51 and since was content to take over what were regarded as '*the commanding heights*' of the economy. From the list of new state industries above, it can be seen that these commanding heights included at its core the *fuel*, *power*, and *transport* industries. The influence these state-owned industries could have over the remainder of the economy in private hands should be obvious enough. The supporters of **nationalization** in the early 1950s argued that only the co-ordination resulting from unified (geographical) ownership could produce really efficient industries as in the case of the railways. However, it was not too clear whether it was intended that these state-owned industries should be run on a commercial basis: the 'social service' argument was never far in the background. In other words, was the profitability of railways secondary in importance to the availability of rail services especially in rural areas?

In Chapter 2 we pointed out that in the capitalist model competition between rival suppliers results in pressures to increase efficiency. But it has long been argued that in some industries, by their very nature, only one supplier can exist. This argument holds that costs per unit of output are lowest when just one single firm supplies say electricity, gas, or water to all consumers within a locality. For example, if there is more than one supplier of electricity then duplication in cable systems and generating capacity, the argument runs, results in a waste of scarce economic resources. In these special cases competitive forces are held to be inappropriate as a monopoly supplier minimizes resource use. We shall examine these arguments closely in Chapter 29 but for the moment we just need to be aware of how the **natural monopoly** argument has been one part of the case for an increase in state intervention in many economies and not just in the UK.

In the case of these 'natural monopolies' nationalization was regarded by the Labour government as essential in order to prevent abuse of the consumer. If economic factors pointed to a monopoly situation then it should be publicly rather than privately owned.

In addition to the general arguments just discussed Attlee's administration held that there were sometimes specific reasons for taking industries into public ownership. Thus in the case of the coal-mines there was a strong belief in the need for state ownership as a means of both improving technical methods and industrial relations since it was judged that industry's record up to 1939 was particularly deficient in these respects. But the steel industry was, in the late 1940s and long afterwards very much at the heart of the political divide. The incoming Conservative government denationalized the industry in 1953 but retained a measure of central control concerning pricing and investment policies over the industry. There was a change yet again when in 1967 the Wilson government nationalized the biggest fourteen steel-making firms. This is not the place to assess the economic performance of the nationalized industries (see Chapter 29) but we can offer the non-contentious comment that the post-war relationship between government and state corporation has, for various reasons, been a rather troubled one.

It has not been found easy to square autonomy for the managers of these undertakings with the need both for accountability to Parliament and an appropriate measure of Ministerial direction.

Public ownership is, of course, not the only alternative to private enterprise. In the US, for example, a third option has long been used. This is leaving energy and transportation in private hands but leaving price and output decisions to public utility regulatory bodies.

The Private Sector in the UK

The previous section has pointed out that the line drawn between the public and private sector is one at the centre of political debate. It has also indicated the precise difficulty of defining what constitutes the public sector.

At first sight the private sector element in the mixed economy seems to be free of definitional difficulties. Surely we mean firms owned and controlled by individuals independently of the state? In fact there is a rich variety in the forms of private enterprise in an economy like the UK. We have at one end of this spectrum owner-managed businesses, such as corner shops and partnerships. (We formally define types of businesses in the UK in Chapter 22.) At the other end of the spectrum are giant companies like ICI and Shell with operations in more than just one country (multinationals). Some giant companies like BP have shares owned by the government, a fact that illustrates the blurred state–private sector divide! There are many distinctive types of institutions having quite varied objectives and constraints on their operations. These institutions include the building societies, insurance companies, and the co-operative movement. In their various ways they differ from the imagined nineteenth-century concept of the capitalist enterprise somewhat aloof from the legislative powers of government. Thus the private sector today itself contains a very mixed group of institutions, and they have been increasingly affected by the predisposition of post-war governments to constrain their behaviour through legislation.

Post-war UK governments have legislated freely on many aspects of industry and trade. They have concerned themselves with the location and physical growth of firms through planning controls and regional policies. Governments have shown increasing concern with the quality and condition of goods and services produced (consumer protection measures). The terms and nature of employment practices – wages and safety aspects – have given rise to much legislation. In short, the varied institutions within the private sector are now much more constrained and answerable than was the case of the nineteenth-century capitalist firm. Some parts of the private sector are very dependent on central and local government buying their goods and services – for example, publishers of school books and firms making electrical generating equipment. Similarly government support for research through contracts with companies making technologically advanced goods such as computers and military hardware illustrates how employment in private industry can be sensitive to state patronage.

Modern governments thus affect private enterprise even with small shifts in public expenditure. This

---

Key Points 4.3

▶ **In the UK there has been prolonged debate on the desirability of public ownership or nationalization of the energy and transport sectors of the economy on political and economic grounds.**

▶ **The problem of natural monopolies – where economic activity tends to be undertaken by a single producer – can be approached by nationalization or public regulatory supervision.**

shows how truly mixed now is the character of economic activity in the UK economy.

Other Western Economies

We have already tried to show that the UK today has a very mixed economy. It is even more difficult to quantify how much more or less mixed is the UK economy as compared with some other European economies because of national variations in the forms of enterprise as found, say, in France or Italy. The extent of state control is not easily inferred from the proportions of capital held by the government. Thus in the case of France a number of government agencies are significant shareholders in industry. Being active participants in the affairs of those companies such institutions have an influence that often exceeds what would be suggested by nominal share ownership. Indeed France illustrates the point that actual public *ownership* is not essential for the state to have much influence on private industry. France has a long history of contractual relationships between the state and private industry and since 1946 there have been five-year plans specifying targets for various industries. These plans have aimed at improving information between those involved in economic activity and have not required compliance from particular firms to fulfil specified levels of output. On the other hand, indirect financial assistance to industry has enabled French governments to exert considerable *control* over institutions not in state ownership.

Public ownership is usually held to be desirable for political reasons but is sometimes justified on historical and essentially pragmatic grounds, such as the need to preserve jobs in what are considered key parts of the economy. As a result, countries in Western Europe exhibit considerable differences even within one sector of the economy as to the extent of state ownership. Before the nationalization of British Leyland, state ownership of the motor industry in the UK was insignificant whereas in France Renault has long been nationalized. In West Germany and Italy the state has had virtual total domination in match production in sharp contrast with the UK and France. Tobacco manufacture is essentially a state-owned industry in France but in neither West Germany nor the UK is this the case.

Key Points 4.4

▶ **The influence of government on the economy is varied in Western European countries and is not simply related to the number of industries in public ownership.**

▶ **Western European economies exhibit a varied pattern of state ownership even within one sector of the economy.**

CASE STUDY

Markets and the Public Interest

Post-war governments of both parties have responded to the emergencies of inflation and unemployment, poverty and inequality, falling standards in education and medical care, communal divisiveness and environmental damage by measures of regulation and restriction that closed more doors in transport, fuel, heavy industry, manufacturing, welfare and personal services, science and technology.

Behind these closed doors, established positions and interests were being consolidated. While private industry was exposed to internal and external competition, especially since the abolition of the EEC tariffs, in services like transport, fuel, education and health, protected from competition by economies of scale or legal enactment, people at all levels of seniority or skill were battening down the hatches, prepared to defend what they held against all comers.

The universal implication of economic scarcity is that resources have continually to be switched from less urgent to more urgent objects and so denied to worthy objects. 'Confrontation' is therefore inevitable. The choice for public policy and individuals in a free society is whether confrontation is on a small scale and frequent, or infrequent and on a large scale. People can either argue and hassle daily about using human and material resources here rather than there, to satisfy 'market forces' – shoppers and housewives, parents and patients, owner-occupiers and pension-savers, travellers and leisure customers –

or we can have the basic decisions made on a grand scale by experts, specialists, public officials, 'representatives' of all kinds (local, regional, national) and politicians. The smaller the scale and the more frequent, the less disturbing or abrasive the confrontations. The larger the scale and the less frequent, the more disturbing and abrasive the confrontations.

From this anlysis we have argued that markets, where decisions are small and change gradual, should be used whenever possible, and government, in which decisions are large and change discontinuous, should be used only where unavoidable.

This is the 'political' argument for the market, for the free economy, for 'capitalism' wherever possible, and against state ownership, 'socialism', or control or regulation in the wide range of personal goods and services which government, central and municipal, has enveloped in the last century for reasons that, if they were ever relevant, are now out of date.

The earlier assumption was that politicians and their 'obedient' civil servants deployed the wisdom of Solomon in performing three main tasks that economic markets could not achieve through the mechanism of individual payment for choice between competing suppliers. The first classical function of government was the duty of supplying 'public goods' like defence and law enforcement that

have to be arranged collectively and compulsorily financed through general taxation. The second was the shaping of a legal framework that compelled competitive markets to serve the sovereign consumer without the risks of force and fraud associated with the popular caricature of *laissez-faire*. The third classical function of government – dating from the supplementation of charity by the Elizabethan Poor Law – was the provision of a minimum income for individuals who were poor through no fault of their own.

Such fundamental duties of government are, of course, capable of varying interpretation. But the economic analysis of politics and bureaucracy helps to explain the remorseless tendency for any system of 'representative' government to err progressively in the direction of over-government.

Its starting-point is that politicians are in the business of seeking power, at best to advance the 'public interest' as they conceive it. To achieve or retain power, they are increasingly tempted to buy the support of sectional interests, by methods ranging from outright subsidies to the protection of the incomes of specified groups – whether of capitalists, consumers, employees, trade union leaders, tenants or owner-occupiers – against the less comfortable consequences of generally beneficial competition and adaptation to change.

As the favoured exceptions to the market discipline multiply, the queue of 'special cases' lengthens. And as political interventions distort and disrupt the self-correcting mechanism of changing relative prices, governments are drawn deeper into still more damaging 'solutions'.

The baneful consequences of the 'vote motive' – the political substitute for the profit motive – are made worse by competition in the political market. On the supply side – in the absence of constitutional limits on the power of transient majorities – the parties will always be tempted to promise more than they can deliver after the votes are safely in the bag. On the demand side – in the absence of market prices for 'free' services and other favours – the electorate will be tempted to vote for more government than they are prepared to finance when the bills come home to roost.

Source: Extracts from R. Harris and A. Seldon, 'You Pay Your Money, Who makes Your Choice?' *The Guardian*, 6 Aug. 1979.

Questions
1. The authors stress the use of market forces to achieve social and economic ends. Why?
2. Do you think the authors are too pessimistic about the successful working of a mixed economy in the UK?

CASE STUDY

Reform in Beijing

The inertness of Russia in 1984, so different from the recovered vitality of America, looks even more peculiar by contrast with what has

happened in China this year. By October, when the Chinese extended the radical reform of their economy from agriculture to a

large part of their industry, it had become clear that Mr Deng Xiaoping's policy of 'building socialism with capitalist methods'

continued overleaf

amounted to a super-revisionism not far short of a counter-revolution. When Mr Deng took the salute in October at Peking's first military march-past in almost 20 years, on the 35th anniversary of the Liberation of 1949, he was saluting a different liberation of his own.

The aim of Mr Deng and his two chief lieutenants – the prime minister, Mr Zhao Ziyang, and the Communist party leader, Mr Hu Yaobang – is to pull China's peasant economy into the modern age by the year 2000. He means to do this by dismantling much of the bureaucracy that has stifled growth in China – as in the rest of the communist world – and by making communist planners accept the heresy of the market-place. A political liberalization it is not. But 'socialism with Chinese characteristics', as Mr Deng's mandarins call their plans, is something new under the Marxist sun. Not even Hungary, the most adventurous of the east European reformers, has tackled economic reform with such gusto. Mr Deng has begun to wean his countrymen away from Chairman Mao's brand of all-poor-together socialism. The 'iron rice bowl', which guaranteed every Chinese a rudimentary living no matter how much or how little he worked, has been thrown away. So have the Soviet textbooks on central planning that China's bureaucrats learned from in the 1950s. As Chinese officials explain, for many years they paid too much attention to the theory of who owned what and too little to the reality of what people needed. Now China is writing its own version of do-it-yourself socialism.

The target is to quadruple the value of industrial and agricultural output by 2000. It sounds wildly ambitious. But the growth rates achieved in industry and on the farms over the past four years are impressive. So is the lucidity of the ideas on which the hopes for 2000 are based.

With four times the population of the Soviet Union, and only half its arable land, China cannot afford the squeeze-the-peasants approach to industrialization that bled the Soviet Union white in the 1930s. With 80 per cent of Chinese still working on the land, Mr Deng made agriculture the first priority of his 'four modernizations' plan, with industry, science and defence following along in that order.

The old commune system, under which peasants could grow only what they were told and how they were told, has all but disappeared. The new 'responsibility' system, introduced tentatively in 1978, has been confidently shoved forward in the past two years. It isn't a return to agricultural capitalism. Legally speaking, the land is still collectively owned. But peasant households now sign contracts for both land and equipment, and they use these as they think best.

Last January the land contracts were extended from three years to 15 years – which gives peasants more sense of proprietorship, and encourages them to tend the land carefully rather than work it to death. The crops they grow can be sold freely on the open market, once they have filled the quotas that still have to be delivered to the state. Equally important, the prices the state pays for these quotas have been raised. The result has

been a remarkable food boom.

In October, encouraged by the success on the farms, Mr Deng moved on to China's factories. Those newly flush peasants want to buy themselves televisions and trucks, houses and even the odd grand piano.

The industrial reform is designed to reorganize the relationship between ministries and factories, and between factories and workers. Parts of the economy, including heavy industry and energy, will remain firmly under the central planners' thumb. Most other firms will be able to vary the prices they charge within certain guidelines, and will have to learn to produce what their customers want: it will be harder to dump unsellable goods in state warehouses. Some small firms, and the growing number of businesses owned by individuals or small groups, will be able to offer their wares at whatever price the market will stand. There is even talk of a stock market.

This will transform the planners' lives.

Source: 'China Notes that Marx is Dead', *The Economist*, 22 Dec. 1984

Questions

1. In what ways do the reforms change the role of the central planners of the economy of China?
2. The article suggested that the economic reforms would strain the social fabric of China. It made clear that many are worried that the Deng reforms are 'fostering a nation of capitalist fat cats'. Why should such reforms cause social tensions?

Exam Preparation and Practice

MULTIPLE CHOICE QUESTIONS

1. The main difference between a fully planned and a mixed economy is the existence in the latter of both
A supply and demand situations ✓
B commercial and industrial workers
C private and public sector
D consumers and producers

One or more of the options given in Questions 2, 3, and 4 may be correct. Select your answers by means of the code set out in the grid:

A	B	C	D
1,2,3	1,2	2,3	1
all	only	only	only
correct	correct	correct	correct

2. In mixed economies
  1 both private and public sectors exist
  2 government legislation modifies the operation of markets
  3 the profit motive does not operate at all

3. In a mixed economy like that in the UK
  1 there is political debate about the desirability of an increase in government ownership and intervention in the economy
  2 at least some part of the economy is state-controlled
  3 resources are allocated entirely by the free market mechanism ✓

4. In mixed economies there is
  1 debate about how much modification there should be of a free market system
  2 no consistent pattern to be found in the extent to which governments influence particular industries
  3 difficulty in defining precisely what constitutes the extent of government regulation of the economy ✓

RELATED ESSAY QUESTIONS

1. Discuss the economic justification for government involvement in the provision of education and health services.

†2. How are resources allocated in a free market and in a planned economy? Examine the relative merits, in terms of economic efficiency, of each method of resource allocation.

3. Discuss the view that a mixed economy is an inevitable practical compromise between a free market and a command economy.

4. Suppose you are required to assess the economic performance of alternative economic systems. What issues would be involved in your assessment?

5. Contrast the free enterprise and centrally planned approaches to solving the economic problem. Consider whether or not the growth of living standards in an economy might be significantly influenced by the type of economic system.

6. Do planned economies perform better than free market economies?

7. Explain what is meant by 'an economy'. Discuss what functions the following economies have in common: the household economy; the city economy; the UK economy; the world economy.

5 Demand and Supply

Key Points to Review

▶ Scarcity (1.1)
▶ Increasing relative costs (1.3)

▶ Models (1.4)

Questions for Preview

1 The theory of demand indicates that an inverse relationship exists between price and quantity demanded, other things constant. Why?

2 Distinguish between (a) a change in demand and (b) a change in quantity demanded, with a given demand curve. Use graphs to aid you.

3 There is generally a direct relationship between price and quantity supplied, other things constant. Why?

4 Why will the market-clearing (equilibrium) price be set at the point of intersection of supply and demand, and not at a higher or lower price?

One corner-stone of economic analysis is the simple demand and supply model. Understanding what demand is, what supply is, and the relationship between the two is essential for understanding virtually all economics. Demand and supply are two ways of categorizing the influences on the price of goods that you buy. This chapter is an introduction to the study of demand and supply. First, we will look at demand, then supply, and then put them together. In the Case Study section of this chapter, we will use demand and supply analysis to examine the market for home computers and compact discs.

Theory of Demand

The **theory of demand** can be stated succinctly as follows:

At higher prices, a lower quantity will be demanded than at lower prices, other things being equal.

Or, looked at another way:

At lower prices a higher quantity will be demanded than at higher prices, other things being equal.

The theory of demand, then, tells us that the

quantity demanded of any commodity is *inversely* related to that commodity's price, other things being equal. Thus, the theory of demand states that the price and the quantity demanded move in opposite directions. Price goes up, quantity demanded goes down; price goes down, quantity demanded goes up.

Other Things being Equal

Notice that at the end of the theory of demand, there is the phrase *other things being equal** Otherwise stated, we are assuming that 'other things are held constant'. Price is not the only thing that affects purchases. There are many others, which we will look at in detail later on. One, for example, is income. If, while the price of a good is changing, income is also changing, then we would not know whether the change in the quantity demanded was due to a change in the price or to a change in income. Therefore, we hold income

---

*This is the **ceteris paribus** assumption where *ceteris paribus* means other things being equal or constant.

constant, as well as any other factor that might affect the quantity of the product demanded.

Since we are holding all other things equal, or constant, that obviously means that we are holding the prices of all other goods constant when we state the theory of demand. Implicitly, therefore, we are looking at a price change of the good under study *relative* to all other prices. An understanding of the concept of *relative prices* is important in the study of economics.

Relative Prices

The **relative price** of any item is its price compared to the price of other goods, or relative to a (weighted) average of all other prices in the economy. The prices that you and I pay in sterling for any good or service at any point in time are called **absolute**, or **nominal**, prices. Consumer-buying decisions, however, depend on relative, not absolute prices. To drive this point home, let us consider the hypothetical absolute and relative prices of LPs and cassette tapes, which we do in Figure 5.1. We show the absolute prices of LPs and tapes in 1978, 1981, and 1984. They have both gone up in price since 1978. In 1984 a popular ('pop') 33 rpm record sold for the same price as a recording on cassette tape. But in 1978 the LP was cheaper by 0.41p. In the six-year period, while both prices had gone up absolutely, the relative price of tapes had fallen (and, conversely, the relative price of LPs has risen). If the law of demand holds, then over this six-year period, a larger quantity of tapes will have been demanded, while a smaller quantity of LPs will have been demanded, other things being equal.

Once this distinction is made between absolute and relative prices, there should be no confusion about the meaning of price (increases) during a period of generally rising prices. Someone not familiar with this distinction may contend that the theory of demand clearly does not hold because, say, the price of washing-machines went up last year by 5 per cent, but the quantity demanded did not go down at all. Assuming that other things in the economy did not change, this indeed may have been a possible refuta-tion of the theory of demand, except for the fact that last year's prices in general may have gone up by as much as or more than 5 per cent. It is the price of washing-machines *relative* to all other prices that is important for determining the relationship between price and the quantity demanded.

Two Reasons Why We Observe the Theory of Demand

There are two fundamental reasons that explain why the quantity demanded of a good is inversely related to its price, other things being equal.

SUBSTITUTION EFFECT

Let us assume now that there are several goods, not exactly the same, or perhaps even very different from one another, but all serving basically the same pur-pose. If the price of one particular good falls, we most likely will substitute in favour of the lower-priced good and against the other similar goods we might have been purchasing. Conversely, if the price of that good rises relative to the price of the other similar goods, we will substitute in favour of them and not buy as much of the higher-priced good. Consider an example: the prices of pizzas, hamburgers, and hot dogs are all about the same. Each of us buys a certain amount (or none) of each of these three substitutable fast foods. What if the price of pizzas increases considerably, while the prices of hamburgers and hot dogs do not? What will we do? We will buy more hamburgers and hot dogs and fewer pizzas, since they are relatively more expensive, while hot dogs and hamburgers are now relatively cheaper. In effect, we will be substituting hamburgers and hot dogs for pizzas *because* of the relatively higher price of pizzas. Thus, you can see how the **substitution effect** affects the quantity demanded of a particular good.

REAL INCOME EFFECT

If the price of something that you buy goes up while your money income and other prices stay the same, then your ability to purchase goods in general goes down. That is to say, your effective purchasing power

Figure 5.1
Absolute versus Relative Price. The absolute price of both LPs and tapes has risen. But the relative price of tapes has fallen (or, conversely, the relative price of LPs has risen).

	Absolute Price (£)			Relative Price (%)		
	1978	*1981*	*1984*	*1978*	*1981*	*1984*
LPs	3.79	4.49	5.25			
				110	102	100
Cassette tapes	4.20	4.59	5.25			

Source: British Phonographic Industry Yearbooks.

is reduced even though your money income has stayed the same. If you purchase ten pizzas a week at £1 apiece, your total outlay for pizzas is £10. If the price goes up by 50p, you would have to spend £15 in order to purchase ten pizzas. If your money income and the prices of other goods remained the same, it would be impossible for you to purchase ten pizzas a week at £1.50 apiece (as you used to do at the lower price) and still purchase the same quantity of all other goods and services that you were purchasing. You are poorer, and hence it is likely that you will buy less of a number of things, including the good whose price rose. The converse will also be true. When the price of one good that you are purchasing goes down without any other prices changing and without your money income changing, you will feel richer and undoubtedly will purchase a bit more of a number of goods, including the lower-priced good.

In general, the **real income effect** is usually quite small. After all, unless we consider broad categories, such as housing or food, a change in the price of *one* particular item that we purchase will have a relatively small effect on our total purchasing power (given a limited income). Thus, we expect that the substitution effect is usually more important in causing us to purchase more of goods that have become cheaper and less of goods that have become more expensive.

The Demand Schedule

Let us take a hypothetical demand situation to see how the inverse relationship between the price and the quantity demanded looks. What we will do is consider the quantity of wheat demanded *per year*. Without stating the *time dimension*, we could not make any sense out of this demand relationship, because the numbers would be different if we were talking about the quantity demanded per month or the quantity demanded per decade.

In Figure 5.2(a) we show the price per constant quality tonne of wheat. The words 'constant quality' take care of the problem of varying qualities of wheat actually sold or that could be sold every year. By taking an average quality at an average price of wheat we recognize differences in the qualities of wheat purchased.

We see in Figure 5.2(a) that if the price were £10 per

Figure 5.2(a)
The Demand Schedule and Demand Curve for Wheat. Column 1 represents the price per constant-quality tonne of wheat. Column 2 represents the quantity demanded in constant-quality tonnes of wheat per year. The last column merely labels these price-quantity demanded combinations. As the price rises, the quantity demanded per year falls.

Price per tonne of constant-quality wheat	Quantity demanded of constant-quality (million tonnes) wheat per year	Combination
£50	2	A
£40	4	B
£30	6	C
£20	8	D
£10	10	E

tonne, 10 million tonnes would be bought each year; but if the price were £50 per tonne, only 2 million tonnes would be bought each year. This reflects the theory of demand. Figure 5.2(a) is also called a **demand schedule** because it gives a schedule of alternative quantities demanded per year at different possible prices.

The data in Figure 5.2(a) is shown as a demand curve in Figure 5.2(b) where the price per constant-quality tonne is plotted on the vertical axis and the quantity measured in constant-quality tonnes per year on the horizontal axis. All we have to do is take combinations *A*, *B*, *C*, *D*, and *E* from Figure 5.2(a) and plot those points in Figure 5.2(b). Now we connect the points and we have a **demand curve.** * It is downward-sloping (from left to right) to indicate the *inverse* relationship between the price of wheat and the quantity demanded per year.

---

*Even though we call them curves for the purposes of exposition, we only draw straight lines. In many real-world situations, demand and supply 'curves' will in fact be lines that do curve. In order to connect the points in Figure 5.2(b) with a smooth line, we assume that for all prices in between the ones shown, the quantities demanded will be found along that line.

Key Points 5.1

▶ **There is an inverse relationship between the quantity demanded of a good and its price, other things being equal.**

▶ **We hold constant other determinants of quantity demanded, such as income.**

▶ **The theory of demand holds because when the price of a good goes down: (a) we substitute in favour of it and (b) we are now richer and buy more of everything, including it.**

Figure 5.2(b)

We measure the quantity of wheat in millions of constant-quality tonnes per year on the horizontal axis and the price per constant-quality tonnes on the vertical axis. We then take the price-quantity combinations from Figure 5.2(a) and put them in this diagram. These points are A, B, C, D, and E. When we connect the points, we obtain a graphic representation of a demand schedule. It is downward-sloping to show the inverse relationship between quantity demanded and price.

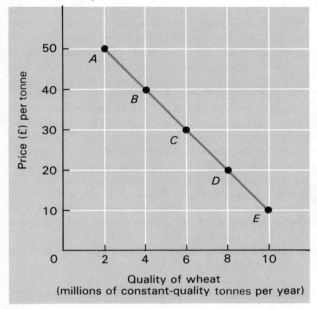

Quality of wheat
(millions of constant-quality tonnes per year)

Determinants of Demand

The demand curve in Figure 5.2(b) is drawn with other things held constant, that is, with all of the other *non-price* factors that determine demand held constant. There are many such determinants. The major non-price determinants are: (1) income, (2) tastes and preferences, (3) the price of related goods, (4) changes in expectations of future relative prices, and (5) population (that is, market size). Other non-price determinants of demand are, for example, the season of the year for some goods and the cost of financing the purchase of some very expensive consumer items.

Changes in Demand

If one of the above five determinants of demand changes, then the entire demand curve *shifts*, either to the right or the left. Consider, for example, how we might represent a dramatic increase in the quantity of wheat demanded at *all* prices because of a medical discovery that, say, bread consumption increased life expectancy! The demand curve would shift outwards, or to the right, to represent an increase in demand. That is to say, there will now be an increase in the quantity demanded at *each and every possible price*. We do

Figure 5.3

A Shift in the Demand Curve. If only the price of wheat changes, we move to a different point (co-ordinate) along a given demand curve. However, if some factor other than price changes, the only way we can show its effect is by moving the entire demand curve from DD to D'D'. We have assumed in our example that the move was precipitated by a medical discovery showing bread consumption led to a greater life expectancy. That meant that at *all* prices a larger quantity would be demanded than before. For example, at a price of £30 instead of 6 million tonnes per year being demanded, 10 million would be demanded. If there were a medical discovery indicating shorter life because of bread consumption, the demand curve would shift inwards to D''D''. At a price of £30 for example, now only 4 million tonnes per year would be consumed. Curve D''D'' represents reduced demand.

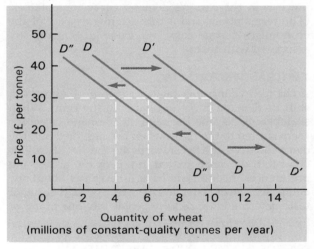

Quantity of wheat
(millions of constant-quality tonnes per year)

this in Figure 5.3. The demand curve has shifted from DD to D'D'. Take any price, say £30. Originally, before the great medical discovery, the quantity demanded at £30 was 6 million tonnes per year. Thus, we have witnessed a shift in the demand for wheat. We could use a similar analysis when discussing a shift inwards, or to the left, of the demand curve for wheat. This might happen, for example, in the case of a medical discovery that bread consumption actually decreased life expectancy. The demand curve would shift to D''D''; quantity demanded would now be less at each and every possible price.

The Determinants of Demand

We mentioned that there are five major non-price determinants of demand.

INCOME

For most goods, an increased income will lead to an increase in demand. The phrase *increase in demand* always refers to a comparison between two *different* demand curves. Thus, an increase in income for most goods will lead to a rightward shift in the position of the demand curve from, say, *DD* to *D'D'* in Figure 5.3. You can avoid confusion about shifts in curves by always relating an increase in demand to a rightward shift in the demand curve and a decrease in demand to a leftward shift in the demand curve. Goods for which the demand increases when income increases are called **normal goods**. Most goods are 'normal' in this sense. There are some goods for which demand *decreases* as income increases. These are called **inferior goods**. Potatoes might be an example. Assume that we are in a very poor nation and that potatoes are eaten in large quantities by most families as the staple diet. Incomes are typically too low for it to be possible to eat meat instead of potatoes. If now we assume people have higher incomes then more people will be able to afford meat. Thus, instead of buying *more* potatoes as their income rises, the nation will substitute more meat. An increase in income will have caused a shift inwards in the nation's demand curve for potatoes. (The terms *normal* and *inferior* are merely part of the economist's terminology; no value-judgements are associated with them.)

TASTES AND PREFERENCES

A change in consumer tastes in favour of a good can shift its demand curve outwards to the right. When skateboards became the rage, the demand curve for them shifted to the right; when the rage died out, the demand curve shifted inwards to the left. Fashions depend to a large extent on people's tastes and preferences. Economists have little to say about the determination of tastes and have few 'good' theories of taste determination or why people buy one brand of product rather than others.

PRICE OF RELATED GOODS: SUSBSTITUTES AND COMPLEMENTS

Demand schedules are always drawn with the prices of all other commodities held constant. When we draw the demand curve for butter, we assume that the price of margarine is held constant. When we draw the demand curve for stereo speakers, we assume that the price of stereo amplifiers is held constant. When we refer to *related goods* we are talking about those goods whose demand is interdependent. In other words, if a change in the price of one good shifts the demand for another good, we say that those two goods are related.

There are two types of related goods: **substitutes** and **complements**. We can define and distinguish between substitutes and complements in terms of how the change in price of one commodity affects the demand for its related commodity.

Consider butter and margarine. Generally, we think of butter and margarine as substitutes. Let us assume that each originally costs £1 per pound. If the price of butter remains the same and the price of margarine falls from, say, £1 per pound to 50p per pound, people will buy more margarine and less butter, the demand curve for butter will shift inwards to the left. If, on the other hand, the price of margarine rises from £1 per pound to £2 per pound, people will

buy more butter and less margarine. The demand curve for butter will shift outwards to the right. In other words, an increase in the price of margarine leads to an increase in the demand for butter, and an increase in the price of butter will lead to an increase in the demand for margarine. Thus, for substitutes, a price change in the substitute will cause a change in the same direction in the demand for the good under study.

With complementary goods, the situation is reserved. Consider stereo speakers and stereo amplifiers. We draw the demand curve for speakers with the price of amplifiers held constant. If the price per constant-quality unit of stereo amplifiers decreases from, say, £500 to £200, that will encourage more people to purchase component stereo systems, and they will now buy more speakers, at any given price, than before. The demand curve for speakers will shift outwards to the right. If the price of amplifiers, on the other hand, increases from £200 to £500, fewer people will purchase component stereo systems. The demand curve for speakers will shift inwards to the left. In sum, a decrease in the price of amplifiers leads to an increase in the demand for speakers. An increase in the price of amplifiers leads to a decrease in the demand for speakers. Thus, for complements, a price change in a product will cause a change in the opposite direction in the demand for its complement.

The relationship between price and related goods is shown in Figure 5.4.

CHANGES IN EXPECTATIONS ABOUT FUTURE RELATIVE PRICES

Expectations about future relative prices play an important role in determining the position of a demand curve because many goods are storable. If suddenly there is an expectation of a rise in the future relative price of *x*, then we might predict, all other things held constant, that people will buy more now and the present demand curve will shift from *DD* to *D'D'* in Figure 5.3. If, on the other hand, there is a new expectation of a future decrease in the price of *x*, then people will buy less now and the present demand curve will shift instead to *D"D"* in Figure 5.3.

Note that we are talking about changes in expectations of future *relative* prices rather than *absolute* prices. If all prices have been rising at 10 per cent a year, year in and year out for 100 years, this *now fully anticipated* price rise has no effect on the position of the demand curve for a particular commodity (if the price is measured in *relative* terms on the vertical axis)* Consider, for example, what would happen to the demand curve for new motor cars if it were known that their price would rise by 10 per cent next year. If it were anticipated that the prices of all other goods would also rise by 10 per cent, then the price of new cars relative

---

*We assume that *all* prices have been rising, including the value of all the things that you own and the price you are paid for your labour, that is, your income.

Figure 5.4
Related Goods

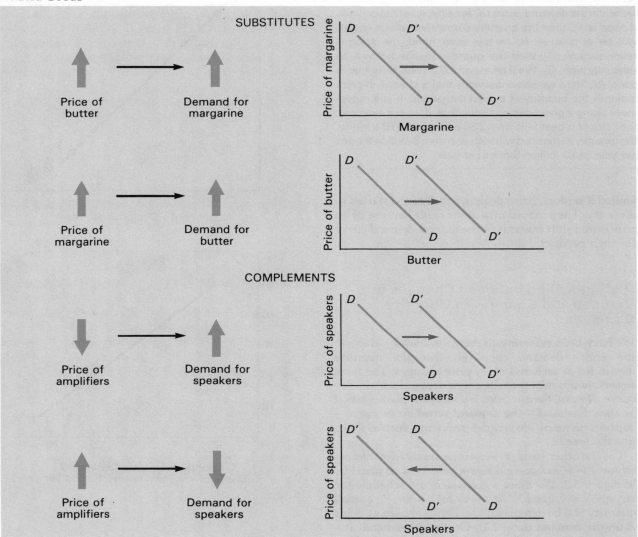

SUBSTITUTES

COMPLEMENTS

to an average of all other prices would not be any different next year from what it is this year. Thus, the demand curve for new cars this year would not increase just because of the *anticipated* 10 per cent price rise in absolute price.

POPULATION

Often an increase in the population in an economy (holding per capita income constant) shifts the market demand outwards for most products. This is because an increase in population leads to an increase in the number of buyers in the market. Conversely, a reduction in the population will shift most demand curves inwards because of the reduction in the number of buyers in the market. An example of the impact of a change in the number of consumers in a market is the effect of birth-rates on the baby food industry. As birth-rates have recently dropped in the

---

Key Points 5.2

▶ **Demand curves are drawn with non-price determinants held constant. The major non-price determinants are: (1) income, (2) tastes, (3) prices of related goods, (4) expectations of future relative prices, and (5) population (number of buyers in the market). If any one of these determinants changes, the demand schedule will shift to the right or to the left.**

Figure 5.5

Movement along a Given Demand Curve. In panel (a), we show the demand curve DD for a hypothetical good, X. If price is P_1, then the quantity demanded will be Q_1; we will be at point A. If, on the other hand, the price is relatively low, P_2, then the quantity demanded will be relatively high, Q_2. We'll be at point B on DD. Now look at panel (b). Here we show distinctly that a change in price changes the quantity of a good demanded. It is a movement along a given demand schedule. If, in our example, the price of wheat falls from £30 a tonne to £10 a tonne, the quantity demanded will increase from 6 million tonnes per year to 10 million tonnes per year.

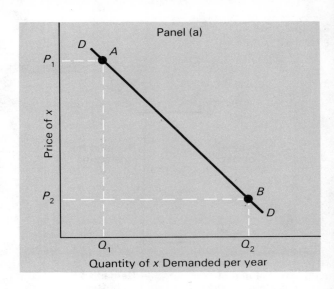

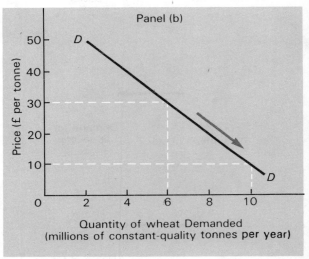

United Kingdom, firms dealing in baby food started to diversify. They moved into other fields because of an anticipated shift inwards in the market demand curve for their product.

Distinguishing between Changes in Demand and Changes in Quantity Demanded

We have been referring to *changes in demand* – shifts in the entire demand curve so that the quantity demanded at each and every price changes. The term *demand* always relates to the entire demand schedule or curve. *Demand, therefore, refers to a schedule of planned rates of purchase.* Demand – the demand schedule or curve – depends on many *non-price* determinants, such as those just discussed.

On the other hand, *a change in the quantity demanded can only come about because of a change in price.* Look at panel (a) in Figure 5.5. We draw a given demand schedule for any good, say, good X. At a very high price, P_1, a small quantity will be demanded Q_1. This is shown as point A on the demand curve DD. On the other hand, at a very low price, say P_2, a very large quantity will be demanded, Q_2. We show this on the demand curve as point B. *A change in the quantity demanded occurs when there is a movement to a different point (co-ordinate) along a given demand curve.* This movement occurs because the price of the product changes. In panel (b) of Figure 5.5, let us assume that we start off at a price of £30. If the price falls to £10, the quantity demanded will increase from 6 million tonnes per year to 10 million tonnes per year. You can see the arrow moving *down* the given demand curve DD in panel (b).

In economic analysis, we cannot emphasize too much the following distinction that must be constantly made:

A change in price leads to a change in quantity demanded.

A change in the non-price determinants of demand leads to a change in demand.

Supply

Just as there is a relationship between price and quantity demanded, so, too, is there a relationship between price and quantity supplied. This relationship is called **supply** and involves the following:

At higher prices, a larger quantity will generally be supplied than at lower prices, all other things held constant.

Or, stated otherwise:

At lower prices, a smaller quantity will generally be supplied than at higher prices, all other things held constant.

In other words, there is generally a direct relationship between quantity supplied and price. This is the opposite of the relationship we saw for demand. There, price and quantity demanded were inversely related. Here they are directly related. For supply, as the price rises, the quantity supplied rises; as the price

> ## Key Points 5.3
> ▶ **A change in demand comes about only because of a change in the non-price determinants of demand.**
> ▶ **A change in the quantity demanded comes about only when there is a change in the price.**
> ▶ **A change in demand shifts the demand curve and is caused by changes in the determinants of demand; a change in quantity demanded involves a movement along a *given* demand curve and is caused by a change in price.**

falls, quantity supplied also falls. Producers are normally willing to produce and sell more of their product at a higher price than at a lower price, other things being constant.

Why a Direct, or Positive, Relationship?

There are a number of intuitive reasons why there is normally a direct, or positive, relationship between price and quantity supplied. These involve the incentives for increasing production facing suppliers and the law of increasing costs, discussed in Chapter 1.

INCENTIVES FOR INCREASING PRODUCTION

Consider a situation in which nothing else changes except the price per tonne of wheat obtainable in the market-place. If this occurs, farmers will find it more rewarding monetarily than it was before to spend more of their time and resources producing wheat than they used to. They may, for example, *switch* more of their production from barley production to wheat production because the market price of wheat has risen. The wheat farmer may even find it now profitable to add the use of *more* labour and machines to the production of wheat because of its higher market price.

THE THEORY OF INCREASING COSTS

In Chapter 1, we explained why the production possibilities curve is bowed outwards. The explanation basically involved the theory of increasing costs – as society takes more and more resources and applies them to the production of any specific item, the opportunity cost for each additional unit produced increases at an increasing rate. The law of increasing

costs exists because resources are generally better suited for some activities than for others; and therefore, when we shift less well-suited resources to a particular production activity, more and more units of it will have to be used to get the same increase in output as we expand production.

Now apply this analysis to a wheat-farmer wishing to increase quantity of wheat supplied. That farmer will eventually find that each additional output of wheat production will involve higher and higher costs. Hence, the only way that a wheat-farmer would be induced to produce more and more wheat would be because of the lure of a higher market price that that wheat could fetch. For example, only if a higher market price of wheat could be fetched would a farmer be willing, for example, to pay overtime rates for workers and to pay the extra costs involved in, for example, tilling stony, less desirable land. In a sense, then, it is because of the law of increasing costs that price has to go up in order to create a situation in which the quantity supplied will also go up.*

Supply Schedule

Just as we were able to construct a demand schedule, so we can construct a **supply schedule**, which is a table relating prices to the quantity supplied at each price.

---

*Strictly speaking, the theory of increasing costs can be used as an explanation for the generally positive relationship between quantity supplied and price only in the short run, when there is no possibility that improved production techniques resulting from the increased production will actually lower costs.

> ## Key Points 5.4
> ▶ **There is normally a direct, or positive, relationship between price and quantity of a good supplied, other things being constant.**
> ▶ **Because of the law of increasing costs, suppliers can only be induced to incur higher additional production costs if the market price they receive for their product goes up.**

It is a set of planned production rates that depends on the price of the product. In Figure 5.6 panel (a), we show the supply schedule of wheat.

Supply Curve

We can convert the supply schedule in panel (a) of Figure 5.6 into a **supply curve**, just as we earlier created a demand curve in Figure 5.2. All we do is take

the price–quantity combinations from panel (a) of Figure 5.6 and plot them in panel (b). We have labelled these combinations F through J. The curve is upward-sloping to show the normally direct relationship between price and the quantity supplied. Again, we have to remember that we are talking about quantity supplied *per year*, measured in constant-quality units.

The Determinants of Supply

When supply curves are drawn, only the price changes, and it is assumed that other things remain constant. The other things assumed constant are: (1) the prices of resources (inputs) used to produce the product, (2) technology, (3) taxes and subsidies, (4) price expectations of producers, and (5) the number of firms in the industry. These are the major *non-price* determinants of supply. If any of them changes, there will be a shift in the supply curve.

Shifting Supply

A change in the price of the good itself will cause a movement along the supply curve. A change in the non-price determinants, however, will shift the entire curve.

Consider an example: If a new method of fertilizing and planting wheat reduces the cost per tonne of growing wheat by, say, 50 per cent, farmers will supply more wheat *at all prices* because their cost of so doing has fallen dramatically. Competition among farmers to produce more at each and every price will shift the supply schedule of wheat outwards to the

Figure 5.6

The Supply Schedule and Supply Curve for Wheat. In panel (a) at higher prices, suppliers will be willing to provide a greater *quantity* of wheat. We see, for example, in column 1 that at a price per constant-quality tonne of £10 only 2 million tonnes will be supplied; but at a price of £50 per tonne, 10 million will be forthcoming from suppliers. We label these price-quantity combinations in the third column. In panel (b) the horizontal axis measures the quantity of wheat supplied, expressed in millions of constant-quality tonnes per year. The vertical axis, as usual, measures price. We merely take the price-quantity combinations from panel (a) and plot them as points F, G. H, I, and J. Then we connect these points to find the supply curve for wheat. It is positively sloped. At higher prices, a larger quantity will be forthcoming.

Panel (a)

Price per constant-quality tonnes	Quantity supplied of wheat (millions) of constant-quality tonnes per year)	Combination
£10	2	F
£20	4	G
£30	6	H
£40	8	I
£50	10	J

Figure 5.7

A Shift in the Supply Schedule. If only the price changes, we move along a given supply schedule. However, if for example the cost of production of wheat were to fall dramatically the supply schedule would shift rightwards from SS to S'S' so that at all prices a larger quantity would be forthcoming from suppliers. Conversely, if the cost of production rose, the supply curve would shift leftwards to S"S".

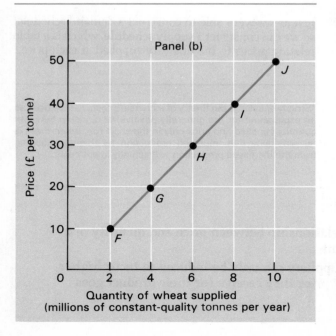

Panel (b)

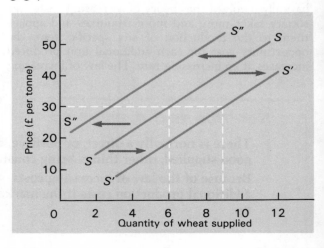

right from *SS* to *S'S'* as we see in Figure 5.7. At a price of £30, the quantity supplied was originally 6 million tonnes per year; but now the quantity supplied (after the reduction in the costs of production) at £30 a tonne will be 9 million tonnes per year. This is similar to what has happened to the supply curve of electronic calculators and computers in recent years.

The opposite case will make the point even clearer. Suppose that a new and totally unknown disease caused a blight on wheat throughout the UK such that 60 per cent of the UK's total crop is destroyed. Users of wheat products will find a reduced supply. They – in competition with one another – will bid up its price. Ultimately, the users of wheat for wheat-based products will pay greatly increased prices. The supply curve will have shifted inwards to the left to *S"S"*. At each and every price, the quantity of wheat supplied will fall dramatically, due to the crop-destroying disease.

The Determinants in Detail

THE PRICES OF INPUTS USED TO PRODUCE THE PRODUCT

If one or more input prices fall, the supply curve will shift outwards to the right; that is, more will be supplied at each and every price. The opposite will be true if one or more inputs become more expensive. In other words, when we draw the supply curve of cars, we are holding the price of steel (and other inputs) constant.

TECHNOLOGY

Supply curves are drawn on the assumption of a given technology or 'state of the art'. When the types of production techniques available change, the supply curve will shift. For example, if a better production technique becomes available, the supply curve will shift to the right. A larger quantity will be forthcoming at each and every price because the cost of production will have fallen.

TAXES AND SUBSIDIES

Certain taxes, such as sales taxes, are effectively an addition to production costs and therefore reduce the supply. Thus, if the supply curve were *SS* in Figure 5.7, a sales tax increase would shift it to *S"S"*. A subsidy would do the opposite; it would shift the curve to *S'S'*. Every producer would get a 'gift' from the government of, say, a few pence for each unit produced.

PRICE EXPECTATIONS

A change in the expectation of a future relative price of a product can affect a producer's current willingness to supply, just as price expectations affect a consumer's current willingness to purchase. Farmers may withhold from market part of their current wheat crop if they anticipate a higher wheat price in the future. In either example, the current quantity supplied at each and every price will decrease.

THE NUMBER OF FIRMS IN THE INDUSTRY

In the short run when firms can only change the number of employees they use, we hold the number of firms in the industry constant. In the long run, the number of firms may change. If the number of firms increases, the supply curve will shift outwards to the right. If the number of firms decreases, it will shift inwards to the left.

Change in Quantity Supplied and Change in Supply

We cannot overstress the importance of distinguishing between a movement along the supply curve – which occurs only when the price changes – and a shift in the supply curve, which occurs only with changes in other non-price factors. A change in price always brings about a change in quantity supplied. We move to a different co-ordinate on the existing supply curve. This is specifically called a change in quantity supplied.

But a change in technology, for example, will shift the curve such that there is a change in the quantity supplied at each and every price. This is called a change in supply. A rightward shift represents an increase in supply; a leftward (inward) shift represents a decrease in supply.

A change in price leads to a change in quantity supplied.

A change in the non-price determinants of supply leads to a change in supply.

Putting Demand and Supply together

In the preceding sections on supply and demand, we tried to confine each discussion only to supply or to demand. There is an interaction between the two. In this section, we will discuss how they interact and how

---

Key Points 5.5

▶ The supply curve is drawn with other things held constant. If non-price determinants of supply change, then the supply curve will shift. The major non-price determinants are: (1) input costs, (2) technology, (3) taxes and subsidies, (4) expectations of future relative prices, and (5) the number of firms in the industry.

Figure 5.8

Putting Demand and Supply together. In panel (a) we combine Figures 5.2(a) and 5.6(a). Column 1 is the price per constant-quality tonne, column 2 is the quantity supplied, and column 3 is the quantity demanded, both on a per year basis. The difference is expressed in column 4. For the first two prices, we have a negative difference; that is, there is an excess quantity demanded (a shortage) as expressed in column 5. At the price of £40 or £50 we have a positive difference; that is, we have an excess quantity supplied (a surplus). However, at a price of £30 the quantity supplied and the quantity demanded are equal, so there is neither an excess quantity demanded nor an excess quantity supplied. We call this price the equilibrium, or market-clearing, price. In panel (b) the intersection of the supply and demand curves is at *E* where there is neither an excess quantity demanded nor an excess quantity supplied. At a price of £10 the quantity supplied will be only 2 million tonnes per year, but the quantity demanded will be 10 million. The difference is excess quantity demanded at a price of £10. There are forces that will cause the price to rise, so we will move from point *A* up the supply curve to point *E*. At the other extreme, £50 elicits a quantity supplied of 10 million, with a quantity demanded of 2 million. The difference is excess quantity supplied at a price of £50. Again, forces will cause the price to fall, so we will move down the demand and the supply curves to the equilibrium price, £30 per tonne quantity supplied, but quantity demanded would drop to 2 million, leaving a difference of (plus) 8 million, which we call an excess quantity supplied (surplus).

(1) Price(£)	(2) Quantity supplied (tonnes per year)	(3) Quantity demanded (tonnes per year)	Panel (a) (4) Differences (2)–(3) (tonnes per year)	(5) Excesses
10	2 million	10 million	–8 million	Excess quantity demanded
20	4 million	8 million	–4 million	Excess quantity demanded
30	**6 million**	**6 million**	**0**	**Market-clearing price – equilibrium**
40	8 million	4 million	4 million	Excess quantity supplied
50	10 million	2 million	8 million	Excess quantity supplied

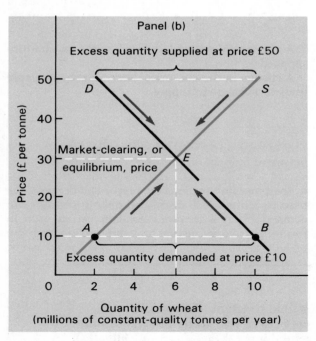

Panel (b)

Excess quantity supplied at price £50

Market-clearing, or equilibrium, price

Excess quantity demanded at price £10

Quantity of wheat
(millions of constant-quality tonnes per year)

that interaction determines the prices that prevail in our economy. So knowing, understanding how demand and supply interact is essential to understanding how prices are determined in our economy and other economies where the forces of supply and demand are allowed to work themselves out.

Let us first combine the demand and supply schedules, and then we will combine the curves.

The Demand and Supply Schedules Combined

Let us place Figure 5.2(a) (the demand schedule) and panel (a) from Figure 5.6 (the supply schedule) into Figure 5.8(a). Column 1 shows the price; column 2, the quantity supplied per year at any given price; and column 3, the quantity demanded. Column 4 is merely the difference between columns 2 and 3, or the difference between the quantity supplied and the quantity demanded. In column 5, we label those differences as either an excess quantity demanded (shortage/surplus) or an excess quantity supplied. For example, at a price of £10 there would be only 2 million tonnes supplied, but the quantity demanded would be 10 million. The difference would be a negative 8 million, which we label an excess quantity demanded (shortage). At the other end of the scale, a price of £50 per tonne would elicit a 10 million quantity supplied, but quantity demanded would drop to 2 million,

> ### Key Points 5.6
> ▶ If the price changes, we *move along* a curve – there is a change in quantity demanded and/or supplied. If something else changes, we *shift* a curve – there is a change in demand and/or supply.

leaving a difference of (plus) 8 million, which we call an excess quantity supplied (surplus).

At the price of £30 both the quantity supplied and the quantity demanded per year are 6 million tonnes of wheat. The difference then is zero. There is neither an excess quantity demanded (shortage) nor an excess quantity supplied (surplus). Hence, this price of £30 is very special. This is the **market-clearing price** since it clears the market of all excess supply or excess demand. The market-clearing price is the **equilibrium price**, or the price at which there is no tendency for change. Demanders are able to get all they want at that price; and suppliers are able to sell the amount that they want at that price.

The Concept of Equilibrium

We have used the term 'equilibrium price'. The concept of equilibrium is important in and of itself because we will frequently be referring to equilibrium situations in different markets and in different parts of the economy. **Equilibrium** in any market is defined as a situation in which the plans of buyers and the plans of sellers exactly mesh, causing the quantity supplied to equal the quantity demanded at the price in the market-place for the good. Equilibrium prevails when opposing forces are in balance. In any market, for a given supply curve and a given demand curve, the intersection gives an equilibrium price. For any given supply and demand, if price were to drift away from equilibrium – say, because of firms groping about for the 'right' price – forces would come into play to push price back to equilibrium. Such a situation is one of **stable equilibrium** An unstable equilibrium is one in which, if there is a movement away from the equilibrium, there are forces that push price and/or quantity even further away from equilibrium (or at least do not push price and quantity back towards the equilibrium level or rate).

The difference between a stable and an unstable equilibrium can be illustrated by looking at two balls: one made of hard rubber, the other made of soft putty. If you were to squeeze the rubber ball out of shape, it would bounce back to its original form. On the other hand, if you were to squeeze the putty out of shape, it would remain out of shape. With respect to the shape of the two balls made out of different materials, the former illustrates a stable equilibrium (in terms of physical form) and the latter an unstable equilibrium.

Now consider a shock to the system. The shock can be represented either by a shift in the supply curve or a shift in the demand curve or a shift in both curves.

Thus, any shock to the system will result in a new set of supply-and-demand relationships and a new equilibrium; forces will come into play to move the system from the old price – quantity equilibrium (which is now a disequilibrium situation) to the new one.

The Demand and Supply Curves Combined

Perhaps we can better understand the concept of an equilibrium, or market-clearing, price by looking at the situation graphically. What we want firmly established is the understanding that in the market, a commodity's price will tend towards its equilibrium, or market-clearing, price. Once that price is reached, the price will remain in effect unless either supply or demand changes.

Let us combine panel (b) in Figure 5.2 and panel (b) in Figure 5.6 into panel (b) in Figure 5.8. The only difference now is that the horizontal axis measures both the quantity supplied and the quantity demanded per year. Everything else is the same. The demand curve is labelled *DD*, the supply curve *SS*. We have labelled the intersection of the supply curve with the demand curve as *E*, for equilibrium. That corresponds to a price of £30 at which both the quantity supplied and the quantity demanded per year are 6 million. There is neither an excess quantity supplied nor an excess quantity demanded. Point *E*, the equilibrium point, always occurs at the intersection of the supply and demand curves. Now let us see why we said that this particular price is one towards which the market price will automatically tend to gravitate.

SHORTAGES

The demand and supply curves depicted in Figure 5.8 represent a situation of stable equilibrium. In other words, a non-market-clearing, or disequilibrium, price will put into play forces that cause the price to change towards the market-clearing price where equilibrium will again be sustained. Look again at panel (b) in Figure 5.8. Suppose that, instead of being at the market-clearing price of £30 per tonne, for some reason the market price is £10 per tonne. At this price, the quantity demanded exceeds the quantity supplied, the former being 2 billion tonnes per year and the latter, 10 million tonnes per year. We have a situation of an excess quantity demanded or **shortage** at the price of £10. Demanders of wheat would find that they could not buy all that they wished at £10 per tonne. But forces will cause the price to rise: demanders will bid up the price and/or suppliers will raise the price and increase output, whether explicitly or implicitly. We would move from points *A* and *B* towards point *E*. The process would stop when the price again reached £30 per tonne.

SURPLUSES

What happens if the market price was at £50 per tonne of wheat, rather than at the market-clearing price of £30 per tonne? Clearly, the quantity supplied will exceed the quantity demanded at that price. The result will be an excess quantity supplied at £50 per tonne. This excess quantity supplied is often called a **surplus**. However, given *DD* and *SS*, there will be forces pushing the price back down towards £30 per tonne: suppliers will attempt to reduce their inventories by cutting prices and reducing output, and/or demanders will offer to purchase more at lower prices. The reason that suppliers will want to reduce inventories is that the latter will be above their optimal level; that is, there will be an excess over what each farmer believes to be the most profitable stock of wheat. After all, inventories of corn are costly to hold. On the other hand, demanders may find out about such excess inventories of wheat and see the possibility of obtaining increased quantities of corn at a decreased price. It induces demanders to attempt to obtain a good at a lower price, and they will therefore try to do so. If the two forces of supply and demand are unrestricted, they will bring the price back to £30 per tonne.

The point is that any disequilibrium situation automatically brings into action correcting forces that will cause a movement towards equilibrium. The market-clearing price and quantity will be stable as long as demand and supply do not change (that is, as long as the non-price determinants of demand and supply do not change). This is what occurs in a stable-equilibrium situation. And, of course, we are ignoring the possibility of restrictions in the market-place that might prevent the forces of supply and demand from changing price.

Price Flexibility and Adjustment Speed

We have used as an illustration for our analysis a market in which prices are quite flexible. In reality, there are markets in which this is the correct analysis. There are others, however, where price flexibility may take the form of indirect adjustments such as by way of hidden payments or quality changes. For example, the published price for an airline seat may remain the same throughout the year. None the less, the price per constant-quality unit of airline services differs, depending on *how crowded* the airplane is. In a sense, then, you pay a higher price for airline services during the peak holiday periods than during off-peak periods.

One must also consider the fact that markets do not get back into equilibrium immediately. There is an adjustment time that must take place. A shock to the economy in the form of a sudden rise in imported prices, a drought, a long strike, and so on will not be absorbed overnight. That means that, even in unrestricted market situations where there are no restrictions on changes in price and quantities, temporary excess quantities supplied and excess quantities demanded may appear. Our analysis simply indicates where, ultimately, the market-clearing price will be, given a demand curve and a supply curve. Nowhere in the analysis is there any indication of the *speed* with which a market will, for example, get a new equilibrium if there has been a shock. This *caveat* should be remembered as we examine changes in demand and changes in supply because of changes in their non-price determinants.

Changes in Demand and Supply

Now that we have combined both demand and supply on one graph, we can analyse the effects of changes in supply and changes in demand. In Figure 5.9 there are

---

Key Points 5.7

▶ When we combine the demand and supply curves we can find the market-clearing, or equilibrium, relative price at the intersection of those two curves. The equilibrium price is one from which there is no tendency to change and towards which price will gravitate if it is higher or lower.

▶ At prices above the market-clearing price, there will be an excess quantity supplied, or a surplus.

▶ At prices below the market-clearing price, there will be an excess quantity demanded, or a shortage.

▶ Equilibrium in a market exists whenever the separate plans of buyers mesh exactly with the separate plans of sellers, so that quantity demanded equals quantity supplied at the market-clearing price.

▶ For any stable equilibrium situation, any movement of price away from the market-clearing price will put into play forces that will cause the price to gravitate towards the market-clearing price.

four panels. In panel (a), the supply curve remains stable, but demand increases from DD to $D'D'$. Note that the result is both an increase in the market-clearing price from P_e P_e' and an increase in the equilibrium quantity from Q_e to Q_e'.

In panel (b) there is a decrease in demand from DD to $D'D'$. This results in a decrease in both the relative price of the good and the equilibrium quantity.

Panels (c) and (d) show the effects of a shift in the supply curve while the demand curve is stable. In panel (c), the supply curve has shifted rightwards – supply has increased. The relative price of the product falls; the equilibrium quantity increases. In panel (d) supply has shifted leftwards – there has been a supply decrease. The product's relative price increases; the equilibrium quantity decreases.

Figure 5.9

Shifts in Demand and in Supply. In panel (a), the supply curve is stable at SS. The demand curve shifts out from DD to $D'D'$. The equilibrium price and quantities rise from P_e Q_e to P_e' Q_e' respectively. In panel (b), again, the supply curve remains stable at SS. The demand curve, however, shifts inwards to the left showing a decrease in demand from DD to $D''D''$. Both equilibrium price and equilibrium quantity fall. In panel (c), the demand curve now remains stable at DD. A supply increase is shown by a movement outwards to the right of the supply curve from SS to $S'S'$. The equilibrium price falls from P_e to P_e'. The equilibrium quantity increases, however, from Q_e to Q_e'. In panel (d), the demand curve is stable at DD. Supply decreases, as shown by a leftward shift of the supply curve from SS to $S''S''$. The market-clearing price increases from P_e to P_e''. The equilibrium quantity falls from Q_e to Q_e''.

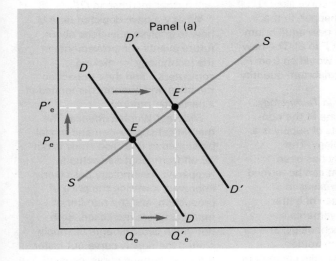

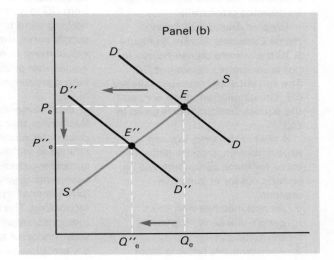

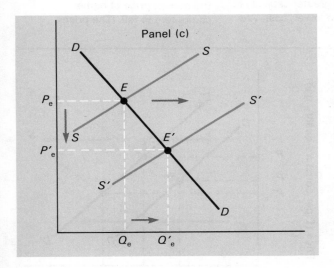

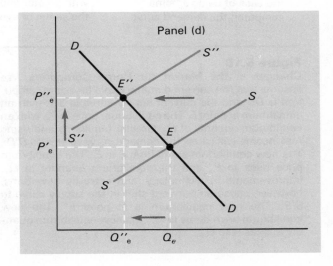

CASE STUDY

The Market for Home Computers

Buy a Pet or an Apple? A Vic or a Spectrum? In other words, should you buy a home computer, otherwise known as a microcomputer? This question would not have made much sense to most individuals ten years ago, for the market for home computers actually did not exist then. But now virtually a new industry has appeared. The situation today can be depicted graphically.

Graphic Analysis of Today's Home Computer Market. In Figure 5.10 the current demand curve for home computers is labelled *DD*. The current supply curve is labelled *SS*. The equilibrium price is P_e and the equilibrium quantity is given by Q_e.

A shift in demand. We can expect, though, that the demand curve for home computers will be shifting out for at least two reasons:

1. As real incomes rise, more people will be willing to buy microcomputers.
2. As individuals become more familiar with the capacity and the ease of using a home computer, the demand curve

will also shift outwards, to the right. After all, many younger people are becoming familiar and unafraid of computers very early in their schooling. Older individuals whose friends and neighbours own micros are finding out how quickly they can use this new technology.

We would expect the demand curve to shift outwards to the right from *DD* to a new curve like *D'D'*. If nothing were to happen to the supply curve, the new equilibrium would move from *E* to *E'*. The new equilibrium price would go from P_e', with a greater equilibrium quantity of Q_e'.

Improvements in Technology. Remember that one of the non-price determinants of supply is a change in technology. The computer industry has been experiencing what can be termed 'phenomenal' increases in technology. The use of better memories, improvements in semiconductor technology, and so on, are allowing computer manufacturers to make computers with greater and greater capacity at the same, or even lower, cost. We

can predict, therefore, that as a result of these technological advances and because high profits in existing firms will cause more and more firms to enter the industry that there will be a significant increase in the supply curve from *SS* to *S'S'*. The new equilibrium will shift from *E'* to *E"*. The equilibrium price will fall from P_e' to $P_e"$. The equilibrium quantity will further increase to $Q_e"$.

What we have depicted here is how to analyse questions about future events – improvements in the technology for making computers – and their impact on the price and quantity demanded of a particular product.

The Real-World Evidence. The theoretical supply–demand model presented in this case study is not far off from what has actually happened. Technology has clearly improved, lowering the price of production; and the number of manufacturers increased. Both non-price determinants of supply shifted the supply curve out faster than the demand curve, causing the market price of home computers to fall. (The prices

---

Figure 5.10
Changes in the Market for Home Computers. We assume that the current demand curve for home computers is *DD* and the current supply curve is *SS*, with an equilibrium at point *E*. The equilibrium price is P_e, with an equilibrium quantity of Q_e. Greater familiarity and rising real income will cause the demand curve to shift to *D'D'*. The new equilibrium shifts from *E* to *E'*. The equilibrium price rises to P_e' and the equilibrium quantity to Q_e'. Improvements in technology, and entry by new firms, however, cause an outward shift in the supply curve to *S'S'*. The new equilibrium is at point *E"*. The new equilibrium price drops to $P_e"$; the new equilibrium quantity increases to $Q_e"$.

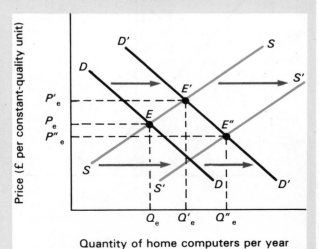

shown do not include the price of peripherals, such as monitors, printers, and the like.) Indeed the decline in the price of microcomputers has been so marked as to cause some manufacturers to cease production. An example is Texas Instruments which announced in 1984 that it would terminate the manufacture in the US of its TI-99/4A computer. This model was introduced into the UK in 1981 at a price of £299. Within a year the price of this micro had been reduced to £199.99. Between mid-October 1982 and February 1983 each person who purchased a TI-99/4A at this price could obtain a refund of £50, implying a further saving of 25 per cent. Texas Instruments faced keen competition for its model in the home computer market and by 1984 felt obliged to withdraw from the market. In 1986 the TI-99/4A can be purchased at a price of just £85.

Questions

1. How does the experience of Texas Instruments in the home computer market illustrate the operation of a free market economic system?

2. In what circumstances, even given dramatic improvements in the technology of making home computers, could our prediction about a lower price in the future be wrong?

CASE STUDY

RIP for LPs

The day stereo became *de rigueur* millions of mono record-players were left spinning impotently as switched-on sophosticates headed for high street hi-fi stores. After plugging in both speakers and placing them the regulation six feet apart, they placed their seats smack bang in the middle and bathed in the luxury of true sound.

Stereo. Wow! What a gas. Groups like Led Zeppelin, Supertramp and Yes started incorporating gimmicky little breaks into their music, just to let you know that, yes man, you had stereo and no mistake. A plane took off, a train went through a tunnel, echoing footsteps and duelling banjos went from speaker to speaker. It was as if you were actually there. Stereo was the best thing.

Until the compact disc. A silver salver that won't warp, won't scratch, won't deteriorate no matter how many times you play it. Although you could have trouble if you cover it in porridge since it relies on a beam of laser light to pick up the sound track.

In the last two-and-a-half years, since compact discs were introduced, reaction has been slow to change from initial suspicion (remember what a donkey quadrophonic turned out to be?) to a late but powerful drop in the price of a good unit. It was the classical music buffs who led the way – drawn to compact discs by the purity of the sound. Now prices of players have fallen from the £700–£800 launch mark to just under £300 and the discs are dropping steadily from their original £10–11 ceiling. A discount CD in W. H. Smiths or Woolworths now costs just £6.99.

'In the early days, people tended to dismiss CD as something for the hi-fi enthusiast and not really for the person in the street', says Polydor's CD manager, George McManus. 'But now most people outside the industry are definitely aware of CD.'

The British phonographic industry project that by 1990 the compact disc will be the dominant medium. Albums will be redundant, although cassettes will still be in use (somehow ghetto-blasters don't fit in with the sophistication of compact disc land). And ten years from now it will be virtually impossible to buy a replacement stylus for your stereo.

It only takes 38 seconds to press a compact disc, yet record companies have been slow to gear up to CD and to commit themselves to the medium, despite the fact that demand far outstrips present supply. However, things are changing. There are more pressing plants in operation and record companies are seeing the sense in releasing the CD simultaneously with the LP.

Pioneers in popular CD and the most successful group on CD to date, is Dire Straits, who illustrate another advantage of CD over LP on their latest album *Brother in Arms*. The album lasted just 43 minutes while the CD was approximately 57 minutes long. And the difference in quality is awesome.

At first I was dubious of the maker's claims as I slipped Tears for Fears's brilliant *Tales from the Big Chair* into my Philips CD104. There's no faffing around with blowing the fluff off the stylus or

continued overleaf

lining it up. Just push two buttons and turn up the volume. My ears rejoiced. I've never heard such a pure sound from my system. No crackle, no hiss, no static, nothing except superb sound. Add to this the machine's ability to play tracks in any order you wish and what more could you ask for? A remote control perhaps? Don't worry, they've already got it covered.

Some Machines to Toy with
The excellent Philips CD104 is remarkable value at just £299.99 as is its newer stable-mate, the CD 104B (£330) with its snazzier black-and-grey trim. Steady but sure are the Ferguson CD-01 (£299) and Hitachi DA-800 (£299). *Which Compact Disc?* magazine calls the Marantz CD-54 (£289), 'one of the best midi-sized models currently available', while the Mitsubishi DP-105 is a no-frills solid player for £299. Pioneer's P-DX500 at £300 gives great value but for £339 you can get the excellent Sansui PC-V100. It was the Sentra 880 (299), though, which received *Which CDs* 'highest value rating' and a rave review. Instead of our Walkman why not move up to a Sony D50? A portable compact-disc player for £280 which will also plug into your system. Hot on their heels are Technics who will soon launch the 'smallest CD in the world' – the Technics SL-XP7 which fits into the palm of the hand.

As you move up in price, the quality, the look and the technology improve, and as time goes by the price will come down further. Make no mistake, we are witnessing final vinyl and entering a new era where the multiple audio orgasm can finally be achieved.

Prices can be reduced by 10% if you buy from electrical discount shops.

Source: A. French, 'Final Vinyl', *Cosmo-Man*, Nov. 1985, p. 62.

Question
1. Given the introduction of the compact disc what repercussions now seem probable in the record industry?

Exam Preparation and Practice

INTRODUCTORY EXERCISES

1. Construct a demand curve and a supply curve for electronic calculators based on the data provided in the following tables.

Price per calculator	Quantity demanded per year (million)
£75	3
£50	6
£35	9
£25	12
£15	15
£10	18

Price per calculator	Quantity supplied per year (million)
£75	18
£50	15
£35	12
£25	9
£15	6
£10	3

What is the equilibrium price? What is the equilibrium quantity at that price?

2. Give factors, other than price, that affect the demand for a good. Place each of the following events in its proper category, and state how it would shift the demand curve in question.
(a) New information is disclosed that large doses of vitamin C prevent common colds. (The demand for vitamin C.)
(b) A drop in the price of cassette recorders occurs. (The demand for LPs—long-playing records).
(c) A significant fall in the price of English lamb chops occurs. (The demand for mint sauce.)

3. Examine the table below, then answer the following questions.

Price (per unit) last year	Price (per unit) today
Heating oil £100	£200
Natural gas £80	£320

What has happened to the absolute price of heating oil? Of natural gas? What has happened to the price of heating oil relative to the price of natural gas? What has happened to the relative price of heating oil? Will consumers, through time, change their relative expenditures?. If so, how?

4. Suppose that the demand for oranges remains constant but that a frost occurs in Florida that could potentially destroy one-third of the Florida orange crop. What will happen to the equilibrium price and quantity for oranges?

MULTIPLE CHOICE QUESTIONS

1. Assuming normal sloping demand and supply curves, the effect of any tax on the price of a good in the short run, all other things remaining equal, can be shown diagrammatically by a shift of the
A demand curve to the right
B demand curve to the left
C supply curve to the right
D supply curve to the left
E demand and supply curves

2. The demand curve for a normal good will shift to the left if
A the incomes of consumers rise
B the price of the good rises
C the prices of complementary goods rise
D advertising expenditure on complementary goods increases
E taxes on the good are increased

3. In a typical demand schedule, quantity demanded
A varies directly with price
B varies proportionately with price
C is determined by the quantity offered for sale
D is independent of price
E varies inversely with price

continued overleaf

†4. In the following diagram the equilibrium price for a normal good is at *X*, given the existing demand and supply curves D_1 and S_1. Which point (**A, B, C, D** or **E**) indicates the new equilibrium price if there is now marked increased efficiency in the production of this good and simultaneously a rightward shift in demand?

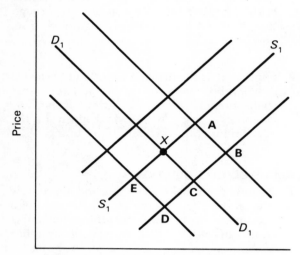

Quantity per period

Which of the above intersection points **A, B, C, D**, or **E** represents the equilibrium point resulting from the introduction of a new and cheaper production technique for the commodity?

5. In the following diagram, S_1 and D_1 represent the initial supply and demand curves for a normal commodity and *X* the initial equilibrium. The remaining curves represent possible shifts in the supply and demand curves.

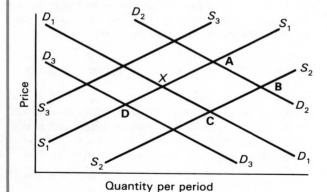

Quantity per period

Which of the above intersection points (**A, B, C,** or **D**) represents the equilibrium point resulting from a rise in the price of a substitute commodity?

One or more of the options given in Questions 6 and 7 may be correct. Select your answer by means of the code set out in the grid:

A	B	C	D
1,2,3	**1,2**	**2,3**	**1**
all	only	only	only
correct	correct	correct	correct

†6. Cotton lint and cotton seed are produced under conditions of joint supply in proportions which cannot be altered. Other things being equal, the effect(s) of an increase in demand for cotton lint will be
1   a rise in the price of cotton seed
2   a rise in the price of cotton lint
3   an increase in the quantity supplied of cotton seed

7. The diagram shows the demand curves for a product.

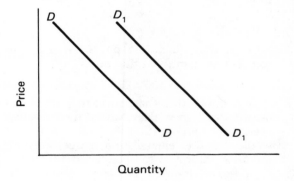

Quantity

The shift in the curve from *D* to D_1 could have been caused by a fall in
1   the price of a substitute good
2   the general level of prices
3   the price of a complementary good

6 The Price System

Key Points to Review

▶ Scarcity (1.1)

▶ Capitalism (2.1)

▶ The three key questions facing any economy: what, how and for whom (2.2)

▶ Types of economy (3.1)

▶ Demand (5.1)

▶ Supply (5.4)

▶ Changes in demand lead to changes in price (5.3, 5.6)

Questions for Preview

1   What are some costs and benefits of specialization?

2   How do markets lower the transactions costs of exchange?

3   What is consumer sovereignty? Is consumer sovereignty worth while?

4   What is the difference between technical efficiency and economic efficiency?

The model of supply and demand in Chapter 5 was a model of price determination. As such, it gave us the tools of analysis to explain the structure of relative prices within our economy. Now we need to delve into the economic system and look at it as a whole. We would like to answer questions about what determines the kinds of products that are produced and the quantities in which they are produced. In other words, how do we end up using our resources to produce motor cars instead of trains? By what mechanism was the paper, ink, and glue funnelled into the publishing industry for this very book to be published? To answer these questions, we must understand how a **price system**, or market system works in more detail than was offered in Chapter 2. We now define a price or market system as an economic system in which (relative) prices are constantly changing to reflect changes in supply and demand for different commodities. In addition, the prices of those commodities are the *signals* to everyone within the system about what is relatively expensive and what is relatively cheap. As we shall see, it is the signalling aspect of the price system that provides the information to buyers and sellers about what should be bought and what should

be produced. This chapter analyses the way in which the pure market economy works. In Chapter 4 we showed that many Western economies are not examples of this idealized economic system and so we reconsider the problems that have prompted state intervention in market economies.

Resource Allocation

Because we live in a world of scarcity, decisions must be made, whether implicitly or explicitly, about how resources shall be allocated. The problem of **resource allocation** is solved by the economic system at work in a nation. As Chapter 2 indicated, resource allocation involves answering the three questions of *what, how,* and *for whom* goods and services will be produced. Throughout this chapter, we will show how the price system answers these three basic resource allocation questions.

1. *What and how much will be produced?* There are literally millions of different things that could be produced with society's scarce resources. Some mechanism

must exist that causes some things to be produced and others to remain as either inventors' pipe-dreams or individuals' unfulfilled desires.

2. *How will it be produced?* There are many ways to produce a desired item, once the decision has been made to produce it. It is possible to use more labour and less capital and vice versa. It is possible to use lots of unskilled labour or fewer units of skilled labour. Somehow, some way, a decision must be made as to the particular mix of inputs and the way they should be organized.

3. *For whom will it be produced?* Once a commodity is produced, who will get it? In other words, what mechanism is there to distribute commodities (and income) once they are produced?

We shall see that in a price system, literally millions of individuals are involved in solving these three fundamental questions. The interaction among the individuals within the price system is done without the use of centralized decision-making. Rather, the price system involves *de*centralized decision-making. Each decision in a price system is made by the interaction of the millions of people involved in the decision. In many parts of Western economies much of the decision-making that goes on about *what, how,* and *for whom* is carried out in markets by voluntary exchange.

Exchange Takes Place in Markets

As a society we have unlimited wants, but we must make choices among the limited alternatives available to us. When you start trading with other individuals, choices arise because you have to pick among alternative **exchanges** that you could make. Individuals in societies have been exchanging goods and services for hundreds of years. For example, archaeologists tell us that during the Ice Age, hunters of mammoths in the Great Russian Steppe were trading for Mediterranean shells.

VOLUNTARY EXCHANGE

For the most part, our discussion of exchange will centre on voluntary exchanges among individuals and among nations. By necessity, prior to the undertaking of every voluntary exchange, the act of exchange itself appears to make both parties to the exchange better off. In other words, exchange is mutually beneficial or it would not be entered into. By assumption, if it were not mutually beneficial, individuals and nations would not bother exchanging.

To be sure, involuntary exchanges do occur and some are quite unpleasant for the losing parties. Involuntary exchanges occur where coercion is used to alter the behaviour of another person or nation. When individuals are robbed, they suffer exchange of goods that must be deemed involuntary. We make the assumption that only a very small part of all exchanges are involuntary and, hence, such involuntary exchanges will not affect our analysis of the price system.

The **terms of exchange** – the opportunity cost or price we pay for the desired item – are determined by the interaction of the forces underlying demand and supply. This statement, of course, relates only to an unrestricted price system. Many of the terms of exchange – the prices consumers pay – are determined by laws and regulations that are a result of the political process. Additionally, some items of exchange are determined by custom and by tradition. While custom does not play a significant role in determining prices in developed economies, in traditional societies it has been an important determinant. Customs, regulations, and laws are established by individuals acting in some type of collective manner. Thus, in a sense, all terms of exchange are determined ultimately by individuals.

In our economy, the allocation of resources takes place through voluntary exchanges in *markets*.

Markets and Information

Economists talk about markets a lot. The concept of a **market** is abstract, for it encompasses the exchange arrangements of both buyers and sellers that underlie the forces of supply and demand. In other words, demand and supply work themselves out in markets. As a general term, the word *market* refers to any arrangement or arrangements that individuals have for exchanging with one another. Economists, therefore, typically talk about product and factor markets: for example, the sugar and housing markets are examples of the former and the capital market is one of the latter types of market.

One of the major factors involved in the market is the exchange of information about prices, quantities, qualities, and so forth. Indeed, markets are collectors of information that reflect the choices of consumers, producers, and the owners of resources. All this information is given by one summary statistic – the market price of goods and services. Markets with a price system also involve co-ordination without the help of a central decision-making unit. Market prices are the aids to the co-ordination of the choices of buyers and sellers. Market prices also establish a signalling system to indicate when a correct choice has been made – higher profits are made or a commodity is purchased at a 'good' price. In other words, market prices create a penalty/reward system.

Different markets have different degrees of information and speed with which that information is transmitted. The stock market in any Western economy, for example the UK, has information about the prices and quantities of stocks being bought and sold. This information is transmitted almost instantaneously throughout the country at least, if not the world. Profit-seeking entrepreneurs are constantly looking for ways to make more profits by improving on the information network within markets. That is why every stockbroker can now tell you instantly the last price of any stock listed on a major stock exchange.

Why We Turn to Markets

The reason individuals turn to markets to conduct economic activities or exchanges is that markets reduce the costs of exchanging. These costs are generally called **transactions costs** because they are associated with transacting economic exchange. We can define transactions costs as all of the costs enabling exchanges to take place. Thus, they include the cost of being informed about the qualities of a particular product, its price, its availability, its durability record, its servicing facilities, its degree of safety, and so on. Consider, for example, the transactions costs in shopping for a portable microcomputer. Such costs would include phone calls or actual visits to sellers in order to learn about product features and prices. In addition to these costs, we must include the cost of negotiating the sale. The specification and execution of any sales contract is thus included, and ultimately transactions costs must include the cost of enforcing such contracts.

The transactions costs in the most highly organized markets are relatively small. Take, for example, the London Stock Exchange. It is quite easy to obtain immediate information on the price of listed shares, how many have been bought and sold in the last several hours, what the prices were the day before, and so on.

Generally, the less organized the market, the higher the transactions costs. No market can completely eliminate transactions costs, but some markets do a better job of reducing them than do others. Historically, as it has become less costly to disseminate information through technological improvements, transactions costs have fallen.

In a price system where there is voluntary exchange, we observe the phenomenon called **specialization**. Specialization involves working at a relatively well-defined, limited endeavour, such as accounting, selling, teaching, writing, making shoes, and so on. Most individuals in a price system specialize – they are not jacks of all trades – and they exchange the results of their specialized production activities with others who have also specialized. Just consider a typical UK household that consumes literally thousands of different commodities a year. But the members of that household who work certainly do little if anything to aid in the actual production of the commodities used by the household over a year's period. The fact is that specialization leads to greater productivity, not only for each individual but for each nation. The best way to see the benefits of specialization (and then exchange) is to look at a simple numerical example.

Look at Figure 6.1. Here we show total output available for two teams of workers in a small world where they are the only ones around. At first, they do not specialize; rather, each team works 8 hours a day

Figure 6.1

Before specialization. Here we show the relationship between team A's and team B's daily work-effort and the production of computers and wheat. When team A works on its own without specialization in either activity, it devotes 4 hours a day to computer production and 4 hours a day to wheat production. For its efforts, it obtains 2 computers per day and 2 tonnes of wheat per day. On the other hand, team B, again not specializing, will, during the same two 4-hour periods, produce 3 computers, but only 1 tonne of wheat. The total output of the 2 teams will be 5 computers and 3 tonnes of wheat per day.

Daily work-effort	Team A
4 hours	2 computers
4 hours	2 tonnes of wheat
	Team B
4 hours	3 computers
4 hours	1 tonne of wheat
Total = 5 computers, 3 tonnes of wheat per day	

After Specialization. If team A specializes in the production of wheat, it can harvest 4 tonnes of wheat for every 8 hours of work-effort. Team B, specializing in the production of computers, will produce 6 per day. Their grand total of production will be 6 computers and 4 tonnes of wheat per day, which means the benefit of specialization is increased production of 1 more computer per day and 1 more tonne of wheat per day than before they specialized.

Daily work-effort	Team A
8 hours	4 tonnes of wheat
	Team B
8 hours	6 computers
Total = 6 computers, 4 tonnes of wheat per day	

Key Points 6.1

▶ Within a price system, supply and demand determine the prices at which exchanges shall take place.

▶ The price system is also called a market system because exchanges take place in markets where market mechanisms have reduced transactions costs, defined as all costs associated with exchange.

producing both computers and wheat. Team A can produce two computers in 4 hours of work and 2 tonnes of wheat with the additional 4 hours. Team B can produce three computers in its first 4 hours of work, but only 1 tonne of wheat in its second 4 hours. The total amount that the two teams can, and choose to, produce without specialization is five computers and 3 tonnes of wheat per day.

Now look at what happens when each team specializes. We see in Figure 6.1 that after specialization, when team A spends all its time producing wheat, it can harvest 4 tonnes (since it can harvest 2 tonnes in 4 hours). Team B, on the other hand, spending all its work-day producing computers, can produce six computers per day (since it can produce three computers in just 4 hours). The total 'world' output has now increased to six computers per day and 4 tonnes of wheat per day. With the same two sets of teams using the same amount of resources, the total output of this economy has increased from five computers per day to six, and from 3 tonnes of wheat per day to 4. Obviously, the two teams would be better off (in a material sense) if they each specialized and then exchanged their products. Team A would exchange wheat for computers, and team B would do the reverse. You should note that our discussion has not dealt with the disadvantages of specialization – monotony and drudgery in one's job. But if we assume that after specialization each individual is indeed doing what he or she could do *comparatively* better than the other, then we have an appreciation of the concept of comparative advantage.

Comparative Advantage

Specialization, as outlined in the example above, rests on a very important fact: different individuals, communities, and nations are indeed different, at least when it comes to the skills of each in producing goods and services. In our simple two-team example, if these teams could do both jobs equally well, there would be no reason for specialization, since total output could not have been increased. (Go back to Figure 6.1 and make team B equally physically productive in the production of both computers and wheat, producing, say, one computer in 4 hours and 1 tonne of wheat in 4 hours, and then see what happens to our example after specialization.)

In fact, people are not uniformly talented. Even if individuals or nations had the talent to do everything better (for example, by using fewer resources, especially labour hours), they would still want to *specialize in the area of their greatest advantage*, that is, in their **comparative advantage**. To continue the example, consider the hypothetical dilemma of the managing director of a large company. Suppose that he or she can type better than any of the typists, drive a lorry better than any of the lorry-drivers, and wash windows better than any of the window-washers. That just means that the director has an **absolute advantage** in all these

endeavours – he or she uses fewer labour hours for each task than anyone else in the company. However, his or her *comparative* advantage lies in managing the company, not in doing the aforementioned tasks. How is it known that that is where the comparative advantage lies? The answer is quite easy: the managing director is *paid* the most for being a managing director, not for being a typist or a lorry-driver or a window-washer for the company.

Basically, *one's comparative advantage is found by choosing that activity that has the lowest opportunity cost*. Consider the example given in Figure 6.1 before specialization. Team A in 4 hours can produce two computers or 2 tonnes of wheat. That means, the opportunity costs for two computers is 2 tonnes of wheat, so that the opportunity cost for one computer is 1 tonne of wheat. In other words, team A has to give up 1 tonne of wheat in order to produce one computer. What about team B? Since it can produce three computers in 4 hours, or 1 tonne of wheat, its opportunity cost for producing one computer is only 1 divided by 3, or 1/3 of a tonne of wheat. That is to say, the opportunity cost of team B for one computer is 1/3 of a tonne of wheat. Since one's comparative advantage is found by choosing that activity that has the lowest opportunity cost, it is clear that team B should specialize in computer production because it incurs the lowest opportunity cost. Indeed, that is what we show when the teams specialize. Team B spends all 8 hours producing computers.

Although this discussion of specialization and comparative advantage has been couched in terms of labour it applies equally well to all factors of production.

The Division of Labour

Within any given firm that includes specialized human and non-human resources, there is a **division of labour** among those resources. The most famous example of all time comes from one of the earliest and perhaps one of the most famous economists of all time, Adam Smith, who illustrated the benefits of a division of labour with this example:

One man draws out the wire, another straightens it, a third cuts it, a fourth points, a fifth grinds it at the top for receiving the head; to make the head requires two or three distinct operations; to put it on is a peculiar business, to whiten the pins is another; it is even a trade by itself to put them into the paper.*

Making pins this way allowed ten workers without very much skill to make almost 48 000 pins 'of a middling size' in a day. One worker, toiling alone, could have made perhaps 20 pins a day; therefore, ten workers could have produced 200. Division of labour allowed for an increase in the daily output of the pin factory from 200 to 48 000! (Smith did not attribute *all*

---

*Adam Smith, *The Wealth of Nations* (1776), Bk. I, Ch. 1, Everyman edn. (1964), p 5.

> ## Key Points 6.2
> ▶ With a given set of resources, specialization results in higher output; in other words, there are gains to specialization in terms of higher material well-being.
> ▶ Individuals and nations specialize in their comparative advantages in order to reap the gains of specialization.
> ▶ Comparative advantages are found by determining which activities have the lowest opportunity cost or, otherwise stated, which activities yield the highest return for the time and resources used.
> ▶ A division of labour occurs when different workers are assigned different tasks. Together, the workers produce a desired product.

of the gain to the division of labour according to talent, but also to the use of machinery, to the fact that less time was spent shifting from task to task, and so on.)

What we are referring to here involves a division of the resource called labour into different kinds of labour. The different kinds of labour are organized in such a way as to increase the amount of output possible from the fixed resources available. We can therefore talk about an organized division of labour within a firm leading to increased output.

Relative Prices Revisited

We have often referred to prices as relative prices. This is even more important in understanding how the price system solves the basic allocation of resources problem. In the broad sense of the term, the relative price of a good is defined as the price of that good expressed in terms of how much of other goods must be given up to purchase a unit of the good in question. To establish relative prices, comparison with other prices must be made. Virtually all economic models, like supply and demand, relate individual behaviour to changes in relative, not absolute, prices.

Prices and Information

Relative prices are the conveyors of information in the market-place. For the buyers, the relative price of a good indicates what the individual purchaser must give up in order to obtain that good. Suppose that you are told that a loaf of bread will cost you £100 and this you regard as an incredibly high price. But then you are told that you are assumed to be earning £500 per hour? Does that £100 load of bread still sound so expensive? Is it any more expensive than, say, a price of £1 for the loaf and a wage-rate of £5 per hour? In both cases, you only have to work one-fifth of an hour to pay for the loaf of bread. It is the relative price of the loaf of bread – in this case, relative to the price of your labour – that tells you how expensive it *really* is (or what your real purchasing power is).

Now consider the relative value of the resources used to produce the bread. Its relative price will, in most cases, indicate the amount of resources given up to produce that good. Hence, when the relative price of a commodity goes up, that bit of information tells the buyer and the seller that the good is now relatively scarcer. Note that neither the producer nor the consumer has to know *why* that particular commodity has become relatively scarcer. It may not matter to you as a consumer, when allocating your budget, whether the price of petroleum has gone up *because* of a restriction on imports or *because* of a new law that requires petrol companies to install more expensive pollution abatement equipment. The only thing that definitely matters to you is the higher relative price, for that is the basis on which you will make your decision about the quantity to purchase. The message is transmitted by the higher relative price. Of course, how you respond to the message is impossible to predict on an individual basis, for there are probably an infinite number of ways that a consumer can 'conserve' on a relatively scarcer good.

Changes in relative prices convey information on changing relative scarcity to both buyers and sellers. Of course, buyers respond differently from sellers. Sellers may see a rise in the relative price of a particular good as an opportunity to increase profits, and eventually such information may be translated into a larger amount of resources going to the production of that now relatively higher-priced good. It is in this manner that resources are allocated in a system that allows prices to convey the information about relative scarcities. In a market system prices convey the information to the individuals – both sellers and buyers – in the market-place. There is no need for a central agency to produce information or to allocate resources. This does not mean that problems will not arise and that certain economic activities could not be better handled by other than unrestricted market processes. What it does mean is that spontaneous co-ordination occurs in a decentralized price system and resource allocation requires no outside management. This is what Adam Smith meant by an invisible hand at work.

Markets, Prices, and the Determination of *What* Is To Be Produced

The decision about *what* is to be produced depends on the incentives generated within an economic system. Within the price system, the incentive that is foremost is *profit*: the search for higher profits causes decision-makers to produce a mix of goods whose total effective demand is the greatest relative to the scarce resources available for the production of all goods and services.

Profits

A business person seeks **profits**. We define profits as the difference between the cost of producing something and the price that it fetches in the market-place. (Remember: The only way we are strictly able to define cost is *opportunity cost* – the value of the resources in their next highest, or best, alternative use.) Another way of looking at profits is as the income generated by buying cheap and selling dear. A business person buys factors of production – land, labour, and capital – at a cost that is less than the price obtainable when the finished product is sold. This definition of profit also includes the income received by the buying of anything at a lower price than the price for which it is sold.

We take two examples to see how changes in profitability cause resources to be *re*allocated, and hence determine what is to be produced. In the previous chapters we used the market for wheat to show how demand and supply come together in a free market to determine an equilibrium price. Now let us imagine several farmers who just grow, say, carrots and potatoes. We shall now follow through the consequences of a change in one of the determinants of the demand for these goods – a change in consumer tastes.

Suppose that there is suddenly an increased and sustained demand for potatoes because it is believed that eating potatoes – whether boiled, roasted, or fried – is good for one's health. This shift in tastes would result in an outward movement in the demand curve for potatoes and their relative price rise in Figure 6.2 from P_e to P''_e. If we suppose also that carrot-eating has become less popular this is translated into an inward shift in the demand curve for carrots. The relative price of carrots falls from P_e to P'_e. Assuming now that the cost of inputs into carrot production has not

Figure 6.2

Shifts in Demand Cause Prices to Change. In panel (a) we show the supply and demand for carrots. At the original equilibrium, the market-clearing relative price is P_e. When, because of a shift in tastes, the demand curve shifts leftward from DD to $D'D'$, the relative price, and hence profitability, of carrot-growing. The new market-clearing price after adjustment would become P'_e with the smaller quantity Q'_e produced. In panel (b), just the opposite has happened for potatoes. The demand curve has shifted from DD to $D''D''$. The market-clearing price has gone up from P_e to P''_e with the larger quantity Q''_e produced. The profitability of growing potatoes has risen. More resources will flow into potato-growing and fewer will be used in growing carrots.

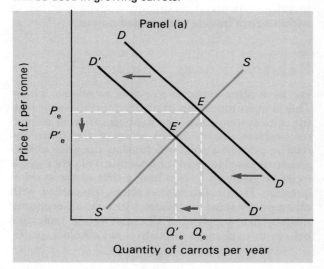

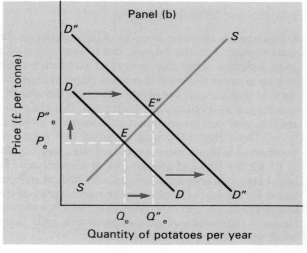

changed, the lower market-clearing price will mean less profit (or maybe even losses) in growing carrots. On the other hand, assuming again that there has been no change in input prices, when the market-clearing price of potatoes goes up, the profit per unit will also rise. The price adjustments and ensuing changes in profitability will lead to resource reallocation. There is a profit incentive for farmers to devote more of their land and labour to growing potatoes. The incentive to minimize losses causes a cutting back on the use of these resources in carrot-growing. Thus the change in consumers' tastes results here in a response by producers to alter their production of carrots and potatoes in favour of the more profitable product – potatoes – since it is in their best interest to do so.

Moving Resources from Lower- to Higher-valued Uses

The above examples relate to agriculture but the principle involved – resource reallocation – is generally applicable. The movement of resources in search of higher profits for businesses is simultaneously a movement of resources from lower- to higher-valued uses. When consumers no longer wanted to buy as many carrots, the demand curve shifted inwards to the left (panel (a) of Figure 6.2). Thus, carrots were no longer as valuable from a subjective point of view as they were prior to the shift in demand. Had all the resources remained in carrot-growing they would be generating a lower subjective value to consumers than they could elsewhere in the economy.

Another incentive to shift production would involve the piling up of unsold stocks of carrots. Unsold carrots due to falling orders from vegetable wholesalers and retailers provides information which encourages growers to switch resources to the production of something else.

When some of these resources were moved from carrot- to potato-growing, they were, by necessity, being moved to a use that generated a higher value to consumers. How do we know this? Because the demand curve for potatoes shifted outwards to the right. With a given supply curve, this dictated a higher relative price, which gave an indication that consumers now valued an additional unit of resources in the carrot industry more than in the past.

Note that we have stressed that consumers are the decision-makers that prompt transfers in resources. We will now examine this decision-making process more closely.

Consumer Sovereignty

The movement of resources from lower- to higher-valued uses depends crucially on consumer sovereignty. Consumer sovereignty means that the ultimate determiners of how much of what is produced are consumers, not politicians or businesses. In other words, in a world of consumer sovereignty, consumers are the decision-makers. Final production is destined to fulfil their wants and no one else's. In a pure market economy, or price system, each consumer expresses his or her desires (constrained by income) by 'voting' in the market-place with their pounds and pence. When fewer consumers were voting for carrots, this was translated into a shift leftward of the demand curve. When more consumers were expressing their votes for potatoes, this was shown by a shift rightward of the demand curve for potatoes.

The consumer voting system is, of course, not the same as a majority voting system. No firm has to receive 51 per cent of the available spending votes in order to produce a particular product. There are, for example, specialty car companies like Porsche and Alfa Romeo that receive of the order of just a few per cent of the total 'votes' for new cars in the UK each year. But they continue to exist because there is a sufficient demand to make them profitable. On the other hand, there are many products that are not produced even though they could receive 100 per cent of all of the votes by all of a small group of people who desire those goods. This is because even with 100 per cent of the votes, there would not be enough buyers for a business person to make a profit on the product. This is also another difference between political voting and money voting. In a market system you do not have to 'vote' for an entire package at one single time. Rather, you 'vote' for different parts – goods and services – of your total consumption package a little at a time. In the political arena you make your decision, at most, once a year, and sometimes only once every five years.

In sum, in a pure market economy, consumers vote with their money but it is proportional (as opposed to majority rule) voting. Manufacturers will respond and resources will be allocated proportionally to the way the total population spends its money, or votes with its income.

The Market System and Efficiency

Consumer sovereignty in a pure price system means that resources will be used as efficiently as possible. The efficient use of resources will occur because

---

Key Points 6.4

▶ Within a market economy, businesses seek profits. In their quest for profits, they move resources out of declining industries into expanding industries.

business persons in each industry are competing for the money 'votes' of consumers. Consequently, each firm (and hence the economy taken as a whole) will fully utilize its available resources and will generate maximum consumer satisfaction by fulfilling the largest number of consumer desires reflected by money income spent.

There are really two parts of efficiency – **technical efficiency** and **economic efficiency**, both of which are satisfied in a pure market economy, or price system.

TECHNICAL EFFICIENCY

Technical efficiency relates to utilizing production techniques that do not waste inputs. In other words, we can assume that within the market economy businesses will never waste inputs: they will never use 10 units of capital, 10 units of labour, and 10 units of land when they could produce the same amount of output with only 8 units of capital, 7 units of labour, and 9 units of land. Technical efficiency refers to decisions within a production unit. Managers respond to the prices that are given to them from outside the firm for the resources they must use. Technical efficiency, therefore, relates to managers responding 'correctly' to the input prices facing them.

ECONOMIC EFFICIENCY

This concept relates to maximizing the total subjective valuation (sometimes called utility) of our available resources. That means that resources are moved to their highest-valued uses, as evidenced by consumers' willingness to pay for the final products. As we saw above, profits signal resources to move around so that economic efficiency occurs. The forces of demand and supply guide resources to their most efficient uses. In a sense, it is the invisible hand concept again. Individuals as business persons seeking their own self-interest end up, consciously or unconsciously, generating maximum economic value from their activities.

Economic efficiency refers to relationships outside each firm. That is to say, economic efficiency refers to market price determination within an economy. Whenever a price system is in operation, market price determination will create the 'proper' signals to market participants so that they will indeed be able to

make the correct choices about resource allocation.*

Of course, an economic system can never attain economic efficiency unless within each firm or production unit technical efficiency has already been attained. That is to say, technical efficiency is implicitly a part of economic efficiency.† Usually, when discussing economic efficiency, economists assume that all profit-maximizing firms are operating technically efficiently.

How can we apply these two efficiency concepts?

1. Technical efficiency means that resources will never be wasted in producing a given output.
2. Economic efficiency means that resources will be used in their highest-valued uses.

Technical efficiency. Colour television sets will be packed to shops using the minimum amount of cardboard necessary. They will not, for example, be made 3" thick when ⅜" will do just as well (and also save on distribution costs because it is ligher).

Economic efficiency. Corrugated board will be used rather than oak or mahogany which have a higher-valued use today for, say, furniture. Furniture-makers will be willing to pay a lot more for that type of wood than will the makers of colour television set assemblers.

Organizing Production – *How* Will Goods Be Produced?

The second function of an economic system, which was mentioned at the beginning of this chapter, relates to *how* goods will be produced.

How Output Will Be Produced

The question of how output will be produced in a price system relates to the efficient use of scarce resources. Consider the possibility of only using two types of resources – capital and labour. A firm may have the

---

*Even in a pure price system, it is possible for market prices to generate incorrect signals. We look at this problem later.
†Technical efficiency is a necessary but not a sufficient condition for economic efficiency.

Key Points 6.5

▶ If consumers sovereignty exists, proportional money voting by consumers determines the output mix. Thus, within a pure market economy, resources flow from lower- to higher-valued uses. In the process, the price system attains both technical and economic efficiency.

▶ With technological efficiency, inputs are not wasted.

▶ With economic efficiency, total subjective valuation of all resources is greatest. Resources are used in their highest-valued uses.

following options given in Figure 6.3. It can use various combinations of labour and capital in order to produce the same amount of output. Two hypothetical combinations are given in that exhibit. The *least-cost combination* (which is technique B) will in fact be chosen, because in this manner, profits will be the highest possible. If any other technique were chosen, firms would then be sacrificing *potential* profit.

Moreover, in a price system, competition will in effect *force* firms to use least-cost production techniques. Any firm that fails to employ the least costly technique will find that other firms can undercut its price. Other firms that choose the least-cost production technique will be able to offer the product at a lower price and still make a profit. The lower price that they offer the product for will induce consumers to shift sales to them from the firm with the higher prices. Inefficient firms will be forced out of business.

All this discussion assumes that technology and resources prices are held constant. But if, say, the cost of capital remained the same and the cost of labour were to decrease considerably in our example in Figure 6.3, another production technique such as A might then be less costly. Firms would shift to that production technique in order to obtain the highest profits possible.

The Distribution of Total Output

The last question that any economic system must solve is distribution – *how* is total output distributed among competing claimants? The problem of distribution of total output can be separated into two parts, one relating to the distribution of products to consumers and the other relating to the distribution of money income to individuals. It should not surprise you that the second part of this problem of distribution quickly takes us into the world of normative economics.

Which Consumers Get What?

In a price system the distribution of finished products to consumers is based on the consumers' ability and willingness to pay the market price for the products. If the market-clearing price of a bottle of wine is £2.50, those consumers who are able and willing to pay that price will get their wine. Those consumers who are not, will not.

Here we are talking about the *rationing* function of market-clearing prices in a price system. Rather than have a central political figure decide which consumers will get which goods, those consumers who are willing to pay the market-clearing price obtain the good. That is to say, relative prices ration the available resources, goods, and services at any point in time among those who would like to have the scarce items. If scarcity did not exist, then we would not need any system to ration available resources, goods, and services.

The Determination of Money Income

In a price system, a consumer's ability to pay for consumer products is based on the size of his or her money income. That, in turn, depends on the quantities, qualities, and types of the various human and non-human resources that the individual owns and supplies to the market-place. Additionally, the prices, or payments, for those resources influence total money income. When you are selling your human resources as labour services, your money income is based on the wage-rate, or salary, that you can fetch in the labour market. If you own non-human resources – capital and land, for example – the level of interest and rents that you would be paid for your capital and land will clearly influence the size of your money income and thus your ability to buy consumer products.

What are the implications of these observations? Well, if labour services are not paid for at a common wage-rate and also not everyone has capital to invest to advantage, then we will soon face normative issues. How fair is such a system when some people have more money than others? The 'for whom' question quickly makes us strain away from the world of positive economics.

Figure 6.3
Production Costs for 100 Units of Product X. Technique A or B can be used to produce the same output. Obviously, B will be used because its total cost is less than A's.

Inputs	Input unit Price	A Production technique A (input units)	Cost	B Production technique B (input units)	Cost
Labour	£10	5	£50	4	£40
Capital	£ 8	4	£32	5	£40
Total cost of 100 units of product X			£82		£80

A 'perfectly performing' price system may not provide for much equality in income. That is to say, an efficient price system could still be one in which some people were starving to death. If one of the social goals in a society is to provide more income equality, then something other than the price system must be utilized. Indeed, most Western economies have a taxation system that attempts to reduce the high levels of income of the highest-income-earning individuals; and we also have a system of welfare, in which we attempt to transfer some of those revenues collected by taxes to the lowest-earning (or non-earning) members of our society.

Related to the social goal of income equality is the goal of income security. The price system may not guarantee income security to all. A non-market system, using government, may therefore be (and is) an alternative. For example, the provision of government-provided unemployment insurance benefits (paid by taxes) is an attempt to reduce income insecurity among the economy's participants.

This recognition of the shortcomings of a market economy concerning the distribution of goods and services prompts the need for a more general reappraisal of the price system. What perhaps have we too readily assumed in the above analysis?

Evaluating the Price System

It is possible to evaluate the price system in terms of what it can and cannot do. When a price system alone cannot satisfy certain social goals, then government or voluntary solutions to problems need to be examined.

What the Price System Can Do

Throughout this chapter we have seen that the price system can communicate information concerning relative scarcity and opportunity costs. And, in a world in which individual preferences are self-determined (rather than programmed), individual preferences can be expressed via the purchase or non-purchase of commodities. The communication-of-information function of the price system, as we have seen, leads to efficiency.

EFFICIENCY

The price system does lead to both technical and economic efficiency. Competition among firms forces them to choose the least-cost production techniques, thus avoiding waste (technical efficiency). In the absence of restraints and imperfections in the system (to be discussed below), maximum economic value is obtained from a given set of resources at any point in time (economic efficiency). In some sense, then, the price system harnesses self-interest in order to provide society with the greatest possible output of desired goods. The price system leads to a movement of resources from lower- to relatively higher-valued

uses. Thus, resources will not stay in an industry, the demand for whose product has withered away because of a change in consumer tastes.

INDIVIDUAL FREEDOM

Another aspect of the price system which can be listed as something it can do involves maximizing individual, or personal, freedom. Since the co-ordination of social organization through a price system does not require central direction or the use of force by any governmental authority, individual freedom presumably obtains. The price system allows for a type of spontaneous co-ordination that has been described as 'an invisible hand'. The price system permits, as it were, the freedoms of choice and enterprise. Individuals are free to further their self-interest. One of the contemporary champions of the price system has said that

So long as effective freedom of exchange is maintained, the central feature of the market organization of economic activity is that it prevents one person from interfering with another in respect of most of his activities. The consumer is protected from coercion by the seller because of the presence of other sellers with whom he can deal. The seller is protected from coercion by the consumer because of other consumers to whom he can sell. The employee is protected from coercion by the employer because of other employers for whom he can work, and so on. And the market does this impersonally and without centralized authority.*

GROWTH

A price system can (and historically has) led to economic growth. Remember from Chapter 1 that we defined economic growth as an increase in the productive capacity of a nation over time (a shifting outwards to the right of the production possibilities curve). Since the price system offers a reward-and-penalty signalling system to its participants, there is an incentive to increase productivity because of the reward (profits). No centralized authority must decide which innovations should be utilized to increase productivity; rather, market participants make the decisions and those who make the correct decisions are rewarded by increased profits. Consequently, one can argue that a price system provides the setting for economic growth because of its reward system for those who choose correctly. Moreover, because of the penalty of reduced profits, or even losses, resources do not stay in areas where consumer demand no longer exists.

What the Price System Cannot Do

The 'market' does not always work. That is to say, there are market failures that prevent the price system from actually attaining economic efficiency and individual freedom – as well as other social goals. And, of course, every case in which the price system cannot

---

*Milton Friedman, *Capitalism and Freedom* (Chicago: University of Chicago Press, 1962), pp. 14–15.

attain a social goal is a case in which non-market alternatives must be considered.

EXTERNALITIES

If the price system does not register all the costs and benefits associated with the production and/or consumption of commodities, then an externality arises. We define an **externality** as a cost or benefit external to an exchange. In other words, the external benefits or costs accrue to parties other than the immediate seller and buyer in a transaction. An obvious example of an external cost is the pollution of air and water. These are externalities because they result from production and consumption activities in which the parties involved do not take account of such ill effects on others. The point to be made is that whenever supply and demand do not fully reflect all costs and all benefits of production and consumption, the price system cannot be expected to bring about an efficient allocation of resources. (Externalities are an extremely important topic in economics; we treat them in detail in Chapter 10.)

PUBLIC GOODS

The price system relates to the tabulation of individual wants only. Many goods and services are not, however, financed by individuals through the marketplace. Flood control programmes and national defence cannot be purchased in small amounts by households and individuals. They can be consumed only on a public, or collective, basis. The price system, then, is considered to be incapable of providing such public goods in optimal quantities. (We treat them in more detail in Chapter 10.)

COMPETITION

Implicit in much of the discussion of supply and demand in Chapter 5 and of the price system in this chapter is the notion of competition, where there are many buyers and sellers of products. But even in a price system, there may be a lack of competition because of, for example, successful efforts on the part of business persons to restrict competition. Adam Smith realized that 'people of the same trade seldom meet together for fun and merriment, but the conversation ends in a conspiracy against the public, or in some contrivance to raise prices'.*

Smith's fear of conspiracies and monopolies that would hurt consumers is a fear that still is with us today. For many, this fear has taken on the form of reality, for they believe that there is little competition left in many parts of the UK economy. The price system cannot work to its fullest advantage if there are restraints on trade through monopoly. Whenever the degree of competition declines, the price system becomes less of a perfect mechanism for efficiently allocating resources.

If there is a recognition of the need to ensure a fully competitive market system then some scope for government intervention is implied. Governments may, for example, wish to restrict the willingness of large firms in particular markets to merge together and dominate them. (We consider policies in the UK to make product markets more competitive in chapter 30.)

UNEQUAL INCOME DISTRIBUTION

We have already recognized that the market system may operate in a technical sense well but do so in the context of what some see as an unfair distribution of income and wealth. Government policies to redistribute income and wealth can try to 'correct' this shortcoming of the market mechanism.

FACTOR IMMOBILITY

We showed earlier in the chapter how shifts in the demand for potatoes and carrots brought about price adjustments and ensuing changes in profitability for farmers. The end result was that there would be a reallocation of resources and it was implicitly assumed that this process would take place readily and without difficulty. If we now broaden our horizons we can recognize that in the real world the factors of production will not, in practice, be re-allocated as easily as in this theoretical example. Labour cannot readily move from one industry to another since retraining and relocation of work are likely to be involved.

A second dimension to this problem of the less than perfect mobility of factors of production is the phenomenon of *structural change*. It is not just shifts in demand that prompt the need for resource re-allocation but also the process of technological change as represented, for example, by the appearance of microprocessors and robotic equipment. Industries such as steel and motor vehicle manufacturing are undergoing major change in terms of the character of the industrial process. Can a purely market economy handle the reallocation of capital and labour without some government intervention?

Manufacturing in the UK is exposed to foreign competition both in the home market and in overseas markets, whereas the service industries, by their very nature face no international competition at all. We must recognize that the problem of resource allocation is now more crucial than ever before due to the rapid pace of technological change and the growing competition in manufactured goods from the more advanced developing countries.

The Results of the Evaluation

The price system it seems satisfy some social goals, and, at the same time, it cannot satisfy numerous others. As you might expect, therefore, the actual economic system that exists in the United Kingdom and most developed countries is a combination of the price system and a non-price system – and that is what we will examine in Chapter 8.

---

*Adam Smith, *The Wealth of Nations* (1776), Bk. I, Ch. 10, Everyman edn., p. 117.

Key Points 6.6

▶ Within a price system competition forces producers to seek least-cost techniques of production. Competition is thus the driving-force behind the free market solution of how goods and services are to be produced.

▶ The actual distribution of goods and services is dependent on the ability and willingness of consumers to make payments for these outputs. This ability to pay will be dependent on the size of money incomes. Money incomes are unequal since there is not an even ownership of human and non-human resources.

▶ A pricing system can lead to technical and economic efficiency while permitting individual freedom within a dynamic economy. However, a price system may in practice lack strong competitive pressures to promote efficiency.

▶ A pricing system cannot, without non-market intervention, easily take care of externalities. Nor can it provide a sufficient amount of public goods. A pricing system can also operate in a society where income disparities are so great that government intervention to achieve the social goal of income equality is widely accepted as being desirable.

CASE STUDY

The Just Price in Cigarettes

Supply and demand operate at any time that transactions are made, even when money is not present. When supply and demand interact, prices may change. How can prices be determined if no coin or currency is used in the trading? During World War II in prisoner-of-war camps in Germany, barter replaced the kind of exchange described in this chapter, and as time passed, more complex exchange systems developed in the camps. In the article that is quoted in the following paragraphs, you can read about what actually took place. It is a fascinating and instructive first-hand account of how markets, money, and supply and demand developed *spontaneously* in prisoner-of-war camps:

We reached a transit (prisoner-of-war) camp in Italy about a fortnight after capture and received a quarter of a Red Cross food parcel each a week later. At once

exchanges, already established, multiplied in volume. Starting with simple direct barter, such as a non-smoker giving a smoker friend his cigarette issue in exchange for a chocolate ration, more complex exchanges soon became an accepted custom. Stories circulated of a padre who started off round the camp with a tin of cheese and five cigarettes and returned to his bed with a complete parcel in addition to his original cheese and cigarettes; the market was not yet perfect. Within a week or two, as the volume of trade grew, rough scales of exchange values came into existence. Sikhs (followers of an Indian monotheistic religion that rejects idolatry and the caste system of India) who had at first exchanged tinned beef for practically any other foodstuff began to insist on jam and was worth ½ lb. of margarine plus something else; that a cigarette issue was worth several chocolates issues, and a tin of diced carrots

was worth practically nothing.

In this camp we did not visit other bungalows very much and prices varied from place to place; hence the germ of truth in the story of the itinerant priest. By the end of a month, when we reached our permanent camp,* there was a lively trade in all commodities and their relative values were well known, and expressed not in terms of one another – one didn't quote bully (canned beef) in terms of sugar – but in terms of cigarettes. The cigarette became the standard of value. In the permanent camp people started by wandering through the bungalows calling their offers – 'cheese for seven'

*Notice the difference between a transit camp and a permanent camp. A transit camp is where prisoners-of-war were first taken but not where they were permanently going to stay. After they were at the transit camp for some time, it was decided where their permanent 'home' would be in a permanent prisoner-of-war camp.

(cigarettes) – and the hours after parcel issue were Bedlam. The inconveniences of this system soon led to its replacement by an exchange and mart notice board in every bungalow, where under the headings 'name', 'room number', 'wanted' (bid) and 'offered' (offer) sales and wants were advertised. When a deal went through, it was crossed off the board. The public and semi-permanent records of transactions led to cigarette prices being well known and thus tending to equality throughout the camp ... With this development everyone, including non-smokers, was willing to sell for cigarettes, using them to buy at another time and place. Cigarettes became the normal currency, though, of course, barter was never extinguished.

The unity of the market and the prevalence of a single price varied directly with the general level of organization and comfort in the camp. A transit camp was always chaotic and uncomfortable: people were overcrowded, no one knew where anyone else was living, and few took the trouble to find out. Organization was too slender to include an exchange and mart board, and private advertisements were the most that appeared. Consequently, a transit camp was not one market but many. The price of a tin of salmon is known to have varied by two cigarettes in 20 between one end of a hut and the other. Despite a high level of organization in Italy, the market was (broken up) ... in this manner at the first transit camp we reached after our removal to Germany in the autumn of 1943. In this camp – Stalag VIIA at Moosburg in Bavaria – there were up to 50 000 prisoners of all nationalities. French, Russians, Italians and Yugo-Slavs were free to move about within the camp; British and Americans were confined to their compounds, although a few cigarettes given to a sentry would always procure permission for one or two men to visit other

compounds. The people who first visited the highly organized French trading centre with its stalls and known prices found coffee extract – relatively cheap among the tea-drinking English – commanding a fancy price in biscuits or cigarettes, and some enterprising people made small fortunes that way. (Incidentally we found out later that much of the coffee went 'over the wire' and sold for phenomenal prices at black market cafés in Munich: some of the French prisoners were said to have made substantial sums in RMs (Reich marks, the German currency). This was one of the few occasions on which our normally closed economy came into contact with other economic worlds.)

Eventually public opinion grew hostile to these monopoly profits – not everyone could make contact with the French – and trading with them was put on a regulated basis. Each group of beds was given a quota of articles to offer and the transaction was carried out by accredited representatives from the British compound, with monopoly rights. The same method was used for trading with sentries elsewhere, as in this trade secrecy and reasonable prices had a peculiar importance, but as is ever the case with regulated companies, the interloper proved too strong.

The permanent camps in Germany saw the highest level of commercial organization. In addition to the exchange and mart notice boards, a shop was organized as a public utility, controlled by representatives of the Senior British Officer, on a no-profit basis. People left their surplus clothing, toilet requisites and food there until they were sold at a fixed price in cigarettes. Only sales in cigarettes were accepted – there was no barter – and there was no higgling. For food at least there were standard prices: clothing is less homogeneous and the price was decided around a norm by the seller and the shop

manager in agreement; shirts would average say 80, ranging from 60 to 120 according to quality and age. Of food, the shop carried small stocks for convenience; the capital was provided by a loan from the bulk store of Red Cross cigarettes and repaid by a small commission taken on the first transactions. Thus the cigarette attained its fullest currency status, and the market was almost completely unified.

Public opinion on the subject of trading was vocal if confused and changeable, and generalizations as to its direction are difficult and dangerous. A tiny minority held that all trading was undesirable as it engendered an unsavoury atmosphere; occasional frauds and sharp practices were cited as proof. Certain forms of trading were more generally condemned; trade with the Germans was criticized by many. Red Cross toilet articles, which were in short supply and only issued in cases of actual need, were excluded from trade by law and opinion working in unshakable harmony. At one time, when there had been several cases of malnutrition reported among the more devoted smokers, no trade in German rations was permitted, as the victims became an additional burden on the depleted food reserves of the Hospital. But while certain activities were condemned as antisocial, trade itself was practised, and its utility appreciated, by almost everyone in the camp.

More interesting was opinion on middlemen and prices. Taken as a whole, opinion was hostile to the middleman. His function, and his hard work in bringing buyer and seller together, were ignored; profits were not regarded as a reward for labour, but as the result of sharp practices. Despite the fact that his very existence was proof to the contrary, the middleman was held to be redundant in view of the existence of an official shop and the exchange and mart.

continued overleaf

Appreciation only came his way when he was willing to advance the price of a sugar ration, or to buy goods spot and carry them against a future sale. In these cases the element of risk was obvious to all, and the convenience of the service was felt to merit some reward ... Opinion notwithstanding, most people dealt with a middleman, whether consciously or unconsciously, at some time or another.

There was a strong feeling that everything had its 'just price' in cigarettes. While the assessment of the just price, which incidentally varied between camps, was impossible of explanation, this price was nevertheless pretty closely known. It can best be defined as the price usually fetched by an article in good times when cigarettes were plentiful. The 'just price' changed slowly; it was unaffected by short-term variations in supply, and while opinion might be resigned to departures from the 'just price', a strong feeling of resentment persisted. A more satisfactory definition of the 'just price' is impossible. Everyone knew what it was, though no one could explain why it should be so.

Source: R. A. Radford, 'The Economic Organization of a POW Camp', *Economica*, New Series, vol. 12, Nov. 1945, pp. 189–201.

Questions

1. What substitutes for currency and coin were used by the prisoners? Did the fact that substitutes were used mean that a price system was not operating?
2. How did supply and demand operate within the prisoner-of-war camp?
3. Were non-smokers better off than smokers?
4. What factors influenced (a) the structure of prices and (b) the general level of prices?

Exam Preparation and Practice

INTRODUCTORY EXERCISES

1. Assume that in 1980 a pint of beer cost 50p while a pint of whisky cost £5. By 1984, the respective absolute prices had risen to 70p and £6.30. What happened to the relative price of whisky in relation to beer? Suppose that the average of all other prices rose by 70 per cent over the same period. That is to say, in 1984 it cost £170 to buy the same goods and services that would have cost £100 in 1980. What has happened to the relative prices of beer and whisky in comparison to all other consumer goods and services?

2. List the types of transaction costs that are involved in locating and buying a home. After you have listed them, can you think of ways to economize on such transaction costs?

3. Assume that a business has found that its most profitable output occurs when it produces £172 worth of output of a particular product. It can choose from three possible techniques, A, B, and C, that will produce the desired level of output. We see the amount of inputs these techniques use along with each input price in the following table.

Price of input (per unit)		Production techniques		
		A (units)	B (units)	C (units)
£10	Land	7	4	1
£ 2	Labour	6	7	18
£15	Capital	2	6	3
£ 8	Entrepreneurship	1	3	2

(a) Which technique will the firm choose and why?
(b) What would the firm's maximum profit be?
(c) If the price of labour increases to £4 per unit, which technique will be chosen and why? What will happen to profits?

4. *Daily work effort*   *Mrs Jones*
        4 hours   8 jackets
        4 hours   12 ties

                                Mr Jones
        4 hours   8 jackets
        4 hours   12 ties

        Total daily output = 16 jackets, 24 ties.

Given the above information, answer the following questions.
  (a) Who has an absolute advantage in jacket production?
  (b) Who has a comparative advantage in tie production?
  (c) Will Mrs and Mr Jones specialize?
  (d) If they specialize, what will total output equal?

5. *Daily work effort*   *Mrs Jones*
        4 hours   8 jackets
        4 hours   12 ties

                                Mr Jones
        4 hours   4 jackets
        4 hours   12 ties

        Total daily output = 12 jackets, 24 ties.

Given the above information, answer the following questions.
  (a) In what does Mrs Jones have an absolute advantage?
  (b) In what does Mr Jones have an absolute advantage?
  (c) In what does Mrs Jones have a comparative advantage?
  (d) In what does Mr Jones have a comparative advantage?
  (e) If they specialize according to their comparative advantages, what will total output equal?

MULTIPLE CHOICE QUESTIONS

1. Markets are important to economic exchanges because they reduce transactions costs. Transaction costs are defined as:
  A the price of the product
  B all of the costs enabling exchanges to take place
  C a market mechanism to disseminate price information
  D those costs suppliers consider when determining the quantities they will put on the market

2. The term 'relative price' refers to a price relative to:
  A people's income
  B people's wealth
  C other prices
  D what the price was in the past

3. Use of the least-cost production technique for a given output is characteristic of:
  A economic efficiency
  B technical efficiency
  C production possibilities
  D the transformation curve

4. Economic efficiency means that:
  A least-cost methods of production are used
  B resources move to their highest-valued uses via the price system
  C consumer sovereignty is irrelevant in determining the outcomes of markets
  D individuals and business people cannot rely on their own self-interests but must rely on the government's determination of economic decisions

5. Opponents of the price system criticize the system for all but one of the following reasons:
  A the market does not register all of the costs and benefits associated with production or consumption
  B the price system is incapable of providing social goods in adequate quantities
  C competition is promoted among firms which forces them to choose the least-cost production techniques
  D all of the above

RELATED ESSAY QUESTION

What are the economic strengths and weaknesses of a free market economy?

7 Demand and Supply Elasticity

Key Points to Review

▶ **Demand (5.1, 5.2)**
▶ **Shifts versus movements along demand curves (5.3, 5.6)**

▶ **Supply (5.4, 5.5)**

Questions for Preview

1 What is price elasticity of demand?

2 How is total revenue related to price elasticity of demand?

3 What are the determinants of price elasticity of demand?

4 What is cross price elasticity of demand?

5 What is income elasticity of demand?

6 What is price elasticity of supply?

The corner-stone of microeconomic analysis is supply and demand, concepts already discussed in Chapter 5. Microeconomic analysis concerns itself with decision-making by individuals in their capacity as consumers, workers, and business persons. Our analysis of micro-economic decision-making involves an examination of how the various decisions made by individuals ultimately determine prices and quantities in the real world.

Remember from Chapter 5 that the fundamental theory of demand is that there is an inverse relationship between prices and quantity demanded, holding other things constant. If price goes up, less will be consumed or used than before. If price goes down, more will be consumed or used than before. If you are a decision-maker in a top-management position at, say, Sinclair Research, will knowing the theory of demand help you in any way to decide whether you should change the price of one of your products? The answer is obviously 'no'. You can predict the *direction* of change in quantity demanded if you raise price or lower price, but you will not be able to tell *by how much* quantity demanded will change. In August 1985

Sinclair announced a 50 per cent reduction in the price of its QL computer called Spectrum. Since its intro-duction Spectrum had not sold as well as anticipated. Management at Sinclair decided that it was necessary to reduce the price to induce more people to purchase it and meet competition from the new Amstrad system priced at £199. Clearly, management had to have some idea of the increase in the quantities of the QL model sold per year that would result from the 50 per cent drop in price. If potential consumers were not going to respond much to the lower price – if quantity demanded was going to remain about the same – then management at Sinclair would have made a critical business error, for the drop in price of the QL would not have been matched by much increase in quantity demanded, and the total revenues from the sale of QL would fall.

In other words, some measure of the *responsiveness* of consumers to changes in price is necessary in order to estimate the effects of changes in price. Not only management in private firms, but decision-makers within government have to have an idea of how responsive people in the real world will be to changes in price. Economists have given a special name to price-responsiveness – *price elasticity*. Elasticity is the subject of this chapter.

Price Elasticity

To begin to understand what 'elasticity' is all about, just keep in mind that it means 'responsiveness'. Here we are concerned with the price elasticity of demand and the price elasticity of supply. We wish to know the extent to which a change in the price of, say, petroleum products will cause the quantity demanded and the quantity supplied to change, other things held constant. Let us restrict our discussion at first to the demand side.

Price Elasticity of Demand

We will formally define the **price elasticity of demand**, which we will label e_d, as follows:

$$e_d = \frac{\text{percentage change in quantity demanded}}{\text{percentage change in price}}$$

What will price elasticity of demand tell us? It will tell us the relative amount by which the quantity demanded will change in response to a change in the price of a particular good.

Consider an example where a 10 per cent rise in the price of petrol leads to a reduction in quantity demanded of only 1 per cent. Putting these numbers into the formula, we find that the price elasticity of demand of oil equals the percentage change in quantity demanded divided by the percentage change in price, or,

$$e_d = \frac{-1 \text{ per cent}}{+10 \text{ per cent}} = -0.1$$

Notice that this number is pure – that is, dimensionless, a percentage divided by a percentage.*

---

*Miles divided by gallons gives the ratio 'miles per gallon'. But when you see a ratio without such a dimension, that means that the ratio is comparing two identical dimensions.

An elasticity of –0.1 means that a 1 per cent *decrease* in the price would lead to a mere one-tenth of 1 per cent *increase* in the quantity demanded. If you were now told that the price elasticity of demand for oil was, say, –1, then you would know that a 1 per cent increase in the price of petrol would lead to a 1 per cent decrease in the quantity demanded.

Basically, the greater the numerical price elasticity of demand, the greater the demand responsiveness to relative price changes – small change in price has a great impact on quantity demanded. The smaller the numerical price elasticity of demand, the smaller the demand responsiveness to relative price changes – a large change in price has little effect on quantity demanded.

PRICE ELASTICITY OF DEMAND IS ALWAYS NEGATIVE

Remember that the theory of demand states that quantity demanded is *inversely* related to the relative price. Thus, in the preceding example, an increase in the price of oil led to a decrease in the quantity demanded. Alternatively, we could have used an example of a decrease in the relative price of oil, in which case the quantity demanded would increase a certain percentage. The point is that price elasticity of demand will always be negative. By convention, *we will ignore the negative sign in our discussion from this point on.*

RELATIVE QUANTITIES ONLY

Notice that in our elasticity formula, we talk about *percentage* changes in quantity demanded divided by percentage changes in price. We are not, therefore, interested in the absolute changes, but only in relative amounts. This means that it does not matter if we measure price changes in terms of pence, pounds, or hundreds of pounds. It also does not matter whether we measure quantity changes in, for example, ounces, grams, or pounds. The percentage change will be the same. However, if the concept of price elasticity is really quite a simple one we find that in practice the arithmetical calculation is not quite so straightforward. We now explain what the problem is confronting us and how it can be resolved.

Key Points 7.1

▶ **Price elasticity is a measure of the responsiveness of the quantity demanded and supplied to a change in price.**

▶ **The price elasticity of demand is equal to the percentage change in quantity demanded divided by the percentage change in price.**

▶ **The theory of demand states that quantity demanded and price are inversely related. Therefore, the price elasticity of demand is always negative, since an increase in price will lead to a decrease in quantity demanded and a decrease in price will lead to an increase in quantity demanded**

▶ **Price elasticity of demand is calculated in terms of relative percentage changes in quantity demanded and in price. Thus, we end up with a unitless, scaleless number.**

Calculation of Elasticity

In order to calculate the price elasticity of demand, we have to compute percentage changes in quantity demanded and in relative price. To obtain the percentage change in quantity demanded, we can look at

$$\frac{\text{change in quantity demanded}}{\text{original quantity demanded}} \times 100 \text{ per cent}$$

To find the percentage change in price, we can look at

$$\frac{\text{change in price demanded}}{\text{original price demanded}} \times 100 \text{ per cent}$$

There is a slight problem with computation of percentage changes in this manner. We get a different answer depending on whether we move up the demand curve or down the demand curve.

Consider the hypothetical data presented in Figure 7.1 for the quantities of petrol demanded by UK consumers at various prices. For the moment we are just looking at these first four columns.

Columns 1 and 3 of Figure 7.1(a) are simply the quantity demanded and price data for the demand curve represented graphically as Figures 7.1(b) and (c). Columns 2 and 4 show changes in quantity demanded corresponding to changes in price.

Let us start with a quantity of one unit demanded at the price of £10 per unit and *move down the demand curve*. If we start at a price of £10 with 1 unit demanded, price then falls to £9. Quantity demanded increases to 2. The percentage change in price is:

[(£10 – £9)/£10] × 100 per cent, or:
(£1 ÷ £10) × 100 per cent = 10 per cent

The percentage change in quantity demanded is:

[(2 – 1)/1] × 100 per cent, or:
(1 ÷ 1) × 100 per cent = 100 per cent

Thus, price elasticity of demand is equal to:

100 per cent ÷ 10 per cent = 10

Now let us calculate the price elasticity of demand when *we move up the demand curve*. We start at a price of £9 with 2 units demanded. The price goes up to £10 and 1 unit is demanded. The percentage change in price is now equal to:

[(£10 – £9)/£9] × 100 per cent =
(£1 ÷ £9) × 100 per cent = 11.11 per cent.

The percentage change in quantity demanded is:

[(2 – 1)/2] × 100 per cent, or:
(1 ÷ 2) × 100 per cent = 50 per cent

Thus, the price elasticity of demand is now equal to:

50 per cent ÷ 11.11 per cent = 4.5

Quite a difference! We show this in Figure 7.1(b).

USING AVERAGE VALUES

For the same segment of the demand curve, we get different values of price elasticity of demand because the original prices and quantities depend on whether we move up or down the demand curve. The *absolute* changes in price and quantity are the same size regardless of direction. But when moving down the demand curve, the *original* price is higher than when moving up the demand curve. When moving up the demand curve, the original quantity demanded is greater. Since a percentage change depends on the size of the original value, the percentages we calculate for price elasticity of demand will be affected by choosing a higher price and smaller quantity, or a lower price and greater quantity. One way out of this difficulty is to *take the average of the two prices and the two quantities* over the range we are considering and compare the change to the average, instead of comparing it to the price or quantity at the start of the change.

The formula for computing price elasticity of demand then becomes:

$$e_d = \frac{\text{change in quantity}}{\text{sum of quantities}/2} \times 100 \text{ per cent}$$
$$\div \frac{\text{change in price}}{\text{sum of prices}/2} \times 100 \text{ per cent}$$

We can rewrite this more simply if we do two things: (1) We can let Q_1 and Q_2 equal the two different quantities demanded before and after the price change, and P_1 and P_2 equal the two different prices; and (2) because we will be dividing a per cent by a per cent, we simply use the ratio, or the decimal form, of the per cent. Therefore,

$$e_d = \frac{\text{change in } Q}{(Q_1 + Q_2)/2} \div \frac{\text{change in } P}{(P_1 + P_2)/2}$$

Look again at the example that showed a price elasticity of demand equal to 10 when moving from a £10 price to a £9 price, but gave an elasticity of 4.5 when moving from £9 to £10. We insert our numbers in the average formula just given, so that price elasticity of demand becomes in either case:

$$e_d = \frac{1}{\left(\frac{1+2}{2}\right)} \Bigg/ \frac{1}{\left(\frac{9+10}{2}\right)} = \frac{1}{\left(\frac{3}{2}\right)} \Bigg/ \frac{1}{\left(\frac{19}{2}\right)}$$
$$= \frac{2}{3} \Bigg/ \frac{2}{19} = \frac{38}{8} = 6.33$$

We show this in Figure 7.1(c).

Thus, calculating the price elasticity of demand, using the mid-point (or average) formula, yields, $e_d = 6.33$. This calculation is not affected by the direction of movement along the demand curve; that is, $e_d = 6.33$ whether we move up or down the demand curve over the range we have been considering.

If we now look again at Figure 7.1 we note that columns 5 and 6 give us the average quantities and the average prices. And finally, in the last column, a numerical example of price elasticity of demand is given.

Figure 7.1(a)

Numerical Calculation of Price Elasticity of Demand for Petrol. Column 1 is the quantity demanded at different prices. Column 2 is the change in the quantity demanded. In other words, we merely subtract the smaller from the larger quantity. In each case, the change is 1 million gallons per day. Column 3 is the price per gallon, and column 4 is the change in the price, which happens to be £1 in each case. Columns 5 and 6 are the average quantities and prices, e.g. $(Q_1 + Q_2)/2 = (0 + 1)/2 = 0.5$ and $(P_1 + P_2)/2 = (£11 + £10))/2 = £10.5$ for the first row. Column 7 presents an approximation of the price elasticity of demand, e_d.

(1) Quantity demanded Q (millions of gallons per day	(2) Change in Q millions of gallons per day	(3) Price (P) (£)	(4) Change in P (£)	(5) $\dfrac{Q_1 + Q_2}{2}$	(6) $\dfrac{P_1 + P_2}{2}$	(7) $\dfrac{\text{Change in Q}}{(Q_1 + Q_2)/2} \Big/ \dfrac{\text{Change in P}}{(P_1 + P_2)/2}$
0		11				
	1		1	0.5	10.5	$1/0.5 \div 1/10.5 = 21$
1		10				
	1		1	1.5	9.5	$1/1.5 \div 1/9.5 = 6.333$
2		9				
	1		1	2.5	8.5	$1/2.5 \div 1/8.5 = 3.4$
3		8				
	1		1	3.5	7.5	$1/3.5 \div 1/7.5 = 2.143$
4		7				
	1		1	4.5	6.5	$1/4.5 \div 1/6.5 = 1.444$
5		6				
	1		1	5.5	5.5	$1/5.5 \div 1/5.5 = 1$
6		5				
	1		1	6.5	4.5	$1/6.5 \div 1/4.5 = 0.692$
7		4				
	1		1	7.5	3.5	$1/7.5 \div 1/3.5 = 0.467$
8		3				
	1		1	8.5	2.5	$1/8.5 \div 1/2.5 = 0.294$
9		2				
	1		1	9.5	1.5	$1/9.5 \div 1/1.5 = 0.158$

Figure 7.1(b)
Two Different Elasticities

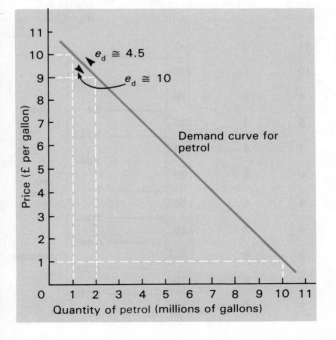

$e_d \cong 4.5$

$e_d \cong 10$

Demand curve for petrol

Figure 7.1(c)
Using Average Values

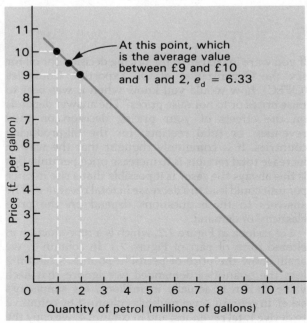

At this point, which is the average value between £9 and £10 and 1 and 2, $e_d = 6.33$

We see that the computation of elasticity ranges from 21 down to 0.158. What does that mean? Simply that at very high prices for petrol, such as between £10 and £9 a gallon, the response to a 1 per cent decrease in price will be a 21 per cent increase in the quantity demanded. At the other extreme, at relatively low prices for petrol – say, between £2 and £1 per gallon – the elasticity of 0.158 means that a 1 per cent reduction in price will be followed by only 0.158 of a 1 per cent increase in the quantity demanded. Thus, in our example, elasticity falls as price falls.

Different Kinds of Price Elasticities

We have definitions for the varying ranges of price elasticities, depending on whether a 1 per cent change in price elicits more or less than a 1 per cent change in the quantity demanded:

1. **Price-elastic demand**. We say that a good has a price-elastic demand whenever the price elasticity of demand is greater than 1. A 1 per cent change in price causes a response greater than 1 per cent change in quantity demanded. Candidates for elastic-demand sections of our demand schedule in Figure 7.1 are obviously an e of 1.444 and above.
2. **Unitary price elasticity of demand**. In this situation, a 1 per cent change in price causes a response of exactly 1 per cent change in the quantity demand.
3. **Price-inelastic demand**. Here, a 1 per cent change in price causes a response of less than 1 per cent change in quantity demanded. An elasticity of 0.692 and below in the last four rows of Figure 7.1(a), represents a situation of inelastic demand. In brief, a 1 per cent change in price causes a less than 1 per cent change in quantity demanded.

Elasticity and Total Revenues

If you were in charge of the pricing decision for oil for say the Organization of Oil Exporting Countries (OPEC), how would you know when it was best to raise prices or to not raise prices? The answer depends on the effects of your pricing decision on total revenues, or total receipts, for the oil-producing countries. It is commonly thought that the way to increase total receipts is to increase price per unit. But is this always the case? Is it possible that a rise in price per unit could lead to a decrease in total revenues? The answers to these questions depend on the price elasticity of demand.

Let us look at Figure 7.2, which is a reproduction in altered form of part of Figure 7.1. In column 1, we again show the price of petrol in pounds. Column 2 lists the quantities demanded (we ignore that each value shown is actually in millions, for simplicity's sake). In column 3, we multiply column 1 by column 2 to derive total revenues; and in column 4, we copy the

values of elasticity from Figure 7.1. Notice what happens to total revenues throughout the schedule. They rise steadily as the price rises from £1 to £5 per unit; then, when the price rises further to £6 per unit, total revenues remain constant at £30. At prices per unit higher than £6, total revenues actually fall as price is increased. So it is not safe to assume that a price increase is always the way to greater revenues. Indeed, if prices are above £6 per unit in this example, total revenues can only be increased by cutting prices – not by raising them.

Labelling Elasticity

The relationship between price and quantity on the demand schedule is given in columns 1 and 2 of panel (a) in Figure 7.2. In panel (c), the demand curve, DD, representing that schedule, is drawn. In panel (b), the total revenue curve representing the data in column 3

Figure 7.2

The Relationship between Price Elasticity of Demand and Total Revenues. Here we reproduce in different form, parts of Figure 7.1. In panel (a), we show the elastic, unit elastic, and inelastic sections of the demand schedule according to whether a reduction in price increases total revenues, causes them to remain constant, or causes them to decrease, respectively. In panel (b), we show graphically what happens to total revenues, and we have labelled the sections elastic, unit elastic, and inelastic, which we have also done in the accompanying demand curve shown in panel (c).

Panel (a)

(1) Price of petrol (£ per unit)	(2) Units demanded (per time period)	(3) Total revenue $TR = P \times Q$ [(1) × (2)]	(4) Elasticity $e_d = \dfrac{\text{change in } Q}{\dfrac{(Q_1 + Q_2)/2}{\text{change in } P}}$ $\dfrac{}{(P_1 + P_2)/2}$
11	0	0	
10	1	£10	21
9	2	18	6.333
8	3	24	3.4 } elastic
7	4	28	2.143
6	5	30	1.444
5	6	30	1 } unit elastic
4	7	28	0.692
3	8	24	0.467
2	9	18	0.294 } inelastic
1	10	10	0.158

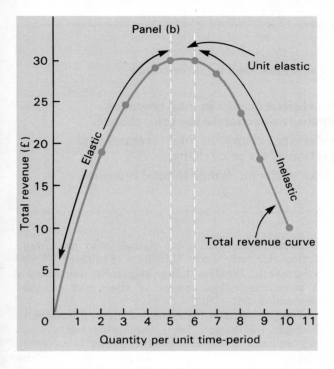

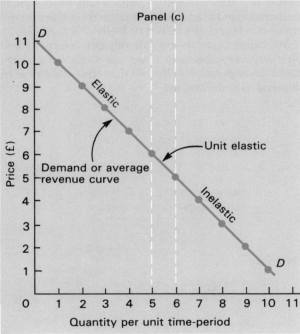

is drawn. Notice first the level of these curves at small quantities. The demand curve is at a maximum height, but total revenue is zero, which makes sense according to this demand schedule – at maximum price, no units will be purchased and therefore total revenue will be zero. As price is lowered, we travel down the demand curve, total revenues increase up to a price of £6 per unit, remain constant from £6 to £5 per unit, and then fall for lower unit prices. Corresponding to those three sections, demand is price elastic, unit elastic, and price inelastic. Hence, we have three relationships among

the three types of price elasticity and total revenues.

1. *Price-elastic demand.* A negative relationship between small changes in price and changes in total revenues. That is to say, if it lowers price, total revenues will rise when the firm faces demand that is price elastic. And if it raises price, total revenues will fall. Consider an example: if the price of Coca-Cola were raised by 25 per cent, and the price of all other soft drinks remained constant, the quantity demanded of Coca-Cola would probably fall dramatically. That is to say, the decrease in quantity demanded due to the increase in the price of Coca-Cola would be more than in proportion. Hence, such an increase in the price of Coca-Cola would lead, in this example, to a reduction in the total revenues of the firms that bottle Coca-Cola.

2. *Unit price-elastic demand.* Small changes in price do not change total revenues. In other words, when the firm is facing demand that is unitary price elastic, if it increases price, total revenues will not change; if it decreases price, total revenues will not change either.

3. *Price-inelastic demand.* A positive relationship between small changes in price and total revenue. In other words, when the firm is facing demand that is price inelastic, if it raises price, total revenues will go up; if it lowers price, total revenues will fall. Consider an example: imagine that you are managing director of a company which has just invented a cure for the common cold that has been approved by the health authorities for sale to the public. Your company is not sure what price you should charge. It decides on a price of £1 per pill. The firm sells 20 million pills at that price over a year. You feel the price could be raised without too much effect on sales. So next year, you decide to raise the price by 25 per cent. Suppose that the number of pills sold dropped to 18 million per year. The price increase of about 25 per cent has led to approximately a 10 per cent decrease in quantity demanded. However your total revenues will have risen because of the price increase.

We can see in Figure 7.2 the areas in the demand curve that are elastic, unit elastic, and inelastic. For prices from £11 per unit to £5 per unit, as price decreases, total revenues rise from zero to £30. Clearly, demand is price elastic. When prices change from £6 to £5, however, total revenues remain constant at £30; demand is unit elastic. Finally, when price falls from £5 to £1, total revenue decreases from £30 to £10; demand is price inelastic. In panels (b) and (c) of Figure 7.2, we have labelled the sections of the demand curve accordingly, and we have also shown how total revenues first rise, remain constant, and then fall.

The relationship between the price elasticity of demand and total revenue brings together some important microeconomic concepts. Total revenue, as we have noted, is the product of price per unit times quantity of units sold. The theory of demand states

Key Points 7.2

- **Price elasticity of demand is related to total revenues (and total consumer expenditures).**
- **When demand is elastic, the change in price elicits a change in total revenues (and total consumer expenditures) in the opposite direction to the price change.**
- **When demand is inelastic, a change in price elicits a change in total revenues (and in consumer expenditures) in the same direction as the price change.**
- **When demand is unit elastic, a change in price elicits no change in total revenues (or in total consumer expenditures).**

that, along a given demand curve, price and quantity changes will move in opposite directions: one increases as the other decreases. Consequently, what happens to the product of price times quantity depends on which of the opposing changes exerts a greater force on total revenue. But this is just what price elasticity of demand is designed to measure – responsiveness of quantity to a change in price.

The relationship between price elasticity of demand and total revenue, *TR*, is summarized in Figure 7.3.

Figure 7.3
The Relationship between Elasticity and Total Revenues.

	Price Elastic Demand	Unitary Elastic Demand	Price Inelastic Demand
Price Increase	↑ × ↓ → ↓ P × Q = TR	↑ × ↓ → No Change P × Q = TR	↑ × ↓ → ↑ P × Q = TR
Price Decrease	↓ × ↑ → ↑ P × Q = TR	↓ × ↑ → No Change P × Q = TR	↓ × ↑ → ↓ P × Q = TR

Changing Price Elasticity

We have seen in the example of the demand for petrol that the price elasticity changes as we move along the demand curve. That is to say, price elasticity is high when price is high and low when price is low. (Look again at columns 3 and 7 in Figure 7.1(a).) As a general rule, along any demand curve that is a straight line, price elasticity declines as we move down that demand curve. Consider the reason why. In our example in Figure 7.1(a), the change in price was always £1 and the change in the absolute quantity demanded was always 1 million gallons per day. Remember that here we are talking about absolute changes only. What about percentage changes? At the upper end of the demand curve, a £1 price change is in percentage terms relatively small (£1/[(£9 + £10)/2] = 10.5%) whereas the 1 million change in quantity demanded is a large percentage change of the small quantity demanded (1/[1 + 2)/2] = 66.7%).

Thus, at the top of the demand curve, the elasticity formula will have a large numerator and a small denominator; therefore, price elasticity is relatively elastic (66.7%/10.5% = 6.33). At the lower end of the curve, the price elasticity formula will have a small numerator and a large denominator; thus, the demand curve is relatively inelastic (10.5%/66.7% = 0.158).

We can indicate the relationship between price and elasticity very concisely if we use some basic arithmetic manipulations. Recall that the elasticity of demand, e_d is defined as:

$$e_d = \frac{\text{percentage change in quantity demanded}}{\text{percentage change in price}}$$

$$= \frac{\dfrac{\text{change in quantity demanded}}{\text{original quantity demanded}}}{\dfrac{\text{change in price}}{\text{original price}}}$$

therefore

$$e_d = \frac{\text{change in quantity demanded}}{\text{original quantity demanded}} \times \frac{\text{original price}}{\text{change in price}}$$

$$e_d = \frac{\text{change in quantity demanded}}{\text{change in price}} \times \frac{\text{original price}}{\text{original quantity demanded}}$$

But the slope of a demand curve is given as*

$$\text{slope} = \frac{\text{change in price}}{\text{change in quantity demanded}}$$

$$\text{so } e_d = \frac{1}{\text{slope}} \times \frac{\text{original price}}{\text{original quantity demanded}}$$

*Refer to Chapter 1 on graphical analysis for a refresher explanation on the meaning of slope.

Note that because we assumed a linear (straight-line) demand curve, slope (and therefore 1/slope) is a constant. However, as price falls, quantity demanded rises; therefore the *ratio* of price to quantity demanded must fall. As price falls we calculate e_d by multiplying a constant (1/slope) times a decreasing ratio (price : quantity demanded); as price falls e_d falls.

Elasticity and Slope

Students often confuse elasticity and slope. As the preceding analysis clearly indicates, however, they are *not* the same. We demonstrated that along a linear demand curve (that is, a straight line that has a *constant* slope, by definition) elasticity continuously falls with price. As a matter of fact, the calculated elasticity along a downward-sloping *straight-line* demand curve goes numerically from infinity to zero as we move down the curve. We therefore must always specify the *price range* when discussing price elasticity of demand, since most goods have ranges of both elasticity and inelasticity. The only time we can be sure of the elasticity of a straight-line demand curve by looking at it is if it is either perfectly horizontal or perfectly vertical. The horizontal straight-line demand curve has infinite elasticity at every quantity (it has only one price for every quantity). The vertical demand curve has zero elasticity at every price (it has only one quantity demanded at every price). Then we know that it has infinite elasticity or zero elasticity, respectively.

Extreme Elasticities

There are two extremes in price elasticities of demand: one is total unresponsiveness, which is called a **perfectly inelastic demand** situation or zero elasticity, and the other is complete responsiveness, which is called an unlimited, infinite, or **perfectly elastic demand** situation.

We show perfect inelasticity in panel (a) of Figure 7.4. Notice that the quantity demanded per year is 8 million units, no matter what the price. Hence, for any percentage price change, the quantity demanded will remain the same, and thus the change in the quantity demanded will be zero. Look at our formula for computing elasticity. If the change in the quantity demanded is zero, then the numerator is also zero, and anything divided into zero results in an answer of zero, too. Hence, perfect inelasticity.

At the opposite extreme is the situation depicted in panel (b) of Figure 7.4. Here we show that at the price of 30p, an unlimited quantity will be demanded. At a price that is only slightly above 30p, none will be demanded. In other words, there is complete, or infinite, responsiveness here, and hence we call the demand schedule in panel (b) of Figure 7.4 infinitely elastic.

Most estimated demand-schedule elasticities lie between the two extremes. For example, in Figure 7.5

Figure 7.4

Two Extreme Price Elasticities. In panel (a), we show complete price unresponsiveness. The demand curve is vertical at the quantity of 8 million units per year. That means that price elasticity of demand is zero. Consumers demand 8 million units of this particular commodity no matter what the price. In panel (b), we show complete responsiveness. At a price of 30p in this example, consumers will demand an unlimited quantity of the particular good in question. This is a case of infinite price elasticity of demand.

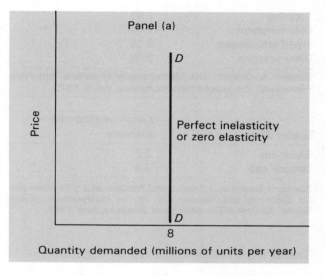

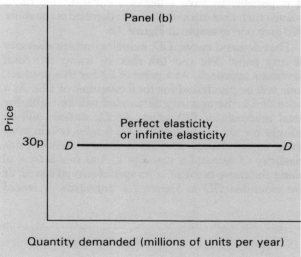

we present demand elasticities for selected goods. None of them is zero, and the largest one is 3.4 – a far cry from infinity. Remember, again, that though we are leaving off the negative sign, there is an inverse relationship between price and quantity demanded and that the minus sign is implicit. Also, remember that these elasticities represent average elasticities over *given* price ranges. Presumably, different price ranges would yield different elasticity estimates for these goods.

Figure 7.5

Demand Elasticity for Selected Items. Here we have obtained the estimated demand elasticities for selected items. All of them are negative, although we have not shown a minus sign. For example, the price elasticity of demand for dairy produce is 0.05. That means that a 1 per cent increase in the price of dairy produce will bring about a 0.05 per cent decrease in the quantity of dairy produce demanded.

Great Britain Commodity or service	Estimated elasticity in 1970
Catering	2.61
Entertainment	1.40
Bread and cereals	0.22
Dairy produce	0.05

Source: A. Deaton, 'The Measurement of Income and Price Elasticities', *European Economic Review*, Vol. 6, 1975.

United States	Long-run elasticity estimate
Electricity	2.2
Natural gas	3.4

Source: J. Beierlein, J. Dunn, and J. McConnan Jr., 'The Demand for Electricity and Natural Gas in the Northeastern United States', *Review of Economics and Statistics*, Aug. 1981.

Constant Price Elasticity of Demand

It is possible to have a demand curve that actually curves such that price elasticity of demand is constant. We give one example in Figure 7.6

That demand curve, *DD*, exhibits unitary elasticity at any point. We can tell this by using the total revenues approach. At a price of £8 for this product, four will be purchased for total revenues of £32. At a price of £4, the quantity demanded will be eight, for total revenues of £32 again. At £2, sixteen will be bought for total revenues of £32. A reduction in price leads to no change in total revenues; hence, price elasticity of demand is equal to 1. And this is true all along the curve because of its special curved shape. (If we extended *DD* in Figure 7.6 outwards, it would

Figure 7.6

Constant Price Elasticity of Demand. If the demand curve is curved in such a way that total revenues (and consumer expenditures) remain constant no matter what the price, then we have a demand curve that is everywhere unit elastic. This is what we show here.

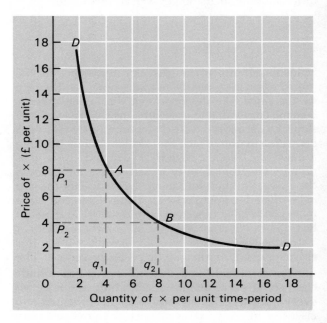

become a very flat line at the extreme ends, but, none the less, the elasticity at the extreme ends would be just the same as anywhere else on the curve.)

The way in which we found out the total revenues is an important tool that you should understand for the rest of this section. Remember the formula for total revenues:

total revenues = price × quantity

Thus, in Figure 7.6, we measured total revenues by looking at the *rectangle* formed from the price to the demand curve to the quantity axis. The vertical side of the rectangle was always equal to the price, and the horizontal side of the rectangle was always equal to the quantity. Thus, if asked how to determine total revenue for any price–quantity combination from a

---

Key Points 7.3

► The price elasticity of demand changes as we move down a straight-line demand curve; it becomes relatively more inelastic.

► Price elasticity of demand cannot be determined by looking at the *slope* of a straight-line demand curve. There are two extreme exceptions:

► When a demand curve is perfectly vertical, it has zero price elasticity of demand; it is completely inelastic.

► When a demand curve is perfectly horizontal, it has completely elastic demand; its price elasticity of demand is infinite.

demand curve, you simply form the appropriate rectangle. The *area* of that rectangle is equal to total revenues for the particular quantity under consideration.

The Determinants of the Price Elasticity of Demand

We have learned how to calculate the price elasticity of demand. We know that it ranges numerically from zero – completely inelastic – to infinity – completely elastic. What we would like to do now is come up with a list of the *determinants* of the price elasticity of demand. The price elasticity of demand for a particular commodity at any price depends on

1. The existence and closeness of substitutes
2. The length of time allowed for adjustment to changes in the price of the commodity.

Existence of Substitutes

The closer the substitutes for a particular commodity, the greater will be its price elasticity of demand. At the limit, if there is a perfect substitute, the price elasticity of the commodity will be infinity. Thus, even the slightest increase in the commodity's price will cause an enormous reduction in the quantity demanded; quantity demanded will fall to zero. We are really talking about two goods that the consumer believes are exactly alike and equally desirable, like five pound notes, whose only difference is serial numbers. When we talk about less extreme examples, we can only speak in terms of the number and the closeness of substitutes that are available. Thus, we will find that the more narrowly we define a good, the closer and greater will be the number of substitutes available. Take an example. If we talk about food and drinks in general, there are not many substitutes. If we talk about tea, there are certainly lots of substitutes, including coffee, milk, soft drinks, and so on. Thus, the more narrowly we define the good, the more substitutes there are available and the greater will be the price elasticity of demand. In this example, the price elasticity of demand for all beverages will be numerically much less than it is for, say, PG Tips tea. If the price of PG Tips tea increased by 20 per cent, a lot of people might switch over to another brand of tea such as Typhoo. On the other hand, if the price of all beverages went up on average by 20 per cent, certainly a smaller percentage of beverage consumers would switch over to beverage substitutes, such as food or recreation or whatever else might conceivably be considered a substitute for beverages. The availability of an alternative product for a particular commodity is, however, not the only relevant factor in determining the sensitivity of demand. In the real world consumers do not all react instantaneously to price changes and so we must recognize the importance of time.

The Time for Adjustment in Rate of Purchase

When the price of a commodity changes and that price change persists, more people will learn about it. Further, consumers will be better able to revise their consumption patterns, the longer the time they have to do so. And, in fact, the longer the time they do take, the less costly it will be for them to engage in this revision of consumption patterns. Consider a price decrease. The longer the time that the price decrease persists, the greater will be the number of new *uses* that consumers will 'discover' for the particular commodity, and the greater will be the number of new *users* of that particular commodity.

It is possible to make a very strong statement about the relationship between the price elasticity of demand and the time allowed for adjustment: *The longer any price change persists, the greater the price elasticity of demand.* Otherwise stated, price elasticity of demand is greater

---

Figure 7.7
Short-run and Long-run Price Elasticity of Demand. The longer the time allowed for adjustment, the greater the price elasticity of demand. In other words, for any given increase in price, the longer the time allowed for adjustment, the greater the reduction in quantity demanded; and for any given decrease in price, the longer the time allowed for adjustment, the greater the increase in quantity demanded. Consider an equilibrium situation in which the market price is P_e and the quantity demanded is Q_e. Then there is a price increase to P_1. In the short run, as evidenced by the demand curve D_1D_1, we move from equilibrium quantity demanded, Q_e, to Q_1. After more time is allowed for adjustment, the demand curve rotates at original price P_e to D_2D_2. Quantity demanded falls again, now to Q_2. After even more time is allowed for adjustment, the demand curve rotates at price P_e to D_3D_3. At the higher price P_1 in the long run, the quantity demanded falls all the way to Q_3.

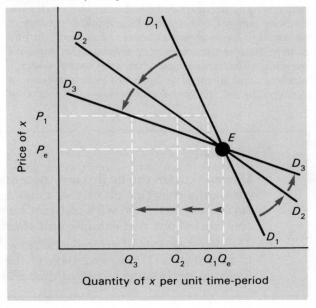

in the long run than in the short run.

Let us take an example. Suppose the price of electricity goes up 50 per cent. How do you adjust in the short run? You can turn the lights off more often, you can stop running the stereo as much as you used to, and so on. Otherwise, it is very difficult to cut back on your consumption of electricity. In the long run, though, you can devise methods to reduce your consumption. If your house has electric central heating you could contemplate switching to gas heating. If you are about to move house, one with gas-fired heating would have rather greater attraction than previously. The next time you move house you will have a gas cooker installed. You may even purchase fluorescent bulbs because they use less electricity. The longer you have to figure it out, the more ways you will find to cut electricity consumption. We would expect, therefore, that the short-run demand curve for electricity would be highly inelastic (in the price range around P_1), as demonstrated by D_1D_1 in Figure 7.7. However, the long-run demand curve may exhibit much more elasticity (in the neighbourhood of P_1), as demonstrated by D_3D_3. Indeed, we can think of an entire family of demand curves such as those depicted in that diagram. The short-run demand curve is for that period when there is no time for adjustment. As more time is allowed, the demand curve becomes flatter, going first to D_3D_3. Thus, *in the neighbourhood of P_1 elasticity differs for each of these curves*. It is greater for the less-steep curves (but remember, slope alone does not measure elasticity for the *entire* curve).

HOW TO DEFINE THE SHORT AND THE LONG RUN

We have mentioned the short run and we have mentioned the long run. Is the short run one week, two weeks, a month, two months? Is the long run three years, four years, five years? The answer is that there is no one answer! What we mean by the long run is that period of time necessary for consumers to make full adjustment to a given price change, all other things held constant. In the case of the demand for electricity, the long run will be however long it takes consumers to switch over to cheaper sources of heating, to buy houses that are more energy-efficient, to purchase manufactured appliances that are more energy-efficient, and so on. The long-run price elasticity of demand for electricity therefore relates to a period of

at least several years. The short run – by default, as it were – is any period less than the long run.

Cross-price Elasticity of Demand

We have already talked about the effect of a change in the price of one good on the quantity demanded of a related good back in Chapter 5. We defined substitutes and complements in terms of whether a reduction in the price of one caused a shift leftward or rightward, respectively, in the demand curve of the other. If the price of butter is held constant, the amount of butter demanded will certainly be influenced by the price of a close substitute like margarine. If the price of cassette players is held constant, the quantity of cassette players demanded is most likely to be affected by changes in the price of cassette recordings.

What we need to do is come up with a numerical measure of the price responsiveness of demand to the prices of related goods. This is called **cross-price elasticity of demand**, which is defined as the percentage change in the demand for one good divided by the percentage change in the price of the related good. Hence, the cross-price elasticity of demand is a measure of the responsiveness of one good's quantity demanded to changes in a related good's price.

When two goods are *substitutes*, the cross-price elasticity of demand will be *positive*. For example, when the price of margarine goes up, the quantity demanded of butter will go up too. A producer of margarine could use a numerical estimate of the cross-price elasticity of demand between butter and margarine. For example, if the price of butter went up by 10 per cent, and the margarine producer knew that the cross-price elasticity of demand was 1, he or she could estimate that the demand for margarine would also go up to 10 per cent. Plans for increasing margarine production could then be made.

When two related goods are *complements*, the cross-price elasticity of demand will be *negative*. To use an earlier example, when the price of cassette recordings goes up, the quantity demanded of cassette players is likely to fall. Any manufacturer of cassette players must take this into account in order to make production plans.

Key Points 7.4

▶ Demand curves can be linear or non-linear. Linear demand curves have constantly changing elasticities as we move along them. Non-linear demand curves *may* be drawn with constant elasticities of any desired value. We have constructed one that exhibits unit elasticity everywhere on the curve.

▶ The determinants of price elasticity of demand are: (1) the number and closeness of substitutes, (2) the percentage of the total budget spent on the good in question, and (3) the length of time allowed for adjustment to a change in prices.

Income Elasticity of Demand

In Chapter 5, we talked about the determinants of demand. One of those determinants was income. Using the same approach as we did in measuring the sensitivity of demand to changes in price we can apply our understanding of elasticity to the relationship between changes in income and changes in demand. We measure the responsiveness of quantity demanded to income changes by the **income elasticity of demand**:

e_y = income elasticity of demand

$$= \frac{\text{percentage change in the amount of good purchased}}{\text{percentage change in income}}$$

We will denote the income elasticity of demand by e_y.

Income elasticity of demand refers to a *horizontal shift* in the demand curve in response to changes in income (while price elasticity of demand refers to a movement *along* the curve is response to price changes). Shifts in demand curve will obviously have major implications for business persons. Those goods whose income elasticity is positive will be ones where markets will grow as consumers have more income to spend. Conversely, goods and services whose income elasticity is negative will be ones which will experience declining markets as consumer incomes increase. Before elaborating on this important matter let us be clear how to calculate income elasticity of demand.

A simple example will demonstrate how income elasticity of demand can be computed. In Figure 7.8, we give the relevant data. The product in question is stereo records. We assume that the price of stereo records remains constant relative to other prices. In period 1, six records per month are purchased. Income per month is £200. In period 2, monthly income is increased to £300 and the quantity of records demanded per month is increased to eight. We can apply the following calculation:

income elasticity of demand = e_y

$$= \frac{(8-6)/6}{(300-200)/200} = \frac{1/3}{1/3} = \frac{2}{3} = 0.667.$$

Hence, measured income elasticity of demand for record albums for the individual represented in this example is 0.667. Note that this holds only for the move from six records to eight records purchased per month. In the move for decreased income from £300 to £200 per month and from eight to six records per month, the calculation becomes:

$$\frac{(6-8)/8}{(200-300)/300} = \frac{2/8}{100/300} = \frac{1/4}{1/3} = \frac{3}{4} = 0.75$$

Thus, the measured income elasticity of demand is equal to 0.75.

To get the same income elasticity of demand over the same range of values, regardless of which direction the change (increase or decrease), we can use the same mid-point formula that we used in computing the price elasticity of demand. When doing so, we have the following:

$$e_r = \frac{\dfrac{\text{change in quantity}}{\text{sum of quantities}/2}}{\dfrac{\text{change in income}}{\text{sum of income}/2}}$$

Figure 7.8
How Income Affects Quantity of Records Demanded

Time-period	Quantity of stereo albums demanded per month	Income per month
Period 1	6	£200
Period 2	8	£300

This example involves just one product when there is a major increase in one person's income. Now let us consider the economy as a whole and how consumers alter their spending habits as they have more money available to spend. We might reasonably expect to find that spending on some goods and services is very sensitive to quite small changes in income. With yet other goods and services this income elasticity is less marked. We need something to classify the different reactions of consumers.

Different Kinds of Income Elasticity

We have the following definitions for the varying ranges of income elasticities depending on whether a 1 per cent change in income results in more or less than a 1 per cent change in the quantity demanded.

1. **Income elastic demand**. We say that a good or service has an income elastic demand whenever the income elasticity is greater than 1. A 1 per cent change in income causes a greater than 1 per cent change in quantity demanded. In these cases we are talking about *luxury goods*.
2. **Income inelastic demand**. Here a 1 per cent change in income causes a change of less than 1 per cent in quantity demanded. If the income inelasticity is less than 1 but above zero then this implies that the good or service is not one that is strongly sensitive to changes in consumer incomes. In other words it is a consumer *necessity*.
3. **Negative income elasticity**. Where the income elasticity is negative then it implies that in the case of these goods, consumers are prepared to reduce their spending as they get richer. In these situations the relevant goods are *inferior goods*. In Chapter 5 we suggested potatoes might be an example of an inferior good.

The Importance of Income Elasticity

As incomes increase and consumers adjust their patterns of spending there are important repercussions for those engaged in business activity. Figure 7.9 shows some real-world estimates of income elasticities in the UK.

Figure 7.9
Estimates Income Elasticities of Demand in 1970

Commodity or service	Elasticity e_y
Coal	-2.02
Bread	-0.49
Cigarettes and tobacco	-0.03
Beer	1.22
Catering	1.63
Recreational goods	1.98
Wines and spirits	2.59
Expenditure abroad	1.14

Source: A. S. Deaton, 'The Measurement of Income and Price Elasticities', *European Economic Review*, Vol. 6, 1975, p. 266.

Figure 7.9 points out clearly the depressing market situation facing British Coal as compared with purveyors of alcoholic drink. It also indicates that the demand for bread was declining but that in 1970 makers of sports equipment had the encouraging prospect of rising sales. So Britons appeared to wish to eat less bread and seek more healthy exercise! Households 'voted' with their money not for an increase in cigarette smoking but for more lager and 'short' drinks.

Figure 7.9 includes just one food commodity, that of bread. If we now examine the income elasticities for some other items of food we can begin to realize the implications for food processors in the UK economy (Figure 7.10). Let us have in mind the following question: do particular food markets expand or contract as households have more income to spend?

You will note that in none of these twelve groups of foodstuffs is the income elasticity as high as 1.0 and in most cases it is closer to zero than 1.0. In two food groups it is negative. What does this mean for food processors (and indeed farmers)? It means that as households have more income available to spend they devote very little to extra food consumption. As a

Figure 7.10
Estimates of Income Elasticities of Expenditure in 1982

Milk and cream	0.09
Cheese	0.29
Carcass meat	0.32
Fish	0.26
Fats	0.08
Sugar and preserves	-0.13
Fresh fruit	0.59
Fresh potatoes	-0.12
Fresh green vegetables	0.30
Bread	-0.04
Cakes and biscuits	0.20
Beverages	0.16

Source: Ministry of Agriculture, Fisheries and Food

result food processors in most of the individual food markets do not experience steadily rising sales of food. Thus processing firms like United Biscuits cannot expect that the consumption of biscuits *in volume terms* will show any encouraging growth. So if Britons show little or no willingness to munch more biscuits as each year passes by the only course open to United Biscuits in seeking higher sales is to obtain a bigger share of the static biscuit market. By offering new varieties of biscuit in well-planned marketing campaigns United Biscuits might then prompt households to switch some of their biscuit buying to United Biscuits brands. Rival firms would, as a result, face declining sales and lose some of their share of the market.

Elasticity of Supply

The **price elasticity of supply** is defined in a similar way as the price elasticity of demand. Supply elasticities are generally positive; this is because at higher prices, larger quantities will generally be forthcoming from suppliers. Our definition of the price elasticity of supply, e_s, is the following:

$$e_s = \frac{\text{percentage change in quantity supplied}}{\text{percentage change in price}}$$

Key Points 7.5

► The sensitivity of the quantity demanded to changes in income is called the income elasticity of demand. For luxury goods the income elasticity is greater than 1: for inferior goods the income elasticity is negative. The degree of income elasticity is a major determinant of how the market for a good or service is growing over time.

Figure 7.11

Calculating the Price Elasticity of Supply for Petrol. We use some hypothetical data to demonstrate how to calculate price elasticity of supply. We use the mid-point, or average, formula. Column 2 gives the change in quantity of petrol supplied derived from column 1. Column 4 gives the change in price derived from column 3. Columns 5 and 6 give the average quantity and price values. Column 7 presents the price elasticity of supply, which is constant and equal to one because the curve intercepts the origin.

(1) Quantity supplied (millions) of gallons	(2) Change in Q (millions) of gallons	(3) Price (£)	(4) Change in P (£)	(5) $\dfrac{Q_1 + Q_2}{2}$	(6) $\dfrac{P_1 + P_2}{2}$	(7) $e_s = \dfrac{\text{Change in } Q}{(Q_1 + Q_2)/2} \Big/ \dfrac{\text{Change in } P}{(P_1 + (P))/2}$
0		.00				
	2		1.0	1	0.5	$(2/1) \div (1.0/0.5) = 1.00$
2		1.00				
	2		1.0	3	1.5	$(2/3) \div (1.0/1.5) = 1.00$
4		2.00				
	2		1.0	5	2.5	$(2/5) \div (1.0/2.5) = 1.00$
6		3.00				
	2		1.0	7	3.5	$(2/7) \div (1.0/3.5) = 1.00$
8		4.00				
	2		1.0	9	4.5	$(2/9) \div (1.0/4.5) = 1.00$
10		5.00				

We use some hypothetical data to illustrate the price elasticity of supply for petrol. This is done in Figure 7.11. Note that the price elasticity of supply remains constant and equal to 1 in this particular example. This is a special feature of any *straight-line* supply curve that passes through the origin, that is, whose intercept is zero.*

Classifying Supply Elasticities

Just as with demand, there are different types of supply elasticities. They are similar in definition.

If a 1 per cent increase in price elicits a greater than 1 per cent increase in the quantity supplied, we say that at the particular price in question on the supply schedule, *supply is elastic.*

If, on the other hand, a 1 per cent increase in price elicits a less than 1 per cent increase in the quantity supplied, we refer to that as an *inelastic supply* situation.

If the percentage change in the quantity supplied is just equal to the percentage change in the price, then we talk about *unitary elasticity of supply.*

We show in Figure 7.12 two supply schedules, SS and S'S'. Can you tell at a glance, without reading the caption, which one is infinitely elastic and which one is perfectly inelastic?

As you might expect, most supply schedules exhibit elasticities that are somewhere between the range of zero to infinity.

*If the straight-line supply curve has a vertical intercept, then price elasticity of supply is greater than 1 (elastic throughout); if a straight-line supply curve intersects the horizontal axis, then its price elasticity of supply is less than 1 (inelastic throughout).

Price Elasticity of Supply and Length of Time for Adjustment

We pointed out earlier that the longer the time allowed for adjustment, the greater the price elasticity

Figure 7.12

The Extremes in Supply Curves. Here we have drawn two extremes of supply schedules: *SS is a perfectly elastic supply curve, S'S' is a perfectly inelastic one.* In the former, an unlimited quantity will be forthcoming at the price P_1. In the latter, no matter what the price, the quantity supplied will be Q_1. An example of S'S' might be the supply curve for fresh fish on the morning the boats arrive back in dock.

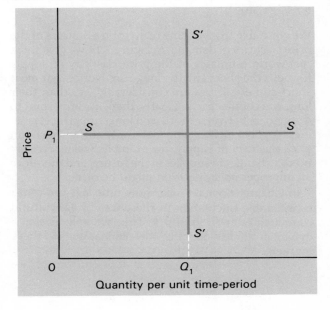

of demand. It turns out that the same proposition applies to supply. The longer the time for adjustment, the more price elastic is the supply curve. Consider why this is true:

1. The longer the time allowed for adjustment, the more firms are able to figure out ways to increase production in an industry.
2. The longer the time allowed, the more resources can flow into an industry through expansion of existing firms.

We therefore talk about short- and long-run price elasticities of supply. The short run is defined as the time-period during which full adjustment has not yet taken place. Thus, the long run is the time-period during which firms have been able to adjust fully to the change in price.

Consider an example – an increase in the price of housing. In the very short run, when there is no time allowed for adjustment, the amount of housing services offered for rent or for sale is relatively inelastic. However, as more time is allowed for adjustment, current owners of the housing stock can find ways to increase the amount of housing services they will offer for rent from given buildings. The owner of a large house can decide, for example, to have two of his or her children move into one room so that a 'new' extra bedroom can be rented out. This can also be done by the owner of a large house who decides to move into an apartment and rent each floor of the house to a family. Thus, the quantity of housing services supplied will increase. We can show a whole set of supply curves similar to the ones we generated for demand. In Figure 7.13 when nothing can be done in the short run, the supply curve is vertical, $S_1 S_1$. As more time is allowed for adjustment, the supply curve rotates to $S_2 S_2$ and then $S_3 S_3$ becoming more elastic as it rotates.

Real-world Estimates of Price Elasticity of Supply

We were able to give some real-world estimates of the price elasticity of demand. In Figure 7.14 we give some real-world estimates of the price elasticity of supply for both the short and the long run. Notice that most short-run elasticities are considerably less than their long-run counterparts. Clearly, then, it is important to distinguish between short- and long-run price elasticities. A policy-maker who looks only at the short-run price elasticity of supply, for example, will incorrectly predict changes in supplies in the future, and therefore an improper policy decision might be made.

In Chapter 8 we consider how time lags can cause considerable fluctuation in the prices of agricultural commodities and foodstuffs. Thus we will develop a dynamic model of price determination in these markets.

Figure 7.13
Short-run and Long-run Price Elasticity of Supply. The longer the time allowed for adjustment, the greater the price elasticity of supply. Consider a given situation in which the price is P_e and the quantity supplied is Q_e. In the short run, we hypothesize a vertical supply schedule, $S_1 S_1$. In other words, we assume that suppliers are unable to do anything in the very short run, even when there is a price increase. With the given price increase to P_1, therefore, there will be no change in the short run in quantity supplied; it will remain at Q_e. Given some time for adjustment, the supply curve will rotate at price P_e to $S_2 S_2$. The new quantity supplied will shift out to Q_1. Finally, the long-run supply curve is shown by $S_3 S_3$. The quantity supplied again increases out to Q_2.

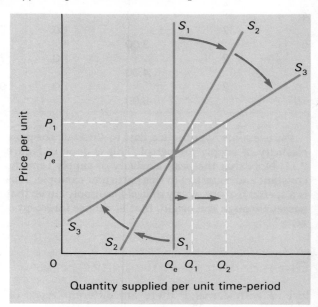

Figure 7.14
Estimates Price Elasticities of Supply of Some Commodities in the United States

Commodity	Elasticity e_s	
	Short run	Long run
Cabbage	0.36	1.20
Carrots	0.14	1.00
Cucumbers	0.29	2.20
Onions	0.34	1.00
Green peas	0.31	4.40
Tomatoes	0.16	0.90
Cauliflower	0.14	1.10
Celery	0.14	0.95

Source: M. Nerlove and W. Addison, 'Statistical Estimation of Long-run Elasticities of Supply and Demand', *American Journal of Agricultural Economics* (formerly *Journal of Farm Economics*), Vol. 40 (Nov. 1958), pp. 861–80.

Key Points 7.6

▶ Price elasticity of supply is given by the percentage change in quantity supplied divided by the percentage change in price.

▶ Usually, price elasticities of supply are positive – higher prices yield larger quantities supplied.

▶ Long-run supply curves are more elastic than short-run supply curves because the longer the time allowed, the more resources can flow into or out of an industry when price changes.

CASE STUDY

Shipowners Encounter Rough Water

There are some long, grey beards in the world's shipping markets. The demise of Sanko Steamship comes when second-hand ships are worth little more than the scrap value of their steel and when freight rates barely cover operating costs, let alone interest payments. So heavy is the fall in both rates and second-hand values from already depressed levels that many shipowners say the worst cannot be far off.

They are wrong. World shipping is likely to remain long in the doldrums – perhaps beyond the rest of this decade. The continuing huge imbalance between low demand and potential supply seems to defy ordinary business cycles. The tanker market has remained in recession ever since the 1974 oil-price rise. Bulk carriers have fared little better, save for a speculative ordering boom between 1979 and 1981.

Born of the second oil crisis, it was based on misguidedly optimistic projections of future coal demand.

The world has too many ships. In the dry cargo market, some 35 per cent of the world bulk fleet of 230m deadweight tonnes (dwt) is surplus capacity. The picture is no better for heavy tankers, those of 175 000 dwt and above. Demand is not strong enough to reduce the glut. World trade has grown at above-average rates in the past

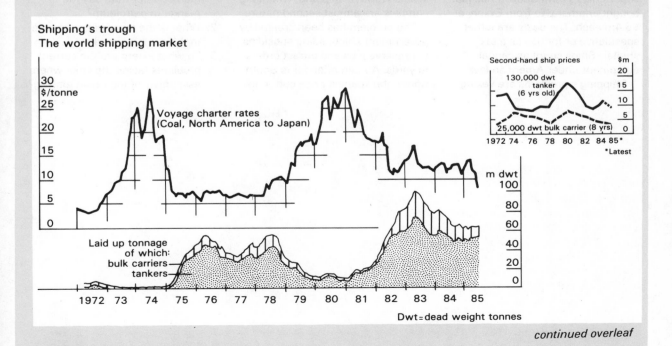

Shipping's trough
The world shipping market

continued overleaf

two years because of huge American imports. Yet that has barely touched the underlying overcapacity. The growth in world trade is slowing now.

Recovery is not necessarily brought any nearer when shipping companies go out of business. A shipowner may go bust but his ships survive. A creditor bank, which nearly always secured its loan against a much higher market value of the vessel, may arrest the ship, but there is little it can then do except sell it, depressing the second-hand market further.

There are nearly always punters willing to buy a ship in these circumstances, gambling on what they view as a cheap asset. A 1976-built Panamax (the biggest sort of bulk carrier that can get through the Panama canal), which in early 1981 was worth $25m, now costs less than $5m. Today's buyer can operate the ship at a profit on much lower freight rates than an established owner who bought the ship five years ago. So the underlying glut of tonnage continues as marginal operators – often new to shipping – enter the market. Last year, Loews, an American hotel group, bought two supertankers from Shell. It has just bought another two from Exxon, at $5.4m each. The deals are either speculative or for use as a tax shelter. Ships count as capital equipment under American law.

Shipping's problems are vexing

banks. As in their sovereign debt and energy lending, banks rushed to lend to ship owners. They took as security the then-high value of a vessel (and sometimes up to 100 per cent of it). As the market has soured, banks have turned reluctant shipowners. It is estimated that they have had to seize 500 vessels since mid-1983 – not counting arrests that will occur as a result of Sanko.

Wherever possible, which means wherever there is enough cash flow being generated from charter income to justify not taking a loss, banks have hung on in the forlorn hope that the value of their security will recover. Now, with no sign of recovery at hand, banks are increasingly having to write off the loans.

One shipowner who is not in hock to his bankers is Hongkong's Sir Yue-kong Pao. Over the past few years he has prudently sold ships. In 1980, he was the world's largest independent shipowner, with a fleet of 202 vessels, weighing 20.5m dwt. Today, the fleet of his Worldwide group, both the public and private parts, is only 84 vessels, weighing 9.9m dwt.

Such caution is rare in the high-stakes world of shipping, where big gambles are almost second nature.

The problem has been created by government shipbuilding subsidies to preserve jobs and attract orders to yards. A main offender is South Korea, the keenest price cutter. In

1984, world shipbuilding production exceeded 18.3m gross registered tonnes – the highest level of output since 1977, an insane situation given the glut of ships. The world order book in 1984 was less than one quarter of its level 10 years earlier.

Some of the surplus can be cut by pulling existing ships to pieces. Scrapping of tankers has been on the increase since 1980, and that of bulk carriers since 1982. Last year, according to Drewry Shipping Consultants, 21m dwt-worth of tonnage was scrapped. One problem is that four-fifths of the world's shipbreaking capacity is in east Asia, mostly in Taiwan, South Korea, and, more and more, China. But many of the world's laid-up ships are anchored off Scandinavia or Greece. The International Maritime Industries Forum, a ship-industry club, wants the World Bank to finance a scrapyard half-way, in Liberia. The World Bank is not keen.

Source: 'It is an ancient Mariner, and He Laid Up One of Three', *The Economist* 17 Aug. 1985 pp. 51–2.

Questions
1. How does the world's shipping market differ from say the market in petroleum?
2. What is the significance of time in the shipping market?
3. To what extent are the current problems facing the shipowners essentially of their own making?

Exam Preparation and Practice

INTRODUCTORY EXERCISES

1. In 1957 the firms in the US car industry sold approximately 6 million cars for an average price of about $2500. Mr Walter Reuther, president of the United Auto Workers, suggested that all of the major automobile companies reduce their prices by $100; he estimated that an increase in sales of one million units would result and that aggregate industry profits of about $2 billion would not be reduced. What is Mr Reuther's estimate of the elasticity of demand for automobiles in the US?

In discussing Mr Reuther's proposals, Mr Theodore O. Yntemna of the Ford Motor Company called attention to statistical studies which estimated the elasticity of demand for cars as being between –0.5 and –1.5. What would be the result of the $100 price reduction upon sales under each of these demand conditions?

(From J. S. Duesenberry and L. E. Preston, *Cases and Problems in Economics*, Allen & Unwin, 1960, pp. 47–8.)

The following exercises are, strictly speaking, multiple choice questions. However, they are all numerical in content and thus very suitable for inclusion as rests of a quantitative understanding of the concept of elasticity.

2. A manufacturer produces two products, X and Y. Market prices of both products go up by the same percentage and his supply of X is increased by 100%, and that of Y by 50 per cent. What can be deduced about the elasticity of supply of X and Y?
A the elasticity of X is 2, and that of Y is 1
B the elasticity of X is 1, and that of Y is $\frac{1}{2}$
C the elasticity of X is between 1 and 2, and that of Y between $\frac{1}{2}$ and 1
D the elasticity of X is 1, while that of Y cannot be determined
E neither of the elasticities can be determined

3. The demand function for good A is written as follows:

$$Q_D = 300 - 3P_A + 2P_B - 0.2Y,$$

where Q_D is the quantity demanded of good A in millions of tonnes,
where P_A is the price of good A in dollars,
P_B is the price of good B in dollars,
Y is the level of national income in millions of dollars.

Initially, when $P_A = 10$, $P_B = 15$ and $Y = 500$, the demand for A is 200. If Y increases to 1000 what is the income elasticity of demand
A $-\frac{1}{10}$
B $-\frac{1}{5}$
C $-\frac{1}{2}$
D –1
E –2

4. Assume that the cross-elasticity of demand for cars with respect to changes in the price of petrol is –0.5. At an average price per car of £5000, the number of cars sold per week is 10000. If the average price of cars remains unchanged, but the price of petrol increases from 40p to 44p per litre, the number of cars sold per week will fall to
A 5000
B 7500
C 8500
D 9000
E 9500

5. The demand for butter is negatively related to the price of butter:

elasticity = –0.43

The demand for butter is also affected by the prices of flour, margarine, cakes, and meat. Cross-elasticities of demand for butter with respect to the prices of these goods are:

flour	–0.23
margarine	–0.10
cakes	0.59
meat	0.56

Which one of the following can be predicted from this information?
A a rise in the price of flour will lead to a rise in the demand for butter
B a fall in the price of margarine will lead to a rise in the demand for butter
C a fall in the price of cakes will lead to a rise in the demand for butter
D a fall in the price of meat will lead to a fall in the demand for butter
E a fall in the price of butter will lead to a more than proportionate rise in the demand for butter

continued overleaf

MULTIPLE CHOICE QUESTIONS

†1.

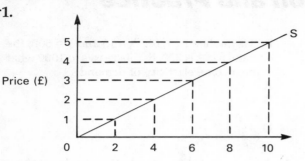

Quantity supplied per period

The elasticity of the supply curve shown in the above diagram is

A zero
B between zero and unity
C unity
D between unity and infinity
E infinity

†2.

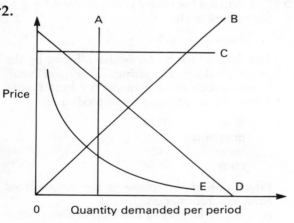

Which of the curves labelled **A–E** on the above diagram illustrates unitary elasticity of demand throughout its length?

†3. The elasticity of a downward sloping straight line demand schedule is

A zero
B unity
C positive
D variable along its length
E infinity

One or more of the options given in Questions 4, 5 and 6 may be correct. Select your answer by means of the code set out in the grid:

A	B	C	D
1,2,3	1,2	2,3	1
all correct	only correct	only correct	only correct

†4. In the diagram below, line 0Z represents the income/consumption curve for a particular good.

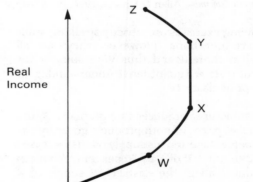

Income-elasticity of demand for the good is

1 negative from Y to Z
2 positive from 0 to W
3 unity from X to Y

5. Cross-elasticity of demand is a measure of the responsiveness of demand for commodity X to a change in the

1 price of a substitute for X
2 real income of consumers
3 price of X

6.

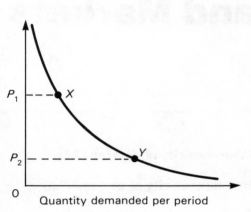

Quantity demanded per period

The above demand curve for a commodity is a rectangular hyperbola. It follows that
1 the price elasticity of demand is greater at X than at Y
2 a fall in price from OP_1 to OP_2 will cause a proportionate rise in the quantity demanded
3 consumer outlay on the good is the same at price OP_1 as at OP_2

RELATED ESSAY QUESTIONS
1. Explain what is meant by the elasticity of supply. What factors are likely to influence the elasticity of supply of fresh fish in
   (a) the market period
   (b) the short period
   (c) the long period

2. What factors determine the elasticity of supply of a product?

3. Describe briefly the conditions (or determinants) of demand and supply. Explain why and how price changes may occur when the conditions of demand and supply
   (a) change
   (b) are constant

4. Consider the effect of an increase in the price of oil on the demand for petrol, diesel, and heating oil. How might the response vary between different types of user, both in the short run and in the long run?

5. Define price elasticity of demand and outline the factors which determine its value. Show the relevance of price elasticity in analysing the effects of a rise in the price of petrol on the demand for different forms of transport.

8 Governments and Markets

Key Points to Review

▶ **Shifts in demand (5.3, 5.6)**

▶ **Shifts in supply (5.3, 5.6)**

▶ **Surpluses and shortages (5.7)**

▶ **Price elasticity of demand (7.1)**

▶ **Income elasticity of demand (7.5)**

▶ **Price elasticity of supply (7.6)**

Questions for Preview

1 How do the concepts of price and income elasticity help explain why agriculture is the subject of government intervention?

2 How do controls on rents charged by landlords affect the market for rented accommodation?

3 Who benefits from government policies which raise the minimum level of wages which employers must pay their employees?

The pricing system answers three basic questions of resource allocation: *what* goods will be produced? *how* will they be produced? and *for whom* will they be produced? The forces of supply and demand acting through the pricing system (i.e. the market) affect the bulk of decisions that answer these three questions. But as Chapter 4 pointed out developed countries like the UK and US are not purely private market economies. In addition to market forces, there are many other forces at work that affect the allocation of resources. One of the most important of these non-market forces is government. In this chapter we will look at the impact on markets of various forms of government intervention and in doing so draw on the concepts of demand and supply elasticity explained in Chapter 7. Our aim is to show some applications of supply and demand analysis. We will firstly draw on the concepts in the previous chapters to show why agriculture in developed economies is not left to unregulated market forces. Using our theory of free market pricing we can explain why, in the absence of government intervention, the operation of forces on the demand and supply side results both in a low income and an unstable income situation for the farming community.

In the second part of this chapter we show how the concepts of price elasticity of demand and of supply are helpful in understanding the repercussions of taxes imposed by government. Of course governments need tax revenues in order to help finance a wide range of expenditure programmes. The rationale of government spending takes us firmly into the macro field and is the subject of our first chapter in Part B.

The final part of this chapter considers the impact of government policies which control the prices that would operate in a free market. We consider specific policies which fix a maximum price level and appraise the impact in the market for rented accommodation. The labour market provides us with an illustration of another form of government intervention with the price mechanism. We study the effect of minimum wage legislation. Finally we briefly preview the problems facing governments attempting general restraints on upward price movements. But first we consider how the free market operates in the agricultural sector. Having considered in turn the demand for and supply of food we see why governments are so willing to regulate agricultural markets.

The Agricultural Problem

The Demand Side

The root cause of the problem facing the farming community is the fact that there is a limit to how much food people can eat! Adam Smith recognized this in the *Wealth of Nations.*

The rich man consumes no more food than his poor neighbour. In quality it may be very different, and to select and prepare it may require more labour and art; but in quantity it is very nearly the same. But compare the spacious palace and great wardrobe of the one with the hovel and few rags of the other, and you will be sensible that the difference between their clothing, lodging and household furniture is almost as great in quantity as it is in the quality. The desire for food is limited in every man by the narrow capacity of the human stomach; but the desire for the convenience and ornaments of building, dress, equipage and household furniture, seems to have no limit or certain boundary.*

Even if people who are rich can 'afford' to buy huge quantities, they do not do so. We expect, therefore, that as households get richer, the percentage of their budget spent on food will fall. This occurs because the income elasticity of demand for food is less than 1. We have previously defined income elasticity of demand as follows:

income elasticity

$= \dfrac{\text{percentage change in amount of good purchased}}{\text{percentage change in income}}$

If the income elasticity of demand for agricultural products is less than 1, for every 1 per cent increase in income there will be a *less*-than-1 per cent increase in quantity demanded, *other things being constant.* Look at Figure 8.1, where we show the income elasticity for food products in various countries. We see that income elasticity is quite low for the richer nations in the world. In fact, the richer the nation, the lower the income elasticity of demand for agricultural products. All nations seem to exhibit income elasticities for food products that are less than 1. Therefore, we predict that agriculture will be of declining importance in all nations as each becomes richer. (We are ignoring the possibility of *exports* of food becoming more and more important. If that were to happen because of increased world demand, the agricultural sector could conceivably even grow as a nation became richer.)

Figure 8.2 shows the volume of some items of food consumption in the UK. It shows that on a per capita basis consumption of seven of the twelve categories of food products was lower in 1980 than in 1977. In some of these food products the fall in consumption was a continuation of a long-term trend, i.e. grain products

*A. Smith, *Wealth of Nations*, Bk. 1, Ch. 11, Everyman edn., 1964, pp. 149–50.

Figure 8.1
Income Elasticity for Food Products. The income elasticity of demand for food is defined as being equal to the percentage change in the quantity demanded divided by the percentage change in real income. This income elasticity is quite low for the richer nations in the world.

(a) *Data for Great Britain*

	Income elasticity
Liquid milk	0.03
Cream	1.21
Mutton and lamb	0.07
Eggs	–0.034
Fresh potatoes	–0.24
Large white sliced bread	–0.50
Tea	–0.12

Source: Household Food Consumption and Expenditure: 1982.

(b) *Comparative data for ten countries* (all food products)

	Income elasticity
United States	0.08
Canada	0.15
Britain	0.24
Germany	0.25
France	0.25
Ireland	0.23
Italy	0.42
Greece	0.49
Spain	0.56
Portugal	0.60

Source: Charles L. Schultze, *The Distribution of Farm Subsidies: Who Gets the Benefits?* (Washington, DC: The Brookings Institution, 1971).

(mainly bread). Clearly, changing views on what constitutes a healthy diet and many other factors besides rising incomes have affected food consumption habits in the UK but surely we can now appreciate Adam Smith's point about the 'narrow capacity of the human stomach'. As real incomes rise consumers prefer to spend their money on foreign holidays, colour televisions, and motor cars. The higher *income elasticity* values for these products compared with those for items of food indicates how society is registering its market preferences. Unhappily for farmers the slow rate of population growth in the UK does not offset the disappointing growth in demand due to rising incomes: an increase in the sheer numbers (of mouths to feed) does not counteract the basically sluggish market situation resulting from the income determinant. In 1977 the UK population was 55.91 million: three years later it had grown only to 56.01 million.

The income inelasticity of demand for food means

that society does not want the same number of farmers to continue in production: if numbers do remain constant their incomes relative to other groups in society must fall.

Figure 8.2

Food Supplies Moving into Consumption in the United Kingdom. Consumption on a per head basis was lower in 1984 as compared with 1975 in six of the twelve categories of foodstuffs. This decline was not just a phenomenon of recent years but part of a longer-term decline in consumption.

	1 lb per head per annum 1975	kilos per head per annum 1980	1984
Dairy products (excluding butter as milk solids)	26.7	22.8	23.3
Meat (as edible weight)	56.3	56.4	53.5
Fish (as edible weight)	7.9	7.7	7.0
Eggs and egg products (number)	244	235	224
Oils and fats (fat content)	24.5	24.4	26.2
Sugar and syrups (sugar content)	43.0	43.4	44.3
Potatoes and potato products	101.9	99.3	102.7
Pulses and nuts	4.6	4.6	4.9
Fruit (as fresh equivalent)	61.7	71.6	83.5
Other vegetables (as fresh equivalent)	68.8	71.7	80.6
Grain products	72.3	69.9	67.4
Tea	3.5	3.3	3.1

Source: Ministry of Agriculture, Fisheries and Food.

Figure 8.3

Estimated Average Yields of Crops and Livestock Products. In the case of all four crops average yields for the period 1978–82 were higher than in 1973–82. Thus over the second half of the decade the tonnes per hectare of wheat, barley, oats, and sugar beet was increasing. A similar picture of increased productivity is evident in the case of milk and egg production.

Crop	Tonnes per hectare		
	10-year average 1973–82	5-year average 1978–82	5 year average 1980–84
Wheat	5.16	5.71	6.47
Barley	4.08	4.39	4.78
Oats	3.95	4.34	4.38
Sugar beet	33.9	37.8	40.9

Livestock products	Average of 1971–3	1978	1981
		(litres per cow)	
Milk	3968	4618	4728
		(no. per bird)	
Eggs	227.5	242.0	249.5

Source: Ministry of Agriculture, Fisheries and Food.

The Supply Problem

On the supply side technical progress – 'making two blades of grass grow where one grew before' – exacerbates the problems facing the farming community in developed economies. The agricultural sector has exhibited throughout history an impressive record of rising crop yields and improved productivity in livestock production due to improvements in animal husbandry. Figure 8.3 shows farming's recent record of improved productivity.

The Problem of Farm Prices

Let us now bring together both of our observations concerning the demand for and the supply of food. If the demand curve shifts horizontally only slowly over time while the supply curve shifts very perceptibly to the right due to technical progress we must surely conclude that there will be downward pressure on prices if there is an unregulated market in the pricing of agriculture. Falling prices for farm output should be the market signal for resources to move out of agriculture. But if resources do not flow out of

farming then the working of the price mechanism is to that extent flawed. If the process of resource reallocation as explained in Chapter 6 does not take place then there may be grounds for governments to help *some* farmers who are receiving incomes below those in the non-farm sector of the economy.

You will note that we have just referred to the size of some farmers' *incomes*. We have seen that the interaction of supply and demand has the effect of depressing farm *prices*. Now of course for an *individual* farmer his income is the product of output times prices received per unit. Those farmers who produce little agricultural output will of course have lower incomes than those farmers whose sheer volume of production gives them much larger incomes. This simple point – that some farmers produce little output whereas other farmers who are very large and account for a significant proportion of total output – in fact is the nub of 'the farm problem' in developed economies like the UK and US. Some farmers whose production is relatively small may never be able to generate enough receipts from the sale of output to be large enough to be economically viable. In short, the low-income problem is not so much because of depressed farm prices but really the small size of farming operations. Before examining what aid government might offer farmers let us examine another aspect of farm incomes, that is their instability.

Unstable Incomes

The pressure on prices in an unregulated agriculture are however only part of the pricing problems facing farmers. Farmers in an unregulated market also suffer from unstable prices. Year-to-year fluctuations in weather and livestock production result in price instability – unless there is government intervention. Once more simple demand and supply theory can be used to show the effect on price of, for example, a bumper harvest and one where there is a poor crop harvest. Note that we here are using the concept of elasticity again – this time concerning price and not income elasticity of demand.

Low Price Elasticity of Demand

Not only is the income elasticity of demand for agricultural products low; so too is the price elasticity – it is relatively price inelastic. Whereas the low-income elasticity was important for explaining the long-run downward trend in the farm sector, the low-price elasticity of demand is important for understanding the high variability of farmers' incomes in the short run.

Let us consider the change in price that results from an increase in supply due to abnormally good weather conditions. In Figure 8.4 we show the supply schedule shifting from SS to $S'S'$. It has shifted out to the right, indicating a large increase in production. Notice that the supply schedule here is fairly vertical, indicating that the *price elasticity of supply* in the short-run period under consideration is also quite small (at E). After all, once farmers have planted and cultivated their crops, they can supply no more and no less – unless, of course, they decide to store or destroy the crops.

What if the demand schedule is in addition relatively elastic, such as DD (at E)? The new equilibrium price in this case will be set at the intersection of the new supply curve $S'S'$ and the demand curve DD, or at point E'. The old equilibrium price was established at point E, or at a price of P_e. The new price of P_e' obviously lies below the old price.

What if the demand curve is relatively *less* elastic, such as $D'D'$ (at E)? The new equilibrium price will

---

Figure 8.4

Consequences of a Relatively Inelastic Demand. The quantity of food produced per time-period is on the horizontal axis and the price per unit on the vertical axis. Assume that the original supply curve is SS – relatively inelastic supply in the short run at the current price. If the demand curve facing farmers is DD, a shift in the supply curve from SS to $S'S'$ due to good weather will lower the equilibrium price from P_e to P_e'. But if the demand curve is instead $D'D'$, when the supply curve shifts to $S'S'$, the new equilibrium price falls to P_e''. This accounts for the large variability in incomes of farmers in different years.

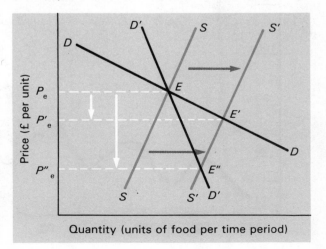

Quantity (units of food per time period)

then be established at E'', and the new equilibrium price will be P''_e, which is even lower than P'_e. We see, therefore, that when there is a given shift rightwards in the supply curve, the more price inelastic the demand for agricultural products, the greater the decline in the market price. Conversely, for any shift leftwards in the supply curve of agricultural products, the greater the price inelasticity of demand, the greater the rise in the market price of agricultural products. For example, if there is a drought, we expect prices to rise rather substantially due to the relative inelasticity of demand for food. Thus, we see that the relative price inelasticity of demand for agricultural products has also been one of the reasons that prices, and therefore farm incomes, have fluctuated more in agriculture than they have in other industries from year to year.

The Effect on Farmers' Incomes

So far we have only demonstrated that for any given shift in the supply curve, the more price inelastic the demand for food products, the greater will be the resultant change in the market-clearing price. Thus, when there is a bumper crop, the relatively price-inelastic demand for food results in a relatively substantial drop in the market-clearing price for food products.

What, though, happens to farmers' incomes? Well, you have to go back to our discussion of the relationship between changes in price and changes in total revenues and consumer expenditures. This was discussed in Chapter 7. There we showed that any firm facing an inelastic demand would suffer a *decrease* in total revenues if it lowered price. This analysis holds for the total income in farming. Because farmers are facing a price-inelastic demand for food (that is, as a

group they are undoubtedly operating in the inelastic portion of the *market* demand for food), a reduction in price – for example, from P_e to P''_e in Figure 8.4 – will result in a reduction in total farm income.

The Cobweb

Agriculture differs from manufacturing industry due to the biological character of its form of production. Because of this the problem of price instability as just outlined is not an irregular phenomenon of this sector of the economy. Indeed we shall see that price fluctuations can take the form of fairly *regular* cycles over time. Figure 8.5 shows the ups and downs in the size of the cattle herd in the US. How can the successive expansion and contraction in the number of cattle be explained using simple price theory? We need only specify three conditions for such cyclical movements in farm output, and hence prices.

Assumption 1. There is a time-lag before an intended expansion in production actually is available for sale in market.

Assumption 2. The decision by producers to change their output is essentially taken on the basis of the current market price. Thus supplies in Year 2 are dependent on prices actually received in Year 1

Figure 8.5

The Ups and Downs in America's Cattle Herd. The apparent regularity of the movement in the size of the cattle herd in the US is striking. The cobweb theory helps explain this alternate expansion and contraction in cattle numbers.

Source: 'Herd Instinct', *The Economist*, 26 Nov. 1977 p. 49.

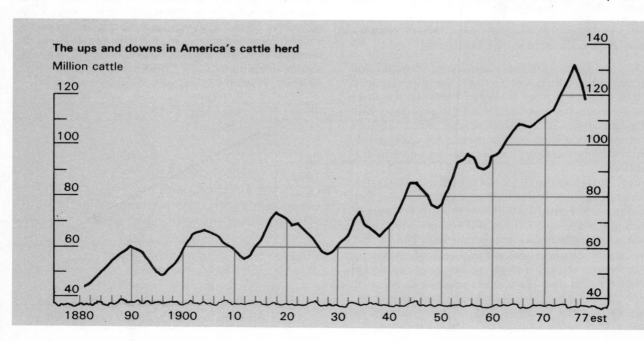

rather than what is expected to be received in Year 2.

Assumption 3. Producers are many and they each take decisions to adjust their scale of production in isolation from each other.

The result of these three conditions is that if supplies happen to be scarce in one time-period the high level of the market-clearing price will prompt producers to begin a major expansion of production. This rise in production will in due course depress market prices which sets off a major contraction in the

scale of production. Let us show how this is explained. In Figure 8.6 the fixed amount available in the short run means that the market-clearing price is OP_1. The supply curve indicates that at price OP_1 farmers would like to produce OP_2. But they cannot do so until the next harvest (assumption 1). Suppose farmers plan to adjust output to the current market price and try to produce OP_2 (assumption 2). If each farmer's micro decision overlooks the consequences for total industry output – the macro situation – then assumption 3 is fulfilled. If indeed output OQ_2 is actually harvested the market-clearing price will then be OP_2. Now the fulfilment of our assumptions will result in a contraction in production and higher prices. Note that in this example market prices move above and below the equilibrium level OP and are not stable. Depending on the nature of the supply and demand curves this instability of prices could be greater or lesser than as shown in Figure 8.6.

Can Anything Be Done to Help Farmers?

If farmers suffer from such major fluctuations in prices and hence incomes what can be done about the problem? Is it a problem anyway?

Many economists would agree that price instability in an unregulated agricultural sector results in a poorly working mechanism to effect resource reallocation. Where cobweb-type swings in production occur there is either an excessive expansion of production or an excessive reduction in production. Greater price 'stability' would avoid unnecessary changes in production and perhaps give farmers greater confidence about the future. We can recognize at once however that measures which aim at giving farmers greater price stability should not be confused with other policies that are explicitly intended to raise the incomes of farmers above free market levels. In fact the two issues tend to be difficult to separate completely from each other. We can show this in examining the **buffer stock** approach to meeting the problem of price instability.

Figure 8.6

How Agricultural Prices Can Fluctuate. The market equilibrium is *OP* and quantity *OQ* but if there is a poor wheat harvest and no supplies are available from any other source it will be next year before extra supplies can be forthcoming. The fixed amount available – Q_2 – means a market, or short-run supply curve, effectively exists – the dashed line above OQ_1. The supply curve indicates that at price OP_1, farmers would like to produce OQ_2 but they cannot until the next harvest. If farmers try to produce OQ_2 and all of OQ_2 is harvested (note the assumption) then in the next year a big wheat crop will be harvested. The price will be OP_2. The price *could* oscillate around the equilibrium level *OP* but *never* actually at that level. A pattern can be drawn which looks like a spider's web, hence the **cobweb**.

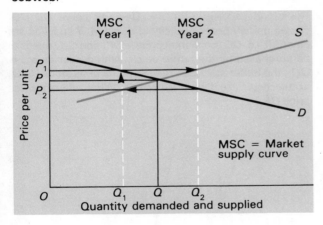

Key Points 8.2

▶ For any shift in the supply schedule, a firm facing a relatively inelastic demand curve will experience a larger fluctuation in the price of the product. It is argued that since the demand for food is relatively price inelastic, the prices farmers receive for their products fluctuate more than in other sectors of the economy when there are shifts in supply.

▶ Farmers operate in an environment rather different from other sectors of the economy. When there are many, geographically separate decision-making units quite independent of each other and time-lags exist before planned changes in output are realized, market-clearing prices will be unstable.

Buffer Stocks

Price fluctuations might be minimized if an organization exists that buys in supplies in times of plentiful harvests and sells these when harvests are poor. Its purchases and sales could help to smooth out the course of market prices. In Figure 8.7 we show how such a buffer stock scheme might work.

Figure 8.7
The Operation of a Buffer Stock. Buffer stock aims at maintaining the price of OP_3. If the harvest is plentiful buying QR could ensure a market price of OP_3 rather than OP_1. If the crop is poor, selling SQ would reduce the market price to OP_3 from OP_2.

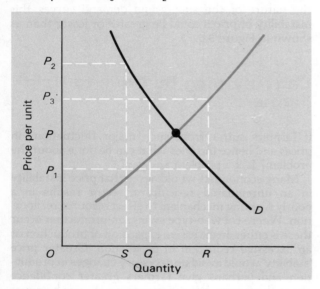

If the buffer stock aims at maintaining the target price of OP_3 then it would buy up supplies which would otherwise result in lower market-clearing prices. In Figure 8.7 buying QR would avoid the fall in the market equilibrium price to OP_1. If, however, supplies were scarce then in the absence of intervention the market price would be OP_2. By selling SQ output at a price of QP_3 then the buffer stock organization would help to make the market price conform to its target price.

Such a scheme is assumed just to eliminate price fluctuations arising from variations in supply. If the target price is set at a level which corresponds to what the average free market price would have been for several time-periods then it should find its purchases and sales balance out. It is neither a net gainer of stocks, i.e. needs more storage capacity, nor is short of funds in order to purchase stocks when there is a bumper harvest.

Clearly those commodities that cannot be stored over time are immediately ruled out of consideration for any buffer stock scheme. But even where this problem of perishability does not exist such a scheme assumes that the target price is set at the appropriate level. If the target price turns out to have been set too high, i.e. above the actual average free market price, the buffer stock managers will find more activity in purchasing than selling. They will in fact need more physical space to store such production which has been bought in for stockpiling. The managers of a buffer stock scheme would also of course be facing the need of more financial resources. In order to keep prices stable by buying up excess supplies they might well need almost unlimited funds to carry on with the task! Perhaps you can appreciate therefore why buffer stocks while simple in concept involve tricky problems concerning their financing. Should farmers be left to finance the buffer stock or should their customers also be involved? Quite apart from their opposing viewpoints neither producers nor consumers have the perfect foresight possessed by Joseph of Old Testament times. Look up Chapter 41 in Genesis!

A buffer stock scheme may stabilize prices somewhat but does not solve the fluctuating income problem. Remember income is price multiplied by quantity sold. Variations in production will thus result in similar variations in income if the buffer stock is 'successful' in keeping its target price unchanged. How then can the unstable income problem be tackled? Here we can again deploy the concept of elasticity, this time unitary price elasticity. You should recall from Chapter 7 that when price elasticity is unitary total

---

Figure 8.8
Price and Income Stability. Demand curve DD–DD_1 shows unitary price elasticity of demand. If supplies are plentiful, i.e. OQ the market price is OP_1 and Q_1Q needs to be purchased by the buffer stock. With a poor crop, i.e. OQ_2, the buffer stock can release some of its stocks Q_2Q_3 at the required selling price of OP_2. What relevance has price OP_4?

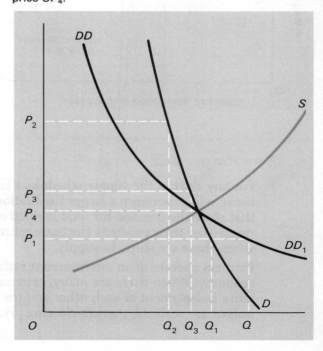

Key Points 8.3

▶ **In theory the problem of price instability facing farmers can be solved by a buffer stock buying in supplies when harvests are plentiful and selling its stocks when harvests are poor. In practice buffer stocks neither operate with ease nor solve the basic problem facing farmers which is variable incomes.**

revenue is unchanged when there is a change in prices. In Figure 8.8 the rectangular hyperbola, DD–DD_1, where price elasticity is constant and equal to 1 shows how stability of farmers' incomes could in theory be achieved. If production was OQ the market price has to be OP_1 in order that the aim of fixed total income is fulfilled. At market price OP_1 demand is OQ_1 so the buffer stock buys in quantity Q_1Q over and above this market demand. If production is OQ_2 due to a poor crop, stability of income requires a price of OP_2 to exist. Given the demand curve at market price OP_2 the buffer stock needs to sell Q_2Q_3 from previously stored output.

Government Policies to Help Farmers

So far we have used simple supply and demand analysis to illustrate the problem of price instability facing farmers. Let us now turn to use our understanding of price determination to show the implications of government intervention.

During the 1930s the farm sector in the United States suffered falling prices and incomes. The US government created the Federal Farm Board to begin price stabilization operations for poor farmers. The Farm Board was supposed to use the money to support the price of farm products so that farmers' incomes would not fall so much. Essentially it bought crops to keep their prices from falling. Then, when the Great Depression got into full swing, a system of **price supports** came into being. There have been some forms of price supports for wheat, feed grains, cotton, tobacco, rice, peanuts, soybeans, dairy products, and sugar. A type of price support system was also introduced into the UK after 1945 and remained at the heart of British agricultural policy until entry into the EEC. So let us now graphically analyse the effect of a price support system.

Price Supports

A price support system is precisely what the name implies. Somehow the government stabilizes or fixes the price of an agricultural product so that it cannot *fall* below a certain level. Look at the supply and demand curves in Figure 8.9, showing the market demand and market supply of wheat. Competitive forces would yield an equilibrium price of P_e and an equilibrium

Figure 8.9
Price Supports. The quantity of wheat is measured on the horizontal axis and the price on the vertical axis. The domestic market demand and supply curves are given by DD and SS. Equilibrium is established at E with an equilibrium price of P_e, and an equilibrium quantity of Q_e. However, the government steps in and sets a support price at P_s. At P_s the quantity demanded is Q_d and the quantity supplied is Q_s. The difference is the excess quantity supplied, or surplus, which the government must somehow take care of. One course of action actually adopted by the US government is to distribute surplus stocks of food to developing countries.

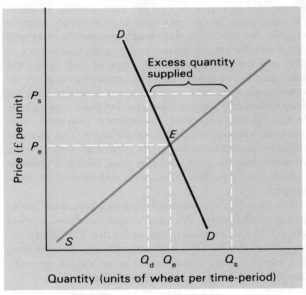

Quantity (units of wheat per time-period)

quantity of Q_e per unit time-period. If the government sets the support price at P_e or below, obviously there will be no change, because the farmers can sell all they want at the market-clearing price, P_e.

Thus to achieve any help for farmers the government will set the support price above P_e – say, at P_s. At P_s the quantity demanded is only Q_d, but the quantity supplied is Q_s. That is, at the higher price, there is a smaller quantity demanded but a larger quantity supplied. The difference is the *excess quantity supplied* – a 'surplus'. Producers respond to higher market prices by producing more. That is why we show the supply schedule as upward sloping. At the higher prices, farmers are able to incur higher production costs and still make a profit. They will keep producing up to the point where the support price cuts the supply curve.

Since the government guarantees to purchase every-thing the wheat-farmers want to sell at the price P_s. The government is therefore pledged to acquire the quantity of wheat represented by the distance between Q_s and Q_d in Figure 8.9.

The price support system just described gives farmers the benefit of a guaranteed price and there is now not much significance of the market equilibrium – OP_e in Figure 8.9. But suppose the government wishes to allow market forces to operate more fully while still committing itself to assisting farmers? The guaranteed or target price system is one such answer. In the case of the UK a **guaranteed price** support system began after World War II and was at the heart of agricultural policy until British entry into the EEC. In 1973 the US government introduced a **target price** system which incorporates the same principles as the former UK policy. Let us explain how the guaranteed price system operates again with reference to a diagram.

Guaranteed prices differ from price supports in that the government guarantees that each farmer (who qualifies for inclusion in the system) will receive at least the guaranteed price. If the guaranteed price for wheat, for example, is £50 per ton, and the market-clearing price is £40 per ton, farmers may become eligible for so-called **deficiency payments** that will equal the difference between the guaranteed price of £50 and the market-clearing price of £40 times the total number of tonnes that the farmer has sold on the open market. A deficiency payment is simply another way to describe a direct *subsidy* paid to the farmer so the terms 'guarantee price', 'deficiency payment', and 'subsidy' are just what they seem to be. The government promised to make up the difference between the market-clearing price and the price which it deemed was appropriate that farmers should receive for their output.

Figure 8.10 shows the working of guaranteed prices in a graphic format. We have already analysed market price and the support price in Figure 8.9 where we showed that when the support price was greater than the market price, there would be an excess quantity supplied ('surplus') at the support price.

The concept of a guaranteed price is slightly differ-ent because it involves no direct purchase by govern-ment and, thus, no storage of the crop by government. In Figure 8.10 we show the market demand as *DD* and market supply as *SS*. At price P_T the quantity supplied will be equal to Q_T. At that quantity, however, consumers will only purchase it at P_c. Therefore, the subsidy to each farmer is equal to the vertical differ-ence between P_T and P_c times the number of units that the farmer sells. We have labelled it 'per unit subsidy'. Guaranteed prices, therefore, lead to a greater use of resources, greater output, and greater consumption than in an unrestricted market. With this understand-ing of the effects of a guarantee system at work we need to pose the question who pays for this interven-tion? The funds required to pay farmers these *subsidies* obviously had to come from somewhere: using tax-

payers' money meant that taxpayers were assisting consumers. In so far as rich people paid more in tax than poorer persons the farm support system in the UK was viewed by many as being socially acceptable. It was regarded as fair and enabled consumers to enjoy lower prices for food than would otherwise have been the case.

Figure 8.10

Guaranteed Prices. We show the market demand curve, *DD*, and the market supply curve as *SS*. The intersection of *DD* and *SS* is at point *E*, yielding a market equilibrium price of P_e and an equilibrium quantity of Q_e. The government, however, sets the target price, P_T, above the market equilibrium price. The total market quantity pro-duced will be Q_T. But that quantity, Q_T, can only be sold if the price, P_c is charged. Hence the market clearing price is labelled P_c. This means that the government must pay a subsidy on each unit produced and sold of the vertical difference between P_c and P_T. This is labelled 'per unit subsidy'. Each farmer therefore receives a total subsidy of the per unit subsidy times the number of units sold.

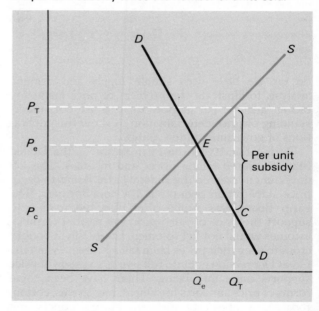

How did the price support system affect Britain's overseas supplies of foodstuffs? We can now modify our diagram to show the effect of guaranteed prices on imports of food.

If we assume that overseas suppliers of, say, butter are willing to supply an unlimited quantity of food to the British market at a particular price then the supply curve will be perfectly elastic. If, for example, New Zealand was able to offer Great Britain butter at prices below which British farmers could not compete then the market price would be determined by the imported product.

Figure 8.11 shows that at the market price of *OW* imports of butter from New Zealand amount to *AD* and home-produced supplies to *OA*. The effect of the deficiency payment system is to raise the proportion of total supplies accounted for by home-produced supplies and diminish that of imports. The quantity of butter from New Zealand is now BE rather than AD. Thus the price support system did not shut off supplies from abroad and deny British consumers the benefit of cheap food from countries who for geographical and climatic reasons were able to produce food at low cost. On the other hand the result of the price guarantees was to increase the degree of self-sufficiency of British food supplies.

The EEC System

On her entry into the European Community the UK began to move the basis of her agricultural support system over to an **import levy** system. Under this

method of agricultural support the prices of imported foodstuffs are raised by levies to bring them into line with *target* prices. Figure 8.12 is a simple illustration of this system indicating how this policy results in consumers of food supporting farmers directly through high market prices. The levies on imported food are paid into a common farm fund known as FEOGA (the initials of its French title) which are partly used to subsidize the disposal of excess stocks. In so far as the EEC's target prices have generally been well above world prices the cost of this method of agricultural support has been considerable. For some commodities the output of the Community's farmers has vastly exceeded consumption at the targeted price – hence the infamous butter 'mountains' and wine 'lakes'. The costly storage and subsequent disposal of

Figure 8.11
The Impact of Deficiency Payments in an Open Economy. In the absence of guaranteed prices the world market price is determined by the lowest-cost supplier. If we assume that New Zealand could supply butter at a price of OW (the world price) then British farmers will supply OA at this price. Imports of butter thus dominate the UK market, being AD. The supply curve for both the UK and imports is thus VYZ. However, the effect of the guaranteed price OG stimulates home production and the UK share of the butter market increases from OA to OB. Imports are now BE. The supply curve for both the UK and imports is thus VYPFZ. Can you work out what the area OGPB means?

Figure 8.12
The Impact of Levies in an Open Economy. In the absence of a levy on, say, butter, the world market price is OW determined by the lowest-cost supplier. If we assume that New Zealand could supply butter at a price of OW (the world price) then British farmers will supply OA at this price. Imports of butter thus dominate the UK market, being AD. The supply curve for both the UK and imports is thus JKM. However, the effect of imposing a levy WL stimulates home production and the UK share of the butter market increases from OA to OB. Imports are now BC. The new supply curve for both the UK and imports is JKGF. Can you work out what the area GFEH means?

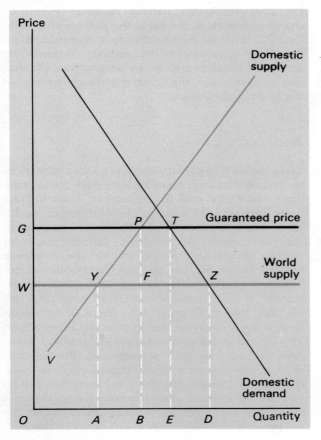
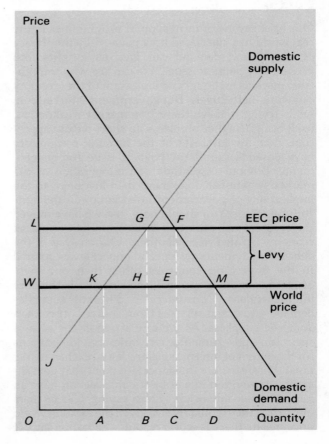

Key Points 8.4

▶ Governments in developed economies have tried several methods to resolve the problem of low and unstable farm incomes in a free market.

▶ Price supports can give farmers a stable price but leave a problem for the government to dispose of surplus stocks at the supported price.

▶ Guaranteed prices ensure that each farmer will receive the price determined by the government, and thus qualify for a subsidy or deficiency payment in excess of the newly determined market price.

▶ A guaranteed price system has an impact on the use of resources as well as the levels of domestically produced output, domestic consumption, and share of the market accounted for by imports.

▶ A farm support system can be based on making food imports more expensive by imposing levies or taxes. This system means consumers bear the burden of the policy rather than taxpayers.

---

these stockpiles has, not surprisingly, been a controversial one. Should excess butter supplies be offered at a substantial discount on world prices to the Russians? Why should low-cost suppliers like New Zealand who are non-members of the Community find their trade unfairly disrupted by the disposal of such stocks?

The Agricultural Problem in a Wider Context

Our brief review of farm support programmes in the real world has illustrated how powerfully the theory of supply and demand can give us insights into present-day political issues. We can see why unregulated markets in the agricultural sector of the economy can work ineffectively. But government intervention, while trying to solve these free market weaknesses, itself brings further problems. In short we can appreciate that the interests of the farming community have posed a significant political issue for governments. But our case study of the operation of the market system has done more than just point to the implications of government intervention in the agricultural sector. You should note that we have moved the focus of our attention away from just one *closed* economy isolated from all others. Our analysis of the deficiency payments system and import levies pointed to the impact on countries other than our own. Modern economies are *open economies*, that is they are interdependent. Consumers in different countries demand goods and services from sources other than domestic suppliers. As we saw above in the case of agriculture government intervention has implications for the extent of international trade and exchange. We must therefore note the important point that government intervention in a domestic market can have an international dimension. Thus paying UK farmers more than they would receive given the existing world price means there is world resource allocation impact

to be considered. We must look at the whole picture and not just the immediate and local part.

A second point to note about the case study of the agricultural sector is that it raises the important matter of how government intervention in markets is to be financed. We referred both to subsidies and levies on imports. The latter are, in effect, taxes on goods. Under the pre-1973 system the UK used tax revenues to subsidize domestic production. Where did these revenues come from? Under the current system the UK along with her EEC partners raises tax revenue by charging importers of food at the point of entry into the EEC. What we now need to do is examine in more detail how governments impose taxes on goods and services. Such taxes are known as *indirect taxes*. We shall aim to do this with the demand and supply model at the heart of the analysis.

Indirect Taxes

Taxes imposed by governments on goods and services are so-called indirect taxes because they are in some form eventually paid by consumers. Such indirect taxes contrast with a tax on one's income or wealth (direct taxes) which are paid directly by the taxpayer to the government. An employer deducts tax from weekly or monthly wages before the employee receives his or her pay packet. The amount of tax deducted depends on the taxpayer's individual circumstances. It is a personal matter in each case (we consider this in Chapter 10). There is no option concerning non-payment of income tax. However, an item on sale in a supermarket which is subject to tax does not vary in price according to the personal circumstances of the potential purchaser of the good. If someone does not buy the good then they pay no tax. Even if someone does purchase the good that is taxed then that consumer may not be paying all the tax per unit imposed on the good. How can this be?

The Supply Side

When government imposes a tax on a good or service the effect is to shift the supply schedule upwards and to the left. This is because it is the responsibility of a supplier to collect an indirect tax when goods are manufactured or sold and to pay over the tax to the government. In Figure 8.13 we assume a good not previously subject to tax now has a tax of $£P_1P_3$ per unit imposed. This shifts the supply schedule upwards and leftwards by an equal amount throughout the length of the original supply curve.

The Demand Side

The tax paid by the supplier to the government can be recovered from the consumer by adding the tax on to the price charged. The effect of the tax upon the price and quantity demanded of the good will depend on the price elasticity of demand for that good. Figure 8.13 shows two demand schedules with quite different sensitivities of demand to the prices charged. What difference do the two demand curves make to the situation?

Figure 8.13

The Impact of Indirect Taxes. Demand schedule D_1 shows quantity demanded is more price sensitive than is D_2. If the pre-tax price for both goods is OP_1 the price, post-tax, is OP_2 in the case of D_1 but OP_3 in the case of D_2.

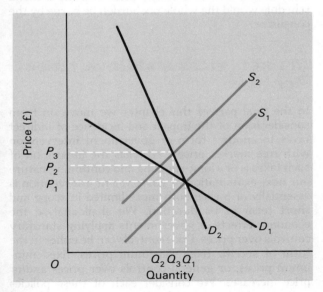

The Effect of the Indirect Tax

The imposition of the tax results in the supply schedule moving from S_1 to S_2. In the case of the demand schedule D_1 the market price now rises from OP_1 to OP_2 and quantity demanded falls from OQ_1 to OQ_2. But if the demand curve D_2 is now considered we note the price rises from OP_1 to OP_3 which is much

greater. The fall in the quantity demanded is less – from OQ_1 to OQ_3 – than in the case of demand schedule D_1. Why is this? It is simply because D_1 indicates that consumers are more sensitive in their willingness to buy quantities of the good as the price is altered. In the case of D_2 the price elasticity of demand is, broadly speaking, lower reflecting a relatively greater insensitivity of consumers to upward movements in prices charged.

Let us set out the conclusion from this analysis. A government which wishes to raise tax revenue should impose indirect taxes on those goods the consumption of which is relatively insensitive to a tax-based increase in price. If demand for a good is highly price elastic when the tax is imposed then the tax revenue obtained is less than where demand is less price elastic.

Our conclusion may not seem too surprising. Thus cigarettes may seem to you to be a more obvious item to tax than say a tax on works of art. But a moment's reflection should make you realize that low price elasticity of demand for the commodity is not the only relevant aspect in selecting suitable bases for indirect taxes. Consumption of a good has to be sufficiently large for a tax to raise much revenue. Some foodstuffs as we saw in Chapter 7 have a low price elasticity of demand but taxing say butter and cheese may not be acceptable to a government. The price of basic necessities such as food has long been of political importance and thus governments have seen a more promising base for an indirect tax in the 'optional necessities' of tobacco and alcohol. Thus for many years the price charged for cigarettes, beer, wines, and spirits includes a large element of tax. These commodities need not be purchased although few citizens are total abstainers! Leaving aside the moral question of a government's revenues being at least partially dependent on the addiction of citizens to smoking and drinking the choice of tobacco and alcoholic drinks as suitable bases for an indirect tax is quite understandable. But do smokers pay all the tax per unit that is imposed? This takes us to the matter of **tax incidence**.

Tax Incidence

The term 'tax incidence' refers to the burden on whom a tax falls. Does it fall wholly on the consumer or does the supplier pay part of a tax?

Figure 8.14 shows the demand for two goods which have differing sensitivities of quantity demanded to prices charged. If a tax is now imposed on both goods which is of the same rate per unit what happens? In the case of good T the market price is now OP_2 rather than OP_1. The tax per unit is BD of which the consumer pays BC. In the case of good W the rise in the market price is from OP_3 to OP_4. Here the consumer pays GH of the same tax per unit GI. Clearly in the case of good T the consumer pays only a small part of the tax burden. The supplier has to bear most of the tax burden since demand is relatively price elastic. In the case of good W the reverse happens: the supplier bears

Figure 8.14
The Incidence of Indirect Taxes.

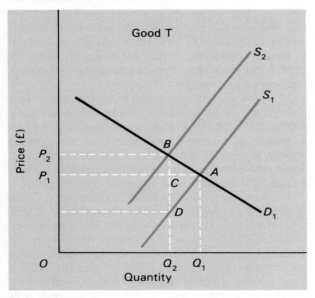

Good T

Good T		Good W	
Pre-tax price	OP_1	Pre-tax price	OP_3
Tax per unit	BD (=GI)	Tax per unit	GI
Post-tax price	OP_2	Post-tax price	OP_4
Consumer's burden	BC	Consumer's burden	GH
Supplier's burden	CD	Supplier's burden	HI

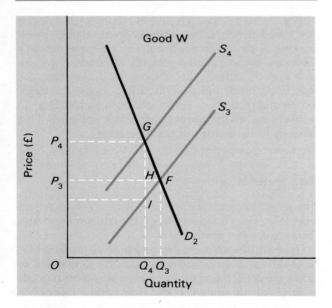

Good W

just the amount HI of the tax burden. The supplier is the more able to pass on the tax burden since demand for W is less sensitive than is the case with good T. The supplier of good W faces less of a difficulty in trading since his profit margin in selling good W is that much less squeezed. Both suppliers however bear some burden and face the issue whether they can somehow reduce the costs of selling these goods.

What would happen if the demand curve was perfectly inelastic rather than either of the two situations in Figure 8.14? Here you should satisfy yourself that the full impact of a flat-rate (or specific) indirect tax falls wholly on the consumer.

An *ad valorem* Tax

Our example of an indirect tax has been a flat-rate tax, such that the post-tax supply curve shifted to the left throughout its length by the same amount. If the tax varies according to the value of the item as charged by suppliers the tax is called an **ad valorem tax**. Thus a 10 per cent *ad valorem* tax would result in a higher tax being payable on an item when sold at £10 as compared with £5. The effect of an *ad valorem* tax is to make the post-tax supply curve diverge from the pre-tax supply curve as we move from left to right. This divergence is explained of course by the direct relationship of the tax with the prices that producers seek to obtain for their goods. Our earlier example of a flat-rate tax is the simplest form of indirect tax but in the real world *ad valorem* taxes are exemplified by Value Added Tax (VAT) which is charged on many goods and services at a rate of 15%. Can you think of reasons why governments might favour a tax on such a sliding-scale basis?

Let us now sum up on the matter of the relative burden of an indirect tax: where demand for a good is relatively price sensitive the burden of an indirect tax will be shared between the consumer and producer. Only in the case of a totally price-inelastic demand schedule would the whole tax burden be borne by the consumer.

Market Prices and Government Controls

In the final part of this chapter we move on from consideration of the impact and incidence of indirect taxes to another form of government intervention with free market prices. Whereas the imposition of such taxes is of a long-standing and continuing nature our next examination of government intervention is essentially of a type both more limited in scope and short term in its duration. We shall analyse the economic effects of governments applying statutory controls over prices. Price controls can be either in the form of specific fixed maximum prices, fixed minimum prices, or general controls over prices and/or price increases. We consider each of these policies against a background that intervention is deemed necessary because the existing free market price (or prices) is (are) for one or more reasons not appropriate.

Specific Fixed Maximum Prices

If the government fixes a maximum price in a given market below the existing market equilibrium price then that newly established price will have profound implications for the operation of that market. Why? Let us look again at the supply and demand dimensions with reference to Figure 8.15. In the UK and in several other countries rents that can be charged for property rented from landlords are subject to controls. The rationale for a maximum price to be charged is that it is necessary to keep the cost of housing as low as possible. Control of rents charged by landlords is usually one interference with the housing market: tax benefits for owner-occupiers paying for their houses with long-term loans or mortgages is yet another illustration of the social and political concern of governments with housing. Our concern here is not to query the motivation to influence the prices people have to pay for occupying either the houses they own or the property in which they are temporarily residing. But we can point out as an exercise in positive economics that Rent Acts and other policies which permit rent reductions have significant repurcussions on both sides of the housing market – landlords and tenants.

In Figure 8.15 the demand for rented accommodation at the maximum rent that can be charged – price OP_1 – is OQ_3. But at this price – below an equilibrium price of OP_2 – landlords only supply OQ_1 and the distance Q_1Q_3 is unsatisfied demand at the rent OP_1. Those unable to obtain privately owned property can only try to buy a house or seek accommodation within the public sector. Landlords who are not prepared to make rented housing available at the controlled price may sell their property, leave it empty, or use it for purposes other than temporary accommodation. Whatever response the upshot is that the supply side contracts and thus a maximum rents policy really only benefits those fortunate to find and live in rented accommodation. Our analysis thus points to maximum rent policies discouraging the supply of rented private housing. In the UK we find this proposition has been borne out. Since the 1967 Rent Act the percentage of the total stock of dwellings accounted for by rented private accommodation has fallen sharply. Whereas in 1967 the figure was 24 per cent it fell steadily each year to 11 per cent by 1984.

Of course, maximum prices only have effects such as in Figure 8.14 if they are set below the equilibrium market price. If set at or above the equilibrium price

Figure 8.15

The Market for Private Rented Accommodation. The free market equilibrium price is OP_2. A maximum price for rented property of OP_1 means demand is OQ_3 but supply available is only OQ_1.

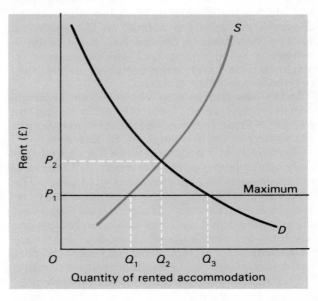

then a maximum price will be of no consequence. You should convince yourself why this must be so: consider what the equilibrium price means.

Specific Fixed Minimum Prices

In contrast to maximum prices governments may fix a price which they deem is necessary because the free market price is 'too low'. Again setting a minimum price above what would be the free market price has important effects and our example is taken from the labour market. In the UK there has been concern expressed by the government about the operation of Wage Councils which regulate minimum wage-rates. A debate has arisen between those who support such minimum rates and those critical of them. The former argue employment would be greater if wage-rates were lower than at the regulated levels. Opponents argue that such state controls are a safety net to prevent exploitation of workers by private employers.

In the US there has been a long running debate on the operation of minimum wage rates. Let us see how we can understand the nature of the debate. As was pointed out earlier in this chapter, in the UK the regulation of minimum wage rates is effected by Wage Councils. These Councils set legal minimum rates of pay for about 3 million workers employed in the manufacture of clothing and in several service sectors of the economy, such as hairdressing, laundries, catering and retailing. Whether Wage Councils in these industries are actually desirable has recently become a political issue.

If you look at Figure 8.16 you can see that in an unrestricted labour market there will be an equilibrium wage-rate at which equal quantities of labour are demanded and supplied. What if a legal **minimum wage-rate** were set above the equilibrium wage-rate? Who benefits and who loses from the imposition of a minimum wage-rate above W? If a minimum wage w_m, which is higher than w_e, is imposed the quantity demanded for labour is reduced to Q_D, and some workers now become unemployed. Some of these workers may be unemployed, but others may be employed at a lower wage elsewhere in the non-covered sectors of the economy.

In the long run, some of the reduction in labour demanded will result from the reduction in the number of firms, and some will result from changes in the number of workers employed by each firm.

The effects of a minimum wage law depend crucially upon whether or not it is enforced. If the law is not enforced, it may have no effect whatsoever. The analysis of minimum wages is identical with the analysis of price controls. Although it is easy to analyse the effects of minimum wage legislation because the law spells out specifically which kinds of labour are covered and what exemptions are allowed, it still does not always follow that the minimum wage is effective.

Our analysis suggests that minimum wage legislation, like price controls, benefits some but not others. In the United States a fair amount of empirical evidence has been gathered to demonstrate the unemployment effects of minimum wages on specific groups, such as teenagers. One study showed, for example, that there was a statistically significant reduction in the ratio of teenage:adult employment associated with increased minimum wage-level or coverage. The investigator estimated that a 1 per cent increase in the effective minimum wage reduces the teenage share of employment by 0.3 per cent. Teenage workers in the low-wage category clearly lose as a result of an increase in minimum wage-rates because high minimum wage-rates substantially reduce full-time employment, forcing teenagers into part-time employment or unemployment. Those teenagers who become unemployed are further disadvantaged because they have a very low probability of qualifying for unemployment benefit. Other studies suggest that only low-wage adult women appear to have gained from the minimum wage. They receive, as a group,

Figure 8.16

The Effect of Minimum Wages. The market-clearing wage-rate is w_e. The market-clearing quantity of employment is Q_e and is determined by the intersection of supply and demand at point E. A minimum wage equal to w_m is established. The quantity of labour demanded is reduced to Q_D; the reduction of employment from Q_e to Q_D is equal to the distance between B and A. That distance is smaller than the excess quantity of labour supplied at wage-rate w_m. The distance between B and C is the increase in the quantity of labour supplied that results from the higher minimum wage-rate.

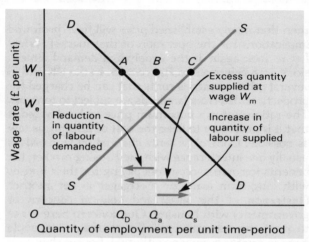

higher wages than they would have received in the absence of the minimum wage.

Other studies have shown that minimum wage legislation weakens the economic status of those at the bottom of the distribution of earrings. The apparent redistribution of income that occurs as a result of the minimum wage appears to be from some 'have nots' to other 'have nots'. Additionally, low-wage workers who are the most skilled are the very ones who are not put out of work by increases in the minimum wage-rate. The group with the greatest degree of poverty – those workers who are least productive – are the most likely to become unemployed due to minimum wage-rate increases.

As one can imagine the debate tends to become highly charged and highlights the political implication of intervening in the market for human resources. Legislation to eliminate sexual discrimination in the labour market in the UK has also inevitably been a contentious matter.

General Price Controls

Our consideration of interventions in the markets for housing and labour illustrate how governments have a concern to modify the operation of certain free market prices. But governments also have a general concern about the pace at which *all* prices move upward. This concern is not new. In 1800 BC the ruler of Babylonia decreed that anyone caught violating his wage and price freeze would be drowned. In AD 301 the Roman Emperor Diocletian fixed the maximum price on beef, grain, eggs, and clothing and prescribed the death penalty for violators.

Moving to more recent times we should note that during World War II many countries imposed **price controls** on a wide range of goods and services. Such controls gave rise to the problem of their enforcement and thus control of **black markets**. We can analyse the effect of a black market by reference to the supply and demand diagram in Figure 8.17.

Assume that Figure 8.17 represented the market in, say, sugar in 1938. On the outbreak of war the UK government took over the allocation of the now scarcer raw materials with the result that sugar producers in the UK (in common with many other manufacturers) were unable to produce as freely as in 1938. The supply curve then shifted to the left with the result that, left to market forces, the price would rise from OP_1 to OP_2. The market mechanism rations the scarcer commodity but at a price. If the government prescribes a maximum price of say OP_1 then a black market in sugar can develop. The price in the illegal black market will be bid up to OP_3 because that is the price at which all available supplies can be sold. The distance CE represents the shortage at the controlled 'white market' price. If, as seems likely for social reasons, the government is unable to accept the working of the price mechanism in distributing available supplies what can it do? If it rejects a 'first-come-first-served' method by which the scarce supplies are distributed then some **rationing** system is necessary. What this means is that households are allocated coupons on a regular basis by which they are entitled to claim at least some sugar per week or per month. The quantities may be less than many are prepared to pay. But at least the rationing system meets the objection that because there is not an equal distribution of incomes the free working of the price system is unjust in its operation. How else can it be ensured that pensioners and those on low incomes obtain some sugar and other basic foodstuffs?

Price controls thus tend to require the introduction of rationing systems. But in a normal peacetime market economy neither is necessary. But that does not mean that the issue of food and other prices are not still politically important.

As we shall see in Chapter 11 the rate of movement of prices in general has been the key aspect of the Thatcher government's economic policies. But the concern is not new since nearly all post-war UK governments have resorted to policies to control the rate of price inflation. By inflation we mean a sustained and persistent rise in prices. Sometimes governments have used statutory or formal means to moderate the pace of inflation. At other times the policies used have been informal and relied on voluntary co-operation rather than legal sanctions to achieve results. Sometimes the emphasis is on controlling the rate of increase in wages in the belief that wage costs are the key element in determining prices. Yet other policies have been almost solely concerned

Figure 8.17

Black Market and Rationing. The market-clearing price is OP_1 in peacetime and OP_2 in a wartime economy. Price control at the level OP_1 means the black market price is OP_3. At the controlled price CE is the excess demand. Rationing distributes the available supplies OB (P_1C) when demand at the controlled price is OA (P_1E).

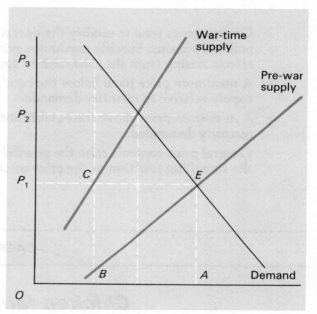

with limiting price rises irrespective of any justification. The proper place to appraise general policies affecting the whole or greater part of the economic system is within the macro section of this book and hence is deferred till Part E. But we can from a micro perspective emphasize the need to examine the supply and demand aspects of a rise in the price whether it be of one good or many goods. There is, as we have seen, upward pressure on the price level if the demand schedule moves to the right and/or the supply schedule shifts to the left. Artificial limits on prices prevent *market forces* from working themselves out. A kettle of boiling water cannot be controlled by fixing down the lid if there is a force of heat at work be it gas or electricity. At some point the build-up of pressure will force off the lid and have possibly serious effects. The market system adjusts to supply and demand pressures and there are dangers if the government pursues a policy of allowing only uniform rates of increases in wages and prices. Why is this? If prices cannot move according to the circumstances of particular markets then the resource allocative function of prices cannot operate properly. If relative prices get out of line then inappropriate signals are being conveyed. For example if the government has a statutory policy which permits only a flat-rate increase in wages then those who receive lower wages than the average for all workers are relatively better off. This effect may be viewed as socially desirable but there will be, by definition, a narrowing of the wage differentials between the wages for different occupations. Firms who seek people in skilled jobs cannot pay them more in order to attract them. If there is a shortage none is indicated by the wage signal in the labour market. The same difficulty arises with a statutory prices policy. In practice, governments recognize such policies need to

be flexible and allow for special circumstances. They have always learned that everyone claims to be a special case requiring relaxation from the general adherence to the norm! How many exceptions can there be before no policy is left in force?

Key Points 8.6

▶ **Governments tend to modify the operation of equilibrium prices for social and political reasons. Specific maximum price and minimum price controls have effects arising from the mismatch of supply and demand.**

▶ **A maximum price fixed below the equilibrium level results in a shortage of supply relative to quantity demanded.**

▶ **A minimum price above the equilibrium results in a surplus of supply relative to quantity demanded.**

▶ **General price controls raise the possibility of relative prices being distorted and the signalling function of the price mechanism not working effectively.**

CASE STUDY

Chicken farming in Riyadh

Question: who gets more in subsidies – a farmer in the European common market or in Saudi Arabia? Answer: Saudi Arabia's farmer, several times over. By throwing petrodollars at its agriculture, Saudi Arabia has turned itself from a land of peasant farmers into the wheat bowl of the Gulf. It is now a net exporter of

wheat. Thanks mainly to government subsidies, the past decade has seen a phenomenal increase in the country's farm output.

Here are some of the figures. In 1975–6. Saudi Arabia grew about 3000 tonnes of wheat; by the 1983–4 harvest, this had multiplied more than four-hundredfold to

1.3m tonnes, going on for twice as much as the 8½m people in the country needed to feed themselves. Saudi Arabia eats more chickens per head of population than any other country. In striving to meet this demand, its farmers reared 250m chickens in 1984, four times as many as they did in 1981. During the same period, the

Figure 8.18
Growing More by Borrowing More All years to end-November

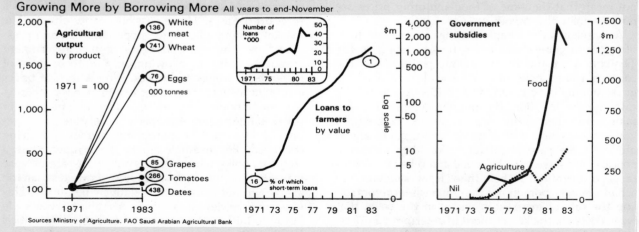

Sources Ministry of Agriculture. FAO Saudi Arabian Agricultural Bank

number of eggs laid by these birds doubled to 2 billion. Saudi Arabia now exports eggs to Kuwait and the United Arab Emirates. The increase in production has cost a fortune.

Since 1980, the beginning of its third five-year plan, Saudi Arabia has spent a total of $20 billion on developing its farming. The bulk of this was paid out by the government in price subsidies. In its defence, the government says that the huge amount it has spent on farming has brought wealth to the outlying provinces and has helped slow the drift off the land to the cities which is the curse of so many developing countries.

The government notes that Saudi Arabia is still the world's third biggest food importer; so it argues that it is not unduly protectionist. The Reagan administration does not buy the argument. As recently as 1979 Saudi Arabia imported 1.5m tonnes of wheat, most of it from the United States. American agronomists splutter that growing cereals at exorbitant cost in the desert makes about as much economic sense as planting bananas under glass in Alaska.

The Americans have a point. Saudi farmers are among the most cossetted in the world. Consider: a Saudi farmer is usually given the land he wants to farm by the government. He then receives a cash subsidy of between 20–50% of the cost of all machinery (except irrigation equipment) bought to till the land. If he still needs extra cash, the farmer can raise an interest-free loan repayable over 10 years from the Saudi Arabian Agricultural Bank (SAAB). In theory, the loans are supposed to cover half the cost of equipping the farm, and repayments do not start for two years. In practice, most farmers bump up their invoices so that the loan pays for most things not already covered by subsidies.

Spoonfed

The spoonfeeding does not end there. SAAB or the Saudi Ministry of Agriculture and Water offer the farmer extra help in producing his crop – e.g., by airlifting milking cows from abroad, by supplying free seed potatoes, free pesticides, and paying for half the cost of most fertilisers and animal feeds.

In consequence, Saudi agriculture has become big business. Lavish government aid has attracted the richest as well as the poorest of Saudi Arabia's population and attracted many foreigners to enter into agricultural joint ventures in Saudi Arabia. These foreigners include Danish Turnkey Dairies, the Irish Dairy Board, and Masstock Systems from Northern Ireland.

Chicken farming is one way Saudi farmers have made money. They have benefited even more from the subsidised price of wheat. Until the price was belatedly cut in November 1984, the government guaranteed farmers $1 000 for each tonne they harvested – more than twice as much as it cost them to produce it ($430 a tonne) and five times as much as it costs to import a tonne (up to $200 cif) at the port of Jeddah.

Saudi wheat production took off in 1979, when guaranteed prices were first introduced. Nearly all the country's wheat is grown on the central plateau (the Najd) in the provinces of Qassim and Hail, and around Kharj, south of the capital Riyadh. In a country that has one of the driest climates in the world, this area gets an average of 4" of rainfall a year.

Saudi wheat is sold at the official price to the Saudi Arabian Grain Silos and Flour Mills Organisation. Buying it cost the Saudi government more than $1 billion in 1984. The cost of importing the same amount of wheat through the port of Jeddah? A mere $160m. Until it slashed the official price last year, Saudi Arabia was starting to build up a wheat mountain. In 1983 the American secretary of agriculture, Mr John Block, described its burgeoning wheat output as 'crazy'.

Source: 'Green Grow the Deserts O', *The Economist*, 6 Apr. 1985, p 74–5.

Questions

1. How does the case study illustrate that agricultural production can be responsible to government intervention?
2. In what way can the concept of opportunity cost be applied in this case study?
3. What international repercussions are apparent from the Saudi government's agricultural policies?

CASE STUDY

Keeping Control of the GIs in Yokohama

Late in 1945 I was sent to Japan as part of a military government team stationed in Yokohama. I was put in charge of rationing, price control, forestry, fishing, and mining for Kanagawa Prefecture. That meant I had nothing to do. The occupation was being run exclusively by General MacArthur's headquarters in Tokyo. But we in the military government at lower levels didn't know we weren't supposed to do anything. Neither did the local Japanese officials. We – and they – took ourselves quite seriously.

One day the medical officer of our company came to see me. He was worried about the heatlh of the American troops. They were picking up girls on the street instead of patronizing the brothels' where the girls were given a medical inspection once a week. The medical officer thought the soldiers were picking up girls on the street because the brothels' prices were too high. Since I was in charge of price control, he wanted me to take action.

I sent for the chief of the Yokohama police, asked for a report on prices charged by every brothel in Yokohama, and naïvely told him why. The conversation was conducted through an interpreter. The chief spoke no English, and the Japanese language instruction provided by the Army program at Northwestern had not taught me the vocabulary needed for the conversation. At the end of the interview, the interpreter informed me that the chief, who was not naïve, would like to give me a party, and he wanted my friend the medical officer to come too.

I got to quite a few good parties before the Japanese learned I had no power, but the police chief's party was by far the best. By the time it took place, I had had second thoughts. What if American newspapers got hold of the story that a United States Army Officer was reducing prices in brothels for the benefit of American troops? I quietly abandoned the project. A bulky report on Yokohama brothels went unused. The chief must have thought his party had been a great success.

Years later, when I finally saw the light, I became shocked at the deficiency of my economic training. To be sure, I had been away from economics for three and a half years before this incident, but that was hardly an excuse. I had majored in economics as an undergraduate at Harvard, received an MA in economics from Columbia, taught economics for two years at Harvard, passed the qualifying examination for the PhD, and worked briefly for the Office of Price Administration. Yet it had not occurred to me to apply elementary economic analysis to the problem. The medical officer's proposal would have had exactly the opposite effect from what he intended. But if I had figured that out, I would have missed a hell of a good party.

Source: R. Fels, 'The Price of Sin', in Rendigs Fels, Stephen Buckles, and Walter Johnson, *Casebook of Economic Problems and Policies*, 4th edn., West Publishing Co., St Paul, United States, pp. 26–7.

Questions
1. What economic concepts and principles are applicable to this case?

2. (a) Draw a supply and demand diagram for the services of the brothels. Indicate the equilibrium price.
   (b) Show on the diagram a price representing the result of carrying out the medical officer's proposal.
   (c) Use the diagram to explain why the medical officer's proposal would have had the opposite effect from the one intended.

3. Suggest a better approach to the medical officer's objective.

Exam Preparation and Practice

INTRODUCTORY EXERCISES

The following letter appeared in the letters page of *The Times* on 22 November 1985.

Mobility of labour
From Mr A. G. Cadman

Sir, Having just completed a visit to the United Kingdom I was struck by the terrible limitation which lack of rented accommodation places upon skilled but unemployed Northern craftsmen who seek to work in the more prosperous South.

America has succeeded in guaranteeing the mobility of labour and has enabled skilled workers to go immediately to where the jobs are to be found at short notice because there is in that country now ample provision of short-term rental accommodation, both furnished and fully vacant.

In the UK, on the other hand, I recently observed Southern shortages, such as decorative plasterwork craftsmen, which attracted over 100 applicants from the North, which were blocked by lack of vacant flats or houses.

Surely the simple act of the Government declaring all new rental space from a given future date to be made free of the Rent Acts would open up a golden opportunity for the enterprise of the property and building industries and do much to soften the frustration and despair of the numerous unemployed Northern craftsmen who could apply their skills in London and the Home Counties, where they are indeed urgently needed.

As a former Director General of the Brick Development Association in the UK and now concerned mainly with housing for the middle and lower income groups overseas I know that this technique is a potent weapon in the fight against unemployment almost everywhere in the industrialised world.

Assuming that you were a Government Minister responsible for housing how would you write a response to the writer of this letter?

MULTIPLE CHOICE QUESTIONS

†1. Which diagram (**A, B, C** or **D**) illustrates the effect on the price and sales of tobacco of an increase in the specific duty per tonne?

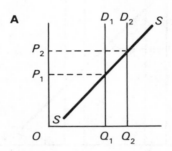

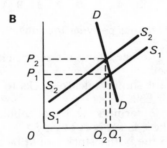

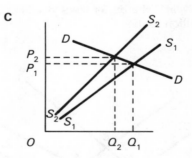

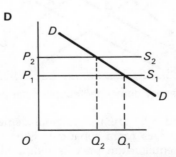

continued overleaf

†2. The diagram below shows the supplies of an agricultural crop in each of five years in relation to the demand for it. Assume that the government wishes to maintain the price paid to farmers at £50 per tonne by purchasing and selling from a buffer stock. Which of the following statements is *untrue*?

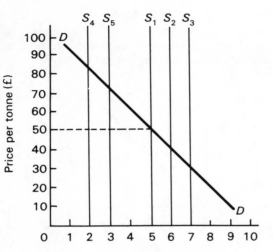

No. of tonnes per year (millions)

A in year 1 it need take no action either to buy or sell
B in year 4 it should release stocks to ensure a price of £50
C in year 2 farmers will not obtain £50 unless there is support buying
D in year 5 the buffer stock would be a seller of stock
E in year 3 the buffer stock needs to buy in 1 million tonnes

3.

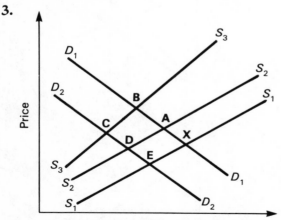

Quantity demanded/supplied per period

D_1D_1 and S_1S_1 are the original demand and supply curves for a consumer good, and the original equilibrium price is indicated by the letter X. If the government imposes an *ad valorem* tax on the good, which of the points labelled **A–E** will be the new equilibrium price?

4. If a government imposes a maximum price on a commodity, then
A there will be an excess quantity supplied
B conditions for a black market will be created
C illegal price cutting will be encouraged
D stocks of the commodity will increase
E the new price will be above the equilibrium price.

5. If, when the 100 per cent *ad valorem* tax on a commodity is doubled, the tax revenue doubles, the price elasticity of demand for the commodity must be
A 0
B 0.5
C 1.0
D 2.0
E 4.0

6. The diagram below shows the market supply and demand schedules for a particular agricultural product.

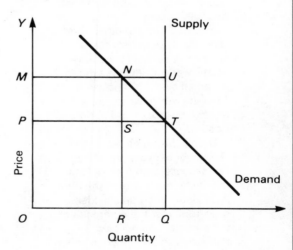

Quantity

The government decides to fix the price at *OM* by buying in the open market. Which area in the diagram represents the government's expenditure?
A *OMNR*
B *RNUQ*
C *PMNT*
D *RNTQ*
E *NUTS*

RELATED ESSAY QUESTIONS

1. Show how buffer stocks may be used to stabilize commodity prices and outline the possible effects on producers' incomes.

2. Explain fully what is meant by price elasticity of demand. How would knowledge of demand assist a government wishing to levy indirect taxes?

3. 'Government intervention in the free market inevitably gives rise to problems.' Discuss this statement with reference to minimum wage legislation and rent controls.

4. How can the basic concepts of supply and demand contribute to an understanding of the problems facing producers of primary products?

5. 'Agriculture is one of the few examples where there is a strong case for government intervention.' Discuss.

9 Demand and Supply in an Open Economy: International Trade and Exchange

Key Points to Review

▶ Opportunity cost (1.2)

▶ Production possiblities curve (1.3)

▶ Demand (5.1)

▶ Supply (5.4)

▶ Equilibrium, surplus, shortage (5.7)

▶ Specialization and comparative advantage (6.2)

▶ Price elasticity of demand (7.1)

Questions for Preview

1 What is a foreign exchange rate?

2 What is a floating exchange rate system?

3 What is a fixed exchange rate system?

4 What is the difference between the balance of trade and the balance of payments?

5 What are some arguments against free trade?

Thus far in this book we have noted differences between countries how their economic systems operate and perform. But we have not examined the interrelationships *between* countries in the sense of how international transactions take place. It is the purpose of this chapter to move on from examining markets in a domestic or internal context to analysing international markets.

When we talk about international trade, we refer to the movement of goods and services from one country to another. We must now make reference to the way in which world trade in goods, services, and financial assets is financed. How does the UK pay for its imports? How does the rest of the world pay for exports from the UK? These are questions that we will cover in this chapter. We will describe several alternative international financial systems. We will look at flexible (or floating) exchange rates and fixed exchange rates. Additionally, we will examine the measurement and the components of the balance of

payments. We will follow the same approach as earlier in this book. At the outset of our analysis we assume a world where foreign exchange markets are not affected by government intervention. Then, as in Chapter 8, we will examine the nature of such intervention in international markets.

Floating, or Flexible Exchange Rates

When you decide to buy foreign products, such as French wine, you have pounds with which to pay the French wine-maker. The French wine-maker, however, would be hard pressed to pay his or her workers in pounds. The workers are French, they live in France, and they need francs to buy goods and services in that country. There must therefore be some way to exchange pounds for the francs that the wine-maker will accept. That exchange occurs in a **foreign**

exchange market, which, in this case, specializes in exchanging francs and pounds. The particular exchange rate between francs and pounds that would prevail depends on the interaction of the demand for and supply of francs and pounds. In a sense, then, our analysis of the exchange rate between pounds and francs will be familiar for we explained supply and demand in Chapter 5. If it costs you 20p to buy one franc, that is the **foreign exchange rate** determined by the demand and supply of francs in the foreign exchange market. The French person going to the foreign exchange market would find that he or she needs 5 francs to buy one pound. The numbers we will use here are hypothetical. We will later show the actual exchange rate of major currencies relative to the pound. We will continue our two-country example in which the only two countries in the world are the UK and France. Now let us consider what determines the demand and supply of foreign currency in the foreign exchange market.

Our analysis will initially restrict itself to the market in foreign exchange arising from the import and export of *goods*. In the real world, exchange rates are determined, not only by the demand and supply of currency arising from international trade, but also flows of capital. We acknowledge this important aspect of foreign exchange markets later in the chapter.

The Demand and Supply of Foreign Currency

You wish to buy some Bordeaux wine. To do so, you must get French francs. You go to the foreign exchange market. Your desire to buy the French wine therefore provides a supply of pounds sterling to the foreign exchange market. In other words, your demand for French francs is equivalent to your supply of pounds in the foreign exchange market. Indeed, every transaction concerning the importation of foreign goods constitutes a supply of pounds and a demand for some foreign currency and vice versa. In this case, it constitutes a demand for French francs.

In our example, we will assume that only two goods are being traded – French wine and Shetland lamb's-wool sweaters. Thus, the UK demand for French wine creates a supply of pounds and a demand for francs in the foreign exchange market. Similarly, the French demand for Shetland sweaters creates a supply of francs and a demand for pounds in the foreign exchange market. In a **freely floating (or flexible) exchange rate** situation, the supply and demand of pounds and francs in the foreign exchange market will determine the equilibrium foreign exchange rate. The equilibrium exchange rate will tell us how many francs a pound can be exchanged for – that is, the sterling price of francs – or how many pounds (or fractions of a pound) a franc can be exchanged for – that is, the franc price of pounds.

The Equilibrium Foreign Exchange Rate

In order to determine the equilibrium foreign exchange rate, we have to find out what determines the demand and supply of foreign exchange. We will ignore for the moment any speculative aspect of buying foreign exchange; that is, we assume that there are no individuals who wish to buy francs because they think the price will go up in the future.

The idea of an exchange rate is not different from the idea of paying a certain price for something you want to buy. If you like to buy coffee, you know you have to pay, say, 35p a cup. If the price went up to £1, you would probably buy fewer cups. If the price went down to 15p, you might buy more (assuming you are a coffee-drinker). In other words, the demand curve for cups of coffee, expressed in terms of pounds, slopes downwards following the theory of demand. The demand curve for francs slopes downwards also, and we will see why.

THE DEMAND SCHEDULE FOR FRANCS

Let us think more closely about the demand schedule for francs. Let us say that it costs you 20p to purchase one franc; that is the exchange rate between pounds and francs. If tomorrow you had to pay 25p for the same franc, then the exchange rate would have changed. Looking at such an increase with respect to the franc, we would say that there has been an **appreciation** in the value of the *franc* in the foreign exchange market. But this increase in the value of the franc means that there has been a **depreciation** in the value of the *pound* in the foreign exchange market. Previously, the pound could buy 5 francs; tomorrow, the pound will be able to buy only 4 francs at a price of 25p per franc. In any event, if the sterling price of francs is higher, you will probably demand fewer francs. Why? The answer lies in looking at the reason why you demand francs in the first place.

You demand francs in order to buy French wine. Your demand curve for French wine, we will assume, follows the theory of demand and is therefore downward sloping. If it costs you more pounds in order to buy the same quantity of French wine, presumably you will not buy the same quantity; your quantity demanded will be less. We say that your demand for French francs is *derived* from your demand for French wine. In Figure 9.1 we show the hypothetical demand schedule for French wine in the UK by a representative wine-drinker. In panel (b) we show the UK demand curve for French wine in terms of pounds.

Let us assume that the price per litre of French wine in France is 20 francs. Given that price, we can find out the number of francs required to purchase one, two, three, and four bottles of French wine. That information is given in panel (c) of Figure 9.1. One bottle requires 20 francs, four bottles require 80. Now we have a sufficient amount of information to determine the derived demand curve for French francs. If 1 franc costs 20p, a bottle of wine would cost £4 (20 francs per bottle/5 francs per pound = £4 per bottle). At £4 per

Figure 9.1

Deriving the Demand for French Francs. In panel (a), we show the demand schedule for French wine in the UK, expressed in terms of pounds per bottle. In panel (b), we show the demand curve *DD*, which is downward sloping. In panel (c), we show the number of francs required to purchase one, two, three, and four bottles of wine. If the price per bottle of wine in France is 20 francs, we can now find the quantity of francs needed to pay for the various quantities demanded above. In panel (d), we see the derived demand for francs in the UK in order to purchase the different quantities of wine given in panel (a). The resultant demand curve *D'D'* is shown in panel (e). It is the derived demand for francs in the UK.

Panel (a)

DEMAND SCHEDULE FOR FRENCH WINE IN THE UK PER WEEK

Price per bottle	Quantity demanded
£10	1 bottle
£ 8	2 bottles
£ 6	3 bottles
£ 4	4 bottles

Panel (c)

Quantity demanded	Francs required to purchase quantity demanded (at P = 20 francs per bottle)
1 bottle	20
2 bottles	40
3 bottles	60
4 bottles	80

Panel (d)

DERIVED DEMAND SCHEDULE FOR FRANCS IN THE UK WITH WHICH TO PAY FOR IMPORTS OF WINE

Price of 1 franc	Quantity of francs demanded per week
50p	20 francs
40p	40 francs
30p	60 francs
20p	80 francs

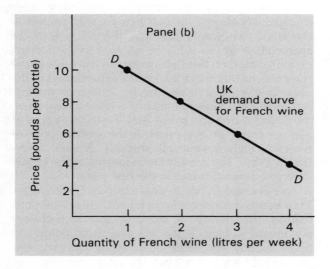

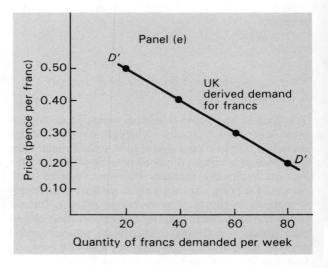

bottle, our representative wine-drinker would, we see from panel (a) of Figure 9.1, demand four bottles. From panel (c), we see that 80 francs would be demanded to buy the four bottles of wine. We show this quantity demanded in panel (d). In panel (e), we draw the derived demand curve for francs. Now consider what happens if the price of francs goes up to 30p. A bottle of French wine costing 20 francs in France would now cost £6 in the UK. From panel (a), we see that at £6 per bottle, three bottles will be imported into the UK by our representative wine-drinker. From panel (c), we see that three bottles would require 60 francs to be purchased; thus, in panels (d) and (e), we see that at a price of 1 franc per 30p, the quantity demanded will be 60 francs. We do

this all the way up to a price of 50p per franc. At that price, a bottle of French wine costing 20 francs in France would cost £10 in the UK, and our representative wine-drinker would import only one bottle.

DERIVED DEMAND IS DOWNWARD SLOPING

As can be expected, as the price of francs falls, the quantity demanded will rise. The only difference here from the demand analysis used in Chapter 5 is that the demand for francs is derived from the demand for a final product, French wine in our example.

THE SUPPLY OF FRENCH FRANCS

The supply of French francs is a derived supply in the sense that it is derived from a French person's demand for Shetland sweaters. We could go through an example similar to the one above to come up with a supply schedule of French francs in France. It is upward sloping. Obviously, the French need pounds in order to purchase the sweaters. If we offer more pounds for the same amount of francs, the sterling price of francs would go up. In principle, the French would be willing to supply more francs when the sterling price of francs goes up, because they can then buy more sweaters with the same quantity of francs; that is, the franc is worth more in exchange for UK goods than when the sterling price for francs was lower. Let us take an example. A sweater in the UK costs £10. If the exchange rate is 25p for one franc, the French have to come up with 40 francs (= £10 at 25p per franc) to buy a sweater. If, on the other hand, the exchange rate goes up to 50p for one franc, the French must come up with only 20 francs (= £10 at 50p per franc) to buy a sweater. At a lower price (in francs) of sweaters, they will demand a larger quantity. In other words, as the price of French francs goes up in terms of pounds, the quantity of sweaters demanded will go up, and hence the quantity of French francs supplied will go up. Therefore, the supply schedule of foreign currency (francs) will be upward sloping.

We draw an upward-sloping schedule in Figure 9.2. In our hypothetical example, assuming that there is only one wine-drinker in the UK and one demander of sweaters in France, the equilibrium exchange rate will be set at 20p per franc, or 5 francs to £1. Let us now look at the aggregate demand and supply of French

francs. We take all demanders of French wine and all demanders of sweaters and put their demands and supplies of francs together into one diagram. Thus, we are showing an aggregate version of the demand and supply of French francs. The horizontal axis in Figure 9.3 represents a quantity of foreign exchange – the number of francs per year. The vertical axis represents the exchange rate – the price of foreign currency (francs) expressed in pounds (per franc). Thus, at the foreign currency price of 25p per franc, you know that it will cost you 25p to buy 1 franc. At the foreign currency price of 20p per franc, you know that it will cost you 20p to buy 1 franc. The equilibrium is again established at 20p for 1 franc. This equilibrium is not established because the British like to buy francs or because the French like to buy sterling. Rather, the equilibrium exchange rate depends upon how many sweaters the French want and how much French wine the British want (given their respective incomes, tastes, and the relative price of wine and sweaters). (Remember however, our assumption that we have excluded from consideration the relevance of flows of capital in determining the exchange rate.)

Figure 9.3
The Aggregate Demand and Supply of French Francs.
Here we have drawn the demand curve for French francs. It is a derived demand schedule – that is, a schedule derived from the demand by the British for French wine. We have drawn the supply curve of French francs, which results from the French demand for sweaters. The demand curve, DD, slopes downwards like most demand curves, and the supply curve, SS, slopes upwards. The foreign exchange price, or the sterling price of francs, in millions, is represented on the horizontal axis. If the foreign exchange rate is 25p – that is, if it takes 25p to buy 1 franc – then the British will demand 80 million francs. The equilibrium exchange rate is at the intersection of DD and SS. The equilibrium exchange rate is 20p. At this point, 100 million French francs are both demanded and supplied each year.

Figure 9.2
The Equilibrium Exchange Rate for Two Individuals.
Here we assume that there are only two individuals – one representative British wine-drinker and one representative French purchaser of sweaters. The derived demand curve for French francs is taken from Panel (e) of Figure 9.1. The derived supply curve SS results from the representative French purchaser of sweaters who supplies francs to the foreign exchange market when he or she demands pounds in order to buy sweaters. The intersection of D'D' and SS is at E. The equilibrium exchange rate is 20p for 1 franc. The equilibrium quantity of francs in the foreign exchange market will be 80 per week.

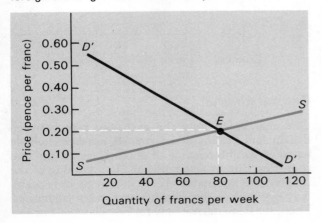

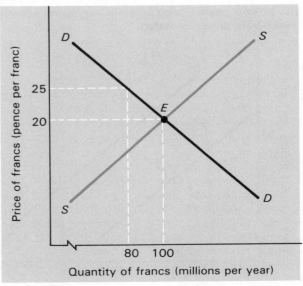

A SHIFT IN DEMAND

Assume that a successful advertising campaign by British wine importers has caused the British demand (schedule) for French wine to double. We now demand twice as much wine at all prices. Our demand schedule for French wine has shifted out and to the right. (Can you draw this?)

The increased demand for French wine can be translated into an increased demand for francs. Our thirst for bottles of Bordeaux wine means we will supply more pounds to the foreign exchange market while demanding more French francs to pay for the wine. Figure 9.4 presents a new demand schedule, D'D', for French francs; this demand schedule is to the right and outward from the original demand schedule. If the French do not change their desire for sweaters, the supply schedule of French francs will remain stable. A new equilibrium will be established at a higher exchange rate. In our particular example, the equilibrium is established at an exchange rate of 30p. It now takes 30p to buy 1 franc, whereas it took 20p before. This is translated as an increase in the price of French wine to UK drinkers and as a decrease in the price of sweaters to the French.

Figure 9.4

A Shift in the Demand Schedule. The British experience a shift in their taste in favour of French wine. The demand schedule for French wine shifts to the right, causing the derived demand schedule for francs to shift to the right also. We have shown this shift as a movement from DD to D'D'. We have assumed that the French supply schedule of francs has remained stable – that is, their taste for sweaters has remained constant. The old equilibrium foreign exchange rate was 20p. (It cost 20p to buy one franc.) The new equilibrium exchange rate will be at the intersection of D'D' and SS – or E'. The new exchange rate will be higher than the old one. It will now cost 30p to buy 1 franc. The quantity of francs demanded is greater even at this higher price because the demand schedule has shifted out. The higher price of francs will be translated into a higher sterling price for French wine and a lower French franc price of sweaters.

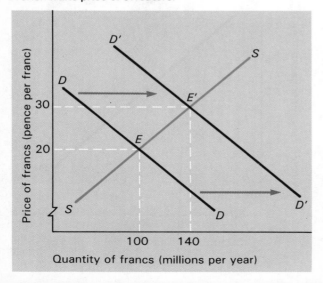

A SHIFT IN SUPPLY

In the preceding example, we assumed that the British taste for wine had shifted. Since the demand for French francs is a derived demand by the British for French wine, that caused a shift in the demand curve for francs. Now let us assume that the supply curve of French francs shifts outwards to the right. This may occur for many reasons, the most probable one being a relative rise in the French price level. For example, if the price of all French-made clothes went up 100 per cent in francs, Shetland sweaters would become relatively cheaper. That would mean that French people would want to buy more sweaters. But remember that when they want to buy more sweaters, they supply more francs to the foreign exchange market. Thus, we see in Figure 9.5 that the supply curve of French francs moves from SS to S'S'. In the absence of restrictions – that is, in a system of floating exchange rates – the new equilibrium exchange rate will be 1 franc equals 10p, or £1 equals 10 francs. The quantity of francs demanded and supplied will increase from 100 million per year to 200 million per year. We say, then, that in a free (or floating) international exchange rate system, shifts in the demand and supply of foreign currencies will cause changes in the equilibrium foreign exchange rates. Those rates will remain in effect until supply and/or demand shift.

Figure 9.5

A Shift in the Supply of French Francs. For whatever reason, there has been a shift in the supply curve of French francs. The new equilibrium will occur at E'. Ten pence, rather than 20p, will now buy 1 franc. After the exchange rate adjustment, the amount of francs demanded and supplied will be 200 million per year.

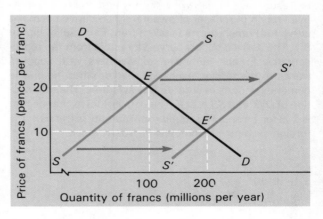

Capital Flows

Our analysis of how the exchange rate between Britain and France is determined has been wholly based on an interchange of goods between the two countries. But, as was noted at the beginning of the chapter, this international exchange in goods provides only one part of the demand for foreign currencies. There is a demand, not only for French wine, but also

---

Key Points 9.1

▶ The foreign exchange rate is the rate at which a unit of one country's currency can be exchanged for another's.

▶ The demand for foreign exchange is a derived demand; it is derived from the demand for foreign goods and services (and in the real world also for financial assets).

▶ The supply of foreign exchange is derived from foreigners' demands for our goods and services.

▶ In general, the demand curve of foreign exchange slopes downwards and the supply curve of foreign exchange slopes upwards. The equilibrium foreign exchange rate occurs at the intersection of the demand and supply curves.

▶ A shift in the demand for foreign goods will result in a shift in the demand for foreign exchange. The equilibrium foreign exchange rate will change.

▶ A shift in the supply of foreign currency will cause a change in the equilibrium exchange rate.

---

for francs, by those UK residents who travel to France for their holiday. They need francs in order to buy food (and wine!) when in France. A further demand for francs arises when, say, a UK firm wishes to acquire a firm in France, or if a UK resident wishes to buy a holiday flat in, for example, Cannes. In these cases we are referring to transactions in *financial assets*. Those involved in making decisions whether to invest abroad will be sensitive to the actual and *expected* situation in foreign exchange rates. The timing of an investment abroad may be affected by a view on how the foreign exchange rate is expected to change in the future. But once we recognise the relevance of expected changes in exchange rates, we have then come to realise that *speculation* is one aspect in the market for foreign currencies. In short, we should expect transactions in foreign currencies for their own sake.

Dealings in the foreign exchange market reflect the willingness of individuals, firms and financial institutions to shift funds for financial gain. Thus our initial assumption that foreign exchange markets merely serve to satisfy the needs of trade in goods is now seen to be a very limited one.

Fixed Exchange Rate System

We have just described the workings of a freely floating, or flexible, exchange rate system in international finance. Now we consider a situation in which central banks intervene in order to prevent foreign exchange rates from changing. This is a system of **fixed exchange rates**. As with most systems where a price of a particular good or service is fixed, the only way that it can remain so is for the government to intervene.

Let us take our two-country example again. Sup-

pose that the price of sweaters has increased as part of everything made in the UK. The French now will buy fewer sweaters than before. They supply fewer francs to the foreign exchange market and demand fewer pounds at the fixed exchange rate. But UK wine-drinkers continue to demand French wines. In fact, they will demand more, because at the fixed exchange rate, the relative price of French wines has fallen. So the UK will now supply more pounds in the foreign exchange market and demand more francs. As in Figure 9.6, the demand curve for francs will shift to *D'D'*. In the absence of any intervention by central banks, the exchange rate will change. The price of French francs in terms of pounds will go from 20p per franc to 25p. That is, the value of a pound in terms of francs will go down. The pound will suffer a *depreciation* in its value relative to the franc, and the franc will experience an *appreciation* in its value in terms of the pound. But the UK government is committed to maintaining a fixed price of pounds in the foreign exchange market. When the French take their excess pounds and put them onto the foreign exchange markets, the UK central bank will be forced to go into the foreign exchange market and buy up those excess pounds. The Bank of England has to have foreign currency (or gold) to buy up the excess pounds. That is, it has to have a reserve of francs or gold in its coffers to buy the pounds that the French want to sell. It must supply 25 million francs per year to keep the exchange rate fixed, as seen in Figure 9.6.

The only way for the UK and other countries to support the price of the pound is to buy up excess pounds with foreign reserves – in this case, with French francs. But the UK might eventually run out of francs. It would no longer be able to stabilize the price of the pound, and a **currency crisis** would ensue. A currency crisis occurs when a country can no longer support the price of its currency in foreign exchange markets. Many such crises have occurred in the past several decades when countries have attempted to maintain a fixed exchange rate that was in disequilibrium.

Devaluation

One alternative to a currency crisis or to continuing to try to support a fixed exchange rate is to unilaterally devalue. **Devaluation** is the same thing as depreciation except that it occurs under a fixed exchange rate regime. A particular country unilaterally lowers the price of its currency in foreign exchange markets. The opposite of devaluation is **revaluation**. This occurs when, under a fixed exchange rate regime, there is pressure on a country's currency to rise in value in foreign exchange markets. Unilaterally, that country can declare that the value of its currency in foreign exchange markets is higher than it has been in the past. Revaluation is the same thing as appreciation except that it occurs under a fixed exchange rate regime.

In 1973 most of the world's major nations adopted floating exchange rates. However central banks were still prepared to intervene in foreign exchange rates in order to counter sudden shifts in the demand for or supply of currency. Thus an intermediate system of **dirty floating** was introduced. This system allows a 'pure' floating system to be modified by occasional central bank intervention in order to smooth out sharp short-run changes in exchange rates while allowing market forces to determine the prices of currencies over the long term.

The Balance of Trade and the Balance of Payments

We have talked about a flexible exchange financial system and a fixed exchange rate system. With either system, countries are concerned with both their balance of trade and their balance of payments. The

Figure 9.6

Supporting the Value of the Pound in the Foreign Exchange Market. If there is inflation in the UK, all prices go up. We assume that prices remain constant in France, so French goods become cheaper. The demand schedule for French goods shifts to the right, as does the derived demand schedule for French francs, from DD to D'D'. Without exchange rate controls, the exchange rate would rise to 25p – it would then cost 25p instead of 20p to buy a franc. The UK government, however, is committed to supporting the price of the pound. Instead of allowing the £ to equal 4 francs, the government maintains the price of a £ at 5 francs – it keeps the price at 20p per franc. But at that exchange rate there is an excess quantity demanded for francs at the fixed exchange rate of 25 million per year. The UK government must step in and supply 25 million francs from its coffers annually in order to support the £ in the foreign exchange market.

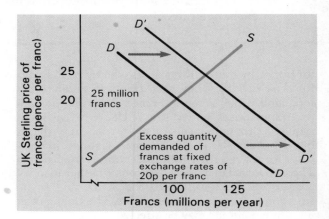

balance of trade is defined as the difference between the value of merchandise or visible exports and the value of merchandise or visible imports. When the balance of trade is in balance, the value of exports will equal the value of imports. The **balance of payments** is a more general term used to reflect a summary of all economic transactions between two nations, usually for a period of one year. In a flexible exchange rate

---

Key Points 9.2

▶ **Fixed exchange rates are a system where countries determine that their exchange rates should not alter and central banks support the declared rates by intevening in foreign exchange markets.**

▶ **Currency crises occur when a country can no longer support the price of its currency and under a fixed exchange rate system is obliged to devalue, that is lower, the price of its currency in foreign exchange markets. When a country declares that the value of its currency is now higher than it has been it has adopted a policy of revaluation, the opposite of devaluation.**

▶ **Depreciation is the same as devaluation except that it occurs when exchange rates are floating.**

system, the balance of payments is always in balance because of automatic adjustments in exchange rates. But since we do not have a *truly* freely floating exchange rate system the balance of payments is an important topic in international finance.

The balance-of-payments transactions of the UK can be grouped into three categories: current account transactions, capital account transactions, and official financing transactions. We now examine these.

Current Account Transactions

During any designated period, all payments and gifts that are related to the purchase or sale of both goods and services constitute the current account in international trade. Within any current account, there are three major types of current account transactions: the exchange of visible or merchandise goods, the exchange of invisibles or services, and, third, investment earnings plus transfers.

VISIBLE TRADE TRANSACTIONS

The largest portion of any nation's balance-of-payments accounts is typically the importing and exporting of merchandise goods. During 1984, for example, as can be seen in Figure 9.7 (p. 132), the UK exported £70 409 million of visible goods and imported £74 510 million. As we pointed out above, the balance of trade is defined as the difference between the value of visible exports and the value of visible imports. For 1984, the UK had a balance-of-trade deficit because the value of its visible imports exceeded the value of its visible exports. During 1984, this deficit was £4 101 million.

SERVICE EXPORTS AND IMPORTS

The balance of trade has to do with tangible items – you can feel them, touch them, and see them. The service exports and imports have to do with invisible or intangible items that are bought and sold, such as shipping, insurance, tourist expenditures, and banking services. As Figure 9.7 shows the UK enjoyed a net surplus on transactions in services in 1984.

INVESTMENT TRANSACTIONS AND TRANSFERS

The third type of current account transactions comprises net earnings arising from overseas assets owned plus transfers of funds to and from the UK. Some of these transfers are made by private individuals but the UK's entry into the EEC has caused the proportion accounted for by government to increase supply.

BALANCING THE CURRENT ACCOUNT

The balance on current account is a summary statistic that takes into account the three transactions that form current account transactions. In 1984, even though the balance of trade was a negative £4 101 million (there was a balance-of-trade deficit), the balance on current account was £935 million. That

meant that, even though the UK imported more visible goods than it exported and there was a net deficit on transfers, our service earnings plus overseas income were so much greater than our service payments plus investments income paid to foreigners that our balance on current account was positive.

Capital Account Transactions

In addition to buying and selling goods and services in the world market, it is also possible to buy and sell financial assets. There is really no difference in terms of the foreign exchange market. If, on the one hand, some people decide to buy shares in French companies, the demand for French financial assets will create a derived demand for francs and a supply of pounds. On the other hand, if the French decide they want to buy ICI shares, that demand will result in a derived demand for pounds and a supply of francs.

Capital account transactions thus comprise investment activity by private individuals, banks, companies, and publicly owned undertakings. One would expect that a wide range of persons engaged in this investment activity to vary in their motives. For some the intention is profit-seeking over the long term while for others funds may be quickly moved in the light of changing conditions. Our earlier analysis of exchange rates excluded the possibility of transactions in financial assets. If we recognized the reality of such activity then participants in capital transactions may alter their behaviour in the light of anticipated movements of the exchange rate.

Official Financing Transactions

The third type of balance-of-payments transactions concerns movements of capital that involve the UK's central bank, the Bank of England. As we noted earlier in this chapter the Bank of England engages in activity to influence the exchange rate. The Bank may draw on its reserves to buy pounds in the foreign exchange market and in doing so record a credit to balance this activity. This would be *drawings on official reserves*. If the Bank sells pounds it records a debit under its entry *additions to official reserves*. The Bank of England has dealings with other central banks and the **International Monetary Fund** (IMF) which was set up to manage the world's monetary system in 1945. We need therefore to understand how the IMF was supposed to operate. Briefly, the role of the IMF was to help member countries experiencing balance-of-payments difficulties by lending from its gold and currency holdings. These holdings arose out of the subscriptions of the members set by reference to a formula that took into account a country's importance in the world economy. After 1945 members of the IMF established fixed exchange rates for their currencies in terms of dollars and were obliged to maintain the values of their currencies in foreign exchange markets within a 1 per cent band of their declared par values. In 1970 the IMF created a new reserve asset,

Figure 9.7
Current Account of the UK Balance of Payments, 1984 (£m)

	Credits	Debits		Net difference
Visibles				
food, beverages, tobacco	4672	8199		-3527
basic materials	2014	4866		-2852
oil	14910	7774		7137
other fuels and lubricants	457	2002		-1547
semi-manufacturers	18266	18405		-138
finished manufactures	28306	31953		-3647
other	1783	1310		-474
Total goods	70409	74510	Visible balance	-4101
Invisible services				
general government	473	1396		
sea transport	3235	4386		
civil aviation	3016	2547		
travel	4169	4617		
financial and other services	10434	4396		
Total services	21327	17342	Services balance	+3985
Interest, profits, and dividends	50744	47440	balance	+3304
Transfers				
general government	2370	4460	balance	-2090
private	1438	1601	balance	-163
Total invisibles	75879	70843	Invisible balance	+5036
Current total			Current balance	+935

Capital Account of the UK Balance of Payments, 1984 (£m)

	Credits		Debits		
Investment and other capital transactions					
Overseas investment in the UK	3619	UK private investment overseas	14585		
Foreign currency transactions by UK banks	8865	Official long-term capital	361		
sterling transactions by banks and other financial institutions	5163	Sterling lending by UK banks	4716		
Import credit	172	Export credit	646		
Capital transactions in British government securities	1277	Other miscellaneous items	2079		
Total	19096		22387	Balance on capital account	-3291

Official Financing Transactions

Balance on current account	+935	Balance on capital account	-3291
Balancing item	+1040		
Requiring official financing	+1316		
	+3291		-3291
Drawings on official reserves	908		
Other official financing through borrowing in foreign currencies	408	Requiring official financing	1316
	1316		1316

Source: UK Balance of Payments, 1985, HMSO.

Special Drawing Rights, which countries could use to settle international payments.

Now although the Bank of England has the potential to influence the exchange rate it must be understood that the *changes in the official reserves* and *other official financing* merely represent the accommodating changes that are required given all the other transactions that we have previously identified. Thus the item *total official financing* is merely the sum of the overall change in official reserves and the change in other official financing. That figure should, of course, equate with the sum requiring official financing arising from the first two groups of transactions that we have defined above – current and capital transactions. In practice in the real world difficulties in identifying certain of these latter transactions result in ignorance in the detail of the sums crossing the exchanges. To ensure that the current balance plus capital balance equals the sum for official financing we find an item is added that ensures that this is so! This item is *the balancing item*.

Figure 9.7 shows that in 1984 the UK had a current account surplus of £935m. The balance on investment and other capital transactions was a deficit of £3 291m. Allowing for the balancing item the total sum requiring official financing was £1 316m. This was financed by running down the official reserves by £908m and taking in capital from central banks of sums amounting to £408m. This had to be so since the balance of payments must, by definition, always balance.

The Rationale of International Trade

We have now examined the ways in which trade in goods, services, and financial assets is financed with particular reference to the UK. We began with the simple example of the interchange of French wine and Shetland lamb's-wool sweaters. Having considered how the foreign exchange market exists for the buying and selling of currencies to make such an interchange possible we should now examine what is the rationale of such trade between two countries. We need to consider questions such as what are the gains from such trade? What are the costs involved? As consumers we appear to gain when we can purchase foreign products at lower prices than those made by domestic manufacturers. But what if foreign suppliers put UK firms out of business and so put some of the UK's labour force out of work? Are the gains from international trade worth the costs?

Putting Trade in Its Place

Trade among nations must somehow benefit the people of each nation by more than it costs them. World trade volume, measured in terms of exports, increased at a compound growth rate of between 5 and 8 per cent per year in the period. Figure 9.8 shows that in the period after 1955 world trade expanded at a much more rapid rate than the rate of increase in world output. Clearly the world's trading nations showed an enthusiasm to participate in international exchange. However, in the past decade the international monetary and trading system has been subject to strain most notably due to OPEC's increase in oil prices in early 1974 and 1979. This in turn exacerbated the balance-of-payments situation of many oil-importing developing countries. Their attempts to borrow funds from banks in the US and Western Europe have subsequently given rise to problems of indebtedness. Thus since 1973 the rate of growth of

---

Key Points 9.3

▶ The balance of payments reflects the value of all transactions in international trade, including the trade in goods, services, transfers, and financial assets.

▶ The visible trade balance gives us the difference between exports and imports of tangible items.

▶ The invisibles account presents the export and import in tangible items, i.e services.

▶ The current account includes both goods and services and also earnings on investments abroad less payments on investments in the UK owned by foreigners, plus net government and net private transfers.

▶ The capital account includes investment flows by private individuals and the public sector. In contrast to the current account it records transactions in financial assets.

▶ The overall balance of payments is given by adding together the current and capital account plus the balancing item. The total thus found denotes the sum (with sign reversed) of official financing that the government is required to undertake given all the other balance-of-payments transactions.

Figure 9.8
World Trade by Volume 1955–84

Source: The Economist, 5 October 1985.

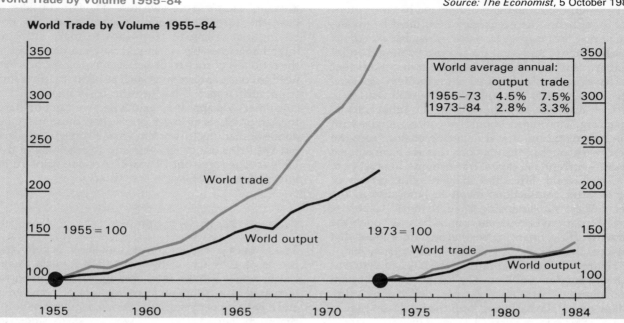

World Trade by Volume 1955–84

World average annual:		
	output	trade
1955–73	4.5%	7.5%
1973–84	2.8%	3.3%

1955 = 100

World trade

World output

1973 = 100

World trade

World output

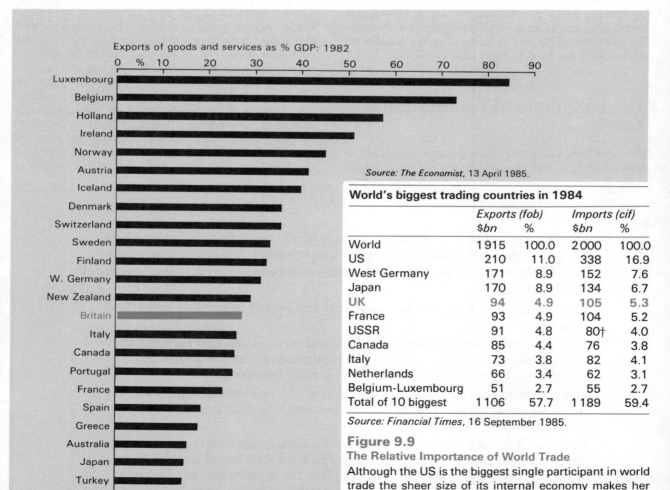

Exports of goods and services as % GDP: 1982

Source: The Economist, 13 April 1985.

World's biggest trading countries in 1984

	Exports (fob)		Imports (cif)	
	$bn	%	$bn	%
World	1915	100.0	2000	100.0
US	210	11.0	338	16.9
West Germany	171	8.9	152	7.6
Japan	170	8.9	134	6.7
UK	94	4.9	105	5.3
France	93	4.9	104	5.2
USSR	91	4.8	80†	4.0
Canada	85	4.4	76	3.8
Italy	73	3.8	82	4.1
Netherlands	66	3.4	62	3.1
Belgium-Luxembourg	51	2.7	55	2.7
Total of 10 biggest	1106	57.7	1189	59.4

Source: Financial Times, 16 September 1985.

Figure 9.9
The Relative Importance of World Trade

Although the US is the biggest single participant in world trade the sheer size of its internal economy makes her international trade exchange with other countries of relatively minor significance.

international trade has fallen markedly and reflected the world-wide recession in world output. Rising unemployment in the US and Western Europe has strengthened the demands for restrictions on world trade. So part of the less buoyant growth in world trade since 1973 is actually explained by measures to restrict imports so that jobs are protected. These curbs on imports illustrate that international exchange does have an impact on the use of domestic resources. Where governments have restricted international trade they have judged that the costs incurred from an unrestricted exchange of goods are unacceptably high. We must therefore examine the arguments in favour of restraining the importation of goods and services from other countries.

Before we examine both the disadvantages of international exchange and its advantages we should note that international trade is of more significance to some countries than others. Figure 9.9 shows the marked variation between developed countries in the proportion of gross domestic product accounted for by exports. Some countries export more than one-third of their GDPs. The United States ranks near the bottom of the list. In fact, the United States is the Western country that would suffer the least if we imagine the unlikely event of international trade ceasing to take place. In contrast the UK is a much more *open economy* or one dependent on relationships with other countries.

The pattern of the UK's trade with other countries has, historically, been an exchange of exported manufactured goods and services for imported raw materials and foodstuffs. Since the mid-1970s North Sea oil and gas has developed into a major aspect of the UK's trading position. In 1984 the UK enjoyed a balance on trade in oil of £7.1bn. Looking at the UK's trade it is reasonable to ask the following question: how did this trade pattern become established? The answer lies in the principle of comparative advantage that we explored in Chapter 6. We now re-examine that principle in an open economy context.

Comparative and Absolute Advantage

The reason there are gains from trade lies in one of the most fundamental principles of economics: a nation gains by doing what it can do best relative to other nations. The UK benefits by specializing in only those endeavours in which it has a **comparative advantage**.

The concept of comparative advantage was first explained by the economist, David Ricardo, nearly two hundred years ago and his own example cannot be bettered. Figure 9.10 shows the number of man-hours per unit required to produce cloth and wine in a two-country world comprising England and Portugal. It is evident that Portugal has a superior position to England in the production of both cloth and wine. Portugal has an **absolute advantage** over England in both commodities.

Figure 9.10
Ricardo's Model of Comparative Cost Advantage man-hours per unit of output)

	Cloth	Wine
Portugal	90	80
England	100	120

Why? The cost of producing cloth in Portugal is 90 per cent of the cost in England. In the case of wine Portugal can produce wine at two-thirds of the cost in England. But of the two commodities clearly it is in wine that Portugal has the greater or *comparative* advantage over England. But does this mean Portugal gains nothing from trade with England? This at first sight seems to be the case. What Ricardo showed was that England could *specialize* in cloth production and trade cloth exports for wine imports from Portugal – to the benefit of both countries. How was this possible?

In England labour costs per unit are higher than in Portugal for both cloth and wine, but her comparative cost disadvantage is least in the case of cloth. The cost ratios are respectively 10 : 9 and 12 : 8. Thus it costs England about 1.1 times as much to manufacture cloth and 1.5 times as much to produce wine as in Portugal.

Ricardo showed that if the two countries exchanged a unit of English cloth for a unit of Portuguese wine both countries gained. England gains by 20 man-hours on each unit of cloth exchanged for wine since it costs her 100 man-hours to manufacture cloth but another 20 man-hours to produce wine. How does Portugal gain? Trading a unit of wine costing 80 man-hours for a unit of cloth that would domestically require 90 man-hours means she gains a saving of 10 man-hours. So although she is able to make the cloth at a lower cost than England Portugal would still gain by specializing in the production of wine. Her comparative advantage is greater in wine than cloth.

Ricardo's model is, of course, a simple one. It assumes there are no transport costs incurred in shipping cloth and wine between England and Portugal. But it indicated that trade could be advantageous at a certain rate of international exchange. Ricardo's model was later modified to explain how the nature of the rate of exchange was actually determined.

Comparative Advantage and Opportunity Cost

An alternative approach to the concept of comparative advantage is to relate it to another concept that we met in the very first chapter of this book. There we noted that comparative advantage emphasizes the fact that cost means opportunities that must be forgone. If the UK decides to produce military goods it forgoes part of its opportunity to produce civilian goods because the resources used in producing guns and tanks cannot be used simultaneously in producing butter. We drew a production possibilities curve reflecting a society's choice between guns and butter. We can now draw on the concept of a production possibilities curve to show the gains from trade.

Figure 9.11 shows the limiting situations for production possibilities for the UK and US in the case of wheat and cloth. From this data we can draw the two straight-line production possibilities curves. In the absence of trade the two domestic price ratios are as follows:

UK   1 unit of wheat exchanges for 4 units of cloth (or ¼ unit wheat for 1 unit cloth)

US   1 unit of wheat exchanges for 2 units of cloth (or ½ unit wheat for 1 unit cloth)

If the UK, which has no superior or absolute advantage in either wheat or cloth compared to the US, could trade cloth on more favourable terms than one-quarter unit of wheat, she would gain. An international exchange of say 0.3 units of wheat for one unit of cloth would be advantageous to the UK. The dashed line on Figure 9.11 shows this ratio.

If the UK now produces say *OX* cloth (rather than *OW* when no trade takes place) she can purchase *UX* of wheat from the US. The UK in this case is now totally specializing in cloth and importing all her requirements of wheat. Imports of wheat of *UX* equal her cloth exports of *SU*. International exchange has enabled the UK to move outside the range of possibilities that were present before trade took place. Point *S* is beyond point *P* which was the situation before trade.

Figure 9.12 shows the price ratios before trade in the UK and US. For international exchange to be beneficial the rate of exchange must lie between the two domestic opportunity cost ratios. The UK would gain from trade if she could trade 8 units of cloth for 3 units of wheat. This would be better than the domestic price ratio of 8 units of cloth exchanging for 2 units of wheat. Likewise the US would gain from an international exchange such as 3.5 units of cloth for one of wheat. As long as the UK and US can agree on a basis of exchange both countries can gain.

Of course, as in Ricardo's model, we have assumed away the matter of transport costs. For some items these might be so high compared with the cost of the good itself that international exchange is not worth while. We have also implicitly assumed that imported goods do not face any increase in price due to the imposition of a tax or tariff. In the previous chapter we noted how international trade in foodstuffs was indeed affected by such measures. But none the less we have shown how, in a simple example of two countries and two products, differences in opportunity cost ratios provide the basis for countries to trade because they specialize in those commodities in which they have a comparative advantage.

You may now be thinking why comparative costs should differ between countries. The basic reason for the existence of comparative advantage – whether among individuals, companies, cities, counties, states, countries, or continents – lies in the fact that opportunity costs vary. It costs less for different parties to engage in different types of economic activities. Opportunity costs for different countries vary just as they vary for different individuals. Let us consider some of the reasons why opportunity costs and, hence, comparative advantages differ among nations.

Figure 9.11

	Wheat	Cloth	Wheat	Cloth
UK	40	0	0	160
US	80	0	0	160

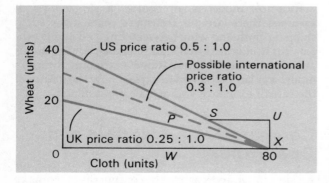

OP =   pre-trade production and consumption

OX =   cloth production (total specialization) if trade takes place at given international price ratio

UX =   wheat imports

SU =   cloth exports

Differing Resource Mixes

We know that different nations have different resource bases. Australia has much land relative to its population, whereas Japan has little land relative to its population. All other things being equal, one would expect countries with relatively more land to specialize in products that use more land. One expects Australia, for example, to engage in extensive sheep-raising but not Japan, because the opportunity cost of raising sheep in Japan is much higher. Since land in Japan is relatively scarce, its use carries a higher opportunity cost.

There are also differences in climates. We do not expect countries with cold, dry climates to grow bananas. Our earlier examples illustrate the natural resource and climatic differences between countries. Portugal's comparative advantage in wine is not surprising given her easier ability to grow grapes as compared with the situation in England, both at the time Ricardo was trying to explain his theory of

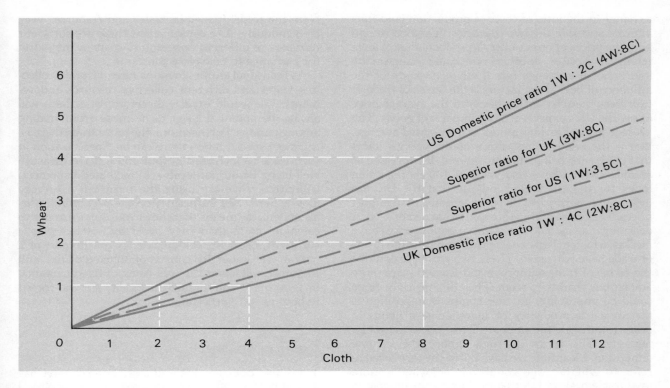

Figure 9.12
Price Ratios: can the UK and US do a deal? The solid
lines indicate the pre-trade price ratios in the UK and the
US. The two dashed lines indicate price relationships
between wheat and cloth that would make trade between
the two countries worthwhile.

comparative advantage and today. Our approach to
explaining trade by reference to opportunity cost
assumed that the US was relatively better suited to
growing wheat than to manufacturing cloth as compared with the UK.

A third reason why costs differ is quite simply
because some countries have superior knowledge of
the techniques of manufacturing goods. You will note
we have moved away from primary commodities like
wheat and wool and now have man-made products
such as synthetic fibres and electronics in mind. Some
developing countries, for example, cannot yet effectively compete with countries in Western Europe in
the manufacture of clothes made of polyester and
computers since as yet they lack the technology.
Remember, back in Chapter 1 we recognized how
improved technology can over time help push out the
production possibilities curve.

Other Factors Explaining Comparative Costs

The thoughtful student will reflect that the above
reasons explaining why comparative costs can differ
between countries are quite simply the inherent
characteristics of a nation's factor endowment. They

are supply-based aspects: Australia is a wool-
producing nation since she is relatively well endowed
with land, a factor of production that is essential for
extensive sheep-farming. But demand conditions can
also help explain why countries differ in comparative
advantage. Some manufactured goods such as motor
cars and household electrical goods are traded
between developed countries. The UK imports cars
from France, West Germany, and Japan – Renaults,
Mercedes, and Toyotas – and also sells British Leyland
cars to these countries – the Montego and Maestro.
Clearly there are differences in the design, specification, and performance of all these motor vehicles.
Note that we do not have one nation just specializing
in motor cars. This is because such consumer goods
are not viewed by consumers as being homogeneous
(like wheat and wine as in our earlier examples).
Consumers throughout the world like different types
of modern consumer goods so that it is not the case
that one industry is based in one country. Within an
industry countries specialize on different types of
goods: this trade is known as 'intra-industry trade'.

The Terms of Trade

Our earlier example of trade between the UK and US
in wheat and cloth assumed that an international
exchange rate between the two commodities would be
established such that both countries gained from
being open economies. In the real world the terms on
which a country exchanges its exports for imports are,
of course, measured in monetary terms – as prices.
These prices alter for two reasons. First, there may be

a change in the ratio of costs of production (and thus internal prices) in the two countries. A second reason why the prices of one country's products may change relative to those of the other country is a change in the international exchange rate itself. A measure of the influence of both these factors is the **terms of trade**. It expresses the relationship between the average price of say the UK's exports and our imports of goods. The average prices are determined as a weighted average, that is the relative importance of the various items that are traded being duly recognized. If expressed as an index with a base-year value of 100 then a rising index for the UK would indicate that the UK has increased export prices on average faster than import prices. The terms of trade are said to have improved. A declining index would indicate that import prices have increased faster than export prices and thus the terms of trade have worsened. These two words to describe the terms of trade – improve and worsen – are more ambiguous than they seem. The UK's terms of trade could be improving, but her competitive position is threatened if producers of manufactured goods in other countries offer more attractive prices in foreign markets. The terms of trade ignore the volume dimension. Meantime we have noted the term used to refer to whether one country is enjoying a more favourable basis of international exchange compared with the past. This picture of whether a country is relatively gaining from trade makes it appropriate to realize that trade may not benefit every country equally. What are the disadvantages of international exchange?

Advantageous Trade Will Always Exist

From before the beginning of recorded history, there have been examples of trade among individuals. Since these acts of exchange have usually been voluntary, we must assume that individuals generally benefit from the trade. Individual tastes and resources vary tremendously. As a consequence, there are sufficient numbers of different opportunity costs in the world for exchange to take place constantly.

As individual entities, nations have different collective tastes and different collective resource endowments. We would expect, therefore, that there will always be potential gains to be made from trading among nations. Furthermore, the more trade there is, the more specialization there can be. Specialization in turn leads to increased output and – if we measure well-being by output levels – to increased happiness. (Admittedly, we are using the term *well being* very loosely here.) Self-sufficiency on the part of individuals undeniably means that they forgo opportunities to consume more than they could by not being self-sufficient. Likewise, self-sufficiency on the part of a nation will lower its consumption possibilities and therefore will lower the well-being of its inhabitants. Imagine life in your immediate locality if it was forced to become self-sufficient!

Costs of Trade

Trade does not come without cost. If one country has a comparative advantage in producing agricultural crops, other countries may not be able to succeed as sources of agricultural production. Farm-workers in these latter countries that are less efficient at agricultural production will suffer decreases in their incomes until they find other occupations or move to where alternative jobs are.

As tastes, supplies of natural resources, prices, and so on change throughout the world, different countries may find their areas of comparative advantage changing. One example of this is the production of steel. Japan has become increasingly competitive in steel products, and steelmakers in western Europe are losing sales to imports. They are feeling the pinch

---

Key Points 9.4

▶ Countries can be better off materially if they specialize in their comparative advantage.

▶ It is important to distinguish between absolute and comparative advantage; the former refers to the ability to produce a unit of output with fewer physical units of input; the latter refers to producing that output that has the lowest opportunity cost for a nation.

▶ Different nations will always have different comparative advantages because of differing opportunity costs due to different resource endowments, technical knowledge, and different tastes.

▶ The relationship between average export prices and average import prices is the terms of trade.

▶ Foreign trade can adversely affect certain groups in each country because of increased competition from abroad.

from Japan's ability to produce steel products at lower costs. The same competitive threat from Japan is to be found in the case of many other consumer goods exported to countries in Western Europe.

Arguments against Free Trade

There are numerous arguments against free trade but many on closer inspection turn out to be incomplete. They mainly point out the costs of trade; they do not consider the benefits or the possible alternatives for reducing costs while still reaping benefits.

Infant Industry Argument

A nation may feel that if a particular industry were allowed to develop domestically, it could eventually become efficient enough to compete effectively in the world market. Therefore, if some restrictions were placed on imports, native producers would be given the time needed to develop their efficiency to the point where they would be able to compete in the domestic market without any restrictions on imports. In terms of the concept of the supply curve, we would expect that if the protected industry truly does experience technological breakthroughs toward greater efficiency in the future, then the supply curve will shift outwards to the right so that the domestic industry can produce larger quantities at each and every price. This **infant industry argument** has some merit in the short run and was used to shelter several UK industries in 1918 under the Safeguarding of Industries Act. The year is significant since the Act was a policy response to the UK's experience during the First World War. When hostilities began in 1914 the UK was dependent on German supplies in several key industrial sectors. Our dependence on a country which became a foreign enemy had highlighted the need for certain industries to be protected at least in the short term. This strand of the infant industry argument is very close to the case for protection on grounds of national security which we discuss next. However, in principle the infant industry case could be applied to industries *not* of strategic significance in a wartime economy. The general application of the infant industry case can be easily criticized. Often the protective import-restricting arrangements remain even after the infant has grown up. If other countries can still produce more cheaply, the people who benefit from this type of situation are obviously the owners of the firms (and specialized factors of production) in the industry that is still being protected from world competition. The people who lose out are the consumers, who must pay a price higher than the world price for the product in question. In any event, it is very difficult to know *beforehand* which industries will eventually survive. In other words, we cannot predict very well the specific 'infant' industries that should be protected. Note that when we talk about which

industry *should be* protected, we are in the realm of normative economics. We are stating a value-judgement that comes from our heart.

National Security

It is often argued that we should not rely on foreign sources for many of our products because in time of war these sources might well be cut off and we would have developed few, if any, substitute sources. Such an argument was part of the case for the post-war expansion of UK agriculture. The Second World War had shown the dependence of UK consumers on foreign suppliers who were thousands of miles away. The uncertain passage of ships from the Southern Hemisphere across the North Atlantic due to the threat from German U-boats appeared to underline the case for the more certain presence of home-grown foodstuffs. On the face of it the argument looked appealing. But as we noted in Chapter 8 post-war agricultural policy which offered some protection for UK farmers had an impact on the use of resources. Guaranteed prices for UK farmers had the effect of limiting the market for food imports. In so far as sales of food to the UK were restricted, there was a reduced capacity of countries like New Zealand to import items like manufactured goods. Increased UK food production certainly reduced food imports. But the overall impact on the balance of payments was not just on the flow of imported butter and lamb but also the sales of motor cars and electrical equipment to overseas buyers.

Protecting a Way of Life

Free world trade may destroy certain industries in a particular economy as comparative advantages change throughout the world. A society may wish to protect a certain group of individuals who are threatened by international competition because they believe that their particular way of life should be maintained.

Of course, there are always alternative ways to protect particular livelihoods and individual groups. For example, if a country wished to protect watchmakers, rather than restricting foreign trade, it could simply give a subsidy directly to watchmakers. This would not raise the price of watches for consumers, but it would serve as a protection of a particular way of life. Our discussion of the method of protecting UK farmers in the period 1948–73 illustrated one merit of deficiency payments over tariffs.

Stability

Many people argue that foreign trade should be restricted because it introduces an element of instability into our economic system. They point out that the vagaries of foreign trade add to the ups and downs in our own employment level. However, if we follow this argument to its logical conclusion, we would restrict trade within a country itself. After all, the vagaries of trade among particular areas of the UK sometimes cause employment in other areas. Things are sorted out over time, but workers suffer during the adjustment period. As regards the international sphere, however, people somehow change their position. They feel that adjusting to the vagaries of *international* trade costs more than adjusting to the vagaries of domestic trade. Perhaps people believe foreign trade really does not benefit us that much, and thus they argue against it, claiming that the stability of aggregate economic activity is at stake. We should note one difference between the domestic and international situations, however, that lends some truth to this argument. Labour is more mobile within a country than between countries. Immigration laws prevent workers from moving to countries where they can earn the most income. There are also many differences in language and customs that prevent workers from freely moving from country to country. Therefore, the adjustment costs to a changing international situation may in fact be higher than the adjustment costs to a changing domestic situation.

Protecting Jobs

Perhaps the most frequently used argument against free trade is that unrestrained competition from other countries will eliminate jobs at home because other countries have lower-cost labour than we do. This is indeed a compelling argument, particularly for politicians from areas that might be threatened by foreign competition. For example, a Member of Parliament from an area with textile or shoe factories would certainly be upset about the possibility of constituents losing their jobs because of competition from lower-priced cotton shirt manufacturers in Hong Kong or shoe manufacturers in Brazil and Italy. Again we note that limitations on imports may help employees in such industries but at the expense of consumers. And as we have also recognized, attempts at protecting jobs by imposing tariffs, quotas, and other restrictions on international trade lead to retaliation by our trading partners. In other words, they start imposing similar restrictions on trade with the UK. We may end up saving less productive employment at the expense of more productive employment.

Countering Foreign Subsidies and Dumping

Another strong argument against unrestricted foreign trade has to do with countering other nations' subsidies to their own producers and to dumping. When a foreign government subsidizes its producers, our competing producers claim that they cannot

compete fairly with these subsidized foreigners. To the extent that such subsidies fluctuate, one can argue that unrestricted free trade will seriously disrupt domestic producers. After all, they will not know when foreign governments are going to subsidize their own producers and when they are not. Our competing industries, then, will be expanding and contracting too frequently.

Occasionally, the phenomenon called **'dumping'** takes place and is used as an argument against unrestricted trade. Dumping occurs when a producer sells its products abroad at a price below its cost of production. Although cries of dumping against foreign producers are often heard, they typically only occur when the foreign nation is in the throes of a serious recession. The foreign producer does not want to slow down its production at home because it anticipates an end to the recession and it does not want to bear large costs of financing. Therefore, it dumps its product abroad at prices below its costs. This does, in fact, disrupt foreign trade.

SOME NEWER WAYS TO RESTRICT WORLD TRADE

The late 1970s and 1980s will be known in world trade history as the era of new restrictions. Consider the following barriers to world trade that have occurred in the last few years.

France: French-language customs documents; restrictions on Japanese video-cassette recorders; delays in allowing the import of Swiss cheese.

Britain: Severe restrictions on foreign insurance firms, banks, and law firms; limits on the number of Japanese cars imported.

Japan: Excessive red tape against cosmetics produced elsewhere.

United States: 'Voluntary' limits on European steel and Japanese cars; 'buy American' rules for new bridges and roads.

These restraints on trade form a reversal to the post-war commitment by the world's trading nations to dismantle tariffs and trade restrictions. Since 1945 members of the General Agreement on Tariffs and Trade (GATT) have agreed to rounds of tariff cuts and helped stimulate the growth in world trade that we noted in Figure 9.8. Some fear that the growing number of these trade restrictions prompted by the world recession could multiply and threaten the whole basis of international exchange.

Counter-purchases. One of the newest impediments to world trade are the requirements of a **counter-purchase**, which is a set of parallel cash sales agreements in which a supplier sells a plan or product and orders unrelated products to offset the cost of the buyer. Consider the following two examples of counter-purchase requirements:

1. Canada bought $2.4 billion worth of F-18 aircraft from McDonnell Douglas, but required that McDonnell Douglas helped find customers for goods and services worth $2.9 billion.

2. Hughes Aircraft and Canada's Spar Aerospace won

Key Points 9.5

▶ The infant industry argument against free trade contends that new industries should be allowed protection against world competition so that they can become technically efficient in the long run.

▶ The national security argument against free trade contends that we should not rely on foreign sources for crucial materials needed during time of war.

▶ Unrestricted foreign trade may allow foreign governments to subsidize exports or foreign producers to engage in dumping – selling products in other countries below their cost of production. To the extent that foreign export subsidies and dumping create more instability in domestic production, they may impair our well-being.

▶ In the 1970s and 1980s a number of new ways to restrict world trade have been instituted, such as voluntary limits on exports, counter-purchase, and buy-back agreements.

---

a $130-million space satellite contract from Brazil but had to agree to arrange to import an equal amount of products from Brazil into Canada.

Buy-back Agreements. Another impediment to world trade is a **buy-back agreement** in which, under separate agreement to the sale of a plant, the supplier agrees to purchase part of the plant's output for up to 20 years. For example, Russia made a $20-billion deal with Occidental Petroleum whereby the latter built ammonia plants and agreed to buy part of the output. China awarded a $500-million contract to a company in Italy to expand China's mines and to modernize its railroads. In return the Italian firm had to agree to buy coal from China.

Does the increase in these **non-tariff barriers** to international trade mean that the future of international trade is in jeopardy? Some believe so, but others point out that the increased restrictions in world trade have occurred mainly during periods of world-wide recession. Therefore, we might expect during the next period when most countries are experiencing economic growth that such trade barriers will shrink, even if only slowly. New restraints on trade might then come back again during the next serious recession that hurts the majority of world countries.

CASE STUDY

The Dollar Problem

The dollar is certainly the most frequently discussed economic phenomenon of our times. Why is there so much discussion about the dollar? There are three reasons.

First, the dollar's exchange rate is at present the most important price in the world economy (while ten years ago one would probably have attributed this role to the oil price). The high dollar has had an enormous impact on the world economy. It has affected the competitive position of other industrial countries versus the United States, the US trade balance, the structure and development of world trade, the prices of commodities and other internationally traded goods, and price inflation both in the United States and elsewhere. More recently the high dollar has been called the major drag on the American economy. And it has certainly been the foremost cause of protectionist pressures which threaten to undermine our trading system. No wonder that the high dollar has been a subject of discussion and complaints at several economic summit meetings.

A second reason why the dollar is so ardently discussed is because it is such a controversial subject. Its behaviour has seemed to defy all conventional wisdom. At least until the beginning of 1985, we could watch a rather paradoxical, if not 'perverse', spectacle: the more the American budget deficit and trade

continued overleaf

deficit increased, the higher rose the dollar. What would have made all other currencies weak seems to have strengthened the dollar.

A third reason for the world-wide keen interest in the dollar is concern about the future. What will happen to the world economy if and when a definitive reversal of the dollar trend should lead to a much lower level of the dollar's exchange rate?

The powerful position of the dollar is not only based on its being the currency of the largest and most powerful economy. It goes beyond that because the dollar fulfils a unique role as a world currency.

Second, the dollar has remained the main currency for trade and financial transactions. More than 50 per cent of world trade is priced in dollars, and that comprises most of the internationally traded commodities including oil. Thus the ups and downs of the dollar in the exchange markets have a much more than proportionate effect on the import prices in other currencies. In Germany nearly 30 per cent of total imports are priced in dollars (while direct imports from the United States are only about 7

per cent), and in France about 40 per cent.

The dollar's position is even more pronounced in the financial sphere. It has become the dominating currency in the international financial markets, and this position has been built up particularly during the 1970s. As a consequence, 80 per cent or more of the external debt of the Third World is expressed in dollars. A large part of this debt bears variable interest rates tied to dollar interest rates. Thus, large movements of the dollar exchange rate and, in particular, of dollar interest rates, have a big impact on the international debt situation.

Third, high dollar interest rates have not only been a heavy burden on the high-debt countries, but also an attraction for foreign investors, and thus an important reason for the high dollar.

Fourth, a further distinctive feature of the dollar is the predominant role which capital movements play, both in the US balance of payments and for the dollar's exchange rate. There is no other currency with a similar predominance of capital movements over the so-called

'traditional fundamentals' (like inflation differences or the trend of the current account balance). Capital movements may vary quickly under the influence of changing expectations or shifting confidence. This makes the exchange rate of the dollar so volatile and unpredictable, like a 'Russian roulette'. The fact that in the case of the dollar, the key currency, the capital balance completely overwhelms trade and current account flows is a major problem and a weak point in the present international monetary system for it is bound to lead not only to great volatility, but to long-lasting misalignments measured against cost and price differences.

The overwhelming influence of capital movements and the huge amount of liquid dollar holdings in the world explain another unique feature of the dollar: it is the only currency for which it can be said with certainty that under conditions of capital mobility it can function only as a fully floating currency.

Source: O. Emminger, 'The International Role of the Dollar', in *Economic Review*, Federal Reserve Bank of Kansas City, Sept./Oct. 1985, pp. 17–20.

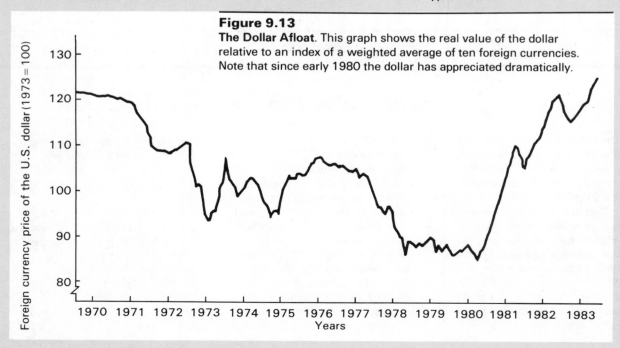

Figure 9.13

The Dollar Afloat. This graph shows the real value of the dollar relative to an index of a weighted average of ten foreign currencies. Note that since early 1980 the dollar has appreciated dramatically.

Questions
1. Why would a fixed exchange rate for the dollar be very unlikely to last if the US government attempted to impose one?

2. What are the implications for the world's international trade and monetary system of the importance of the dollar?

3. Can you think what factors might have accounted for the appreciation of the dollar in the period between 1980 and 1983 as shown in Figure 9.13?

CASE STUDY

The Pit and the Pandemonium

It is 8 o'clock on a wintry morning at the Chicago International Monetary market. Yet the heating is deliberately controlled at 10 degrees below the normal 70F – to help prevent temperatures on the trading floor getting too volatile. This, and a $3000 fine for striking another trader, is designed to stop trouble breaking out.

In the 'pit', the money-changers shout, scream, push, elbow, bite, punch and kick, laugh and cry. They leap up and down, stamp their feet, roar bids at one another, throw contract notes in the air. It looks more like the start of a football riot than a business in which millions of dollars, pounds, marks, francs, pesos, are changing hands.

Chicago is the world's most flamboyant money market, but London is still the largest. New York is not far behind, and there are new markets flourishing not just in old centres like Frankfurt, but also in Sydney, Singapore and Hong Kong. Advanced communications technology means that the market never closes. When traders go home in London, they pass business to New York, then Chicago, then, briefly, to the West Coast, before moving on to South-east Asia and then back to London.

It is a huge business that has grown up in the past decade largely unnoticed – despite the fact that the price of foreign currencies affects most things we do, from eating cornflakes to buying petrol. These markets are a major influence on the ebb and flow of inflation. Yet the only experience most of us ever have of it is going to the bank to buy traveller's cheques.

The new money-changers are an anonymous bunch, but they are the people who decide how many dollars we get for our pounds, marks or yen. They make decisions that used to be reserved for governments. Money trading was once a monopoly of the banks, which bought and sold currencies for their commercial customers. Speculation was discouraged by exchange controls.

That ended in 1973, when the free market in currency opened. Now, at least 90 per cent of the deals done in foreign exchange are not to facilitate import or export trade, but for speculation.

In Chicago, at 7.19 a.m. local time, a pale figure in his early thirties hurries to the 'pit', where British pounds are traded after 7.20. His name is Andy Schreiber. He earns his basic income trading as a broker for banks. (They buy £1 million at $1.4245 in Chicago and sell it to another bank in London or New York at $1.4250. This is arbitraging.) Schreiber's real money is made trading on his own account: last December, for example, selling two £25000 contracts at $1.4760 and buying at $1.4200 – a profit of $2200 in three days' trading.

The pressure is intense, and Schreiber has developed an aversion to crowds. 'I don't know how much more I can take of it. I'm 33 now, but I've got the insides of a man of 70.'

As Schreiber's dealing makes clear, the last thing a trader wants is to have to take delivery of the money he has bought or to deliver the money he has sold. He is hoping that he will be able to buy or sell it before the delivery date and make a profit. To illustrate how it is done, and to show the enormous sums of money involved, the experience we had in the trading room of Lloyds Bank in the City of London is illuminating.

The deal we are about to describe was in pounds and US dollars, but it could equally well have been in pounds and yen, or Swiss francs and German marks. It began purely as a demonstration of how the Reuters Monitor trading screen works. This is a video terminal with a telex-type keyboard connected to the telephone system. 'Suppose I want to call up another

continued overleaf

bank,' the trader giving the demonstration said. 'I just tap out his call-sign like this.'

He called another London bank, but it could easily have been any other Monitor subscriber in the world. When the bank answered, the trader, continuing the demonstration, said, 'I'll ask him what his rates are for buying and selling dollars for delivery in a month's time.'

The other bank replied. Suddenly we were forgotten. A gleam came into the trader's eye. His fingers flew over the keyboard. It was all over in 30 seconds. 'Too good to miss,' he said. 'I just bought and sold 15.' Fifteen what? 'Fifteen million pounds!' Then he explained. He knew that earlier in the day a colleague had bought £15 million-worth of dollars on the spot (immediate) market at $1.4410 to the pound. His colleague had then sold these for delivery in a month's time at $1.4365.

Our trader had sold the dollars his colleague was holding at cost price, $1.4410. Then he had bought them back for delivery in a month's time at $1.436575. His profit was the difference between this price and the price at which his colleague had contracted to deliver in a month, $1.4365, namely $0.000075 on £15 million – £545.16. This seemed a small return on a turnover of £60 million, but, as the trader pointed out, all it had taken was two calls, about a minute, and the nerve to risk millions of your employer's money.

If the deal seems too complicated for the trader to have recognized so quickly that it would produce a profit, then consider this. On the face of it, the first deal, the one made by the trader's colleague, would have produced the greater profit. But the second deal left our trader still in control of the pounds – either to use for further deals, or to earn interest. So, in addition to

recognizing in seconds a favourable circumstance for a deal, the foreign exchange trader has to weigh constantly the profit from that deal against the current rate of interest for short-term bank deposits.

Source: S. Fay and P. Knightley, 'The Pit and the Pandemonium', *The Observer*, 12 Jan. 1986.

Questions

1. What does the above passage indicate about the character of the market in international currencies?
2. What factors have influenced the development of this market?
3. What qualities do you imagine are required to be a successful trader in international currencies?
4. What is meant by arbitrage?
5. How does the passage offer an illustration of the concept of opportunity cost?

Exam Preparation and Practice

MULTIPLE CHOICE QUESTIONS

†1. Using all available resources, country X can produce 1 tonne of food or 3 tonnes of cloth, while country Y can produce ½ tonne of food or 1 tonne of cloth. Each country will benefit from trade if the price of food in terms of cloth is

A 1 tonne of food for 1 tonne of cloth
B 1 tonne of food for 1½ tonnes of cloth
C 1 tonne of food for 2 tonnes of cloth
D 1 tonne of food for 2½ tonnes of cloth

2. The following is a table showing a country's international transactions

	Units
Value of visible imports	1 000
Value of visible exports	800
Value of private invisible imports	200
Value of private invisible exports	400
Net government current expenditure abroad	–100

What is the balance of trade?
A –200
B –100
C 0
D +100

3. Country X and country Y both produce cars and cabbages and their production possibilities curves are as shown below.

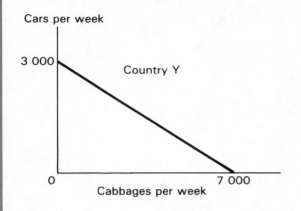

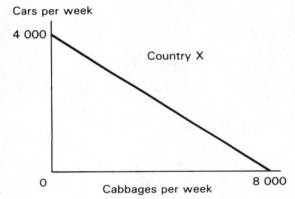

On the basis of this information we can say that
A country X should produce cars and cabbages for its home market and export any surplus
B country X should export cars to country Y and import cabbages from country Y
C country Y should export cars to country X and import cabbages from country X
D country Y should import both cars and cabbages from country X

4. The following table shows the relationship between import and export prices for a country.

	1976	1983
Index of import prices	100	240.1
Index of export prices	100	288.6

From this information it is possible to conclude that between 1978 and 1983 the
A terms of trade improved
B terms of trade worsened
C current balance improved
D current balance worsened

5. Which of the following items is *not* a credit item in the United Kingdom balance of payments?
A goods sold overseas
B visitors' expenditure in United Kingdom
C the carriage of foreign goods in United Kingdom ships
D Capital invested overseas

6. If a country has a balance-of-payments surplus on current account, this means that
A the total for official financing must be a negative value
B the value of goods exported must be greater than the value of goods imported
C there must be an equal and opposite deficit on capital account
D the aggregate of the balance of trade and the invisible balance must be positive

RELATED ESSAY QUESTIONS
1. What are the gains from international trade? Who receives them?

2. What are the main components of the overseas trade accounts? How might a country finance a persistent balance-of-trade deficit?

†3. Analyse the probable economic consequences of import controls.

4. Evaluate the case for free trade. Discuss the possible effects of the current spread of trade agreements among nations.

Part B

Introductory Macroeconomics

10 The Role and Size of Government

Key Points to Review

▶ Opportunity cost (1.2)
▶ Public expenditure and transfer payments (4.2)
▶ Shifts in demand (5.3)

▶ Shifts in supply (5.5)
▶ Market forces (5.7)
▶ Indirect taxes (8.5)

Questions for Preview

1 What is a public good and what examples can you think of?

2 What is the difference between a private good and a merit good?

3 Pollution is considered to be an example of a negative externality. Why?

4 What are the main economic objectives that *all* post-war UK governments have striven to achieve?

5 What has been happening to the percentage of public spending in recent years, in the United Kingdom?

6 (a) What is the difference between a progressive and regressive tax?
  (b) Can you identify some specific examples of each?

The pricing system answers three basic questions of resource allocation; *what* goods will be produced? *how* will they be produced? and *for whom* will they be produced? The forces of supply and demand acting through the pricing system (that is, the market) affect the bulk of decisions that answer these three questions. But we do not live in a free market world. In addition to market forces, there are many other forces at work that affect the allocation of resources. One of the most important of these non-market forces is government. In this chapter *first* we will look at *the role* that government plays in our economy. *Then* we will look at *its size*; this will be mainly achieved by analysing government *expenditure*, as knowing how big a govern-

ment is relative to the total economy is an indicator of its importance in resource allocation. *Finally*, we will complete the chapter by briefly looking at the related topic of *taxation* – as taxes also affect resource allocation.

The Economic Functions of Government

In this section we will discuss five important economic functions of the UK government. They are:

1. Providing public goods.

2. Providing merit goods, and regulating demerit goods.
3. Trying to correct externalities.
4. Carrying out cost-benefit analysis.
5. Striving to achieve economic objectives and stability.

Providing Public Goods

Up to this point we have generally described goods called **private goods**, such as chips, hamburgers, and manufactured commodities. Private goods are defined as those for which the **principle of exclusion** applies. That is to say, if you use a private good, *I cannot use it.* And conversely, if I use a private good *you cannot use it.* When I use the services of a mechanic, he or she cannot be working at the same time on your car. Mechanics' services are a private good. An apple is a private good. If I eat an apple, you cannot eat the same apple. You must get your own apple.

There is an entire class of goods that are not private goods. These are called **public goods**. The principle of exclusion does not apply to them. That is, they can be *jointly* consumed by many individuals simultaneously. National defence, policy protection, and street lighting, for example, are public goods. If you partake of them, you do not necessarily take away from anyone else's share of those goods.

CHARACTERISTICS OF PUBLIC GOODS

We can list several distinguishing characteristics of public goods that set them apart from all other goods.

1. *Public goods are usually indivisible.* You cannot buy or sell £5 worth of our ability to annihilate the world with bombs. Public goods cannot be produced or sold very easily in small units.
2. *Public goods can be used by increasing numbers of people at no additional cost.* Once a television signal has been transmitted from a station, turning on your set does not cost the station anything; the opportunity cost of you receiving the signal is zero.
3. *Additional users of public goods do not deprive others of any of the services of the good.* If you turn on your television set, your neighbours don't get weaker reception because of your action.
4. *It is very difficult to charge people for a public good on the basis of how much they use.* It is nearly impossible to determine how much any person uses or values national defence. It cannot be bought and sold in the market-place.

FREE RIDERS

This last point leads us to the **free-rider problem**. It is a problem because it involves a situation in which some individuals believe that others will take on the burden of paying for public goods such as national defence. Alternatively, 'free riders' will argue that they receive no value from such government services as national defence or overseas representation

and, therefore, really should not pay for it. Consider a hypothetical example: citizens will be taxed directly in proportion to how much they tell an interviewer that they value national defence for the following year. Some people will probably tell interviewers that they are unwilling to pay for national defence because they do not want any of it – it is of no value to them. Many of them would end up being free riders especially when they assume that others will pay for the desired public good anyway. We all want to be free riders when we believe that someone else will provide the commodity in question.

Look at the problem as it is represented in Figure 10.1. Here we show the different possible outcomes depending on whether you decide to pay your share of the annual national defence budget and whether others decide to pay. If everyone else pays and you pay also, the total amount of money spent on national defence would be £18 000 000 100 per year. If you do not pay, the total amount for national defence will only fall by £100 to £18 000 000 000 per year. The difference does not seem to be very much, and, expressed as a percentage of the total defence budget, it is very small indeed. There are two other possibilities. If no one else pays and you pay, national defence spending will be only £100 per year, and then if you do not pay and no one else pays either, there will be no money spent on national defence that year.

Figure 10.1

Scoreboard for National Defence. The free rider is the one who will gladly let everyone else pay the bill. If you do not pay your share of national defence but everyone else does, there will still be £18 billion per year available for the country's defence. Whether you pay or not seems to make very little difference.

	If you pay	If you do not pay
And if everybody else pays	£18 000 000 100/yr	£18 000 000 000/yr
And if no one else pays	£100/yr	£0.00/yr

What is a probable choice that you might make in such a situation? If you pay, either others will or they will not. If they do not, your £100 is not going to matter much; if they do, your £100 will still not matter much. Why not take a free ride? That's exactly what the free-rider problem is all about. Public goods, therefore, may be provided in too small amounts if left to the private sector.

Many products and services in our economy are public goods. For example: the fire services, the maintenance of law and order, and overseas representation and there is a very strong case for having the government finance them. In fact even Adam Smith the arch-apostle of free market forces recognized that the government must provide them and in most countries today this is the case.

Merit Goods and Demerit Goods

Merit goods by comparison differ from country to country. As what constitutes a merit good is defined by the political process according to what the government deem is socially desirable. Once this decision has been taken those goods that are selected are made available free, or almost free, to all citizens, either by the government subsidizing the production or more commonly actually organizing the output themselves. Some examples of merit goods in the UK are: museums, ballet and the arts, health services, education, and library provision. Note that there is nothing inherent in any of these particular goods that makes them different from private goods. They *can be supplied through the market* and in some countries they actually are (e.g. medical care in America).

It is clearly a political decision, therefore, as to what constitutes a merit good, but in general terms they serve two objectives. Firstly, they facilitate a redistribution of real income; as merit goods are largely financed out of progressive taxation – the result is that the poorer citizens get access to a standard of service that they could not otherwise afford. Secondly, by making these goods readily available to all citizens at well below the market-clearing price individuals become better educated and healthier, and thus provide a more effective labour force and ultimately a higher standard of living for the country as a whole.

Demerit goods are the opposite of merit goods. They are goods that, through the political process, are deemed socially undesirable. Heroin, morphine, and

LSD are just some examples of so-called demerit goods. The way the government exercises its role in the area of demerit goods is by taxing, regulating, or prohibiting their manufacture, sale, and use. Partly, the relatively high taxes on alcohol and tobacco are justified by governments on the basis that these are demerit goods.

In Britain it is claimed that we have developed a 'caring society' that looks after each of us from 'the cradle to the coffin'. In consequence more than a third of our government spending goes into the provision of these various merit goods and the regulation of demerit goods. (Now read Key Points 10.1.)

Correcting Externalities

In a pure capitalist system, competition generates economic efficiency only when individuals are faced with the true opportunity cost of their actions. In some circumstances, the price that someone actually pays for a resource, good, or service is higher or lower than the opportunity cost that all of society pays for that same resource, good, or service.

Consider a hypothetical world where there is no government regulation against pollution. You are living in a town that so far has clean air. A steel mill moves into your town. It produces steel for which it has paid for the inputs – land, labour, capital, and entrepreneurship. The price it charges for the steel reflects, in this example, only the costs that the steel mill incurred. In the course of production, however, the mill gives off smoke – free by simply dispersing it. This is indeed taking a liberty. The steel mill does not have to pay the cost of cleaning up the smoke; rather, it is the people in the community who pay that cost in the form of dirtier clothes, dirtier cars and houses, and perhaps even more respiratory illnesses. The effect is similar to what would happen if the steel mill could take coal or oil free. There has been a spillover effect,

---

Key Points 10.1

▶ Public goods can be jointly consumed. The principle of exclusion does not apply as it does with private goods.

▶ Public goods have the following characteristics: (1) they are indivisible; (2) once they are produced, there is no opportunity cost of additional consumers using them; (3) your use of a public good does not deprive others of its simultaneous use; and (4) there is difficulty in charging consumers on the basis of use.

▶ Merit and demerit goods do not have any inherent characteristics that qualify them as such; rather, we collectively, through the political process, make judgements about which goods and services are 'good' for society and which are 'bad'.

▶ The provision of public goods and merit goods contributes to a nation's standard of living. In the UK a substantial part of government spending involves the provision of these goods.

or an **externality**. Actually, there has been an *external cost*. Some of the costs associated with the production of the steel have *spilled over* to **third parties**, that is, parties other than the buyer and the seller of the steel. A negative spillover is called a *negative externality* because there are costs that you and your neighbours pay – dirtier clothes and cars plus respiratory problems – even though your group is external to the market transaction between the steel mill and the buyers of steel.

Not all externalities are negative. Using a classic example, even people who *do not* receive inoculations against polio, smallpox, whooping cough, and diphtheria benefit from everyone else being inoculated, for epidemics will not break out. Thus there are benefits that are external to each individual's decision to be inoculated. We call the existence of such benefits a *positive* externality.

ATTEMPTING TO MEASURE EXTERNAL COSTS

Look at panel (a) in Figure 10.2. Here we show the demand curve for steel to be DD. The supply curve, as observed by the steel mill in your town, is SS. That supply curve includes only those costs that the firm has to pay. The equilibrium, or market-clearing, situation will occur at a quantity of Q_e. Let us take into account the fact that there are external costs. These are the spillover costs that you and your neighbours pay in the form of dirtier clothes, cars, houses, and increased respiratory disease due to the air pollution emitted from the steel mill. Let us include these costs in our graph. We do this to find out what the full cost

of steel production really is. This is equivalent to saying that the price of some other input into steel production has increased. Remember that in Chapter 5 we showed that an increase in input prices would shift the supply curve inwards to the left. Thus, in panel (a) of Figure 10.2 the supply curve shifts from SS to $S'S'$. If the spillover costs were somehow taken into account, the equilibrium quantity would fall to Q'_e and the price would rise to P'_e. That price is implicitly being paid for, but by two different groups of people. The lower price P_e is being explictly paid for by the purchasers of steel and steel products. The difference between P'_e and P_e represents the cost that third parties are bearing in the form of dirtier clothes, houses, cars, and increased respiratory illnesses.

ATTEMPTING TO MEASURE EXTERNAL BENEFITS

To demonstrate external benefits in graphic form, we will use the example already mentioned concerning inoculations against various diseases. In panel (b) of

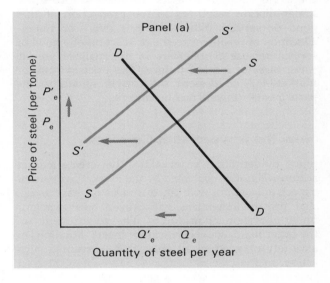

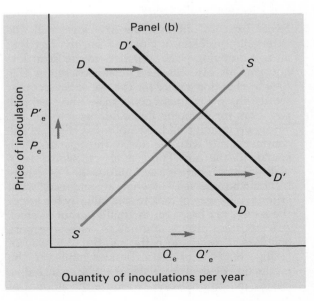

Figure 10.2
External Costs and Benefits. In panel (a) we show a situation in which the production of steel generates external costs. If the steel mill ignores pollution, at equilibrium the quantity will be Q_e, where the demand curve, DD, intersects the supply curve SS. If we include the additional cost borne by nearby residents that is caused by the steel mill's production, the supply curve would shift inward to the left to $S'S'$. This shows that the society is devoting too many resources to steel production if external costs are not taken into account, for if consumers were forced to pay a price that reflected the environmental cost of the spillover costs the quantity demanded would fall to Q'_e. In panel (b) we show the situation in which inoculations against diseases generate external benefits to those individuals who may not be inoculated but who will benefit because epidemics will not break out. If each individual ignores the external benefit of inoculations, the market-clearing quantity will be Q_e, where DD intersects SS. If external benefits are taken into account, however, the demand curve would shift rightward to $D'D'$. The new equilibrium quantity would be Q'_e and the price would be higher, P'_e. With no corrective action, however, this society is not devoting enough resources to inoculations against contagious diseases.

Figure 10.2, we show the demand curve, without taking account of any external benefits as *DD* and the supply curve as *SS*. The equilibrium price is P_e and the equilibrium quantity is Q_e. We assume, however, that inoculations against contagious diseases generate external benefits to those individuals who may not be inoculated but who benefit because epidemics will not break out. If such external benefits are taken into account, the demand curve would shift out from *DD* to *D'D'*. The new equilibrium quantity would be Q_e' and the new equilibrium price would be P_e'. With no corrective action, this society is not devoting enough resources to inoculations against diseases.

SUMMARY OF EXTERNALITIES

We have seen that when there are external costs the market will tend to over-allocate resources to the production of the good in question (as these costs are not borne by the producer). In our example, too much steel was being produced. On the other hand, when there are external benefits the market forces will under-allocate resources to the production of that good or service. When there is over- or under-allocation of resources to the production of a good or service because of spillovers, or externalities, we call these cases of **market failure**. The price system, or market, fails to present the correct signals to the participants – buyers and producers.

How the Government Corrects

Since, by definition, externalities that create market failure will not be corrected by the market, we cannot expect, at least not with the examples we have given, that private individuals will prevent the over- or under-allocation of resources. The government, on the other hand, could correct externality situations in a variety of ways in all cases that warranted such action. In the case of negative externalities, at least two avenues of action are open to the government – special taxes and/or legislation.

1. *Special Taxes.* In our example of a steel mill, the externality problem originates from the fact that air as a dumping-place is costless to the firm. The government can, however, compensate for this flaw by charging a price for the use of air. In other words, the government could make the steel mill pay a tax for dumping its pollutants into the air. The government could attempt to tax the steel mill commensurate with the cost to third parties from smoke in the air. This, in effect, would be a pollution tax. There is a serious question as to how it should be assessed – at what rate and using what criteria. One way of making the mill pay for use of the air is a tax based on the mill's output of steel. After all, the more steel the mill produces, the more pollution it dumps into the air. But this way of taxing creates a problem. Besides inhibiting the production of steel, it would *not provide* an incentive for the mill to find ways to reduce the amount of

pollution per unit of output. For example, let us assume that for every ton of steel produced, ten grams of pollutants are spewed into the atmosphere. If the steel mill is taxed according to the number of tons of steel produced by it, it may reduce its total yearly output, but it will certainly not seek ways to reduce the number of grams of pollutants produced *per ton* from ten down to, let us say, five. Therefore, an alternative tax system would be one based on the amount of the pollution dumped into the air rather than just a tax on output itself. Then if the steel mill came up with various methods to reduce air pollution, it would pay a lower tax.

No matter what type of tax is used, the supply curve will move leftwards as it did in panel (a) of Figure 10.2. The ultimate effect would be to raise the price to consumers. The equilibrium quantity of steel would fall in our example.

2. *Legislation.* In order to correct a negative externality, or negative spillover, arising from steel production, the government could simply specify a maximum allowable rate of pollution. This action would require that the steel mill install pollution-abatement equipment within its facilities, or that it reduce its rate of output, or some combination of the two. In any event, the steel mill's supply curve would again shift leftwards as it did in panel (a) of Figure 10.2.

In this section about the role of government, we have talked in terms of negative externalities and what to do about correcting them. Now we shall discuss very briefly the case of positive externalities. Here the question is: What can the government do when the production of one good spills benefits over to third parties? There are several policy options facing the government: (1) financing the production of the good or producing the good itself, (2) special subsidies (negative taxes), and (3) legislation.

1. *Government Financing and Production.* If the positive externalities seem to be extremely large, the government has the option of financing the desired additional production facilities so that there will be the 'right' amount of the good produced. In the previous example of inoculations against contagious diseases, the government could finance campaigns to inoculate the population. It could even produce and operate centres for inoculation.

2. *Special Subsidies.* A **subsidy** is a negative tax; it is a payment made either to a business or to a consumer when the business produces or the consumer buys a good or a service. For example, in the case of youth training, the government subsidize everyone who is on a youth training scheme by making payments to private firms that provide the schemes. Subsidies, in this case, reduce the net price to employers, thereby causing a larger equilibrium quantity of training and more skilled workforce for the future community.

> ## Key Points 10.2
>
> ► Negative externalities, or negative spillovers, lead to an over-allocation of resources to the specific economic activity. Two possible ways of correcting these spillovers are by taxation or government legislation.
>
> ► Positive externalities, or positive spillovers, result in an under-allocation of resources to the specific activity. Three possible government corrections are: (1) financing the production of the activity, (2) subsidizing private firms or consumers to engage in the activity, or (3) legislation.

---

3. *Legislation.* In the case of certain positive externalities, the government can require by law that a certain action be undertaken by individuals in the society. For example, there are regulations requiring all school-age children to be inoculated prior to entrance into schools. Some people believe that state eduction itself generates positive externalities. Indeed, we have regulations – laws – that require all children aged 5–16 to attend school.

A more elaborate way of accounting for both positive and negative externalities at once is via **cost-benefit analysis** and this is introduced next.

Moving Towards Cost-benefit Analysis

PRIVATE COSTS

Up until this chapter we have been dealing with situations where the costs of an individual's actions are borne directly by the individual. When a business firm has to pay wages to workers, it knows exactly what its labour costs are. When it has to buy materials or build a factory, it knows quite well what these will cost. When an individual has to pay for car repairs, or shoe repairs, or for a concert ticket, he or she knows exactly what the cost will be. These costs are what we term **private costs**. Private costs are those borne solely by the individuals who incur them. They are *internal* in the sense that the firm or household must explicitly take account of them.

SOCIAL COSTS

What about the situation discussed in this chapter relating to the steel mill that dumps waste products from its production process into the air? Obviously a cost is involved in these actions. When the steel mill pollutes the air people in the neighbouring community suffer the consequences. In other words, the cost of the steel mill's actions are borne by people other than those who own the steel mill. That is, the creator of the cost is not the sole bearer. The costs are not internalized by the individual or firm; they are external. When we add these *external costs* to *internal*, or private costs, we get **social costs**. Pollution problems and, indeed, all problems pertaining to the environment may be viewed as situations where social costs

are greater than private costs. Since some economic agents do not pay the full social costs of their actions, but rather only the smaller private costs, their actions are socially 'unacceptable'. In such situations where there is a divergence between social and private costs, we therefore see 'too much' steel production, car-driving, and beach-littering, to pick only a few of the many examples that exist.

EXTERNALITIES

When private costs differ from social costs we have used the term *externalities* – because individual decision-makers are not internalizing *all* the costs. Rather, some of these costs are remaining external to the decision-making process. Remember that the full cost of using a scarce resource is borne one way or another by others who live in the society. That is, society must pay the full opportunity cost of any activity that uses scarce resources. The individual decision-maker is the firm or the customer, and external costs and benefits will *not* enter into that individual's or firm's decision-making processes.

Cost-benefit Analysis (CBA)

To overcome this problem government economists are increasingly employing an investment appraisal technique known as **cost-benefit analysis**. In such analysis external costs and benefits are considered alongside the internal (private) costs and benefits. In brief, the *total* social costs and benefits are considered. The *problem* with this technique is that all issues need to be expressed in a common denominator for a 'total price' to be arrived at. The 'total (social) price' will incorporate internal and external costs and benefits.*

Cost-benefit analysis has been carried out for the siting of London's third airport, the building of motorways, the Channel Tunnel, and the construction of the Victoria underground line in London – to

---

* *Important note*: rather confusingly, some authors will employ the terms 'social' costs or benefits in *the same way* as we have used the terms 'external' costs and benefits. This confusion of terms simply represents the developmental nature of this concept in terms of exposition. (To illustrate this point attempt the first multiple choice question in the exam preparation and practice section.)

> ## Key Points 10.3
> ► Internal costs + external costs = Total (Social) Costs.
> ► Internal benefits + external benefits = Total (Social) Benefits.
> ► CBA involves identifying monetary values for *all* the internal and external costs and benefits of a project allowing a total (social) price to be arrived at.
> ► The use of CBA in government departments is increasing.

cite just a few of the examples available from recent public investment projects. We shall return to this theme of CBA in one of the case studies at the end of this chapter.

Striving to Achieve Economic Objectives and Stability

The government attempts to stabilize the economy by smoothing out the ups and downs in overall business activity. It aims to maintain full employment, keep prices steady, sustain economic growth, achieve an equilibrium on the balance of payments, and redistribute income and welfare. Indeed, the economy seems to be plagued with many problems. British governments have taken on the task of attempting to solve these problems in order to stabilize the economy. The order of priority in which these economic objectives are attacked depends on the government in office – but *all* governments ultimately desire the same objectives in their quest for economic stability.

This notion that the government should undertake actions to stabilize business activity is in historical terms a relatively new idea. In Winston Churchill's budget speech of 1929 he said: 'it is the orthodox Treasury dogma that, whatever the social and political advantages, ... no permanent additional employment can ... be created by state borrowing and public expenditure'. Since then, however, economic advisers and economic graduates have been appointed by the government to measure and analyse economic trends and suggest policy for their manipulation. The turning-point to governments being responsible for economic objectives became pronounced after World War II. For example, the White Paper on Employment published in May 1944 stated that the government accept 'as one of their primary aims and responsibilities the maintenance of a high and stable level of employment after the war'.

Since this statement of intent in 1944 employment policy has been an important criteria for all governments. Recently, however, it has been dropped from the number one spot to allow a more concentrated effort on curbing inflation – which ultimately, it is hoped, will have a desirable effect on the other objectives including the reduction of unemployment.

The discussion on employment and inflation as key variables will be picked up again in the forthcoming chapters. And later on in the text the question of growth will also be discussed more fully.

Finally, before closing this introductory section on the maintenance of economic objectives, we shall make some brief remarks on redistributing income and welfare.

INCOME AND WELFARE REDISTRIBUTION

Again this is a largely post-war phenomenon, supported by *all* governments – although with differing levels of commitment. In general terms redistribution uses *three* systems: the *system of taxation*, especially progressive income tax which involves taxing high-income earners progressively more than the lower paid (see closing section of this chapter for more details); the *provision of merit goods* as discussed above, which makes essential services freely available to all; and *transfer payments*.

Transfer payments are those payments made to individuals for which no services or goods are concurrently rendered. The main transfer payments in our system are social security, old age pensions, and various grants. Some of these income redistribution payments are specifically *means tested* to assure that only the poor benefit. Others, however, are available to all as a basic human right, regardless of financial position.

Increased expenditure on these welfare-type policies have 'knock-on' and 'knock-off' effects on the other objectives. For example, further inflationary pressures are generated due to increases in public expenditure and/or increased unemployment may follow as incentives to work become a less attractive alternative to life on social security. In fact several of the objectives discussed above interlink and even conflict with one another. This will become more apparent when we look at policies in Part E of the book, as often one government policy affects several government objectives, and unfortunately these results may not all be symmetrical. Indeed it is the incompatibility of the various objectives discussed above that leads to debates regarding their order of priority.

> ## Key Points 10.4
>
> ► Economic stability is a responsibility accepted by *all* post-war governments.
> ► To achieve economic stability various objectives are worked towards, mainly: full employment, stable prices, equilibrium on the balance of payments, steady growth, and a redistribution of income and welfare.
> ► The various economic objectives identified are incompatible with one another and in consequence their order of priority changes according to the government in office.

The Size and Growth of Government

When considering the role of governments in an economy its public expenditure is a key variable for concern.

In Figure 10.3 we present a breakdown of the UK's public (government) expenditure for the years 1983–8. Basically Figure 10.3 reflects the theme of this chapter. In fact the expenditure pattern for the various public goods, merit goods, and policy manoeuvres that the UK government is presently involved in could be calculated as separate categories. It is clear from Figure 10.3 that large increases in the health and social security areas have been experienced and are expected to continue, while spending on government housing and subsidies to agriculture, industry, trade, and employment will be reduced. Such observations about individual programmes provide some idea of a government's priorities, policies, and philosophy.

However, a more significant variable to discover is public spending expressed as a percentage of the total spending occurring in the country as a whole. That is, in determining whether £120.3 billion of public spending in the year 1983–4 is a lot, or not, depends on the level of spending committed by all sectors of the economy in the same year. In formal terms we need to see public expenditure expressed as a percentage of national income (which is similar to *gross domestic expenditure*). In 1983–4 the £120.3 billion of public expenditure represented approximately 42½ per cent of national income. By 1987–8 this proportion, it is hoped, will have fallen to around 39½ per cent of national income.

If one looks at Figure 10.3 again the final sentence of the previous paragraph may seem bewildering. You will certainly notice that in cash terms public spending in 1987–8 is the highest of all years. Yet, once inflation and the anticipated increase in national income is brought into the picture the public sector is expected to experience a reduction in size; and certainly this is the desired intention of the present (1986) government.

In their very first White Paper on public spending (in 1979) the present government opened with the statement that 'public spending is at the heart of Britain's economic difficulties'. They believe this to be

the case as they have a great respect for market forces and obviously if the public sector is cut back the market forces of the private sector may increase. In other words, the converse of reduced public expenditure is that more resources become available for the

Figure 10.3
Public Expenditure by Programme 1983-88 (in cash terms)

	1983–4 out-turn (£bn)	1985–6 plans (£bn)	1986–7 plans (£bn)	1987–8 plans (£bn)
Social security	35.2	40.1	41.9	44.0
Defence	15.5	18.1	18.6	18.9
Health and personal social services	14.8	16.5	17.4	18.1
Education and science	13.4	13.6	14.0	14.2
Scotland	6.7	7.2	7.3	7.3
Industry, energy, trade, and employment	5.9	4.7	3.7	3.5
Law, order, and protective services	4.6	5.2	5.5	5.6
Transport	4.4	4.5	4.8	4.8
Northern Ireland	3.7	4.3	4.5	4.6
Other environmental services	3.7	3.5	3.6	3.5
Housing	3.1	2.3	2.5	2.6
Wales	2.6	2.7	2.9	2.9
Overseas aid and other overseas services	2.6	2.6	2.5	2.8
Agriculture, fisheries, food, and forestry	2.1	2.1	1.9	1.9
Other public services	1.7	1.9	2.0	2.0
Common services	0.9	1.1	1.1	1.2
Arts and libraries	0.6	0.6	0.7	0.7
Adjustments				
Special sales of assets	–1.1	–2.5	–2.2	–2.2
Reserve		3.0	4.0	5.0
Total	120.3	131.5	136.7	141.5

Source: Economic Progress Report, Jan. 1985.

Note: In this table a programme-by-programme breakdown of public expenditure is shown (although in this instance National Debt interest payments have not been included). Any differences between totals and the sum of their component parts are due to rounding.

private market sector. Therefore, more decisions relating to resource allocation would become left to market forces. Whether public sector expenditure can be continually cut back (e.g. even into the 1990s) is a theme of the first Case Study, at the close of this chapter. (Now read Key Points 10.5.)

Taxation

Related to public expenditure is taxation – since taxation may be defined as the main source of income from which governments finance their spending. Theoretically, therefore, cut-backs in public expenditure in the UK could ultimately lead to cut-backs in taxation. From the market mechanism point of view such reductions would be good, as taxes also distort market forces. This is because taxes are imposed on Land, Labour, Capital, and Interest (i.e. all factor payments) as well as most Goods and Services (i.e. product payments).

Categories of Taxation

In the UK it is traditional to envisage two forms of taxation: *direct* and *indirect*. **Direct taxation** is largely the tax of one's income, i.e. the tax one is billed for directly and liable to pay as a named individual. **Indirect taxation** by contrast, is largely tax on spending, i.e. the tax that one may not be aware of. Since it is the seller of the good or service who is liable and therefore it has an indirect nature.

Examples of Direct Taxes

All forms of income on which tax is liable fall into this category. The most obvious, and most significant example, is **income tax** (often paid through the PAYE* scheme via the employer) but there are various other forms of income and consequently various other examples, the main ones being:

Corporation tax which is paid by firms on their profits.

Capital gains tax which is paid by individuals who profit by selling a capital asset at a higher price than they originally paid.

Inheritance tax which was formerly called 'Death Duties' and should therefore be self-explanatory.

Petroleum revenue tax which is paid by firms operating in the North Sea as an extra burden for them. A kind of payment for the benefits they gain from extracting the UK natural assets.

Examples of Indirect Tax

Most taxes on spending are indirect since it is the seller of the good who is ultimately liable for the tax bill. The most obvious, and most significant, example is **Value Added Tax** (VAT) which is presently charged on most goods and services sold in the UK at a rate of 15%†.

Other examples of indirect tax include the various duties obtained from specific products, for example:

oil duties which are paid on petrol, diesel and other hydrocarbon oils.

tobacco tax which is paid on cigarettes, cigars, and pipe tobacco.

excise duties on alcohol which is paid on wines, spirits, and beers.

Each of these specific taxes are charged per unit (e.g. per pint, per gallon, per packet of twenty, per litre, or whatever) and it is not entirely clear who carries the tax burden. The seller of the products will usually strive to pass on the tax incidence to the purchaser by raising the price accordingly.

OTHER TYPES OF TAX

It may be worth recognizing that other forms of taxation also exist, which are not always collected by the central government. For example, local rates which are calculated according to the value of property are the responsibility of the local authorities to assess and collect. Similarly water rates, airport taxes, motor vehicle and TV licences are not the direct responsibility of central government but are administered by appointed public authorities acting on their behalf as revenue collectors. Finally, National Insurance contributions made by employers and employees should also be recognized as a tax, especially as both are payments which affect the demand and supply of labour.

Types of Taxation Systems

All of the taxes mentioned above can fit into one of three types of taxation system – proportional, progressive, or regressive.

Proportional Taxation

A system of **proportional taxation** means that as an individual's income goes up, so, too, do his or her taxes in exactly the same proportion. A proportional tax system can also be called a *flat rate tax*. Taxpayers at all income levels end up paying the *same percentage* of their income in taxes. In other words, if the proportional tax rate were 20 per cent, an individual with an income of £10 000 would pay £2000 in taxes while an individual making £100 000 would pay £20 000, the identical 20 per cent rate being levied on both.

---

*PAYE is the standard abbreviation for Pay As You Earn.

†Some essential goods and services are zero-rated.

> ## Key Points 10.5
>
> ▶ Public spending can be analysed in two forms: in absolute terms by analysing the breakdown of total public expenditure programme by programme; or in terms that show government expenditure in proportion to the rest of the nation's spending, i.e. public expenditure expressed as a percentage of national income.
>
> ▶ In the UK public spending is presently around 40 per cent of our nation's national income. (In 1900 it was approximately 15 per cent.)
>
> ▶ The present Conservative government wish to reduce the proportion of government spending in order to allow market forces to operate.
>
> ▶ Remember that as the role of the government increases it is probable that the role of market forces decrease.

Progressive Taxation

Under **progressive taxation**, as a person's income increases, the percentage of income paid in taxes increases; or to express it formally, the *marginal tax rate* is greater than the *average tax rate*. To understand this we need to examine these terms. The **marginal tax rate** is expressed as

$$\text{marginal tax rate} = \frac{\text{change in tax bill}}{\text{change in income}}$$

The word *marginal* merely means incremental here.

We should compare the marginal tax rate with the **average tax rate**, which is defined as

$$\text{average tax rate} = \frac{\text{total tax bill}}{\text{total income}}$$

The difference between the marginal and the average tax rate can be seen in Figure 10.4. In this example of a progressive tax system the first £100 in income is taxed at 10 per cent, the next £100 at 20 per cent, and the third £100 at 30 per cent.

Regressive Taxation

With **regressive taxation**, a smaller percentage of income is taken in taxes as income increases. The marginal rate is *below* the average rate. The following is an example of regressive taxation. Assume that the more income a family earns, the lower the percentage of its income is spent on food purchases. Now assume further that the government obtains *all* of its revenues from a 20 per cent sales tax on food purchases. Since food purchases constitute a larger proportion of total expenditures for poor people than for rich people, the percentage of total income that would be paid in food taxes under such a system would *fall* as income rose. It would be a regressive system.

The relative importance of these various taxes and how they will affect the economy will be dealt with more specifically in Chapter 32.

Figure 10.4
Progressive Tax System. The percentage of tax taken out of each additional pound earned goes up; that is, the marginal tax rate increases progressively with income.

Therefore, the average tax rate is less than the marginal tax rate in a progressive tax system. Whereas, in a proportional tax system, the marginal tax rate is constant and always the same as the average tax rate.

Income	Marginal rate	Tax	Average rate
£100	10%	£10	$\frac{£10}{£100} = 10\%$
£200	20%	£10 + £20 = £30	$\frac{£30}{£200} = 15\%$
£300	30%	£10 + £20 + £30 = £60	$\frac{£60}{£300} = 20\%$

Key Points 10.6

► Taxes are mainly levied by central government and enable it to finance a large part of its spending.

► The two main forms of tax are direct and indirect. The former being taxes on income (of which there are many forms) and the latter being taxes on spending.

► We can identify other forms of tax which are not necessarily administered or collected by the central government, e.g. local authority rates.

► We can classify tax systems into proportional, progressive, and regressive, depending on whether the marginal tax rate is the same as, greater than, or less than the average tax rate as income rises.

► Marginal tax rates are those applied to marginal tax brackets, defined as spreads of income over which the tax rate is constant.

CASE STUDY

The Chancellor's Problem

Nigel Lawson's exasperated look is due to the fact that, according to his analysis, public spending as a percentage of national income needs to go down still further.

Question

1. Why is his objective difficult to achieve?

2. How would you suggest he went about achieving his aim?

3. Does public spending, in your view, have a minimum below which it is impossible to fall?

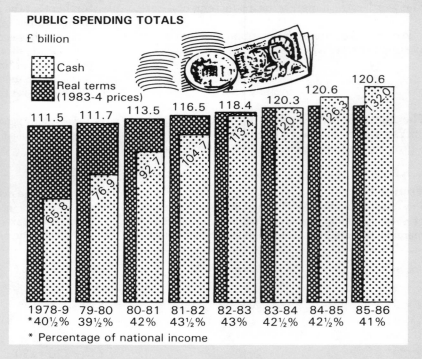

PUBLIC SPENDING TOTALS

£ billion

Cash

Real terms (1983-4 prices)

	1978-9	79-80	80-81	81-82	82-83	83-84	84-85	85-86
Cash	65.8	76.9	92.7	104.1	113.4	120.3	126.3	132.0
Real terms	111.5	111.7	113.5	116.5	118.4	120.3	120.6	120.6
*%	40½%	39½%	42%	43½%	43%	42½%	42½%	41%

* Percentage of national income

Source: The Guardian, 13 November 1984.

CASE STUDY

An Example of Cost-benefit Analysis in Action

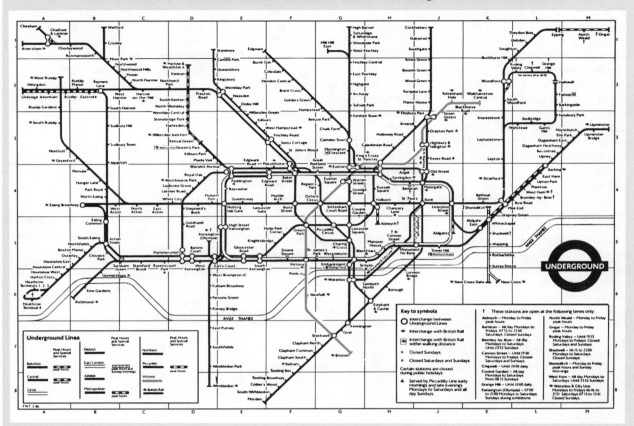

Figure 10.5
A map of London's Underground

London's underground had a new length of line added in the late 1960s and early 1970s, namely the Victoria Line. Intriguingly, as shown by the map in Figure 10.5, this line, to a large extent, went nowhere new – its main purpose was to link several parts of the existing network. In conventional accounting terms the 'Victoria Line project' was deemed to make a loss. However in cost-benefit analysis terms the Victoria underground line was viable, and so it was built.

Questions

1. Reduced journey times to work and reduced costs to those remaining in their cars were both recorded as external benefits during the Victoria Line cost-benefit analysis. Can you explain why?

2. In cost-benefit analysis terms what do you think was considered during the appraisal of the Victoria Line project? (Hint: Consider private [internal] costs and the external costs, and compare these to the private [internal] benefits and the external benefits.)

3. How may monetary values be attached to the items listed for consideration in Question 2? (Hint: opportunity cost is an important concept here.)

CASE STUDY

Now The Acid Test!?

'The international row over acid rain began with nothing more dramatic than a few rain gauges in Sweden just after World War Two. In 1968 Professor Swante Oden, one of the Swedish scientists monitoring the effects of acid rain, published a brilliant study linking the jigsaw of acidity readings from the rain gauges with wind patterns.

The prevailing winds blow Europe's acid rain and pollution northwards, much of which comes from Britain's power stations. The rainfall over the southern coast of Norway has 40 times more acid than natural rain. The salmon have vanished from the seven big rivers of southern Norway and the four southern-most counties contain an amazing 2840 lakes many of which are now extinct of all fish. Next door in Sweden, fish have been affected in 9000 lakes and wiped out in a third.

In the UK, the House of Commons' Environment Committee emphasised that the threat was not only to the natural environment but also to historic buildings including Westminster Abbey, Lincoln Cathedral, York Minister and St Paul's.

So far it looks as if cleaning up this mess would cost Britain alone billions of pounds. It could put up electricity prices from now until the end of the century. It could affect the future of the coal-mining industry, because the extra cost of removing acid gases from the smoke of coal-burning power stations would make nuclear plants an even better buy. It could dictate the power and speed of our cars, because pollution from our present car engines is one of the major causes of the damage.

The House of Commons' Environment Committee said that Britain should clean up its

chimneys: pledge itself to an immediate 30 per cent cut and work towards a 60 per cent cut in sulphur emissions by 1993.'

Source: The Sunday Express Magazine, 9 September 1984

Questions
1. Using illustrations from the above article, distinguish between the private and external costs of electricity supply.
2. What criteria would economists use in advising the Government concerning a decision on whether to reduce or eliminate sulphur emissions from UK power stations?
3. Evaluate the effectiveness of alternative policy instruments which could be used in reducing this form of pollution.

Source: University of London, 'S' Level Paper. June 1986.

Exam Preparation and Practice

MULTIPLE CHOICE QUESTIONS
(NB: Before attempting Question 1 read the important footnote on page 153.)

1. If a firm's private costs of production are not equal to the social costs of its production, the government could increase economic welfare by
   A taxing the firm if its social costs exceed its private costs
   B taxing the firm if its social costs are less than its private costs
   C subsidizing the firm if its social costs exceed its private costs
   D taxing other firms if social costs are less than private costs in the firm in question
   E subsidizing other firms if social costs are less than private costs in the firm in question

2. Public goods, such as street lighting, are not supplied through the ordinary market mechanism because
   A the initial capital cost would be prohibitive
   B some households would not be able to afford to make their full contribution towards the cost
   C the benefits would not be confined to the buyers, but would automatically be available to non-buyers
   D the provision of public goods is essential, and therefore cannot be left to private initiative
   E monopolies would earn excess profits

For Questions 3, 4, and 5 – one or more of the options given may be correct. Select your answers by means of the code set out into grid:

A 1,2,3	B 1,2	C 2,3	D 1
all correct	only correct	only correct	only correct

3. Because of the deficiencies of the market mechanism the state might intervene to ensure an adequate supply of
1 public goods
2 merit goods
3 inferior goods

4. In using cost-benefit analysis to assess the economic need for a Channel Tunnel, account would need to be taken of the
1 construction costs of the tunnel
2 effects of the tunnel on the environmental amenities at Dover
3 effects of the tunnel on air traffic at London Airport

5. Where a private sector activity generates significant external costs then the community may benefit following
1 a government take-over of the activity
2 the legal restriction of the activity
3 the subsidization of the activity

6. Which one of the following forms of taxation is most regressive?
A a progressive income tax
B a proportional income tax
C motor vehicle tax
D tobacco tax

7. Which one of the following taxes is most likely to affect the supply of labour?
A income tax
B a tax on corporate profits
C death duties
D an increase in employers' National Insurance contributions

8. The term 'Marginal Rate of Tax' is applied to the
A proportion of income which is paid in tax
B amount of tax payable after allowances have been deducted
C rate of tax paid on unearned income
D tax paid out of an increment to income
E rate of tax which gives the highest yield

RELATED ESSAY QUESTIONS

1. Distinguish between public goods and merit goods. What are the arguments for and against the provision by the state of merit goods?

2. What are externalities in economics? If an externality has an adverse effect, how might it be controlled?

3. Discuss the economic justification for government involvement in the provision of education and health services.

4. Why do governments supply certain goods and services at zero prices whereas other commodities and services are supplied via the market mechanism?

5. 'Reducing inequalities of income by progressive taxation penalises initiative and enterprise.' Discuss.

6. In what sense can river pollution and traffic congestion be viewed as economic problems? Can economics make any contribution to the solution of these problems?

11 Economic Indicators: Unemployment and Inflation

Key Points to Review

▶ Labour as a resource (1.1)

▶ Excess demand (5.7)

▶ Relative prices (6.3)

▶ Price controls (8.6)

Questions for Preview

1 What is a recession?

2 What is unemployment?

3 Why is frictional unemployment not necessarily harmful?

4 What are some of the problems associated with measuring inflation?

5 Who is affected by inflation?

Sometimes the overall business climate is buoyant – few workers are unemployed, businesses are expanding, and not many firms are going bust. At other times, however, the business situation is not so good – there are many unemployed workers, businesses are cutting back in their production, and a significant number of firms are going out of business. These ups and downs in economy-wide economic activity can be called **business fluctuations** or **business cycles**.

When we talk about these fluctuations or cyclical patterns in economic activity we are suggesting that many **economic indicators** or variables are moving at once. For example: prices, employment, money supply, stocks, return on capital, savings, interest rates, balance of payments, output, exchange rates etc. These indicators are measured and presented in many ways. One readily accessible source is the free monthly Treasury publication entitled *Economic Progress Report*. The table presented in their July 1985 issue is reproduced in Figure 11.1 with charts (from the same publication) giving a more detailed breakdown of similar information.

Of these various indicators changes in unemploy-

ment and inflation are important aspects affecting most of the other variables in one way or another. In this chapter we will take a brief look at business cycles and their uses in general before tackling unemployment and inflation specifically.

Business Cycles

During most years the UK economy is growing – output, income, and employment are increasing. In other words, the trend in business and general economic activity is upward. But there are fluctuations around what we might call the 'growth-path' line. We have terms for the periods when business activity temporarily pulls us below our upward growth-path, and others for periods when business activity moves with, or in excess of, our normal growth path. We call the former **recessions** or **depression*** and the latter **expansions** or **booms**. Think of

---

*For a more accurate understanding of when to use which term see the dictionary inclusion for recession.

this in terms of a growing child. The child is on a long-term growth trend in regard to body weight and height. There are, however, temporary fluctuations. The child can become sick or can experience malnutrition and deviate from the long-term trend towards maturity. This would be the equivalent of a recession in the economy. When the child experiences growth spurts this would be equivalent to an expansion in the economy.

Figure 11.1
Economic Indicators

Panel a

Published monthly		1980	1981	1982	1983	1984	1985 Apr.	May
Output of production industries	1980 = 100	100.0	96.5	98.6	101.9	102.9	107.4	—
Unemployment (adult)	millions	1.56	2.42	2.97	2.97	3.05	3.18	3.18
Sterling index[2]	1975 = 100	96.1	95.0	90.5	83.2	78.7	78.0	78.7
PSBR[2,3]	£ billion	12.7	8.6	8.9	9.7	10.1	1.8	1.0
Interest rate: 3 months interbank[2]	%	16.6	13.9	12.3	10.2	9.9	12.7	12.7
Retail prices index[2]	% increase	18.1	11.9	8.7	4.6	5.0	6.9	7.0
Average earnings, whole economy[4]	over same period a year earlier	20.7	13.1	9.4	8.4	6.1	9.4	—

Published quarterly		1980	1981	1982	1983	1984	1985 Q1
Balance of payments, current account	£ billion	3.5	6.9	5.5	2.5	0.1	0.1
GDP (average)[5]	1980 = 100	100.0	98.6	100.6	103.6	106.4	108.9
GDP (average)[5]		−2.3	−1.4	2.0	3.0	2.7	2.8
Total fixed investment[5]		−5.1	−8.8	6.7	3.8	7.4	3.7
Consumers' expenditure[5]	% increase	−0.3	−0.3	0.8	3.99	1.6	1.3
Exports of goods and services[5]	over same	−0.1	−1.8	1.0	1.2	6.6	8.6
Imports of goods and services[5]	period a	−3.9	−3.4	3.9	5.5	8.9	9.6
Employed labour force[6]	year earlier	−0.3	−3.9	−1.8	−1.3	1.6	—
Productivity: whole economy		−2.2	1.9	4.1	3.8	1.0	—
Gross trading profits of industrial and commercial companies[7]		12.3	14.3	18.3	20.5	23.6	26.2

1. Seasonally adjusted unless otherwise stated. Many of the most recent figures are provisional and subject to revision. 2. Not seasonally adjusted. 3. Annual figures refer to financial years ending in the following March. 4. GB, not underlying series. 5. 1980 prices. 6. Annual comparisons are for June. 7. Net of stock appreciation.

Panel b

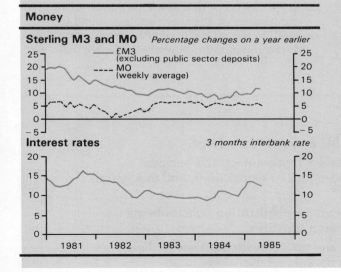

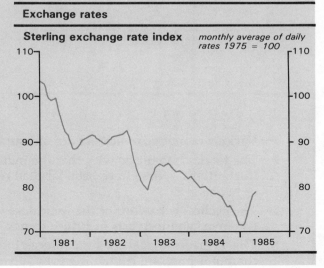

Source: Economic Progress Report, July 1985

In Figure 11.2 we show a typical business cycle fluctuating around a smooth upward-sloping growth-line. Over the last 100 years the economy has averaged about a 1.5 per cent annual increase in the material standard of living of the average UK citizen. Alongside this overall upward trend we have experienced booms and depressions. Indeed, economists have long recognized that *left to its own devices* an economy has a built-in cyclical pattern of its own. There are many explanations for this cycle of which the following is only one. Boom situations lead to circumstances of 'over-heating' characterized by 'shortages' of labour, capital, and stock and a consequent rising of prices. This leads into a depression characterized by falling output, and profits, rising unemployment and stocks, and a stabilizing of prices. This eventually generates a potential upswing situation to another boom.

This business cycle of boom and depression was

first identified in 1860 by an economist named Juglar – he referred to it as a 'trade cycle' and some still employ this original phrase. He claimed that it took eight to eleven years for a cycle to progress from one boom through a depression to another boom. Other economists have challenged this measurement to both extremes, with Kitchin claiming three-and-a-half-year cycles and N. Kondratieff (a Russian economist) conceiving of long-wave fifty-year cycles. Which of these measurements is correct is a matter of academic debate. What is important is that cyclical economic behaviour can be perceived. Furthermore, the cyclical movement of these economic indicators interact sufficiently to enable stabilization policies to be employed if desired, and forecasts of general economic behaviour to be attempted.

Consequently, various models of economic behaviour exist and again, whether one is more accurate than the other is arbitrary. What is important is that economic indicators can be used to make important economic forecasts.

In Figure 11.3 the Treasury model of 1978 is presented in the form of a flow chart. Obviously this model is continually revised and the conscientious student may like to reflect on which variables would need to have been added to today's model. In fact, in its present computer format the Treasury have identified some 700 economic relationships which contribute to determining the main variables. This model is used for estimating the effects of policy and for forecasting. Often forecasts are wrong due to false assumptions about policy changing and due to unforeseen developments (e.g. strikes), misinterpreted relationships, or faulty figures. Nevertheless forecasts do provide a guide and even the errors are useful in so far as they provide further understanding and insight into the interrelationship of the various economic variables.

The last point is important as economic forecasting is still a relatively young science – Whitehall has only been involved for approximately forty-five years and refinements are continually being made. What is ironic, however, is that some forecasts prove to be wrong because of the way people respond (or over-respond) to the reliability of economists' predictions.

Most commentators, however, do agree that unem-

Figure 11.2

The Business Cycle. The coloured line depicts the long-term 'growth-path' around which the economic activity fluctuates – moving in some consistent pattern from expansion to recession and back again.

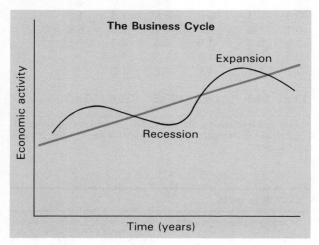

Key Points 11.1

► Various economic indicators are measurable and can be analysed.

► The total economic activity that the indicators represent exhibit periodic fluctuations – these have been labelled recessions or depressions, and expansions or booms.

► The cyclical behaviour of the indicators leads to stabilization policies being employed and forecasts of future trends being identified.

► The Treasury model used for forecasting and policy evaluation is based on a computer program containing over 700 economic relationships.

Figure 11.3
Flow Chart of the Treasury Model

The direction of the arrow between the boxes represent the Treasury's interpretation of the direction of causation between variables. Those variables at the top of the page in circles are those known as **exogenous** variables, i.e.

they are external to the system, determined by policy or world events. The remaining indicators in boxes are called **endogenous** variables. i.e. they are internal to the system and affect one another.

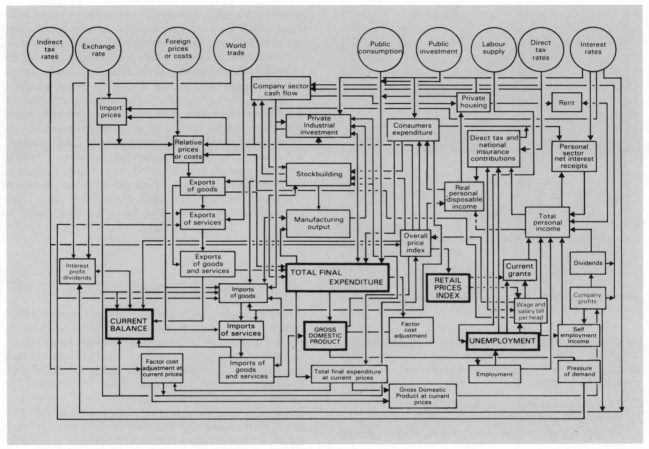

Source: H M Treasury Macroeconomic Model Technical Manual, 1978.

ployment and inflation are two central economic variables. They *affect* many aspects of the economy and are *affected* by many other economic variables including each other. These will now be examined in depth.

Unemployment

One of the major consequences of fluctuating business activity is the ensuing unemployment, particularly of workers, but also of other factors of production (non-human resources). Unemployment has many costs – in human suffering, in loss of dignity, in loss of output and savings – the list goes on and on. That is why policy-makers in our economy closely watch the unemployment figures published by the Department of Employment each month. Unemployment is considered to be a social evil that must be kept at an 'acceptable' level. We can see from Figure 11.4 (page 166) that the rate of unemployment in the United Kingdom during the post-war period averaged

around 2 per cent of the working population for most of the 1950s and 1960s and never above 3 per cent until 1971. Since then, however, the trend has been towards an ever-increasing unemployment rate and it has become an economic and social problem of great magnitude. Remember that the 13.5 per cent unemployment rate plotted for 1985 represents three and a quarter million people.

The rate of unemployment is measured by dividing the total number of persons defined as unemployed by the total number of persons defined as being within the labour force. Determining who is truly unemployed and who is effectively in the labour force is no easy task.

How Official Measurements Are Defined

The working population is presently defined by the Department of Employment as 'persons over sixteen

Figure 11.4
The UK Unemployment Record since 1950

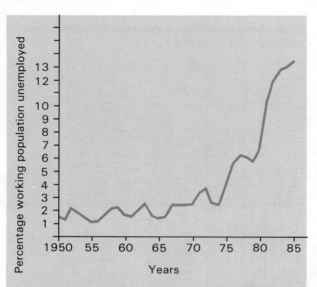

Note: The figures plotted are annual averages, except for 1985 which has been estimated from figures for the first six months of the year only.

Source: British Labour Statistics, Historical Abstract 1886–1968 and *Department of Employment Gazette.*

who work for pay or gain or register themselves as "available" for such work and meanwhile claim benefit'. In less formal terms therefore the working population includes:

1. Employees in employment
2. Employers and the self-employed
3. Those registered as unemployed and claiming benefit
4. Members of military forces.

Obviously this is not the same as all those of *working age* – which would include those involved in full-time education, those in early retirement, housewives, and those who are seeking work but have not registered for unemployment benefit.

In numerical terms for 1984 the following figures collated from the *Department of Employment Gazette* and the *Monthly Digest of Statistics* may help clarify matters a little further:

Total population of working age	35 113 000
minus those not involved in labour force	8 048 000
equals working population	27 065 000
minus unemployed	3 030 000
equals employed labour force	24 035 000

Until 1990 the number of people in the working-age group is expected to increase by about 1.2 million, of whom it is expected that 950 000 will join the working population. This could make our unemployment figures still higher, unless job opportunities happen to increase as well.

Registered Unemployment

It must be recognized that to become part of the unemployment statistics in the UK one must be officially registered as a claimant at an Unemployment Benefit Office. This official measure is recognizably suspect: it *excludes* all those who are not eligible for benefits; it *officially excludes* all men aged over sixty who since April 1983 no longer have to sign on to claim benefit; and it also *excludes* those who register as desiring work at commercial agencies but not with the official offices as owing to marriage or similar status circumstances they are not eligible for benefit. Indeed, a labour force survey of 1983 identified some 820 000 people seeking work but not claiming benefit. Many estimates put the 'true' level of unemployment beyond four million. In textbook terms the official unemployment statistics contain a certain amount of **hidden unemployment** incorporating the many categories who are falsely excluded, plus those on the other side who are wrongly included, e.g. those that claim unemployment benefit but have no real desire to work.

Measuring Unemployment Sensitively

Apart from the problem of hidden unemployment which by its very nature makes reliable statistics of those truly wanting work most difficult to ascertain, there is also the problematic question of *who* is actually unemployed? The pool of unemployed labour is not a stagnant lake of humans crying for work. The monthly unemployment statistics are a snapshot of those registered claimants who are unemployed when the count occurs (on the second Thursday of each month). This group will obviously change its characters, as there are constantly large numbers of people joining and leaving the official books each month. Those joining the pool are referred to as the **inflow** and those leaving it are referred to as the **outflow**. By result any increase in unemployment represents inflow minus outflow. As Figure 11.5 highlights the problems during the 1970s and 1980s stem largely from sharp drops in outflow rather than rises in inflow. The corollary of this is that people have to wait far longer before leaving the unemployment pool. In formal terms the **duration** of unemployment is now longer. For example, in 1955 when unemployment was down to 1.1 per cent of the working population the average period of each case of unemployment was three and a half weeks. In 1985 the average period of unemployment is far longer – in fact over 50 per cent have been unemployed for six months or more (see Figure 11.6).

However, the idea of *average* unemployment duration no longer makes much sense, as some groups in our economy are far more vulnerable than others. For example, the young (under twenty-five) and the old (over fifty-five) endure longer unemployment periods

Figure 11.5

The Inflows and Outflows of Male Unemployment (Monthly averages in thousands). It is important to remember that these figures are *monthly averages* of only those men who move into or from the official unemployment statistics.

	Inflow ('000s)	Outflow ('000s)
1970	248	244
1971	252	236
1972	226	235
1973	207	222
1974	222	215
1975	238	208
1976	218	214
1977	203	200
1978	189	197
1979	180	183
1980	217	173
1981	220	183
1982	222	214
1983	246	243
1984	248	241

Source: Department of Employment Gazette

than their middle-aged counterparts (see the table in Figure 11.6 for details).

Similarly one's gender, occupation, regional location, social class, and even marital status affect one's chances of unemployment. Indeed, the white, male, owner-occupier, London-based, managerial type, with two children is statistically less likely to experience unemployment than the coloured youth who is unskilled and lives in Teeside. To a large extent this is

Figure 11.6

Unemployment by Age and Duration

		Duration of unemployment (weeks)			Total (= 100%) thousands
		Up to 26	Over 26 up to 52	Over 52	
		(%)	(%)	(%)	
Males aged:	under 25	51.6	17.4	31.0	791.9
	25–54	35	14.9	50.2	1 225.7
	55 and over	30.9	18.8	50.3	298.5
	All ages	40.1	16.3	43.6	2 316.0
Females: aged:	under 25	57.5	18.2	24.2	494.3
	25.54	46.4	22.6	31.0	462.0
	55 and over	23.5	14.3	62.1	68.6
	All ages	50.2	20.0	29.8	1 024.9

Source: Department of Employment Gazette, May 1985. (Totals do not sum due to rounding.)

due to the way that the labour market operates which is the theme of a Case Study at the end of this chapter.

Finally, in undertaking a sensitive interpretation of unemployment statistics it is also necessary to recognize what adjustments have been made to the portrait presented. **Seasonally adjusted** is the most common and this means that the figures incorporate an adjustment to allow for those seasonal quirks which regularly cause unemployment to be particularly high or low during certain months.

Similar adjustments are made for:

(i) **School-leavers** (i.e. young persons seeking their first job).

(ii) **Adult students** (who have registered for vacation work and/or benefit).

Key Points 11.2

▶ Unemployment rates in the United Kingdom during the post-war period have risen from a low of 1 to 2 per cent in the 1950 and 1960s to levels above 10 per cent in the 1980s.

▶ The working population in official terms includes: (1) employees in employment, (ii) employers and the self-employed, (iii) HM Forces, and (iv) unemployed persons claiming benefit. The first three of these groups make up the employed labour force.

▶ When the outflow from the unemployment books decreases, the duration of unemployment increases.

▶ The unemployment statistics contain certain problems and some of these are catered for by the concept of hidden unemployment.

▶ All unemployment statistics should be analysed carefully, noting if possible source, adjustments, age-categories etc.

Figure 11.7

Unemployment Statistics – The Great Divide. People interpret the unemployment figures differently. Those on the left of the political chamber wish to highlight the under-counting by adding omissions, while those on the right stress the over-counting by making subtractions. Which final figure do you agree with?

Official Total: 3 094 000 (Nov '83)

Left-wing critics add:		Right-wing critics subtract:	
Unemployed over-sixties (no longer required to register)	199 000	School leavers	168 000
		Claiments who are not really looking for jobs	490 000
Short-time working	43 000		
		Severely disabled	23 000
Students on vacation	27 000		
		'Unemployables' – mentally or or physically incapable	135 000
Effect of Special Employment Measures	395 000		
		'Job changers' – out of work for four weeks or less	360 000
Unregistered unemployed	490 000		
		'Black economy' – workers, illegally claiming benefit	250 000
Total additions	1 154 000	Total subtractions	1 426 000
Total unemployed	4 248 000	Total unemployed	1 668 000

(iii) **Temporarily stopped** (i.e. those workers who have been laid off due to bad weather or someone else's strike and are claiming benefit until they can return to work).

These three special groups are important to remember as the unemployment figures are often presented as *the number of wholly unemployed excluding the temporarily stopped, school-leavers, and adult students*. These three groups are excluded as it is felt that they do not form part of the long-term unemployed – though this may be difficult to justify in the case of present school-leavers.

This section has served to highlight the sensitive nature of unemployment statistics and before closing we would like to draw your attention to Figure 11.7 which appeared in a similar form in *The Sunday Times* in 1983. It summarizes concisely some of the problems with unemployment statistics. (See Key Points 11.2.)

The Major Types of Unemployment

Unemployment can be categorized into four basic types: frictional, cyclical, seasonal, and structural. You may hear about these different types of unemployment, so you might want to know what they mean.

Frictional Unemployment

Of the 27 million people in the working population more than 4 million persons will have reported themselves unemployed at one time or another during each year. What we call **frictional unemployment** is this continuous flow of individuals from job to job in and out of employment. It used to be called **'transitional unemployment'** which as the name suggests merely involves people *moving* or *changing* from one job to another. The modern phrase places the emphasis on 'time taken' to change as a result of certain frictions in the labour market. Indeed, there will always be some frictional unemployment as resources need time to be redirected within the market. To eliminate frictional unemployment completely, we would have to prevent workers from leaving their present jobs until they had already lined up other jobs at which they would start working immediately. A complete elimination of frictional unemployment would probably reduce the rate of growth of our economy. One important source of advances in productivity is the movement of workers from sectors of the economy where labour productivity and wages are low, to sectors where productivity and wages are high. The search for better job-offers is the process by which workers discover areas where their productivity is highest, that is, where they can make the most income. Frictional unemployment can, therefore, be reduced by the provision of better information services and employment agencies but it could never be eliminated altogether.

CYCLICAL UNEMPLOYMENT

Cyclical unemployment is related to the business cycle. In fact, cyclical unemployment is defined as unemployment associated with changes in business conditions – primarily recessions and depressions. The way to lessen cyclical unemployment would be to reduce the intensity, duration, and frequency of ups and downs of business activity. Economic policy-makers attempt, through their policies, to reduce cyclical unemployment by keeping business activity on an even keel, and these policies will be discussed in Part E, the final section of the book.

Seasonal Unemployment

Seasonal unemployment is just that. It comes and goes with seasons of the year in which the demand for particular jobs rises and falls. For example, construction workers often can work only during the warmer months. They are seasonally unemployed during the winter. Resort workers usually can only get jobs in resorts during the summer season. They, too, become seasonally unemployed during the winter; the opposite is true for ski resort workers. There is little we can do to reduce seasonal unemployment.

Structural Unemployment

Presumably, there have been structural changes in our economy that have caused some workers to become permanently unemployed, or at least unemployed for very long periods of time, because they cannot find jobs that use their particular skills. Structurally unemployed persons are usually those who simply cannot find *any* job they can do. **Structural unemployment** has often been associated with **technological unemployment**, that is, unemployment resulting from the increased use of labour-saving machines.

Unlike cyclical unemployment, structural unemployment is not caused by the business cycle, although the business cycle may affect it. And unlike frictional unemployment, structural unemployment is not related to the movement of workers from low-paid to high-paid jobs. Rather, structural unemployment results when the consuming public no longer wants to buy an individual's services in that location. Instead of going through retraining, that individual persists in his or her search for employment with 'obsolete' skills in a market with limited demand. Some of these people eventually will go into new industries. In most urban settings this is precisely what happens. However, in some settings this does not happen. Often people refuse to move. They wait for times to improve. The result is a permanent depression in some geographic areas due to labour immobility.*

---

*See Dictionary inclusion for mobility of labour.

In fact in some instances structural unemployment is very closely related to **regional unemployment** too. When an industry concentrated in one area declines as a result of changes in the pattern of demand the whole area becomes full of workers with nothing to do. To illustrate this you simply need to look at a chart showing regional unemployment (such as that in Figure 33.2) and you will notice that in those areas that have rates high above the national average, the local economy had previously been based on one industry which has undergone decline. We will return to this theme in Chapter 33.

From Unemployment Types to Policy

By categorizing unemployment in the ways above, solutions to the various problems become easier to discern. It is clear that the most serious forms of unemployment are those due to a *general* decline in demand – namely cyclical unemployment. In the post-war period advances in economic theory and policy have helped to moderate this cycle in many ways which are discussed in forthcoming chapters.

More specifically, structural, technological, or regional unemployment is due to the decline in demand for a *specific* skill or product. These can be remedied in various ways by attempting to improve regional and occupational mobility. The policies aimed at achieving these ends are discussed in Chapter 33.

Finally, the recognition that frictional and seasonal unemployment exists alters the government's perception of what level of full employment to expect. For example, no government policy would ever aim at 100 per cent of the working population being employed. This theme will be developed in the next section.

Defining Full Employment

As already stated full employment does not mean that everybody is employed. It is obvious that in any dynamic economy some unemployment is unavoidable. The question is, what level of unemployment is unavoidable and at what level does it become a problem?

According to Lord Beveridge's influential work *Full Employment in a Free Society* (published 1944), an unemployment rate of 3 per cent would be compatible with the aims of full employment. His figure allows 1 per cent for frictional unemployment, 1 per cent for seasonal unemployment, and 1 per cent for overseas factors. His inclusion of overseas factors is interesting as many economists ignore the interdependence of one economy's trends with another. Furthermore, Beveridge's target was effectively adhered to during the post-war period in the UK until 1971. However, other formulas of what constitutes full employment are also possible. For example, during the same period of time as we were adhering to Beveridge's criteria, the US employed a different formula. For them post-war full employment represented 96 per cent employment. Their 4 per cent unemployment was to account for frictional unemployment and the various forms of structural unemployment. Yet they, too, have been way off target since 1970.

This raises the question: what does full employment in the 1980s and 1990s represent? Clearly the variables have changed. Technology has improved, more people have entered into the search for work, unemployment benefits have increased, and so on. Consequently neither Britain nor the US have come anywhere near their previous full employment targets in the last decade. The 'correct' level needs to be redefined, but economists are hesitant to do so. The US, under political pressure, has recently suggested a target of 5½ per cent unemployment. In the UK targets of 6 per cent and higher are suggested by politicians.

Economists themselves seem to have become disinterested in this isolated target for employment, and they are presently placing more emphasis on the concept of a **natural rate of unemployment**. This is a constantly moving rate which relates the preferable level of unemployment to that which is compatible with constant prices. It is based on the principle that every market, including labour, has an equilibrium rate. This concept will be discussed in full in Chapter 18 after inflation and related ideas have been explored.

Inflation

The persistent increase in most prices in the United Kingdom has affected all of us. Rising prices now seem as inevitable as death and taxes. We are constantly reminded by newspapers and magazine articles that the pound of twenty years ago is worth only 16p today. In the remainder of this chapter, we will examine what inflation is, how it is measured, and how it affects each of us in our simultaneous roles as consumers, taxpaying citizens, and income earners.

A Definition of Inflation

At the outset, we must have a precise definition of the phenomenon called **inflation**. We will technically define it as a situation in which there is a *sustained* rise in a weighted average of all prices. An alternative definition would be a relatively *persistent* general increase in prices. Notice the emphasis on the words *sustained* and *persistent* in our definitions. A one-time increase in the (weighted) average of all prices is not, under these definitions, an inflationary phenomenon. Rather, it is just a one-off event. When the (weighted) average of all prices is rising year in and year out as it has in the United Kingdom in recent years, that is definitely inflation.

Official measurements of inflation are made monthly by the Department of Employment. They use a technique which involves buying the same 'basket' of goods and services each month, thereby enabling them to assess the purchasing power of money. In recent years to physically buy the goods (which they do not do – they merely get 'price

---

Figure 11.8
Inflation Rates in the UK 1935 –1985

Years	Average annual increase in prices (%)
1935–9	2.1
1953–69	3.3
1970–5	12.0
1976–9	13.5
1980–5	9.0

Key Points 11.3

▶ There are many types of unemployment including frictional, cyclical, seasonal, structural, technological, and regional.

▶ Frictional unemployment occurs because workers do not have all the information necessary about vacancies nor do employers know about all of the qualified workers to fill those vacancies. Consequently, 'job search' time must be allowed for when people wish to change jobs.

▶ Structural unemployment occurs when the demand for a commodity permanently decreases so that workers in an industry are permanently barred from the job they are used to doing.

▶ The level of frictional, seasonal, and/or structural unemployment can be used to arrive at an (arbitrary) definition of full employment.

▶ The various types of unemployment need to be identified in order to consider policy options.

quotations') would have required more and more money, as inflation has become a marked problem. For an historical portrait of inflation rates see Figure 11.8.

Types and Causes of Inflation

There are many different explanations for inflation. Here we will hypothesize that inflation occurs either because an increase in total demand pulls up prices ('demand-pull' inflation) or because an increase in the cost of production pushes up the prices of final products ('cost-push' inflation).

Demand-pull Inflation

When total demand in the economy is rising while the available output of goods is limited, **demand-pull inflation** occurs. Goods and services may be in 'short' supply either because the economy is being fully utilized or because the economy cannot grow fast enough to meet the increasing level of demand. As a result of either, the general level of prices rises. This type of inflation is often experienced as an economy approaches and reaches its full employment level.

Consider the following possibility: total demand rises and the economy gets closer and closer to full capacity output; in fact some firms may well reach full capacity (but not all). Any further increases in demand, especially if experienced by the firms that have reached full capacity, will cause them to raise prices. Moreover, if these firms supply intermediate goods to other firms, then the increased price of these intermediate goods means that the cost of production rises for the firms using those intermediate goods. Thus, increases in demand tend to pull up prices, and hence the term *demand-pull inflation*.

Cost-push Inflation

The **cost-push inflation** theory of price increases has emerged as a popular theory. It attempts to explain why prices rise when the economy is nowhere near full employment. Cost-push inflation apparently explains 'creeping' inflation and the inflation that Britain experienced during the 1973–5 recession. There are essentially three explanations of cost-push inflation: union power, big business power, and higher raw materials prices.

UNION POWER— OR THE 'WAGE - PRICE SPIRAL'

Many people feel that unions are responsible for inflation. Their reasoning is as follows. Unions decide to demand a wage rise that is not warranted by increases in their productivity. Since the unions are so powerful, employers must give in to union demands for higher wages. When the employers have to pay these higher wages, their costs are higher. To maintain their usual profit margin, these business people

raise their prices. This type of cost-push inflation seemingly can occur even when there is no excess demand for goods, and even when the economy is operating below capacity at under full employment.

The union-power argument rests on the unions having a strong hold over their particular labour markets. In terms of evaluating this argument one may resort to statistics on days lost in industrial disputes and trade union memberships. As Figure 11.9 suggests both these variables showed upward trends during the 1970s when inflation became a major problem.

Figure 11.9
Trade Union Power 1972–82. The figures in the right-hand column represent millions of working days lost from industrial disputes in the year concerned. During the 1960s the average number of days lost for similar reasons averaged 3 million. The other figures show the total number of union members at the end of each year. These increased by 2–3 per cent a year between 1972 and 1979 (which is significantly faster than the 1960s), yet since 1979 the number of members has begun to decline quite markedly – between 1979 and 1982 alone there was a 14 per cent decline.

Year	Number of union members	Working days lost (millions)
1972	11 359 000	24
1973	11 459 000	7
1974	11 764 000	15
1975	12 193 000	6
1976	12 386 000	3
1977	12 846 000	10
1978	13 112 000	9
1979	13 289 000	29
1980	12 947 000	12
1981	12 106 000	4
1982	11 445 000	5

Source: Department of Employment Gazette, Jan. and July 1984.

BIG BUSINESS POWER, OR THE 'PRICE - WAGE SPIRAL'

The other variant of the cost-push theory is that inflation is caused when the monopoly power of big business pushes up prices. Powerful corporations are presumably able to raise their prices whenever they want to increase their profits. Each time the corporations raise prices to increase their profits, the cost of living goes up. Workers demand higher wages to make up for the loss in their standard of living, thereby giving the corporations an excuse to raise prices again, and so a vicious price-wage cycle is established.

RAW MATERIALS COST-PUSH INFLATION

Since the 1973 beginning of higher and higher prices for all forms of energy, a relatively new type of cost-push inflation has been suggested. It is raw materials cost-push inflation because the cost of raw materials seems to keep rising all the time. Coal is more expensive, so is petroleum, so is natural gas, and so are many other basic inputs into production processes.

Few economists would deny the impact of the OPEC oil prices in the early 1970s contributing to the inflationary surges experienced by most oil-importing countries in the mid-1970s. In fact it is easy to distinguish an international pattern to inflation in most developed capitalist countries. Figure 11.10 shows the marked peaks around 1975 which followed the quadrupling of oil prices in the 1973–4 period.

SUMMARY AND A MOVE TOWARDS POLICY

Whether it be union power, big business power, or higher prices for raw materials, the resultant increased cost of production pushed prices up; hence the term *cost-push inflation*. One solution offered as a way to stop, or at least slow down, cost-push inflation is wage and price controls. In the UK these controls have largely been employed in the form of **prices and incomes policies**. In 1965 a National Board for Prices and Incomes was established and after monitoring several policies this was abolished in 1971. From 1971 to the late 1970s the emphasis became more focused on controlling incomes directly either through government policy or public sector wage negotiations. In all cases the policies and negotiations proved difficult to manage, and even those policies that were enforced effectively only acted as a stop-gap, temporary measure to curbing inflation. This theme will be returned to in Chapter 30. (Now read Key Points 11.4.)

Measuring Inflation

If inflation is defined as a sustained rise in the general price level, how do we come up with a measure of the rate of inflation? This is indeed a thorny problem for government statisticians. It is easy to determine how much the price of an individual commodity has risen: if last year a light bulb cost 50p and this year it costs 75p, there has been a 50 per cent rise in the price of that light bulb over a one-year period. We can express

Figure 11.10
Inflation Rate in the UK and the Rest of OECD. From this graph it is clear that over the last twenty years, although the trends of inflation have been similar in most OECD countries the UK has experienced a higher than average rate of price inflation. (For a list of these countries the reader should look up OECD in the dictionary at the end of the book.) It is also notable that since 1980 both foreign and UK inflation rates have been falling, but the UK inflation rate has been falling faster.

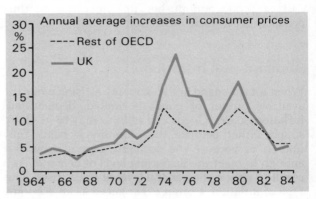

Source: OECD.

the change in the individual light bulb price in one of several ways: (i) the price has gone up 25p; (ii) the price is one-and-a-half (1.5) times as high; (iii) the price has risen by 50 per cent; (iv) by using an index number.

INDEX NUMBERS

An index number of the price rise just discussed is simply the second choice multiplied by 100, that is, the index number would be 150. All we need to do now is select a base year to compare prices.

Computing a Price Index

Of course, the problem becomes more complicated when we are dealing with a large number of goods, some of whose prices have gone up faster than others, and some may have even fallen. What we have to do is

---

Key Points 11.4

▶ **Inflation represents a persistent increase in prices. This has been the UK experience in the post-war period. It became a major problem in the 1970s.**

▶ **Demand-pull inflation occurs when the total demand for goods and services rises faster than the rate of growth of supply.**

▶ **Cost-push inflation is due to one or more of the following: (1) union power, (2) big business power and/or (3) raw materials price increases.**

▶ **Price and incomes policies have been used to attempt the control of inflationary pressure for short periods of time.**

pick a representative selection, a so-called 'basket' of goods and services and compare the cost of that 'basket' of goods and services over time. When we do this, we obtain a **price index**, which is defined as the cost of our representative basket of goods today, expressed as a percentage of the cost of the same basket of goods in some starting, or base, year. In other words,

$$\text{price index} = \frac{\text{cost today of 'basket'}}{\text{cost of 'basket' in base year}} \times 100.$$

A simple numerical example of a price index calculation is given in Figure 11.11. In this example there are only two goods in the basket – corn and microcomputers. The quantities in the basket remain the same between the base year 1980 and 1986. Only the prices change.

STATISTICAL WEIGHTS

So far in this section on measuring inflation we have discussed three goods: light bulbs, corn, and microcomputers. Obviously price rises in corn will affect the general public more than the price rises in light bulbs and microcomputers (especially microcomputers as these are a luxury item). To some extent this was catered for in our simple example by having a larger quantity of corn.

In official measurements, however, each item that is measured is allocated a 'statistical weight' according to its importance for the average family – this is ultimately determined by the percentage of average income that is spent on each good. Therefore, the statistical weight for food will be far higher than that for cigarettes, as changes in food prices affect everybody, whereas cigarette prices only affect smokers.

Real-world Price Indexes

A number of price indexes are used in the United Kingdom. We shall discuss the three official ones that

are most commonly referred to, namely the Retail Price Index, Producer Price Index, and Tax and Price Index.

The Retail Price Index

The most often quoted of all price indexes is the Retail Price Index (RPI). The Department of Employment uses essentially the same techniques as outlined above for this index, but of course they measure the movement of far more prices. In fact, approximately 600 goods and services are 'priced' each month in the various retail outlets up and down the country. This is administered by the 200 or so local employment offices, who end up, between them, with a total of 150 000 price quotations.

These price movements are averaged out for the country as a whole by the Department of Employment. Their relative importance is then accounted for by the average price changes for each group of goods multiplied by the statistical weights. The index is then published in percentage form displaying its monthly change. Some representative figures have already been presented in Figure 11.1

Those 600 items that are chosen for measurement and the statistical weights allocated are meant to represent the *average* households, that is, those in which the main breadwinner is neither a pensioner nor earning an income in excess of £300 per week. In fact, separate price indexes are calculated for pensioners.

The official comments on these various retail price indexes seem keen to stress that *price changes only* are being measured. This is because income tax payments, National Insurance contributions, payments to pension funds, and subscriptions to trade unions etc. are *not* included. The Retail Price Index cannot, therefore, be equally synonymous with a Cost of Living Index. To overcome this problem, to some extent, the Tax and Price Index was introduced in 1979.

Figure 11.11

Calculating a Price Index for a Basket Containing Two Goods Only. In this simplified example, there are only two goods – corn and microcomputers. The base-year quantities and prices are given in columns (2) and (3). The cost of the 1980 basket is calculated in column (4) and totals £1 400. The 1986 prices are given in column (5). The price of the basket in 1986 is calculated in the last column and is £1 700. The price index of 1986 compared to 1980 ends up as 121.43.

(1) Commodity	(2) 1980 basket quantity	(3) 1980 price per unit (£)	(4) Cost of basket in 1980 (£)	(5) 1986 price per unit (£)	(6) Cost of basket at 1986 prices (£)
Corn	100 bushels	4.00	400.00	8.00	800.00
Microcomputers	2	500.00	1 000.00	450.00	900.00
Totals			1 400.00		1 700.00

$$\text{Price index} = \frac{\text{Cost of basket in 1986}}{\text{Cost of basket in base year 1980}} \times = \frac{1\,700.00}{1\,400.00} \times 100 = £121.43$$

The Tax and Price Index (TPI)

This is also published monthly. It attempts to measure the changes in income before tax that Mr Average would need to maintain his purchasing power. For example, if the TPI were 120 Mr Average would need a 20 per cent increase in gross income compared to his base-year income (1978) to maintain his standard of living. To undertake this calculation the Retail Price Index is combined with changes in an employee's direct tax liability (including his National Insurance contributions).

The Tax and Price Index may be promoted, therefore, as a more comprehensive index. Yet non-taxpayers such as pensioners and those with high incomes are again excluded from the calculations. Furthermore, many regard the introduction of this index as a purely political tool, as the Conservative governments in office from 1979 onwards were committed to switching from direct to indirect taxation. This inevitably played havoc with the Retail Price Index which measures prices inclusive of any indirect taxes. They hoped, therefore, to switch people's attention to the more favourable Tax and Price Index which would highlight their reduced direct tax burden. As it turned out, however, the Retail Price Index is still the one that most commentators refer to. A possible explanation for this traditional preference is that the idea of an 'average income-earner' is less relevant than the idea of 'an average shopping-basket' that everyone spends on.

The Producer Price Index

The **Producer Price Index** (PPI), formerly called the Wholesale Price Index (until August 1983) is similar to the RPI in terms of how it is calculated. The PPI measures changes in the average prices of goods sold in primary markets by producers of commodities in all stages of processing. Price quotations for about 10 000 items representative of goods purchased and manufactured by the UK industrial sector are used. This constitutes the entire 'basket' for calculating the PPI. Just as the RPI is organized into categories which are weighted according to importance, so too is the PPI.

Often journalists and economists – as well as government officials – will make note of an increase in the PPI because it represents the prices of goods in their earlier stages of production. The reasoning is that if the PPI goes up an increase in later months may well be signalled in the RPI.

The Accuracy of Price Indexes

There is continuous debate about how accurate the measured price indexes really are. Do we have an accurate view of the 'rate' of inflation? We cannot answer that question completely, but we can point out the potential biases in the two main price indexes that the government actually uses.

The Retail Price Index and the Producer Price Index allow for comparisons between years. The latter index uses base-year quantities evaluated at today's prices. Yet, is there sufficient attempt to find out if the actual quantities purchased by the average consumer changes through the years? In the case of the PPI the answer is negative. The basket of goods used at the time of writing dates back to 1979. However, in the case of the RPI, the answer is more positive. Each January the statistical weights of the basket of goods and services are revised. This revision is based on information arising from the annual Family Expenditure Survey, which is undertaken by about 6 500 homes in the UK each year.

More important, perhaps, is the bias imparted to these two indexes because of improper accounting for changes in quality. For example, at the same nominal price a good is actually cheaper if its quality has been improved. Conversely, at the same nominal price a good is actually more expensive if its quality has fallen. It is difficult for government statisticians to take quality into account.

It is also difficult for government statisticians to take into account at once the introduction of new

---

Key Points 11.5

▶ Once we pick a 'basket' of goods, we can construct a price index which compares the cost of that basket today with the cost of the same basket in a base year.

▶ The Retail Price Index (RPI) is the most often used price index in the UK. The Producer Price Index (PPI) is the second most often mentioned. The latter gives information on changes in the weighted average of the prices of goods sold in primary markets by producers of commodities (goods sold at wholesale). Finally, there is also the new and rather underrated Tax and Price Index.

▶ All price indexes suffer from certain inaccuracies. For example, they have a hard time taking into account quality changes and the 'baskets' may not always be entirely representative of the purchases actually made.

products, such as personal home computers, compact discs, and other consumer products that may not have been widely marketed when the original basket of goods was surveyed during the base year. But as we have noted the composition of the basket measured by the RPI is adjusted annually.

The Effects of Inflation

Everybody complains about inflation. Just about everybody assumes that inflation is 'bad'. In order to determine how bad it is for you, you have to figure out what happens to earnings during inflation, what happens to the value of the things you own and the debts you owe. In a moment we shall examine these general effects, but first it will help if we distinguish between 'anticipated' and 'unanticipated' inflation.

We define **unanticipated inflation** as that inflation rate which comes as a surprise, as it were, to individuals in the economy – or at least to the majority of them. For example, if the inflation rate in a particular year turns out to be 10 per cent when the majority of people thought it was going to be 5 per cent, there will have been unanticipated inflation – or an inflation greater than that which was anticipated.

Anticipated inflation is that rate of inflation that the majority of individuals believe will occur. If the rate of inflation this year turns out to be 10 per cent, and that is about what most people thought it was going to be, then we are in a situation of fully anticipated inflation. Many of the problems caused by inflation are due to the fact that it is unanticipated. For when it is anticipated, some people are able to protect themselves from its 'ravages'. With this distinction between anticipated and unanticipated inflation in mind, we can move on to see the relationship between inflation and interest rates.

Inflation Effects and Interest Rates

Let us start in a hypothetical world in which there is no inflation and no anticipated inflation. In that world, you may be able to borrow – in order to buy a house or a car – at some **nominal, or market, rate of interest** of, say, 6 per cent. If you borrow the money to purchase a house or a car and your anticipation of inflation turns out to be accurate, then you will not have been fooled, and the lender will not have been fooled either. The money you pay back in the years to come to pay the interest on that loan will be just as valuable in terms of purchasing power as the money that you borrowed.

But what about a situation in which you borrow at 6 per cent and the following year there is unanticipated inflation of, say, 6 per cent? Lucky you! For you will be able to pay back the lender in pounds that are depreciating at the rate of 6 per cent a year. In effect, the **real rate of interest** that you will be paying will fall to practically zero. But of course, the lender will not be

quite so happy. Consequently, if you, the lender, and everyone else now anticipate that inflation will remain at 6 per cent per year, the next time the lender offers a loan, he or she will add on a 6 per cent inflationary premium to cover the depreciation in the purchasing power of the pounds repaid by borrowers.

CREDITORS LOSE AND DEBTORS GAIN WITH UNANTICIPATED INFLATION

Now you are in a position to understand why creditors lose and debtors gain with unanticipated inflation. In the above example, unanticipated inflation caused the debtor to benefit. Why? Because the debtor was not initially charged a nominal, or market, interest rate that covered the rate of inflation that actually occurred. Why? Because the lender did not anticipate inflation correctly. The point to understand is that creditors lose and debtors gain whenever inflation rates are *underestimated* for the life of a loan. In the last several decades, there have been apparently periods in which there was considerable unanticipated inflation – as in the late 1960s, early 1970s, and the late 1970s. When we say unanticipated inflation, we mean higher-than-anticipated inflation. During those years, creditors did, on balance, lose, and debtors did, on balance gain.

In general, the elderly are net creditors because they have paid off their mortgages and have built up savings. They are hurt by unanticipated inflation. On the other hand, younger people who are borrowing a lot for homes, cars, and the like are net debtors and therefore have been beneficiaries of recent periods of unanticipated inflation.

It is, of course, possible that the rate of inflation be overestimated. When unanticipated inflation is therefore negative, creditors gain and debtors lose. Some economists argue that the abrupt drop in the rate of inflation in 1983, for example, created just such a situation.

Obviously, whenever inflation is correctly anticipated by both creditors and debtors, neither class of individuals loses (or gains).

Inflation Effects on Fixed Income Earners

Besides the transfer of wealth from creditors to debtors during periods of unanticipated inflation, there is a similar redistribution of income away from those on fixed incomes. Fixed incomes constitute student grants, old age pensions, dole money, and long-term contracts. Inevitably these payments do not cater for unanticipated inflation. Consequently, persons who are solely dependent on fixed incomes lose purchasing power during periods of inflation. Indeed, even during periods of anticipated inflation these groups are in a weak negotiating position, and for most of them the only hope is that the annual review of their situation will help them catch up.

The only exceptions to this fixed income effect are those who have negotiated index-linked contracts. This is becoming more and more common for those who work on long-term contracts, and also for some pension schemes. Index-linking, basically links income changes to movements in the Retail Price Index, thereby overcoming problems of leaving people on totally fixed incomes as inflation increases.

Inflation Effects on Business Environment

Some economists believe that the main cost of an unanticipated inflation is the resources used to protect against inflation, and the distortions introduced as firms attempt to plan for the long run. In other words, business men have to spend time and resources to figure out ways to 'cover themselves' in case inflation is different from what it has been in the past. This may involve spending a longer time working out more complicated contracts for employment, for purchases of goods in the future, and for purchases of raw materials, or it may simply make any business decision impossible. The outcome is that business becomes more complex, expectations alter, and many firms may falter during inflationary periods. These problems are further compounded when the businesses concerned are heavily involved with imports or exports as exchange rates have to be estimated and these too are affected by inflation.

Inflation Effects on Holding Cash

Most individuals carry some cash in their wallets in the form of notes. Many individuals keep bank accounts that may average several hundred or even several thousand pounds. All of us use some form of cash and/ or bank account balance because of the convenience they provide. All of us therefore lose value whenever there is inflation. That is, the purchasing power of the cash held in our wallets or bank account balances falls at the rate of inflation.

Take a simple example. Assume that you have stashed £100 away underneath your mattress. If, by the end of one year, there has been an increase in inflation of 10 per cent, the purchasing power of that £100 will be only about £90. You will have lost value equal to the 10 per cent times the amount of cash you kept on hand. In essence, then, the value of the cash we keep on hand depreciates at the rate of inflation. The only way we can avoid this type of inflationary tax, as it were, on the cash that we hold is by reducing our cash balances and purchasing valuable objects that will retain their value. Or by moving any spare cash into index-linked saving schemes.

Key Points 11.6

▶ Whenever inflation is greater than anticipated, creditors lose and debtors gain.

▶ Whenever the rate of inflation is less than anticipated, creditors gain and debtors lose.

▶ Individuals on fixed incomes are clearly hurt by inflation.

▶ Business men become involved in protecting themselves against unanticipated inflation. This imposes a resource cost in terms of time and often entails problems of forecasting, especially if exchange rates are involved.

▶ Holders of cash will lose during periods of inflation because the purchasing power of their cash depreciates at the rate of inflation.

CASE STUDY

The Labour Market

Labour is bought and sold almost like anything else and can be analysed as if it were any commodity. The following extract will help highlight this point.

Markets are made up of a supply side and a demand side. On the one hand there are suppliers of labour – those who wish to sell their labour for a wage. And on the other hand there are the demanders of labour – those who wish to hire workers and pay wages.

Supply
From the point of view of suppliers the amount of labour for sale will depend upon:

(a) the financial reward for working
(b) the taste for leisure, and
(c) the number of persons in the working age-group.

We can represent the supply side of the market by a supply curve. This curve takes (b) and (c) as given and shows how the supply of man-hours of labour increases as the wage-rate is increased. This supply curve is shown in Figure 11.12.

The upward-sloping line represents the case when population, unemployment benefit and 'tastes' remain constant. The whole line will move if any of these are changed. If, for example, there is a decrease in unemployment benefit, the need to work will increase and the curve will move to the right. Hence for any given wage there will be more man-hours offered. Some point on this line has been adjudged to represent the potential 'workforce'. The potential 'workforce' will of course depend on the position of the supply curve *and* the choice of a point on it.

Demand
The demand curve for labour depends upon the employment decisions of employers. The employer's aim is to make profits, and he will hire someone only if he 'makes' more than he costs. His 'cost' to the employer is the wage-rate which must be paid. At very high wages there are few employees who can make enough to cover their costs. But as the wage-rate falls more and more employees become profitable. The demand curve for labour will therefore slope downwards as shown in Figure 11.13.

If employers find the demand for their products falling then they will be unable to employ many workers and the whole demand curve moves to the left. On the other hand, if workers become more productive – say by becoming skilled – then they 'make' more and at any given wage more of them would be profitable. In this case, the whole demand curve moves to the right.

Demand and Supply
In the usual way of economists, we can superimpose these two diagrams onto one and yield the market diagram. This is shown in Figure 11.14.

We can see that the market for labour will 'clear' at wage-rate W^* and employment L^*. (The market is said to be clear when the amount supplied equals the amount demanded.)

Thus in this model there will be an employed labour force of L^* and a workforce of $\bar{L}$ (L^* is also called the 'natural rate' of employment). We can now begin to understand our 'facts'. The employed labour force depends upon the shapes and positions of both the supply curve and the demand curve. The workforce is determined solely by the supply curve.

Source: pp 37–9. *Economic Review*. Vol. 2 No. 1, Sept. 1984. D. Heathfield 'Facts, Theories and Economic Policies'.

Figure 11.12

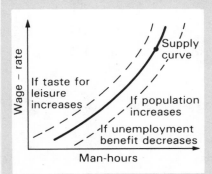

Figure 11.13

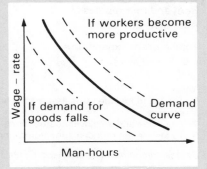

Figure 11.14

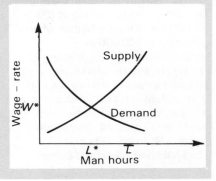

Questions
1. The analysis presented above suggests that there is a certain amount of voluntary unemployment in the labour market.

(a) Identify this voluntary unemployment on the diagram.
(b) Consider whether any other forms of unemployment may exist within this category

identified as voluntary unemployment.
2. What forces does this supply and demand type approach to the labour market overlook?

CASE STUDY

The Economic Costs of Unemployment: (A Secret Affair?)

Apart from the psychological and social costs of unemployment that one can read about in the popular press – several economic costs exist too! Unfortunately explicit information on these economic costs is hard to come by. The Treasury published an estimate of the cost of an increase in unemployment by 100 000 in 1980–81. This gave rise to a similar exercise carried out by the Manpower Services Commission (MSC) for the year 1981–82. However, since then, despite direct requests from members of parliament, no official up-dating of these figures has been carried out (although it is thought that the treasury may have some unpublished information).

Consequently the following extract is largely based on the original rather obsolete data. The case study questions that follow, however, redress the balance by helping us to consider how far we can project and use this type of information in today's terms.

The Treasury's original costing exercise involved looking at the direct cost to the Exchequer of an increase of 100 000 in unemployment in the private sector. This exercise took into account losses of income tax and national insurance contributions, the payment of various benefits and their related administration costs, and so on. In fact the detailed chart presented by the treasury economists is laid out in Figure 11.15.

It is evident from this information that in 1980–81 an increase in the number of people out of work by 100 000 would have a *direct* cost to the exchequer of £340 million (i.e. £3 400 per year for each unemployed person).

The MSC estimate for the following year (1981–1982) worked out that every extra person drawing unemployment benefit cost the Exchequer £4 380 a year. This higher figure was to a large extent accounted for by the MSC including the loss of indirect taxes – such as VAT – since they

Figure 11.15
Direct Exchequer Costs of an increase of 100 000 in Registered Unemployment (Excluding School-Leavers) in 1980–81. At 1980–81 out-turn prices

	Exchequer costs for 1980–81 (£m)
Monies Lost in Revenue	
Income Tax[1]	115
National insurance contributions[2]	75
National insurance surcharge	15
Total	205
Expenditure Incurred[3]	
National insurance benefits (including earnings related supplement)	65
Other social security benefits	55
Rent and rate rebates	5
Administrative costs	10
Total current expenditure	135
Exchequer cost	340

Notes
1. The fall in income tax is assumed to be 23 per cent of the fall in wages and salaries.
2. Employee and employer contributions.
3. Totals are the rounded sum of unrounded components.

Source: Economic Progress Report, Feb. 1981.

assumed that the unemployed worker will spend less than they would if working.

Questions

1. The above estimates discuss *'direct'* costs. Can you define this concept in the context of the above exercise?
2. Added to the economic costs discussed above there are the less measurable psychological and social costs; technically these can be regarded as the indirect or external costs of unemployment.
   (a) What external costs of unemployment can you think of?
   (b) Could you put some monetary values to these?
   (c) Could Government economists take into account these indirect costs.
3. As suggested in the introduction to this Case Study the official available figures are rather dated. Can you change these costs into more recent terms? (Hint: you will need a series of up-to-date inflation figures, such as the Department of Employment Gazette or similar publication.)
4. What problems are there in forecasting today's Exchequer costs for unemployment by simply projecting forward from 1981 data, as suggested in question 3.
5. Could you estimate the *total* direct cost of unemployment for the current year? (Hint: Two economists at Edinburgh University – N. Fraser and A. Sinfield – calculated the total direct Exchequer costs of unemployment in 1984/85 to be approximately £20 billion, i.e. £6600/person).
6. (a) Why do you think the Treasury were hesitant to up-date their figures during the years 1981–86?
   (b) Has there been any up-dating since these years?

CASE STUDY

Top Managers' Pay Soars

Britain's top managers enjoyed pay rises up to 25 per cent last year, well over three times the national average pay settlement.

Dick Giordano, the chairman of BOC, emerged as the highest-paid British executive for the second year running, with £772000, 48 per cent up on 1983. This year, Giordano is set to be the first director of a British company to break £1m.

In a survey of the 100 highest-paid directors, produced by Datastream, the City research body, the average pay rose nearly £30000 last year to £156000 (see Figure 11.16). Even Giordano's rise was dwarfed by other well-known City figures. Ralph Halpern of the Burton Group took his pay to £348000, a rise of 75 per cent and Trevor Chinn, the chairman of Lex Services, was not far behind with a 62 per cent rise. John Harvey-Jones, the ICI chairman, matched the 67 per cent growth in his

company profits with a 68 per cent increase in earnings.

The biggest increase went to Michael Ashcroft, the Hawley chairman – a climb of 114 per cent to £199000. The secretive merchant banks did very well on the back of takeover fever and the government privatisation programme. An unnamed director of Kleinwort Benson, bankers to the British Telecom issue, had a 96 per cent rise to £186000. Another anonymous director, at Hill Samuel, had a 92 per cent increase to take his pay to £242000.

The top British executives still have a long way to go to catch their American counterparts. T Boone Pickens, the celebrated Wall Street corporate raider, topped the American business pay league last year, with total remunerations of £19m as chairman of Mesa Petroleum. This is nearly 100 times the amount paid to the two top British oil company directors, Sir

Peter Walters at BP and Sir Peter Baxendell at Shell Transport.

More conventional American executives are far better paid than their British counterparts. Philip Caldwell, the chairman of Ford, received over £4m last year. Yet the head of his British operation, Sam Toy, received just £157000 – albeit a 67 per cent rise on the previous year. Many British companies with large American subsidiaries, such as Reed International, are having to pay directors of local American offshoots more than their British chairmen.

This will only add to the competitive strain on British companies to hold on to their best people, forecasts Barry Curnow, managing director of Hay-MSL, management consultancy. 'There's nothing specific to the UK about the talents of a John Harvey-Jones. That man would be earning several million dollars a year in America,' he says. Not all the top earners

continued overleaf

head public companies. Gerald Ronson, the chairman of the privately owned Heron group, paid himself £446000 last year, a modest increase on his 1983 earnings of £438000.

British managers do not do so badly in comparison with politicians and executives in nationalised industries. Mrs Thatcher's salary is £53600, though she draws only £42980, the same as her cabinet ministers. Ordinary MPs make do with £16904. A full general or admiral does a little better, drawing £45500, while Robin Leigh-Pemberton, the governor of the Bank of England, earns £82000.

Salaries of the chairmen of nationalised industries can vary from the £44600 for Fred Clarke of Royal Ordnance to well over £120000 in the case of the late Sir William Duncan at Rolls-Royce.

For a few of the top British earners in the Datastream survey, a pay increase is just loose change. Tiny Rowland of Lonrho may earn £323000 from the company but his 45m shares in the company netted him well over £4m in dividends. And the value of that shareholding is around £76m.

Source: The Sunday Times, 19 May 1985

Questions

1. There are many causes of inflation. Which ones do the statistics in the article and Figure 11.16 suggest may arise in the late 1980s?
2. What is unusual about the suggestion that directors' salaries may cause inflation, and do you think it is right or wrong?
3. What other economic consequences may the structure of directors' salaries have on our economy?
4. What other statistics would you like to aid your interpretation of these questions?

Figure 11.16
Big League Bosses: The Top 100 and How They Performed

	Name	Company	1984 salary £'000	% pay increase 1983–4	% rise in pre-tax profits		Name	Company	1984 salary £'000	% pay increase 1983–4	% rise in pre-tax profits
1	Dick Giordano	BOC	772	48	30	52	Roger Foster	ACT	127	74	150
2	N Stewart & B Christopher	BSR	526	6	29	53	Sir Austin Pearce	British Aero	125	43	46
3	Gerald Ronson	Heron	446	2	53	54	Derek Birkin	RTZ	124	9	16
4	Ralph Halpern	Burton	348	75	44	55	Phillip Birch	Ward White	124	19	80
5	Tiny Roland	Lonrho	323	22	19	56	David Rowland	Steward Wrightson	122	37	27
6	Trevor Chinn	Lex	308	62	24	57	Dominic Cadbury	Cadbury Schweppes	121	37	27
7	Sir Kenneth Corfield	STC	297	48	53	58	Stanley Kalms	Dixons	121	–5	16
8	John Harvey-Jones	ICI	287	68	677	59	Howard Hicks	IDC Group	121	14	50
9	W Sinsheimer	Plessey	248	6	20	60	Peter Levene	USH	121	–14	–20
10	Sir Peter Walters	BP	242	32	33	61	David Plaistow	Vickers	121	49	63
11	—	Hill Samuel	242	92	—	62	Sir Kenneth Durham	Unilever	120	49	63
12	Sir Peter Baxendell	Shell Transport	210	4	32	63	Carol Mosselmans	Sedgwick	119	–6	–2
13	Patrick Sheehy	BAT	200	33	43	64	—	Standard Charter	119	25	8
14	Alan Woltz	LRC	200	28	25	65	—	Marley	118	–19	18
15	Michael Ashcroft	Hawley	199	114	121	66	Phillip Wilkinson	Nat West	118	19	18
16	—	Tate & Lyle	198	46	21	67	Lord Weinstock	GEC	116	4	—
17	—	Kleinworts	186	96	—	68	Manny Fogel	Home Charm	116	23	57
18	Arnold Lorbeer	Ultramar	182	23	84	69	John Beckett	Woolworths	114	—	45
19	Lord Hanson	Hanson	177	26	86	70	Sir Jeremy Morse	Lloyds Bank	113	6	12
20	Sir Arthur Bryan	Wedgwood	174	61	266	71	Derek Palmer	Bass	112	10	25
21	Sir Graham Wilkins	Beacham	172	12	13	72	Geoffrey Taylor	Midland Bank	112	18	66
22	—	Ass Newspapers	169	28	37	73	John West	Reckitt & Colman	110	12	19
23	Lord Roll	Mercury Sec	164	45	—	74	James Longcroft	Tricentrol	110	13	–11
24	Chris Greentree	LASMO	159	46	25	75	Cecil Harris	Commercial Union	109	10	—
25	Lord Rayner	Marks & Spencer	159	322	17	76	David Palmer	Willis Faber	109	13	24
26	Murray Gordon	Comb Eng Stores	156	95	240	77	Sir Lawrie Barratt	Barratt Dev	108	–22	31
27	Geoffrey Kent	Imps	156	12	13	78	Sir William Barlow	BICC	108	6	10
29	Ephraim Margulles	S & W Berlsford	152	49	43	80	—	Prudential	108	93	4
30	Sir Ernest Harrison	Racal	152	3	4	81	Aylmer Lenton	Bowater	107	15	–47
31	Saatchi Bros	Saatchi & Saatchi	152	8	82	82	Sir Derrick Holden-Brown	Allied-Lyons	106	18	22
32	Ernest Saunders	Guinness	151	36	19	83	Peter Cowell	Dubilier	106	54	83
33	Rudolph Agnew	Cons Gold	148	17	17	84	—	Dalgety	105	10	29
34	Peter Laister	Thorn EMI	147	28	29	85	Samuel Oxford	Magnet & Southerns	105	17	33
35	Raymond Miquel	Arthur Bell	145	20	13	86	—	Sears	105	36	41
36	Stanley Grinstead	Grand Met	144	30	13	87	—	Farnell	104	14	60
37	Roy Messervy	Lucas	144	8	1550	88	Colin Corness	Redland	104	25	45
38	Sir Owen Green	BTR	142	46	66	89	Alastair Morton	Guinness Peat	102	62	—
39	—	Glaxo	142	35	31	90	Jimmy Gulliver	Argyll Group	101	–23	54
40	—	Howden Group	142	29	10	91	Stephen Marks	French Connection	100	75	300
41	Sir Eric Sharp	Cables & Wireless	137	22	21	92	Kenneth Horne	Robert Horne	100	—	48
42	Vernon Brink	Rothmans	137	19	15	93	Sir Jeffrey Sterling	P&O	100	32	23
43	Peter Goodall	Hepworth Ceramic	136	6	3	94	Lord & Rocco Forte	THF	100	32	23
44	Eric Parker	Trafalgar House	135	22	43	95	Dr Peter Main	Boots	99	22	18
45	Sir Timothy Bevan	Barclays	133	7	18	96	George Helsby & Eric Grayson	Burnett & Hallam	99	15	–70
46	Sir Trevor Holdsworth	GKN	132	14	36	97	Sir Christopher Hogg	Courtaulds	99	27	87
47	John Kerridge	Fisons	131	17	55	98	Sir Robin Cater & John Connell	Distillers	99	–5	–4
48	Denis Allport	Metal Box	131	41	35	99	David Wickins	BCA	98	8	50
49	Michael Gifford	Rank	131	64	36	100	Chris Bryant	Bryant Holdings	98	8	37
50	—	Laing Properties	130	94	18						
51	—	Reed	129	25	57						

Source: The Sunday Times (Business News), 19 May 1985 by P. Beresford.

Exam Preparation and Practice

MULTIPLE CHOICE QUESTIONS

One or more of the options given in Questions 1 and 2 may be correct. Select your answer by means of the code set out in the grid:

A	B	C	D	E
1,2,3 correct	1 & 2 only	2 & 3 only	1 only	3 only

1. A rise in house prices can be caused by
   1 a decline in house building
   2 an increase in lending by building societies
   3 a rise in mortgage rates

2. Cost-push inflation may occur, other things remaining equal, as a result of
   1 higher import prices
   2 higher domestic wage rates
   3 higher consumer spending

3. The Tax and Prices Index will rise at a faster rate than the Retail Price Index if there is an increase in
   A Value Added Tax
   B income tax allowances
   C specific import duties
   D standard rate of income tax

4. Which group would *not* be included in the official definition of the working population
   A school-leavers on a Youth Training Scheme
   B people who are overseas in the British Army
   C someone claiming unemployment benefit
   D married women who register themselves as available for temporary work with a commercial agency
   E persons over retirement age but still working

5. Which one of the following policies is most likely to *reduce* the level of structural unemployment
   A reduce the level of interest rates
   B lower unemployment benefits
   C increase the level of consumer expenditure
   D increasing research and development grants for technology
   E increasing labour mobility

6. Which group would *not* normally be included in the official (unadjusted) unemployment figures
   A persons temporarily laid off
   B unemployed school-leavers
   C persons over sixty seeking work and claiming benefit
   D persons who are claiming benefit and working illegally
   E a student signing on for benefit and work during his holidays

RELATED ESSAY QUESTIONS

1. What economic grounds exist for government intervention in an economy? Describe and explain the forms which such intervention may take.

2. Discuss the economic argument that government should curb the power of trade unions.

3. Discuss the statement that 'inflation is undesirable only if it runs at a higher rate than in other countries'.

4. What are the main characteristics and causes of unemployment in the UK at present? What are the costs of unemployment to the economy?

5. 'The costs incurred from the current level of unemployment in the United Kingdom are unacceptably high.' Discuss.

12 The Circular Flow of Income, Output, and Expenditure

Key Points to Review

▶ Factors of production (1.1)

▶ Money as a medium of exchange (2.3)

▶ Trade-off of consumer goods and capital goods (2.4)

▶ Equilibrium, surplus, shortage (5.7)

Questions for Preview

1 How do economists define profit?

2 Why does total income equal total output?

3 How does the existence of economy-wide saving and investment affect our simple circular flow model?

4 What happens to an economy if the total planned rate of production exceeds the total planned rate of expenditures?

We now make a distinct move into pure macro-economics – 'the world of totals'. You have already been introduced to the basic idea that goods and services are produced by bringing together various factors of production. The **total output** (production) that arises is organized in millions of firms (owned by the public or private sector). The **total expenditure** on these goods and services emanates from millions of households (both at home and abroad). In this chapter we shall analyse the interrelationship of these various economic units (i.e. firms and households) to understand how a country arrives at a certain level of output, expenditure, and income. Therefore, we shall begin to appreciate how the behaviour of one sector of the economy directly affects another.

The ideas developed here have already been briefly encountered in Chapter 2, where the circular flow for a monetary economy was introduced. We shall now build on this model and thereby provide an important framework for our interpretation of the forthcoming chapters on understanding how to measure and manipulate economic activity.

The Simple Circular Flow

To *begin* our detailed analysis of the circular flow of income we ignore the government sector, the financial institutions sector, and the overseas sector. Technically such a model economy could be called a closed economy with no government sector. That is, it represents a simplified starting-point in which we analyse only the relationships between households and businesses. The complications of the real world will be built in later. (To appreciate the need for such modelling consider the chaos if we started by discussing all the interrelated sectors at once as illustrated in Figure 12.3.) Consider briefly Figure 12.1 therefore as our starting-point.

To make our starting model effective it is *assumed*: that households receive their income by selling the use of whatever factors of production they own, that businesses sell their entire output immediately to households, and that households spend their entire income on consumer products. These assumptions are reasonably realistic. Businesses will only make what they can sell. Production will involve buying in land, labour, capital, and enterprise, and these factor (of production) services will generate their respective income payments: rent, wages, interest, and profit.

The concept of the circular flow of income as outlined has identified three basic principles:

(i)   *In every economic exchange, the seller receives exactly the same amount that the buyer spends.*

(ii) *Goods and services flow in one direction and money flows in the other.*

(iii) *There is a close relationship between income, output and expenditure.*

These principles are laid out in their traditional format in Figure 12.1.

Figure 12.1

The Circular Flow of Income. This diagram shows a simple economy comprised of only households and businesses. The two upper flows indicate the **product markets** wherein businesses provide *final* consumer goods and services to households (upper clockwise loop) that pay for them with money (upper anti-clockwise loop). The monetary value of these consumer goods is referred to as *total expenditure*. The two lower flows indicate the **factor markets**, wherein households exchange their factor services with businesses (lower clockwise loop) that pay for them with money (lower anti-clockwise loop). The total household receipts for services is referred to as *total income*.

Money represented in the outer loops flows anti-clockwise – from businesses to households to businesses and so on, highlighting the circular flow of income (and expenditure). Thus one man's income can be considered as another man's expenditure and vice versa.

The inner loop indicates that total output is identical to total income because for every factor involved in output there is an income: rent for the landowner, wages for the labourer, interest for the provider of capital, and profit for the entrepreneur. Again there is a circular flow involved.

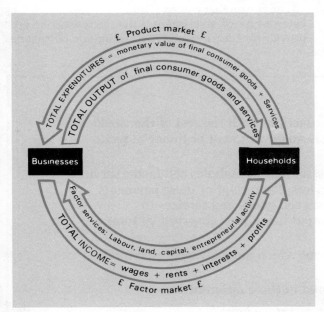

From Figure 12.1 it is possible to appreciate that the amount of economic activity in an economy can be measured in three ways:

1. By adding up the value of all the goods and services produced (in given period of time).
2. By adding up the value of all the income received (during that time-period).
3. By adding up the value of all the spending that occurred (during that period of time).

In each case the result obtained should be identical as

total income ≡ total production ≡ total expenditure.

These symmetrical identities will be discussed below.

NOTE ON PROFITS

We have indicated in Figure 12.1 that profit is a cost of production. You are probably under the impression that profits are not part of the cost of producing goods and services; but profits are indeed a part of this cost because entrepreneurs must be rewarded for providing their services, or they will not provide them. Their reward, if any, is profit. The reward – that is, the profit – is included in the cost of the factors of production. If there were no expectation of profit, entrepreneurs would not incur the risk associated with the organization of productive activities. That is why we consider profits a cost of doing business.

*Total Income ≡ Total Output ≡ Total Expenditure

On the arrow that goes from businesses to households in Figure 12.1 are the words *total income*. What would be a good definition of **total income**? If you answered 'the total of all individuals' income', you would be right. But all income is actually a payment for something, whether it be wages paid for labour services, rent paid for the use of land, interest paid for the use of capital, or profits paid to entrepreneurs. It is the amount paid to the resource suppliers. Total income, therefore, can be alternatively defined as the annual cost of producing the entire output of *final* goods and services. In other words, another method for calculating the level of economic activity would be to sum up the value of all the output generated in that year. Either way the result should be identical as all output generates income and vice versa.

Notice that we have stressed the word *final*. That is because we are referring to the actual goods and services that consumers consume. An example of a final good would be a loaf of bread. Many things went into making that loaf of bread, such as wheat and salt.

---

* The symbol ≡ means 'is identical with'. It is used to distinguish an identity from an equation. An identity is a relationship that is always equal, as a matter of definition.

The wheat and salt are not considered final goods because they are not consumed themselves, but rather used in the production of some other good. Remember in this chapter and in the next that income, expenditure, and output measurements relate to *final* goods and services.

On the arrow going from households to businesses are the words *total expenditure*. Now what would be your definition of **total expenditure**? Would it not involve the aggregate (total) of everything that was spent? Yes, it would. Total expenditure then can be formally defined as the total monetary value of all the *final* goods and services bought in the simple economy that we are considering. Alternatively, this spending can be regarded as total business receipts from the sale of all goods and services produced by these businesses and consumed by all households. These business receipts, of course, are the opposite side of household expenditures; when households *purchase* goods and services with money, that money becomes a business *receipt*. In every transaction, there is an expenditure and a receipt. Therefore one man's income (receipt) is another man's expenditure and vice versa. Consequently economic activity can be measured/calculated by summing up income or expenditure – the answer should be the same in either case. (See Key Points 12.1.)

The Circular flow with Saving, and Investment

Saving

Now we wish to take account of the‚ fact that not everything that is earned by households is spent on goods and services. Rather, households do save part of their income. **Saving** can be defined as the act of *not* consuming. Whatever is not consumed is, by definition, saved. Thus, the rate of saving by households in this simplified model is the difference between total income and household consumption expenditures.

Investment

When economists refer to investment, they are referring to additions to productive capacity. **Investment** may be thought of as an activity that uses resources now in such a way that they allow for greater production in the future and, hence, greater consumption in the future. When a business buys new equipment or puts up a new factory, it is investing; it is increasing its capacity to produce in the future.

The lay person's notion of investment often relates to the purchase of stocks and shares. For our purposes, such transactions simply represent the *transfer of ownership* of assets called stocks and shares. Thus, you must keep in mind the fact that investment in economics refers *only* to additions to productive capacity.

THE TWO COMPONENTS OF INVESTMENT

In our analysis we will consider the two basic components of investment. We have already mentioned the first one, which involves a firm buying equipment. This is known as a **capital good**. A capital good is simply a good that is purchased not to be consumed in its current form but to be used in order to make other goods and services. The purchase of equipment and factories – capital goods – is called **fixed investment**.

The other type of investment has to do with the change in stocks of raw materials and finished goods. Firms do not immediately sell off all their products to consumers. Some of the final product is usually held in warehouses waiting to be sold. Firms hold stocks to meet future expected orders for their products. When a firm does increase its amount of stock of finished products it is engaging in what may be called investment in working capital. **Working capital** consists of all finished goods on hand, goods in process, and raw materials. In short, goods not yet used up in production.

The reason that we can think of a change in stock as being a type of investment is that increases one year provide for future increased consumption possibilities

---

Key Points 12.1

▶ A closed economy is one which has no transactions with the rest of the world. In *our* rather simplified starting model there is no government of financial sector either.

▶ The simple circular flow model highlights: (a) that households sell factor services to businesses that pay for those factor services, the receipt of these payments generating total incomes: (b) that businesses sell goods and services to households that pay for them, the total output being thus absorbed by total expenditure.

▶ Total income must always equal total output which must always equal total expenditure.

▶ Economic activity can therefore be measured in three different ways.

another year. In fact stock changes are a good indicator to business prospects.

If a firm's planned output is greater than actual sales, it will have to indulge in unplanned stock building and vice versa. This, in turn, will affect production plans in the forthcoming year.

(Finally, it may be interesting to note that the unplanned increases or decreases in stock enable the accounting identities of expenditure, output, and income to be maintained. In accounting terms what is produced is always bought if not by the households (this year) then by the businesses themselves. Conversely, when households desire more than is made in a particular year stocks are run down, disinvestment occurs. And once more, in accounting terms, the relationship between income, expenditure, and output is maintained.)

Saving and Investing Linked by Financial Institutions

What are the resources necessary for investment? And from where do they come? Basically, they come from saving that in our simplified example is provided by households. (Businesses can save, too, and thereby provide themselves with the funds necessary for investment, but for the moment we will ignore business saving.) The saving that households do each year is not directly handed over to the businesses wishing to engage in investment. Rather, the flow of saving passes through various financial institutions. These institutions include, but are not limited to, commercial banks, insurance companies, pension plans, building societies, and the stock market. In essence, households are providing funds through the financial market from which businesses obtain funds, which then become expenditures for things they invest in.

Here we can see more clearly, then, the link between saving and investment. Saving is identically equal to forgone current consumption. But since saving in our model is funnelled through financial institutions into investment, then there is a clear connection between investment and forgone current consumption.

Figure 12.2 is, therefore, a more accurate representation of the circular flow: it takes into account saving and investment.

Savings can be formally regarded as a **leakage** (sometimes termed *withdrawals*) from the circular flow. In this definition savings represent income generated by output that is *not* passed on directly in spending. It is likely as suggested in Figure 12.2 that most savings will be passed back into the system. But savings in a tin box under the bed could cause problems to the levels of economic activity. Conversely, *investment* can be regarded as an **injection**. This may be defined as an addition to the circular flow *which does not* relate to present consumer spending. An injection, therefore, could also cause changes to the level of economic

activity, especially if it were funded by money from past hoardings/forgery. Theoretically, for the model economy represented in our circular flow to retain its present equilibrium the total leakage should equal the total injection. The supporting text to Figure 12.2 suggests this is the case.

Figure 12.2

The Circular Flow *with* Saving and Investment. To make the circular flow diagram more realistic, we must consider that households save. Therefore, we must represent in the diagram financial institutions (as shown by a rectangle) through which households' saving passes to businesses. Businesses use the investment funds obtained from these financial institutions to make investment expenditures on capital goods and stocks. Once businesses make these expenditures they are included as part of the monetary value of consumer and investment goods combined. This is shown by the arrow that goes from businesses to the flow line of total expenditure. In this more realistic circular flow, total output equals the monetary value of all consumer and investment good expenditures. Of course, the actual production of investment goods *also* generates total income in the form of wages, rents, interest, and profit receipts to households. This is shown by the flow line on the bottom of the circular flow diagram. So once again income, expenditure, and output are still at the same level.

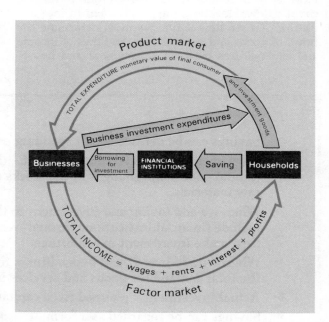

Furthermore, academic theory highlights that *actual* (realized) investment must by its very nature be equivalent to the *actual* (realized) level of saving. The former is inherently related to the latter and this relationship will be briefly identified in the following section.

The Relationship between Savings and Investments

Firstly, income (Y) can be disposed of in only two ways: by consumption (C) or by saving (S), i.e. Y = C + S. Secondly, income can be generated in only two areas of production (output): by producing consumer goods (C) or producing investment goods (I), i.e. Y = C + I. Therefore using this standard notation one can prove that

$$Y \equiv C + I$$
$$Y - C \equiv S$$

Therefore

$$I \equiv S$$

It may help your comprehension if you remember what was said about unplanned stockbuilding being a form of investment. (Now read Key Points 12.2.)

We have started to explore the basis of some theoretical questions relating to managing the economy. These will be raised again in Chapters 15 and 16. Meanwhile we must continue to open up our model economy and identify the remaining interrelationships.

The Circular Flow now with Government Added

Now let us introduce government to our 'picture' of circular flow. How does the government fit into this picture? To see how it fits, we must determine the flows of goods and services and the flows of income and expenditures between government and households, businesses and financial institutions.

We know certainly that there is a flow of money from households to government in the form of taxes. We also know that households receive money from government in the form of social security payments, old age pensions, grants, and other payments. These forms of payments are called transfer payments, which we have previously defined as those payments made from government to individuals for which no goods or services are concurrently provided in exchange. The government borrows from financial institutions to finance its deficits when its spending exceeds its revenues. In other words the government sells gilt-edged securities and similar instruments to cover its debts. When it has a surplus (when revenues exceed expenditures), it buys back some of the securities that it issued. Finally, the government adds to total expenditures when it *purchases* goods and services.

Look at Figure 12.3. We have put government above and to the right of the financial institutions. From these financial institutions to government there is an arrow that is labelled government *net* borrowing. Net government borrowing takes account of the fact that some government departments run a surplus while others may run a deficit. The arrow going from households to government is labelled *net taxes*. It is the difference between taxes paid and transfer payments. That is why the term *net* was added.

Then there is an arrow going from the government to the consumption expenditure arrow, which leads into the product markets. This shows that government purchases of goods and services (excluding transfer payments) add to the total amount of expenditures in any one year.

Key Points 12.2

► Savings can be defined as not spending on consumer goods.

► Investment includes fixed investment – the purchase of plant and equipment (capital goods) and changes in the stocks of finished goods, goods in process, and raw materials.

► When we add saving and investment to the circular flow model, we must also include financial institutions through which the savings flow to firms which in turn make investment expenditures.

► When we add investment expenditures to consumption expenditures, we obtain the total demand for goods and services in the product markets.

► Actual investment = planned fixed capital, planned and unplanned stockbuilding.

► Savings can be regarded as a form of 'leakage'.

► Investment can be regarded as a form of 'injection'.

► In our model, we have assumed that households save and business firms invest. Thus, the savers and the investors are different groups of people who have different motivations.

► Actual saving must always equal actual investment; unplanned stock changes will cause this identity to hold.

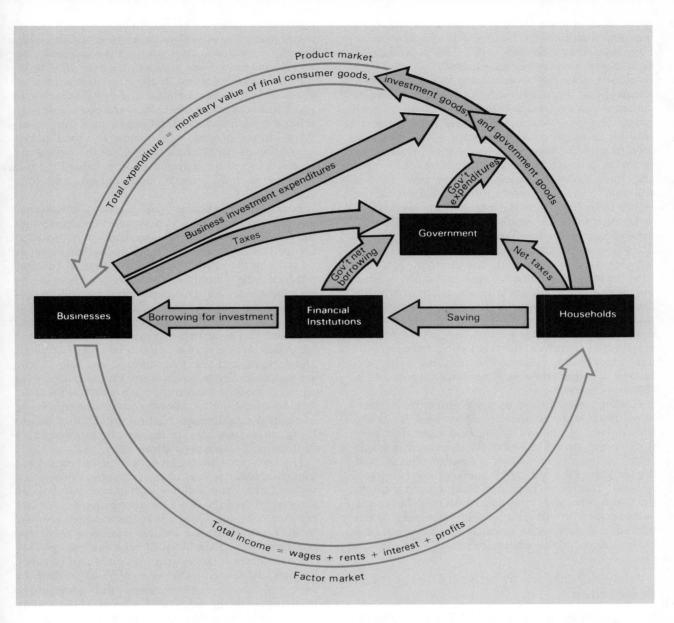

Figure 12.3

The Circular Flow of Income and Product with Government. When we add government to the picture the product market is affected (as shown by the government expenditure arrow) because governments also make expenditures on goods and services. Hence, output increases; it equals the monetary value of total consumer, investment, and government goods purchased. Of course, wages, interest, rents, and profits are generated from the production of government goods; therefore, total income increases correspondingly. The diagram also indicates that households and businesses pay net taxes to the government, and that the government may also borrow from the financial institutions. Only the money flows appear in this figure.

Once again one can sense the process of 'injections' and 'leakages' being incorporated into the flow. For example, injections in the form of government expenditure, and leakages in the form of taxation. Ideally to maintain the present level of economic activity government spending and government revenue (income) should be balanced. Government deficits and surpluses will affect the level of economic activity, unless counterbalanced by a corresponding deficit or surplus in another sector – for example, the foreign trade sector which will be briefly considered next.

The Circular Flow now with Foreign Trade

Now we will open up our model to include foreign trade. Consequently, domestic households may now spend part of their income on goods produced by businesses overseas (i.e. buy imports), while domestic businesses may now sell part of their produce to households overseas (i.e. sell exports).

Imports, therefore, constitute a leakage from our circular flow, because households spend their money abroad which in effect boosts another country's total output and total income. Conversely, exports constitute an injection into the domestic circular flow, foreign spending boosts employment of the domestic factors of production thereby increasing total output and total income. Consequently we now have a situation where the domestic total expenditure may be less or more than domestic total output.

To retain the identities of total income $\equiv$ total expenditure $\equiv$ total output it would be necessary to draw several hundred circular flows for all the countries involved in trade with one another. You may have the imagination to envisage this complexity – but our pages are certainly not large enough to portray the diagram. Nevertheless it is possible to conceptually understand that one country's trade deficit is its overseas partner's trade surplus. In terms of international trade, therefore, the relationship between output, expenditure, and income remains. (This will become apparent when analysing national accounts in the next chapter.)

Another complication once we enter the international trade scene is currency differences. Thus the financial institutions will be involved again. This time to exchange currencies so that the movement of goods from one country to another is possible. This in itself does not upset the domestic monetary flow. However, *speculators* in currency hoping to make a profit through fluctuating exchange rates may complicate the income–expenditure–output relationship, especially when viewed in *domestic* terms alone. It is the one-country analysis that we now wish to return to.

Equilibrium

In Chapter 5 we talked about the concept of equilibrium, that is, where supply and demand are in equilibrium. The equilibrium price, or market-clearing price, occurred at the intersection of the demand curve and the supply curve. The special feature about equilibrium is that there is no tendency for price or quantity to change once supply and demand are in equilibrium. Remember that when the market price is greater than the equilibrium price, forces start in action that push the price back down toward equilibrium. Unsold 'surpluses' are offered for sale by producers and retailers, for example, at lower prices. Producers will also reduce output. Remember also that when the price is below the equilibrium price, there is an excess quantity demanded at that price. Forces are set in motion that cause the price to go up. More-than-willing demanders bid up the price. Producers respond by increasing the quantity supplied.

Thus, the important thing to remember from

equilibrium analysis is that when we are *not* in equilibrium, forces will work to re-establish equilibrium. The same is true whether we are analysing equilibrium for a single product market or equilibrum for the entire economy. If the total demand for all goods and services is not equal to the total supply of all goods and services, market forces will operate so as to bring total demand and total supply back into equilibrium. In the process, total income and total output may either rise or fall. Indeed, much of this part of the text is designed to analyse the forces behind the rise and fall of total income, total output, and total expenditure.

Equilibrium is a concept that pervades all economic analysis. We have actually assumed that equilibrium prevails within the circular flow model represented in Figure 12.1. By requiring that all household earnings be spent in the product market and that all business production be offered for immediate sale, there can be no discrepancy in the basic circular flow model between the total demand and the total supply of goods and services. Thus, the basic circular flow model in Figure 12.1 accurately represents the total demand for goods and services and the total supply of goods and services, and that total demand and total supply are automatically in equilibrium. Provided we never alter this model it will continue to function at the same level for ever. Such an economy can be classed as being in **neutral equilibrium**. Neutral equilibrium means there are no pressures for change, the established set of flows will simply persist forever.

However, we then began to open up our model and introduce other sectors of the economy. Within each sector *if* the various flows of injection and leakage were equal then the flow of income around the circuit remains constant. Only when the leakages are perfectly counterbalanced by the injections could the economy be said to be in equilibrium. For example, say we have three leakages from expenditures (savings, imports, and tax) with the values of $5 + 2 + 3$ and three injections (investment, exports, and government spending) with the values of $2 + 2 + 6$. The economy would still be in equilibrium, because the total value of the injections (10) equals the total value of the leakages (10). However, as our analysis has suggested the various decisions affecting the leakages and injections of funds are carried out by different groups of individuals with different motivations. Therefore, it is unlikely that year after year leakages and injections will remain the same.

However, due to the income–output–expenditure relationship the economy will adjust to new equilibrium levels. For example, if leakages exceed injections, expenditure will be less than factor incomes. Consequently, firms will not receive sufficient revenue to cover their output costs. Stocks will accumulate and firms will cut back output and income until they equal expenditure again. A new level of equilibrium will have been established. In short, equilibrium means a 'balanced state'.

It is the character of the imbalances between

leakages and injections that prompts changes in output from year to year. These changes lead to different amounts of income circulating within the economy – which represent different levels of economic activity. (Note, therefore, that all economies will tend towards an equilibrium but the equilibrium point is not necessarily the point of full employment.) Measuring these yearly changes in economic activity is the topic of the next chapter.

Conclusion

The theme that will recur in the next chapter is that total income $\equiv$ total expenditure $\equiv$ total output. In fact national accounts are based on these identities. The logic behind them, therefore, will be briefly restated once more before closing.

All income is generated by selling factor services. Owners of labour gain wages, the providers of land receive rent, the persons providing capital receive interest, and the entrepreneurs taking the risks gain any profits. These factors of production when combined provide output, the cost of which is identical to the payment for factor services. In fact it may help if the *prices* of final goods and services are regarded as *bundles of incomes* that have been paid out during the course of their production.

Another way of looking at the value of output is from the angle of expenditure. Indeed, you must recognize that all output is sold, even if only to the business's warehouse. Expenditure, therefore, absorbs the final goods and services either in the form of consumer goods or capital goods and sets the cycle off again. The outcome is that total expenditure $\equiv$ total income $\equiv$ total output.

Key Points 12.3

▶ **When we add government to the circular flow we add government goods to the product market. These goods are purchased out of tax revenue from households and firms.**

▶ **When we incorporate foreign trade to our model the flow of income becomes complicated by import, export, and currency manoeuvres.**

▶ **Imports represent a form of leakage. Exports represent a form of injection.**

▶ **All economies tend towards an equilibrium.**

▶ **The equilibrium point is a 'balanced state', not necessarily a point of full employment.**

▶ **Total expenditure $\equiv$ total income $\equiv$ total output – these are national accounting identities.**

Exam Preparation and Practice

INTRODUCTORY EXERCISE

(a) Copy the diagram below.

(b) Identify the following sectors and locate them in appropriate boxes: households, businesses, government, financial institutions, and foreign trade.

(c) Distinguish each sector's main leakage and injection in appropriate boxes remaining.

A model of income flows

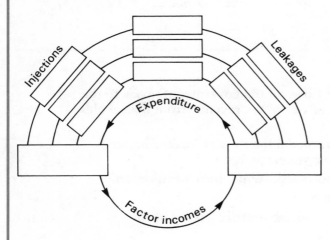

MULTIPLE CHOICE QUESTIONS

†1. Total injections into the circular flow of income within a country during any given year consist of

  A saving + imports + tax
  B exports + government expenditure + saving
  C government expenditure + exports + consumer spending
  D investment + saving + exports − imports
  E exports + investment + government expenditure

†2. Which of the following would be correctly regarded as a withdrawal from the circular flow of real national income?

  A a rise in consumption
  B a surplus on the balance of visible trade
  C a rise in public investment
  D a rise in private investment
  E a deficit on the balance of visible trade

3. Which of the following sets a limit to the real output of an economy in the long run?

  A the supply of money
  B the supply of factors of production
  C the size of the government sector
  D the volume of international trade
  E the level of effective demand

4. Which of the following represents a leakage from the circular flow of income?

  A current expenditure of nationalized industries
  B purchases of vehicles by firms
  C imports of machine tools
  D payments of rents by local authority tenants
  E interest received on capital invested abroad

†5. This question is based on the following diagram:

Which of the flows labelled A-E illustrates transfer incomes?

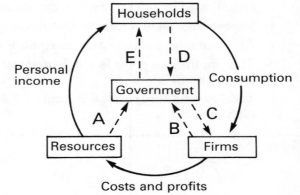

RELATED ESSAY QUESTIONS

1. Explain the circular flow of income in an economy with government and foreign trade sectors.

2. State the conditions for the circular flow of income in an economy to be in equilibrium. Show how the equilibrium is reached.

3. (a) Distinguish between injections into and withdrawals from the circular flow of income.

  (b) Explain carefully the relationship between injections, withdrawals and changes in the national income.

4. In a macroeconomic model, what are injections and withdrawals? Examine the consequences of changes in injections and withdrawals in an open economy.

13 Measuring Economic Activity: National Income

Key Points to Review

▶ Relative prices (6.3)
▶ Price index (11.5)
▶ Effects of inflation (11.6)

▶ The circular flow of income (12.1)
▶ Actual investment (12.2)

Questions for Preview

1 What is gross national product (GNP) and what does it measure?

2 What are the three approaches to measuring GNP and why do they yield identical results?

3 What must be added to gross domestic product (GDP) to arrive at a GNP figure?

4 What is the basic difference between GNP and National Income (i.e. NNP)?

5 How does correcting GNP for price level and population changes improve the usefulness of GNP estimates?

Governments must know how the economy is performing in order to decide when, how, and how much stimulus or constraint should be applied. That is, policy-makers need a statistical knowledge of the nation's performance. Furthermore, a historical statistical record aids economists in testing their theories about how the economy actually works. Thus, **national income accounting** is an important topic in the study of economics. It involves attaching actual numbers to the elements of the circular flow of income, product and expenditure that we went through in detail in Chapter 12. Consequently, it can be measured in the three ways identified (in Chapter 12) by adding up each year all the expenditure, or all the income, or all the output.

For a precise idea of the magnitude of numbers involved and the areas actually measured the student can do no better than actually look at the *United Kingdom National Accounts*.* These are published annually by the Central Statistical Office, around September, and your local reference library should have a copy. For those who cannot make it to the library some extracts from this publication are included in this chapter.

However, before becoming involved with these tables of figures we must understand what it is we are actually measuring, i.e. we must examine what gross national product involves.

Gross National Product

Gross national product (GNP) represents the total money value of the nation's annual final product, or output, produced per year. We can formally define

---

*Prior to 1984 this publication was titled: *'The National Income and Expenditure Blue Book'*.

GNP as the total market value of all *final* goods and services produced in an economy during a year. We are referring here to a **flow** of production. A nation produces at a certain rate, just as you receive income at a certain rate. Your income flow might be at a rate of £5000 per year or £50000 per year. Suppose you are told that someone earns £500. Would you consider this a good salary? There is no way you can answer that question unless you know whether the person is earning £500 per month or per week or per day. Thus, you have to specify a time period for all flows – income received is a flow. You must contrast this with, for example, your total accumulated savings, which are a **stock** measured at a point in time, not across time. Implicit in just about everything we deal with in this chapter is a time-period – usually a year.

The Stress on *Final* Output

As we noted, GNP measures the value of *final* output. GNP ignores intermediate goods, or goods used up entirely in the production of final goods, because to include them would be to **double-count**.

We can use an example to clarify this point. Our example will involve determining the value added at each stage of production. *Value added* is the amount of value added to a product by each stage of its production. In Figure 13.1 we see the difference between total value of all sales and value added in the production of a doughnut. We also see that the sum of the values

added is equal to the sale price to the final consumer. It is the 15p that is used to measure GNP, not the 32p. If we used the 32p, we would be double-counting, for we would include the total value of all of the intermediate sales that took place prior to the doughnut being sold to its final consumer. Such a double-counting would grossly exaggerate GNP if it were done for all of the goods and services sold.

Excluding Non-productive Transactions

Not only is the stress in measuring GNP on the word *final*, but it also relates to productive transactions only. Productive transactions involve some *final* purchases of *newly* produced goods or services. However, daily economic activity also involves numerous non-productive transactions. These non-productive transactions are typified by transfers of money (or the ownership of used goods). Technically these are referred to as **transfer payments** – and we shall illustrate them with four typical examples.

TRANSFER PAYMENTS

1. *Buying and selling shares.* When you purchase shares on the Stock Exchange in a public limited company, e.g. ICI or Marks & Spencer, someone else must sell them to you. In essence there is merely a transfer of ownership rights you pay to obtain a share certificate. Someone else, via the Stock Exchange, received your payment and gave up the

Figure 13.1

Sales Value and Value Added in Pence per Doughnut at Each Stage of Production

Stage 1: A farmer purchases a penny's worth of fertilizer and seed that are used as factors of production in growing wheat.

Stage 2: The farmer grows the wheat, harvests it, and sells it to a miller for 2p. Thus, we see that the farmer has added 1p worth of value. That 1p represents income paid in the form of rent, wages, interest, and profit by the farmer.

Stage 3: The flour miller purchases the wheat for 2p, and adds 2p to the value added; that is, there is 2p for him as income to be paid as rent, wages,

interest, and profit. He sells the ground wheat flour to a doughnut baking company.

Stage 4: The doughnut-baking company, buys the flour for 4p and adds 6p as the value added. It then sells the doughnut to the final retailer.

Stage 5: The dougnut retailer sells fresh hot doughnuts at 15p apiece, thus creating additional value of 5p.

We see that the total value of sales resulting from the production of one doughnut was 32p, but the total value added was 15p which is exactly equal to the retail price. The total value added is equal to the sum of all income payments, including payments to rent, wages, interest, and profit.

(1) Stage of production	*(2)* Value of sales (p)	*(3)* Value added (p)
Stage 1 Fertilizer and seed	1	1
Stage 2 Growing wheat	2	1
Stage 3 Flour milling	4	2
Stage 4 Doughnut baking	10	6
Stage 5 Doughnut retailing	15	5
Total value of all sales	32p	Total value added 15p

share certificate. No productive activity is generated and consequently the bulk of the monies involved in this transaction are not included in our measurements of gross national product (only the brokerage fees for the *productive services* involved in deed transfers etc. need to be counted).

2. *Government transfer payments.* We have already referred to transfer payments as payments for which no productive services are concurrently provided in exchange. The most obvious *government* transfer payments are social security payments, old age pensions, student grants, and interest payments on the National Debt. The recipients make no contribution to current production in return for such transfer payments (although they may have made contributions in the past in order to receive them).

3. *Private transfer payments.* Are you receiving money from your parents in order to live at school? Has a wealthy relative ever given you a gift of money? If so, you have been the recipient of a *private* transfer payment. This is merely a transfer of funds from one individual to another. As such, it does not constitute productive activity and is not included in gross national product.

4. *The transfer of used goods.* If I sell you my two-year-old car, there is no current production involved. Rather, I transfer to you the ownership of a car that was produced several years ago; in exchange, you transfer to me, say, £3 000. The original purchase price of the car was included in the GNP in the year I purchased it. To include it again when I sell it to you would be counting the value twice.

However, if the car was bought from a second-hand car dealer, the mark-up between the price he bought it in at and the selling price would be included. The profit represents the salesman's income and is a return for a service. This final example brings us back to the central issue – gross national product calculations must incorporate payments for productive services. The car salesman will be very willing to tell you how he has improved the car before putting it out for display on his forecourt – in a way one may sense that his work has added value and is therefore part of new annual output.

The Three Methods of Measuring GNP

GNP has been defined as the total market value of all goods and services produced in an economy during a year. Consequently, government statisticians can use one of three methods to measure its size. They can either:

1. Add up the *flow of expenditures* made on all goods and services during each year. This is known as the **expenditure approach**.
2. Add up the *flow of income* received in the same year by everybody involved in the production of these goods and services. This is known as the **income approach**.
3. Add up the specific value of the *flows of output* arising from each sector of the economy. This is known as the **output approach**.

In Britain we use *all* three methods of measurement. This is not too much of a problem, because as identified in Chapter 12 in each case the measurements should be identical. Therefore, the theory of Chapter 12 will now be revisited with the application of actual figures.

Furthermore, by analysing each of these methods of measurement, in turn, we will get an insight into the UK economy from three perspectives; according to the types of income being earned; according to the types of goods being produced; and according to the nature and purpose of our nation's expenditure.

PLAN OF ATTACK

In order that the large number of concepts and definitions involved in this section can be understood, we shall move through the calculations in three separate stages:

Firstly, by calculating GDP via each method.
Secondly, by moving from GDP to GNP figures.
Thirdly, by moving from GNP to net National Income.

Key Points 13.1

▶ GNP is the total money value of final goods and services produced in an economy during a one-year period.

▶ GNP also represents the flow of production over a one-year period.

▶ In order to avoid counting, we look only at final goods and services produced or, alternatively, at value added.

▶ In measuring GNP we must exclude transfer payments, these are merely transfer of monies which do not correspond to any type of productive economic activity.

Measuring GDP with the Expenditure Approach

By acquiring statistical information from a wide range of industrial enquiries, household surveys and government accounting data, the Central Statistical Office is able to produce annually tables of national expenditure. This is laid out in its traditional format in Figure 13.2.* The relevant categorizations and terminology are clarified in the following section where each numbered item in Figure 13.2 is explained.

Figure 13.2
Gross Domestic Product by the Expenditure Approach

At Market Prices	1985 (£m)
(1) Consumers' expenditure	213 208
(2) General government final consumption	74 012
(3) Gross domestic fixed capital formation	60 118
(3) Value of physical increases in stocks and works-in-progress	528
Total domestic expenditure	347 866
(4) Exports of goods and services	102 304
Total final expenditure	450 170
(4) *Less* imports of goods and services	–98 603
Gross domestic product at market prices	351 567
Factor Cost Adjustments:	
(5) *Less* taxes on expenditure	–56 812
(5) *Plus* subsidies	7 710
Gross domestic product at factor cost	302 465

Source: United Kingdom National Accounts, 1986 (London: HMSO)

(1) Consumers' Expenditure

Consumer spending falls into three categories: **durable consumer goods, non-durable consumer goods,** and **services**. Durable goods are *arbitrarily* defined as items that last more than a year; these include cars, TVs, furniture, and household appliances. Non-durable goods are all the rest, such as food, fuel, and clothes. Services are just what the name suggests: insurance, bank charges, funeral expenses, rents, and rates.

You should be aware of the fact that there are some goods and services that do not pass through the

market-place. For example, food grown on the farm for household consumption by farmers' families is certainly a consumption expenditure, but it does not show up in the usual way, because it does not pass through an organized market. The £213bn spending represents therefore only official consumer spending; there will be some transactions that do not go through any official books.

(2) Government Expenditures

In addition to personal consumption expenditures, there are local and central government purchases of goods and services (these are grouped under the formal heading of *general government final consumption*). It is evident from the figures that the government sector is an important spender in our economy, and this is not at all surprising when one remembers that in Britain it provides many of our services, e.g. health, education, parks, libraries, police, and defence etc. Because many of these services are provided free or below cost they are valued in the National Accounts at their cost of provision.

(3) Investment Expenditures

Gross domestic fixed capital formation is *not* the name of a northern dance team, but is the official term for investment expenditure. In Chapter 12 we explicitly pointed out what economists mean when they say investment expenditures: it is worth repeating here because the point is so important.

First of all, investment in economics does not relate to simple *transfers* of asset ownership among individuals. Thus, if you buy a stock or a bond, that is *not* investment from the economic point of view; you have simply traded money and received in exchange a piece of paper entitling you to something. Such transfers are not investment.

Investment, therefore, relates to expenditure on our future productive capacity. It relates to newly produced goods that are carried over into the next time-period. The bulk of this £60bn worth of expenditure is therefore on items such as industrial buildings, domestic dwellings, plant, and machinery.

Apart from these items of fixed investment you will remember that we also made a reference to investment of working capital. Indeed it is important to remember that for accounting purposes businesses buy into stock any output that is not sold to the public. Consequently, we can identify a second component of investment expenditure, namely the *value of physical increases in stock*. One would expect some stock building to occur in any dynamic economy. However, in 1980, 1981, 1982 and 1984 the UK actually experienced negative values for this category as stocks were run down during the recession. To some extent stock levels are an indicator of demand for a nation's products.

Note: The bracketed numbers per item are the only modifications made to the table. The authors have incorporated them to support their text.

Key Points 13.2

▶ In the UK we use three methods for measuring GNP. Namely, the expenditure approach, the income approach, and the output approach.

▶ The expenditure approach to measuring GDP requires that we add up: consumers' expenditure (C), government expenditures (G), investment expenditures (I), and net exports (NX). In *general terms*, therefore GDP = C + G + I + NX.

▶ Included in consumer expenditures are consumer durables, consumer non-durables, and services.

▶ We include government expenditures at their cost, since we do not usually have market prices at which to value government goods and services.

▶ Gross investment *excludes* transfers of asset ownership. It includes only additions to the productive capacity of a nation, plus repairs and replacements of existing capital goods, and any changes in business stocks.

▶ Overseas expenditures must be incorporated into GDP. Foreigners buying exports are spending on our nation's produce and therefore these monies must be added as they represent domestic economic activity. Conversely imports must be subtracted.

▶ GDP at factor cost involves removing the market price distortions of indirect taxes and subsidies.

---

(4) Overseas Expenditures

To get an accurate representation of gross domestic product, we must also include the foreign sector. That is, we must *add* to our total domestic expenditure what foreigners spend on our goods and services when they purchase export items. To get some idea of the *net* expenditures emanating from this overseas trade we must also subtract the value of imports (as these represent another country's GDP) from the value of our exports to obtain net exports for a year:

net exports ≡ total exports – total imports

In numerical terms for 1985 this would involve subtracting 98 603 from 102 304 (as indicated in Figure 13.2). Once this calculation has been accounted for we can arrive at a figure for gross domestic product at market prices.

(5) From Market Prices to Factor Costs

The next manoeuvre is to remove the distortions caused by taxes on expenditure and subsidies. Indirect taxes, i.e. taxes on expenditure (e.g. VAT), merely increase the price of goods and services, while subsidies (e.g. the rent on certain properties) reduce market prices. Businesses are actually acting on behalf of the government when they collect VAT or claim a subsidy. Therefore, movements in expenditure taxes or subsidies move market prices for the purchasers, but the amount received by producers (other things remain-

ing constant) will remain unaltered. In other words, the rewards to the actual factors of production remain the same, while governments move their rates of expenditure tax and or subsidies. As our aim is to measure real economic activity, i.e. assess the productivity of our resources, it makes more sense to measure GDP at factor prices (or factor costs) and this is a common practice in National Income accounting in the UK. Thus we can arrive at another formula:

GDP at factor prices =
GDP at market prices – taxes on expenditure + subsidies

Consequently, in Figure 13.2, there are two ways of looking at expenditure: spending in the market-place (i.e. GDP at market prices) and spending that represents the value that the firms receive by result (i.e. GDP at factor cost). Now read Key Points 13.2.

Measuring GDP with the Income Approach

By acquiring statistical information from the Inland Revenue (who collate and organize tax returns) the CSO is able to produce annually tables of national income. This is set out in its standard format in Fig. 13.3.

The figures are expressed as factor incomes. In other words, in terms of what it costs in total to employ each factor at face value. Therefore income tax and other deductions are included.

It is interesting to note that as anticipated the final

Figure 13.3
Gross Domestic Product by the Income Approach

Factor incomes	1985 (£m)
(1) Income from employment	195 350
(1) Income from self-employment	29 859
(2) Gross trading profits of companies	52 977
(2) Gross trading surplus of public corporations	7 106
(2) Gross trading surplus of general government enterprises	264
(3) Rent	20 541
(4) Imputed charge for consumption of non-trading capital	2 681
(5) Total domestic income	308 778
less stock appreciation	−3 037
Gross domestic product (income-based)	305 741
(6) Residual error	−3 276
Gross domestic product (expenditure-based)	302 465

Source: United Kingdom National Accounts, 1986 (London: HMSO).

Note: The numbers in brackets (1–6) are the only modification made to this official table. They have been included to assist with the cross-references in the text.

figure for GDP at factor cost is identical with that on the expenditure table. This is because while producing the things they sell firms incur costs which when totalled are identical to the sale price of their products. These costs are rewards (payments) to the factors of production, namely (1) wages, (2) profit, (3) rent, and (4) interest. Indeed the table may largely be summarized using these four payments and consequently the bulk of the items in the table (Figure 13.3) have been numbered (1)–(4) respectively. These numbers (along with (5) and (6)) will provide a means of cross-reference.

(1) Wages

The most important category in Figure 13.3 is, of course, 'wages', including wages, salaries, and other forms of labour income. In the table, the relevant formal categories total £225 209m – this constitutes approximately 75 per cent of all income in 1985. In these figures we include: National Insurance payments (both the employees' and the employers' contributions), payments to pension schemes and union subscriptions etc., as we wish to know the factor reward before deductions.

(2) Profits

This category includes total gross profits *before deductions* of tax, interest payments, and allowances for depreciation. The bulk of these profits arise from companies, in the private sector, involved in finance, commerce, and industry. It is interesting to note, however, the significant surplus of public corporations, as many commentators assume that nationalized industries lose money – this is obviously not the case when the sector is taken as a whole. Similary, general government enterprises such as passenger transport, docks and harbours etc. run on behalf of local and central government also gross up a small trading surplus when considered as a whole group.

(3) Rent

Rent includes all the receipts earned by individuals from their ownership of land and buildings, such as farms, houses, and stores.

(4) Interest

Interest payments do not equal the *sum* of all payments for the use of money capital in a year – such an inclusion would simply involve double-counting, as implied above in the section on profits. Interest is being used here to express a return on those fixed capital assets owned by the government in a non-trading form. For example, local authority offices and the Houses of Parliament are owned and occupied by

---

Key Points 13.3

▶ To derive GDP using the income approach, we add up all factor payments, including wages, interest, rent, and profits.

▶ Stock appreciation is the increased value of stock due to inflation that needs to be subtracted from our measurements of economic activity.

▶ Residual error is a 'balancing item' (it may be positive or negative) incorporated for the inevitable mistakes that occur when calculating national accounts.

government. This generates a form of intangible service income (in terms of saved rent); consequently an estimated (imputed) figure is included at this juncture.

Now we can arrive at a figure which reflects the total domestic income for the year concerned. However, you will notice that in Figure 13.3 this is still not classifiable as GDP; before we can arrive at this figure **stock appreciation** must be accounted for.

(5) Stock Appreciation

In their accounts businesses include in their profits any stocks which have gone up in value during the year due to inflation. In short, a situation where the physical volume of stock produced has not changed but its money value has. To be consistent with the other 'flows' measured, we must only take account of those incomes resulting from economic activity; therefore inflated stock values due to inflation must be estimated and subtracted, before arriving at an income-based GDP figure.

(6) Residual Error

It may not surprise you, given the thousands of figures involved and the various estimates that have to be made, that the final GDP figure *based on income* is slightly different from the GDP figure *based on expenditure*. However, you must remember that these two estimates of GDP are built up largely from independent data, and although *in theory* the total should be identical in *reality* they are not.* The residual error is therefore merely a 'balancing item' to allow identical totals to be presented for each method of measurement. (Now read Key Points 13.3.)

Measuring GDP with the Output Approach

The various values for this calculation are derived from censuses of production, and statistics on the different forms of income. These enable the CSO to produce annually a table showing national output. This table is broken down into various industrial sectors to show the proportional contributions made within the UK economy. The output table is presented in its standard format in Figure 13.4.

Again you will notice that the final GDP figures are identical to those appearing in the income and expenditure tables presented in Figures 13.2 and 13.3. This is because output is only made possible by generating rewards (income) to the factors of production

involved. Correspondingly, all output is assumed to be sold (even if it is only in the form of stock building).

What is involved, therefore, is an adding-up of all the contributions to domestic output made by each producing unit in the country (*after allowing for stock appreciation*). It is important to remember, however, that the emphasis must be on the **value added** by each producing unit, otherwise some output may be counted twice. To avoid such double-counting the value of 'intermediate' products (i.e. the value of products brought in for the production process) must be subtracted from the value of the final product. This concept has already been illustrated in Figure 13.1.

Alternatively it is possible to concentrate solely on the value of *final* goods and services, as is done largely in the (public) service sector, where the value of all the input costs are totalled up to measure the final value of the output. For example, education and health services are listed in Figure 13.4 as producing £26 187m worth of output. This is simply what it costs in total to provide these services in terms of staff wages, and maintenance etc.

Having made these prepatory remarks Figure 13.4 should now be self-explanatory.

Figure 13.4
Gross Domestic Product by the Output Approach

	1985 (£m)
Agriculture, forestry, and fishing	5 485
Energy and water supply	34 335
Manufacturing	76 800
Construction	18 651
Distribution, hotels, and catering; repairs	40 384
Transport	12 913
Communication	8 044
Banking, finance, insurance, and business services	42 473
Ownership of dwellings	17 775
Public administration and national defence	21 599
Education and health services	26 187
Other services	17 978
Total	322 624
Adjustment for financial services*	–16 883
Gross domestic product at factor cost (income-based)	305 741
Residual error	–3 276
Gross domestic product at factor cost (expenditure-based)	302 465

Source: United Kingdom National Accounts, 1986 (London: HMSO).

---

*Although given the complexity of these national accounts a residual error of approximately 1 per cent seems quite amazing.

*These are interest payments that need to be deducted to avoid double-counting.

> ## Key Points 13.4
>
> ▶ To derive GDP using the output approach, we sum up the 'value added' by each industry producing a good or service in our economy.
>
> ▶ To avoid double-counting we must *not* look at the total sales from each sector, but what has been *added* in value terms to those component products bought in (see Figure 13.1 for example).
>
> ▶ The output of some service industries is measured in terms of the value of their *final* cost.

Moving from GDP to GNP

We have seen that GDP figures measure the total spending, income, and or output made from *home-based resources*, and therefore exports are included. In contrast GNP (gross *national* product) figures measure the total economic activity generated by our *nation's* resources both at home and *abroad*. This may sound complex, but in national accounting terms the only calculation involved is to add to our tables a net figure for property income from abroad – in 1985 the figures were as shown in Figure 13.5.

Figure 13.5
Moving from GDP to GNP

	£m
Gross domestic product at factor cost	302 465
Net property income from abroad	3 400
Gross national product at factor cost	305 865

Source: United Kingdom National Accounts, 1986 (London: HMSO).

All we need to do now is clarify this new item and GNP will (then we hope) make sense. In addition to the movement of goods and services across frontiers explicitly accounted for within the expenditure table (see discussion of item (4) on page 195) there is the movement of interest, profit, and dividend resulting from assets owned overseas (e.g. UK oil companies have various investments in capital abroad). To arrive at a figure for *net* property income it is necessary to offset our credits from abroad against the corresponding payments made for foreign investment in the UK. The specific situation in 1985 was as follows:

	£m
Property income *from* abroad	53 032
Property income *paid* abroad	49 632
∴ *Net* property income from abroad =	3 400

Thus we have identified another important definition.

GNP = GDP + net property income from abroad.

Moving from GNP to NNP

We have used the terms *gross* national product and *gross* domestic product without really indicating what *gross* means. The dictionary defines it as 'without deductions', as opposed to 'net'. Deductions for what? you might ask. Deductions for something we call **depreciation**. In the course of a year, machines and structures wear out, become outdated, or are 'used up' as they are used in the production of national product. For example, machines need repairs, or replacement, even if firms are only going to continue production at the same rate. That is, most fixed capital depreciates. An estimate of this is subtracted from gross national product to arrive at a figure called **net national product** (NNP).

Alternatively, depreciation can be thought of as that portion of the current year's GNP that is used to replace any physical capital *consumed* in the process of production. Indeed, another term for depreciation is **capital consumption**.

Consequently, gross investment can be expressed in the following way:

gross investment = replacement investment + expansion investment

This is a useful formula as it highlights that if we are attempting to measure a country's progress (development) we should ignore replacement investment. Consequently, in official statistics net figures are more important. This moves us towards yet another definition:

NNP = GNP – depreciation (capital consumption allowances)

To see this in numerical terms see Figure 13.6.

Obviously capital consumption does not represent an easily identifiable set of transactions, and by result it is an estimated amount arrived at using a system of accounting conventions. Depreciation does not vary greatly, therefore, from year to year as a percentage of GNP, and you will get a similar picture about what is happening to our economy by looking at either NNP or GNP data. However, the final line in all official accounts is the 'net' figure. In other words, to measure

---

Key Points 13.5

▶ By adding property income from abroad into our accounts we can move from a GDP figure (which measures economic activity arising from *domestic* – home – based resources) to a GNP figure which measures economic activity from the broader perspective of all *national* resources both at *home* and *abroad*.

▶ Capital consumption (depreciation) represents an estimated figure to allow for the nation's fixed capital that has been 'used up' during the production process.

▶ GNP – capital consumption = NNP.

▶ NNP is officially referred to as national income.

Figure 13.6
Moving from GNP to NNP

	£m
Gross national product at factor cost	305 865
less Capital consumption	–41 846
National income (i.e. net national product)	264 019

Source: United Kingdom National Accounts, 1986 (London: HMSO).

a country's progress it is best to look at *net* figures, as these indicate spending, output and/or income made on behalf of 'additional' goods to a nation's economic flow. Indeed *net national product* is most commonly what economists are referring to when they talk of **national income**. (Now read Key Points 13.5.)

Uses of These National Accounts

As implied at earlier junctures in this chapter these accounts have four main uses:

1. **MEASURING ECONOMIC GROWTH.** As these figures are a measure of economic activity, the annual national income can be compared with previous years and an impression is thereby gained about changes in the standard of living. Indeed, economic growth rates are worked out from these accounts and this is illustrated in the second Case Study at the end of this chapter.

2. **COMPARING COUNTRIES.** Apart from comparisons across time, these national accounts also offer opportunities to make comparisons between countries in terms of development, affluence, policies, and so on. In fact, contributions to international agencies such as the IMF, Red Cross, World Bank, and the EEC are often assessed as a percentage of a country's GNP.

3. **GOVERNMENT PLANNING.** As stated in the opening lines of this chapter, the statistical tables on expenditure, output, and income provide an important analytical tool to those economists who are involved in recommending and evaluating policies on behalf of government.

4. **EVALUATION OF ECONOMIC CLIMATE.** Similarly businessmen, research students, trade union representatives, and journalists involved in interpreting economic trends will find the statistical breakdowns provided in the various tables most useful for their forecasts and work in general.

Is National Income Accounting Sufficient?

We have now completed our run-down of the different ways that the national accounts are compiled, the various totals that can be arrived at, and the main uses of these statistical presentations. What we have not yet touched on though is how reliable these figures are. Inevitably there are some limitations, and we shall deal with these next.

Key Points 13.6

▶ National income accounts can be seen to have *two general* uses: (1) to make comparisons (between countries and across time) and (2) for planning and evaluation (by government, business men, and related parties).

Once this is complete you will recognize how to interpret national income statistics and be in a position to answer questions relating to 'How sufficient national income accounting is?' This is a common theme of academic debate and often the central issue within an A-level question.

Correcting National Income for Price Changes

If a video tape costs £5 this year, ten tapes will have a market value of £50. If next year they cost £10 each, the same ten tapes will have a market value of £100. There will have been no increase in the total quantity of tapes produced and sold, but the market value will have doubled. Apply this to every single good and service produced and sold in the United Kingdom and you realize that national accounts measured in 'current' values may not be a very useful indication of economic activity. After all, we are really interested in variations in the *real* output of the economy. What we have to do, then, is correct GNP for changes in general prices from year to year. This is done by converting all money values to a common base year via a price index (at present the government's base year is 1980). Consequently, two sets of figures are produced each year: *money* national income and *real* national income.

Money national income is formally referred to as **current price** or **nominal national income**, and it represents the measurements of economic activity expressed in current 'face value' terms. **Real national income**, by contrast, represents the same measurement but expressed in value terms of a specific base year. This technique of employing constant price measurements makes comparisons across time far more meaningful. For example, consider the following figures:

UK national income *1975 prices*	£85060m
UK national income *1985 prices*	£264019m

These figures suggest that in ten years the UK has become nearly 300 per cent richer. However, if we now account for inflation in this ten-year period and express both figures again in *constant price* terms, as follows:

1975 UK national income *1980 prices*	£163062m
1985 UK national income *1980 prices*	£189552m

we can see that in real terms we have only increased our economic activity from 1975 to 1985 by approximately 16 per cent.

For most purposes *real* values are more indicative of economic performance. Indeed, the chart shown in Figure 13.7 was used by the Chancellor of the Exchequer in April 1985 when making an academic presentation relating his budget proposals to economic strategy. The chart clearly shows how the general growth of nominal (money) GDP is simply a reflection of inflation rather than a rapid growth of real output.

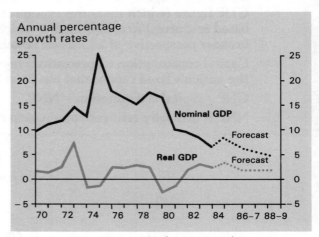

Figure 13.7
The Difference between Real and Nominal GDP

Source: Economic Progress Report, May 1985.

Per Capita GNP

Even by looking at changes in *real* national income one still may be subject to deception, especially if changes in population size have been significant. For example, if 'real' GNP over a ten-year period went up 100 per cent, you might immediately jump to the conclusion that the material well-being of the economy had increased by that amount. But what if, during the same period, population increased by 200 per cent? Then what would you say? Certainly, the amount of GNP per person, i.e. **per capita** GNP would have fallen, even though *real* GNP has risen. What we must do therefore is try and be precise by accounting for price changes and population size changes.

A significant economic variable therefore in RGNP per head (real gross national product per head). More conveniently National Income per head may at times suffice. These can be calculated quite simply by the following formulas:

$$\frac{\text{RGNP}}{\text{Total Pop.}} = \text{RGNP per head.}$$

$$\frac{\text{NNP}}{\text{Total Pop.}} = \text{national income per head.}$$

With these formulas in mind one can look at population growth in the Third World and begin to sense why many of the people are starving even though their national income may increase marginally each year.

A further complication arises when income distribution is added to the picture. To appreciate this you may care to calculate UK's Money National Income per head for 1985 (taking the UK population as approximately 56m) and compare the results to *your* income in that year.

Black Economy

Another complication that the last suggested exercise brings to mind is that some student incomes will be of the 'unofficial' variety; for example, 'casual' jobs over the summer, bar work, helping in the corner shop, painting and decorating, etc. Many of these jobs are sometimes organized on a 'cash-in-hand' basis, so that the employer can avoid certain legislation and/or the employee avoids paying tax. This type of unofficial economic activity is seen as constituting an 'informal', 'hidden', or 'shadow' economy and is referred to by economists as the **black economy**.

With the general increase in unemployment and the increase in VAT many commentators feel that the black economy may be expanding relative to the 'official' economy. Indeed, the discrepancy between official recorded expenditure and declared incomes is increasing and this whole area is one of recent investigation. For some examples of these investigations and their findings see Figure 13.8.

Figure 13.8
Estimated percentage of GDP that Escapes Official Detection in the UK

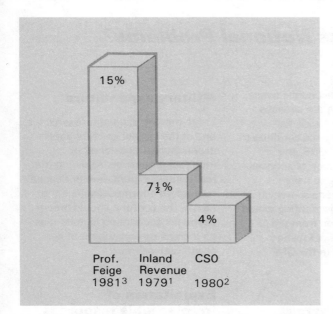

Sources: [1]Sir William Pile, Former Chairman of the Inland Revenue; [2]'A glimpse of the Hidden Economy in the National Accounts', CSO (*Economic Trends*) 1980. [3]'The UK's unobserved Economy', *Journal of Economic Affairs*, July 1981.

The existence of the black economy is not only worrying in terms of undermining national income statistics but in terms of lost tax revenue. For example, the former chairman of the Board of Inland Revenue estimated that the black economy may represent $7\frac{1}{2}$ per cent of GDP. This would imply that a significant unofficial sector exists. In fact, if he were correct it would suggest that approximately £6 billion is being

lost in tax revenue per year from these 'underground' or 'cash' activities.

Difficulties Comparing Countries' Accounts

As the last section suggests, a country's national income figures largely reflect what is recorded. In different countries official interpretations of what is eligible for recording changes according to circumstances. For example, the attempts to prohibit alcohol in the United States in the 1920s led to a large illegal bootlegging industry. This replaced a former legitimate industry, and national income figures were affected accordingly. Similarly, 'prostitutes' in those countries where they are state organized will provide an economically measurable service, whereas in other countries this will not be the case.

Not only do laws affect the figures but so does accounting convention. For example, in the US government statisticians add to their GNP figures an estimated amount for those foods which farmers have grown and their families have eaten, i.e. those foods that inevitably do not pass through a market-place. In contrast, self-sufficiency in the Third World represents a major form of existence yet these self-consumed products normally remain unrecorded for official purposes.

These problems are further compounded when there is the need to express world national incomes figures in a common currency, as this brings in problems of exchange rates. The $ and £ values, which are normally used for international comparisons, alter daily against other currencies. Therefore converted figures from the currency of measurement to the common currency are often suspect.

Measuring Welfare

We have presented in this chapter several measures of economic activity and obviously each measure has a different purpose. This raises the question, however, do any of them effectively measure well-being?

The critics of national accounting contend that it glorifies the materialistic society in which we live. They believe that the numbers cannot capture our true overall well-being as a nation. They point out that many forms of economic activity also produce external costs, such as pollution, noise, and accidents. These are not officially measured within national income, but they do affect welfare. Similarly, leisure, happiness, and health cannot be measured simply in terms of income, output, or expenditure.

Consequently new measures of welfare are being developed (especially in the US), and our next Case Study will explore some of these new concepts. The subsequent questions raised thereafter will help you to investigate further this difficult issue of national accounting and what it actually measures.

Key Points 13.7

▶ National income is best expressed each year in a common value. At present nominal (money) national income is converted into real national income by expressing all values in 1980 prices.

▶ Ideally changes in population size should be considered to arrive at a per capita figure. For example, if you did the calculation suggested on page 200, you would have found that in 1985 UK national income per head was approximately £4714.

▶ Studies of the 'black economy' estimate the amount of 'unrecorded' or 'unofficial' economic activities that go on. These reduce the size of a country's official national income.

▶ What is officially recorded as economic activity will differ from country to country.

▶ Finally, there are the critics who contend that national income accounting is not a sufficient measure of welfare and this issue is raised in the next Case Study.

CASE STUDY

Does GNP Mean Gross National Problems?

Given the deficiencies in our national income accounts, is it possible to come up with a new measure of GNP? Ed Mishan, a former professor at the London School of Economics, would sincerely hope so. There follows an edited extract from an article of his that was published in November 1984 – which will prompt some interesting questions.

How easy is it to estimate real growth?

Role of women

Let us turn first to the increased participation of women in the workforce over the last thirty years which has increased output in the private and public sectors of the economy and to that extent has increased the estimated growth in real GNP and also in per capita real income. A good part of this apparent contribution to the GNP

statistics is, in an economic sense, fictitious. For while the services that women now provide for industry and commerce continue to add to the value of GNP, the concomitant reduction of services they would otherwise have provided in their homes – which on proper economic accounting would enter as a deduction from the nation's aggregate of finished goods – is ignored in the GNP computation.

Public sector versus private sector

Second, since public goods tend to be overvalued as compared with those produced by the private sector, and since the output of the public sector over the last thirty years has grown appreciably as a component of GNP, it follows that the real growth of GNP over the period will be overestimated.

Military expenditure

Third, military expenditure which is one of the largest items of public expenditure, raises another interesting question. Allowing that real military expenditure per capita has grown enormously since the turn of the century, should proper economic accounting include it as an increasing component of per capita real income?

Exploitation of irreplaceable resources

Fourth, an increasingly significant source of error arises from the global exploitation of irreplaceable resources. If the total stock of capital is taken to include not only man-made capital but also 'nature-made' capital such as fossil fuels, mineral reserves, ocean fisheries, tropical forests etc., it is entirely possible for current rates of global consumption to be reducing the stock of nature-made capital faster than it is increasing the stock of man-made capital, which implies that we are currently consuming beyond our real income – in effect, eating into the total capital we have inherited to the detriment of our future and our children's future.

Environmental considerations

A fifth factor related to the preceding one is the propensity of modern industry and its products to pollute air, soil, and water and generally to degrade the environment, which acts to reduce real income below the official figures. If, to begin with, nothing is done to curb the industrial overspill which damages the health and amenity of people, GNP is overstated to the extent of the cost of the damage that is borne – this being the value of the 'bads' that accompanies the production and distribution of the goods.

Concluding thought

If these and other deficiencies in the conventional methods of estimating changes in GNP were recognized, and allowance made for them, the real standard of living in the West as compared with that of other 'less-developed countries' would look much less impressive.

Source: E. J. Mishan, 'GNP-Measurement or Mirage', *National Westminster Bank Review*, Nov. 1984.

Questions
1. Mishan's statements imply a need for recording minuses as well as pluses to national accounts. What do you think should be taken off national accounts to arrive at a real measure of progress?
2. Professors Tobin and Nordhaus in a similar article in an American publication argue that there is also a need for *adding* activities that are not traditionally included in GNP figures. List the kind of things you think they may have in mind.
3. In the mid-1970s the Economic Development Council of Washington, DC created an entirely new measure of wealth and health, namely, the PQLI. **The Physical Quality of Life Index** bases its terms of reference on figures for life expectancy, literacy, and infant mortality. From these figures countries are rated on a scale of 1 to 100. Critically evaluate this index as a measure of welfare.
4. Suggest what you would like to use as a measure of welfare.
5. What does national income in its standard UK format actually measure?

CASE STUDY

Economic Growth: Spot the Trend

Figure 13.9

Expenditure on the gross domestic product (£m, 1980 prices)

	Gross domestic product at market prices	Consumers' expenditure	General government consumption		Gross domestic fixed capital formation	Value of physical increase in stocks and work-in-progress	Exports of goods and services	Imports of goods and services
			Central government	Local authorities				
1964	164380	98636	22909	11649	31581	3366	28418	31520
1965	168142	100124	23281	12172	33095	2194	29822	31805
1966	171384	101907	23628	12748	33907	1383	31159	32594
1967	176181	104360	24969	13479	36902	1071	31434	34851
1968	183574	107273	24697	13871	39191	1702	35377	37455
1969	185981	107880	23878	13948	38932	1886	38867	38653
1970	190158	110777	23878	14528	39925	1413	40996	40713
1971	195272	114211	24338	15219	40700	376	43789	42838
1972	199836	121204	24785	16403	40594	−90	44302	47101
1973	215599	127436	25548	17608	43535	5023	49451	52693
1974	213332	125630	26452	17406	41734	2837	53072	53350
1975	211827	124748	27939	18329	41808	−2969	51657	49578
1976	220050	125175	28533	18336	42434	1035	56282	51641
1977	222215	124564	28252	17857	41323	2566	59939	52251
1978	230290	131373	28579	18546	42938	2054	61067	54267
1979	235221	137256	29097	19010	43925	2474	63367	59908
1980	230197	136789	29851	18959	41628	−2899	63298	57429
1981	227555	136714	30058	18753	38075	−2739	62140	55446
1982	231895	138135	30286	18936	40645	−1247	62729	57591
1983	239626	144008	30910	19613	42348	207	63329	60789
1984	242300	145455	31066	19623	45391	68	68528	67831

Note. For the years 1964–77 each separate series is adjusted by a price index appropriate to the specific category of expenditure. Consequently GDP figures for these years will differ slightly from the sum of their components.

In this Case Study we look at some data on UK GDP (see Figure 13.9). The various items listed have been taken from a more general table presented in the CSO publication *Economic Trends* (1985 and 1986 editions).

It must be emphasized that all component items are evaluated in constant price terms. Thus one of the exercises will be to calculate some 'real' growth rates for the UK. Other uses of such data is for interpreting past events and forecasting future ones. These issues will form the themes of Questions 2 and 3.

Questions

1. Calculate the economic growth rate for the last six years. This is derived in percentage terms by taking each year separately using the following formula:

$$\frac{\text{GDP of year to be measured (e.g. 1980)} - \text{GDP of previous year (e.g. 1979)} \times 100}{\text{GDP of previous year}}$$

2. Try and account for the economic downturn since 1979.

3. Suggest what the UK GDP may be in 1990 and give economic reasons for your estimate.

Exam Preparation and Practice

INTRODUCTORY EXERCISES

In the following four questions fill in the items that are missing to complete the formulas. Although this is a seemingly simple exercise the different definitions are important and this should help you to focus on the distinguishing features.

   (i) GDP (at market prices) = $C + I + G + \underline{\hspace{1cm}}$.
   (ii) GDP at factor cost =
   (iii) GNP = GDP + $\underline{\hspace{2cm}}$.
   (iv) NNP = GNP $\underline{\hspace{2cm}}$.

MULTIPLE CHOICE QUESTIONS

†1. From the following information calculate the gross national product (GNP).

	£m
Wages	= 9 000
Salaries	= 7 000
Government pensions	= 1 500
Unemployment pay and other social benefits	= 1 500
Rent and interest	= 1 500
Profits	= 1 500

		£m
A	=	18 500
B	=	19 000
C	=	19 000
D	=	20 500

2. Why are the GNP (gross national product) figures of a nation *not* considered to be accurate indicators of the welfare of its people?
  A the GNP figures do not allow for depreciation
  B welfare includes non-marketable goods and services enjoyed by the community
  C GNP figures do not include social security benefits
  D payments for social workers and doctors are made out of taxpayers' money

3. The slower rate of growth of the British economy as compared with that of her main competitors can best be seen from comparison of
  A per capita gross national product at constant prices
  B total volume of production
  C rate of capital investment
  D balance of payments position

†4. The following figures are extracted from the national income accounts of Country X for a particular year:

	£'000m
Consumers' expenditure	65
Fixed capital formation	20
Net addition to stocks during year	5
Government expenditure	10
Exports of goods and services	10
Imports of goods and services	12
Property income received from abroad	6
Property income paid abroad	4
Taxes on expenditure	6
Subsidies	1
Capital consumption	5

What is the value of Country X's national income (at factor cost)?
  A £90 million
  B £95 million
  C £105 million
  D £100 million

5. Which of the following would *not* give the value of the UK's gross national income?
  A gross domestic product + net property income from abroad
  B gross national product
  C net national income + depreciation
  D gross national expenditure – exports
  E total factor incomes earned by UK residents

6. A director becomes redundant as a result of a company merger. His salary in employment was £10 000 per annum. He is entitled to a redundancy payment of £5 000 (£4 000 as a lump sum and £1 000 as 10 per cent of his salary). His wife takes up employment at a wage of £1 000 per annum and his daughter increases the contribution to the family housekeeping by £500 from her earnings.

    The net reduction in the contribution of the family to the measured national income in the first year of the father's redundancy is
  A £5 000
  B £6 500
  C £7 500
  D £8 500
  E £9 000

continued overleaf

RELATED ESSAY QUESTIONS

1. Explain concisely *three* methods of measuring national income. For what purposes might national income statistics be used?

2. What are the main conceptual and measurement problems involved in constructing national income accounts?

3. Explain carefully what is meant by value added and show how it is used in arriving at a figure for the national product.

4. In 1972 the gross national product of the UK was estimated to be £55.9 bn. By 1982 it had risen to £228.4 bn. To what extent does this increase indicate an improvement in the standard of living?

5. 'National income accounting tells us where we think we have been, around six months after we were there: it cannot show us where we are now, nor can it tell us where we are about to go.' Discuss.

6. How adequate a measure of social and material welfare are the UK National Accounts?

14 Aggregate Supply and Aggregate Demand

Key Points to Review

▶ Supply and demand (5.7)

▶ Inflation (11.4, and 11.6)

▶ Unemployment (11.2, and 11.3)

▶ Real versus nominal (13.7)

Questions for Preview

1 Why is the aggregate demand curve downward sloping?

2 Why does the aggregate supply curve have three ranges?

3 What is demand-pull inflation?

4 Can aggregate demand–aggregate supply analysis explain stagflation?

5 How is supply-side economics related to the *AS* curve?

In Chapter 5, a model of price determination using supply and demand analysis was given, but the prices that we were referring to were individual commodity prices relative to all other prices. Concern over prices at the economy-wide level is much more general, for it is a concern about why there have been continuous increases in the price level, or why there has been inflation. In Chapter 11, we found out that the UK rate of inflation has varied dramatically over time. We also found out that we have had varying periods of growing prosperity and recession, with accompanying periods of expanding employment and then unemployment.

Why, for example, was it that in 1977 the rate of inflation was 15.9 per cent but the rate of economic growth was only 2.6 per cent, whereas, in 1984 the rate of inflation was 4.6 per cent and the rate of economic growth was 2.3 per cent? We have to construct a model in our attempt to explain these variations. We will use the tools of supply and demand but with a major change: instead of looking at the price of *one* commodity, we will look at the price level (an index of general prices) and how it relates to aggregate demand and aggregate supply. The definition of the

price level and how we measure changes in the price level have been given in Chapter 11. The definition of **aggregate demand** is the sum total of all *planned* expenditures in the economy. In Chapter 12, we already discussed total planned expenditures on a theoretical level in an economy that had no government and no foreign sector. In that situation, aggregate demand was equal to planned consumption expenditures by households plus planned investment expenditures by business firms. **Aggregate supply** is defined as the sum total of *planned* production in the economy. Again, going back to our simplified economy in Chapter 12, total planned production consisted of consumer goods for households and investment goods for businesses.

Given the above definitions, we can now proceed to construct an aggregate demand curve and then an aggregate supply curve.

The Aggregate Demand Curve

The **aggregate demand curve**, *AD*, gives the various quantities of all commodities demanded at various price levels. Otherwise stated, the aggregate demand curve gives the relationship between the total amount, of income, or real national output that will be purchased and the price level. Remember from Chapter 13 that *real* national income consists of the output of final goods and services in the economy – it is everything that is produced for final use, either by businesses or households. Look at Figure 14.1. On the horizontal axis is measured real national income. On the vertical axis is measured the price level. At a price level of P_1, aggregate demand will be £300 billion per year. At a price level of P_2. aggregate demand will decrease to £200 billion per year. The higher the price level, the lower will be the total real output demanded by the economy, and vice versa.

Why the Aggregate Demand Curve Slopes Down

We cannot explain the downward-sloping demand curve for all commodities in the same way as we explain the downward-sloping demand curve for individual commodities. After all, a change in the price level changes the average price of all goods and services, on average. Other reasons must be given. They include the following:

1. Interest rate effects
2. Wealth effects
3. Substitution of foreign-produced goods.

INTEREST RATE EFFECTS

Remember in Chapter 11, when we discussed inflation, we pointed out that one result of inflation is a rise in nominal interest rates because inflationary premia are added to all interest rates. But a rise in interest rates will reduce the quantity demanded of interest-rate-sensitive goods. These goods are those that must be financed by borrowing, such as cars, homes, and new factories. Thus, the link is as follows:

Price level up → Interest rates up → Quantity demanded of interest-rate-sensitive goods down → Total real income (production) demanded falls

WEALTH EFFECTS

In Chapter 11 we saw that an increase in the price level reduces the purchasing power of cash balances. In essence, then, those individuals who hold part of their **wealth** in cash balances will find a reduction in the purchasing power of their wealth. Actually, every part of a person's wealth that is denominated in money terms only, such as government bonds with fixed interest rates, will suffer a reduction in real wealth when the price level increases. After all, if you own a £100 bond, and the price level doubles, when you cash in that bond, the £100 will buy only £50's worth of goods and services at the higher price level.

Consequently, whenever there is a rise in the price level, the real value of all assets denominated in money

Figure 14.1

The Aggregate Demand Curve. On the horizontal axis we measure real national income in £ billion per year. On the vertical axis we measure the price level. The aggregate demand curve (*AD–AD*) is downward sloping for three reasons: (1) an increase in the price level increases interest rates, which decrease the quantity demanded of interest-sensitive goods, such as cars and factories; (2) an increase in the price level reduces the real wealth of all individuals holding cash, thereby causing them to want to spend less; and (3) an increase in the UK price level causes us to buy more imports and sell fewer exports therefore reducing the demand for real output in the UK. Therefore, at price level P_1 real national income demanded will be £300 billion per year, but when the price level increases to P_2, real national income decreases to £200 billion per year, other things being equal.

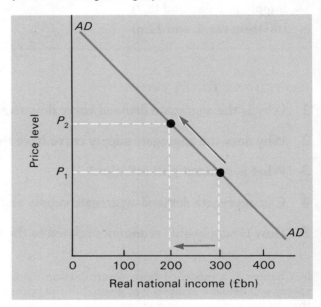

terms falls. Individuals will therefore tend to spend less. Planned purchases (real national income) will fall.

FOREIGN GOODS SUBSTITUTION

Any increase in the price level in the UK will make domestically produced goods relatively more expensive compared to foreign-produced goods. That means that an increase in the UK price level will cause planned purchases of domestically produced goods to fall and planned purchases of foreign-produced goods (imports) to rise. It also means that foreigners will no longer want to purchase as much of UK production as before. In sum, the demand for UK domestic real output (production) will fall when the UK price level rises.

The Aggregate Supply Curve

The **aggregate supply curve** represents the relationship between real income, or output, and the price level. It would be nice to say simply that the aggregate supply curve slopes up, because the higher the price level, the more producers are willing to produce – because producers have a greater incentive and they can cover any additional costs incurred in the increased output. But remember, just as with our discussion of the aggregate demand curve, we are talking about changes in the price level – the index of the weighted average of *all* prices. Every price is allowed to vary. In order to understand the true nature of the aggregate supply curve, we have to examine three situations:

1. Large amounts of unused capacity and significant unemployment
2. Full capacity
3. Intermediate range between the two.

UNUSED CAPACITY AND SIGNIFICANT UNEMPLOYMENT

When the economy has many factories operating at less than capacity, numerous individuals unemployed, and a general underutilization of the productive capabilities of the nation, it is possible to increase output without there being any pressure on prices. Under such a setting, producers can increase supply at will without having to pay any higher prices for factors of production. In other words, per-unit costs of output will remain the same, no matter what the volume of output is, so long as significant amounts of unemployment and unused capacity remain. Under such a setting, we would expect the aggregate supply curve to be a horizontal line at the current price level. Consider that the current price level is P_0, as given on the vertical axis of Figure 14.2. The horizontal line labelled 'excess capacity' represents that part of the aggregate supply curve, *AS–AS*, that exists when there is no pressure on prices with any increase in output. Within this range, supply is perfectly elastic.

NO EXCESS CAPACITY

Now consider the other extreme situation where there is absolutely no excess capacity. In other words, the economy is at full employment. It is impossible, by definition, for any additional output to be produced. What will the shape of the aggregate supply curve look like now? Obviously, it has to be a vertical line, as shown at output rate Q_1 in Figure 14.2. It is a vertical line because there is only one thing that can happen in such a situation – the price level can rise, but no further increases in output are physically possible. Supply can be said to be perfectly inelastic.

The vertical portion of the aggregate supply curve in Figure 14.2 is also a representation of aggregate supply in the long run. That is to say, in the long run, when all prices are flexible, the potential level of real national income (total output) is independent of the price level. Rather, it depends only on the supply of resources and the economy's technology. As technology advances, more can be produced so the vertical

Figure 14.2

The Three Ranges on the Aggregate Supply Curve. Starting out at a price level of P_0, the aggregate supply curve, *AS–AS*, is a horizontal line up to quantity of real national income, Q_0. It is a horizontal line because there is excess capacity such that any increase in production does not raise per-unit costs. Output level Q_0–Q_1 is where some sectors experience excess capacity but others do not. In other words, bottle-necks appear as the economy moves closer and closer to maximum capacity. Those sectors experiencing near-full capacity will find that their per-unit costs are rising, and therefore the prices charged for their commodities will rise. The general price level will therefore rise as output increases from Q_0 to Q_1. This is called the intermediate range, where there is some excess capacity. At Q_1, there is no excess capacity – the economy is experiencing full employment of all its resources, and using its technology to its fullest. The only thing that can happen, therefore, is for prices to rise. Output cannot increase, by definition, past Q_1.

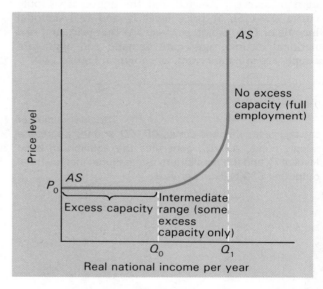

line showing full capacity output will shift gradually to the right. (This will be pursued in Chapter 34.)

INTERMEDIATE RANGE

When there is some excess capacity in some parts of the economy, but no excess capacity in other parts of the economy, then, as production is increased, the price of some goods and services will be pushed up (but not the price of *all* goods and services).

This is the beginning of demand-pull inflation. So-called bottle-necks, or supply constraints may develop. As firms try to increase output they may experience shortages of certain inputs, most frequently, certain kinds of skilled labour. When this happens, firms can try to attract more of the scarce input by paying a higher price for it – in this case, wages. Their costs rise and they put prices up.

The intermediate range of the aggregate supply curve is, in essence, based on this bottle-neck explanation. As the aggregate supply curve starts to slope up, it will become steeper and steeper as maximum capacity is approached, because, as this happens, more and more bottle-necks appear. As bottle-necks appear, certain prices increase. Also in this situation sellers can anyway put prices up, without losing customers. Since the price level is a weighted average of all prices, if some prices stay constant and some go up the price level will rise, too. That means that if we start at the end of the excess capacity rate of output, Q_0 in Figure 14.2, and increase production, the price level will rise along with real national income. In this range, there is a positive relationship between real national income and the price level. As supply constraints become more numerous, supply becomes less and less elastic.

Putting Aggregate Demand and Aggregate Supply Together

Equilibrium occurs at the intersection of the aggregate demand curve (AD–AD) and the aggregate supply curve (AS–AS), at price level P_0 and real national income of £300 billion per year. At that price and real national income, aggregate demand and aggregate supply are in equilibrium, as shown in Figure 14.3.

Figure 14.3
Equilibrium Price Level and Output. The intersection of the aggregate demand curve, *AD–AD*, and the aggregate supply curve, *AS–AS*, generates the equilibrium price level at P_0 and the equilibrium real national income (total output) at £300 billion per year.

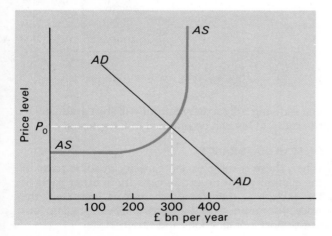

Applying Aggregate Demand/ Aggregate Supply Analysis – Explaining Inflation

In Chapter 11 there was a discussion of demand-pull inflation. Using shifts in the aggregate demand curve and the aggregate supply curve shown in Figure 14.4

Figure 14.4
Demand-pull Inflation. The aggregate supply curve, *AS–AS*, is shown as first a horizontal line, then a positively sloped line, then a vertical line, to represent output rates with excess capacity, declining excess capacity (bottle-necks), and no excess capacity. If the aggregate demand curve intersects the aggregate supply curve prior to output rate Q_0, then any increase in demand will *not lead* to a rise in the price level. Thus, a shift from AD_1 to AD_2 leaves the price level unaltered at P_0. A shift from AD_2–AD_2 to AD_3–AD_3, however, will cause the price level to increase to P_1. After output rate Q_1, any increase in demand will simply result in a higher price level, since, by definition, at full employment, no more output is physically possible. An increase in demand from AD_3–AD_3 to AD_4–AD_4 will increase the price level to P_2. Demand-pull inflation occurs any time the aggregate demand curve increases and intersects the aggregate supply curve at some output rate greater than Q_0 per year.

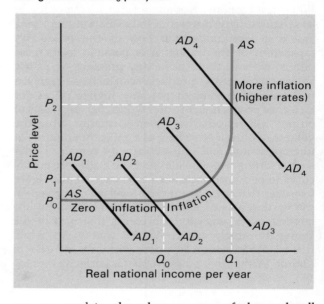

we can explain the phenomenon of demand-pull inflation. Start out at price level P_0. Assume that the aggregate demand curve is AD_1–AD_1. An increase in the aggregate demand curve to AD_2–AD_2 will not alter the price level. There will be no inflation. However, as given in Figure 14.4, at any point past real national income of Q_0 per year, there will be some sectors experiencing full employment or no excess capacity. Therefore, an increase in demand from AD_2–AD_2 to AD_3–AD_3 will cause the price level to increase from P_0 to P_1, and any further increase will cause an even higher price level. If the demand curve shifts to AD_4–AD_4, the price level will rise to P_2. Indeed, no output rate greater than Q_1 per year is physically possible. That means that any increase in demand after that output rate will simply result in a higher price level (inflation).

Demand-pull inflation can be defined as any increase (rightward shift) in the aggregate demand curve after output rate Q_0.

Aggregate Supply and Demand Analysis – Explaining the Great Depression

The Depression of the 1930s affected business everywhere, but probably most dramatically in the United States. From 1929 to 1933, real GNP fell by 29.4 per cent. Unemployment had reached 25 per cent of the civilian labour force. Prices fell by 23.6 per cent during that same period.

Aggregate supply and aggregate demand analysis can help us to understand what happened during the Great Depression. Look at Figure 14.5. Here we show an aggregate supply curve, AS–AS, with the three ranges discussed above. Assume that during the period 1929–33, nothing happens to shift the aggregate supply curve. In 1929, aggregate demand is AD_1–AD_1. For a variety of reasons – falling international demand for goods produced in the United States, less desired investment by businesses, less desired consumption by households, and for other reasons – the aggregate demand curve decreases – shifts inwards to the left – to AD_2–AD_2. In 1929, the price level was P_1 and the real national income per year was Q_1. By 1933, the price level had fallen to P_2 and the real national income per year had fallen to Q_2.

Short-run versus Long-run Aggregate Supply Curves

In our discussion of the aggregate supply curve, we mentioned that the vertical portion is really equivalent to the long-run aggregate supply curve, since it indicates maximum potential output possible with given resources and given technology.

It would logically follow, then, that the horizontal and positively sloped section of the aggregate supply curves, as given in Figures 14.2, 14.3, 14,4, and 14.5 should properly be labelled short-run aggregate

Figure 14.5

Explaining the Great Depression. The supply curve for the period 1929–33, is assumed to remain stable at AS–AS. In 1929, the aggregate demand curve is given by AD_1–AD_1. The intersection of this aggregate demand curve and the aggregate supply curve yields an equilibrium price level of P_1 and an equilibrium output level or real national income per year of Q_1. For a variety of reasons, and, in particular, a collapse in planned investment by businesses, the aggregate demand schedule decreased, that is, it shifted inwards to the left to AD_2–AD_2. It intersected the aggregate supply schedule at an equilibrium price of P_2 and an equilibrium output of Q_2 per year. Prices fell, and so, too, did output.

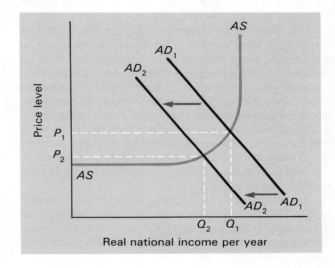

supply curves. In other words, it is only in the short run that an increase in total output in the economy is possible simply because aggregate demand has increased. Therefore, from now on, since we will be examining – for the most part – only the horizontal

---

Key Points 14.1

► Aggregate demand is the sum of all planned expenditures for both consumption and investment purposes, by both the private and the public sector.

► Aggregate demand will fall when the price level rises, because of interest rate and wealth effects, and because of the substitution of foreign for domestic goods.

► The aggregate supply curve shows the relationship between the price level and total output.

► So long as there is excess capacity, output can be increased. As more and more sectors of the economy reach full capacity, increasing output brings successively larger price increases.

► At full capacity, increasing aggregate demand fails to stimulate increasing output and leads only to rising prices.

and positively sloped sections of the full aggregate supply curve, we will label our aggregate supply curves as short run, or *SRAS*. This will avoid any confusion with questions relating to economic growth, which properly apply only to the long-run vertical supply curve and our ability to shift it outwards over time through saving and investment as well as more efficient use of our resources.

Supply-side Economics

The two examples we have already given to demonstrate the use of aggregate supply and aggregate demand related to shifts in the aggregate demand schedule. Those shifts are often called **aggregate demand shocks**. We can now look at an example in which there is an attempted shift in the short-run aggregate supply curve. This is sometimes called an **aggregate supply shock**. The example we wish to discuss concerns the government policy referred to as supply-side economics. **Supply-side economics** involves creating incentives to increase productivity. Recent governments have argued that a reduction in *marginal* tax-rates would induce individuals to work harder. This would improve efficiency and increase real income. The short-run aggregate supply curve would shift to the right and there could be a reduction in the rate of inflation.

Look at Figure 14.6. The aggregate demand curve is *AD–AD*. The aggregate supply curve is given as *SRAS*. The equilibrium price level is P_1, and the equilibrium real national income per year is Q_1. The short-run aggregate supply curve moves outwards so that the equilibrium price level would fall to P_2 (i.e. lower the rate of inflation, in a dynamic setting), and the equilibrium level of real national income would increase to Q_2 per year.

The historical evidence is not overwhelmingly supportive of this supply-side argument. While the rate of inflation fell in the early 1980s, it seemed to take longer than predicted for the rate of output to increase.

Figure 14.6
Supply-side Economics in Theory. The equilibrium price level, P_1, and real national income, Q_1 per year, is given by the intersection of the short-run aggregate supply curve, $SRAS_{1980}$, and the aggregate demand curve. For simplicity's sake we keep the aggregate demand curve stable. A reduction in marginal tax-rates presumably was to increase incentives for workers to work harder and longer. This increase in productivity was to increase short-run aggregate supply so that $SRAS_{1984}$ would be to the right of $SRAS_{1980}$. The new equilibrium would be at an increased output of Q_2 per year, and a reduced price level, P_2. This would be an example of an aggregate supply shock with a stable aggregate demand curve.

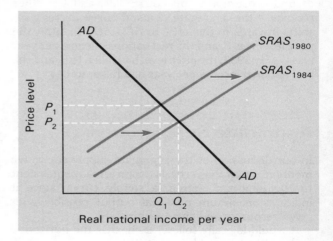

Key Points 14.2

▶ Only in the short run can output be increased simply because aggregate demand has increased.

▶ In the long run, the growth of output depends on the level of investment and the state of technology.

▶ If people can be induced to work harder or move efficiently, the aggregate supply curve will shift to the right.

CASE STUDY

Supply Constraints, Rising Costs, and Inflation

One way of estimating the likely extent of supply constraints at any given time is to look at figures for vacancies. Only a proportion of vacancies which occur are notified to employment offices. But when there is a sharp increase in the number of vacancies, it does indicate that employers are having difficulty in recruiting the kind of labour they require.

Consider the increase in vacancies in 1973–4. This suggests that the economy in 1973 was at point A in Figure 14.7. As demand increased, and employers sought to increase output, they would be faced with a shortage of suitable labour. They would offer higher wages, costs would rise and so would prices. Any increase in aggregate demand would lead to a movement of AS_1.

Vacancies notified to employment offices (000s)

1970	188.3
1971	130.9
1972	147.3
1973	307.0
1974	297.5
1975	154.4
1976	122.0
1977	154.5
1978	210.3
1979	241.3
1980	143.0
1981	97.0
1982	111.3
1983	145.1

Source: CSO, *Economic Trends*, 1985.

But, meantime, there were dramas on the international scene. OPEC countries were able to raise oil prices fourfold. This increased costs sharply – it meant that any given level of output would be produced at a higher price level.

Aggregate supply shifted from AS_1 to AS_2. The new equilibrium is at B; a lower output is being produced at a higher price level. This, of course, is stagflation.

Figure 14.7
The Oil Price Rise. Rising oil prices meant that any given output would be produced and sold at a higher price than previously. There would be a shift from AS_1 to AS_2. With given aggregate demand the economy moves to B with lower output and a higher price level.

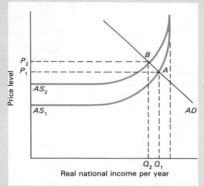

Turning to the 1980s, Figure 14.8 shows capacity utilization in the major industrial countries. The evidence suggests increasing supply constraints during 1986. If inflation does not accelerate then other, more favourable factors are simultaneously at work.

Figure 14.8
Focus: Spare Capacity. The economic recovery of the past three years has put much idle plant back to work in the main industrial economies. But in none of them has capacity utilization in manufacturing yet reached the heights it was at during the

1979–80 boom, just before the second oil shock pushed the world into recession. The biggest increase in the use of capacity has been in Canada, but its industry still has the farthest to go to be working flat out. In Britain, by contrast, manufacturers are almost back to the workloads they had in 1979 – even though their output has yet to regain that earlier level. So much plant has been scrapped that bottle-necks are appearing when more than 13 per cent of the workforce is still unemployed. The main moral of the chart is the need for more investment to expand capacity, rather than just to save on labour.

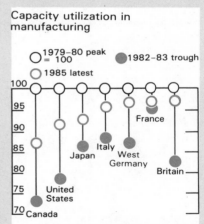

Capacity utilization in manufacturing

Source: The Economist, 11 Jan 1986.

Questions
1. Aggregate demand may change with government policy. How would decreasing aggregate demand, due to cuts in government expenditure, affect the economy?
2. How did the 1979 oil price rise affect the UK?

Exam Preparation and Practice

INTRODUCTORY EXERCISE

1. Given the curves in the diagram below, discuss why the equilibrium price level will be at P_e and not at P_1 or P_2.

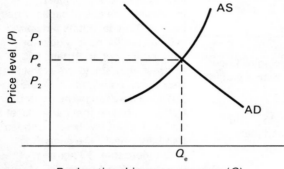

Real national income per year (Q)

MULTIPLE CHOICE QUESTIONS

1. If aggregate demand has risen output will not increase if
   A productivity is rising
   B there are some supply constraints
   C the aggregate supply curve is vertical
   D there is underutilized capital in the economy

2. Inflation will decelerate if
   A aggregate demand is constant and input costs rise
   B aggregate demand stays constant and productivity increases
   C aggregate supply falls
   D aggregate supply is constant

RELATED ESSAY QUESTIONS

1. 'Inflation is due to excess demand.' Discuss.
2. Explain how aggregate supply can be increased (a) in the short run, and (b) in the long run.
3. Distinguish between a movement along the aggregate supply curve, and a shift of the curve to the right.

15 Aggregate Demand: Consumption, Savings, and Investment

Key Points to Review

▶ Shift versus movement along a curve (5.6)

▶ Equilibrium, surplus, shortage (5.7)

▶ Actual versus planned saving and investment (12.2)

▶ Nominal versus real values (13.7)

Questions for Preview

1 What determines real national income in the Keynesian model?

2 How are saving, consumption, and income related in a closed private economy?

3 What are the determinants of investment?

Aggregate demand was defined as the sum total of all planned expenditures over a year's period. We found that the aggregate demand curve was downward-sloping – there is an inverse relationship between the price level and aggregate quantity demanded. In order to find the equilibrium price level and the equilibrium level of real national income per year, it was also necessary to use the aggregate supply curve. But supposing we are dealing only with that portion of the aggregate supply curve that is a horizontal line? If there are large amounts of unused productive capacity and unemployment, an increase in aggregate demand will not raise prices, and a decrease in aggregate demand will not cause firms to reduce prices. In such a situation, the equilibrium level of real national income per year is completely *demand-determined*. Thus, in order to construct a model of income determination, we need only to understand the determinants of aggregate demand. In the simple models that we have used so far, aggregate demand determinants have been limited to planned consumption expenditures on the part of households, and planned investment expenditures on the part of firms. In this chapter, we

will examine what determines the rate of planned consumption expenditures and what determines the rate of planned investment expenditures.

Keynesian Economics

John Maynard Keynes, who wrote *The General Theory of Employment, Interest, and Money* suggested that many prices, and especially the price of labour (wages), are sticky downwards. Therefore, even in situations of excess capacity and large amounts of unemployment, we will not necessarily observe the price level falling. Rather, all we will observe is continuing unemployment and a reduction in the equilibrium level of real national income per year. Keynes argued that, to some extent, the lengthy duration of the Great Depression could be explained by the sticky-downward nature of prices and wages. Thus, a general economy-wide equilibrium can occur, and last for a long time, even when there is excess capacity. Keynes and his followers argued that capitalism was therefore not necessarily a self-regulating system, sustaining eternal prosperity and full employment. Keynes, at the time, was attacking the so-called classical view of the world, which argued that markets would all clear. Prices and wages would adjust; as wages fell, more people would be employed and full employment would never be far away.

Some Simplifying Assumptions

We have already assumed that prices will not rise when output rises, so for the time being, we need not concern ourselves with inflation. We will be seeing the economy in real terms. In order to simplify the income-determination model that follows, a number of other assumptions are made:

1. Businesses pay no indirect taxes (for example, VAT).
2. Businesses distribute all of their profits to shareholders.
3. There is no depreciation (capital consumption allowance) so that gross private domestic investment equals net investment.
4. The economy is closed, i.e. there is no foreign trade.

Given all of these simplifying assumptions, real disposable income will be equal to real national income minus taxes.

Definitions and Relationships

There are literally only two things you can do with a pound's worth of income (in the absence of taxes). You can consume it or you can save it. If you consume it, it is gone for good. However, if you save the entire pound you will be able to consume it (and perhaps more if it earns interest) at some future time. That is the distinction between **consumption** and **saving**. Consumption is the act of using income for the purchase of consumption goods. **Consumption goods** are those goods that are purchased by households for immediate satisfaction. Consumption goods are such

things as films, food, clothing, and the like. By definition, whatever you do not consume you *save* and can consume sometime in the future.*

The Difference between Stocks and Flows

It is important to distinguish between saving and savings. Saving is an action that occurs at a particular rate such as £5 a week. This rate is called a flow. It is expressed per unit of time, usually a year. Implicitly, then, when we talk about saving we talk about a flow or rate of saving. Savings, on the other hand, is a stock concept measured at a certain point or instant in time. Your current savings are the result of past saving. You may presently have savings of £1000 that are the result of four years' saving at a rate of £250 per year. Consumption, being related to saving, is also a flow concept. You consume from after-tax income at a certain rate per week, per month, or per year.

Relating Income to Saving and Consumption

The relationship of saving, consumption, and disposable income is therefore:

consumption + saving ≡ disposable income.

This is called an 'accounting identity'. It has to hold true at every moment in time. From it we can derive the definition of saving:

saving ≡ disposable income − consumption.

---

*A definitional problem arises when a household purchases a consumer durable. Part of the expenditure is consumption and the other part is saving. The part that is consumption is the implicit, or implied, stream of services consumed within one year; the remainder is therefore considered a form of saving because it allows the household to consume more in the future.

Key Points 15.1

▶ **If we assume that prices will not rise as output increases, the equilibrium level of real national income is demand-determined. (The economy is on the horizontal section of the aggregate supply curve.)**

▶ **Saving is a flow concept, something that occurs over time. Savings, on the other hand, are a stock. They are the accumulation due to saving.**

▶ **Saving equals disposable income minus consumption.**

▶ **Investment is a flow concept, also. It includes expenditures on new machines, buildings and equipment, new houses, and changes in the level of stocks.**

JOHN MAYNARD KEYNES
(1883–1946)

Mechanic of the Market

'The ideas of economists and political philosophers ... are more powerful than is commonly understood ... Practical men, who believe themselves to be quite exempt from any intellectual influences, are usually the slaves of some defunct economist. Madmen in authority, who hear voices in the air, are distilling their frenzy from some academic scribbler of a few years back.' The most important 'defunct economist' of the twentieth century is the man who penned these words – John Maynard Keynes. Over the twenty-five years following the end of World War I, Keynes transformed the way in which economics was viewed as a discipline and as an aspect of government policy.

During the 1920s, Keynes studied European finance and wrote *The Treatise on Money* (1930), efforts on which he would later build as British representative to the 1944 Bretton Woods conference on international monetary policy. At the same time, Keynes amassed a considerable

sum by speculating on the stock market, handling his transactions by telephone before getting out of bed each morning.

It was in 1936, in the midst of the Great Depression, with millions throughout Europe and the United States unemployed, that Keynes's masterwork, *The General Theory of Employment, Interest, and Money*,

appeared. The market is not a self-regulating mechanism, Keynes argued, because when depression strikes, people tend to use up the savings that could be employed to fuel business investment. To bring the economy quickly out of depression and end high unemployment, some way of stimulating investment and capital expansion is needed; only by maintaining 'effective demand' – a desire for goods and services among people who have the money income to pay for them – can recessions be warded off. The natural entity to stimulate aggregate demand, Keynes asserted, is the government using a combination of deficit spending and regulation of tax-rates and money supply.

Just as Keynes predicted, his theories – those of an academic scribbler – were not really utilized by government policy-makers for many years after the publication of his *magnum opus*. Indeed, Keynesian economics, as it is called, has, since the 1950s, been a dominant force in government policy-making in this country and elsewhere.

Investment

Investment is also a flow concept. Investment is defined as expenditures by firms on new machines and buildings – **capital goods** – that are expected to yield a future stream of income. This we have already called *fixed investment*.* Additionally, we included in our definition *changes* in stocks. When some of current output is not sold, stocks increase. Similarly if demand exceeds current production, firms will run down stocks, to meet the demand.

Determinants of Planned Consumption and Planned Saving

The major determinant of planned real consumption expenditures is clearly expressed in Keynes's 1936

---

*Fixed investment should also include expenditures by households on *new* houses. For convenience' sake, we will usually ignore this aspect of investment in this chapter.

book. According to Keynes's General Theory, when we look at consumption, we find that:

the fundamental psychological law, upon which we are entitled to depend with great confidence both *a priori* from our knowledge of human nature and from the detailed facts of experience, is that men are disposed, as a rule and on the average, to increase their consumption as their income increases, but not by as much as the increase in their income.

A relationship is suggested here between the planned consumption expenditures of households and their current income. This relationship is called the **consumption function**. It shows how much all households plan to consume per year with each level of real disposable income per year. The first three columns of Figure 15.1 show a consumption function for a hypothetical group of households.

We see from Figure 15.1 that as real disposable income goes up, planned consumption rises also, but by a smaller amount, as Keynes suggested. Planned saving also increases with disposable income. Notice, however, that below an income of 5000 units the

Figure 15.1

Hypothetical Real Consumption and Saving Schedules. At levels of disposable income below 5000 units, planned saving is negative. In column (4), we see the average propensity to consume, which is merely planned consumption divided by disposable income. Column (5) lists average propensity to save, which is planned saving divided by disposable income. Column (6) is the marginal propensity to consume, which shows the proportion of additional income that will be consumed, ΔC (the change in consumption) over ΔY (the change in income). And finally, column (7) shows the portion of additional income that will be saved, or the marginal propensity to save.

Combination	(1) Real disposable income Y_d (Units per year)	(2) Planned real consumption C (Units per year)	(3) Planned real saving $S \equiv Y_d - C$ (1) – (2) (Units per year)	(4) Average propensity to consume $APC \equiv C/Y_d$ (2)÷(1)	(5) Average propensity to save $APC \equiv S/Y_d$ (3)÷(1)	(6) Change in consumption $MPC \equiv \dfrac{\Delta C}{\Delta Y_d}$	(7) Change in saving $MPS \equiv \dfrac{\Delta S}{\Delta Y_d}$
A	0/yr	1000/yr	–1000/yr	...	...	...	...
B	1000	1800	– 800	1.80	–0.8	0.8	0.2
C	2000	2600	– 600	1.30	–0.3	0.8	0.2
D	3000	3400	– 400	1.133	–0.133	0.8	0.2
E	4000	4200	– 200	1.05	–0.05	0.8	0.2
F	5000	5000	0	1.00	0.00	0.8	0.2
G	6000	5 800	200	0.967	0.033	0.8	0.2
H	7000	6600	400	0.943	0.057	0.8	0.2
I	8000	7400	600	0.925	0.075	0.8	0.2
J	9000	8200	800	0.911	0.089	0.8	0.2
K	10000	9000	1000	0.9	0.1	0.8	0.2

planned saving is actually negative. The more income drops below that level, the more people dissave, either by going into debt or by drawing on past savings.

We can see the relationship between C, S, and Y in Figure 15.2.

Figure 15.2

The Relationship between C, S, and Y. Here we show graphically that $C + S \equiv Y$. In panel (a) the consumption shedule is drawn. In panel (b) the saving schedule is drawn. When we add the two schedules together we get panel (c). Consumption plus saving must equal income.

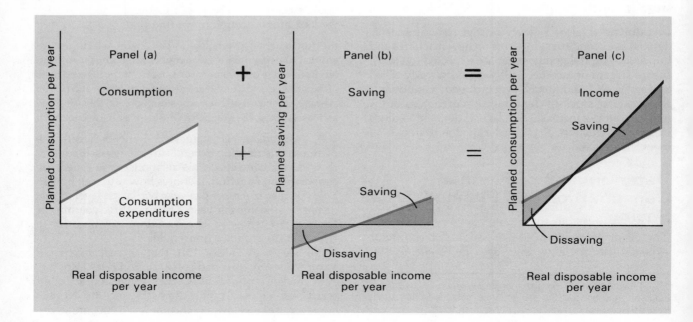

Graphing the Numbers

In Figure 15.3 the vertical axis measures the level of planned consumption per year, and the horizontal axis measures the level of real disposable income per year. In Figure 15.4 the horizontal axis is again real disposable income per year, but now the vertical axis is planned saving per year. All of these are on a pounds per year basis, which emphasizes the point that we are measuring flows, not stocks.

As you can see we have taken the income–consumption and income–saving combinations in Figure 15.1. Figure 15.3 shows the consumption function and Figure 15.4 the savings function. The savings function is the complement of the consumption function because consumption plus saving always equal disposable income. What is not consumed is, by definition, saved. The difference between actual disposable income and the planned level of consumption per year must be the planned level of saving per year.

Figure 15.3 shows the consumption function intersecting **the 45-degree line**. Along the 45-degree line, expenditure is exactly equal to income, so at point F, where the consumption function intersects the 45-degree line, real disposable income equals planned consumption. Point F is sometimes labelled the break-even income point because there is neither positive nor negative saving. This can be seen in Figure 15.4 as well. The planned annual rate of saving at a real disposable income level of 5000 units is indeed zero.

Dissaving and Autonomous Consumption

To the left of point F on Figures 15.3 and 15.4 this hypothetical family engages in dissaving. The amount of saving or dissaving in Figure 15.3 can be found by measuring the vertical distance between the 45-degree line and the consumption function. This simply tells us that if real disposable income temporarily falls below 5000 units, consumption will not be cut back by the full amount of the reduction. People will instead go into debt or consume existing assets in some way to compensate for the loss.

Now look at the point on the diagram where real disposable income is zero but planned consumption per year is 1000 units. This amount of planned consumption, which does not depend at all on actual disposable income, is called **autonomous consumption**. In other words, the autonomous consumption of 1000 units is *independent* of the level of disposable income. (We are, of course, assuming here that real disposable income does not equal zero year in year out.) It seems reasonable to assume that some spending continues in order to preserve life.

There are, of course, many possible types of autonomous expenditures. We generally take investment to be autonomous – existing independently of the model. We can assume that government expenditures are autonomous depending as they often do on

political forces. We will do just that at various times in the following chapters, in order to simplify our analysis of income determination.

___

Figure 15.3

The Consumption Function. If we plot the combinations of real disposable income and planned consumption from columns (1) and (2) in Figure 15.1 we get the consumption function. Every point on the 45-degree line bisecting this diagram is equidistant from the horizontal and the vertical axes; thus, at every point on it, consumption equals real disposable income. Where the consumption function crosses the 45-degree line, we know that consumption equals real disposable income and there is zero saving. The vertical distance between the 45-degree line and the consumption function measures the rate of saving or dissaving at any given income level.

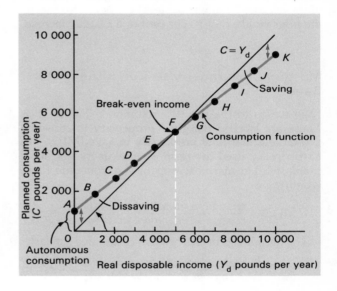

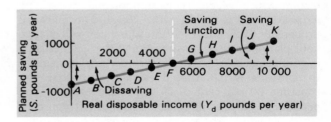

Figure 15.4

The Saving Function. If we plot the relationship between column (1), real disposable income, and column (3), planned saving, from Figure 15.2, we arrive at the savings function shown in this diagram. It is the complement of the consumption function presented in panel (d), Figure 15.3.

Average Propensity to Consume and to Save

Columns (4) and (5) of Figure 15.1 show the **average propensity to consume** (APC) and **average propensity to save** (APS). They are defined as:

$$APC \equiv \frac{consumption}{real\ disposable\ income}$$

$$APS \equiv \frac{saving}{real\ disposable\ income}$$

Notice that the average propensity to consume decreases as real income increases. This decrease simply means that the fraction of the family's real disposable income going to saving rises as income rises. The same fact can be found in column (5). The average propensity to save, which at first is negative, finally hits zero at an income level of £5000 and then becomes positive. In this example, it reaches a maximum value of 0.1 at income level £10000. This means the household saves 10 per cent of a £10000 income.

Marginal Propensity to Consume and to Save

Now we go to the last two columns in Figure 15.1. These are labelled **marginal propensity to consume** (MPC) and **marginal propensity to save** (MPS). We have already used the term *marginal*. It means 'small change in'. The marginal propensity to consume, then, is defined as:

$$MPC \equiv \frac{change\ in\ planned\ consumption}{change\ in\ real\ disposable\ income} \equiv \frac{\Delta C}{\Delta Y}$$

The marginal propensity to save is defined similarly:

$$MPS \equiv \frac{change\ in\ planned\ saving}{change\ in\ real\ disposable\ income} \equiv \frac{\Delta S}{\Delta Y}$$

What do the MPC and the MPS tell you? They tell you the percentage of an increase or decrease in income which will go to consumption and saving. The emphasis here is on the word *change*. The marginal propensity to consume indicates how you will change your planned rate of consumption if there is a change in your disposable income. If your marginal propensity to consume is 0.8, that does not mean that you consume 80 per cent of *all* disposable income. The percentage of your disposable income that you consume is given by the average propensity to consume, or APC, which is not, at most income levels, equal to 0.8. An MPC of 0.8 means that you will consume 80 per cent of any *increase* in your disposable income. In general, we assume that the marginal propensity to consume is between zero and one. In other words, we assume that individuals increase their planned consumption by more than zero and less than 100 per cent of any increase in real disposable income that they receive.

Some Relationships

By definition, consumption plus saving must equal income. Thus, both your disposable income and the change in disposable income are either consumed or saved. The proportions of either measure must equal 1, or 100 per cent. This allows us to make the following statements:

    1. APC + APS = 1 (100 per cent of total income)
and
    2. MPC + MPS = 1 (100 per cent of the change in income)

In other words, the average propensities as well as the marginal propensities to consume and save must total 1, or 100 per cent.

We can also show some of the key relationships in the theory of income and employment in graphical terms. These are set out Figure 15.5 in panels (a), (b), and (c) which show how to measure geometrically the average and marginal propensities to consume and to save. As can be seen in panels (b) and (c), the marginal propensity to consume is equal to the slope of the consumption function, and the marginal propensity to save is equal to the slope of the saving function.

Distinguishing between a Movement and a Shift

In Chapter 5 we made a clear distinction between a *movement along* a supply or demand curve and a *shift in* either of those curves. This same distinction applies when considering the consumption or saving function. Since the saving function is the complement of the consumption function, let us simply talk in terms of movements along, or shifts in, the consumption function.

In Figure 15.6 (on page 222) we show the effect on consumption of a rise in real disposable income of, for example, 2500 units per year, starting from the break-even income at 5000 units per year. We move upward along the consumption function, now labelled C, from point A to point B. Planned consumption per year will increase by the marginal propensity to consume (0.8) times the increase in real disposable income, or 0.8 × 2500 units= 2000 units; that is, planned consumption will rise from 5000 units to 7000 units per year. The same analysis holds for a decrease in disposable income. These represent movements along a given consumption function, CC.

How do we represent a decrease in *autonomous* consumption? In Figure 15.6 the autonomous part of planned consumption was 1000 units. If we wish to represent a decrease in the autonomous component of planned consumption, we must shift the entire consumption function downwards by the amount of this decrease. For example, a 500 units decrease in the autonomous component of consumption will shift the consumption function C down to C'. The break-even point moves from point A, or 5000 units, to point F, or

Figure 15.5

Marginal and Average Relationships. In panel (a), we show the relationship between the average propensity to consume (APC) and the average propensity to save (APS). Start off in panel (a) with real disposable income level equal to OA. This is identically equal to the horizontal distance EB and DC. Consumption at all real disposable incomes is given by the consumption function CC. Thus, consumption at real disposable income OA is equal to the vertical distance AB. We can now find the average propensity to consume. It is merely consumption ÷ real disposable income, or $AB ÷ OA$. To find the average propensity to save, we look at the difference between real disposable income and consumption. This is shown as the

vertical distance CB, which is also equal to the vertical distance DE. In any event, the APS is equal to saving ÷ real disposable income or $CB ÷ OA$.

In panel (b), we can find the marginal propensity to consume (MPC). It is defined as the change in consumption associated with a change in real disposable income. We show that with the change in real disposable income of NP, consumption will increase by PQ. Thus, the marginal propensity to consume is $PQ ÷ NP$.

The marginal propensity to save is defined as the change in saving due to a change in real disposable income. In panel (c), the change in real disposable income is the horizontal distance TU; the change in saving is the vertical distance UV. Thus, MPS is equal to $UV ÷ TU$.

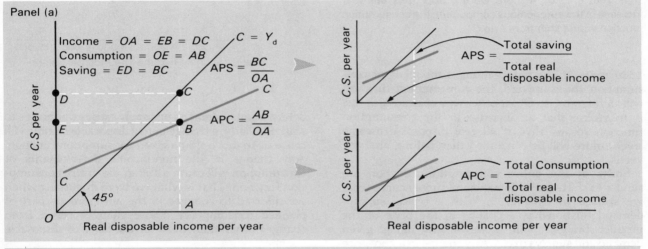

Panel (a)

$$Income = OA = EB = DC$$
$$Consumption = OE = AB$$
$$Saving = ED = BC$$

$C = Y_d$

$$APS = \frac{BC}{OA}$$

$$APC = \frac{AB}{OA}$$

$$APS = \frac{Total\ saving}{Total\ real\ disposable\ income}$$

$$APC = \frac{Total\ Consumption}{Total\ real\ disposable\ income}$$

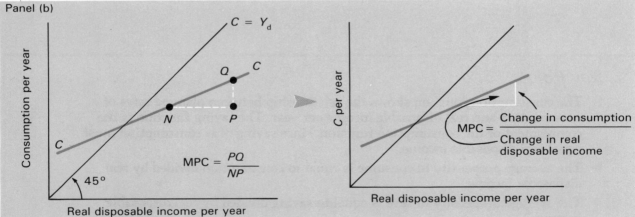

Panel (b)

$C = Y_d$

$$MPC = \frac{PQ}{NP}$$

$$MPC = \frac{Change\ in\ consumption}{Change\ in\ real\ disposable\ income}$$

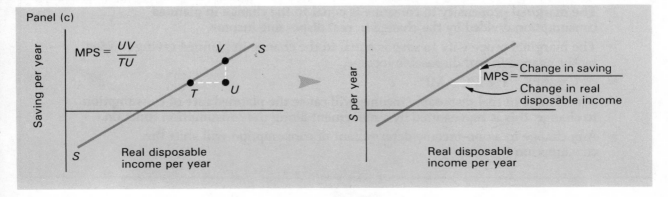

Panel (c)

$$MPS = \frac{UV}{TU}$$

$$MPS = \frac{Change\ in\ saving}{Change\ in\ real\ disposable\ income}$$

Figure 15.6

Distinguishing between Movements along and Shifts in the Consumption Function. Starting at the break-even real disposable income at point *A* on line *C*, if real disposable income increases by 2 500 units per year, then we will experience a movement from point *A* to point *B* along that consumption function. Planned consumption will go up by the product of marginal propensity to consume and the increase in real disposable income, or by 0.8 × 2 500 units = 2 000 units. Planned consumption will rise from 5 000 units to 7 000 units. On the other hand, if there were a 500 units per year decrease in autonomous consumption, the entire consumption function would shift from *C* to *C'*. If there were a 500 units per year increase in the autonomous component, the consumption function would shift from *C* to *C''*.

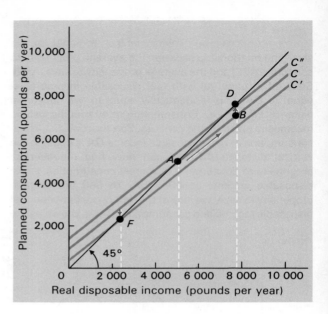

2 500 units. If the autonomous component of consumption shifts upward, the consumption function will shift from *C* to *C''*. Another way of looking at this is to realise that an increase in the consumption function means that at *all* real disposable income levels, more will be consumed than before, and vice versa.

Shifts in the entire consumption function are similar to shifts in the demand and supply curves that we studied in Chapter 5. With a typical supply–demand relationship, a change in the price of the product brings about a movement along given demand and supply curves. Any change in a non-price determinant of demand or supply causes the curves to shift. Similarly, a change in real disposable income will cause us to move *along* a given consumption function. Any change in the non-income determinants of consumption will cause a *shift* in the entire consumption function. That is what we were discussing when we referred to changes in the autonomous part of planned consumption. Those changes result from changes other than those in the level of disposable income.

Key Points 15.2

▶ The consumption function shows the relationship between planned rates of consumption and real disposable income per year. The saving function is the complement of the consumption function, since saving plus consumption must equal real disposable income.

▶ The average propensity to consume is equal to consumption divided by real disposable income.

▶ The average propensity to save is equal to saving divided by real disposable income.

▶ The marginal propensity to consume is equal to the change in planned consumption divided by the change in real disposable income.

▶ The marginal propensity to save is equal to the change in planned saving divided by the change in real disposable income.

▶ APC + APS = 1, MPC + MPS = 1

▶ Any change in real disposable income will cause the planned rate of consumption to change; this is represented by a movement along the consumption function.

▶ Any change in a non-income determinant of consumption will shift the consumption function.

The Non-income Determinants of Consumption

So far, the only determinant of spending in our theory of consumption has been income. There are, of course, other determinants of real consumption. They include the following: (1) wealth, (2) expectations, (3) interest rates and the ease with which credit can be obtained, and (4) the distribution of income.

Wealth

Other things being equal, the position of the consumption function will depend partly on the real wealth that an individual has. Wealth includes all the cars, houses, stereos, and bonds that a household possesses. We predict that when the real wealth of a household increases, the consumption function will shift upwards, and when it decreases the converse will hold.

Inflation can affect one's real wealth and, therefore, the position of the consumption function. Inflation can erode the value of money-denominated assets (all other things being held constant), causing the consumption function to fall.

Expectations

Particularly in the short run, expectations can influence the position of the consumption function. If households anticipate better times ahead (higher income) than currently, the consumption function may shift upwards. If they are pessimistic, it may shift downwards. The expectation of the future rate of inflation relative to today's rate of inflation may also have a bearing on planned consumption expenditures. If we expected that the rate of inflation might rise in the years to come, we might increase consumption now.

The Interest Rate

An increase in the interest rate typically leads to a reduction in interest-sensitive purchases such as cars and houses. Most of these are financed by borrowing. Therefore, the higher the rate of interest, the more expensive it becomes to buy a car or a house. Other things being equal, an increase in the rate of interest will lead to a decrease in planned consumption expenditures at every level of real disposable income.

A credit squeeze, in which it is made harder for people to obtain loans for consumer purchases, may be associated with higher interest rates. Before they could buy durable goods, some people would have to save up, and their consumption levels will be lower than they would have been if credit had been easy.

The Distribution of Income

Income distribution becomes more unequal when some groups of the population become wealthier while others become poorer. A more equal distribution of income may result from redistributive tax and benefit systems, which tax high incomes heavily in order to pay benefits to those on low incomes. The rich will tend to have a lower marginal propensity to consume than the poor. Some of the income taken from the rich might have been saved. Practically all the income transferred to the poor will be spent on consumption. So a more equal distribution of income will, other things being equal, shift the consumption function upwards.

IS THE MPC CONSTANT?

So far we have assumed that the MPC is constant, which means that the consumption function will be a straight line. Is this reasonable? In practice, it is highly likely that the MPC will fall if income rises. Growth in the standard of living will generally cause people to save a larger proportion of increased income and consume a smaller proportion. A fall in the MPC as income rises would lead to the consumption function levelling off (rising less steeply) as income rises.

When the MPC is constant, so that the consumption function is linear, it can be stated in the form $C = a + bY$, where a is the autonomous element in consumption and b is the MPC (and the gradient of the consumption function).

Permanent-income Hypothesis

In recent years a rather different view of the consumption function has been developed. Basically, the **permanent-income hypothesis** holds that consumption doesn't depend on *current* disposable income but rather on some measure of expected, or permanent, income. The planning period may be anywhere from two to five years, or even longer, depending upon people's expectations. According to this theory, consumption will not drop drastically even if, for some reason, people's income falls below what they think their permanent income is. Conversely, consumption will not increase very much even if people's income suddenly jumps above the level they consider to be permanent. The permanent income hypothesis suggests that the level of consumption will stay fairly stable over time. (It is part of the theory underlying those views concerning inflation which stress the importance of money.)

Determinants of the Level of Saving

Since saving is inversely related to consumption, everything which influences consumption will similarly influence saving – but in the opposite direction.

In particular, people consider interest rates, inflation rates and expectations about the future, when taking decisions about saving. Low rates of interest give a poor return on savings held in the form of financial assets such as bank accounts, and may reduce the level of saving. Inflation however, leads to a reduction in the value of an individual's stock of savings. If people want to keep their savings at a particular level of purchasing power (e.g. one year's income), they will have to save more for a while in order to rebuild their savings. Or they may be encouraged to save if they can buy granny bonds (index-linked bonds), the value of which is linked to the rate of inflation so that they do not lose their purchasing power. Both interest rates and inflation have been found to be important in determining the level of saving in the UK in the past decade.

Expectations would seem to be important in affecting savings decisions. However, the threat of increasing unemployment has not in practice caused increased saving in the UK. The world's thriftiest people are the Japanese, who save roughly a third of their incomes – almost twice the European average. The threat of unemployment in Japan is comparatively low. Cultural factors, and habit, probably play a major part in determining the level of saving.

Determinants of Investment

Investment, you will remember, is defined as expenditure on new plant and capital equipment and changes in stocks. Investment levels can be quite volatile, especially net investment, i.e. gross investment less depreciation or capital consumption. Figure 15.7 shows how both have fluctuated.

If we compare investment expenditures historically with consumption and saving expenditures, we find that the latter are relatively less variable over time than the former. Investment decisions are based on highly variable, subjective estimates of how the economic future looks. We just discussed the role of expectations in determining the position of the consumption function. Expectations play an even greater role in determining the position of the investment function. This could account for much of the instability of investment over time. Given this chronic instability, it is more difficult to derive a satisfactory theory of planned investment expenditures. None the

Figure 15.7
Trends in Gross and Net Investment. Net investment is particularly volatile. Note that these figures give absolute values. Gross investment as a percentage of GDP has grown less rapidly.

Year	Gross investment	Net Investment
	(£m, 1980 prices)	
1963	27095	13117
1964	31581	16945
1965	33095	18004
1966	33907	18215
1967	36902	20420
1968	39191	21853
1969	38932	20882
1970	39925	20854
1971	40700	20759
1972	40594	19748
1973	43535	21909
1974	41734	20063
1975	41808	18271
1976	42434	18070
1977	41323	16324
1978	42938	16531
1975	43925	16809
1980	41628	13688
1981	38075	8943
1982	40645	10516
1983	42348	11633
1984	45693	14349
1985	46104	14455

Source: CSO, *Economic Trends*; 1985 Blue Book, Tables 11.4 and 11.5; and Treasury, *Economic Progress Report*, Mar. 1986.

less, we shall attempt to construct an investment function.

The Planned Investment Function

Consider that at any time there is a range of investment opportunities that firms can identify. These investment opportunities have rates of return ranging from zero to very high, with the number (or value) of all such projects inversely related to the rate of return. That is to say, there are certainly fewer investment opportunities with high rates of return than there are with low rates of return. Since each project is profitable only if its rate of return exceeds the opportunity cost of the investment – the rate of interest – it follows that, as the interest rate falls, planned investment spending increases, and vice versa.* There will be an increasing number of projects which yield a rate of return sufficient to cover interest charges, as interest rates fall. In other words, a fall in interest rates leads to a movement down the investment function.

A hypothetical investment schedule is given in Figure 15.8 and plotted in Figure 15.9. If the rate of interest is 13 per cent, then the quantity of planned investment will be £225 million per year. Notice, by the way, that planned investment is also given on a per year basis, showing that it represents a flow, not a stock. (The stock counterpart of investment is the accumulated stock of capital in the economy.)

The rate of return on investments is sometimes called the marginal efficiency of capital (MEC), or the marginal product of capital. Keynes recognised that although interest rates and investment would be related, their relationship (i.e. the marginal efficiency of capital or the investment function) could be unstable.

Other Determinants of Investment

We saw that the consumption function could be related to the level of real disposable income. We also saw that there were other determinants that would shift the schedule up or down. The same analysis can be applied to planned investment. The rate of interest and the rate of planned investment are related. At the same time, there are many other determinants of planned investment. Increased demand in the economy would increase the rate of return. At any given interest rate more investment would take place and the MEC schedule would shift to the right. Other major influences on investment are expectations, the cost of capital equipment, innovation and technology, and the tax treatment of investment expenditure.

EXPECTATIONS

Firms estimate the future demand for their products, in order to assess the likely future profitability of their investments. If higher future sales are expected, then

Figure 15.8
Planned Investment Schedule. The rate of planned investment is asserted to be inversely related to the rate of interest in this hypothetical schedule.

Rate of interest (per cent per year)	Planned investment (£m per year)
15	175
14	200
13	225
12	250
11	275
10	300

Figure 15.9
Planned Investment. If we plot the interest rate/planned investment data pairs from panel (a), we obtain the investment function *II*. It is negatively sloped.

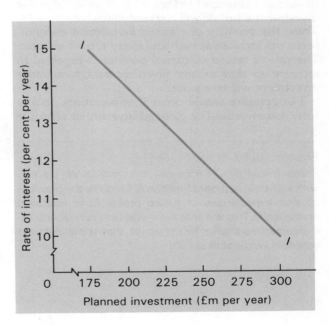

more machines and bigger plants will be planned for the future. More investment will be undertaken.

Each investment undertaken will yield an income stream in the future, which is the profit from the project. This will be total revenue, less total cost. Estimating revenue means deciding the likely level of sales, at the price which the market will bear. Estimating total cost requires knowledge of the costs of all necessary inputs, and of any technological problems which are likely to arise. The resulting estimate of likely profit, for each year of the life of the investment can then be discounted (i.e. reduced by an amount corresponding to market rates of interest) in order to

---

*Even if firms use retained earnings (corporate savings) to finance an investment, the higher the market rate of interest the greater the *opportunity cost* of using those retained earnings, which could have been earning interest, at no risk, in the bank. Thus, it does not matter in our analysis whether the firm must seek financing from external sources or can obtain such financing by using retained earnings.

find its present value. If the present value of the total future income stream, yielded by the investment, is greater than the cost of the capital to be invested, then the project looks profitable enough to be viable. (Chapter 27 explains this in more detail.)

Of course there are risks involved in any investment project. One of these is the risk that unforeseen events, such as inflation, may cause costs and revenues to be less favourable than the firm's estimates suggested they might be. Technical problems may raise costs unexpectedly. Fashions may change the level of demand. The riskier the project, the greater the likelihood of profit must be before the firm goes ahead with the investment.

When firms have rosy expectations, and a high level of confidence about the prospects for their sector of the economy, the investment function will shift outwards to the right; that is, at each interest rate, more will be invested than before. If they expect the future to be grim, the investment schedule will move inwards, to the left, reflecting less desired investment at each and every interest rate.

Consider the possibility that expectations have improved dramatically. What will this do to the investment schedule? In Figure 15.10 we see that the investment schedule will shift outwards from II to $I'I'$. Thus, the quantity of planned investment expenditures will increase at each and every rate of interest. The rate of return on capital invested is expected to increase so that at any given interest rate, more investment will take place.

The opposite would occur if expectations took a turn downwards. The planned investment schedule

would therefore shift leftwards to $I''I''$. In other words, the planned rate of investment expenditures would fall at each and every rate of interest. Appendix B to Chapter 16 looks in more detail at the effect of changing demand on investment.

COST OF NEW CAPITAL GOODS

If the cost of new plant and equipment suddenly were to increase (*relative* to the price at which output can be sold), firms' investment plans may change. In fact, we would expect the investment function to shift leftwards. The opposite would occur if there were an abrupt, unanticipated fall in the relative cost of capital goods. Investment goods become *relatively* cheaper, even if the price remains the same, if labour costs rise. Labour-saving investment may then increase.

INNOVATION AND TECHNOLOGY

Both improvements in current productive technology and innovations could generally be expected to shift the investment function to the right, since both would stimulate a demand for additional capital goods. In other words, we would see an increase in the demand for capital goods.

Profits Taxes

Firms estimate rates of return on investments on the basis of expected after-tax profits. If there is an increase in tax-rates on profits, other things being equal, we expect a shift in the planned investment function leftwards. If there is a decrease in tax-rates, we expect a shift rightwards.

In the UK, taxes have been designed to encourage firms to plough back profits into the business. For any given rate of interest, investment is likely to be higher if expenditure on capital reduces the tax due.

Figure 15.10

Shifts in the Planned Investment Schedule. We start off with a given investment function *II*. Consider the possibility that expectations of future profits have improved dramatically. This will shift the investment schedule to *I'I'*. If expectations change for the worse, then the investment schedule would shift to *I''I''*.

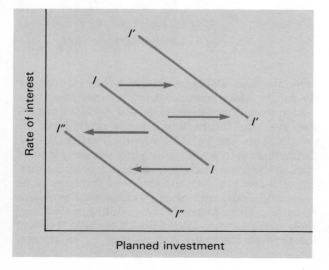

Planned investment

Figure 15.11
Tax Subsidy Rates on Manufacturing Fixed Investment

	% of asset price
UK	13.1
USA	12.8
Netherlands	6.2
Italy	5.0
France	4.4
Belgium	−2.4
Japan	−3.4
Germany	−5.5

Source: IMF Survey 1981.

At least this is the logic. In the UK, rather low levels of profitability caused governments to give generous investment allowances in calculating corporation tax. This led to a substantial subsidy for capital investment (see Figure 15.11). In the 1984 budget the system was changed in order to give more encouragement to investments generating a high rate of return, and to sectors which had not benefited under the old rules. Also, the rate of tax was reduced from 42 per cent to 35 per cent (or 30 per cent for small companies). It was also recognized that subsidizing capital investment makes little economic sense at a time when there is a large excess supply of labour.

Key Points 15.4

► **Saving depends primarily on the rate of interest, the rate of inflation, and sometimes, expectations about future economic well being.**

► **Investment is related though not always closely, to interest rates.**

► **Investment is significantly affected by profits or by expectations about future profitability; by the cost (supply price) of capital; by the cost of investment relative to that of labour; and by changes in technology and profits tax.**

CASE STUDY

The Consumption Function in the UK

Figure 15.12 shows consumption plotted against disposable income in the UK, 1974–84. A line has been drawn along the points, which can be regarded as the UK consumption function. All the points fall below the 45-degree line, which shows that every year, aggregate saving was positive.

Keynes's theory seems to have been borne out by the empirical evidence. Real consumption is greatly dependent on real disposable income, and as real income changes, so too does real consumption, though by a smaller amount. However, there seems to be a difference between this historical consumption function and the hypothetical household consumption function represented in Figures 15.3 and 15.4. In Figure 15.12 there is no autonomous consumption; that is, the

consumption function never crosses the 45-degree $C = Y_d$ reference line. In fact, it intersects

---

Figure 15.12
The UK Consumption Function

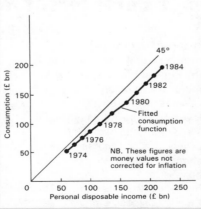

Source: Annual Abstract of Statistics, 1985, pp. 3 and 37.

the vertical axis at zero. How can this be? These two different consumption functions can be reconciled by distinguishing between the short and the long run.

Short-run versus Long-run Consumption Functions

The consumption function in Figure 15.12 represents the long-run consumption behaviour in this country and goes through the origin. It shows no autonomous consumption, since it starts at zero. In Figures 15.3 and 15.4 there was an autonomous component to consumptiion. Also, the slope of the consumption function in Figure 15.12 and the slope of the

continued overleaf

consumption functions in the previous figures are quite different. The hypothetical consumption functions that we have been drawing in our graphs are similar to *actual* short-run consumption functions; the empirical evidence suggests that distinct short-run and long-run consumption functions exist. The long-run consumption function shows a marginal propensity to consume of about 0.9. (Incidentally, the average propensity to consume is also 0.9.) We see, then, a basic inconsistency between the short-run consumption functions used in our examples and the historical long-run consumption function. One way to reconcile this inconsistency involves the permanent-income hypothesis.

When we get data on families with different incomes and different levels of spending, we can assume that many high-income people are experiencing those levels of earnings only temporarily,

not permanently. On the one hand, their APS appears high because they assume they will not be able to maintain a high spending level when the income goes back to normal. Their APC, on the other hand, appears to be relatively low. Conversely, many people with low incomes may be at earning levels that are abnormally low for them, when compared to a higher level that they consider to be more permanent. These people will probably be saving very little, or even dissaving. Thus, we can imagine plotting a consumption relationship like the one in Figure 15.3. The permanent-income hypothesis would predict such a consumption relationship at any one point in time.

This hypothesis also predicts the long-run consumption function found in Figure 15.12, since the permanent-income hypothesis assumes that the marginal propensity to consume is the same in the long run as the average

propensity to consume. Proponents of the hypothesis contend that there is no difference between marginal and average propensities to consume if one looks at *permanent* income rather than *current* income. Accordingly, we would not expect to see the 'permanently' rich saving a larger percentage of their income (in the long run) than the 'permanently' poor – other things being equal.

Questions

1. Does the consumption function in the UK behave as economic theory would predict?

2. In the UK the APC is approximately 0.9. This is the same as the MPC. Can you explain why?

3. In what way does a Keynesian consumption function differ from the consumption function suggested by the permanent income hypothesis?

CASE STUDY

Are Levels of Investment Sensitive to Changes in Interest Rates?

Figure 15.13 shows estimated real interest rates, the average rate of discount used by the Bank of England (as a representative interest rate), and the level of gross domestic fixed capital formation for the years 1966 to 1985.

The nominal interest rates paid by firms on money borrowed for investment are usually well above the Bank of England's discount rate. This nevertheless gives us a good idea of how the general level of nominal interest rates has

changed over the years. The estimated real rate of interest is the Bank of England's discount rate minus the inflation rate.

What can we deduce? Investment grew steadily up till 1973 when the oil price rise caused business confidence to slump. It grew again during the boomlet of 1977–9 and slumped horribly in the recession of 1980–1. Clearly business expectations are crucial in determining the level of investment. Nevertheless it would

be a mistake to discount the role of the rate of interest. *Relatively* low interest rates during the late seventies may have encouraged investment in 1978–9. And there is no doubt that the high nominal interest rate in 1980 played a major part in the slump in investment in 1980–1. Firms were quick to point out their problems to the government through such mouthpieces as the CBI.

While it is unlikely that the level of investment will respond to small changes in interest rates, either real or nominal, major and sustained changes may have a substantial effect.

Figure 15.13
Investment and the Rate of Interest

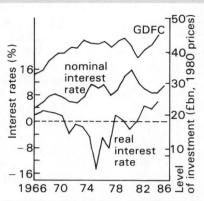

Source: Blue Book 1985; CSO *Economic Trends, 1985; Financial Statistics*, Oct. 1985.

Question
1. How is investment affected by (a) business expectations and (b) interest rates?

CASE STUDY

The Savings Ratio in the UK

Figure 15.14
The Savings Ratio 1976-85

Personal saving as a percentage of personal disposable income

1976	12.1
1977	11.6
1978	12.7
1979	13.5
1980	15.0
1981	13.3
1982	12.8
1983	11.5
1984	12.1
1985	11.9
1986	13.4 (est.)

Sources: CSO: Economic Trends, 1986 Financial Statistics, July 1986

The savings ratio varies considerably from year to year. There are a number of possible influences at work, often simultaneously. The level of income may influence saving in two ways. There may be a simple direct relationship. Income rises so people save more. Or, the permanent income hypothesis suggests that an increase in income which is temporary will lead to higher savings because consumption will remain stable. The interest rate may have some effect on savings at times, e.g. in 1984 when interest rates were high. Periods of high inflation reduce the value of assets held in money terms (e.g. building society deposits) and induce people to save more (as in 1979-81).

Questions
1. Use data in Chapter 11 to relate inflation rates to savings.
2. How would you explain the slowly rising savings from 1984 onwards?

Exam Preparation and Practice

INTRODUCTORY EXERCISES

1. Complete the following table.

Disposable income (£)	Consumption (£)	Saving (£)
500	510	—
600	600	—
700	690	—
800	780	—
900	870	—
1 000	960	—

(a) Plot the consumption and saving schedules on graph paper.

(b) Determine the marginal propensity to consume and the marginal propensity to save.

(c) Determine the average propensity to consume and the average propensity to save for each level of income.

2. Consider the following table, then answer the questions below it.

Annual consumption (£)	Annual income (£)
5	0
80	100
155	200

(a) What is the APC at annual income level £100? At £200?

(b) What happens to the APC as annual income rises?

(c) What is the MPC as annual income goes from £0 to £100? From £100 to £200?

(d) What happens to the MPC as income rises?

(e) What number is the APC approaching?

(f) What is the equation for the consumption function in this table?

3. Consider the following table, then answer the questions below it.

Annual consumption (£)	Annual income (£)
0	0
80	100
160	200

(a) What is the APC at annual income £100? At £200?

(b) What happens to the APC as annual income rises?

(c) What is the MPC as income rises from £0 to £100? From £100 to £200?

(d) What happens to the MPC as income rises?

(e) What is the equation for the consumption function in this table?

(f) In what way has consumption changed in this question, compared to the situation in Question 2?

MULTIPLE CHOICE QUESTIONS

1. The marginal propensity to consume can be expressed as

A $\dfrac{\text{total consumption}}{\text{total income}}$

B $\dfrac{\text{change in consumption}}{\text{total income}}$

C $\dfrac{\text{change in income}}{\text{change in consumption}}$

D $\dfrac{\text{change in consumption}}{\text{change in income}}$

2. The following data represent a consumption function for an economy.

Income (£m)	Consumption (£m)
120	116
140	132
160	148
180	164
200	180
220	196

What is the value of the marginal propensity to consume in this economy?

A 0.00
B 0.80
C 0.90
D 0.91
E 0.98

3. If the marginal propensity to consume is rising as income rises, then the

A marginal propensity to save is rising
B marginal propensity to save is constant
C average propensity to consume is rising
D average propensity to consume is constant
E average propensity to save is rising

4. An analysis of expenditure by households at different income levels suggests that average propensity to consume (APC) is equal to the marginal propensity to consume (MPC) over low income levels. However, at high income levels, MPC declines with income and is less than the APC. Which one of the following describes these findings?

RELATED ESSAY QUESTIONS

1. Explain why, in the short run, the marginal propensity to consume is less than the average propensity to consume, but tends to equal it in the long run.

2. 'Aggregate consumption is mainly a function of the level of income.' Discuss.

3. Distinguish between saving and investment. What are the determinants of saving?

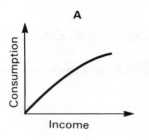

A

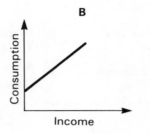

B

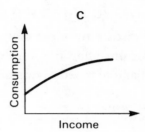

C

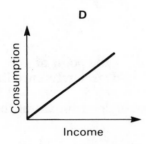

D

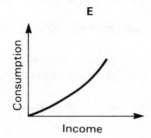

E

16 Income and Employment Determination: A Simple Model

Questions for Preview

1 What does the total *planned* expenditure curve indicate?

2 What is the interpretation of the 45-degree line?

3 Why does the equilibrium level of real national income occur at the point of intersection of the total planned expenditure curve and the 45-degree reference line?

4 What is the multiplier, how does it work, and what is the main determinant of the multiplier?

5 What is the paradox of thrift?

Why is the equilibrium level of real national income what it is? We can answer this question using a Keynesian model of income determination subject to simplifying assumptions. The most important assumption is that the short-run aggregate supply curve is horizontal at the existing price level. The implication of this is that the equilibrium level of real national income is demand-determined. We do not have to worry about either supply constraints or changes in the price level, at least not initially.

In Chapter 12 we found that the circular flow was only in equilibrium when total planned expenditures were equal to total national output. Also, in equilibrium planned saving must equal planned investment. Whenever such was not the case, there would be unplanned changes in stocks. The unplanned changes would either cause a contraction or an expansion of the circular flow. We can now determine when the circular flow will be in equilibrium. We need to determine when aggregate (total) planned expendi-

ture equals planned production. Since, for the moment, we are ignoring government expenditures as well as the foreign sector (net exports), our analysis involves only planned consumption expenditures and planned investment expenditures.

Consumption as a Function of Real National Income

We are interested in determining the equilibrium level of real national income. But when we examined the consumption function in the last chapter, it related planned consumption expenditures to the level of real disposable income per year. Disposable income is national income less taxes plus transfer payments.

If we assume that real disposable income is the same proportion of real national income every year, then we can substitute real national income for real disposable income in the consumption function.

Figure 16.1

Combining Consumption and Investment. This graph is simply the consumption function with autonomous investment, *I*, added. The arrow, labelled *I*, shows by how much investment raises expenditure. The result is the consumption plus investment line, *C* + *I*, or the total planned expenditure function relating planned expenditures to different levels of real national income, under the assumption that there is no government or foreign sector.

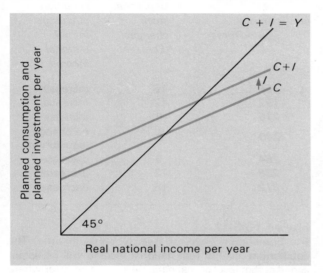

The 45-degree Line

Along the **45-degree line**, planned expenditures equal real national income per year. In Figure 16.1, at the point where the consumption function intersects the 45-degree line, planned consumption expenditures will be exactly equal to real national income per year.

Adding the Investment Function

We add now the other component of private aggregate demand: investment spending (*I*). We simplify our model by considering all planned investment to be autonomous, that is, independent of income. Firms plan to invest a given, constant *amount* and will do so no matter what the level of income. How do we add this amount of investment to our consumption function? We simply add a line above the *C* line in Figure 16.1 that is higher by the vertical distance equal to the amount of autonomous investment. This distance is shown by the arrow connecting the consumption function *C* to the expenditure function, *C* + *I*.

If we ignore government expenditures and net exports (the foreign sector), the *C* + *I* line represents total planned expenditures for the economy at different levels of real national income per year.

Determining the Equilibrium Level of Real National Income

We continue to assume that a Keynesian short-run horizontal aggregate supply curve exists, that there is no government or foreign sector, and that investment is autonomous, and that planned consumption expenditures are determined by the level of real national income.

Assume that the consumption function has an autonomous component equal to £33 billion per year, and that the marginal propensity to consume, out of real national income, is 0.8, or four-fifths.

Using this consumption function gives us the values for consumption in column (2) of Figure 16.2 (page 234), and also the values of savings in column (3).

Planned investment, in column (4) is assumed to be autonomous at a level of £15 billion per year no matter what the level of national income. Column (5) is the sum of planned consumption and planned investment. In Figure 16.3 (page 234) the horizontal axis measures real national income and the vertical axis measures consumption and investment expenditure. The consumption figures in column (2) are used to plot the consumption function *C*.

Equilibrium will occur when total planned expenditures equal total production. In Figure 16.3 total planned expenditures are given by the *C* + *I* line, which is also equivalent to aggregate demand. Total planned expenditures will equal total production, or real

Figure 16.2

The Determination of Equilibrium Real National Income. Given that prices are constant and the short-run aggregate supply schedule is horizontal at the current price level, the equilibrium level of real national income is demand-determined only. Consequently, whenever total planned expenditures – planned consumption plus planned investment – equal real national income, equilibrium will occur. In our hypothetical example, equilibrium occurs at £240 billion per year. At this level of real national income, planned expenditures equal real national income, planned saving equals planned investment, and there are no unplanned changes in stocks.

(1) Real national income (£bn)	(2) Planned consumption (£bn)	(3) Planned saving (£bn)	(4) Planned investment (£bn) (2) + (4)	(5) Total planned expenditures	(6) Unplanned stock changes (£bn)	(7) Direction of change in real national income
150	153	–3	15	168	–18	increase
180	177	3	15	192	–12	increase
210	201	9	15	216	–6	increase
240	225	15	15	240	0	no change (equilibrium)
270	249	21	15	264	6	decrease
300	273	27	15	288	12	decrease
330	297	33	15	312	18	decrease

national income, where the C + I line intersects the 45-degree line at E, because points along that line are equidistant from both axes. At point E, there is no tendency for the equilibrium level of real national income to change. Thus at £240 billion per year, we have the equilibrium level of real national income.

What about Employment?

What will be the level of employment associated with the equilibrium level of income? This figure depends on the number of employees required to produce £240 billions' worth of output annually. It may or may not be the number of people wanting work. Given a fixed amount of capital and a steady state of technology – reasonable assumptions in the short run, as it takes time to increase capital and improve technology – we can predict that an increase in output will be associated with a higher level of employment, and vice versa.

What Happens When There is Disequilibrium?

What happens if total planned expenditures exceed real national income (total planned production) or vice versa?

TOTAL PLANNED EXPENDITURES EXCEED REAL NATIONAL INCOME

If we start with real national income at £180 billion, in Figure 16.3, we see that at this real national income level, annual planned consumption will be £177 billion. Adding planned investment of £15 billion, we get total planned expenditures of £192 billion, which exceeds real national income by £12 billion. The planned

Figure 16.3

The Equilibrium Level of Real National Income. The equilibrium level of real national income will be established at that level of real national income per year where total planned expenditures, as evidenced by the C + I line, intersect the 45-degree line, because that is where total planned expenditures will exactly equal real national income (production). In this diagram, equilibrium occurs at point E with an equilibrium level of real national income of £240 billion per year.

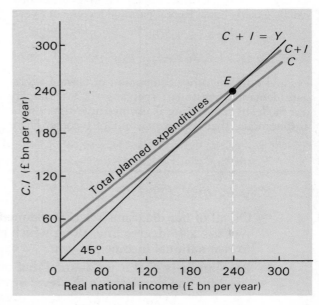

investment of firms exceeds the planned saving of households. In other words, goods and services are being bought at a faster rate than they are being produced. The result of this is seen in column (6) of Figure 16.2. Stocks are being run down at the rate of £12 billion a year, exactly the rate by which total planned expenditures exceed real national income (planned production). As a result, firms will seek to expand their production; they will take on more labour. This will create an increase in real national income and employment. Real national income will rise toward its equilibrium level.

TOTAL PLANNED EXPENDITURES ARE LESS THAN REAL NATIONAL INCOME

Now take the opposite situation. Real national income is at the £300-billion level. At that level of real national income, planned consumption is £273 billion and planned investment is still £15 billion. Total planned expenditures, $C + I$, now equal £288 billion, which is less than real national income (planned production) of £300 billion. In other words, the rate at which households plan to save exceeds the rate at which firms plan to invest. This means that firms will find their sales less than they had expected. Stocks will accumulate, as we see in column (6), at the rate of £12 billion per year. This *unplanned* accumulation of stocks causes firms to cut back on their production and, therefore, lay off employees. The result will be a drop in employment toward the equilibrium level, £240 billion.

Another Approach: Leakages and Injections

We can look at the determination of the equilibrium level of real national income using leakages and injections.

In Chapter 12, we defined **leakages** as withdrawals of potential planned expenditures from the income–expenditures stream. Leakages are saving, purchases of goods from other countries (imports),

and taxes. Whenever there is a leakage, consumption necessarily falls. Leakages tend to reduce the equilibrium level of national income, unless, of course, leakages are offset by injections.

Injections are additions of potential planned expenditures to the income-expenditures stream. They add spending to the flow. Injections are investment, government spending, and foreign purchases of UK goods (exports). Injections tend to increase the equilibrium level of real national income, and they offset leakages.

To simplify, we must continue to assume that there is one leakage – saving – and one injection – investment. Chapter 17 introduces the other leakages and injections.

ATTAINING EQUILIBRIUM

When planned leakages equal planned injections, total planned expenditures will equal real national income. Equilibrium will occur because the total planned amount of non-consumption (leakages) equals the total planned amount of supplemental expenditures (injections).

GRAPHICAL ANALYSIS

In our model so far in this chapter, investment has been autonomous, that is, fixed at some level and not a function of aggregate income. In Figure 16.4 we show real national income per year on the horizontal axis and saving and investment per year on the vertical axis. At point E, the intersection of II and SS, the equilibrium level of real national output is determined.

THE BATH-WATER THEOREM

One can vizualize a bath with a specified level of water already in it. The drain is open; this is clearly a leakage. Unless there is an injection, the level of the water will fall. The injection will be water from the tap. The leakage represents saving; the injection represents investment, and the level of the bath-water represents

---

Key Points 16.2

▶ **The equilibrium level of real national income is at the intersection of the total planned expenditure line with the 45-degree line. At that level of real national income, planned consumption plus planned investment will equal real national income.**

▶ **When total planned expenditures exceed real national income, there will be unplanned decreases in stocks; the size of the circular flow of income will increase and the economy will expand.**

▶ **Whenever planned expenditures are less than real national income, there will be unplanned increases in stocks, the size of the circular flow will shrink – a lower equilibrium level of real national income will prevail.**

▶ **If we know the relationship between real national income and the required labour force, then we can determine the level of employment consistent with any given equilibrium level of real national income.**

national output (which is exactly equal to real national income).

Figure 16.4
Leakages-Injections Approach to Equilibrium. On the horizontal axis we measure real national income per year. On the vertical axis we measure saving and investment per year. Saving constitutes a leakage. Investment constitutes an injection. Leakages equal injections where the saving schedule *SS* intersects the investment schedule *II*. This occurs at point *E*, yielding an equilibrium level of real national income per year of Y_e.

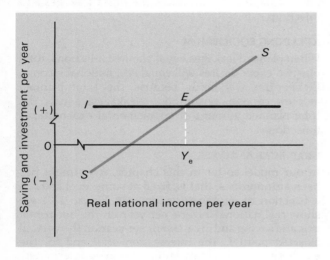

Real national income per year

Figure 16.5
Planned and Actual Rates of Saving and Investment. Only at the equilibrium level of real national income of £240 billion per year will planned saving equal actual saving, planned investment equal actual investment, and therefore planned saving equal planned investment. At higher income levels, planned investment will be less than actual investment, the difference being made up of unplanned increases in stocks. The opposite is true for all income levels less than £240 billion per year.

Using the Leakages–Injections Approach

The leakages–injections approach can show us the reasons why the equilibrium level of real national income may be different from levels of real national income that policy-makers might consider acceptable. Leakages in our simplified example are represented by *desired* rates of saving. Injections, on the other hand, are represented by *desired* rates of investment. Desired (or planned) saving and desired (or planned) investment are carried out by different parts of society and for different reasons. Basically, households save in order to provide for emergencies, retirement, and so on. Firms on the other hand invest in order to increase plant and equipment, as well as to build up stocks. Since savers and investors are often different groups of people acting for different reasons, we have no assurance that desired saving will equal desired investment at a national output and income level that results in an acceptable rate of employment. Suppose, for example, that we start off in equilibrium, where planned investment equals planned saving. Planned investment might then rise. But since investment decisions are frequently made by individuals different from those making saving decisions, there is no guarantee that *planned* saving will also rise by an equivalent amount. As another example, suppose that after starting out initially in an equilibrium where planned investment equals planned saving, savers, for whatever reason, increase their planned saving. Firms cannot be expected to automatically increase planned investment by an equal amount. Indeed the resulting loss of demand for consumer goods may make their prospects quite gloomy.

Saving and Investment: Planned versus Actual

Figure 16.5 shows planned investment as a horizontal line at £15 billion per year. Investment is constant and does not depend on the level of income.

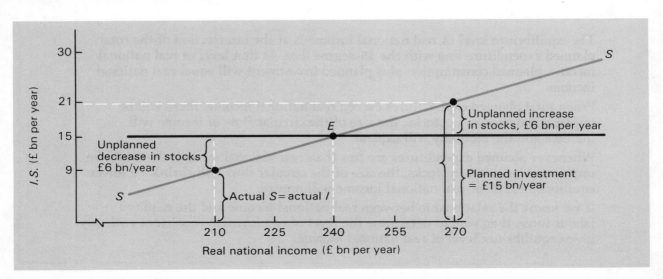

Real national income (£ bn per year)

Planned saving is represented by *SS*. It is taken directly from Figure 16.2 which shows planned saving in column (3) and real national income in column (1). The planned saving schedule is the complement of the planned consumption schedule, represented by the *C* line in Figure 16.3.

Why does equilibrium have to occur at the intersection of the planned saving and planned investment schedules? If we are at *E* in Figure 16.5, planned saving equals planned investment. There is no tendency for firms to alter the rate of production or level of employment, because they are neither increasing nor decreasing their stocks in an unplanned way.

However, if output is at £270 billion, planned investment is £15 billion as usual, but planned saving is £21 billion. This means that consumers will purchase less of total output than firms had anticipated. There will be an unplanned increase in stocks of £6 billion bringing actual investment into line with actual saving. But this rate of output cannot continue for long. Firms will respond to this unplanned increase in stocks by cutting back production and employment, and we will move towards a lower level of real national income.

On the other hand, if the real national income is £210 billion per year, planned investment continues annually at £15 billion; but at that output rate, planned saving is only £9 billion. This means that households and firms are purchasing more of the real national income than firms had expected. They must run down stocks below the planned level by £6 billion bringing actual investment into equality with actual saving. This situation cannot last forever either. In their attempt to increase stocks to the desired previous level, firms will increase output and employment, and real national income will rise towards its equilibrium value of £240 billion. Figure 16.5 demonstrates the necessary equality between actual saving and actual investment. Stocks adjust so that saving and investment, after the fact, are *always* equal.

Every time the saving rate planned by households differs from the investment rate planned by firms, there will be an expansion or contraction in the circular flow in the form of unplanned changes in stocks. Real national income and employment will change until there are no unplanned stock changes, that is, until we have attained the equilibrium level of real national income.

Changes in Equilibrium Real National Income and the Multiplier

The actual level of real national income is not in fact very stable. We have had long-run growth along with the ups and downs of the trade cycle. We will try now to explain *why* the equilibrium level of real national income fluctuates and *how* it fluctuates.

In our simplified model a change in autonomous investment will clearly change the equilibrium level of

real national output. Figure 16.6 shows the determination of the equilibrium level of real national income per year using the two approaches previously given. In panel (a), we find that with schedule $C + I_1$, the equilibrium level of real national income will be Y_1, shown on the horizontal axis. Given the consumption function implicit in panel (a), we have its complement,

Figure 16.6

Changes in Equilibrium Real National Income. In panel (a) the $C + I_1$ curve intersects the 45-degree line at point *E*. Therefore, the equilibrium level of real national income is Y_1. This is also shown in panel (b). Leakages are shown by the saving schedule, *SS*; injections are shown by the autonomous investment function, I_1I_1. Those two functions intersect also at point *E*, giving the same equilibrium level of real national income per year of Y_1. A shift upwards in the investment schedule to I_2I_2 causes the total planned expenditures curve to shift upwards to $C + I_2$. The new equilibrium level of real national income per year is Y_2 in both panels (a) and (b). A decrease in the investment schedule to I_3I_3 causes the total planned expenditures curve to drop to $C + I_3$. The new equilibrium level of real national income per year is Y_3 in both panels (a) and (b). Notice that the change in the equilibrium level of real national income per year was greater than the change in autonomous investment.

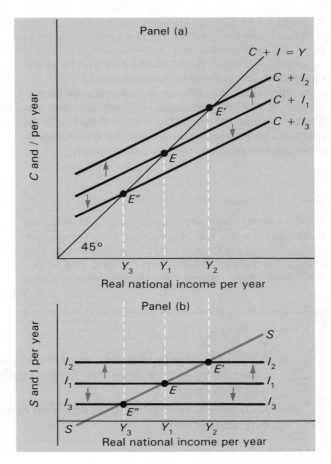

the saving function, shown as SS in panel (b). Given a level of investment I_1, the equilibrium level of real national income per year is also Y_1. In panel (b), we use the leakages–injections approach. Note that the total planned expenditures in panel (a) consists of two parts – consumption and investment. Initially, investment is at I_1.

Consider an increase in autonomous investment from I_1 to I_2. This *shifts* the aggregate expenditure or demand schedule to $C + I_2$. The equilibrium level of real national income increases to Y_2 in panel (a). In panel (b), the intersection of SS with the new autonomous investment line I_2I_2, is also at that equilibrium of Y_2.

Consider now a decrease in autonomous investment from I_2 to I_3. The aggregate expenditure line will shift downwards in panel (a) to $C + I_3$.
The aggregate expenditure line will shift downwards in panel (a) to $C + I_3$. The equilibrium level of real national income will fall to Y_3. The same is shown in panel (b), where the new autonomous investment schedule I_3I_3 intersects the saving function SS at the equilibrium level of real national income of Y_3.

In sum, then, any change in autonomous investment will *shift* the aggregate expenditure line and thereby change the equilibrium level of real national income. This same analysis will hold for any change in autonomous spending, such as consumption.

Shifts in Aggregate Expenditure

Total planned expenditures depend, certainly, on more than just real national income. For example, we talked about desired consumption expenditures also being a function of wealth, expectations, and so on. We talked about planned investment expenditures

also being a function of other variables, such as firms' expectations of future profitability. None of those determinants, however, is given in our current diagrams, just as income, population, the price of related goods, and expectations were not given on the supply and demand curves we developed in Chapter 5. Hence, if there is a change in any of these other non-income determinants of total planned expenditure, those changes will cause a shift in the $C + I$ curve similar to those shifts that we just demonstrated graphically in Figure 16.6. Basically, then, changes in total planned expenditures that arise from reasons other than changes in real national income are represented by shifts in the $C + I$ curve.

The Multiplier Effect of Changes in Autonomous spending

In Figure 16.6, the change in investment that caused the $C + I_1$ curve to shift up and down is relatively small compared to the resulting change in the equilibrium level of national income and output. It turns out that the change in the equilibrium level of real national income will always be larger than the change in autonomous investment. In Figure 16.7 an increase in investment of £5 billion shifts the $C + I$ line upwards. The new equilibrium level of income has increased by much more than the initial increase in investment, in fact by five times that amount.

The Multiplier

What is operating here is the **multiplier** effect of changes in autonomous spending. The multiplier is the number by which a change in autonomous investment or autonomous consumption is multiplied to get the change in the equilibrium level of real national income. In other words, any increases in autonomous investment will cause a larger increase in real national income.

Figure 16.7

The Multiplier Effect. Investment, and total expenditure, rise by £5 billion. As a result real national income increases by £25 billion.

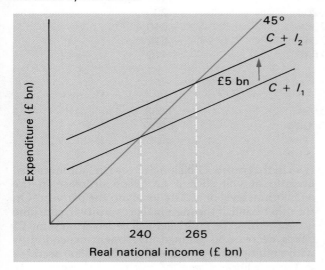

To get an idea of how a larger increase in income results from a given increase in investment, we can follow the progress of the increased injection around the circular flow of money. If investment rises by £5 billion, some firms are buying more plant and machinery. In doing so they increase demand for other firms' products. These other firms will need to increase their output of investment goods and to do so, will take on more labour. The new employees (assuming they were previously unemployed) will now have wages, profits will have increased, and total income will have risen by the £5 billion spent. If we assume, as before, an MPC of four-fifths and an MPS of one-fifth, we know how households will allocate their increased income: consumption will rise by £4 billion and savings by £1 billion.

This addition to consumption adds further to aggregate demand. This time, firms producing consumer goods find sales rising and stocks falling. They will increase output, taking on more labour, pay more in wages, and earn more profit. Again incomes have risen and a further increase in consumption will occur. If we continue to calculate the increase in induced expenditure occurring as a result of this expansion in the economy, the general extent of the total increase in income becomes apparent. Figure 16.8 (page 240) gives the figures involved.

The Multiplier Formula

It is possible to find the full extent of the multiplier effect by extending Figure 16.8 (page 240) through many more rounds. In each successive round, aggregate expenditure increases by the previous increase in income, multiplied by the MPC, 0.8. See if you can work out the effect of three more rounds of the circular flow. You will find that the sum of all the successive increases in income will be five times the initial increase in investment, if the MPC is 0.8, and the MPS 0.2.

Alternatively, we can find the formula for the multiplier by comparing the original equilibrium position with the new equilibrium position, after the full multiplier effect has worked its way through the economy. First we define the multiplier:

The multiplier is the amount by which we would multiply an initial change in expenditure to find the ultimate change in income. Stated another way, that is the ratio of the change in income to the change in expenditure which brought it about.

We can call this change in expenditure ΔI: the Greek letter Δ means 'a change in'. Similarly we call the change in income ΔY. The multiplier is therefore:

$$\Delta Y / \Delta I$$

ΔY is the difference between the initial equilibrium level of income and the ultimate equilibrium level of income, once the multiplier has fully worked through the system.

What do we know about the equilibrium level of income? We know that planned injections and planned leakages will be equal. It follows that the size of the *increase* in planned injections must be equal to the amount by which planned leakages have increased when the new equilibrium has been reached. Stated symbolically:

$$\Delta Y \times \text{MPS} = \Delta I$$

$\Delta Y \times$ MPS is equal to the increase in savings, because the increase in savings is determined by the MPS and the increase in income.

We can now rearange the equation to arrive at the multiplier. Dividing both sides by the MPS, we get

$$\Delta Y = \frac{\Delta I}{\text{MPS}}$$

And dividing both sides by ΔI,

$$\frac{\Delta Y}{\Delta I} = \frac{1}{\text{MPS}}$$

An alternative way of stating this uses the fact that, in a closed economy with no government,

$$\text{MPC} + \text{MPS} = 1$$

or $\text{MPS} = 1 - \text{MPC}$

Then the multiplier can be written:

$$\frac{\Delta Y}{\Delta I} = \frac{1}{1 - \text{MPC}}$$

Figure 16.8

The Multiplier Effect of a £5 billion per year Increase in *I* – the Multiplier Process. We trace the effects of a £5 billion increase in investment spending on the equilibrium level of real national income. If we assume a marginal propensity to consume of 0.8, such an increase will eventually elicit £25 billion increase in the equilibrium level of real national income. Notice that with each successive round income increases, but by slightly less than before.

Round	Increase in real national income (millions of £/yr)	Increase in planned consumption (millions of £/yr)	Increase in planned saving (millions of £/yr)
1 (£5 billion/yr increase in *I*)	5 000 _____	4 000	1 000
2	4 000 _____	3 200	800
3	3 200 _____	2 560	640
4	2 560 _____	2 048	512
5	2 048 _____	1 638	410
.	.	.	.
.	.	.	.
.	.	.	.
All later rounds	8 192	6 554	1 638
Totals (*C* + *I'*)	25 000	20 000	5 000

The greater the MPS, and the lower the MPC, the lower will be the multiplier. The common sense of this is that with a high marginal propensity to save, more of any given increase in expenditure leaks away in savings, and therefore does not add to consumption demand. Equally the lower the MPS, the more any given increase in expenditure adds to consumption and therefore to demand.

If we calculate the multiplier using data on the MPC, we can use it to predict how much a given change in expenditure will affect income.

> multiplier × change in expenditure = change in equilibrium level of real national income.

The multiplier, as we mentioned, works both for an increase and a decrease in expenditure. If there has been a decrease, we speak of a downward multiplier effect.

The Significance of the Multiplier

As we just stated, the larger the marginal propensity to consume, the larger the multiplier. If the marginal propensity to consume is one-half, the multiplier is two. In that case a £1 billion decrease in (autonomous) investment will elicit a £2 billion decrease in the equilibrium level of real national income per year. On the other hand, if the marginal propensity to consume is nine-tenths, the multiplier will be ten. That same £1 billion decrease in planned investment expenditures with a multiplier of 10 will lead to a £10 billion decrease in the equilibrium level of real national income per year. Presumably an economy with such a multiplier is less stable.

The Paradox of Thrift

The paradox of thrift refers to the outcome of an increase in the savings function. Figure 16.9 shows a shift upwards in the savings function. At any given income, a larger proportion of income will be saved, because people have decided to behave more thriftily. Any of the reasons given earlier in the chapter, as to why consumption or savings might change, could account for this.

With the initial increase in savings, planned leakages

Key Points 16.5

► Any change in autonomous expenditure causes a multiplier effect on the equilibrium level of real national income per year.

► The multiplier is equal to the reciprocal of the marginal propensity to save.

► The smaller the marginal propensity to save, the greater the multiplier. Otherwise stated, the greater the marginal propensity to consume, the larger the multiplier.

Figure 16.9

The Paradox of Thrift. With the new savings function $S'S'$, there is a new, lower, equilibrium level of income, Y_2. Here planned saving is again equal to planned investment.

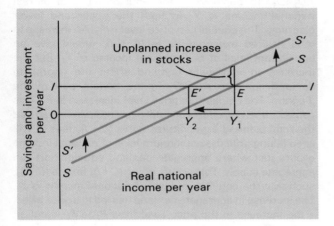

exceed planned injections. Consumption must fall; aggregate expenditure will be less than current output and firms will find that stocks are rising. They will cut production and after a time reduce employment too. So incomes will fall. But of course a fall in income means that savings will gradually fall back again – hence the paradox.

So long as planned savings exceed planned investment, income will continue to fall because there is a leakage from the circular flow which is not balanced by injections. Incomes will cease falling once the new lower level of saving is again equal to planned investment, at Y_2.

The outcome is that an intention to save more, in macroeconomic terms, leads to falling income and employment, and therefore, ultimately, to falling savings.

Is Increased Thriftiness always 'Bad'?

This argument seems to indicate that increased thriftiness on the part of individuals may end up being bad for the nation. The equilibrium level of real national income per year falls, as does the amount of saving. Whether this is bad or not depends on the general level of employment. If people are saving more because unemployment is rising and they are fearful for the future, then increased saving is bad in that it will reduce real incomes. But supposing unemployment is low. That which is saved is not consumed. More saving means that resources can be reallocated away from consumption and devoted to investment in new plant and equipment. Investment adds to the future productive capacity of the nation. As we will see in Chapter 34 more investment typically leads to a higher rate of economic growth. The prime example has been Japan, a country that has saved and invested at a rate nearly double that of the UK. Not surpris-

ingly, Japan has experienced a rate of economic growth that is the envy of most of the world.

Only when there is a serious problem of less than full employment should we worry about the problem of individuals wanting to save too much.

Expansionary and Output Gaps

These are sometimes termed inflationary and deflationary gaps. It is possible that the equilibrium level of real national income per year is greater than potential output, perhaps because all the resources needed are fully employed. In Figure 16.10 we see that this has occurred. Full-capacity output is given as Y_f per year, but the intersection of the total planned expenditures curve with the 45-degree line is at a greater level of real national income per year. There exists, at the full employment level of real national income, therefore, an **expansionary gap**. An expansionary gap exists whenever the equilibrium level of real national income exceeds the full-capacity level of output. Clearly, an expansionary gap means that there will be pressure on the price level and that we would have to abandon our assumption of a fixed price level. The implication is that the economy would be on the upward-sloping part of the aggregate supply curve.

It is also possible for the equilibrium level of real national income per year to be less than the full-capacity level. When this occurs, we talk in terms of an **output gap**. We show an output gap in the bottom part of Figure 16.10. There the intersection of the total planned expenditures curve with the 45-degree line is at a level of real national income that is below the full-capacity level. As we will see in the next chapter, various proposed government policies can be used to fill the output gap.

Relaxing the Assumption of a Fixed Price Level – The Determination of Output and Prices

For the moment, let us assume that we are no longer in the horizontal portion of the aggregate supply curve, but rather in the upward-sloping portion. How would an increase in aggregate demand affect the price level and real national income (total output)?

The total expenditure curve (which we have labelled $C + I$) relates total planned spending to real income, holding all other things constant. But, as real national income rises towards equilibrium following an initial rise (shift) in the $C + I$ curve, some prices will rise. This will simply cause the $C + I$ curve to then shift down, partially offsetting the initial rise in the $C + I$ curve, until a new equilibrium is reached. In other words, when prices are allowed to rise because of an increase

Figure 16.10
Expansionary and Output Gaps. In the top diagram, at the full-capacity level of real national income per year, Y_f, total planned expenditures exceed real national income per year. There is therefore an expansionary gap. In the bottom diagram, total planned expenditures fall short of real national income at the full-capacity level of real national income. Thus there is an output gap.

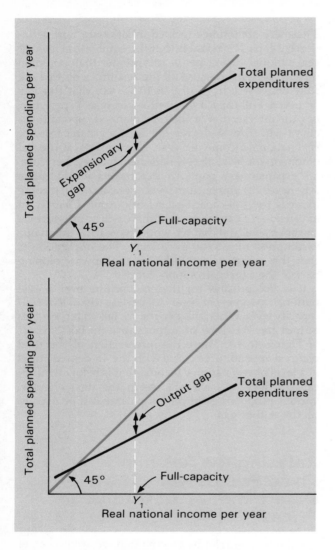

Figure 16.11
The Output and Price Effects of an Increase in Aggregate Demand. Assume that total desired spending is $(C + I)_1$. Assume further that short-run aggregate supply is given by SRAS and aggregate demand is given by AD_1AD_1. To begin with, the equilibrium level of real national income is Y_1 in both the upper and lower diagrams. The equilibrium price level is P_1. An increase in total desired expenditures to $(C + I)_2$ would give an equilibrium level of real national income of Y_2. But the increase in aggregate demand shifts the aggregate demand curve to AD_2AD_2 in the bottom part of the diagram. The equilibrium price level increases to P_2. This causes offsetting effects on total planned spending so that the total planned expenditures curve $(C + I)_2$ falls. It will keep falling until the equilibrium level of national income occurs just where aggregate demand equals short-run aggregate supply. This occurs when $(C + I)_2$ falls to $(C + I)_3$, such that the equilibrium level of national income is Y_3. The increase in aggregate demand has led to a price effect – the increase in the price level from P_1 to P_2 – and an output effect – the increase in the equilibrium level of real national income from Y_1 to Y_3.

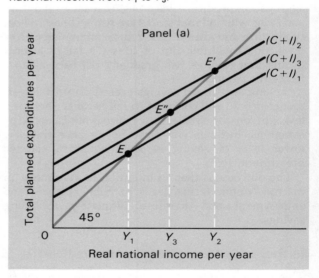

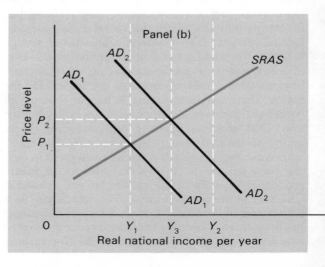

in total desired spending (aggregate demand), there will be a feedback mechanism. Consider Figure 16.11. Initially, total planned spending (expenditures) rise from $(C + I)_1$ to $(C + I)_2$. The initial equilibrium is shown at E and it moves to E'. Ignoring other things (prices) that might change, the equilibrium level of real national income seems to rise from Y_1 to Y_2.

But look what happens on the aggregate supply–aggregate demand curves in the lower diagram (b). Aggregate supply in the short run is given as *SRAS* – it is upward-sloping rather than horizontal. If we start out in equilibrium with aggregate demand as AD_1AD_1, then the price level is P_1. But the increase total planned expenditures also causes the aggregate demand curve to shift to AD_2AD_2. This will cause the price level to increase from P_1 to P_2. But an increase in the price level has an interest-rate effect, a wealth effect, and a trade effect, such that $(C + I)_2$ will fall. This process continues until the new equilibrium is reached where $(C + I)_3$ intersects the 45-degree line at that equilibrium level of real national income per year where the new aggregate demand curve, AD_2AD_2, intersects $SRAS$. This occurs when the $(C + I)_2$ curve falls to $(C + I)_3$ and intersects the 45-degree line at E''. The equilibrium level of real national income is Y_3, and the new equilibrium price level is P_2.

Thus an increase in total desired expenditures (aggregate demand) has had a price effect and an output effect. Output went up from Y_1 to Y_3, and prices went up from P_1 to P_2.

What we can say for any increase in aggregate demand is the following: the closer we are to full-capacity output, the more there will be an offsetting effect due to an increase in prices and therefore less of an output effect. The greater the amount of unemployment (the flatter the short-run aggregate supply curve), the less will be the offsetting price effect and the greater will be the output effect.

Key Points 16.6

▶ The paradox of thrift shows how an increase in the savings function produces contraction in the economy and therefore a fall in the level of savings.

▶ An expansionary (or inflationary) gap exists when planned expenditure exceeds full capacity output.

▶ An output (or deflationary) gap exists when planned expenditure is less than full capacity output, i.e. there are unemployed resources in the economy.

▶ The closer the economy is to full capacity the more likely it is that increased expenditure leads to accelerating inflation rather than rising output.

The Acceleration Principle and the Interaction between the Accelerator and the Multiplier

It was obvious during the nineteenth century that investment fluctuated more than output as a whole. While, for example, expenditure on food is continuous, expenditure on investment can be postponed or brought forward according to circumstance.

The Acceleration Principle

As sales rise, firms want to increase output. To do so they need a larger capital stock. This is known as the *acceleration principle*, or the accelerator:

The level of planned investment varies with *changes in the level* of output itself. Otherwise stated, the level of planned investment is related to the *rate of change* of output or sales.

If the capital stock – the value of the machines, equipment, and buildings – is related to the sales of a company, then we relate the *change* in sales to the *change* in capital. But the change in the capital stock – additions to or subtractions from the total amount of equipment, machines, buildings – is what we have called investment. Therefore, the change in sales is related to the *level* of investment.

We can see a simple example of the acceleration principle at work in the planned investment of the A & B Heater Company. Figure 16.12 (page 244) shows the relationship between the company's investment and sales. We begin by assuming that in 1972 the firm started with just the necessary amount of capital stock, that is, machinery valued at £5 million (column (4), row 1972).

Now, if you look at the financial data across the row for 1972, you will see that in this first year of

Figure 16.12
Relationship between Investment and Sales for A & B Heater Company.

(1) Year	(2) Sales (£m)	(3) Required stock of machines (£m)	(4) Actual stock of machines (£m)	(5) Replacement investment (£m per year)	(6) Net investment in new capital (£m per year)	(7) = (5) + (6) Gross investment (£m per year)
1972	10	5	5	1	0	1
1973	12	6	5	1	1	2
1974	14	7	6	1	1	2
1975	16	8	7	1	1	2
1976	16	8	8	1	0	1
1977	16	8	8	1	0	1
1978	14	7	8	0	0	0
1979	14	7	7	1	0	1
1980	14	7	7	1	0	1
1981	18	9	7	1	2	3
1982	18	9	9	1	0	1

operation, £10 million in sales (column (2)) were produced from £5 million of capital stock (shown as 'Actual stock of machines' in column (4)). We assume that the actual stock of machines in 1972 was also equal to the required, or optimal, stock of machines in 1972, so that there is basically a 2-to-1 relationship between sales and the value of the stock of machines necessary to produce that amount of water heaters. This information lets us know how much to invest in new machinery to produce the expected increase in sales. For this example, we can do this by looking at the expected amount of sales and dividing that amount by 2 to find out the desired capital stock to produce those sales.

What happens when sales are expected to increase by £2 million per year, as they did in fact increase from 1972 to 1973? The 'Required stock of machines' (column (3)) was increased by £1 million to (£6 million from £5 million).

Depreciation

Before we proceed further, we have to consider depreciation. In this example, we assume that £1 million worth of machinery wears out every year and must be completely replaced. This means that £1 million must be spent on 'Replacement investment' (column (5)) every year just to produce the same amount of sales each year. Therefore, the A & B Heater Company will have to spend:

£1 million in *replacement investment* to take care of *depreciation* in machines and to produce the same sales as before;
and
£1 million in new machines (shown as 'Net investment in new capital' in column (6)) to produce the additional £2 million in expected sales.

The sum of those two is what we call gross investment; that is, *gross investment* equals the sum of replacement investment and net investment. In this example, for 1973 £1 million in 'Replacement investment' (column (5)) plus £1 million in 'Net investment' (column (6)) equals £2 million in 'Gross investment' (column (7)).

Notice, the *level* of sales increases by another £2 million per year from 1973 to 1974 and from 1974 to 1975, but that 'Gross investment' (column (7)) remains constant at £2 million per year. This is a demonstration of the *acceleration principle*. Gross investment is a function of the *rate* of change of sales. If that rate of change is a constant amount, then gross investment will be a constant amount.

Now look at what happens when sales decline from £16 million a year to £14 million as they did from 1977 to 1978. The *required* capital stock on hand is still £8 million. In other words, there is more capital on hand than needed to produce the lower rate of sales. Furthermore, £1 million of actual machinery will wear out and need to be replaced. But since sales fell by £2 million, that means that £1 million less of machinery is needed. Thus, in this year, it is not necessary even to pay for depreciation or replacement machinery.

Therefore, we see for 1978 that the replacement investment is, in effect, zero; the net investment is zero; and, consequently, the total gross investment is also zero. In other words, if the rate of capital formation – investment – is a function of the *rate of change* of sales, a decline in sales can lead to a zero amount of gross investment (and in some cases, to a *negative* net investment).

We can also see that small changes in sales result in large changes in planned (gross) investment. For example, from 1972 to 1973, sales for the A & B Heater Company went up by 20 per cent, but gross investment went up by 100 per cent. From 1980 to

1981, sales increased by 28.57 per cent {[(18 – 14) ÷ 14] × 100 per cent = 28.57 per cent}, while gross investment increased by 200 per cent {[(3 – 1) ÷ 1] × 100 per cent = 200 per cent}.

In sum, as long as the level of investment is related to the level of sales, small changes in sales may lead to magnified changes in investment. The longer the life of the capital equipment, the more marked these changes will be.

The Interaction between the Accelerator and the Multiplier

Investment is a key determinant of the equilibrium level of national income in the model that we have been using in Part B. If the rate of planned investment follows the acceleration principle, this could explain, to some extent, the rather dramatic swings in business activity that we have experienced from time to time. After all, any change in investment, according to our theory in Chapter 16, leads to a multiplier effect in which there is a multiple change in the equilibrium level of income and employment. The evidence suggests that in both the UK and the US, the accelerator, combined with the multiplier, may produce the business fluctuations that are experienced in the real world.

The accelerator and multiplier interact, affecting business as follows. We assume that the economy is moving towards full employment, national income is rising, and sales are expanding at an *increasing* rate. Because of the acceleration principle, this growth – meaning expected increases in sales – results in a relatively high level of planned investment. Furthermore, because of the multiplier, this relatively high level of planned investment provokes *even greater* increases in the equilibrium level of national income. Thus, the accelerator and the multiplier tend to reinforce each other, resulting in a strong upward movement in national income. This is shown in Figure 16.13.

Eventually, however, the economy nears some level of full-capacity. That is to say, since we have only a certain amount of labour, land, and other factors of production, it is impossible to continue increasing national income at the rapid rate that was experienced during the expansion phase of the business cycle. At some point, supply constraints must become a problem and growth of all of the components of the economy has to slow down. Sales will not increase forever at the same fast rate; they will begin to increase at a slower rate. This slow-down in the growth of sales means that the rate of growth of planned investment is going to turn down abruptly, just as it did, for example, when sales of the A & B Heater Company were maintained at £16 million a year. However, because of the multiplier effect, this decrease in planned investment will lead to a magnified, or multiplied, decrease in the equilibrium level of income. This is shown pictorially in panel (b) of Figure

Figure 16.13

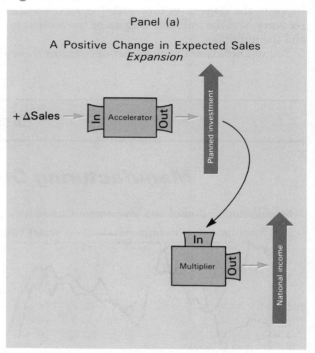

Panel (a)

A Positive Change in Expected Sales
Expansion

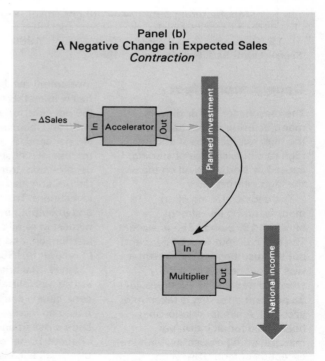

Panel (b)
A Negative Change in Expected Sales
Contraction

16.13. The reduction in the rate of growth of national income will mean a further reduction in the rate of sales growth, leading to a further reduction in gross investment, and so on. Eventually, the economy will experience a recession and the cycle will start again.

At some point, the capital stock of firms, that is, their actual stock of machinery, buildings, and manufacturing equipment, gets into line with their reduced sales rates. This is what happened between 1978 and 1980 for the A & B Heater Company. When this happens, the stage is set for another upturn, another recovery, and the interaction again of the accelerator and the multiplier.

You will note that the multiplier–accelerator theory

of the business cycle is one in which business cycles are self-starting and self-terminating. Each phase of the business cycle automatically leads into the next. In practice, this kind of fluctuation occurs together with changes brought about by shocks such as oil price changes.

CASE STUDY

Manufacturing Output and Investment

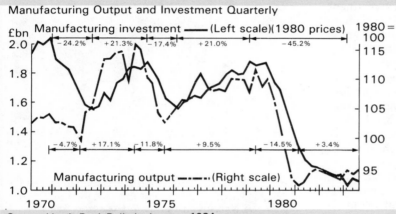

Manufacturing Output and Investment Quarterly

Source: Lloyds Bank Bulletin January 1984.

Decelerator effect

The reasons for the decline in manufacturing output have been the high rate of interest and the high rate of exchange of sterling, caused by North Sea oil on top of the high interest rates.

The decelerator effect on manufacturing investment between 1979 and 1982 is evident. The fall in output was 14 per cent, but the resulting fall in investment was 40 per cent, with a fairly standard multiple of 2.8 times, (or 33 per cent if leasing is taken into account). A similar relationship holds good for all individual manufacturing industries, with the exception of food. The fall in

investment has been particularly heavy in metals – mainly steel – (59 per cent), chemicals (50 per cent) and mechanical engineering (49 per cent). A number of traditional industries, such as construction, transport and distribution also had falls in investment. The fall in investment and in output have both been modest in retail and wholesale distribution, and investment began to recover in 1981 in these sectors.

Since industrial investment as a whole has fallen by only 10 per cent, clearly some sectors must have had increases. There has been a rise in energy investment, of about 10 per cent; this sector is untypical, because North Sea Oil

investment peaked in 1976, and has been recovering from a trough in 1980, and the strong rise in output in recent years has been determined by the investment made in the first half of the 1970s. In the service industries, the big increases in investment have been in business and financial services, telcommunications, and to a lesser extent in hotels and catering, with standard accelerator effects showing investment rising by a multiple of the rise in output. Investment in 'business services', which includes computer services, has risen by 70 per cent in real terms, reaching £2.7bn in 1982 – about as much as in retail and wholesale distribution, nearly as much as in North Sea oil and gas, and half as much as in the whole of manufacturing industry.

Questions
1. What changes in investment took place?
2. In what way has the accelerator affected investment in (a) industries with declining output and (b) industries with increasing output?

Exam Preparation and Practice

INTRODUCTORY EXERCISES

1. You are given the following information for a hypothetical economy: Assume that the marginal propensity to consume is constant at all levels of income. Further assume that investment is autonomous.

Real national income	Consumption expenditures	Saving	Investment
£1 000	£1 100	_____	£100
2 000	2 000	_____	_____
3 000	_____	_____	_____
4 000	_____	_____	_____
5 000	_____	_____	_____
6 000	_____	_____	_____

APC	APS	MPC	MPS
_____	_____	_____	_____
_____	_____	_____	_____
_____	_____	_____	_____
_____	_____	_____	_____
_____	_____	_____	_____
_____	_____	_____	_____

(a) Draw a graph of the consumption function. Then add the investment function, giving you $C + I$.

(b) Right under the first diagram, draw in the saving and investment curves. Does the $C + I$ curve intersect the 45-degree line in the upper diagram at the same level of real national income as where saving equals investment in the lower diagram? (If not, redraw your diagrams.)

(c) What is the multiplier effect from the inclusion of investment?

(d) What is the numerical value of the multiplier?

(e) What is the equilibrium level of real national income and output without investment? With investment?

(f) What will happen to income if autonomous investment increases by £100?

(g) What will the equilibrium level of real national income be if autonomous consumption increases by £100?

2. Assume a closed, private economy.

(a) What is the multiplier if the MPC = $\frac{1}{2}$? If the MPC = $\frac{3}{4}$? If the MPC = $\frac{9}{10}$? If the MPC = 1?

(b) What happens to the multiplier as the MPC rises?

(c) In what range does the multiplier fall?

3. Consider a closed, private economy, in which

(a) $C = £30 + \frac{3}{4}Y$

(b) $I = £25$.

What will the equilibrium level of real national income (Y) be equal to in this economy? (*Hint:* In equilibrium, real national income must equal total planned expenditures, or $Y = C + I$.)

4. Using the model in question 3:

(a) What is the multiplier?

(b) What will the *new* equilibrium level of real national income be if investment increases by £5?

5. Using the model in question 3, calculate the new equilibrium level of real national income if the consumption function becomes $C = £35 + \frac{3}{4}Y$ (the consumption function shifts upward by £5).

MULTIPLE CHOICE QUESTIONS

For Questions 1 and 2 refer to this diagram.

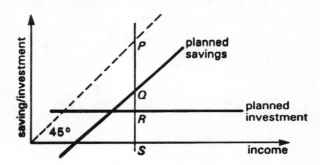

1. Which distance represents unplanned increase in stocks?

A *PQ*
B *PR*
C *PS*
D *QR*
E *RS*

2. Which distance indicates consumption expenditure?

   A PQ
   B PR
   C PS
   D QR
   E QS

3. In a macroeconomic economy where Y = national income, C = aggregate planned consumption, and I = aggregate planned investment

$$Y = C + I$$
$$C = 30m + \tfrac{2}{3}Y$$
$$I = 60m$$

If the existing level of income is £300m, what is the level of realized investment?

   A £90m
   B £70m
   C £60m
   D £50m

†4. The multiplier effect of public investment is likely to be high where there is
   A a preference for foreign goods
   B a high level of stocks
   C excess productive capacity in the private sector
   D heavy taxation of companies
   E a high propensity to consume

5. A new firm requires one machine for every 2 million units of consumer goods it produces each year. The machines last for four years including the year in which they are bought and then are replaced. Demand for the consumer goods is shown in the schedule.

Year	Quantity demanded (millions)
1	10
2	20
3	30
4	40
5	40
6	48

Total investment by the firm will be (in number of machines)

	Year					
	1	2	3	4	5	6
A	5	5	5	5	5	9
B	5	5	5	5	5	4
C	5	5	5	5	0	4
D	5	5	5	5	0	9

RELATED ESSAY QUESTIONS

1. Compare and contrast the multiplier process with the accelerator process.

2. What is the accelerator principle? Discuss the weaknesses of the accelerator principle in explaining fluctuations in the level of aggregate investment.

3. (a) Explain why the Keynesian theory of employment, related to a closed economy, depends on the assumption that divergencies can exist between planned investment and planned savings.
   (b) For what reasons did Keynes consider that instability in planned investment was likely to be a major cause of depressions?
   (c) Why have economists often used the phrase 'the paradox of thrift' when discussing savings behaviour in depressions?

4. Examine the effects of a rise in consumers' expenditure upon national income, investment, and savings.

5. If savings are always identical with investment in a closed economy, how can we refer to saving and investment having different values?

17 Income and Employment Determination: Government and Trade

Key Points to Review

▶ The circular flow with a government and foreign trade (12.3)

▶ Equilibrium via leakages–injections (16.3)

▶ Multiplier effect (16.5)

Questions for Preview

1 What is fiscal policy?

2 What is an output gap, and how can fiscal policy eliminate it?

3 What is an expansionary gap, and how can fiscal policy eliminate it?

4 What are automatic stabilizers and how do they lend stability to an economy?

5 How do imports and exports affect national income?

So far we have left government out of our model of real national income determination. The tools learned already still apply when making the basic model more realistic. In this chapter, we will consider how changes in government spending and taxation will alter the equilibrium level of real national income. We will go on to examine the effects of foreign trade.

Adding Government Spending and Taxes

We now include government spending in our macroeconomic model, but we will assume that the level of government purchases is determined by political processes outside the economic system under study. In other words, we will consider G to be autonomous, just as in the last chapter we considered I, for simplicity's sake, to be autonomous.

Panel (a) in Figure 17.1 shows the new aggregate expenditure function, $C + I + G$. Equilibrium income Y occurs where planned expenditure and real income and output are equal, that is at the intersection with the 45-degree line.

Alternatively, we can find the equilibrium level of real national income by using the leakages–injections approach. Remember that for equilibrium to occur, leakages must equal injections. In this present analysis, we have an additional injection into the system, autonomous government spending. Therefore, in panel (b) we show a new injections line that is investment plus government spending, or $I + G$. Since investment and government spending are both autonomous, or given, the $I + G$ line is horizontal. Within the model we are using, we have treated savings as induced, depending directly on the level of income. Similarly, taxes constitute a leakage and are dependent on income. They are a leakage because they reduce the level of disposable income, and therefore the level of personal consumption. They very obviously depend on income. Both direct taxes (taxes levied on income itself, such as income and profits tax) and indirect taxes, or expenditure taxes (such as VAT and excise duties), rise with income. So we have a new leakage function, the $S + T$ line in panel (b). The equilibrium level of income is that which generates a level of savings and tax revenue which is equal to planned investment and government expenditure.

It should be noted that the level of taxes set by the government will influence savings. An increase in taxes will generally lead to both a fall in consumption *and* a fall in savings. In order to pay the higher taxes, people will save somewhat less. So a given increase in tax-rates will lead to a somewhat smaller increase in leakages.

Figure 17.1

Equilibrium Income with a Government. Aggregate expenditure is $C + I + G$. Equilibrium income is Y, the level at which expenditure is exactly equal to income and output. Panel (b) shows the injections leakages approach, with equilibrium occurring where planned $I + G = S + T$.

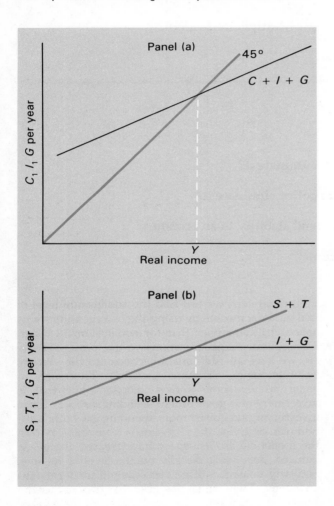

The Multiplier with a Government

Our original derivation of the multiplier was based on there being one leakage only, savings. With another leakage, taxes, the story changes. The more of any given increase in expenditure which leaks away as either savings or taxes, the smaller the multiplier.

We can of course use the original alternative formula for the multiplier, $1/(1 - MPC)$. But this only raises the question, what is the MPC when there is the further leakage of taxes?

When households decide how much to spend on consumer goods, they examine not gross income (before tax) but disposable income (income after tax). Disposable income (Y_d) can be defined as national income less taxes:

$$Y_d = Y - T$$

Taxes will be levied at particular rates. If the marginal rate of taxation (MRT) and the average rate are both equal to 0.2, then

$$Y_d = Y - 0.2Y$$
$$= 0.8Y$$

If we assume that the average and marginal propensities to consume out of disposable income are 0.9, then

$$C = 0.9Y_d$$
$$= 0.9 \times 0.8Y$$
$$= 0.72Y$$

Thus if the MRT is 0.2, and the MPC out of disposable income is 0.9, the MPC out of national income is 0.72. The multiplier is then 3.6.

Possible Discretionary Fiscal Policies

Governments can choose to vary spending or taxes, or both, in order to expand or contract aggregate expenditure.

Filling the Output Gap

Figure 17.2 shows an economy in which, initially, expenditure is insufficient to buy all of potential output. Real income, Y, can be produced by fewer people than are actually seeking work. There is some cyclical, or demand-deficiency unemployment.

If expenditure can be increased then real income and output can expand and employers will take on more labour. (The implication of there being unemployed resources is that the economy is on the horizontal section of the aggregate supply curve. Aggregate supply can expand to meet any increase in aggregate demand.)

In Figure 17.2, the increased expenditure is shown as arising from increased government expenditure. Aggregate expenditure rises from $C + I + G_1$, to $C + I + G_2$. The resulting level of real national income is Y_2. This corresponds to the level of income at which planned $I + G_2$ is equal to $S + T$ in panel (b). An alternative possibility would have been to reduce taxes. This would increase disposable income and therefore consumption. Both increasing spending and decreasing taxes serve to increase the level of the

---

> ## Key Points 17.1
>
> ▶ **Government spending is politically determined and is therefore autonomous, that is, determined outside the model.**
>
> ▶ **Taxes, though the rates are set by governments, depend directly on incomes, that is, they are induced.**
>
> ▶ **In equilibrium planned injections equal planned leakages, so $G + I = S + T$.**
>
> ▶ **In using the multiplier it must be remembered that its level is determined by *all* leakages.**

---

government's deficit so that injections increase in relation to leakages. Or a package of measures would

be possible, perhaps including monetary policies. All are discussed in more detail in Part E.

It should be noticed that the eventual increase in income and output is much larger than the initial increase in government spending. This is precisely what we would expect, with the multiplier at work. It means that it is important for the government to be able to predict the multiplier effect of its change in spending. Otherwise it might overdo its expansionary policy, income could increase by more than the output gap and create the reverse problem.

Figure 17.2

Reducing Unemployment with Fiscal Policy. At real income level Y_1 there is substantial demand deficiency unemployment. Increasing government expenditure from G_1 to G_2 adds to aggregate demand, causing firms to try to expand output and take on labour. The new equilibrium real income Y_2 is achieved when aggregate expenditure, $C + I + G_2$, is exactly equal to real income and output, and when $I + G_2$ (injections) equal $S + T$ (leakages).

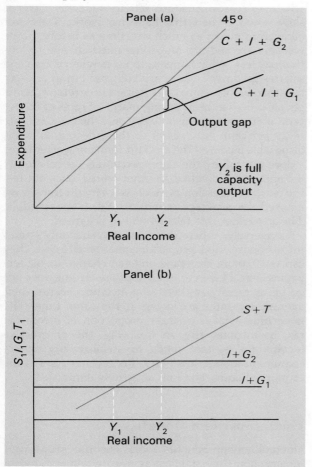

Reducing the Expansionary Gap

Figure 17.3 (page 252) shows an economy in which, initially, aggregate demand or expenditure exceeds output or aggregate supply. This excess demand arises because the economy is incapable of producing real income Y_1 – there simply are not enough suitable resources available to do the job. The most that can be produced – the maximum potential, or full-capacity output, of the economy – is Y_2. Supply constraints are preventing the economy from expanding and unless expenditure is reduced, prices will rise. (The economy is on the upward-sloping section of the aggregate supply curve.) This is sometimes known as overheating.

Figure 17.3 shows the effects of increasing taxes to reduce expenditure. The reduced disposable income causes consumption to fall, as shown in panel (a). Panel (b) shows the increase in taxes. This reduces the government's deficit, increasing leakages relative to injections. The reduced expenditure should remove the excess demand and the upward pressure on prices. An alternative would have been to reduce government spending, or some policy combination. Note again, because of the downward multiplier effect, the eventual decrease in expenditure will be greater than the initial change in spending. In this case the importance of accurate forecasting is even greater. The government needs to have good estimates not only of the multiplier but also of the extent to which a tax increase affects the level of consumption. It must know the marginal propensity to consume out of disposable income.

Figure 17.3

Reducing Inflationary Pressure with Fiscal Policy. At Y_1, planned expenditures exceed full capacity output. Prices will rise due to aggregate excess demand. To reduce expenditure, taxes can be raised from T_1 to T_2. Disposable income is thus reduced and consumption falls from C_1 to C_2. There is a downward multiplier effect as expenditure falls and equilibrium real income falls from Y_1 to Y_2.

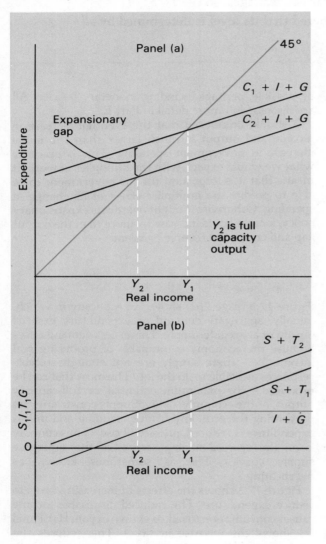

The Balanced Budget Multiplier

There are times when a government may wish to increase spending, and finance the increase by raising taxes to match. The increased spending is an injection into the circular flow. All of it will be spent and be subject to the multiplier effect.

The increase in taxation will reduce disposable income. This will almost certainly mean that both consumption and savings fall. But savings are a leakage. Because they diminish somewhat the *total* increase in leakages will be less than the increase in taxes.

The net effect of this is that although both government spending and taxes have increased by an equal amount, total leakages increase by less than total injections. So the effect on the economy will be expansionary. Provided there are suitable unemployed resources available, income and output will increase.

Automatic or Built-in Stabilizers

In contrast to discretionary fiscal policy, automatic stabilizers need no new legislation in order to make them effective. The system of taxes and benefits works to counteract cyclical changes in the level of expenditure automatically.

Progressive Income Taxes

As taxable income rises so does the marginal tax rate – to a maximum of 60 per cent. Thus, income tax is progressive: the higher the income, the larger the proportion of it which is paid in tax. Or we can say that as taxable income decreases, the marginal tax rate goes down. Think about this for the entire economy. Initially, personal income taxes may yield the government, say, £50 billion per year. Now suppose that, for whatever reason, business activity suddenly starts to slow down. When this happens, workers are not allowed to put in as much overtime as before. Some workers are laid off, and some must change to jobs that pay less. What happens to taxes when wages and salaries go down? Taxes are still paid but at a lower rate than before, since tax-rates are progressive. Some people who had been paying marginal rates of 50 per cent or 60 per cent will now pay only the standard rate of 29 per cent. As a result of these decreased taxes, disposable income – the amount remaining after taxes – does not fall by the same percentage as before-tax income. The individual, in other words, does not feel the pinch of recession as much as we might think if we ignored the progressive nature of our tax schedule. The *average* tax-rate falls when less is earned.

Conversely, when the economy suddenly comes into a boom period, people's incomes tend to rise. They can work more overtime and can change to higher-paying jobs. However, their *disposable* income does not go up as rapidly as their total income, because their average tax-rates are rising at the same time. The government takes a larger proportion of income in tax, as incomes rise. In this way, the progressive income tax system tends to stabilize any abrupt changes in economic activity. Tax revenue rises as the economy booms, and falls as activity diminishes.

Unemployment Benefits

Unemployment benefits work like the progressive income tax: they stabilize aggregate demand. When business activity drops, most laid-off workers automatically become eligible for unemployment benefits. Their disposable income therefore remains positive, although less than when they were working. During boom periods, there is less unemployment and consequently fewer unemployment payments made to the labour force. Less purchasing power is being added to the economy. So government expenditure automatically offsets fluctuations in income.

The Stabilizing Impact

Progressive taxes and the benefit system reduce the impact of changes in demand on disposable income, consumption, and the equilibrium level of national income. We presented a model in which disposable income – take-home pay – is the main determinant of how much people desire to spend. Hence, if disposable income is not allowed to fall as much as it would otherwise during a recession, the downturn will be moderated. On the other hand, if disposable income is not allowed to rise as rapidly as it would otherwise during a boom, the boom will not get out of hand, causing prices to rise, among other things. The government automatically swings into deficit when there is a recession, and back towards surplus when the economy booms. Figure 17.4 shows this graphically.

Fiscal Policy and a Full-employment Budget

We earlier discussed the government increasing expenditures, but we did not discuss how such expenditures would be financed. If we assume no increase in taxes, and if the budget is initially balanced, we can conclude that when the government spends more it ends up with a deficit. If the government is already running a deficit, it will have an even larger one. Fiscal policies have therefore been associated with **deficit spending** on the part of the government. Fiscal policy advocates point out that an increase in the deficit stimulates the economy, whereas a decrease in the deficit has the opposite effect. The government can also run a **surplus**. That is, it can take in more revenues than it spends. An increase in the government's budget surplus would have a depressing effect on the economy, just as would a decrease in government expenditures or an increase in taxes. The existence of, or an increase in, the government budget surplus presumably reduces total aggregate demand and thereby depresses economic activity.

Some economists do not like to look only at the government's *actual* deficit or surplus. They do not think it is useful to look at current levels or taxes and expenditures or the current budget deficit or surplus that results. Consider for a moment the following situation. Suppose the economy is at full employment and the government budget is in balance – no deficit

Figure 17.4
Automatic Stabilizers. Assume that government expenditures remain constant no matter what the level of real national income. Thus they are fully autonomous and represented by *GG*. Taxes, on the other hand, vary directly with national income. Thus we see that when real national income increases from Y_0 to Y_1, taxes will exceed government expenditures as shown by the vertical distance between *GG* and the tax line, *TT*. This government budget surplus, which occurs *automatically* during expansion, could assist in offsetting possible inflationary pressures. Alternatively, when real national income falls from Y_0 to Y_2, the resultant automatic budget deficit could help offset or alleviate the recession.

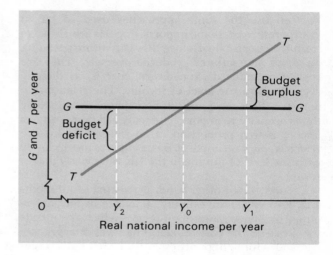

and no surplus. Then the economy goes into a recession, and incomes fall. The government, however, does nothing. Spending on its part, *G*, remains the same. But since some taxes, *T*, are based on income, government revenues fall. A formerly balanced budget goes into deficit, since *G* is now greater than *T*. The budget deficit should certainly not be regarded here as an active policy decision on the part of the government. It is a *result* of the recession. Therefore, economists now make calculations to determine whether *at full employment* the government budget *would be* in a deficit or a surplus position. The result is called the **full-employment government budget**. We define it as what the budget deficit or surplus would be if the economy were operating at full employment throughout the entire year.

The Budget and Fiscal Policy

Fiscal policy is set out at two annual events: the Chancellor's Autumn Statement, and the budget each spring. In the Autumn Statement, the economy is surveyed and forecasts published. In the budget, actual changes in tax rates are decided. Underlying both, there is the policy of the government of the day, which determines what, if any, changes will be made to discretionary policies.

If policy is expansionary the government's deficit (i.e. expenditure minus tax revenue) will increase. This means that **P.S.B.R.** (the public sector borrowing requirement) will rise: more borrowing must take place, for the year in hand. Also, the **National Debt** will rise; this is the sum total of all outstanding government debt, past and present. However, an expansionary policy may cause real income to rise, so that tax revenues then rise. This will reduce the deficit somewhat.

These issues will be taken up again in Chapter 32.

Adding Exports and Imports

We can use the same approaches used so far to incorporate exports and imports. Imports are a leakage from the circular flow, since they constitute spending on goods and services produced overseas. They are treated as induced expenditure, that is, as directly dependent on the level of income. The relationship between the level of imports and income is defined by the propensity to import. The marginal propensity to import is that proportion of an increase in income which is spent on imports. Since imports move closely with the level of income in the UK this clearly makes sense.

Exports, on the other hand, are treated as autonomous. Rather like investment, they are in fact determined by a wide range of influences which are outside the scope of the basic model. The level of aggregate demand in foreign countries with which the UK trades extensively; the exchange rate; and non-price competitiveness (factors such as design, reliability, and after-sales service) all affect the level of demand for UK exports.

As always, the equilibrium condition is that planned injections be equal to planned leakages.

$$S + T + M = I + G + X.$$

Figure 17.5

The Effect of Rising Imports. As imports rise, leakages increase, expenditure on domestic output falls and there is a downward multiplier effect on income.

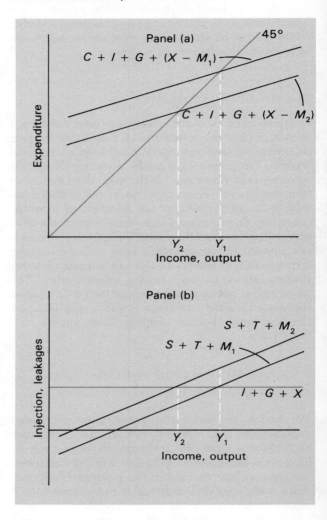

Key Points 17.2

▶ Fiscal policy can be used to regulate the level of expenditure in the economy.

▶ Demand deficiency unemployment can be reduced by increasing government spending or reducing taxes.

▶ Inflationary pressures can be reduced by increasing taxes or reducing government spending

▶ Built-in stabilizers automatically moderate changes in disposable income resulting from changes in overall business activity.

▶ Some economists make a distinction between the actual government budget and the so-called full-employment government budget, where the latter gives us what the budget deficit or surplus *would be* if the economy were operating at full employment throughout the entire year.

▶ The annual deficit, expenditure minus tax revenue, is known as P.S.B.R.

It is not necessary that any one, or all, pairs of injections and leakages be equal – only that total planned injections equal total leakages – for equilibrium to occur. The economy could be in overall equilibrium with a government deficit (G exceeding T), balanced by a private sector surplus (S exceeding I), with perhaps also a balance-of-trade surplus (X exceeding M). Or both government and trade may be in deficit, with the private sector surplus balancing both deficits. Both these situations, and many other such combinations, are consistent with overall equilibrium. (This does not mean that a balance-of-trade deficit could be ignored indefinitely.)

Figure 17.5 shows the effect of an increase in imports. Just as when any other change occurs in injections or leakages, the fall in expenditure brings about a fall in income which is larger than the initial increase in imports, because of the downward multiplier effect.

With foreign trade the expenditure function includes the net balance of exports and imports, ($X - M$), or net exports. This will be negative if imports exceed exports, creating a net leakage. Panel (a) shows how in equilibrium, planned expenditure from all sources must be equal to planned output, that is, the expenditure function must intersect with the 45-degree line. A rise in imports reduces expenditure leading income to fall from Y_1 to Y_2.

Total expenditure $= C + I + G + (X–M)$

Because imports are a rising function of income, low levels of income will generate a low level of imports. With exports autonomous, the likelihood is that when incomes are low there will be a **trade surplus**. Similarly, high levels of income generate increased imports, and probably a trade deficit. If high levels of expenditure lead to excess demand and supply constraints, it is inevitable that both firms and households find themselves unable to purchase all the goods and services they want from domestic producers. Obviously they will turn to imports to fill the gap, and a **trade deficit** will develop. This is another good reason for not allowing aggregate demand and expenditure to grow beyond aggregate supply, or the capacity of the economy to provide a growing output to meet that demand.

The Multiplier in an Open Economy

Our original formula for the multiplier

$1/\text{MPS}$

was based on there being a single leakage, savings. With an open economy with a government this can be amended to

$1/(\text{MPS} + \text{MRT} + \text{MPM})$

where MRT is the marginal rate of taxation and MPM is the **marginal propensity to import.** (Care must be taken that these marginal rates of leakage are all expressed as a proportion of national income, as a whole, when using this formula.)

Clearly with three leakages, the multiplier will be smaller than we have tended to suggest before. An economy which has a large public sector and is very open, in that a substantial proportion of output is traded, will have a relatively small multiplier. This clearly applies to the UK. The effect of increasing expenditure on imports and the balance of trade can often be a major factor in considering future policy. Roughly 30 per cent of UK output is exported. Imports take a similar proportion of expenditure. The balance, net exports, tends to be a relatively small part of total demand.

Rising imports will tend to reduce employment in domestic firms, and rising exports to increase it. If a rising level of export demand is to be satisfied there must be suitable unemployed resources available to expand output. If there are not, rising demand will lead to rising prices rather than increased output. This is likely to reduce foreign demand for domestically produced goods anyway, as price rises erode competitiveness.

Key Points 17.3

▶ Imports are induced, that is they depend directly on the level of income. They are a leakage from the circular flow.

▶ Exports are autonomous, being determined by a wide range of factors. They are an injection into the circular flow.

▶ In an open economy with a government, equilibrium requires that all planned injections equal planned leakages, $I + G + X = S + T + M$.

▶ The multiplier depends on the marginal rate of leakage.

CASE STUDY

Keynesian Demand Management in Practice

Initially deficit financing was Keynes's response to the 1930s depression. Whereas governments at that time were intent on policies of austerity, Keynes argued that increased spending would stimulate the economy, bringing growth and reduced unemployment.

After World War II these ideas became the conventional wisdom. From the end of the war until 1974 there was not a single year in which output fell. Until 1970, inflation was very seldom higher than 5 per cent, and averaged 3.3 per cent for the period 1953–69; unemployment was generally in the range of 1½ per cent to 2½ per cent, and was never higher than 2.6 per cent. So it must be concluded that in certain circumstances, demand-management policies can reduce cyclical fluctuations in the economy. They can provide an economic framework which is conducive to steady growth.

Unfortunately, demand-management policies were probably oversold. In the early 1960s, Chancellors of the Exchequer said they could 'fine-tune' the economy. They would set the level of aggregate demand just so as to get the balance between unemployment, inflation, and growth exactly right. They would be able to use fiscal and monetary policies to achieve their target level of aggregate demand. To be fair to the politicians, economists encouraged them to think that their promises could be made good.

There were two specific problems. It is usually not possible to achieve satisfying growth-rates and unemployment levels without a tendency for inflation to accelerate. And forecasting techniques are not so accurate that the fiscal and monetary policies can be set to produce a predicted outcome with any precision. A common failing with counter-cyclical policy is that governments take too much action, too late, and so overshoot their targets. Partly this is because there are time-lags involved. By the time the statistics have been collected they are already out of date. So reflating when unemployment was high could lead later to more inflation. And deflating, to control inflation, reduced growth and employment. It has been said that demand-management policies of this sort could make the economy less, rather than more, stable.

More generally, demand-management policies do not of themselves help much with problems which have structural causes. Monopolistic wage bargaining processes, immobilities of labour and capital, and poor quality management, make it difficult for an economy to produce desirable products at competitive prices. So if these sorts of problems are causing supply constraints and difficulty in competing with foreign producers, demand management will hold no magic answers. Neither can fiscal and monetary policies protect economies from unexpected supply-side shocks such as oil price changes.

For all sorts of reasons, simple adherence to the 1950s- and 1960s-style fiscal policies became increasingly inappropriate after 1970. But we must be careful not to throw out the baby with the bathwater. Fiscal policy remains an extremely powerful tool for controlling the level of aggregate demand in the economy.

Question

Look at Figures 11.4 and 11.10 earlier in the book. Can you deduce, from the figures for the mid-1960s, what the government's fiscal policy would have been in 1965?

Exam Preparation and Practice

INTRODUCTORY EXERCISES

1. Redraw Figure 17.2 showing the effect of reduced taxes on real national income.

2. Redraw Figure 17.3 showing the effect of reducing government expenditure on real national income.

MULTIPLE CHOICE QUESTIONS

1. A deflationary policy is most likely to cause
   - **A** a reduction in the volume of exports
   - **B** increased monetary demand
   - **C** a reduction in the level of taxation
   - **D** an increase in the level of unemployment
   - **D** a fall in the value of money

2. Assume that investment rises by £500 million and that exports rise by £1 300 million. Given that the marginal propensity to consume is $4/5$, by how much will national income increase?
   - **A** £1800 million
   - **B** £3 000 million
   - **C** £4050 million
   - **D** £6000 million
   - **E** £9 000 million

†3. Which of the following is likely to be deflationary?
   - **A** index-linking of consumers' savings
   - **B** failing to increase tax allowances in line with inflation
   - **C** failing to balance the Budget during recessions
   - **D** funding the deficits of nationalized industries
   - **E** reducing the external value of the currency

†4. If an open economy with government activity is in equilibrium and imports are greater than exports, which of the following *must* be true?
   - **A** savings are greater than investment
   - **B** investment plus government spending is greater than savings plus taxation
   - **C** taxation is greater than government spending
   - **D** investment plus government spending is less than savings plus taxation
   - **E** government spending is greater than taxation

5. The government of a country could seek to raise aggregate demand by increasing the
   - **A** marginal propensity to save
   - **B** budget surplus
   - **C** general level of interest rates
   - **D** level of private investment

6. In an economy with full employment, which of the following policies will be least suitable for the controlling of inflationary tendencies in the economy?
   - **A** Encouraging saving
   - **B** Increasing taxation
   - **C** Increasing exports
   - **D** Increasing productivity

RELATED ESSAY QUESTIONS

1. Discuss some of the macroeconomic consequences of a reduction in personal taxation.

2. (a) Given the assumption of a closed economy, explain carefully the working of the multiplier.
   (b) How is the working of the multiplier affected if the economy engages in foreign trade?

3. (a) Explain the theory underlying proposals that governments should use discretionary fiscal policy to stabilize fluctuations in aggregate monetary expenditure.
   (b) For what reasons has it been asserted that such policies in practice run the risk of destabilizing the economy?
   (c) Explain why the actual budget deficit (or surplus) may not be a reliable indicator of discretionary changes in fiscal policy.

4. Either (a) Explain the circular flow of income in an economy with government and foreign trade sectors.
   Or   (b) State the conditions for the circular flow of income in an economy to be in equilibrium. Show how this equilibrium is reached.

5. What is meant by the management of the economy?

18 Income and Employment Determination: Some Alternative Views

Questions for Preview

1 What is supply-side economics?

2 What is the Laffer curve?

3 What is a Phillips curve?

4 What is the adaptive-expectations hypothesis?

The income-determination models presented in the previous chapters are a good start at understanding how the macroeconomy works. But the real world presents some problems in analysis and prediction. For example, the simplified Keynesian model used throughout most of Chapter 16 assumed that demand determined the level of output, that wages and prices were inflexible, and that inflation only occurred when we hit full employment. These theoretical assumptions have all led to controversies regarding the actual determination of income and employment. Therefore, some alternative views need to be examined and these will be considered next via the concepts of:

Supply-side economics
The Phillips curve
Adaptive expectations
The natural rate of unemployment
Rational expectations.

Supply-side Economics Revisited

In Chapter 14, we presented a simplified model of so-called supply-side economics. Supply-side economics involved shifting the aggregate supply curve outwards and to the right, as in Figure 14.6. We pointed out in Chapter 14 that there are two sides to fiscal policy, one of them being the effects of changes in the tax structure on the position of the aggregate supply curve. Supply-side economics is nothing more nor less than a belief in the ability to affect incentives enough to actually shift the aggregate supply curve. As an example we can follow the use of one supply-side policy, e.g. lowering marginal tax-rates. Such a policy allows the government to pursue expansionary demand-management policies – shifting the aggregate demand curve out – without suffering increased inflation, because it is simultaneously shifting the aggregate supply curve outwards. A similar supply-side economics argument is presented graphically in Figure 18.1.

Of course, supply-side economics is not new. Any attempt at increasing productivity can be labelled supply-side economics. Governments throughout the world have attempted to increase productivity by: setting up training schemes, by providing advisory services to business persons, by lowering unemployment benefit, by abolishing complex legislation relating to work and wages, by providing various tax incentives, and so on. For a more specific idea of the

Figure 18.1

Supply-side Economics. Viewed in a favourable light, the use of supply-side policies can create an increase in the equilibrium level of real national income per year without an increase in the price level. Start in equilibrium with aggregate demand as $AD_1 AD_1$ and short-run aggregate supply as $SRAS_1$. The equilibrium price level is P_1 and the equilibrium level of real national income per year is Y_1. The government simultaneously engages in two manoeuvres: (1) expansionary fiscal policies which shift out the aggregate demand curve to $AD_2 AD_2$, and (2) supply-side productivity-increasing policies, such as reductions in marginal tax-rates and/or training programmes, which shift out the short-run aggregate supply curve to $SRAS_2$. The new equilibrium price level remains at P_1, but the new equilibrium level of real national income per year has increased to Y_2.

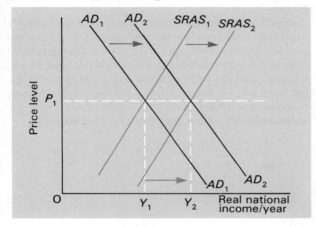

UK government's interpretation of supply-side theory and policy see the first Case Study at the end of this chapter.

The Effect of Changes in Tax-rates

Reform of tax-*rates* is central to any supply-side package. Notice the word *rates* is italicized. This is because supply-side economics deals primarily with changes in tax-*rates*, as opposed to changes in total tax revenues. The underlying assumption is that individuals, in their capacities as workers, savers, and investors, will respond to changes at the margin. What is important to the worker contemplating more or less work is the after-tax, or take-home pay (especially as there is always the choice of more or less leisure to trade this against). Similarly, what is important for the saver and the business person is the expected rate of return on their savings and investments after tax has been deducted. Therefore, the higher the marginal tax-rate, the greater the incentive to avoid paying taxes, either through legal tax avoidance, illegal tax evasion, or simply less work, less saving, and less investment. This simple proposition dates back perhaps several thousand years. It was reborn in the

1970s as the **Laffer curve**, named after Arthur Laffer, an American economist.

The Laffer Curve

Laffer's basic argument rests on the premise that zero tax-rates would obviously produce zero tax revenues, while tax rates of 100 per cent would also produce zero revenues, as taxpayers would cease to work (at least for money), since their incomes would be entirely taxed away. Maximum revenue would, therefore, be achieved by some rate in between. This idea is best illustrated graphically. Look at Figure 18.2. We measure tax-rates, T, on the vertical axis and tax revenues, R, on the horizontal axis. Tax-rate T_1 is the maximum rate that the government can impose before the relationship between tax-rates and revenues becomes negative, or inverse. For example, at tax-rate T_2 revenues will have dropped from R_{max} to R_2.

Figure 18.2

The Laffer Curve. The Laffer curve is a representation of the relationship between *tax-rates* and tax revenues collected. We put tax revenues on the horizontal axis and tax-rates on the vertical axis. The maximum tax revenues collectable, R_{max}, result when the tax-rate, T_1, is utilized. If the government insists on having a tax-rate of T_2 tax revenues collected fall from R_{max} to R_2 Thus, the Laffer curve policy implication is that if we believe that the real-world relationship between tax-rates and tax revenues is as depicted here, and we believe that we are above tax-rate T_1, then a reduction from current tax-rates of, say, T_2 towards tax-rate T_1 will *increase* tax revenues from R_2 to some greatear amount, with the maximum reachable at R_{max}. In other words, a tax-rate reduction leads to an increase in tax revenues. The validity of this proposition rests on the empirical relationship between reductions in tax-rates and changes in the amount of work effort, investment, saving, and attempts at avoiding the payment of taxes.

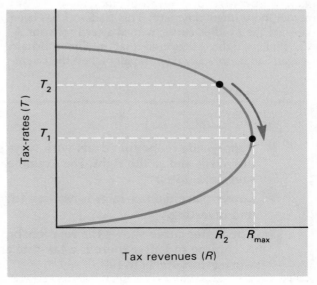

The policy implications of the Laffer curve are that if the economy is already at tax-rate T_2, a reduction in tax-rates will actually lead to an increase in tax revenues. This kind of reasoning has formed the basis of many tax changes since 1979 in the UK.

Criticisms of the Laffer Curve

While one cannot argue with the theoretical possibility of the existence of the Laffer curve, one can argue about where an economy is on the Laffer curve. For example, are the government correct in assuming that the UK economy has already exceeded the point at which maximum revenue would be derived (T_1)? Furthermore, can one be certain that reductions in marginal rates of taxation will stimulate the economy sufficiently actually to increase the total government tax revenue? Indeed, it is difficult to estimate how much of the underground economy will come above ground if marginal tax-rates are reduced.

Another complication is that in the UK, while direct taxes have been reduced to some extent to encourage incentives to work and invest, indirect taxes – taxes on spending – have been increased to maintain government expenditure. In some way this highlights the classic problem of lowering inflation and unemployment at the same time and this will be dealt with next.

The Phillips Curve in Theory and Reality

Another important controversy that is presently debated has arisen because inflation does not only occur at full employment. In fact, some economists argue that there is a constant *trade-off* between the rate of employment and the rate of inflation. Their argument is that in order to obtain less unemployment, we have to suffer greater rates of inflation. Or, conversely, in order to reduce the rate of inflation, we have to accept more unemployment. This trade-off has been labelled the **Phillips curve**, named after Professor A. W. Phillips, who discovered that in Great Britain wages had historically risen rapidly when the unem-

ployment rate was low and had risen more slowly when the unemployment rate was high. His empirical evidence was for the years 1861–1957.

Although Phillips's original analysis published in 1958 was in terms of *wage-rate* increases and the unemployment rate, economists have contended that the relationship also holds between *price increases* and the unemployment rate. Indeed, there does seem to be a close relationship between wage-rate changes and the Retail Price Index.

Figure 18.3 shows a hypothetical Phillips curve. With the hypothetical Phillips curve, if we are, for example, at an unemployment rate of 6 per cent and want to reduce the unemployment rate to 4 per cent, we have to accept an increase in the rate of inflation of 2 percentage points. If only the world were so simple!

Figure 18.3

A Hypothetical Phillips Curve. The Phillips curve shows the relationship between the unemployment rate and the rate of inflation. If we want a 3 per cent unemployment rate, we presumably have to live with 5 per cent annual inflation. If we do not want to live with 5 per cent inflation but insist on only 3 per cent, we will have to 'buy it' with more unemployment, since a 3 per cent rate of inflation is associated with a 4 per cent rate of unemployment.

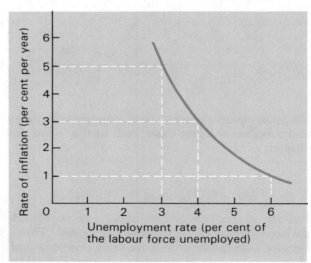

Key Points 18.1

► Supply-side economics deals with ways of shifting the aggregate supply curve outwards and to the right. For example, by improving the incentives to work, save, and invest.

► Lower marginal tax-rates is *one* way to improve the rewards for working, saving, and investing.

► The Laffer curve shows the relationship between the tax-rates and tax revenues. According to Laffer there is a tax-rate above which tax revenues start to fall as work effort starts to fall.

If it were, policy-makers could simply set a trade-off menu. Each year they could vote on whether they wanted to have less or more unemployment with concomitantly more or less inflation. Indeed, that is the way many policy-makers talked during the late 1960s and the mid-1970s.

The Phillips Curve in Reality Today

In Figure 18.4 we plot the rate of inflation and the rate of unemployment that has actually occurred since Phillips's publication. Instead of there being a *negative* trade-off relationship between the rate of unemployment and the rate of inflation, in recent times there has been a *positive* one. That is to say, over time, higher rates of inflation have been, more or less, associated with higher rates of unemployment. To understand why this trade-off between the rate of inflation and the rate of unemployment has diminished, we must first understand the role of expectations.

Expectations and the Phillips Curve

The hypothetical Phillips curve presented in Figure 18.3 assumes rigid expectations of future changes in the rate of inflation. Actually, the original specifications of the Phillips curve worked well for about a century in the United States and in Great Britain. Fluctuations in the rate of inflation were, to a large degree, symmetrical with unemployment, yet as time progressed this relationship changed.

With the developments of increased unemployment benefit people took longer to search for work. Union strengths helped generate better wages. Employment legislation, such as minimum wages and redudancy payments, also had its effects on employment opportunities and inflationary pressure. Inflation itself became a problem, especially as its rate seems to fluctuate from year to year. Consequently, it

Figure 18.4
The Phillips Curve Relationship in Reality 1960–85. In this diagram we plot the average annual unemployment rate against the average inflation rate for the period 1960–85. You will notice that the smooth line of the Phillips curve has been displaced by a scatter diagram. The various points no longer show the purported negative trade-off relationship. In fact at points it displays combined high rates of inflation and unemployment – a situation that some economists term **'stagflation'**.

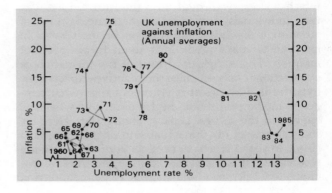

Source: The figures are taken from the *Department of Employment Gazette*. (Those plotted for 1985 are an estimate based on the first half of the year only.)

was no longer rational for individuals to hold rigid expectations about future changes in the rate of inflation. That is changes in the expected (anticipated) rate of inflation became as important as changes in the actual rate of inflation. The new relationship between inflation and unemployment required a new explanation. This explanation developed via the accelerationist Phillips curve which complements the presentation of a natural unemployment rate. Both of these more

Key Points 18.2

▶ Since 1969, this country has seen simultaneous bouts of high unemployment and inflation, usually called 'stagflation'.

▶ The Phillips curve is named after A. W. Phillips who discovered that wages in Great Britain had risen rapidly when unemployment was low, and slowly when unemployment was high (during the period 1861–1957).

▶ The theoretical negative trade-off between the rate of unemployment and the rate of inflation has, in the last few decades, not been validated by the real world; rather, there seems to be a positive relationship between the rate of inflation and the rate of unemployment.

▶ Basically, the Phillips curve trade-off between the rate of inflation and the rate of unemployment only works when there is a constant relationship between the *actual* and *expected* rate of inflation.

recent concepts will be explained below, after exploring the idea of expectations a little further.

Adaptive Expectations

The main observation here is that workers cannot be fooled forever. Everyone can be assumed to adapt eventually to a changed situation if that adaptation is beneficial. Figuring out what the rate of inflation is going to be next year is beneficial to anybody attempting to make economic decisions, the consequences of which will carry through into the future. One way that individuals can adapt to a changing rate of inflation is by using information on past rates of inflation to make predictions about future rates of inflation. This simplistic theory of the formation of expectations has been called the **adaptive-expectations hypothesis**. It states that workers gauge what happened in the past as the best indicator of what will happen in the future. Look at Figure 18.5. Here we show, in panel (b) the actual rate of inflation. It is rising. In year 1 it is 6 per cent per annum, during the second year it is 8 per cent, during the third year it jumps to 12 per cent, and stays at 12 per cent during the fourth, fifth, and sixth years.

In the simplest adaptive-expectations model, the expected rate of inflation this year is simply whatever the rate of inflation was last year. This is shown in panel (a). During the second year, workers believed inflation would be 6 per cent because that is what it was the year before. During the third year they believed it would be 8 per cent (because that is what it was the year before). In this simplified adaptive-expectations model, workers are always behind in their expectation of inflation. When the rate of inflation is rising, they will always believe it is going to be less than it actually turns out to be; when the rate of inflation is falling, they will always believe it is going to be more than it actually turns out to be. Only when the rate of inflation remains constant for a period of time do expectations come into line with reality.

A more sophisticated model of the adaptive-expectations hypothesis will have workers forming their expectation of inflation on the basis of some combination of, say, the last three, four, or five years' rates of inflation, with more weight being given to rates of inflation in the immediately preceding years.

Adaptive Expectations and a Series of Short-run Phillips Curves

Using the adaptive-expectations hypothesis, one can posit that there still exists a series of *short-run* Phillips curves. Each short-run Phillips curve will relate to each expected rate of inflation. In order to understand the argument completely, one must first understand the concept of the natural rate of unemployment, which is typically associated with full employment.

Figure 18.5
The Adaptive-expectations Hypothesis. According to the simplest version of the adaptive-expectations hypothesis, individuals formulate their expectation of inflation solely on what the rate of inflation was in the previous year. Consider panel (b), where we show the actual rate of inflation as being 6 per cent during year 1, 8 per cent during year 2, and 12 per cent during years 3, 4, 5, and 6. According to the simplified adaptive-expectations hypothesis, in year 2 people will predict that inflation will be 6 per cent, because that is what it was in year 1. We show this in panel (a). In year 3, even though the actual rate of inflation is 12 per cent (as shown in panel (b) the expected rate of inflation is 8 per cent (as shown in panel (a). Finally, in year 4, the expected rate of inflation is equal to the actual rate of inflation because inflation has levelled off.

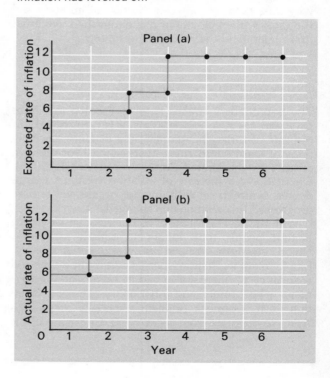

The Natural Rate of Unemployment

The **natural rate of unemployment** is the amount of unemployment which would prevail when inflation is correctly anticipated. The natural rate of unemployment is that unemployment which continues even when the economy is operating at full capacity (i.e. when it is on the vertical section of the aggregate supply curve). We might attempt to measure statistically the natural rate of unemployment by looking at what the average rate of unemployment has been when booms have been at their height, e.g. 1978–79.

Each economy will have its own natural rate of unemployment. This will depend upon the amount of frictional unemployment, a topic that we discussed in Chapter 11. If the labour market is functioning smoothly, with workers able to find out quickly about the availability of job vacancies, then, other things being equal, the natural rate of unemployment might be relatively low. If there are a large number of effective impediments to a smoothly functioning labour market, then the natural rate of unemployment might be high. We surmise, for example, that the more restrictions there are in the labour market, the higher the natural rate of unemployment. These restrictions might be minimum wages legislation, occupational training requirements, strict union membership requirements, and so on. For the present consider a natural rate of unemployment to be an average unemployment rate for a couple of decades.

Keeping the Rate of Unemployment below Its Long-run Natural Rate

Using the adaptive-expectations hypothesis, the only way to keep the unemployment rate below its long-run natural rate is to have the *actual* rate of inflation exceed the *expected* rate. In this way workers will suffer from a 'money illusion' and believe that wage-rates are going up – making work far more worth while. But since workers adapt, in order to maintain the gap between the actual and expected rates of inflation, the rate of inflation would have continually to accelerate. What is needed to consistently increase output and reduce unemployment permanently, then, is an inflation rate that is always greater than anticipated. This can be called an **accelerationist view** of the Phillips-curve analysis.* It suggests that the only way to produce deviations from the natural rate of unemployment is to have accelerating or decelerating inflation.

GRAPHIC ANALYSIS OF THE ACCELERATIONIST VIEW

In Figure 18.6, we see two curves similar in appearance to the standard Phillips curve (thus the alternative name in the footnote.) On the horizontal axis, we measure unemployment; on the vertical axis, we measure the *actual* rate of inflation. The Phillips curves, however, are drawn for two different levels of *expected* rates of inflation. The left one is drawn for an expected rate of inflation of 3 per cent; the right one is drawn for an expected rate of inflation of 6 per cent. The vertical line labelled U^* represents the so-called natural rate of unemployment, which we will assume to be 5 per cent.

Figure 18.6

An Expectations-augmented Phillips Curve, showing Natural Rate of Unemployment. Here we show two Phillips curves. On the horizontal axis, the unemployment rate is measured. On the vertical axis is the rate of inflation. We assume that the 'natural' or long-run level of unemployment is at U^*, or 5 per cent of the labour force. There are two separate Phillips curves: one is for an expected rate of inflation of 6 per cent per year, and the other is for an expected rate of inflation of 3 per cent per year. If the expected rate of inflation is 6 per cent per year and the actual rate of inflation (which is measured on the vertical axis) is also 6 per cent per year, then the long-run equilibrium unemployment level will be maintained at point A. However, if the expected rate of inflation remains at 6 per cent per year, but the *actual* rate of inflation is only 3 per cent per year, we will find ourselves at point D, where there is excess unemployment – that is, unemployment over and above the normal long-run U^* of 5 per cent. Here we see that an actual rate of inflation less than the expected rate of inflation leads to unemployment. Now take the innermost curve, where the expected rate of inflation is 3 per cent per year. If the actual rate of inflation is also 3 per cent, then there will be no excess unemployment – that is, unemployment will be at its 'normal' long-run level of 5 per cent. We will be at point B. Suppose, however, that the actual rate of inflation is 6 per cent. We will find ourselves at point C. We will be over full employment – that is, unemployment will be less than its long-run or normal level of 5 per cent. At point C, individuals *underestimate* the actual rate of inflation. Contrast this with point D, where individuals *overestimate* the actual rate of inflation. The underestimate causes unemployment rates to fall below U^*. The overestimate causes unemployment rates to be greater than U^*.

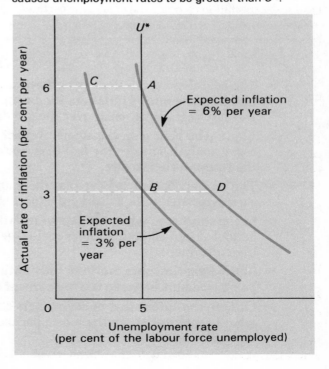

Those who believe in the accelerationist theory assume that the unemployment rate will eventually settle at U^* when the future inflation rate is correctly anticipated, that is, when the *actual* rate of change in prices is equal to the *expected* rate of change in prices. This would occur either at point A, if the actual rate of inflation were 6 per cent, or point B, if the actual rate of inflation were 3 per cent. Look at point C, however. Here the anticipated rate of inflation is 3 per cent, but the actual rate is 6 per cent. Point C represents 'over full' employment. Now look at point D. The actual rate of inflation is 3 per cent, but the anticipated rate is 6 per cent. Unemployment exceeding the natural rate thus occurs.

The accelerationist theory says that you can keep unemployment down only by increasing (creating an acceleration in) the rate of inflation. Hence, high inflation does not keep unemployment down. Only rising inflation does. If the accelerationists are correct, it does not matter much in the long run what the rate of growth of the money supply is, provided that the rate remains stable. Those who believe in the accelerationist theory believe that a continuous rate of inflation of 4 per cent per year will yield the same long-run level of unemployment as a continuous rate of change of prices of 10 per cent. The only prerequisite for this outcome is that the rate of change of prices be correctly anticipated. (Now read Key Points 18.3.)

Another Modern School of Thought – Rational Expectations

Finally, it is worth looking at the criticism made by the rational-expectations school. They make the pertinent point that adaptive-expectations theorists always have workers being one step behind what is actually occurring, or what policy-makers are actually doing. This implies that workers can be fooled. No learning from experience is allowed for, which somehow strikes a false chord in the minds of this final school. Their notion is that eventually rational individuals will modify their forecasting equation to produce unbiased estimates of the rate of inflation (or whatever). Taken to its ultimate conclusion supporters of rational expectations would claim that eventually there will not even be a short-run trade-off between unemployment and inflation. (The long-run Phillips curve would thus become U^* in Figure 18.6.)

The Rational-expectations Hypothesis

The **rational-expectations hypothesis** therefore is most concerned with human behaviour, it emphasizes the rational sifting and weighing of all available information that can be undertaken.

Rather than simply looking at what has happened in the previous year, rational individuals will form *rational expectations*. They will look at what happened in the past and combine it with their predictions of *current* government policies that they think are being pursued and *future* government policies that they think are likely to be introduced and pursued. In other words, rational expectations require a judgement about the future effects of current and future policies that are combined with lessons from whatever has happened in the past.

Consider a simple example. *Suppose* that a government is worried about being re-elected as, although it has kept inflation constant at 5 per cent a year for the previous four years, unemployment has risen to a

---

Key Points 18.3

▶ The adaptive-expectations hypothesis argues that workers will make predictions of this year's rate of inflation, for example, based on what the rate of inflation was last year, or, at most, over the previous few years.

▶ Those who believe in the accelerationist theory argue that the original Phillips-curve analysis ignores the fact that workers will eventually correctly anticipate the future inflation rate.

▶ The accelerationists believe that there are numerous short-run Phillips curves, each associated with a different expected rate of inflation.

▶ In the short run, when the rate of inflation exceeds its expected rate, workers can be fooled into accepting lower real-wage increases; hence, there is a reduction in unemployment.

▶ In the long run, once workers fully anticipate future rates of inflation, there will be no trade-off between unemployment and inflation.

▶ Only to the extent that policy-makers can keep the rate of inflation higher than what is anticipated can there be a permanent trade-off between unemployment and inflation.

high level. Common sense tells this government that if they can cut unemployment quickly their chances of re-election will be far better. The Prime Minister, therefore, puts pressure on the Bank of England to increase the money supply. It is known from past experience that this action may increase inflation but it should also temporarily reduce unemployment.

Certainly, under the adaptive-expectations hypothesis, there is a short-run Phillips-curve trade-off between the rate of inflation and the rate of unemployment. Using just the adaptive-expectations hypothesis, one would predict that on using this policy the government could succeed in its desires. On the other hand, if the rational-expectations hypothesis is correct, decision-makers – such as union leaders – will understand the relationship between the rate of growth of the money supply and the rate of inflation (and, hence, the potential reduction in their members' real wages and those of any other employees freshly recruited from the unemployed or otherwise). They will certainly not be fooled into accepting a prediction of a 5 per cent rate of inflation in the coming year, just because that is the way inflation has gone for the previous few years. They will use the information that they have about current government policy. The union leaders will demand wage increases consistent with the higher anticipated rate of inflation. The desired reduction in unemployment will not, therefore, materialize.

Now, of course, not all decision-makers will get their predictions right. It is impossible to know exactly the relationship between the rate of increase in the money supply and the rate of inflation; or, at best, it is impossible to figure out the '**time-lag**' between changes in monetary policy and changes in the rate of inflation. What the rational-expectations hypothesis suggests, however, is that workers and other decision-makers in the economy will not *consistently* and *systematically* make a forecasting error by simply basing the future on the past.

Which side you find yourself taking in this concluding scenario is not too important. What is important, however, is that you recognize the difficulties that the economist faces. You should certainly appreciate that *expectations* of one sort or another definitely influence economic behaviour; that time-lags compound the problems of economic analysis; and that there are no easy answers but many complex alternative possibilities. Indeed, this whole chapter has, it is hoped, opened up the supply-side of the economy generally, and thus put you in a better position to understand existing policy and the debates emanating from it.

Key Points 18.4

▶ **The rational-expectations hypothesis predicts that individuals will form their expectations rationally by examining all information. That means that economic agents will look not only at such things as the past rate of inflation but also at present government policies that can affect the current and future rate of inflation.**

▶ **The rational-expectations hypothesis simply predicts that decision-makers in the economy will *not* consistently and systematically make a forecasting error by basing the future on the past.**

CASE STUDY

The Supply-Siders

Supply-side Economics

The basic premise here is that *supply will create its own demand*. The supporters of this school believe, therefore, that it is necessary to allow the private (market) sector sufficient freedom and incentive to expand the range of goods and services that they feel it worth their while to produce. Consequently, the policies orientated towards the supply-side are aimed at making business and employment rewarding. Once supply increases, income increases (for the owners of the factors of production) and thus spending and

continued overleaf

employment, in turn, also increase.

The prime objective of any government wishing to promote these supply-determined increases in national income and employment, would be to remove the market distortions that reduce an individual's willingness to supply labour or a firm's willingness to supply goods. These policies have been at the core of the Conservative Manifesto since they came to office in May 1979. As reported in the *Economic Progress Report* of June that year their Economic Strategy is:

based on four principles: first, the strengthening of incentives, particularly through tax cuts, allowing people to keep more of their earnings in their own hands, so that hard work, ability and success are rewarded; second, greater freedom of choice by reducing the state's role and enlarging that of the individual; third, the reduction of the borrowing requirement of the public sector to a level which leaves room for the rest of the economy to prosper; and fourth through firm monetary and fiscal discipline, bringing inflation under control and ensuring those taking part in collective bargaining are obliged to live with the consequences of their actions.

The model upon which this policy is based is very different from the Keynesian presentation in most 'A'-level texts. Explanations for variations in employment and output are being made by reference to the factors which determine *Aggregate Supply* (as opposed to Aggregate Demand). The factors which can be seen to determine Aggregate Supply are: Level of profit, ease of movement into and out of markets, the level of wages, the marginal efficiency of capital, the marginal revenue product, the level of fixed costs etc. – i.e. mainly microeconomic factors. Furthermore, it is assumed that the correct level of aggregate supply will be determined by market forces and not government intervention.

The ideas outlined above date back to a French economist – Jean Baptiste Say – who lectured at the turn of the nineteenth century. (Say formulated his law of markets in 1803.) At the beginning of the 1970s Professor Lucas and T. Sargeant, both American economists, popularized these classic ideas once again. In the mid-1970s British institutions such as Liverpool University, the London Business School, and the Institute of Economic Affairs (IEA) started to add their support.

Following these academic developments governments in the USA and UK today are very much under the influence of supply-side economics. In fact, some would argue that the policies pursued by the present Conservative government should lose the title 'Monetarist' and gain the broader label 'New Classical Macroeconomics'. Indeed the various faces of monetarism that the Conservatives present all have classical roots. Supply-side economics is merely one of those roots

Source: D. Myers, 'The Supply Siders' *Economics* (Journal of the Economic Association) Vol XX part 4, No. 88, Winter 1984, p. 17.

Questions

1. What are the other classical roots that Monetarism contains?
2. 'More detailed government intervention or greater trust in market forces'. Which policy would you promote as economic adviser to the Prime Minister?
3. Supporters of supply-side economics make frequent reference to the existence and size of the black economy. Can you explain why?

CASE STUDY

Surely among the Millions Out of Work There's Someone Who Can Make Tights

Yesterday saw publication by the CBI of some figures on labour shortages. Labour shortages? Do we really have labour shortages with three million plus unemployed?

Well, yes. Or at least that is what companies say. The CBI's Employment Affairs Report shows that 12 per cent of firms expect labour shortages to restrict output, the highest since 1980.

In the capital goods industries it is worse: no less than 19 per cent of firms expect shortages of skilled labour to restrict output in the next four months. Almost one-third of firms in the electronic and instrument engineering industry have skill shortage problems.

Fine, you might say: that is hi-tech – you would expect skill shortages given our lamentable record in technical training. What about more basic products?

Products don't come much more basic than hosiery and knitwear, and there 39 per cent of firms expect skill shortages to limit output.

You can draw two very different sets of conclusions from this data. The first would be that we must have a dreadfully inefficient labour market, poor industrial training, and a dreadful geographical mis-match of people, skills, and jobs.

That is probably quite right, though anyone assuming it is a new problem should recall that in Glasgow in the 1930s – in the depths of a depression which struck Glasgow particularly hard – there were shortages of bricklayers. The reason was technological change. Glasgow had a tradition of building in stone, and so there were plenty of stonemasons. But this form of building had been priced out by bricks. All the spare brickies were presumably down in the South-East building the semi-detached houses which were being strung out along the arterial roads.

But there is an alternative set of conclusions, which is that companies are very adept at finding reasons why they cannot do things. Look at the way company chairmen fuss about the pay increases of their workforce, while handing themselves rises which in percentage terms are far in excess of anything they would countenance for their workers.

Perhaps companies which claim that they cannot get skilled workers simply are not paying enough for them.
Source: The Guardian, 16 July 1985, p. 19.

Questions

1. How could the employed labour force be increased?
2. The need for wage increases seems to be an important argument used by this journalist.
   (a) How could you as an economist support his argument?
   (b) How could another economist challenge these arguments?

Exam Preparation and Practice

INTRODUCTORY EXERCISES

1. Answer the following questions based on the graph below.

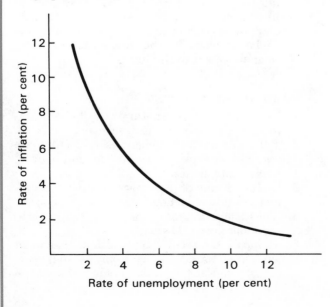

(a) In order to reduce inflation to 2 per cent per year, unemployment will 'cost' what per cent?
(b) In order to reduce unemployment to 4 per cent, what is the minimum rate of inflation that must be accepted?
(c) What would cause this curve to 'worsen'; that is, shift to the right?

continued overleaf

2. Answer the following questions based on the graph below.

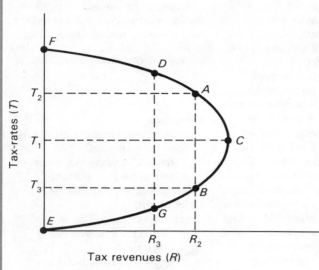

Tax revenues (R)

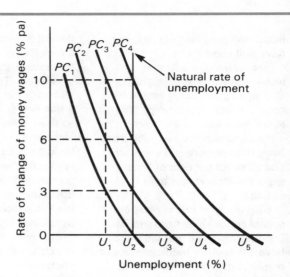

Unemployment (%)

(a) What two letters indicate zero tax revenues? How can this situation exist?
(b) What two letters indicate tax revenues equal to R_2?
(c) If the economy is at point A (tax-rate T_2 yielding tax revenues R_2), what will happen to tax revenues if the tax-rate falls below T_2?
(d) What letter indicates the highest tax-rate above which further tax-rate increases will yield lower tax revenues?

MULTIPLE CHOICE QUESTIONS

1. The term 'marginal rate of tax' is applied to the
 A proportion of income which is paid in tax
 B amount of tax payable after allowances have been deducted
 C rate of tax paid on unearned income
 D tax paid out of an increment to income
 E rate of tax which gives the highest yield

2. Which one of the following would not constitute a supply-side policy?
 A Business start-up schemes
 B Laws reducing trade unions' power to picket and strike
 C Introduction of minimum wage legislation
 D Liberalization of the laws relating to who can provide electricity supply

Questions 3 and 4 refer to the following diagram of the expectations-augmented Phillips curve, in which U_2 is the natural rate of unemployment, and PC_1 to PC_4 are Phillips curves associated with successively higher inflationary expectations.

3. When there are no inflationary expectations, what will be the effect of a government attempt to reduce unemployment to U_1? One or more of the three responses given are correct. Select your answer from the code set out in the grid.
 1 in the long run, unemployment remains at U_2
 2 the rate of change of money wages rises to 3 per cent per annum
 3 the natural level of unemployment rises

A	B	C	D	E
3 only	1 and 2 only	1 and 3 only	2 and 3 only	1,2,3 only

4. With expectations of 3 per cent inflation, the government uses fiscal policy to reduce unemployment to U_1. Subsequently, a new government is elected which determines to eliminate wage inflation. It would be necessary, if this was to be achieved in the short run, to allow unemployment to rise to:
 A U_1 B U_2 C U_3 D U_4 E U_5

RELATED ESSAY QUESTIONS

1. Explain the term 'the natural rate of unemployment' and discuss how its level may be reduced.
2. 'Both supply and demand side factors are required to explain how an economy works'. Explain and discuss.
3. Discuss some of the macroeconomic consequences of a reduction in personal taxation
4. 'The Phillips curve is no longer a useful guide to economic policy.' Discuss.
5.. Compare the relative costs of unemployment and inflation to the economy. Can policy-makers choose the level of unemployment and inflation for an economy?

19 Money and Related Financial Institutions

Key Points to Review

▶ Money as a medium of exchange (2.3)
▶ Specialization and comparative advantage (6.2)
▶ Exchange rates (9.1)

▶ Types and causes of inflation (11.4)
▶ Retail Price Index (11.5)
▶ The meaning of GNP (13.5)
▶ Black economy (13.7)

Questions for Preview

1 What is money?

2 How is money narrowly defined in the United Kingdom?

3 Which institutions constitute the monetary sector in the UK?

4 What are the functions of the Bank of England?

If someone were to ask you, 'How much money do you make?' you might answer in terms of so many pounds per week or per year. In this context, the term *money* really means income or the ability to purchase goods and services – in fact, the term is most generally used to mean income. But in this sense it is being used incorrectly. Counterfeiters 'make money'; as we shall see in this chapter, the banking system also 'makes money'. What you make is income. In this chapter and throughout the rest of the text, we will use the term *money* to mean anything which we use as a medium (means) of exchange. You use your cheque-book as a medium of exchange. The money in your building society can be regarded as a medium of exchange. Even a premium bond, which can be sold, can ultimately be regarded as a medium of exchange. Therefore, money is more than just the notes and coins that you have in your wallet or purse, or hidden in a tea caddy. Consequently, the official money supply includes more than just **currency** – paper notes and coins.

In this chapter, we will examine the functions that money serves, the different types of money that are in existence, and the financial system generally. In the

Case Studies section, we will look at the future of the cashless society.

The Functions of Money

There are four traditional functions of money. The one that most people are familiar with and the one that we referred to above is as a *medium of exchange*. However, money also serves as a *unit of accounting*, a *store of purchasing power*, and a *standard of deferred payment*.

When we say that money serves as a medium of exchange, what we mean is that sellers will accept it as a means of payment in market transactions. Without some generally accepted medium of exchange, we would have to resort to barter. In fact, before money was used, transactions took place by means of barter. Barter is simply a direct exchange – no intermediary good called money is used. Economic historians often suggest that the switch from barter to the use of money allowed for more rapid economic growth of the Western world, since increased specialization was then possible. It was extremely costly – that is, the transactions costs were high – to make all exchanges by barter. Imagine the difficulty you would have today if you had to exchange your labour directly for the fruits of someone else's labour. Imagine the many exchanges that would have to take place for you to get from a position where you owned, for example, twenty-five pairs of shoes to a position where you owned only two pairs but now also had bread, meat, a pair of pants, and so on. The use of money facilitates exchange. Indeed, the existence of money means that individuals no longer have to hold a diverse collection of goods as an exchange inventory. Hence, more specialization can occur.

Money as a Medium of Exchange

As a **medium of exchange**, money allows individuals to specialize in any area in which they have a comparative advantage and to receive money payment for the fruits of their labour. Money can then be exchanged for the fruits of other people's labour. The usefulness of money as a medium of exchange causes more specialization. Moreover, we see that money is more important the larger the amount of trade. Thus, money would not be as important in self-sufficient family units as it is in modern commercial economies.

Money as a Unit of Accounting

A **unit of accounting** is a way of placing a specific value on economic goods and services. Thus, as a unit of accounting, the monetary unit is used to measure the value of goods and services relative to other goods and services. It is the common denominator, or measure. It thus enables individuals to compare, easily, the relative value of goods and services. Governments use money prices to measure national income each year. A firm uses money prices to calculate profits and losses; and a typical household budgets daily its regular expenses using money prices as its unit of accounting.

Another way of describing money as a unit of accounting is to say that it is a *standard of value* that allows economic transactors to compare the relative worth of various goods and services. In short, it acts as an economic yardstick.

Money as a Store of Value

To see how money is a **store of value**, consider the following simple example. A fisherman comes into port after several days of fishing. At the going price of fish that day, he has £1000's worth of fish. These fish are not a good store of value, because, if the fisherman keeps them too long, they will rot. If he attempts to exchange them with other tradespeople, some of the fish may rot before he can exchange the entire catch for the goods and services that he desires. On the other hand, if the fisherman sells the entire catch for

money, he can store the value of his catch in the money that he receives. (Of course, he can freeze the fish, but that is costly.)

Money as a Standard of Deferred Payment

The fourth function of the monetary unit is as a **standard of deferred payment**. In less technical terms this simply means that money can be used as a means of entering into agreements regarding *future* payments. This function, therefore, simultaneously involves money as a medium of exchange and a unit of accounting. For example, debts are typically stated in terms of a unit of account and are paid with a monetary medium of exchange. The negotiation of future payments is an essential feature of any complex society. Workers negotiate a salary for payment on completion of a job; landlords negotiate a rent that will be paid at regular intervals in the future; shareholders will be given a portion of the profits each year, and so on.

It is interesting to note that not all countries will use their own national monetary unit to specify future payments. Often the dollar or pound is used as the unit of account, as these are more acceptable as international mediums of exchange. Failing their reliability some contracts are still negotiated in terms of gold.

Liquidity

Money is an asset – something of value – that accounts for part of one's wealth. Wealth in the form of money can be exchanged later for some other asset. Although it is not the only form of wealth that can be exchanged for goods and services, it is the one most widely accepted. This attribute of money is called **liquidity**. We say that an asset is liquid when it can easily be acquired or disposed of without high costs and with relative certainty as to its value. Notes and coins are by definition the most liquid asset there is. Just compare it, for example, to a share listed on the Stock Exchange. To buy or sell that share you must call a stockbroker who will place the buy or sell order for you. This must be done during normal business hours. You have to pay a percentage commission to the broker. Moreover, there is a distinct probability that you will get more or less for the share than you originally paid for it. This is not the case with notes and coins which can be easily converted to other asset forms.

However, when we hold notes and coins, we pay a price for this advantage of liquidity. That price is the interest yield that could have been obtained had the asset been held in another form, for example, in the form of a savings account. In other words, the cost of holding money (its opportunity cost) is measured by the alternative interest yield obtainable by holding some other asset. Notes and coins therefore, are merely one of a whole range of assets which can represent a person's wealth. Of all the assets, however, they are certainly the most liquid.

Why Money Has Value

Today in the United Kingdom all of us accept coins, notes, and cheques in exchange for items sold, including our labour services. The question remains as to why we are willing to accept for payment some bits of paper or metal that have no *intrinsic* value. The reason is that in this country we have a **fiduciary monetary system**. This means that the value of our currency rests upon the public's confidence that money can be exchanged for goods and services. *Fiduciary* comes from the Latin *fiducia*, which means trust or confidence. In other words, in our fiduciary monetary system, money, whether in the form of currency or cheques, is not convertible to a fixed quantity of gold, silver, or some other precious commodity. The money that people hold in their wallets or purses, or bank accounts cannot be exchanged for a specified quantity of some specified commodity. The various bank notes are just pieces of official paper that cost a fraction of their face value to produce. Similarly, coins have a value stamped on them that is normally greater than the market value of the metal in them. Regardless, currency and bank cheques are money because of their acceptability and predictability of value.

Acceptability

Bank accounts, cheques, and currency are money because they are accepted in exchange for goods and services. They are accepted because people have confidence that they can later be exchanged for other goods and services. This confidence is based on the knowledge that such exchanges have occurred in the past without problems. Even during a period of relatively rapid inflation, we would still be inclined to accept money in exchange for goods and services. Why? Because it is so useful. Barter is a very costly, time-consuming alternative.

Predictability of Value

For money to have a predictable value, the relationship between the quantity of money supplied and the quantity of money demanded must not change frequently, abruptly, or in great magnitude. In this sense, the value of money is like the economic value of anything else. Supply and demand determine what it 'sells' for. What is the selling price of a pound coin? It is what one has to give up in order to 'purchase' a pound. What do you have to give up? You must give up the goods and services that you could have instead. In other words, in order to own a one-pound coin, you give up the *purchasing power* inherent in that pound. That purchasing power might be equal to a magazine or a small hamburger. The purchasing power of the pound (that is, its value) therefore varies inversely with the price level. Thus, the more rapid the rate of increase of some price index, such as the Retail Price Index, the more rapid is the decrease in the value, or purchasing power, of a pound. Money still retains its usefulness even if its value – its purchasing power – is declining year in and year out. In other words, money is still useful and accepted even during periods of inflation. Why? Because it still retains the characteristic of predictability of value. If you believe that the inflation rate is going to be around 10 per cent next year, you know that any pound you receive a year from now will have a purchasing power equal to 10

Key Points 19.1

▶ Money is defined by its functions, which are: (1) a medium of exchange, (2) a unit of accounting or standard of value, (3) a store of value, and (4) as a standard of deferred payment.

▶ Since notes and coins are widely accepted in exchange for goods and services, currency is a highly liquid asset. It can be disposed of without high transactions costs and with relative certainty as to its value.

▶ The United Kingdom has a fiduciary monetary system because our money is not convertible into a fixed quantity of a commodity such as gold or silver.

▶ The reason that money is accepted in exchange for goods and services is because people have confidence that money can later be exchanged for other goods and services.

▶ Also, the reason that we continue to accept money is because it has a predictable value.

▶ The purchasing power, or value, of money is inversely related to the price level.

per cent less than that same pound this year. Thus, you will not refuse to use money or accept it in exchange simply because you know that its value will decline by the rate of inflation next year.

The Relationship between the Money Supply and the Price Level

The idea that changes in the money supply result in changes in the price level was a fundamental tenet of classical economic reasoning. In fact, this relationship is one of the oldest known in the history of economic thought. We can look at the link between money and prices by means of the **equation of exchange** formally developed by an American economist, Irving Fisher, at Yale University in the early 1900s (also known as the Fisher equation).

The Equation of Exchange

Bank notes that you have in your wallet, purse, or bank account usually do not just sit there. They are eventually spent and in the process change hands. It is difficult to see how fast each individual five-pound note is spent, but we can compute an average velocity of the number of times that five-pound notes generally change hands to purchase final goods or services during the year. We call this the **income velocity of money***, which is designated by V. The income velocity of money is defined as the average number of times per year that the nation's stock of money is spent on purchasing the economy's annual flow of output (or its GNP).

If we let M stand for the total money supply, then our formula for the income velocity of money is:

$$V = \frac{\text{GNP}}{M}$$

Let us take an example. In 1983 GNP was approximately £260 billion and the money supply (£M3) was approximately £100 billion. The income velocity of money, V, therefore equated £260 billion divided by £100 billion, or 2.6. In other words, each pound changed hands an average 2.6 times that year. We might say, then, that the income velocity of money is a measure of the economy's output per pound.

TRANSPOSING THE EQUATION

Let us multiply both sides of the equation by M. This gives us:

$$MV \equiv \text{GNP}$$

Now let us break down GNP into its separate components – quantities and prices. We will let P stand for the average price of final products produced during the year in question. We let Q stand for the physical, or real, quantities of final outputs. Thus, the value of final output is price times quantity, or GNP = $P \times Q$. Now the equation can be rewritten as:

$$MV \equiv PQ**$$

In fact, this is the standard notation and form in which the **equation of exchange** is presented.

Consider a simple numerical example in which we consider a one-commodity economy. In this economy, the total money supply, M, is £100. The quantity of output, Q is 50 units of a good. The average price of this output is £10 per unit. Thus, using the equation of exchange we have:

$$
\begin{aligned}
MV &= PQ \\
£100\ V &= £10 \times 50 \\
£100\ V &= £500 \\
V &= 5
\end{aligned}
$$

Therefore, each pound is spent an average of five times a year.

EQUATION OF EXCHANGE IS AN IDENTITY

The equation of exchange is an identity. It always has to be true. It is what we call an *accounting identity*, which tells us that the total amount of money *spent* on final output, MV, is equal to the total amount of money *received* for final product, PQ. Thus, we can look at a given flow of money from either the buyers' or the producers' side of the picture. The value of goods purchased is equal to the value of goods sold.

Now we can use the equation of exchange to derive the quantity *theory* of money and prices.

Quantity Theory of Money and Prices

If we make some assumptions about certain components of the equation of exchange, we can actually come up with one of the oldest theories about inflation – the **quantity theory of money and prices**. That theory states that the level of prices in the economy is directly proportional to the quantity of money in circulation per unit of output. To state this theory in symbols, we divide both sides of the equation of exchange by **Q**. Thus **MV = PQ** becomes:

$$P = M \times \left(\frac{V}{Q}\right).$$

To derive the quantity theory of money and prices, we now have to make an assumption. If we assume that both V and Q are fairly constant, then as M increases or decreases, so, too, does P, and at the same rate. In fact classical economists believed that V was constant because it was determined by the long-run money-holding habits of firms and households, which seemed to them to be fairly stable. Q was also assumed fairly constant because of their prediction that the

---

*Sometimes termed velocity of circulation.

**Sometimes Q for quantity is represented by T for transactions.

economy tended toward full employment. Given that V and Q are constant one could predict therefore that a 10 per cent increase in M would cause a 10 per cent increase in P. To some extent this type of thinking affects monetarist governments' policies.

The Empirical Evidence

Evidence for the quantity theory of money and prices seems relatively favourable if we look at fairly long periods of time. For example, the inflation that occurred in England during 1750–1800 was probably due to the rapid expansion of banks and the resultant increase in money supply during that period. The inflation of the 1970s is similarly explained as a possible by-product of the money supply expansions caused by deficit financing by governments striving to maintain full employment. Thus it may be said that M and P are correlated – but they are certainly *not* proportional to the extent that if M is doubled P will rise twofold.

Furthermore, V does seem to vary from period to period and Q certainly is not constant as evidenced by recessions. Regardless, if one allows for time-lags of 12–18 months, money supply changes may explain movements in RPI – but this is very much dependent on choosing an appropriate definition of money supply – which is the next problem we shall concern ourselves with.

Defining and Measuring the Money Supply

Money is important. Changes in the total **money supply**, and changes in the rate at which it is growing affect important economic variables, such as the rate of inflation, interest rates, and employment. Although there is widespread agreement among economists that money is important they have never agreed on how to define and how to measure money. For example, the OECD published a table in 1977 showing how, at that time, its twenty-four members already used twenty-three different definitions of money supply. In the UK we have employed various definitions at different times. And today there are eight alternative versions of money supply published on a regular basis (see Figure 19.1, on p. 274). These measures do not move in line with one another as they all measure slightly different things.

A basic difference between these eight UK definitions of money supply is that some tend towards measuring narrow money and some tend towards broad money. The **broad measures** (M3, £M3, PSL1, and PSL2) include various types of money on which interest is paid and therefore to some extent they indicate changes in liquidity. The **narrow measures** (M0, M1, NIM1, and M2) focus more specifically on money held primarily for transaction purposes. In other words the former stresses the role of money as a temporary store of value and the latter the role of money as a medium of exchange.

The Narrow Measures (M0, M1, NIM1, M2)

The narrow measures consist of the following components.

1. Notes and coins
2. Operational balances at the Bank of England
3. Sight deposits
4. Retail deposits

1. NOTES AND COINS

Notes and coins are the most liquid component of any money supply. In the UK in 1984 there were approximately £12.8 billion worth of notes and coins in circulation. Taking the narrowest measure of money supply (M0) they account for approximately 99 per cent of its total. Taking a broader measure, e.g. M3, notes and coins would only account for approximately 10 per cent of the total. Movements in M0 are said to

---

Key Points 19.2

▶ In its simplest form the equation of exchange states that MV = GNP (which suggests that expenditures by one person will equal income receipts by another).

▶ Viewed as an accounting identity the equation of exchange is always correct, since the amount of money spent on final output must be equal to the total amount of money received for final output.

▶ If we transpose the equation of exchange, it can be made into $P = M \times (V/Q)$. If one assumes that V (the income velocity of money) and Q (output) are fairly constant, then any change in the money supply (M) will change the price level (P) by the same proportion.

▶ Monetarists believe that changes in rate of growth of the money supply to a large extent will affect the rate of inflation.

Figure 19.1
Money Supply Definitions

M0	Notes and coin in circulation with the public and held by the banks plus banks operational deposits held at the Bank of England. Operational deposits are total deposits held at the Bank of England less the volume required in order to satisfy the officially imposed cash ratio.
M1	Notes and coin in circulation with the public plus sterling sight deposits held by the UK private sector with the monetary sector.
Non-Interest M1 (NIM 1)	M1 excluding those sight deposits which pay interest.
M2	Notes and coin in circulation with the public plus sterling cheque accounts plus retail deposits (i.e. sums of £100000 or less with a maturity of one month or less) held by the UK private sector with UK banks, building societies, and in the National Savings Bank Ordinary Account.
£M3	Notes and coin in circulation with the public plus *all* sterling bank accounts (including certificates of deposit) held by UK residents in the private sector with the monetary sector.
M3	£M3 plus all foreign currency deposits held with UK banks by the UK private sector.
PSL1	£M3 less deposits with a maturity of more than two years plus private sector holdings of specified money market instruments.
PSL2	PSL1 plus most building society shares and deposits, and deposits with the National Savings Bank and National Savings instruments.

Source: D. T. Llewellyn 'The Difficult Concept of Money', p. 19. *Economic Review*, Vol. 2, No. 3, January 1985.

be a good indicator of the 'Black Economy' as this relies heavily on cash transactions.

2. OPERATIONAL BALANCES AT THE BANK OF ENGLAND

The remaining 1 per cent of M0 are the various commercial banks' operational balances held at the Bank of England – commonly referred to as the **bankers' balances**. That is, all commercial banks hold deposits (balances) at the Bank of England for the purposes of settling debts between themselves (they are *also* formally obliged to hold some 'cash-ratio deposits' at the Bank of England but these cannot be withdrawn and are not included in M0 – these non-operational deposits will be discussed later).

3. SIGHT DEPOSITS

Sight deposits in banks are those which can be withdrawn without notice. They are commonly referred to as current accounts which people can draw on by making out a cheque. These obviously represent a ready means of payment or medium of exchange and should be incorporated in any definition that wishes to measure money available for transaction purposes. In general terms approximately 70 per cent of M1 constitutes sight deposits. Of this 70 per cent, nearly 30 per cent represents interest-bearing sight deposits; these are a special type of bank account which offer normal cheque facilities, immediate access, and some interest on monies held. This final qualification should help you comprehend NIM1 itemized in figure 19.1, indeed the first three definitions should now make some sense.

4. RETAIL DEPOSITS

This is a general name for all bank accounts which can be readily used for transaction purposes. Broadly, these are all bank deposits of less than £100000 and any building society deposits, which are withdrawable within one month. These accounts can be regarded as 'active balances' which respond to patterns of consumer spending. The term 'retail deposits' is important for understanding the measure of money supply called M2. This recent definition represents an important development as it is the only narrow measure of money supply that is not restricted solely to deposits at banks. (In fact bank balances account for less than half of the total of M2.)

The Broad Measures (£M3, M3, PSL)

As already stated the broad measures are concerned with money in a fuller sense. That is, not only as a medium of exchange but also as a store of value. Consequently these broader measures involve all the above, plus varying forms of interest-earning assets, that can be converted into money given some time-period. The broader measures of money chiefly incorporate the following:

5. Time deposits
6. Foreign currency bank deposits
7. Money market instruments.

5. TIME DEPOSITS

Time deposits represent all those bank accounts which require a period of notice before withdrawal. These may take several forms and for our purposes it is best to think of them as bank deposit accounts, some building society accounts, and Certificates of Deposit. **Certificates of Deposit** are primarily an alternative way of storing large amounts of money (between £50000 and £500000) for long periods of time (up to five years) in return for a receipt (Certificate) which may be sold before maturity.

By adding private sector time deposits held at banks in the form of an account or as a Certificate of Deposit we arrive at a definition for £M3 (known as 'Sterling M3'). This measure is over twice the size of M1. For example, in June 1984 M1 totalled approximately £49 billion while £M3 totalled approximately £106 billion. This shows the significant amount of money that is held in interest-yielding deposit accounts or Certificates. Consequently this measure of money supply is seen to be responsive to changes in interest rates.

6. FOREIGN CURRENCY BANK DEPOSITS

Obviously foreign currency is not generally part of the UK money supply. But some residents of the UK do hold bank deposits in currencies other than sterling. These foreign currency deposits do represent potential stores of value, expecially if speculators are hoping to gain interest from fluctuating exchange rates. And these foreign currency deposits represent a medium of exchange for overseas expenditure. In consequence we have a measure of money supply that also takes these monies into account, namely M3 (see Figure 19.1 for details). Money balances, such as those discussed above, held in countries other than those of its origin, are known as *eurocurrency*.

7. MONEY MARKET INSTRUMENTS

In an attempt to make a full assessment of a nation's total liquidity, items classed as '**near-money**' should also be incorporated in a broad definition of money supply. These items of *near-money* include things such as **bank bills**, **Treasury bills**, and **local authority bills**. These bills are forms of 'paper money' as they are sold by banks (on behalf of firms), the Treasury, and local authorities at a price below their face value. The

holder reaps the reward when they mature by being paid the face value. However, they may sell, or pass the bill on, to someone else before it matures. Consequently, these bills represent a claim to money as a medium of exchange and they certainly form a store of value. Thus any truly comprehensive broad measure of money supply should include these instruments which accounts for the development of PSL1. PSL aptly stands for 'Private Sector Liquidity'. Once this concept has been conceived the need to incorporate any other savings instrument that represents a potential claim to funds can be appreciated. Thus we arrive at the broadest measure of all PSL2. This is defined in Figure 19.1, with all the other measures – they should all now make sense.

From Narrow to Broad and Back Again

We have seen by now a whole series of monetary aggregates, and in order to summarize how these relate to one another a table adapted from a Bank of England publication is presented as Figure 19.2. This table gives the impression that money supply definitions have evolved by simply adding more and more assets to the basic definition each time a revision is made. However, this is an entirely wrong impression. In historical terms the broader measures were defined first. M3 has been measured since 1963. M0 by comparison was introduced more recently, in June 1982. You may ask, does this shift towards a narrower measure imply that this measure is more correct. The answer is certainly No! For different purposes, different definitions are best. For example, if one wishes to know which definition of the money supply is most controllable by the government, it is probably £M3. If one wants to use a definition that seems to correlate best with economic activity on an economy-wide basis PSL2 is probably better. The appropriate definition depends on the question being asked.

Key Points 19.3

▶ There are two basic approaches to measuring money supply – the narrow measures and the broader measures. The former give us M0, M1, NIM1, M2, and represent the transaction balances, and the latter gives us £M3, M3, PSL1, and PSL2 and represents stores of value or liquidity.

▶ M0, M1, NIM1, and M2 consist of one or more of the following items: notes and coins, operational balances at the Bank of England, sight deposits, and some building society accounts.

▶ £M3, M3, PSL1, PSL2 include most of the above plus varying proportions of time deposits, foreign currency, and money market instruments.

▶ There is no one correct definition, each definition measures something slightly different. At present the UK regularly measures eight different definitions – these are summarized in Figure 19.2 (on p. 276).

Figure 19.2
Relationships between the UK Measures of Money Supply

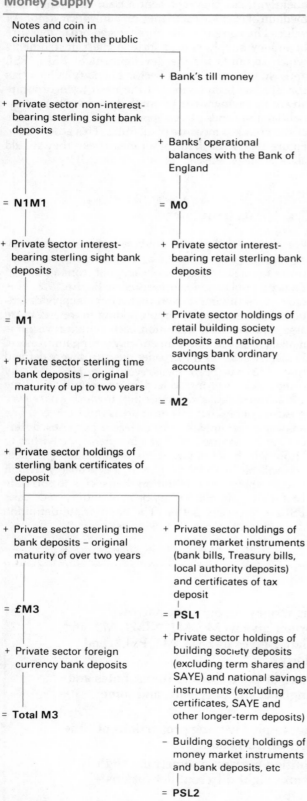

Notes and coin in circulation with the public

+ Bank's till money

+ Private sector non-interest-bearing sterling sight bank deposits

+ Banks' operational balances with the Bank of England

= **N1M1**

= **M0**

+ Private sector interest-bearing sterling sight bank deposits

+ Private sector interest-bearing retail sterling bank deposits

= **M1**

+ Private sector holdings of retail building society deposits and national savings bank ordinary accounts

+ Private sector sterling time bank deposits – original maturity of up to two years

= **M2**

+ Private sector holdings of sterling bank certificates of deposit

+ Private sector sterling time bank deposits – original maturity of over two years

+ Private sector holdings of money market instruments (bank bills, Treasury bills, local authority deposits) and certificates of tax deposit

= **£M3**

= **PSL1**

+ Private sector foreign currency bank deposits

+ Private sector holdings of building society deposits (excluding term shares and SAYE) and national savings instruments (excluding certificates, SAYE and other longer-term deposits)

= **Total M3**

– Building society holdings of money market instruments and bank deposits, etc

= **PSL2**

Source: Bank of England Quarterly Bulletin, March 1984

The British Banking Structure

So far we have looked at the functions of money, of its relationships to other economic variables, and its definition. We have thus seen that a major component of the money supply is the various bank accounts that are held at the 15 000 commercial bank branches scattered throughout the UK, and the various other savings accounts organized with other financial intermediaries.

Commercial Banks

A **commercial bank** is a privately owned, profit-seeking institution. Examples include: Barclays, Lloyds, Midlands, National Westminster (and its subsidiary, Coutts), and Williams & Glyn's (sometimes these six are grouped under the heading London Clearing Banks); Bank of Scotland, Clydesdale, and Royal Bank of Scotland (sometimes these three are grouped under the generic title Scottish Clearing Banks); the Co-operative Bank and the Yorkshire Bank.

Apart from accepting funds from their customers and using them to make profits, these commercial banks have other common features. They all have extensive branch networks and are major participants in the clearing system (this involves the daily settling of debts between banks that is generated by customers' cheques). In fact these banks between them transmit large amounts of cash through the economy each year. Over 6 million cheques alone are processed each day amounting to billions of pounds in value each year, while further billions are transferred by electronic methods, for example, all those payments made by direct debit, standing order, or credit cards.

Other Financial Intermediaries

Although the commercial banks ultimately act as a link between thousands of lenders and borrowers, they still have to compete with other financial intermediaries to attract their deposits. These other financial intermediaries undertake similar functions to banks, but do not necessarily offer the services of a cheque system. Examples of such intermediaries include: **discount houses, building societies, finance houses**, the **National Savings Bank, merchant banks**, and **foreign banks**. Each of these has specialized areas of interest as detailed below.

Discount Houses

Here we are *not* talking of Comet, Trident, Asda, or any other household name, but an élite group of ten institutions that are unique to Britain. Their names (e.g. Gerrard & National; Seccombe, Marshall & Campion; King & Shaxson; Carter Allan) are by no means commonplace as their trading-place lies in the heart of the financial city. Their main area of interest is to act as a **financial intermediary** between the commercial banks and the Bank of England. They borrow from the commercial banks for very short periods of time (taking advantage of what is termed **'money at call'**) perhaps over night or just for a few days, and lend to those with short-term cash flow problems by investing in short-term bills, especially **Treasury bills** sold by the Bank of England. In return for servicing this link, the Bank of England at times may even lend money direct to the discount houses if problems arise elsewhere in the system and their access to funds dries up. The discount houses' specialization is, therefore, interbank lending and borrowing for very short periods of time often just overnight and rarely for longer than ninety-one days.

Building Societies

Now we are certainly talking about common high-street names, regardless of where that high street is. There are some 200 building societies in the UK at present, with approximately 6500 branches. The biggest of these are the Halifax and the Abbey National who between them represent over one-third of the total building society assets.

Building societies gain their deposits (as many readers will know from personal experience) by gathering the savings of millions of short-term savers. These are then lent to house-buyers for longer periods of time, normally twenty-five years. Seventy-five per cent of the mortgage loans for house purchase in 1983 were provided by building societies. Their specialism is certainly the area of private house purchase.

Finance Houses

These institutions are responsible for financing hire purchase agreements for periods of two to three years. However, the man-in-the-street often accesses the funds through the retailer from whom he is buying the product. In other words, the retailer is often the agent for the finance house. However, finance houses can be approached directly and often are by firms, especially when firms wish to take advantage of their leasing facilities.

In the UK there are about forty finance houses (e.g. Mercantile Credit, Forward Trust, United Dominions Trust, and Lombard North Central). They gain their funds largely from the financial and banking sector, and partly from the public. These funds are then lent out to those involved in hire purchase agreements at quite high rates of interest.

The National Savings Bank

This used to be called the Post Office Savings Bank and even under its new name it is still government run

and processed through the Post Office. Sixteen per cent of all savings are presently handled through this bank. Ordinary accounts, investment accounts, savings certificates, and premium bonds are all offered to entice depositors. These deposits are then lent to the government.

The Merchant Banks

The merchant banks specialize in the affairs of large commercial and industrial companies. Indeed, one of their specialisms is issuing new shares. Thus they are sometimes called *issuing houses*. Another of their alternative titles is *accepting houses* arising out of their other specialism, namely accepting commercial bills issued by commercial organizations. This involves the merchant bank guaranteeing owners against loss on **commercial bills**, in return for a commission calculated as a percentage of the face value of the bill*.

In summary, therefore, merchant banks are very much a bank for entrepreneurs, as they organize and administer large-scale loans on behalf of companies. Interestingly, they do not necessarily provide the funds themselves. Their specialism is largely service through their knowledge of the relevant markets. There is a limit to this knowledge and in consequence the number of merchant banks is quite small – approximately twenty at present.

Foreign Banks

The number of foreign banks has risen steadily in the last decade. At present there are certainly over 400. The majority of these are located in London, as one of their main purposes is to administer the financial aspects of trade between Britain, their home country, and any other country where their interests are represented. They are therefore primarily concerned in international banking activities. London is very much a centre for such activity and these banks hold large stocks of foreign currency reserves. In fact over 80 per cent of the liabilities of these foreign banks (based in London) are held in foreign currency (this would represent somewhere in the region of 350 billion in sterling terms). Their main specialism, therefore, is to act as a link between those who have foreign currency deposits and those who want them (and they certainly have more than anyone else in the UK financial system). To a large extent these foreign currency funds may simply be demanded for speculative purposes on the foreign exchange market – which will be considered next.

---

*See Dictionary reference for commercial bills.

Related Networks and Institutions Overseas

Foreign Exchange Market

The domestic financial framework identified above coexists alongside a similar international network. An important example is the existence of the foreign exchange market. This is *not* one big building in a specific country, but a network of bank telephones and telexes communicating from one country to another – making efforts to buy and sell one another's currencies. The pressures of demand and the available supplies of each currency determine its daily price and this is illustrated in Figure 19.3.

Although the diagram suggests that movement of currency across the foreign exchange market relates to imports and exports, currency also moves because of speculation. In fact, it is estimated that 95 per cent of daily currency movements relate to speculative dealings. The principal operators in this market are, therefore, central banks, commercial banks, and foreign banks whose telephones and telexes are employed on behalf of their clients and/or governments who wish to buy or sell currency.

International Monetary Fund (IMF)

A broader and less commercial organization is the IMF. (This was briefly referred to in Chapter 9.) Again the principal concern is international exchange. But, in this instance, the international banking community is not left entirely to its own devices. The IMF has its head office in Washington, America, which has the potential back-up of 130 member states (i.e. most non-communist countries are members) and they have funds today totalling $10 000 million. Their original brief, dating back to 1945, was to provide a kind of world bank for international finance and thus maintain exchange rate stability. Primarily, they were intended to assist member countries by lending to them in times of deficit from the IMF's holdings of gold and currencies which were accumulated from subscriptions by its members in relation to their *quotas*. Each member's quota was set according to a formula that took into account its importance in the world economy.

The problems were that countries with a history of balance-of-payments deficits constantly had to draw funds, while those with a surplus had to provide funds. Increasingly, these imbalances made it impossi-

---

Figure 19.3

A Simple Representation of the Foreign Exchange Market. Assume a shop in the UK wishes to purchase some French wine. The shop must pay the French supplier in francs. Consequently, sterling is pushed onto the foreign exchange market and francs are pushed out. As a result of this exchange, francs decrease in supply and

pounds increase in supply. Their exchange rates could move accordingly. Obviously, these changes in supply will be offset by trade with other areas. For example, on the left-hand side of the diagram we see an American paying (selling) in dollars to push out (buy) pounds in order to purchase some British produce. Ultimately such movements will affect the daily exchange rates.

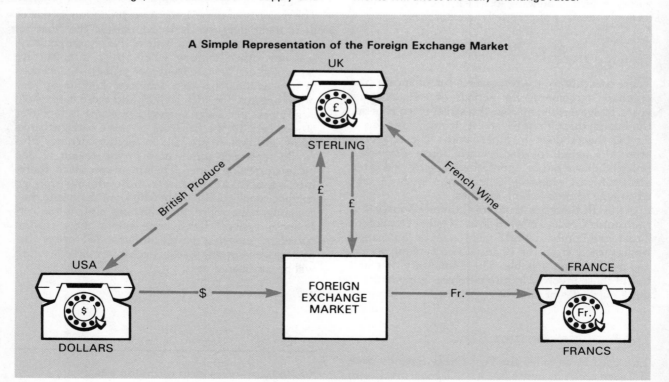

A Simple Representation of the Foreign Exchange Market

ble to maintain the fixed exchange rate system that the IMF was meant to maintain. Consequently over the years a floating exchange rate regime has evolved. This responds to pressures of supply and demand, as outlined opposite in Figure 19.3.

The IMF's next move may be to regain status by development of an independent international currency. This would be a rather ironic development as our representative, J. M. Keynes, at the Bretton Woods Convention that set up the IMF was very much in favour of what he called 'Bancor' – an international currency.

World Bank

The other international organization that was set up at Bretton Woods in 1945 was the **International Bank for Reconstruction and Development**, informally referred to in most texts as the World Bank. Some of its funds are borrowed and some are subscribed by developed member countries. As its official title suggests its funds were largely meant to promote the development of countries' economies, especially those in the Developing World (see Chapter 35). Projects such as dams, roads, and power-stations have been undertaken, as well as monies being provided for private enterprise. Similar to the IMF, the World Bank works on a subscription basis, larger funds coming from countries of higher status, and more votes going their way too. (Now read Key Points 19.4.)

The Central Bank

At the head of our entire monetary sector there is a **central bank**. Every country in the world has a central bank, and it is either implicitly or explicitly owned and operated by the government. In the UK we have one of the oldest central banks; it originated in 1694 when a group of business men grouped together to form a bank to raise a loan for the government. This bank–government relationship continued to develop and in 1844 this bank was given the power to control note issue. In 1946 this bank – the Bank of England – was nationalized, making it ultimately responsible to the Treasury and government for the monetary sector and its constituent money supply.

Monetary Sector

We have just used the term monetary sector without really defining it. The monetary sector has been officially identified since 1979 as comprising two main groups of financial institutions, namely **recognized banks** and **licensed deposit-takers**.

RECOGNIZED BANKS

To be a recognized bank a deposit-taking institution must apply to the Bank of England for recognition, and deposit ½ per cent of its eligible liabilities in non-interest-earning accounts held at the Bank of England. Criteria that the Bank of England applies in allocating the status of recognized bank is based on an assessment of the range and depth of services offered and the reputation the institution has developed over time. This definition obviously includes all the 'high street' commercial banks, merchant banks, and many foreign banks.

LICENSED DEPOSIT-TAKERS (LDTS)

Licensed deposit-taking institutions are the smaller, less established, financial institutions that offer a narrower range of services. Obvious examples are finance houses and some smaller foreign banks. These LDTs also have to deposit ½ per cent of their eligible liabilities in non-interest-earning accounts held at the Bank of England.

Facts of the Monetary Sector

The number of institutions comprising the monetary sector is quite substantial. At the time of writing there

---

Key Points 19.4

▶ The current financial network in the UK involves many financial intermediaries competing for funds, which can then be lent out, in order to make profit.

▶ Some examples of British financial intermediaries are: commercial banks, discount houses, building societies, National Savings Bank, finance houses, merchant banks, and overseas banks.

▶ Each of these financial intermediaries tends to have a specialism to offer. Each, therefore, caters for specific market needs.

▶ Alongside the domestic financial network exists an international framework. Some of the important organizations on this international scene are: the foreign exchange market, the IMF, and the World Bank.

are over 600 institutions, and an up-to-date list of these is always available from the Bank of England on request. To give some idea of the growth patterns and division between these two groups Figure 19.4 shows the number of recognized banks and licensed deposit-takers for the years 1981–85.

Figure 19.4
The Bank of England's Authorized Institutions

For financial year ending:	1981	'82	'83	'84	'85
Number of recognized banks:	281	293	295	290	290
Number of licensed deposit-takers:	286	300	295	308	315

Source: Bank of England Report and Accounts, 1985.

Finally, it is interesting to note that the only real omission from this official monetary sector is the building societies and the National Savings Bank. These anomalies are accounted for, to some extent, by the fact that the former are supervised by the Chief Registrar of Friendly Societies and the latter is owned and run by the government. (See Key Points 19.5.)

Functions of the Bank of England

Here we will set out in detail the most important functions that the Bank* carries out for this country.

Control of the Note Issue

The Bank of England is responsible for issuing new bank notes and withdrawing worn ones. It is the only note-issuing bank in England and Wales, and ultimately it could print as many notes as it liked. This is because today's currency is not backed by gold but by

---

* Whenever 'Bank' is spelt with a capital B it refers to the Bank of England.

government securities (i.e. it is entirely fiduciary). The amount of notes in circulation at any one time, therefore, is largely dependent on public demand, for example, just before Christmas it normally reaches a peak of around £14 000 million (in various denominations). The Bank is more concerned with money supply as a whole than its specific note component.

The Bankers' Bank

Apart from the mandatory deposit of ½ per cent of their eligible liabilities that all recognized banks and LDTs must make to non-operational, non-interest-bearing accounts, all banks and licensed deposit-takers hold operational accounts at the Bank of England as well. The Bank of England also holds accounts for other central banks, the IMF, and the World Bank. In short the Bank of England are bankers for the whole financial community.

Of these accounts the most important are those belonging to the clearing banks who make settlements amongst themselves after each day's clearing by drawing on their Bank of England accounts.

Finally, as with any other bank–customer relationship the Bank of England may lend money to the banks – normally via the discount houses – if times get really difficult. In this context the Bank of England is described as the *lender of last resort*.

The Government's Bank

As we are all aware the government collects large sums of money through taxation. The government also spends and distributes equally large sums. Consequently, the government, like any other commercial concern, needs a bank. And it does in fact have several accounts at the Bank of England. Furthermore, when these accounts run low it is also the Bank that arranges and finances any borrowing. In fact, it is the Bank of England that administers the National Debt, making sure that holders of gilts receive their dividends and that Treasury bills are paid on maturity.

Key Points 19.5
▶ Our central bank in the UK is the Bank of England, it was set up in 1694, and formally nationalized in 1946.
▶ The Bank of England supervises and controls the monetary sector on behalf of the government.
▶ The monetary sector comprises two main groups of institutions, namely recognized banks and licensed deposit-takers. The main difference between these groups is the range of services offered, the number of years since establishment, and general financial status.

POLICY ADVICE

Additionally, like any other bank, the Bank of England will advise its customers. Thus, there is a very close relationship between the Bank of England and the government when it comes to the formulation of monetary policy. This is particularly important to maintain as it is the Bank that will ultimately have to execute any monetary policy that is passed.

Controls Foreign Exchange Affairs

As agents for the government the Bank of England supervises the nation's gold and foreign currency reserves. According to the exchange rate policies of the government the Bank will use these reserves to buy and sell currency on the foreign exchange market. This is done through the aptly named **exchange equalization account**. Any excessive movement in sterling and this account is brought into action. Therefore, our so-called free-floating exchange rate is best regarded as one of 'managed flexibility' – which we note in Chapter 9, has been termed **dirty floating**. 'Dirty' because governments step in to stabilize the value of their currency – which is assumed to be freely floating on the exchange market – by operating their exchange equilization account, and thereby offsetting the natural market forces.

Supervises the Monetary Sector

The Bank of England has a responsibility to assure that the financial system is sound. Indeed, it administers a Deposit Protection Fund for the safeguarding of the nation's depositors, and will step in whenever a widespread banking collapse seems imminent.

The Bank takes this role responsibly by vetting all recognized banks' and LDTs' accounts at least every three months and meeting with their senior management regularly. Each institution is, therefore, judged individually and any business which is not conducted in a responsible manner could eventually lead to the Bank removing its authorization to take deposits, and this has happened in some cases.

Finally, if this qualitative type of control is not sufficient the Bank of England can impose certain quantitative controls. For example, they have the existing right to call in a small percentage of banks' and LDTs' eligible liabilities into **special deposit** accounts; these are then held at the Bank of England and earn a low rate of interest for as long as the Bank feels it is necessary to reduce liquidity in the system. Similar attacks on monetary sector assets could be designed and applied if circumstances demand it, as one must remember that the Bank of England always has the power to call in government backing if necessary.

Key Points 19.6

▶ The main functions of the Bank of England are: (1) to control the issue of notes, (2) to be a bank for the financial community, (3) to be the government's bank and help advise on policy, (4) to control foreign exchange affairs, and (5) generally to supervise the whole monetary sector.

CASE STUDY

Are We Headed for a Cashless Society?

In recent years, a tremendous technological change has taken place in our monetary system and in financial markets in general. It will soon be possible to have funds electronically transferred from a private bank account to a local retailer. The technology involved is simply an extension of the existing cash-dispenser machines. In fact in America such a system has already been developed. It is aptly named as an **electronic funds transfer system (EFTS).***

An electronic funds transfer system is a cheque-less money transfer system in which sums of money are transferred from one account to another by means of electronic signals. In this way,

---

* If you think this is a mouthful, the term EFTPOS has been suggested as the name for the potential English equivalent. EFTPOS standing for: Electronic Funds Transfer System at Point of Sale.

continued overleaf

individuals' banking accounts are automatically credited and/or debited. Paper bills, notes, coins, and cheques are required far less. An EFTS allows people to (1) make deposits or withdrawals using computer terminals located in stores, and (2) transfer funds (equal to the value of purchases) from their own accounts to the store's account by using a computer terminal located at check-out counters.

Electronic banking verifies that the customer has the proper computer identification card and that there are sufficient funds in the customer's account. Moreover, the customer's account is instantly debited and the store's account simultaneously credited for the value of the purchase. Electronic transfer systems almost completely eliminate the problem of bad debts in the banking system. Cheques that cannot be met due to lack of funds will no longer be a problem.

The number of cheques made out illegally by using a stolen cheque-book and cheque-card will similarly be reduced and, finally, having to wait three days before the value of a cheque is actually credited and debited to and from the appropriate accounts will no longer pose cash-flow hiccups.

Currently, there are about 6 million cheques written a day. All these cheques have to be cleared. That is, all of them have to be sent to different banking institutions so that some accounts can be credited and some accounts can be debited. An EFTS eliminates the physical necessity of having this endless paper flow throughout the banking system. Thus, the use of electronic banking will reduce the overall cost of banking transactions. For example, the commercial banks estimate that it costs them approximately 32p to process a cheque, and only 12p to process a similar withdrawal via a cash-dispenser.

Clearly, an EFTS reduces the need to hold note and coins, and it cuts down on the use of physical cheque-writing. Because of this, some people maintain that electronic banking eliminates the need for money. They feel that in the future, we will have a cashless society, with all or most transactions handled by some form of electronic transfer system.

We will not, however, end up with a cashless, moneyless society. Only the *form* of money will change; the total money supply will still be the same. Though its components may be different, money is here to stay!

Questions
1. Why is there a demand for money?
2. Who will benefit from an EFTS? Who will lose?

Exam Preparation and Practice

INTRODUCTORY EXERCISE

In the UK at present eight measures of money supply are officially identified. Distinguish in the table below which assets are included in each. Use a ✓ to designate included and P for partially included.

(Non-interest M1 has already been done as an example.) Ideally you should copy the chart, complete it, and then check it against the answers at the back of the book.

		M0	NIMJ	M1	M2	£M3	M3	PSL1	PSL2
1.	Notes and coin with public		✓						
2.	Notes and coin with banks								
3.	Banks' operational deposits at Bank of England								
4.	Private sector non-interest-bearing sight deposits		✓						
5.	Private sector interest-bearing sight deposits								
6.	Private sector retail sterling deposits at UK banks		P						
7.	Private sector sterling time deposits at UK banks < 2 years								
8.	Private sector sterling time deposits at UK banks > 2 years								
9.	Private sector holdings of Certificates of Deposit								
10.	Private sector foreign currency deposits at UK banks								
11.	Private sector holdings of Treasury bills								
12.	Private sector holdings of Local Authority bills								
13.	Private sector holdings of bank bills								
14.	Building society deposits								

MULTIPLE CHOICE QUESTIONS

1. Lending by the monetary sector to the government is represented by one of the following:

A mortgages
B special deposits
C money at call
D Treasury bills

One or more of the options in Question 2 may be correct. Select your answer by means of the code set out in the grid:

A	B	C	D	E
1,2,3 correct	1,2 only	2,3 only	1 only	3 only

2. The demand for money may be expected to vary
  1. positively with the level of real income
  2. positively with the general price level
  3. negatively with the rate of interest

3. If the variables are expressed as index numbers with a base for all dates of 100, the money supply is 140, the velocity of circulation is 100, and the number of transactions is 110, then, using the Fisher quantity theory identity, the approximate index for the price level is:
A 100   B 127   C 130   D 154

4. Which one of the following is *not* a function of money?
A unit of account
B source of credit
C store of value
D medium of exchange
E standard for deferred payments

RELATED ESSAY QUESTIONS

1. How is the efficiency with which money fulfils its functions affected by the rate of inflation?
2. What are the main functions of commercial banks? Why may they need to be supervised, and if necessary, controlled?
3. 'Inflation is entirely a monetary phenomenon that can only be overcome by effective control of the money supply.' Discuss.

20 The Supply of Money

Key Points to Review

▶ Opportunity cost (1.2)

▶ Definition of money (19.1, 19.3)

▶ UK banking system (19.4)

Questions for Preview

1 What is a fractional reserve banking system?

2 What is the composition of the banking system's reserve assets?

3 What happens to the overall money supply when the supply of reserve assets increases?

4 What forces reduce the money multiplier?

5 How does the Bank of England control credit creation?

The money supply, as given in the definition £M3, was defined in the previous chapter as notes and coin, and sight and time deposits. In this chapter we will find that the Bank of England and the banks together determine the stock of money in the banking system at any one time.

Fractional Reserve Banking System

Predecessors to modern-day banks were goldsmiths and moneylenders. These individuals had the strongest vaults. Other people who had gold (and other valuables), but no means of protection, began to ask goldsmiths and moneylenders to store their gold and valuables) for safekeeping. The goldsmiths and moneylenders charged a fee for this safekeeping service. It turned out that only a fraction of the total

amount of gold and other valuables left with these guardians was ever requested to be withdrawn over any time-period. That is to say, only a small fraction of clients would ask for their deposits at any one time. Thus, to meet the requests of those clients, the vault owners needed to keep only a relatively small fraction of the total deposits 'on reserve'.

Now, if you were a vault-owner and knew that only a certain percentage of deposits would be requested in any one time-period, you could lend the remainder out at interest and make additional income, besides the fee for the use of your vault. This is how banks grew up as part of a **fractional reserve banking system**. In other words, in such a system, reserves on hand to meet net withdrawal demands by depositors are some fraction less than 100 per cent of total deposits. Nowadays, reserves are not kept in the form of gold, but rather in the form of deposits with the Bank of England and other very liquid assets.

Reserves

Banks must maintain a percentage of their customer deposits as **reserves**. Take a hypothetical example. If the required level of reserves, the **reserve asset ratio**, is 20 per cent and the bank has £1 billion in customer deposits, then it must hold at least £200 million as reserves. It can hold these reserves in the form of notes and coin, balances with the Bank of England and a range of liquid assets, which can easily be turned into cash if required. These include money lent at call to the discount houses, and Treasury bills (short-term loans) to the government. If a bank has reserves in excess of £200 million, then it will wish to make more loans (or advances) to customers. If it does not, then it is forgoing interest which could be earned on loans backed by the reserves in excess of £200 million. If, on the other hand, the bank's reserves fall below the £200-million mark, it will have to call in some of its loans. This reduces deposits to the point where the level of reserves is again 20 per cent of total deposits.

In the analysis that follows, we examine the relationship between the level of reserves and the size of the money stock. This analysis shows that whatever affects reserves also affects the money supply.

The Relationship between Reserves and Total Bank Deposits

To show the relationship between reserves and bank deposits, we first analyse a single bank (existing alongside many others). A single bank is able to make loans to its customers only to the extent that it has reserves above the level required to cover the new deposits. When an individual bank has excess reserves, it can make loans.

How a Single Bank Reacts to an Increase in Reserves

To examine the behaviour of a single bank after its reserves are increased, the following simplifying assumptions are made.

1. The required reserve asset ratio is 10 per cent for all transactions deposits: the government requires that an amount equal to 10 per cent of all demand deposits be held on reserve.
2. Transactions deposits are the bank's only liability; reserves and advances to customers are the bank's only **assets**. Advances to customers are promises made by customers to repay some amount in the future; that is, they are IOUs.

3. There is such a ready demand for advances that the bank has no trouble lending additional money.
4. Every time a loan is made to an individual (consumer or firm), all the proceeds from the loan are put into a transactions deposit; no cash (currency or coins) is disbursed.
5. Banks desire to keep their excess reserves at a zero level because reserves earn little if any interest.

Look at the initial position of the bank in Figure 20.1. Liabilities consist of £1 million in demand deposits. Assets consist of £100 000 in reserves, and £900 000 in loans to customers. Total assets of £1 million equal total liabilities of £1 million.

Figure 20.1
Bank +1

Liabilities		Assets	
Demand deposits	£1 000,000	Total Reserves	£100000
		Required reserves (£100000)	
		Excess Reserves (–0)	
		Loans	£900000
Total	£1 000000	Total	£1 000000

The principle of double-entry accounting, showing both assets and liabilities, is that they are two sides of the same coin.

Assume now that a *new* depositer writes a £100 000 cheque and deposits it in bank +1. Demand deposits in bank +1, therefore, immediately increase by £100 000, bringing the total to £1.1 million. At the same time, total reserves of bank +1 increase to £200 000. A £1.1 million total in demand deposits means that required reserves will have to be £110 000. Bank +1 *now has* excess reserves equal to £200 000 minus £100 000, or £90 000. This is shown in Figure 20.2.

Figure 20.2
Bank +1

Liabilities		Assets	
Demand deposits	£1 100 000	Total Reserves	£200000
		Required reserves (£110000)	
		Excess Reserves (£90000)	
		Loans	£900000
Total	£1 100000	Total	£1 100000

Look at excess reserves in Figure 20.2. Excess reserves were zero before the £100 000 deposit. After they are £90 000, that is, £90 000 worth of assets not earning any income. By assumption, bank +1 will now lend out this £90 000 in excess reserves in order to obtain income. Loans will increase to £990 000. The borrowers who receive the new loans will not leave them on deposit in bank + 1. After all, they borrow money to spend it. As they spend it, actual reserves eventually will fall to £110 000 (as required), and excess reserves will again become zero, as indicated in Figure 20.3.

Figure 20.3
Bank +1

Liabilities		Assets	
Demand deposits	£1 100 000	Total Reserves	£110 000
		Required reserves (£110 000)	
		Excess Reserves (–0)	
		Loans	£990 000
Total	£1 100 000	Total	£1 100 000

WHAT HAS HAPPENED TO THE MONEY STOCK?

The new deposit in bank +I may have been a payment from a customer of *another* bank. Therefore, the other bank suffered a *decline* in its demand deposits and its reserves. While total assets and liabilities in bank +1 have increased by £100 000, they have *decreased* in the other bank by £100 000. Thus, the *total* amount of money and credit in the economy is unaffected by the transfer of funds from one bank to another.

Each individual bank can create loans (and deposits) only to the extent that it has excess reserves. In the above example, bank +1 had £90 000 of excess reserves after the deposit of £100 000. On the other hand, the bank on which the cheque was written found that its excess reserves were now a *negative* £90 000 (assuming it had zero excess reserves previously). That bank now has less reserves than it should. It will have to call in loans in order to make actual reserves meet required reserves. So long as the level of total deposits and

reserves in the banking system remains unchanged, deposits moving from one bank to another have no effect on the money stock.

Credit Expansion by the Banking System

Consider now the entire banking system. For all practical purposes, we can look at all banks taken as a whole. To understand how money is created, we must understand how banks respond to Bank of England actions that increase reserves in the entire system.

The Bank of England Purchases UK Government Securities

The banks have a continuous relationship with the discount houses. They lend them money at call because they can in so doing use their surplus funds to make a loan, which will bring in interest. But because they can call the loan back any time, it is a very liquid asset. The interest on it will be relatively low because it is so liquid.

The discount houses use these funds to buy commercial and Treasury bills, and to make other short-term loans. They charge a slightly higher interest rate than they must pay on their borrowed funds. If the banks run short of cash to make good customer demands for withdrawals, they can always recall the money they have lent to the discount houses. But this will leave the discount houses, in turn, short of funds to carry on their normal business. Then they must turn to the Bank of England, which will lend to them, in order to ensure that there is enough liquidity in the banking system to maintain customer confidence that requests for withdrawals will always be met. In other words, it is the Bank of England which ultimately underpins the banking system's operations. (In this context it acts as lender of last resort.)

What actually happens when the discount houses borrow from the Bank of England? The discount houses borrow by *selling* Treasury and commercial bills to the Bank of England, which pays for the bills with a cheque drawn on itself. When, over time, the Bank of England increases its lending in this way, the cash base

---

Key Points 20.1
► We have a fractional reserve banking system in which banks hold a percentage of deposits as reserves.
► When a bank's holdings of reserves increase, that bank can expand its lending.

of the monetary system increases. The overall effect is that the Bank of England pumps extra liquidity into the banking system by itself creating credit.

The cash base of the monetary system has already been defined as M0, or notes and coin plus banks' balances with the Bank of England. The result of the Bank of England's lending to the discount houses is that the discount houses have been able to pay for a commercial or a Treasury bill. The previous holder of this bill now has cash and will deposit it in a bank account. The bank will place the cash in its account with the Bank of England.

M0 has increased by the amount of the Bank of England's credit creation. In other words, the cash base of the banking system, sometimes known as the **monetary base** or high-powered money has increased. The monetary base is the foundation on which bank lending rests; it includes the banks' most liquid reserve assets.

WHAT HAS HAPPENED TO THE MONEY STOCK?

If the Bank of England bought £100000 of bills from the discount houses the money stock has increased by £100000 immediately. Why? The money becomes part of the demand deposits held by the public. The reserves of the banks involved have increased. No bank has *lost* reserves.

Figure 20.4
Bank +1

Liabilities		Assets	

Demand deposits	£1 200 000	Total Reserves
		  Required reserves
		  (£120000)
			£210000

		Excess Reserves (90000)	
		Loans	£990000
Total	£1 200 000	Total	£1 200 000

THE PROCESS DOES NOT STOP

The process of credit creation will continue. Figure 20.4 shows total reserves of £210000. This is £100000 more than bank +1 had in Figure 20.3. That £100000 is the proceeds of the Bank of England's purchase of bills. Demand deposits have increased by that £100000, so the bank's holdings of reserves have increased by that amount too. Now bank +1 needs to keep 10 per cent or £120000 in reserves, and therefore has £90000 excess reserves. The bank will want to increase lending by this amount in order to maximize

Figure 20.5
Bank +1

Liabilities		Assets	

Demand deposits	£1 200 000	Total Reserves
		  Required reserves
		  (£120000)
			£120000

		Excess Reserves (–0)	
		Loans	£1 080000
Total	£1 200000	Total	£1 200000

the interest it can earn. The outcome is shown in Figure 20.5: loans increase to £1 080000.

The individuals who have received the £90000 of new loans will spend these funds, which will then be deposited in other banks. To make this example simple, assume that the £90000 in excess reserves was lent to a single firm for the purpose of buying a franchise from McDonald's. After the firm buys the franchise, McDonald's deposit the £90000 in their account at bank +2. For simplicity, ignore the previous assets and liabilities in bank +2 and concentrate only on the *changes* resulting from this new deposit, as shown in Figure 20.6. A plus sign indicates an increase, and a minus sign indicates a decrease. For bank +2, the £90000 deposit, after the cheque has been deposited in the bank's account at the Bank of England, becomes an increase in reserves (assets) as well as an increase in demand deposits (liabilities). Because the reserve requirement is assumed to be 10 per cent, or £9000 required reserves, bank +2 will have excess reserves of £81000. But, of course, excess reserves are not income-producing, so bank +2 will reduce them to zero by making loans of £81000 (which will earn interest income) as Figure 20.7 shows. When the borrower has spent this, it will be deposited in bank +3, increasing both assets and liabilities for that bank.

Figure 20.6
Bank +2

Liabilities		Assets	

New Demand
Deposits
	+£90000	Total Reserves
		  Required reserves
		  (+9000)
			+£90000

		Excess Reserves (+81000)	
Total	+90000	Total	+90000

Key Points 20.2

- **The Bank of England can increase the level of banks' reserves (the cash base of the monetary system) by buying securities from the discount houses.**
- **As banks' reserves increase they can expand their lending by a multiple of the initial increase in reserve assets. Thus the money stock increases correspondingly.**

Figure 20.7
Bank +2

Liabilities		Assets	
Demand Deposits	£90000	Total Reserves	£9000
		Required reserves (9000)	
		Excess Reserves (–0)	
		Loans	+81000
Total	90000	Total	90000

Remember that in this example the original £100000 deposit originated from the Bank of England. That £100000 constituted an immediate increase in the money stock of £100000. The deposit-creation process (in addition to the original £100000) occurs because of the fractional reserve banking system, coupled with the desire of banks to maximize interest earned (given a sufficient loan demand).

THE PROCESS CONTINUES TO BANKS +3, +4, +5, ETC.

This process will continue. Each bank obtains smaller and smaller increases in deposits because 10 per cent of each deposit must be held in reserve; therefore, each succeeding bank makes correspondingly smaller loans.

What Has Happened to Total Deposits?

In this simple example, deposits increased initially by the £100000. They were further increased by a £90000 deposit in bank +2. And they again increased by an £81000 deposit in bank +3. Eventually, total deposits will increase by a total approaching £1 million. The money stock has expanded by ten times the initial increase in reserve assets. The size of this **money multiplier** is determined by the reserve asset ratio – in this case taken to be 10 per cent.

Overall Reserves Must Increase for the Multiple Expansion to Occur

Even with fractional reserve banking and zero excess reserves, *deposits cannot expand unless overall reserves are increased, that is, unless the monetary base is enlarged.*

The example would work the same way if banks used their excess reserves to acquire interest-earning securities (bonds, certificates of deposit, etc.) instead of making loans directly. The owners of those securities would receive cheques from the purchasing bank; the sellers of securities would then deposit these cheques into their own banks. The deposit expansion process would continue in the same manner.

The Money Multiplier

In the example just given, a £100000 increase in excess reserves yielded an £1000000 increase in total deposits; the money multiplier was 10.

We can now make a generalization about the extent to which total deposits will increase when the banking system's reserves are increased. If we assume that no excess reserves are kept and that *all* loan proceeds are quickly deposited in banks, then the following equation applies:

$$\text{maximum money multiplier} = \frac{1}{\text{reserve asset ratio}}$$

Credit Creation in the Real World

So far we have simplified our view of credit creation. In reality a variety of institutional factors affect the extent to which the banking system creates credit.

We have assumed that the entire loan from one bank is always deposited in another bank. But, when deposits increase, the public may want to hold more currency. Currency that is kept in a person's wallet or purse or in a safe-deposit box or hidden underneath a mattress remains outside the banking system. The greater the amount of cash leakage, the smaller will be the money multiplier. Similarly banks may not, in fact, always keep excess reserves at zero. To the extent that they want to keep extra reserves, the multiplier will be smaller.

Maintaining Confidence: Prudential Standards of Liquidity

In practice the Bank of England no longer retains a single reserve asset ratio applicable to all banks. Instead it requires banks to observe **prudential standards of liquidity**. Banks must keep specified proportions of their assets in the form of liquid reserves. The proportions, or ratios, required vary according to the type of lending involved. Riskier kinds of business require a high level of reserve assets to back them. The Bank of England monitors the performance of the banks through its supervision process. While banks obviously must hold reserves of notes and coin, the amount they hold is left by the Bank of England to the individual bank's own discretion. Banks generally keep about 2 per cent of their assets in notes and coin.

Maintaining confidence is crucial to the efficient functioning of the banking system. If people lose confidence in a bank they will all want to withdraw their deposits. Since banks operate on a fractional reserve system they could not satisfy all their customers' demands at once, and the bank would crash. The Bank of England maintains confidence first by trying to ensure that banks are well managed, and second by providing liquidity in the form of loans to the banking system, when funds are short.

Any increase in reserve asset ratios will reduce the money multiplier and limit credit creation.

Monetary Policy: Open Market Operations

When governments want to pursue tight monetary policies, they will seek to restrain the growth of the monetary base. To the extent that the Bank of England avoids increasing its level of lending, over time, to the discount houses, the money stock will be prevented from expanding.

If the Bank of England wants actually to restrict monetary growth, it can sell government securities, that is, engage in **open market operations**. When it sells a **government bond**, the buyer pays with a cheque drawn on a bank account. The bank transfers the cash from the customer's account to the government's account in the Bank of England. In making this transfer, the bank must reduce its own balance with the Bank of England, by the price of the bond. This reduces the level of the bank's reserve assets by a corresponding amount. If the bank has no excess reserves, it will have to reduce its lending by an amount equal to the loss of reserves times the money multiplier. This method of reducing the reserve assets available to banks can restrict the growth of credit substantially, therefore. Figure 20.8 shows the growth of monetary aggregates from 1981–86.

Monetary policy will be dealt with in more detail in Chapter 31.

Figure 20.8
Monetary aggregates 1981–86. £ million, June each year.

Years	M0	£M3	PSL2
1981	—	71 460	129 706
1982	—	87 620	142 668
1983	—	95 920	160 671
1984	13 425	106 070	180 405
1985	14 122	118 450	204 631
1986	14 566	138 661	239 050

Source: CSO, *Financial Statistics*, July 1986.

Figure 20.9
Summary Balance Sheet for UK banks, 15 February 1985. The two sides to a bank's balance sheet reflect two different aspects of the flow of funds through the bank. As financial intermediaries, banks have liabilities to their lenders, and assets in the form of loans.

Liabilities	£m	Assets	£m
Sterling		**Sterling**	
Sight deposits	73 511	Notes and coin	2 170
Time deposits	143 987	Balances with the	
CDs	19 341	Bank of England:	
Items in transmission	5 832	Cash ratio deposits	713
Capital and other	30 439	Other	165
funds		Loans to Discount	
		Houses	6 415
		Treasury bills	463
		Local authority bills	337
		Other bills	4 687
Other currencies		Other Market loans:	
Sight and time	511 818	(Interbank, CDs)	78 399
deposits		Advances:	
CDs	69 703	UK public sector	1 368
Other	20 581	UK private sector:	129 317
		overseas	12 406
		Net lending by BoE	
		to government	497
		Investments	17 431
		Other currency assets	
		(Mainly loans on	
		London and	
		overseas money	
		markets.)	534 956

Sources: CSD: *Financial Statistics*, July 1986.

Assets and Liabilities: The Full Story

Besides notes and coin, and balances with the Bank of England, there are other assets which qualify as reserves although they are slightly less liquid. These are Treasury, local authority, and commercial bills.

Taking the assets in descending order of liquidity, we come to the more profitable assets, those which earn higher interest rates. There is an inverse relationship between liquidity and profitability: the greater the liquidity, the lower the interest rate; the lower the profitability, vice versa. Advances to customers are the most profitable form of business, but the loans are not liquid because in general they will take time to be paid off. Figure 20.9 shows these on the summary balance sheet for the UK banking system.

Bank of England Regulations: the Full Story

In 1981 the Bank of England reorganized its requirements of the banking system.

1. Prudential standards of liquidity were introduced.
2. The ½% rule: banks must keep ½% of their liabilities in non-interest-earning balances with the Bank of England.
3. Banks must keep a minimum of 2½% of their liabilities in the form of money lent at call to the discount houses.
4. Special Deposits: the Bank of England retains the right to require banks to make Special Deposits with it. These would then be frozen, reducing the banks' stock of liquid assets, and therefore, their capacity to lend.

This is the *background* against which monetary policy operates. The details of *how* it operates must wait until Part E.

Key Points 20.3

▶ **The maximum money multiplier is the reciprocal of the reserve asset ratio.**
▶ **Bank of England regulations, including prudential standards of liquidity should ensure that banks do not overlend.**
▶ **Monetary policy limits credit creation.**
▶ **The liquidity of banks' assets and their profitability are inversely related.**

CASE STUDY

Will There Ever be a Run on the Banking System?

During the 1930s depression, many US banks failed. As an increasing number of depositors withdraw their funds, more and more banks became insolvent. They were unable to meet customers' demands for withdrawals. When a bank fails, its customers lose their money and will in many cases become bankrupt. So bank failure can have a very detrimental effect on economic activity. Hence the importance of maintaining confidence.

In 1972–73 there was a boom in property prices. Property developers were anxious to borrow and buy property which, once bought, provided excellent security for the loan. A number of banks lent considerable amounts to property developers. The increased demand for property generated price increases which made property deals very profitable, and so increased the demand for further loans. When the bubble burst – property was changing hands at prices in excess of its real

long-term value – some banks found they had overlent to property companies. These companies' assets were no longer saleable at prices high enough to cover the loan. So the banks which had overlent had to be rescued by the Bank of England, with loans to tide them over.

As a result of this, the 'lifeboat' scheme was introduced. It is a deposit insurance scheme in which the banks participate. In future, if a bank fails, its depositors will get their money back. To some extent, the very existence of the lifeboat ensures that confidence in banks is maintained.

In fact, when the next bank failure occurred, with Johnson Matthey Bankers in late 1984, the Bank of England simply took the bank over completely. JMB had made too many risky loans and had become encumbered with bad debts (which would never be repaid). Suspecting bad

management, the Bank of England took over rather than lend to the existing management team. Subsequent disclosures of fraud confirmed the view that the bank had been mismanaged. The only question was, why had not the Bank of England detected the mismanagement earlier, in the course of its normal supervision process?

Questions
1. Why is maintaining confidence in banks so vitally important?
2. Why do banks sometimes lend too much?
3. How can bank failures be prevented?

Exam Preparation and Practice

INTRODUCTORY EXERCISES

Round	Deposits	Reserves	Advances
Bank 1	£1 000 000	£	£
Bank 2			
Bank 3			
Bank 4			
Bank 5			
All other banks			
Totals			

1. Bank 1 has received a deposit of £1 million. Assuming the banks retain no excess reserves, answer the following:
   (a) The reserve requirement is 25 per cent. Fill in the blanks. What is the money multiplier?
   (b) Now the reserve requirement is 5 per cent. Fill in the blanks. What is the money multiplier?
2. Arrange the following items on the proper side of the member bank's balance sheet:
   (a) demand deposits
   (b) notes and coins
   (c) time deposits
   (d) balances with Bank of England
   (e) advances to customers
   (f) holdings of government, bonds
   (g) bank buildings and fixtures
   (h) borrowings from other banks

Liabilities	Assets

MULTIPLE CHOICE QUESTIONS

1. If the Bank of England sells securities for £10 million on the open market, then the commercial banks
   A need take no action because their assets and liabilities are both reduced by the same amount
   B must reduce their existing liquid assets
   C must reduce their advances by an amount dependent upon their existing liquid reserves
   D can increase advances by £10 million, provided there is a sufficient demand for credit
   E can increase advances by more than £10 million if their liquid assets exceed the required minimum

2. Which one of the following is a liability of a UK commercial bank?
   A loans to discount houses
   B money at call
   C deposit accounts of customers
   D special deposits at the Bank of England
   E overdrafts incurred by small traders

3. If all banks observe a 20 per cent reserve asset ratio, by how much can the banking system increase deposits in response to a new deposit of £100?
   A £100
   B £200
   C £400
   D £500
   E £2 000

continued overleaf

†4. British commercial banks usually do all of the following EXCEPT
   A buy long-term government securities
   B pay interest on some of the money deposited with them
   C re-discount Treasury bills
   D lend for very short periods to the money market
   E subscribe to new issues of ordinary shares

5. The official selling of government securities in the open market might result in any of the following *except*
   A an expansion of credit
   B an increase in interest rates
   C an increase in saving
   D a decrease in investment

RELATED ESSAY QUESTIONS

1. Explain what is meant by the discount market of the City of London and discuss its functions and importance.

2. How does the Bank of England control the operations of commercial banks? Why is it necessary to have more than one type of control?

3. What is the main function of commercial banks? Why might they need to be supervised and, if necessary, controlled?

4. What factors determine the level of advances made by commercial banks?

Part C

Product Markets

21 Consumer Choice

Key Points to Review

▶ Trade-offs (1.2, 1.3)
▶ Demand, income, and substitution effects (5.1)

▶ Change in demand versus change in quantity demanded (5.3)

Questions for Preview

1 What is utility?

2 What is the theory of diminishing marginal utility?

3 How does a consumer maximize his or her total utility?

4 What happens to consumer equilibrium when price changes?

5 How can the theory of diminishing marginal utility account for the law of demand?

When we first discussed the theory of demand in Chapter 5, we gave several reasons why the quantity demanded went up when the price of something went down. We pointed out that as the price of a good falls, individuals will *substitute* some of that good for other things. Additionally, when the price of one good in a consumer's budget goes down with all other prices remaining the same, that person's buying power will actually be greater. A person not only *feels* better off, he or she *is* better off. With a constant money income, when the price of one good falls, the person clearly has more real spending, or purchasing power.

The theory of demand is important and so, too, is its derivation, because it allows us to arrange the relevant variables, such as prices, incomes, and tastes, in such a way as to generate predictions about the real world.

How do we *derive* the theory of demand? We examine two explanations: first the traditional **utility analysis** and second the more comprehensive indifference curve analysis. Utility theory appears conceptually attractive on the grounds of its simplicity but it soon turns out to be rather wanting. Hence we resort to indifference curves as a more rigorous derivation of downward-sloping demand curves.

Utility Theory

When you buy something, you buy it because of the satisfaction you expect to receive from having and using it. For just about everything that you like to have, the more you have of it, the higher the level of satisfaction you receive. Another term can be used for satisfaction, namely **utility**, or want-satisfying power. This is a property that is common to all goods that are desired. However, the concept of utility is purely subjective. There is no way that you or I can measure the amount of utility that we or another consumer might be able to obtain from a particular good, for utility does not mean 'useful', 'utilitarian', or 'practical'. For this reason, there cannot be true accurate scientific assessment of the utility that someone may receive by consuming, say, a Mars bar or a packet of crisps relative to the utility that another person might receive. Thus we must recognize at the outset that the theory of utility presents us with an immediate problem of measurement.

Economists used to believe that utility could be measured. They therefore first developed utility theory in terms of units of measurable utility, to which they applied the term **util**. Thus, the first chocolate bar that you eat might yield you four utils of satisfaction; the first bag of crisps, six utils; and so on. Today, no one believes that we can actually measure utils, but the ideas forthcoming from such analysis will prove useful in our understanding of the way in which consumers choose among alternatives. Economists are not alone in using simple but inherently suspect concepts. Teachers of physics have used the concept of force. No physicist has ever seen a unit of force just as no economist has ever seen a unit of utility. But in both subject areas a rather nebulous concept has none the less proven useful for analytical purposes. Indeed we might note that even though illegal activities may be considered morally wrong by many people, they can still be analysed in terms of the utility that those activities generate for their consumers.

Total and Marginal Utility

Consider the satisfaction, or utility, that you might receive each time that you hire and watch a video-cassette on your home VCR. There are many video-cassettes to choose from each year and we might reasonably assume that each of them is of the same quality. Suppose you normally hire one video-cassette per week. You could, of course, hire two, three, or four per week. Presumably each time you hire another video-cassette per week you will get additional satisfaction, or utility. The question, though, that we must ask is, given that you are already hiring one per week, will the next one give you the same amount of additional utility? That additional, or incremental utility is called *marginal utility*, where *marginal* is another term for incremental, or additional. Understanding the concept of marginal is important in economics, because we make decisions at the margin. This means that at a particular point, we compare additional benefits with additional costs.

The way to understand the concept of marginal utility is to take the specific example presented in Figure 21.1. Here we show the total and marginal utility of watching video-cassettes each week. The marginal utility is seen to be the difference between the total utility derived from a specific quantity of video-cassettes, say, Q, and the total utility derived from one more, $Q + 1$. In our example, when a person has already watched two video-cassettes in one week, and then watches another, total utility increases from 16 utils to 19. Therefore, the marginal utility (of watching one more video cassette after having watched two already) is equal to three utils.

Graphic Analysis

We can transfer the information in Figure 21.1 onto a graph, which we do in panels (a) and (b) of Figure 21.2. Total utility, which is represented in column 2 of Figure 21.1 is transferred in blocks (represented by dashed outlines) to panel (a) of Figure 21.2.

Total utility continues to rise until four video-cassettes are watched per week. This measure of utility remains at 20 utils through the fifth video-cassette, and at the sixth video-cassette per week falls to 18 utils, because we assume that at *some* quantity consumed per unit time-period, dislike sets in. If we connect the tops of the total utility blocks with a smooth line, we come up with a representation of the total utility curve associated with watching video-cassettes during a one-week period. This is shown in panel (a) of Figure 21.3.

Marginal Utility

If you look carefully at both panels (a) and (b) of Figure 21.2, the notion of marginal utility and what it is can be seen very clearly. In economics, marginal always refers to a change in the total. The marginal utility, for example, of watching three video-cassettes a week as opposed to two video-cassettes a week is the increment in total utility and is equal to three utils per day. Marginal utility is represented by the shaded portion of the blocks in panel (a) of Figure 21.2.

We can transfer these shaded portions down to panel (b) of Figure 21.2 and come up with a graphic

Figure 21.1
Total and Marginal Utility of Watching Video Cassettes.
If we were able to assign specific numbers to the utility derived from watching video-cassettes each week, we could then obtain a marginal utility schedule that would probably be similar in pattern to the one below. In column 1 is the quantity of video-cassettes watched per week, in column 2, the total utility from each quantity; and in column 3, the marginal utility, which is defined as the change in total utility due to a change of one unit of watching video-cassettes per week.

(1) Quantity of video-cassettes	(2) Total utility (utils per week)	(3) Marginal utility (utils per week)
0	0	
		10
1	10	
		6
2	16	
		3
3	19	
		1
4	20	
		0
5	20	
		−2
6	18	

> ### Key Points 21.1
> ► Utility is defined as want-satisfying power; it is a property common to all desired goods and services.
> ► We artificially try to measure units of utility in utils.
> ► It is important to distinguish between total utility and marginal utility. Total utility is the total satisfaction derived from the consumption of a given quantity of a good. Marginal utility is the change in total utility due to a one-unit change in the consumption of the good.

Figure 21.2
Total and Marginal Utility in Discrete Units

In panel (a), the dashed outline indicates a total utility for each rate of viewing of video-cassettes per week. The shaded portion of each dashed box indicates a marginal utility for each video-cassette watched per week. When we transfer the shaded boxes to panel (b), we have a diagram of discrete marginal utility.

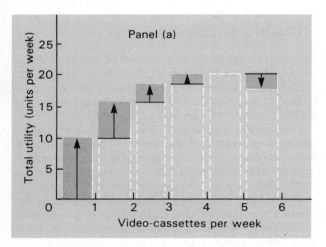

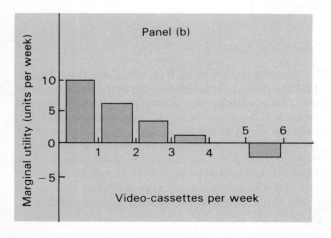

representation of marginal utility. When we connect the tops of these marginal utility rectangles in panel (b) of Figure 21.2 we come up with a smoothly sloping marginal utility curve. Notice that that curve hits zero when more than four video-cassettes are watched per week. At zero marginal utility, the consumer has watched all the video-cassettes that he or she wants to and does not want to watch any more. The last video-cassette watched at zero marginal utility gives the consumer no additional satisfaction, or utility.

When marginal utility becomes negative, such as it does in this example after more than four video-cassettes per week are watched, it means that the consumer is fed up with watching video-cassettes and would require some form of compensation to watch any more. When marginal utility is negative, the additional unit consumed actually lowers total utility by becoming a 'nuisance'.

Diminishing Marginal Utility

Notice that in panel (b) of Figure 21.3, marginal utility is continuously declining. This property of marginal utility has been named **diminishing marginal utility**. There is no way we can prove diminishing marginal utility; none the less, economists and lay-persons for years have believed strongly in the assertion of diminishing marginal utility. Diminishing marginal utility has even been called a 'law'. This supposed law concerns a psychological, or subjective, utility that you receive as you consume more and more of a particular good. Stated formally, the law is:

As an individual consumes more of the same good per unit of time, utility increases (up to a point at least). However, the extra utility added by an extra (marginal) unit of that good does not increase at a constant rate. Rather, as successive new units of the good in question are consumed, after some point that total utility will grow at a slower and slower rate. Otherwise stated, as the amount of a good consumed per unit of time increases, the marginal utility of the good tends to decrease.

Figure 21.3

Total and Marginal Utility. If we take the total utility units from column 2 in Figure 21.1, we obtain rectangles like those presented in Figure 21.2(a). If we connect the tops of those rectangles with a smooth line, we come up with a total utility curve that peaks somewhere between four and five video-cassettes per week and then slowly declines (panel (a)). Marginal utility is represented by the increment in total utility, shown as the shaded blocks in panel (b) of Figure 21.2. When these blocks are connected by a smooth line, we obtain the marginal utility curve.

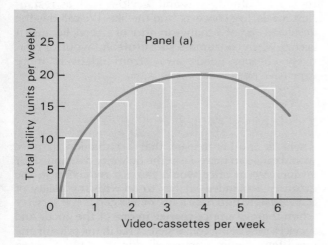

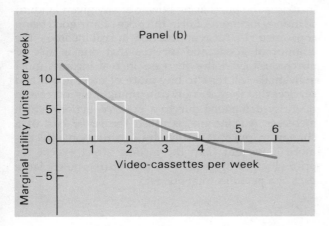

Optimizing Consumption Choices

Every consumer has a limited income. Choices must be made. When a consumer has made all his or her choices about what to buy and in what quantities, and the total level of satisfaction, or utility, from that set of choices is as great as it can be, we say that the consumer has optimized his or her consumption choices. The consumer has attained an *optimum consumption* basket of goods and services.

Consider a simple example that involves two goods. The consumer has a choice between spending income on the rental of video-cassettes and the purchase of

food. Suppose that the last po[...] yielded three utils of utility, but th[...] on video-cassette rentals yielded te[...] Would this consumer not increase to[...] pounds were taken away from food co[...] allocated to videotape rentals? The a[...] Given diminishing marginal utility, more [...]ey spent on video-cassette rentals will reduce marginal utility per last pound spent, whereas fewer pounds spent on food consumption will increase marginal utility per last pound spent. The optimum – where total utility is maximized – might occur when the satisfaction per last pound spent on both food and video-cassette rentals per week is, say, five utils.

We can put this optimum consumption situation in a clearer manner as follows: total utility of the consumer is maximized (**consumer optimum** is reached) when a fixed money income is spent on goods and services such that:

$$\frac{\text{marginal utility of } x}{\text{price of } x} = \frac{\text{marginal utility of } y}{\text{price of } y} \ldots$$

$$= \frac{\text{marginal utility of } n}{\text{price of } n}$$

$x, y \ldots n$ indicate the different goods and services that the consumer might purchase.

Optimization typically refers to individual decision-making processes. When we deal with many individuals interacting in the market-place, we talk in terms of an equilibrium in the market-place. Generally speaking, equilibrium is a property of markets rather than of individual decision-making.

We can apply the theory of consumer optimum to the way in which people use their time. Every individual must make a choice among all possible uses of time. For example, the marginal utility received from the last minute used to study economics should not be radically different from the marginal utility received from the last minute used to study geography (assuming, of course, that the student is maximizing grades while faced with a time constraint). If these marginal utilities are greatly out of line, then obviously the student should change the time-mix. He or she should spend more or less time with one than the other.

Remember here that clearly we are not assuming that the student receives utility from spending time studying either economics or geography (although this is a possibility). Rather, it is the outcome of the time spent studying – higher grades and perhaps a better job in the future – that generates the utility.

Consumption decisions are summarized in the theory of demand, which you will recall from Chapter 5, states that the amount purchased is inversely related to price. We can now see why by using the theory of diminishing utility.

Decisions to purchase are made such that marginal utility of the last unit purchased and consumed is just equal to the price that had to be paid, that is, the

...ortunity cost for that last unit. No consumer will, when optimizing, buy ten units of a good per unit time-period when the subjective valuation placed on the tenth unit is less than the price of the tenth unit.

If we start out with the consumer optimum and then observe a price decrease, we can predict that consumers will respond to the price decrease by consuming more. Why? Because, before the price change, the marginal utility of the last unit was about equal to the price paid for the last unit. Now with a lower price, it is possible to consume more than before. If the theory of diminishing marginal utility holds, the purchase and consumption of additional units will cause marginal utility to fall. Eventually, it will fall to equate marginal utility with the price of the final unit consumed. The limit to this increase in consumption is given by the theory of diminishing marginal utility. At some point, the marginal utility of an additional unit would be less than what the person would have to give up (price) of that additional unit.

Look at a hypothetical demand curve for video-cassette rentals per week for a typical consumer in Figure 21.4. At a price of £5 per video-cassette rental, the marginal utility of the last video-cassette rented per week is MU_1. At a price of £4 per video-cassette rental per week, the marginal utility is represented by MU_2. Because of the theory of diminishing marginal utility, MU_2 must be less than MU_1. What has

happened is that, at a lower price, the number of video-cassette rentals per week increased from two to three; marginal utility must have fallen. At a higher consumption rate, marginal utility falls down to meet the lower price for video-cassette rental per week.

The Substitution Effect

What is happening all along, as the price of, say, video-cassette recorder rental falls, is that consumers are substituting the now relatively cheaper video-cassette rentals for other goods and services, such as restaurant meals, live concerts, and the like. We call this the *substitution effect* of a change in price of a good, because it occurs when consumers substitute in favour of relatively cheaper goods away from relatively more expensive ones.

The Income Effect

There is another reason that a reduction in price would cause an increase in the quantity demanded (or an increase in price would cause a reduction in the quantity demanded). It has to do with the ability of individuals to purchase more or less goods and services when there is a price change in one of the goods and services now being consumed. A fall in the price of any one item being purchased during, say, a week increases the purchasing power of any given amount of money income. A fall in the price of any good being consumed results in an increase in real income – the amount of goods and services that one is able to purchase. Given this increase in real income, most individuals will tend to buy more of most goods and services that they are now consuming. This increase in quantity demanded due to a price reduction, which increases real income, is called the *income effect* of a change in price. (Usually the substitution effect is more important than the income effect except for price changes of goods that constitute a fairly large part of a person's total budget.)

Figure 21.4
Changing Video-cassette Rental Prices and Marginal Utility. The rate of video-cassette rentals per week will increase as long as the marginal utility per last video-cassette rental per week exceeds the cost of that rental. Therefore, a reduction in price from £5 to £4 per video-cassette rental will allow consumers to increase consumption until marginal utility falls from MU_1 to MU_2 (because of the theory of diminishing marginal utility).

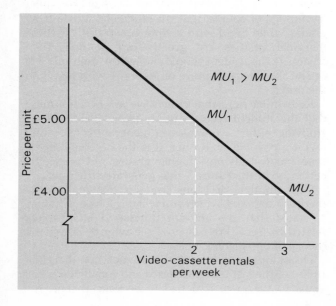

The Demand Curve Revisited

Linking together the theory of diminishing marginal utility and the theory of equal marginal utilities per pound gives us a negative relationship between the quantity demanded of a good or service and its price. As the relative price of video-cassette rental goes up, for example, the quantity demanded will fall; and as the relative price of video-cassette rental goes down, the quantity demanded will rise. Figure 21.4 shows this demand curve for video-cassette rentals. As the relative price of video-cassette rental falls, the consumer can maximize total utility only by purchasing more of them, and vice versa. In other words, the relationship between price and quantity desired is simply a downward-sloping demand curve. Note,

Figure 21.5(a)

Video-cassette Rentals Demanded per Week. Individuals A, B, and C present us with the various quantities of video-cassette rentals they intend to rent at various relative prices: £2, £3, and £4. When we add quantities demanded by these individuals, we get the total or market quantity demanded at each of these various prices.

	£2	£3	£4
Individual A's quantity demanded	4	3	2
Individual B's quantity demanded	2	1	0
Individual C's quantity demanded	1	0	0
Market quantity demanded	7	4	2

Figure 21.5(b)

Deriving the Market Demand Curve. Individual A's demand curve is shown first, then individual B's and individual C's. By adding these three demand curves horizontally, we obtain the market demand curve represented by the heavily shaded line in the right-hand graph.

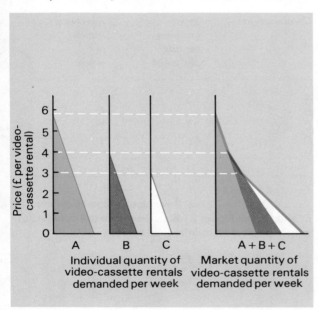

though, that this downward-sloping demand curve (the theory of demand) is derived under the assumption of constant tastes and incomes. You must remember that we are keeping these important determining variables constant when we simply look at the relationship between price and quantity demanded.

Deriving the Market Demand Curve

The demand curve we have been talking about is one that relates directly to an individual. But what about a *market* demand curve, that is, the demand curve that represents the entire market for a particular good or service? How can we derive a market demand curve from the individual ones we have analysed?

Actually, deriving a market demand curve from individual demand curves is not difficult. What we have to do is add together all the individual demands horizontally (assuming that each individual's decisions are made independently of others'). We know that not all people are alike. We know, for example, that even at very low prices, certain individuals will demand no video-cassette rental whatsoever. So, to derive a demand curve for the entire market, we must add up each individual's demand. This is what we do in Figure 21.5. The figure shows explicitly that the market demand curves are fitted together to obtain the market demand curve for video-cassette rental by what we call 'horizontal addition'. Notice that the good's demand is expressed in quantity per time-period. We include a time-period to the demand analysis because we are talking about a flow through time of a demand for a specific good.

Consumer Surplus

Figure 21.5(b) provides us with the basis of an understanding with the concept of consumer surplus. It shows the market demand curve for a society of three individuals. Suppose now that the rental charge for video-cassette hire is £2. At that price the quantity demanded is seven per week. We note from Figure 21.5(a) that individual A would have been prepared to pay £4 for video hire. Presumably he considered that he would have received at least £4 of utility from viewing a video. Individual B was prepared to pay £3 for video hire and again we can presume that this reflects the utility obtained from watching a particular film. Individual C is not prepared to pay more than £2 for the rental of a video. What significance is there if this latter price is indeed that which all three members of our imaginary society actually have to pay for video rental? If the charge made to all three individuals of £2 is the same then both individuals A and B could be said to have received extra utility for which they have not had to pay. It is only individual C who actually equated his utility with the price. Thus in terms of Figure 21.5(b) the whole of the area above the horizontal line marking the price charged (£2) and below the demand curve is the measure of 'surplus' utility obtained by individuals A and B but not paid for. This area is called **consumer surplus**. The term is of relevance to us when we come to consider whether all consumers do indeed pay a common price. It might be possible for a product to charge some individuals more than others, i.e. discriminate between them and thus transfer some of this consumer's surplus to himself. We examine this possibility in Chapter 24.

Utility Analysis – A Summary

The analysis of consumer demand using utility theory may appear abstract. That, of course, must be true every time we attempt to hypothesize anything about people's behaviour. But utility theory was developed for a very specific reason. It allowed economists to understand the importance of the factors that influence demand and the quantity demanded.

The theory of consumer choice is a theory that helps economists predict how consumers will react to changes in price, income, and so on. The goal of this analysis, as well as of any other in this text, is to allow the reader to predict what will happen when an important determining variable changes. Because we have used an example concerning consumer choice about video-cassette rentals that does not mean that the analysis stops there. It can be extended to any good or service.

Indifference Curve Analysis

While the theory of diminishing marginal utility can be fairly well accepted on intuitive grounds and by introspection, if we want more elegant theorizing we can translate our discussion into graphic analysis with what are called 'indifference curves' and 'the budget constraint'. Here we discuss these terms and their relationship and demonstrate consumer equilibrium in geometric form.

On Being Indifferent

What does it mean to be indifferent? It usually means that you don't care one way or the other about something: you are equally disposed to either of two alternatives. With this interpretation in mind, we will turn to the two choices, video-cassette rentals and restaurant meals. In Figure 21.6(a), we show several combinations of video-cassette rentals and restaurant meals per week that our representative consumer

Figure 21.6(a)
Combinations that Yield Equal Levels of Satisfaction. The combination A, B, C, and D represent varying combinations of video-cassette rentals and restaurant meals per week that give an equal level of satisfaction to this consumer. In other words, the consumer is indifferent about these four combinations.

Combination	Video-cassette rentals per week	Restaurant meals per week
A	1	7
B	2	4
C	3	2
D	4	1

Figure 21.6(b)
An Indifference Curve. If we plot the combinations A, B, C, and D from Figure 21.6(a), we obtain the curve ABCD, which is called an indifference curve.

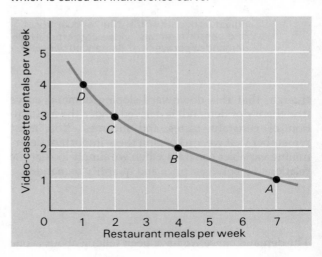

considers to be equally satisfactory. That is to say, for each combination, A, B, C, and D, this consumer will have exactly the same level of total utility.

This simple numerical example that we use happens to concern video-cassette rentals and restaurant meals per week, but this example is used to illustrate general features of indifference curves and related analytical tools that are necessary for deriving the demand curve. Obviously, we could have used any other two commodities. Just remember that we are using a *specific* example to illustrate a *general* analysis.

We can plot these combinations graphically in Figure 21.6(b), with restaurant meals per week on the horizontal axis and video-cassette rentals per week on the vertical axis. These are our consumer's indifference combinations – the consumer finds each combination as acceptable as the others. Each one carries the same level of total utility. When we connect these combinations with a smooth curve, we obtain what is called the consumer's **indifference curve**. Along the indifference curve, every combination of the two goods in the equation yields exactly the same level of total utility. Every point along the indifference curve is equally desirable to the consumer; for example, four video-cassette rentals per week and one restaurant meal per week will given our representative consumer exactly the same total satisfaction as, say, two video-cassette rentals per week and four restaurant meals per week.

Properties of Indifference Curves

Indifference curves have special properties relating to their slope and shape.

INDIFFERENCE CURVES USUALLY SLOPE DOWN

The indifference curve that we showed in Figure 21.6(b) sloped down. That is to say, it had a negative slope. Consider Figure 21.7. Here we show two points, A and B. Point A represents four video-cassette rentals per week and two restaurant meals per week. Point B represents five video-cassette rentals per week and six restaurant meals per week. Clearly, B is always preferred to A, because B represents more of everything. If B is always preferred to A, then it is impossible for points A and B to be on the same indifference curve, because the definition of the indifference curve is a set of combinations of two goods that are equally preferred.

INDIFFERENCE CURVES ARE RARELY STRAIGHT LINES

The indifference curve that we have drawn in Figure 21.6(b) is special. Notice that it is curved. Why did we not draw a straight line as we have usually done for a demand curve? To find out why we do not posit straight-line indifference curves, consider the implications. We show such a straight-line indifference curve in Figure 21.8. Start at point A. The consumer has no restaurant meals and five video-cassette rentals per week. Now the consumer wishes to go to point B. He

Figure 21.7
Indifference Curves Cannot Slope Up. Point B represents a consumption with more video-cassette rentals per week and more restaurant rentals per week than point A. B is always preferred to A. Therefore A and B cannot be on the same indifference curve, which is positively sloped, because an indifference curve shows *equally* preferred combinations of the two goods.

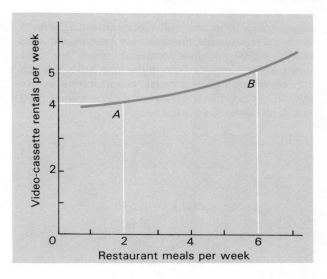

or she is willing to give up only one video-cassette rental in order to get one restaurant meal. Now let us assume that the consumer is at point C. That consumer is consuming one video-cassette rental and four restaurant meals per week. If the consumer wants to go to point D, he or she is again willing to give up one video-cassette rental in order to get one more restaurant meal per week. In other words, no matter how many video-cassettes the consumer rents, he or she is willing to give up one video-cassette rental in order to get one restaurant meal per week. That does not seem to be plausible. According to the theory of diminishing marginal utility, the more of something that a consumer has, the lower will be its marginal utility. Thus, does it not make sense to hypothesize that the more video-cassettes the consumer rents per week, the less he or she will value an additional video-cassette rental? Presumably, when the consumer has five video-cassette rentals and no restaurant meals per week, he or she should be willing to give up more than one video-cassette rental in order to get one restaurant meal. Therefore, once we accept diminishing marginal utility of video-cassette rental consumption, a straight-line indifference curve as shown in Figure 21.8 no longer seems possible. Diminishing marginal utility implies curved indifference curves like the one shown in Figure 21.6(b). In mathematical jargon, an indifference curve is convex with respect to the origin. The reason for this is the theory of diminishing marginal utility. As the individual consumes more of a particular item, the marginal utility of consuming one

Figure 21.8

The Implications of a Straight-line Indifference Curve. If the indifference curve is a straight line, the consumer will be willing to give up the same number of video-cassette rentals (one for one in this simple example) to get one more restaurant meal per week, whether the consumer has no restaurant meals or a lot of restaurant meals per week. For example, the consumer at point A has five video-cassette rentals and no restaurant meals per week. He or she is willing to give up one more video-cassette rental in order to get one more restaurant meal per week. At point C, for example, the consumer has only one video-cassette rental and four restaurant meals per week. Because of the straight-line indifference curve, this consumer is willing to give up the last video-cassette rental in order to get one more restaurant meal per week, even though he or she already has four.

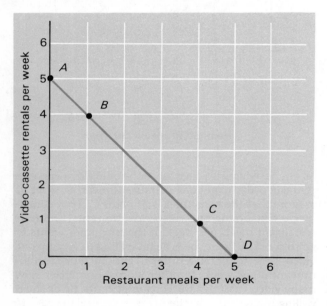

additional unit of that item falls, or, conversely, as the person consumes less of it, that good will have a higher marginal utility.

We can measure the marginal utility of something by the quantity of a substitute good that would leave the consumer indifferent. Let us look at this in Figure 21.6(a). Starting with combination A, the consumer has one video-cassette rental but seven restaurant meals per week. To remain indifferent, the consumer would be willing to give up three restaurant meals to obtain one more video-cassette rental (as shown in combination B). However, to go from combination C to combination D, notice that the consumer would be willing to give up only one restaurant meal for an additional video-cassette rental per week. In other words, the quantity of the substitute considered acceptable changes as the relative scarcity of the original item changes.

Diminishing marginal utility exists throughout this set of choices and consequently the indifference curve

in Figure 21.6(b) will be 'bowed in' (convex when viewed from below). If it were a straight line marginal utility would not be diminishing but constant; if it were 'bowed out' (concave when viewed from below), marginal utility would be increasing.

The Marginal Rate of Substitution

Above we discussed marginal utility in terms of the marginal rate of substitution between restaurant meals and video-cassette rentals per week. More formally, we can define the consumer's marginal rate of substitution as follows:

> MRS = the change in the quantity of one good that just offsets a one-unit change in the consumption of another good, such that total well-being remains constant.

We can see numerically what happens to the marginal rate of substitution in our example if we rearrange Figure 21.6(a) into Figure 21.9. Here we show restaurant meals in the second column and video-cassette rentals in the third. Now we ask the question: What change in the consumption of restaurant meals per week will just compensate for a one-unit change in the consumption of video-cassette rentals per week and leave the consumer's total utility constant? The movement from A to B reduces restaurant meal consumption by one. Here the marginal rate of substitution of restaurant meals for video-cassette rentals is 1 to 3. If we do this for the rest of the table, we find that, as video-cassette rental consumption increases, the marginal rate of substitution goes from 1 to 3 to 1 to 1. The marginal rate of substitution of restaurant meals for video-cassette rentals per week rises, in other words, as the consumer obtains more video-cassette rentals.

In geometric language, the slope of the consumer's indifference curve (actually, the 'negative of the slope') measures the consumer's marginal rate of substitution. Notice that this marginal rate of substitution, or MRS, is purely subjective or psychological. We are not

Figure 21.9

Calculating the Marginal Rate of Substitution

Combination	Restaurant meals per week	Video-cassette rentals per week	Marginal rate of substitution of restaurant meals for video-cassette rentals
A	7	1	
			1/3
B	4	2	
			1/2
C	2	3	
			1/1
D	1	4	

talking about financial capabilities, merely about a consumer's particular set of preferences.

The Indifference Map

Let us now consider the possibility of having both more video-cassette rentals *and* more restaurant meals per week. When we do this, we can no longer stay on the same indifference curve that we drew in Figure 21.6. That indifference curve was drawn for equally satisfying combinations of video-cassette rentals and restaurant meals per week. If the individual now has the possibility of attaining *more of both*, a new indifference curve will have to be drawn *above* and to the right of the one shown in Figure 21.6(b). Alternatively, if the individual is faced with the possibility of having *less of both* video-cassette rentals and restaurant meals per week, an indifference curve would have to be drawn *below* and to the left of the existing one in Figure 21.6(b). Thus, we can map out an entire set of indifference curves corresponding to these different possibilities. What we come up with is an indifference map.

Figure 21.10 shows several possible indifference curves. Indifference curves that are higher than others necessarily imply that more of both goods in question can be consumed. Looked at another way, if

one goes from, say, indifference curve I_1 to I_2, it is possible to consume the same number of restaurant meals but be able to rent more video-cassettes per week. This is shown as a movement from point A to point B in Figure 21.10. We could do it the other way. When we move from a lower to a higher indifference curve, it is possible to rent the same number of video-cassettes and to consume more restaurant meals per week. Thus, the higher a consumer finds himself or herself on the indifference curve map, the greater that consumer's total well-being – assuming, of course, that the consumer does not become satiated.

The Budget Constraint

Our problem here is to find out how to maximize consumer satisfaction. In order to do so, we must consult not only our *preferences* – given by indifference curves – but also our *opportunities* – given by our available incomee, called our **budget constraint**. We might want more of everything, but for any given budget constraint we have to make choices or trade-offs among possible goods. Everyone has a budget constraint; that is, everyone is faced with a limited consumption potential. How do we show this graphically? We must find the prices of the goods in question and determine the *maximum* consumption of each allowed by our consumer's budget. For example, let us assume that video-cassettes rent for £5 each and restaurant meals cost £10. Let us also assume that our representative consumer has a total budget of £30. What is the maximum number of video-cassettes the consumer can rent? Obviously, six. And the maximum number of restaurant meals per week he or she can consume? Three. So we now have, in Figure 21.11, two points on our budget line, which is sometimes called the 'consumption possibilities curve'. The first point is at b on the vertical axis; the second at b' on the horizontal axis. The line is straight because the prices do not change.

Any combination along line bb' is possible; and, in fact, any combination in the grey area is possible. We will assume, however, that the individual consumer completely uses up his or her available budget, and we will consider as possible only those points along bb'.

The Slope of the Budget Constraint

The budget constraint is a line that slopes downwards from left to right. The slope of that line has a special meaning. To see this, look carefully at the budget line in Figure 21.11. Remember from our discussion of graphs in the Appendix to Chapter 1 that we measure a negative slope by the ratio of the fall in Y over the run in X. In this case, Y is video-cassette rentals per week and X is restaurant meals per week. In Figure 21.11, the fall in Y is minus two video-cassette rentals per week (a drop from four to two) for a run in X of one restaurant meal per week (an increase from one to

Figure 21.10

A Set of Indifference Curves. There are an infinite number of indifference curves that can be drawn. We show three possible ones. You should realize that a higher indifference curve represents the possibility of higher rates of consumption of both goods. Hence, a higher indifference curve is preferred to a lower one because 'more' is preferred to 'less'. Look at points A and B. Point B represents more video-cassette rentals than point A; therefore, indifference curve I_2 has to be a preferred one, since the number of restaurant meals per week is the same at points A and B.

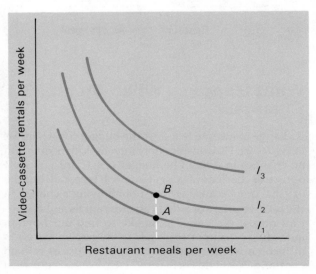

Figure 21.11

The Budget Constraint. The line *bb'* represents this individual's budget constraint. Assuming that video-cassette rentals cost £10 each and restaurant meals cost £20 each and that the individual has a budget of £60, a maximum of six video-cassette rentals or three restaurant meals can be bought. These two extreme points are connected to form the budget constraint. All combinations within the shaded area are feasible.

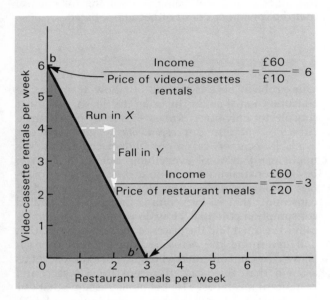

two); and therefore the slope of the budget constraint is –2/1, or –2. This slope of the budget constraint represents the rate of exchange between video-cassette rentals and restaurant meals: it is the realistic rate of exchange, given their prices.

Now we are ready to determine how the consumer achieves his or her optimum consumption rate.

Consumer Optimum Revisited

Consumers, of course, will attempt to attain the highest level of total utility possible, given their budget constraint. How can this be shown graphically? We draw a set of indifference curves similar to those in Figure 21.10 and we bring in reality – the budget constraint, *bb'*. Both are drawn in Figure 21.12. Now, since a higher level of total satisfaction is represented by a higher indifference curve, we know that the consumer will strive to be on the highest indifference curve possible. However, the consumer cannot get to indifference curve I_3, because his or her budget will be exhausted before any combination of video-cassette rentals and restaurant meals represented on indifference curve I_3 is attained. This consumer can maximize total utility, subject to the budget constraint, only by being at point *E* on indifference curve I_2, because here the consumer's income is just being exhausted.

Mathematically, point *E* is called the tangency point of the curve I_2 to the straight line *bb'*.

Consumer equilibrium is achieved when the marginal rate of substitution (which is subjective) is just equal to the feasible, or realistic, rate of exchange between video-cassette rentals and restaurant meals. This realistic rate is the ratio of the two prices of the goods involved. It is represented by the absolute value of the slope of the budget constraint. At point *E*, the point of tangency between indifference curve I_2 and budget constraint *bb'*, the rate at which the consumer wishes to substitute video-cassette rentals for restaurant meals (the numerical value of slope of the indifference curve) is just equal to the rate at which the consumer *can* substitute video-cassette rentals for restaurant meals (the slope of the budget line).

Figure 21.12

Consumer Optimum. A consumer reaches an optimum when he or she ends up on the highest indifference curve possible, given a limited budget. This occurs at the tangency between an indifference curve and the budget constraint. In this diagram the tangency is at *E*.

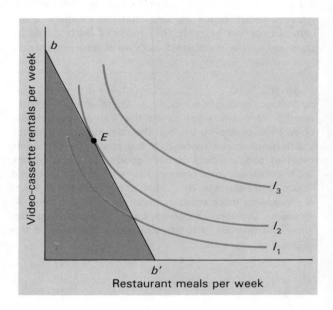

What Happens When Income Changes?

A change in income will shift the budget constraint *bb'* in Figure 21.12. Consider only increases in income and no changes in price. The budget constraint will shift outwards. Each new budget line will be parallel to the original one because we are not allowing a change in the relative prices of video-cassette rentals and restaurant meals. We would now like to find out how an individual consumer responds to successive increases in income when nominal and relative prices remain constant. We do this in Figure 21.13. We start out with an income that is represented by a budget line *bb′*. Consumer optimum is at point *E*, where the consumer attains his or her highest indifference curve *I*, given the budget constraint *bb′*. Now we let money income increase. This is shown by a shift outwards in the budget line to *cc′*. The consumer attains a new optimum at point *E′*. That is where a higher indifference curve, *II*, is reached. Again, the consumer's income is increased so that the new budget line facing him or her is *dd′*. The new optimum now moves to *E″*. This is where the indifference curve, *III*, is reached. If we connect the three consumer optimum points, *E*, *E′*, and *E″*, we have what is called an income consumption curve. The **income consumption curve** shows the optimum consumption points that would occur if income for that consumer were increased continuously, holding the prices of video-cassette rentals and restaurant meals constant.

Figure 21.13

The Income Consumption Curve. We start off with income sufficient to yield budget constraint *bb′*. The highest attainable indifference curve is *I*, which is just tangent to *bb′* at *E*. Next we increase income. The budget line moves outwards to *cc′*, which is parallel to *bb′*. The new highest indifference curve is *II*, which is just tangent to *cc′* at *E′*. Finally, we increase income again, which is represented by a shift in the budget line to *dd′*. The new tangency point of the highest indifference curve, *III*, with *dd′*, is at point *E″*. When we connect these three points, we obtain the income consumption curve.

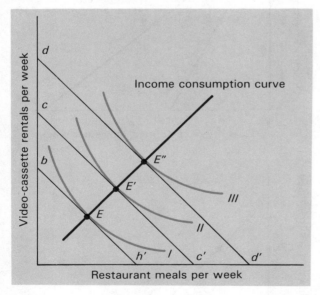

Normal and Inferior Goods

We have shown in Figure 21.13 that as income increases, the consumer purchases more of both video-cassette rentals and restaurant meals. This may not necessarily be the case. As income increases, the consumer could purchase more restaurant meals and rent fewer video-cassettes, or purchase fewer restau-

rant meals and rent more video-cassettes. We show these possibilities in Figure 21.14.

Figure 21.14

We define an inferior good as one for which the quantity demanded decreases as income increases. We define a normal good as one for which the quantity demanded increases as income increases. In panel (a) we show that as income increases, the quantity of video-cassettes rented increases, while the quantity of restaurant meals consumed decreases. In panel (a) video-cassette rentals are a normal good and restaurant meals are an inferior good. In panel (b) the quantity of video-cassettes rented decreases as the quantity of restaurant meals consumed increases. In panel (b) video-cassette rentals are an inferior good and restaurant meals are a normal good.

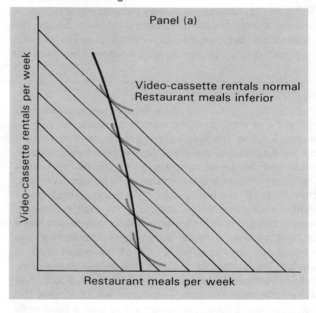

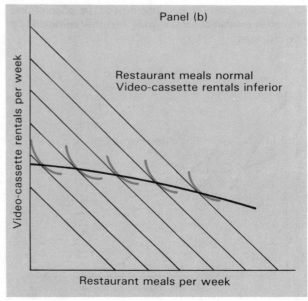

In Figure 21.14 panel (a), we show that as income increases, the consumption of video-cassette rentals increases, but the consumption of restaurant meals decreases. In this situation, we call video-cassette rentals a normal good and restaurant meals an inferior good. The definition of a **normal good** is one for which quantity demanded increases as income increases. The definition of an **inferior good** is one for which quantity demanded decreases as income increases. In panel (b), we show the opposite situation. As income increases, fewer video-cassettes are rented and more restaurant meals are consumed. Thus, video-cassette rentals become an inferior good and restaurant meals become a normal good.

Price Consumption Line

In Figure 21.15 we hold money income and the price of video-cassette rentals constant while we change the price of restaurant meals. Specifically, we keep lowering the price. As we keep lowering the price of restaurant meals, the quantity of meals that could be purchased if all income were spent on restaurant meals clearly increases; thus, the extreme points for the budget constraint keep moving outwards to the right as the price of restaurant meals falls. In other words, the budget line rotates outwards from *bb* to *bb'*.

Figure 21.16
Deriving the Demand Curve. In panel (a) we show the effects of a decrease in the price of restaurant meals from £20 to £10. At a price of £20 the highest indifference curve touches the budget line *bb'* at point *E*. The quantity of restaurant meals consumed is two. We transfer this combination – the price of £20, quantity demanded two – down to panel (b). Next, we decrease the price of restaurant meals to £10. This generates a new budget line, or constraint, which is *bb''*. Consumer optimum is now at *E'*. The optimum quantity demanded of restaurant meals at a price of £10 is five. We transfer this point – the price of £10, quantity demanded five – down to panel (b). When we connect these two points, we have a demand curve, *DD*, for restaurant meals.

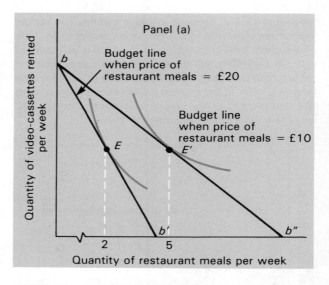

Figure 21.15
Price-consumption Curve. In this experiment we hold the price of video-cassette rentals constant, as well as money income. We keep lowering the price of restaurant meals. As we lower the price of restaurant meals, income measured in terms of restaurant meals per week increases. We show this by rotating the budget constraint from *bb'* to *bb''* and finally to *bb'''*. We then find the highest indifference curve that is attainable for each successive budget constraint (which is drawn with a lower and lower price of restaurant meals). For budget constraint *bb'*, the highest indifference curve is *I*, which is tangent to *bb'* at point *E*. We do this for the next two budget constraints. When we connect the optimum points, *E*, *E'*, and *E''*, we derive the price consumption curve, which shows the combinations of the two commodities that a consumer will purchase when money income and the price of one commodity remain constant while the other commodity's price changes.

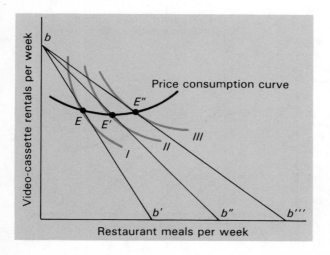

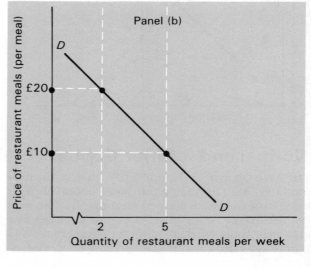

Each time the price of restaurant meals falls, a new budget line is thus formed. There has to be a new optimum point. We find it by locating on each new budget line the highest attainable indifference curve. This is shown at points E, E', and E''. We see that as price decreases for restaurant meals, the consumer purchases more and more restaurant meals per week. We call the line connecting points E, E', and E'' the **price-consumption curve**. It connects the tangency points of the budget constraints and indifference curves, thus showing the amounts of two goods that a consumer will buy when his or her income and the price of one commodity are held constant while the price of the remaining good changes.

Deriving the Demand Curve

We are now in a position to derive the demand curve by using difference curve analysis. In panel (a) of Figure 21.6 we show what happens when the price of restaurant meals decreases, holding the price of videocassette rentals constant and income constant. If the price of restaurant meals decreases, the budget line rotates from bb' to bb''. The two optimum points are given by the tangency at the highest indifference curve that just touches those two budget lines. This is at E and E'. But those two points give us two price–quantity pairs. At point E the price of restaurant meals is £20; the quantity demanded is two. Thus we have one point that we can transfer to panel (b) of Figure 21.16. At point E' we have another price–quantity pair. The price has fallen to £10. The quantity demanded has increased to five. We therefore transfer this other point to panel (b). When we connect these two points (and all the others in between), we derive the demand curve for restaurant meals; it is downward sloping.

Key Points 21.3

▶ An indifference curve is a set of consumption alternatives each yielding the same total amount of satisfaction.

▶ By definition an indifference curve cannot intersect with another one and each curve is usually convex with respect to the origin.

▶ Convex-shaped indifference curves reflect diminishing marginal rates of substitution between the relevant two items.

▶ Purchasers of goods and services face a budget constraint and the optimum point of consumption is reached where the slope of the budget line and the highest indifference curve possible is the same.

▶ If income changes while prices remained fixed the new series of optimum consumption points is termed 'an income consumption curve'. When consumers buy more of a good as income rises it is a normal good: if they buy less it is an inferior good.

▶ If relative prices alter but income remains unchanged the new series of optimum consumption points is termed 'a price-consumption curve'. The demand curve can be derived from the price-consumption curve.

CASE STUDY

Why are Diamonds more Expensive Than Water?

Water is essential to life. Diamonds are quite unessential to life. None the less, water is cheap relative to diamonds. In economics this is called the diamond–water paradox. For many years there was no acceptable solution to this paradox, particularly during the period when economists used to explain the value of things by the amount of labour that was required to produce them. This was called the labour theory of value. If five hours of a given quality of labour were required to produce one hat, but 10 hours were required to produce a pair of shoes, the labour theory of value would indicate that the shoes were twice as valuable as the hat. We know now that such a theory is inadequate and inaccurate. Goods that require countless hours of labour to produce will have little or no market value if few people desire to consume them.

We can use marginal utility analysis to solve the diamond–water paradox. In so doing, we must distinguish between total and marginal utility.

Total versus marginal utility

It is not the total utility of water or of diamonds that determines the price of either. To be sure, the total utility of water greatly exceeds the total utility derived from diamonds. However, in economics what determines price is what happens on the margin, and what happens on the margin is quite simple. Since we have so much water, its marginal utility (because it is diminishing) is quite small, given the total quantity that we consume. Because we have relatively few diamonds, the marginal utility of

Figure 21.17
The Diamond–Water Paradox. We pick kilograms as a common unit of measurement for both water and diamonds. The demand curve for water is way to the right of the demand curve for diamonds. To demonstrate that the demand for water is immense, we have put a break in the demand curve, D_{water} D_{water}. We have also put a break indication on the vertical axis to show that it goes much higher than indicated on this graph. Although the demand for water is much greater than the demand for diamonds, the marginal valuation of water is given by the marginal value placed on the last unit of water consumed. To find that, we must know the supply of water, which is given as SS. At that supply, the price of water is P_{water}. But the supply for diamonds is given by $S'S'$. At that supply, the price of diamonds is $P_{diamonds}$. The total valuation that consumers place on water is tremendous relative to the total valuation consumers place on diamonds. What is important for price determination, however, is the marginal valuation, or the marginal utility received.

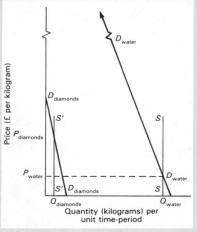

Quantity (kilograms) per unit time-period

that last diamond consumed is quite high. Moreover, the price of water is the same, more or less, for everyone who buys it in a particular market situation. We find also that the price of a diamond, in another market situation, is the same for everyone who buys it. In other words, every unit must be sold for what the last (marginal), and hence least useful, unit sells for. We mean *least useful* in terms of individual subjective or psychological marginal utility.

So the diamond–water paradox is only a paradox if one confuses total utility with marginal utility. Total utility does not determine what people are willing to pay for a particular commodity. Marginal utility does.

Graphic Analysis

Let us examine Figure 21.17. Here we show the demand curve for diamonds, labelled $D_{diamonds}$ $D_{diamonds}$. The demand curve for water is labelled D_{water} D_{water}. We plot quantity in terms of kilograms per unit time-period on the horizontal axis. On the vertical axis is plotted price in pounds per kilogram. We use kilograms as our common unit of measurement for water and for diamonds. We could just as well have used gallons or litres.

Notice that we have drawn the demand curve for water with a break in it to illustrate that the demand for water is many, many times the demand for diamonds. We draw the supply curve of water as SS at a quantity of Q_{water}. The supply curve for diamonds is given as $S'S'$ at quantity $Q_{diamonds}$. Clearly, at the intersection of the supply curve of water with the demand curve of water, the price per kilogram is P_{water}. The intersection of the supply curve of diamonds with the demand curve of diamonds is at $P_{diamonds}$. Notice that $P_{diamonds}$ exceeds P_{water}. Diamonds sell at a higher price than water.

Measuring Marginal Valuation

If we assume that at any point along the demand curve we can infer marginal valuation of that particular quantity of the good,

then we can make a determination of relative value. In other words, the point gives an indication of the consumer's monetary evaluation of the last unit consumed. The marginal valuation (marginal utility) of diamonds exceeds the marginal valuation of water. Clearly, the total value of water has got to be huge. After all, look how far over to the right the demand curve is. But price is determined by marginal utility, or marginal valuation. Since water is plentiful, as indicated by the supply curve SS, it intersects demand at a relatively low price.

If for some reason the supply

curve of water shifted inwards to the left from SS in Figure 21.17, then its price could eventually far exceed the price of diamonds. In other words, what is important is relative scarcity, that is, supply relative to demand. That is how we explain the diamond–water paradox.

Questions
1. Would the analysis just presented apply to other 'necessities' such as food?
2. Why is the marginal utility of diamonds so high?

Exam Preparation and Practice

INTRODUCTORY EXERCISES

1. Suppose that a rational man has £1 to spend on a pub lunch. Beer costs him 20p per pint and sandwiches are 10p each.

His utility from consumption is as follows:

Beer			Sandwiches	
Pints	Total utility		No.	Total utility
1	30		1	13
2	55		2	25
3	75		3	36
4	90		4	46
5	100		5	55
			6	63
			7	70
			8	76
			9	81
			10	85

How should this person use his money to obtain the highest possible level of welfare?

2. Suppose that you are standing in the check-out line of a supermarket. You have 5 lb of oranges and three ears of sweetcorn. Oranges cost 30p a pound; so, too, does one ear of corn. You have £2.40 to spend. You are satisfied that you have reached the highest level of satisfaction, or total utility. Your sister comes along and tries to convince you that you have to put some of the corn back and replace it with additional pounds of oranges. From what you know about utility analysis, how would you explain this disagreement?

3. In order to increase marginal utility, the consumer must decrease consumption (other things being constant). This sounds paradoxical. Why is it a correct statement, none the less?

4. Assume that Mr Warfield's marginal utility is 100 utils for the last beer he drank. If the price of beer is £1 a pint, what is Warfield's marginal utility per pound's worth of beer? What is his marginal utility per pound's worth if the price were 50p per pint? If the price were £2? How do we calculate marginal utility per pound worth of specific commodities?

Source: S. Charles and A. Webb, *The Economic Approach to Social Policy*, Wheatsheaf Books, 1986.

continued overleaf

5. Consider a two-person economy in which the following table indicates each person's demand for beer.

Price per pint of beer	Mr Smith: quantity demanded per week	Mr Johnson: quantity demanded per week
£2.00	2	0
1.50	3	1
1.00	4	2
.50	5	3

(a) Construct a group demand schedule (table).
(b) Graph Mr Smith's, Mr Johnson's, and the group's demand curves.
(c) Why might Mr Smith and Mr Johnson have different demand curves for beer?

MULTIPLE CHOICE QUESTIONS

1. A downward-sloping demand curve
  A has constant price elasticity throughout its length
  B shows the effects of increasing income of consumers
  C can be derived from the theory of diminishing marginal utility
  D shows the effects of changes in the price of substitutes
  E indicates the response of demand to changes in price expectations

2. Assume that a person with a fixed income spends it on only two goods, X and Y. Total utility will be maximized when the total income is distributed so that the
  A average utility of the last unit of X purchased equals the average utility of the last unit of Y purchased
  B marginal utility of the last unit of X purchased equals the marginal utility of the last unit of Y purchased
  C marginal utility of the last unit of X purchased divided by the price of X equals the marginal utility of the last unit of Y purchased divided by the price of Y
  D marginal utility of the last unit of each good purchased is equal to zero
  E total utility of good X is equal to the total utility of good Y

3. Consumers' surplus is
  A the difference between the quantity demanded and the quantity supplied
  B unsatisfied consumer demand
  C unspent disposable income
  D excess demand
  E the difference between the aggregate amount consumers are prepared to pay and the amount they do pay

4.

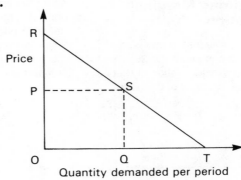

In the above diagram, at output OQ consumer surplus is represented by the area
  A RSQO
  B PSTO
  C PSQO
  D RSP
  E STQ

5.

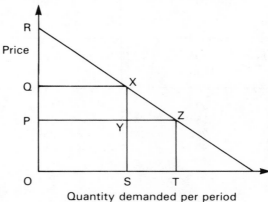

The diagram represents the market demand schedule for a product. The increase in consumer surplus enjoyed as a result of a price reduction from OQ to OP is shown by the area
  A PQXY
  B PRZ
  C PQXZ
  D YXZ
  E SXZT

For questions 6 and 7 select your answers from the following grid:

A	B	C	D	E
1,2,3 all correct	1, 2 only correct	2, 3 only correct	1 only correct	3 only correct

†6. A consumer maximizes his satisfaction from spending a given income when
   1 he maximizes his total utility
   2 the marginal utility from the last penny spent on each good is identical
   3 he equalizes the ratio of the marginal utility of each good purchased to its price

†7. Assume that a consumer behaves rationally in buying 3 packets of crisps each costing 16p. This behaviour indicates that this consumer
   1 obtained marginal utility from the third packet at least equal to its price
   2 would have obtained greater utility from purchasing a fourth packet of crisps
   3 derived a total utility from purchasing the 3 packets equal to 48p

RELATED ESSAY QUESTIONS

1. Discuss and illustrate the relevance of total and marginal utility for the determination of consumer demand in the cases of water and gold.

2. Why are demand curves normally thought to be downward sloping? Why is this not always the case?

22 Businesses and Their Costs

Key Points to Review

▶ Opportunity cost (1.2)

▶ Resource allocation and costs (6.6)

▶ Supply (5.4)

▶ Indirect tax (8.5, 10.6)

Questions for Preview

1 How does the economist's definition of profit differ from the accountant's?

2 What distinguishes the long run from the short run?

3 What is the law of diminishing returns?

4 Why is the average total cost (ATC) curve U-shaped?

5 How are the marginal cost (MC) and the average total cost (ATC) curves related?

The last chapter dealt with a theory of the behaviour of consumers. We were looking at the behind-the-scenes elements that affected the demand side of microeconomics. But, as highlighted in Chapters 14 and 18, knowing about the demand side is not sufficient to understand how the world works; we also have to know about the supply side. Therefore we now develop a theory of how suppliers behave. We look at what is known in economics as the **theory of the firm**. How do owners of businesses react to changing taxes, changing input prices, and changing government regulations? In order to answer these questions, we have to understand the nature of production costs and revenues for each firm owner. In this chapter, we examine the nature of productivity and costs, and in the following chapters, we look at the revenue side of the picture.

Defining a Business

What is a business? Everybody knows the answer. It is the supermarket down the street, the dress shop around the corner, British Leyland, the market stall,

Marks & Spencer etc. The list will get very large indeed if we attempt to name every business in the United Kingdom. Everybody also knows that there is a difference between a corporate giant like Coca-Cola and the local dress shop. In terms of our analysis, however, we will not usually make a distinction between these types of firms, except with regard to the market power they have, that is, the extent to which they control the prices of commodities they sell.

There are legal differences, of course, among the various types of businesses, and these are briefly summarized in Figure 22.1.

The Firm

In general terms we can define a business, or **firm**, as follows:

A firm is an organization that brings together different factors of production, such as labour, land, and capital, to produce a product or service which it is hoped can be sold for a profit.

The actual size of a firm would affect its precise

Figure 22.1
Types of Business Ownership

Type of business	No. involved in ownership	Examples	Sources of finance	Liability for debts	Profit distribution	Authority and control
Sole proprietor	1	newsagent, corner shop, butcher, baker	Bank loans and/or personal savings, HP finance, credit, etc.	Owner is fully liable for all debts incurred	Owner keeps all profits	Full control by proprietor
Partnership	2 to 20	doctors, solicitors, dentists, builders	Bank loans and/or personal savings, HP finance, mortgages, etc.	At least one partner is fully liable for all debts	Profits shared according to deed of partnership	All partners have equal power (except sleeping-partners)
Private joint-stock company	2 to ∞	small local breweries*	All the above + the issue of shares to agreed members	Limited liability for debts. Each shareholder only risks the amount put in to buy shares	Distributed between all shareholders – dividends being paid per share	Normally directed by shareholders (In proportion to the number of shares held)
Public joint-stock company	2 to ∞	ICI, Shell, banks, Sainsbury*	All the above. But the ownership of shares is open to all via the stock exchange.	As for private joint-stock company. But annual general report must be available to the public and accounts publicized in the national press. (A minimum amount of share capital is another prerequisite.)		Shareholders appoint a board of directors to act on their behalf. (These directors are voted in/out at the AGM.)

Note: All the above types of business organization are owned and controlled by private individuals, that is, they form part of the private sector. In contrast government-funded and -organized firms (not detailed above) constitute the public sector.

* Since the 1980 Companies Act, a private joint-stock company must include the word 'limited' in its title, and a public joint-stock company must have the words 'public limited company' at the end of its name (this is commonly abbreviated plc).

structure, but a common set-up would involve: entrepreneur, managers, and workers. The entrepreneur is the person who takes the chances. Because of this, the entrepreneur is the one who will get any profits that are made. The entrepreneur also decides who to hire to run the firm. Some economists maintain that the true quality of an entrepreneur becomes evident when he or she can pick good managers. Managers, in turn, are the ones who decide who should be hired and fired and how the business should generally be set up. The workers are the ones who ultimately use the machines to produce the products or services that are being sold by the firm. Workers and managers are paid contractual wages. They receive a specified amount for the specified time-period. Entrepreneurs are not paid contractual wages. They receive no specified 'reward'. Rather, they receive what is left over, if anything, after all expenses are paid. Profits are, therefore, the reward paid to the entrepreneur for taking risks.

Profit

The costs of production must include an element of

profit to pay for the entrepreneur's services. If the level of profits falls in one area of activity entrepreneurs may move their resources to an industry where the returns are higher. To illustrate this behaviour economists employ a concept of **normal profit**. Normal profit may be defined as:

The minimum level of reward required to ensure that existing entrepreneurs are prepared to remain in their present area of production.

Normal profit is included in the cost of production, as it is an essential minimum reward necessary to attract the entrepreneur into economic activity. Normal profit also highlights that all resources can be employed in several ways (i.e. all resources have alternative uses). Consequently, what is meant by 'profit' in economics differs from its general meaning.

To portray the general meaning of profit the following formula could be used:

profits = total revenues − total costs

For economists an alternative formula is required:

Economic profits = total revenues *minus* total opportunity cost of all inputs used

What the economic profits formula actually involves will become clearer by looking at two areas of resource allocation and the related cost accounting calculations. The first resource is capital and the second resource is labour.

Opportunity Cost of Capital

Firms enter or remain in an industry if they earn, at a minimum, a *normal rate of return* (NROR), i.e. normal profit. By this term, we mean that people will not invest their wealth in a business unless they obtain a positive competitive rate of return, that is, unless their invested wealth pays off. Any business wishing to attract capital must expect to pay at least the same rate of return on that capital as all other businesses of similar risk are willing to pay. For example, if individuals can invest their wealth in almost any publishing firm and get a rate of return of 10 per cent per year, then each firm in the publishing industry must *expect* to pay 10 per cent as the normal rate of return to present and future investors. This 10 per cent is a *cost to the firm*. This cost is called the **opportunity cost of capital**. The opportunity cost of capital is the amount of income, or yield, forgone by giving up an investment in another firm. Capital will therefore not stay in firms or industries where the expected rate of return falls below its opportunity cost.

Opportunity Cost of Labour

Sole traders often grossly exaggerate their profit rates because they forget about the opportunity cost of the time that they personally spend in the business. For example, you may know people who run small grocery stores. These people, at the end of the year, will sit down and figure out what their 'profits' are. They will add up all their sales and subtract what they had to pay to other workers, what they had to pay to their suppliers, what they had to pay in taxes, and so on. The end-result they will call 'profit'. However, they will not have figured into their costs the salary that they could have made if they had worked for somebody else in a similar type of job. For somebody operating a grocery store, that salary might be equal to £6 an hour. If so, then £6 an hour is the opportunity cost of the grocery-store owner's time. In many cases, people who run their own businesses lose money in an economic sense. That is, their profits, as they calculate them, may be less than the amount of labour income they *could* have earned had they spent the same amount of time working for someone else. Take a numerical example. If an entrepreneur can earn £6 per hour, it follows that the opportunity cost of his or her time is £6 × 40 hours × 52 weeks, or £12 480 per year. If this entrepreneur is making less than £12 480 per year in accounting profits, he or she is actually losing money. (This does not mean that such entrepreneurs are 'stupid'. They may be willing to pay for the non-

pecuniary benefits of 'being the boss'.)

We have spoken only of the opportunity cost of capital and the opportunity cost of labour, but we could have spoken in general of the opportunity cost of all inputs. Whatever the input may be, its opportunity cost must be taken into account in order to figure out true economic profits.

Another way of looking at the opportunity cost of running a business is that opportunity cost consists of all explicit (direct) and implicit (indirect) costs. Accountants are only able to take account of explicit costs, though. Therefore, accounting profit ends up being the residual after only explicit costs are subtracted from total revenues.

Accounting Profits Are not Equal to Economic Profits

You should have a good idea by now of the meaning of profits in economics.

The term *profits* in economics means the income that entrepreneurs earn, over and above their own opportunity cost of time, plus the opportunity cost of the

---

Figure 22.2
Simplified View of Economic and Accounting Profit. Here we see that on the right-hand side, total revenues are equal to accounting costs plus accounting profit. That is, accounting profit is the difference between total revenues and total accounting costs. On the other hand, we see in the left-hand column that economic costs are equal to accounting costs plus a normal rate of return (NROR) or normal profit on invested capital, which is the opportunity cost of capital.

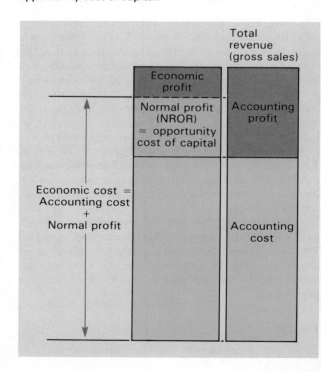

capital they have invested in their business. Profits can be regarded as total revenues minus total costs – which is how the accountants think of them – but we must now include *all* costs.

We indicate this relationship in Figure 22.2. We are assuming that the accountants' bookkeeping costs for all factors of production except capital are correct.

The Goal of the Firm

In most instances we will use a model that is based on maximization of profits. In other words, the firm's goal is to maximize profit; it is expected to attempt to make the positive difference between total revenues and total cost as large as it can. We use a profit-maximizing model because it allows us to analyse a firm's behaviour with respect to quantity supplied and the relationship between cost and output. Whenever this profit-maximizing model produces poor predictions, we will examine our initial assumption about profit maximization. We might have to conclude that the primary goal of *some* firms is not to maximize profits but rather to maximize sales, the number of workers, the prestige of the owners, and so on. However, we are primarily concerned with generalizations. Therefore, provided the assumption of profit maximization is correct for *most* firms, then the model will suffice as a good starting-point (Key Points 22.1).

The Relationship between Output and Inputs

A firm takes numerous inputs, combines them using a technological production process, and ends up with an output. There are, of course, many, many factors of production, or inputs. We classify production inputs into two broad categories (ignoring land) – labour and capital. The relationship between output and these two inputs is as follows:

output per unit time period = $\dfrac{\text{some function of capital}}{\text{and labour inputs}}$

Short Run versus Long Run

The time-period here is important. Throughout the rest of this chapter we will consider a 'short' time-period as opposed to a 'long' time-period. In other words, we are looking at *short-run* production relationships and *short-run* costs associated with production.

Any definition of the short run will, necessarily, be arbitrary. We cannot talk in terms of the short run being a specific time-period such as a month, or even a year. Rather, we must deal in terms of the short run having to do with the ability of the firm to alter the quantity of its inputs. For ease of understanding, we will simply define the **short run** as any time-period when there is at least one factor of production that has a fixed cost. In the **long run**, therefore, all costs are variable. That is all factors are variable.

How long is the long run? That depends on each individual industry. For McDonald's (hamburgers), the long run may be four or five months – because that is the time-period during which they can add new franchises. For British Steel the long run may be several years – because that is how long it takes to plan and build a new plant.

In most short-run analyses, the factor that has a fixed cost, or is fixed in quantity, is capital. We therefore state that in our short-run model, capital is fixed and invariable. That is not unreasonable: in a

---

Key Points 22.1

▶ The basic forms of private enterprise in the United Kingdom are sole trader, partnerships, private and public joint-stock companies.

▶ A firm is an organization that brings together production inputs in order to produce a good or service that can be sold for a profit.

▶ Accounting profits differ from economic profits.

▶ Economic profits are defined as total revenues minus total costs, where costs include the full opportunity cost of all the factors of production.

▶ Single-owner proprietorships often fail to consider the opportunity cost of the labour services provided by the owner.

▶ The full opportunity cost of capital invested in a business is generally not included as a cost when accounting profits are calculated. Thus, accounting profits overstate economic profits.

▶ Profit maximization is regarded as the main objective when considering a firm's behaviour.

typical firm, the number of machines *in place* will not change over several months, or even over a year. After all, the input that changes the most is labour. The production relationships that we use, therefore, holds capital constant, or given, and labour is variable.

The Production Function – A Numerical Example

The relationship between physical output and the quantity of capital and labour used in the production process is sometimes called a **production function**. The term 'production function' in economics, owes its origin to production engineers for it is used to describe the technological relationship between inputs and outputs. It depends therefore on the available technology.

Figure 22.3(a)
Diminishing Returns: A Hypothetical Case in Agriculture. In the first column, we measure the number of workers used per week on a given amount of land with a given amount of machinery and fertilizer and seed. In the second column, we give their total product, that is, the output that each specified number of workers can produce in terms of bushels of wheat. The last column gives the marginal product. The marginal product is the difference between the output possible with a given number of workers minus the output made possible with one less worker. For example, the marginal product of a fourth worker is 8 bushels of wheat. With four workers, 44 bushels are produced, but with three workers only 36 are produced; the difference is 8.

Input of labour (no. of worker-weeks)	Total product (output in bushels of wheat per week)	Marginal physical product (in bushels of wheat per week)
0	0	
		10
1	10	
		16
2	26	
		10
3	36	
		8
4	44	
		6
5	50	
		4
6	54	
		2
7	56	
		–1
8	55	

Look at Figure 22.3(a). Here we show a production function relating total output in column 2 to the quantity of labour measured in worker-weeks in column 1. When there are no worker-weeks of input, there is no output. When there are five worker-weeks of input (given the capital stock), there is a total output of 50 bushels per week. (Ignore for the moment the rest of that Figure.) In Figure 22.3(b) we show this particular hypothetical production function graphically. Note, again, that it relates to the short run and that it is for an individual firm.

Figure 22.3(b)
A Production Function. A production function relates outputs to inputs. We have merely taken the numbers from columns 1 and 2 of Figure 22.3(a) and presented them here.

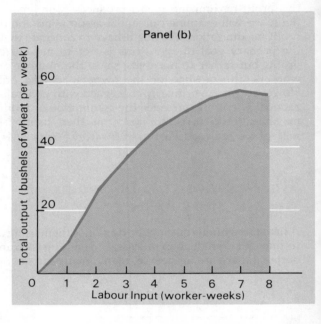

Figure 22.3(b) shows a total physical product curve, or the amount of physical output that is possible when we add successive units of labour while holding all other inputs constant. The graph of the production function in Figure 22.3(b) is not a straight line. In fact, it peaks at seven worker-weeks and starts to go down. To understand why such a phenomenon occurs with an individual firm in the short run, we have to analyse in detail the **law of diminishing (marginal) returns***.

Diminishing Returns

The concept of diminishing marginal returns applies to many different situations. If you put one seat belt

---

*Other names for this law are diminishing marginal productivity, diminishing marginal returns, diminishing marginal physical productivity, and the law of variable proportions.

over your lap, a certain amount of additional safety is obtained. If you add another seat belt, some more safety is obtained, but less than when the first belt was secured. When you add a third seat belt, again the amount of *additional* safety obtained must be even smaller. In a similar way, Winston Churchill apparently believed that there were diminishing returns to dropping more and more bombs on German steel mills during the Second World War; extra bombs, he felt, merely moved about the wreckage from prior bombs.

The same analysis holds for firms in their use of productive inputs. When the returns from hiring more workers are diminishing, it does not necessarily mean that more workers will not be hired. In fact, workers will be hired until the returns, in terms of the *value* of the extra output produced, are equal to the additional wages that have to be paid for those workers to produce the extra output. Before we get into that decision-making process, let us demonstrate that diminishing returns can be represented graphically and can be used in our analysis of the firm.

Measuring Diminishing Returns

How do we measure diminishing returns? First, we limit the analysis to only one variable factor of production (or input). Let us say that factor is labour. Every other factor of production, such as machines, must be held constant. Only in this way can we calculate the marginal returns from using more workers and know when we reach the point of diminishing marginal returns.

Marginal returns for productive inputs are sometimes specifically referred to as the **marginal physical product**. The marginal physical product of a worker, for example, is the change in total product that occurs when that worker joins an already existing production process. It is also the *change* in total product that occurs when that worker resigns or is laid off an already existing production process. The marginal productivity of labour therefore refers to the change in output caused by a one-unit change in the labour input.

The marginal productivity of labour may increase at the very beginning. That is, a firm starts with no workers, only machines. The firm then hires one worker, who finds it difficult to get the work started. When the firm hires more workers, however, each is able to *specialize*, and the marginal productivity of those additional workers may actually be greater than it was with the previous few workers. Therefore, at the outset increasing marginal returns are likely to be experienced. Beyond some point, however, diminishing returns must set in; each worker has (on average) fewer machines with which to work (remember, all other inputs are fixed). Eventually, the firm will become so crowded that workers will start running into one another and will become less productive. Managers will have to be hired to organize the workers.

Using these ideas, we can define the law of dimin-

ishing returns. For example consider the two following possible definitions:

As successive equal increases in a variable factor of production, such as labour, are added to other fixed factors of production, such as capital, there will be a point beyond which the extra or marginal product that can be attributed to each additional unit of the variable factor of production will decline.

or more formally:

As the proportion of *one* factor in a combination of factors is increased, after a point, the marginal product of that factor will diminish.

Put simply diminishing returns merely refer to a situation in which output rises less than in proportion

---

Figure 22.3(c)

Marginal Product – Diminishing Marginal Return. On the horizontal axis, we plot the number of workers; starting from 0 and going to 8. On the vertical axis, we plot the marginal physical product in bushels of wheat. When we go from no workers to one worker, marginal product is 10. We show this at a point between 0 and 1 worker-weeks to indicate that marginal product relates to the change in the total product as we add additional workers. When we go from one worker to two workers, marginal product increases to 16. After two workers, marginal product declines. Therefore, after two workers, we are in the area of diminishing marginal physical returns. Since total product, or output, reaches its peak at seven workers, we know that after seven workers, marginal physical product is negative. In fact when we move from seven to eight workers, marginal product becomes –1 bushel. (Note, again, that we have approximated the curve by using the *mid-points* between the number of worker-weeks; that is why the curve peaks between 1 and 2 worker-weeks rather than exactly at 2 worker-weeks.

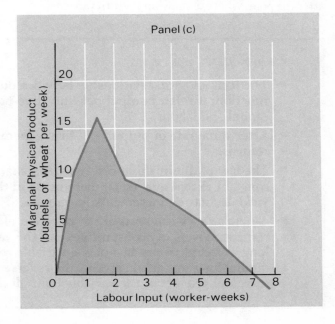

to an increase in, say, the number of workers employed.

An Example

An example of the law of diminishing returns is found in agriculture. With a fixed amount of land, fertilizer, and tractors, the addition of more people eventually yields decreasing increases in output. A hypothetical set of numbers illustrating the law of diminishing marginal returns is presented in Figure 22.3(a). The numbers are presented graphically in Figure 22.3(c) (page 317). Marginal productivity (returns from adding more workers) first increases, then decreases, and finally becomes negative. When one worker is hired, total output goes from 0 to 10. Thus, marginal physical product is equal to 10. When another worker is added, marginal physical product increases to 16. Then it begins to decrease. The point of diminishing marginal returns occurs after two workers are hired.

The Relationship between Diminishing Marginal Returns and the Theory of the Firm

If we now introduce business costs one can begin to sense the central importance of the law of diminishing returns.

For example, consider the relationship between marginal cost, i.e. the cost of an extra unit of output, and the incidence of diminishing marginal physical returns as illustrated in Figure 22.3(a). Let us assume that each unit of labour can be purchased at a constant price. Further assume that labour is the only variable input. We see that as more workers are hired, marginal physical product first rises and then falls after the point where diminishing returns are encoun-

tered. Thus, the marginal cost of *each extra unit* of output will first fall as long as marginal physical product is rising, and then it will rise as long as marginal physical product is falling. Consider specifically Figure 22.3(a). Assume that a worker is paid £100 a week. When we go from zero labour input to one unit, output increases by 10 bushels of wheat. Thus, each of those 10 bushels of wheat has a marginal cost of £10. Now the second unit of labour is hired, and it, too, costs £100. Output increases by 16. Thus, the marginal cost is £100 ÷ 16 = £6.25. We continue the experiment. We see that the next unit of labour yields only 10 additional bushels of wheat, so that marginal cost starts to rise again back to £10. The following unit of labour increases marginal physical product by only 8, so that marginal cost becomes £100 ÷ 8 = £12.50.

Marginal costs in turn effect the pattern of other costs, e.g. average variable costs and average total costs. Once these other costs have been discussed the importance of marginal cost analysis (and the above section) will become clearer (see Key Points 22.2).

Short-Run Costs to the Firm

In the short run, a firm incurs certain types of costs. Economists label all costs incurred as **total costs**. Then we divide total costs into total fixed costs and total variable costs, which we explain below. The relationship, or identity, is, therefore:

total costs ≡ total fixed costs + total variable costs.

After we have looked at the elements of total costs, we will find out how to compute average and marginal costs.

Total Fixed Costs

Let us look at a business such as the Ford Motor Company. The decision-makers in that corporate

---

Key Points 22.2

▶ The technological relationship between output and input is called the production function. It relates output per unit time-period to the several inputs, such as capital and labour.

▶ After some rate of output, the firm generally experiences diminishing marginal returns.

▶ The law of diminishing returns states that if all factors of production are held constant except one, equal increments in that one variable factor will eventually yield decreasing increments in output.

▶ A firm's short-run costs are a reflection of the law of diminishing marginal returns. Given any constant price of the variable input, marginal costs decline as long as marginal product of the variable resource goes up. At the point of diminishing marginal returns, the reverse occurs. Marginal costs will rise as the marginal product of the variable input declines.

giant can look around and see big machines, thousands of parts, huge buildings, and a multitude of other pieces of plant and equipment that are in place, that have already been bought. Fords have to take account of the wear and tear of this equipment, no matter how many cars it produces. The payments on the loans taken out to buy the equipment and the rates on the land have to be paid regardless of output. All these costs are unaffected by variations in the amount of output. That is they are mainly the overhead costs. This leads us to a very straightforward definition of fixed costs:

All costs that do not vary, that is, costs that do not depend on the rate of production, are called fixed costs, or sunk costs.

Let us take as an example the fixed costs incurred by a manufacturer of leather handbags. This firm's total fixed costs will equal the cost of the rent on its equipment and the insurance it has to pay. We see in panel (a) of Figure 22.4 (page 320) that total fixed costs per day are £10. In panel (b), these total fixed costs are represented by the horizontal line at £10 per day. They are invariant to changes in the output of handbags per days: no matter how many are produced, fixed costs will remain at £10 per day.

The difference between total costs and total fixed costs is total variable costs (total costs − total fixed costs = total variable costs).

Total Variable Costs

Total **variable costs** are those costs whose magnitude varies with the rate of production. One obvious variable cost is wages paid. The more the firm produces, the more it has to pay. There are other variable costs, though. One is materials. In the production of leather handbags, for example, leather must be bought. The more handbags that are made, the more leather must be bought. Part of the rate of depreciation (the rate of wear and tear) on machines that are used in the production process can also be considered a variable cost, if depreciation depends partly on how long and how intensively the machines are used. Total variable costs are given in column 3 of panel (a) of Figure 22.4. These are translated into the total variable cost curve in panel (b). Notice that the variable cost curve lies below the total cost curve by the vertical distance of £10. This vertical distance represents, of course, total fixed costs.

Short-run Average Cost Curves

In panel (b) of Figure 22.4, we see total costs, total variable costs, and total fixed costs. Now we want to look at average cost. The average cost concept is simply one in which we are measuring cost per unit of output. It is a matter of simple arithmetic to figure the averages of these three cost concepts. We can define them simply as follows:

$$\text{Average total costs} = \frac{\text{total costs}}{\text{output}}$$

$$\text{Average variable costs} = \frac{\text{total variable costs}}{\text{output}}$$

$$\text{Average fixed costs} = \frac{\text{total fixed costs}}{\text{output}}$$

The arithmetic is done in columns 5, 6, and 7 in panel (a) of Figure 22.4, while the numerical results are translated into graphical format in panel (c). Let us see what we can observe about the three average cost curves in that graph.

AVERAGE FIXED COSTS (AFC)

Average fixed costs continue to fall throughout the output range. In fact, if we were to continue the diagram further to the right, we would find that average fixed costs would get closer and closer to the horizontal axis. That is because total fixed costs remain constant. As we divide this fixed number by a larger and larger number of units of output, the result, AFC, has to become smaller and smaller.

AVERAGE VARIABLE COSTS (AVC)

We assume a particular form of the **average variable cost** curve. The form that it takes is U-shaped: first it falls; then it starts to rise. It is certainly possible to have other shapes of the average variable cost curve.

AVERAGE TOTAL COSTS (ATC)

This curve has a shape similar to the average variable cost curve. However, it falls even more dramatically in the beginning and rises more slowly after it has reached a minimum point. It falls and then rises because **average total costs** is the summation of the average fixed cost curve and the average variable cost curve. Thus, when AFC plus AVC are both falling, it is only logical that ATC would fall, too. At some point, however, AVC starts to increase while AFC continues to fall. Once the increase in the AVC curve outweighs the decrease in the AFC curve, the ATC curve will start to increase and will develop its familiar U-shape.

Marginal Cost

We have stated repeatedly in this text that the action is always on the margin – movement in economics is always determined at the margin. This dictum holds true within the firm also. Firms, according to the analysis we use to predict their behaviour, are very interested in their **marginal cost**. Since the term *marginal* means additional or incremental, marginal costs refer to those costs that result from a one-unit change in the production rate. For example, if the production of 10 leather handbags per day costs a firm £48 and the production of 11 leather handbags costs it £56 per day, then the marginal cost of producing that eleventh leather handbag per day is £8.

We find marginal cost by subtracting the total cost of producing all but the last unit from the total cost of producing all units, including the last one. Marginal costs can be measured, therefore, by using the formula:

$$\text{marginal cost} = \frac{\text{change in total cost}}{\text{change in output}}$$

We show the marginal costs of handbag production per day in column 8 of panel (a) in Figure 22.4, where marginal cost is defined as the change in total cost divided by the change in output. In our particular example, we have changed output by one unit every time, so we can ignore the denominator in that particular formula.

This marginal cost schedule is shown graphically in panel (c) of Figure 22.4. Like average variable costs and average total costs, marginal costs first fall and then rise. It is interesting to look at the relationship between marginal costs and average costs.

Figure 22.4
An Example of the Costs of Production

Panel (a)

Total output (Q/day) (1)	Total fixed costs (TFC) (2)	Total variable costs (TVC) (3)	Total costs (TC) (4) = (2) + (3)	Average fixed costs (AFC) (5) = (2) ÷ (1)	Average variable costs (AVC) (6) = (3) ÷ (1)	Average total costs (ATC) (7) = (4) ÷ (1)	Total costs (TC) (4)	Marginal cost (MC) (8) = Change in (4) / Change in (1)
0	£10.00	0	£10.00	—	—	—	£10.00	
								£5.00
1	10.00	£5.00	15.00	£10.00	£5.00	£15.00	£15.00	
								3.00
2	10.00	8.00	18.00	5.00	4.00	9.00	18.00	
								2.00
3	10.00	10.00	20.00	3.33	3.33	6.67	20.00	
								1.00
4	10.00	11.00	21.00	2.50	2.75	5.25	21.00	
								2.00
5	10.00	13.00	23.00	2.00	2.60	4.60	23.00	
								3.00
6	10.00	16.00	26.00	1.67	2.67	4.33	26.00	
								4.00
7	10.00	20.00	30.00	1.43	2.86	4.28	30.00	
								5.00
8	10.00	25.00	35.00	1.25	3.13	4.38	35.00	
								6.00
9	10.00	31.00	41.00	1.11	3.44	4.56	41.00	
								7.00
10	10.00	38.00	48.00	1.00	3.80	4.80	48.00	
								8.00
11	10.00	46.00	56.00	0.91	4.18	5.09	56.00	

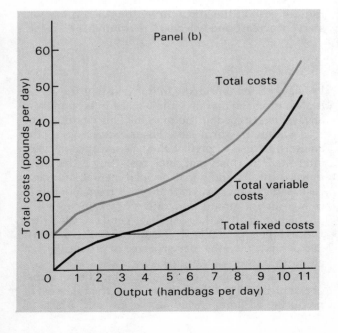

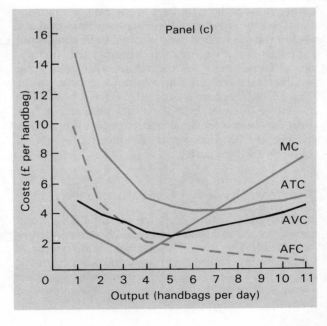

The Relationship between Average and Marginal Costs

There is always a definite relationship between averages and marginals. Consider the example of ten football players with an average weight of 200lb. An eleventh player is added. His weight is 250lb. That represents the marginal weight. What happens now to the average weight of the team? It must increase. Thus, when the marginal player weighs more than the average, the average must increase. Likewise, if the marginal player weighs less than 200lb, the average weight will decrease.

There is a similar relationship between average variable costs and marginal costs. When marginal costs are less than average costs, the latter are falling. Conversely, when marginal costs are greater than average costs, the latter are rising. When you think about it, the relationship is obvious. The only way for average variable costs to fall is for the extra cost of the marginal unit produced to be less than the average variable cost of all the preceding units. For example, if the average variable cost for two units of production is £4 a unit, the only way for the average variable cost of three units to fall is for the variable costs attributable to the last unit – the marginal cost – to be less than the average of the past units. In this particular case, if average variable costs falls to *£3.33 a unit*, then total variable cost for the three units would be three times £3.33, or (to round it off) £10. Total variable cost for two units is two times £4, or £8. The marginal cost is therefore £10 minus £8, or £2, which is less than the average variable cost of £3.33.

A similar type of computation can be carried out for rising average variable costs. The only way for average variable costs to rise is for the average variable cost of additional units to be more than that for units already produced. This incremental cost is the marginal cost. Therefore, in this particular case, the marginal costs have to be higher than the average variable costs.

There is also a relationship between marginal costs and average total costs. Remember that average total cost is equal to total cost divided by the number of units produced. Remember also that marginal cost does not include any fixed costs. Fixed costs are, by definition, fixed and cannot influence marginal costs. The above example can be repeated substituting the term *average total cost* for the term *average variable cost*.

In other words, the marginal cost curve is uniquely related to both the average total cost curve and the average variable cost curve because marginal cost is defined as the *change* in total cost. As we increase production, fixed costs do not change. Therefore, the average total cost curve is changing because of a change in variable costs. This means that the preceding discussion can be applied in terms of the relationship between marginal costs and average total costs. In other words, when marginal costs are less than either average total costs or average variable costs, the latter two are falling. Conversely, when marginal costs are greater than either average total costs or average variable costs, the latter two are rising. Finally, marginal costs will equal both average total costs and average variable costs at their respective minimum points. These rising and falling relationships can be seen in Figure 22.4. You can also see there that MC intersects AVC and ATC at their respective minimum points.

Finding Minimum Costs

At what rate of output of leather handbags per day does our representative firm experience the minimum average total costs? Column 7 in panel (a) of Figure 22.4 shows that the minimum average total cost is £4.28, which occurs at an output rate of seven leather handbags per day. We can find this minimum cost also

---

Key Points 22.3

▶ **Remember the short run is that period of time during which the firm cannot alter its existing plant size.**

▶ **Total costs equal total fixed costs plus total variable costs.**

▶ **Fixed costs are those that do not vary with the rate of production; variable costs are those that do vary with the rate of production.**

▶ **Average total costs equal total costs divided by output, or ATC = TC ÷ Q.**

▶ **Average variable costs equal total variable costs divided by output, or AVC = TVC ÷ Q.**

▶ **Average fixed costs equal total fixed costs divided by output, or AFC = TFC ÷ Q.**

▶ **Marginal cost equals the change in total cost divided by the change in output.**

▶ **The marginal cost curve intersects the minimum point of the average total cost curve and the minimum point of the average variable cost curve.**

by finding the point in panel (c) of Figure 22.4 at which the marginal cost curve intersects the average total cost curve. This should not be surprising. When marginal cost is below average total cost, average total cost falls. When marginal cost is above average total cost, average total cost rises. At the point where average total costs are neither falling nor rising, marginal cost must then be equal to average total cost. When we represent this graphically, the marginal cost curve will intersect the average total cost curve at its minimum.

The same analysis applies to the intersection of the marginal cost curve and the average variable cost curve. When are average variable costs at a minimum? According to panel (a) of Figure 22.4 average variable costs are at a minimum of £2.60 at an output rate of five leather handbags per day. This is exactly where the marginal cost curve intersects the average variable cost curve in panel (c) of Figure 22.4. (Key Points 22.3.)

Long-run Cost Curves

The long run, as you will remember, is defined as a time-period during which *full* adjustment can be made to any change in the economic environment. That is, *in the long run, all factors of production are variable.* For example, in the long run the firm can alter its plant size. Consequently, there may be many short-run curves as a firm develops over the years but only one long run. Long-run curves are sometimes called planning curves, and the long run may be regarded as the **planning horizon**.

We start out our analysis of long-run cost curves by considering a single firm contemplating the construction of a single plant. The firm has, let us say, three alternative plant sizes from which to choose on the planning horizon. Each particular plant size generates its own short-run average total cost curve. Now that we are talking about the difference between long- and short-run cost curves, we will label all short-run curves with an *S*; short-run average (total) costs will be labelled SAC, and all long-run average cost curves will be labelled LAC.

Look at Figure 22.5(a). Here we have shown three short-run average cost curves for three plant sizes that are successively larger. Which is the optimal plant size to build? That depends on the anticipated rate of output per unit time-period. Assume for a moment that the anticipated rate is Q_1. If plant size 1 is built, the average costs will be C_1. If plant size 2 is built, we see on SAC$_2$ that the average costs will be C_2, which is greater than C_1. Thus, if the anticipated rate of output is Q_1, the appropriate plant size is the one from which SAC$_1$ was derived.

Note, however, that if the anticipated permanent rate of output per unit time-period goes from Q_1 to Q_2, and plant size 1 had been decided upon, average costs would be C_4. However, if plant size 2 had been decided upon, average costs would be C_3 which are clearly less than C_4

Figure 22.5(a)

A Preferable Plant Size. If the anticipated permanent rate of output per unit time-period is Q_1, the optimal plant to build would be the one corresponding to SAC$_1$ because average costs are lower. However, if the rate of output increases to Q_2, it will be more profitable to have a plant size corresponding to SAC$_2$. Unit costs fall to C_3.

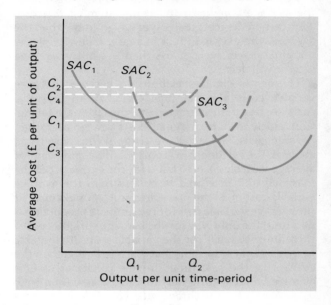

Figure 22.5(b)

Deriving the Long-run Average Cost Curve. If we draw all the possible short-run average cost curves that correspond to different plant sizes and then draw the envelope to these various curves, SAC$_1$ ... SAC$_8$, we obtain the long-run average cost curve, or the planning curve.

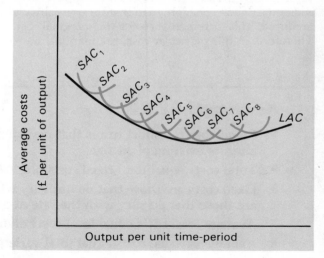

Long-run Average Cost Curve

If we make the further assumption that during the development of a firm the entrepreneur is faced with an infinite number of choices regarding plant size then we can conceive of an infinite number of SAC curves similar to the three in Figure 22.5(a). We are not able, of course, to draw an infinite number; we have drawn quite a few, however, in Figure 22.5(b).

By joining the minimum points of these various SAC curves we plot the long-run average cost curve (LAC). The long-run average cost curve, by result, represents the cheapest way to produce various levels of output, i.e. provided the entrepreneur is prepared to change the size and design of his plant. Consequently long-run average cost curves are sometimes referred to as **planning curves**.

Why the Long-run Average Cost Curve is U-Shaped

Notice that the long-run average cost curve, LAC in Figure 22.5(b) is U-shaped, similar to the U-shape of the short-run average cost curve developed previously in this chapter. The reason for the U-shape of the long-run average cost curve is not the same as that for the short-run U-shaped average cost curve. The short-run average cost curve is U-shaped because of the law of diminishing marginal returns. However, that law cannot apply to the long run, because in the long run all factors of production are variable, so there is no point of diminishing marginal returns since there is no fixed factor of production. Why, then, do we see the U-shape in the long-run average cost curve? The reasoning has to do with changes in the scale of operations. When the long-run average cost curve slopes downwards it means that average costs decrease as output increases. Whenever this happens the firm is experiencing **economies of scale**. If, on the other hand, the long-run average cost curve is sloping upwards, the firm is incurring increases in average costs as output increases. That firm is said to be experiencing **diseconomies of scale**. Finally, if long-run average costs are invariant to changes in output, the firm is experiencing **constant returns to scale**. In Figure 22.6, we show three panels (a), (b), and (c). The first one is for a firm experiencing economies of scale; the second one, constant returns to scale; and the third one, diseconomies of scale.

Reasons Why We See Economies of Scale

Here we list some of the reasons why a firm might be expected to experience economies of scale. Following Professor E. A. G. Robinson's approach we shall consider five possible categories.

TECHNICAL ECONOMIES
Large firms can take advantage of increased capacity machinery. For example, a double-decker bus can carry twice as many passengers as a single-decker bus. But the purchase costs and the running costs are not doubled. Similarly with boats and planes the larger the

Figure 22.6
Economies of Scale, Constant Returns to Scale, and Diseconomies of Scale. Long-run average cost curves will fall when there are economies of scale, as shown in panel (a). They will be constant when the firm is experiencing constant returns to scale, as shown in panel (b). And, finally, long-run average costs will rise when the firm is experiencing diseconomies of scale, as shown in panel (c).

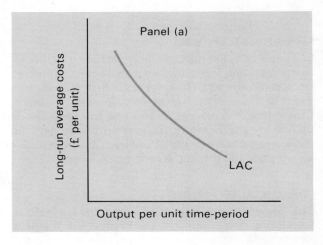

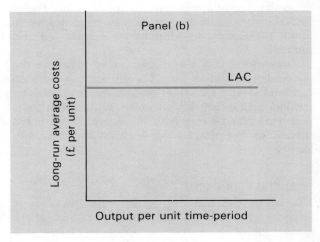

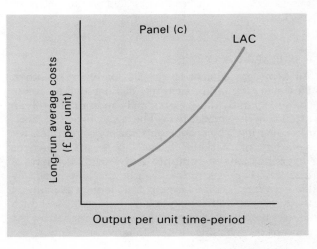

carrier the greater the saving. This economy is often linked to the principle of increased dimensions, because the volume of a sphere increases more than proportionately with its circumference. Consequently, as oil tankers and storage containers increase in size they become relatively cheaper to maintain and run. In fact a management consultancy agency once estimated that the day-to-day running costs of a 90 000-tonne oil tanker was £1 870 compared with £996 for a 30 000-tonne oil tanker. In short, the costs were barely doubled, while the capacity was trebled.

MANAGERIAL ECONOMIES

In a small firm the manager may perform the role of cost accountant, foreman, salesman, personnel officer, stock controller etc. However, as a firm increases in size it can take advantage of specialization of labour. Each managerial role can be allocated to a specialist in that field. Furthermore, bigger firms can buy in management services and afford large in-house salaries to entice and retain the best management.

COMMERCIAL ECONOMIES

The large firm can buy its raw materials in bulk at favourable rates. Similarly, the products of the firm can be sold in bulk with reduced costs. It is only necessary to pay a salesman marginally more wages for taking an order of 5 million units compared to 5 000; packaging and administration costs are also reduced.

Large firms can also afford to advertise in the national press and on TV. This can lead to some kind of brand loyalty for larger organizations where one product of the firm leads to sales of other products with that brand name. Much of Marks & Spencer's success, for example, is owed to this type of customer loyalty.

FINANCIAL ECONOMIES

The larger the firm the greater the number of financial advantages. The larger firm can negotiate loans from banks and related institutions easily and at favourable rates. Shares may be sold on the new issue market.

RISK-BEARING ECONOMIES

All firms are subject to risk at sometime or other. However, the larger firm has distinct advantages in this area. Firstly changes in supply and/or demand can often ruin the smaller firm. The larger firm, however, can cover itself by producing a variety of products for a variety of markets. These tactics are known as 'diversification of output' and 'diversification of markets'. For illustration, list the products made by Heinz, Walls, and/or Dunlop and identify as many of their market outlets as possible – an exercise which should help you to appreciate what is meant by the concept of 'diversification'. Similarly, one section of a

large conglomerate can lean on other parts of the company when developing or going through some irregular phase. For example, one bank branch may gain funds from another in the group. Finally, larger firms can afford to spend money on research and development. This type of expenditure can yield particularly high returns by securing footholds in tomorrow's market, whereas small firms face the risk of going out of business.

Why a Firm Might Experience Diseconomies of Scale

One of the basic reasons that the firm can expect to run into diseconomies of scale is that there are limits to the efficient functioning of management. Moreover, as more workers are hired, a more-than-proportionate increase in managers may be needed, and this could cause increased costs per unit. For example, it might be possible to hire from one to ten workers and give them each a shovel to dig ditches; however, as soon as ten workers are hired, it may also be necessary to hire an overseer to co-ordinate their ditch-digging efforts. Thus, perhaps constant returns to scale will remain until ten workers and ten shovels are employed; then decreasing returns to scale set in. As the layers of supervision grow, the costs of information and communication grow more than proportionately. Hence, the average per unit cost will start to increase.

A Final Note on Technical Jargon

The economies (listed above) are all *internal* to the firm. That is to say, they do not depend on what other firms are doing or what is happening in the economy. They are formally referred to as **internal economies (or diseconomies) of scale**. This phrase is necessary to distinguish them from **external economies** which arise through the growth of the whole *industry*.

EXTERNAL ECONOMIES OF SCALE

When expansion of a *whole industry* occurs *all* the comprising firms benefit. Firms can buy in services easier; firms can collude to fund research and/or training; firms often become more specialized; and a trade association and/or journal may be started. These developments normally lead to savings for *all* the firms involved.

Therefore it is possible to envisage a firm benefiting from internal and external economies of scale; the former being the direct result of internal company policy, and the latter the by-product of being a firm involved in an expanding industrial sector.

Key Points 22.4

► The long run is often called the planning horizon.
► The long-run average cost is the planning curve. It is found by drawing a line tangent to one point on a series of short-run average cost curves, each corresponding to a different plant size.
► The firm can experience economies of scale, diseconomies of scale, and constant returns to scale, all according to whether the long-run average cost curve slopes downwards, upwards, or is horizontal (flat). Economies of scale refer to what happens when all factors of production are increased.
► We can classify internal economies of scale into five sections: (i) managerial, (ii) commercial, (iii) financial, (iv) technical, and (v) risk-bearing.
► The firm may experience diseconomies of scale because of limits to the efficient functioning of management.
► Internal economies of scale arise from the growth of one firm, regardless of what is happening to other firms.
► External economies of scale relate to the whole industry.

CASE STUDY

Do Economies of Scale Make Musical Sense?

One way the big record companies cope with being out of touch musically is to pinch good new bands and ideas from the smaller rather more idealistic, independent labels.

Over the past ten years UB40, The Damned, Dire Straits, Motorhead, Ruby Turner and Adam Ant – to name but a few – have all been enticed away by the promise of larger cheques and limitless appearances on Top of the Pops.

'You can't blame the bands, but we're fed up acting as unpaid A & R men for the majors,' says Ian McNay, managing director of Cherry Red Records and a founder member of 'Umbrella', a new loose collection of indie labels which aims to keep its groups longer by offering them better deals and a better chance of hit singles. They are lobbying for more airtime, improving their distribution and adopting a much more pragmatic approach in the knowledge that if they fail the kind of adventurous

risk-taking music they stand for could be set back considerably.

Some things are looking bad for the indies. A hard core of about 70 labels (rising to 2000 if you count those eccentric individuals who release records from their bedrooms) account for 50 per cent of the weekly UK single releases, but their share of the market, never more than 9 per cent at their peak, has fallen to 4 per cent over the past three years. Sales of 4000 to 5000 are usually an excuse to throw a party.

Even so, quite how far this new commercial approach should go in defending members' ideals is already a source of some dispute within 'Umbrella'.

This was clear during the debate at last Monday's meeting about whether indie labels which use sales reps from the major companies should be considered independent at all.

That may seem a bit pedantic, but it's quite important for anyone

trying to drive an indie-shaped wedge into mainstream music since at present only the major companies have sufficient clout and personnel to ensure that all 500 shops used by the Gallup chart pollsters never run out of stock at vital moments.

Source: Colin Shearman, 'They'll do it their way', *The Guardian*, 19 May 1986.

Questions
1. What economic advantages do established record labels have over small independents? (Try to think of some specific examples.)
2. Is 'Umbrella' an example of an internal or external economy of scale?
3. What economic advantages may small independent labels have?
4. What do you think fixed costs would be like for companies producing records? (Try to incorporate some examples to illustrate your answer.)

CASE STUDY

How Does a Tax Affect a Firm's Cost Curves

Figure 22.7
The Effects of a Per-Unit Tax.
Here we change panel (a) of Figure 22.4 to take into account the effects of a tax on each unit produced. The government, for example, charges 20p per handbag to the handbag manufacturer. This changes the handbag manufacturer's cost curves. The average variable cost curve moves up to AVC_1. It moves up by the vertical distance equal to the amount of the tax. After all, the tax is on each unit of production. That means that the marginal cost curve will move up also. It moves from MC to MC_1. And finally, the average total curve, ATC, moves to ATC_1.

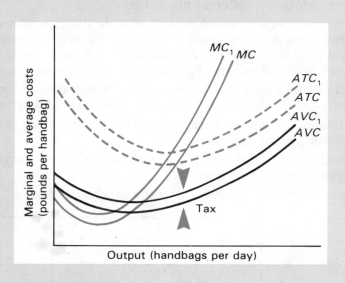

It might be useful at this point to show how to represent the effects of a tax on a firm. Let us talk about a tax on each unit of production. This will be a unit tax. It is not based on the value of the output, but rather on the mere fact that output is being produced. What do you think happens to all of those curves in Figure 22.4, panel (c) – which related to handbags – when a per unit tax is put on the production of handbags?

Let us ask ourselves what happens to fixed costs. The tax is incurred only if the firm produces handbags. If it produces nothing, it does not have to pay the tax. This means that fixed costs do not change; average fixed costs will remain the same also, so the AFC curve does not change. When it comes to the average variable costs, things do change. Each time a new unit is produced, the tax has to be paid. This means that the average variable cost curve will move up vertically by the amount of the tax. We show this in Figure 22.7. Since average variable cost moves up, so does the average total cost curve, and by the same amount.

What about marginal costs? Marginal costs will have to move up also. The marginal cost curve, up also. The marginal cost curve, MC, will move up vertically by the amount of the tax on each unit of production. After all, marginal cost is defined as the increment in costs. If the firm must pay a tax when it produces one more handbag, this means the marginal cost will go up by that tax also.

Questions
1. What would a lump-sum tax on each firm do to each firm's marginal cost curves?
2. How does a lump-sum tax affect the average fixed cost curve?

Exam Preparation and Practice

INTRODUCTORY EXERCISE

Data response and multiple choice questions often involve defining the various cost curves and/or their interrelationships. The following exercise, therefore, is designed to help students consolidate their understanding of these various business costs. The task is to copy and complete the 30 squares from the seven clues given.

Complete the table from the clues given below it

Output	Total Cost	Marginal Cost	Average Total Cost	Average Fixed Cost	Average Variable Cost	Total Variable Cost
2	±8	8			30	
3	)	28	-			
4			+2⁵			
5	258					
6				9		+100

CLUES

1. Average fixed cost for 6 units of output is £9.
2. Average variable cost for 2 units of output is £30.
3. Total cost is increased by £28 when the third unit of output is added.
4. Average total cost of 4 units of output is the same as the average total cost of 3 units of output.
5. Total cost for 5 units of output is £258.
6. Total variable cost is increased by £100 when the sixth unit of output is added.
7. Total cost increases by £8 when the second unit of output is added.

Source: Michael Seales, 'So you think you understand the theory of costs ...', *Economics* (Journal of the Economics Association) Vol XX, Part 4, No. 88.

MULTIPLE CHOICE QUESTIONS

1. If marginal cost is increasing
   A average cost must also be increasing
   B average cost must be greater than marginal cost
   C marginal cost must be equal to average cost
   D marginal cost must be greater than average cost
   E none of the above is necessarily true

2. The following table relates the total output and the total costs of a firm.

Output (units)	Costs (£)	Output (units)	Costs (£)
100	125	400	275
200	200	500	290
300	250		

The firm's production shows
A increasing returns throughout
B decreasing returns throughout
C increasing returns for output between 100 and 300 units and decreasing returns for output larger than 300 units
D decreasing returns for output between 100 and 300 units and increasing returns for output larger than 300 units
E constant returns throughout

3. Each curve in the diagram below describes the different combinations of capital and labour capable of producing the level of output indicated.

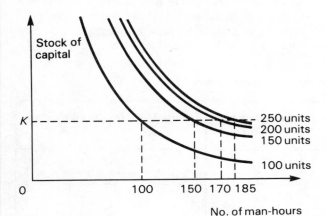

It may be deduced from the diagram that, with a fixed stock of capital, K, as output increases
A   the average product of capital diminishes
B   short-run average costs fall faster than long-run average costs
C   there are diseconomies of scale
D   the marginal product of labour is constant
E   the marginal product of labour increases

†4. In the table below, a firm producing 'widgets' displays its short-run total costs for differing levels of output.

Quantity of widgets	Short-run total costs (£)
0	1000
10	1200
20	1400
30	1600
40	1800

The variable cost per unit at an output of 20 is

A   £1000
B   £70
C   £400
D   £20
E   none of the above

5. An increase in the size of a manufacturing plant resulting in an increase in unit costs is an example of
A   internal diseconomies of scale
B   internal economies of scale
C   external diseconomies of scale
D   constant returns to scale

RELATED ESSAY QUESTIONS
1. What is normal profit? Explain why its level is likely to vary between industries.
2. Explain what is meant by economies of scale and how they arise. What factors are likely to determine the scale of production chosen by a firm?
3. How would you use the law of variable proportions to explain the theoretical shapes of a firm's cost curves?

23 Pricing and Output Decisions in Perfect Competition

Key Points to Review

▶ Demand (5.1)
▶ Supply, changes in supply versus changes in quantity supplied (5.6)
▶ Price elasticity of demand (7.3)

▶ Accounting and economic profits (22.1)
▶ Economies and diseconomies of scale (22.4)

Questions for Preview

1 What are the characteristics of the market structure of perfect competition?

2 How much will a perfect competitor produce in the short run?

3 What is the perfectly competitive firm's short-run supply curve?

4 Can a perfectly competitive firm earn economic profits?

5 Why is a perfectly competitive market structure considered to be economically efficient?

Firms have to know not only about costs, discussed in the last chapter, but also about revenues when they make pricing and output decisions. In order to understand, for example, the relationship between output, revenues, and price, a firm has to know the structure of the market, or industry, in which it is selling its product. There are various **market structures**, all dependent upon the extent to which buyers and sellers can assume that their own buying and selling decisions do not affect market price. At one extreme, when buyers and sellers indeed can correctly assume that they cannot affect market price, the market structure is one of **perfect competition** – the subject of this chapter. Whenever buyers and sellers must take into account how their individual actions affect market price, we are not in a market structure of perfect competition and have entered an *imperfectly competitive market*. We examine such markets in Chapters 24 and 25.

The Meaning of Competition

Economists use the term competition to mean two different things. In its most general sense, the term competition relates to a relatively relaxed view of the competitive process that focuses on the concept of rivalry among economic transactors. After all, in a world of scarce resources, there will be **rivalry** among sellers and among buyers. Behaviour among sellers where rivalry exists takes many forms: advertising, improvement in the quality of the product, sales promotion, development of new products, modification of old products, and so on. Rivalry among buyers also takes many forms: finding better deals, figuring out ways to take advantage of quantity discounts, offering a higher price to obtain a product that is in fixed supply, and so on. Rivalry is the real-world aspect of competition that is happening all around, because competition in the real world is a dynamic process.

The second use of the term competition is much more specific and well defined, for it relates to a particular model of market organization in which buyers and sellers do not and cannot affect the market price because there are so many of them. In this sense, competition means perfect competition. For the remainder of the chapter the term perfect competition will relate specifically to a particular market structure, the characteristics of which we will set out below.

The Characteristics of Perfect Competition as a Market Structure

In this chapter we are interested in studying how a firm acting within a perfectly competitive market structure makes decisions about how much to produce. Before we go ahead with this analysis, we want to give the characteristics of the market structure called perfect competition. These characteristics are:

1. The product that is sold by the firms in the industry is *homogeneous*. That means that the product sold by each firm in the industry is a perfect substitute for the product sold by each other firm. In other words, buyers are able to choose from a large number of sellers of a product that the buyers believe to be the same. The product is thus not in any sense differentiated as a result of whoever is the source of supply.
2. Any firm can enter or exit the industry without serious impediments. Resources must be able to move in and out of the industry without, for example, government legislation that prevents such resource mobility to occur.
3. There must be a large number of buyers and sellers. When this is the case, no one buyer or one seller has any influence on price, and also when there are large numbers of buyers and sellers, they will be acting independently.
4. There must be the fullest information available for both buyers and sellers about market prices, product quality and cost conditions.

Now that we have defined the characteristics of a perfectly competitive *market* structure we can consider the position of an individual constituent unit. We define a **perfectly competitive firm** as follows: it is one that is such a small part of the total industry in which it operates that it cannot significantly affect the price of the product in question. Since the perfectly competitive firm is a small part of the industry, that firm has no control over the price of the product. That means that each firm in the industry is a **price taker** – the firm takes price as given, as something that is determined *outside* the individual firm.

The price that is given to the firm is determined by the forces of market supply and market demand. That is to say, when all individual consumers' demands are added together into a market demand curve, and all

the supply schedules of individual firms are added together into a market supply curve, the intersection of those two curves will give the market price, which the purely competitive or price-taking firm must accept.

This definition of a competitive firm is obviously idealized, for in one sense the individual firm *has* to set prices. How can we ever have a situation where firms regard prices as set by forces outside their control? The answer is that even though every firm, by definition, sets its own prices, a firm in a perfectly competitive situation will find that it will eventually have no customers at all if it sets its price above the competitive price. Let us now see what the demand curve of an individual firm in a competitive industry looks like graphically.

Single-firm Demand Curve

In Chapter 7 we talked about the characteristics of demand schedules. We pointed out that for completely elastic demand curves, if the individual firm raises the price one penny, it will lose all its business. Well, this is how we characterize the demand schedule for a purely competitive firm – it is a horizontal line at the going market price. That is, it is completely elastic (see Chapter 7). And that going market price is determined by the market forces of supply and demand. Figure 23.1 is the hypothetical market demand schedule faced by an individual leather handbag producer who sells a

Figure 23.1
The Demand Curve for an Individual Leather Handbag Producer. We assume that the individual handbag producer is such a small part of the total market that he or she cannot influence the price. The firm accepts the price as given. At the going market price it faces a horizontal demand curve, *dd*. If it raises its price even one penny, it will sell no handbags. The firm would be foolish to lower its price below £5, because it can sell all that it can produce at a price of £5. The firm's demand curve is completely, or perfectly, elastic.

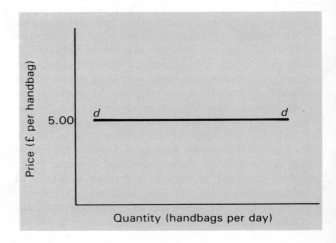

very, very small part of the total leather handbag production in the industry. At the market price, this firm can sell all the output it wants. At the market price of £5 each, which is where the horizontal demand curve for the individual producer lies, people's demand for the leather handbags of that one producer is perfectly elastic. If the firm raises its price, they will buy from some other producer. (Why not worry about lowering the price?) We label the individual producer's demand curve *dd*, whereas the market demand curve is always labelled *DD*.

How Much Does the Perfect Competitor Produce?

As we have shown, a perfect competitor has to accept the given price of the product. If the firm raises its price, it sells nothing. If it lowers its price, it makes less money per unit sold than it otherwise could. The firm has only one decision variable left: How much should it produce? We will apply our model of the firm to this question to come up with an answer. We shall use the *profit maximization* model and assume that firms, whether competitive or monopolistic, will attempt to maximize their total profits, that is, the positive difference between total revenues and total costs.

Total Revenues

Every firm has to consider its **total revenues**. Total revenues are defined as the quantity sold multiplied by the price. (They are also the same as total receipts from the sale of output.) The perfect competitor must take the price as given.

Look at panel (a) of Figure 23.2. Much of the information comes from panel (a) of Figure 22.4, but we have added some essential columns for our analysis. Column 3 is the market price of £5 per handbag, which is also equal to average revenue (AR), since

$$AR = \frac{TR}{Q} = \frac{P \times Q}{Q} = P$$

Column 4 shows the total revenues, or TR, as equal to the market price, *P*, times the total output in sales per day, or *Q*. Thus, TR = *P* × *Q*. We are assuming that the market supply and demand schedules intersect at a price of £5 and that this price holds for all the firm's production. We are also assuming that since our handbag maker is a small part of the market, it can sell all it produces at that price. Thus, panel (b) of Figure 23.2 shows the total revenue curve as a straight line. For every unit of sales, total revenue is increased by £5.

Total Costs

Revenues are only one side of the picture. Costs must also be considered. **Total costs** are given in column 2 in panel (a) of Figure 23.2. Notice that when we plot total costs on panel (b) the curve is not a straight line but rather a wavy line that is first above the total revenue curve, then below it, and then above it again. When the total cost curve is above the total revenue curve, the firm is experiencing losses. When it is below the total revenue curve, the firm is making profits. (When we refer to profits, we will always mean economic profits.)

Comparing Total Costs with Total Revenues

By comparing total costs with total revenues, we can figure out the number of leather handbags that the individual competitive firm should produce per day. Our analysis rests on the assumption that the firm will attempt to maximize total profits. In Figure 23.2(a) we see that total profits reach a maximum at a production rate of between seven and eight leather handbags per day. We can see this graphically in Figure 23.2(b). The firm will maximize profits at that place on the graph where the total revenue curve exceeds the total cost curve by the greatest amount. That occurs at a rate of output and sales of either seven or eight handbags per day; this rate is called the **profit-maximizing rate of production**.

We can also find this profit-maximizing rate of production for the individual competitive firm by looking at marginal revenues and marginal costs.

Using Marginal Analysis

Marginal cost was introduced in Chapter 22. It was defined as the change in total cost due to a one-unit change in production. This leaves only **marginal revenue** to be defined.

Marginal Revenue

What amount can our individual handbag-making firm hope to receive each time it sells an additional (marginal) leather handbag? Since the firm is such a small part of the market and cannot influence the price, it must accept the price determined by the market forces of supply and demand. Therefore, the firm knows it will receive £5 for every handbag it sells in the market. So the additional revenue the firm will receive from selling one more handbag is equal to the market price of £5; marginal revenue, in this case, equals price.

Marginal revenue presents the increment in total revenues attributable to producing one additional unit of the product in question. Marginal revenue is also defined as the change in total revenue resulting from a one-unit change in output. Hence, a more formal definition of marginal revenue is:

$$\text{marginal revenue} = \frac{\text{change in total revenue}}{\text{change in output}}$$

Total output and sales per day (1)	Total cost (TC) (2)	Market price (P) (3)	Total revenue (TR) (4) = (3) × (1)	Total profit = (TR) − (TC) (5) = (4) − (2)	Average total cost (ATC) (6) = (2) ÷ (1)	Average variable cost (AVC)* (7)	Marginal cost (MC) (8) = $\frac{\text{Change in (2)}}{\text{Change in (1)}}$	Marginal revenue (MR) (9) = $\frac{\text{Change in (4)}}{\text{Change in (1)}}$
0	£10.00	£5.00	0	−£10.00	—	—		
							£5.00	£5.00
1	15.00	5.00	£ 5.00	− 10.00	£15.00	£5.00		
							3.00	5.00
2	18.00	5.00	10.00	− 8.00	9.00	4.00		
							2.00	5.00
3	20.00	5.00	15.00	− 5.00	6.67	3.33		
							1.00	5.00
4	21.00	5.00	20.00	− 1.00	5.25	2.75		
							2.00	5.00
5	23.00	5.00	25.00	2.00	4.60	2.60		
							3.00	5.00
6	26.00	5.00	30.00	4.00	4.33	2.67		
							4.00	5.00
7	30.00	5.00	35.00	5.00	4.28	2.86		
							5.00	5.00
8	35.00	5.00	40.00	5.00	4.38	3.12		
							6.00	5.00
9	41.00	5.00	45.00	4.00	4.56	3.44		
							7.00	5.00
10	48.00	5.00	50.00	2.00	4.80	3.80		
							8.00	5.00
11	56.00	5.00	55.00	− 1.00	5.09	4.18		

* Taken from Figure 22.4.

Figure 23.2(a)
The Costs of Production and the Revenues from the Sale of Output: Finding the Profit-maximization Rate of Output and Sales. Profit maximization occurs at a rate of sales of either seven or eight handbags per day.

Figure 23.2(b)
Finding Maximum Total Profits. Total revenues are represented by the straight line, showing that each handbag sells at £5. Total costs first exceed total revenues, then are less than total revenues, and then exceed them again. We find maximum profits where total revenues exceed total costs by the largest amount. This occurs at a rate of production and sales per day of seven or eight handbags.

Figure 23.2(c)
Profit Maximization Using Marginal Analysis. Profit maximization occurs where marginal revenue equals marginal cost. Marginal revenue is represented by the individual firm demand curve, *dd*, which is a horizontal line at £5. The marginal cost curve is represented by MC. It intersects the marginal revenue curve at a rate of output and sales of somewhere between seven and eight handbags per day.

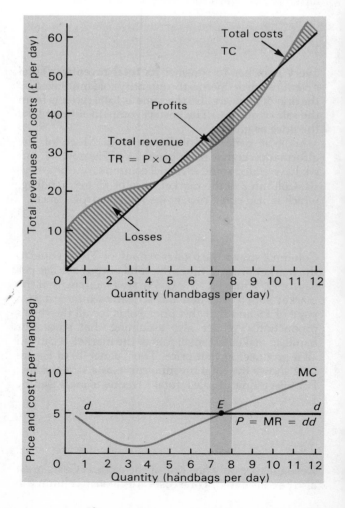

In a perfectly competitive market, the marginal revenue curve is exactly equivalent to the price line or, in other words, to the individual firm's demand curve, since the firm can sell all of its output (production) at the market price.

Thus, in Figure 23.1 the demand curve, *dd*, for the individual producer is at a price of £5 – the price line is coincident with the demand curve. But so, too, is the marginal revenue curve, for marginal revenue in this case also equals £5.

The marginal revenue curve for our competitive leather handbag producer is shown as a horizontal line at £5 in Figure 23.2(c). Notice again that the marginal revenue curve is equal to the price line, which is equal to the individual firm's demand curve, *dd*.

When Profits Are Maximized

Now we add the marginal cost curve, MC, taking from column 8 in Figure 23.2(a). As shown in Figure 23.2(c), the marginal cost curve first falls and then starts to rise, eventually intersecting the marginal revenue curve and then rising above it. Notice that the numbers for both the marginal cost schedule and the marginal revenue schedule in Figure 23.2(a) are printed *between* the figures that determine them. This indicates that we are looking at a change between one rate of output and the next.

In Figure 23.2(c), the marginal cost curve intersects the marginal revenue (or *dd*) curve somewhere between seven and eight handbags per day. Consider a rate of production that is less than that. At a production rate of, say, six handbags per day, marginal cost is clearly below marginal revenue. That is, the marginal cost curve at an output of six is below the marginal revenue curve at that output. Since it can receive £5 per handbag, and since marginal cost is less than this marginal revenue, the firm has an incentive to increase production. In fact, it has an incentive to produce and sell until the amount of the additional revenue received from selling one more handbag just equals the additional costs incurred from producing and selling that handbag. This is how it maximizes profit. Whenever marginal cost is less than marginal revenue, the firm will always make more profit by increasing production.

Now consider the possibility of producing at an output rate in excess of eight – say, at ten handbags per day. The marginal cost curve at that output rate is higher than the marginal revenue (or *dd*) curve. The individual producer would be spending more to produce that additional output than it would be receiving in revenues. The firm would be foolish to continue producing at this rate.

Where, then, should it produce? It should produce at point E, where the marginal cost curve intersects the marginal revenue curve from below. Since the firm knows it can sell all the handbags it wants at the going market price, marginal revenue from selling an additional handbag will always equal the market price. Consequently, the firm should continue production until the cost of increasing output by one more unit is just equal to the revenues obtainable from that extra unit. Profit maximization is always at the rate of output at which marginal revenue equals marginal cost. (To be strictly correct, we should add: 'and the MC curve cuts the MR curve from below'.)* For a perfectly competitive firm, this is at the intersection of the demand schedule, *dd*, and the marginal cost curve, MC. In our particular example, our profit-maximizing, perfectly competitive leather-handbag producer will produce at a rate of between seven and eight handbags a day.

Notice that this same profit-maximizing rate of output is shown in both Figure 23.2(b), where the total revenue and total cost curves are drawn and in Figure 23.2(c) where the marginal revenue and marginal cost curves are drawn. We can find the profit-maximizing output solution for the perfectly competitive firm by looking at either diagram.

Profits in the Short run

To find what our individual, competitive leather-handbag producer is making in terms of profits in the short run, we have to add the average total cost curve

---

* The marginal cost curve, MC, also cuts the marginal revenue curve (*dd*) from above at an output rate of less than one.

Key Points 23.1

▶ **A perfectly competitive firm is a price taker. It takes price as given. It can sell all that it wants at the existing market price.**

▶ **The demand curve facing a perfect competitor is a horizontal line at the going market price. The demand curve is also the perfect competitor's marginal revenue curve, since marginal revenue is defined as a change in total revenue due to a one-unit change in output.**

▶ **Profit is maximized at the rate of output where the positive difference between total revenues and total costs is the greatest. Using a marginal analysis, the perfectly competitive firm will produce at a rate of output where marginal revenue equals marginal cost. Marginal revenue, however, is equal to price. Therefore, the perfectly competitive firm produces at an output rate where marginal cost equals the price of the output.**

to Figure 23.2(c). We take the information from column 6 in Figure 23.2(a) and add it to Figure 23.2(c) to get Figure 23.3. Again, the profit-maximizing rate of output is between seven and eight handbags per day. If we have production and sales of seven handbags per day, total revenues will be £35 a day. Total costs will be £30 a day, leaving a profit of £5 a day. If the rate of output in sales is eight handbags per day, total revenues will be £40 and total costs will be £35, again leaving a profit of £5 a day.

Figure 23.3

Measuring Total Profits. The profit-maximizing rate of output and sales is where marginal revenue equals marginal cost. Profits are the difference between total revenues and total cost. Total revenues will equal the rate of output and sales times the market price of £5. Total costs will equal the quantity produced and sold multiplied by average total cost (ATC). Profits are represented by the shaded area.

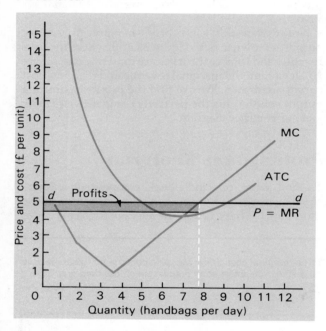

It is certainly possible, also, for the competitive firm to make short-run losses. We give an example in Figure 23.4. Here we show the firm's demand curve shifting from dd to $d'd'$. The going market price has fallen from £5 to £3 per handbag because of changes in market supply and/or demand conditions. The firm will always be better off by producing where marginal revenue equals marginal cost. We see in Figure 23.3 that the marginal revenue (or $d'd'$) curve intersects the marginal cost curve at an output rate of about 5½ handbags per day. The firm is clearly not making profits, because average total costs at that output rate are greater than the price of £3 per handbag. The losses are shown in the shaded area. Here, by producing where marginal revenue equals marginal cost, the firm is minimizing its losses.

Figure 23.4

Minimizing Short-run Losses. In cases where average total costs exceed the average revenue or price, profit maximization is equivalent to loss minimization. This again occurs where marginal cost equals marginal revenue. Losses are shown in the shaded area.

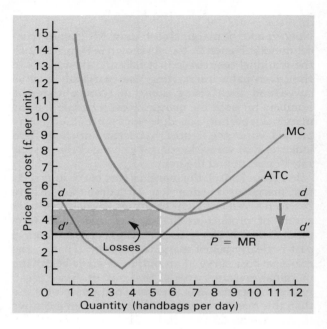

Closing down in the Short run

In Figure 23.4, the firm is making economic losses. Will it go out of business? Certainly in the long run it will, for the owners of the firm will not incur economic losses forever. But in the short run, the firm may not go out of business. So long as the loss from staying in business is less than the loss from going out of business, the firm will continue to produce. Now how can we tell when that is the case; that is, when sustaining economic losses in the short run is still worth while? We must compare the cost of staying in business (with losses) with the cost of closing down. The cost of staying in business in the short run is given by the average variable cost curve, or AVC. As long as average variable costs are covered by revenues ($P \times Q$), the firm is better off staying in business. In other words, if average unit variable costs are exceeded even a little by the price of the product, then staying in business produces something that can be applied towards covering fixed costs.

A simple example will demonstrate this situation. Let the price of a product be £8. Let average total costs equal £9 at an output of 100. In this hypothetical example, average total costs are broken up into average variable costs of £7 and average fixed costs of £2. Total revenues, then, equal £8 × £800, and total costs equal £9 × 100, or £900. Total losses therefore equal £100. However this does not mean the firm will shut down. After all, if it does shut down, it still has fixed costs to pay. And in this case, since average fixed costs equal £2 at an output of 100, the fixed costs are £200. Thus, the firm has losses of £100 if it continues to produce, but it has losses of £200 (the fixed costs) if it shuts down. The logic is fairly straightforward: As long as the price per unit sold exceeds the average variable cost per unit produced, the firm will be paying for at least part of the opportunity cost of capital invested in the business. Although the price is below average total cost and the firm is not making a normal or competitive rate of return on its investment, at least it is making *some* return. A small rate of return on an investment is better than no rate of return at all.

If the firm continues to sustain economic losses, it will not replace any capital. In the long run, capital becomes a variable input. The reason capital becomes variable is that the firm can decide how much it should purchase and replace, given a long enough time-period. In the long run, therefore, any cost associated with capital becomes a variable cost because the firm can decide how much it wants to purchase. Otherwise stated, in the long run, all costs are variable. Hence, in the above example, in the long run the firm will not be covering average variable costs and will therefore go out of business (if demand remains at *d'd'*).

The Short-run Break-even Point

Let us look at demand curve *dd* in Figure 23.5. It just touches the minimum point of the average total cost curve, which, as you will remember, is exactly where the marginal cost curve intersects the average total cost curve. At that price, which is about £4.30, the firm will be making exactly zero short-run economic profits. Thus, that particular price is called the short-run break-even price. And point *E* is therefore called the **short-run break-even point** for a competitive firm. It is the point at which marginal revenue = marginal cost = average total cost. The break-even price is the one that yields zero short-run profits or losses.

Calculating the Closing-down Point

In order to calculate the firm's shut-down point, we must add the average variable cost (AVC) to our graph. In Figure 23.5 we have taken the AVC curve from column 7 in Figure 23.2(a). For the moment, consider two possible demand curves, *dd* and *d'd'*, which are also the firm's respective marginal revenue curves. Therefore, if demand is *dd*, the firm will produce at *E*, where that curve intersects the marginal cost curve. If demand falls to *d'd'*, the firm will produce at *E'*. The special feature about the hypothetical demand curve *d'd'* is that it just touches the average variable cost curve at the latter's minimum point, which is where the marginal cost curve intersects it also. This price is labelled the short-run shut-down price. Why? Below this price the firm is paying out more in variable costs than it is receiving in revenues from the sale of its

Figure 23.5

Short-run Close-down and Break-even Prices. We can find the short-run break-even price and the short-run close-down price by comparing the price with average total costs and average variable costs. If the demand curve is *dd*, then profit maximization occurs at output *E*, where MC = marginal revenue (the *dd* curve). Since the ATC curve includes all relevant opportunity costs, point *E* is the short-run break-even point, and zero economic profits are being made. The firm is earning a normal rate of return. If the demand curve falls to *d'd'*, then profit maximization (loss minimization) occurs at the intersection of MC and MR (the *d'd'* curve) or *E'*. Below this price, it does not pay the firm to continue in operation, because its average variable costs are not covered by the price of the product.

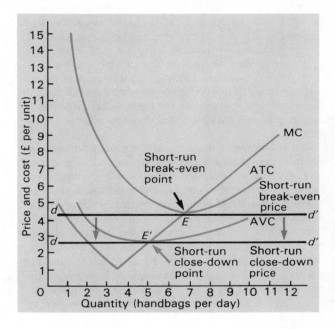

product. On each unit it sells, it is adding to its losses. Clearly, the way to avoid incurring these additional losses, if price falls below the closing-down point, is in fact to shut down operations. (Of course, if price falls below the short-run shut-down price, a firm may still continue in business in the short run if it decides it can afford to wait until the price moves up again, and it can profitably re-enter production.)

The intersection of the price line, the marginal cost curve, and the average variable cost is labelled *E'*. We called it the **short-run close-down point**. This point is labelled short run because, of course, in the long run, the firm will not produce below a price that yields a normal rate of return and, hence, zero economic profits.

THE MEANING OF ZERO ECONOMIC PROFITS

Perhaps the fact that we labelled point *E* in Figure 23.5 the break-even point may have puzzled you. At point *E*, price is just equal to average total cost. If this is the case, why would a firm continue to produce if it were making no profits whatsoever? If we again make the distinction between accounting profits and economic profits, then at that price the firm has zero economic profits but positive accounting profits.

Accounting versus Economic Profits Revisited

Think back to the last chapter when we discussed how an accountant must total up costs. The accountant adds up all of the expenses, subtracts them from all of the revenues, and calls the result profit. What is ignored is the reward offered to investors. Those who invest in the firm, whether they be proprietors or shareholders must anticipate a rate of return that is at least as great as could be earned in similar investments of equal risk. Looking at capital alone, we know that the cost of capital is its opportunity cost. Accountants, in conforming with tax laws, do not enter the opportunity cost of most of the capital involved as a cost of doing business. (Moreover, accountants do not have an exact figure on the opportunity cost of capital; therefore, it is appropriate for them to talk in terms of profits without making the distinction that we make here.)

In our analysis, the average total cost curve includes the full opportunity cost of capital. Indeed, the average total cost curve includes the opportunity cost of *all* factors of production used in the production process.

We have defined economic profits as those profits over and above what is required to keep capital in the firm. At the short-run break-even price, economic profits are, by definition, zero. However, accounting profits at that price are not equal to zero; they are positive. Let us consider an example different from the one used in Figure 23.5. A squash-racket manufacturer sells rackets at a particular price. The owners of the firm have invested only their own capital in the business: they have borrowed no money from anyone else. Moreover, assume that they explicitly pay the full opportunity cost to all factors of production, including any managerial labour that they themselves contribute to the business. In other words, they pay themselves salaries that show up as a cost in the books, and those salaries are equal to what they could have earned in the next-best alternative occupation. At the end of the year, the owners find that after they subtract all explicit costs from total revenues, they have earned £100 000. Let us say that their investment was £1 million. Thus, the rate of return on that investment is 10 per cent per year. We will assume that this turns out to be equal to the rate of return that, on average, all other squash-racket manufacturers make in the industry.

This £100 000, or 10 per cent rate of return, is actually, then, a competitive, or normal, rate of return on invested capital in that industry or in other industries with similar risks. If the owners had only made, say, £50 000, or 5 per cent on their investment, they would have been able to make higher profits by leaving the industry. Thus, we say that the 10 per cent rate of return is the opportunity cost of capital. The accountant shows it as a profit; we call it a cost. We also include that cost in the average total cost curve similar to the one shown in Figure 23.5. Thus, at the short-run break-even price, average total cost, including this opportunity cost of capital, will just equal that price. The firm will be making zero economic profits but a 10 per cent accounting rate of return.

Now we are ready to derive the firm's supply curve.

The Firm's Short-run Supply Curve

What does the supply curve for the individual firm look like? Actually, we have been looking at it all along. We know that when the price of handbags is £5, the firm will supply seven or eight handbags per day. If the price falls to £3, the firm will supply five or six handbags per day. And if the price falls below £3, the firm will shut down in the short run. Hence, in Figure 23.6 the firm's supply curve is the marginal cost curve above the short-run close-down point. This is shown as the heavily shaded part of the marginal cost curve. The definition, then, of the individual firm's supply curve in a competitive industry is its marginal cost curve equal to and above the point of intersection with the average variable cost curve.

Figure 23.6
The Individual Firm's Short-run Supply Curve. The individual firm's supply curve is that portion of its marginal cost curve above the average variable cost curve.

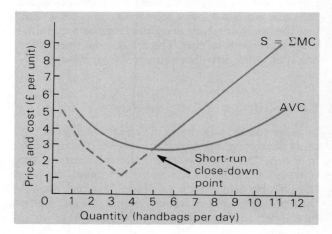

The Industry Short-run Supply Curve

Now let us see what the market supply curve, or the supply curve for the entire industry, looks like. First, what is an industry? Isn't it merely a collection of firms producing a particular product? Yes, and therefore we have a way to figure out the total supply curve of, for example, leather handbags. To do this, we merely add, for every possible price, the quantitites that each firm will supply. In other words, we *horizontally* sum the individual supply curves of all the competitive firms. But the individual supply curves, as we just saw, are simply the marginal cost curves of each firm. Consider doing this for a hypothetical world in which there are only two handbag producers in the industry, firm A and firm B. These two firms' marginal cost curves are given in panels (a) and (b) of Figure 23.7. The marginal cost curves for the two separate firms are presented as MC^a in panel (a) and MC^b in panel (b). Those two marginal cost curves are drawn only for prices above the minimum average variable cost for each respective firm. Hence, we are not including any of the section of the marginal cost curves below minimum average variable cost. In panel (a) for firm A at price P_1, the quantity supplied would be q_1^a. At price P_2, the quantity supplied would be q_2^a. In panel (b), we see the two different quantities corresponding to those two prices that would be supplied by firm B. Now we horizontally add for price P_1 the quantity of q_1^a and q_2^a. This gives us one point, F, for our **industry supply curve**, SS. We obtain the other point, G, by doing the same horizontal adding of quantities at P_2. When we connect points F and G, we obtain industry supply curve SS, which is

also market as Σ (the summation sign) MC, or horizontal summation of the marginal cost curves (above the respective minimum average variable cost of each firm).

Factors that Influence the Supply Curve

As you have just seen, the industry supply curve is the horizontal summation of all of the individual firms' supply curves above their respective minimum average variable cost points. That means that anything that affects the marginal cost curves of the firm will influence the industry supply curve. Therefore, the individual factors that will influence the supply function in a competitive industry can be summarized as those factors that affect the individual marginal cost curves, such as changes in factor costs – the wages paid to employees and the prices of raw materials. Changes in productivity on the part of the individual firm, taxes, and anything else that would influence the individual firm's marginal cost curves also determine the industry supply curve.

All of these are non-price determinants of supply. Since they affect the position of the marginal cost curve for the individual firm, they indeed affect the position of the industry supply curve. A change in any of the above-mentioned non-price determinants of supply will shift the market supply curve. Thus, once we are given the market demand curve in the perfectly competitive industry, if we know there has been a shift in a non-price determinant of the market supply curve, we can predict what will happen to the equilibrium price and quantity of the product being produced by the perfectly competitive industry.

Figure 23.7
Deriving the Industry Supply Curve. We assume there are only two firms in this industry. Marginal cost curves above average minimum variable cost are presented in panels (a) and (b) for firms A and B. We horizontally sum the two quantities supplied, q_1^a and q_1^b at price P_1. This gives us point F. We do the same thing for the quantities at price P_2. This gives us point G. When we connect those two points, we have the industry supply curve, SS, which is the horizontal summation of the firms' marginal cost curves above their respective average minimum costs.

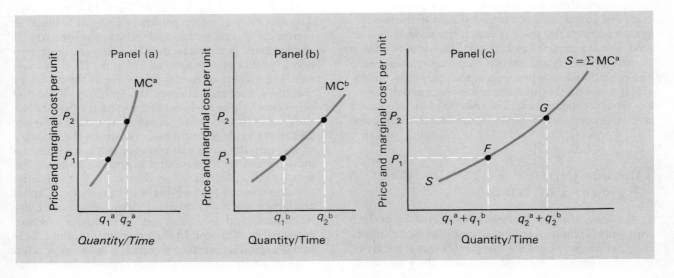

> ## Key Points 23.2
>
> ▶ Short-run profits and losses are determined by comparing average total costs with price at the profit-maximizing rate of output. In the short run, the perfectly competitive firm can make economic profits or economic losses.
>
> ▶ The competitive firm's short-run break-even output occurs at the minimum point on its average total cost curve, which is where the marginal cost curve intersects the average total cost curve.
>
> ▶ The competitive firm's short-run shut-down output is at the minimum point on its average variable cost curve, which is also where the marginal cost curve intersects the average variable cost curve. Close-down will occur if price falls below average variable cost.
>
> ▶ The firm will continue production at a price that exceeds average variable costs even though the full opportunity cost of capital is not being met; at least some revenues are going towards paying some rate of return to capital.
>
> ▶ At the short-run break-even price, the firm is making zero economic profits, which means that it is just making a normal rate of return in that industry.
>
> ▶ The firm's short-run supply curve is that section of its marginal cost curve equal to or above minimum average variable costs.
>
> ▶ The industry short-run supply curve is a horizontal summation of the individual firms' marginal cost curves above their respective minimum average variable costs.

Competitive Price Determination

How is the market, or 'going', price established in a competitive market? This price is established by the interaction of all the firms and all the demanders. The market demand schedule DD in Figure 23.8(a) represents the demand schedule for the entire industry, and the supply schedule SS represents the supply schedule for the entire industry. Price P_e is established by the forces of supply and demand at the intersection of SS and DD. Even though each individual firm has no control or effect on the price of its product in a competitive industry, the interaction of *all* the producers determines the price at which the product will be sold. We say that the price P_e and the quantity Q_e in Figure 23.8(a) constitute the competitive solution to the pricing/quantity problem in that particular industry. It is the equilibrium where suppliers and demanders are both maximizing. The resulting individual firm demand curve dd is shown in Figure 23.8(b) at the price P_e.

The Long-run Industry Situation – Exit and Entry

In the long run, we surmise that firms in perfect competition will tend to have average total cost curves that just touch the price = marginal revenue curve, or individual demand curve dd. That is, in the long run in

a competitive situation, firms will be making zero economic profits. How does this occur? It is through an adjustment process that depends on economic profits and losses. In Chapter 6 we referred to changes in demand and technological progress having the effect of changing prices and profits, signalling resource owners about where their resources should flow. Now we can be more precise about this process.

Exit and Entry of Firms

Go back and look at Figures 23.3 and 23.4 (page 334). The existence of either profits or losses is a signal to owners of capital within and outside the industry. If the industry is characterized by firms showing economic profits as represented in Figure 23.3, this will signal to owners of capital elsewhere in the economy that they, too, should enter this industry. If, on the other hand, there are firms in the industry that are like those suffering economic losses represented in Figure 23.4, this signals resource owners outside the industry to stay out. It also signals resource owners within the industry not to reinvest and if possible to leave the industry. It is in this sense that we say that profits direct resources to their highest-valued use. Capital and labour will flow into industries where profitability is highest, and will flow out of industries where profitability is lowest. In the price system, the allocation of capital is therefore directed by relative expected rates of return on investment. It should be noted that

Figure 23.8(a)

The Industry Demand and Supply Curves. The industry demand curve is a representation of the demand curve for all potential consumers. It is represented by *DD*. The industry supply curve is the horizontal summation of all those sections of the marginal cost curves of the individual firms above their respective minimum average variable cost points. We show it as *SS* and mark it as equal to Σ MC. The intersection of the demand and supply curves at *E* determines the equilibrium or market price at P_e.

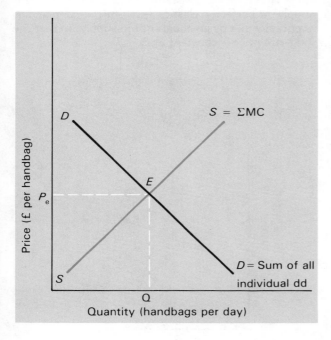

Figure 23.8(b)

Individual Firm Demand Curve. The individual firm demand curve is set at the going market price determined in Figure 23.8(a). That is, the demand curve facing the individual firm is a horizontal line, *dd*, at price P_e.

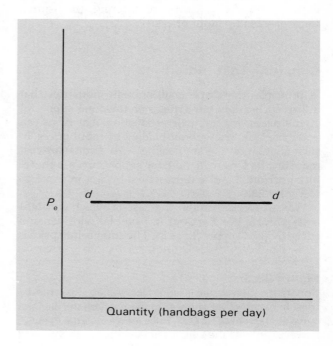

when resources are immobile the signalling mechanism becomes ineffective.

In addition, when we say that in a competitive long-run equilibrium situation firms will be making zero economic profits, we must realize that at a particular point in time it would be pure coincidence for a firm to be making *exactly* zero economic profits. Real-world information is not as exact as the curves we use to simplify our analysis. Things change all the time in a dynamic world, and firms, even in a very competitive situation, may, for many reasons, not be making exactly zero economic profits. Remember, in any event, that the concept of long-run zero economic profits in a competitive industry is a long-run concept. We say that there is a *tendency* towards that equilibrium position, but firms are adjusting all the time to changes in their cost curves and in their (horizontal) *dd* curve.

Long-run Supply Curves

In Figure 23.8(a), we drew the summation of all of the portions of the individual firm's marginal cost curve above each firm's respective minimum average variable costs as the upward-sloping supply curve of the

entire industry. We should be aware, however, that a relatively steep upward-sloping supply curve may only be appropriate in the short run. After all, one of the prerequisites for a competitive industry is that there be no restrictions on entry. We expect, therefore, that if the consumer demand schedule shifts out to the right (there is increased demand for the product in question), eventually more firms will enter the market so that the quantity supplied can also be expanded. In fact, each time the demand curve shifts to the right, the price can be expected to rise, other things being constant. But this means positive economic profits for the current producers. Therefore, existing firms will expand, and more producers will enter the market, thus eventually forcing the price down to its old equilibrium level, assuming costs in the industry remain constant.

Remember our definition of the long run is one in which adjustments can be made. Our definition of the **long-run industry supply curve** is a supply curve showing the relationship between quantity supplied by the entire industry at different prices after firms have been allowed to either enter or exit from the industry, depending on whether there have been positive or negative economic profits. The long-run industry supply curve is drawn under the assumption that entry and exit have been completed.

There are three possible types of long-run industry supply curves, depending on whether input costs stay

---

constant, increase, or decrease. What is at issue here is the effect on input prices of a change in the number of firms in the industry. In the last chapter, we assumed that input prices remained constant to the firm, no matter what the firm's rate of output was. When looking at the entire industry, that assumption may not be correct if, for example, when all firms are expanding and new firms are entering, they simultaneously bid up input prices.

Constant-cost Industries

In principle, there are small enough industries that utilize such a low percentage of the total supply of inputs necessary for their production that firms can enter the industry without bidding up input prices. In such a situation we are dealing with a **constant-cost industry**. Its long-run industry supply curve is therefore horizontal and is represented by $S_L S_L$ in panel (a) of Figure 23.9.

We can work through the case in which constant costs prevail. We start out in panel (a) with demand curve DD and supply curve SS. The equilibrium price is P_e. There is a rightward shift in market demand to $D'D'$. In the short run, the supply curve remains stable. The equilibrium price rises to P_e. This generates positive economic profits for existing firms in the industry. Such economic profits induce capital to flow into the industry. The existing firms expand and/or new firms enter. The supply curve shifts out to $S'S'$. The new intersection with the new demand curve is at E''. The new equilibrium price is again P_e. The long-run supply curve is obtained by connecting the intersections of the corresponding pairs of demand and supply curves, E and E''. It is labelled $S_L S_L$ and is horizontal. Its slope is zero. In a constant-cost industry, long-run supply is perfectly elastic. Any shift in demand is eventually met by an equal shift in supply, so that the long-run price is constant at P_e.

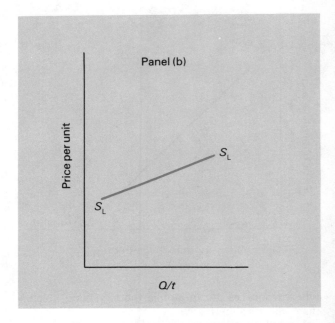

Panel (b)

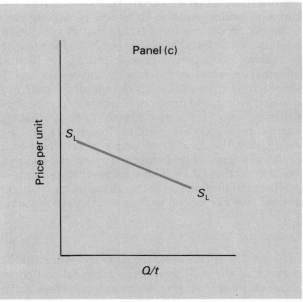

Figure 23.9

Constant-, Increasing-, and Decreasing-cost Industries. In panel (a), we show a situation where the demand curve shifts from DD to $D'D'$. Price increases from P_e to P_e'; however, in time the supply curve shifts out to $S'S'$, and the new equilibrium shifts from E to E''. The market-clearing price is, again, P_e. If we connect points such as E and E'', we come up with the long-run supply curve $S_L S_L$. This is a constant-cost industry. In panel (b), costs are increasing for the industry, and therefore the long-run supply curve is upward sloping; in panel (c), costs are decreasing for the industry as it expands, and therefore the long-run supply curve is downward sloping.

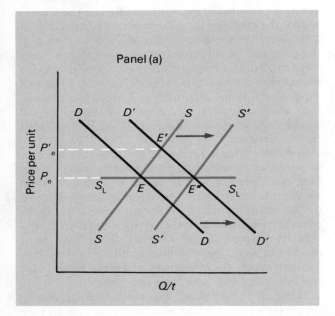

Panel (a)

Increasing-cost Industries

In an **increasing-cost industry**, expansion by existing firms and the addition of new firms causes the price of inputs within that industry to be bid up. As costs of production rise, short-run supply curves (each firm's marginal cost curve) shift inwards to the left. The result is a long-run industry supply curve that is upward-sloping and is represented by $S_L S_L$ in panel (b) of Figure 23.9.

Decreasing-cost Industries

It is possible that an expansion in the number of firms in an industry leads to a reduction in input costs. When this occurs, the long-run industry supply curve will be downward-sloping. An example is given in panel (c) of Figure 23.9. This is a **decreasing-cost industry**.

Industry-wide Economies and Diseconomies of Scale

An industry can be other than constant-cost if there are industry-wide economies or diseconomies of scale. If there are industry-wide economies of scale, the long-run supply curve shown in panel (c) of Figure 23.9 would result. If there are industry-wide diseconomies of scale, the upward-sloping long-run industry supply curve, as presented in panel (b) of Figure 23.9, would result. The concept of economies and diseconomies of scale at the *firm* level was introduced in Chapter 22. Economies and diseconomies of scale at the firm level resulted from factors *internal* to each separate firm.

Industry-wide economies of scale concern themselves with changes in input prices that are *external* to each individual firm. Industry-wide economies of scale occur when an increase in the output of the entire industry (not just one firm) allows suppliers to the industry to engage in increased specialization or innovative activities, which help to lower the unit costs of inputs to that industry. Take an example. One firm starts a business in a small residential area that has been set aside for offices and light industrial activity. This firm has photocopying needs but not enough to justify the purchase of its own equipment. The firm must take its originals to be photocopied some distance away. If, on the other hand, many firms move into the same area, it may become profitable for a specialist photocopying firm to start business. There will at least be a reduction for the original firm in the time cost of having its photocopying done because it will not have to go so far. Additionally, the new photocopying firm may be able to use large, lower-cost-per-unit machines, which will additionally lower the monetary outlay involved in getting photocopies. The result will be a downward-sloping long-run industry supply curve, as represented in panel (c) of Figure 23.9.

Industry-wide diseconomies of scale occur when input prices rise because the expansion in the industry puts pressure on all the suppliers to the industry. No individual firm has control over this phenomenon. It is all firms taken together that cause the input prices to rise. In such a situation, industry-wide diseconomies of scale will cause an upward-sloping long-run industry supply curve, similar to the one depicted in panel (b) of Figure 23.9.

Long-run Industry Response: What if Demand is Declining or Increasing?

One of the reasons we attempt to develop a model of a market structure is to predict what will happen when there are changes in the economy. Figure 23.9 can be used to predict what will happen when there are changes in a perfectly competitive industry.

In the case of increasing demand, we first need to determine whether we are dealing with a constant, increasing, or decreasing-cost industry. Once we have determined that, we can then tell what will happen to price as industry demand increases. The simplest case is when we are dealing with a constant-cost perfectly competitive industry. This situation is, in fact, depicted in panel (a) of Figure 23.9. An increase in industry demand leads to a larger output being sold in the long run at a constant price, P_e. If, however, we are dealing with an increasing-cost industry, increasing demand will, in the long run, lead to increased production and also an increased price. Finally, if we are dealing with a decreasing-cost industry, in the long run, an increase in demand will lead to an increase in output and a *decrease* in price.

Our predictions can be made in a similar fashion if we are dealing with a declining, perfectly competitive industry – one in which market demand is falling. If we are dealing with a constant-cost perfectly competitive industry, then in the long run, output will be reduced but price will remain constant at P_e, as in panel (a) of Figure 23.9. If we are dealing with an increasing-cost industry, a decline in industry demand will eventually lead to a reduction in output and a *reduction* in price. And, finally, if we are dealing with a decreasing-cost industry, a reduction in market demand will lead to a long-run reduction in output and an *increase* in price.

The Perfectly Competitive Firm in Long-run Equilibrium

In the long run, the firm can change the scale of its plant. In the long run, the firm will adjust plant size in such a way that it has no further incentive to change. It will do so until profits are maximized. Figure 23.10 shows the long-run equilibrium of the perfectly competitive firm. Long-run average costs are at a minimum and so too are short-run average costs. Price is set equal to both marginal costs and minimum average costs. In other words, the long-run equilibrium position is where 'everything is equal', which is

Figure 23.10

Long-run Firm Competitive Equilibrium. In the long run, the firm operates where price equals marginal revenue equals marginal cost equals short-run minimum average cost equals long-run minimum average cost, or, where 'everything is equal'. This is given at point E.

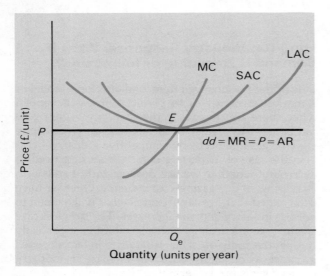

at point E in Figure 23.10. There, *price* equals *marginal revenue* equals *marginal cost* equals *average cost* (minimum, short run, and long run).

Perfect Competition and Minimum Average Total Cost

Look again at Figure 23.10. In the long-run equilibrium, the perfectly competitive firm finds itself producing at output rate q_e. At that rate of output, the price is just equal to the minimum long-run average cost as well as the minimum short-run average cost. In this sense, perfect competition results in no 'waste' in the production system. Goods and services are produced using the least costly combination of resources. This is an important attribute of a perfectly competitive long-run equilibrium, particularly when we wish to compare the market structure of perfect competition with other market structures that are less than perfectly competitive. We examine these other market structures in Chapters 24 and 25.

Competitive Pricing Equals Marginal Cost Pricing

In a perfectly competitive industry, each firm produces where its marginal cost curve intersects its marginal revenue (or *dd*) curve from below. Thus, perfectly competitive firms always sell their goods at a price that just equals marginal cost. For many economists, this represents a 'desirable' pricing situation because the price that consumers pay just reflects the opportunity

cost to society of producing the good. In order to understand this, consider what marginal cost represents. It represents the cost of changing production by one incremental unit. Suppose a marginal cost curve shows that an increase in production from 10 000 leather handbags to 10 001 leather handbags will cost £1.50. That £1.50 represents the *opportunity cost* to society of producing one more leather handbag. Thus, the marginal cost curve gives a graphic representation of the opportunity cost of production.

The competitive firm produces up to the point where the market price just equals the marginal cost. Herein lies the element of the 'desirability' of a competitive solution. It is called **marginal cost pricing**. The competitive firm sells its product at a price that just equals the cost to society – that is, the opportunity cost – for that is what the marginal cost curve represents.

When an individual pays a price equal to the marginal cost of production, then the cost to the user of that product is equal to the sacrifice or cost to society of producing that quantity of that good as opposed to more of some other good. (We are assuming that *all marginal social* costs are accounted for.) The competitive solution, then, is called *efficient*. It is efficient in the economic sense of the word. Economic efficiency means that it is impossible to increase the output of any good without lowering the total *value* of the output produced in the economy. No juggling of resources, such as labour and capital, will result in an output that is higher in value than the value of the goods and services already being produced. In an efficient situation, it is impossible to make one person better off without making someone else worse off. All resources are used in the most advantageous way possible. All goods and services are sold at their opportunity cost, and marginal cost pricing prevails throughout.

Is Perfect Competition Possible?

The analytic model presented here represents a situation that, by definition, can never be seen in reality. Perfect competition can exist only if information is also perfect. After all, the only way for a price to be uniform at every moment in time (corrected for quality changes and transportation costs) is for everybody to know what is happening everywhere at every moment in time. Obviously, information is never perfect. In fact, the cost of trying to achieve perfect information would be prohibitive and therefore undesirable.

A profit-maximizing firm will produce at the point where the additional revenues obtained from producing more goods exactly cover the additional costs incurred (where marginal revenue equals marginal cost). Similarly, if we are concerned to maximize the state of market information we would never spend more than we get in return for improving information flows. We would improve information in the market-place only up to the point where the value of doing so is equal to the marginal cost. That is certainly at a point well below *perfect* information.

A purely competitive industry has been defined as one with many sellers. To satisfy the criterion of perfect competition where each seller has *no* control whatsoever over the price of his or her product, we would have to have a tremendous number of firms. Free entry into an industry would have to be possible and firms operating with constant returns to scale production functions. However, in the real world we quickly observe that the number of firms is not large and therefore individually each firm has – at least in the short run – some control over its price. But analyzing the industry in the long run, we might say that it was *tending* toward a competitive solution all the time because there were a sufficient number of firms *on the margin* attempting to increase their total sales by undercutting the other firms. Notice we said that the industry might tend toward a competitive solution at all times. That is a *dynamic* process – which is to say that it operates through time and never ends. At any time,

an investigation of the particular industry would reveal that the industry was tending toward a competitive solution, but the industry would probably never reach that point.

Even if an industry is not perfectly competitive, it does not necessarily follow that steps should be taken to make it more competitive so as to ensure efficiency. After all, it is not possible to change an industry's structure from non-competitive to competitive without using resources. We will discuss some of the ways of doing this, such as legislation against restrictive business practices and regulation of non-competitive industries in Chapter 30.

The fact that we use the model of perfect competition in economic analysis does not mean that perfect competition is accepted as the only type of industry structure to be tolerated. It is, as you should have recognized throughout this chapter, a theoretical abstraction. But it does provide us with a reference point in considering the use of scarce resources as we have seen in discussing the 'desirability' of marginal cost pricing.

Key Points 23.3

▶ The competitive price is determined by the intersection of the market demand curve with the market supply curve; the market supply curve is equal to the horizontal summation of those sections of the individual marginal cost curves above their respective minimum average variable costs.

▶ In the long run, competitive firms make zero economic profits because of entry and exit of firms into and out of the industry whenever there are industry-wide economic profits or economic losses.

▶ Economic profits and losses are signals to resource owners.

▶ A constant-cost industry will have a horizontal long-run supply curve. An increasing-cost industry will have a rising long-run supply curve. A decreasing-cost industry will have a falling long-run supply curve.

▶ In the long run, a competitive firm produces where price equals marginal revenue equals marginal cost equals short-run minimum average cost equals long-run minimum average cost.

▶ Competitive pricing is essentially marginal cost pricing, and therefore the competitive solution is called efficient because marginal cost represents the social opportunity cost of producing one more unit of a good; when consumers are faced with a price equal to the full opportunity cost of the product they are buying, their purchasing decisions will lead to an efficient use of available resources.

CASE STUDY

Lead Astray

The Snailbeach Company worked a vein of ore in West Shropshire which was once described as being one of the most productive in Europe per acre of ground. The company first took its lease on the vein in 1783 and continued to work it without interruption until 1912. It illustrates how a firm, working in a perfect market, responded to external and internal factors in an industry traditionally unstable and noted for its high-risk element. Before analysing the behaviour of the firm it is worth while to outline the essential feature of lead-mining which made for a perfect market.

Firstly, there were a large number of firms which ranged from fairly large joint-stock companies operating in Cornwall and Wales, to small partnerships of miners operating in all regions, and the further back in time one went, the smaller and more numerous became the firms. In the early years of the eighteenth century most mines worked were in effect little more than shallow holes in the ground. Enterprises of this kind were active in all the major lead-producing areas of the country – Derbyshire, the Mendips, the North Pennines, North Wales, and West Shropshire. Similar partnerships had worked tin in Cornwall from earliest times. The produce of the mines, in the form of concentrated ore, was sold at markets which were held at regular intervals in a wide number of centres. The normal method of sale was for the company or partnership to put a small sample of their ore into the market, and having inspected it buyers would then make offers for the complete lot. The price of the

lead was, therefore, determined by 'the market' thus satisfying the second condition of perfect competition in that the firm had no control over the price at which its produce was sold. In times of scarcity the price of lead was high, and in times of surplus, or of demand deficiency, it fell. In consequence the price of lead exerted an enormous influence over the whole structure of the industry, determining profits, wages, and the opening up and closing down of marginal enterprises. This perfect market for lead was the framework within which the British lead-mining industry worked throughout the eighteenth and nineteenth centuries.

At the end of the Napoleonic Wars the Snailbeach Company was in a sound position. The general price increases which had occurred during that time prompted increased output which was sold at prices averaging around £12 per ton. Prices fell slightly after the wars but the continuation of industrialization and urbanization maintained a buoyant market for lead throughout the country although short price recessions accounted for many casualties among the more marginal enterprises. From the records it appears that the Snailbeach Company was looking for a profit of around £2 per ton of ore, and if the price of lead increased it increased output accordingly, at the same time increasing wages. If the price of lead fell it reduced output and reduced wages.

By the 1860s improved mining techniques allowed increased output from fewer workers and

profits began to rise. At the same time large deposits of lead were beginning to be exploited in Australia, Mexico, and North America, and were paying handsome returns to their shareholders. Demand also increased to such an extent that, in the early 1860s a shortage of ore occurred. These conditions were highly conducive to creating a major boom in this country and one of the results was the setting up of many 'bubble' companies, several of which worked the West Shropshire orefield. The Snailbeach Company itself was reconstituted in 1867 as a joint-stock company, though it did not become public. By the middle of the 1870s there were over fifteen companies working this orefield.

As mining techniques had improved during the eighteenth century the presence of the small partnership became less and less practical since only larger enterprises organized as joint-stock companies had sufficient funds to pay for the equipping of mines with steam-engines for drainage and crushing of ores, and to expend large sums of money on such things as sinking shafts and driving drainage adits, none of which paid immediate returns. But although the companies needed to raise large sums of money for working the mines, they did not create assets of an equal sum, since most of the money was spent on labour costs in making wider, deeper, and longer holes in the ground. Only a small proportion of the total capital involved in floating the company actually created physical assets – usually at the surface and consisting of pumping-engines and crushing-plant together with their housing buildings. The fixed costs of the company were very small, whereas the variable costs were high. Most of the mining companies purchased machinery either out of revenue or by drawing on capital and did not set aside sums for depreciation. Therefore, when looking for a fixed cost element which, in the long run, determined shut-down if total costs exceeded total revenue, one is hard pressed to find one. There was one cost, however, which could be regarded as fixed, and this was the cost of keeping the mine dry. If pumping stopped the mine flooded, and so we shall regard pumping costs as the main fixed cost even though it consisted of expenditure on fuels and labour.

After 1870 prices plummeted (see Figure 23.11) and by 1895 were hitting a low floor of around £7 per ton, by which time all the West Shropshire mines, with the sole exception of Snailbeach, had closed. The reason for the falling price of lead is generally held to be the increased supply into world markets from overseas sources, the success of which had originally started the boom. With falling

prices it was impossible for the majority of mines to stay profitable. The reaction of the company to the falling prices is interesting in that it chose to maintain average profit rather than total profits. With falling prices it abandoned the working of all but the most productive parts of the vein where ore could still be worked at a profit. In doing this the Snailbeach Company stood out in sharp contrast to most other mining enterprises, since the normal reaction, given falling prices, was to increase output in order to maintain total revenue. However, this action, taken independently by all companies, produced in aggregate an even greater supply which depressed the price still further and forced the mines into a position of regular losses and, inevitably, closure.

The Snailbeach Company did not cease production until 1912. By 1910 the shareholders were unwilling to spend any more money with little or no chance of profits and so in 1911 the giant Cornish engine, which had kept the mines dry was stopped and the mine allowed to flood to adit level.

Questions
1. Show by means of a supply and demand diagram how the price of ore changed in the latter part of the nineteenth century. Assume that the depression in the UK economy was reflected in the demand for lead.
2. What type of cost is critical to determining the close-down of a firm? In the case of the Snailbeach Company what is unusual about determining this cost?
3. Why would joint-stock mining firms wish to increase output as ore prices fell after 1870?
4. If the Snailbeach Company tried to maintain average profit rather than total profits how would this be shown with reference to a diagram? (Hint: the reference to average should point you towards considering average revenue and average cost.)
5. The company ceased to continue mining lead in 1912. What factors explain this situation?

Figure 23.11

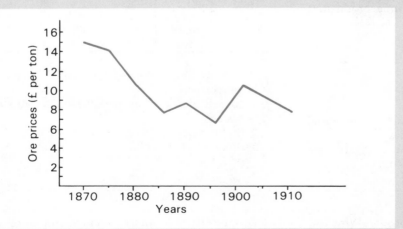

Source: F. Brook, 'Perfect Competition in the Lead Mining Industry – a nineteenth-century Case-study', *Economics* (Journal of the Economics Association), Vol. VIII, Pt. 5, no. 35, Autumn 1970, pp. 248–55.

Exam Preparation and Practice

INTRODUCTORY EXERCISE

1. Explain, with diagrams, what happens to the firm in a perfectly competitive industry when the demand curve shifts to the right. Assume that the firm is a producer of carrots which become more popular as a result of increased vegetarian diets!

MULTIPLE CHOICE QUESTIONS

†1. Which of the following statements regarding a firm in long run equilibrium operating under conditions of perfect competition is NOT correct?
A marginal cost is equal to marginal revenue
B average revenue is equal to marginal cost
C average revenue is equal to average cost
D price is equal to marginal revenue
E average variable cost is equal to marginal cost

†2. Which of the following is the most conclusive evidence that a firm is NOT in a perfectly competitive industry?
A marginal cost is below average cost
B average fixed cost is falling as output increases
C average variable cost is rising
D average revenue is above average cost
E marginal revenue is below average revenue

†3. Which of the following types of costs has to be covered for a firm to continue production in the short run?
A overhead
B fixed
C marginal
D total
E average variable

4. Which of the following is *not* an essential prerequisite of perfect competition?
A each buyer and seller must regard the market price as beyond his control

B buyers will have no incentive to restrict their purchases in order to drive down prices
C sellers will have no incentive to restrict output in order to maintain or increase prices
D the profits of each seller must be normal in the short run
E the demand for the product of any one firm must be perfectly elastic

5. A firm in a perfectly competitive market will necessarily have a
A perfectly elastic supply curve
B perfectly inelastic supply curve
C supply curve of unitary elasticity
D perfectly elastic demand curve
E perfectly inelastic demand curve

†6. If a profit-maximizing firm is operating under conditions of perfect competition, it can be predicted that in the short run
A there will be no incentive for other firms to enter the industry
B only normal profits will be earned
C average fixed costs will be constant
D price must equal minimum average total cost
E price will equal marginal cost

For Question 7 select your answers from the following grid:

A	B	C	D	E
1,2,3 all correct	1,2 only correct	2,3 only correct	1 only correct	3 only correct

7. Which of the following prevent(s) markets being perfect?
1 advertisers claiming special characteristics of goods
2 the number of producers being small
3 there is imperfect knowledge of products and prices

RELATED ESSAY QUESTIONS

1. What is meant by 'normal' profit? Why are profits normal in the long run under conditions of perfect competition?

†2. Discuss the relevance of average and marginal costs for the determination of prices in the short and in the long run.

24 Pricing and Output Decisions in Monopoly

Key Points to Review

▶ Total revenue and elasticity (7.2)
▶ Perfectly elastic demand (7.3)

▶ The long run (22.4)
▶ Perfect competition (23.1)

Questions for Preview

1 What is a monopolist, and how can a monopoly be formed?

2 For the monopolist, marginal revenue is less than selling price. Why?

3 What is the profit-maximizing rate of output for the monopolist?

4 What is the cost to society of monopoly?

The world, of course, does not consist of *perfectly* competitive industries. In this chapter, we will present a model of a monopoly business and discuss how a monopolist decides what prices to charge and how much to produce. Most of the analytical tools needed here have already been introduced. In the Case Study we will look at the creation of monopoly profits by restricting entry into the taxi-cab business.

Definition of a Monopolist

The word *monopoly* or *monopolist* probably brings to mind a business that takes undue advantage of the consumer, sells faulty products, gets rich, and any other bad thoughts that one can have about big business. If we are to succeed in analysing and predicting the behaviour of non-competitive firms, however, we will have to be somewhat more objective in defining a monopolist. Our definition of monopoly is one that will be as applicable to small businesses as it is to companies selling on a nation-wide basis. Thus, a **monopolist** is defined as a *single supplier* that constitutes the entire industry.

We must be careful in our definition of monopoly, for the more narrowly we define a product, the more easily we come up with a monopoly situation. Consider a small town with a single newspaper. By our definition of monopoly, the owner of the newspaper is a monopolist. He or she sells the only newspaper printed in the locality. What if we consider this product – the only local newspaper – as part of the news media industry? Do the owners of this newspaper have a monopoly in all news media? Certainly not, for they are in competition with radio, television, magazines, newspapers from nearby towns, as well as national newspapers. Thus the uniqueness about the monopolist is indeed one of degree and few monopolists are likely to face no competition at all.

As we shall see in this chapter, a seller prefers to have a monopoly rather than to face competition. In general, we think of monopoly prices as being higher than competitive prices, and of monopoly profits as being higher than competitive profits (which are, in the long run, merely equivalent to a normal rate of return). How does a firm obtain a monopoly in an industry? Basically, there must be **barriers to entry** that enable firms to receive monopoly profits in the long run. We define barriers to entry as those difficulties facing potential new competitors in an industry. What sort of difficulties might a new competitor face?

Barriers to Entry

For monopoly power to continue to exist in the long run, there has to be some way in which the market is closed to entry. Either legal means or certain aspects of the industry's technical or cost structure must somehow prevent entry. Below, we will discuss several of the barriers to entry that have allowed firms to reap monopoly profits in the long run.

Ownership of Resources without Close Substitutes

Preventing a newcomer from entering an industry is often difficult. Indeed, there are some economists who contend that no monopoly acting without government support has been able to prevent entry into the industry unless that monopoly has had the control of some 'essential' natural resource. Consider the possibility of one firm owning the entire supply of a raw material input that is essential to the production of a particular commodity. The exclusive ownership of such a vital resource serves as a barrier to entry until an alternative source of the raw material is found or an alternative technology not requiring the raw material in question is developed. A good example of control over a vital input is the Aluminum Company of America (Alcoa), a firm that prior to the Second World War controlled the world's bauxite, the essential raw material in the production of aluminium. (Such a situation is rare, though.)

Government Restrictions – Licences

In many industries it is illegal to enter without a licence provided by the government. For example, in the UK you could not operate an unlicensed postal service or radio service. In the US you cannot simply set up in business and supply electricity in competition with the existing supplier in an area. You would first have to obtain a 'certificate of convenience and public necessity' from the appropriate authority, which is usually the state's public utility commission. However, public utility commissions rarely, if ever, issue a certificate to a group of investors who want to compete directly in the same geographic area with an existing electric utility; hence, entry into the industry in a particular geographic area is prohibited, and long-run monopoly profits could conceivably be earned by the electric utility already serving the area.

It is necessary to obtain the equivalent of a certificate of convenience and public necessity in the case of the regional independent television service in the UK. The Independent Broadcasting Authority allots franchises and successful applicants to receive monopoly rights to the sale of TV advertising space in their areas for eight years. Since these franchises or licences are not granted very often, long-run monopoly profits can be earned by those firms already in the industry.

Historically, TV franchises have been very profitable to own. One franchise-holder described it as 'a licence to print money'!

Another example of a licence that creates a monopoly has to do with taxi-cabs. In many major cities, it is illegal to operate a taxi-cab without first having obtained a permit to do so. We discuss this example in the Case Study at the end of the chapter.

Patents

Closely related to the franchise required for entry is a patent. A patent is issued to an inventor to protect him or her from having the invention copied for a period of years. At the end of the patent period the patented invention is no longer private property but public property which anyone can copy or reproduce. Patents were first enacted in the UK as long ago as 1623 so as to encourage the process of invention by giving short-term reward for promoting scientific discovery. As one would expect patent owners jealously guard their interests and try to enforce their exclusive rights. If, in fact, the costs of enforcing a particular patent are greater than the benefits, the patent may not bestow any monopoly profits on its owner – the policing costs are then too high.

Problem in Raising Adequate Capital

Certain industries require a large initial capital investment. The firms already in the industry can, according to some economists, obtain monopoly profits in the long run because no competitors can raise the large amount of capital needed to enter the industry. This is the 'imperfect' capital market argument employed to explain long-run, relatively high rates of return in certain industries. These industries generally are ones in which large fixed costs must be incurred in order merely to start production. Their fixed costs generally are for expensive machines necessary in the production process.

Certainly, it is more difficult, at any given level of risk, to raise a larger rather than a smaller amount of capital. But a sufficiently high-risk premium can presumably be added to the anticipated rate of return from investing in the risky industry to enable a newcomer to raise the needed capital. It may be, of course, that the anticipated rate of return offered to investors in such an industry would have to be so high that it would not be profitable for an entrepreneur to undertake entry into the industry. It is not clear why such a situation is called an imperfect capital market or why it should be considered a barrier to entry any more than any other high-risk premium, but it often is.

Economies of Scale

Sometimes it is not profitable for more than one firm to exist in an industry. Such a situation may arise

---

because of a phenomenon we have already discussed known as economies of scale. When economies of scale exist, costs increase less than proportionately to the increase in output. If the long-run average cost curve continues to fall as output increases then a situation of *natural monopoly* might arise. The first firm that is established is able to enjoy very low average costs per unit. If it charges a price that reflects this favourable cost situation then no rival firm can threaten its position. It is sure not to be undercut and thus is assured of being a monopolist. We examine the natural monopoly case further in Chapter 29 and how governments face up to the questions of whether such monopolies should be privately owned and left free to fix prices as the monopolists see fit. We must now examine how a monopolist determines how much output to produce and what price to charge, assuming, as in Chapter 23, that the aim is to maximize profits.

The Demand Curve Facing a Monopolist

How does a monopolist determine how much to produce? To answer this question let us briefly recap on the situation for the firm in perfect competition. You will recall that a competitive firm has a horizontal demand curve. That is, the competitive firm is such a small part of the market that it cannot influence the price of its product. It is a *price taker*. Each time production is changed by one unit, total revenue changes by the going price, and price is always the same. Marginal revenue never changes; it always equals price, or average revenue. Average revenue is total revenue divided by quantity demanded, or:

$$\text{average revenue} = \frac{\text{TR}}{Q} = \frac{P \times Q}{Q} = P$$

Monopolists' Marginal Revenue

What about a monopoly firm? Since a monopoly is the entire industry, the monopoly firm faces the entire market demand curve. The market demand curve is downward sloping, just like the others that we have seen. Therefore, in order to sell more of a particular product given the industry demand curve, the monopoly firm must lower the price. Thus, the monopoly firm moves *down* the demand curve. If all buyers are to be charged the same price, the monopoly must lower the price on all units sold in order to sell more. It cannot just lower the price on the last unit sold in any given time-period in order to sell a larger quantity.

Imagine that you are a monopoly ferry-boat owner. Assume that you have a government-granted legal franchise, and no one else can compete with you in operating a service ferry between two islands. If you are charging, say, £1 per crossing, there will be a certain quantity demanded of your services. Suppose that you are ferrying 100 people a day each way at that price. If you decide that you would like to ferry more individuals, you must lower your price to all individuals – you must move *down* the existing demand curve for ferrying services. In order to calculate the marginal revenue of your change in price, you must first calculate the total revenues you received at £1 per passenger per crossing, and then calculate the total revenues you would receive at, say, 90p per passenger per crossing.

The only way the monopolist can increase sales is by getting consumers to spend more of their incomes on the monopolist's product and less on all other products combined. Thus, the monopolist is constrained by the entire market demand curve for its product. We see this in Figure 24.1 which compares the perfect competitor's and monopolist's demand curves.

Here we see the fundamental difference between the monopolist and the firm in perfect competition. The latter does not have to worry about lowering prices to sell more. In a purely competitive situation, the competitive firm sells such a small part of the market that it can sell its entire output, whatever that may be, at the same price. The monopolist cannot. The more the monopolist wants to sell, the lower the price it has to charge on the last unit (and on *all* units put on the market for sale). Obviously, the extra revenues the monopolist receives from selling one more unit are going to be smaller than the extra revenues received from selling the next-to-last unit. The monopolist has to lower the price on the last unit to sell it because it is facing a downward-sloping demand curve. The only way to move down the demand curve is to lower the price.

Figure 24.1
Comparison of the Perfect Competitor's and the
Monopolist's Demand Curves. The perfect competitor
faces a horizontal demand curve *dd* in panel (a). The
monopolist faces the entire industry demand curve in
panel (b), and it is downward sloping.

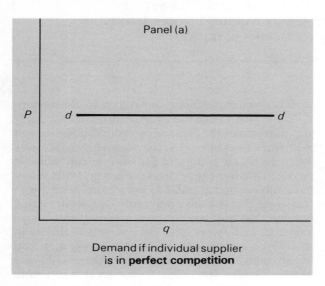

Demand if individual supplier
is in **perfect competition**

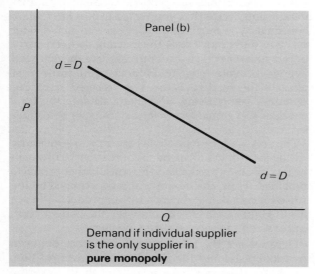

Demand if individual supplier
is the only supplier in
pure monopoly

The monopolist's marginal revenue therefore is
going to be falling. But it falls even more than one
might think, because to sell one more unit the
monopolist has to lower the price on *all* previous units,
not just on the last unit produced and sold. This is
because information flows freely; the monopolist will
not usually be able to charge one consumer £2 and
another consumer £3 for the same item. The consumer who could buy the product for £2 would buy lots
of it and resell it to the one who was willing to pay £3
for a price of, say, £2.50. Unless the monopolist is
successful in somehow separating *discriminating*
between the different markets to prevent secondary
transactions among the consumers in those markets,

it will have to sell all goods at a uniform price. (We
examine this possibility of discriminatory pricing later
in the chapter but for the moment we assume a
common price is charged to all buyers.) Therefore,
when a monopolist increases production, he must
charge a lower price on the last unit *and on all previous
units*.

The Monopolist's Marginal Revenue is less than Price

An essential point in the above discussion is that for
the monopolist marginal revenue is always less than
price. To understand why, look at Figure 24.2. Here
we show a unit increase in sales due to a reduction in
the price of, say, handbags from P_1 to P_2. After all, the
only way that sales can increase, given a downward-
sloping demand curve, is for price to fall. The price P_2
is the price received for the last unit. Thus, that price
P_2 times the last unit sold represents what is received
from the last unit sold. That would be equal to the
horizontally shaded column showing the effects of a
one-unit increase in sales. The area of the horizontally
shaded column is one unit wide times P_2.

But the price times the last unit sold is not the
addition to total revenues received from selling that
last unit. Why? Because price was reduced on all
previous units sold (OQ) in order to sell the larger
quantity $Q + 1$. The reduction in price is represented
by the vertical distance from P_1 to P_2 on the vertical
axis. We must therefore subtract the vertically gridded
row from the horizontally shaded column in order to
come up with the *change* in total revenues due to a one-
unit increase in sales. Clearly, the change in total
revenues, i.e. marginal revenue, must be less than
price, because marginal revenue is always the difference between the two shaded areas in Figure 24.2.

Elasticity and Total Revenues

The monopolist faces a downward-sloping demand
curve. That means that it cannot charge just *any* price
(a common misconception) because, depending on the
price charged, a different quantity will be demanded.
In other words, there is a unique relationship between
the price the monopolist charges and total revenues,
which equal price times quantity. Thus, there is a
relationship between the total revenues and the price
elasticity of the demand curve. We have already
discussed this relationship, but it is worth going over
again briefly. The demand curve of a monopolist has
varying elasticities, depending on where we are on the
demand curve. Remember that a straight-line demand
curve has a price elasticity of demand that goes from
infinity to zero as we move down the demand curve.
(Thus, it is *not* true that a monopolist faces an inelastic
demand curve.)

We earlier defined a monopolist as the single seller
of a specific good or service with no *close* substitutes.

Figure 24.2

Marginal Revenue is always Less than Price. The only way to sell one more unit when facing a downward-sloping demand curve is to lower the price. The price received for the last unit is equal to P_2. The revenues received from selling this last unit are equal to P_2 times one unit, or the area of the horizontally shaded vertical column. However, if a single price is being charged for all units, total revenues do not go up by the amount of the area represented by that column. The price had to be reduced on all the previous OQ units that were being sold at price P_1. Thus, we must subtract the vertically lined area [the rectangle $(P_1 - P_2)$ high and OQ wide] from the horizontally lined area in order to derive marginal revenue. Marginal revenue is therefore always less than price.

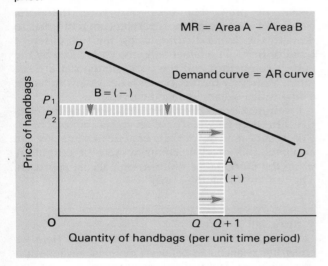

That does not mean, however, that the demand curve facing a monopoly is vertical, or exhibits zero-price elasticity of demand. (Indeed, as we shall see below, the profit-maximizing monopolist will *never* operate in a price range in which demand is inelastic.) After all,

consumers have limited incomes and alternative wants. The downward slope of a monopolist's demand curve occurs because individuals compare the marginal satisfaction they will receive to the cost of the commodity to be purchased. Take the example of telephone service. Assume that there is absolutely no substitute whatsoever for telephone service. The market demand curve will still slope downwards. At lower prices, people will add more phones and separate lines for different family members.

Additionally, the demand curve for telephone service slopes downwards because there are at least several *imperfect* substitutes, such as letters, telexes, and for some persons even CB radios. Thus, even though we defined a monopolist as a single seller of a commodity with no *close* substitutes, we can talk about the range of *imperfect* substitutes. The more such imperfect substitutes there are, the more elastic will be the demand curve facing the monopolist, all other things held constant.

We can see the relationship now between the price elasticity of demand for a monopolist, marginal revenue, and total revenues. This relationship is presented in Figure 24.3 (a) and (b). At point A' on the demand schedule, the point corresponding to zero marginal revenues, we have marked $e_d = -1$. That is, the elasticity of demand is such that a change in price elicits a proportional and opposite change in quantity demanded. That portion of the demand schedule to the right of point A' we have labelled *inelastic*. That is, to the right of point A', a change in price elicits a proportionately smaller change in quantity demanded. That portion of the demand curve to the left and above point A' (above price P_m) we have labelled *elastic*. This means that to the left of A' a change in price will cause a proportionately larger change in quantity demanded.

We show the relationship between elasticity and total revenue graphically in Figure 24.5(b). Obviously, total revenues are zero at a zero price and at P_{max} where no units are sold. Between these points, total revenues rise and then fall. The maximum revenue is

Key Points 24.2

▶ The demand curve facing a monopolist is downward sloping by definition.

▶ The monopolist must consider the marginal revenue curve, where marginal revenue is defined as the change in total revenues due to a one-unit change in quantity sold.

▶ For the perfect competitor, price equals marginal revenue equals average revenue. For the monopolist, price is always greater than marginal revenue. Otherwise stated, for the monopolist, marginal revenue is always less than price because of the downward slope of the demand curve.

▶ The price elasticity of demand facing the monopolist depends on the number and closeness of substitutes. The more numerous and the closer the substitutes, the greater the price elasticity of demand of the monopolist's demand curve.

▶ The monopolist will never produce on the inelastic portion of its demand curve.

where the elasticity of demand is unity, as shown in Figure 24.3(b).

Costs and Monopoly Profit Maximization

In order to find out at what rate of output the perfect competitor would be maximizing profits, we had to add cost data. We will do the same thing now for the monopolist. We assume profit maximization is the goal of the pure monopolist, just as we assumed it was the goal of the perfect competitor. With the perfect competitor, however, we had only to decide on the profit-maximizing rate of output, because price was given. The competitor is a price taker. For the pure monopolist, we must seek a profit-maximizing *price–output combination*. The monopolist is a *price maker*. We can determine the profit-maximizing price–output combination in either of two ways: by looking at total revenues and total costs, or by looking at marginal

revenues and marginal costs. Both approaches are given here.

Total Revenue–Total Costs Approach

We show hypothetical demand (rate of output and price per unit), revenues, costs, and so on in Figure 24.4(a). In column 3 we see total revenues for our hypothetical monopolist, and in column 4 we see total costs. We can transfer these two columns to Figure 24.4(b). The only difference between this total revenue and total cost diagram (Figure 24.4(b)) and the one we showed for a perfect competitor in the last chapter is that the total revenue line is no longer straight. Rather, it curves. For any given demand curve, in order to sell more, the monopolist must lower the price. The basic difference, therefore, between a monopolist and a perfect competitor has to do with the demand curve facing the two different types of firms. Fundamentally, the costs faced by the perfect competitor and the pure monopolist are the same. Monopoly market power is derived from facing a downward-sloping demand curve.

Profit maximization involves maximizing the positive difference between total revenues and total costs. This occurs at an output rate of about 4 units. We can also find this profit-maximizing rate of output by using the marginal revenue–marginal cost approach. The results will be the same.

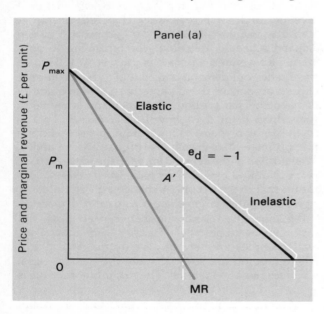

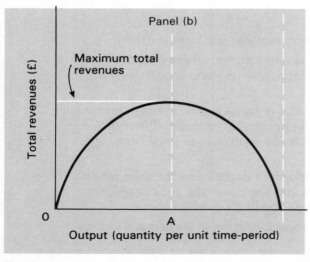

Figure 24.3(a)

Elasticity of Demand and Total Revenues. Here we show the relationship between marginal revenue, the demand curve, and the elasticity of demand. From the point where marginal revenue equals zero – that is, point A' – demand is inelastic to the right and below, and elastic to the left and above. At point A', demand has unitary elasticity, or equals –1. To the right, the monopolist would find that if it lowered price, the quantity demanded would increase less than proportionally. To the left of A' as it raised price, the quantity demanded would fall more than proportionally.

Figure 24.3(b)

Total Revenues and the Demand Curve. Here we show the relationship between the demand curve, elasticity of demand, and total revenue. When the price is set at P_{max} in Figure 24.3(a), the total revenues are, of course, zero. When the price is set at zero, total revenues are also zero. In between these two ends of the price possibilities scale, we will find some price that maximizes total revenues. That price happens to be where marginal revenue equals zero, or at point A' in Figure 24.3(a). We have shown here that the maximum occurs at the output at which marginal revenue equals zero. If the monopolist had no variable costs at all, it would obviously want to produce at point A because that is where it would maximize its total revenues, which under *that* condition would maximize total profits.

Figure 24.4(a)
Monopoly Costs, Revenues, and Profits.

Rate of Output	Price per Unit	Total Revenue	Total Costs	Total Profit	Marginal Cost	Marginal Revenue
	£	£	£	£	£	£
0	31.50	0	10	–10		
					19	29
1	29.00	29.00	29	0		
					13	13
2	26.00	52.00	42	10.00		
					11	17
3	22.90	68.70	53	15.70		
					12	12
4	20.25	81.00	65	16.00		
					14	5.50
5	17.30	86.50	79	7.50		
					17	1.10
6	14.60	87.60	96	–8.40		
					20	–7.10
7	11.50	80.50	116	–35.50		
					22	–11.70
8	8.60	68.80	138	–69.20		
					24	–16.60
9	5.80	52.20	162	–109.80		

Figure 24.4(b)
Profit Maximization: The TR-TC Approach. The mono-polist maximizes profits where the positive difference between TR and TC is greatest. This is at an output rate of 4 units. Notice the difference between the TR curve here and the one shown in the last chapter for a perfect competitor. This one is curved to reflect a downward-sloping linear demand curve.

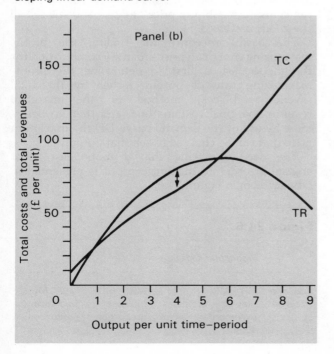

Figure 24.4(c)
Profit Maximization: The MR-MC Approach. Profit maximization occurs where marginal revenue equals marginal cost. This is at an output rate of 4 units. (Also, the MC curve must cut the MR curve from below.)

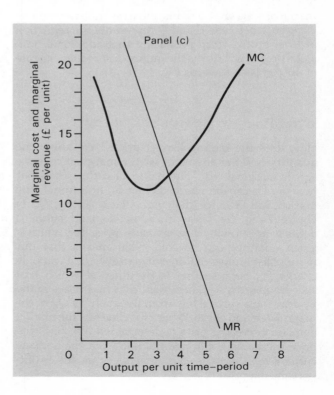

Marginal Revenue–Marginal Cost Approach

Profit maximization will also occur where marginal revenue equals marginal cost. This is as true for a monopolist as it is for a perfect competitor (but the monopolist will charge a higher price). When we transfer marginal cost to marginal revenue information from columns 6 and 7 in Figure 24.4(a) to Figure 24.4(c), we see that marginal revenue equals marginal cost at an output rate of about 4 units. Profit maximization occurs at the same output in Figure 24.4(b).

If the monopolist goes past the point where marginal revenue equals marginal cost (4 units of output), marginal cost will exceed marginal revenue. That is, the incremental cost of producing any more units will exceed the incremental revenue. It would not be worth while, as was true also in perfect competition. On the other hand, if the monopolist produces less than that, then it is not making maximum profits. Look at output rate Q_1 in Figure 24.5. Here the monopolist's marginal revenue is at A, but marginal cost is at B. Marginal revenue exceeds marginal cost on the last unit sold; the profit for that *particular* unit Q_1 is equal to the vertical difference between A and B, or the difference between marginal revenue and marginal cost. The monopolist would be foolish to stop at output rate Q_1 because if output is expanded, the marginal revenue will still exceed marginal cost and therefore total profits will rise. In fact, the profit-maximizing monopolist will continue to expand output and sales until marginal revenue equals marginal cost, which is at output rate Q_m. The monopolist will not produce at rate Q_2 because here we see that marginal costs are C and marginal revenues are D. The difference between C and D represents the reduction in total profits from producing that additional unit. Total profits will rise as the monopolist reduces its rate of output back towards Q_m.

What Price to Charge for Output?

How does the monopolist set prices? We know the quantity is set at the point where marginal revenue equals marginal cost. The monopolist then finds out how much can be charged, that is, how much the market will bear for that particular quantity, Q_m in Figure 24.5. We know that the demand curve is defined as showing the *maximum* price for which a given quantity can be sold. That means that our monopolist knows that in order to sell Q_m it can only charge P_m, because that is the price at which that specific quantity, Q_m, is demanded. This price is found by drawing a vertical line from the quantity Q_m to the market demand curve. Where that line hits the market demand curve the price is determined. We find that price by drawing a horizontal line from the demand curve over to the price axis; that gives us the profit-maximizing price of P_m.

Figure 24.5

Maximizing Profits. Here we show the monopolist's demand curve *DD*, as before and its marginal revenue curve, MR, with its margingal cost curve, MC. The monopolist will maximize profits where marginal revenue equals marginal cost; it will produce up to the point where MC equals MR and then will find the highest price at which it can sell that quantity. The profit-maximizing production rate is Q_m, and the profit-maximizing price is P_m. The monopolist would be unwise to produce at the rate Q_1, or at the rate Q_2. You should satisfy yourself why this is so with reference to points A, B, C, and D.

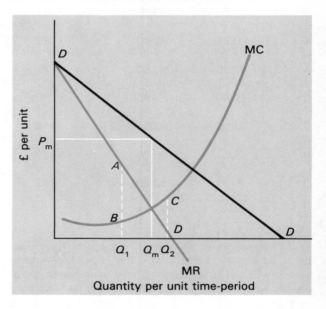

In our detailed numerical example, at a profit-maximizing rate of output of 4 in Figure 24.4, the firm can charge a maximum price of £21.5 and still sell all the goods produced.

The basic procedure for finding the profit-maximizing short-run price–quantity combination for the monopolist is first to determine the profit-maximizing rate of output, either by the total revenue–total cost method or the marginal revenue–marginal cost method, and then to determine by use of the demand curve *DD* the maximum price that can be charged to sell that output.

The decision-making that a monopolist must engage in order to maximize profit is presented in tabular form in Figure 24.6.

Figure 24.6

	Production decision		
Situation	MR = MC	MR > MC	MC < MC
Decision	Stay put = profit-maximization rate of output	Increase production	Decrease production

Calculating Monopoly Profit

We have talked about the monopolist making profit, but we have yet to indicate how much profit the monopolist makes. We have actually shown total profits in column 5 of Figure 24.4(a). We can also find total profits by adding an average total cost curve to Figure 24.4(c). We do that in Figure 24.7. When we add the average total cost curve, we find that the profit that a monopolist makes is equal to the shaded area. Given the demand curve and a uniform pricing system, there is no way for a monopolist to make greater profits than those shown by the shaded area. The monopolist is maximizing profits where marginal cost equals marginal revenue. If the monopolist produces less than that, it will be forfeiting some profits. If the monopolist produces more than that, it will be forfeiting profits.

The same is true of a perfect competitor which produces where marginal revenues equal marginal costs because it produces at the point where the marginal cost schedule intercepts the horizontal dd curve. The horizontal dd curve represents the marginal revenue curve for the pure competitor, for the same average revenues are obtained on all the units sold. Perfect competitors maximize profits at MR = MC, as do pure monopolists. But the perfect competitor makes no true economic profits in the long run. Rather, all it makes is a normal competitive rate of return.

Monopoly Does not Necessarily Mean Profits

The term *monopoly* conjures up the notion of a greedy firm ripping off the public and making exorbitant profits. However, the mere existence of a monopoly does not guarantee high profits. In the United States the Penn Central railroad had a virtual monopoly in railroad service along all its routes but none the less went bankrupt as a result of competition from road transport. Numerous other monopolies have gone bankrupt, too. In the UK, Rolls Royce became bankrupt in 1971 as a result of problems in developing a new type of aero-engine. Look at Figure 24.8. Here we show the demand curve facing the monopolist as DD and the resultant marginal revenue curve as MR. It does not matter at what rate of output this particular

Figure 24.7
Monopoly Profit. We find monopoly profit by subtracting total costs from total revenues at an output rate of 4 units, which is approximately the profit-maximizing rate of output for the monopolist. Monopoly profit is given by the shaded area. This diagram is similar to Figure 24.4(c) except that we have added the short-run average total cost curve (ATC).

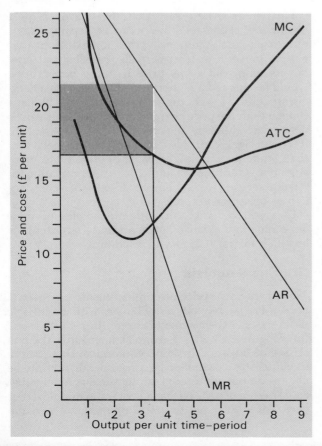

Figure 24.8
Monopolies Are not Always Profitable.
depicts the situation confronting some monopolists. The average total cost curve ATC is everywhere above the average revenue or demand curve DD. In the short run, the monopolist will produce where MC = MR at point E. Output Q_m will be sold at price P_m, but cost per unit is C_1. Losses are the shaded rectangle.

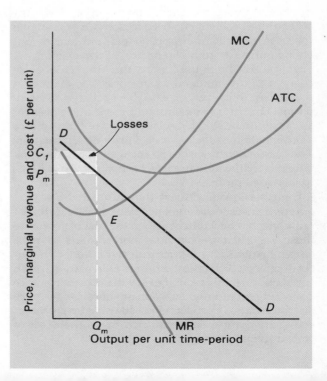

> ## Key Points 24.3
>
> ► The monopolist must choose the profit-maximizing price–output combination.
> ► It is found by choosing that output where marginal revenue equals marginal cost and then charging the highest price possible as given by the demand curve for that particular output.
> ► The basic difference between a monopolist and a perfect competitor is that a monopolist faces a downward-sloping demand curve and therefore marginal revenue is less than price.
> ► Monopoly short-run profits are found by looking at average total costs compared to the price per unit. When this difference is multiplied by quantity, monopoly profit is determined.
> ► A monopoly does not necessarily mean profit. One could have a monopoly, but if the average total cost curve lies everywhere above the monopoly demand curve, it will not pay to produce because there will be losses.

monopolist operates; total costs cannot be covered. Look at the position of the average total cost curve. It lies everywhere above *DD* (the average revenue curve). Thus, there is no price–output combination that will allow the monopolist profits.

Price Discrimination

In a perfectly competitive market, each buyer is charged the same price for every unit of the particular commodity (corrected, of course, for quality differences and differential transportation charges). Since the product is homogeneous, and since we also assume full knowledge on the part of the buyers, a difference in price per constant-quality unit cannot exist. Any seller of the product who tried to charge a price higher than the going market price would find that no one would purchase from him or her. In this chapter, we have assumed up until now that the monopolist charged all consumers the same price for all units. A monopolist, however, may be able to charge different people different prices and/or different unit prices for successive units sought by a given buyer. Either one or a combination of these is called **price discrimination**. The reason a firm wishes to engage in price discrimination is that, where feasible, such a practice will lead to increased profits.

It must be made clear at the outset that charging different prices to different people and/or for different units which reflect differences in the cost of service to those particular people does not amount to price discrimination. This is **price differentiation**: differences in prices which reflect differences in marginal cost.

We can turn this around to say that a uniform price does not necessarily indicate an absence of price discrimination. If production costs vary by customer and all are charged the same price, this is also a case of price discrimination.

Necessary Conditions for Price Discrimination to Exist

There are three necessary conditions for the existence of price discrimination:

1. The firm must have some market power (i.e. it is not a price taker).
2. The firm must be able to separate markets.
3. The buyers in the different markets must have different price elasticities of demand.

Further, it is necessary that these two or more identifiable classes of buyers can be separated at a reasonable cost. Additionally, the monopolist must be able to prevent, at least partially, reselling by those buyers who paid a low price to those buyers who would be charged a higher price. For example, charging students a lower admission price to see a film at a cinema than the price charged to non-students can be done relatively easily: the cost of checking out student IDs is not significant. Also, it is fairly easy to make sure that students do not resell their tickets to non-students. As another example, price discrimination for medical services is easy. The resale value of a coronary bypass operation is zero!

Can you think of any other examples of price discrimination? What about discos that charge females less than males? It is easy to discriminate here!

Graphic Analysis

We can see how a price-discriminating monopolist will act if there are two classes of buyers with identifiable differences in their demand curves. In panels (a) and (b) of Figure 24.9 we see group I and group II, the two classes of buyers. To simplify, marginal cost for the monopolist is assumed to be constant. For profit to be at a maximum, we know that marginal revenue must equal marginal cost. We have a common marginal cost here, MC. We have two sets of marginal revenue curves, MR_I and MR_{II}. Thus, for profit maximization, $MR_I = MR_{II} = MC$. It is as if the goods sold to class I and class II were two *different* goods having exactly the same marginal cost of production. In other words, to maximize total profits, the monopolist wants to set marginal revenue equal to marginal cost in all markets in which it is selling. If marginal revenue in market I exceeded marginal cost, profits could be increased by expanding output (lowering price) in market I. The same holds for market II. On the other hand, if marginal revenue in market I (or market II) were less than marginal cost, profit could be increased by reducing output (raising price) in market I (or II).

We show this in Figure 24.9. Group I buyers are presented in panel (a), group II buyers in panel (b). We assume for simplicity's sake that the marginal costs for servicing both classes of consumers are both equal and constant. Marginal cost equals marginal revenue for group I at quantity Q_1. The price at which this quantity can be sold is P_1. On the other hand, for buyers in group II who have a more elastic demand curve (at *any* given P) than buyers in group I, the intersection of marginal cost with MR_{II} is at quantity Q_{II}. The price at which this quantity is sold is P_{II}, which is lower than P_I. In other words, the price-discriminating monopolist will sell that same product to the group of buyers having a relatively less elastic demand curve at a higher price than that charged to the other group of buyers having a relatively higher elasticity of demand.

The Cost to Society of Monopolies

We now consider the desirability of a monopolistic market structure as compared with a perfectly competitive industry. In Figure 24.10 we show an industry where long-run marginal costs are constant. From our analysis in Chapter 23 we know that in a perfectly competitive industry the equilibrium price would be P_c – price equals marginal cost. Now let us assume that the industry is suddenly transformed into a monopoly *and there is no change in the cost situation facing the monopolist.* The monopolist would charge a price of P_m: output would be reduced from Q_c to Q_m. A monopolist therefore produces a smaller quantity and sells it at a higher price. This is the reason usually given when one attacks monopolists. Monopolists raise the price and restrict production, compared to a competitive situation. For a monopolist's product, consumers are forced to pay a price that exceeds the marginal cost of a production. Resources are misallocated in such a situation – too few resources are being used in the monopolist's industry and too many are used elsewhere. As we have pointed out before, this difference between monopoly and competition arises not because of differences in costs, but rather because of differences in the demand curves facing the individual firms. The monopolist has monopoly because it faces a downward-sloping demand curve. The individual perfect competitor does not have any market power.

Figure 24.9

Price Discrimination. Here the monopolist has separated buyers into those with relatively less elastic demand curves (group I) and those with relatively more elastic demand curves (group II). Profit maximization occurs when marginal revenue equals marginal cost. Therefore, our monopolist sets marginal revenue equal to marginal cost in each individual category. We find that the monopolist sets a price of P_I for group I and a price of P_{II} for group II. Those with the relatively less elastic demand end up paying more than do those with the relatively more elastic demand for the same service. In such a situation, the monopolist earns a greater income than it would by charging a single price to all customers.

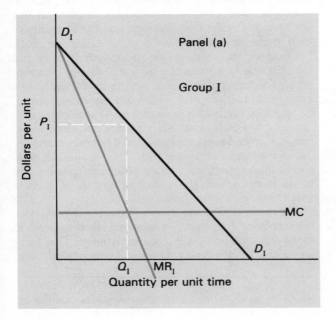

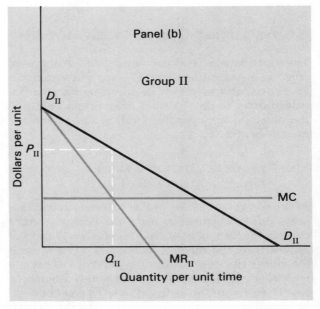

Figure 24.10

The Effects of Monopolizing an Industry. If there are constant long-run marginal costs in a perfectly competitive industry then the equilibrium price would be P_c and the equilibrium quantity supplied and demanded would be Q_c. Now we assume that the industry is suddenly monopolized. We assume that the costs stay the same; the only thing that changes is that the monopolist now faces the entire downward-sloping demand curve. The monopolist will produce at the point where marginal revenue equals marginal cost. The monopolist therefore produces at Q_m and charges a price P_m. We see, then, that a monopolist charges a higher price and produces less than an industry in a competitive situation.

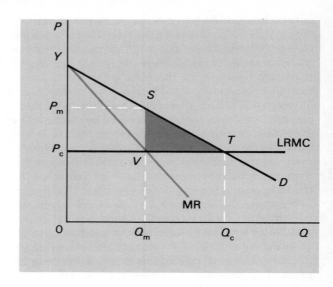

Consumer Surplus and Product Surplus

We can examine the adverse impact of monopoly on resource allocation still further using the concept of consumer surplus that was defined in Chapter 21. In Figure 24.10 the area of consumer surplus is YTP_c in the case of the perfectly competitive industry. If the industry is suddenly monopolized and there is no change in the cost situation facing the monopolist then the area under the demand curve shrinks to YSP_m. The monopolist has gained the area $P_m SVP_c$ at the expense of consumers: this area is defined as *producer surplus*. The remaining part of the former area of consumer surplus is, of course, the triangular area STV. Neither consumers nor the monopolist now obtain this as a surplus: it is lost to either party. Because of this it is called the **deadweight welfare loss** arising from monopolization of the competitive industry. This very term highlights how we can build up a strong case against monopoly and a presumption in favour of competition. However, there are several other aspects that still need to be considered.

Some Other Costs of Monopoly

There are at least two additional costs in terms of resource misallocation that may occur when monopolies exist. One involves the resources used by individuals in order to obtain and maintain monopoly, and the other involves possible inefficiencies within the monopoly firm.

The Resource Cost of Obtaining and Maintaining a Monopoly Firm

As we recognized earlier in this chapter some monopolies can be obtained by using the help of government in the form of restrictive licences, certificates of convenience, and the like. Individuals, in their quest for higher-than-normal rates of return, will expend resources to obtain government-bestowed monopolies. These resources can (from society's point of view) be considered wasted. As an example the Federal

Communications Commission in the US has announced that it will allow only three new FM radio stations in a particular city. The *full* procedure by which an individual or a firm obtains one of the new licences is not explicitly stated in any government documents, but it certainly involves lobbying and offering hospitality to important civil servants agreeing to do public-service programmes, and the like. All of those activities of course use scarce resources. If, on the other hand, new FM licences were simply sold to the highest bidder, virtually no resources would be spent wining and dining FC officials and lobbying on behalf of potential station owners.

Efficiency Loss in Monopoly

We have assumed that all firms – whether they be perfect competitors or monopolists – will seek to minimize their costs of production. Implicit in our discussion of perfect competition was the necessity of each perfectly competitive firm to minimize costs. Because of the competitive process, if it does not minimize costs – given the large number of competitors minimizing their costs – then it will go out of business in the long run. This same argument cannot be applied directly to a monopolist. A monopolist can, in principle, not be completely minimizing the costs of production and that monopolist will not necessarily go out of business in the long run. To be sure, such non-cost-minimization will reduce monopoly profits, but bankruptcy is not the consequence, as it is in a perfectly competitive firm.

The notion that costs are not minimized by effective management or that *organizational slack* occurs in monopoly has been called **x-inefficiency**. This term was used by Professor Harvey Leibenstein,* who

*Harvey Leibenstein, 'Allocative Efficiency versus -Inefficiency', *American Economic Review*, Vol. 56 (June 1966), pp. 392–415.

ascribed X-inefficiency to a lack of motivational efficiency and to an inefficient market for knowledge. According to Leibenstein, X-inefficiency arises largely from losses of output due to motivational deficiency of resource owners:

(With a given) … set of human inputs purchased and … knowledge of production techniques available to the firm, a variety of outputs are possible. If individuals can choose, to some degree the APQT bundles (Activity, Pace, Quality of work, Time spent) they like, they are unlikely to choose a set of bundles that will maximize the value of output.*

One of Leibenstein's favourite examples from the field of economic development involves two identical inefficient petroleum refineries in Egypt. The introduction of a new manager at one of the refineries (the one that produced less output) apparently brought about an immediate improvement in output. After some time passed, there was a *spectacular* improvement in output. The increase in output was attributed to the new manager. In the case of the UK there is evidence that X-inefficiency exists as evidenced by the dramatic improvement in efficiency in those firms which have experienced major changes in senior management. The British Oxygen Company, while not now enjoying a monopoly in the production of gases as it once did, is a good example of how a new managing director cut out wasteful use of resources including raw materials, expense accounts, and other management fringe benefits.

---

*Harvey Leibenstein, 'Competition and X-Inefficiency: Reply', *Journal of Political Economy*, Vol. 81 (May–June 1973), pp. 765–77.

The Benefits of Monopoly

Our analysis has indeed built up a critical picture of a monopoly. Both from a consumer viewpoint and in general terms of resource allocation we do not end up with a favourable view of the single seller. But if you recall our analysis of the monopolization of a perfectly competitive industry we must repeat that our analysis was based on an heroic assumption. That assumption was that the monopolization of the perfectly competitive industry does not change the cost structure. Of course if monopolization results in higher marginal cost, then the cost to society is even greater. On the other hand, if monopolization results in cost savings, then the cost, if any, to society of monopolies is less than we infer from the above analysis. Indeed, we can present a hypothetical example in which monopolization leads to such a dramatic reduction in cost that society actually benefits.

Figure 24.11 shows such a possibility. If the monopolist can enjoy scale economies and thus operate on a lower short-run marginal cost curve he can produce cost savings to set against the deadweight welfare loss. The perfectly competitive price is OP_c and the monopolist charges a profit-maximizing price of OP_m. The deadweight welfare loss is now STV – a smaller area than in Figure 24.10. The rectangle P_cVWZ represents the saving in resource costs achieved by the monopolist. If this area exceeds the area STV then our antipathy to the monopolist looks less well founded.

A further point is that the monopolist may not actually charge the profit-maximizing price of P_m but one nearer P_c. Why might he do so? Simply he would be drawing less attention from government and his customers if his price does not appear 'excessive'. If he

---

Key Points 24.4

▶ A monopolist can make higher profits if it can price discriminate. Price discrimination requires that two or more identifiable classes of buyers exist whose price elasticities of demand for the product are different, and that these two classes of buyers can be cheaply separated.

▶ Price differentiation should not be confused with price discrimination. The former occurs when there are differences in prices which reflect differences in marginal cost.

▶ The three necessary conditions for price discrimination are (1) the firm has some market power; (2) the firm must be able to separate markets; and (3) buyers in different markets have different price elasticities of demand.

▶ If we compare a perfectly competitive industry in which the cost curves are essentially the same as those facing the monopolist, then that industry's output is greater than that produced by the monopolist and also the price charged is lower.

▶ Besides raising price and restricting output, monopoly creates a situation in which resources are spent to obtain and to maintain monopoly status. Additionally, there may be organizational slack within a monopoly; this has been called X-inefficiency.

Figure 24.11

Deadweight Welfare Loss – Reconsidered. If the mono-polist is able to reduce costs from SMC_c to SMC_m then resource savings can offset the deadweight welfare loss of STV. The profit-maximizing price is OP_m and output OQ_m. P_cVWZ is the area representing cost savings due to the lower SMC of the monopolist not available to the perfectly competitive firm.

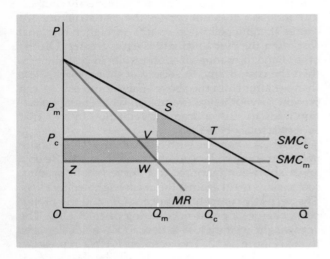

charges a price resulting in high profits he may attract the concern of government which may investigate his business with ensuing possible adverse publicity. A rival may be encouraged to compete with him with explicit government financial support. Better there-fore not to charge too much above the competitive price and enjoy the benefit of continued security of at least some monopoly profits. If therefore P_m is nearer to P_c the magnitude of consumer surplus that is diverted and enjoyed by the monopolist is diminished and our case against the single seller thereby again weakened.

The Process of Innovation

Our discussion of the monopolist has so far concerned the costs and prices of existing products. What about development of new products? Joseph Schumpeter, the distinguished Austrian economist, argued strongly that the process of innovation is best encour-aged by monopolists who can afford to take a long-term view and finance expensive – and uncertain – research and development programmes. The security offered to the monopolist thus benefits society through the appearance of new products. The monop-olist enjoys profits in the short term but sooner or later competition forces down prices and the monopo-list finds his dominant position eroded away. Consider the ball-point pen. In October 1945, Milton Reynolds patented a new writing instrument, tipped with a ball-bearing instead of a nib. It cost about 80 cents to make but sold at Gimbels, the New York department store for $12.50. On the first day the pen was on sale, Gimbels sold 10000. By March 1946, the Reynolds International Pen Company had been making profits of $500000 a month. However, by Christmas 1946, there were roughly 100 makers of ball-point pens in production, some of them selling models for as little as $2.98. Production costs had fallen below 30 cents a pen. By mid-1948, pens were selling for 39 cents, and costing 10 cents to make.

Thus the monopolist creates a new market ulti-mately only to see his dominance destroyed. Society can gain from the appearance of the new product and expect competitive forces to temper the monopolist charging a price well above the costs of production.

What can we offer as a comment on this dynamic case for monopoly? Firstly, it has to be said that there is no certainty that the monopolist will innovate. As the Nobel Laureate, Lord Hicks, once put it the greatest benefit of a monopoly can be 'the quiet life'. The security of very limited competition means that there are no immediate market pressures on the monopolist to reduce costs and innovate at all: he can sit back and enjoy at least some monopoly profits. Secondly, the Schumpeterian case needs to be sup-ported by empirical evidence. If the process of innova-tion is not strongly related to the sheer size of firm then the basis of arguing that only very large firms are innovators looks suspect. Current evidence indeed hardly provides one with a confident basis for viewing small firms as unwilling agents seeking technical change. Schumpeter's argument is thus relevant in considering government policy towards monopoly and size of firm but in itself not a conclusive one that justifies a monopolistic structure. We consider the development of UK government policy towards monopoly in Chapter 30.

> ## Key Points 24.5
>
> ▶ By price discrimination, a monopolist can divert part of consumer surplus to himself and enjoy producer surplus.
>
> ▶ Deadweight welfare loss refers to the loss of welfare arising from the monopolization of a competitive industry. It is a measure of society's loss of welfare due to the misallocation of resources arising from the presence of monopoly.
>
> ▶ As monopolist may not charge the profit-maximizing price in order to avoid the disadvantage of government scrutiny and stimulating competition from rivals.
>
> ▶ Monopoly has been held to be desirable in order to foster innovation but the empirical evidence appears to be not yet convincing.

CASE STUDY

How to Get Taken by a Taxi-cab

One way to attempt to obtain monopoly profits is to close entry into the market by legal means. If a law can be passed that requires a licence to be obtained in order to do business in a particular profession or industry, those in the industry prior to the licensing restriction and who are automatically granted a licence will obtain monopoly profits. A clear-cut case can be seen if we examine the market for taxi services in many countries. In many, if not most cities, in order to operate a taxi a licence must be obtained. In New York City, this licence is called a medallion.

In 1937 the city sold medallions at $10 a piece to cab-operators. The city issued 11 787. Since 1937 that is the total number that have remained in existence. As demand for taxi-cab services grew, the market value of a tax medallion increased from its original price of $10 to its mid-1980s price of about $62 000. Those who invested $10 in a taxi-cab medallion earned about a 21 per cent compound rate of return.

What does this price represent? It represents the fully discounted present value of the expected stream of monopoly profits that can be obtained by owning a legal taxi-cab in New York City.

Owners who purchased or received the medallions in the late 1930s and early 1940s obtained 'monopoly' profits. However, buyers *today* receive no more than a competitive rate of return on their labour and capital. Why? Because they have already paid the market price for their medallions, and the opportunity cost of that money capital has been added to their other costs. An elimination of the restrictions on entry into the New York taxi-cab market would immediately subject all the present owners of medallions to a large windfall loss. The emergence of 'gypsy' cabs (whose owners do not have medallions) in New York City has already partially reduced the market value of medallions from what it would be without 'gypsies'. The 'gypsy' cab-drivers have no *legal* right to pick up passengers for hire. None the less, New York

authorities have, for the most part, allowed these illegal cabs to operate in the city in recent years.

Figure 24.12
The Rise in Value of Medallions. If the city of New York sets the number of medallions at Q_1, then the supply curve is vertical, SS. If the demand curve a number of years ago was DD, then the going price was P_1. As population and real incomes rise, however, the demand curve shifts outward to the right to $D'D'$. The price or value of a medallion rises to P_2 because the quantity supplied is fixed.

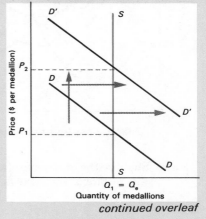

continued overleaf

We can understand this situation by looking at Figure 24.12. Here we show that the city of New York has issued a fixed number of medallions equal to Q_1. The supply curve of medallions is thus completely price inelastic at Q_1, and is represented by SS. As the city has grown and real income has increased, the demand curve for taxi services and hence for medallions has increased from DD to $D'D'$. The price of medallions has risen from P_1 to P_2. If free entry were allowed into the tax-cab industry, the supply curve of medallions would shift to the right so as always to intersect the demand curve at a price of zero. (This is a point not lost on current owners!) In other words, the authorities would issue medallions to anyone who wanted them at a zero price. Whatever the quantity demanded at that zero price, the quantity supplied would be equal – this would merely mean producing some more medallions that authorized the bearer to operate a taxi in New York City.

In 1977 a market for taxi licences came into existence in Dublin soon after the government in Ireland decided not to issue any new licences. In the classified columns of the evening newspapers published in Dublin one can identify asking prices for a taxi licence:

October 1977	£1 200
February 1979	£2 000
November 1980	£4 000

Source: M. Keane, 'Monopoly Profits: the Market for Taxi Licences, *Economics* (Journal of the Economics Association) Vol XVII, Part 4 No. 76, Winter 1981, pp. 108–110.

Questions

1. Using a demand and supply analysis outline what has happened to the price of a taxi licence in Dublin in recent years.

2. What does this price represent?

3. Interpret the statement found in the Report of the National Prices Commission that 'taxi operators, under current fare rates as of March 1977, are in a position to earn substantially more than the levels of income which they themselves would regard as typical'.

4. Who benefits from the licensing of taxi-cabs in New York City (or in other cities)?

5. How is it possible for a barrier to entry to remain in existence for such a long time?

Exam Preparation and Practice

Introductory Exercises

1.

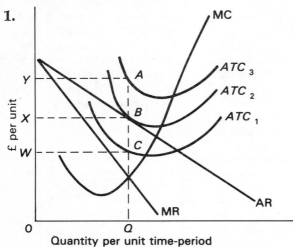

rectangle showing total revenue. Is the monopolist showing an economic loss, a break-even (normal profit), or an economic profit situation? What is the significance of the MC = MR output?

(b) Suppose the monopolist faces ATC_2. Define the rectangle that shows the monopolist's total costs. Also, define the rectangle showing total revenue. Is the monopolist showing an econdomic loss, a break-even (normal profit), or an economic profit situation? What is the significance of the MC = MR output?

(c) Suppose the monopolist faces ATC_3. Define the rectangle that shows the monopolist's total costs. Also, define the rectangle showing total revenue. Is the monopolist showing an economic loss, a break-even (normal profit), or an economic profit situation? What is the significance of the MC = MR output?

(a) Suppose the monopolist faces ATC_1. Define the rectangle that shows the monopolist's total costs at output rate Q. Also, define the

2. Suppose that a monopolist is faced with the following demand schedule. Compute marginal revenue.

Price	Quantity demanded	Marginal revenue
£1 000	1	£_____
920	2	_____
840	3	_____
760	4	_____
680	5	_____
600	6	_____
520	7	_____
440	6	_____
350	9	_____
260	10	_____

MULTIPLE CHOICE QUESTIONS

†1. If a profit-maximizing monopolist is in equilibrium and a profits tax is imposed, what action will he take in order to maintain his profit-maximizing position?
   A raise his price
   B reduce his output
   C raise his price *and* reduce his output
   D alter neither price nor output
   E reduce his price and raise his output

2. Other things being equal, an increase in variable costs will cause a monopolist to
   A reduce his output and increase his prices
   B increase his output and reduce his prices
   C advertise more extensively in order to increase his sales
   D discriminate between different markets
   E do none of the above

3. Price discrimination represented by cheap day return rail tickets is financially sound provided the reduced fares at least
   A cover operating costs
   B cover fixed costs
   C equal the amount of subsidy received per passenger
   D equal overheads
   E cover labour costs

For Questions 4 and 5 select your answer from the following grid:

A	B	C	D	E
1, 2, 3 all correct	**1, 2** only correct	**2, 3** only correct	**1** only correct	**3** only correct

4. A monopolist with no costs of production maximizes revenue by fixing price where
   1 marginal revenue is zero
   2 the point elasticity of demand is unity
   3 total revenue is neither rising nor falling

5. Which of the following is/are necessary for the charging of discriminatory prices by a profit maximizing monopolist?
   1 purchasers cannot buy in one market and resell in another
   2 different markets have different price elasticities of demand
   3 some markets cost more to supply than others

RELATED ESSAY QUESTIONS

1. What are the main determinants of monopoly power? Why might a firm choose not to maximize its monopoly profits?

2. Discuss the factors which (a) encourage and (b) discourage the development of monopolies.

3. Under what conditions will price discrimination be effective? Does price discrimination operate in the interests of the consumer?

4. What are the sources of monopoly? What is the economic case for and against patents?

5. Under what conditions can a profit-maximizing firm successfully operate a policy of price discrimination? In what circumstances could such a policy benefit the consumer?

25 Pricing and Output Decisions in Monopolistic Competition and Oligopoly

Key Points to Review

▶ Perfect price elasticity of demand (7.3)
▶ Average total cost curve (22.3)

▶ Perfect competition (23.1)
▶ Monopoly (24.1)

Questions for Preview

1 What are the characteristics of the market structure of monopolistic competition?

2 How is the equilibrium price–output combination decided by the monopolistic competitor?

3 How does the monopolistic competition market structure differ from perfect competition?

4 What are the characteristics of the oligopoly market structure?

5 How do oligopolies compete?

Up to this point, we have discussed the two extremes in market structure – perfect competition and pure monopoly. In the perfectly competitive model, we assume that there are numerous firms that produce the same product and that have no influence over price: they are *price takers*. In the pure monopoly model, we assume that the firm is a single seller of a good to the entire market: the firm is a *price maker*. There are obviously market situations that fall between these two extremes. Indeed, almost all the UK economy is characterized by firms that are neither perfectly competitive nor purely monopolistic. After all, most firms have some control over price, that is, individually they do not face a perfectly elastic (horizontal) demand curve, but they really are not pure monopolists. In this chapter, we will look at market structures that lie in between competition and monopoly. The first market structure of such an 'in-between' situation that we must look at is monopolistic competition, i.e. a situation where each seller has a small amount of market power but is in competition with a large number of others selling *almost* identical products. We then exam-ine oligopolistic market structures where the number of competitors is small and their market power is considerable.

Monopolistic Competition – Its Origin

Back in the 1920s and 1930s, economists became increasingly dissatisfied with the polar extremes of market structure mentioned above. There seemed to have been many industries for which both the per-fectly competitive model and the pure monopoly model did not apply and did not seem to yield very accurate predictions.

Theoretical and empirical research was instituted to develop some sort of middle ground. Two separately developed models of **monopolistic competition** resulted. In the US Edward Chamberlin published *The Theory of Monopolistic Competition* in 1933. The same year, Britain's Joan Robinson published *The Economics of Imperfect Competition*. The following account is based on their important contributions to the theory of the firm.

The Characteristics of Monopolistic Competition

We define monopolistic competition as a market structure in which there are a relatively large number of producers offering similar but differentiated products. Monopolistic competition therefore has the following characteristics.

1. Significant numbers of sellers in a highly competitive market due to the freedom of entry into the industry.
2. Differentiated products.
3. The existence of advertising.

We will analyze these characteristics in turn.

Number of Firms

In a perfectly competitive situation, there is an extremely large number of firms; in pure monopoly there is only one. In monopolistic competition, there is a somewhat large number of firms, but not as many as in perfect competition.

Several important implications for monopolistically competitive industry follow.

1. Small share of market. With so many firms, each firm has a relatively small share of the total market. Thus, it has only a very small amount of control over the market-clearing price.
2. Collusion difficult. With so many firms, it is very difficult for all of them to get together to collude, that is, to set a pure monopoly price (and output!) Rigging price in a monopolistically competitive industry is virtually impossible.
3. Independence. Since there are so many firms, each one acts independently of the others. That is to say, no firm attempts to take into account the reaction of all its rival firms – that would be impossible with so many rivals. Rivals' reactions to output and price changes are largely ignored.

Product Differentiation

Perhaps the most important feature of the monopolistically competitive market is **product differentiation**. In a sense, we can say that each individual manufacturer of a product has an absolute monopoly over its own product, which is slightly differentiated from other similar products. Consider the abundance of brand names for such things as toothpaste, soap, and shampoos. Should you buy SR, or any of the numerous rival brands?

Indeed, it appears that product differentiation characterizes most markets for consumer goods in the UK. Consumers are not obliged to buy just one make of television set, toothpaste, sweatshirt or motor car. There are usually a number of similar but differentiated products from which to choose. We note that the greater the success at product differentiation, the greater the monopoly power.

REAL VERSUS ARTIFICIAL DIFFERENTIATION

Some economists like to distinguish between product differentiation that is 'real' and that which is 'artificial'. Real product differentiation involves variations in physical characteristics, such as an actual chemical difference between two brands of washing-machine detergents. Artificial product differentiation would involve no significant differences in products but different packaging materials, brand names, and advertising outlays. The above examples of 'real' and 'artificial' product differentiation, of course, represent only the tip of an iceberg. Firms can also differentiate their products on the basis of location and service provided with the products sold. Therefore in practice it is difficult to draw the line between real and artificial product differentiation.

SUBSTITUTES

However we wish to define product differentiation, the fact remains that each separate differentiated product has numerous close substitutes. This clearly has an impact on the price elasticity of demand facing the individual firm. Remember when we discussed the determination of the price elasticity of demand, we mentioned that one determinant was the availability of substitutes. The greater the number of substitutes available – other things being equal – the greater the price elasticity of demand. In other words, if the consumer has a vast array of alternatives that are just about as good as the product under study, a relatively small increase in the price of that product will lead consumers to switch to one of the many close substitutes. Thus, the ability of a firm to raise the price above the price of close substitutes is very small.

PRODUCT GROUPS

Up until now we have defined an industry as a collection of firms producing a homogeneous commodity. However, it is difficult to maintain this definition of an industry when we talk in terms of differentiated products. Each firm has a distinct product and thus in a sense constitutes an industry. But this is not a very practical approach and we can solve this problem by lumping together firms producing very closely related products. These are called product groups. Some product groups that come to mind are breakfast cereals, motor cars, toilet paper, and hand soap.

Sales Promotion – Advertising

Monopolistic competition differs from perfect competition in that in the latter there is no sales promotion. By definition, the perfect competitor is selling a product that is identical to the product that all other firms in the industry are selling.

But such is not the case for the monopolistic competitor. Since the monopolistic competitor has at least some monopoly power, advertising may result in increased profits. How much advertising should be undertaken? As much as is profitable. It should be carried to the point where the additional revenue from one more pound of advertising just equals one pound of marginal cost.

SHIFTING THE DEMAND CURVE

The goal of advertising is to shift the demand curve to the right. Advertising, it is hoped, will lead to a larger volume of business that more than covers the cost of the advertising. This is shown in Figure 25.1. In that exhibit, assume that the market-clearing price is P_1. At that price with demand curve dd, the quantity sold will be q_1. If, however, advertising succeeds in shifting the demand curve over to $d'd'$, then at that same price the quantity q_2 will be sold.

It is possible, on the other hand, that advertising is necessary just to keep the demand curve at dd. Without advertising, the demand curve might shift inwards to the left. This presumably is the case with competitive advertising. For example, cigarette manufacturers may have to expend large outlays on advertising merely to keep the share of the market they now have. If they discontinue advertising, they would lose ground to all the other companies that are engaged in heavy advertising.

ADVERTISING AND ECONOMIES OF SCALE

An alleged reason for advertising is that the subsequent increased sales can lead to economies of scale. This is possible only if the economies of scale outweigh the advertising costs. Look at Figure 25.2. Here we find that the hypothetical average total cost curve without advertising is ATC. With advertising, it is ATC'. If production is at q_1, then without advertising average total costs will be ATC_1. If advertising campaigns shift demand and increase the profit-maximizing output to q_2, then average total costs will fall to ATC_2. The reduction in average total costs will more than outweigh the increased expenses due to advertising. If the advertising campaign were not successful and demand and production remained where they were, then the firm would stop advertising. It would not be profitable to continue.

Price and Output for the Monopolistic Competitor

Now that we have presented the assumptions underlying the monopolistic competition model, we can analyze the price and output behaviour of each firm in a monopolistically competitive industry. We assume in the analysis that follows that the desired product type

Figure 25.1

Advertising's Desired Effect. The firm that advertises hopes that the advertising will shift the demand schedule for its product to the right. In other words, before advertising, the demand schedule is at dd; after advertising takes place, the demand schedule should shift to $d'd'$.

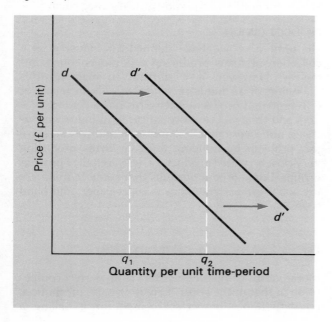

Figure 25.2

Another Desired Effect of Advertising. Advertising may be able to more than pay for itself. For example, in this diagram we start out on the average total cost curve ATC at point A with production of q_1. Here average total costs are ATC_1. Advertising is added, and the average total cost curve shifts up to ATC'. However, if we move out to point B, the quantity produced will be q_2 with an average total cost of only ATC_2, which is lower than ATC_1.

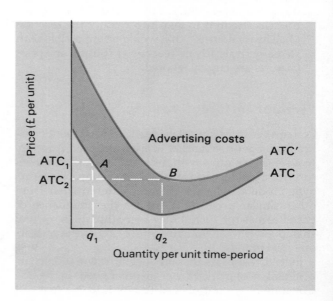

Key Points 25.1

▶ **Monopolistic competition is a market structure that lies in between pure monopoly and perfect competition.**

▶ **A monopolistically competitive market structure has (1) a large number of sellers, (2) differentiated products, and (3) advertising.**

▶ **Because of the large number of firms, each has a small share of the market and collusion is difficult; firms ignore the reactions of rivals to changes in prices.**

▶ **The goal of advertising is to shift the demand curve outwards to the right and at the very least maintain existing market share.**

▶ **Proponents of advertising argue that it leads to increased sales, which allow firms to take advantage of economies of scale.**

---

and quality have been chosen. Further, we assume that the budget and the type of promotional activity have already been chosen and do not change.

The Individual Firm's Demand and Cost Curves

Since the individual firm is not a perfect competitor, its demand curve is downward sloping, as is shown in panels (a), (b), and (c) of Figure 25.3. Thus, it faces a marginal revenue curve that is also downward sloping and below the demand curve. To find the profit-maximizing rate of output and the profit-maximizing price, we go to the output where the marginal cost curve intersects the marginal revenue curve from below. That gives us the profit-maximizing output rate. Then we draw a vertical line up to the demand schedule. That gives us the price that can be charged to sell exactly that quantity produced. This is what we have done in panels (a), (b), and (c) of Figure 25.3. In each of those panels, a marginal cost curve has been drawn in. It intersects the marginal revenue curve at E. The profit-maximizing rate of output is q_e and the profit-maximizing price is P.

The Short-run Equilibrium

In the short run, it is possible for a monopolistic competitor to make economic profits, that is, profits over and above the normal rate of return, or profits over and above what is necessary to keep that firm in that industry. In panel (a) of Figure 25.3, we show such a situation. The average total cost curve is drawn in below the demand curve dd at the profit-maximizing rate of output q_e. Economic profits are shown by the shaded rectangle in that panel.

Losses in the short run are clearly also possible. They are presented in panel (b) of Figure 25.3. Here the average total cost curve lies everywhere above the individual firm's demand curve dd. The losses are marked as the shaded rectangle.

As with any market structure or any firm, in the short run it is possible to observe either economic profits or economic losses. In the long run, however, such is not the case with monopolistic competition.

The Long Run – Economic Profits are Competed Away

The long run is where the similarity between perfect competition and monopolistic competition becomes more obvious. In the long run, since there are so many firms making substitutes for the product in question, any economic profits will be competed away. They will be competed away either through entry by new firms seeing a chance to make a higher rate of return than elsewhere, or by changes in product quality and advertising outlays by existing firms in the industry. (Profitable products will be imitated by other firms.) As for economic losses in the short run, they will disappear in the long run because those firms that suffer them will leave the industry. They will go into another business where the expected rate of return is at least normal. Thus, panels (a) and (b) of Figure 25.3 represent only short-run situations for a monopolistically competitive firm. In the long run, the average total cost curve will just touch the individual firm's demand curve dd at the particular price that is profit maximizing for that particular firm. This is shown in panel (c) of Figure 25.3.

A word of warning. This is an idealized, long-run equilibrium situation for each firm in the industry. That does not mean that even in the long run we will observe every single firm in a monopolistically competitive industry making *exactly* zero economic profits or *just* a normal rate of return. We live in a dynamic world. All we are saying is that if this model is correct, the rate of return will *tend* towards normal, that is, economic profits will tend towards zero.

Figure 25.3

Long-run Equilibrium with Monopolistic Competition.
In panel (a), we show the typical monopolistic competitor making economic profits. If that were the situation, there would be entry into the industry, forcing the demand curve facing the individual monopolistic competitor leftward. Eventually firms would find themselves in the situation depicted in panel (c), where zero economic profits are being made. At the profit-maximizing rate of output, where marginal cost equals marginal revenue, price equals average total cost. In panel (b), we show a situation where the typical firm in a monopolistically competitive industry is making economic losses. If that were the case, firms would leave the industry. The demand curve would shift outward to the right. Eventually the average industry firm would find itself in the situation depicted in panel (c).

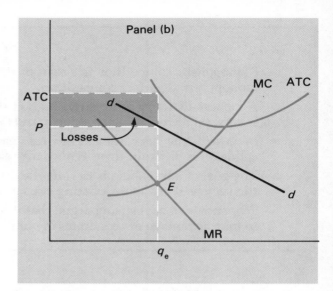

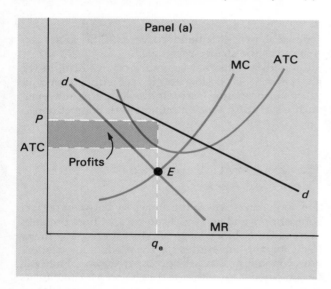

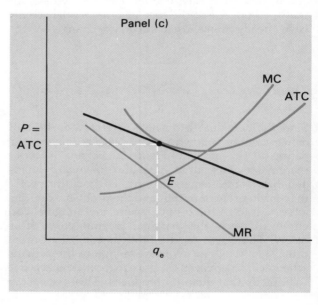

Comparing Perfect Competition with Monopolistic Competition

If both the monopolistic competitor and the perfect competitor make zero economic profits in the long run, then how are they different? The answer lies in the fact that the demand curve facing the individual perfect competitor is horizontal, that is, the price elasticity of demand is infinity. Such is not the case for the individual monopolistic competitor. The demand curve has *some* slope to it. This firm has some control over price; it has some market power. Price elasticity of demand is not infinite. We see the two situations in panels (a) and (b) of Figure 25.4. Both show average total costs just touching the respective demand curves at the particular price at which the firm is selling the product. Notice, however, that the perfect competitor's average total costs are at a minimum. This is not the case with the monopolistic competitor. The equilibrium rate of output is to the left of the minimum point on the average total cost curve where price is greater than marginal cost. (The monopolistic compet-

itor cannot expand output to the point of minimum costs without lowering price; and then marginal cost would exceed marginal revenue.)

It has been argued, therefore, that monopolistic competition involves waste because minimum average total costs are not achieved and price exceeds marginal cost. There are too many firms producing too little output. According to critics of monopolistic competition, society's resources are being wasted.

In his book *The Economics of Monopolistic Competition* Chamberlin had an answer to this criticism. He contended that the difference between the average cost of production for a monopolistically competitive firm in an open market and the minimum average total cost represented what he called the cost of producing 'differentness'. In other words, Chamberlin did not label this difference in cost between perfect competition and monopolistic competition necessarily a waste. In fact, he argued that it is rational for

Figure 25.4

Comparison of the Perfect Competitor with the Monopolistic Competitor. In panel (a), the perfectly competitive firm has zero economic profits in the long run. Its long-run average total cost curve is tangent to the demand curve dd just at the point of intersection with the marginal cost curve. The price is set equal to marginal cost, and that price is P_1. There are zero economic profits. Also, its demand curve is just tangent to the minimum point on its average total cost curve, which means the firm is operating at its optimum rate of production. With the monopolistically competitive firm in panel (b), there are also zero economic profits in the long run, because the average total cost curve is tangent to the individual monopolistic competitor's demand curve, $d'd'$, at the output where production occurs. The price, however, is greater than marginal cost; the monopolistically competitive firm does not find itself at the minimum point on its average total cost curve. It is operating at a rate of output less than is optimal – that is, to the left of the minimum point on the ATC curve.

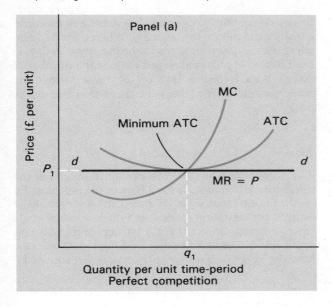

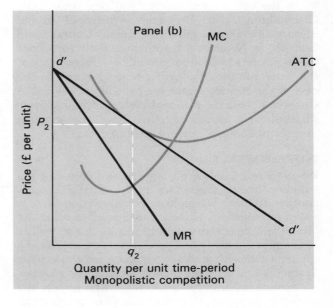

consumers to have a taste for differentiation; consumers willingly accept the resultant increased production costs in return for choice and variety of output.

Oligopoly – A World of Interdependence

The second form of market structure that we have yet to discuss is an important one indeed. It involves a situation where there are several large firms that dominate an entire industry. They are clearly not competitive in the sense that we have used the term; they are clearly not even monopolistically competitive. We call such a situation on **oligopoly**, which means few sellers that are interdependent.

Characteristics of Oligopoly

There are several characteristics of oligopoly that we now comment on.

Key Points 25.2

▶ **In the short run, it is possible for monopolistically competitive firms to make economic profits or economic losses.**

▶ **In the long run, monopolistically competitive firms will make zero economic profits, that is, they will make a normal rate of return.**

▶ **Because the monopolistic competitor faces a downward-sloping demand curve, it does not produce at the minimum point on its average total cost curve. Thus, a monopolistic competitor has higher average total costs per unit than a perfect competitor would have. Some have called this a 'waste'.**

SMALL NUMBER OF FIRMS

We have already mentioned that there is a small number of firms in an oligopolistic industry. Does that mean more than two but less than 100? The question is not easy to answer. Basically, though, we are interested in several firms dominating the entire industry so that these several firms really are able to set the price. By domination, we must be specific, however. We are referring to the percentage of total industry output accounted for by the few top firms.

You can probably think of quite a few examples of an oligopolistic market structure. The brewing industry in the UK is dominated by six large firms. Bass Charrington, Allied Breweries, Whitbread, Grand Metropolitan (Watney, Mann Truman), Courage, and Scottish & Newcastle together account for about three-quarters of UK beer production and own about the same number of all public house licences. In the case of the clearing banks we have already noted in Chapter 19 that the National Westminster, Barclays, Midland, and Lloyds together have the greatest number of domestic current accounts.

INTERDEPENDENCE

When there are only a few large firms dominating the industry, they cannot act independently of one another. In other words, they recognize that there is *mutual interdependence*. Each firm will react to what the other firms do in terms of output and price, as well as to changes in quality and product differentiation. To specify a complete model of oligopoly, we would have to somehow specify the manner in which an oligopolist expects his or her rivals to react. Remember, in a perfectly competitive model each firm ignores the reactions of other firms because each firm can sell all that it wants at the going market price. In the pure monopoly model, the monopolist does not have to worry about the reaction of rivals, since, by definition, there are none.

We must stress here that the mutual interdependence results from the small number of firms in the industry that produce the largest share of total industry output. In fact, we might state that in an oligopoly market structure, the firms must try to predict the reaction of rival firms. Otherwise, poor business decisions could be made that would spell lower profits.

Why Oligopoly Occurs

Why is it that some industries are dominated by a few large firms? What are the reasons that will cause an industry that might otherwise be competitive to tend towards oligopoly?

Economies of Scale

Perhaps the strongest reason that has been offered for the existence of oligopoly is economies of scale. Remember that economies of scale are defined as a production situation in which a doubling of output results in less than a doubling of the total costs. When economies of scale exist, the firm's average total cost curve will be downward sloping as it produces more and more output. That is, average total cost can be reduced by continuing to expand the scale of operation. Smaller firms will have a tendency in such a situation to be inefficient; their average total costs will be greater than those incurred by a large firm. They will tend to go out of business (or be absorbed into the larger firm, which we discuss below). Historically, in many of the industries that have become oligopolistic in the United States, it has been technical progress that has made economies of scale obtainable. For example, consider the motor-car business. When it started out, there were numerous firms in the industry. Today, in the UK and in most developed nations the number of competitors is but a fraction of those pioneering makers of motorized transport: there are three major ones.

Minimum Efficient Scale

The number of firms must be examined in light of the **minimum efficient scale** for a firm in the industry. By minimum efficient scale we mean the lowest rate of output per unit time-period at which average costs reach a minimum point for a particular firm. If you recall our discussion of costs in Chapter 22 we saw how the long-run average cost curve is determined by

Figure 25.5

Minimum Efficient Scale. This long-run average cost curve reaches a minimum point at *A*. After that point, long-run average costs remain horizontal, or constant, and then, at some later rate of output, rise. Point *A* is called the minimum efficient scale for the firm because at that point it reaches minimum costs. It is the lowest rate of output at which the average long-run cost curves are minimized.

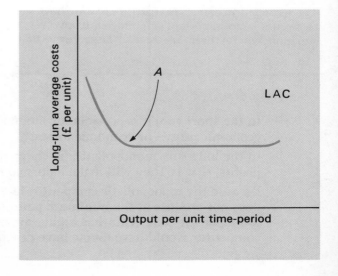

the nature of the returns to scale. In Figure 25.5 we show how economies of scale initially determine a declining long-run average cost curve before such economies become exhausted. When scale economies are exhausted and constant returns to scale begin the minimum efficient scale for the firm is encountered.

Minimum efficient scale is thus concerned with that rate of output where the long-run average cost of the firm flattens out. The relevant issue now is whether firms suffer a significant cost disadvantage if they are unable to sell a sufficienty large volume of output so that they can enjoy all possible internal economies of scale. Empirical evidence on this is now much more extensive in the United States than in the UK. Figure 25.6 shows that in the case of products like refined sugar, aluminium semi-manufactures, and detergents we should indeed be surprised to find anything other than an oligopolistic market structure. Quite simply, scale economies explain why the number of efficient competitors will be relatively few.

Figure 25.6
Some Estimates of Minimum Efficient Scale of Plant.
The data show that for some products efficient production in the supply of that product is likely to require an appreciable degree of concentration of output in few plants.

Product	MES as a percentage of UK sales
Flour	About 1%
Oil refining	9%
Potato crisps	About 10%
Detergent powder	10%
Refined sugar	About 20%
Cigarettes	About 21%
Sulphuric acid	26%
Ethylene	34%
Aluminium semi-manufacturers	36%
Industrial diesel engines	56%
Tractors	76%

Source: A Review of Monopolies and Mergers Policy: A Consultative Document, Cmnd 7198, HMSO, May 1978.

Barriers to Entry

It is possible that certain barriers to entry have prevented more competition in oligopolistic industries. We defined barriers to entry in Chapter 24. They include legal barriers, such as patents, control and ownership over critical supplies, all of which can result in a pure monopoly situation existing. But there may be entry barriers of a less overwhelming kind which may result in the presence of some competitors but not as many as would create a monopolistic competi-

tive market structure. The sort of difficulties of becoming a new entrant into an industry that we have in mind are the large sums of finance that may be required in order to set up in production, advertise heavily, and create a new brand awareness – to product differentiate – and also to build up a national distribution system.

In the 1950s Professor Joe Bain began pioneering research into the nature of entry barriers into a wide range of US manufacturing industries. The problem of capital requirements was one of the barriers that Bain tried to quantify. He found that the capital requirements barrier was the highest in cigarettes, automobiles, steel, petroleum-refining, and tractor production. However, the capital requirement difficulty was almost non-existent in flour, shoes, and meat-packing, and relatively small in canned foods and vegetables, fountain pens, and metal containers.* In Bain's view the problem of product differentiation was the most important source of entry barriers for firms contemplating entry into many consumer goods markets. From this we have something to reflect on in Chapter 30 where government policies to make markets more competitive are considered. But there is one more aspect about the creation of oligopolistic markets that has public policy implications. This is the slimming down in the number of competitors through merger activity.

Oligopoly by Merger

Another reason that explains the development of oligopolistic market structures is that a number of firms have merged. A merger is the joining of two or more firms under a single ownership or control. There are two types of merger – horizontal and vertical.

HORIZONTAL MERGERS
Horizontal mergers involve firms selling a similar product. If two shoe manufacturing firms merge, that is a horizontal merger. If a group of firms all producing, say, cars merge into one, that is also a horizontal merger.

VERTICAL MERGERS
Vertical mergers occur when one firm merges with either a firm from which it purchases an input or a firm to which it sells its output. Vertical mergers occur, for example, when a shoe manufacturer purchases retail shoe outlets. (Obviously, vertical mergers do not create oligopoly as we have defined it.)

The Rationale for Mergers

We must presume that the decision by, say, the board of directors of two firms to merge is not taken lightly.

---

* Joe S. Bain, *Barriers to New Competition* (Cambridge, Mass.: Harvard University Press, 1956).

There must be some rationale for the firms involved to wish to give up their independence. One would assume that the directors perceive benefits from the merger which outweigh any of the disadvantages involved. The wish to take advantage of scale economies by combining outputs is clearly one such potential gain from merger activity. Mergers allow companies to grow and indeed to expand in size overnight. An alternative method of company growth is for a firm to win some of the market held by its rivals. As compared with a merger, this method of growth is typically slow since it takes time to win new customers. Mergers permit a quick and more certain expansion. However, sometimes a firm is reluctant to lose its independence and is faced not with a merger option but a take-over bid from a rival. It is then a matter of persuading the shareholders of the desirability of staying independent rather than accept an attractive offer for their shares. In this case we are referring to a take-over bid, which may be contested by an unwilling recipient and the desirability of a merger keenly disputed by the two parties.

Sometimes the enthusiasm for mergers and take-overs appears to be based less on the quest to realize scale economies and more on jockeying for position by the senior management of large firms to build ever-larger companies. 'Empire-building' for its own sake and the attempt by senior managers to keep competition restricted by eliminating awkward competitors are motives for mergers that are indeed well documented. We must therefore not assume that the merger process is necessarily always in the interests of consumers. This point will be a major matter for us to consider in Chapter 30 in our review of what policies government might wish to adopt in seeking the promotion of competitive markets.

We have so far been considering the creation of oligopolies in a theoretical manner and we must now look at the actual picture of oligopolies in the UK.

Industry Concentration

We have seen that the definition of oligopoly is a situation in which a very few interdependent firms control a large part of total output in an industry. Output of the industry is *concentrated* in a few hands. How do we measure this concentration of industry output?

Concentration Ratio

The most frequent way to compute industry concentration is to determine the percentage of total sales or production accounted for by, say, the top four or top eight firms in an industry. This then gives the four- or eight-firm **concentration ratio**. An example of an industry with 25 firms is given in Figure 25.7. We account for 90 per cent of total output in the hypothetical industry which certainly describes an oligopoly situation.

Figure 25.7
Computing the Four-firm concentration Ratio

	Annual sales (£m)	
Firm 1	150 ⎫	
Firm 2	100 ⎬ = 405	
Firm 3	85	
Firm 4	70 ⎭	
Firm 5–25	45	
	450	

4-firm concentration ratio	=	$\dfrac{405}{450}$	= 90 per cent

Figure 25.8
Market Concentration by UK Manufacturing Sector Measured by Employment in 1980

Minimum list heading sectors	No. of industries	Average 5-firm concentration ratio
Vehicles, transport equipment	7	65
Extraction, metal manufacture	4	59
Food, drink, tobacco	15	58
Electrical & electronic engineering	7	57
Non-metallic mineral products	8	54
Chemicals	8	53
Textiles	9	42
Instrument engineering	4	41
Mechanical engineering	11	36
Paper, printing	3	30
Other	6	30
Leather, footwear, clothing	6	23
Timber, wooden furniture	7	21
Metal goods	5	22
	100	44

Source: Calculations based on Summary Tables, 1980 Census of Production by R. Clarke, *Industrial Economics*, Basil Blackwell, 1985, p. 22.

Note: Figure 25.8 shows the average five-firm concentration ratio as measured by employment using the 1980 Census of Production Minimum List Heading definition of industries. This definition of an industry is a very broad one but the data do illustrate the variation in concentration in UK manufacturing industry. Can you establish any relationship between the level of concentration and the nature of production in this table?

Key Points 25.3

▶ Oligopoly means few sellers; an oligopoly is a market situation in which there are few interdependent sellers.

▶ An oligopolistic market structure can come about because of (1) returns to scale, (2) barriers to entry, and (3) horizontal mergers.

▶ Horizontal mergers involve firms selling a similar product.

▶ Vertical mergers involve the merging of one firm with either the supplier of an input or a firm to which it sells its output.

▶ Industry concentration can be measured by the percentage of total sales accounted for by the top four or five firms.

UK Concentration Ratios Over Time

Figure 25.8 shows the five-firm concentration ratios for various industries in 1980. But is there any way we can show or determine which industries we classify as oligopolistic? There is no definite answer. If one arbitrarily picks a five-firm concentration ratio of 2 per cent, then one could indicate that just half of the 100 industries were oligopolistic. But one would always be dealing with an arbitrary definition of what constitutes an oligopolistic industry. See in Figure 25.8 how the proportion changes if our cut-off point is raised from 52 to, say, 58 per cent.

The concept of an 'industry' is necessarily arbitrary. As a consequence, concentration ratios rise as we narrow the definition of an industry and fall as we broaden it. Thus, we must be certain that we are satisfied with the definition of the industry under study before we jump to conclusions about whether the 'industry' is truly 'too' concentrated, as evidenced by a high measured concentration ratio.

Oligopoly Price and Output Determination

When we analysed perfect competition, pure monopoly, and monopolistic competition, we were able explicitly to present the profit-maximizing rate of output and price combination. In each case, we were able to draw a demand curve, a marginal revenue curve, and a marginal cost curve. (For all three cases, profit maximization occurred when marginal revenue equalled marginal cost.) We cannot so easily do the same thing for oligopoly. Indeed, it is impossible for us to draw any one specific demand curve facing the oligopolist. Remember that we pointed out that each oligopolist had to take account of the reaction of other oligopolists. How can a demand curve be known or even guessed without specifying the way that the other oligopolists will react? The answer is, it cannot. In each oligopoly model, we must take account explicitly of other rivals' reactions. As you might expect, economists have come up with a multitude of

oligopoly models, each one depending on a different type of reaction by rivals.

The Simplest Oligopoly Model

To begin this discussion of oligopoly on its most general level, we make six assumptions.

1. The industry has only a small number of firms. The position and shape of the long-run average cost (LAC) curve relative to the industry demand curve is such that the industry can support only a small number of efficient plants and firms.

2. The firm (and plant) LAC is upward sloping over the relevant range of outputs. The total cost curve of each firm is continuous and normal in the sense that marginal costs will always be positive and above LAC.

3. Single-plant firms are the only possibility. This would in fact be the case if there are large diseconomies at the firm level and/or the possibility of government policies precluding the operation of plants under common ownership and control.

4. Free entry. There are no barriers to entering into or exiting from the industry.

5. Homogeneous product. The firms produce similar products.

6. Profit maximization. We continue to analyse price and output determination assuming that firms strive to make the highest possible aggregate profits.

The Oligopolist's Demand Curve

Now we are faced with the difficult task of drawing the demand curve for an oligopolist. We cannot use the industry demand curve because the oligopolist is not a monopolist. We cannot use a horizontal demand curve at the market-clearing price because the oligopolist is, by definition, not a perfect competitor. We can say nothing about the demand curve of an oligopolist until we make an assumption about the interaction among oligopolists. We have to know something about the **reaction function** that we are looking at.

Does each oligopolist believe that others will not react to changes in its price and/or output? If the typical oligopolist believes that they will react, we must specify the manner in which the oligopolist *expects* them to react. Remember that in a perfectly competitive model, each firm ignores the reactions of other firms because each firm can sell all that it wants at the going market price. In the pure monopoly model, the monopolist does not have to worry about the reaction of rivals, since by definition there *are* none.

Being able to ignore what other firms are doing in an industry – whether it be perfectly competitive or purely monopolistic – is therefore the key distinction to be made between those two forms of market structure and the one under study, oligopoly. We are referring here to interdependence. This interdependence lies at the heart of every oligopoly model, and thus every time a new assumption about interaction among oligopolists for a reaction function is made, a new oligopoly model is born. For this simplest of oligopoly models, we will assume the following:

Each firm expects that any change in price will be matched by all other firms in the industry.

We can see in Figure 25.9 the result of this assumption. The industry demand curve is *dd*. If the industry has only two firms of equal size, each firm will believe that its demand curve is equal to the one labelled ½D½D. This follows from our assumption

that whatever price it chooses will be matched by its rivals. If we assume three equal-sized firms in the industry, each individual demand curve, as perceived by the individual oligopolist, will be ⅓D⅓D. The demand curves ½D½D and ⅓D⅓D are called **proportionate demand curves**, since they represent equal proportions of the industry.

The Equilibrium Number of Firms

We have assumed unrestricted entry and exit. Further, we assume that all firms have cost curves exactly alike. We can determine the number of firms that will be in the industry by comparing the long-run average cost curve with the firms' demand curves. This is shown in Figure 25.10. If there were one firm in the industry, other firms would be attracted because the long-run cost curve lies below the industry demand curve DD for a large range of outputs. If there were two firms in the industry, there would still be an incentive to enter. Finally, if three firms were in the industry, a fourth firm would not desire to enter because the LAC curve is everywhere above the proportional demand curve ¼D¼D. If four firms were in the industry, by our assumptions, none could cover long-run average costs. They would all suffer economic losses.

Figure 25.9
Proportionate Demand Curves. If each firm expects that any change in price will be matched by all other firms in the industry, and if there are two equal-sized firms in the industry, each will face a demand curve that is ½D½D. If there are three equal-sized firms in the industry, each will face a demand curve that is ⅓D⅓D.

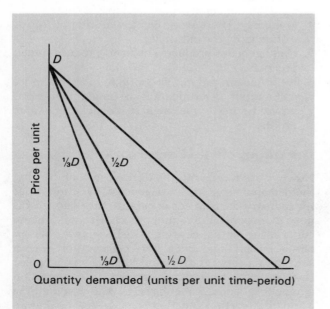

Figure 25.10
Establishing the Equilibrium Number of Firms. If the long-run average cost curve for the industry is LAC, only three firms can be supported in this industry. If a fourth enters, each will face a demand curve equal to ¼D¼D. The LAC curve is everywhere above that proportionate demand curve; all firms make losses.

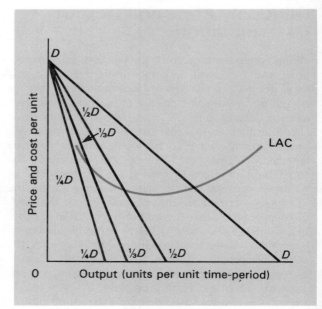

Long-run Economic Profits

It is possible in this simple model that in the long run, economic profits will be obtained. This can be seen by transferring the proportional demand curve for an individual oligopolist when there are three firms to Figure 25.11. The demand curve facing each of the three individual firms is $\frac{1}{3}D\frac{1}{3}D$. The long-run average cost curve is given as LAC, and the long-run marginal cost curve is LMC. The profit-maximizing rate of output for each individual oligopolist is at the intersection of marginal revenue and long-run marginal cost, or at a rate of output q_1. The price that the product will sell for is identically equal for each firm at P_1. Unit cost, given LAC, is C_1. Economic profits per unit time-period are equal to the shaded area in Figure 25.11.

Given the assumption in this model, this is the long-run equilibrium situation.

Figure 25.11

Long-run Economic Profits. We have assumed that three equal-sized firms will exist in this industry. Each faces a proportionate demand curve $\frac{1}{3}D\frac{1}{3}D$. The marginal revenue curve facing each firm is MR, the output for each firm is q_1, and the price is P_1. Costs are equal to C_1 and, thus each firm's profit is the shaded area.

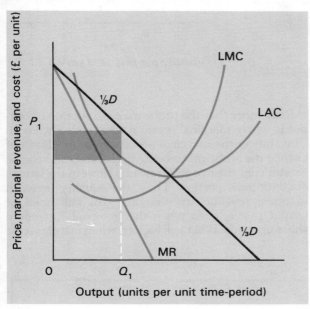

Price Rigidity and the Kinked Demand Curve

We can offer yet another solution to the oligopoly pricing situation. Suppose now that the decision-makers in an oligopolistic firm assume that rivals will react in the following way : they will match all price *decreases* (in order not to be 'undersold'), but not price *increases* (because they want to capture more business). The implications of this reaction function, as it were, are rigid prices and a **kinked demand curve**, which we will explain now.

In Figure 25.12 we draw a kinked demand curve, which is implicit in the assumption that oligopolists follow price decreases but not price increases. We start off at a given price of P_0 and assume that the quantity demanded at that price for this individual oligopolist is q_0. The oligopoly firm assumes that if it lowers its price, rivals will react by matching that reduction to avoid losing their respective shares of the market.

Figure 25.12

The Kinked Demand Curve. Start with the price of P_0. The quantity demanded will be q_0. Now assume that if the firm raises the price above P_0, no firm (or at least only a few firms) will follow suit. Therefore, at a price of P_0, the individual oligopolist's demand curve is relatively elastic – it will lose large amounts of business if it raises price. The demand curve is relatively flat, as shown in the portion d to E. If we were to extend it out, it would follow the broken line after point E. Now consider a reduction in price by the individual oligopolist. The rest of the firms will follow suit, so that a drop in price will result in very little increase in business. Demand will be relatively inelastic below price P_0, as shown by the steeper demand-curve portion from E to d as we move downwards. That demand curve, if it continued, would go up the broken line past point E toward the vertical axis. We can now draw marginal revenue curves for these two separately sloped demand curves. Only those portions of the two marginal revenue curves that are relevant are shaded in colour. There is a discontinuous portion shown with the coloured dots. That is where the kink occurs in the kinked demand curve.

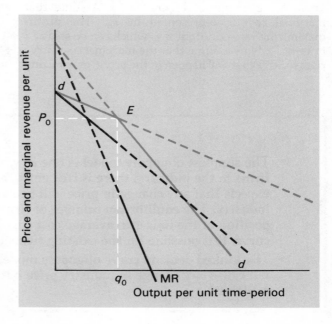

Thus, the oligopolist that lowers its price will not increase its quantity demanded greatly. The portion of its demand curve to the right of and below point E in Figure 25.12 is much less elastic. On the other hand, if the oligopolist increases price, no rivals will follow suit. Thus, the quantity demanded at the higher price for this oligopolist will fall off dramatically. The demand schedule to the left of and above point E will be relatively elastic. This is the flatter part of the curve to the left of point E. Consequently, the demand curve facing the oligopolist is dd, which has a kink at E.

The Marginal Revenue Curve

To draw a marginal revenue curve for the kinked demand curve in Figure 25.12, we first draw a marginal revenue curve out from the vertical axis for the elastic portion of the demand curve (from the upper d to a point directly below E). At quantity q_0, however, the demand curve abruptly changes slope and becomes steeper. The marginal revenue curve will have a discontinuous part in it that corresponds to the kink at quantity q_0 in the demand curve dd. To the left of that 'step', marginal revenue is relatively high. This indicates that revenues will be lost rapidly if the firm moves up (raises price) the relatively elastic portion of its demand curve. To the right of the 'step', on the other hand, marginal revenue is relatively lower. This indicates that little extra revenue can be obtained when the oligopolist moves down (lowers price) the relatively less elastic portion of the demand curve.

Price Rigidity

Over the discontinuous portion of the marginal revenue curve, the oligopolist does not react to changes in marginal cost (unless they are really large). Look, for example, at Figure 25.13. Assume that marginal cost is represented by mc. The profit-maximizing rate of output is q_0 which can be sold at a price of P_0. Now assume that the marginal cost curve rises to mc'. What will happen to the profit-maximizing

rate of output? Nothing. Both quantity and price will remain the same for this oligopolist.

Figure 25.13
Changes in Cost May Not Alter the Profit-maximizing Price and Output. As long as the marginal cost curve 'intersects' the marginal revenue curve in the latter's discontinuous portion, the profit-maximizing price P_0 (and output q_0) will remain unchanged. (However, the firm's rate of profit will change.)

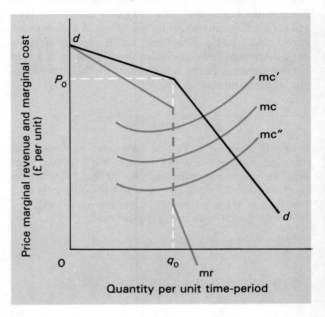

Remember that the profit-maximizing rate of output is where marginal revenue equals marginal cost. The shift in the marginal cost curve to mc' does not change the profit-maximizing rate of output, because mc' still 'cuts' the marginal revenue curve in the latter's discontinuous portion. Thus, the equality between marginal revenue and marginal cost still holds at output rate q_0 even when the marginal cost curve shifts upwards. What will happen when marginal cost

---

Key Points 25.4

▶ The simplest oligopoly model is one in which there are only a small number of firms in the industry, there is free entry, and a homogeneous product. Each firm expects that any change in price will be matched by all other firms in the industry. The equilibrium number of firms in the industry will depend on the position of the long-run average cost curve relative to the proportionate demand curve. It is possible for the existing firms to have long-run economic profits.

▶ The kinked demand curve oligopoly model predicts that major shifts in costs will not cause any change in industry price but the existing price is not satisfactorily explained.

falls to mc''? Nothing. This oligopolist will continue to produce at a rate of output q_0 and charge a price of P_0. Thus, whenever the marginal cost curve cuts the discontinuous portion of the marginal revenue curve, fluctuations (within limits) in marginal cost will not affect output or price, because the profit-maximizing condition MR = MC will hold. Thus, prices are seen to be rigid in oligopolistic industries if they react the way we assumed in this model.

The theory is thus an application of the revenue functions that are now familiar to us. But one of the criticisms that has been waged against the kinked demand curve is that we have no idea how the existing price, P_0, came into being. Seemingly, if every oligopolistic firm faced a kinked demand curve, it would not pay for it to change prices. The problem is that the kinked demand curve does not show us how supply and demand originally determine the going price of an oligopolist's product.

Collusion

Our discussion of the kinked demand curve highlighted the basic problem of the oligopolist – trying to estimate how rivals will react. In short the world of oligopoly is one of *uncertainty*. This is in contrast to the situation both in pure monopoly and in perfect competition. In the case of the former where there is only one firm the question of considering rivals does not arise. At the other end of the spectrum where the number of firms is large the decisions made by an insignificant single producer are trivial to the outcome of the whole industry. Interdependence means that oligopolists are, in a freely competing market, always unsure what will be the impact of one firm's change in market behaviour. One firm's decisions has consequences for all.

Uncertainty was seen in Chapter 16 as one basis for individuals to hold money. In a micro-context the presence of uncertainty provides managers of firms with an incentive to reduce the risks inherent in business life. How can managers in an oligopolistic market structure try to minimize the uncertainties they all face? Well they can try to agree on restraints on their independent decision-making. If they *collude* they limit their ability to use the crucial variable of price to try to gain sales from rivals.

Study of the business environment in the UK in the nineteenth century shows a 'natural' tendency for firms in concentrated industries to try to act in concert. Indeed, the operation of capitalism seems to prompt efforts by businessmen to reach either implicit or explicit agreement on prices which should be charged. This raises the very relevant issue of government policy towards such restraints on price competition and is discussed in the next chapter. For the moment we need to consider what are the possible advantages of oligopolists of engaging in **collusion**. First of all we need to define what we mean by collusion. Collusion that takes place in a **cartel** is an agreement made by a number of independent entities to co-ordinate decisions. The purpose of the cartel is that the cartel will earn monopoly profits. Thus the operation of a cartel that fixes prices takes us back to our discussion of the behaviour a monopolist who attempts to increase total revenue by restricting output. The analysis of a profit-maximizing monopolist is the same as a cartel which seeks to maximize the joint profits of its member firms.

Duopoly

The simplest way to approach the operation of cartel pricing is to consider the case of just two firms in an industry. This situation is called **duopoly**. Suppose the two firms, Smith plc and Jones plc each account for half of an industry's output which is not differentiated by product and produce under identical cost conditions. These two assumptions mean the costs and revenue functions for both Smith plc and Jones plc are as in Figure 25.14. Profits are maximized for both firms at the level of output OQ and the shaded area $PRST$ indicates the short-run economic profits accruing to both Smith plc and Jones plc. Neither firm has any incentive to charge a price other than OP. A cut in price by say Smith plc would result in both firms suffering reduced profits. The interests of Smith plc square with those of Jones plc if the price is OP.

Figure 25.14

Duopoly with Identical Costs and Market Shares. The two firms, Jones and Smith are assumed to have similar costs in producing the same product and equally share the output of the industry. They each maximize profits at output OQ and each gains the short-run profits of $PRST$. Neither firm has any reason to undercut the other: they would both charge the common price of OP.

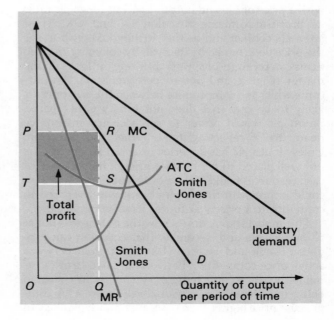

Figure 25.15
Duopoly: Costs Differ but Equal Market Shares. When one firm in a duopoly has lower costs than its rival it would wish to charge a price that differs from its competitor. Here Smith would select an output of *OW* and charge *OS* while Jones, the higher cost firm, would wish to set a higher price *OJ*. The duopolists have no common view and face a difficulty in resolving their individual outlooks.

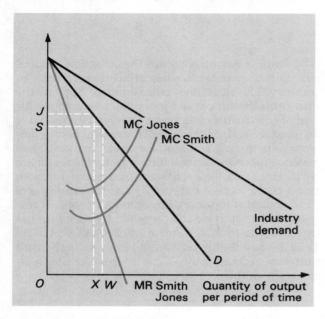

But what happens if in our duopoly model Jones plc is now a higher-cost producer perhaps because its production facilities are older and less productive or even because of managerial inefficiency. Figure 25.15 shows that the two firms cannot sell at a price that will equate their individual interests with that of the industry as a whole. Smith plc gains maximum profits with a price of *OS* and output *OW* but Jones plc finds its profit-maximizing situation *OJ* and *OX*. Their interests conflict and neither firm would wish to see the price determined by its rival. By colluding the two firms can try to resolve their differing outlooks on the matter of price and output determination. An outcome which is a compromise between the two prices is likely to be one that does not satisfy either party. Smith plc would prefer to see a compromise price nearer to *OS* reflecting its favourable cost situation. Unless Jones plc has superior financial resources it is not well placed to try to set a price. The presence of cash resources could make a difference since Jones plc could impress on Smith plc that it was prepared to contemplate a price war unless its view prevailed.

This model shows firstly how the outcome is not at all predictable and, secondly, that collusion can produce a fragile and uncertain lasting interlude between active price competition between the two firms. Our model points to any temporary success in collusion being threatened by individual self-interest. A compromise price higher than *OX* leaves Smith plc likely to concede secret price cuts to a few customers. Collusion is thus threatened since prices are undercut by a member of the price arrangement not upholding to what was agreed. Once price cuts become apparent and all parties engage in price concessions the effectiveness of the cartel is eroded until common cause is again established. Thus cartels are beset by the problem of its members being prompted to *cheat* on what they promise to uphold in common cause: self-interest clashes with the wider interest of the industry as a whole.

The recent difficulties of the oil-producing countries to agree on a common pricing policy illustrate the difficulties that face a cartel like OPEC. But at least one major oil producer has tried to provide some stability to the oil cartel and achieved some success through its relative importance in this market. This stabilizing role as performed by Saudi Arabia as a major oil-producer takes us on to yet another form of price determination within the world of oligopoly, that of price leadership.

Price Leadership

This term refers to the possibility of one firm within an oligopolistic market acting as the leader in effecting changes in prices. One firm may wish to raise its prices because its costs have risen and its profitability thus fallen. Its rivals facing common cost pressures, such as higher wages, could thus be in a similar position and content to follow suit. Thus the lead given by the first firm is one the rest of the industry is more willing to accept. As long as the leader has carefully judged the magnitude of the price rise the problem of the kinked demand curve would not then arise. The price leadership model thus describes how in an oligopolistic market virtual simultaneous changes in prices (so-called **parallel pricing**) can occur. The result appears to point to collusive behaviour but may well simply reflect how all firms await a suitable lead by one firm which acts as a *barometer* for the rest of the industry. The **barometric leader** need not be the same firm on every occasion of a change in price. On the other hand it could be the case that the largest firm in the industry is accepted as the price leader. In this case as the **dominant firm** it might be recognized as the appropriate guide for the rest of the industry. Much smaller firms may hesitate to challenge the determination of market price by the most powerful firm within the industry for fear of starting a challenge from which it may ultimately be the loser.

Non-price Competition

By their very nature, oligopolistic firms do not exhibit active price competition. The benefits from cutting prices tend to be small given the reactions of rivals. Hence a situation where rivals keep trying to undercut one another in the battle for supremacy in the market in a so-called *price war* is unlikely to persist. The likelihood of becoming a victor is slim if costs conditions are similar. Thus price wars do erupt occasionally, but these are only temporary. Therefore, competition for an increased percentage of total sales in the market must take some other form. The alternative form is what is generally called **non-price competition**. Non-price competition cannot be neatly subdivided into categories because it takes on a large number of aspects. The only thing that we can say about non-price competition is that it is an attempt by one oligopolistic firm to attract customers by some means other than a price differential. Here we will consider only the two types of product differentiation that we have explicitly or implicitly referred to when discussing monopolistic competition.

Advertising

As we pointed out previously, the primary purpose of advertising is to shift the demand curve to the right. This allows the seller, whether it be an oligopolist, a monopolistic competitor, or a monopolist, to sell more at each and every price. Advertising may also have the effect of differentiating the product and of making the product's availability better known. A firm will advertise as a way of gaining a non-price competitive advantage over other firms. Whatever can be said about advertising, its effect on the oligopolistic firm is certainly not completely predictable.

Quality Variations

Quality differentiation results in a division of one market into a number of sub-markets. We talked earlier about differentiating product through quality variation when we discussed monopolistic competition. Now we can apply the same discussion to oligopoly. The prime example of product differentiation is the motor vehicle industry. There are specific physically definable differences between different automobile models within one single firm. A Maestro and a Montego are certainly not the same product. If we examine cars, we see that competition among oligopolistic firms creates a continuous expansion and redefinition of the different models that are sold by any one company. There is competition to create new quality classes and thereby gain a competitive edge. Being the first in the market in a new quality class has often meant higher profits. Thus oligopolists are always looking for best-selling new models. New products can promise higher sales and profits in a way that avoids the alternative risk of engaging in price competition with rivals.

Comparing Market Structures

Now that we have looked at perfect competition, pure monopoly, monopolistic competition, and oligopoly, we are in a position to compare the attributes of these four different market structures. We do this in summary form in Figure 25.16, where we compare the number of sellers, their ability to set price, and whether product differentiation exists.

Figure 25.16
Comparing Market Structures

Market structure	Number of sellers	Unrestricted entry and exit	Ability to set price	Long-run economic profits possible	Product differentiation
Perfect competition	Numerous	Yes	None	No	None
Monopolistic competition	Many	Yes	Some	No	Considerable
Oligopoly	Few	Partial	Some	Yes	Frequently
Pure monopoly	One	No	Considerable	Yes	The product is unique

Key Points 25.5

▶ Because the world of oligopoly is one of uncertainty there is an incentive for oligopolists to try to collude such that competition in price is at least partly eliminated.

▶ In a duopoly situation the equilibrium price and industry output could be equivalent to the pure monopoly profit-maximizing price and output combination. Differences in their cost situation makes collusion between duopolists difficult to effect.

▶ Price leadership may be one method by which oligopolists avoid the uncertainties in price determination when they do not collude. The leader may be the largest firm in an industry or simply one firm that hopes its rivals will accept its proposed change in price.

▶ Non-price competition is typical of oligopolistic market structures since if one firm tries to expand sales through price competition it is unlikely to be successful without damage to its profit situation. Advertising campaigns are the means by which oligopolists try to differentiate their products. Such expenditures highlight the new products that oligopolists strive to develop in order to win consumer support.

CASE STUDY

Whisper It Not

The gigantic brands in the 'pure' chocolate market had, without exception, origins dating back to before the Second World War. Cadbury's Dairy Milk was launched in 1905 and has sold prodigiously ever since. Some 20 years later Cadbury launched Flake, which was discovered as a by-product of manufacturing milk chocolate.

These two products set the pace in the market for 80 years. There have been many attempts to launch a product to stand alongside CDM and Flake. None succeeded until the late 1970s when Cadbury started work on a project code named P.46.

This is the story of P.46, a remarkable management success:

Mount Everest

It's widely acknowledged that the Mount Everest of chocolate product development is to invent a bar which is new and different yet still comprised solely of pure chocolate.

Such an achievement is rare indeed. Flake, which is now legend, was something of an accident; the crumbly extrusions were a by-product of manufacturing milk chocolate.

In fact, in the last twenty years, only five new brands have achieved lasting success in the intensely competitive confectionery market.

The opportunity was there and it was decided that Cadbury, the first name in chocolate, was going to be the company to realise that opportunity.

Enter P.46

It all started with a secret company R & D project in the mid-seventies. It was found that the latest technology applied to chocolate manufacturing could confer a different texture and new eating characteristics on the classic milk chocolate product.

The formula was refined and given the codename P.46. When you realise that this product has now achieved an RSP value of no less than £70 million you'll realise why the whole project was shrouded in secrecy.

All the pre-launch research suggested that the product was a winner. However, as years of bitter experience have taught many manufacturers in this market, having a product that the public likes is not always enough. The complete marketing package is just as critical.

Nothing new under the sun

This was the attitude of most consumers to chocolate products.

They simply didn't believe you could produce anything new. Reversing this belief was the problem facing the Young and Rubicam advertising agency when Cadbury brought them the product, now named 'Wispa', in 1980.

The Account Director, Clive Holland, who worked on the launch recalls 'We couldn't have been more clearly briefed.'

And, of course, it's the ideal stage in a product's development for the agency to become involved.

The sheer professionalism of Cadbury's management team greatly assisted in developing what turned out to be a textbook advertising solution.'

The 'Whispering Duos' campaign, a wittily simple device, was made ready for the Tyne Tees test market launch in September 1981.

Fist fights

It is not an overstatement to say that the Geordies went mad for Cadbury's 'Wispa'. The television advertising had to be stopped after just three weeks because the limited capacity pilot plant at Bourneville couldn't cope with the demand.

Eight weeks after the launch, five weeks after the end of advertising, the product was on allocation. Strange reports of black market trading and even a 4p price premium began to filter back.

Weirdest of all was the serious fist fight which broke out over the last two cases at a major cash and carry outlet.

Withdrawal and investment

It was obvious to Cadbury management that here at last was

the long awaited 'breakthrough' chocolate bar. So what did they do? They withdrew it. Then, false rumours of being unable to produce the product consistently and profitably spread, which confused the opposition.

Next, a massive £12 million was budgeted for plant investment. A large area of the factory was secretly cleared and the relevant components of a large and as yet, unproven plant were obtained. A high-tech plant, controlled by 24 microprocessors was then built from scratch – all inside 20 months.

At the same time, the staff was selected and trained and new working practices adopted in order to ensure a competitive cost structure.

The advertising and media plan was finalized and the Company prepared itself for the launch that would make marketing history.

Marketing history

On Monday 24 October 1983, the product was relaunched in Tyne-Tees. Cadbury could now spend heavily on advertising with complete confidence, and spend they did, at a national equivalent of £6 million.

The launch comprised 10-second teaser commercials followed by three 40-second TV commercials and a massive poster campaign. In a quite unprecedented blitz launch, 90 per cent distribution was achieved in just one weekend – a feat normally requiring 4–6 weeks.

In just two days a major department store in Newcastle sold no less than 36 000 bars.

With a start like that there was no looking back.

Success where others settle for survival

Cadbury's 'Wispa' is now the third largest brand in the *total confectionery market*. The multipack is now the third biggest brand in grocery and multiple outlets.

Customers, who were so closely involved in the launch of the brand, have rated it as one of the greatest ever new products.

Eleven weeks after launch, spontaneous awareness of the brand among consumers reached 73 per cent, and trial now exceeds 80 per cent.

Whichever way you look at it, Cadbury's 'Wispa' is a superb technical and marketing accomplishment unique in a fiercely competitive market.

The Cadbury management team feel justifiably pleased with the results. Cadbury Managing Director Neville Bain says 'Whereas a product like "Flake" came to us by accident, the whole team feels extremely proud of being able to claim an even greater success with "Wispa", a new brand developed by innovative and resourceful management.'

Source: Observer, 9 Feb. 1985.

Questions
1. Why do you think Cadbury felt the need to plan the whole project 'shrouded in secrecy'?
2. Why would Cadbury have tried to test the new product just in the Tyne Tees television area?
3. What does the case study mean by the critical importance of 'the complete marketing package'?

CASE STUDY

OPEC Over a Barrel?

It has not been a good week for producer cartels. That most famous of them, OPEC has been further battered, as Yamani's latest comments underline. It is a far cry from the days when people made jokes about 'Yamani or your life'.

But does this mean that producer cartels serve no function? Are they ultimately self-defeating? Do they work inevitably against the interests of the consumers? And why, in any case, have these two cartels failed?

OPEC has always tried to set its oil price in relation to market conditions. It has, to be sure, sought to bend those conditions in its favour. But it is a loose organization and has never had the internal discipline to try to hold a price which is far out of line with what the market will bear.

And the method of operation of OPEC has been essentially for the dominant members to restrict production while the smaller members maintain the price structure of the large. Its weapon has been production cuts.

There have been periods where OPEC got its prices out of line. Between the two oil shocks, it was having great difficulty holding its official price. It was saved in that instance by the collapse of Iranian oil production, after the Shah was toppled. But it has never persistently tried to oppose the market. That quadrupling of the oil price at the end of 1973 was a response by OPEC to market conditions, rather than an imposition by the producers of a price which the market could not sustain.

In a sense, then, the thing which has saved OPEC is what most people perceive as its weakness: lack of internal discipline. That very weakness has checked it from getting its prices too far out of line.

For all the impact which new producer areas like the North Sea and Alaska have had, the fact remains that the OPEC members are the lowest-cost oil producers in the world. In the Middle East the stuff just floods out of the ground. Compare that with the cost of erecting something like the Eiffel Tower in the middle of the North Sea. Moreover, OPEC has played a very important educative role. It owes a lot to the intelligent and sensitive leadership of its most important member, Saudi Arabia, which increased its production to the limits in the middle 1970s to try not to damage the industrial fabric of the West, and which subsequently cut production drastically to try to preserve the economic fabric of debtor nations such as Mexico and Nigeria.

The plunge in OPEC's share of the world oil market does not necessarily imply any diminution in its ability to control prices. This apparent paradox follows from one of the most elementary observations of market economics which is sometimes forgotten by over-enthusiastic free marketeers: a market price is determined by the marginal transaction, not the average one. In layman's terms, a cartel does not require 60 per cent, or even 40 per cent, of the world's oil output to succeed in fixing prices; it needs only to control increases in production.

The reasoning is easy to understand. Suppose Britain, for instance, was currently pumping every barrel of oil which its wells could produce. It would then be completely impossible for Britain to undercut OPEC by reducing the price of British oil; Britain's price cut would raise the demand for British oil, but because the North Sea oilfields could not actually meet this extra demand, Britain could not lure a single customer away from OPEC. Thus, if Britain is already producing its maximum available output, the British National Oil Corporation's price cuts can have nothing more than a psychological effect on OPEC or the world oil price.

Precisely the same argument applies to every other oil-producing country. And the fact of the matter is that all the non-OPEC producers are at present pumping every barrel of oil they have. In the short term (which means one to three years for the oil industry) Britain cannot produce much more than its current 2.7 m barrels a day (mbd) without geological damage to the oilfields. US oil production has been stuck at the 8.6-mbd mark since the 1970s, with rising output from Alaska only just offsetting the rapid depletion of the traditional fields.

Of the non-OPEC countries, only Mexico is believed to have significant unused potential, but even this would require massive investment in production facilities to tap; the government's current energy plan forecasts an increase of only 0.4 mbd from its present 2.7-mbd level between now and 1988.

Sources: Hamish McRae, 'If you really want your cartel to work, you have to keep an eye on the markets', *The Guardian*, 9 Nov. 1985; Anatole Kaletsky, 'OPEC can beat the markets', *Financial Times*, 26 Oct. 1984.

Questions

1. What are the key points that explain how OPEC has been able to influence the price of oil?
2. Why is it that the UK which is not a member of OPEC has not weakened OPEC's influence on oil prices?
3. The case study suggests that 'cartels can work very successfully if they genuinely seek to match supply to demand'. What problems arise for OPEC if demand for oil falls?
4. How could members of OPEC gain a larger share of the oil market?
5. Why might Mexico and Nigeria threaten the cohesiveness of the cartel?

Exam Preparation and Practice

INTRODUCTORY EXERCISES

1. Read the following extract* and complete the final sentence:

Joe Doakes was in the prune-juice business. He grew his own prunes, put them through his own squeezer, bottled the juice and sold it for 10p a bottle. He sold the residual pulp for fertilizer. Joe had competition from four other prune-juice squeezers in his area, but they each had their own steady customers, they all charged a fair price and all made a good living.

One day one of Joe's bright young men pointed out that the new squeezer they had built a couple of years ago was not operating at full capacity. 'Boss,' he said, 'the cost of turning out more juice will only be marginal. We won't need any more men at the plant, the same salesmen can handle it, there won't be any increase in overheads. We can make the extra juice for 5p a bottle instead of the 7½p the regular stuff costs us.' So Joe knocked 1p off the price of the juice and the boys got rid of the extra production by taking away accounts from the competitors. As soon as they found out, the competitors promptly retaliated by reducing their prices too by 1p a bottle.

Meanwhile, the prune pulp from Joe's additional production mounted up and Joe had to cut prices to dispose of it. Once again his competitors reacted and soon the prune-pulp market was in as bad a state as the prune-juice market. Joe's financial position became desperate and he searched frantically for a means of making some more profit. His squeezer still had surplus capacity. He succumbed to the suggestion that he buy up the distressed

production of a prune-grower with surplus prunes on his hands. However, to market the additional prune juice he had to cut prices yet again. Once again his competitors reduced prices in retaliation and so the market went into a descending price spiral. The story came to a sad end with poor Joe in the bankruptcy court and a nasty smelly pile of prune pulp in his backyard.

The moral of this fable was not lost on many managers. The dangers of marketing on the basis of marginal cost were overemphasized and misinterpreted. What was not revealed in the fable was that the mistake Joe had made was not in basing his marketing decisions on marginal costs, but . . . . .
. . . .

2. Suppose you own a monopolistically competitive firm that sells car tune-ups at a price of £25 each. You currently are selling 100 per week. You are the owner-operator and you initiate an ad campaign in the local newspaper. You promise to smooth out any ill-running car at a price of £25. The result is that you end up tuning 140 cars per week. What is the 'marginal revenue' of this ad campaign? What additional information do you need to determine whether your profits have risen?

---

* K. Mackrell, 'Marginal costs and the price of prunes', *Financial Times*, 17 June 1969.

continued overleaf

3. In the graph below we depict long-run equilibrium for a monopolistic competitor.

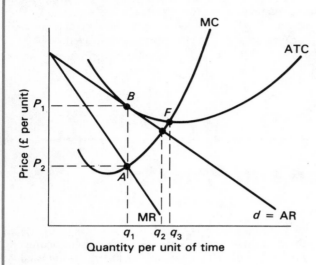

(a) Which output rate represents equilibrium?
(b) Which price represents equilibrium?
(c) Which letter indicates that economic profits are zero?
(d) Which letter indicates minimum ATC?
(e) Is ATC at equilibrium higher than or equal to minimum ATC?
(f) Is the equilibrium price greater than, less than, or equal to the marginal cost of producing the equilibrium output?

4. The table below indicates some information for Industry A.

Annual sales

Firm 1	£200 000 000
Firm 2	150 000 000
Firm 3	100 000 000
Firm 4	75 000 000
Firms 5–30	300 000 000

(a) What is the four-firm concentration ratio for this industry?
(b) Assume that Industry A were the 'steel industry'. What would happen to the concentration index if we redefined Industry A as the 'rolled steel industry'? As the 'metal industry'?

MULTIPLE CHOICE QUESTIONS

†1. In which of the following market forms would a price taker certainly be found?
A monopoly
B duopoly
C oligopoly
D imperfect competition
E perfect competition

†2. When the total revenue function of a firm is shown by a straight line passing through the origin, it illustrates
A monopoly in the short or in the long run
B perfect competition in the short or in the long run
C imperfect competition in the short or in the long run
D all firms in the short run

3. If the five-firm concentration ratio for an industry is 20 per cent this indicates that the
A largest five firms in the industry have a market share of 20 per cent each
B largest firm in the industry has a 20 per cent market share
C average market share of the largest five firms is 20 per cent
D largest five firms have a total market share of 20 per cent

4. In an imperfectly competitive market, a profit-maximizing firm will try to equate
A marginal cost and price
B marginal revenue and average cost
C marginal revenue and marginal cost
D average cost and price
E average cost and marginal cost

5. The organization of the commercial banks in the UK is best described as one of
A duopoly
B oligopoly
C monopsony
D monopoly
E perfect competition

†6. Which of the following is NOT a condition of perfect competition?
A differentiated products
B lack of barriers to entry to the industry
C large number of firms in the industry
D no one firm large enough to influence the market
E no discrimination by buyers between sellers except on the basis of price

For Questions 7 — 10 select your answers from the following grid:

A	B	C	D	E
1,2,3 all correct	1,2 only correct	2,3 only correct	1 only correct	3 only correct

†7. In equilibrium in the long run, normal profit may be earned by firms operating under conditions of
   1   perfect competition
   2   monopolistic competition
   3   monopoly

†8. A firm in conditions of monopolistic competition will, in the long run, usually
   1   make normal profit
   2   produce at optimum capacity
   3   equate marginal revenue with average cost

†9. When a monopolist maximizes his profits
   1   the demand for his product will be price elastic
   2   marginal cost will equal marginal revenue
   3   marginal revenue will be positive

10. Which of the following statements about price, marginal revenue, and marginal cost is/are true?
   1   Under conditions of perfect competition profits are maximized when price equals marginal revenue equals marginal cost
   2   Under imperfect competition marginal cost equals marginal revenue when profits are maximized
   3   Under imperfect competition, price equals marginal revenue

RELATED ESSAY QUESTIONS

†1. 'Oligopoly involves interdependence in a way unlike any other market structure.' Explain this statement and discuss its implications.

2. Why might there be a tendency in conditions of oligopoly towards price rigidity? How may an individual oligopolist attempt to increase his share of the market?

3. Why do firms compete other than by price? Is such competition preferable to price competition?

4. Discuss whether the assumption of profit maximization is consistent with the actual behaviour of monopolistically competitive firms.

5. Describe the characteristics of an oligopolistic industry and examine the different explanations of oligopolistic price and output determination.

6. Why do firms advertise their products? Examine the possible effects that advertising expenditures may have upon the price and output of a product.

7. One finds marked differences between various United Kingdom industries in terms of the way firms compete with each other, e.g. price, advertising, design, after-sales service, delivery dates etc. What economic reasons are there for these various types of competition?

8. 'When an industry contains only a few firms, the behaviour and performance of those firms will differ from what would be the case if the number of firms were greater.' Discuss.

Part D

Factor Markets

26 Demand and Supply in the Labour Market

Key Points to Review

▶ Substitution and income effect (5.1)
▶ Determinants of elasticity (7.4)
▶ Law of diminishing returns (22.2)

▶ Profit maximization (23.1)
▶ Monopolist's demand, marginal revenue less than price (24.2)

Questions for Preview

1 In hiring labour, what general rule will be followed by employers who wish to maximize profits?

2 What is the profit-maximizing rate of employment for (a) a perfectly competitive firm? and (b) an imperfectly competitive firm?

3 What is the shape of the supply of labour curve?

4 How is an industry wage-rate determined?

5 What effect do trade unions have on wages?

6 In what ways is the labour market imperfect?

How much people are paid, and the extent to which their labour resources are used, are crucial issues in economics because they determine who is rich and who is poor. These factors determine what percentage of national income goes to wages and what percentage goes to interest, profits, and dividends.

Before analysing the distribution of income, we try to predict the amount of a particular input that firms will demand and the price they will pay for it. We assume that there is only one variable factor of production: labour, and that all other factors of production are fixed; in other words, the firm has a fixed number of machines but can hire or fire workers.

A firm's demand for inputs can be studied in much the same manner as we studied the demand for output in different types of market situations. Our analysis will always end with the conclusion: a firm will hire employees up to the point where it is not profitable to hire any more. It will hire employees to the point

where the marginal benefit of hiring a worker will just equal the marginal cost. We will start our analysis under the assumption that the market for input factors is perfectly competitive, and that the output market is perfectly competitive, also. This provides a bench-mark against which to compare other situations where labour markets and/or product markets are not perfectly competitive.

A Competitive Market

Let us take as our example a prerecorded-tape manufacturing firm that is in competition with many companies selling the same kind of product. Assume that the labour hired by our tape manufacturing firm needs no special skills. This firm sells its product in a perfectly competitive market and also buys its variable input – labour – in a perfectly competitive market. The

Figure 26.1(a)

(1) Labour input	(2) Total physical product (per week) ≡ TPP	(3) Marginal physical product ≡ MPP	(4) Price of tape (P = £2.50) × Marginal physical product ≡ MRP (£ per additional worker)	(5) Wage rate (£ per week) Marginal factor cost ≡ MFC ≡ change in total costs change in labour
6	882		295	£200
7	1000	118	277.50	£200
8	1111	111	260	£200
9	1215	104	242.50	£200
10	1312	97	225	£200
11	1402	90	207.50	£200
12	1485	83	190	£200
13	1561	76		

firm can influence neither the price of its product nor the price that it must pay for its variable input; it can purchase all the labour it wants at the going market wage without affecting that wage. The 'going' wage is established by the forces of supply and demand in the labour market. The total labour demand is the sum of all the individual firms' demands.

Marginal Physical Product

Look at Figure 26.1(a). In column 1, we show the number of worker-weeks that the firm can hire. In column 2, we show total physical product (TPP) per week. In other words, column 2 shows the units of total *physical* production, or real output that different quantities of the labour input will generate in a week's time. In column 3, we show the additional output gained when a tape-manufacturing company adds additional workers to its existing capacity. You will notice that the third column, **marginal physical product (MPP)**, represents the extra (additional) output attributed to employing additional units of the variable input factor, which in this case is labour. Thus, if this firm adds a seventh worker, the marginal physical product is 118. You will recall that the law of diminishing marginal returns predicts that additional units of a variable factor will, after some point, cause the marginal physical product to decline, other things being equal.

Why Does Marginal Physical Product Decline?

If our tape-manufacturing firm wants to add one more worker to an assembly line, it has to crowd all the existing workers a little closer together because it does not increase its capital stock (the assembly line equip-

Figure 26.1(b)

Marginal Revenue Product Curve. The employer hires workers up to the point where the marginal revenue product equals the wage-rate. In our case it is 12 worker-weeks. If the employer hired only 11 worker-weeks, potential profit represented by triangle *A* would be lost. If 13 worker-weeks are hired, profit is reduced by an amount shown in triangle *B*. *E* is the equilibrium at the intersection of demand and supply, or the point where the MRP equals the going wage.

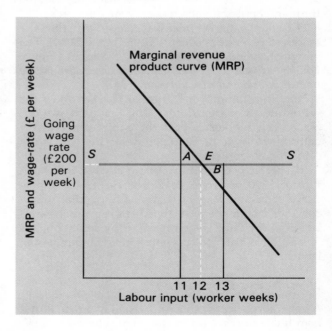

ment) at the same time that it increases the work-force. Therefore, as we add more workers, each one has a smaller and smaller fraction of the available capital stock with which to work. If one worker uses one machine, adding another worker will not normally double the output, because the machine can run only so fast for so many hours per day.

ALL WORKERS PAID SAME WAGE

What additional information do we need to determine the number of workers to be employed? Since we have assumed that labour is employed in a competitive market, then every worker we employ is paid the same wage-rate. Figure 26.1(b) assumes that this wage-rate is £200 per week.

In addition, we need to know the price of the product. Since we have assumed perfect competition, the hypothetical market equilibrium price established in Figure 26.1 is £2.50. Our firm will employ workers up to the point where the marginal revenue, or benefit, of hiring a worker will equal the additional (marginal) cost.

The marginal cost of workers is the extra cost we incur in employing that factor of production. We recall that

$$\text{marginal cost} = \frac{\text{change in total cost}}{\text{change in amount of resource used.}}$$

In our example, one additional worker can be hired at a constant cost of £200 per week.

Marginal Revenue Product

We now need to translate the physical product into a money value. This is done by multiplying the MPP by the market price of tapes. If the seventh worker's MPP is 118, and the market price is £2.50 per tape, then the **marginal revenue product** is £295 (118 × £2.50). The marginal revenue product is shown in column 4 Figure 26.1(a). *We call the individual worker's contribution to total revenues the marginal revenue product or MRP.*

Now in column 5 of Figure 26.1(a), we show the wage-rate or marginal cost (MC) of each worker. Since each worker is paid the same competitively determined wage of £200 per week, the MC is the same for all workers.

In a perfectly competitive labour market, the wage-rate of £200 per week really represents the supply curve of labour. It is, of course, a horizontal supply curve of labour, because that firm can purchase all labour at the same wage-rate since, by definition, it is a minuscule part of the entire market purchasing labour.

How Many Employees?

A general rule for the hiring decision of a firm is: the firm hires workers up to the point where the additional cost associated with hiring the last worker is equal to the additional revenue generated by that worker.

In a perfectly competitive situation, this is the point where the wage-rate just equals the marginal revenue

product. If the firm hired more workers, the additional wages would not be sufficiently covered by additional increases in total revenue. If the firm hired fewer workers, it would be forfeiting the contributions that those workers could make to total profits.

Therefore, referring to columns 4 and 5 in Figure 26.1 (a), we see that this firm would certainly employ the seventh worker, because the MRP is £295 while the MC is only £200. The firm would continue to employ workers up to the point where MC = MRP because as workers are added, they contribute more to revenue than to cost.

We can also use Figure 26.1 (b) to find how many workers our firm should hire. The horizontal supply curve, *ss*, intersects the marginal revenue product curve at 12 worker-weeks. At the intersection *E*, the wage-rate is equal to the marginal revenue product. This MRP curve is also a *factor demand curve*, assuming only one variable factor of production and perfect competition in both the factor and product markets, because it shows how much labour employers want at each level of wages. The firm in our example would not hire the thirteenth worker who will only add £190 to revenue but £200 to cost. If the firm were to hire the thirteenth worker, its net income would be reduced by £10 (shown by triangle B). If the firm hired only 11 workers it would be forgoing £7.50 of revenue over and above the cost of a 12th worker (shown by triangle A).

Derived Demand

This demand curve is *derived*, that is, it shows a **derived demand**, because the tape firm does not want to purchase the services of workers simply for the services themselves. Factors of production are rented or purchased not because they give satisfaction but because they can be used to produce products that can be sold at a profit. This is different from a consumer's desire to buy a product.

The MRP curve, because it is derived, will shift whenever there is a change in the demand for and price of the final product. If, for example, the demand for tapes goes down, the price will go down, and the marginal revenue product curve will shift inwards to the left, to MRP' in Figure 26.2. If demand for, and the price of, tapes go up, the MRP curve will shift outwards to the right, since MRP = MPP × price of product. If output and price fall, so, too, does the demand for labour; at the same going wage-rate, the firm will require fewer workers. Conversely, if output and price rise, the demand for labour will also rise, and the firm will want to hire more workers at each and every possible wage-rate. Hence wages will generally be higher in industries with growing demand than in industries with declining demand. Growing demand may be associated with a rise in the relative price of a substitute, with rising incomes, with shifts in tastes and fashions, or with a fall in the price of a complement. Changing technology may be an integral part of the picture.

Equally, a change in productivity (output per worker) can change MRP. If marginal physical product rises, e.g. because of more efficient management or technology, MPP × price, or MRP, will be higher for any given quantity of labour. In other words the MRP curve will have shifted to the right.

Figure 26.2
Demand for Labour, a Derived Demand. The demand for labour is a derived demand – derived from the demand for the final product being produced. Therefore, the marginal revenue product curve will shift whenever the price of the product changes.

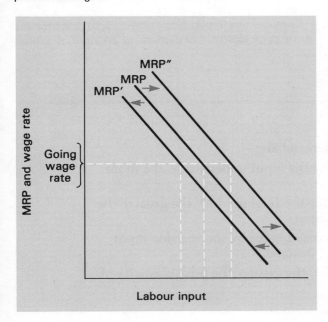

Determinants of Demand Elasticity for Inputs

Just as we were able to discuss the price elasticity of demand for different commodities in Chapter 7, we can discuss the price elasticity of demand for labour. The price elasticity of demand for labour is the percentage change in quantity demanded divided by the percentage change in the price of labour (the wage-rate). When this ratio is less than 1, it is considered inelastic; when it is 1, unitary; and when it is greater than 1, elastic.

There are four principal determinants of the price elasticity of demand for an input:

1. The easier it is for a particular input to be substituted for by other inputs, the more price elastic the demand for that variable input will be.
2. The greater the price elasticity of demand for the final product, the greater the price elasticity of demand for the variable input.
3. The smaller the proportion of total costs accounted for by a particular variable input, the lower its price elasticity of demand.
4. The price elasticity of demand for a variable input will be greater in the long run than in the short run.

Substitute Factors

If it is technically possible to substitute capital for labour, an increase in real wages will probably lead to an increase in labour-saving capital investment; more capital-intensive methods of production will be adopted. So an increase in wages may lead to a more than proportional decrease in quantity demanded: the demand for labour is elastic. Equally if the price of capital falls, wage costs rise relatively and the outcome will be similar. In some situations no substitution of capital is possible and demand for labour will be inelastic. Another way of stating the case is to relate the availability of substitute factors to their elasticity of supply. If the supply of substitute factors is elastic, it will be possible to increase the use made of them.

Final Product Elasticity

The second determinant of factor demand elasticity is the elasticity of demand for the final product. We have already seen that the demand for an input is a *derived* demand. Since it is derived from the demand for the final output, we would expect the elasticity of the derived demand to mirror the elasticity of the demand for the final product, other things being equal.

Assume the elasticity of demand for electricity is very low. If the wages of skilled workers in the electricity industry are forced up by a strong union, the companies will pass on part of the increase in costs to customers in the form of higher prices. But since the elasticity of demand for electricity is relatively low, customers will not reduce by very much the quantity of electricity demanded. The electricity companies will lay off very few workers. The low elasticity of demand for the final product leads to a low elasticity of demand for the factors of production. The converse is also true. If firms cannot pass on increased costs to the consumer, because quantity demanded would fall sharply if they did, they will be unable to pay higher wages without a substantial cut in employment.

Proportion of Total Input Costs

The third elasticity determinant is the proportion of total costs accounted for by the input under study. This determinant merely points out that if a factor of production accounts for only a very small part of the total cost of the product, any given price change will not affect total costs by much. Take the example of electricity as an input of manufacturing. On the average, the cost of electricity accounts for about 1 per cent of the total cost of manufactured goods. If electricity accounts for exactly 1 per cent and prices now double, only 1 per cent more would be added to total costs. Hence, demand for electricity will not fall by very much. This may explain the relative amount of power that a union has in raising wage-rates. If the labour input constitutes a very small percentage of the total cost of producing a commodity, then an increase in wages will not add very much to total cost. In such situations, unions will be able to get their members higher wage-rates than they would when labour input constitutes a significantly greater percentage of total production costs.

Length of Time Allowed for Adjustment

The fourth determinant concerns the difference between the short run and the long run. The long run is usually defined as the time-period during which people adjust easily to a change in their business environment. The more time there is for adjustment, the more elastic both the supply and the demand curves will be. This assertion holds for *input* demand curves as well. The longer the time allowed for adjustment to take place, the more responsive firms will be to a change in the price of a factor of production. Particularly in the long run, firms can reorganize their production process to minimize the use of a factor of production that has become more expensive relative to other factors of production.

Consider one implication of this fourth determinant of the price elasticity of demand of an input. A union,

---

Key Points 26.2

The determinants of input price elasticity of demand are:

▶ **The easier it is to substitute other inputs for the input under study, the more price elastic will be that input's demand.**

▶ **The greater the price elasticity of demand for the final product, the greater the price elasticity of demand for the variable input.**

▶ **The smaller the proportion of total costs accounted for by the variable input under study, the lower its price elasticity of demand.**

▶ **The greater the time allowed for adjustment, the greater the price elasticity of demand for an input.**

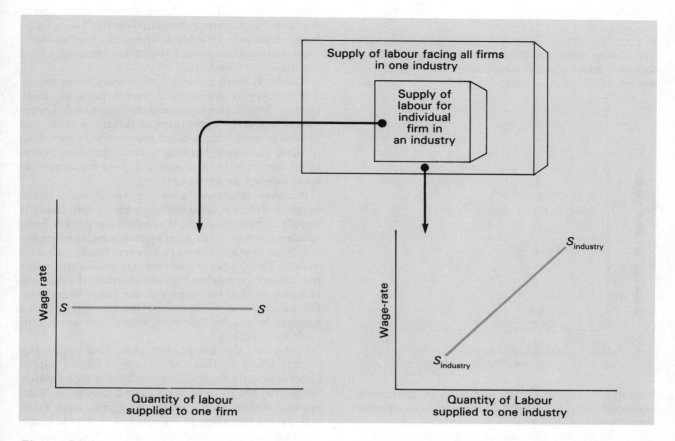

Figure 26.3
Two Supply Curves of Labour. The individual firm that represents a very small part of the total market faces a horizontal supply curve of labour at the going wage-rate. This firm's supply curve of labour is represented by *ss* on the left-hand side of the diagram. The industry, on the other hand, faces an upward-sloping supply curve, similar to the one labelled $S_{Industry}\ S_{Industry}$ on the right-hand side of this diagram.

for example, could succeed in raising workers' wage-rates – the price of the labour input – considerably above what they are without immediately experiencing a substantial cut-back in employment. The short-run price elasticity of demand for labour might be relatively small. If, however, time is allowed for adjustment, the union may find that the large increase in wage-rates will result in significant cut-backs in employment, that is, in the quantity of the labour input demanded, as firms invest in more labour saving capital.

The Supply of Labour

Having developed the demand curve for labour in a particular industry, let us turn to the labour supply curve. By adding supply to the analysis, we can come up with the equilibrium wage-rate that workers earn in an industry. We can think in terms of a supply curve

for labour that is upward sloping in a particular industry. At higher wage-rates, more workers will want to enter that particular industry – in our example, tape manufacturing. The individual firm, however, does not face the entire *market* supply curve. Rather, in a perfectly competitive case, the individual firm is such a small part of the market that it can hire all the workers that it wants at the going wage-rate. We say, therefore, that the industry faces an upward-sloping supply curve but that the individual *firm* faces a horizontal supply curve for labour. Figure 26.3 shows the difference.

The market supply curve of labour is simply the summation of the individual supply curves of labour. We do, however, assume that we are only operating in that range where the individual supply curve of labour if upward sloping. That is why we show the industry supply curve to be only upward sloping.

THE LABOUR/LEISURE CHOICE AND THE INDIVIDUAL LABOUR SUPPLY CURVE

All work involves an opportunity cost – the highest-valued alternative non-work choice. As such, analysing the individual decision about how much to work is similar to analysing the consumer's decision about what to buy in the product market. In essence, the individual is choosing between leisure (not working) and the consumption of commodities that can be bought in the market-place (because that is what one can do with the income earned from working). A

Figure 26.4

The Individual's Backward-bending Labour Supply Curve. After wage rate W_1, higher wage-rates lead to a backward-bending labour supply curve, such that a lower quantity of labour is supplied.

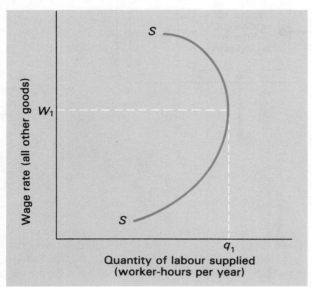

decision to increase the consumption of purchased commodities is, by necessity, a decision to reduce the consumption of leisure.

In order for an individual to make a decision, that individual must know the opportunity cost of leisure. That opportunity cost is best represented by the wages that could have been earned (after taxes). Assume that the worker can make, after taxes, £4 an hour. A decision to work four hours less, therefore, represents a decision not to be able to consume £16 of purchased commodities.

Consider, then, the effect of an increase in wages. The worker is given an incentive to work more because leisure has become more expensive. Therefore, the worker substitutes in favour of work and against leisure. This is called the *substitution effect* of an increase in wages. Looking only at the substitution effect, any increase in wages will cause the worker to want to work longer hours.

But there is also an *income effect*, and it works in the opposite direction. A higher wage-rate means that, for any given number of hours worked, the worker has a greater income. With a greater income, the worker will tend to purchase more of everything, including leisure. Thus, a wage increase has an income effect that causes the worker to want to reduce the number of hours worked because he or she wants to increase the purchase of leisure. The income effect of an increase in wages, therefore, causes the worker to want to work less.

Generally, the substitution effect outweighs the income effect so that the individual labour supply curve is upward sloping. Eventually, at a high enough wage-rate, the income effect may dominate, so that, above a certain level, higher and higher wage-rates will cause a reduction in the number of labour-hours worked. In Figure 26.3 this *backward-bending* supply curve of labour shows that, up to wage rate W_1, the substitution effect overrides the income effect, and

Figure 26.5

Civilian Labour Force Economic Activity Rates: by Age and Sex in Great Britain (percentages).

	16–19	20–4	25–44	45–59	60–64	65+	All aged 16 or over
Males							
1971	69.4	87.7	95.4	94.8	82.9	19.3	80.5
1976	63.8	86.1	95.7	94.9	80.4	14.5	78.3
1979	71.4	86.5	95.8	93.8	73.0	10.3	77.3
1981	74.3	85.1	95.6	93.0	69.4	10.3	76.7
1983	73.9	84.2	94.6	90.2	59.5	8.5	74.7

	16–19	20–24	25–44	45–54	55–9	60+	All aged 16 or over
Females							
1971	65.0	60.2	52.4	62.0	50.9	12.4	43.9
1976	61.3	65.0	60.0	66.5	54.3	10.3	46.4
1979	70.7	67.5	61.7	67.0	53.8	7.4	47.3
1981	70.7	67.9	61.6	68.1	53.4	8.3	47.5
1983	70.2	68.6	62.5	68.3	50.8	8.1	47.6

Source: Dept. of Employment.

above wage-rate W_1, the income effect overrides the substitution effect.

The Supply of Labour in Practice

The size of the labour force as a whole depends on the number of people available for work. This number in turn depends primarily on the number of people in full-time education, the retirement age, the participation of women in the labour force, and, not least, the population of working age. Quite sharp changes in this occur over time. For example, the loss of many young men during the First World War and the relatively low birth-rate subsequently, have meant that relatively few people have been retiring during the 1980s.

Figure 26.5 shows economic activity rates by age and sex, that is, the proportion of the population in each age group which is available for work. The increasing participation of women in the labour force during the 1970s has levelled off during the 1980s. Earlier retirement is reducing activity rates for older members of the labour force.

The Elasticity of Supply of Labour

In practice wage-rates can depend very crucially on the elasticity of supply of labour. In some circumstances a relatively small increase in wages will provide a substantial incentive and will attract many extra employees. In other circumstances an increase in supply will not be forthcoming unless a large pay

---

Figure 26.6
Perfectly Inelastic Supply of Labour. If supply is perfectly inelastic, it has no effect on wages, which are determined solely by the level of demand.

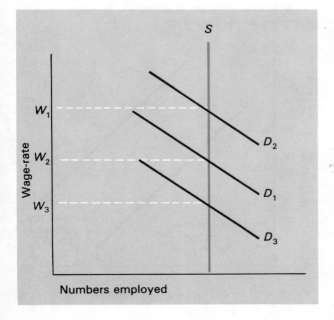

increase is offered. Supply is then inelastic. The supply curve will slope steeply upwards from left to right.

There is a special case in which supply is perfectly inelastic. The reward to labour is then said to be demand determined. Figure 26.6 shows how wages may rise or fall depending solely on the level of demand.

When the supply of a particular kind of labour is inelastic because there is some form of restriction upon it, **economic rent** is earned. Economic rent is that part of earnings which is in excess of what could be earned in an alternative occupation. This opportunity cost, of working in any given occupation, is what could be earned elsewhere, and is known as **transfer earnings**. Thus:

Economic rent = Total earnings – Transfer earnings.

A typical situation in which economic rent is earned occurs when the supply of labour is inelastic in the short-to-medium run because there is a long training period needed to generate the skills for the job. Equally, if supply can be restricted by unions or professional associations, economic rents can be earned. The supply of doctors, barristers, and some crafts skills can be restricted by both factors. Economic rent is usually highest of all for people whose characteristics are unique, as in the case of pop stars, comedians, and other star performers.

In general, both geographical and occupational immobility can restrict the supply of labour to particular occupations. For example, there may easily be shortages of computer repair specialists in the Thames Valley. House prices are high, deterring suitable workers from moving into the area. It takes time to train an increased supply of workers with the necessary skills. Substantially higher incomes may be needed to attract additional labour with these scarce skills. Differentials between wages in different areas, and between wages in different occupations (generating a similar marginal product) will persist so long as geographical and occupational immobilities prevent the labour market from adjusting to employers' demands.

Wage-rate Determination

Going back to the tape industry, we put down the demand curve for labour in that industry as DD in Figure 26.7 (page 396), and the supply curve of labour is shown as SS. When we put supply and demand of labour in the tape industry together on one graph, we find that the equilibrium wage rate of £200 a week is established at the intersection of the two curves. The quantity of workers both supplied and demanded at that rate is Q_1. If for some reason the wage-rate fell to £150 a week, we would find in our hypothetical example that there was an excess quantity of workers demanded at that wage-rate. Conversely, if the wage-rate rose to £250 a week, there would be an excess quantity of workers supplied at that wage-rate.

1. The alternative wage-rate offered in other industries changes.
2. Non-monetary aspects of the particular occupation change.

Consider the first reason for a shift in the supply curve of labour. If wage-rates for factory workers in the prerecorded-tape industry remain constant, but wage-rates for factory workers in the laser compact disc industry go up by 50 per cent, the supply curve of factory workers in the prerecorded-tape industry will shift inwards to the left.

If working conditions in the prerecorded-tape industry improve markedly because of some new production technique, then the supply curve of labour in the prerecorded-tape industry will shift outwards to the right. The converse will be true if working conditions deteriorate.

Shifts in Demand and the Problem of Labour Market Shortages

Labour markets do not adjust instantaneously. When there is an increase in demand, wage-rates do not change immediately. Consider Figure 26.8. Here we

Figure 26.7
The Equilibrium Wage-rate and the Tape Industry. The intersection of demand and supply curves is at point E, giving an equilibrium wage-rate of £200 per week and an equilibrium quantity of labour demanded of Q_1. At a price above £200 per week there will be an excess quantity of workers supplied. At a price below £200 per week there will be an excess quantity of workers demanded.

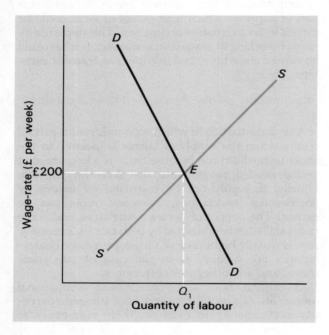

Shifts in the Supply and Demand of Labour

Just as we discussed shifts in the supply curve and the demand curve for various products in Chapter 5, we can discuss the effects of a shift in supply and/or demand in labour markets.

Reasons for Shifts in the Labour Demand Curve

These include:

1. The demand for final product shifts.
2. The price of a related factor of production changes (a substitute or a complement).
3. Labour becomes more or less productive.

If any one of these determinants of the position of the demand curve for labour changes, then the demand curve for labour will shift.

Determinants of the Supply Curve of Labour

There are several reasons why the supply curve of labour in a particular industry will shift. They include:

Figure 26.8
Adjustments to Increases in Demand for Computer Programmers. We start out in equilibrium at point E, where the wage-rate is w_1 and the quantity of employment of computer programmers is Q_1. Assume demand increases to $D'D'$. The new market-clearing equilibrium occurs at point E'. The wage-rate would be w_2, and the amount of employment of computer programmers would be Q_2. However, because of lags in adjustment, the wage-rate at first only rises to w_3. At that wage-rate, the quantity demanded of computer programmers will be Q_3, but the quantity supplied of computer programmers will be Q_4. Firms will experience a 'shortage' of computer programmers at that wage-rate.

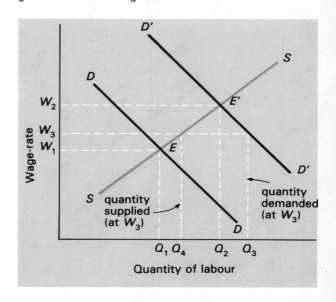

show the supply curve of computer programmers as *SS*. The demand curve is *DD*. The wage rate is w_1, and the equilibrium quantity of programmers is Q_1.

Consider that a big break-through has occurred in the computer industry so that 50 per cent more businesses want computers and, therefore, more computer programmers. The demand curve shifts outward to *D'D'*. There would be no shortage if the wage-rate increased to w_2, because at w_2 the new demand curve intercepts the stable supply curve at *E'*. The equilibrium quantity of computer programmers would be Q_2.

But the wage-rate does not rise instantaneously to its equilibrium rate. It moves gradually, and during this period of transition, shortages do indeed exist at the lower-than-equilibrium wage-rates. Take, for example, the wage-rate w_3. Those organizations desiring to hire computer programmers during this period will experience what they call a 'shortage'. They will not be able to hire all the computer programmers they want *at the going wage-rate*. A shortage of this sort can take many years to be eliminated when the demand curve continues to shift to the right faster than the wage-rate and people adjust.

Monopoly in the Product Market

We now continue our assumption that the firm purchases its factors of production in a perfectly competitive factor market, but assume that the firm sells its product in an *imperfectly competitive* output market. In other words, we are considering an output market structure of monopoly, oligopoly, or monopolistic competition. In all such cases, the firm faces a downward-sloping demand curve for its product. Throughout the rest of this chapter, we will simply refer to a monopoly output situation for ease of analysis. The analysis does, certainly, hold for all industry structures that are less-than-perfectly competitive. The fact that the firm faces a downward-sloping demand curve for its product means that if it wants to sell more of its product it has to reduce the price, *not only on the last unit, but on all preceding units. The marginal revenue received from selling an additional unit is continuously falling as the firm attempts to sell more and more.*

The Monopolist's Input Demand Curve

Now, in considering the demand for an input, we must account for the facts that (1) the marginal *physical* product falls because of the law of diminishing returns as more workers are added, *and* (2) the price (and marginal revenue) received for the product sold also falls as more is produced and sold. That is, for the monopolist firm, we have to account for *both* the diminishing marginal physical product, *and* the diminishing marginal revenue. In other words, marginal revenue is always less than price for the monopolist. The marginal revenue curve is always below the downward-sloping demand curve.

Key Points 26.3

▶ **The individual competitive firm faces a horizontal supply curve – it can buy all the labour it wants at the going market wage-rate.**

▶ **The industry supply curve of labour is upward sloping.**

▶ **Each individual faces a labour/leisure choice. The individual may have a backward-bending labour supply curve.**

▶ **When we put on the same diagram an industry-wide supply curve for labour and an industry-wide demand curve for labour, we obtain the equilibrium wage-rate in that industry.**

▶ **The supply of labour is affected by the population, and the age of entering and leaving the labour force.**

▶ **When the supply of labour is inelastic, a part of earnings is termed economic rent, being that part which is in excess of transfer earnings (the opportunity cost of earnings in an alternative occupation).**

▶ **The labour demand curve can shift because (1) the demand for final product shifts, (2) the price of a related (substitute or complementary) factor of production changes, or (3) labour changes in its productivity.**

▶ **The supply curve of labour will shift if the alternative wage–rate offered in other industries changes and if the non-monetary aspects of the job change.**

▶ **Abrupt changes in demand in a particular industry may lead to temporary 'shortages' as wage-rates move gradually to their long-run equilibrium level.**

How Many Employees?

For the monopolist, marginal revenue product (MRP) will tend to fall off more sharply as sales increase. Nevertheless the profit-maximizing output continues to be that at which the MRP is equal to the going wage. That is, the monopolist stops hiring when the wage-rate is equal to the marginal revenue product, since additional workers add more to cost than to revenue. (It stops hiring when MR = MC.) But since marginal revenue may diminish sharply, both output and employment may be lower under monopoly than they would be in a competitive industry.

Cost Minimization

How can the firm minimize its total costs for a given output? Assume you are an entrepreneur attempting to minimize costs. Consider a hypothetical situation in which if you spend £1 more on labour, you would get, say, twenty more units of output, but if you spend £1 more on machines, you would get only ten more units of output. What would you want to do in such a situation? Most likely, you would wish to hire more workers or sell off some of your machines for you are not getting as much output per last pound spent on labour. In other words, you would want to employ relative amounts of every factor of production so that the marginal products per last pound spent on each are equal.

To minimize total costs for a particular rate of production, the firm will hire factors of production up to the point where the marginal physical product per last pound spent on each factor of production is equalized, or:

$$\frac{\text{marginal physical product of labour}}{\text{price of labour}} = \frac{\text{marginal physical product of machines}}{\text{price of machines}} = \frac{\text{marginal physical product of land}}{\text{price of land}}$$

All we are saying here is that the profit-maximizing firm will always use *all* resources in *such combinations* that cost will be minimized for any given output rate. We are referring here to what is commonly called the *least-cost combination of resources*.

An Imperfect Labour Market

So far, we have assumed that employers compete to hire workers. We also have assumed that workers are actively competing in the sale of their labour services to employers. There are at least two situations in which these assumptions must be altered. The first one involves restraints on the competition among workers arising from trade union activities. Then we look at restraint among employers in their bidding for workers.

Trade Union Power and the Labour Movement

The concept of **unions** goes back at least as far as the Middle Ages when guilds were formed. By the twelfth century, Western European guilds were of two broad types: merchant and craft. The medieval craft guilds were the original occupational associations, formed by the artisans in a particular field.

Modern trade unions use their bargaining power to influence wage-rates, working conditions and, often, the actual production arrangements. The majority of unions are relatively small: only eleven are larger than 250 000, although they account for 62 per cent of all union members. **Craft unions** include workers with similar skills from many industries, such as the electricians' union (EETPU). General unions attract a wide range of occupations, mainly from the semi-skilled and unskilled groups. The Transport and General Workers Union (TGWU) is one of these. **Industrial unions** cover all or most of the employees in one industry, such as the National Union of Mine-workers (NUM). White collar unions restrict membership to professional, administrative, and clerical occupations. ASTMS (the Association of Scientific, Technical and Managerial Staffs) exists for supervisory and managerial staff in industry. This type of union membership has tended to grow in recent years; most other unions face falling membership except where they have amalgamated. Increasing unemployment has caused union membership to fall.

Key Points 26.4

▶ When a firm sells its output in a monopoly market, it must take account of marginal revenue, which is less than price.

▶ As under perfect competition, the profit-maximizing combination of factors will occur when each factor is hired up to the point where its MRP is equal to its unit price.

▶ In order to minimize total costs for a given output, the profit-maximizing firm will hire each factor of production up to the point where the marginal physical product per last pound spent on each factor is equal to the marginal physical product per last pound spent on each of the other factors of production.

Unions and Collective Bargaining

Unions can be looked at as setters of minimum wages. Through collective bargaining, unions establish minimum wages below which no individual worker can offer his or her services. Collective bargaining is collective in the sense that the union leaders bargain for all workers in the bargaining unit. Typically, collective bargaining contracts between management and the union apply also to non-union members who are employed by the firm or the industry.

While it is still true to say that the strike is an important source of union power, its use has greatly diminished during the 1980s (apart from the miners' strike of 1984–5). Figure 26.9 shows the days lost through strike action in recent years.

Figure 26.9
Industrial Disputes – Working Days Lost and Number of Stoppages: by Cause (UK)

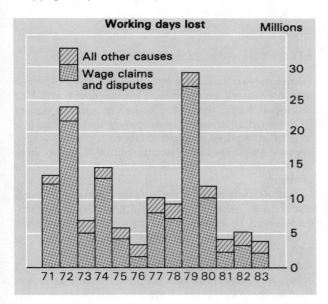

Source: Social Trends, 1985

Closed Shops

Quite a few management–labour contracts contain a provision requiring all workers to join the same union. This is a closed shop. It gives the union greater bargaining power but it also may suit the employer, who is saved the necessity of negotiating with a number of unions.

Negotiated Wage-rates

We have already pointed out that unions can be looked at as setters of minimum wages. In many situations, any wage-rate set higher than a competitive market-clearing wage-rate will reduce total employment in that market. This can be seen in Figure 26.10. We have a competitive market for labour. The market demand curve is DD and the market supply curve is SS. The market-clearing wage-rate will be w_1; the equilibrium quantity of labour will be Q_e. If the union establishes by collective bargaining a minimum wage-rate that exceeds w_1, there will be an excess quantity of labour supplied (assuming no change in the demand schedule). For example, if the minimum wage established by collective bargaining is w_2, the quantity supplied would be Q'_e; the quantity demanded would be Q_D. The difference is the excess quantity supplied, or 'surplus'. The union which establishes a wage-rate above the market-clearing price may try to ration available jobs among the excessive number of workers who wish to work in unionized industries. In order to reduce the excess quantity supplied, the union may lengthen the apprenticeship period for new entrants to the trade. There is a trade-off here that must be faced by any union.

Figure 26.10
Union Wage Rates. If demand for Labour is DD and supply is SS, the equilibrium wage rate is W_1 and the number employed Q_e. If the Union negotiates higher wages, W_2, demand for Labour will be Q_d and supply will be Q'_e. There will be an excess supply of labour equal to $Q_e - Q_d$.
Restricting Supply Over Time. As demand increased, that is, as the demand schedule shifted out to $D'D'$ from DD, the union restricted membership to its original level of Q_e. The new supply curve is SS', which intersects $D'D'$ at E', or at a wage-rate of w_3. Without the union, equilibrium would be at E'' with a wage-rate of w_2 and employment of Q'_e.

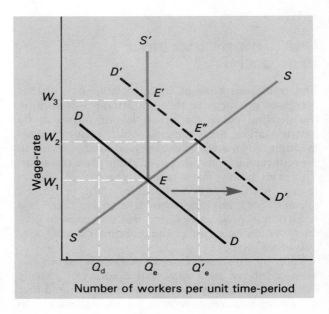

Limiting Entry over Time

Unions may limit the size of their membership to the size of their employed work force when the union was first organized. No workers are put out of work at the time the union is formed. If demand for labour in the industry increases, these original members receive larger wage increases than otherwise would be the case. We see this in Figure 26.10. If the supply of labour can be restricted from then on, these higher wages will continue to be paid.

Have Unions Raised Wages?

Unions are able to raise the wages of their members if they are successful in limiting the supply of labour in a particular industry. They are also able to raise wages above what wages would otherwise be to the extent that they can shift the demand for labour outwards to the right. This can be done through overmanning agreements, which include a specified number of workers for any given job, e.g. requiring a pilot, co-pilot, and engineer in the cockpit of a jet airplane, even if an engineer is not required on short flights. Economists have done voluminous amounts of research to determine the actual increase in union wages relative to non-union wages. They have found that, in certain industries, such as construction, and in certain occupations, such as pilots in commercial airlines, the union wage differential can be as high as 50 per cent or more. That is to say, unions have, in some industries and occupations, been able to win wage-rates 50 per cent or more above what they would otherwise be in the absence of unions.

Finally, on average, unions appear to be able to raise the wage-rates of their members relative to non-union members by between 10 and 20 per cent.

Can Unions Increase Productivity?

The traditional view of union behaviour is that it decreases productivity through attempts at shifting the demand curve for union labour outwards by having staffing arrangements which result in over-manning. Also, unions have been accused of trying to prevent capital from being used in the place of labour. The print unions have resisted the use of labour-saving machinery, in some cases right up to the present. Also, anytime there is a strike, there is a reduction in productivity, and this reduction in productivity in one sector of the economy can spill over into other sectors.

Recently, this traditional view against unions has been countered by a view that unions can actually increase productivity. Some economists contend that unions act as a collective voice for their members. In the absence of a collective voice, any dissatisfied worker simply remains at his job and works in a disgruntled manner. But unions, as a collective voice, can listen to worker grievances on an individual basis and then apply pressure on the employer to change working conditions. The individual worker does not run the risk of being singled out by the employer and harassed. Also, the individual worker does not have to spend his or her time in trying to convince the employer that some change in the working arrangement should be made. Given that unions provide this collective voice, worker turnover in unionized industries should be less, and this should contribute to productivity. Indeed, there is strong evidence that worker turnover is reduced when unions are in place. Of course, this evidence may also be consistent with the fact that wage-rates are so attractive to those in unions they will not change jobs unless working conditions become unbearable. It has been found that output losses during strikes are quickly made up after the return to work.

Other Market Imperfections

Sometimes there will be only one employer of significance within a given area. This employer will be a monopoly buyer of labour, known as a **monopsonist**. In these circumstances the employer may well be able to get the required amount of labour for lower wages, because employees have no alternative. This would be most likely if geographical immobility was a serious problem.

Exploitation may be defined as paying a resource less than its value. By one definition, labour exploitation would be equal to the difference between the wage-rate and the marginal revenue product of labour.

It will be possible for exploitation to occur if employers have more market power than employees, that is where employers have a degree of monopsony while employees are competing to obtain work. Exploitation allows a larger proportion of total revenue to accrue as profit while a smaller proportion of revenue accrues to labour.

Sometimes a monopsony can be created by an **employers' association**. While there may be many employers, they can agree to negotiate as a unified association, all paying the same wage-rate. **Bilateral monopoly** exists in the labour market when a single employer or employers' association negotiates with a single union which covers all the employees in the industry. An example of this occurs when British Coal faces the National Union of Mineworkers. The establishment of the Union of Democratic Mineworkers could alter this.

Wages councils set wages nationally for low-paid, poorly unionized sectors such as catering. Effectively, they set a minimum wage for the occupations they cover.

Key Points 26.5

► Unions negotiate minimum wage-rates, and working conditions.

► Union activity can lead to higher wages but may lead also to fewer jobs being available.

► On average, unions appear to raise wage-rates for their members relative to non-union members by between 10 and 20 per cent.

► Some economists believe that unions can increase productivity by acting as a collective voice for their members, thereby freeing members from the task of spending their time trying to convince their employers that some change in their working arrangements should be made. Unions may reduce employee turnover, thus adding to productivity also.

► Exploitation may occur if there is a monopsony, or a single employer (buyer of labour).

► Bilateral monopoly exists when a single employer deals with a single union, so that there is one buyer and one seller.

CASE STUDY

Do Labour Markets Clear?

Competitive markets usually clear, in the sense that the price changes until it reaches an equilibrium in which there is neither excess supply nor excess demand. In theory, wage-rates are free to find their own level in the market-place. In practice since human beings are sometimes slow to react to stimuli, even financial ones, there may be time lags before markets adjust to new situations. For example, a shortage of high technology skills may lead to high rates of pay being offered. But because training takes time, it may take some while for the scarce skill to become less so. In the long run, however, we would expect freely functioning markets to clear so that excess supply and demand are eliminated.

What is the evidence? First, we must remember that the labour market is not one, but many markets, for different types of labour in different places. Then we can look at the signs of excess supply: large numbers of unemployed people. Simultaneously we can see unfilled vacancies where employers are seeking people with scarce skills. The culprit here is easily spotted: it is geographical and occupational immobility of labour. These prevent a free flow of labour to employers who require it.

Other distortions include the various monopolies which exist among both employers and sellers of labour. Consider the Health Service. There is an excess supply of young people willing and able to become doctors (visible among the well-qualified applicants for medical school). Selection restricts the supply to less than it otherwise would be, thus raising pay. The market clears, but it is a constrained equilibrium – constrained by the limited supply. Employment may well be less than it would be if the supply were allowed to increase and pay were reduced. So market-clearing does not necessarily maximize employment.

For all labour markets to clear, it would be necessary for wages sometimes to fall. Among other things, J. M. Keynes pointed out that money wages are inflexible downwards – there is a ratchet effect. This can mean that people sometimes have little incentive to move from a job which is poorly paid, because the differential obtainable by moving to a better paid job is not sufficient to justify the effort involved. This would make for an inflexible labour market, slow to adjust to employers' new needs.

Questions

1. How has inflation affected wage differentials?
2. Are real wages inflexible downwards?
3. Are people inflexible?
4. What data would you need to show that labour markets do not clear?

CASE STUDY

Minimum Wages and Employment

The basic link between pay and jobs is clear. If people cost less to employ, more of them will be employed. (Treasury.)

This quotation aptly summarizes the objective of the current government policy of attempting to reduce real wages or their growth. Ministerial statements present this as the most important means of achieving an improvement in employment. But how useful is this policy likely to be? It may be contested on two levels – the macro and the micro. At the macro-level we ask whether cutting wages increases the aggregate number of jobs. Here we will focus on the micro-consequences of government wage policy in individual markets. This is particularly appropriate, for a careful examination of government policy makes it clear that reducing aggregate real wages is not the primary wage objective. The policies which have been adopted in recent years, including controls of public sector wages, privatization, and the abolition of the Fair Wages Resolution, the measures to reduce youth pay and the serious weakening of the Wages Councils, are directed at attempts to reduce real wages *at the lower end* of the pay scale.

Reducing Wages at the Lower End

These policies have reflected themselves in a widening dispersion in earnings. Between April 1980 and April 1984 the lowest decile of male workers received an increase in earnings of 37 per cent, only marginally above the increase in prices of 35 per cent. The average male wage-earner, meanwhile, received increases in gross pay of 46 per cent. The highest decile saw their gross pay rise by 52 per cent (Low Pay Unit 1984).

There are two aspects of the policy on which we focus here: *the weakening of the Wages Council system of minimum rates of pay and the attempt to reduce the relative pay of young people.* Neither of these policies can be justified in terms of a reduction in the aggregate level of real wages or their growth.

Wages Councils set legal minimum rates of pay for almost 3 million workes employed mainly in retailing, catering, clothing manufacture, hairdressing, and laundries. The workers in this sector account for only 8 per cent of the nation's total hourly wage bill, so that reductions in the earnings of this group would have an almost imperceptible effect on the level of wages in the economy as a whole. Nor can Wages Councils be accused of contributing significantly to the growth of real wages.

The first challenge comes from within the theory itself. The wage is said to be equal to the marginal product of labour (i.e. the amount which each additional worker contributes to total output). Yet the marginal product of labour is something which cannot be measured. So many take it as an act of faith that, whatever is the wage, this is the marginal product.

In the textbook world of competitive labour and product markets, this may indeed be the case. Under these circumstances, the wage may equal the marginal product of labour, so that artificially induced wage increases will lead to unemployment. However, where workers have restricted mobility or job opportunities, the wage offered is likely to be below the marginal product – a situation of technical exploitation – and an enforced minimum wage need have no effect on the numbers employed.

The marginal productivity theory therefore suggests that certain groups are low paid because they have lower productivity. When applied to ethnic minority workers or women – to groups which are disproportionately affected by low wages, and which very often receive lower rates of pay even when education, job status, and experience are held constant – the implications are disturbing. The theory would seem to suggest that these groups are less productive because of their race or sex, a suggestion which most people would find as abhorrent as it is lacking in credibility.

A more credible explanation for the lower pay of these groups is that they find themselves at a disadvantage in the labour market relative to other groups. Especially at times of high unemployment, the chances open to women, ethnic minority workers, and young people are severely restricted. Employers find themselves in a 'buyers market', able to recruit labour, in the short term at least, at a wage below that justified by the workers' productivity. If these workers were able to organize themselves into unions, or if a minimum wage existed, the wages received might move closer to the marginal revenue product of their labour.

The alternative model is the non-competitive model. It assumes that market imperfections are the norm rather than the exception, and that the labour market is characterized by structural divisions and persistent inequalities in bargaining strength which ensure *in the long term* that certain groups are trapped into low-wage employment. While the orthodox competitive model places emphasis on the quality of the labour supply, this model (sometimes described as the 'labour market segmentation' approach) considers more closely the factors which determine the patterns of demand for labour. This requires examination of the industrial and institutional characteristics of low-paying industries. Using this approach, the policy implications are quite the opposite of those recommended by orthodox theory.

Wages Councils and Unemployment: The Evidence

We have noted that Wages Council rates of pay represent a small proportion of the aggregate wage bill. The rates of pay are low in absolute terms, ranging in 1985 between £63 a week and £72 a week for full-time adult workers. The question must therefore be asked: if wages at this level are too high in real terms, what level of real pay is necessary to ensure the establishment of full employment? This is both an economic and a moral question. As yet no answer has been forthcoming from those who advocate Wages Council abolition.

Some estimates have been made of the possible employment effects of abolishing Wages Councils. Some have been encouraged to make extravagant claims. However, the House of Commons Select Committee on Employment, having considered the evidence, came to the conclusion that:

The direct effect that could be achieved by abolition of the Wages Councils is estimated through econometric evidence to be relatively small in terms of jobs. (House of Commons.)

Young People's Pay and Employment

The marginal productivity theory is often used in support of the notion

that young people have priced themselves out of jobs. It is argued that wages for this group have exceeded their worth to the employer, given their relative lack of experience. The government has proposed taking young people out of the scope of Wages Councils (which set legal minimum pay rates for about one-fifth of young people in work). Some have proposed that adult rates should not be paid until the age of 22 or 23, instead of at age 18.

The marginal productivity approach may help to justify some age differentials, for instance in jobs where training and experience take time to acquire. However, in many of the jobs that young people do, they act as direct substitutes for adult workers. For example, about one in three young people find their first job in the distributive trades (including shopwork) and miscellaneous services (including hairdressing and catering). Very often such jobs require little skill, experience, or training before the worker is fully productive. Once again the lower earnings of this group, as with women and ethnic minorities, are very often associated less with productivity and more with bargaining power. Hence, the House of Commons Select Committee reporting recently on the effects of Wages Councils commented that 'any young persons employed on the Wages Council rates is likely to be engaged in jobs that are unskilled and for which they may be competing directly with adults. A significant cut in these rates could therefore result in a direct substitution of young people for adults'. (House of Commons)

An implicit acceptance of this fact appears to emerge from the Department of Employment which, in its Consultative Paper on Wages Councils, appears not to rely on marginal productivity theory:

There is a growing body of evidence that the employment prospects of young people are adversely affected by the level of

their pay relative to adults. (Department of Employment)

Here we have a new proposition: that it is young people's pay *relative* to adults which is significant, rather than their real wage relative to their productivity. The argument is therefore analogous to that applied to capital –labour substitutions: the lower the pay of young people, the more will be employed.

However, this is not an argument about how many jobs will be created by reducing pay; it is about who will get the jobs that are available. The Department of Employment's own research suggested that eight out of ten new jobs created for young people as a result of reductions in youth pay would be at the expense of adult workers. The Public Accounts Committee found that 77 per cent of the jobs subsidized under the Young Workers Scheme (which offers a subsidy to firms paying low wages to young people) would have existed anyway.

Even on the basis of substitution, there appears to be little evidence that increases in the relative pay of young people are to blame for youth unemployment. Since 1979, youth unemployment has doubled, yet the relative pay of young males has fallen by 23 per cent in comparison to adults, while young women's pay has fallen by 30 per cent (Low Pay Unit). This would seem to support the earlier findings of research undertaken by the Department of Employment demonstrating that 'variations in youth unemployment do not appear to have any systematic relationship with changes in the relative earnings of young people'. (Department of Employment).

Source: Chris Pond, 'The Case for Minimum-Wage Protection', *Economic Review*, Vol. 3, No. 1, Sept. 1985.

Questions overleaf

Exam Preparation and Practice

INTRODUCTORY EXERCISES

1.

Quantity of labour	Total product per week	MPP	MRP
1	250	____	____
2	450	____	____
3	600	____	____
4	700	____	____
5	750	____	____
6	750	____	____

Assume the above product sells for £2 per unit.
(a) Use the information above to derive a demand curve for labour.
(b) What is the most that this firm would be willing to pay each worker if five workers were hired?
(c) If the going salary for this quality of labour is £200 per week, how many workers would be hired?

2. Below are some production function data for a firm in which the only variable input is capital; the labour input is fixed. First fill in the other columns. What quantity of capital will the firm use if the price of capital is £90 per machine-week? If the price of capital is £300 per machine-week, what quantity of capital will the firm use?

Explain.

Quantity of capital (machine-weeks)	Total product (units/week)	Marginal product of capital (units/week)	Product price (£/unit)	MRP (£/week)
0	0	____	£10	____
1	25	____	10	____
2	45	____	10	____
3	60	____	10	____
4	70	____	10	____
5	75	____	10	____

3. The graph below indicates the supply and demand for labour in the construction industry.

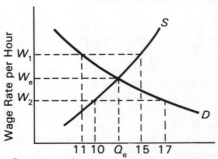

(a) When wage-rates are W_1 per hour, how much do labourers intend to offer per unit?

(b) How much do businesses intend to buy at this wage-rate?

(c) Which group is able to realize its intentions and which can't?

(d) What forces will be set in motion at wage rate W_1, given a free market for labour?

4. Using the graph in Question 3 above, answer the following questions.

(a) At wage-rate W_2, how many labour-hours do labourers intend to offer?

(b) At W_2, how many labour-hours do businesses intend to purchase?

(c) Which group can realize its intentions and which can't?

(d) What forces will be set in motion at W_2, if a free market for labour exists in this industry?

(e) What will the equilibrium wage-rate be?

5. Some people argue that the extraordinary earnings of entertainment and sports 'superstars' are not pure economic rents at all, but merely the cost of ensuring that a steady stream of would-be stars and starlets continues to flow into the sports and entertainment fields. Outline the argument.

MULTIPLE CHOICE QUESTIONS

1. The marginal productivity theory of wages maintains that

A the amount of labour employed determines its wage

B the value of labour depends upon its marginal productivity

C productivity can be the result and not the cause of wages

D marginal changes in wage levels have little effect on employment.

2. The elasticity of demand for a factor of production will be high when

A it is difficult to substitute some other factor for it in production

B the cost of a factor is a small part of total cost

C the factor is highly specific to the production of the final product.

D the elasticity of demand for the final product is high.

3. Transfer earnings are most accurately defined as

A payments which are excluded from National Income calculations

B unearned income derived from the ownership of a factor

C earnings from overseas assets

D payment to a factor to keep it in its present use

E payments to the government for taxes or National Insurance.

For question 4 select your answer from the following grid:

A	B	C	D	E
1,2,3 all correct	**1, 2** only correct	**2, 3** only correct	**1** only correct	**3** only correct

†**4.** The elasticity of demand for a factor of production is likely to be low where the

1 price elasticity of demand for the final product is low

2 factor accounts for a small proportion of total costs

3 factor has no alternative uses

5. 'Economic rent' is

A an alternative term for 'transfer earnings'

B a rent allowing reasonable incomes to landlords

C income in excess of a factor's supply price

D characteristic of perfectly competitive conditions

E reduced when supply is inelastic.

6. A trade union wishes to increase the wages of its members in a given industry without causing unemployment among them. Which of the following would weaken the union's bargaining position?

A The labour force is highly skilled.

B Employers have no central bargaining organization.

C There is a low degree of elasticity of substitution of alternative factors of production.

D The price elasticity of demand for the workers' product is high.

E Wages form a low proportion of total production costs.

Continued overleaf

RELATED ESSAY QUESTIONS

1. What determines the total supply of labour in the UK and the supply of a particular type of skilled labour?
2. How are factor earnings related to productivity?
3. What factors determine a producer's demand for labour *either* in the short run *or* in the long run?
4. Give examples of low-paid workers in Britain and suggest reasons why they are low paid. Would a national minimum wage improve the position of the low paid in Britain?
5. (a) What factors affect the ability of trade unions to increase the real wages of their members relative to other groups?
   (b) In what sense, if any, could it be argued that trade unions protect workers from 'exploitation' by employers?
6. Outline the theory of relative pay determination in a freely competitive market. How far is it possible to explain salary differentials within the teaching profession and between teaching and other professions in terms of labour supply and demand analysis?
7. It has been suggested that the incentive to work in the UK will be increased by (a) a reduction in social security payments, and (b) a reduction in the higher rates of taxation. Explain and evaluate the reasoning underlying these views.

27 Rent, Interest, and Profits

Key Points to Review

▶ Trade-off between consumer and capital goods (2.4)

▶ Profit as a resource allocator (6.4)

▶ Elasticity of supply (7.6)

▶ Credit creation (20.2)

▶ Accounting versus economic profits (22.1)

Questions for Preview

1 What is rent?

2 What is interest?

3 What is the economic function of interest rates?

4 What is the economic function of profits?

We have talked about four factors of production – labour, land, capital, and entrepreneurship. So far in Part D, we have discussed only the demand and supply of labour and the factor payments to labour – wages and salaries. The other three factors of production and their respective factor payments – rent, interest, and profits – are also important. In this chapter, we will look at the determination of each of these factor payments.

Rent

Land, in general, is in completely *inelastic* supply. Thus, the supply curve for land is a vertical line. That is to say, no matter what the prevailing market price for land, the quantity supplied will remain the same. The term **rent** has been associated with the payment for the use of land, for land seems to be the best example of a resource that is in fixed supply. When, indeed, no matter what the price, the quantity and quality of a resource will remain at its current levels, then we say there is **pure economic rent**. (Chapter 26 examined this in relation to labour.) We define pure economic rent as that price paid to, in this case, land (or any other

productive factor) that is in completely inelastic supply.

Does Economic Rent Have an Allocative Function?

In a price system, changes in prices usually cause people to change their behaviour. If the price of petroleum products goes up relative to other prices, suppliers are induced to supply more, and consumers are induced to consume less. Does economic rent have a similar allocative function? Some economists would answer yes, and others would answer no. Those who do not believe economic rent serves an allocative function point out that, by definition, it is associated with unique properties of a resource that cannot be changed. If an exceptionally productive tract of land exists, does this property's high economic rent mean that somehow additional tracts with the same high productivity will come into being? The answer is no. After all, if economic rent exists, it means that it is attributed to a factor's qualities that cannot be altered in the long run. Therefore, by definition, if economic rent is being earned, it cannot serve an allocative function.

Those who believe that economic rent does serve an allocative function indicate that it serves the purpose of regulating the use of society's resources, particularly its natural resources that are fixed in supply. In a competitive market-place, economic rent serves as a guide by rationing the available supply to the most efficient use.

Since the value of bare, urban land has nothing to do with the talents or effort of the owner, but with the presence of other people, some have argued that the pure economic rent of land should be taxed.

Quasi-Rents

A **quasi rent** is defined as a payment over and above what is necessary to keep a factor of production in existence *in the short run* in its current quantity and quality. In the long run, if the quasi-rent is inadequate, the factor of production will be allowed to depreciate and not be replaced. Consider a factory that has a fixed amount of plant and machinery. Assume that nothing can be done with the capital equipment; it can be used only to continue producing the same product. In the short run, it is possible for the owners of that fixed capital not to be paid very much at all. In the long run, however, if those owners of fixed capital are not paid at least a normal rate of return for their investment, they will keep the equipment running until it wears out, but will not then replace it.

Economic Rents to Other Factors of Production

This analysis is equally applicable to any other factor of production that is fixed in supply. Economic rents accrue to individuals possessing scarce natural talents. It is defined as any payment over and above what is necessary to maintain a factor of production in its current activity. Natural talents that human beings possess will be more significant in some occupations than in others. They seem to be particularly important in athletics, acting, music, and other entertainment endeavours. In some cases, pure economic rents can explain a great part of the difference between the extraordinary earnings of highly successful musicians, for example, and the average musician.

Interest

Interest is the price paid for the use of capital. Capital is the factor of production that is typically considered man-made. Capital exists because individuals, as a group, have been willing in the past to forgo consumption – to save. Those resources not consumed were usually used by firms for investment purposes, which added to our stock of capital. The production of capital goods occurs in our society because of the existence of credit markets, where borrowing and lending take place.

Owners of capital, whether directly or indirectly, obtain income in the form of interest. They receive a specific interest rate. Thus, we can look at the interest rate as either the rate earned on capital invested or the cost of borrowing – the two sides of the credit market. For the moment, we will look only at the cost of borrowing.

Interest and Credit

When you obtain credit, you actually obtain money to have command over resources today. We can say, then, that interest is the payment for current rather than future command over resources. Thus, interest is the payment for obtaining credit. If you borrow £100 from me, you have command over £100 worth of goods and services today. I no longer have that command. You promise to pay me back £100 plus interest at some future date. The interest that you pay is usually expressed as a percentage of the total loan calculated on an annual basis. Thus, if at the end of one

---

Key Points 27.1

▶ **Pure economic rent is defined as any payment to a factor of production that is completely inelastic in supply.**

▶ **Pure economic rent is a payment to a resource over and above what is necessary to keep that resource in existence at its current level in the long run.**

▶ **Economic rent serves an allocative function by guiding available supply to the most efficient use.**

▶ **A quasi-rent is that payment over and above what is necessary to keep a resource in its current quality and quantity in the short run, but not sufficient to do so in the long run.**

▶ **Factors of production other than land can earn pure economic rents if their supply is completely price inelastic.**

year, you pay me back £110, the annual interest is £10 ÷ £100, or 10 per cent. When you go out into the market-place to obtain credit, you will find that the interest rate charged differs greatly. A loan to buy a house (a mortgage) may cost you 10–15 per cent annual interest. An instalment loan to buy a car may cost you 15–25 per cent annual interest. The government, when it wishes to obtain credit (by selling bonds) may have to pay 10–13 per cent annual interest. Variations in the rate of annual interest that must be paid for credit depend on the following factors.

LENGTH OF LOAN

In some (but not all) cases, the longer the loan will be outstanding, other things being equal, the greater will be the interest rate charged.

RISK

The greater the risk of non-repayment of the loan, other things being equal, the greater the interest rate charged. Risk is assessed on the basis of the credit-worthiness of the borrower. It is also assessed on the basis of whether the borrower provides collateral for the loan. Collateral consists of any asset that will automatically become the property of the lender should the borrower fail to comply with the loan agreement. Typically, when you borrow to purchase a car, the car itself is collateral for the loan. Should you default on payments to the lending institution, it can, in most cases, repossess the car, sell it, and pay off the loan that way. The more and the better the collateral offered for a loan, the lower the rate of interest charged, other things being equal.

ADMINISTRATIVE CHARGES

It takes resources to set up a loan. Papers have to be filled out and filed, credit references have to be checked and so on. It turns out that the larger the amount of the loan, the smaller will be the administrative charges as a percentage of the total loan. Therefore, we would predict that, other things being equal, the larger the loan, the lower the interest rate.

Loans are taken out both by consumers and by firms. It is useful for us to separate the motives underlying the demand for loans by these two groups of individuals. We therefore will treat consumption loans and investment loans separately. But before we do that, we will examine the relationship between interest rates and present value – or how to relate the value of future sums of money to the present.

In the discussion that follows, it will be assumed that there is no inflation; that is, that there is no consistent increase in general prices.

The Interest Rate, the Present, the Future, and Present Values

Interest rates are used to link the present with the future. After all, if you have to pay £110 at the end of the year when you borrow £100, that 10 per cent interest rate gives you a measure of the price of things one year from now compared to the price of things today. If you want to have things today, you have to pay the 10 per cent interest rate in order to have purchasing power.

Turned around somewhat, the question could be put this way: What is the present value (the value today) of £110 that you could receive one year from now? That depends on the market rate of interest, or the rate of interest you could earn in a bank account. To make the arithmetic simple, let us assume that the rate of interest (also called the **rate of discount**) is 10 per cent. Now you can figure out the **present value**, as it were, of £110 to be received one year from now. You figure it out by asking the question, 'How much money must I put aside today at the market rate of interest of 10 per cent to receive £110 one year from now?' Mathematically we represent this question by the following:

$$(1 + 0.10)P_1 = £110$$

where P_1 is the sum that you must set aside now.

Let us solve this simple equation to obtain P_1:

$$P_1 = £110 ÷ 1.10 = £100.$$

That is to say, £100 will accumulate to £110 at the end of one year with a market rate of interest of 10 per cent. Thus, the present value of £110 one year from now, using a rate of interest of 10 per cent, is £100. The formula for present value of any sums to be received one year from now thus becomes:

$$P_1 = \frac{A_1}{(1 + i)}$$

where

    P_1 = present value of a sum one year hence
    A_1 = future sum of money paid or received one year hence
    i = market rate of interest.

The same method can be used to calculate the present value of income expected in the more distant future. We call this **discounting**. It enables firms to assess the present value of the income they are likely to receive from an investment project. This helps them in deciding whether a given capital expenditure is likely to be worth while.

What Determines Interest Rates?

The overall level of interest rates in the economy is determined by the supply of loanable funds and the demand for loanable funds. Let us first look at the supply and then the demand.

THE SUPPLY OF CREDIT, OR LOANABLE FUNDS

The supply of loanable funds depends on individuals' willingness to save. To induce people to save more, one must offer a higher rate of interest. Thus, we expect that the supply curve of loanable funds will be upward sloping. At higher rates of interest, savers will be willing to offer more current consumption to borrowers, other things being equal.

The supply of credit will also depend on how much credit banks can create, and therefore on the Bank of England's operation of monetary policy. (This is dealt with in more detail in Chapters 20 and 31.)

THE DEMAND FOR LOANABLE FUNDS

There are three major sources of the demand for loanable funds:

1. Households that want funds for the purchase of services, non-durable goods, and consumer durables, such as cars and houses.
2. Firms that want funds for investments.
3. Governments that want to cover their deficits – the excess of government spending over tax revenues, or PSBR.

THE CONSUMER DEMAND FOR LOANABLE FUNDS

On average, consumers prefer earlier consumption to later consumption. By borrowing, consumers can spread out purchases more evenly during their lifetimes. Consider that sometimes individual household income falls below the average income level expected over, say, the next few years. Individuals will go to the credit market to borrow whenever they perceive a temporary dip in their current income – assuming they expect their income to go back to normal later on.

The demand by consumers for loanable funds will be inversely related to the cost of borrowing – the rate of interest. Why? For the same reason that all demand curves slope down: a higher rate of interest means a higher cost of borrowing, and a higher cost of borrowing must be weighed against alternative uses of limited income. At higher costs of borrowing, consumers will forgo current consumption.

FIRMS' DEMAND FOR LOANABLE FUNDS

Firms demand loanable funds to make investments in new plant and machinery, new production techniques, research and development, new types of organizations, and any other type of investment that they believe will increase productivity. Any time a business believes that, by making an investment in its production process, it can increase revenues (net of other costs) by more than the cost of capital (the rate of interest on loanable funds), it will borrow and invest. Firms compare the interest rate that they must pay in the loanable funds market with the rate of return, or profit that they think they can earn by investing. This comparison helps them to decide whether to invest.

At higher interest rates, fewer investment projects will make economic sense to firms – the cost of capital will exceed the rate of return on the capital investment. Conversely, at lower rates of interest, more investment projects will be undertaken because the cost of capital will be less than the expected rate of return to the capital investment. (We can relate this to the planned investment function in Chapter 15. J. M.

Keynes called the rate of return on capital the 'marginal efficiency of capital'.)

The demand for loanable funds by households, firms, and the government, and the supply of loanable funds, interact to produce an equilibrium interest rate. (In practice there are, as we have seen, a number of interest rates for loans of different duration and for different purposes.) Funds are traded, that is to say, lenders lend, and borrowers borrow, on the capital or money markets. This consists of a wide range of financial intermediaries, including banks, building societies, insurance companies and pension funds, discount houses, merchant banks and finance houses. These institutions aim to provide a very wide range of loans for borrowers with different needs and similarly varied ways of saving for potential lenders. They will compete to offer their customers the most favourable terms and interest rates. This is one market which will clear all the time. Interest rates are flexible and the institutions can lend to one another on a short-term basis should there be excess supply of or demand for their funds. The theory relating to the supply of and demand for money is examined in Chapter 31.

Real versus Nominal Interest Rates

Up to now, we have assumed that there is no inflation. In a world of inflation – a consistent rise in all prices – **nominal**, or market, **interest rates** will be higher than they would be in a world with no inflation. Basically, market rates of interest eventually rise to take account of the anticipated rate of inflation. If, for example, there is no inflation and no inflation expected, the market rate of interest might be, say, 5 per cent for mortgages. If the rate of inflation goes to 10 per cent a year and stays there, then everybody will anticipate that inflation rate. The market, or nominal, rate of interest will rise to 15 per cent to take account of the anticipated rate of inflation. We generally say that the real rate of interest is equal to the nominal rate of interest, minus the rate of inflation. When loans are made in terms of a fixed sum of money, the purchasing power of that money declines if there is inflation so that the lender is repaid a smaller amount of real purchasing power. The higher nominal interest payments compensate for this. In short, you can expect to see high nominal rates of interest in periods of high and/or rising inflation rates. **Real rates of interest** may not necessarily be high, though. We must correct the nominal rates of interest for inflation, before determining whether real interest rates are, in fact, higher than normal.

The Allocative Role of Interest

Interest is a price that allocates funds (credit) to consumers and to firms. Within the business sector, interest allocates funds to different firms and therefore to different investment projects. Those investment, or capital, projects whose rates of return are

---

> ## Key Points 27.2
>
> ▶ Interest is the price paid for the use of capital. It is also the cost of obtaining credit.
>
> ▶ In the credit market, the rate of interest paid depends on, among other things, the length of the loan, the risk, and the administrative charges.
>
> ▶ In order to express a future sum of money (or income stream) in terms of today's pounds, we must discount the future sum back to the present by using the appropriate discount rate. The result is the present value.
>
> ▶ The interest rate is determined by the interaction of the supply of credit, or loanable funds, and the demand for credit, or loanable funds.
>
> ▶ The demand for loanable funds comes from households, firms, and governments.
>
> ▶ Nominal, or market, interest rates adjust to take account of inflation. Therefore, during periods of high anticipated inflation, nominal, or market, interest rates will be historically high. Real interest rates, on the other hand, may not, because they are defined as the nominal interest rate minus the anticipated rate of inflation.

higher than the market rate of interest in the credit market will be undertaken, given an unrestricted market for loanable funds. For example, if the expected rate of return on the purchase of a new factory in some industry is 20 per cent and loanable funds can be acquired for 15 per cent, then the investment project may take place. If, on the other hand, that same project had only an expected rate of return of 9 per cent, it would not be undertaken. In sum, the interest rate allocates loanable funds to those industries where resources will be the most productive.

It is important to realize that the interest rate performs the function of allocating money capital – loanable funds – but that what this ultimately does is allocate real physical capital to various firms for investment projects. Often, non-economists view the movement of loanable funds (credit) simply as something that has to do with 'money' and not with the 'real' world of machines and factories.

Profits

In Chapter 1, we called entrepreneurship, or entrepreneurial talent, the fourth factor of production. Profit is the reward that this factor earns. You may recall that entrepreneurship involves engagement in the risk of starting new businesses. In a sense, then, nothing can be produced without an input of entrepreneurial skills.

We cannot easily talk about the demand and supply of entrepreneurship. For one thing, we have no way to quantify entrepreneurship. What measure should we use? First we will point out what profit is *not*. Then we will examine the sources of true, or economic, profit. Finally, we will look at the functions of profits in a market system.

Distinguishing yet again between Economic Profits and Business, or Accounting Profits

In Chapter 22 we saw a distinction between economic and accounting profit. The accountant calculates profit for a business as the difference between total explicit revenues and total explicit costs. Consider an extreme example. You are given a large farm as part of your inheritance. All the land, fertilizer, seed, machinery, and tools are fully paid for. You take over the farm and work on it diligently with half a dozen labourers. At the end of the year you sell the output for, say, £200 000. Your accountant then subtracts your *explicit* expenses.

The difference is called profit, but it is not economic profit because no accounting was taken of the implicit (as opposed to the explicit) costs of using the land, seed, tools, and machinery. The only explicit cost that was considered was the labourers' wages. As long as the land could be rented out, the seed could be sold, and the tools and machinery could be leased, there was an opportunity cost of using them. To derive the economic profits that you might have earned last year from the farm, you must subtract from total revenues the full opportunity cost of all factors of production used (which will include both implicit and explicit costs).

As a summary, then, accounting profits' main use is the definition of taxable income and, as such, includes returns to both owner's labour and capital. Economic profit, on the other hand, represents a return over and above the opportunity cost of all resources (including a normal profit to the owner's entrepreneurial abilities and labour).

When viewed in this light, it is possible for economic profits to be negative, even if accounting profits are positive. Using the farming case again, what if the opportunity cost of using all the resources turned out to be £220000? Then you would have suffered economic losses.

In sum, the accountant's definition and the economist's definition of profits usually do not coincide. Economic profits are a residual. They are whatever remains after *all* economic, or opportunity, costs are taken into account.

Is Economic Profit a Payment for Managerial Skill?

It is often argued that profit is a payment for 'managing' a business venture well. Clearly, better managed firms will earn higher rewards than poorly managed ones, but *profit* cannot be called the reward for good management, because managerial skill is a *service* available on the market. Any entrepreneur can hire a manager, in other words. Better managers, typically, earn higher salaries than poorer ones. The good entrepreneur who apparently earns high profits because of his or her good management is only earning an *imputed salary*, in effect, what he or she could have earned *elsewhere* by managing *someone else's* business.

Economic profit, strictly speaking, cannot be called the reward for managerial skill. For the firm which prospers owing to good management, payment for management is a cost of production rather than profit.

Is Economic Profit a Payment for Taking Risk?

Unlike a manager who might be employed by the owner, the person owning the enterprise takes the *risk* that the enterprise may fail. It is often argued, therefore, that profits are the reward for bearing such risks. After all, if the business fails, it is the owner who suffers a reduction in net worth. However, many risks can be reduced by purchasing an *insurance policy*. Small and big businesses alike may purchase strike insurance, crop failure insurance, and so on.

So What Is Profit?

Profit is a residual. But it does not arise accidentally; it is a consequence of the unique capabilities of the firm's owner. It rewards the taking of risks which cannot be spread by insurance. It can be explained in other ways too.

Exploitation

The classical economists' view of profit was indistinguishable from what we would now call interest. This is because their concern was not for individual markets and individual factor prices, but rather for the *share of national income* earned by various *social classes*.

Karl Marx argued that the source of profits was **exploitation**. His definition of exploitation was phrased quite carefully, and was different from our normal use of the word. As he used the word, firms actually 'exploited' workers by paying them precisely what their labour was *worth*.

Marx based his entire argument upon the **labour theory of value** – a theory accepted by all the classical economists – which stated that the force underlying the value of all goods was the amount of labour to produce them. This amount included 'direct' labour – the actual amount of work expended by a labourer of average skill – and 'indirect' labour – the labour-value of the portion of the *tools* used in producing the commodity.

Marx put forward his exploitation thesis by asking: if the value of any commodity is measured by the direct and indirect labour-time needed to produce it, what can the value of *labour-time* itself be? He answered that it must be *subsistence*, the amount of goods and services needed to enable a worker and his family to keep body and soul together. This is what it cost, in other words, for society itself to 'produce' one worker. Therefore, when the worker earned subsistence, he or she was earning a 'fair wage', because the labour power provided by the worker was priced in a fashion similar to that of all other commodities.

Marx was restating (albeit in a highly potent, political fashion) what all the classical economists believed: owners of firms earned profit because they could legitimately claim anything 'left over' after all costs of production had been paid. But Marx went on to extend this restatement. Even though the source of profit was 'exploitation', in that workers produce goods of much higher value than the price of their subsistence, by the rules of the game of capitalism itself, 'exploitation' was a perfectly *fair* wage. When workers 'sold their labour power', as Marx put it, if they earned subsistence they received the *full* value of the service they provided. This argument led to Marx's conclusion that a complete revolutionary change in, rather than reform of, the capitalist system was in the best interest of the working class.

Restrictions on Entry

We pointed out in Chapter 24 that monopoly profits – a special form of economic profits – are possible when there are barriers to entry. Monopoly profits due to entry restrictions are often called monopoly rents by economists. Entry restrictions exist in many industries, including taxis, cable television franchises, prescription drugs and spectacles, and numerous others. Basically, monopoly profits are capitalized into the value of the business that owns the particular right to have the monopoly.

Innovation

A number of economists have maintained that economic profits are created by innovations, which is defined as the creation of a new organizational strategy, new marketing strategy, or a new product. The innovator creates new economic profit opportunities by his or her innovations. The successful innovator obtains a temporary monopoly position, allowing him or her to have temporary economic profits. When other firms catch up, those temporary economic profits disappear. In order to encourage innovation this temporary advantage may be extended by granting patents, which prevent copying of the innovation for a certain length of time.

The Function of Economic Profit

In a market economy, the expectation of profits induces firms to discover new products, new production techniques, and new marketing techniques – literally all the new ways to make higher profits.

Profits in this sense spur innovation and investment.

Additionally, as we pointed out in Chapter 6, profits cause resources to move from lower-valued to higher-valued uses. Prices and sales are dictated by the consumer. If the demand curve is close to the origin, then there will be few sales and few, if any, profits. The lack of profits therefore means that there is insufficient demand to cover the opportunity cost of production. In the quest for higher profits, firms will take resources out of areas where either accounting losses or lower-than-normal rates of return are being made and put them into areas where there is an expectation of higher profits. The profit incentive is an inducement for an industry to expand when demand and supply conditions warrant it. The existence of economic losses, on the other hand, indicates that resources in the particular industry are not as valued as they might be elsewhere. These resources therefore move out of that industry or, at a minimum, no further resources are invested in it. Therefore, resources follow the firm's quest for higher profits. They allocate resources, guiding them towards production of the goods and services which consumers most want.

Key Points 27.3

- ▶ Profit is the reward to entrepreneurial talent, the fourth factor of production.
- ▶ It is necessary to distinguish between accounting profits and economic profits.
- ▶ Accounting profits are measured by the difference between total revenues and all explicit costs.
- ▶ Economic profits are measured by the difference between total revenues and the total of all opportunity costs of all factors of production.
- ▶ There are numerous theories of why profits exist. These include the notions that profits are (1) a reward to risk taking, (2) a result of disequilibrium in the market-place, and (3) a result of imperfect competition.
- ▶ The function of profits in a market economy is to allocate scarce resources. Resources will flow to where profits are highest.

CASE STUDY

The Landlords' Retreat

How a Political Consensus Would Revive Britain's Housing Market

For a government committed to sweeping away market rigidities, the British Tories have been extraordinarily reluctant to tackle the most basic of all: the rigidity of the housing market. If people are to move house to look for work, they need an adequate and flexible supply of rented homes. In Britain, this does not exist. The rented market is split between the local authorities, which rent one-third of the country's homes, mainly to people who have had their names on waiting lists for years; and a few private landlords, who are a disappearing breed because they are not allowed to charge market rents. The housing minister, Mr John Patten, has promised to scrap rent controls for new tenancies if the Conservatives win the next election. But reviving the supply of rented housing will take more than one daring deed. The government needs to persuade Labour politicians that its housing policy is worth preserving if they come to power.

The controls on private sector tenancies are a blatant nonsense. Agree on a rent with a landlord today, and you can ask the rent officer tomorrow to fix a 'fair' rent – that is, one that, by law, must be set taking no account of scarcity. Once in, you and your heirs are in for ever. Little wonder that private rentals have shrunk, to about 2½m houses and flats out of 22m. The Tories have kept rent controls mainly because they fear that the Labour party, still obsessively hostile to private landlords, would threaten to reverse any decontrol, and so drive away potential investors.

That Tory fear may be out of date. Realists in the Labour party know that local authorities can house people just as miserably in the public sector as a Rachman slum-landlord ever did in the private. A rented sector monopolized by local authorities lacks qualities which many Labour activists now favour: like choice, and control over one's life, and smallness. Labour politicians are still nervous of some types of private landlord. But other would-be landlords, like building societies and housing associations, might offer tenants choice without bullying, and quality without exploitation. There is lots of money, too, in the hands of institutional investors such as pension funds, which might be lured into paying for more rented housing. Between them, pension funds, building societies, and housing associations might lay the foundations for a new and acceptable form of private rented housing. Two obstacles stand in their way. One is rent control: the other is the tax incentives to owner-occupiers. No sensible housing policy can address one without the other.

A Tory government could make the removal of rent controls credible, and acceptable to Labour. To do so, it would need to stick to its plans to decontrol new lettings only. That is bad economics, but it could be good politics: with full decontrol, all rents in Tory-voting southern England would certainly go up, perhaps sharply before the supply of new rented housing did. The Conservatives would also need to muster all the enthusiasm of the building societies and housing associations to show how big and flexible the rented sector might be, if rents could be relied on to rise in line with inflation. And the

government ought to accept – publicly – that if poor tenants are not subsidized through the destructive device of rent conrols, they may be helped by more housing benefit.

Tackle all the Distortions Together

Such a policy will be more convincing if it is part of a wider attempt to free the housing market. It is not just private rents that have been held down: many public rents are ludicrously low. Last April, the average rent of a three-bedroom council house was under £20 a week, even in London. Yet that is not the biggest distortion. Income tax relief on mortgage loans up to £30000 makes buying a house more attractive than renting it. The relief will cost £4.8bn in forgone revenue this year. The only political consensus on housing in Britain is that this giant, market-distorting subsidy to the better-off should stay. As long as it does, the Labour party cannot honestly claim it wants to house the poorest well, and the Tories cannot boast of their commitment to a more efficient jobs market.

Source: The Economist, 22 Feb. 1986.

Questions
1. Is there any connection between rent for housing and economic rent?
2. In what ways are market forces distorted in the housing market? Why have these distortions developed?

CASE STUDY

Finding Finance for Investment

When a firm wants to invest, it can seek funds either internally, or externally, or both. **Internal finance** is generated from the firm's own savings. This is known as corporate saving, or retained profit, or sometimes as depreciation allowances. Its purpose is to provide for the replacement of existing capital, and expansion of productive capacity. Typically a profitable firm saves for several years, during which it will seek to obtain the best interest rate it can on its surplus funds. (It may obtain a CD or some other high-interest-yielding asset.) When it has accumulated assets, it will try to identify the most profitable investment project open to it. This may be a replacement of existing productive capacity, perhaps with more technically advanced machinery. Or it may add to existing capacity: this would be expansion, or net investment. The more profitable the firm is, the more profit it can retain for future investment, and the more likely it is to have dynamic plans for the future. In general, firms may often be more willing to take risks if they have substantial retained profits. They do not have to justify the use of internal funds to their bankers and so may undertake riskier projects. Perhaps 75 per cent of total finance for expansion typically comes from internal finance.

In addition to internal finance, the firm may seek **external finance**. This may come from a number of sources, all of which are part of the capital or money markets. **Debt finance** involves borrowing fixed amounts on which a predetermined rate of interest is paid. **Equity finance** involves issuing shares in the company; the returns will be not interest but dividends, a share of the profit which will vary from year to year depending on the performance of the company.

Debt Finance

Companies can borrow either short or long term. Much the most important source of short-term finance or working capital is the bank overdraft. The advantage of this is that interest is payable only on the amount outstanding; the disadvantage is that the company must regularly review its position with the bank, and may have to pay more for the loan when interest rates rise. An alternative source of short-term finance is the commercial bill. This is a promise to pay a stated sum on a certain date, usually three months hence. There is a market in commercial bills, which are *discounted*, i.e. bought for less than their face value. (See Chapter 19.)

Long-term loan finance may involve the issue of corporate bonds or debentures. These allow the firm to borrow at a fixed rate of interest; repayment at maturity may be twenty years hence. The company then has an assured source of finance which may be linked to the life of its capital equipment. However, it must be able to offer reasonable security to lenders, and of course the interest must be paid irrespective of whether the firm is making profits. The other sources of long-term loans are banks and finance houses. Such loans would normally be tied to the life of a particular investment project, so that both interest and repayments are paid from the income generated by the investment. Such loans may extend over five to ten years.

Equity Finance

When people buy equities, or shares in a company, they buy, literally, an entitlement to a share of the future profits of the company. When a firm needs more capital, it will make a **new issue** of shares through a merchant bank acting as an issuing house. The latter will advertise the new issue; alternatively, the company may offer a **rights issue** to existing shareholders. This gives each one the right to buy a certain number of the new shares usually in proportion to their existing holdings. A rights issue is cheaper than a new issue; the latter is likely to be used only if large amounts of capital are being sought.

From the company's viewpoint, the attraction of equity finance is that the buyer shares the risks. In a bad year little or no dividend need be paid. From the shareholders' viewpoint, precisely *because* they have carried the risk, they can expect to get a higher rate of return over the long run than they would from a fixed interest loan. Also they may make capital gains. Inflation erodes the value of assets denominated in money terms, so that the lender loses some of the real value of the loan, and the interest paid. Meanwhile, profits will tend to be at least stable in the long term, or perhaps will grow. In money terms the value of the share will grow, provided the firm is healthy. If the firm is very profitable then, of course, the share price will rise further. So inflation may increase the attractions of equities as assets, provided business

Continued overleaf

confidence does not suffer.

At the same time, inflation can lead to high nominal interest rates and this can cause firms with extensive loan finance to have difficulty in meeting interest payments. They will have a **cash flow problem**. This can further enhance the attractiveness of using equity finance for investment.

Markets

When we speak of the capital market, we refer to the market in funds for investment, that is, for loans and new issues, both of which provide long-term finance. When we speak of the money market, we refer to the market in short-term funds, lent by selling commercial and Treasury bills and by other similar means, through banks and discount houses. The **Stock Exchange** is separate and has particular functions: it allows the *exchange* of stocks (bonds and equities), that is, the transfer of ownership of stocks from one body to another. It does not lead to the creation of *new* loans or equities. Just to confuse you though the Stock Exchange does handle new issues of government bonds; they are issued through the twenty-nine primary dealers on the Stock Exchange who have been accepted as such by the Bank of England.

These very many ways of lending and borrowing money, of putting money productively to work means that there are many different rates of return to be had, depending on the circumstances. Blue chip companies can be relied upon to pay dividends. Firms seeking venture capital are going to be adventurous with your capital, probably in an area of high technology. They will pay little in dividends, but may provide substantial capital growth (i.e. the share price will go up) if the companies themselves grow rapidly. The government will pay relatively low rates of interest, but is very safe – hence, gilts. Other sorts of loans will have interest rates falling between the extremes, but higher for longer loans and vice versa.

Banks which are buying shares in the stockbroking firms which trade on the Stock Exchange will become **financial conglomerates**. They will be offering many different kinds of financial products through their different departments.

Questions
1. Why do interest rates vary at an given time?
2. In what circumstances will firms seek external finance?
3. What factors will savers take into account when deciding how to invest their funds?

Exam Preparation and Practice

INTRODUCTORY EXERCISES

1. 'All revenues obtained by the Italian government from Renaissance art museums are pure economic rent.' Is this statement true or false, and why?

MULTIPLE CHOICE QUESTIONS

†1. A man earns £100 per week. The next most highly remunerative job available to him would carry a wage of £95 per week. The £95 is known as his
A economic rent
B quasi-rent
C rent of ability
D transfer earnings
E transfer payments

†2. If the demand for a factor in absolutely inelastic supply were to increase, then the
A transfer earnings would fall
B transfer earnings would rise
C economic rent would fall
D economic rent would rise
E quasi-rent would fall

†3. Quasi-rent is
A a fringe benefit received by workers
B the interest charged on hire purchase transactions
C the rent of a piece of land as distinct from the property built on the land
D the surplus payment received by factors whose supply is fixed in the short run
E the rent charged for the hire of durable consumer goods

RELATED ESSAY QUESTIONS

1. 'Since land is fixed in supply, land values can be varied without affecting either the use or the development of land.' Discuss.
2. What are the economic functions of profit?
3. Why are borrowers willing to pay a rate of interest to obtain a loan? Why do lenders require a payment for making a loan?
4. Distinguish between transfer earnings and economic rent. Discuss the contention that economic rent may be earned by any factor of production.
5. What is meant by economic rent? Why might it continue to exist in the long run?
6. Are profits rent?

28 How Income is Distributed

Key Points to Review

▶ **Positive versus normative economics (1.4)**

▶ **Marginal revenue product (26.1)**

▶ **The elasticity of supply of labour (26.3)**

Questions for Preview

1 How are factor and product markets related?

2 How does structural change affect the labour market?

3 Is marginal productivity an important influence on income distribution?

4 What other factors influence wages?

5 How equal is the distribution of income in the UK?

We know that there are many rich and many poor people, and some of us think we know why. The real reasons are more complex than most of us care to admit. In this chapter we will present some of the more obvious reasons why in the UK the **distribution of income** is uneven. And we will examine the relationship between factor and product markets.

The Functional Distribution of Income

Income accrues to factors of production in return for their services. Figure 28.1 shows the share of total income arising from labour, capital, and property respectively, that is, wages, profit, and rent. 1975 illustrates an exceptionally bad year for profits. Rising oil prices and rising wage costs combined to reduce company profits substantially: they had been running at around 18 per cent of total income. Since 1983 the share of profits may have risen as economic growth increased. And high levels of unemployment have made it possible for employers to hire some kinds of labour (mainly unskilled) at relatively low rates of pay.

Factor and Product Markets

So far, we have kept factor and product markets separate. We examined supply of and demand for products in Part A. To some extent supply-and-demand analysis is applicable to labour and capital markets, which appeared in Chapters 26 and 27. We call this **partial equilibrium analysis**. The meaning of partial equilibrium analysis can best be expressed by a particular qualifying statement that we have tacked on to most of our 'laws' and theories. That particular statement is: 'other things being equal'. In partial equilibrium analysis, it is assumed that, aside from whatever else we are analysing, almost everything else is held constant. In essence, partial equilibrium analysis allows us to focus on a single market and view it in isolation. For analytical purposes, the market is viewed as independent and self-contained. That is, it is independent of all other markets.

General Equilibrium Analysis

General equilibrium analysis regards all sectors as important. General equilibrium analysis recognizes

Figure 28.1
Factor Incomes

	1975 (£m)	%	1979 (£m)	%	1983 (£m)	%
Income from employment	68656		115734		170072	
		77.9		73.5		73.1
Income from self-employment	9388		16442		23123	
Gross trading profits of companies (private sector)	11741		28942		41530	
Gross trading surplus of public corporations (public sector)	3095	14.9	5587	19.2	9661	19.3
Gross trading surplus of government enterprises	79		102		−109	
Rent	6375	6.4	11483	6.4	17424	6.6
Total domestic income*	100243		179929		264157	

*Includes some capital consumption and stock appreciation.

Source: CSO Annual Abstract 1985, p. 246.

the important fact that everything depends on everything else. It takes account of the interrelationships among prices and quantities of various goods and services. It is a more precise analysis than partial equilibrium analysis, but also a more difficult one to undertake. Just as partial equilibrium analysis does not require that *all* other things be held constant, general equilibrium analysis does not permit *all* other things to vary. There is a limit to how many markets can be taken into account in any analysis. That limit is reached either by the cerebral limits of the economist doing the analysis or by the capacity of the computer that he or she is utilizing. When economists talk of general equilibrium analysis in dealing with practical problems, they are taking account of *several markets* and the relationships among them. If the goal of the economist is to predict what will happen when the economic environment changes, his or her choice of general equilibrium analysis depends on (1) the question being asked, and (2) the degree to which the answer will change if several markets are *not* considered. One would want to use general equilibrium analysis when analysing the effects of, say, a new law requiring the producers of steel to pay a 300 per cent tax on the value of all steel produced. There would be important interrelationships among the steel industry, the car industry, and the labour markets involved in both industries, as well as effects on and from a multitude of other industries in the economy.

Let us now look at the simplest general equilibrium model. We will go back to the world of guns and butter discussed in Chapter 1.

THE CIRCULAR FLOW IN A TWO-GOOD WORLD

Assume that there are only two goods available – guns

and butter. Nothing else is produced, nothing else is consumed. All income is spent on either guns or butter. Thus, there are two industries. We show the circular flow of income and product in Figure 28.2. We have broken the factor markets and the product markets into two industries – guns and butter. We have also assumed that there is only one factor of production – labour. (Of course, there have to be others, but we want to make the model simple to show the interrelationships involved.) Let us start off in equilibrium in both labour markets and both product markets. The equilibrium prices and quantities of guns and butter are P_G, P_B, Q_G and Q_B, respectively. The equilibrium wage-rates and quantities of labour are W_G, W_B, L_G, and L_B, respectively.

Now, to show how the interrelationships work, we will assume an increase in the demand for guns. This is shown by a shift in the demand schedule in the product market from $D_G D_G$ to $D'_G D'_G$. The short-run equilibrium price, given the supply curve of $S_G S_G$, will rise from P_G to P'_G. This means that firms in this industry will be making higher than normal profits. (We assume they were in equilibrium before; thus, they were making normal profits, or a competitive rate of return.) That is why output expands to Q'_G.

THE LABOUR MARKET

There is one way for firms in the guns industry to expand, however. More resources must be obtained. Considering labour alone, the demand curve for labour in the gun industry must shift from $d_G d_G$ to $d'_G d'_G$. It will shift outwards to the right because, as you will remember, the demand for labour is a derived demand. Now that output (guns) can be sold at a higher price (P'_G), the marginal revenue product curve

Figure 28.2

A Simplified General Equilibrium Model: Guns and Butter. In this world we have just two products, guns and butter. We have a simplified circular flow diagram in which firms purchase resources in the labour market and sell goods and services in the product market. Households sell factor services to the labour market and receive national income as factor payments. Households purchase goods and services in the product market and make consumer expenditures. We assume that there is a shift in tastes in favour of guns. In the diagrams below we use lower-case d's and s's for the demand and supply curves in the labour markets and upper case D's and S's for the demand and supply curves in the product markets. The demand curve for guns shifts out to $D_G' D_G'$. The price increases to P_G'. This causes the derived demand curve for labour in the gun industry to shift outwards to $d_G' d_G'$. Wage-rates in the gun industry increase to W_G'. Concurrently, the demand curve for butter shifts inwards to $D_B' D_B'$. The price of butter falls to P_B'. The derived demand for labour in the butter industry decreases to $d_B' d_B'$. Wage-rates fall in the butter industry to W_B'. In the long run, further shifts occur. Labour and resources flow into the gun industry so that the supply curve shifts outwards. The supply curve in the butter industry shifts inwards. Prices move to P_G'' in the gun industry and to P_B'' in the butter industry. Workers move into the gun industry so that its supply curve of labour shifts outwards. The supply curve of labour shifts inwards in the butter industry. The equilibrium wage-rate in the gun industry goes to W_G''. The equilibrium wage-rate in the butter industry goes to W_B''. There are further adjustments that then take place, which we do not show.

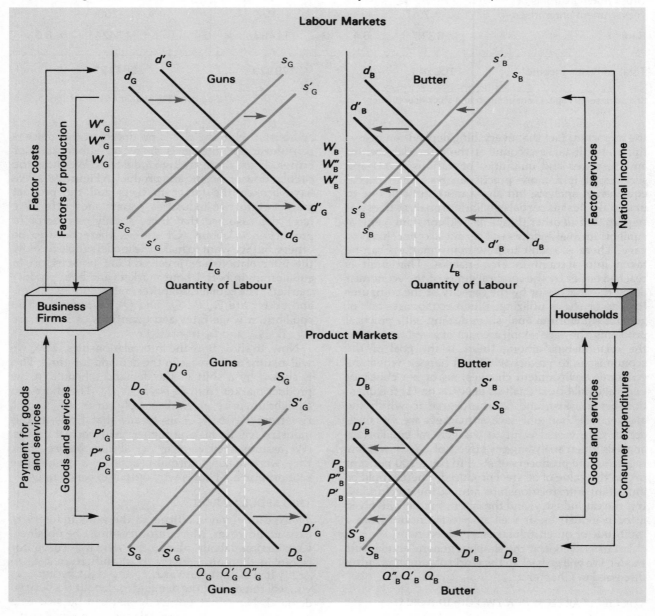

shifts outwards to the right, and so too does the demand curve for labour in the gun industry. The only way the industry can attract more workers is for the wage-rate to increase. That is why we show an upward-sloping labour supply curve of $s_G s_G$. The wage-rate rises to W'_G.

WHAT ABOUT THE BUTTER INDUSTRY?

The opposite short-run adjustments will occur in the butter industry. The product demand curve will shift leftwards from $D_B D_B$ to $D'_B D'_B$. This is so because we are living in a two-good, full-employment world. The only way for the population to demand and consume more guns is to reduce its demand and consume less butter. Given the supply curve $S_B S_B$, the short-run equilibrium price will fall in the butter industry to P'_B. Looking at the labour market, since the demand for labour is a derived demand, the demand curve will shift leftwards from $d_B d_B$ to $d'_B d'_B$. The market-clearing wage-rate will fall to W'_B, and labour will leave the butter industry and enter the gun industry.

General Equilibrium in the Long Run

What we have done is trace the short-run adjustments to a shift in demand in favour of guns and away from butter. This is only a short-run situation because at the new equilibrium, economic profits are being made in the gun industry while economic losses are being made in the butter industry. Resources will flow out of the butter industry into the gun industry. That is to say, firms may go out of business in the butter industry; they or others will quickly see a place to make higher profits and move into the gun industry even before bankruptcy threatens. Thus, the supply curve in the gun industry will shift outwards from $S_G S_G$ to $S'_G S'_G$. Simultaneously, the supply curve will shift inwards in the butter industry. A new long-run equilibrium price will prevail in both industries. It will fall in the long run from P'_G to P''_G in the gun industry. In the butter industry, it will rise from P'_B to P''_B.

There will be long-run adjustments also taking place in the resource markets. Workers will shift out of the butter industry and into the gun industry. The supply curve in the former will shift leftwards while simultaneously the supply curve in the latter will shift rightwards. The new equilibrium wage-rate in the long run will fall slightly in the gun labour market from W'_G to W''_G. It will simultaneously rise in the butter labour market to W''_B.

FURTHER ADJUSTMENTS

The process does not end there, for the demand curve for labour in both markets will have to shift again. Remember, the demand for labour is a derived demand. When the price of guns and the price of butter change again to P''_G and P''_B, this will cause the marginal revenue product to change also. We do not show these further changes, but they will continue with the demand and supply curves shifting until the long-run equilibrium is established in both the labour

markets and the product markets. If we were to consider the possibility of other markets existing, that is, a world in which there were more than two goods, we would also take into account shifts in the demand for other goods due to a change in the price of guns and of butter. We would then have to find out what would happen to the resources used in other industries. A true general equilibrium analysis would take account of every relevant market.

A Short Digression: Perfect Competition and Economic Efficiency

Underlying this description is a perfectly competitive economy. It turns out that the perfectly competitive price system has a very special quality. There is a correspondence between an efficient allocation of resources and the results of the allocation from a perfectly competitive price system. Indeed, this correspondence is exact. Every perfectly competitive allocation in long-run equilibrium yields an economically efficient allocation of resources. The definition of economic efficiency is a situation in which the economy is deriving maximum economic value from the economy's given resources. Once we have attained a position of economic efficiency, it is impossible to make any person better off without making another person worse off. Costs are kept to a minimum and each pound spent on inputs yields output of equal value.

THE MEANING OF A PERFECTLY COMPETITIVE PRICE SYSTEM

Let us be specific about what we mean by a perfectly competitive price system. In such a system, each good has an equilibrium price that is established by the interaction of supply and demand. The equilibrium price clears each market; the quantities demanded and supplied of each good are equal.

Consumers take the price of the goods and services they buy as given. Subject to their budget constraints, they adjust their behaviour to maximize satisfaction, or utility. Firms, of which there are a large number, each operate to maximize profits. Under these conditions, three things happen:

1. Profit-maximizing competitive firms produce at an output rate at which price equals marginal cost. Price reflects the worth to consumers, because they are willing to pay the price of a product. Marginal cost reflects the social opportunity cost of the resources needed in production. Thus, when price is set equal to marginal cost, the extra value placed on goods and services by consumers is just equal to the extra social opportunity cost of producing those goods and services. We say, then, that the optimal output of each commodity gets produced.
2. Perfect competition results in each good or service being produced at minimum long-run average total cost. Thus, there is no 'waste' in the system. Goods and services are produced using the least costly

combinations of resources. Specifically, for each industry, the last pound spent on each factor input generates the same marginal physical product. Additionally, perfect competition results in every factor of production being paid its marginal revenue product (MRP).

3. Consumers will choose in competitive markets so that the distribution of output will maximize consumer satisfaction, or utility. That is to say, each consumer will buy goods and services in such amounts that the last pound spent on each good or service yields the same amount of extra satisfaction, or marginal utility.

The Real World: Market Failure and Structural Change

We have explained the relationship between factor and product markets in terms of perfect competition. This approach is useful in two ways. First, it shows us how resources are reallocated *across many markets* when changes in demand take place. And second, it reminds us that keeping markets competitive whenever possible can help to promote an efficient allocation of resources. However, the real world is full of instances of market failure. These are situations in which market forces either cannot work freely, or cannot respond to all the economic forces at work.

For example, it is clear that any kind of change in demand will require changes in the structure, or composition, of output. We call this process **structural change**. Resources must move out of lines of production which face lower demand (and losses), and into production of goods and services for which demand is growing. Because human beings often find change difficult and disruptive, structural change can be a painful process. In particular, if resources are not very mobile, it may produce **structural unemployment**. People who are made redundant from declining

industries may lack the skills needed by growing industries, or may live far away from them. The market fails to ensure an easy reallocation of resources. They may be unemployed for some time, especially if the declining industry is a localized one such as shipbuilding: heavy unemployment will then persist. Similarly, capital must move also, in the long run.

When capital equipment wears out, it will not be replaced unless it has been making a profit. Instead, the owners of the capital will seek to reinvest in a more profitable enterprise. So we see whole factories closing down altogether, and new ones opening up.

Because the demand for labour is *derived* from the demand for the product, structural change is a major source of income differentials. Firms in growing industries will pay more to attract the labour they need. So pay in the electrical and electronics industries is usually higher than it is in the textile trade. Electronics firms are often located in places with relatively low unemployment (e.g. the Thames Valley) and may have difficulty in recruiting all the labour they need. They will have to pay well to attract and to keep people with scarce skills. A textile firm in Bolton which has been laying off its employees will pay less well. Some of them may be without work years after they were made redundant. Their skills are abundant in relation to the demand for them, and their market power is therefore very limited.

Marginal Productivity Theory

When trying to determine how many workers a firm would hire, we had to construct a marginal revenue product curve. We found that as more workers were hired, the MRP fell due to diminishing marginal returns. If the forces of supply and demand established a certain wage-rate, workers would be hired until marginal revenue product was equal to the going wage-rate. Then the hiring would stop. This analysis

---

Key Points 28.1

▶ The functional distribution of income describes the shares of total income forming rewards to land, labour, and capital.

▶ Partial equilibrium analysis is one that does not take account of interrelationships among markets.

▶ General equilibrium analysis attempts to take into account the interrelationships among different markets.

▶ A change in the demand for one good will elicit changes in the demand for another good and also cause changes in the corresponding factor markets.

▶ It is possible to show that there is a correspondence between perfect competition and economic efficiency.

▶ Changing patterns of demand lead to structural change in the composition of output, and to differentials in incomes between different industries.

suggests what *all* workers can expect to be paid in the labour market. *They can each expect to be paid the value of their marginal product* or MRP, assuming, of course, that there are low-cost information flows and that the labour and product markets are competitive.

We have already seen that rising demand for a product will result in higher prices, and therefore increasing MRP. Other things being equal, wages will rise as MRP rises.

Rising demand may occur for a number of reasons. Improved competitiveness with substitutes, whether on price or non-price factors, will increase demand. Rising incomes will be important for products with high income elasticity of demand. Falling demand will be associated with the development of efficient production of a substitute abroad, or of new substitutes. Shifting tastes and fashions can work both ways.

Process of Competition

In most situations, the marginal productivity theory gives us a rough idea of what workers will be paid. In a competitive situation, with mobility of labour resources (at least on the margin), workers who are being paid less than their MRP will be bid away to better employment opportunities. This process will continue until each worker is paid his or her MRP. In general, employers will not want to keep workers if their wage-rates are greater than their MRPs. In such a situation, it would pay an entrepreneur to fire or lay off those workers who are being paid more than the worth of their contribution to total output.

Full Adjustment is Never Obtained

Individuals are not always paid their MRPs. This can be because we do not live in a world of perfect information, or in a world with perfectly competitive input and output markets. Employers cannot always seek out the most productive employees available. It takes resources to research the past records of potential employees, their training, their education, and their abilities. You may know musicians, artists, photographers, singers, and other talented people who are being paid much less than well-known, publicized 'stars'. But this does not mean that marginal productivity theory is invalid. It merely indicates that information is costly. Furthermore, we must distinguish carefully between the *market* evaluataions of an individual worker's worth and *subjective* evaluations. You may subjectively believe that the output of a particular artist is extremely valuable. Unfortunately for the artist and perhaps for your sense of fairness, few other people may share your subjective evaluation. Therefore, the artist is unable to sell his or her work very easily or at very high prices. Finally, the marginal productivity theory of wages applies in the large, that is, on average. It will not necessarily explain every single case.

Bearing in mind that it is sometimes very difficult to determine what an employee's contribution to production actually is, we would expect to find many cases where the connection between pay and product is not obvious.

If we accept marginal productivity theory, then we have a way to find out how people can, in fact, earn higher incomes. If they can manage to increase their marginal physical product, they can expect to be paid more. Some of the determinants of marginal product are innate intelligence, education, experience, and training. Most of these are means by which marginal product can be increased.

INNATE ABILITIES AND ATTRIBUTES

These factors are obviously the easiest to explain and the hardest to acquire if you do not possess them. Innate abilities and attributes can be very strong, if not overwhelming, determinants of a person's potential productivity. Strength, good looks, co-ordination, mental alertness, and so on are all facets of non-acquired human capital and, thus, have some bearing on one's ability to earn income.

EDUCATION AND TRAINING

Education is usually placed under the heading of 'investment in human capital', a topic we will discuss later. For the moment, suffice it to say that education improves one's productivity by increasing the human capital one has available for use in the labour market. Education usually allows an individual to be more versatile in the things he or she can do. On-the-job training can be as important as basic education in increasing producitivity.

EXPERIENCE

Additional experience at particular tasks is another way to increase one's productivity. Experience can be linked to the well-known *learning curve* that occurs when the same task is done over and over. Take an example of a person going to work on an assembly line at Ford Motor Company. At first, he or she is able to screw on only three bolts every two minutes. Then the worker becomes more adept and can screw on four bolts in the same time plus insert a rubber guard on the bumper. After a few more weeks, even another task can be added. Hence, we would expect experience to lead to higher rates of productivity. And we would expect people with more experience to be paid more than those with less experience. More experience, however, does not guarantee a higher wage-rate. The *demand* for one's services must also exist. Spending a long time to become a first-rate archer in modern society would probably add very little to the income of the person who becomes an archer. As another example, a more experienced pianist in a society uninterested in music may earn the same as an inexperienced pianist, for they both may earn virtually nothing at all, since there is little demand for their talents. Experience only has value if the output is demanded by society.

CAPITAL INVESTMENT

The more capital people have to work with, the higher will be their productivity. A better machine will enable its operator to increase marginal physical product. In the long run, increases in real wages come from the increase in marginal revenue product resulting from this improved productivity.

Problems with Marginal Productivity Theory

Marginal productivity theory can help us to understand *why* some differentials in wages exist and persist. It does not imply that people *should* be paid any particular wage. It may, in fact, lead to some people being paid very poorly indeed. But this is not all. A weakness of the theory is that, for many people, it is very difficult to determine what their marginal physical product is. How would we evaluate the productivity of a railway signalman, a restaurant cleaner, or a primary-school teacher?

It is vitally important to consider both whatever marginal productivity theory can tell us, *and* all other relevant features of the labour market, including the market imperfections which exist. Immobilities, restrictions on supply, monopoly buyers and sellers of labour, and special conditions relating to individual occupations and localities, are all important.

DISCRIMINATION

It is possible – and, indeed, quite obvious to most – that discrimination affects the distribution of income. Certain groups in our society do not receive wage-rates comparable to those received by other groups, even when we correct for productivity. Some argue that all of these differences are due to discrimination against, for example, non-whites and women. We cannot simply accept *all* differences in income as due to discrimination, though. What we need to do is discover why differences in income across groups exist, and then determine if explanations other than discrimination in the labour market can explain at least some of those differences in incomes. That part of income differences across groups that is not explained is what we can rightfully call the result of discrimination.

Which People Have the High-paying Jobs?

White males, on average, occupy jobs in the highest-paying occupations more than non-white males and all females. As for the lowest-paying jobs, they are dominated by females, white and non-white, and by non-white males. Clearly, the distribution of groups across occupations is one of the major reasons why there are income differentials among whites and non-whites and males and females.

Some argue that this uneven distribution of jobs among groups is the result of past and current discrimination in the job market. In any society where white males dominate management positions, if there is racial and sexual prejudice, then white males will tend to hire white males, rather than non-white males or females.

Other Determinants of Income Differences

There are a multitude of determinants of income differences. They have to do with age, talent, education, productivity, and the like.

The Age–earnings Cycle

Within every class of income-earners, there seem to be regular cycles of earning behaviour. Most people earn more when they are middle-aged than when they are younger or older. This is called the **age–earnings cycle**. Every occupation has its own age-earnings cycle, and every individual will probably experience some variation from the average.

When individuals start working at a young age, they typically have no work-related experience. Their ability to produce is lower than that of more experienced workers. That is, their productivity is lower. As they become older, they attain more training and more experience. Their productivity rises, and they are therefore paid more. Moreover, they start to work longer hours, in general. At the age of forty-five or fifty, the productivity of individual workers usually peaks. So, too, do the number of hours per week that are worked. After this peak in the age–earnings cycle, the detrimental effects of ageing usually outweigh any increases in training or experience.

Trade Unions

Sometimes employers pay good wages because of market forces. Trade unions may then appear to be quite successful while in fact making relatively little difference. There are some circumstances, however, in which unions can be successful in raising wages, irrespective of market forces. Where large numbers of employees work on one site, it is easy for unions to recruit and communicate with their members. It will be easy to organize industrial action and this will give the union extra muscle. Similarly, if the production process is highly integrated, so that a large number of people contribute in varied and specialized ways, strike action by a very few people can disrupt production. In the car industry, where production involves many people contributing parts for and working on an assembly line, quite small groups of people can halt production if they withdraw their labour. This sort of union power is much reduced by the threat of unemployment.

Inelastic Demand for the Product

When wage costs are rising, the firm can pass the cost on to the consumer in the form of higher prices for the product. If demand is inelastic then consumers will continue to buy the product despite the higher price. If on the other hand demand is elastic, people will switch to a cheaper substitute or do without the product altogether. So the firm cannot raise prices without facing a substantial drop in demand, and will therefore try to avoid paying higher wages.

Restricted Supply of Labour

In Chapter 26 we considered various reasons why the supply of labour may be inelastic. Whenever labour is scarce in relation to the demand for it, wages will tend to rise. Supply may be kept scarce by shortages of training facilities (reflecting occupational immobility) or by entry restrictions (as with barristers, reflecting some monopoly power) or by individuals' unique qualities.

When particular skills are in scarce supply, there are said to be **supply constraints**.

Investment in Human Capital

Investment in human capital is just like investment in any other thing. If you invest in a building, you expect to realize a profit later on by receiving a rate of return for your investment. You expect to receive some reward for not consuming all your income today. The same is true for investment in human capital. If you invest in yourself by going to college, rather than going to work after school and earning more money, you presumably will be rewarded in the future by a higher income and/or a more interesting job.

On average, the rate of return to investment in human capital is similar to the rate of return to investment in other areas. The main cost of education is the income forgone, or the opportunity cost, through not working. The extra income earned over a lifetime is almost always more than enough to compensate for this.

Technology, Jobs, and Wages

Increasing capital investment, using better technology, and investment in human capital, are processes which go hand in hand. They all increase labour productivity and, together, they are the source of long-run economic growth. All three can be seen to lead to increasing wages.

But there are other factors which make the connections complex. For example, in agriculture there has been an enormous amount of capital-spending on machines, and much technical progress in seeds, fertilizers, and production methods. What has happened to employment? Many jobs have been lost, and agricultural work is still very poorly paid compared to the rest of the economy.

In order to understand this, we must allow for the nature of demand for the product, and of the supply of labour. The demand for food products grows slowly, if at all. Food has a low income elasticity of demand –

Key Points 28.2

▶ There are numerous determinants of income differences.

▶ If we accept the marginal productivity theory of wages, workers can expect to be paid their marginal revenue product. Note, however, that full adjustment is never obtained, so that some workers may be paid more or less than their marginal revenue product. The marginal productivity theory does not necessarily explain every single individual case.

▶ Marginal revenue product rises when the price of the product rises.

▶ Marginal productivity depends on: (1) innate abilities and attributes, (2) education, (3) experience and training, (4) capital invested per employee.

▶ Wages and salaries may be greatly affected by factors other than marginal productivity, such as labour market imperfections.

▶ Most people follow an age–earnings cycle in which they earn relatively small incomes when they first start working, increase their incomes until about age fifty, then slowly experience a decrease in their real incomes.

▶ Trade unions may be able to influence wages.

most of us in the UK already eat more than enough; higher incomes mean only modest increases in demand for some more expensive foods. So improved technology in agriculture leads to the substitution of capital for labour rather than to expansion of production. The labour needs of the industry then diminish; at any given wage there will be excess supply of labour. Agricultural workers are widely separated geographically and therefore have a weak union structure. They live on the job and are geographically rather immobile. So inevitably their wages have remained low in spite of massive increases in productivity. Farm workers have moved into other occupations but not fast enough to create conditions of scarcity for themselves.

Figure 28.3 shows how different the effects of investment, technical progress, and education may be. If demand for the product is static or slow-growing, then employers' labour needs will be progressively reduced and wages will probably stay low. If on the other hand the fall in costs and prices leads to a growing market, then the industry may expand rapidly and create new jobs. This is what happens whenever a new product is created, using modern technology to mass produce and develop a large market. Televisions, calculators, and VCRs all fol-

lowed this path. In the initial period of expansion, the wages paid to attract labour to the new line of production may be above average. In the long run the wages paid will depend partly on whether the skills needed are still scarce.

Wealth and Income Are not the Same

So far we have looked at income distribution primarily as a matter of differentials in earnings, the return to labour. Individuals also receive a return for the ownership of land. We have called this rent. Individuals receive income as a return to the ownership of capital. We have called this interest. And, finally, entrepreneurs receive economic profits as a return to entrepreneurial ability, again a form of human wealth. Income is a flow received year in and year out. It is the flow received from wealth, which is a stock of both human and non-human capital.

Therefore, the discussion of the distribution of income is not the same thing as a discussion of the distribution of wealth. A complete concept of wealth would include tangible objects, such as buildings, machinery, land, cars, and houses – non-human

Figure 28.3
The Effect of Technology, and Investment on the Labour Market

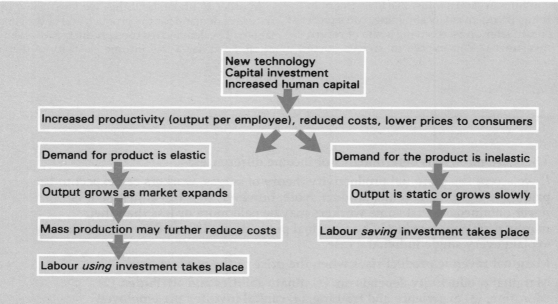

Consequences

1 People spend more on the product than they did previously
2 Demand for labour rises
3 Wages rise, unless the labour is unskilled and abundant in supply

Consequences

1 Real incomes rise – people spend less on the product, more on other things
2 Demand for labour falls, leading to excess supply
3 Wages fall, relative to other industries, unless supply of labour adjusts rapidly

wealth – as well as people who have skills, knowledge, initiative, talents, and so on – human wealth. The total of *human* and non-human wealth gives us our nation's capital stock. (Note that the terms *wealth* and *capital* are often used *only* with reference to non-human wealth.) The capital stock refers to anything that can generate utility to individuals in the future. A fresh ripe tomato is not part of our capital stock. It has to be eaten before it turns rotten, and after it is eaten it can no longer generate satisfaction.

Stocks and Flows – a Digression

The wealth that you have is a **stock**. (Note here that we are not talking just about stock in a company, shares of which are sold on, say, the Stock Exchange.) Lots of other things are stocks, too, such as a building that you might own. Stocks are defined independently of time, although they are assessed at a point in time. A car dealer can have a stock of cars that may be worth £50000. A timber company may have five acres of trees worth £10000; this is a stock of trees.

On the other hand, the income you make is a flow. Remember, a **flow** is a stream of things through time. It is a certain number of things per time-period. You receive so many pounds per month or so many pounds per year. The number of cars that a car dealer sells per week is a flow; the number of cars he has is a stock. Flows, in other words, are defined as occurring over a given *period* of time; stocks are defined at a *point* in time.

If you want to add to your stock of wealth or capital, you must save. That is, you must not consume part of your income. The act of saving is a flow that makes your stock of wealth larger. You should not confuse the act of saving with how much you have in savings. 'Savings' is a stock concept akin to wealth, as we have defined it.

People build up their wealth positions by saving. Savings can be held as cash (not such a good idea if there is inflation), or put into stocks, bonds, businesses, precious metals, or consumer durable goods. The purchase of a house, for example, adds to one's accumulated savings, or wealth.

What Determines Differences in Wealth

Each of us either *inherits* a certain amount of wealth, or otherwise has some of our parents' generation's wealth transferred to us in some form. Some people, for example, inherit a home or large estate consisting of stocks and bonds, cash, diamonds, and other assets. Some people inherit a small amount – perhaps just a parental contribution to a university grant. And it may be a negative amount – if, for example, we have to support our parents in their old age or take over their debts when they die.

No matter what its initial size, you can only add to your wealth by saving: you must set your flow of

spending at a level lower than your flow of after-tax income.

Do the rich get richer 'automatically'? A favourite saying is that the 'rich get richer and the poor get poorer'. This is not a very accurate or well-thought-out theory of wealth differences. In fact, the classical economists such as Thomas Malthus, David Ricardo, Adam Smith, and Karl Marx were satisfied that this simple theory was an explanation not only of wealth distribution but also of income distribution. They believed that wealth 'bred' more wealth, and therefore, once one's endowment was established, so was one's income. After all, income – as we pointed out before – is simply the 'return' to wealth. In particular, rent is the return to land and interest is return to ownership of capital. Clearly, people who own more land and more capital will receive more rent and more interest than those who own no land or no capital. The children of wealthy parents, in other words, are far more likely – all other things being equal – to have an increase in their stock of wealth and hence have higher incomes than are the children of poor parents.

This simple classical theory is outmoded in any modern democratic society, according to many economists. Wealth, as we pointed out before, includes non-tangible assets, such as people's skills, knowledge, initiative, and talents. The stock of society's human wealth is important in determining income differences. From this point of view, entrepreneurs receive profits as a return to their endowment of entrepreneurial ability, workers receive wage and salary income from their endowment of ability to work.

The Distribution and Redistribution of Income in the UK

Figure 28.4 shows how earnings are distributed in the UK. Earnings consist of wages and salaries and exclude all 'unearned income', that is income from profits, interest, and rent. Neither does wealth in any form appear here. Average earnings are given for each fifth, or quintile of the population, from the poorest to the richest fifth.

Also shown are the taxes and benefits which redistribute income. Taken together with earnings, these give figures for disposable income – the average amounts which families in each quintile have to spend. Three-fifths of the families surveyed have below-average disposable incomes. Most of the poorest fifth have no economically active family member: they are retired, unemployed or disabled, or caring for the young or the sick. On average, the richest fifth have two economically active family members.

As far as earnings are concerned, a fair amount of redistribution takes place. Because wealth has never been redistributed very effectively or systematically (in spite of death duties), the distribution of total income is much more uneven.

Figure 28.4

Redistribution of Income through Taxes and Benefits, all Households (UK), 1982[1]. A quintile is one-fifth of the sample. One-fifth of the population surveyed had almost no income of their own and relied on benefits. They include many retired people and some young families. The total effect of taxes and benefits is progressive.

	Quintile groups of households ranked by original income					All house-holds
	Bottom fifth	Next fifth	Middle fifth	Next fifth	Top fifth	
Average per household (£s per year)[2]						
Earnings of main earner	20	1540	5420	7550	11100	5120
Earnings of others in the household	–	90	630	1880	5070	1540
Occupational pensions, invest-ment income, annuities, etc.	130	990	640	600	1220	710
Total original income	150	2620	6690	10040	17390	7380
+Benefits in cash						
Age-related	1340	1110	280	160	110	600
Child-related	100	150	280	290	230	210
Income-related	990	480	200	140	130	390
Other benefits in cash[3]	250	230	130	100	60	150
Gross income	2830	4580	7580	10720	17920	8730
–Income tax and NIC[4]	10	430	1430	2280	4100	1650
Disposable income	2820	4160	6150	8440	13820	7080
–Indirect taxes[5]	740	1220	1710	2190	3050	1780
+Benefits in kind						
Education	290	440	620	710	730	560
National Health Service	680	610	580	540	550	590
Welfare foods	30	30	20	20	20	30
Housing subsidy	120	90	80	50	40	80
Other allocated benefits[6]	10	30	60	90	150	70
Final income	3220	4130	5790	7670	12260	6620
Average per household (numbers)						
Adults	1.4	1.7	2.0	2.2	2.7	2.0
Children	0.4	0.5	0.9	0.9	0.7	0.7
Economically active people[7]	0.1	0.7	1.4	1.7	2.2	1.2
Retired people	0.9	0.7	0.2	0.1	0.1	0.4
Number of households in sample	1486	1485	1486	1485	1486	7428

[1] These estimates are based on the Family Expenditure Survey. See Appendix. Part 5: Redistribution of income.
[2] Rounded to nearest £10.
[3] Mainly related to sickness and disability.
[4] Employees' National Insurance contributions.
[5] Domestic rates, VAT, excise duties, etc., *plus* taxes paid by industry and passed on to consumers, such as employers' National Insurance contributions and commercial rates.

[6] Rail travel subsidy, option mortgage expenditure, and life assurance premium relief.
[7] Comprising employees, the self-employed, and others not in employment but who were seeking or intending to seek work, but excluding those away from work for more than one year.

Source: Social Trends, 1985.

> ## Key Points 28.3
>
> ► Capital is invested in human beings as they develop skills and knowledge through education and training.
>
> ► The effect of improvements in technology on wages and employment depends partly on demand for the product and the supply of labour to produce it.
>
> ► Wealth is not the same thing as income. Wealth is a stock concept, such as your accumulated savings at a point in time.
>
> ► Stocks must be distinguished from flows; flows are measured over time. You have a flow of saving, which might be so many pounds per month that you put into your savings account.
>
> ► Earnings undergo some redistribution through the tax and benefit system of the UK.

CASE STUDY

Women in the Labour Force

Female services

Women tend to work predominantly in the service industries (see Figure 28.5). They make up 70 per cent of those employed in professional and scientific services, such as teaching and nursing. There is a higher than average proportion of women in consumer goods industries, such as clothing and footwear, in hotels and catering, and in retailing. Part-time women play a particularly large part in lower grades of service industries, as cleaners, shop assistants, and secretaries. All women are relatively less numerous higher up the promotion ladder. Only 7 per cent of managers are women, only 23 out of 650 MPs, and only one out of 45 permanent secretaries in the Civil Service. Only a quarter of engineering workers and only 7 per cent of engineering technology undergraduates are women.

The lower grades of women's jobs partly explain the fact that women's pay is lower than men's. In anticipation of the 1975

implementation of the Equal Pay Act, women's hourly rates rose to 75 per cent of men's in the few years up to 1976, but have tended to slip back slightly since then; taking overtime and thus total earnings into account, the figure is closer to 65 per cent. The Sex Discrimination Act also passed in 1975 may have done a small amount to improve women's

earnings by opening up higher-grade jobs to them, and the Employment Protection Act of the same year by making it easier for them to return to work after childbearing. The 1983 Act giving women equal pay for work of equal value rather than only for the same job may also, with a recent prompt from the courts, result in higher relative pay for women.

Figure 28.5
Women's Occupations: Distribution by Industry, Great Britain, 1984

Industry	% of all women working in it	Women as % of labour force
Professional and scientific services	28.7	69.9
Retail distribution and repairs	12.1	54.9
Financial and business services	10.6	48.5
Public administration and defence	7.2	41.3
Hotels and catering	4.3	65.5
Engineering	4.0	25.8
Footwear, clothing and leather	n.a.	69.1
Other (inc. above)	33.1	Various

Source: New Earnings Survey 1984. Part E, Table 138.

continued overleaf

The rise in women's relative pay has not prevented the increase in the female labour force, because women are still cheaper than men, and many of the growing service industries are offering jobs normally done by women in any case. While the growth in total labour force may appear to have increased the unsatisfied demand for jobs, the rise in the number of low-paid part-time women available for work has expanded the effective demand for labour.

The increase of 1.5m in the labour force between 1971 and 1984 was the same as the rise in the population of working age (Figure 28.6). The drop in male activity rates offset either the increase in the male population or the rise in female activity rates, according to which comparison is made. The labour force increase thus consisted entirely of women.

The difficulty of reducing unemployment is compounded by the fact that the labour force is expected to increase faster in the five years to 1989 than in the previous period by half a per cent each year. The Department of Employment's labour force projections have had to be revised upwards. After falling in 1982 and 1983, the female activity rate rose sharply in 1984, and is expected to rise by half a percentage point each year for the next five years. The male activity rate, is not expected to fall any further, and the population of working age will stop increasing only after 1989. So if the rise in unemployment is to be halted, another 750 000 jobs must be found over the next five years to satisfy the growth in the labour force – 40 per cent of it due to higher female activity, 60 per cent of it to demographic factors.

An increase in the husband's income, or in the family's unearned income, makes it less likely that the wife will work, or at least work full time. An increase in the wife's rate of pay makes it more likely that she will work. If both the husband's and the wife's income rise by the same amount the net effect seems to be a rise in female work. The move towards equal pay in the early 1970s increased female activity, and equal pay for work of equal value may now be increasing it further. The differential between men and women's pay rises sharply with age, as men earn more, and women the same or less, rising from only 10 per cent for under 18s to 40 per cent for over 50s. So women are less likely to work as they get older, and their husbands earn more.

The cuts in National Insurance contributions carried out in October, will increase female activity because they are directed at the lower paid, among whom women predominate. If the reforms of family taxation to be published in a Green Paper at the end of this year give households a transferable tax allowance for wives who stay at home, it will have the opposite effect.

Women's relative pay prospects have improved because of legislation, but their total earnings are still only two-thirds those of men, partly because of their lower grades of work.

Source: Lloyds Bank Bulletin, Nov. 1985.

Questions
1. Why is women's pay generally less than that of men?
2. What effect is equal pay legislation having?

Figure 28.6
Why the Labour Force is Rising Faster: Great Britain, Labour Force, (thousands)

| | 1971–84 changes due to: | | | 1984–9 changes due to: | | |
	Population	Activity	Total	Population	Activity	Total
Male	923	−1014	−91	288	5	293
Female	527	1080	1608	152	300	452
Total	1450	66	1517	440	305	745
Activity rates	**1971**		**1984**		**1989**	
Male	80.5		74.2		74.3	
Female	43.9		48.4		49.7	
All	61.3		60.8		61.5	

Source: Employment Gazette, July 1985.

Exam Preparation and Practice

MULTIPLE CHOICE QUESTIONS

1. *For Question 1 select your answer from the following grid:*

A	B	C	D
1,2,3 all correct	1,2 only correct	2,3 only correct	1 only correct

The table below is reproduced from a report by the Diamond Commission on the distribution of income and wealth.

Most wealthy (% of adult population)	% of total wealth owned	
	1971	1977
5	51.8	46.4
10	65.1	61.1
25	86.5	83.9
50	97.2	95.0

From the data it is evident that from 1971–7

1 a slightly more equal distribution of wealth occurred
2 the wealthiest 10% became poorer
3 incomes became more evenly distributed

†2. Which of the following statements is *untrue* in the UK?
 A wealth is more equally distributed than income
 B inheritance leads to major differences in income
 C government expenditures tend to lead to a more equal distribution of income
 D a larger proportion of gross national product constitutes returns to labour than to land or capital

3. The proposition that 'each worker receives the value of his marginal physical product' is correct if the
 A product and factor markets are both perfect
 B product market only is perfect
 C factor market only is perfect
 D wage paid is equal to unit price in the product market

4. The theory of distribution in economics is concerned with
 A how goods reach consumers from factories
 B how government fiscal policies redistribute income
 C how rewards are allocated to factors of production
 D where consumers live
 E the localization of industry.

5. The government imposes a minimum wage upon a particular industry above the level of the lowest-paid workers. Which of the following conditions is *most* likely to minimize redundancies?
 A The supply of labour is inelastic.
 B The demand for labour is elastic.
 C The demand for the final product is elastic.
 D The original wage of the lowest-paid workers was below their marginal revenue productivity.
 E Capital and labour can be easily substituted.

RELATED ESSAY QUESTIONS

1. Assess the ways by which the UK's tax and benefit system could be used to reduce inequalities in the distribution of income.

2. How does economic theory account for differences in wages? Discuss briefly whether the theory adequately accounts for the differences between male and female wages.

3. Discuss the economic argument that government should curb the power of trade unions.

4. 'Although wage differentials have an economic, purpose, differences in income may have none.' Discuss.

5. What is meant by 'Economic Efficiency'? What effect, if any, is the privatization of large sections of the public sector likely to exert on the efficiency of the economy?

Part E

Economic
Policies and Issues

29 Nationalized Industries and Privatization

Questions for Preview

1 What are the distinguishing features of goods produced by nationalized industries?

2 Which industries are *presently* nationalized in the UK?

3 What is a natural monopoly and how could one arise?

4 What does privatization mean and which industries have undergone this process?

5 What arguments have been put forward to support privatization?

In Chapter 10 we explained that due to certain characteristics some goods were best provided by the government – these goods were called 'Public Goods' or 'Merit Goods'. We now turn our attention to another type of good produced and administered on behalf of the government, namely goods produced by **nationalized industries**. (See Chapter 4 for a discussion of Nationalization.) The distinguishing feature of these goods is that they are 'private-type goods' but produced by the government sector and charged for through the market mechanism.

Examples of such goods and services in the UK include: electricity, coal, steel, and the Post Office. The proportion of output arising from nationalized industries differs from country to country and across time. In France, for example, Renault cars, the tobacco industry, and the match industry are existing nationalized industries. In the past the UK's list included the British Sugar Corporation, Thomas Cook, and Jaguar cars.

Industries come under national ownership for various political and economic reasons. The arguments for include: they are responsible for a lot of employment, their existence is central to the rest of the economy, they need financial help, they offer government control over the economy, they increase efficiency, they encourage industrial democracy, and they enable the government to accommodate externalities.

Obviously each of these arguments could be challenged and it is feasible and possible for most industrial assets to be privately owned and controlled (as they are largely in the US). This explains why the list of nationalized industries varies across time and between countries. Indeed, the present (1986) British government has been committed to a policy of privatization since taking office in 1979 and this will be dealt with at the end of this chapter. First of all, however, we begin our overview by looking at why nationalized industries exist and their importance in the UK.

Nationalized Industries in the UK: The Arguments For

In total there are sixteen nationalized industries in the UK. In 1983 they accounted for approximately 10 per cent of national output, employed approximately 7 per cent of the total working population and represented approximately 17 per cent of total investment in fixed capital. These figures highlight the fact that nationalized industries are often more than proportionately capital intensive. Consequently very few entrepreneurs in the private sectors could meet the capital costs of setting up. Indeed, it is the distinctive cost structure that has led economists to develop the **natural monopoly** argument as an underlying reason for certain industries to be nationalized. This argument will be explored first.

The Natural Monopoly Argument

In many industries a tremendous amount of capital is required to produce a product or service. Think about how much money you would require to start a railway network or an electricity-generating grid. Once you have started, however, the *marginal cost* of providing the service is relatively small. Thus, in industries where large capital requirements are needed just to get started, average fixed costs fall dramatically with higher and higher production rates. That is, the average total cost curve would be downward sloping throughout a very large range of production rates.

In Figure 29.1, we have drawn a downward-sloping long-run average total cost curve (LAC) for electricity. (A long-run cost curve is one that relates to a time-span long enough for all inputs, including all fixed costs, to be freely variable.) When we explained the relationship between marginal costs and average costs we pointed out that when average costs are falling, marginal costs are less than average costs; and when average costs are rising, marginal costs are greater than average costs. We can apply the same analysis to the long run. Thus, when long-run average total costs are falling, the long-run marginal cost curve (LMC) is below the average total cost curve. In our example, long-run average costs are falling over such a large range of production rates (relative to demand) that we would expect that only one firm could survive in such an industry. That firm would be the natural monopolist. It would be the first one to take advantage of the decreasing average costs, that is, it would construct the large-scale facilities first. As its average total cost curve fell, it would lower prices and get increasingly larger shares of the market. Once that firm had driven all other firms out of the industry, it would set its price to maximize profits. Let us see what this price would be.

A profit-maximizing monopolist will set the output rate where marginal revenue is equal to marginal cost. Let us draw in the market demand curve, *DD*, and the marginal revenue curve, *MR*, in Figure 29.2. The

Figure 29.1

The Cost Curves that Might Lead to a Natural Monopoly. Here we show the long-run average cost curve falling over a very large range of electricity production rates. The long-run marginal cost curve is, of course, below the average cost curve when the average cost curve is falling. A natural monopoly might arise in this situation. The first firm to establish the low-unit cost capacity would be able to take advantage of the lower average total cost curve. This firm would drive out all rivals by charging a lower price than the others could sustain at their higher average costs.

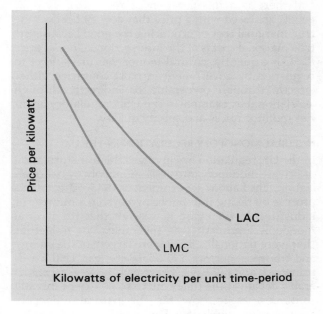

Figure 29.2

Profit Maximization. The profit-maximizing natural monopolist here would produce at the point where marginal cost equals marginal revenue, that is, at point *A*, which gives the quantity of production Q_m. The price charged would be P_m.

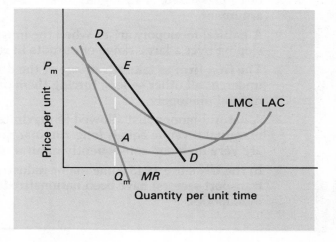

intersection of the marginal revenue curve and the marginal cost curve is at point A. The monopolist therefore would produce quantity Q_m and charge a price of P_m.

What do we know about a monopolist's solution to the price–quantity question? When compared to a competitive situation, we know that consumers end up paying more for the product, and consequently they purchase less of it than they would purchase under competition. The privately owned monopoly solution is therefore economically inefficient from society's point of view; the price charged for the product is higher than the opportunity cost to society, and there is a misallocation of resources. That is, people are faced with a price that does not reflect the true marginal cost of producing the good because the true marginal cost is at the intersection A, not at price P_m. Consequently, natural monopolies are subject to regulation by government in most countries; either directly through ownership or indirectly through legislation. For example in the USA regulatory agencies monitor prices and specify quality.

NATURAL MONOPOLY REGULATION IN THE UK

In the UK regulation has involved the transformation of private monopoly into *public* monopoly by nationalization. The Labour government of 1945–50 *started* this process by taking into public ownership a number of industries. In each case it was felt that the natural monopoly argument was applicable. The industries that were nationalized *first* were largely in the energy and transport sectors, i.e. electricity, gas, coal, road-transport, and railways. There was, however, considerable debate at the time (and to some extent this still continues) as to how far the natural monopoly argument was applicable. For example, it is debatable whether in these industries the technical characteristics of production point to single producers only. Is it not possible that the market is so large that *some* form of competitive production is possible? While contemplating these issues of debate relating to the number of *producers* in each industry, one final point should be raised, namely *distribution*.

The distribution aspect of gas, electricity, and water provides a further impetus to the natural monopoly argument. The supply channels required for such services – pipes – certainly suggest that one common network is most desirable for all users. A system of competing services would involve the road being opened up for a lot of time to access pipes for maintenance work etc. (Now read Key Points 29.1.)

The Price Arguments

If we take for the moment as given the desirability of, say, the electricity industry being nationalized, we still have to consider how those appointed to manage its affairs are to fix the price to be charged. Let us assume that the government decides to make the natural monopolist produce as in a perfectly competitive situation. Where is that perfect competitive solution in Figure 29.3? It is at the intersection of the long-run marginal cost curve and the demand curve, i.e. point A. However, given the different character of a natural monopolist's costs at this point it cannot make a profit. Indeed it makes a loss equal to the shaded area of Figure 29.3.

SUBSIDIZATION

How do we get out of such a dilemma? There are several possible answers. The first is to have the

---

Key Points 29.1

▶ A nationalized industry is a state-owned and administered corporation, producing goods for the public and charging the consumer for the product.

▶ There is no agreed national policy whether nationalized industries should remain or be privatized. A strong argument used in their favour is the natural monopoly argument.

▶ A natural monopoly arises when the long-run average cost curve is downward sloping over a large range of outputs in relation to industry demand.

▶ The first firm to take advantage of the declining long-run average cost curve can undercut all other sellers, forcing them out of business, thereby obtaining a natural monopoly.

▶ A natural monopolist allowed to maximize profit will set quantity where marginal revenue equals long-run marginal cost. At this point prices and profits are very high and consequently natural monopolies are often state regulated.

▶ In the UK since 1945 some major industries (especially in the energy and transport sectors) have been nationalized on the basis of being natural monopolies.

Figure 29.3

Regulating Natural Monopolies – Marginal Cost Pricing. If the government attempted to regulate natural monopolies so that a competitive situation would prevail, it would make the nationalized industry set production at the point where the marginal cost curve intersects the demand schedule, because the marginal cost schedule would be the competitive supply schedule. The quantity produced would be Q, and the price would be P_1. However, average costs at Q_1 are equal to P_2. Losses would ensue, equal to the shaded area. It would therefore be self-defeating for the government to force a natural monopolist to produce at a competitive solution without subsidizing some of its costs.

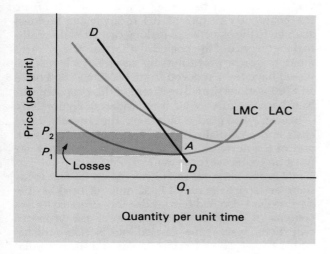

nationalized industry price at marginal cost and then subsidize production. That is, the government could give the industry a subsidy that will allow it to break even (including a normal rate of return on investment). The subsidy per unit of output in this particular case would have to be equal to the difference between P_2 and P_1; it would have to match the industry's per unit losses. The government would have to pay an amount $(P_2 - P_1)$ on every unit produced and sold to keep output at this level.

Marginal cost pricing thus involves the issue of how desirable it is to use taxpayers' money to finance subsidies in public enterprises.

PRICE DISCRIMINATION

Another possible solution is to allow the monopoly in public ownership to **price discriminate**. This means it could charge different prices to different customers who have different elasticities of demand for the product. The state-owned undertaking would charge a lower price to those who have very elastic demands and a higher price to those who have relatively less-elastic demands. Essentially, then, the demanders with relatively less-elastic curves would allow the public body to recover sufficient revenues to cover fixed costs. You might say that those with less-elastic demands would be subsidizing those with more-elastic

demands. (This would still be a misallocation of resources.)

As mentioned in previous chapters, *any* monopolist can earn higher profits if it can discriminate among the demanders of the product. Assume the monopolist is not discriminating but instead is charging everyone the same price. Now assume the monopolist begins to discriminate. First, the monopolist raises the price to less-elastic demanders and lowers the price to more-elastic demanders. When the price to less-elastic demanders is raised, the total revenue received from them will rise because the fall in the quantity demanded is proportionately smaller than the increase in price. When the price to more-elastic demanders is lowered, total revenues from them will rise also. The increase in the quantity demanded will be proportionately greater than the decrease in price. The monopolist therefore improves profits in both areas, and total revenues rise.

As to the *desirability* of price discrimination the economist can only point out that it is 'unfair' that those with less elastic demands are forced to pay more than those with more elastic demands, i.e. problems of equity arise. Regardless of this observation it is commonplace for many nationalized industries in the UK to price discriminate. For example, British Rail discriminates against business men and in favour of other customers (especially students and OAPs) by lowering prices (often in the form of special offers) in between the rush hours.

TWO-PART TARIFF

Another solution adopted by the gas and electric industries in the UK is the principle of a two-tier pricing system. Firstly, the user pays a fixed sum for access to the service and, secondly, a price per unit consumed. The fixed sum (standing charge) is intended to cover the fixed costs of production and distribution and the marginal charges are intended to cover the variable costs which alter with the amount provided. Supporters of nationalized industries would argue that standing charges will be lower if you only have to cover the fixed costs of *one* government-organized industry.

VARYING TARIFF RATES

Nationalized industries do use a form of price discrimination that favours their bigger customers. This is based on a principle which may be called **declining block pricing** – a name derived from its graphic presentation. Look at Figure 29.4. If the nationalized industry concerned wanted to sell the quantity Q_3, it could do so by charging the same price of P_3 to everyone for each unit purchased. Its total revenues would be represented by the rectangle OP_3CQ_3. However, if it engages in declining block pricing or price discrimination, it might charge P_1 for the first Q_1 of units sold per month. It could charge P_2 for those units sold between Q_1 and Q_2. And then finally it could charge P_3 for the units sold between Q_2 and Q_3. The revenues it would receive would be the sum of the

Figure 29.4

Declining Block Pricing. Nationalized industries often use declining block pricing in which separate 'blocks' of the service or product can be purchased at declining prices. If the industry charges a uniform price of P_3, its revenues will be OP_3CQ_3. If, however, it charges a price of P_1 for the first Q_1 of units used, and then P_2 for the next 'block' used up to quantity Q_2, and then price P_3 for the next 'block' up to Q_3, its total revenues will equal $OP_1AQ_1 + Q_1DBQ_2 + Q_2ECQ_3 = OP_1ADBECQ_3$.

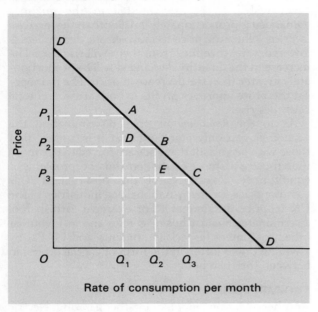

Rate of consumption per month

areas of the rectangles OP_1AQ_1 plus Q_1DBQ_2 plus Q_2ECQ_3, or $OP_1ADBECQ_3$. The sum of these three areas of the rectangles exceeds the area of the rectangle given by uniform pricing of P_3 times the quantity sold, Q_3.

Whether varying tariff rates are more effectively administered by a centralized monopoly is again debatable. But at least nationalized industries have the capacity to offer a range of varying prices that ultimately stem from the principles of economies of

scale. These economies of scale were discussed in Chapter 22 and provide another argument in favour of nationalized industries. The various pricing options discussed above illustrate this to some extent.

The Externalities Argument

Apart from the considerations of direct cost and direct revenue discussed above, there are the broader indirect costs and indirect benefits to consider. These indirect or external considerations are formally referred to as **externalities**.

A classic example of how externalities contribute to the argument for nationalized industries come from a 1963 report, *The Reshaping of British Railways*. This report was drafted by Dr Beeching, who was recruited from the board of directors of ICI to apply his business acumen to the objective of making British Rail a profit-making service. He concluded that for the government to run a profit-making service track mileage would have to be reduced from 17000 to 8000 miles and 700 stations shut. The extent of this proposed cutback becomes more vivid by considering Figure 29.5.

Beeching had used as his criteria the potential direct costs and potential direct revenues of running each part of the network – those lines that would not pay went on to his list for axing.

His proposals were *not* fully acted on (in fact today there are approximately 11000 miles of track) as the government also had to consider the *external* costs and benefits of doing so. For example, if the proposed reductions were fully carried out social hardship would have followed: certain areas and their populations would have become remote (see Figure 29.5 for exact areas); there would have been more road congestion, a loss of local jobs, and a waste of social capital if people were forced to move because of a reduction in transport facilities.

Some key industries are seen to be best run by the government, as they can employ broader terms of reference when appraising investment. Indeed, most nationalized industries since the 1970s have been subject to the broader cost benefit analysis criteria

---

Key Points 29.2

▶ If the nationalized industry is forced to set a price equal to long-run marginal cost, the industry will sustain losses. One way to compensate for the losses is to introduce a government subsidy.

▶ Another way for the nationalized industry to avoid losses is for it to be allowed to price discriminate.

▶ A two-part tariff system provides a way of covering the high fixed costs by a standing charge and adding a unit charge for consumption thereafter.

▶ Price discrimination can take the form of varying tariffs in which successive blocks are sold to buyers at lower and lower rates. This principle illustrates the economies of scale.

Figure 29.5
Making British Rail a Profit-making Service.

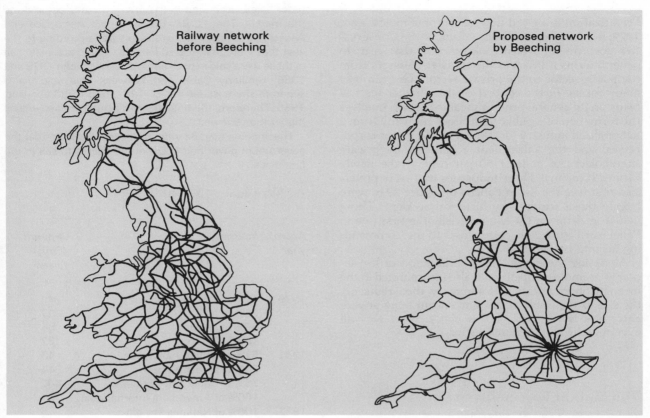

when decisions have been made regarding investment and disinvestment. For example, Rolls Royce and British Leyland were nationalized in 1971 and 1976 respectively as 'lame ducks'. They may have been financially bankrupt, but in terms of being important employers to local communities, potential 'flag ships' for British exporters, and big traders with other firms involved in British manufacturing, they could not be allowed to collapse, as their external benefits outweighed their private costs.

Similarly when making out a case for wishing to nationalize the 'commanding heights' of the economy the Labour government can do so largely on the grounds of social virtue, or more formally by analysing externalities.

MOVING TOWARDS ARGUMENTS AGAINST

In these last three sections we have tried to show that if the state does nationalize industries there are major issues to be resolved concerning the definition of a natural monopoly, the structure of prices charged, and the evaluation of investment programmes. All these aspects are largely affected by value-judgements and although we have tried to discuss the issues in economic terms, political values do cloud these policies. In fact each argument *for* nationalization can be *challenged* in some way or other. The points put forward would represent the views of those who support privatization and it is these that we shall consider next in lieu of a list of arguments against.

Key Points 29.3

▶ Externalities involve accounting for the *indirect* costs and benefits of projects. When these are considered the value to the community as a whole is brought into the picture. For example, some loss-making railway lines are economically justifiable.

▶ The arguments *against* nationalized industries are equally numerous, and these will be considered next via the arguments for privatization.

Privatization in the UK: The Arguments For

Privatization is a word that has become topical since 1979; it forms a central policy plank of the Conservative government which took office in that year. In general terms it involves the transfer of assets from the public sector to the private sector. This can take many forms. In the context of this chapter we will focus on its general present meaning which involves the formation of a public Joint Stock company from a nationalized industry (or, similar public sector corporation) and the subsequent acquisition by private shareholders of at least 50 per cent of the newly formed company. Those industries that were privatized first (see the list in Panel a of Figure 29.6) were largely those acquired by historical accident. Those industries later on the list, especially the first two in Panel b of Figure 29.6, come closer to the 'commanding heights' concept.

Alongside these sales, the liberalization of legislation to promote competition is also incorporated in the meaning of privatization. In summary, then, reducing, the size of the public sector and encouraging private enterprise is the goal of this policy. Next we will overview the main arguments for.

The Market Forces Argument

To a large extent *unsuccessful* public sector organizations will continue to operate regardless of their finances; whereas private firms which perform poorly cease to trade. This is because in the private sector firms are subject to the market forces, they seek maximum profit for their owners and if they fail their resources are directed elsewhere. In the public sector efficiency is interpreted differently, goals are altered through government intervention, and state backing disturbs the incentives to maximize profit.

Once privatized, firms become subject to direct market forces in both the capital and product markets. Within the product market suppliers would have to become sensitive to price to gain consumers' preferences; this may entail altering quality, lowering costs, adapting quickly to changes in taste etc. Within the capital market firms would become accountable to shareholders. If these shareholders became disappointed with their returns on investment, they would be hesitant to purchase any further shares when the firm attempted to raise capital for new projects. Shareholders clearly have alternative investment opportunities. Indeed, to a large extent the commercial world of finance is far more concerned with profits and repayments than the open purse of the government treasury, which in the final resort will always honour any debts generated. As some reviewers on this topic have neatly put it: 'the government as banker is a softer touch than a commercial bank.'*

Figure 29.6

The Privatization Programme. The list is laid out in the order sales, according to the *first* time they came on to the market. That is; BP, Britoil, British Aerospace and Associated British Ports are only listed according to the year they were *first* offered for sale – but in actual fact all of these were sold in two separate lots between 1979 and 1985. Similarly Cable and Wireless was sold via 3 separate share issues in Oct. 1981, Dec. 1983 and Dec. 1985. Therefore, the final amount actually raised will be higher than shown.

Those items marked with an asterisk indicate that the government never had 100% of the shares to sell in the first place.

(a) Sales during 1979–85

Approx. year	Industry	Amount (£m) raised
1979	12% of British Petroleum*	841
	25% of ICL*	37
	50% of Ferranti*	55
	100% of Fairey	22
1981	51% of British Aerospace	43
	24% of British Sugar*	44
	75% of Cable and Wireless	442
	100% of Amersham International	64
1982	100% of National Freight Corporation	5
	51% of Britoil	627
1983	49% of Associated British Ports*	46
	100% of British Rail Hotels	35
1984	50.2% of British Telecom	3900
	100% of Enterprise Oil	380
	100% of Sealink Ferries	66
	100% of Jaguar cars	297

(b) Proposed Sales 1986 (until General Election 1987)

British Gas, British Airways, National Bus Co., British Airports Authority, Royal Ordnance Factories and the Water Authorities.

Source: Financial Times, 7 Feb. 1984 and various newspaper articles.

The PSBR Argument

The PSBR is an important indicator for any monetarist government, for example, the Conservative government from 1979 onwards. It is important to them that their annual targets for PSBR should not be

---

* Kay and Silberston, *Midland Bank Review*, Spring 1984.

exceeded and ultimately the overall size of the PSBR should be reduced.

By selling off assets the government obviously gains a short-term boost to revenue. For example, the 1979–85 sales listed in Figure 29.6 represent an income of at least £6 bn. Obviously this has diverted needs to raise funds through gilt sales, to print money, or increase tax. In fact some opponents of privatization scornfully regard the policy as a short-sighted process which entails selling off 'the family silver' to cover present financial embarrassments. However, a standard response to this kind of argument is that in the long term the transfer of nationalized industries to the private sector will reduce government responsibilities which should facilitate a fall in the tax burden. Finally, some claim that a reduction in the PSBR may stimulate private investments which had previously been 'crowded out' by government borrowing. These issues are all revisted in the closing Case Study to this chapter which is intended to highlight the contentious nature of this argument.

The Diseconomies Argument

To paraphrase the famous economist Lord Hicks: the best thing about monopoly is a quiet life. This statement is even more apt when the monopoly concerned is a nationalized industry. There is no pressure from competitors, there is no pressure to reap rewards and in the case of the nationalized industries there are strings of government White Papers and administrative machinery behind which the management can hide. It can be argued that making these organizations cost-effective, therefore, entails opening them up to competition, making them accountable to market criteria, and generally providing a freer framework to work within. Indeed, along with privatization run the possibilities of decentralization and franchise. Whether these potentials will actually be fulfilled, however, is difficult to judge at the time of writing. In fact, some fear that in most cases a private monopoly will simply replace the public monopoly. Whether this will be the actual result only time will tell.

Key Points 29.4

► Privatization is a policy of the Conservative government which involves the transfer of assets from the public sector to the private sector.

► A case for privatization can be made by respecting market forces. Once privatized, firms are directly affected by market forces in both the capital and product markets and consequently they should become more efficient.

► The PSBR argument for privatization is based on the need to balance the government books, ultimately reduce the annual government borrowing, and 'crowd in' private investment.

► The diseconomies argument follows the line that monopoly power is not necessarily efficient, especially if that monopoly is centralized.

► Those who favour privatization believe, therefore, that it will provide a set-up where managers and employers will have greater freedom and better motivation.

CASE STUDY

Southern Electricity

Electricity Prices
Domestic tariffs from 1 April 1985
The following prices will apply to all electricity used after the normal meter reading next following 31 March 1985:

Domestic tariffs	Quarterly charge (£)	Unit price (p)
General		
Credit meter	7.02	5.07
Slot meter	10.60	5.07
Economy 7	8.84	
Day		5.43
Night		2.04

Non-domestic (quarterly) tariffs from 1 April 1985

	Block			Day/Night		
	Quarterly charge (£)	Units	Unit price (p)	Quarterly charge (£)	Units	Unit price (p)
Standard tariff	7.02			8.84		
Primary units		1000	6.72		1000	6.72
Additional units			5.07			5.43
Night units						2.04

Question
1. How can the structure and variety of these charges be explained?

CASE STUDY

Forty Years Can Make a Lot of Difference

Nationalization   *versus*   Privatization

'Amalgamation under public ownership will bring great economies in operation and make it possible to modernize production methods ... Public ownership ... will lower charges, prevent competitive waste, open the way for co-ordinated research and development ... **Only if public ownership replaces private monopoly can industry become efficient.**'

Labour Party Manifesto 1945

'Privatization is bringing about a fundamental change in the operation and efficiency of key sections of the UK economy. Its success ... is self-evident ... Privatization liberates managers and employees and allows them to reach their full potential ... **Privatization increases productive efficiency whether or not a monopoly is involved.**'

Financial Secretary to the Treasury 1985

Questions
1. What was nationalized after the 1945 Labour manifesto statement?
2. What has been privatized since (in keeping with the tone of the 1985 statement)?
3. What economic arguments complicate these two statements?
4. Both statements refer to 'efficiency' – what do economists mean by this term?

CASE STUDY

Swings and Roundabouts
An Academic Story of Privatization

Any claim (from government or opposition) that the revenue gained from asset sales has had any real macroeconomic significance should be treated with scepticism. The effect on the public sector borrowing requirement of the sale of British Telecom was certainly to reduce it. But it is not clear what effects that had on real interest rates or the real economy. Selling shares in British Telecom required the extraction of funds from the private sector (e.g. funds withdrawn from building societies) in precisely the same way as increased government borrowing (e.g. through more attractive interest rates for national savings). Either way of financing the shortfall of government tax receipts from government expenditure would have put upward pressure on interest rates. Any difference in the size of the effect would only arise to the extent that different methods of tapping private sector savings will always have different levels of appeal to the public.

The longer-run effects of privatization on public finance are likely to be equally small in significance. Future generations of taxpayers have avoided the burden of paying interest on government bonds that would have had to have been issued in the absence of asset sales. However, they have also forgone access to the profits that these assets could have yielded to central government. Net effects on the government's future finances are thus unlikely to be large.

One way in which a sharp effect

continued overleaf

on a given year's borrowing requirement might occur is that, after privatization, government will no longer borrow on behalf of an enterprise to finance its capital expenditure programme. Again, if public sector borrowing were lowered in any one year for this reason, the effect would surely be cosmetic. If capital programmes are the same whether ownership is public or private, similar amounts of borrowing will have to be made, probably (given that the firms are safe monopolist utilities) at similar rates of interest. The effect in displacing alternative investments (crowding out) should therefore not differ greatly between the two cases.

Extract from 'Privatization' by D. Forrest in *Developments in Economics* Vol. 1, 1985, ed. by G. B. J. Atkinson.

Questions

1. What implications does this extract have for the PSBR argument in favour of privatization?

2. How does this extract present the 'crowding-out thesis', and how does this presentation differ from those in favour of privatization?

Exam Preparation and Practice

MULTIPLE CHOICE QUESTIONS

1. Which one of the following public corporations would be classed as a nationalized industry?
  A British Broadcasting Corporation
  B New Town Development Corporation
  C National Coal Board
  D Royal Mint

2. All of the following nationalized industries have been privatized except one. Which is it?
  A British Rail
  B British Telecom
  C British Aerospace
  D Jaguar Cars

3. In order to use its resources efficiently, a city's passenger transport undertaking should charge
  A higher fares during peak periods because much of the equipment needed for peak-period travel is idle for the rest of the day
  B lower fares during peak periods to keep down travel costs for the maximum number of people
  C higher fares during off-peak periods because the cost per passenger is higher during these periods
  D the same fares throughout the day to avoid distorting people's preferences between peak and off-peak travel
  E lower fares in the evening during non-working hours when demand is likely to be more inelastic

For Questions 4 and 5 select your answers from the following grid:

A	B	C	D
1,2,3 all correct	1,2 only correct	2,3 only correct	1 only correct

4. Because of spare capacity at certain times of the day, a nationalized railway may offer lower fares to customers travelling off-peak compared with the fares charged to rush-hour passengers. This is an illustration of
  1 price discrimination
  2 two part tariff
  3 externalities

†5. The cost and revenue curves shown opposite are those of a firm producing a uniform product for sale to industrial and household customers. If the firm sells an output Q_1 at a price of P_1 to industrial customers, and an output Q_2 at a price of P_2 to household customers, it can be deduced that
  1 the household customers are subsidizing the industrial customers
  2 price discrimination is taking place
  3 the firm is maximizing profits

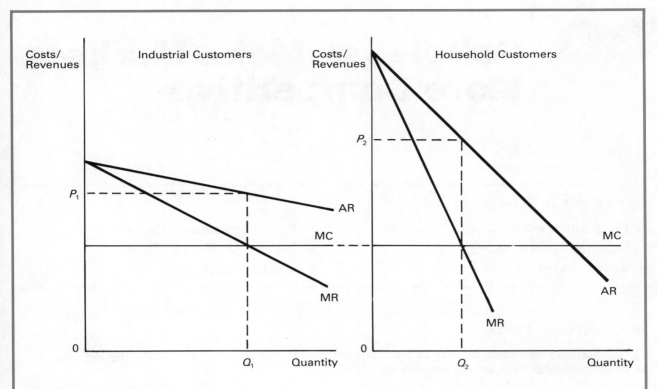

RELATED ESSAY QUESTIONS

1. Explain what is meant by marginal cost pricing and discuss the problems involved in employing it in the nationalized industries.

2. How might the efficiency of a nationalized industry be assessed?

3. 'Privatization represents by far the most effective means of extending market forces and in turn improving efficiency' (Lord Cockfield, 1981). Explain what is meant by efficiency in economics and discuss whether or not you agree with this statement about British industry.

4. Discuss the economic consequences of privatizing nationalized undertakings.

30 Policies to Make Markets More Competitive

Questions for Preview

1 Why would you expect the strength of competitive pressures in a market economy to be influenced by the macroeconomic situation?

2 Why might the government regard a keenly competitive economy as not being a desirable objective?

3 How can competition between firms be influenced by government policy on take-over bids?

4 What is government policy on firms which dominate certain markets?

5 How can governments influence the nature of competition in an open economy?

In the previous chapter we considered the provision of goods and services by nationalized industries. We saw that in the case of the UK the post-war Labour government effected the transformation of several private monopolies into public monopolies. Since 1979 the Thatcher government has begun to return some nationalized industries to the private sector through its privatization policies. Our focus now is to review what have been the policies of successive UK governments towards those firms that have continued to operate within the private sector. Thus we are now concerned with those policies which represent the attempt by government to prevent the creation of monopolies and also the fostering of keen competition between firms. We shall see that the British approach to devising competition policies has been essentially cautious in espousing any of the virtues associated with the competition ethic. We showed in Chapter 6 that competition is the driving force in a capitalist economy. But while competition may be 'a good thing'

governments in the UK have not exhibited a consistent and enthusiastic acceptance of such a viewpoint. To see why this has been the case we need very briefly to consider the course of the economy in the UK during the past century.

The Historical Perspective

In Chapter 25 it was suggested that the operation of capitalism seems to prompt efforts by business men to seek relief from the rigours of a competitive market economy by establishing agreement on prices to be charged. Why should business men behave in this way? It is explained by the wish to reduce the risks inherent in business life. If business men agree not to undercut one another's prices then the possibility of business failure for some firms is considerably reduced. It should not surprise you to learn that the fear of business failure becomes greater when the macro-state of the economy is relatively depressed and firms find themselves operating well below full capacity. In such times firms see a real danger of prices being cut dramatically as each tries to boost sales at the expense of competitors. Competition is thus seen as a process which results in many more losers than winners: in short, in the death of business.

When we look at the state of competition in the UK economy in the early years of the present century we find that most sections of manufacturing industry were characterized by explicit arrangements to restrict competition and control prices. Firms in an industry would often seek to fix prices by discussion in national organizations called **trade associations**. Domestic firms found their common cause a matter of increasing relevance as they faced growing competition in the UK market from imports.

What was the attitude of government to the attempts by business men to restrain the degree of rivalry between themselves? Before showing the changing course of government policy we could usefully note Adam Smith's own view on the matter. In Chapter 6 we referred to his now much-quoted observation that business men were keen in meetings together to uphold their own interests rather than those of consumers (see p. 77). Another of Smith's comments which has been much less well reported reads as follows:

It is impossible indeed to prevent such meetings, by any law which either could be executed, or would be consistent with liberty and justice. But though the law cannot hinder people of the same trade from sometimes assembling together, it ought to do nothing to facilitate such assemblies, much less to render them necessary.*

This view overlooks the political pressures from business interests on the need for behaviour to be co-operative rather than competitive when the economy is in difficulty. The 1920s and 1930s provided an environment for co-operative behaviour to be regarded as not just acceptable but even desirable. We thus find that the response of the Lloyd George coalition government in 1920 to this matter began the cautious approach that has characterized the spirit of British competition policy. Price-fixing arrangements were recognized as having the *potential* for firms to charge excessive prices to the detriment of consumers. But the situation was not so clear-cut that such practices should be *prohibited* by legislation. What was required was a review of the particular situation in individual industries. Thirty industries were investigated by the Board of Trade in 1920 and 1921 as the basis for establishing whether the interests of consumers were *in practice* being adversely affected. But this concern for consumers quickly evaporated during the 1920s and 1930s as the three major political parties

showed increased disenchantment with the desirability of stimulating greater competition. Competition was now seen as a hindrance to the development of strong national concerns capable of meeting foreign competition. Mergers were thus encouraged such that 'wasteful competition' could be eliminated and firms achieve economies of scale while the macro-environment was so depressing.

Thus we see that by 1939 there was very little emphasis in government policy towards industry placed on the desirability of competitive rivalry. This muted enthusiasm for competitive free enterprise contrasted strongly with the explicit presumption in favour of competition which characterized policy in the United States. Let us now see how the UK's post-war legislation concerning competition has continued to reflect an uncertain commitment to the cause of a competitive economy.

The 1948 Monopolies and Restrictive Practices (Inquiry and Control) Act

This Act did not condemn either monopoly or price-fixing outright. Instead a case-by-case approach was adopted such that each situation could be judged on its merits. Monopoly was presumed neither good nor bad and it was up to the newly created Monopolies and Restrictive Practices Commission to investigate particular situations and make a judgement in accordance with some vague expression of 'the public interest'. The Commission was not able to begin an investigation unless at least one-third of the supply of goods was supplied by one person or by two or more persons who restricted competition by agreement (thus including the restrictive activity of trade associations). The Commission consisted mainly of part-time lay persons and they could consider only situations referred to then by the Board of Trade. Action on a report by the Monopolies Commission was left in the hands of the government.

The Act was thus a modest statement on the desirability of a competitive economy. Members of the Commission found the terms of 'the public interest' capable of uncertain interpretation and even a cursory examination of section 14 of the 1948 Act shows why this was so. The public interest was defined as the need to achieve:

1. the production, treatment, and distribution by the most efficient and economical means of goods of such types and qualities, in such volume and at such prices as will best meet the requirements of home and overseas markets;
2. the organization of industry and trade in such a way that their efficiency is progressively increased and new enterprises encouraged;
3. the fullest use and best distribution of men, materials, and industrial capacity in the United Kingdom; and

---

*A. Smith, *Wealth of Nations*, Bk. 1, Ch. X, Pt. II, Everyman edn., p. 233.

4. the development of technical improvements and the expansion of existing markets and the opening up of new markets.

As one member of the Commission, the late Professor G. C. Allen, put it 'The guidance given by the Act consisted of a string of platitudes which the Commission found valueless and it was left for the members themselves to reach their own conclusions by reference to the assumptions, principles or prejudices which their training and experience caused them to apply to economic affairs.'* The Commission worked slowly and between 1948 and 1956 produced just seventeen reports. But these reports did none the less present a clear picture of how widespread were the restrictions on competition throughout British industry. Firms typically agreed common prices for goods sold whether to wholesalers, retailers, or in contracts supposedly subject to secret tendering. Private courts punished individual members of agreements who infringed the rules of the trade.

In a general report on Collective Discrimination published in 1955 the Commission assembled evidence on a variety of restrictive practices and declared itself satisfied that all of them adversely affected the public interest. The Conservative government responded with its 1956 Restrictive Trade Practices Act.

The 1956 Restrictive Trade Practices Act

This Act had three elements to it as Figure 30.1 indicates. On restrictive practices the Act obliged firms to register their agreements with a Registrar of Restrictive Trading Agreements. These registered agreements were to be made open to public inspection and presumed contrary to the public interest unless the parties involved could satisfy otherwise before the Restrictive Practices Court. Thus the legislation represented a much clearer statement in favour of competition than the Monopolies Commission. The Act affected the whole industry and not merely those parts selected for inquiry. There was a precise government commitment against the desirability of price-fixing. The unwillingness to take action by government on Monopolies Commission reports now contrasted with the precise requirement of the Registrar to refer every price agreement to the Court. The judgement of the Court was binding on the respondents if contempt proceedings were to be avoided.

The new Act became the more effective because of the macro-state of the UK economy. The level of unemployment rose in each year between 1955 and 1959 and thus the more competitive climate ushered in by the Act was reinforced by a less buoyant market for many consumer goods. Firms found themselves working at lower levels of capacity than in the recent past. Hitherto many sections of UK industry had enjoyed a sellers' market as the economy recovered from wartime. Where there was excess capacity the price-fixing arrangements had disguised its influence on price levels. Now business men not only had to learn how to price their products but to begin doing so in a more difficult trading environment. The result was predictable – in many manufacturing industries there was a marked downward trend in prices charged. In this respect it has generally been accepted that within a few years of its implementation the 1956 Act was successful in its attack on price-fixing agreements between firms.

A second aspect of the 1956 Act was its prohibition of the collective enforcement of resale price maintenance by the withholding of supplies by a group of manufacturers. This made it no longer possible for a uniform stance to be taken by several manufacturers against a retailer who wished to trade on terms other than those laid down by his suppliers. But the 1956 Act did not have a dramatic impact on the manufacturer–retailer relationship since individual suppliers were able to take action in the courts against traders not maintaining their specified trading terms. The ending of individual retail price maintenance was not brought about till 1964. The Resale Prices Act adopted the same approach as the 1956 Act with the practice of minimum resale prices being prohibited subject to exemptions on specific grounds. As with restrictive practices the Restrictive Practices Court was given the task of hearing applications by manufacturers to continue a form of competitive behaviour now generally deemed unacceptable. Once more the Court began to set a precedent in its early cases on retail price maintenance as with price-fixing which left very few manufacturers expecting to make a successful defence. Thus by the end of the 1960s there was little doubt that two aspects of competition policy had become effective by virtue of the fact that legislation expressed a clear presumption in favour of free competition. Price-fixing and uniform retail prices were no longer seen as desirable practices. In respect of price agreements firms had been given till the end of 1957 to register their existing agreements and the first full case in the Court was not heard until October 1958. Few trade associations chose to take their agreements to the Court when the evidence was clear that the changes of a successful defence were slim. Thus although over 4 000 agreements have now been registered under the Act the vast majority have been voluntarily abandoned and not the subject of a Court case. In respect of retail price maintenance there have been very few cases before the Court and only books and medicines have provided the supporters of fixed trading terms the satisfaction of a costly legal appraisal that survived a Court hearing.

Figure 30.1 makes clear that the 1956 Act had yet a third element – the restricting of the Monopolies and Restrictive Practices Commission. Given the creation of the Restrictive Practices Court the Commission

---

*G. C. Allen, *Monopoly and Restrictive Practices* (1968), p. 66.

Figure 30.1
Monopoly, Merger and Restrictive Practices Legislation 1948–68

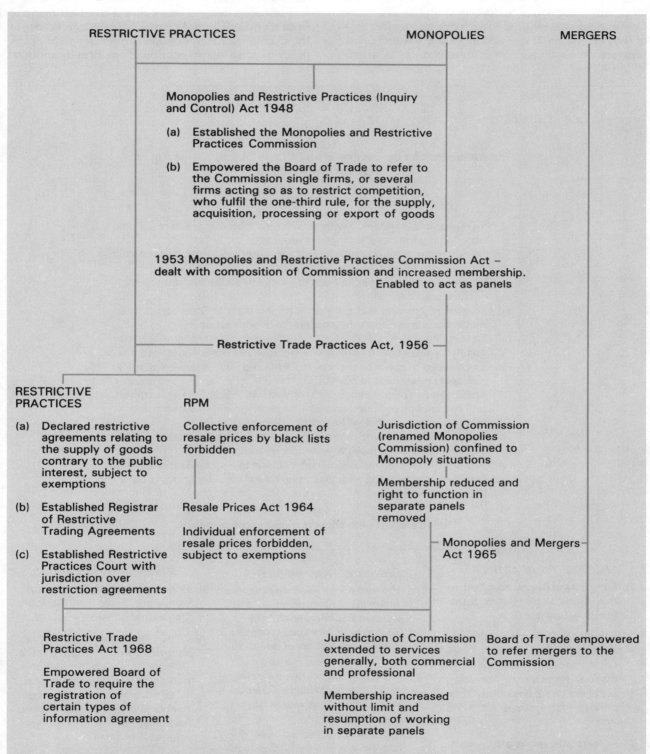

Source: M. C. Fleming, *The Fair Trading Act 1973,* Loughborough Paper in Recent Developments in Economic Policy and Thought., Loughborough University, 1974, p. 2.

was now confined to investigation of monopoly situations and thus appropriately lost two words in its title. But the hesitant nature of UK policy towards large firms continued to manifest itself. The new Commission was reduced to a maximum membership of ten persons and it was no longer able to function in separate panels on particular investigations as it had done since 1953. The Commission may have been viewed in 1956 critically in some quarters as simultaneously 'prosecutor, judge and jury' but at least it was not so actively at work that it troubled many of Britain's major firms. Any revival in the significance of the Commission had to await the development of UK policy towards the acquisition of one firm by another.

Figure 30.2
The Principal Provisions of the Fair Trading Act 1973

The Act provides for the creation of an Office of Director-General of Fair Trading ('The Director')

Responsibilities

(i)   To keep under review 'with a view to becoming aware of and ascertaining the circumstances relating to':
(a) consumer trade practices which may adversely affect the economic interests of consumers,
(b) commercial activities relating to monopoly situations or uncompetitive practices.

(ii) To give information and assistance to Secretary of State about these matters and make recommendations to him for action.

(iii) To keep himself appraised of actual or prospective mergers which may qualify for investigation and advise Secretary of State about them.

(iv) Empowered to make references to CPAC and limited powers to make monopoly references to MMC.

(v)   Empowered to take action to curb conduct which is unfair to consumers and detrimental to their interests – by seeking written assurance or taking proceedings before Restrictive Practices Court.

(vi) Empowered to require information to be provided to assist him in deciding whether to make a monopoly reference.

(vii) Advise Ministers on reports of the MMC and to negotiate (at request of Minister) the securing of undertakings and keep the carrying out of them under review.

Relationships with aspects of competition policy

RESTRICTIVE PRACTICES	*MONOPOLIES AND MERGERS*	*CONSUMER PROTECTION*
(a) Functions of Registrar of Restrictive Trade Agreements transferred to Director	(a) Monopolies Commission renamed Monopolies and Mergers Commission (MMC)	(a) Provides for the appointment of a Consumer Protection Advisory Committee (CPAC)
(b) Empowers Secretary of State to require the registration of certain agreements (including information agreements) between suppliers of services other than professional services (Cf 1965 Act)	(b) Definition of Monopoly reduced from a market share of one-third to one-quarter	(b) CPAC may receive references from the Secretary of State or the Director to report on whether particular consumer trade practices adversely affect the economic interests of consumers (excluding professional services referrable to MMC)
(c) Agreements relating to recommendation of resale prices and patent and design pooling made registrable	(c) Monopoly, but not merger, references may be made by Director (subject to veto) as well as Secretary of State	
	(d) National corporations may be referred but only by Secretary of State and appropriate Minister jointly	
	(e) Restrictive labour practices made referrable	

Source: M. C. Fleming, op. cit., p. 2.

The 1965 Monopolies and Mergers Act

Policy on mergers effectively began in 1965 in the wake of a take-over bid by Imperial Chemical Industries for Courtaulds. The Labour government found itself with no explicit means to declare its position on such a merger. Its solution was to make use of an existing body, the Monopolies Commission, as the appropriate forum where the desirability of a change in the structure of an industry could be examined. The Board of Trade was now able under the Monopolies and Mergers Act to refer a merger proposal to the Commission if the market share of the two firms satisfied the one-third share of the market or if the value of assets taken over exceeded £5m. The government had equipped itself with this new power but neither intended automatic referral to the Commission nor any presumption of hostility to a proposed merger. A Mergers Panel consisting of civil servants was created to advise the appropriate government minister. The Commission, once referred a merger case, had to operate with some speed and normally report back within six months. Its remit was simply whether the proposed merger was against 'the public interest'. Inevitably this same vague principle which had given the Commission such an uncertain orientation back in 1948 was to prove the basis of growing criticism in its handling of merger cases after 1965. Before examining these criticisms we first appraise the many provisions of legislation introduced in 1973.

The 1973 Fair Trading Act

This Act brought about changes not only in the administration of competition policy but also its substance. The newly created office of Director-General of Fair Trading assumed the functions of the Registrar of Restrictive Trading Agreements but with much wider responsibilities. It was charged with keeping under review both commercial activities relating to monopoly situations or uncompetitive practices and also trade practices which might adversely affect the interests of consumers. The Director-General was thus now formally given the task of advising the Secretary of State about all these matters as a continuing brief. Figure 30.2 summarizes the main aspects of the 1973 Act. Of particular significance was the new legal definition of monopoly – the criterion reduced to one-quarter market share – and the broader interpretation of the market as compared with the 1948 Act. The Fair Trading Act made it now possible to refer monopolies of a local character to the Monopolies and Mergers Commission (MMC) rather than those relating to the UK as a whole. Furthermore the monopoly situation of the nationalized industries and other statutory trading bodies were now brought within the scope of the Act. But apart from these extensions of the work of the MMC the Act spelt out a much clearer orientation for the members of that

body. Section 84 now made the promotion of competition a key aspect of its approach to particular investigations. If you compare the following criteria with section 14 of the 1948 Act (see above) you will note the new emphasis on the process of competition as a means of securing economic efficiency.

… the Commission shall take into account all matters which appear to them in the particular circumstances to be relevant and, among other things, shall have regard to the desirability:

(a) of maintaining and promoting effective competition between persons supplying goods and services in the United Kingdom;

(b) of promoting the interests of consumers, purchasers, and other users of goods and services in the United Kingdom in respect of the prices charged for them and in respect of theire quality and the variety of goods and services supplied;

(c) of promoting, through competition, the reduction of costs and the development and use of new techniques and new products, and of facilitating the entry of new competitors into existing markets;

(d) of maintaining and promoting the balanced distribution of industry and employment in the United Kingdom; and

(e) of maintaining and promoting competitive activity in markets outside the United Kingdom on the part of producers of goods, and of suppliers of goods and services, in the United Kingdom.

The 1973 Act thus represented a more confident belief in the virtues of competition than had been the case in the immediate post-war years. Legislation seven years later actually included the word in its title – the 1980 Competition Act.

The 1980 Competition Act

This Act tried to deal with business behaviour which might amount to an *anti-competitive practice*. Responsibility for supervising the investigation of such practices was given to the Director-General of Fair Trading. Figure 30.3 summarizes the procedures laid down in the Act for investigating those courses of business conduct pursued by a person which

of itself or when taken together with a course of conduct pursued by persons associated with him, has or is intended or is likely to have the effect of restricting, distorting or preventing competition in connection with the production, supply or acquisition of goods in the United Kingdom or any part of it or the supply or securing of services in the United Kingdom or any part of it.

You should note that Figure 30.3 provided for the circumstances of each anti-competitive practice to be examined thus continuing the case-by-case approach of the Monopolies Commission. But you must be wondering *what* practices might in specific instances constitute an anti-competitive practice? The Office of

Fair Trading has identified three instances concerning the pricing of goods and six practices relating to their distribution. Since the terms need clarification they are briefly explained in Figure 30.4.

Figure 30.3
The Investigation of Anti-competitive Practices under the 1980 Competition Act

OFT gets complaint, makes inquiries, and investigates whether a particular course of conduct amounts to an anti-competitive practice and then informs

Secretary of State for Trade Company Public

If such a practice is identified in the OFT investigation in a study lasting three months the OFT then

Seeks negotiation of voluntary undertakings

or

If not negotiated, then the OFT refers the matter to the Monopolies and Mergers Commission for its investigation (lasting up to nine months)

If then the MMC reports that the practice is against public interest

then the firm must either voluntarily abandon the practice or anticipate an

Order from Trade Secretary prohibiting the practice.

The provisions of the 1980 Act were not to apply in the case of small firms (those with an annual turnover of less than £5m and which have less than a 25 per cent share of a relevant market). Also specifically exempted from the Act were sectors such as international shipping and civil aviation (where governments have long agreed to regulation of prices and services).

Two further aspects of the 1980 Act illustrate how the public sector was now seen as appropriate for inclusion within legislation concerned with the promotion of competition and efficiency. The Act empowered the Secretary of State for Trade to refer to the MMC questions about the efficiency and costs of, the service provided by, and possible abuse of a monopoly situation by nationalized industries. It also empowered the Secretary of State for Trade to direct the Director-General of Fair Trading to investigate questions about prices of major public concern, either because they are

Figure 30.4
Forms of Competitive Conduct that Might Constitute an Anti-competitive Practice

(a) *Pricing Policy*
Falling into this category would be:
Price discrimination – the practice of selling goods or services, where there are no cost differences, to distinct and separate groups of customers these groups being charged varying prices according to their degree of sensitivity to price levels. Some variants of price discrimination take the form of differential rates of discount or rebate from list prices perhaps in return for loyalty or exclusive supply arrangements. An important variant arises where a purchaser's buying power enables him to insist that suppliers grant him advantageous terms, so artificially enhancing his ability to compete on price in the market in which he sells;
Predatory pricing – which is usually defined as the practice of temporarily selling at prices below cost, with the intention of driving a competitor from the market, so that in the future prices may be raised and enhanced profits extracted;
Vertical price squeezing – which can arise when a vertically integrated firm controls the total supply of an input which is essential to the production requirements of its subsidiary and also its competitors. The input price can be raised and the downstream output price reduced, so that the profits of competitors are squeezed, possibly with a view to driving them from the market.

(b) *Distribution Policy*
There are a number of practices which might serve to restrict, distort, or prevent competition, either at manufacturing or distribution level. These include:
Tie-in-sales – a stipulation that a buyer must purchase part or all of his requirements of a second (tied) product from the supplier of a first (tying) product.
Full-line forcing – which requires a buyer to purchase quantities of each item in a product range in order to be able to buy any of them.
Rental-only contracts – which restrict customers to rental or lease terms only and which can be anti-competitive where there are no alternative methods of acquiring those goods;
Exclusive supply – whereby a seller supplies only one buyer in a certain geographical area, which limits competition between that buyer and his competitors;
Selective distribution – which is the practice of choosing as sales outlets only those which satisfy specific qualitative or quantitative criteria;
Exclusive purchase – which arises when a distributor contracts to stock only the products of one manufacturer, possibly in return for an exclusive supply arrangement.

Source: Office of Fair Trading, 1980.

> ## Key Points 30.1
>
> ▶ UK competition policy has developed from a concern with monopoly (the 1948 Act) to restraints on price competition (the 1956 Act) and only in the late 1960s to take-over bids (the 1965 Act).
>
> ▶ UK policy has been essentially pragmatic rather than doctrinaire. The approach has essentially been to consider individual cases on their merits.

of general economic importance or because consumers are significantly affected. This provision reflected the political concern with the cost of living. This aspect of the 1980 Act provides an appropriate point to indicate that it was not the first time that UK governments have shown their sensitivity to the rate of increase in prices. As a major electoral issue several post-war governments have been prepared if not to take action on prices at least keen to exhibit a willingness to allow a statutory body *other than the MMC* to make a public inquiry into a particular industry. This concern of government with prices was noted in Chapter 10 where we indicated that wage and price controls have been seen as a method of slowing down cost–push inflation.

The Macro-Dimension

As inflationary pressures became more acute in the 1960s governments looked for means other than monetary and fiscal policies to try to contain the upward movement of prices. They perceived that investigation of an industry by a specialist agency offered the possibility of breaking any mechanistic adjustment by firms in determining final product prices whenever they incurred higher labour or raw materials costs. Governments did not accept that manufacturers were necessarily entitled to pass on all higher costs to consumers. Were competitive pressures really strong enough to force at least some containment of costs by increased efficiency? Did parallel pricing by firms amount to a situation where market pressures in some industries were not strong enough to help restrain the upward movement in prices? Investigation of the nature of competition in some major industries by an impartial body like the MMC would not only ascertain the facts but provide the government with evidence that it was 'doing something' tangible to try to achieve some measure of price stability. Obviously the concern with prices assisted the calls for wage restraint being made to the trade union movement. We recognize at once then that single-industry and single-firm inquiries represent a piecemeal micro-approach to the broad goal of macroeconomic policy. But that is not to imply that individual industry inquiries are necessarily insignificant in their ultimate impact. A body that has to examine industries immediately enters a politically

charged world. Neither management nor trade unions are likely to welcome the full glare of publicity brought upon them.

The Labour government's chosen body to implement its prices and incomes policy between 1965 and 1970 was the National Board for Prices and Incomes (NBPI). In several of its reports the NBPI claimed that competitive pressures were weak and also that the competitive process could not always be relied upon to ensure that production was carried out by the most efficient means. The reports on the sweet confectionery industry (1968), margarine and cooking fats (1970), tea (1970), and ice cream (1970) devoted much attention to competition between oligopolists who spent heavily on advertising goods which had a low price sensitivity. The problem that faced the NBPI like the longer-established MMC was its lack of teeth – to see put into immediate effect such remedies as it deemed appropriate in particular cases. Its whole working was set in a political context with its subjects for inquiry not determined by itself but by the government of the day. To this extent its references were seen as being *too* politically motivated. Study of the bread and brewing industries might indeed be justifiable since they were producers of basic consumer goods. But were such choices for NBPI study too easily made by a government anxious to stress to the electorate how items included in the Retail Prices Index were 'being dealt with'?

The Conservative government in 1970 soon abolished the NBPI and preferred to resort to the MMC to handle inquiries where it seemed to have reservations about the strength of competition in particular industries. Like its predecessor the political dimension was not absent as the Heath government had to contend with the escalation in world commodity prices in 1973–4. Food prices became even more a politically sensitive matter and the choice of breakfast cereals, bread and flour, and also frozen foodstuffs undoubtedly reflected the current concern in government quarters. The Heath government set up a Prices Commission as an explicit price control body. Large firms were required to prenotify intentions to increase prices and which could only be permissible under the rules laid down in a Price Code. The work of this Commission under the chairmanship of Lord Cockfield was essentially supervision of an accountancy exercise affecting all firms that fell within its scope. However, the Cockfield Commission was also asked under the provisions of the 1973 Counter-Inflation Act to make such examinations of industries as directed by the Secretary of State. This meant that the Cockfield Commission was asked to undertake studies of the nature of competition in those areas of the UK economy where presumably the government felt unsure about the extent of competitive pressures. The Commission was in effect a surrogate MMC but the attraction to government was its speedy reporting on the nature of pricing without reference to 'the public interest' or the need at the outset to establish whether monopoly conditions existed. In retrospect some of the sectoral studies made in the 1974–7 period have to be seen as a conscious attempt by government to scrutinize the pricing of goods and services at a time when cost inflationary pressures were acute. Lord Cockfield himself saw ample justification for some form of government monitoring of efficiency. He declared

One thing which clearly emerged from the administration of the price control was the extent to which competition is effectively limited in this country. Right at the commencement of the price control the chairman of one of the leading companies in the country accused me of obstructing the free working of competition: the Commission, he said, was preventing him putting up his prices to match those of his competitors. We suffer in this country, from market domination, price leadership, parallel pricing, the lack of effective competition, unwillingness to compete on price, which in many traders is regarded as disreputable or undesirable; and a 'cost plus' mentality under which the instinctive reaction to cost increases is to pass them on in prices rather than absorb them in greater efficiency, with the resulting erosion of resistance to cost increases, particularly unjustified increases in labour costs. There is a tendency in this field to talk of pricing 'abuse'. But my own experience is that it is not so much the active and deliberate abuse which is the problem as a general attitude of non-competitiveness.*

As raw material prices stabilized the need for the strait-jacket to constrain firms in their pricing of final goods disappeared. However, the Callaghan government sought to reach accord with the trade unions on incomes policy. This meant that although cost-related controls might no longer be necessary, prenotification of proposed price increases would serve as the tangible element in government prices policy in support of an understanding on wages. But the 1977 Price Commission Act went further than just requiring firms to continue notifying the new Price Commission under Mr Charles Williams of intended price rises. It gave the Williams Commission *discretion* to select particular companies for investigation. These investigations had to be made in a very short space of time – no more than three months. It had a positive role of 'promoting competition' (1977 Act, section 2) and improving

efficiency ('the desirability of encouraging reductions in costs by improvements in the use of resources'). The work of the new Commission was thus firmly placed within the context of competition policy but operating independently from the existing instruments of this policy (the OFT and MMC). The PC was thus now being asked to make single-firm studies and, unlike either the NBPI or MMC, able to select its own cases for investigations.

In fact the PC made forty-four investigations of notifications of price increases during its lifetime. It also continued to undertake two of the sectoral studies begun by its predecessor of the same name. These studies continued under the terms of the 1977 Act and some nineteen examination reports were undertaken at the request of the newly established Ministry for Prices and Consumer Protection. Thus within a very short period of time the PC issued no less than sixty-five reports. Its rapid rate of working sharply contrasted with the lengthy nature of MMC inquiries. Yet both the PC and MMC were agents of competition policy. The inevitable question arose: was there justification for two separate bodies if each was trying to bring about more competitive markets? Certainly the two agencies had different procedures and philosophy but any enthusiasm by the Labour government for a merger of the MMC and PC had come to nothing by the time of the 1979 General Election.

Of the two Commissions it should not surprise you that the PC found the firms which it chose to investigate much less relaxed about meeting the PC than would have been the case with a MMC-type inquiry. Firms had a particular vital issue under scrutiny by the PC – a proposed price increase – whereas a MMC inquiry has no rationale on such a critical matter as the current financial situation of a firm. Inevitably then companies disliked the PC. It interfered with their freedom of manoeuvre and they looked to a new Conservative government to abolish it.

What did the PC achieve? In fact it is difficult to find little evidence within the private sector of long-term repercussions of the new strand in competition policy in the 1977–9 period. This is not surprising since before it could return to make a second investigation of a firm its days were ended by the incoming Conservative government. We can however argue that the PC documented various elements of competitive behaviour that were a legitimate concern of government. Several of its sectoral studies illustrated the concern in Whitehall about the nature of competition in the markets for car parts, animal feeding stuffs, spectacles, and sanitary protection. In abolishing the PC the new Conservative government was anxious not to be seen as unconcerned about the nature of competition. Its remedy in the 1980 Competition Act for the demise of the PC was the concept of anti-competitive practices which we discussed earlier. Our task now must be to review how competition policy has operated since 1980. We shall see that the subject is still politically contentious.

*Lord Cockfield, 'The Price Commission and Price Control', *Three Banks Review*, March 1978, No. 117, p. 23.

> ## Key Points 30.2
>
> ► In times of escalating inflation there is a tendency for governments to create an agency to help restrain rising prices both directly and indirectly as an element in support of an incomes policy. The NBPI and both the 1973–7 and 1977–9 Price Commissions were all given scope to make micro-studies as part of macroeconomic policies.
> ► These non-specialist agencies of competition policy have made many studies of the nature of competition policy but hitherto have not survived during the life of a Conservative government.

Competition Policies: An Assessment

Our review of the development of competition policy has attempted to show that Labour and Conservative governments in the post-war period have each introduced legislation concerned with the structure of markets and forms of business behaviour. The whole subject-matter appears to be continually debated to establish whether the nature of policy is appropriate to current conditions. In fact this is not just surmise but the very truth of the matter. Competition policy has indeed been the subject of continual review during the last forty years. The question that now needs to be faced is whether the whole panoply of laws since 1948 really amounts to a clear statement by government on the desirability and benefits of competition. Several observers feel that the present stance of competition policy suffers from an ambivalent view of the benefits of competitive markets. The 'every case to be judged on its merits' means that no clear picture is offered of those forms of business behaviour that are regarded as unacceptable. The 'rules of the game' are held to be still too vague to amount to an explicit policy *for* competitive markets. Consequently some have argued that rather than rely on the OFT for redress for those persons who feel aggrieved by forms of anti-competitive conduct we should adopt a more judicial approach. Rather than OFT official action there should be encouragement for *private* actions such that business community is deterred from participating in behaviour such as predatory pricing. The US approach which incorporates criminal penalties and payment of damages amounting to three times the alleged loss (the so-called 'triple damages concept') may be thought too extreme for adoption on this side of the Atlantic but it reflects a view that the aim of competition policy is to stop unfair trading practices in the first place. The UK approach is rather to provide a means whereby problems that do arise can be resolved. Perhaps a change to a 'privatization' in the enforcement of competition would be desirable. Why has such a viewpoint arisen? It seems to have its root in part at least in reservations over the role of the MMC.

The MMC now seems to prompt little public attention in its monopoly inquiries. Its purpose seems essentially dependent on its 'efficiency audits' of public corporations. Its impact on mergers has been minimal. Between 1965 and 1984 2 565 proposed mergers were examined by the Mergers Panel but only 79 referred to the MMC. Twenty-three of these mergers were abandoned during the inquiries made by the MMC and of the remainder fewer were found to be against the public interest than not against it.

It has been argued by some for several years that mergers policy is misdirected. These critics hold that rather than establish whether a merger between two firms would not be against the public interest the MMC should explicitly seek for benefits that might follow from a change in market structure. In other words to apply an explicit weighing-up of the benefits and costs arising from a change in the status quo. Our discussion of consumer surplus in Chapter 24 in appraising the desirability of monopoly is a formal expression of such a neutral approach to mergers.

Of course the MMC can in the meantime only apply itself to those merger situations referred to it by government. Thus it is the political nature of merger decisions that really explains why many now have reservations about the current state of mergers policy. For example *The Economist* has commented as follows:

British anti-trust law is fuzzier than photographs of the Loch Ness monster. Unchanged since 1973, it says that the government should scrutinize all bids which either endanger competition or (here is where the edges blur) may be expected to harm the public interest. The latter clause has given successive governments discretion to refer or veto any bid. Business men whose faces do not fit are the victims.*

and again

In Britain, merger policy is ... politically controversial. The opposition Labour party wants most take-overs banned unless they can be proved to be in the public interest. But in January Mr Leon Brittan, then secretary for trade and industry, reaffirmed that referrals to the monopolies

---

*'Conglomerators' Charter', *The Economist*, 22 February 1986, p.16.

commission should in future be made 'primarily (but not exclusively) on competition grounds.'

In reality, the British government makes up policy as it goes along. On wider-competition grounds, it has gradually ceased to give special protection to Scottish firms (the so-called tartan ring-fence) and has encouraged a take-over approach by General Motors for BL's lorry division in the belief that bigger means more internationaly competitive. Yet it has referred the bid by the General Electric Company for Plessey to the monopolies commission, even though in the world league the merged firm would not be a giant.†

More recently the OFT has found itself caught up in the politically sensitive issue of choosing which take-over bids appear to warrant an MMC study. The proposed merger between United Biscuits and Imperial Tobacco led to determined attempts by these two parties to avoid referral to the MMC. United Biscuits was prepared to dispose of some of its food interests in order to reduce the likelihood of an MMC investigation. (This proposed merger did not proceed since Hanson Trust outbid United Biscuits for Imperial Tobacco.) However, a similar negotiation with the OFT ensured that in early 1986 Guinness could proceed to bid for Distillers. An earlier bid by Guinness had been referred to the MMC but following its proposals to sell off some of Distillers' whisky brands thus bringing down its total market share from 35 to 25 per cent it avoided a second reference to the MMC. Such bargaining between the OFT raises questions about the difficult position in which the OFT is placed and its implications for the relevance of the MMC.

As regards restrictive practices critics feel the ostensible success of the 1956 Act flatters the true position on the enforcement of competitive markets. When firms have defied rulings in the Restrictive Practices Court they have been very modest. This inevitably puts into doubt what deterrence there is when the penalties are far from being penal. Extensive price-fixing and collusive-tendering arrangements have come to light in industries as varied as bread-making, photo-copying equipment, concrete pipes, road black-top materials, and telephone cables. Not surprisingly Sir Gordon Barrie, the Director-General of Fair Trading, has sought tougher sanctions and

---

†'Why Europe's Anti-trusters are a Busted Flush',
The Economist, 8 Mar. 1986, p. 63.

appeared to favour the EEC approach which prohibits anti-competitive practices. At present only trade between the UK and the rest of the EEC is governed by the Common Market's rules. As in mergers the political dimension has intervened in the OFT's handling of restrictive practices.

In 1979 the OFT referred the rules of the Stock Exchange to the Restrictive Practices Court. An agreement was reached between the government and the Stock Exchange in July 1983 whereby special legislation was introduced to exempt the Stock Exchange from the 1956 Act and end the impending court case. As part of the 'deal' the Stock Exchange agreed to give up its minimum commission scales. It was soon realized that increased competition would undermine the traditional separation of functions by brokers and jobbers (single-capacity trading) and plans made to allow dual-capacity trading as from 27 October 1986. Without doubt the court case set in train the possibility of more competitive financial markets. So ultimately one might argue the thrust of the 1956 Act prevailed. This application of the 1956 Act to the service sector of the economy may well, in due course, come to be seen as a major milestone in the evolution of competition policy. But there are other services which have experienced more competitive trading conditions. The two Thatcher administrations have taken the view that in certain professions a more competitive environment was desirable. The monopoly of solicitors in house conveyancing and that of opticians in selling spectacles have been challenged. The committed enthusiast of unfettered competition may, however, point to other areas of the economy where restraints on competition have government backing. For example, imports of cars from Japan are subject to understandings with Nissan, Toyota, and Mazda. Competition for UK textile manufactures is restrained by the Multi-Fibre Agreement. The Central Electrical Generating Board is unable freely to import coal for its power stations. Competition between airline operators in Western Europe has been limited by price-fixing, revenue-sharing, and agreements on capacity. And what about a sector of the economy where there is an import tariff which sometimes reaches 100 per cent and the government agrees to buy all the produce this industry cannot sell abroad at a price well above free market levels? Yes, agriculture. Consider why these deviations from competitive markets are accepted by governments!

Key Points 30.3

▶ **The pragmatic style of UK competition policy has given rise to criticism that it is too uncertain in operation and still lacks a positive commitment to the virtues of competition.**

▶ **The professions have increasingly become the subject of government attempts to foster greater competition but agriculture and some areas of manufacturing industry continue to receive protection from overseas competition.**

CASE STUDY

What's On the Telly?

The Monopolies Commission has a reputation for idiosyncratic decisions. But last week's verdict that the BBC and Independent Television Publication's practice of limiting publication of programme listings does not operate against the public interest was extraordinary. So confused are the report's final conclusions, gainsaying many of its own arguments, that it questions the Commission's ability to play its important part in furthering a more competitive economy.

It has to be said that this newspaper has an interest. As part of the service to readers, we would like to be able to offer a full week's TV programmes. As most other newspapers would like to do so as well, relaxing the restrictions would give us no special advantage.

The need for such publication is there. The BBC confirmed this to the Commission. 'A cheerful publication containing all the TV programmes side by side with considerable editorial material ... could be ... made very popular and would meet the needs of a lot of the central mass of people who like to compare things during the week', was the BBC's view.

In the light of this, how did the Commission, or more strictly speaking, its chairman, Sir Godfray Le Quesne QC, whose casting vote settled the report's recommendation, decide that permitting this cheerful publication to appear was against the public interest?

To a large extent, the Commission's report reflects the Office of Fair Trading's views that such behaviour is anti-competitive. 'There can be no doubt that the relevant policies and practices of the BBC and ITV do in fact prevent or restrict competition in a number of ways and it is clear to us that

they are intended to do so, since a major part of the case in favour of the practice was that it was necessary for *Radio Times* and *TV Times* to be at least to some extent protected from competition' was one clear conclusion.

When the two defendants claimed – as Ford did in an early case about car part designs – that the information was their copyright, the Commission swept this aside. 'We adhere to the view expressed in the Ford report that refusal to grant licences under a copyright can be an anti-competitive practice.'

Having identified a monopolist practice, the Commission then moved on to the issue of the public interest. The second paragraph of this section reinforces the case against the broadcasters. 'In our judgement the most important element of the public interest is the availability of adequate advance information about broadcasting programmes in convenient form.'

How can forcing people to turn to two sources of information rather than one to find out what's happening a week ahead meet this criteria? Nor is the cost insignificant. If the price of the TV licence is a matter of intense public and political debate, the cost of finding out what this brings you each week is over half the annual fee.

The broadcasters claim that waiving their copyright would diminish the quality of service to the public. Free enterprise publications would not necessarily offer the same programme detail and, in the worst case, *Radio Times* and *TV Times* might cut back or cease publication. That life on earth as we know it will end if a little competition arises is the monopolist's stock defence. What they actually mean is that they lack sufficient faith in their product to

let the public have a free choice.

What is just as likely to happen is that the public, given the opportunity to sample the imitators, will decide the original was better. It would need a massive investment to rival *Radio Times* and *TV Times*, which will always enjoy privileged access to programme makers and performers for their feature material. Even now they could probably extend their readership by publishing ITV and BBC programmes as the government has asked them to do. The fact that they have not done so says something about their view of how to serve the public interest.

The three commissioners who wanted to end the monopoly thought the case for giving consumers a choice was paramount. 'We give more weight than do our colleagues to the fact that the form of programme information made available to the public is determined by the producers of the programmes rather than by the viewing public through the operation of competitive forces in the market place.'

Sir Godfray would have none of this. He said he could not make up his mind about the balance of disadvantage and advantage. He therefore voted to keep things as they are. So much for the custodians of competition.

Source: Roger Eglin, 'Why it's time to turn off the TV monopoly', *Sunday Times*, 15 Sept. 1985.

Questions
1. What might be the implications of a wider publication of radio and television programmes for
   (a) the BBC and ITV
   (b) newspapers and magazines?
2. Do you think the MMC is asked to make decisions which inevitably are 'idiosyncratic'?

Taking the Biscuit

Is a crisp a crisp or an 'extruded' snack? Are peanuts plain nuts or substitutes in the £600 million-a-year snacks markets?

Such questions have been the crucial issues dogging those excellent minds at the Office of Fair Trading over the last few weeks as they mulled over the virtues of the £1.2 billion agreed merger between Imperial Group and United Biscuits.

Yesterday's decision by the Department of Trade and Industry – with the full support of the Office of Fair Trading – to refer the Imperial–UB merger to the Monopolies and Mergers Commission has obviously horrified not only the parties concerned but a wide section of the City.

What has staggered the City even more was the decision to give the green light to Hanson Trust's hostile bid for Imperial. For many this smacked immediately as the government's thank you gift to Lord Hanson for his unswerving support throughout the Westlands affair.

With no apparent logic it had been conventional wisdom throughout industry and City that either both bids would be referred – or both cleared.

But in fact if you look at the two issues carefully there was no rational argument – on competition or public interest grounds – to support this view at all. Indeed, the writing was on the wall back in 1982 when the giant US Nabisco group launched its bid for biscuit to snacks group, Huntley & Palmer. The second marker dates back to the former Trade Secretary Norman Tebbit's quite clear ground rules laid down in July 1984.

Nabisco's bid for Huntley & Palmer was cleared by the MMC but with the green light it issued a clear warning for any future mergers in the snack foods market. It said 'Any contemplated

acquisitions by the major suppliers which would further increase the degree of concentration would merit careful scrutiny.' It is inconceivable that the Imperial–UB boards were unaware of this. The MMC dissenters on the Nabisco ruling went further in their arguments against the bid suggesting the merger would be totally detrimental to the industry and would keep out any new entries into the market.

The proposed Imperial–UB merger would give the group a market share of at least 45 per cent of the total snacks market. This includes crisps, peanuts and any other 'extruded' savoury snacks which, in industry terms, are defined as orginating from 'pellets'. But the key here is that they are all substitutes.

This would create a clear duopolistic situation with Nabisco which holds another chunk of about 45 per cent. The OFT claims the structural concentration which would result from this dominance by the two giants would be uncompetitive in terms of pricing, employment, and so on.

The proposed Imperial–UB group would also have a clear niche in the various separate markets. UB already has 50 per cent of the peanut market and Imperial would add another couple of per cent. Imperial, with its Golden Wonder brands and others, has 23 per cent of the crisps market while UB has about 23 per cent. In the 'savoury' snacks market UB has 30 per cent and Imperial's 17 per cent brings this up to just about half the market.

For the OFT it was the new structure which was worrying rather than the actual market shares. The two groups overlap in a few other areas – frozen foods and restaurants – but there is no market share of any significance.

So on straight competition grounds there appears to be a clear case for another MMC study.

Hanson's bid for Imperial is rather more complex. Present government policy is geared simply to competition issues and it is the OFT's job to bring these to their attention. But it is also within its ambit to highlight any mergers which present 'new' issues which merit further investigation.

Prima facie Hanson's bid for Imperial has no competition grounds nor does it raise any particular worries of public interest other than the trend towards conglomerates and the move back to 'big is beautiful'.

Unless the OFT detects a worrying new particular trend – such as it did in Elders' bid for Allied-Lyons – it would have been hard pressed to rationalize a reference recommendation for Hanson. It faced similar problems when looking at the BTR bid for Thomas Tilling but at the end of the day found there were no logical reasons for intervention.

So it should have come as no surprise to anyone that a committed non-interventionist government has decided that it will be the market that now has to make the running.

Source: Margareta Pagano, 'One crisp decision that doesn't take the biscuit', *The Guardian*, 13 Feb. 1986.

Questions

1. How does the case study illustrate the relevance of market structure in UK merger policy?
2. How does the case study illustrate the claim that UK merger policy is unpredictable?
3. Should the fact that some firms have diversified interests make any difference in the determination of mergers policy?

Exam Preparation and Practice

INTRODUCTORY EXERCISES

1. Make a critical appraisal of these opposing views of the desirability of mergers in British industry. Try to make clear the normative aspects in the debate on what matters would you wish to have empirical evidence.

Fashion in mergers

From Mr G. Hall

Sir, – The current fashion for mergers is proving particularly ironic to those of us who are observers of the merger scene. There is an unprecedented consensus among academics that the only people to gain from a take-over are usually the shareholders of the acquired company and often the senior managers of the acquirers. Why should it be that British managements should apparently have exercised such poor judgement? Some possible reasons follow.

They have consistently underestimated the size of the bid premium, that is the amount that the price of the would-be acquired firm rises on announcement (or even in anticipation) of the take-over bid. If the stock market is efficient, and in this respect there would seem little doubt that it is, this premium would rise to exactly equal the expected benefits from a merger.

Managements usually overestimate the expected benefits from a merger and underestimate the problems to which it will give rise. Economies of scale, for instance, are less powerful as an engine for lowering costs than is technological progress. British industry's international uncompetitiveness owes far more to its failure to invest in the latest technology than from its inability to exploit economies of scale. Moreover, severe organizational problems can result from a merger between two sizeable businesses and these can take years to resolve.

Mergers are probably, on the whole, not undertaken for economic reasons. Fashion plays a part and sometimes the desire to pre-empt a less welcome bid. More important, senior management in acquiring firms cannot be oblivious to the greater power and income that an enlarged firm will confer.
G. Hall, *Manchester Business School*

Are mergers good for industry?

From Mr S. Blunt

Sir, – Are take-overs and mergers really in the best interests of British industry? Since 1963 a total of 15 909 companies have been acquired by other companies for a total of £92bn at today's prices (as reported on March 3). If mergers and acquisitions are really so good for industry in Britain, one would have expected British industry to be leading the world today. With the post-war industrial decline continuing, can we afford to allow unbridled merger-mania to continue?

I believe that the Chancellor should include in his Budget changes to make it more expensive for companies to buy shares in other companies, so that leaders in industry direct their energies and talents to improvements in quality, to new product development, to better marketing, and to employee training, instead of to self-aggrandizement by take-over.
S. Blunt, *Winchester, Hants.*

Mergers are good for industry

From Mrs P. Marriott

Sir, – Simon Blunt (March 7) asks: 'Are take-overs really good for British industry?'

It would be foolish to argue that all mergers are in the interests of industry, but it is equally misguided to attribute Britain's decline to take-overs and to conclude that all mergers are wrong.

One particular virtue of a merger is its role in stimulating necessary change. Under-performing companies deservedly attract bids because other firms believe they could make a better job of management and achieve a healthier level of profit.

In a properly conceived acquisition, where the bidding party has a good performance record, the merger will bring a logical operational combination. And if the offer price is realistic and fair it will work to the benefit of both sets of shareholders and employees, and industry and the economy.

Companies which become the targets of bids usually do so because their top management is lethargic and complacent.

A post-acquisition introduction of streamlined and efficient operating systems, responsibility and reward for managers and staff, and an appetite for innovation is far more likely to result in the improvements in quality, new product development, and better marketing and training for which Simon Blunt appeals, than his suggested prescription of protectionist intervention by the Chancellor of the Exchequer.
P. R. Marriott, *London*

Source: Financial Times, 22 Jan., 7 and 11 March 1986.

continued overleaf

2. Study the following table. What do the data for 1980–4 suggest about the likelihood of a merger bid ultimately being successful?

Outcome of References to Monopolies Commission

	No. of references	No. abandoned during investigation	Blocked	Cleared		
				Failed take-over	Successful take-over	
1980	5	1	1	0	3	Blue Circle Industries – Armitage Shanks, S&W Berisford–British Sugar Corporation, Compagnie Internationale Europcar–Godfrey Davis
1981	8	1	5	0	2	BTR–Serck, British Rail Hovercraft–Hoverlloyd
1982	10	2	4	2	2	Nabisco Brands–Huntley & Palmer Foods ICI–Arthur Holden
1983	9	2	4	3	0	
1984	4	1	0	2	1	British Electric Traction–Initial

Source: The Economist, 25 Jan. 1986, p. 65.

RELATED ESSAY QUESTIONS

1. Discuss the proposition that the major weakness of post-war British competition policy has been its focus on non-competitive market conduct rather than an attempt to create competitive market structures.

2. What criteria might be applied when assessing whether a merger between two firms was in the public interest?

3. What are the advantages and disadvantages of policy on mergers in the UK?

4. Has the 1956 Restrictive Trade Practices Act had beneficial effects on the performance of the British economy?

5. In 1983 Mr Roy Hattersley declared that during the 1970s the UK had been operating 'a flaccid competition policy'. Discuss this viewpoint.

6. What criteria may be used by Government policy to stimulate competition? Illustrate your answer from United Kingdom experience.

7. Offer an economic appraisal of Government policies concerned with the maintenance of competition between firms in industry and commerce.

31 Money: Monetary and Exchange Rate Policy

Questions for Preview

1   What is the demand for money and how is it related to the interest rate?

2   Why is the price of bonds* inversely related to the interest rate?

3   What is monetary policy and what are the monetary policy tools of the Bank of England?

4   How do the supply and demand for money determine the interest rate?

5   What is a monetarist?

There is a market for money just as there is a market for goods and services. There is a demand for money – for a number of different purposes. There is a supply of money. The Bank of England's monetary policy seeks to control aggregate monetary demand in the economy. The objectives of policy are to achieve a high level of employment without undue inflation, and to maintain external balance. Monetary policy can be carried out using a range of tools. These can be seen as influencing either the supply of, or the demand for, money. In the main they use interest rate control as a means to an end. We look first at the theory of money, and then at the practicalities of monetary policy.

* See dictionary for clarification.

The Demand for Money

Why do people hold money instead of alternative assets, such as bonds, stocks, and durable goods? Economists like to distinguish three different reasons why we hold money.

1. **Transactions demand.** Households and firms hold a certain amount of money because of its usefulness as a generally acceptable medium of exchange. Holding money facilitates economic exchanges. With money we can buy products and financial assets quickly when and where we want. The transactions demand for money relates to the fact that our receipts of money income do not match our expenditures. For example, throughout a year you may get paid on the first of each month but spend your income at a relatively even rate throughout the entire month.

2. **Precautionary demand.** A certain amount of money holdings are desired by households and firms in order to meet unplanned emergencies. The transactions demand for money relates to planned expenditures. Precautionary demand relates to unplanned expenditures, such as unexpected illness, unemployment, and so on. People like to hold a certain amount of their wealth in the form of very liquid assets, that is, assets denominated in money terms, such as bank balances and building society deposits.

3. **Speculative demand.** The *nominal* value (in money terms) of money is fixed. That is not true for a share of stock in a company or for a bond, a house, or a painting. Thus, compared with other assets that a household could own, there is more safety in holding money because its nominal value does not change. People particularly wish to hold money as an alternative to other assets when the market prices of other assets are falling or when they anticipate that the value of non-money assets such as shares will fall in the future.

The Price of Holding Money

Money, you will remember, is the most liquid of all assets. Clearly though, we pay a price for holding money. The price we pay is the *opportunity cost* involved. What is the opportunity cost? It is the interest that we could have earned on an alternative income-earning asset, such as a bond, a stock or a building society account. Therefore, we state that:

The opportunity cost of *holding* money, or cash, is the interest income forgone.

If you keep £100 in currency under a pillow for one year, what is the cost of holding that currency? If the

best alternative asset you could have purchased with the £100 was an asset that yielded 5 per cent after taxes, then you forfeited £5. Would you think differently about keeping that £100 in currency under your pillow if an alternative asset could yield you a 20 per cent after-tax rate of return? Perhaps you might. You might then decide to put that £100 in an income-earning asset instead of keeping it as part of your wealth in the form of currency under your pillow. We can surmise, therefore, that the higher the cost of holding money, the lower the quantity of money people wish to hold. In other words, there is an inverse relationship between the quantity of money demanded and the cost of holding it, which is the interest rate that you could earn on alternative assets. Money provides the services of liquidity. The higher the opportunity cost of liquidity, the less you will buy. In other words, the higher the alternative interest rate you could earn on money, the less money you will want to hold.

The Money Demand Schedule – Liquidity Preference

Figure 31.1 shows a hypothetical money demand curve where the 'price' of holding money is the interest rate. The higher the interest rate, the lower the quantity of money demanded holding everything else constant. The money demand curve is downward sloping; it has also been called the **liquidity preference function**, because it shows the nation's preference for complete, or perfect, liquidity in the form of money.

THE ALTERNATIVE TO HOLDING MONEY

In the most simplified model, the alternative to holding money is basically financial assets such as bonds. Thus, for a given liquidity preference function, if the interest rate rises, a smaller quantity of money will be demanded, but a larger quantity of other financial assets will be desired. That means that as the interest rate rises, individuals attempt to purchase bonds with some of their money holdings. In other words, they substitute income-earning (or higher income-earning) financial assets for part of the money that they are holding, either in their transactions accounts or as paper currency. Alternatively, for any given liquidity preference function (demand for money function), if the interest rate in the economy falls, a larger quantity of money will be demanded. Individuals will attempt to sell off some of the income-earning financial assets that they own in order to have more cash. They will attempt to substitute cash for some of the bonds and stocks they own.

THE PRICE OF BONDS AND THE INTEREST RATE

Consider the case in which individuals, for whatever reason, feel that they have more money (cash holdings) than they need – there is an excess supply of money. They attempt to replace some of their money holdings with, say, bonds. Thus, the decreased quan-

Figure 31.1

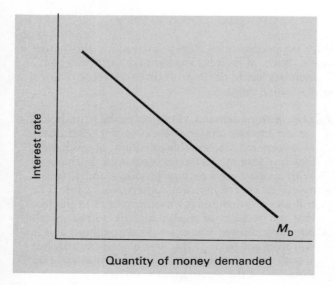

Quantity of money demanded

tity of money demanded leads to an increased quantity of bonds demanded. What will this do to the price of *already existing* bonds? It will cause their price to rise. But this price rise for already existing bonds can only mean one thing – the interest yield on those old bonds will *fall*. How can this be, you might ask, for is not the interest on a bond fixed? The answer is 'yes'. The value of interest payments on a bond are fixed, but the actual *yield* (or rate of return) on a bond is not. Consider a simple example. You have just purchased a £1000 bond that promises to pay you £100 a year for twenty years. That means that your interest yield is £100 ÷ £1000, which equals 10 per cent per year. Now let us say that everyone suddenly demands more bonds, so that the price of all bonds goes up. You find that you can now sell the old bond that you have for £2000. It still pays £100 a year as before, but what has happened to the effective interest yield on that bond received by the buyer of the bond? It has fallen for it is now £100 per year ÷ £2000 which equals 5 per cent per year. The important point to be understood is:

The market price of existing bonds (and all fixed-income assets) is inversely related to the rate of interest prevailing in the economy.

To drive this point home, look at another example taken from the other side of the picture. Assume that the average yield on bonds is 5 per cent. You decide to purchase a bond. You buy a bond that will pay you £50 a year. You will be willing to pay £1000 for it because £50 ÷ £1000 = 5 per cent. Suppose you purchase the bond. Next year something happens in the economy. For whatever reason, you can go out and obtain bonds that have effective yields of 10 per cent. That is to say, the prevailing interest rate in the economy is now 10 per cent. What has happened to the market price of the old bond that you owned – the one you purchased last year? It will have fallen. If you try to sell it for £1000, you will discover that no one will buy it from you. Why should they, for they can obtain £50 a year from someone else by paying only £500? Indeed, unless you offer your bond for sale at a price of £500, no buyers will be forthcoming. Hence, an increase in the prevailing interest rate in the economy has caused the market value of your old bond to fall. Once again, existing bond prices are inversely related to the prevailing interest rate in the economy.

Adding the Money Supply: The Theory

At any given time there is a specific stock of money in the economy. Figure 31.2 shows the quantity of money fixed at the level M_s. This implies that the *supply* of money is completely insensitive to the interest rate. It is assumed to be determined solely by the banking system and the Bank of England. With this supply schedule and a demand schedule (the liquidity preference function), we should be able to find an equilibrium point. It is at the intersection of the supply

schedule and the demand schedule, or point *E*. At point *E*, the equilibrium interest rate happens to be 10 per cent per year. This is the interest rate that equates the quantity of money demanded with the quantity of money supplied.

Figure 31.2
Putting together the Demand and Supply of Money. The demand schedule, $M_D M_D$, is downward sloping; the supply schedule is not only upward sloping, it is vertical at some given quantity of money supplied by the monetary authorities. The equilibrium rate of interest is at 10 per cent. An interest rate of 9 per cent could not prevail for very long, because the quantity of money demanded would exceed the quantity supplied. If people desired more money, they would have to sell bonds. But when they sell bonds, they must lower their price.

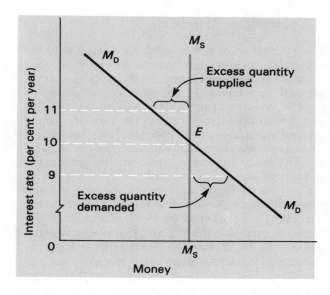

Excess Quantity Supplied

If interest rates were 11 per cent, the quantity of money demanded would be less than the quantity supplied. Excess cash balances would exist; the group – all individuals and firms – would be holding more money than it wanted to hold. People would take those excess cash balances and buy bonds, but the increased demands for bonds would cause the price of bonds to rise. Remember that there is an inverse relationship between the price of bonds and the interest rate. As the price of bonds rises, the interest rate falls. In other words, when more people try to buy bonds, the only way they can do so is by accepting a lower yield, that is, a lower interest rate. Thus, when the interest rate is above the equilibrium level, the excess quantity supplied of money is translated into an increased demand for bonds, which in turn raises the price of bonds, thus lowering the interest rate towards the equilibrium interest rate.

Excess Quantity Demanded

If the interest rate were lower than 10 per cent (the equilibrium rate) there would be an excess quantity demanded for money. People would sell their bonds in an attempt to make up the deficiency between actual cash balances and desired cash balances. As people reduce their demand for bonds, the price of bonds falls, that is, the interest rate rises. Another way of looking at it is that since the demand for bonds has fallen, the only way people can be induced to hold them is by offering them higher yields, that is, higher interest rates. Hence, when the interest rate is below the equilibrium level, there is an excess demand for money that translates into a decreased demand for bonds; this causes the price of bonds to fall and the interest rate to rise until equilibrium is reached in the economy.

Adding Monetary Policy to the Keynesian Model

The interaction of the demand for money with the supply of money determines the interest rate. Changes in the rate of interest will change the rate of planned investment. In Chapter 15, we drew the planned investment schedule as a downward-sloping curve, with the interest rate on the vertical axis and planned investment on the horizontal axis. Figure 31.3 shows a similar planned investment schedule in panel (b). The lower the rate of interest, the greater the quantity of planned investment.

Panel (a) of Figure 31.3 shows the demand and supply of money. Assume that the equilibrium rate of interest, r_1, is established by the intersection of the money supply schedule M_s and the money demand schedule $M_D M_D$. Remember that the money supply in our simplified model is given by the monetary authorities. At interest rate r_1, we can see in panel (b) that the quantity of planned investment per year will be I_1. This quantity of investment will yield – given the consumption function and government expenditures – the total planned expenditures curve labelled $C + I_1 + G$ in panel (c). It intersects the 45-degree line where total planned expenditures are identically equal to real national income (why?) at real national income per year of Y_1.

Now consider expansionary monetary policy. The Bank of England may increase the flow of base money by buying bonds or bills. If banks increase their lending, there is a rightward movement in the money supply curve from M_s to M'_s in panel (a). The increased money supply creates an excess supply of money. The demand for bonds increases thereby driving up their prices and lowering their yields. The equilibrium rate of interest will fall to r_2, as shown in panel (a), for at this interest rate, the quantity of money demanded and the quantity of money supplied is now back into equality.

But at interest rate r_2 in panel (b), we see that there is an increase in the quantity of planned investment per year. That increase is shown by the horizontal arrow moving from I_1 to I_2.

The investment component of the total planned expenditures curve, $C + I_1 + G$ in panel (c) will now have to move upwards by the full amount of the increase in planned investment. This upward movement is shown by the vertical arrow. The new total planned investment curve becomes $C + I_2 + G$. The equilibrium level of real national income per year will increase from Y_1 to Y_2. Note, as always, this change in the equilibrium level of real national income per year is greater than the change in planned investment. This is because there is a multiplier at work – the investment multiplier.

The effects of a contractionary monetary policy can be shown in a similar way. The money supply schedule would shift to the left, causing the equilibrium rate of interest to rise. This would cause a decrease in total planned expenditures and a decrease in the equilibrium level of real national income per year.

Key Points 31.1

▶ **Money is an asset that is desired because of the services of liquidity that it provides.**

▶ **The opportunity cost of holding money is the interest forgone.**

▶ **The demand for money function, or liquidity preference function, is therefore inversely related to the rate of interest.**

▶ **The alternative to money as an asset is considered here to be other financial assets only, such as bonds.**

▶ **There is an inverse relationship between the prevailing rate of interest in the economy and the market price of old (existing) bonds.**

▶ **The intersection of the demand for money function and the supply of money function generates the equilibrium rate of interest.**

Figure 31.3

Adding Monetary Policy to the Keynesian Model. If the money stock is increased for M_s to M'_s there will be an excess supply of money. Demand for bonds will increase, the interest rate will fall, investment will be stimulated, aggregate expenditure increases and income will rise by an amount determined by the multiplier.

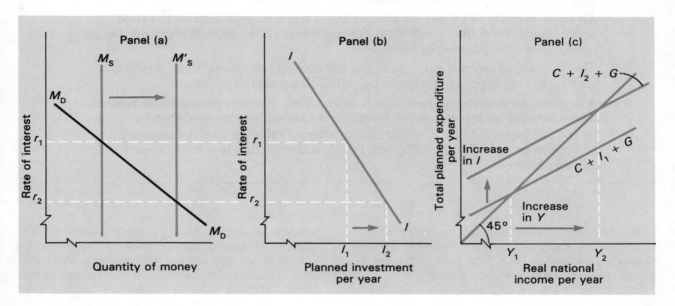

The Keynesian Transmission Mechanism

We are assuming that there is a specific transmission mechanism by which changes in the money supply bring about changes in the equilibrium level of real national income. Specifically, the money transmission mechanism involves changes in the interest rate, which cause a change in investment, which causes a change in income and employment. This transmission mechanism is shown in Figure 31.4.

The overall effect of a change in monetary policy will be somewhat offset by feedback effects. Rising incomes increase the transactions demand for money, shifting the demand for money function rightwards. This will tend to raise interest rates, reversing the original trend, but only by a limited amount.

Alternatives to Keynesian Monetary Theory

The monetary theory presented so far in this chapter is Keynesian in origin. The Keynesian view of monetary theory stresses that the monetary authority (the Bank of England) should target interest rates. When interest rates are changed the demand for funds for investment will change and, hence, total planned expenditures. For many years, monetary theory generally was not held in high regard. Some economists believed that, even though changes in the money supply would affect interest rates, the planned investment schedule was such that the resulting changes in interest rates would have little effect on the quantity of planned investment. In other words, they believed that planned investment was relatively

Figure 31.4

The Keynesian Money Transmission Mechanism

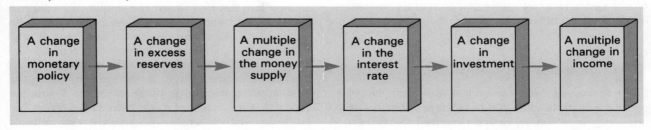

Key Points 31.2

▶ Expansionary monetary policy involves the open-market purchase of government securities, thereby increasing excess reserves and credit creation.

▶ An *excess* quantity of money supplied leads to an attempted shift (at the then prevailing interest rate) away from money in favour of bonds, thereby driving up bond prices and lowering interest rates.

▶ The decrease in interest rates increases the quantity of investment spending, leading to a multiple expansion in output, income, and employment.

▶ A decrease in the money supply leads to an excess quantity of money demanded, which leads to increased sales of bonds, lowering their prices and thereby increasing interest rates. The increase in interest rates reduces the quantity of investment spending, leading to a multiple contraction in output, income, and employment.

---

insensitive, or unresponsive, to interest-rate changes. Consequently, many of their policy recommendations were concentrated on the fiscal side – changes in government spending and/or in taxation.

The view that money *does* matter in influencing the equilibrium level of real national income and the rate of inflation has its origins in the theories which preceded Keynes's work. (The equation of exchange, which relates money to price levels, was outlined in Chapter 19. It shows that *if* the velocity of circulation and the number of transactions are both fairly constant, then price levels will be determined primarily by the stock of money in the economy.) During the 1960s, some economists began again to think that the quantity of money has a major central part to play in the determination of price levels. Professor Milton Friedman at the University of Chicago and others at that time started research on the relationship between changes in the rate of growth of the money supply and changes in macroeconomic variables such as national income and the price level. Not surprisingly, Friedman and his followers took on the name of **monetarists**. The monetarists have stressed the need for monetary policy to be seen in terms of monetary aggregate targets, rather than interest-rate targets. To understand why monetarists have placed so much stress on monetary aggregates, such as M0 or £M3, rather than on interest rates, we must look at an expanded demand-for-money equation that includes more than simply the interest rate. The monetarists have done this by considering money, or cash balances, as only one of a wide range of assets that each of us can hold in our portfolio of wealth.

The Choice among Assets

Given that everyone faces a budget constraint, everyone must decide how to spend on different items. The decision is based on prices and perceived satisfaction

levels from owning or using such different items. The demand for money, or cash balances, can be treated simply as the demand for one particular alternative way of holding one's wealth. People can opt to hold larger cash balances by giving up the purchase of other assets such as bonds, houses, cars, or compact disc players. We acquire cash balances by *not spending* part of our income, that is, by holding part of our income in the bank or in notes and coin.

Modern Monetarist Demand-for-Money Function

The modern monetarist demand-for-money function shows that the demand for money depends on the following:

1. **Nominal income**, because that represents your budget constraint, or how much you have to spend, per time-period, on all items, including liquidity or cash balances.
2. **The rate of return on alternative assets**, such as bonds, that is, the rate of interest on bonds.
3. **The expected rate of inflation**, because as the price level goes up, the purchasing power of the pound goes down. The rate of inflation can be thought of as the rate of depreciation of your cash balances. The faster they depreciate, the more expensive they are to hold.

The modern monetarist view of the demand for money includes more than the simplified Keynesian liquidity-preference function given in this chapter. In other words, it includes more than 'the' interest rate. Additionally, the modern monetarist demand-for-money function includes the rate of return on all alternative assets. So it is inconsistent with the transmission mechanism outlined for the Keynesian model. In the Keynesian model, when households and firms found themselves with an excess quantity of

Milton Friedman
ECONOMIST, FORMERLY OF THE UNIVERSITY OF CHICAGO

The Iconoclast as Institution

Milton Friedman is America's leading conservative economist. A controversial figure, he has seen his views embraced by the libertarian right and dismissed as nonsense by Keynesian liberals; by the left, he has been damned for his opposition to social welfare programmes and for his purported advisory role to the military dictatorship of Chile. For many years an outsider to the Keynesian orthodoxy, Friedman, who won the Nobel Price in 1976 for his monetary theories, has gained so much influence among economists in recent years that he threatens to become a prominent part of the status quo himself.

Friedman's standing among contemporary economists derives primarily from his advocacy of the modern quantity theory of money and prices, of what has come to be known as *monetarism* – the doctrine that the one crucial ingredient shaping short-run economic fluctuations

is change in the amount of money in circulation. The key to a healthy and non-inflationary economy, Friedman has argued persistently over the last three decades, is a constant rate of growth in the money supply. Monetary authorities, Friedman says, instead of tightening money during booms and loosening money during recessions (which is inef-

fective because of the time lags), should simply increase the supply of money at a steady rate of between 3 and 5 per cent per year.

Friedman's work shows quite impressively that, rather than being ineffective, monetary policy *caused* the Great Depression. He pointed out that the money supply was reduced dramatically at the hands of the Fed (the US Central Bank) during that period; that reason, and that reason alone, caused a serious recession to descend into the greatest depression the US has ever had. Friedman, like most monetarists, believes that the macroeconomy is intrinsically stable – if left alone by the prying hand of government.

His philosophy carries over into all areas of government intervention. He has pointed out time and again the unintended, negative effects of government intervention in the economy. His solution to many of society's ills is a more competitive private market-place, rather than increased government regulation, intervention, and spending.

---

money, their only alternative asset was bonds. If the money supply increased, there would be an increased demand for bonds, thus driving up the bond prices and lowering interest rates. So planned investment increased, and there was a multiplier effect on the equilibrium level of real national income.

Modern monetarists do not deny the validity of this indirect transmission mechanism for monetary policy. Rather, they indicate that it is too narrow. Indeed, post-Keynesian economists agree that the traditional simplified Keynesian view of the transmission mechanism is too narrow.

A More Generalized Transmission Mechanism

Money is one asset of a possible range, or portfolio, of assets. If there is an increase in the supply of money, individuals will not simply increase their demand for bonds. Rather, they will increase their demand for bonds, equities, consumer durables, gold, diamonds,

silver, and any other alternative asset. That means that an increase in the money supply, rather than simply increasing the demand for bonds, reducing the interest rate, and thereby increasing planned investment, will increase the demand for a wide variety of assets including consumer and investment goods.

Basically, the increase in the money supply means that the supply of money is greater than the demand for money, and there is a monetary disequilibrium. This excess supply of money causes individuals to attempt to reduce their money balances. In the aggregate, this causes desired expenditures to rise. As in the Keynesian model, this increase in total planned expenditures can initially be satisfied by reducing stocks, but eventually the drop in inventories will cause firms to increase production (or to raise prices). The equilibrium level of national income will increase.

Equilibrium in the aggregate will occur when the demand for money again equals the supply of money. Since the monetarist's demand-for-money function also has income as a component, as national income rises, the demand for money also increases.

Equilibrium is re-established when the demand for money increases sufficiently to equilibrate the supply and demand for money.

So the transmission mechanism that the monetarists use sees an increase in the money suply causing increased spending not just on bonds but on property, equities, and consumer goods. This increased spending causes aggregate demand to increase directly, and it also means that an increase in the money supply will be felt relatively quickly throughout the entire economy. Contrast this transmission mechanism with the simplified Keynesian one, where the increase in the money supply is felt in the bond market and then in the investment market.

The Implications: What Actually Happens?

We have examined two different theories about how money affects the economy. In fact the outcome of a change in the money stock depends crucially on whether *real* income *can* increase. In Chapter 14 we examined the effect of changes in aggregate demand on the price level. We saw that if there were spare capacity in the economy – underutilized labour and capital – then output could increase with little or no increase in the price level. But if the economy is already producing at or near its full capacity output, then increasing demand will lead to rising prices rather than rising output.

In Chapter 16 we examined the Keynesian approach to expansion in the economy. It was pointed out that the simple Keynesian model assumes that output can be expanded, i.e. that the economy is on the horizontal

section of the aggregate supply curve. So a Keynesian view would be that given some unemployed resources, increased spending would lead to increased output and employment.

A crucial factor in the monetarist view of the world is that it sees little scope for such expansion. Generally speaking, unemployment is seen as having its roots in structural problems rather than in the deficiency of aggregate demand. This view suggests that the economy is functioning on the upward-sloping section of the aggregate supply curve. Increasing aggregate demand will lead mainly to rising prices and not, except possibly in the short run, to rising output. In the long run, monetarists believe, output can grow only slowly as the capacity of the economy grows through capital investment and improved technology. The economy will, after a short period of expansion, revert to the level of output associated with the natural rate of unemployment. This is the level of unemployment determined by rigidities in the labour market, such as immobilities and inflexible wages. (This was explained in the discussion of the Phillips Curve in Chapter 18.) Monetary expansion will increase aggregate demand and induce firms to increase output. But at or below the natural rate of unemployment, firms will encounter supply constraints. Efforts to recruit labour with scarce skills, in order to expand, will lead to rising wages as firms try to attract employees. The increased demand will end in rising price levels rather than in increased output.

Of course if unemployment were to be *above* the natural rate at the outset, then resources would be available for at least some increase in output. So the effect of changes in the money stock on the real economy depends on the nature of the unemployed

---

Key Points 31.3

▶ The equation of exchange states that expenditures by one person will equal income receipts by another. In its simplest form, the money supply times velocity (*MV*) equals national income (NNP).

▶ Monetarists are those economists who believe that changes in the rate of growth of the money supply determine, to a large extent, changes in numerous macroeconomic variables such as the equilibrium level of national income and the price level.

▶ A modern monetarist demand-for-money equation includes nominal income, the rate of return on alternative assets (including, but not limited to, bonds), and the expected rate of inflation.

▶ The monetarist transmission mechanism shows that a change in the money supply would change the demand for a variety of assets and thereby be felt as a change in aggregate demand throughout the economy. The simplified Keynesian monetary transmission mechanism has monetary policy directly affecting only the bond market and the investment market.

▶ Increasing the money stock will lead to rising output only if suitable unemployed resources are available within the economy.

work force at the time. In other words, it all depends whether the economy is on the horizontal or the upward sloping section of the aggregate supply curve.

A part of the argument that output will not increase, when the money stock is expanding, involves the permanent income hypothesis (referred to in Chapter 15). Short-run increases in money income will not lead to significant increases in consumption, because consumption depends on expectations about income over the long run rather than the short run. The permanent income hypothesis was developed by Friedman and contrasts with the more short-run view of consumption contained in the Keynesian model.

Whichever theory provides the clearest insights at any particular time, it is clear that the way in which changes in the money stock affect the economy will be much influenced by the availability of underutilized resources and the flexibility of the labour market. If the resources needed to expand output are scarce, then an increase in the money stock will, after a time, lead to a rise in prices.

A Tight Monetary Policy

So far we have been concerned with the effect of an increase in the money stock. What happens if the government imposes a monetary squeeze?

Let us suppose that there is inflation. Rising prices are increasing transactions' demand for money. In Figure 31.5 panel (a), the demand for money function shifts to the right. The government seeks to hold the money stock constant and as a result, interest rates rise. Investment is discouraged (panel (b)) and there is a downward multiplier effect on real income and employment (panel (c)).

This is a Keynesian approach. The monetarist approach, beginning with an excess demand for money, foresees falling demand for a wide range of assets including investment and consumer goods. Irrespective of the approach, it is clear that firms will experience decreased demand for their output, stocks will pile up, and unemployment will rise.

Most frequently, tight monetary policies are introduced in response to inflation. Just how is this very sad fall in output and employment going to reduce the rate at which prices are increasing?

First, the tight monetary policy will reduce any excess demand in the economy. In the simple, aggregate demand – aggregate supply approach developed in Chapter 14, the policy shifts the aggregate demand function to the left, reducing overheating and relieving supply constraints in the economy. But the policy goes beyond this. A component part of inflation is a continuing series of wage increases throughout the economy. As unemployment increases, trade unions become much more wary of negotiating large wage increases. They will do so only if they feel confident that existing employees will not lose their jobs. In 1981–82 inflation fell sharply, partly because many firms were close to bankruptcy. Further wage increases would have brought even more job losses.

Keynesians and monetarists would agree that contractionary policy operates through this effect on output and employment. They would disagree as to how much unemployment is needed to reduce inflation by a given amount.

The Keynesian approach observes that labour markets are not very flexible. Wages seldom fall in real terms. Many people are able to negotiate wage increases, even in hard times, because *their* jobs are not seriously threatened. So output and employment might fall far before expectations of future inflation were much reduced. The experience of 1980–82 when unemployment almost doubled should be considered.

The monetarist approach is more hopeful. It hinges upon the idea of rational expectations, outlined in

Figure 31.5 A Monetary Squeeze

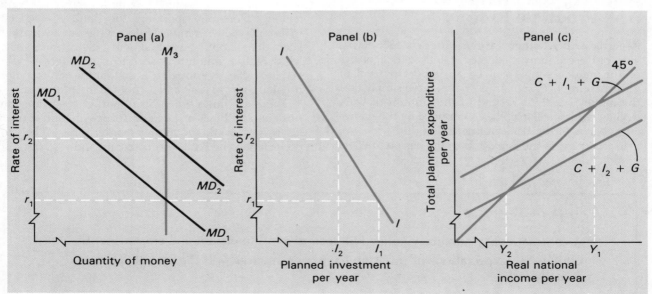

Chapter 18. Its influence can be distinctly heard behind Mrs Thatcher's speeches about firmness in handling the economy. The argument goes like this. If those who negotiate wage bargains (both unions and employers) know from experience that the government intends to control credit creation firmly, then they will know also that employers will not be able to borrow from the banks to pay inflationary wage increases. Faced with a wage increase which it cannot pay, the firm will either contract employment, reducing the number of employees in order to pay more to those remaining, or it will close down altogether. Either way, jobs will be lost. The existence of a declared intention to exert strict monetary control will therefore be sufficient to deter unions from demanding excessive wages.

If unions get the message quickly, then output need not fall very much. Do unions get the message in the UK? The trouble is, not everyone is vulnerable. Consumers will continue to buy many products even if prices rise and incomes fall. Producers of these are not seriously threatened by falling aggregate demand and the employers in these sectors may continue to increase wages and pass on the cost to the consumer.

According to the theory, employers even then need not pay higher wages if there is an adequate supply of unemployed labour willing to work for less. In practice, union-negotiated minimum wage rates and closed shops ensure that the unemployed do not get the chance to work for less. Quite often, existing employees can both retain their jobs and obtain higher wages. The employer cuts the work force by natural wastage – the departure over time of employees who retire or move to other jobs. The penalty then falls upon the young and those made redundant from declining industries who cannot find jobs. Unemployment is much lower among those in their middle years than among the young and the old.

Shifting the Money Supply – The Practical Side

Regardless of whether a Keynesian or a monetarist view of the economy is adopted, it is clear that control of the money supply can be an important tool of government policy. So far, we have stated simply that the money supply is related to the amount of bank lending, which will itself be constrained by the monetary policies of the Bank of England.

In recent years the Bank of England has pursued its monetary policy primarily through controlling interest rates. On a day-to-day basis it intervenes in the money market with 'open-market operations'. If necessary it can change the rate at which it lends to the discount houses. And over the long run, interest rates can be kept from rising by avoiding government borrowing. This last point will be taken up in Chapter 32.

Open-market Operations

The Bank of England sells both short- and long-term government debt, Treasury bills and bonds respectively. When it sells debt the immediate effect is that the buyer pays for it with a cheque drawn on a bank account. In order to make good the payment, that bank will make a transfer from its account with the Bank of England, to the government account. Since the bank's account with the Bank of England is its most liquid reserve asset (other than notes and coin), its reserves have now been reduced. But the bank must still keep adequate reserve assets, so that it may be able to meet customers' requests for withdrawals. The effect of reducing the bank's reserves is to force it to reduce its lending proportionately.

In general, reducing banks' reserves in this way leaves them short of cash. They may have to borrow to make good that day's requests for withdrawals. When they seek to borrow (probably on the inter-bank market), they will be competing for scarce funds and the result will be to drive up interest rates. So the Bank of England, by selling bonds and bills, can exert upward pressure on interest rates.

If, conversely, the Bank of England wants interest rates to fall, it can buy bonds and bills. It will pay for them with cheques drawn on itself. The sellers will deposit these cheques in their bank accounts. Their banks' balances with the Bank of England will increase, giving the banks larger holdings of liquid reserve assets. These can form the basis for increased bank lending. Generally speaking, the Bank of England maintains a level of intervention in the money market such that it both buys and sells bills continuously. Most of the time it will seek to keep interest rates stable: it will buy enough bills, so that the banks do not become short of cash and do not bid up interest rates.

There are times when open-market operations do not give the Bank of England sufficient control over interest rates and the money market. This is likely to occur when the Bank wants to raise interest rates. It

---

Key Points 31.4

▶ **A contractionary monetary policy will lead to a fall in output and employment.**

▶ **Only when expectations of inflation have been reduced will the rate of inflation actually fall.**

can then announce a higher **rate of discount**, or intervention rate. This means that when the Bank of England buys bills it will pay less for them, i.e. charge a higher interest rate: it refuses to discount them at the old rate. This method has been used several times in recent years to steady the market when it has become nervous and unstable. When interest rates are raised in this way, the effect is similar to that of raising minimum lending rate (MLR), before MLR was abolished in 1981. The abolition of MLR and its replacement by an 'undisclosed band' for the interest rates charged by the Bank of England, was intended to make interest-rate changes less dramatic, and to allow more frequent changes.

A tight monetary policy implies that the Bank of England will be seeking to sell as many bonds as possible, and maintaining higher rates of interest. The former acts to reduce the quantity of money *supplied* through credit creation. The latter cuts the quantity of money *demanded* by borrowers.

Monetary Policy in Recent Years

The rapid inflation of the mid-1970s prompted much rethinking of policy. In 1976 the UK found itself with 15 per cent inflation and a massive deficit in the balance of trade, which forced the then Labour government to seek a loan from the IMF. The IMF requires its borrowers to conform to its policy prescriptions. (In fairness, governments are often glad to have an outside body which can be blamed for the necessity of introducing unpopular policies.) In this case the IMF required tighter monetary policy, in effect upgrading its importance as a tool of economic policy. Specifically, monetary targets were introduced for M1 and £M3. These were rolling targets: that is, they were revised every six months and applied to the year ahead. They were part of a package of measures, including fiscal and incomes policies, designed to reduce aggregate monetary demand.

When the Conservatives came to power in 1979, it was their declared intention to control inflation with a much stricter monetary policy. Monetary targets were revised downwards, and interest rates raised. Several different trends became apparent. In spite of tighter monetary policies, £M3 behaved rather badly. It did not begin to grow within its target range until 1982. M1 behaved better until 1982 then grew faster than intended after that. To some extent these divergent growth rates for different measures of the money stock arise from institutional changes, such as the development of different kinds of bank loans, and the increasingly integrated nature of the world banking system. But in the end it was still hard to tell *how* tight monetary policy had been. Whatever the truth of this, the money stock *seemed* to be growing fast, and when we come across inexplicable contradictions it is usually because we are missing a crucial piece of information. In this case, it is the exchange rate. In the two years from the 1979 election, sterling appreciated by more than 20 per cent on average. The reason was twofold. High interest rates in London, relative to other financial centres, attracted capital inflows. This increased the demand for sterling. And the arrival of North Sea oil meant a substantial fall in the supply of sterling as imports of oil were cut. (Also exports of oil developed.) The effect of this appreciation was to make UK output very much less competitive both on foreign markets when exported, and on domestic markets, facing competition from imports. At the same time, because appreciation makes imports cheaper, it was seen as having a very beneficial effect on inflation. Imports form about 30 per cent of total consumer expenditure so their lower prices reduced the growth rate of the RPI for this reason.

Now consider the nature of the exchange rate. It is a price of money in terms of other currencies. A rise in the price of anything normally indicates scarcity. A generally high exchange rate suggests that money is tight, not easy. So some economists, including some of the government's advisers, concluded that from the early 1980s, money was much tighter than the conventional money measures or aggregates, M1 and £M3, suggested.

How did this affect monetary policy? The continued rapid growth of the monetary aggregates has been an embarrassment to the government. The Chancellor's responses have been to stress the importance of paying attention to the full range of money measures rather than just to £M3, as in 1979–80. In addition, the value of an exchange rate target has been considered. When there is a managed float system in operation, the central bank does not disclose its target exchange rate. It just intervenes in the market when the exchange rate floats outside its target range, buying currency when it depreciates and vice versa. Increasingly, it has appeared that the Bank of England has been operating an exchange rate target, at least some of the time. The drawback to controlling the exchange rate as a tool of monetary policy is that the resulting prices of imports and exports are not necessarily those at which domestic producers find it easiest to compete. Further, if interest rates are set at a level which maintains a particular exchange rate, they may be quite high and therefore rather discouraging to potential investors. From 1982 to 1986 real interest rates (i.e. nominal rates minus the rate of inflation) have been exceptionally high. They have undoubtedly kept sterling higher than it would otherwise have been, but at some cost to the economy in terms of forgone borrowing for investment.

The other recent innovation in monetary policy is the introduction of a target range for M0, or the monetary base in 1985. There have been times when M0 was thought to be more closely related to the level of spending than other monetary variables. It replaces M1 as the narrow money target variable.

The emphasis at the time of writing remains upon maintaining a stable exchange rate, through control, mainly, of interest rates, by the methods already described.

The Exchange Rate Changes: the Effect on the Balance of Payments

The exchange rate is subject to both short- and long-run influences. A large payment on either current or capital account (though most often capital) can cause a short-run change. These day-to-day fluctuations, however, are largely ironed out by the Bank of England's management. It intervenes in the foreign exchange market, buying sterling when the rate is falling and vice versa.

Over the medium and long run, trends in market forces may have larger effects which the Bank of England would not try to prevent. Shifting trade patterns result from changes in the international composition of production, as comparative advantages grow and diminish. Capital movements occur as profitable opportunities for investment appear.

If trade patterns shift, the change in the exchange rate acts to restore equilibrium on the balance of payments. Take the case of North Sea oil. As oil became available, less imported oil was needed. The amount of sterling supplied to the foreign exchange market (in order to buy foreign currency) fell. The supply curve of sterling shifted leftwards. The exchange rate appreciated. Figure 31.6 shows this.

What was happening meanwhile to the balance of payments? When less oil was imported, the balance of trade swung into surplus. The subsequent rise in the exchange rate made imports cheaper and exports dearer. Exports (other than of oil and especially of manufactures) fell. Imports rose. The short-term balance-of-trade surplus (disequilibrium), resulting from the reduced oil imports, was eliminated and equilibrium restored.

From time to time a much longer-run trend also is discernible. During this century, the countries which compete with the UK in manufacturing production have grown in numbers and efficiency. For some products – cars and televisions, for example – they have reduced (though not eliminated) the UK's comparative advantage. Over the years, therefore, UK imports have often risen faster than exports. There has been a tendency towards a balance-of-trade deficit.

Figure 31.7 shows that there are shifts in both supply of and demand for sterling. Fewer exports mean reduced demand for sterling to pay for them. More imports mean an increased supply of sterling needed to pay for the foreign currencies to buy the imports. Figure 31.7 shows how the exchange rate depreciates. This depreciation now makes imports dearer and exports cheaper. (Try it: if £1 = $1.50, a £5000 car sells for $7500 in the US. If £1 = $1, the car

Figure 31.6

As less oil was imported, fewer pounds were supplied to the foreign exchange market as less foreign currency was needed. The supply curve of the £ shifted leftwards and the new equilibrium exchange rate was higher.

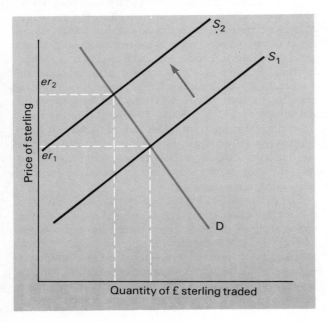

Quantity of £ sterling traded

now sells for $5000: it has become a much better bargain and is more competitive in relation to other countries' cars.) Exports will sell better. There will be fewer imports: the domestic product will be better able to compete on the home market. The balance of trade will improve: the deficit will be gradually eliminated over a period of one to two years.

Figure 31.7

As more imports are demanded the supply of sterling shifts rightwards: at any given exchange rate more sterling will be supplied to pay for foreign currency. As fewer exports are demanded the demand for sterling shifts leftwards. The new equilibrium exchange rate will have depreciated.

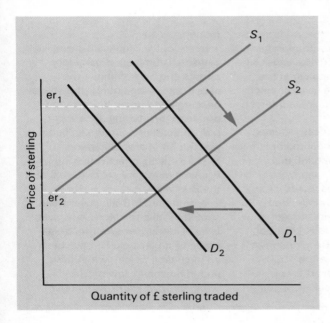

These kinds of exchange rate changes are a response to changes in trade patterns and will serve to prevent long-run balance-of-payments disequilibrium (surplus or deficit). The Bank of England would not, nor could it, prevent market forces from working in this way over the long run. But supposing the exchange rate is responding mainly to capital movements? A major banking and financial centre such as the UK can experience very large capital inflows and outflows. (In recent years capital movements have been the major influence on the sterling exchange rate.) A large capital inflow shifts the demand for sterling to the right. Other things being equal the exchange rate will appreciate. Domestic producers will lose competitiveness; imports will increase and exports decrease. A balance-of-trade deficit will develop. Capital movements can produce an exchange rate at which firms have difficulty in competing. Connect this up with a conclusion we drew just now about monetary policy: a high interest rate, a capital inflow (or less outflow perhaps), a high exchange rate. Tight monetary policy may have its dampening effect on the economy through its influence on the exchange rate. Higher imports mean more leakage. Lower exports mean less injection. The economy will contract.

POSTSCRIPT: ELASTICITIES

When working out the likely effect of an exchange rate change, remember that the exchange rate determines prices of traded goods, and the response to price changes is determined by elasticities. The demand for most UK exports (other than oil) is fairly elastic. Foreigners can go somewhere else on holiday and buy their aircraft engines from Pratt and Whitney instead of Rolls-Royce. UK exports often have good substitutes. So depreciation and improved competitiveness can lead to substantially increased exports of such products, with one proviso. There must be an elastic supply of them. This trend will make them increasingly profitable but if producers actually do not increase output, more cannot be sold. In other words, supply constraints would prevent depreciation from leading to increased production for exports and for home consumption. The chances of output for export increasing are much greater in the long than in the short run.

Looking at imports, the picture is rather different. Where there are good domestic substitutes, i.e. demand is elastic, as with cars, depreciation will encourage falling imports. For products such as iron ore or coffee, demand is rather inelastic because there is no domestic substitute. (Also, for raw materials, they form only a small part of total production costs.) Depreciation will make little difference to the level of imports of raw materials and food products. It will have more effect on imports of manufactures as these compete with UK products.

A PETROCURRENCY

Because 10 per cent of UK exports are now oil, the oil price affects the exchange rate. Rising oil prices strengthen the pound, in the same way as the initial growth of oil output did. Falling oil prices in 1986 led to a lower exchange rate for the pound against most other currencies, and therefore to improved competitiveness for other products.

Key Points 31.6

▶ Exchange rate appreciation will eliminate a balance-of-trade surplus, and vice versa depreciation, a deficit.

▶ Interest-rate changes and capital movements may change the exchange rate and cause balance-of-trade deficit or surplus.

CASE STUDY

Oil, Money, and the Exchange Rate

The pound under pressure, interest rates rising: a government in political trouble can expect no relief from the financial markets. The past month has brought lower oil prices, dearer money and a 15000 increase in unemployment in December, reversing the decline of the previous three months. The economy may still grow by around 2½ per cent this year, with inflation dropping to around 4 per cent. But the government's vote-winning hopes for tax cuts and lower interest rates (i.e. cheaper mortgages) are slipping away.

At one point this week, the Bank of England intervened heavily to stop interest rates rising any further. That steadied the markets for a while, but raised bigger questions about the government's strategy. Last year Mr Lawson dumped his target for sterling M3, the most closely-watched measure of the money supply, saying it had become increasingly misleading. In its place he put an informal exchange rate target, believed to be a range of 78–84 for sterling's trade-weighted index. This week, the pound hit the floor of 78.

The new policy is cruder than the old. The exchange rate has become not just an indicator of monetary conditions, but a weapon to curb inflation directly. A strong pound squeezes companies, which then find it harder to pay big wage increases. But this implies that if

sterling weakens for reasons which have nothing to do with monetary growth and inflation, like lower oil prices or the mishandling of the Westland affair, the government may still be forced to raise interest rates.

If sterling's weakness reflected genuine concern about too much monetary growth and inflation, as was the case a year ago, then higher interest rates would be a good thing. But now inflation is clearly slowing down. Industry's raw material costs fell by 6.1 per cent in the year to December, the biggest decline since the 1950s. Besides, real interest rates of almost 8 per cent look like tight

money, not lax.

Even so, the markets distrust Mr Lawson's dumping of monetary targets and his fudging of the public borrowing figures; they have been demanding an 'uncertainty premium' on sterling. One way to reduce that premium would be to join the European Monetary System (EMS), effectively tying Britain's monetary policy to that of the Bundesbank.

Within the EMS the government should be able to defend any given level of sterling at lower interest rates. Last week would have been an ideal time to join, when the pound touched a low of DM3.50 – a rate with which British industry

Figure 31.8
Oil prices, sterling, and real interest rates.

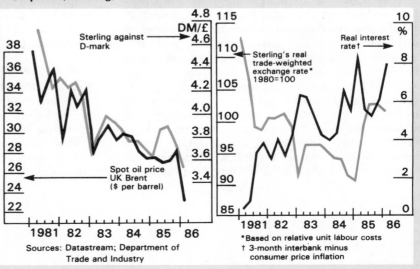

Sources: Datastream; Department of Trade and Industry

*Based on relative unit labour costs
† 3-month interbank minus consumer price inflation

would probably be happy. Watch out for another window in the spring, when the seasonal drop in oil demand could send jitters through the currency markets.

What price sterling?

To the extent that sterling's slide reflects cheaper oil rather than loose money, it needs a different response. A lower oil price both justifies and requires a lower pound. Cheaper oil will offset the inflationary impact of sterling's depreciation. As a rule of thumb, a 10 per cent fall in the oil price at the same time as a 3–4 per cent decline in sterling would be broadly neutral for the retail price index. More important, a drop in the oil price reduces Britain's trade surplus in oil. To compensate, the non-oil deficit must decline – and the surest way for that to happen is through a fall in sterling's real exchange rate. The best route would be via a slower rise in

Britain's unit labour costs compared with those of its trading partners; the more likely way would be a fall in the nominal exchange rate.

Oil prices have fallen by 18 per cent since January 1985, yet sterling's real effective exchange rate has appreciated by 14 per cent. Manufacturers are already feeling the loss of competitiveness. Britain's imports of manufactures are likely to rise at least twice as fast as exports in 1986, and many economists expect the current account to swing into deficit next year. This is worrying for an economy with a £7-billion-a-year oil surplus that is expected to disappear during the next decade.

Sterling's rate against the D-mark (West Germany being an oil importer) has almost always tracked the spot oil price fairly well (see Fig. 31.8). The exceptions have occurred when British interest rates have risen sharply, as in late 1981 and early 1985.

If the government really believes in floating exchange rates, it should accept that the pound can float down as well as up: in which case, lower oil prices are the best reason for letting the pound slide. But if the Treasury prefers the pound to be stable, it should pop it in the EMS and get the market's confidence at lower rates of interest. At the moment, the government is choosing neither of these options – and thus getting the worst of both worlds.

Source: The Economist, 18 Jan. 1986, p. 23

Questions
1. How do oil prices affect the exchange rate?
2. What problems arise from maintaining an exchange rate target when oil prices are falling?
3. How have events since this article appeared changed the situation.

Exam Preparation and Practice

INTRODUCTORY EXERCISES

1. (a) Assume that a bond promises to the holder £1 000 per year forever. If the interest rate is 10 per cent, what is the bond worth now?
   (b) Continue (a) above: what happens to the value of the bond if interest rates rise to 20 per cent? Fall to 5 per cent?
   (c) Suppose there were an indestructible machine expected to generate £2 000 per year in revenues but costing £1 000 per year to maintain – forever. How would that machine be priced relative to the bond described above in (a)?

2. Assume that M = £300 billion, P = £1.72, and Q = 900 billion units. What is the velocity of circulation?

MULTIPLE CHOICE QUESTIONS

1. A rise in the market price of fixed interest securities is an indication that
   A the supply of money has decreased
   B the market rate of interest has fallen
   C the market rate of interest has risen
   D liquidity preference has increased
   E a more restrictive credit policy has been introduced.

†2. All of the following measures would tend to reduce the rate of increase of the money supply EXCEPT
   A an increase in the rate of interest on gilts
   B an increase in the value of Premium Bond prizes
   C a reduction in the Public Sector Borrowing Requirement
   D the sale of long term government bonds to the banking sector
   E the sale of Treasury bills to the discount houses

continued overleaf

†3. If undated government bonds originally sold for £1000 with a nominal interest rate of 3%, and their price has since fallen to £200, their yield is now
   A   3%
   B   9%
   C   15%
   D   18%
   E   25%

†4. Other things being equal, an upward shift in the liquidity preference schedule will tend to drive up interest rates *unless*
   A   there is considerable unemployment
   B   the supply of money increases
   C   retail prices are strictly controlled
   D   the Bank of England increases Special Deposits
   E   wages are prevented from rising

For Questions 5 and 6 select your answers from the following grid:

A	B	C	D	E
1, 2, 3 all correct	**1, 2** only correct	**2, 3** only correct	**1** only correct	**3** only correct

†5. Which of the following motives affect(s) the demand for money which J. M. Keynes termed 'liquidity preference'?
   1   transactions motive
   2   precautionary motive
   3   speculative motive

†6. If a government wished to impose a 'tight' monetary policy, the Treasury might advise the Bank of England to
   1   raise its short term interest rate
   2   call for Special Deposits
   3   increase its purchases of gilt-edged securities on the open market

RELATED ESSAY QUESTIONS

1. 'Monetarism in the UK has been a signal failure.' Would you agree?

2. (a) Distinguish between the money market and the long-term capital market.
   (b) Describe and explain the influence of the Bank of England in each of these markets.

3. What factors determine the general level of interest rates?

4. What methods are used to control the money supply? How successful have they been?

5. What methods may governments use to influence the *demand* for money?

6. Outline the main differences between monetarist and Keynesian views on what determines the supply of money. Explain why the money supply plays a prominent part in economic policy.

32 Fiscal Policy

Key Points to Review

▶ The objectives of government policy (10.4)

▶ Government expenditure (10.5)

▶ Taxation (10.6)

▶ Fiscal policy in the Keynesian model (17.1 and 17.2)

Questions for Preview

1 What are the objectives of fiscal policy?

2 How are taxes levied?

3 What is the PSBR and why does it vary over time?

4 How does fiscal policy affect interest rates and expenditure in the economy as a whole?

5 How does fiscal policy interact with monetary policy?

6 What effect do contractionary policies have on the economy?

Fiscal policy means the use of taxation and expenditure to achieve political ends. These ends are many and varied. A range of them was identified in Chapter 10. One of these – the achievement of economic objectives and stability – can be further broken down into three categories. These are influencing the allocation of resources, redistributing income and wealth, and macroeconomic control of the economy.

The government influences *the allocation of resources* directly through the nationalized industries. It also has a substantial effect on the allocation of resources towards consumption, investment, and exports. It achieves this partly through the operation of the tax system: taxes reduce disposable income and therefore personal consumption. This may affect both the pattern and the level of investment. Further, discriminatory taxes on firms affect the profitability, and therefore the level, of investment. Also, because fiscal policy affects aggregate demand, it influences the levels of imports and, indirectly, of exports.

Both taxation and expenditure can be used to *redistribute income and wealth*. Objectives concerning distribution are at the heart of many of the frequent changes, year by year, in fiscal policy.

In seeking to *control the economy*, the government will try to promote economic growth, stable prices, low levels of unemployment and will try to avoid balance-of-trade deficits. It will usually be difficult to achieve all these at once but governments act according to their priorities at any given time.

Expansionary fiscal policies will promote economic growth and high levels of employment. They may lead to inflation accelerating. They may well lead to increases in imports. Further, the buoyant home market may deter firms from exporting, which demands more effort than home sales. So expansion may produce an external deficit. Contractionary policies reduce inflation, but also growth and employment. However, imports will fall, and firms will turn to export markets to maintain sales. So the balance of trade will improve, and a current account surplus may develop.

Raising Revenue – Taxation

Tax revenues are needed for a range of purposes. They must, first, raise revenue simply to finance expenditure. But they may also be used to redistribute income and wealth, to affect consumption patterns, and importantly to influence the level of aggregate demand. Obviously taxes which raise substantial revenue will also be effective in reducing aggregate demand.

Each tax has its own role to play in meeting government objectives. The composition of tax revenue has important effects on the economy. Figure 32.1 shows the relative contribution of each kind of tax to total tax revenue.

Figure 32.1
UK Tax Revenue 1985

	Revenue (£bn)	% of total revenue
Direct taxes		
Income tax	35.4	26.9
Corporation tax	9.1	6.9
National Insurance	24.1	18.3
Total direct	68.6	52.1
Property taxes		
Rates	13.6	10.3
Inheritance tax	0.8	0.6
Capital transfer tax	0.05	–
Stamp duty	1.2	0.95
Capital gains tax	1.2	0.95
Total property	16.85	12.8
Expenditure taxes		
Excise taxes (alcohol, tobacco, betting, petrol)	16.5	12.6
VAT	21.0	15.9
Customs duties etc.	1.3	1.0
Total expenditure	38.7	29.5
Revenue from North Sea oil	7.4	5.6
Total	131.55	100.0

Source: UK National Accounts, 1986.

Direct taxes

These are levied directly on incomes and profits. **Income tax** is progressive in two respects. The personal allowances are tax free. Subsequent income is taxed at the standard rate of 29 per cent, up to a limit of £17 200. Beyond that, additional tax is payable at marginal rates rising from 40 to 60 per cent, rising by 5 per cent for each of the higher-rate bands of income. So tax as a proportion of income rises as income rises. Income tax applies not only to wages and salaries but also to unearned income from interest, profits, and rent. It is therefore important as a revenue raiser, as a means of redistributing income, and as a means of reducing aggregate demand. In particular, income tax has an important part to play in stabilization policy. It is the progressive nature of income tax which makes it effective as an automatic stabilizer, reducing demand when incomes are high and may exceed output, and increasing demand when incomes are low and unemployment is an increasing problem.

Corporation tax is levied on firms' profits at a rate of 35 per cent; generally it contributes only a small amount to total tax revenue. In the past it was levied with allowances for investment so as to subsidize capital investment. This is probably not advisable at a time of high unemployment and the present arrangements no longer encourage investments with low rates of return.

National Insurance charges (NIC) include both the employers' and employees' contributions. Up to an income level of £14 800 contributions rise with income. (Very low incomes are exempt.) Above that level, contributions are constant. The employees' contributions are not unlike an income tax although they are less progressive. It should be remembered that an increase in income will be subject to both increased tax and increased NIC. So the marginal rate of taxation at some income levels is about 39 per cent. The employer's contribution, by contrast, is in effect a payroll tax. It raises the cost of employing labour. Recent changes in the rates at which it is levied attempt to modify its impact so that employers are encouraged to take on more low-paid labour and reduce unemployment. The main function of NICs is to raise revenue for the payment of benefits.

Property Taxes

Rates contribute substantially to local authority revenue. (The other major component is the Rate Support Grant paid by central government.) Since they are levied on property, their impact on individuals varies according to circumstance. This, and the fact that they are levied on commercial property and create a substantial business cost, has made them unpopular. The proposed replacement – a poll tax on adults – would probably be very regressive in its impact.

Inheritance tax will continue to be levied on the estates of the deceased. **Capital transfer tax** – which was levied on gifts made during a person's lifetime – was abolished in the 1986 budget. It had led to problems in keeping businesses intact over time. This does mean that gifts are once again a means of avoiding death duties. These taxes are (or were) aimed at redistributing wealth by reducing the amount of wealth concentrated in the hands of a few individuals.

Capital gains tax is levied on the increase in the value of property. This means that owners of shares which show substantial capital growth must pay tax on the capital gain when they come to sell the shares.

Expenditure Taxes

Excise taxes are generally levied at a flat rate – so many pence per item. **Value added tax (VAT)**, in contrast, rates 15 per cent of value added at each stage of production. The value added is the revenue from sales minus the cost of inputs other than land, labour, and capital. It is the value added *by* the factors of production.

In principle, expenditure taxes tend to be more regressive than income taxes. They are seen mainly as revenue raisers. They also serve to reduce consumption of harmful goods such as tobacco and alcohol, and of goods which are potentially scarce in the long run, such as petrol. In practice, because VAT is not levied on food for home consumption, fuel, housing, public transport and printed matter, it is not very regressive in its impact.

North Sea Oil Revenue

This includes petroleum revenue tax (PRT), royalties, and licence fees. Falling oil prices have reduced these revenues although some of this reduction can be claimed back if the excise duty on petrol is raised.

The Composition of Tax Revenue

The balance between direct and indirect taxation can be varied to suit circumstances. While income tax must always be the most effective tax for redistributive purposes, it is evaded (illegally) and avoided (legally) in a number of ways, thus losing some of its usefulness. Also it *may* have some disincentive effects although the evidence on this is not at all conclusive. (Except, that is, at levels of income where the poverty trap is a factor. If people simultaneously enter the tax bracket and lose means-tested benefits their effective marginal rate of tax may, in total, be very high indeed.) Expenditure taxes tend to be more regressive because poorer individuals spend a higher proportion of their incomes than do richer individuals. They can be expensive to collect, but are harder to avoid than direct taxes.

During the seventies, with VAT at 8 per cent, the UK was deriving more revenue than now from direct taxes. Other European countries relied more heavily on indirect taxes. The Conservative government shifted the balance markedly in 1979, reducing income taxes and raising VAT. It had many reasons, giving as the primary reason improving the incentive to work. The reduced income redistribution which resulted from the change was in line with Conservative political philosophy of encouraging people to take care of themselves.

If tax evasion and avoidance become more of a problem a further shift towards expenditure taxes might be considered advisable.

Raising Revenue — Borrowing

To the extent that government expenditure exceeds revenue, there must be borrowing. The annual amount needed to cover the difference between spending and tax revenue is the **Public sector borrowing requirement (PSBR)**. The accumulated past debt – the sum total of all government debt outstanding – is the **National Debt**. Borrowing may be financed by selling Treasury bills (for short-term borrowing, or bonds (for long-term borrowing).

Governments no longer try to balance their budgets. They expect to be in deficit if only because they will always be borrowing to finance some capital investment in projects which will generate income in the future. How *much* they borrow will, however, depend on two factors. One is the state of the trade cycle, the other, politicians' views about interest rates.

The Trade Cycle

Automatic stabilizers will reduce the size of the budget deficit as incomes grow, tax revenues rise, and benefits payable to the unemployed fall. In a slump the reverse will be true. Discretionary fiscal policy can be used similarly: taxes can be reduced and government expenditure increased if there are resources in the economy which are unemployed because of a deficiency of demand. Thus we would expect that, other things being equal, PSBR would grow if incomes were falling or stagnating and diminish if incomes are rising.

Key Points 32.1

▶ Taxation is used to raise revenue, to redistribute income and wealth, and to control the level of aggregate demand.

▶ Taxes may be levied by indirect and direct methods and the balance between the two can be varied according to circumstances.

▶ In 1979 there was a shift towards greater emphasis on expenditure taxes in the UK.

Interest Rates

To finance the PSBR the Bank of England will want to sell government bonds. To induce the public to buy them, attractive interest rates must be paid. The government can obtain finance relatively cheaply because it can guarantee repayment, based on its right to tax. (Bonds are often known as gilts – they are as good as gold.) But the more finance it needs, the higher the rate of interest on bonds must be.

The government is always a large borrower. It competes for funds in the money markets with private borrowers contemplating investment projects. Private investment must bring in a rate of return in excess of that of government bonds, otherwise it would not be worth the risks involved. Governments never want to discourage investment. An urge to keep interest rates down for this reason can cause governments to cut PSBR.

How Big is PSBR?

We can examine PSBR in money terms, or as a percentage of GDP. Figure 32.2 shows that PSBR has been falling over time, relative to GDP. The government has achieved its objective, so stated, even though the economy endured its worst post-war slump in 1980–1, and despite the need to spend very large amounts on benefits for the unemployed.

Figure 32.2
PSBR

Sources: CSO *Blue Book*, 1985, *Financial Times*, 19 Mar. 86.

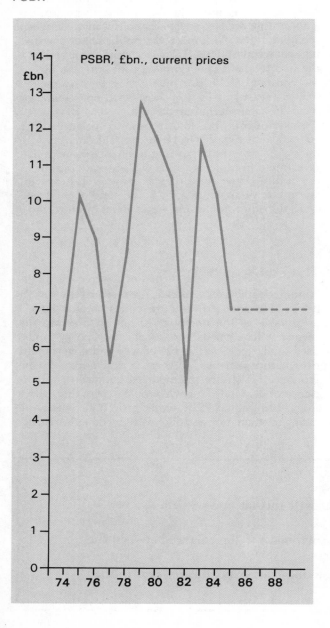

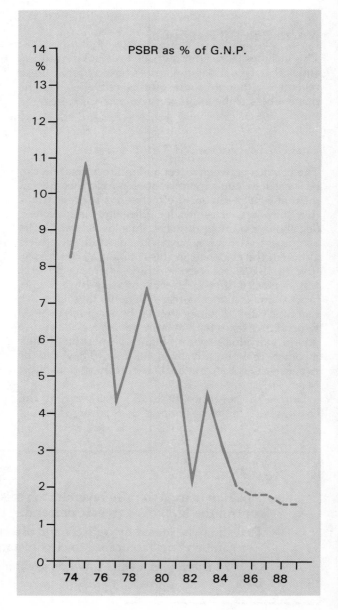

> ## Key Points 32.2
>
> ▶ The PSBR covers the government's deficit. It is the amount which the government must borrow in any given year to cover the difference between expenditure and tax revenue.
>
> ▶ PSBR will tend to rise in a recession and fall in a boom because of automatic stabilizers; discretionary policy may also be used in the same way.
>
> ▶ A large PSBR may require higher interest rates.
>
> ▶ PSBR has fallen in real terms in recent years but this is partly because of privatization and North Sea oil revenues.

Two things have helped in this. One is North Sea oil revenues. The other is privatization. The new private sector owners of those nationalized industries which have been privatized have paid the government substantial sums which have reduced PSBR correspondingly. In November 1985 the Chancellor announced planned asset sales of £4.75 billion in each of the next three years. In addition council house sales could be expected to raise a further £1.7 billion a year. Careful observers of the political scene will have noticed that the PSBR often diverges from the government's planned level. Partly, this is because it is a small difference between two very large numbers; partly also it is because some items of expenditure are hard to control, e.g. spending on unemployment benefits which must rise as the level of unemployment rises.

A Recent Debate: Crowding Out

It is in this context that we turn to the crowding-out issue. If there is a limited supply of credit, and the government offers higher interest rates, it will be able to borrow more. On the other hand, private sector demanders of credit may respond to higher interest rates by demanding a smaller quantity of credit. Then higher interest rates ultimately result in the government obtaining a greater amount of the total credit supplied than previously. Hence the government borrowing has 'crowded out' private borrowing. The reduced growth rate of private investment leads, via

the multiplier, to a reduced growth in income, output, and employment. Offsetting this is a *greater* growth of government spending and, via the multiplier, an increased growth in output, income, and employment. The net effect is to *reduce* the expansionary effect of any government spending. The crowding-out effect is shown in Figure 32.3

Awareness of the crowding-out effect dates back to Adam Smith. Keynes was also concerned with crowding out, as we see in his *General Theory of Employment, Interest and Money*.

If, for example, a Government employs 100000 additional men on public works, and if the multiplier ... is 4, it is not safe to assume that aggregate employment will increase by 400000. For the new policy may have *adverse reactions on investment* in other directions ... The method of financing the policy and the increased working cash, required by the increased employment and the associated rise of prices, may have the effect of increasing the rate of interest and so *retarding investment in other directions*.

It should be pointed out that increased government borrowing does not always require higher interest rates. Increased government spending may occur at a time when private investment is low anyway, because of gloomy business expectations. The evidence that crowding out actually happens is rather scanty.

An Older Debate: Is the National Debt a Burden?

It is true that the National Debt has grown continuously for many years. However, the total National

Figure 32.3 Crowding Out

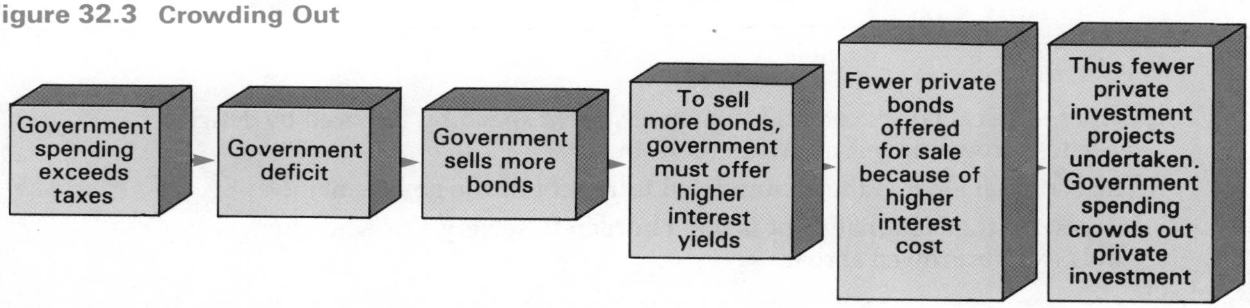

Debt is not what we should look at to analyse the burden of the debt. Figure 32.4 shows that in relation to GDP the National Debt has been falling steadily. One reason for this is that the government borrows in money terms. If it sells a bond it borrows, say, £100. If the bond matures twenty years later, the holder is still repaid £100. But by then inflation has reduced the real value of the repayment to very much less. As a borrower the government gains from inflation. The lenders lose.

Figure 32.4

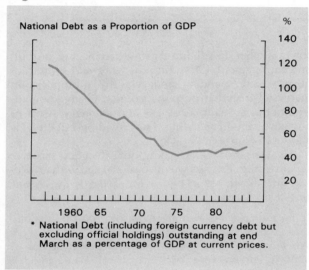

National Debt as a Proportion of GDP

* National Debt (including foreign currency debt but excluding official holdings) outstanding at end March as a percentage of GDP at current prices.

Source: BEQB, Dec. 1984.

It could be argued, however, that the burden consists not of outstanding debt so much as of interest payments. Figure 32.5 shows that although PSBR has been falling, the interest burden is roughly constant. This must reflect the high interest rates prevailing during the 1980s. Again inflation helps to explain. Monetary policy has kept interest rates high; also lenders expect to be compensated for the loss of real value of their loans by better interest rates. In real and nominal terms, interest rates in the 1980s are historically very high.

Figure 32.5
Debt Interest as a Percentage of Total Government Expenditure

1977	10.2
1978	9.8
1979	10.2
1980	10.5
1981	10.9
1982	10.9
1983	10.3
1984	10.7

Source: CSO BLue Book, 1985.

It is possible that more borrowing in the future could increase the interest burden. It should be remembered that this would not be a *national* burden, however. It involves transfer payments from one group of people (taxpayers) to another (holders of government bonds). If on the other hand bonds are sold abroad, then interest payments are made to foreigners, and are an outflow of funds on the invisibles account of the balance of payments. Whether or not increased borrowing makes sense depends partly, therefore, on what sort of spending it will finance. If it is spent on investment it should yield an income in the future which will cover the interest and repayment of the debt. The investment could be in plant and machinery, or in infrastructure – roads, say, – or in education, which is investment in human capital and makes people more productive.

Is Fiscal Policy Effective?

Chapter 17 showed how Keynesian fiscal policies developed. Until the late 1960s, counter-cyclical fiscal policies were quite successful in stabilizing economies. Then unemployment began to rise. The standard Keynesian response would have been to increase aggregate demand by increasing government spending, reducing taxes, and perhaps using expansionary monetary policies as well.

But from the start of the 1970s inflation began to accelerate and remained a major threat. In these circumstances expansionary fiscal policy can lead to accelerating inflation rather than increased output and

---

Key Points 32.3

▶ Critics of fiscal policy contend that government spending financed by deficits leads to a crowding out of private investment.

▶ The National Debt is the accumulated total debt of the government.

▶ Interest on the National Debt is not a burden to society as a whole unless the funds were borrowed abroad.

employment. The crucial question is whether there is underutilized capacity in the economy or whether supply constrains will prevent output from growing further. If there is spare capacity then the unemployment is at least partly due to demand deficiency and expansionary policies may be effective. The implication is that the economy is operating on the horizontal section of the aggregate supply curve. If there is no spare capacity, then the unemployment is rooted in structural problems and immobilities, and will not be reduced by increased aggregate demand: the economy is on the upward-sloping or vertical section of the aggregate supply curve.

While not denying that unemployment can be structural in origin, Keynesians would still see a role for fiscal policy in maintaining a stable economy with good growth prospects and high levels of employment. Expansionary policy would reduce any unemployment caused by the deficiency of aggregate demand rather than by structural problems. This is known as counter-cyclical policy.

Monetarists have drawn different conclusions. They have observed that governments have had some difficulty in forecasting changes accurately and therefore in producing the right amount of change in aggregate demand. They see cyclical unemployment as transient and short-term in nature. Unemployment they see as originating in structural problems or in insufficient incentives. This means that output *cannot* increase rapidly to meet increased aggregate demand and that fiscal expansion will therefore lead to accelerating inflation. So the monetarist policy prescription is the **fixed throttle**: aggregate monetary demand should be allowed to grow at the same rate as productive capacity. So demand would grow exactly in line with the long-run trend in output. Alongside these views on fiscal policy, monetarists hold that control of inflation makes restrictive monetary policy essential. The net effect of this is to downgrade the importance of fiscal policy: it becomes an important buttress to the prevailing monetary policy. It is not used in its own right but as part of an overall package.

This approach calls for unemployment to be dealt with by means of microeconomic measures rather than by expanding aggregate demand. These policies seek to make labour more mobile, to improve information, and to increase generally the efficiency with which the labour market functions. These policies are examined in Chapter 33.

A Policy Package: the Interaction of Fiscal and Monetary Policy

We have already seen that the size of the PSBR may have some effect on interest rates. Financing the PSBR affects monetary growth in other ways also. To see this we must examine the ways in which the PSBR is funded.

Government Borrowing: the Options

We have identified two ways of financing PSBR: the sale of bonds and bills. **Treasury bills** raise finance for three months. They can be used to make good the weekly shortfall between spending and revenue. They are very liquid reserve assets to the banks which are the main providers of bill finance. **Bonds** raise long-term funds from a wide range of sources such as individuals, and from financial institutions such as pension funds. There are two other sources of finance. A major source is **National Savings** (non-marketable debt). For the government, this is very favourable because it pays relatively low interest rates and the funds are cheap and reliable. For savers, funds kept in National Savings are very liquid and convenient. A fourth source of finance is the Bank of England. By itself holding bonds, the Bank can create credit. One way in which it may do this is by **expanding the note issue**. It holds bonds as backing for the note issue. (Where notes are the *liabilities* of the Bank of England, bonds are the corresponding *assets*.) The Bank of England may hold more bonds, making a loan to the government which it then spends. The note issue is increased, the recipients of the government spending place the funds in their bank accounts, and banks' balances with the Bank of England rise. This is base, or high-powered, money and will allow banks to create extra credit by a multiple of the original increase in their liquid reserves.

So increasing government borrowing by this method would lead to expansion of the money stock through credit creation. What of the other sources of finance? The sale of Treasury bills has a similar effect. A Treasury bill bought by a bank gives the government funds to spend. The recipients deposit those funds in their banks. The bank has less cash, but still has the bill, which is a very liquid asset. Overall its reserve asset position is unchanged except that it now has, in addition, the increased deposits resulting from the government's spending. So it can create more credit. Borrowing from the Bank of England, and increasing the issue of Treasury bills, are together known as monetary finance.

The other forms of government borrowing have a very different effect. National Savings involve a straight transfer to the government from the small saver. No banks, and no credit creation, are involved. Bonds sold to people, and institutions other than banks, similarly involve no credit creation. (Remember open-market operations? The sale of bonds reduces banks' balances with the Bank of England. But in this case, the increased government spending will lead recipients to deposit an equal amount with their banks, so there is no change at all in the banks' reserve asset position.)

In conclusion, a government with a tight monetary policy will finance the PSBR either from National Savings or bond sales. The former tend to stay fairly constant over time so any increase in PSBR means more bonds must be sold. If this means raising interest rates, governments will want to avoid increasing PSBR.

Figure 32.6 shows how the National Debt is made up. Since 1976 the use of Treasury bills has diminished substantially. Borrowing from the Bank of England has generally been limited too.

Figure 32.6
Composition of the Sterling National Debt*

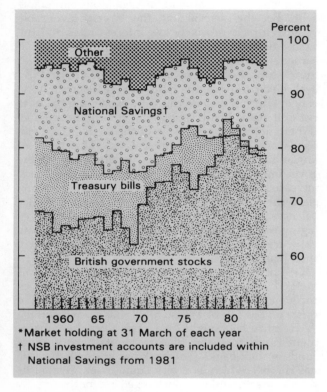

1960   65   70   75   80
*Market holding at 31 March of each year
† NSB investment accounts are included within National Savings from 1981

Source: BEQB, Dec. 1984.

If PSBR must be carefully controlled to make it consistent with monetary policy then there is not much scope for varying fiscal policy to stabilize the economy.

How Have Contractionary Policies Worked?

When fiscal and monetary policies reduce aggregate monetary demand they cut the demand for many firms' products. These firms will begin to make losses. They may contract, making some of their work-force redundant, or they may close, reducing employment still further. If they face rising costs of production they will be unable to pass them on in the form of higher prices, because if they did sales would fall further.

In this situation, with unemployment rising, demands for higher wages will be somewhat reduced. Trade unions will know that higher wages will create more losses and thus contract the number of jobs further. Wage settlements will be gradually reduced. In theory the knowledge that tight fiscal and monetary policies will be introduced and adhered to could induce unions to accept lower wage settlements. In practice unions must advance the interests of their working members, and unemployment may rise substantially before they are pressured into accepting less. So while contractionary policy does reduce inflation, it may do so at quite a high cost in terms of lost output and employment. Also, inflation may have responded favourably to other influences, such as falling commodity or oil prices. This seems to have been a major factor in keeping inflation low during 1986.

Possible alternatives might involve reducing interest rates, and letting the exchange rate depreciate. Both these would help to increase output and perhaps employment. But they might involve a little more inflation.

Key Points 32.4

▶ Keynesians see fiscal policy as having a role to play in reducing unemployment and promoting growth.

▶ Monetarists see fiscal policy as subordinate to monetary policy.

▶ Monetarist policy advocates a 'fixed throttle', a fixed rate of growth of aggregate monetary demand in line with the long-run growth of output.

▶ Government borrowing can be financed with or without affecting the money stock.

▶ Financing the PSBR without increasing the money stock means selling bonds, which may require increased interest rates.

▶ Tight fiscal and monetary policies can reduce inflation but the loss of output and employment may be substantial.

CASE STUDY

Are Our Income Taxes High?

Figure 32.7

Income Tax. The share of earnings docked for tax shows the burden of income taxes, but not their effect on incentives. For that, the marginal tax rate – the amount charged on any rise in income – is a better guide. By either standard, Danes are squeezed: a single person with average earnings pays 46 per cent of them to the taxman, and 63 per cent of any extra goes the same way. West Germans on an average income pay a marginal rate of 59 per cent if single; it drops to 36 per cent for families. For average earners, there is little to choose between America and Britain. Families pay 17 per cent overall in both countries; while America's marginal rates are lower for families, they are higher for single taxpayers.

Questions

1. What is the difference between the proportion of income taken in tax, and the marginal tax rate?
2. Why are marginal rates of tax higher than average rates?
3. How heavily are UK people taxed, relative to other countries?

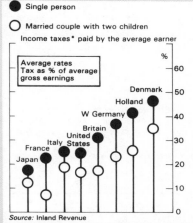
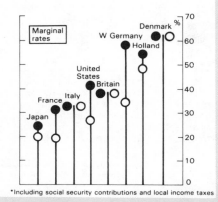

Source: Inland Revenue

*Including social security contributions and local income taxes

Source: The Economist, 25 Jan. 1986.

CASE STUDY

The Medium-term Financial Strategy

The MTFS embodies the government's targets for the money stock and the PSBR. The following quotes from the Chancellor's statement on budget day, 1986, explain the strategy.

'The Medium Term Financial Strategy provides the framework for economic policy, as it has since 1980. It is intended to bring inflation down further over a period of years, and ultimately to achieve price stability. It is complemented by policies which encourage enterprise, efficiency, and flexibility, thus promoting the growth of output and the creation of jobs.

Economic policy is set in a nominal framework in which public expenditure is controlled in cash terms and money GDP growth is gradually reduced by monetary and fiscal policy. As the growth of money GDP declines, inflation is squeezed out, and the division of money GDP growth between output growth and inflation is improved.

Over the past six years, money

continued overleaf

GDP growth has declined from nearly 20 per cent to around 9 per cent. Inflation has come down to around 5 per cent and is set to fall further. And the economy is about to embark on its sixth successive year of growth. For the first time since the 1960s, steady growth is now being combined with low inflation.

If the underlying growth of M0 or £M3 were to move significantly outside their target ranges, the government would take action on interest rates unless other indicators suggested clearly that monetary conditions remained satisfactory.

Experience has shown that a change in short-term rates is unlikely to alter the growth of £M3 significantly within the target period. But such action clearly affects the tightness of monetary conditions, which is what matters, and this would be likely to show up in the behaviour of M0 and the exchange rate.

Public expenditure

Continued restraint in public spending plays a vital role in the government's economic strategy. The cash planning totals set by the government in the White Paper are designed to hold total spending broadly level in real terms.

Conclusion

Events both at home and abroad may modify some of the assumptions on which the projections have been based. But the government is committed to maintaining the progress to lower inflation in the medium term, secured by appropriate financial policies.'

Questions

1. What is the MTFS? How will it reduce inflation and promote growth?
2. What problems have arisen in implementing the MTFS?

Figure 32.8
Growth of Money Supply and Money GDP

	1985–6	1986–7	1987–8	1988–9	1989–90
Money GDP*	9½ (8¼)	6¾	6½	6	5½
M0†	3½	2–6	2–6	1–5	1–5
£M3†	14¾	11–15			

*Per cent change on previous financial year. See table below for assumptions on output and inflation. The figure in parentheses is adjusted for the coal strike. The figure for 1986–7 is a forecast; and in subsequent years the figures describe the government's broad medium-term objective.
†1985–6: percentage change from mid-February to mid-February, 1986–7: target ranges. 1987–8 onwards: illustrative ranges for M0.

Figure 32.9
Public Sector Borrowing*

	1984–5	1985–6	1986–7	1987–8	1988–9	£bn, cash 1989–90
General government expenditure	150.0	158	163	170	175	180
General government receipts	140.9	150	156	164	174	182
Fiscal adjustment from previous years†	–	–	–	–	2	6
Annual fiscal adjustment†	–	–	–	2	4	3
CGBR (Central Govt. Borrowing Requirement)	9.1	8	7	8	7	7
Public corporations market and overseas borrowing	1.0	–1	–	–1	–	–
PSBR	10.1	7	7	7	7	7
Money GDP at market prices	327*	358	382	407	431	455
PSBR as per cent of GDP	3.1	2	1¾	1¾	1½	1½

*Rounded to the nearest £bn from 1985–6 onwards.
†Means lower taxes or higher expenditure than is assumed in lines 1 and 2.

Source: Financial Times, 19 Mar. 1986.

CASE STUDY

Why is Public Expenditure so Hard to Control?

Over the last six years (1978/79 to 1983/84 inclusive) public expenditure has overshot the one-year cash forecasts released at the time of the Budget by an average of £1.8bn p.a. For 1983/84 the figure worked out at £2.5bn. This year the position looks equally unhealthy: the current indications are that public expenditure will overshoot by around £3½ billion. .

Since this expenditure is unaffected by the miners' strike and (with the exception of social security, which appears to be running in line with plans) is cash-limited it has to be concluded that the control of expenditure is as bad as ever. Undoubtedly this is a product of the unrealistic 3% cash limit on pay and overshoots in many of the programmes with heavy subsidy payments.

Just why does the cash planning mechanism fail each year? One answer is that only 40% of expenditure is subject to cash limits and that even some of this (defence, law and order) has a sarcrosanct volume component which tends to have an inbuilt overshoot through inflation. A further answer, however, is summarised in Figure 32.11.

Questions

1. Which kinds of public spending are hardest to control? Why?
2. By what percentage of total expenditure has the government overshot its targets?
3. What is the effect of such overspending?

*Breakdown by function, not programme.

Note: Cash limited means subject to cash limits, i.e. cannot rise above a certain specified limit each year.

Source: Lang and Cruickshank, *Economic and Monetary Review*, October 1984.

Figure 32.10
Public Expenditure this year

Central government overshoot 3%	=	£3bn
Local authority overshoot 2½%	=	£1bn
Public corporations' capital spending undershoot 4%	=	−£½bn
Total forecast overshoot		£3½bn

Figure 32.11
Present Plans * for 1985/86

£bn	1984/85	1985/86	% change
1. Policy-fixed			
Defence: cash limited, strong control, but can't cut	17.03	18.06	6.0
Law and order: only 22% cash limited, some control through specific grants to LAs, can't cut	5.81	6.07	4.6
Employment: strong control, almost all cash-limited, but politically impossible to cut	3.09	3.19	3.3
2. Demand-determined			
Housing subsidies, social security, personal social services: only administration is cash-limited, control only via rates of benefit	41.38	43.71	5.6
3. Semi-discretionary			
Health: 78% cash-limited, 94% is current expenditure, strong control in principle but responsive to demand	16.94	17.86	5.5
Education: 96% current expenditure, only 12% cash-limited, also responsive to demand and local pressures	12.50	12.88	3.0
Agriculture: only 25% cash-limited, weak control, high subsidies, responsive to pressure groups and EEC	2.42	2.31	−4.4
Trade, industry, energy: 70% cash-limited, but large subsidies to industry mean weaker control	3.46	2.31	33.3
Environmental services: only 10% cash-limited, 90% of expenditure by LAs, Scotland, Wales, N Ireland, responsive to local lobbies	4.45	4.54	2.0
Miscellaneous: less than half cash-limited	3.83	3.71	−3.1
4. Discretionary			
Overseas aid: strong control, although EEC budget problem	2.28	2.52	10.4
Arts and libraries: almost all asset expend-iture, but half is by LAs, therefore weak control	0.69	0.71	3.5
Transport: 37% cash-limited, 29% is spending by LAs, large subsidy element	5.32	5.68	6.7
Housing (ex subsidies): almost entirely capital, subject to cash limits, easy to control	2.90	3.14	8.2
Science: mainly grants, cash-limited, easy to control	3.41	3.54	3.8
5. Adjustments			
Asset sales	−2.00	−2.00	
Contingency reserve	2.75	3.75	
Planning Total	126.35	132.08	4.4

Exam Preparation and Practice

MULTIPLE CHOICE QUESTIONS

1. Which of the following methods of financing an increase in the public sector borrowing requirement will lead to an increase in the money supply?
   A sales of securities to the overseas sector
   B a sale of securities to the non-bank private sector
   C sales of Treasury bills that are purchased by the banking system
   D sales of securities to the banking system.

2. Which one of the following measures is likely to be deflationary?
   A a strengthening of the foreign exchange rate
   B a reduction in the rate of income tax
   C a reduction in compulsory deposits with the central bank
   D an increase in investment allowances
   E an increase in the rate of duty on imported goods

3. The increase in the National Debt is best indicated by the
   A level of central government grants to industry
   B level of public expenditure
   C deficit on the balance of payments
   D public sector borrowing requirement

RELATED ESSAY QUESTIONS

1. Distinguish between monetary and fiscal policy. Does monetary policy have any part to play in the Keynesian approach to running the economy and does fiscal policy have any part in the monetarist approach?

2. Examine the case for a major change in the tax base in Britain away from the taxation of earned income and towards the taxation of spending.

3. What is meant by the management of the economy?

4. Discuss some of the macroeconomic consequences of a reduction in personal taxation.

5. 'Increases in public expenditure lead to lower unemployment and eventually to a reduction in public expenditure; public expenditure cuts lead to higher unemployment and to increased public expenditure.' Critically discuss this statement.

6. Why does the PSBR have implications for the Bank of England's ability to control the money supply?

7. Define the term 'budget deficit' and explain how such deficits may arise. Discuss the possible effects on the international economy of a large budget deficit such as that experienced by the USA in recent years.

33 Manpower and Industrial Policies

Questions for Preview

1 What is the aim of manpower and industrial policies and what examples can you cite?

2 What does the immobility of labour mean?

3 Why is manpower and regional policy so difficult to evaluate?

4 Why are the concepts of *enterprise* and *competition* essential for the success of research and development policy and small firms policy?

In the last two chapters we have discussed fiscal and monetary-type policies, and the perceptive student may well feel that the discussion within these chapters on stable prices, full employment, and economic growth etc. effectively covers the matters of industry and manpower. Therefore, the question arises, why a specific chapter on manpower and industrial-type policies? Answer: we shall use this chapter on manpower and industrial policy to cover those measures that are aimed at affecting the structure and performance of industry and labour within specific sectors of the economy. Consequently, there is a clear distinction between this chapter and the last two. Chapters 31 and 32 were essentially macroeconomic in their effect, while the policies to be discussed in this chapter will always be directed at particular sectors of the economy and can thus be regarded as primarily microeconomic in their effects.

A further reason for having a separate chapter on these issues is the extent of expenditure executed on this type of policy. In 1984 the Department of Industry had a budget of approximately £2 000 million and the Manpower Services Commission spent approximately £1 800 million. Furthermore, the Department of Trade, Department of Employment, and the Department of Education and Science also make significant contributions to industrial policy.

In consequence the issues to be discussed within this chapter cover a wide field. However, we shall group them as far as possible into four areas of interest: Regional Policy, Manpower Policy, Research and Development Policy, and Small Firms Policy. These categories largely reflect the emphasis that has occurred as industrial policy has developed.

Regional Policy

Regional policy dates back to 1934. In 1934 the *Special Areas Act* was passed, which identified certain depressed areas as being in need of incentives to promote industrial diversification. Consequently, certain areas today can actually offer firms financial assistance to entice them to develop within their locality. These areas, designated as **assisted areas** were last revised in 1984 and are identified in Figure 33.1. In

Figure 33.1

The Assisted Areas of Great Britain. The areas shown were designated by the Department of Trade and Industry on 29 November 1984 as eligible for regional grants to encourage industrial development. Alongside these general areas, are 25 named *enterprise zones* (e.g. Dudley, Corby, Isle of Dogs, Hartlepool, Wakefield, and Speke). These encourage industrial development largely through local and administrative incentives, e.g. easier planning permission and no rates. The enterprise zones began in the early 1980s and are administered by the Department of the Environment. Generally they are areas that need to become more attractive, as they contain large areas of derelict land.

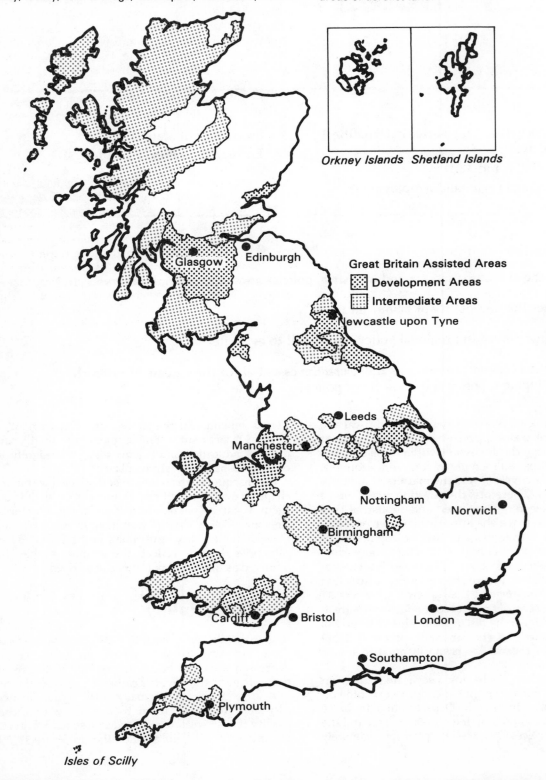

Orkney Islands   Shetland Islands

Great Britain Assisted Areas

  Development Areas
  Intermediate Areas

Glasgow
Edinburgh
Newcastle upon Tyne
Leeds
Manchester
Nottingham
Norwich
Birmingham
Cardiff
Bristol
London
Southampton
Plymouth

Isles of Scilly

the period between this first piece of legislation in 1934 and the most recent in 1984 regional policy experienced its heyday. That is, the 1960s and 1970s were very much a period of regional policies.

What is Regional Policy?

A range of incentives are made available for industries developing in certain areas. Present examples include:

15 per cent of the costs of building or developing new capital.
£3000 for each new job created.
Cash grants for projects providing or safeguarding employment.
Training grants.

Which specific incentive is actually made available depends very much on the nature of the project involved and the geographical area in which it will develop. In very general terms, though, those firms moving into development areas may be able to take advantage of all available incentives, while those moving into an intermediary area may be eligible only for the last two.

The actual list of incentives and the geographical areas for entitlement have been cut back in recent years: to the extent that regional policy now represents a very small percentage of expenditure compared to its previous amounts and those of other industrial policies. For example, in 1984 regional policies cost the government approximately £500 million.

Why Regional Policy Developed

If one looks at Figure 33.1 the remaining areas for assistance all have something in common. They largely represent areas where shipbuilding, textiles, heavy engineering, or coalmining previously took place. These so-called staple industries were important **localized industries** during the UK economy's industrial heyday. A localized industry is one that dominates a whole geographical area, that is, few alternative industries exist in that locality. When a localized industry declines, therefore, so does the regional economy of a whole area. In consequence, the areas designated as areas for assistance also tend to have higher levels of unemployment than the national average (see Figure 33.2).

Furthermore, people tend to stay where they have their social roots. As economists would express it people tend to be **geographically immobile**. Put simply 'Of all baggage human baggage is the most difficult to move.' Consequently the idea of moving work to people becomes an attractive possibility.

Does Regional Policy Work?

Regional policy of one sort or another has been experienced for over fifty years. Yet it is still difficult to evaluate as an effective policy tool. In common with most economic policy there is the problem of not knowing what would have happened without the policy.

Official comments in a government White Paper ('Regional Industrial Development') published in 1983 suggested that the regional policy enforced since 1960 had resulted in there being half a million more jobs in the assisted areas than otherwise would have existed. This is a dubious estimate but it is official! Other commentators look at the figures for regional unemployment, such as those in Figure 33.2 and they recognize, as you can, that those areas that traditionally had higher rates of unemployment than the national average still have them. But again you cannot be sure what kind of statistical portrait would exist if this policy had never been adopted.

Figure 33.2

Regional Unemployment Rates (%). The figures below are annual averages for the various regions designated which should be compared to the national average for the same year, taking the UK as a whole. 1984 has been taken as it is the latest year for which we have complete data at the time of writing and compared to years in the mid-1960s and mid-1970s. 1966 and 1975 seemed the most appropriate as these were years in which major phases of regional policy were introduced. Patterns are evident, e.g. unemployment tends to be consistently above the national average in the northern and western areas (i.e. the first five regions listed) and always well below the national average in the South-east and East Midlands.

	1966	1975	1984
Northern Ireland	5.3	7.9	20.9
Scotland	2.7	5.2	15.1
North	2.5	5.9	18.3
North-west	1.4	5.3	15.9
Wales	2.8	5.6	16.3
West Midlands	0.8	4.1	13.3
Yorkshire and Humberside	1.1	4.0	14.4
East Anglia	1.4	3.4	10.1
South-west	1.7	4.7	11.4
East Midlands	1.0	3.6	12.2
South-east	0.9	2.8	9.5
United Kingdom	1.4	4.1	13.1

Source: Department of Employment Gazette.

What does seem to be agreed, however, is that this policy is not as cost effective as some of its alternatives. If the official estimate that half a million jobs were created between 1960 and 1983 is correct, it means that each job has cost approximately £35000 to create (in 1982 prices). An earlier piece of research by Moore and Rhodes, which was more optimistic about the number of jobs created by regional policy and does not suffer from inflating 1960-type prices into 1982 terms, suggested that the average cost of creating a job between 1960 and 1974 in the assisted areas was approximately £1 250. The gap between these two evaluations is quite wide, but both suggest that the opportunity cost of employing regional policy is high and in consequence alternatives to it are now favoured.

Manpower Policies

Manpower policies are executed by the Manpower Services Commission (MSC). This administrative set-up was conceived of in 1973 and formally established in 1974. During the following ten years the MSC became a major employer of permanent staff and a large spender of public money. In 1985 it employed over 20 000 permanent staff up and down the country and spent over £2 billion. In fact, while regional policy has been on the decline manpower policies have been on the increase; the 1985–6 expenditure of the MSC represents a threefold increase over its expenditure in 1979–80.

The main aims of the Commission are quoted in their *Corporate Plan 1985–1989* as being:

1. To safeguard the provision of skilled manpower for industry's present and future needs.
2. To offer an efficient and cost-effective employment service whose facilities are easily accessible to employers and job-seekers.
3. To offer a range of services to help those job-seekers who have particular difficulty in obtaining suitable work or training.

In brief, they hope to reduce unemployment and assure that each worker has the opportunities and services they need to lead a satisfying working life.

What is Manpower Policy?

To achieve the aims listed above, a whole range of training programmes, schemes, and services is made available – primarily to the unemployed. The chart presented in Figure 33.3 gives a break-down of these various manpower policies according to expenditure. For learning purposes we have numbered the five parts of the key to highlight how these various programmes relate to the aims identified above. Provisions represented by key number 1 are to cater for aim 1; the provisions represented by key number 2 are to cater for aim 2; and the provisions represented partly by key number 3 and wholly by key numbers 4 and 5 cover aim 3.

It is important to recognize that Figure 33.3 is merely a graphic summary of manpower policies; it was designed prior to the 1985 budget and will never be entirely 100 per cent representative of the projected years. Indeed two of the largest schemes, the Community Programme and Youth Training Scheme (YTS), have already been considerably extended in terms of through-put and expenditure for all the forthcoming years illustrated.

Regardless of these modifications, Figure 33.3 gives a good impression of the range of manpower policies and priorities. YTS, the biggest of all the schemes, accounting for over one-third of the MSC budget, will remain the biggest scheme, since the number of unemployed school-leavers that it is meant to cater for will continue to be quite substantial in number, while the employment schemes for the disabled and severely disabled (represented by key number 1) will ultimately remain the smallest programme in expenditure terms because of the smaller numbers in their client group.

Why Manpower Policy Developed

Not only is labour geographically immobile, but it is also said to be **occupationally immobile**. That is,

Figure 33.3
The Various Programmes Constituting Manpower Policy

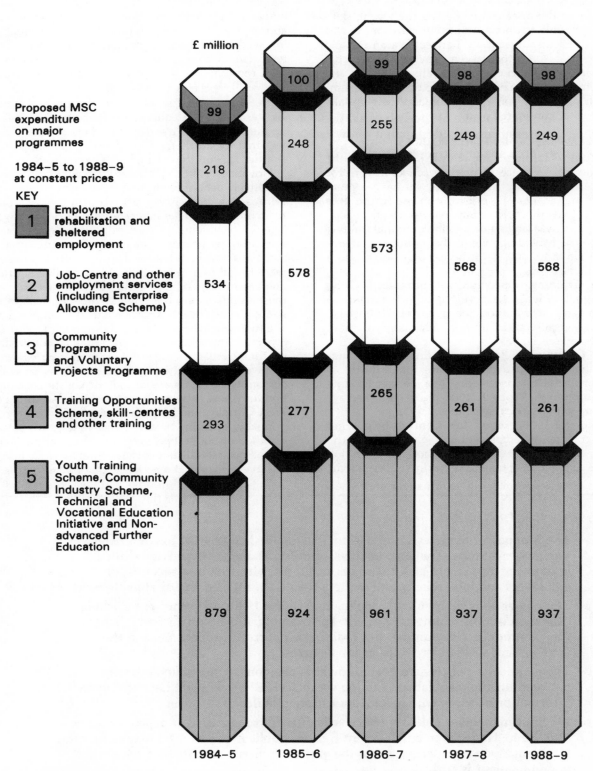

Source: Corporate Plan 1985–1989, published by MSC (May 1985).

people find it difficult to transfer from one job area to another. Yet this is necessary in a dynamic economy. Many government White Papers of the past have highlighted how our problems of unemployment during the 1970s coexisted alongside large numbers of job vacancies. This seemingly odd situation was largely due to the unemployed having the wrong skills and partly due to them lacking information. It was these problems of *mismatch* between vacancies and unemployed labour that largely provided the impetus for manpower policies. To illustrate their aims and move towards evaluating their success, a few examples of manpower policy provision and their up-take rates will be considered next.

SOME EXAMPLES OF MANPOWER POLICIES

The Youth Training Scheme (YTS). This offers the government a chance to prepare school-leavers for work in such a way that Britain will have a more flexible and adaptable work-force in the future. It is evident that the UK, compared to its European neighbours, was lagging behind in vocational training prior to the MSC initiative to the young and unemployed. Up to 400 000 16-to 18-year-olds pass through this scheme a year.

The Training Opportunities Scheme (TOPS). These government schemes offer adults the chance to retrain mid-career in those job areas of skill shortage. On average 65 000 adults take advantage of these opportunities each year.

The Community Programme. Enables the long-term unemployed to avoid becoming totally devoid of the work habit by participating in a job that benefits the community. About 150 000 places per year are taken up with these programmes.

Finally the 1000 or so **Job Centres** help bring together potential employers and job-seekers to the extent that over 14 million contacts between Job Centre staff and the public are encountered each year.

Does Manpower Policy Work?

In numerical terms the various manpower policies seem to be attractive. To provide a snapshot impression – at the end of April 1985 there were 570 000 people participating in youth training and other special employment measures. Alongside these there were approximately 32 500 disadvantaged and disabled involved in employment rehabilitation centres, sheltered employment placements, and similar schemes. This represents a total of over 600 000 involved in manpower policies at one time. This number also represents a great reduction in the unemployment figures and in consequence some criticize the policies as merely being a *cosmetic device*. This phrase is self-explanatory, in that the schemes do certainly put a prettier face on the unemployment statistics.

However, a key question is, how many people effectively benefit from their manpower policy experiences? A sample survey carried out in 1984 of leavers from the YTS scheme suggested that 66 per cent went into employment, further education, or training. Similarly participants on the Community programmes have been followed up and more than a third were found to be gainfully employed following their manpower experiences. The stumbling-block with these evaluations is the same as with regional policy, namely, you never know what the employment situation would have been for these people (and all the others on the schemes) had the schemes not existed.

Other research contains less promising findings, e.g. we are still suffering from shortages of skilled personnel in certain areas, and our vocational education for young people still drags behind the American, West German, and Japanese equivalents.

Finally, in terms of cost effectiveness, we have a situation of 600 000 people involved in various manpower policies, costing the nation around £2 billion; this averages out at a cost per job of around £3 333.

Key Points 33.2

▶ The Manpower Services Commission was established in 1974 to administer manpower policies. The aims of this Commission are: (1) to provide skilled manpower for present and future needs, (2) offer information services for employers and job-seekers, and (3) help the disadvantaged and disabled to work.

▶ Manpower policies are a major policy tool of the 1980s and represent a whole collection of programmes at present. For example, the Youth Training Scheme, the Community Programme, the Training Opportunities Scheme, and the employment services provided at Job Centres.

▶ The manpower policies are geared towards overcoming mismatch problems between unemployed labour and job vacancies, i.e. it is hoped that training and information services will make labour more mobile.

▶ Whether manpower policy is effective is difficult to evaluate. It depends on one's attitude to: training, unemployment figures, public expenditure, job take-up rates after a manpower experience, and the various indirect benefits that arise when unemployment is curbed.

The net cost to the taxpayer is effectively not quite as severe as this figure may at first suggest, since unemployment benefits and other social security payments have been saved and some taxation payments will have been reaped. Finally, these figures will never be able to fully account for the various indirect benefits that are a very important consideration with a social problem such as unemployment.

Research and Development Policy

Research and development – R & D – involves exploring and inventing new product areas. This, by its very nature, is a dodgy affair. Those involved have to take the risk of investing time and money, but can never be sure that the expensive resources used will produce anything. Furthermore, when a product is developed there is little to stop others benefiting from your research; that is, the external benefits often exceed the private benefits.

As detailed in Chapter 10, whenever externalities relating to growth and welfare cannot be absorbed by the market mechanism, the government may step in. R & D is an example of such intervention and the UK government, as most others in the OECD group, are committed to expenditure in this area. In the UK approximately $2\frac{1}{2}$ per cent of our annual GDP is spent on R & D and about one-half of this is met by the government. Similar patterns of expenditure are experienced in the US, Japan, West Germany, and France. Unfortunately, until very recently we fell sadly behind the others once defence-related R & D is subtracted.

What is Research and Development Policy?

Once again there is no simple single answer to cover this section. R & D policy involves a range of government incentives and has been subject to various institutional support.

The institutional support dates back to 1948 when the **National Research and Development Corporation (NRDC)** was established. This Corporation was intended to encourage technical progress through the allocation of funds for the developments of new products that were in the public's interest. In 1981 the NRDC was merged with another government institution, the **National Enterprise Board (NEB)**. The NEB had been a type of state-holding company established in the mid-1970s. The Board had gained some experience with modern technological firms striving to gain a foothold in the market, and had become financially involved with INMOS, a micro-chip company. The merger of NRDC and NEB in 1981 formed the BTG – the **British Technology Group**. This Group presently strives to develop new technologies by exploiting the NEB experiences and participating with the private sector in joint ventures, and building on the previous NRDC contacts in universities and research organizations by licensing out academic findings for development in the commercial field. The group is thereby meant to be self-financing. (A clearer idea of the BTG's function will be gained by reading the Case Study at the end of this chapter.)

Consequently, government incentives to encourage R & D largely take the form of financial assistance either direct to the private sector or via grants for academic research at a government research centre or university. Tax concessions and the law regarding 'patents' also offer some encouragement. Finally, there has been the development of an ad hoc government-sponsored agency to distribute £350 million between 1983 and 1988, specifically to fund research and development in fifth-generation computers. This agency is called the 'Alvey directorate'.

The present government concern over competition and their desire to encourage enterprise has in fact led to more money generally being made available for R & D. The Department of Trade and Industry budget for R & D for the financial year 1985–86 was £394 million which represents approximately a 300 per cent increase since the Conservatives took over in 1979.

Does Research and Development Policy Work?

It seems that in the UK we lack a long-run philosophy to R & D: governments change, institutions come and go, and shifts in emphasis from the public to the private sector are experienced. By result, we have a reputation as a nation of innovating, but not effectively developing and marketing our knowledge (which it is to be hoped the BTG will overcome). In short, an effective and co-ordinated R & D policy still needs to be formulated.

Possibly some solutions may be gained from overseas experience. France, for example, indulges in **indicative planning** in which the government discusses and co-ordinates the direction of the economy over a number of years. The Japanese, similarly, have identified a few key industries in which to concentrate their R & D efforts. In fact, the aforementioned Alvey directorate is a response to the Japanese focus on computers.

Alternatively we may find some way of developing a British R & D strategy by creating a closer link between the policies offered here and those outlined elsewhere in this chapter.

Small Firms Policy

The current emphasis on policy for small firms is not confined to Britain. A whole range of policies to encourage and support the development of small firms is in force throughout Europe, America, and

<hr>

Key Points 33.3

► R & D involves exploring and inventing new product areas, including those involved with defence.

► Most governments, including the UK, are committed to providing assistance for R & D, since one successful development may have many external benefits.

► The British Technology Group is an important organization responsible for developing new technologies. It was formed in 1981 by merging the NEB and NRDC.

► R & D is important in promoting competition and encouraging incentive. Consequently, government incentives are provided in the form of financial assistance, tax concessions, and research grants.

► In many ways R & D policy is still developing. Recent government expenditure has increased and ways of marketing our researched knowledge are being extended through the BTG.

<hr>

Canada. These policies are popular as they encourage enterprise, which many governments presently regard as central to reviving flagging economies.

Apart from specific policies, there is a whole range of institutions developing to support, advise, and represent the small firm. To take just British examples, there exists a small firms division at the Department of Trade and Industry; the regional small firms information and counselling service, training facilities specifically for small firms; the Association of Independent Businesses; and even a parliamentary minister responsible for small firms.

Therefore, although policy for small firms represents the most recent emphasis of UK manpower and industrial policy, it is by no means the least important. In fact between 1979 and 1984, 108 different measures affecting small firms were implemented by the British government. In the next section we shall review *some* of them. But before that we should look at one act specifically in order to gain some idea of what is meant by a small firm. The 1981 Company Act defined small firms as those having less than fifty employees, sales of less than £1.4 million or less than £700 000 of capital employed. Others may define 'small' differently but at least this is a guide.

What is Small Firms Policy?

Much of the small firms policy introduced since 1979 has involved tax benefits, so as to reward enterprise and work in favour of small businesses. For example, the 1984 budget introduced a lower rate of corporation tax for firms whose annual rate of profits did not exceed £100 000.

Another group of measures has been aimed at removing the administrative 'red tape' that seems to complicate the life of so many small firms. For example, the 1980 Employment Act provided for the *exemption* of small firms from requirements relating to

industrial tribunals, maternity reinstatement, and unfair dismissal procedures.

Finally, various financial incentives have been created to encourage the small business. The most innovative of these is the **Enterprise Allowance Scheme**.* This scheme provides an allowance of £40 per week for a year to any unemployed person wishing to set up his/her own business. Since this scheme was launched in August 1983 more than 100 000 people have joined the scheme, and 30 per cent of these had been previously unemployed for over a year. Furthermore, for every two businesses supported one extra job is also created. The other financial incentives cover such things as tax concessions for small businesses wishing to expand, namely, the *Business Expansion Scheme*; and loan schemes, which involve the government acting as guarantor for bank loans to small firms, namely, the *Loan Guarantee Scheme*.

Does Small Firms Policy Work?

Despite the current attention paid to small firms there is at the time of writing little factual information regarding the success of policy in terms of economic activity. Indeed, there is still a lot of debate whether solutions to our unemployment problems lie in the innovating and personalized small firms sector or whether a full economic revival can only come from the large firm sector, where economies of scale will enable them to break into national and international markets. In brief, there seems to be some controversy over the question of whether 'big' or 'small' firms are

<hr>

* In terms of funding this is a Manpower Service Commission responsibility. But inevitably some of these industrial policies overlap and this is a good example.

more beneficial to an economy.

The last few years have certainly seen a huge increase in small business start-ups. But unfortunately many fail. The Enterprise Allowance Scheme may be a way round the problem of small business failure, as people are at least subsidized through their first difficult year. Indeed, the little evaluation that has taken place is encouraging. It suggests that 70 per cent of the businesses set up through this scheme are still continuing after the allowances cease. However, this causes us to close with the question with which we started this evaluation, namely, how significant are small firms in terms of employment and economic activity?

Closing Section: Political Dimension

An answer to the closing question could partly reconcile the divide between the Conservative and Labour parties, and avoid continual further changes to industrial and manpower policy. At present, Conservative strategy seems to rely heavily on the market mechanism, encouraging the independence of firms and a favourable environment for private initiatives. Labour, on the other hand, when in office, have tended towards large-scale organizations and intervention into the market mechanisms. In consequence, no *long-term* co-ordinated industrial policy has ever effectively been developed.

Key Points 33.4

▶ **Policy aimed at encouraging and supporting small firms has been popular with most governments in Europe, America, and Canada in the mid-1980s.**

▶ **In the UK small firms policy has taken three main forms; (1) changes to the tax systems; (2) changes to the administrative 'red tape' requirements, and (3) several financial incentives made available through various schemes.**

▶ **Whether a revival in the small firms sector is sufficient to get the whole economy moving again is the subject of much academic and political debate.**

CASE STUDY

British Technology Group: Press Briefing August 1985

BTG – The Future Role

BTG's objective is to promote the development of new technology into commercial products, particularly where the technology originates from public sector sources such as universities, polytechnics, research councils, and government research establishments.

We shall concentrate our future efforts on technology transfer, helping British industry to exploit technology from UK public sector sources.

More specifically, BTG will:

* offer to take responsibility for patenting, or otherwise protecting, technology derived from universities, polytechnics, and other public sector sources
* provide funding for the development of that technology to the point where it can be taken up by industry
* transfer the technology to industry by seeking licensees
* share the resulting licence income with the source of the technology

* plough back our retained share of the licence income into the development and exploitation of other technology.

As part of its technology transfer role BTG will also offer project finance to companies that want to develop new products and processes based on their own new technology.

Questions

1. What do you understand by the term 'technology transfer'.
2. The BTG is currently funding

continued overleaf

over 375 development projects, has about 500 licence agreements in force, and is involved in approximately 250 joint-ventures with industry.

(a) Do you know about any of these specifically?

(b) Do you know of any invention that may have been developed with BTG funds?

(c) Have you or your educational establishment got a project that may interest the BTG?

3. The BTG expects to be both self-financing and profit-making.

(a) On what does this depend?

(b) What will happen if they are not?

(c) What role can you see for BTG in the year 2000?

CASE STUDY

Small Firms Policy – An Academic's View

A healthy industrial economy will have a mixture of large, medium, and small firms. Although any judgement as to the appropriate proportions will be very subjective, the fact that the UK has a smaller proportion of small firms than other industrial countries and that there have been certain identifiable tax advantages to large firms does suggest that we might aim to enlarge that proportion

Turning to the effects that an increase in the proportion of small firms might have on the economy, our discussion of investment and innovation suggests that the extent of both activities depends to a fairly large extent on the nature of the industry rather than the size of firm. Neither the overall level, nor (for investment) its variability, will be much affected by small shifts in the proportion. However, certain types of innovation are sensitive to firm size, so that any substantial incentives to one size at the expense of the other might well be harmful.

There are, of course, many other factors which would enter into any consideration of policy. *(1) What would happen to the extent of competition*, the level of union power, and, hence (at any level of unemployment) *(2) the degree of inflationary pressure within the economy? (3) What would be the effect on the level and mixture of training and experience acquired by the work-force? (4) Would the encouragement of small firms lead to greater job satisfaction or more opportunities for exploitation?* Unfortunately, we do not have the space to discuss these issues here, but must move on to consider whether the government has any power to influence the size of the small firm sector.

The fact that other countries have appreciably large small firm sectors does suggest the possibility of change, but these larger sectors probably reflect long-established attitudes and institutions, and it is likely that any attempt to produce a *rapid* shift will both be

unsuccessful and do a good deal of harm. The government has very little direct influence over attitudes, and is limited to the indirect effect which shorter-term financial encouragement of small firms might eventually have.

Source: R. Allard 'The Importance and Position of Small Firms', *Economic Review*, Nov. 1983.

Questions
1. In the third paragraph of the extract we have italicized some questions that the author raises, and we have numbered them (1)–(4). Take each point in turn and consider: What would happen if more small firms did develop?
2. Does this author think the government policy for small firms will be successful or not?

Exam Preparation and Practice

MULTIPLE CHOICE QUESTIONS

For Questions 1 — 3 select your answers from the following grid:

A	B	C	D	E
1,2,3 all correct	1, 2 only correct	2, 3 only correct	1 only correct	3 only correct

†1. The 'natural' rate of unemployment can be reduced by
   1 expansionist fiscal policies
   2 retraining schemes
   3 measures designed to reduce imperfections in the labour market

†2. The free-market approach to solving the problem of less prosperous regions assumes that
   1 labour is geographically mobile
   2 wage differentials would reflect regional prosperity
   3 capital would be allocated among regions according to the return it yields

†3. In an under-employed economy, an increase in employment would be likely to follow from
   1 a decrease in government current expenditure
   2 an increase in demand for imports
   3 an increase in fixed capital formation

4. The opportunity cost to society of running manpower policy is
   A the money spent on the schemes
   B the regional policy and R & D policy that could otherwise have been used had the manpower policy option not been adopted
   C the cost of government borrowing needed to finance the schemes
   D the goods and services that could otherwise have been produced by the people on the manpower schemes had the policy not been running

†5. Which of the following is an example of occupational mobility of labour?
   A professional footballers transferring from one football club to another
   B miners moving from South Wales to Lancashire
   C men taking part-time jobs in addition to their normal employment
   D men retraining as plumbers after some years in shipbuilding
   E married women returning to their old jobs after maternity leave

RELATED ESSAY QUESTIONS

1. Discuss the arguments for and against the free market approach to regional economic imbalance.

2. Examine the problems of measuring the costs and benefits of manpower policy schemes.

3. Discuss the ways and means by which discriminatory government policy might affect small business enterprise.

4. Briefly describe the chief characteristics of industrial policy in recent years. Discuss whether, in your opinion, experience supports the view that less direct government intervention is desirable or that more is required.

5. Discuss what is usually meant by 'market failure'. Giving examples, consider what forms of corrective action governments can take to remedy this.

34 Economic Growth

Key Points to Review

▶ Factors of production and society (1.1)

▶ Production possibilities curve (1.3)

▶ Trade-off of present and future consumption (2.4)

▶ Retail Price Index (11.5)

▶ Savings and investment (12.2)

▶ GNP (13.1)

▶ Is national income accounting sufficient? (13.7)

▶ The law of diminishing returns (22.2)

▶ Human capital (28.3)

▶ Regional policies and manpower policies (33.1 and 33.2)

▶ Research and development policies (33.3)

Questions for Preview

1 What is economic growth??

2 What does economic growth measure?

3 What are some of the ways your family could experience economic growth?

4 What are the determinants of economic growth?

5 What government policies may affect the level of economic growth?

Growth is a controversial topic. The business community typically sees economic growth as a means to continuing prosperity. Certain sectors of society see economic growth in this country as the only way that the poor and disadvantaged will ever attain higher standards of living. In direct contrast other sectors of society want economic growth to stop. They argue that we in the UK with only a very small percentage of the world's population use 'too much' of the world's resources. Growth is, therefore, a topic of academic and political debate; and in the Case Studies at the end of this chapter we will return to this opening theme and encourage you to consider whether economic growth is a desirable or undesirable target.

What Is the Meaning of Economic Growth?

As this is the penultimate chapter in the book, most of you probably have a general idea of what the term *economic growth* means. When a nation grows, its citizens are in some ways better off, at least in terms of material well-being. A general definition of **economic growth** might read as follows:

Economic growth is the increase in an economy's level of real output over time.

Generally, economic growth is measured by the *rate of change* of some measure of output. In this nation, and in most other countries today, the most commonly used measure of economic output is gross national product (GNP). In discussing the rate of change of actual output, we have to correct GNP for changes in prices through the use of a price index.

When we do, we get what is called *real* GNP, as discussed and illustrated in Chapter 13. Hence a more formal measure of economic growth may be defined as the rate of change in real GNP over time.

For example, from 1980 to 1984 in the UK, the average annual rate of growth of nominal GNP (i.e. uncorrected for price changes) was 10.3 per cent. During that period, the average annual rate of inflation was 9.6 per cent. Therefore, the approximate average annual increase in *real* GNP was 10.3 per cent minus 9.6 per cent, or 0.7 per cent.*

Correcting for Population Growth

The above measure might be misleading if, for example, the population is growing rapidly at the same time that real GNP is growing. An alternative and perhaps more appropriate definition of economic growth is in terms of per capita output; defined as the total production of goods and services in a one-year period *divided* by the population. The self-explanatory mathematical formula for this calculation has already been presented and discussed in the section headed 'per capita GNP' in Chapter 13. We can therefore move to yet another definition, the fullest and official measure, namely:

Economic growth is the increase in per capita real output; it is officially measured by the percentage rate of changes in *real* GNP *per head* of the population from one time-period to another – normally a year.

Problems of Definition

Nothing is stated in the above definitions about the *distribution* of output and income. A nation might grow very rapidly in terms of increases in total or even per capita real output, while at the same time the nation's poor people remain poor or become even poorer.

Nothing has been said about changes in the leisure time available to the nation. In one sense, 'real' standards of living can open up without there being any positive economic growth as measured by increases in real per capita output.

Similarly, nothing in the above definitions of economic growth relates to the spiritual, cultural, and environmental quality aspects of the 'good' life.

All these themes have already been reviewed in Chapter 13, explicitly, when we discussed the question 'Is National Income Accounting Sufficient'? and implicitly, when we considered the Case Study entitled 'Does GNP mean Gross National Problems'?

Students of economics, therefore, recognize that no measure of economic growth is perfect. Yet, the measures that we do have allow us to make comparisons across countries and through time, and if used judiciously, can provide important insights. In sum, GNP may be a defective measure of well-being, but it is a serviceable measure of productive activity.

The UK Growth Record

If we arranged the countries of the world in a 'league table' each year, with those with the highest growth rates at the top and those with the lowest at the bottom, the UK would show a worrying trend. Once the UK persistently had the highest growth rates in the world, now we are frequently beaten by the USA, Japan, France, and West Germany to name just a few

---

Figure 34.1
The UK Lags behind in OECD League Table for the Years 1970-82. The chart shows approximate growth rates in the twenty-four OECD countries based on their national accounts. They should be regarded as broad approximations only, since they are the official statistics of governments and omit the varying rates of growth of the unrecorded economies, which are substantial in some countries. Nevertheless, they do indicate a very marked divergence in the rates of economic growth in the United Kingdom and other Western industrialized countries. The UK rate of growth for the 12 years shown was less than half the average of 43 per cent.

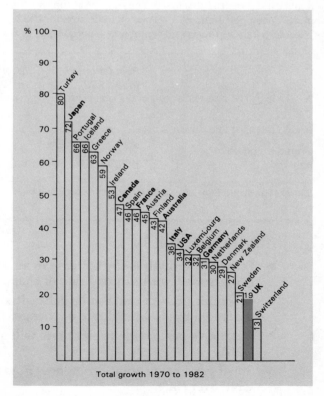

Total growth 1970 to 1982

Source: Economic Affairs, Jan. 1984.

---

*This is only an approximate figure based on the general principle used for converting nominal (money) GNP into real GNP.

of our competitors. This shift in our international league position is reflected in Figure 34.1.

More recent figures, however, suggest a marginal improvement. For example, Nigel Lawson's 1986 budget speech proudly opened with the following lines:

We can now look back to five solid years of growth at around 3 per cent a year ...

In 1985 as a whole, output grew by a further 3½ per cent, the highest rate of growth in the European Community, and higher than the United States too.

The Importance of Growth Rates

The question arises, therefore, of how important these percentage point differences are. The answer is twofold.

Firstly, you must always ask the question, 'percentage of what'? Any developed country's growth rates in percentage terms will traditionally be lower than a developing country. In the developed country you are thinking along the lines of a 2½ per cent increase on £240 000 millions, while in a developing nation one is considering a percentage increase of a far smaller total. It is like comparing a 5 per cent increase of £100 to a 5 per cent increase of £1 billion – even the innumerate will recognize that the latter is far larger.

The second problem is slightly more complex since it relates to compounded rates of growth. If a nation consistently has a low or high rate of growth the time it will take to double its present economic size will vary immensely. The principle is the same as putting a £1 coin in the building society and getting 5 per cent interest a year. If the dividend is added annually and you leave the amount untouched for fifteen years you will recoup £2.08p. If one left another £1 coin in a building society offering only 3 per cent interest per year it would take twenty-four years to double, therefore, just 2 percentage points result in a nine-year difference in 'doubling-time'. These concepts are illustrated in a more international setting in Figure 34.2. (Italy has been chosen because it is similar in population size to Britain.) (Read Key Points 34.1.)

Growth and the Production Possibilities Curve

We can graphically show economic growth by using the production possibilities curve presented in Chapter 1. Figure 34.3 shows the production possibilities curve for 1986. On the horizontal axis is measured the output of agricultural goods, and on the vertical axis,

Figure 34.2
From the income per head column (given the similarity in population size) it is possible to ascertain that the UK is a more developed nation in terms of GNP size in 1982. Therefore Italy's growth rate represents a percentage of a smaller total GNP. However, if these growth trends persist the UK will soon be overtaken in the rate of economic activity by Italy – this is suggested by the shorter doubling-time in the final column.

	Population (mid-1982)	Income per hd. in 1982 ($)	Average yearly growth rate 1960–82 (%)	Doubling-time (if existing growth rate is maintained)
United Kingdom	55.8 m	9.660	2.0	36 years
Italy	56.3 m	6.840	3.4	21 years

Source: The World Bank: *World Development Report*, 1984.

Key Points 34.1

▶ Economic growth is the increase in an economy's real level of output over time. It is measured by the annual rate of change of real output.

▶ Economic growth can also be defined as the increase in real per capita output measured by its annual rate of change.

▶ A nation's percentage growth rate will always be relative to the size of its total GNP.

▶ Small percentage point differences in growth rates lead to large differences in GNP over time.

manufactured goods. If there is economic growth between 1986 and 1990 then the production possibilities curve will shift to the right (or outwards) to the heavy line. The distance that it shifts represents the amount of economic growth, that is, the increase in the productive capacity of the nation.

Potential and Actual Output

Remember that the production possibilities curve represents the maximum rate of output that *can* be achieved with the nation's available resources. It is possible for resources to be underutilized. The production possibilities curve could shift outwards, but the actual utilization of resources might be less than the maximum use represented by the curve. Look at

Figure 34.3

Economic Growth. If there is growth between 1986 and 1990 then the production possibilities curve for the entire economy will shift outwards from the line labelled 1986 to the outer curve labelled 1990. The distance that it shifts represents an increase in the productive capacity of the nation.

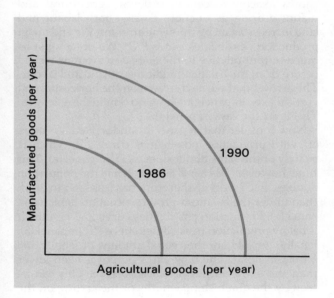

Figure 34.4. Here we show the production possibilities curve for 1986 shifting out as it did in Figure 34.3. We start at point *A*, but find that by the year 1990 we have ended up on point *B* because of underutilization of actual resources in 1990. It is even possible for the economy to have a decrease in actual output if we move inwards to point *C*. Thus, in a sense, the production possibilities curve for 1990 is a representation of maximum **potential output** which is defined as the level of output that a nation could attain if it were operating on the production possibilities curve. **Actual output** will therefore never exceed potential output but it may be smaller. In the long run, it may be

Figure 34.4

Potential versus Actual Output. The production possibilities curve may shift out from 1986 without necessarily ending up on the new potential production possibilities curve for 1990. For example, if we start out at position *A*, we may only progress to point *B*. The 'actual' output rate symbolised by *B* represents an underutilization of resources. We are not producing at our maximum potential rate. Indeed, one could even envisage a situation developing where the economy moves inwards towards *C*: this would represent an 'actual' growth rate well below potential.

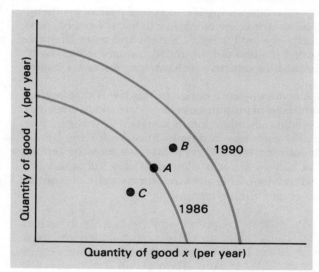

Key Points 34.2

▶ Growth is shown by an outward movement in the production possibilities curve for the entire economy.

▶ Economists make a distinction between potential and actual growth rates. The former represents maximum efficiency with resources and provides a target; the latter represents resource utilization in practice, and illustrates the outcome.

▶ Growth can be achieved in two forms: 1 through increased productive capacity, and 2 by utilizing existing capital equipment more fully. The former should lead to long-term growth, the latter simply represents short-term recovery.

changes in potential output that determine government and business planning, but in the short run it is
changes in actual output that are important.

Let us develop this concept of potential output a
stage further. Potential output can be increased by
enlarging productive capacity which is a long-run
process. In contrast, therefore, economic growth
achieved by simply utilizing existing spare capacity
should be recognized as qualitatively and quantitively
different – and certainly more short-term in nature.
This latter type of growth can be regarded as a kind of
recovery phase. Economic growth built on a recovery
basis only will ultimately lead to full capacity use of the
existing resources. A distinction, therefore, needs to
be drawn between a shorter-term recovery phase
(based on *existing* resources) and a long-term shift in a
nation's potential output. (See Key Points 34.2.)

Growth and the Law of Diminishing Returns

An economy may find it difficult to increase all its
resources in the proportionate manner shown in
Figure 34.3. Certain resources can only be increased
within limits. We now ask the question: what will
happen when one input is increased relative to others?
In other words, we would like to know what happens
when, say, land is held constant and more labour is
applied. To find out, we must re-examine the **law of
diminishing returns** which was introduced in Chapter
22.

A common-sense notion of this law is that beyond
some level of output, successive increases in one input
– holding all other inputs constant – will generate
smaller increases in output. In order for the law of
diminishing returns to operate, we must be certain
that only *one* input is allowed to vary. All others are
held constant. This gives us a formal definition of the
law of diminishing returns:

As successive, equal amounts of one input, such as
labour, are added to other inputs which are fixed
(such as land and technology), beyond some output
the resulting increases in output will diminish in size.

In other words, total output may continue to
increase as we add, say, more and more labour to a
fixed amount of land, but the *rate of increase* in output
will fall after some point. In Chapter 22 when we
discussed this we talked in terms of an average and
marginal product – remember? (If not it may be worth
re-reading that section before continuing any
further.)

An Example: Illustrating the Law of Diminishing Returns

Consider two possible situations: one in which there is
a balanced increase in all production inputs including
land, the other in which land is fixed. In panel (a) of
Figure 34.5 we show the probable effects of balanced
growth: there is a population increase that just
matches the increase in available land. On the vertical
axis, we are measuring manufactured goods per year;
and on the horizontal axis, agricultural goods per year.
We first start out with production possibilities curve
PP in panel (a). Now the population doubles, and so,
too, does the land area on which the population is
producing. The production possibilities curve P'P'
shows exactly twice the scale of agricultural and
manufacturing production. Finally, both labour and
land increase again by the same amount. We end up on
production possibilities curve P''P''. We obtain just as
much output relative to the increased input as we did
before from the balanced additions of land and labour.
The arrows that we have drawn on the horizontal and
vertical axes in panel (a) show no diminishing length.
This is *not* the case in panel (b).

Now consider that in panel (b) land is fixed. We start
off with production possibilities curve ZZ, which is
exactly of the same dimensions as PP in panel (a). This
time, however, *land is held constant*, while the population
doubles. Each worker therefore has less land to work
than under the balanced-growth situation depicted in
panel (a). Production possibilities curve Z'Z' results. It
is below production possibilities curve P'P' in panel (a).
Finally, we add another equal amount of labour, *still
holding land fixed*. The new extra output is even lower
than the extra output produced before. This can be
seen by the diminishing lengths of the arrows on the

Key Points 34.3

▶ The law of diminishing returns tells us that as successive equal amounts of one
  variable input are added to the other *fixed* inputs, the resulting increases in output
  will diminish in size.

▶ The law of diminishing returns can be portrayed by comparing the outward
  movement in the production possibilities curve when all factors of production are
  increased in a balanced manner and when, say, land is fixed. With land fixed, the
  same increase in the variable inputs leads to a smaller and smaller outward shift
  in the production possibilities curve.

Figure 34.5

The Law of Diminishing Marginal Returns. In panel (a), we show balanced growth where population (labour) and land are increased at equal rates. In panel (b), we show a situation where only labour is increased while land is held fixed. In panel (a), proportional increments in labour and land result in proportional increments in potential output, as shown by the increase in the production possibilities curve from *PP* to *P'P'* to *P''P''*. The arrows on the axes labelled 1, 2 and 3 do not diminish in size. In panel (b) they do, however. As we add equal increments of labour, the production possibilities curve shifts out by smaller and smaller amounts. Thus, the arrows 1, 2, and 3 get smaller and smaller in length. In panel (b), we have shown the effects of diminishing marginal returns to labour when land is held constant. As more workers are added, each labourer has less land on which to work. (Of course, technological development may dramatically increase agricultural productivity, making substantial outward shifts in the schedule possible.)

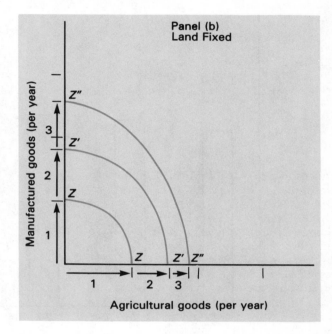

vertical and horizontal axes in panel (b). What has happened in panel (b) resulted from diminishing marginal returns. In other words, equal increments in labour (holding land fixed) resulted in diminishing increments in output. (Read Key Points 34.3.)

Factors Determining Economic Growth

Potential economic growth is largely determined by the factors of production that a nation has at its command. Actual growth, however, is determined by how effectively these factors are developed and combined.

Natural Resources and Economic Growth

A large amount of natural resources is not sufficient to guarantee economic growth. A number of less-developed countries are fantastically rich in natural resources. However, they have not been overly suc-cessful in exploiting these resources. Natural resources must be converted to useful forms. For example, in the United States, the Indians had many natural resources available to them, but they were unable to increase their standard of living or experience economic growth.

People must devise the methods to convert natural resources into usable forms. Countries with similar natural resources vary in their ability to do this.

In short, abundant natural resources are not sufficient in themselves. People are necessary to develop resources into useful things. Less-developed nations require this type of human resource before they are able to exploit the natural resources they possess.

Capital Accumulation and Economic Growth

It is often asserted that a necessary prerequisite for economic development is a large capital stock – machines and other durable goods – that can be used to aid in the production of consumption goods and capital goods in the future. It is true that developed

Figure 34.6
Percentage of GDP Devoted to Investment in Fixed Capital in 1974 and 1984. Japan is the fastest-growing nation in the OECD group at present and it clearly outstrips the others in terms of capital investment.

Of equal importance, however, is the quality of this investment. It should be noted, therefore, that these figures in themselves indicate nothing about how wisely the capital is chosen or how effectively it is used.

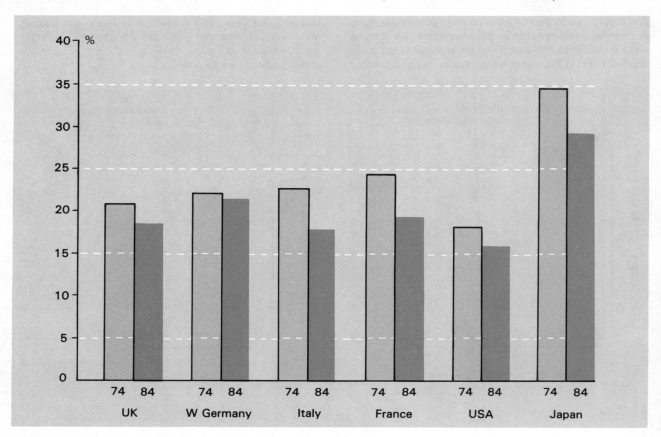

Source: NEDC, *British Industrial Performance* (NEDO, London, 1985).

countries do have large capital stocks per capita. For example, in Figure 34.6 we present a bar chart showing the amounts of fixed capital investment (i.e. plant, machinery, and buildings) that various OECD countries undertook in 1974 and 1984. These figures provide some indication of production potential; however, they say nothing about how wisely the capital investment is chosen or how effectively it is used.

Let us leave these problems relating to the quality and application of capital on one side for a while.

Capital, regardless of the problems outlined, is still seen as a major factor affecting economic growth. The logic is: the larger the capital stock for any given population the higher the possible level of productivity and real income. Obviously, if very few machines are available, a nation will be able to make fewer goods and services and therefore income will be lower. Conversely more machines will mean more income can be generated. Therefore, the larger the capital stock, the larger the income pie.

BUT HOW DOES CAPITAL STOCK GROW?
It grows by people making the decision not to consume all their income today. The more saving by households and the more investment by firms there is, as a percentage of total income, the larger will be the capital stock, and therefore, the higher will be possible future income. We can perhaps demonstrate this decision by again using a production possibilities curve.

In Figure 34.7 we show two potential production possibilities curves for the year 2000. The horizontal axis is labelled as present consumption, and the vertical axis as output of capital goods. We would expect that if our economy is presently operating at A where there are relatively more capital goods being produced than at B, the potential production possibilities curve in 2000 would be farther to the right than if we were producing at B. We have labelled the outside curve AA and the middle curve BB. The rate of growth producing at point A is greater than the rate of growth producing at point B. Therefore the pie gets potentially larger the more people are willing to save today.

Figure 34.7

The Importance of Capital for Growth. Here we show a production possibilities curve with two points on it, A and B. At point A we are consuming less today and providing more consumption for tomorrow in the form of capital goods. At point B, we are consuming more today and providing less for future consumption. If we operate at point A, we may end up on a production possibilities curve of AA in year 2000. However, if we are at point B, we may end up at a production possibilities curve of only BB in year 2000. In other words, there will be less growth during the next decades if we consume more goods today instead of saving and investing in capital goods that provide for more future consumption.

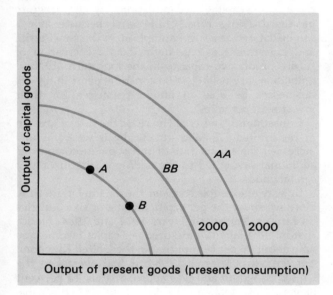

Technological Progress and Economic Growth

When technological progress takes place, it is possible to obtain more output from the same amount of inputs as before. Technological progress or change results in outward shifts in the production possibilities curve. Thus, technological progress determines, at least in part, a nation's rate of economic growth. The ability of a nation to effect and sustain technological change depends on:

1. the scientific capabilities of the population,
2. the quality and size of the nation's educational and training system, and
3. the percentage of income that goes into basic research and development each year.

Technological progress does not occur only in the industrial sector of developed nations. In the less-developed countries, technological change has involved the use of improved pesticides, higher-yielding hybrid seeds, and improved irrigation techniques. Much of the technological change that first occurred in the developed countries has been transferred to the less-developed countries, thereby allowing them to increase their rate of growth. Consider the example of the invention and widespread use of 'miracle' rice, which has caused a 'green' revolution in less-developed countries. Miracle rise, although requiring more fertilizer, has much greater yields per acre planted than any other previously existing strain of rice. The innovation and use of miracle rice has increased the actual output for the limited capital and skilled labour available to less-developed countries.

We can tentatively conclude, therefore, that technological progress, along with the *associated* accumulation of human and physical capital, is important in determining a nation's economic rate of growth.

Can We Tell Which Factor Is Most Important?

Is it possible to find out which factor is most important in determining a nation's economic growth rate? This is indeed difficult to answer. One way to simplify the problem, though, is to talk in terms of two

---

Key Points 34.4

▶ Natural resources are not sufficient to guarantee economic growth; many countries without a large natural resource base have had relatively high growth rates.

▶ Capital accumulation is a possible determinant of growth. The more capital goods we produce today, the higher our potential growth, other things being equal.

▶ There is a trade-off between present goods and future (capital) goods.

▶ Technological progress allows a nation to produce greater output with a given amount of labour and capital.

▶ Technological progress and the accumulation of human and material capital determine, to a large extent, the rate of economic growth.

determinants of economic growth that can be measured – at least in theory:

1. growth of capital stock, and
2. growth of the labour force.

Now if we assume that these two determinants alone will account for all the economic growth that is sustained, it seems relatively straightforward to find out the numerical importance of the factors. The researcher simply estimates the average annual rate of growth in capital and labour.

But the task is not really so easy. Certainly we can measure the value of the number of machines that are put in place and the number of workers that have entered the labour force. But what about the *quality* of the capital we use? And the *quality* of the labour force? Part of the growth in our capital stock and labour force has to do with quality improvement. 'One unit' of a machine today is certainly of a higher quality than the 'same' machine of a hundred years ago. Similarly, the average worker today has much better training and a higher educational attainment level than the worker a hundred years ago. Thus we can say that to a large extent the measurement of the growth in capital and in labour does not take into account the growth in the *quality* of these two factors.

No Growth Theory

Because of the quality/quantity dilemma outlined above, it is most difficult to identify which factor – labour or capital – is the more important contributor to the growth process.

Furthermore, other factors – such as natural resources and technological progress – also need to be brought into the formula. But these two factors *also* have inherent problems of measurement.

Consequently, economists in the 1980s can still not agree on the relative importance of the factors that contribute to economic growth. To paraphrase R. Lipsey from his famous text book *Positive Economics*: of all economic variables growth is the most difficult to control.

Now read Key Points 34.5.

Policies to Promote Growth

Because economists cannot agree on one growth theory, it follows that when governments wish to promote economic growth their advisers have no unanimous policy package to follow. All that exists are several possibilities, *some** of which are outlined below.

Promote Savings

The logic is straightforward: capital is recognized as a key determinant of growth and capital accumulation can depend on the level of savings. If resources are fully utilized increased investment may require reduced consumption. Therefore, increased invest-ment, or capital accumulation, would require increased savings. Why? Quite simply because savings can be defined as *non*-consumption, in the short term, and investment can be defined as the creation of future productive capacity in the long term. Only if individuals are willing *not* to consume everything will businesses be able to obtain resources for their investment activities.

Consequently, we could increase the rate of growth in the United Kingdom drastically if we somehow increased the saving rate of the population, and this additional saving led to the additional production of capital goods.

By way of example consider the data in Figure 34.8. Here we show the per capita income of six countries (in rank order) for the years 1974 and 1984. Notice that in 1974 Japan's measured per capita income was only about 96 per cent of that in the United Kingdom. Yet ten years later, by 1984, it had overtaken the United Kingdom and was approximately 13 per cent bigger. Now look at the lower part of the table (Average Annual Growth Rates) to find out why Japan was able to overtake so fast. Japan's average annual growth rate has been nearly four times greater than that of the United Kingdom during the period under study.

---

*You should be able to identify others, especially if you have read the 33 preceding chapters!

Key Points 34.5

▶ Capital, labour, natural resources, and technological progress all contribute to economic growth. But it is most difficult to identify which is most significant, largely due to problems of measurement.

▶ When considering changes in capital and labour there is a problem distinguishing between quantity and quality aspects. (The same is true of measuring technological progress and natural resources.)

▶ There is no accepted growth theory yet developed.

Figure 34.8

The Changing Positions of the United Kingdom and Japan. The position of Japan relative to other countries has shifted dramatically from 1974 to 1984. This changing position of Japan in the world economy can be found in the economic growth rates displayed in the bottom table.

1974 per capita income		1984 per capita income	
1. United States	$7 245	1. United States	$8 731
2. West Germany	5 599	2. West Germany	6 814
3. France	5 561	3. Japan	6 578
4. United Kingdom	5 050	4. France	6 536
5. Japan	4 845	5. United Kingdom	5 735
6. Italy	4 525	6. Italy	4 921

Average Annual Growth Rates of Real GDP 1974 to 1984

Japan	4.0%	West Germany	1.6%
United States	2.5%	Italy	1.5%
France	2.1%	United Kingdom	1.1%

Source: NEDC, *British Industrial Performance* (NEDO, London, 1985).

Note: Both sets of figures comprising these data are in real terms. The per capita income figures are all expressed in constant 1975 dollar prices. And similarly the percentage increase in real GDP are all based on 1975 prices.

Many have argued that Japan's extraordinary economic growth rate has been due to that country's management system and/or that country's workers' loyalty to their firms. But what is also intriguing is Japan's savings rate. Japan's rate of saving has been approximately 100 per cent higher than that in the United Kingdom. Indeed, current research indicates that the major reason Japan has had such a high growth rate is because it has had such a high rate of saving. If Japan's rate of saving and rate of growth continue unabated, Japan should become the richest country within the next forty years.

Following this trend governments in the UK and France have been changing legislation, tax, and stamp duty to encourage the wider ownership of shares. As Nigel Lawson explicitly remarked during his 1986 budget speech: 'Just as we have made Britain a nation of home-owners, it is the long-term ambition of this government to make the British a nation of share-owners too.' Similarly personal pension schemes in the UK are being made more attractive through legislative changes in social security laws and some minor tax amendments.

These schemes have been designed to increase the savings rate within the UK. However, whether they will now have the desired knock-on effect on capital investment remains to be seen; if they do it *may not* be Japan that becomes the richest country in forty years time.

Promote Mobility

Economic growth implies change and development. Therefore, factors of production will need to be reallocated from industrial sectors that are declining into those that are expanding. However, restrictive practices, such as union-enforced manning levels, prevent some of this reallocation taking place in the UK. Added to this are the universal problems that people are hesitant to uproot themselves or change jobs mid-career. Consequently immobility may cause growth to slow down.

Equally, measures designed to improve mobility may encourage faster growth. Such measures may involve legislation against unions. Alternatively, incentives, such as those discussed in Chapter 33, may be offered to entice labour and capital to be more mobile. These incentives were dealt with under the headings of regional and manpower policies, and may well be worth revisiting at this juncture, in order to glean some relevant sample policy options.

Promote Education and Training

Spending on education and training is regarded by economists as investment in **human capital**, and through this term it can be seen as complimentary, or equally important, as investment in physical capital. Investment in physical capital involves putting time and money into machinery; investment in human capital involves putting time and money into labour. We need specialized labour to operate and develop specialized machinery for we live in a capital-intensive society.

Levels of investment in human capital must, therefore, be maintained and/or increased for economic growth to continue. Consequently we could tabulate the expenditure of education and training from one country to another and assess its importance in the growth process. However, such figures are complicated by the fact that expenditure on education and training is carried out by both the public and private sectors. Furthermore, as with physical capital, how does one measure its effectiveness, especially as the benefits of education and training are often only realized in the long run?

At present the UK government is trying to make the educational process more vocational. It is shifting funds to science and technology subjects and placing an increased emphasis on business training – in this way it is hoped that the quality of our human capital will improve. But only time will tell.

Promote Research and Development

So far in this section we have recognized that investment can be put into human capital or physical capital. We can now complete this by introducing **R & D capital**. R & D capital is the money used for research and development, or to use other words, for invention and innovation. Clearly, such break-throughs would play an important part in the growth process. Consequently, the government engages in funding and undertaking a considerable amount of R & D through research grants and joint projects with business. These government initiatives have already been reviewed in Chapter 33 in some detail and will not be repeated here.

As with all investments in capital the returns can only be measured in the future. Any analysis of R & D investment expenditure is further compounded by the fact that some of it results in no commercial developments. Consequently, economists are still uncertain about the precise importance of R & D policies to the growth process, and this is a question that academics are currently studying.

Promote the Supply Side

As discussed in Chapter 18, present government policies are aimed at improving incentives to encourage businessmen and labour to supply increased amounts of their goods and services. This philosophy is based on a trust in market forces. That is, there is a belief that relying on personal initiative and incentive is the most efficient way to allocate resources. Consequently, various forms of government intervention are presently being reduced and many of these have been explained in Chapter 18.

Before going any further in the text, read Key Points 34.6.

A CLOSING NOTE

Finally, it must be remembered that growth is only one government economic objective. Therefore, spending, legislation, and/or tax cuts to promote growth may cause conflict with the other economic objectives. Consequently, planning and the stage of development are also crucial considerations. These aspects should be a little clearer to the student after the final chapter has been read, and some reflection on the contents of the completed text undertaken.

Key Points 34.6

▶ Several government policies can be envisaged to promote economic growth. There is no agreed policy package. Possible examples include: (1) promoting savings, (2) promoting mobility, (3) promoting education and training, (4) promoting research and development, and (5) promoting the supply side of the economy.

CASE STUDY

Economic Possibilities for Our Grandchildren

John Maynard Keynes wrote an article in the late 1920s under the same title as this Case Study. In this article he concluded that, 'assuming no important wars and no important increase in population, the economic problem may be solved, or be at least within sight of solution within a hundred years'. Keynes felt that within a hundred years, we would be eight times better off economically.

Keynes saw this opulence as *a mixed blessing*. In fact, he felt that 'for the first time since his creation man will be faced with his real, permanent problem – how to use his freedom from pressing economic cares, how to occupy his leisure ... to live wisely and agreeably and well'.

Questions
1. How many times better off do you think we are today compared to Keynes's era and why?
2. How far do you think we have moved towards the idea of 'a mixed blessing'?

A Tale of (at least) Two Nations

Figure 34.9

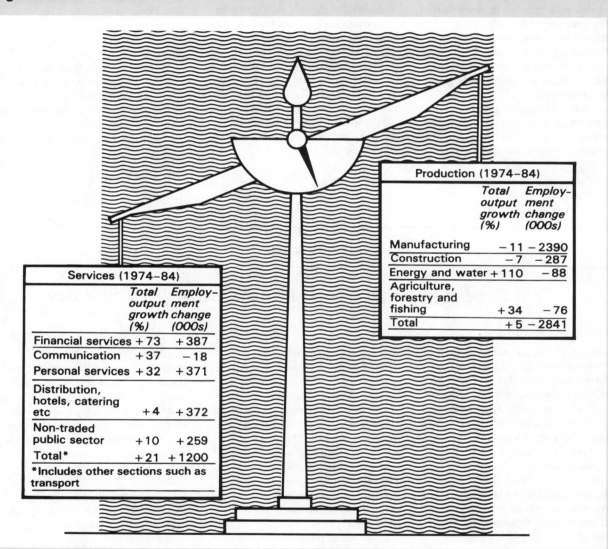

Services (1974–84)	Total output growth (%)	Employment change (000s)
Financial services	+ 73	+ 387
Communication	+ 37	− 18
Personal services	+ 32	+ 371
Distribution, hotels, catering etc	+ 4	+ 372
Non-traded public sector	+ 10	+ 259
Total*	+ 21	+ 1200
*Includes other sections such as transport		

Production (1974–84)	Total output growth (%)	Employment change (000s)
Manufacturing	− 11	− 2390
Construction	− 7	− 287
Energy and water	+ 110	− 88
Agriculture, forestry and fishing	+ 34	− 76
Total	+ 5	− 2841

How radically has the structure of the British economy altered in the past decade? Casual observation suggests there has been a huge upheaval. Indeed, it is hardly an exaggeration to say that there now seem to be two quite separate UK economies, a service-based economy which flourishes in London and the South-east and a production-based economy which languishes in the Midlands and the North.

At the same time, there are now two competing – and compelling – images of British economic life in the 1980s. On the one hand, there is the gloomy vision of those who fret ceaselessly about 'de-industrialization': a grey landscape of deserted factories in what was once the nation's industrial heartland; an endless and depressing vista of dole queues.

On the other, there is the much more encouraging vision of those

who talk airily of a new 'post-industrial society'. A bustling and vibrant, information-based service economy is perhaps best symbolized by the frenetic activity in financial markets or the apparently non-stop growth of business services such as management consultancy. The jobs merry-go-round in the City of London and the seemingly unstoppable inflation of financial sector salaries looks like the icing on a fast-expanding services cake.

Which image is the more representative of the UK's economic health: should we heed the de-industrialists or the post-industrialists? Any judgement has to rest on a detailed examination of the changing structure of the British economy over the last decade, on an analysis of how far casual empiricism about the 'new service economy' is backed up by hard statistics.

Measuring the relative performance of the production and service sectors is by no means straightforward: the output of service industries is notoriously difficult to gauge.

The structural changes occurred against a backdrop of disappointingly slow overall economic growth. Over the whole decade GDP grew in real terms by little more than 13 per cent. In the five years from 1979 GDP grew by barely more than 3 per cent.

The macroeconomic trends were dull and depressing. They are also well understood. Less appreciated, perhaps, is the scale of the variation in the performance of different sectors. The growth rates of service and production industries, and associated changes in employment, over the decade are shown in the two small tables (Figure 34.9).

Source: M. Prowse, 'The tale of (at least) two nations', *Financial Times*, 14 Oct. 1985.

Questions

1. What is de-industrialization?
2. What has possibly caused de-industrialization?
3. Do you think de-industrialization is a problem or not? Give arguments to support your answer.

CASE STUDY

The Problem with Gloom and Doom Predictions

We have to be careful about projections which tell us that the future of the world is one of mass starvation, overwhelming pollution, or total destruction. *The Economist* of London has pointed out, for example, that 'if a Club of Rome had rightly forecast Britain's present quantum of travel, industry, and urban work-force exponentially forward from 1850, it would have proved that this plague-ridden, industrial maimed nation must long since have disappeared beneath several hundred feet of horse manure'.

We just cannot assume that things will not change in the future. It is possible to cite numerous examples of situations that have got better – not worse – such as the pollution level in London. Both air and water pollution have been reduced by 85 per cent in the last twenty years. The reduction in air pollution has doubled the hours of winter sunshine, since there are fewer truly smoggy days to block out the sun. The reduction in water pollution has allowed 55 species of fish to thrive now in the once-mordant Thames. There is even some evidence that in general the average person in the year, say, 1200, absorbed more pollutants than we do now, due to poor ventilation coupled with wood and peat fires.

Concerning the problem of the psychological well-being of the human species, a University of Utah medical sociologist, Dr John Collett, basing his conclusions on the results of a massive study of urban stress, contends that the mental and physical well-being of present-day city dwellers exceeds that of backwoods persons and people who lived in the crop-growing plains areas of the nation a hundred years ago.

In sum, gloom and doom projections about the future of this nation and, indeed, of the world may not be fully warranted. It is not at all clear that today we are worse off physically or mentally than we were a hundred years ago, when we were a poorer nation.

Questions

1. Outline the arguments that would be put forward by those who worry that growth is not a good thing.
2. The Club of Rome* is a group of academics and civil servants from several countries. What line of argument do you think they support? (You may find their book(s) in your library.)

---

*A kind of invisible College founded in April 1968.

Exam Preparation and Practice

INTRODUCTORY EXERCISES

1. List as many costs of economic growth as you can.

2. List as many benefits of economic growth as you can.

3. Using supply and demand curves, show how it is possible for a nation to consume more of a resource over time even though the resource is becoming relatively scarcer.

MULTIPLE CHOICE QUESTIONS

For Questions 1, 2, and 3 select your answers by means of the following grid:

A	B	C	D
1,2,3 all correct	**1,2** only correct	**2,3** only correct	**1** only correct

†1. To calculate the economic growth of a country as measured by changes in the *real* level of National Income, information is required on
   1 social security payments
   2 the retail price index
   3 the Gross National Product less capital consumption

†2. A country may NOT wish to maximize economic growth if this leads to
   1 a reduction in its non renewable resources
   2 a greater inequality of incomes
   3 social costs greatly exceeding private costs

3. Which of the following influence(s) real income per head?

   1 the size of the population
   2 capital investment
   3 technological development.

4. The diagram below shows two production possibility curves.

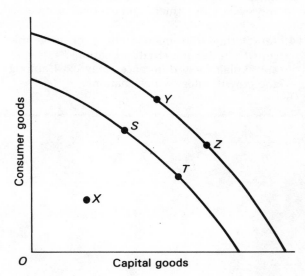

Which movement depicts an increase in the utilization of existing productive capacity?
   A *X* to *T*
   B *S* to *T*
   C *S* to *Y*
   D *S* to *Z*
   E *T* to *Y*

5. Economic growth is most effectively defined as:
   A an increase in money GDP
   B an increase in real GDP
   C an increase in both material welfare and social welfare
   D an increase in real GNP per head.

continued overleaf

RELATED ESSAY QUESTIONS

1. Do the costs of economic growth outweigh the benefits?

2. What are the major determinants of economic growth? To what extent is a policy for growth incompatible with other macroeconomic policy objectives?

3. Explore the nature of the relationship between the level of investment and national income.

†4. (a) Outline the main sources of economic growth in the industrialized nations.
   (b) Explain why differences may exist among the growth rates of these nations.

5. 'Increases in people's welfare can be measured by increases in the economic growth rate.' Discuss this statement with reference to one country only.

6. What factors are likely to increase the level of 'labour productivity' in an economy? Would rapid growth in labour productivity solve the United Kingdom's economic and social problems?

7. Contrast the meaning of 'growth' and 'recovery' when applied to an economy. Discuss whether or not you regard economic growth as desirable.

35 Economic Development

Questions for Preview

1 What is a less developed country (LDC)?

2 Do LDCs all face similar problems in trying to attain fast economic growth?

3 To what extent can LDCs rely on international trade in order to spur economic growth?

4 How can developed nations assist LDCs?

The previous chapter discussed economic growth with reference to countries like the UK. When we examine the same topic in relation to those countries in the world that are not yet developed, we enter the study of economic development. It is hard for us in the UK to realize that what we consider a low level of income in the UK exceeds the average income in a good part of the world. In fact, many of the world's people live at or close to subsistence: just enough to eat for survival. Developed nations encounter problems associated with being relatively rich such as obesity, urban sprawl, and pollution. The **less-developed countries**, or LDCs, are grappling with abject poverty and squalor; in short, with mere existence. The tragic pictures that we have seen of hunger and starvation in Ethiopia have vividly illustrated this contrast with the relative affluence of life in developed nations. Bob Geldof has attempted to bring efforts within the private sector to the aid of the starving in Africa. Can governments do more to assist countries like Ethiopia?

Before considering this we must first examine the nature of developing countries and consider why some countries are more developed than others.

Defining a Developing Country

There are a number of ways to classify nations by level of economic development. The 'three worlds' classification scheme has gained relatively wide acceptance. The **First World** is the highly industrialized, non-communist Western European nations, plus the United States, Australia, Canada, New Zealand, and Japan. The **Second World** includes the communist nations of Eastern Europe, the Soviet Union, and the People's Republic of China (PRC). The **Third World** is the term given to identify remaining countries, i.e. in Africa, Asia, and Latin America. But this classification of the globe has as much a political dimension to it as economics. A more basic distinction has been made between mainly developed countries situated in the Northern Hemisphere – 'the North' – and the vast majority of countries which are less developed and are located below the Equator – 'the South'. The rich North–poor South distinction is necessarily a crude one but still begs the question: what is the definition by which a country is deemed developed rather than developing?

Economists have traditionally used a cut-off point in GNP data to make this distinction. The precise figure used is of course quite an arbitrary one. In 1985 the World Bank defined low-income developing countries as those with a per capita income of less than $400 in 1983. Fifty-nine countries with a per capita income of $400 or more constituted middle-income developing economies.

A fundamental question in looking at different countries is how can we compare the GNP of India measured in rupees with that of a developed country like the UK measured in pounds sterling? We do need a common unit of measurement. Translating all the GNP data into one country's currency seems to solve this problem. As we have just seen, the World Bank

uses dollars as this common currency. Thus India's GNP in terms of dollars is measured as follows

$$\frac{\text{India's GNP per capita in rupees}}{\text{India's exchange rate between rupees and dollars}} = \text{India's GNP per capita in terms of dollars.}$$

The calculation implies that the foreign exchange rate is an international barometer of the cost of living. But a few moments' reflection should make you realize that the exchange rate is determined by the goods and services that are the subject of international exchange. Some items of consumer spending do not enter into world trade, e.g. going to a disco, getting a haircut. Thus our GNP data expressed in dollars (or pounds sterling) present an imperfect picture of the actual cost of living throughout the world. To try and surmount this problem economists have tried to see the differing cost of a common basket of goods and services purchased in various countries. This has revealed that the cost of living in many so-called developing countries can be high relative to countries like the UK,

Figure 35.1

The Cost of Living in 33 Capital Cities. The chart shows the cost of buying a common basket of 126 goods and services and rents in each country weighted by consumer spending in 1985. London is taken as the point of reference with an index of 100. Thus the cost of living in Abu Dhabi was more than twice that in London. Can you suggest a reason why life in Lagos is surprisingly so expensive?

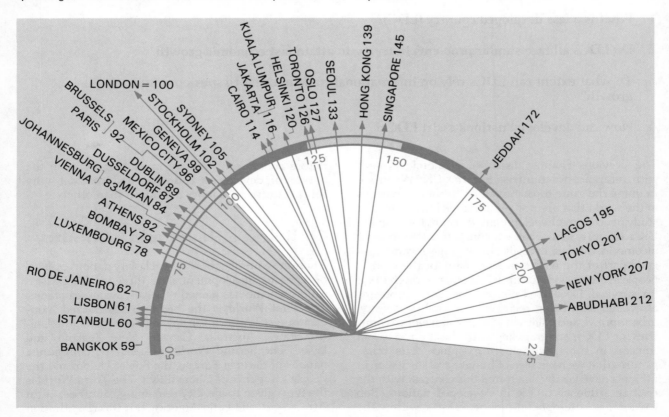

Source: Union Bank of Switzerland survey, *The Economist* 21 Sep. 1985, p. 107.

France, and West Germany. Figure 35.1 presents one such international comparison. Of the sixteen capital cities where the costs of living exceeded that of London nine were to be found in countries outside Western Europe, Japan, North America, and Australia.

We must appreciate that GNP per capita data are thus suggestive of the standards of living rather than precise pictures of differences in the welfare of the world's peoples.

Fortunately we find that other approaches to the definition of development do not really conflict with the broad message of GNP statistics. If we resort to so-called **non-monetary indicators** there is a sufficient correlation between these and GNP data. In Figure 35.2 we see that as we move up through levels of GNP per capita life expectancy as at birth tends to increase. We find that countries with a low level of GNP per

capita suffer from high infant mortality, tend to have low levels of literacy, and typically have a high proportion of their people involved in the primary sector of the economy, that is, engaged in agriculture, forestry, and fishing. Indeed, it is by using some of these alternative measures of development that the **least-developed countries** have come to be defined. In 1971 the UN identified those countries with severe long-term constraints on development using three criteria:

(a) GDP per capita of $100 or less in 1970,
(b) a share of manufacturing in GDP of 10 per cent or less, and
(c) a literacy rate of 20 per cent or less of the population aged 15 years or older.

This definition identified twenty-four countries in 1971 and these are listed in Question 1 of the Introductory Exercises at the end of this chapter.

Figure 35.2
GNP Per Capita and Some Other Indicators of Development in 126 Countries

	Population (millions) mid-1983	GNP per capita[a] Dollars 1983	Average annual growth rate (percent) 1965–83[b]	Percentage of labour force in: agriculture 1965	1981	Life expectancy at birth (years) 1983	Infant mortality rate (aged under 1) 1965	1983	Population per physician 1965[a]	1980[a]	Crude birth rate per thousand population 1965	1983
Low-income economies	2335.4t	260w	2.7w	77w	73w	59w	122w	75w	12419w	5556w	43w	30w
China and India	1752.3t	280w	3.2w	..	73w	62w	115w	61w	..	1858w	42w	25w
Other low-income	583.0t	200w	0.7w	81w	72w	51w	147w	115w	26097	17990w	46w	43w
Sub-Sahara Africa	245.2t	220w	-0.2w	84w	78w	48w	156w	119w	38268	27922w	48w	47w
1 Ethiopia	40.9	120	0.5	86	80	43	166	..	70190	69390	44	41
2 Bangladesh	95.5	130	0.5	87	74	50	153	132	..	7810	47	42
3 Mali	7.2	160	1.2	93	73	45	184	148	49010	22130	50	48
4 Nepal	15.7	160	0.1	95	93	46	184	143	46180	30060	46	42
5 Zaire	29.7	170	-1.3	81	75	51	142	106	39050	13940	48	46
6 Burkina Faso	6.5	180	1.4	90	82	44	193	148	74110	48510	46	47
7 Burma	35.5	180	2.2	..	67	55	143	93	11660	4680	42	38
8 Malawi	6.6	210	2.2	91	86	44	201	164	46900	41460	56	54
9 Uganda	13.9	220	-4.4	88	83	49	126	108	11080	26810	49	50
10 Burundi	4.5	240	2.1	89	84	47	169	123	54930	45020	47	47
11 Niger	6.1	240	-1.2	94	91	45	181	139	71440	38790	48	52
12 Tanzania	20.8	240	0.9	88	83	51	138	97	21840	17740	49	50
13 Somalia	5.1	250	-0.8	87	82	45	166	142	35060	15630	50	50
14 India	733.2	260	1.5	74	71	55	151	93	4860	3690	45	34
15 Rwanda	5.7	270	2.3	94	91	47	159	125	74170	31340	52	52
16 Central African Rep	2.5	280	0.1	93	88	48	184	142	44490	26750	43	41
17 Togo	2.8	280	1.1	81	67	49	158	112	24980	18100	50	49
18 Benin	3.8	290	1.0	52	46	48	193	148	28790	16980	49	49
19 China	1019.1	300	4.4	..	74	67	90	38	..	1740	39	19
20 Guinea	5.8	300	1.1	87	82	37	197	158	54610	17110	46	47
21 Haiti	5.3	300	1.1	77	74	54	160	107	12580	8200	38	32
22 Ghana	12.8	310	-2.1	61	53	59	132	97	12040	7160	50	49
23 Madagascar	9.5	310	-1.2	92	87	49	99	66	9900	10220	44	47
24 Sierra Leone	3.6	330	1.1	75	65	38	230	198	18400	17520	48	49
25 Sri Lanka	15.4	330	2.9	56	54	69	63	37	5750	7170	33	27
26 Kenya	18.9	340	2.3	84	78	57	124	81	12840	7890	51	55
27 Pakistan	89.7	390	2.5	60	57	50	150	119	3160	3480	48	42
28 Sudan	20.8	400	1.3	84	78	48	161	117	23500	8930	47	46
29 Afghanistan	17.2	..	0.5	84	79	36	223	..	15770	16730	54	54
30 Bhutan	1.2	..	..	95	93	43	184	162	3310	18160	43	43

continued overleaf

	Population (millions) mid-1983	GNP per capita[a] Dollars 1983	GNP per capita[a] Average annual growth rate (percent) 1965–83[b]	Percentage of labour force in agriculture 1965	Percentage of labour force in agriculture 1981	Life expectancy at birth (years) 1983	Infant mortality rate (aged under 1) 1965	Infant mortality rate (aged under 1) 1983	Population per physician 1965[a]	Population per physician 1980[a]	Crude birth rate per thousand population 1965	Crude birth rate per thousand population 1983
31 Chad	4.8	..	..	93	85	43	184	142	73040	47640	40	42
32 Kampuchea, Dem.	..	..	..	80	..	..	135	..	22490	..	44	..
33 Lao PDR	3.7	..	..	81	75	44	196	159	26510	..	45	42
34 Mozambique	13.1	..	..	77	66	46	148	109	18700	39140	49	46
35 Viet Nam	58.5	..	..	79	71	64	89	53	..	4190	45	35
Middle-income economies	1165.2t	1310w	3.4w	57w	44w	61w	112w	75w	11388w	5995w	42w	34w
Oil exporters	542.6t	1060w	3.3w	61w	48w	57w	129w	91w	20016w	8089w	46w	39w
Oil importers	622.6t	1530w	3.5w	53w	41w	64w	98w	61w	4146w	3870w	38w	30w
Sub-Saharan Africa	148.2t	700w	1.9w	70w	60w	50w	150w	112w	35517w	11929w	50w	49w
Lower middle-income	665.1t	750w	2.9w	66w	54w	57w	127w	87w	18399w	7555w	45w	362w
36 Senegal	6.2	440	−0.5	82	77	46	172	140	21130	13780	47	46
37 Lesotho	1.5	460	6.3	92	60	53	138	109	22930	18640	42	42
38 Liberia	2.1	480	0.8	78	70	49	149	111	12450	8550	46	49
39 Mauritania	1.6	480	0.3	90	69	46	171	136	36580	14500	44	43
40 Bolivia	6.0	510	0.6	58	50	51	161	123	3310	..	46	44
41 Yemen, PDR	2.0	520	..	68	45	46	194	137	12870	7120	50	48
42 Yemen Arab Rep.	7.6	550	5.7	81	75	44	200	152	58240	11670	49	48
43 Indonesia	155.7	560	5.0	71	58	54	138	101	31820	11530	43	34
44 Zambia	6.3	580	−1.3	76	67	51	137	100	11360	7670	51	44
45 Honduras	4.1	670	0.6	68	63	60	131	81	5450	3120	51	44
46 Egypt, Arab Rep.	45.2	700	4.2	56	50	58	123	102	2260	970	42	34
47 El Salvador	5.2	710	−0.2	59	50	64	120	70	4630	3220	46	40
48 Ivory Coast	9.5	710	1.0	87	79	52	160	121	20690	..	44	46
49 Zimbabwe	7.9	740	1.5	67	60	56	106	69	5190	5900	49	40
50 Morocco	20.8	760	2.9	60	52	52	149	98	12120	10750	49	40
51 Papua New Guinea	3.2	760	0.9	88	82	54	148	97	12520	13590	43	35
52 Philippines	52.1	760	2.9	57	46	64	90	49	1310	7970	46	31
53 Nigeria	93.6	770	3.2	67	54	49	152	113	44990	12550	51	50
54 Cameroon	9.6	820	2.7	86	83	54	155	116	29720	13990	40	46
55 Thailand	49.2	820	4.3	82	76	63	90	50	7230	7100	43	27
56 Nicaragua	3.0	880	−1.8	57	39	58	129	84	2490	1800	49	45
57 Costa Rica	2.4	1020	2.1	47	29	74	74	20	2040	1460	45	30
58 Peru	17.9	1040	0.1	50	40	58	131	98	1620	1390	46	38
59 Guatemala	7.9	1120	2.1	64	55	60	109	67	3830	8610	46	38
60 Congo, People's Rep.	1.8	1230	3.5	47	34	63	116	82	14210	5510	41	43
61 Turkey	47.3	1240	3.0	74	54	63	157	82	2860	1630	41	31
62 Tunisia	6.9	1290	5.0	53	35	62	145	83	8040	3690	46	33
63 Jamaica	2.3	1300	−0.5	34	35	70	51	28	1930	2830	38	28
64 Dominican Rep.	6.0	1370	3.9	64	49	63	103	63	1720	2410	47	33
65 Paraguay	3.2	1410	4.5	55	49	65	74	45	1840	1310	41	31
66 Ecuador	8.2	1420	4.6	54	52	63	124	76	3020	760	45	37
67 Columbia	27.5	1430	3.2	45	26	64	80	53	2530	1710	43	28
68 Angola	8.2	..	..	67	59	43	193	148	12000	..	49	49
69 Cuba	9.8	..	..	35	23	75	54	20	1150	720	34	17
70 Korea, Dem. Rep.	19.2	..	..	59	49	65	64	32	..	430	39	30
71 Lebanon	2.6	..	..	28	11	65	57	48	1240	540	41	29
72 Mongolia	1.8	..	..	66	55	65	89	49	710	450	42	34
Upper middle-income	500.1t	2050w	3.8w	45w	30w	65w	92w	59w	2507w	2018w	38w	31w
73 Jordan	3.2	1640	6.9	41	20	64	117	62	4670	900	48	45
74 Syrian Arab Rep.	9.6	1760	4.9	53	33	67	116	56	4050	2240	48	46
75 Malaysia	14.9	1860	4.5	60	50	67	57	29	6220	..	41	29
76 Chile	11.7	1870	−0.1	26	19	70	103	40	2080	1930	32	24
77 Brazil	129.7	1880	5.0	49	30	64	104	70	2180	..	39	30
78 Korea, Rep. of	40.0	2010	6.7	58	34	67	64	29	2740	1440	36	23
79 Argentina	29.6	2070	0.5	18	13	70	59	36	640	430	22	24
80 Panama	2.0	2120	2.9	46	33	71	59	26	2170	980	40	28

	Population (millions) mid-1983	GNP per capita[a] Dollars 1983	GNP per capita[a] Average annual growth rate (percent) 1965–83[b]	Percentage of labour force in: agriculture 1965	Percentage of labour force in: agriculture 1981	Life expectancy at birth (years) 1983	Infant mortality rate (aged under 1) 1965	Infant mortality rate (aged under 1) 1983	Population per physician 1965[a]	Population per physician 1980[a]	Crude birth rate per thousand population 1965	Crude birth rate per thousand population 1983
81 Portugal	10.1	2 230	3.7	39	28	71	65	25	1 170	540	23	15
82 Mexico	75.0	2 240	3.2	50	36	66	82	52	2 060	..	45	34
83 Algeria	20.6	2 320	3.6	59	25	57	155	107	8 400	2 630	50	47
84 South Africa	31.5	2 490	1.6	32	30	64	124	91	2 140	..	40	40
85 Uruguay	3.0	2 490	2.0	18	11	73	47	38	870	540	21	18
86 Yugoslavia	22.8	2 570	4.7	57	29	69	72	32	1 190	550	21	13
87 Venezuela	17.3	3 840	1.5	30	18	68	71	38	1 270	990	43	35
88 Greece	9.8	3 920	4.0	51	37	75	34	15	710	430	18	14
89 Israel	4.1	5 370	2.9	12	7	74	27	14	410	370	26	24
90 Hong Kong	5.3	6 000	6.2	6	3	76	28	10	2 400	1 210	28	17
91 Singapore	2.5	6 620	7.8	6	2	73	26	11	1 910	1 150	31	17
92 Trinidad and Tobago	1.1	6 850	3.4	23	10	68	47	28	3 820	1 360	33	29
93 Iran, Islamic Rep.	42.5	..	..	50	39	60	150	100	3 770	6 090	50	40
94 Iraq	14.7	..	..	50	42	59	121	71	4 970	1 800	49	45
High-income oil exporters	17.9t	12 370w	3.8w	58w	46w	59w	153w	90w	8 774w	1 360w	49w	42w
95 Oman	1.1	6 250	6.5	..	..	53	175	121	23 790	1 900	50	47
96 Libya	3.4	8 480	–0.9	42	19	58	143	91	3 970	730	49	45
97 Saudi Arabia	10.4	12 230	6.7	69	61	56	164	101	9 400	1 670	49	43
98 Kuwait	1.7	17 880	0.2	1	2	71	66	29	830	570	47	35
99 United Arab Emirates	1.2	22 870	..	..	..	71	104	44	..	910	41	27
Industrial market economies	728.9t	11 060w	2.5w	14w	6w	76w	5.2w	8.0w	752w	554w	19w	14w
100 Spain	38.2	4 780	3.0	34	14	75	7.0	16.7	810	450	21	13
101 Ireland	3.5	5 000	2.3	31	18	73	8.5	14.5	960	780	22	20
102 Italy	56.8	6 400	2.8	24	11	76	5.1	17.1	590	340	19	11
103 New Zealand	3.2	7 730	1.2	13	10	74	7.2	14.2	820	640	23	16
104 Belgium	9.9	9 150	3.1	6	3	73	4.4	6.4	690	400	17	12
105 United Kingdom	56.3	9 200	1.7	3	2	74	6.2	14.3	860	650	18	13
106 Austria	7.5	9 250	3.7	19	9	73	4.5	5.4	550	400	18	12
107 Netherlands	14.4	9 890	2.3	9	6	76	6.4	6.2	860	540	20	12
108 Japan	119.3	10 120	4.8	26	12	77	6.0	4.7	930	780	19	13
109 France	54.7	10 500	3.1	18	8	75	5.3	10.8	810	580	18	14
110 Finland	4.9	10 740	3.3	28	11	73	7.2	10.6	1 280	530	17	14
111 Germany, Fed. Rep.	61.4	11 430	2.8	10	4	75	4.7	4.3	630	450	18	10
112 Australia	15.4	11 490	1.7	10	6	76	5.7	10.5	720	560	20	16
113 Denmark	5.1	11 570	1.9	14	7	74	7.6	9.5	740	480	18	10
114 Canada	24.9	12 310	2.5	11	5	76	4.4	9.4	770	550	21	15
115 Sweden	8.3	12 470	1.9	11	5	78	5.3	10.3	910	490	16	11
116 Norway	4.1	14 020	3.3	15	7	77	6.3	9.7	790	520	18	12
117 United States	234.5	14 110	1.7	5	2	75	4.7	7.5	670	520	19	16
118 Switzerland	6.5	16 290	1.4	10	5	79	5.5	3.9	750	410	19	11
East European nonmarket economies	386.1t	..	..	35w	17w	70w	..	..	564w	345w	18w	19w
119 Hungary	10.7	2 150	6.4	32	21	70	2.6	4.1	630	400	13	12
120 Albania	2.8	..	..	69	61	71	..	..	2 100	..	35	28
121 Bulgaria	8.9	..	..	52	37	70	..	..	600	410	15	14
122 Czechoslovakia	15.4	..	..	21	11	70	..	..	540	360	16	15
123 German Dem. Rep.	16.7	..	..	15	10	71	..	..	870	520	17	14
124 Poland	36.6	..	..	44	31	71	..	..	800	570	17	20
125 Romania	22.6	..	..	58	29	71	..	..	740	680	15	15
126 USSR	272.5	..	..	33	14	69	..	..	480	270	18	20

Notes: t = a total figure; w = a weighted average
Source: World Bank, *World Development Report 1985*, Oxford University Press, Tables 1, 20, 21, and 24.

This consideration of the poverty of some countries in the world underlines the harsh fact of global inequality. When we look at the amount of world output accounted for by developed countries, the inequality is even more striking. The industrialized market economies (the First World) have less than 18 per cent of world population, but none the less generate almost 65 per cent of total world output. The United States, with less than 6 per cent of the world's population, generates almost 30 per cent of total world output!

What is popularly called the Third World is larger in terms of the number of countries than the First World and the Second World combined. But the concept of the Third World is rather vague, because it masks the marked variation *within* it. It lumps together countries that are very different not only in economic terms, but also in cultural, political, racial, and ethnic terms. A look again at Figure 35.1 points to oil as one important determinant of the differences within the Third World. A number of geographic regions and social classes within the Third World have living standards that are closer to Western Europe than to those of other Third World countries. Consider the oil states, for example. Those countries are normally classified as Third World countries, yet the total output per person in the United Arab Emirates in 1983 was over $20 000. The output per person in Kuwait was over $17 000. These figures can be compared with $9 200 for the UK, $14 110 for the USA, and $16 290 for Switzerland!

Some LDCs are developing so rapidly that they have come to be termed **newly industrializing countries (NICs)**. Such countries as Mexico, Brazil, South Korea, and Malaysia are now seen as providing increasingly stiff competition for firms in the manufacturing sectors of the older industrialized countries of Western Europe.

One can identify rather different problems in each of the three continents of Latin America, Africa, and South Asia. In Latin America many economists see the unequal distribution of land as a major problem frustrating the growth of agriculture. While many African countries face major pressing problems in feeding their populations a longer-established constraint on their development has been the relative inefficiency of many institutions within the public sector. In contrast, the key South Asian constraint has been the sheer pressure of population on available land supplies. It is not the quality of the civil service that raises worries but the whole balance of resources.

Geographical Theories of Economic Development

One of the earliest and most simplistic theories of growth concerns geographical location. This might also be called the North–South theory of economic development. According to this theory, nations that are in the colder climates will be more developed than nations in the warmer climates. Most LDCs are between the Tropics of Cancer and Capricorn. This fact offers a robust challenge to the North–South theory of development. One might more convincingly argue an 'equator' theory of development, namely, that countries closer to the equator will develop more slowly than countries farther away from the equator. Basically, though, geographical theories of development cannot be used to predict development with a high degree of accuracy. If the North–South theory had any relevance or validity, it should apply also to the past. It does not. Some of the first civilizations were in the hot southern regions of the world. Look at the Mayas in Central America and all the great civilizations in the Mediterranean area and the Near East. The Germans and the Saxons were far behind the Greeks in development, even though the Greeks enjoyed a warmer climate. As a final example, consider that in AD 1100, the Near East was highly developed relative to the West. By the beginning of the industrial revolution, this was clearly no longer true.

This assessment, however, is in danger of playing down the significance of climatic factors that can hamper development of countries within the tropics. We must at least recognize the problem of agriculture in many LDCs arising from the quality of its soils, the variability of the rainfall, and the multiplicity of pests and diseases. The tropical climate is an important parameter in the development of many LDCs. This point has relevance to our consideration of the nature of the development process which now follows.

Key Points 35.1

▶ **Any definition of a less-developed country (LDC) is arbitrary. Typically, a cut-off point in terms of per capita income of around $400 helps us define an LDC.**

▶ **LDCs can also be defined in terms of so-called non-monetary indicators such as their levels of literacy, education, infant mortality, and life expectancy. In virtually all LDCs, these socioeconomic indicators are quite different from what they are in the developed countries.**

▶ **LDCs differ among themselves almost as much as the differences between them and the countries in the First World.**

Factors in the Development Process

In Chapter 34 we considered the role of natural resources, capital accumulation, and technical progress in determining economic growth. Although our context was then the developed nations such as the UK you should find it helpful to read that review again as much of the analysis is of universal application. We will, however, briefly recap on our earlier conclusions.

We argued that the presence of large natural resources is certainly helpful but not vital for successful economic development. The fastest growing LDCs in the past two decades have been Singapore, Taiwan, South Korea, and Hong Kong. None of these countries is blessed with oil fields.

In any event, it is difficult to find a strong correlation between the natural resources of a nation and its stage of development. Japan has virtually no crude oil and must import most of the natural resources that it uses as inputs into its industrial production. Brazil has huge amounts of natural resources, including fertile soil and abundant minerals. Yet Brazil has a lower per capita income than Japan. Only when we include the human element of natural resources can we say that natural resources determine economic development. This comment takes us neatly into the issue of capital accumulation. Capital is important in both the physical and human sense. Indeed, recent research by the World Bank has pointed to the importance of human development. The Bank now believes better education, nutrition, and family planning can promote development as effectively as capital investment in physical plant.

In the early post-war period the World Bank was keen to help finance the extension of the infrastructure – investment in power, irrigation, and transport. This meant lending funds which were used to buy bricks and mortar and items of capital equipment. Such items are, of course, a means to an end – the improvement in human welfare. By 1980 the World Bank's review of the empirical evidence pointed to the significance of improved health, nutrition, and education as not only another means of bringing about economic development but as being desirable *in themselves*. The World Bank's research points to education, as measured by literacy and primary school attendance, as the main factor linked to the level of human development. In its World Development Report it showed how in one study that educated farmers – defined as those with at least four years of primary education – tended to produce up to 13 per cent more than farmers who had not attended school at all. Expenditure on human capital – better education, health, and nutrition – tends to reduce birth-rates and reduce infant mortality. Thus we find a virtuous circle of self-supporting improvements in human welfare rather than the vicious circle of illiteracy, malnutrition, ill-health, high birth-rates, and low life expectancy for babies. Figure 35.3 identifies the relationships

Figure 35.3
The Dimensions of Human Capital. The chart depicts the interrelated nature of health, education, fertility, and nutrition and their impact on income levels.

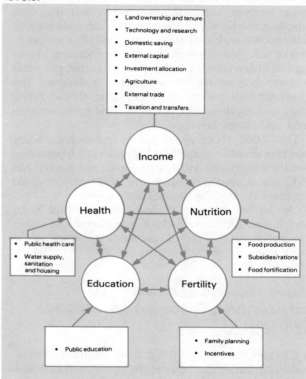

Source: World Bank, *World Development Report*, 1980, p. 69.

between the various dimensions of human capital and their limits with levels of income per head.

When we considered technology in Chapter 34 we noted that there has long been a transfer of technology from the developed world to LDCs. The benefits of this international process have not always been self-evident. The London-based Intermediate Technology has recently illustrated this with a sombre story. Ten years ago when the last dreadful famine gripped the Horn of Africa, 40000 nomads were airlifted from their barren land and set down in a fertile plain in Somalia. They were provided with new brick-built homes and the most sophisticated farming machinery that money could buy. Today ten years on, their 'model' village is deserted. Half the nomads slipped quietly away into the bush to go back to their old way of life. The rest built their traditional stick huts and began to farm the land using the methods of their ancestors. In a vast four-acre compound, row upon row of tractors, bulldozers, and combine harvesters lie idle, corroded with rust. A workshop the size of an aircraft hangar has barely been used since the day it was built.

This spectacular white elephant cost millions. Whatever went wrong? These people who have always lived by the simplest means were suddenly faced with technology that was too complicated and too alien for them to accept. The gap between their knowledge and Western technology was simply too great for them to make use of the 'help' that was offered.

Capital-intensive technology may be, in a technical sense, 'efficient' but LDCs may have as much if not more concern with employment as output. With rapidly growing populations there is an understandable concern with the provisions of jobs. The introduction of a highly automated factory producing plastic sandals in one African country, for example, put 7 000 leather shoemakers out of work. It reduced the incomes of the makers of leather, glue, thread, fabric linings, tacks, dressings, polishes, hand tools, wooden lasts, and carton boxes.

The 7 000 shoemakers were replaced by forty injection-moulding machine operators. Dependence switched to manufacturers of plastic machinery and PVC grains abroad, because the local industry could not meet the new technological demands.

Our earlier example of the capital-intensive 'solution' in Somalia shows how it is important to match the needs and skills of people with appropriate technology.

How Developed Nations Influence LDCs: International Trade

In Chapter 9 we noted the gains from international trade if countries specialize in the production of goods in which they enjoy a comparative advantage. Given their relative abundance of land this would point to LDCs being exporters of primary products exchanged for manufactures and capital equipment. Indeed, many of today's independent countries were sources of raw materials and foodstuffs back in colonial days. But in the 1980s these countries which are now able to determine their own economic policy have reservations about the wisdom of specializing on primary production. They have a basis for hesitating to rely on international exchange to spur economic development. Why is this?

Export Dependence

Several LDCs rely on a single commodity for more than half their export earnings as Figure 35.4 shows. This marked dependence requires broadly stable market conditions for such reliance on one commodity not to cause problems. If for whatever reason export earnings fluctuate then the whole economy is affected. Why should there be fluctuations in these earnings?

Price Inelastic Supply and Demand

A key problem is that, because both supply and demand are insensitive with respect to price, commodity prices fluctuate much more than in the case of manufactured goods. In Chapter 8 we saw that this prompted efforts by governments to try to stabilize agricultural prices in developed economies. We shall thus need, later in this chapter, to reconsider how LDCs can try to stabilize the prices of tea, coffee, and copper on the world's commodity markets.

Technological Progress

A further problem facing some commodity producers is that scientific advance has promoted the development of synthetic substitutes for natural products. In 1970 consumption of natural rubber was already about 2.2m tonnes less than half the consumption of synthetic rubber at 4.6m tonnes. Furthermore, much of the growth in demand in the 1980s was expected to be satisfied by production within the developed economies rather than that arising from South-east Asia. High prices for products like rubber and copper prompt a search in the West for more stable sources of raw materials which tends not to be reversible in any subsequent decline in price of the natural product. Sisal is another example of a natural product that has faced the problem of a synthetic substitute. Furthermore, technological progress in the broadest sense is reducing the volume of metals used. Goods like radios and computers have become smaller and use less

---

Key Points 35.2

▶ Many LDCs are to be found within the equatorial belt of the globe. While any deterministic view of the environment seems misplaced we can recognize certain problems of economic development in this part of the world.

▶ Natural resources are helpful but not critical for economic development.

▶ Health, nutrition, and education expenditures are now considered to be important means of bringing about economic advance.

▶ Capital-intensive technologies may well permit a growth in output but do little to meet the need of LDCs to find jobs for their growing populations.

Figure 35.4
Export Dependence in Some LDCs: Biggest Export as Percentage of Total Exports, 1983. Quite apart from the oil-exporting countries in the Middle East some other countries rely on one commodity for more than 50 per cent of their earnings from exports.

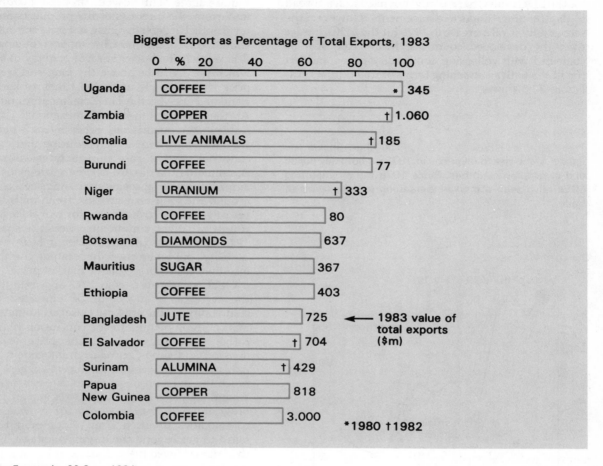

Source: The Economist, 22 Sept. 1984.

materials per unit weight than before. Another example is foodstuffs which are now packed in lighter and thinner cans than a decade or so ago. This has meant some reduction in the demand for tin.

Income Elasticities of Demand

In Chapter 8 we pointed out that the income elasticity of demand for foodstuffs is typically below unity. This means that the growth in demand for foodstuffs shows very little significant growth as time goes by. Indeed, in a country like the US it has reached virtual saturation point. The concern over obesity in Western Europe is encouraging the demand for 'healthy' foods which are often based on synthetic sources. This situation is hardly encouraging for the sugar-cane producers in the Third World! Furthermore, the growth in the market due to population increases in the developed economies also does not provide any sales expansion in commodity markets in terms of sheer volume.

We noted in Chapter 9 that the recession in world output since 1973 had been accompanied by a market fall in the rate of growth of international trade. The sluggish state of manufacturing industry in the West has inevitably had an adverse impact on LDC supplies of industrial raw materials and fuels.

Increased Supply

We noted in Chapter 34 how the adoption of 'miracle' rice has in part contributed to an improved agricultural situation in some LDCs. However, while the enhancement of food supplies at home has been welcome the greater availability of output on world markets has reinforced the downward pressure on commodity prices.

Declining Terms of Trade

We defined the relationship between a country's average export prices in relation to its average import prices as the terms of trade in Chapter 9. In the case of

LDCs the dramatic oil price increases of 1973 pushed down the terms of trade of all oil importers, both LDCs and developed countries. However, the boom in commodity prices partially offset this adverse effect for the LDCs such that they did not need to sell abroad to pay for their import requirements. However, the second OPEC oil increase in 1979 hit the LDCs harder than the developed countries. More expensive oil coincided with collapsing commodity prices and left the LDCs with a worsening terms of trade situation as Figure 35.5 shows.

Figure 35.5

The Terms of Trade for LDCs. The chart shows the impact of the rise in oil prices in 1973 on both developed and developing countries. Since 1978 the oil-importing LDCs have seen a marked worsening in their terms of trade.

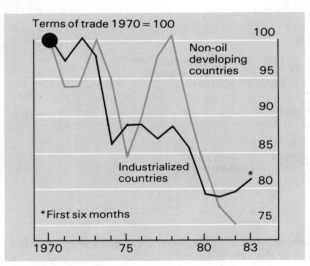

Source: The Economist, 14 January 1984, p. 94.

Given all these depressing factors at work it should not surprise you that LDCs have for many years sought to stabilize world commodity prices. They have seen **international commodity agreements** (ICAs) as a means of effecting this objective. While these are simple in concept they have proved difficult to implement. ICAs are in essence the buffer stock schemes that we examined in Chapter 8 on a world scale. ICAs require agreement between producing countries and importers: the interests of the producers and importers conflict in determining what price the buffer stock should try to maintain by support buying. If it is decided that the buffer stock should try to set a price which proves to be above the long-run free market price level it needs unlimited funds to keep up the regulated price (as the Tin Agreement found in 1985). At the present time the International Coffee and Rubber Agreements are experiencing strains given the differing interests of producing and consuming countries. In the case of the International Cocoa Agreements the discord is even more evident. Is the aim of such an agreement to stabilize cocoa prices around the long-term market trend or is it to raise returns to cocoa-growers as a form of aid to producing countries? When commodity prices rise sharply as in 1973 consuming countries have a keen interest in 'stability', but when they are declining they have little incentive to accept regulated market prices.

OPEC's early success in 1973 appeared to promise the cartel as a model to be emulated by other commodity producers until closer examination of the market in oil pointed to the conclusion that it was a rather untypical product. The price elasticity of demand and supply, product homogeneity, and the religious ties between its producers suggest that oil is much the most promising candidate for cartelization. Ambitious plans in the mid-1970s for an integrated programme of buffer stocks for a wide range of commodities financed from a common fund have failed to get beyond the discussion stage. They have thus not achieved the goal of what LDCs see as being needed – a **new international economic order (NEIO)**, that is, a recasting of the whole basis of international exchange between rich and poor countries.

The Stages of Development

If we look at the development of modern nations we find that they go through three stages. First, there is the agricultural stage when most of the population is

---

Key Points 35.3

▶ As a broad generalization there are some discouraging aspects relating to the demand for and supply of commodities which make international trade appear an uncertain influence on LDCs.

▶ The terms of trade have in recent years moved against the LDCs.

▶ International commodity agreements have been neither easy to arrange nor free from troubles where they have been introduced.

involved in agriculture. Then there is the manufacturing stage when much of the population becomes involved in the industrialized sector of the economy. And, finally, there is a shift towards services which is what is happening in the UK; the so-called tertiary or service sector of the economy is growing by leaps and bounds, whereas the manufacturing sector (and its percentage employment) is declining in relative importance. Figure 35.2 shows that in 1981 the percentage of the labour force in agriculture in the low-income economies was 73 per cent, in the lower-middle-income economies 54 per cent, and in the upper-middle-income economies 30 per cent. In the industrial market economies the figure shrinks to only 6 per

Figure 35.6
Growth of Agriculture and GDP in the 1970s. The data show that out of 17 countries whose GDP grew by less than 3 per cent a year in the 1970s 11 had growth rates of agriculture that were less than 1 per cent. How do you explain the situation of countries in the top left column?

Agricultural growth	GDP growth		
	Above 5%	3–5%	Below 3%
Above 3%	Cameroon China Colombia Dominican Rep. Guatemala Indonesia Ivory Coast Kenya Korea, Rep. of Malawi Malaysia Paraguay Philippines Thailand Tunisia Turkey Yemen Arab Rep.	Bolivia Burma Mali Somalia Tanzania	Liberia Nicaragua Senegal
1–3%	Costa Rica Ecuador Egypt Lesotho	Bangladesh Central African Rep. El Salvador Haiti Honduras India Pakistan Sri Lanka Sudan Upper Volta (Burkina)	Burundi Sierra Leone Zaire
Below 1%	Morocco Nigeria	Togo	Angola Chad Congo Rep. Ethiopia Ghana Madagascar Mauritania Mozambique Nepal Niger Uganda

Source: The Economist, 2 Feb. 1985, p. 95.

cent. Putting the situation another way we could say that one characteristic of many developed countries is their high degree of industrialization, although there are clearly exceptions – Hong Kong and New Zealand, for example. In general, nations with relatively high standards of living are more industrialized than countries with low standards of living. Perhaps it is not too surprising that LDCs have taken this to mean that industrialization can be equated with economic development. The policy prescription seems obvious: so-called backward nations in which a large percentage of total resources are devoted to agricultural pursuits should attempt to obtain higher living standards by industrializing. But the reason why there is a declining agricultural sector and increased industrialization in economies that are experiencing ever higher levels of GNP per capita is to be found in our discussion of elasticity back in Chapter 8. We noted that the income elasticity of demand for food declines as nations get beyond the stage where the basic needs of life are satisfied. The income elasticity of demand for manufactured goods and services promises a growing market for consumer goods and personal services. Thus as incomes grow there is a market signal indicated to farmers and manufacturers. For an LDC to build factories as it were ahead of demand is to confuse the direction of causation. If the agricultural sector is successfully satisfying the basic needs of food of an LDC there is a basis for it to contribute effectively to successful economic development *through its ultimate relative decline in the economy*. The proposition that agriculture can be neglected as industrialization takes a poor LDC into rapid economic development has unhappily been shown to be fallacious thinking. Neglect of agriculture has been a pretty sure recipe for economic stagnation. The data in Figure 35.6 while not necessarily providing conclusive evidence points to the critical importance of a healthy agricultural sector if a significant rate of economic growth is to be enjoyed.

Industrialization through Import Substitution

The worries of today's LDCs concerning world trade as an engine of growth are not new. Latin American countries such as Brazil found the 1930s Depression had a devastating impact on their export earnings. When a country experiences a fall in revenues by one-half it is not surprising that it will not contemplate exposing itself to the dangers a second time. Thus countries such as Brazil, Chile, and Argentina resolved to become less dependent on demand for their coffee, copper, and beef and built up manufacturing industries behind high tariff walls. Imported consumer goods were thus made uncompetitive and domestic manufacture given a basis to encourage through the process of **import substitution**. The rationale was not only understandable given the situation of the 1930s but could draw support from the **infant industry** case for temporary protection that we noted in Chapter 9. The problem in practice has come to be that the growth of the infants has not always been healthy. Behind high tariffs and imports quotas the pressures to become efficient are weak. The opportunity costs incurred in terms of resource use have in some cases been enormous. Thus, on the one hand, we can appreciate that the Ricardian theory of comparative advantage that we saw in Chapter 9 is set in a static context. It follows that LDCs may reject its message on the grounds that they wish to *develop* a comparative advantage and not just accept that they are forever condemned just to be purveyors of fuels and food-stuffs and never participants in manufacturing or services. But, on the other hand, grossly inefficient production of manufactured goods involves a misallo-cation of *today's* resources which cannot be easily discounted. As it happens, inward-looking import substitution is no longer fashionable as it was in the early post-war years. The evidence points to gains being reaped by LDCs who positively seek out markets for manufactured goods on which they can enjoy the benefit of relatively low labour costs. During the last two decades the structure of LDC export trade has been changing with the importance of primary products falling. Figure 35.7 shows how manufactures now provide the dynamic element in LDC exports. The only cloud on the horizon is something we indicated in Chapter 9 – the growing trend towards protectionist policies in developed economies! The LDCs do seem bedevilled with problems on the international front.

Can Aid Help?

The developed economies can also assist LDCs in the form of finance from their government, i.e. aid. This, as its name implies, is help that rich countries can bring to poor countries so as to augment their sparse sources of domestic finance. However, despite the call for rich nations within UNCTAD to make contributions equal to 0.7 per cent of their GNP few countries within the OEDC have consistently met this target as Figure 35.8 shows. They have felt able to plead balance-of-payments reasons as justifying an inability to contribute more generously. In truth Western governments have seen aid programmes as an easy area to effect economies when they have sought cuts in public expenditure programmes. If we try to examine the rationale of official development assist-ance, to give aid its proper name, we find that the case for it is not everywhere taken for granted merely because it is called aid. Critics, notably Professor Peter Bauer, have argued that aid cannot really promote development because it is given to *governments*. Because the flow of funds is put too much into a political arena, they see aid as strengthening the position of govern-ments whose policies in the past have rarely been directed towards the lot of the poorest peoples in LDCs. Furthermore, they argue that aid weakens the

Figure 35.7
The Exports of LDCs. Agricultural products now account for less than one-quarter of all LDC exports. LDCs have enjoyed no volume increase in exports of minerals or fuel since 1980.

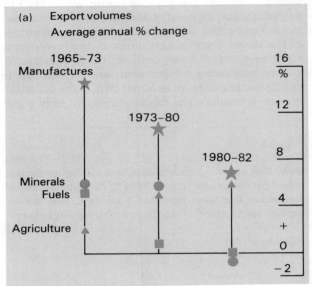

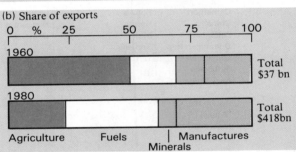

Source: The Economist, 5 May 1984, p. 106.

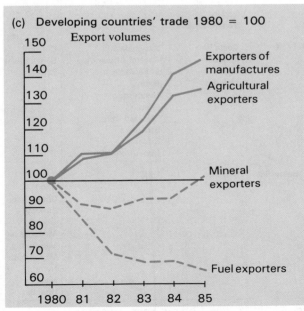

Source: The Economist, 17 May 1986, p. 115.

Figure 35.8

The Aid Programmes of the Developed Countries in 1984. Few of the seventeen members of the OECD donated aid in 1984 that amounted to 0.7 per cent of their GNP.

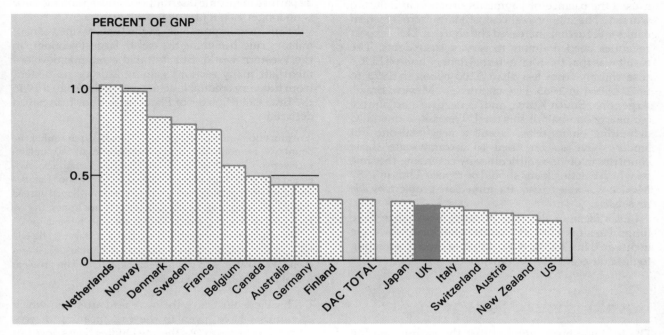

Source: The Financial Times, 6 December 1985.

need for self-reliance and the need to tackle internal problems without relying on the easy option of external help. Even those who feel that the critics overstate their case concede that in LDCs there have been pressures for aid to be directed towards *urban-biased* projects which arguably have been of marginal significance in many LDCs. Professor Michael Lipton has argued that the possibility of rural-based projects has been relatively ignored by Western donors. As a result the supporters of aid have not had the opportunity of pointing to as many success stories as they would have wished to underpin their case.

The fact is that, within LDCs, there has been bias towards large, urban-based prestige investments. Adam Smith noted this more than two centuries ago:

The proud minister of an ostentatious court may frequently take pleasure in executing a work of splendour and magnificence, such as a great highway ... But to execute a great number of little works [that] ... have nothing to recommend them but their extreme utility, is a business which appears in every respect too mean and paltry to merit the attention of so great a magistrate. Such works are almost always entirely neglected.*

Whatever the benefits that aid may have brought about in particular cases this aspect of external finance has been rather overshadowed by another source of finance from developed countries. Major problems of

* A. Smith, *An Enquiry into the Nature and Causes of the Wealth of Nations*, Bk. V, ch. 1 (Everyman edn., p. 217).

Key Points 35.4

► LDCs can turn both to governments in the developed world and also commercial banks for external funds in order to assist their development efforts. Both forms of finance have given rise to difficulties.

► Official aid is a form of external finance from donor governments to recipient governments. Critics argue this means certain types of project are favoured and these are held to be not always the best choice that could be made using overseas finance.

► Borrowing from banks in the 1970s has given rise to a sudden indebtedness in some upper-middle-income developing countries.

indebtedness have arisen due to LDCs having resorted to borrowing from banks in US and Western Europe in order to finance their current account deficits. The rise in oil prices in both 1973 and 1979 caused the balance-of-payments situation in LDCs to worsen. The higher real cost of loans from Western banks still further increased the share of LDC export revenues needed simply to service their debts. The result was that the total external debt of non-oil LDCs rose sharply from less than $200 billion in 1973 to $670 billion in 1983. Five countries – Mexico, Brazil, Argentina, South Korea, and Venezuela – accounted for nearly one-half of this total. The risk of one LDC defaulting on its debts is still a very real one but lenders have so far tried to accommodate those countries in obvious difficulties by extending the time by which existing loans should be repaid. Thus in 1982 Mexico was able to ease its immediate problem by *debt rescheduling*.

LDCs facing a shortage of foreign exchange have found barter trading or **counter-purchase** which we mentioned in Chapter 9 a helpful method of adjusting to difficult economic circumstances.

Development Strategy

The forgoing has suggested that the enthusiasm for industrialization in LDCs has waned in recent years. We have also tried earlier in this chapter to show that economists now believe that human capital is an important element in explaining economic progress.

The shift in thinking is illustrated by the changing character of the lending by the World Bank. Whereas in the financial year 1967 lending on infrastructure projects relating to transportation, power, and communications accounted for 54 per cent of its total lending, by 1977 the figure had fallen to 30 per cent. Agriculture received a much-enhanced share – up from 7 per cent to 32 per cent. Lending for industry increased from 11 per cent to 21 per cent.

We saw earlier in this chapter that the World Bank now regards spending on education, health care, and nutrition as desirable not only as a means to achieve economic growth but as desirable in itself. This view indicates how economists are now aware of the relevance of objectives of policy other than maximization of the growth rate. Until quite recently most economists took the view that in a rapidly growing economy the benefits of faster growth would ultimately *'trickle down'* throughout all sections of society. Thus economic growth would in due course provide a solution to any problems of unemployment and disparities in income distribution. This optimistic view is no longer as popular as it once was.

Brazil grew impressively in the twenty-one years of military rule, becoming the eighth largest economy in the Western world. But its rapid economic development left many sections gaining little or no benefit from this very creditable achievement. In August 1985 the Brazilian Minister of Planning Senhor João Sayad declared:

'We must humanize development. At least 40 per cent of the country's economically active population of 40 million received no benefit whatsoever.' Senhor Sayad acknowledged that after four years of recession, many poor families are simply not getting enough to eat. Senhor Sayad agreed that urgent measures to alleviate poverty are imperative. A respected economist, with a PhD from Yale, he said:

'If you tell an economist that someone is starving, he will tell you that you must first eliminate the public deficit and then take measures to promote employment. The problem is that by then the person is dead.'[*]

This view illustrates the increased attention which economists have given to the real meaning of economic development. As the late Dudley Seers once put it the critical questions in an LDC are:

What has been happening to poverty? What has been happening to unemployment? What has been happening to inequality? If all three of these have declined from high levels then beyond doubt this has been a period of development for the country concerned. If one or two of these central problems have been growing worse, and especially if all three have, it would be strange to call the result 'development' even if per capita income doubled.[*]

In order to try to realize faster growth LDCs have in recent years lost their enthusiasm for the detailed type of planning favoured, as we saw in Chapter 3, by the Soviet Union.

---

[*] Reported in *The Times*, 24 Aug. 1985.

[*] D. Seers, 'The meaning of development', Eleventh World Conference of the Society for International Development, New Delhi (1969), p. 3.

Key Points 35.5

▶ **The post-war enthusiasm for development via import substitution has faded as LDCs have come to find that neglect of agriculture is an almost certain recipe for stagnation.**

▶ **The conventional wisdom in the mid-1980s is that LDCs need to give greater attention to the operation of market forces and place less reliance on planning.**

CASE STUDY

In the Horn of Africa, and the West on the Horns of a Dilemma

'If I must apportion blame for the famine in Ethiopia,' said Dr Keith Griffin, president of Magdalen College, Oxford, 'then I have to blame the Ethiopian Government. They are responsible to a very large degree. The problem was forecast well in advance, remedies were proposed, nothing was done.'

Dr Griffin speaks with more authority than most about the causes of the Ethiopian disaster. In 1982, he led an ILO team of twenty which produced a bulky report on the Ethiopian economy called 'Socialism from the Grass Roots'. The report was suppressed, apparently because the Mengistu regime did not like its recommendations. Yet Dr Griffin is scarcely an unsympathetic observer, being a Keynesian economist of left-wing convictions. Which, perhaps, makes it all the more surprising that his analysis of the present situation makes somewhat glum reading for the toilers at our Western guilt-machine who would have us believe that responsibility for the present tragedy lies essentially with hard-faced governments in Washington and London.

Dr Griffin starts from the view that it is the policy of the Mengistu government and not drought which is the fundamental cause of the Ethiopian famine. Their dereliction of duty has, he believes, been so grave that – far from nourishing the peasants who make up 85 per cent of Ethiopia's population – they have effectively starved them.

They have done this, he explains, in all sorts of ways. Most fundamentally, perhaps, they have ignored the peasantry and their needs by pouring a hugely disproportionate share of the country's resources into industrial development, the relatively small urban population, and the army; and this at a time when their top priority should have been to reverse a long-running fall in food production per head of population.

Such money as has been put into agriculture, says Dr Griffin, has been spent on huge state farms, whose prime purpose, again, is to feed the cities and the army, which make up the regime's political constituency.

'The peasantry don't provide the regime with its political support,' he said, 'so it isn't interested in them. They're not politically organized and, what's more, the government don't want them to be because any political clout they could muster might easily be directed against a Marxist government.'

Nor, Dr Griffin contends, is neglect the only way in which the Mengistu regime discriminates against its peasant farmers. State commodity marketing boards levy what is effectively a 30 per cent export tax on commodities like coffee. Again, the proceeds are largely spent on Ethiopia's three civil wars and urban development. The country's heavily overvalued exchange rate, because the birr is linked to the dollar ('a tremendous irony for a Marxist government', remarks Griffin) has the same effect of discouraging agricultural exports.

'It's crazy', said Griffin, 'because every time the dollar rises, so does the birr. It should be delinked. Who'd be an Ethiopian peasant with the birr overvalued and the state marketing organizations milking you all the time? It isn't merely that the regime neglects the peasantry – they also squeeze them as hard as they can.'

So it is not, he concludes, the low prices paid by Western consumers which burdens Ethiopia's farmers so painfully, but the internal terms of trade: further bad news for our guilt-machine operators.

But is Ethiopia's soil perhaps so poor that even government action would have little effect? Not so, replies Dr Griffin. There is no technical reason why the land in Ethiopia – and all the other drought-affected countries in Africa, for that matter – could not support substantially larger populations if their governments pursued sensible policies. Certainly Ethiopia, with its wide range of soils, should 'very seldom' need international aid.

By 'sensible' Dr Griffin means essentially two things. First, to create food stockpiles in the drought-prone areas during years of good harvests as a cushion against bad times; then link that to a food rationing system which would provide minimum economic security.

The stockpile, he says, should be paid for not by Western donors but by the Ethiopian government itself, because free food from the West might easily act as a disincentive to Ethiopian producers. Even more crucial, the Mengistu regime should put its colonels and civil servants on hard tack for the time being and set in train a rural development programme.

That, says Dr Griffin, does not mean massive injections of scarce capital, merely organization, because there is a vast pool of idle labour in the drought-prone areas during the dry season which could be put to work on irrigation and road-building projects. Unless the Ethiopian and other African governments (such as Chad) did a rapid and complete U-turn of that kind (which he personally doubts is likely), then there was no doubt whatever that each succeeding famine would be worse than the last.

Whatever the West does, adds Dr Griffin, there will unquestionably be more and worse famines in Ethiopia and a dozen other African countries unless their own government's policies change.

To sustain such a view, he says, we only have to look at what happened to the aid given to Ethiopia between 1970 and 1981. In those years, aid as a percentage of GDP went up from 3 to 5.6 per cent, yet investment remained stagnant, savings actually fell and it was public consumption – and that's mainly the army' – which shot up. 'So what can foreign aid do?' asked Dr Griffin theoretically. 'It can help prosecute civil wars.' Nor, he argues, is there any way of stopping a government like

Mengistu's from diverting aid into the wrong channels.

Hence, concludes Dr Griffin, if a government like Ethiopia's is doing the wrong things – 'and it is' – aid merely aggravates the situation because it inevitably sustains and amplifies existing policies. So where does that leave us in the West? According to Dr Griffin, with a clear moral responsibility to try to feed the starving, and bail Ethiopia out of its home-produced mess. In doing even that, he adds, we have to be aware that much of the food we send will end up where the government wants it to end up.

And, since vast numbers of the starving leave their land and congregate along Ethiopia's few roads, we have to plan resettlement programmes now, or a great many may become permanent refugees.

The other thing Dr Griffin would like to see the West do is withdraw its financial support for Ethiopia's three civil wars, but he had to

admit that, even then, under current policies, only a small proportion of the money which the Ethiopian government thus saved would find its way into agricultural development. The irony was that, if Ethiopia's internal policies were sensible, they would not need much support. If they were not, all the support in the world would not solve their problems.

Source: G. Turner, 'Why Ethiopia's rulers let the people starve', *Daily Telegraph*, 24 Nov. 1984.

Questions

1. How does the Case Study suggest that economic development has been misguided in Ethiopia?
2. Why does the Case Study suggest that Ethiopia's internal policies and her need for external aid are related in a difficult manner that presents a dilemma for aid donors?

CASE STUDY 2

All Change at Dar es Salaam?

An era ends in Africa next month as President Julius Nyerere retires as Tanzania's Head of State. No Tanzanian cares to estimate what the change is going to mean except Nyerere himself who says briskly: 'The style is certainly going to change, but not the policies.'

Tanzania's experience over the past fifteen or so years is one of the political landmarks of Third World's governments' attempts to confront the world's most powerful economic institutions. Put simply, there has been a six-year battle

between nationalist ideals and the International Monetary Fund.

Over twenty years Tanzania has poured the bulk of the generous aid funds it has received into social services and education. 'The health services are the best on the continent,' according to United Nations officials. Seventy per cent of children live within 5 km of a health centre, there is universal primary school education, a country-wide vaccination programme will begin next year, adult literacy at 85 per cent is impressive compared with

richer African countries such as Senegal with 10 per cent, Nigeria with 34 per cent, or Kenya with 47 per cent.

But still 600 Tanzanian children under five die every day. Rare is the village with a milling machine or a bio-gas plant. Africa's rural poverty is as degrading in Tanzania as anywhere else. Ujaama villages, where peasants are grouped so that essential services can be shared, have not, in most cases, increased production. Though in Chamwino village, outside Dodoma, where Nyerere will live and till his patch of vines, bananas, maize, and papaya, there is a communal vineyard and a herd of cows and goats, as sleek and well tended as in an English picture-book farm.

The Dodoma region has had a bumper crop this year of sorgum, the staple food, but the foreign exchange crisis means that much of it will never be collected according to the Regional Commissioner Anna Abdallah. 'We have simply no fuel,' she explains. The economic crisis is reflected everywhere. In the University of Dar es Salaam there is no water, no new books, journals, or magazines. Most industries are operating at about 30 per cent of capacity because of lack of spare parts or essential inputs. Agriculture is on a downward spiral and corruption feeds on this atmosphere.

'But we are not facing a *Tanzanian* problem, this is the problem of all sub-Saharan Africa. Unless there is a shift in policy so that massive international resources are poured into this continent the situation will simply get worse,' says Amir Jemal, formerly Finance Minister and now serving his last weeks in government as Minister of State in the president's office.

President Nyerere has said for years that if Tanzania were to implement a classic IMF programme it would mean putting the army on to the streets to control the anger of the population. The IMF riots of Sudan, Egypt, Tunisia, and Morocco are seared deep into Africa's leaders today. 'The

issue in this economic crisis is whether you can keep the democratic process or whether authoritarianism takes over and outside influences are drawn further into this continent,' says Jamal. For more than a decade his voice, like Nyerere's, has been warning that the collapse of producer prices spells catastrophe for a vast section of the poorest of the Third World. The latest World Bank proposals unveiled in Seoul go no way towards meeting this drama.

Tanzania's exports are 90 per cent agricultural. The world drop in producer prices means that the imports they could buy in 1975 were about twice what the same volume could buy today. And, as a result of downward spiral of inputs and efficiency, the volume available for export has dropped by more than one-third.

In addition, the six weeks' Ugandan occupation of northern Tanzania and the subsequent war against Idi Amin cost $400 million in 1979, according to Mr Jamal. That came on top of the collapse of the East African Community which cost about $200 million in new infrastructure. Tanzania's export earnings could not hope to cover costs like these and the second oil shock found the economy with no leeway. Government and people have been squeezed progressively, every year. Two devaluations, cuts in the state sector (18000 civil servants were sacked recently), a rise in producer prices, and cuts in food subsidies have been carried out

gradually since 1981. The World Bank/IMF prescriptions for Tanzania of devaluation, rise in producer prices, privatization, and import liberalization have become the new donor orthodoxy where a commitment to aid the unseen areas of health, education, and budgetary support ruled before.

Salim Salim's infectious confidence is one of the few clear strengths of the uncertain era beginning. 'Agriculture will be the salvation of Tanzania given the change of emphasis we have put on it since last year. We *can* feed ourselves, *can* improve the quality of education and productivity', he says. Agricultural projects are about to begin, with North Korean labour-intensive schemes for cotton and maize with no foreign exchange input.

Nyerere describes the future more cautiously as, 'devising a strategy for survival'. Amir Jamal is more cautious still, 'there is much more belt-tightening to come. The world has turned out to be much harsher than we ever envisaged.'

Source: V. Brittain, 'The dream they could not destroy', *The Guardian*, 18 Oct. 1985.

Question

1. To what extent do you consider that Tanzania has experienced difficulties in its recent economic development that are not of its own making?

Exam Preparation and Practice

INTRODUCTORY EXERCISES

1. The following were those countries which in 1981 were defined as least-developed countries. (The original definition in 1971 included only 24 countries.)

The 31 Least-developed Countries

Afghanistan	Gambia
Bangladesh	Guinea
Benin	Guinea-Bissau
Bhutan	Haiti
Botswana	Laos
Burundi	Lesotho
Cape Verde	Malawi
Central African Republic	Maldives
Chad	Mali
Comoros	Nepal
Ethiopia	Niger

Rwanda
Somalia
Sudan
Tanzania
Uganda
Upper Volta (Burkina)
Western Samoa
Yemen Arab Republic (AR)
Yemen People's Democratic Republic (PDR)

(a) Which continent includes the majority of these countries?

(b) What is the common feature of the Maldives, Comoros, Cape Verde, Haiti, and Western Samoa?

(c) What have Nepal, Bhutan, Lesotho, and Afghanistan got in common?

(d) What have Chad, Botswana, Nepal, and Mali in common?

(e) Do your answers to (b), (c), and (d) have any significance?

---

2. The figure below shows an index of commodity prices between 1950 and 1985 (all-items $ index).

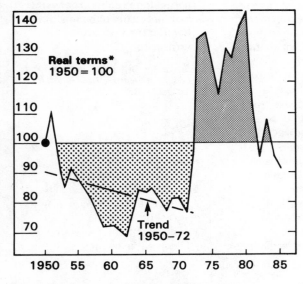

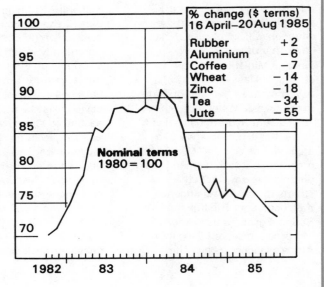

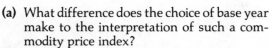

Source: The Economist, 24 August 1985, p. 64.

(a) What difference does the choice of base year make to the interpretation of such a commodity price index?

(b) Why is it important to present such an index in real terms?

(c) Have commodity prices fallen steadily throughout the period?

3. Select any ten countries in Figure 35.2 which are defined as low-income economies plus any ten countries defined as middle-income economies plus any five industrial market economies.
  (a) Plot the data for GNP per capita in 1983 on the horizontal axis and life expectancy at birth in 1983 on the vertical axis. Is there a direct or inverse relationship? (Don't forget the Appendix to Chapter 1!)
  (b) Plot the data for the same countries of population per physician in 1980. What is the nature of the relationship in this case?
  (c) Plot the data for the same countries of the crude birth-rate in 1983. What is the nature of the relationship in this case?

4. In how many low-income countries was the average annual growth rate between 1965 and 1983 a negative one?

5. Is there anything in common about the countries you have identified in answering Question 4?

6. Why are the figures for population per physician in 1980 lower than in 1965?

7. What factors explain the lower figures for infant mortality rates in 1983 compared with 1965?

8. Suggest four non-monetary indicators other than those in Figure 35.2 which might provide a basis for distinguishing between the low-income, middle-income, and industrial market economies? State in each case whether these would be directly or inversely related to GNP per capita.

9. Assume that Ethiopia manages to enjoy an average annual rate of economic growth in its GNP per capita of 2 per cent for each remaining year of this century? What would her GNP per capita be by the year 2000?

10. Do the data in Figure 35.2 suggest that the absolute difference in GNP per capita between Ethiopia and Switzerland will diminish or increase in the next few years?

RELATED ESSAY QUESTIONS

1. 'The most valuable resource any country has is its people, the means and the end of economic advance' (*World Development Report, 1980*). Discuss.

2. Discuss the relative advantages and disadvantages of increases in aid to, and trade with, developing countries.

3. Evaluate the economic arguments for increasing the scale of aid from the developed countries to developing countries.

4. What is the term 'less developed' intended to convey about an economy? Evaluate the following methods of assisting less developed economies: charitable gifts of goods and services (e.g. 'Live Aid'); official aid from governments; credit from the international financial institutions.

Dictionary

absolute advantage   The ability to produce a good or service at an 'absolutely' lower cost, usually (but not necessarily) measured in hours of work required to produce the good.

absolute or nominal prices   The prices that we observe today in terms of today's pounds. Also called nominal or current prices.

accelerationist view   A view, or theory, of inflation that holds that since workers adapt to changing inflation rates, inflation can only reduce unemployment temporarily, the result being that the rate of inflation will tend to accelerate as policy-makers continue to attempt to reduce the unemployment rate by creating more inflation.

accounting profit   The difference between total revenues and total explicit costs.

adaptive-expectations hypothesis   A theory of behaviour which states that people's expectations of the future rate of inflation are formed primarily on the basis of what the rate of inflation has been in the immediate past.

ad valorem **tax**   A duty on a good that increases in relation to the price charged by producers.

aggregate demand   All planned expenditures for the entire economy summed together.

aggregate demand curve   Planned purchase rates for all goods and services in the economy at various price levels.

aggregate demand shock   Any shock that causes the aggregate demand curve to shift inwards or outwards.

aggregates   Total amounts or quantities: aggregate demand, for example, relates to the total quantity demanded within a nation.

aggregate supply   All planned production for the entire economy summed together.

aggregate supply curve   The relationship between planned rates of total production for the entire economy and the price level.

aggregate supply shock   Any shock that causes the aggregate supply curve to shift inwards or outwards.

anticipated inflation   That inflation rate which individuals believe will occur, and when it does, we are in a situation of fully anticipated inflation.

appreciation   The increasing of the value of a domestic currency in terms of other currencies. This occurs in a freely floating exchange market when the quantity demanded for the domestic currency exceeds the quantity supplied at the current price. In a fixed exchange rate market, appreciation cannot occur spontaneously; it must be done officially. Then it is called *revaluation*.

asset   Anything of value that is owned. Customers' deposits create assets in that the bank holds sums of money which it can use until customers withdraw them.

assisted areas   These are geographical areas that have been designated by government as needing industrial development; hence they are assisted by having government incentives available to firms (see Figure 33.1 for actual locations and further details).

automatic, or built-in, stabilizers   Built-in stabilizers do not require initiation and action on the part of the government. Examples are the progressive income tax system and unemployment benefits both of which have built in to the system the ability to modify changes in disposable income caused by the change in overall business activity.

autonomous consumption   That part of consumption that is independent of, or does not depend on, the level of disposable income. Changes in autonomous consumption shift the consumption function.

average fixed costs   Total fixed costs divided by the number of units produced.

average propensity to consume (APC)   Consumption divided by disposable income for any given level of income. The proportion of total disposable income that is consumed.

average propensity to save (APS)   Saving divided by disposable income. The proportion of total disposable income that is saved.

average tax rate   The total tax payment divided by total income. It is the proportion of total income paid in taxes.

average total costs   Total costs divided by the number of units produced.

average variable costs   Total variable costs divided by the number of units produced.

balance of payments   A summary of transactions concerning visible goods and invisibles – services investment earnings and transfers – (the current account) and financial assets (the capital account). Movements of the official reserves and other official flows comprise total official financing. This figure represents the sum requiring official financing arising from both current and capital transactions.

balance of trade   The difference between the value of visible exports and the value of visible imports. Thus a country can be in surplus or in deficit on its visible transactions with one or all countries.

bank bills   See commercial bills.

bankers' balances   The balances, or deposits, that commercial banks keep with the central bank (i.e. Bank of England).

bankruptcy   The situation when a business entity is unable to meet its debts.

barometric price leader   A price increase announced by one firm is quickly followed by rivals. The leader may or may not be the same firm on each occasion of a price increase.

barriers to entry   Barriers that make it either impossible or difficult for firms to enter an existing industry and offer competition to existing producers or suppliers. Some barriers include government restrictions and legislation.

barter   A system of exchange in which goods or services are exchanged for goods or services without the use of money.

base year   The year which is chosen as the point of reference for comparison (e.g. of prices) in other years.

bilateral monopoly   A situation in which the market consists of a single buyer and a single seller.

birth-rate   The number of births per 1000 people in the population per year.

black economy   The unofficial economic activity that cannot be precisely measured because it fails to go through official accounts.

black market   A situation where the official 'white' market price is controlled but buyers are prepared to pay a price which reflects the relative scarcity of the good. Black markets usually exist only in a wartime economy when the availability of civilian goods is curtailed.

bonds   The government issues bonds in order to raise long-term finance (typically for 20 years). (Private companies may issue corporate bonds.) Government bonds are known as gilts because they are 'as good as gold' – there is no risk of default.

British Technology Group (BTG)   The name of the organization formed in 1981 by combining the National Enterprise Board and the National Research Development Corporation. The BTG's primary function is to promote the development and commercialization of inventions arising in the UK.

broad measures   Methods of measuring the money supply by looking at money as a medium of exchange and a temporary store of value. These measures provide a guide to the amount of liquidity in an economy.

budget constraint   The resource constraint imposed on households and firms at any point in time. It represents the set of opportunities facing each decision-maker.

buffer stock   An organization, whether owned and run by a group of producers or financed by the government, that attempts to smooth out fluctuations in prices by the purchase and sale of stocks.

building societies   A group of financial institutions that specialize in providing long-term loans for house purchase (i.e. mortgages).

business fluctuations   The ups and downs in overall business activity, as evidenced by changes in national income, employment, and prices.

buy-back agreement   A commitment to purchase all or part of a plant's output for a specified amount of time in order for the plant to be sold.

capital   All manufactured resources, including buildings, equipment, machines, and improvements to land.

capital consumption   *See* **depreciation** which is another name for the same concept.

capital gains   The positive difference between the purchase price and the sale price of an asset.

capital goods   Goods that are used in the production of other goods. Examples include cranes, factories, and foundries. Consumers do not directly consume capital goods.

capitalism   An economic system in which individuals privately own productive resources; these individuals can use the resources in whatever manner they choose, subject to common protective legal restrictions.

cartel   The most explicit means by which oligopolists effect collusion. A cartel is an association of independent entities that attempts to determine output, sales, and prices such that cartel members can secure monopoly profits. Members of a cartel invariably face a conflict between self-interest and the common cause of all producers.

central bank A banker's bank, usually an official institution that also serves as each country's Treasury's bank. Central banks supervise commercial banks.

certificate of deposit (CD) A time deposit with a fixed maturity date offered by banks and other financial institutions.

ceteris paribus **assumption** The assumption that all other things are held equal, or constant, except those under study.

circular flow model A model of the flows of resources, goods, and services, as well as money, receipts, and payments for them in the economy.

clearing system A mutually agreed system shared by commercial banks in the UK. It refers to the process by which the debts between these banks, generated by their customers' cheques, are settled each day.

closed economy An economic system that has no transactions with any other economy.

closed shop A business enterprise in which an employee must belong to the union before he or she can be employed. That employee must remain in the union after he or she becomes employed.

cobweb A dynamic model which tries to explain why cyclical fluctuations in output and prices can occur such as in the agricultural sector.

collective bargaining Bargaining between management of a company or of a group of companies and management of a union or a group of unions for the purpose of setting a mutually agreeable contract on wages, fringe benefits, and working conditions for *all* employees in the union(s). Different from *individual* bargaining, where each employee strikes a bargain with his or her employer individually.

collusion Price determination by oligopolists which is co-ordinated and aims to avoid the danger of price wars breaking out.

command economic system A system in which the government controls the factors of production and makes all decisions about their use and about the distribution of income. The political character of such a government is indeterminate.

commercial bank This is a privately owned profit-seeking institution, sometimes referred to as a *joint stock bank* to highlight the fact that it has shareholders. Most high street banks, such as National Westminster and Barclays etc. are commercial banks.

commercial bills As the name suggests this is a bill drawn up by a commercial organization, which will be honoured at a stated date in the future (usually 91 days). This helps with cash flow as the seller (often an exporter) is effectively giving a period of 'grace' before payment. A distinguishing feature of these bills is that they may be passed on for cash to another party (at a rate slightly below face value) before the pay due date. The final holder of the bill will then present it for payment on maturity.

Similar bills may be drawn up by banks, local authorities and the Treasury to help with cash flow problems. It may be simpler to regard all these 'bills' as post-dated cheques which may be redeemed for cash at a slight loss before the pay date if necessary.

communism In its purest form, an economic system in which the state has disappeared and in which individuals contribute to the economy according to their productivity and are given income according to their need.

comparative advantage An advantage arising out of relative efficiency, which follows from scarcity of resources. Comparative advantage is the advantage measured in terms of other goods that could be produced, not in terms of factor inputs. If a country has a comparative advantage in one good, it must have a comparative *disadvantage* in another. As long as the opportunity cost of doing the same job differs for different people or different countries, each will have a comparative advantage in something.

competition Rivalry among buyers and sellers of outputs, or among buyers and sellers of inputs (i.e. factors of projection).

complement Two goods are considered complements if a change in the price of one causes an opposite shift in the demand for the other. For example, if the price of tennis rackets goes up, the demand for tennis balls will fall; if the price of tennis rackets goes down, the demand for tennis balls will increase.

concentration ratio The percentage of all sales contributed by the leading four or leading eight firms in an industry; sometimes called the industry-concentration ratio.

constant-cost industry An industry whose total output can be increased without an increase in per-unit costs; an industry whose long-run supply curve is horizontal.

constant prices Sterling expressed in terms of real purchasing power, using a particular year as the base or standard of comparison.

constant returns to scale. A situation in which the long-run average cost curve of a firm remains flat, or horizontal, as output increases.

consumer optimum A choice of a basket of goods and services that maximizes the level of satisfaction for each consumer.

consumer (or consumption) goods Goods that are used directly by consumers to generate satisfaction. To be contrasted with capital goods.

consumer sovereignty The concept of the consumer as the one who, by his or her spending, ultimately determines which goods and services will be produced in the economy. In principle, competition among producers causes them to adjust their production to the changing desires of consumers.

consumer surplus The difference between the amount that a consumer is willing to pay for a commodity and the amount that is actually paid. This surplus utility which is not paid for is measured by the area above the price charged and below the demand schedule.

consumption That which is spent on new goods and services out of a household's current income. Whatever is not consumed is saved. Consumption includes buying food, going to the cinema, going to a concert, and so on.

consumption function The relationship between the amount consumed and disposable income. A consumption function tells us how much people plan to consume out of various disposable income levels.

consumption goods Goods that are bought by households to use up, such as films, food, and clothing.

contractionary policy (or deflation) The use of tax increases and expenditure cuts to reduce inflationary pressure, or overheating, in the economy, or to reduce a balance-of-trade deficit.

cost-benefit analysis (CBA) This is a way of appraising an investment proposal. It is normally undertaken by government departments, since it involves adding the indirect (external) costs and benefits to the conventional direct costs and benefits (revenue). This is done by estimating monetary values for aspects such as health, time, leisure and pollution.

cost-push inflation Rising prices caused by rising production costs, union wage negotiations, or bosses seeking more profits.

counter-cyclical policy The use of fiscal and monetary policy to offset booms and slumps by contractionary and expansionary policy respectively.

counter-purchase An agreement to buy an offsetting amount of unrelated products to counter the cost of buying a particular product; for example, country X can sell to country Y an airplane costing £1m only if country X agreed to purchase £1m worth of some other products in return.

craft unions Labour unions composed of workers who engage in a particular trade or skill, such as baking, carpentry, or plumbing.

cross-price elasticity of demand The percentage change in the demand for one good divided by the percentage change in the price of a related good. Cross-price elasticity of demand is a measure of the responsiveness of one good's quantity demanded to changes in a related good's price.

cross-section data Empirical observations about one or more variables gathered at a particular point in time.

crowding out The expansion of public sector expenditure which reduces private sector spending.

CSO The recognized abbreviation for the Central Statistical Office. This office is responsible for the government's statistical services.

currency Notes and coins – often simply referred to as 'cash'.

currency crisis A situation in the international money market that occurs when a country no longer has the foreign exchange resources to support the price of its currency. A currency crisis brings forced devaluation under a fixed exchange rate system.

cyclical unemployment Unemployment resulting from business recessions that occur when total demand is insufficient to create full employment.

deadweight welfare loss A measure of the reduction in consumer surplus arising from monopolization of a competitive industry which may be partially or even wholly offset by resource savings accruing to the monopolist.

death-rate The number of deaths per 1000 people in the populatiuon per year.

declining block pricing. A system of price discrimination in which consumers are charged different prices per unit of electricity for each 'block' of electricity that they buy. The per-unit price for the first block is higher than the per-unit price for the second block, which is higher than the per-unit price for the third block.

decreasing-cost industry An industry in which an increase in output leads to a reduction in per-unit costs, such that the long-run industry supply curve is downward sloping.

deficiency payment A payment made to qualified farmers for any difference between the target price for their product and the market price that they actually received; a direct subsidy paid to farmers.

deficit spending Government spending that is in excess of government tax revenues.

demand curve A graphic representation of the demand schedule. A negatively sloped line showing the inverse relationship between the price and the quantity demanded.

demand-pull inflation Inflation caused by total demand exceeding the current supply. This is a particular problem when the economy is at full employment.

demand schedule A set of pairs of numbers showing various possible prices and the quantities demanded at each price. This is a schedule showing the rate of planned purchase per time-period at different prices of the good.

demerit good   The opposite of a merit good; one which the political process has decided is socially undesirable.

dependent variable   A variable whose value changes according to changes in the value of one or more independent variables.

depreciation (capital)   Reduction in the value of capital goods over a one-year period due to physical wear and tear and also to obsolescence.

depreciation (currency)   A lessening of the value of a a domestic currency in terms of foreign currencies. Depreciation occurs in a freely floating foreign exchange market when there is an excess supplied of the domestic currency. In a fixed exchange rate market, depreciation can occur if the government allows it.

derived demand   Input factor demand derived from demand for the final product being produced.

devaluation   The same as depreciation except that it occurs officially under a regime of fixed exchange rates.

diminishing marginal utility   The smaller increase in total utility from the consumption of a good or service as more is consumed.

direct relationship   A relationship between two variables that is direct, or positive, such that an increase in one is associated with an increase in the other, and a decrease in one is associated with a decrease in the other.

direct tax   Tax liability targeted at one person on the basis of income.

'dirty' float   A freely floating exchange system that involves governments stepping in to stabilize the value of their currencies. To be contrasted with a 'clean' float, where there is no government intervention in the foreign exchange market.

discount houses   A small group (10 in 1985) of specialized institutions which borrow for very short periods of time from the banks (see **'money at call'**) and invest in 'bills' (see **commercial bills**) and other short-term assets. The discount houses are therefore specialists in the movement of short-term funds between financial institutions. Indeed, they often act as a middle-man between the Bank of England and commercial banks.

discounting   The method by which the present value of a sum or a stream of sums is obtained.

discount rate (intervention rate)   The interest rate at which the Bank of England discounts bills (intervenes in the discount market).

discretionary fiscal policy   Government policy with respect to taxes or spending, or both, that involves a deliberate change legislated by Parliament for the purpose of altering the equilibrium level of real national income.

diseconomies of scale   When increases in output lead to increases in long-run average costs.

distribution of income   The way income is distributed among the population. For example, a perfectly equal distribution of income would result in the lowest 20 per cent of income-earners receiving 20 per cent of national income and the top 20 per cent also receiving 20 per cent of national income. The middle 60 per cent of income-earners would receive 60 per cent of national income.

division of labour   The segregation of a resource into different specific tasks; for example, one car worker puts on bumpers, another doors, and so on.

dominant price leader   The leading firm in an industry which is the first to change prices. A smaller firm may be content either to let the largest firm judge when prices need to be adjusted or feel the kinked demand curve situation could apply if it led an increase in prices.

dumping   The export of products at a price below their cost of production.

duopoly   A market structure in which there are only two sellers of a commodity and thus the matter of interdependence is critical for price determination.

durable consumer goods   Goods used by consumers that have a life-span of more than one year; that is, goods that endure and can give utility over a longer period of time.

economic efficiency   The use of resources that generate the highest possible value of output as determined in the market economy by consumers.

economic goods   Any good or service that is scarce.

economic growth   Defined either as the increase in an economy's real level of output over time or as the increase in the economy's real per capita level of output over time. Economic growth is therefore measured by the rate of change of real output or real per capita output.

economic profit   The difference between total revenues and the opportunity cost of all factors of production.

economic rent   That part of earnings which is in excess of transfer earnings. Economic rent will be earned when the supply of a particular skill or personality is restricted, i.e. inelastic.

economics   A social science studying human behaviour, and, in particular, the way in which individuals and societies choose among the alternative uses of scarce resources to satisfy wants.

economic system   The institutional means through which resources are used to satisfy human wants.

economies of scale   When increases in output lead to decreases in long-run average costs.

electronic funds transfer system   A system whereby bank account balances, credits, and debts are all done via electronic signals rather than through the use of paper memos.

employers' association   A group of employers who negotiate wages jointly with trade unions.

entrepreneurship   The fourth factor of production involving human resources that perform the functions of raising capital, organizing, managing, assembling other factors of production, and making basic business policy-decisions. The entrepreneur is a risk-taker.

equation of exchange   The number of monetary units multiplied by the number of times each unit is spent on final goods and services is identical to the prices multiplied by output (or national income). Formally written as $M \times V = P \times Q$.

equilibrium   A situation in which the plans of buyers and sellers exactly coincide so that there is neither excess quantity nor supply demanded.

eurodollar deposits   Deposits denominated in US dollars but held in banks outside the United States, usually (but not always) in overseas branches of US banks.

exchange   The act of trading, usually done on a voluntary basis, in which both parties to the trade are subjectively better off.

exchange equalization account   An account held and managed by the Bank of England on behalf of the government. It is used to prevent undesirable fluctuations to the sterling exchange rate.

exchange rate target   The Bank of England may set a target range for the exchange rate. Maintaining this may promote stability in the economy more effectively than adherence to a monetary target, which may be subject to change for other reasons than the growth of the money supply.

excise duties on alcohol   *See* **tax**.

exclusive purchase   A distributor contracts to stock only the products of one manufacturer, possibly in return for an exclusive supply arrangement.

exclusive supply   A seller supplies only one buyer in a certain geographical area, which limits competition between that buyer and his competitors.

expansion   A business fluctuation in which overall business activity is rising at a more rapid rate than previously, or at a more rapid rate than the overall historical trend for the nation. This is sometimes referred to as a 'boom'.

expansionary gap   Exists whenever the equilibrium level of real national income exceeds the full-employment level of real national income; the positive difference between total desired spending and the full-employment level of real national income.

expansionary policy (or reflation)   The use of tax cuts and increased government spending (perhaps along with an easy monetary policy) to increase aggregate demand and promote increased economic growth and employment.

expenditure approach   A way of computing national income by adding up the values of all spending at current market prices on final goods and services.

exploitation   Paying a resource less than its value (MRP).

externality   A cost or benefit external to an exchange. In other words, the external benefits or costs accrue to parties other than the immediate seller and buyer in a transaction.

factor markets   In the factor market, households are the sellers; they sell resources such as labour, land, capital, and entrepreneurial ability. Businesses are the buyers in factor markets; business expenditures represent receipts or, more simply, income for households (see Figure 12.1).

fiduciary monetary system   A system in which currency is issued by the government, and its value is based uniquely on the public's *faith* that the currency represents command over goods and services.

finance houses   A group of financial institutions that specialize in providing funds for hire-purchase agreements.

financial intermediaries   Those financial institutions that link up groups of lenders with groups of borrowers, e.g. commercial banks.

financial markets   Those markets through which saving passes before it goes either to governments or to business firms for investment purposes. Included are insurance companies, commercial banks, and pension plans.

firm   An organization that brings together different factors of production, such as labour, land, and capital, to produce a product or service that can be sold for a profit. A firm is usually made up of an entrepreneur, managers, and workers.

First World   The industrialized non-communist countries of Western Europe plus the United States, Australia, New Zealand, Canada, and Japan.

five-year plans   Economic plans set up by the central government in a country that plots the future course of its economic development. The first five-year plan was decised in Russia by Stalin after Lenin's death.

fixed costs   Those costs that do not vary with output.

Fixed costs include such things as rent on a building and the price of machinery. These costs are fixed for a certain period of time; in the long run they are variable.

fixed exchange rates   A system of exchange rates that requires government intervention to fix the value of each nation's currency in terms of every other nation's currency.

fixed investment   Purchases, made by business, of newly produced producer durables, or capital goods, such as production machinery and office equipment.

fixed throttle   Controlled growth of aggregate monetary demand at a constant rate, equal to the long-run growth of productive capacity.

flow   Activities that occur over time. For example, income is a flow that occurs per week, per month, or per year. Consumption is also a flow, as is production.

foreign banks   The name given to banks whose country of origin is overseas. These banks tend to specialize in foreign currency and are often located in London.

foreign exchange market   The market for buying and selling foreign currencies.

foreign exchange rate   The price of foreign currency in terms of domestic currency, or vice versa. For example, if the foreign exchange rate for francs is 25p this means that it takes 25p to buy one franc. An alternative way of stating the exchange rate is that the value of the pound is four francs. It takes four francs to buy one pound.

45-degree line   The line along which planned expenditures equal real national income or output per year; a line that bisects the total planned expenditures–real national income quadrant.

fractional reserve banking system   A system of banking whereby banks keep only a fraction of their deposits on reserve.

free enterprise   A system in which private business firms are able to obtain resources, to organize those resources, and to sell the finished product in any way they choose.

free good   Any good or service that is available in quantities larger than are desired at a zero price.

freely floating (or flexible) exchange rates   Exchange rates that are allowed to fluctuate in the open market in response to changes in supply and demand. Sometimes called free exchange rates or floating exchange rates.

free-rider problem   A problem associated with public goods in which individuals presume that others will pay for the public goods, so that individually they can escape paying for their production without a reduction in production occurring.

frictional unemployment   Unemployment associated with frictions in the system that may occur because of the imperfect job market information that exists.

full-employment government budget   An indication of what the government budget deficit or surplus would be if the economy were operating at full employment throughout the year.

full-line forcing   This requires a buyer to purchase quantities of each item in a product range in order to be able to buy any of them.

general equilibrium analysis   Economic analysis that takes account of the interrelationships among markets; to be contrasted with partial equilibrium analysis, which does not.

GNP deflator   A price index that measures the changes in prices of all goods and services produced by the economy.

geographically immobile   See mobility of labour.

gross domestic investment   The creation of capital goods, such as factories and machines, that can yield production and hence consumption in the future. Also included in this definition are changes in business stocks and repairs made to machines or buildings. In sum, it is investment before depreciation.

gross national product (GNP)   The total market value of all final goods and services produced by the resources of British nationals in a one-year period.

guaranteed (or target) price   A price set by the government for specific agricultural products. If market-clearing prices fall below target prices, a 'deficiency' payment equal to the difference between the market price and the target price is given to each farmer who qualifies.

horizontal merger   The joining of firms that are producing or selling a similar product.

human capital   Investment which has taken place in education and training which enhance the productivity of the individual.

import levy   A tax imposed on a good when landed at a port or other point of entry into a country.

import substitution   The process by which many LDCs have begun to industrialize, i.e. attempt to manufacture consumer goods rather than resort to foreign supplies to meet domestic demand.

income approach   A way of measuring national income by adding up all factor rewards, namely, wages, interest, rent, and profits.

income consumption curve   The set of optimum

consumption points that would occur if income were successfully increased, nominal and relative prices remaining constant.

income elastic demand A given change in income will result in a larger percentage change in quantity demanded in the same direction.

income elasticity of demand The percentage change in the quantity demanded divided by the percentage change in money income; the responsiveness of the quantity demanded to changes in income.

income inelastic demand A given change in income will result in a less than proportionate change in demand in the same direction.

income velocity of money The average number of times per year a pound is spent on final goods and services. It is equal to net national income divided by the money supply.

increasing-cost industry An industry in which an increase in industry output is accompanied by an increase in per-unit costs, such that the long-run industry supply curve is upward sloping.

independent variable A variable whose value can change freely.

indexing Linking a specific nominal sum to the rate of inflation; for example, under some schemes pensions can be indexed so they increase at the rate of inflation.

indicative planning A system which involves the government setting up general targets for the major sectors of the economy to assist the private sector in their decision-taking. This form of planning is used effectively in France.

indifference curve A curve composed of the set of consumption alternatives each yielding the same total amount of satisfaction.

indirect tax The tax imposed on spending. In this case the seller has ultimate responsibility to pay.

industrial unions Labour unions that consist of workers from a particular industry, such as car or steel manufacturing.

infant industry argument An argument in support of tariffs: tariffs should be imposed to protect (from import competition) an industry that is trying to get started. The presumption is that after the industry becomes established and technologically efficient, the tariff can be removed.

inferior good A good of which the consumer purchases less as income increases.

inflation A sustained rise in prices, formally measured by the Retail Price Index.

inheritance tax *See* **tax**.

injections Supplementary expenditures not originating in the household sector; can include invest-

ment, government purchases, and exports.

institutions The laws of the nation as well as the habits, ethics, mores, folkways, and customs of the citizens of that nation.

interest The payment for current rather than future command over resources; the cost of obtaining credit. Also, the return paid to owners of capital.

International Bank for Reconstruction and Development More commonly referred to as the 'World Bank'. An institution which is based in Washington and co-ordinates investment funds on behalf of developing countries.

International Monetary Fund (IMF) An institution set up to manage the international monetary system. It came out of the Bretton Woods Conference in 1944, which established more or less fixed exchange rates in the world.

inverse relationship A relationship that is inverse, or negative, such that an increase in one variable is associated with a decrease in the other, and a decrease in one variable is associated with an increase in the other.

investment The spending by businesses on things like machines and buildings, which can be used to produce goods and services in the future. The investment part of total income is that portion which will be used in the process of producing goods in the future.

joint-stock company A legal entity owned by stockholders. The stockholders are liable only for the amount of money they have invested in the company. These firms are sometimes referred to as *corporations*.

kinked demand curve A model of pricing in an oligopolistic market structure where rivals follow one firm's decision to make a price decrease but not a price increase. The demand curve is thus bent or kinked and the associated marginal revenue curve has a discontinuous part in it.

labour The human resource involving productive contributions of persons who work, which involve both thinking and doing.

labour theory of value A theory that the value of all commodities is equal to the value of the labour used in producing them.

Laffer curve A graphical representation of the relationship between tax rates and total tax revenues raised by taxation.

laissez-faire The viewpoint that government should not intervene in a detailed way in the business life of a country other than remove legal restraints on trade. Adam Smith's *Wealth of Nations* represents this doctrine.

land   The natural resources that are available without alteration or effort on the part of labour. Land as a resource includes only original fertility and mineral deposits, topography, climate, water, and natural vegetation.

law of diminishing (marginal) returns   After some point, successive increases in a variable factor of production, such as labour, added to fixed factors of production, will result in less than a proportional increase in output.

law of increasing relative costs   This law is an economic principle that states that the opportunity cost of additional units of a good generally increases as society attempts to produce more of that good.

leakages   Those parts of national income not used for consumption, e.g. net taxes, saving, and imports.

least developed countries   The poorest of the LDCs defined with reference to three indicators of the state of development.

less developed countries (LDCs)   Those countries that are in the process of development and that have not yet reached an arbitrary per capita living standard which in 1983 the World Bank defined as $400.

liability   Anything that is owed. Customers' deposits create a liability in that the bank must be prepared to repay the customer at any time.

licensed desposit-takers (LDTs)   Institutions permitted (licensed) by the Bank of England to take deposits from the public.

liquidity   A characteristic of any asset; it describes the degree to which the asset can be acquired or disposed of without much danger of any intervening loss in nominal value and with small transaction costs. Money is the most liquid asset.

liquidity preference function   An inverse relationship between the opportunity cost of holding money (interest receipts forgone) and the quantity of money demanded – otherwise called the demand for money function.

local authority bills   *See* **commercial bills**.

localized industry   This is when one industry dominates a whole geographical area, i.e. it is dominant in one locality.

long run   That time-period in which all factors of production can be varied.

long-run average cost curve.   This represents the cheapest way to produce various levels of output given existing technology and current resource prices. It is derived by joining the minimum point of various SAC curves.

long-run industry supply curve   A market supply curve showing the relationship between price and quantities forthcoming after firms have been allowed the time to enter or exit from an industry, depending

on whether there have been positive or negative economic profits.

macroeconomics   The study of economy-wide phenomena, such as unemployment and inflation.

manpower policy   A range of government schemes and services that are made available for the unemployed. A summary of these is given in Figure 33.3.

marginal cost (MC)   The change in total costs due to a one-unit increase in the variable input. The cost of using more of a factor of production.

marginal cost pricing   A system of pricing in which the price charged is equal to the opportunity cost to society of producing one more unit of the good or service in question. The opportunity cost is the marginal cost to society.

marginal physical product (MPP)   The output that the addition of one more worker produces. The marginal physical product of the worker is equal to the change in total output that can be accounted for by hiring the worker, holding all other factors of production constant.

marginal propensity to consume (MPC)   The ratio of the change in consumption to the change in disposable income. A 0.8 marginal propensity to consume tells us that an additional £100 earned will lead to an additional £80 consumed.

marginal propensity to import   The proportion of an increase in income which is spent on imports.

marginal propensity to save (MPS)   The ratio of the change in saving to the change in disposable income. A 0.2 marginal propensity to save indicates that out of an additional £100 earned £20 will be saved. Whatever is not saved is consumed. The marginal propensity to save plus the marginal propensity to consume must always equal 1, by definition (if taxes are ignored).

marginal revenue (MR)   The change in total revenues resulting from a change in output and sale of one unit of the product in question.

marginal revenue product (MRP)   The marginal physical product (MPP) times the price at which the product can be sold in a competitive market.

marginal tax rate   The change in the tax payment divided by the change in income, or the percentage of additional pounds that must be paid in taxes. The marginal tax rate is applied to the last tax bracket of taxable income.

market   An abstract concept concerning all the arrangements that individuals have for exchanging with one another. Thus, we can speak of the labour market, the car market, and the credit market.

market-clearing (or equilibrium) price   The price that clears the market where there is no excess quantity demanded or supplied. The price at which the demand curve intersects the supply curve.

market economic system   A system in which individuals own the factors of production and decide individually how to use them; a system with completely decentralized economic decision-making.

market economy   An economy in which prices are used to signal firms and households about the value of individual resources. It is also called the price system, or one using the price mechanism.

market failure   A situation in which an unfettered market leads to either an under- or over-allocation of resources to a specific economic activity. Externalities are cases of market failure.

market structures   The characteristics of a market which determine the interrelationships between participants in that market. Decision-making in any given market will depend on whether buyers and sellers can assume that they can or cannot affect market price. Thus the type of market structure is determined by the number of buyers and sellers and the ease of entry (and exit) into a market.

market supply curve   The locus of points showing the minimum prices at which given quantities will be forthcoming; also called the short-run industry supply curve.

medium of exchange   Money is anything that is generally accepted for the buying and selling of goods and services. Money, therefore, acts as a means (medium) of payment (exchange).

merchant banks   The name given to a small group of banks whose specialisms involve raising money for companies and advising on portfolio management.

merit good   A good that has been deemed socially desirable via the political process.

microeconomics   The study of the economic behaviour of households and firms and how prices of goods and services are determined.

minimum efficient scale   The lowest rate of output per unit time-period at which average costs reach a minimum point.

minimum wage legislation   Laws which regulate the lowest rates of pay for various occupations that can be paid by employers.

mixed economy   An economic system in which the decision about how resources should be used is made partly by the private sector and partly by the government.

mobility of labour   The ease with which labour can be transferred from one type of employment to another. Mobility of labour can thus be considered in terms of geography and occupation, i.e. labour is discussed in terms of geographical mobility and occupational mobility. The converse concept *immobility of labour* is also often employed by economists.

models, or theories   Simplified representations of the real world used to make predictions or to better understand the real world.

monetarists   Individuals who believe that changes in the money supply are important in the determination of the equilibrium level of nominal national income. Monetarists place money in a more important role in their national income determination model than do Keynesians.

monetary base   The notes and coin in circulation and banks' balances with the Bank of England. Also known as M0 or high-powered money.

money at call   Very short-term lending by commercial banks, ranging from an overnight loan to one that lasts for 14 days. The discount houses are the principal borrowers of these funds.

money multiplier   The reciprocal of the reserve asset ratio, assuming no leakages into currency and no excess reserves. It gives the amount by which credit expands as a result of a given increase in the monetary base.

money supply   A generic term used to denote the amount of 'money' in circulation. There are numerous specific definitions of the money supply. See Figure 19.2 for details of each definition.

monopolist   The single supplier that comprises the entire industry.

monopolistic competition   A market situation where a large number of firms produce similar but not identical products. There is relatively easy entry into the industry.

monopsonist   A single buyer.

multiplier   The ratio of the change in the equilibrium level of real national income to the change in expenditures which brought it about; that number by which a change in investment or autonomous consumption, for example, is multiplied to get the change in the equilibrium level of real national income.

narrow measures   Methods of measuring the money supply by looking at money predominantly as a medium of exchange.

National Debt   The accumulated government debt, the total outstanding.

National Enterprise Board (NEB)   *See* **British Technology Group**.

National Income   The value of the flow of goods and services becoming available to a nation during a given period of time (usually one year).

national income accounting   A measurement system used to estimate national income and its components. This is one approach to measuring an economy's aggregate performance.

nationalization   The taking into public ownership of part or all of economic activity in a key sector of the economy.

nationalized industries Examples of these vary from time to time and country to country. Basically they involve the government owning and running an industry, the products of which are sold through the market and priced accordingly.

National Research and Development Corporation *See* **British Technology Group**.

National Savings Bank A public sector institution that offers banking-type facilities over post-office counters.

natural monopoly A monopoly that arises from the peculiar production characteristics in the industry. Usually a natural monopoly arises when production of the service or product requires extremely large capital investments such that only one firm can profitably be supported by consumers. A natural monopoly arises when there are large economies of scale relative to the industry demand, and one firm can produce at a lower cost than can be achieved by multiple firms.

natural rate of unemployment That rate of unemployment which would prevail when inflation is anticipated correctly, year in and year out.

near monies Assets that are almost money. They have a high degree of liquidity; they can be easily converted into money without loss in value. Deposit accounts held in building societies and Treasury bills are examples.

negative income elasticity A given rise in income will result in a fall in the quantity demanded.

net investment Gross investment minus an estimate of the wear and tear on the existing capital stock. Net investment therefore measures the change in our capital stock over a one-year period.

net national product (NNP) GNP minus depreciation.

new international economic order A proposed international institution to be sponsored by the United Nations that would basically attempt to stabilize raw materials prices and increase the amount of foreign aid given by industrialized nations to LDCs.

newly industrializing countries (NICs) Those upper-middle-income developing countries such as Mexico and South Korea that have developed rapidly over the past decade and are now increasingly significant exporters of consumer goods.

nominal rate of interest The market rate of interest that is expressed in terms of today's pounds.

nominal values The values of variables such as GNP and investment expressed in current pounds. Also called money values. Otherwise stated, measurement in terms of actual market prices at which goods are sold.

non-durable consumer goods Goods used by consumers that are used up within a year.

non-monetary indicators Measures of the state of development such as the number of persons who are literate and average life expectancy. Such measures avoid the problems of using GNP data in making international comparisons.

non-price competition The means by which firms strive to increase sales and increase market share other than by undercutting rivals. Instead of lowering prices and competing by price, firms resort to advertising campaigns, encourage new product development, and regard sales as being sensitive to effective marketing.

non-tariff barriers Restraints on international trade other than import duties.

normal goods Goods for which demand increases as income increases. Most goods that we deal with are normal.

normal profit The normal rate of return to investment; otherwise known as the opportunity cost of capital.

normative economics Analysis involving value-judgements about economic policies; relates to whether things are good or bad. A statement of *what ought to be*.

number line A line that can be divided into line segments of equal length, each associated with a number.

occupationally immobile *See* **mobility of labour**.

OECD The Organization for Economic Co-operation and Development. This could be regarded as a club comprising all the capitalist countries as members who discuss together economic issues of mutual interest. In fact the OECD has 24 member countries, namely, Australia, Austria, Belgium, Canada, Denmark, Finland, France, West Germany, Greece, Iceland, Ireland, Italy, Japan, Luxembourg, The Netherlands, New Zealand, Norway, Portugal, Spain, Sweden, Switzerland, Turkey, the United Kingdom, and the United States. The organization's offices are based in Paris and it produces various economic publications each year.

oil duties *See* **tax**.

oligopoly A market situation where there are very few sellers. Each seller knows that the other sellers will react to its changes in prices and quantities.

open economy An economy that is in some way dependent on one or more other economies. Goods are traded and international exchange takes place.

open-market operations The buying and selling of government securities (e.g. bonds) in the open market by the Bank of England.

opportunity cost The highest-valued alternative that must be sacrificed to attain something or satisfy a want.

opportunity cost of capital The normal rate of return or the amount that must be paid to an investor to induce her or him to invest in a business. Economists consider this a cost of production and it is included in our cost examples.

organization The co-ordination of individuals, each doing different things in the furtherance of a common end.

origin The intersection of the y axis with the x axis in a graph.

output approach A way of measuring national income by adding up the value of the output produced by each specific sector of the economy. (The emphasis is on 'value added'. See Figure 13.1.)

output gap Exists whenever the equilibrium level of real national output is less than the full-employment level; the negative difference between total desired expenditures and the full-employment level of real national income.

paradox of thrift An increased desire to save (an increase in the MPS) will lead to a reduction in the equilibrium level of saving.

parallel pricing The simultaneous changes in prices in an oligopolistic market situation which is explained by collusion or barometric price leadership.

partial equilibrium analysis A way of analysing a market in isolation without taking account of the interrelationships among markets.

partnership A business entity involving two or more individuals who join together for business purposes. In most instances, each partner is liable for the debts of the business to such an extent that he or she can lose his or her personal wealth if the business becomes bankrupt.

perfect competition A market structure in which the decisions of buyers and sellers have no effect on market price.

perfectly competitive firm A firm that is such a small part of the total industry picture that it cannot affect the price of the product it sells.

perfectly elastic supply A supply curve characterized by a reduction in quantity supplied to zero when there is the slightest decrease in price.

perfectly inelastic supply The characteristic of a supply curve for which quantity supplied remains constant, no matter what happens to price.

perfectly price-elastic demand A demand curve that has the characteristic that even the slightest increase in price will lead to a zero quantity demanded.

perfectly price-inelastic demand A demand curve that exhibits zero responsiveness in changes in price, i.e. no matter what the price is, the quantity demanded remains the same.

permanent-income hypothesis A theory of the consumption function that states that people's desire to spend is a function of their permanent or long-run expected income rather than of their current disposable income.

petroleum revenue tax *See* **tax**.

Phillips curve A curve showing the relationship between unemployment and changes in wages or prices. The Phillips curve gives the trade-off between unemployment and inflation.

planning curve Another name for the long-run average cost curve.

planning horizon Another name for long-run cost curves. All inputs are variable during the planning period.

positive economics Analysis that is strictly limited to making either purely descriptive statements or scientific predictions; for example, *If A, then b*. A statement of *what is*. Positive statements can be checked against the evidence.

potential output The maximum level of output achievable if the economy were operating on its production possibilities curve.

predatory pricing The practice of temporarily selling at prices below cost with the intention of driving a competitor from the market, so that in the future prices may be raised and enhanced profits extracted.

present value The value of a future amount expressed in today's pounds; the most that someone would pay today to receive a certain sum at some point in the future.

price–consumption curve The set of consumer optimum combinations of two goods that the consumer would choose as the relative price of the goods changes, while money income remains constant.

price control Government regulation of free market prices such that a legal maximum price is specified.

price differentiation A situation in which price differences for similar products reflect only differences in marginal cost in providing those commodities to different groups of buyers.

price discrimination This is a system of pricing often employed by nationalized industries and other monopolists; it involves charging different prices to different customers who have different elasticities of demand for the product.

price elastic demand A characteristic of a demand curve in which a given percentage change in price will result in a larger percentage change in quantity demanded, in the opposite direction. Total revenues and price are inversely related in the elastic portion of the demand curve.

price elasticity of demand The responsiveness of the quantity demanded for a commodity to changes in its price per unit. The price elasticity of demand is defined as the percentage change in quantity demanded divided by the percentage change in price.

price elasticity of supply The responsiveness of quantity supplied of a commodity to a change in its price. Price elasticity of supply is defined as the percentage change in quantity supplied divided by the percentage change in price.

price index The cost of today's basket of goods expressed as a percentage of the cost of the same basket during a base year.

price inelastic demand A characteristic of a demand curve in which a given change in price will result in a less than proportionate change in the quantity demanded, in the opposite direction. Total revenue and price are directly related in the inelastic region of the demand curve.

price mechanism Prices are used as a signalling system between firms and households concerning the use of resources. Where the price mechanism operates there is a market economy.

price supports Minimum prices set by the government. To be effective, price supports must be coupled with a mechanism to rid the market of 'surplus' production that arises whenever the supported price is greater than the market-clearing price.

price system An economic system in which (relative) prices are constantly changing to reflect changes in supply and demand for different commodities. The prices of those commodities are signals to everyone within the system about what is relatively expensive and what is relatively cheap.

price-taker Another definition of a competitive firm. A price-taker is a firm that must take the price of its product as given. The firm cannot influence its price.

principle of exclusion Stated briefly, when I use a private good, my use excludes the possibility of your using it simultaneously. You and I cannot eat the *same* apple.

private costs Those costs incurred by individuals when they engage in using scarce resources. For example, the private cost of running a car is equal to the petrol, oil, insurance, maintenance, and depreciation costs. Also called explicit costs.

private goods Goods that can only be consumed by one individual at a time. Private goods are subject to the principle of exclusion.

privatization In very general terms this involves the transfer of assets from the public sector to the private sector.

producer price index A statistical measure of a weighted average of prices of those commodities that firms purchase from other firms.

product differentiation When consumers perceive there are differences in the characteristics of products which are alternatives to each other. Product differentiation thus gives producers some freedom in price determination.

production function The relationship between inputs and output. A production function is a technological, not an economic, relationship.

production possibilities curve A curve representing all possible combinations of total output that could be produced assuming (a) a fixed amount of productive resources and (b) efficient use of those resources.

product markets Transactions where households buy goods occur in the product markets, that is where households are the buyers and businesses are the sellers of consumer goods (see Figure 12.1).

profit The income generated by selling something for a higher price than was paid for it. In production, the income generated is the difference between total revenues received from consumers who purchase the goods and the total cost of producing those goods.

profit-maximizing rate of production That rate of production which maximizes total profits, or the difference between total revenues and total costs; also, that rate of production at which marginal revenue equals marginal cost.

progressive taxation A tax system in which, as one earns more income, a higher percentage of the additional pounds is taxed. Put formally, the marginal tax rate exceeds the average tax rate as income rises.

proportional taxation A tax system in which, as the individual's income goes up, the tax bill goes up in exactly the same proportion. Also called a *flat rate tax*.

proportionate demand curve A demand curve that represents the arithmetic portion of an entire industry that an individual firm faces when it sells its product.

public goods Goods for which the principle of exclusion does not apply; they can be jointly consumed by many individuals simultaneously at no additional cost and with no reduction in the quality or quantity of the public good.

public sector The simplest (but rather misleading) definition is to include all forms of public expenditure by all types of government.

public sector borrowing requirement The difference between government expenditure and tax revenue, which must be financed by borrowing.

prudential standards of liquidity The various reserve asset ratios which banks must observe for various types of lending, in line with the Bank of England's supervision requirements.

pure economic rent   The payment to any resource that is in completely inelastic supply. The payment to any resource over and above transfer earnings.

quantity theory of money and prices   The theory that changes in the price level are directly related to changes in the money supply. The quantity theory is based on the equation of exchange.

quasi-rent   A payment over and above what is necessary to keep a factor of production in existence in its same quality in the short run, but not in the long run.

rate of discount   The rate of interest used to discount future income streams back to present value.

rational-expectations hypothesis   A hypothesis or theory stating that individuals combine the effects of past policy changes on important economic variables with their own judgement about the future effects of current and future policy changes.

rationing   A distribution of restricted supplies by the government which is based on some objective criteria (such as numbers per household) at a time when quantity demanded exceeds quantity supplied. Rationing tries to effect a fair distribution of the limited supplies of basic necessities such as foodstuffs in a wartime economy.

reaction function   The manner in which one oligopolist reacts to a change in price (or output or quality) of another oligopolist.

real income effect   The change in people's purchasing power that occurs when, other things held constant, the price of one good that they purchased changes. When that price goes up, real income, or purchasing power, falls; and when that price goes down, real income, or purchasing power, increases.

real rate of interest   The rate of interest obtained by subtracting the rate of inflation from the nominal rate of interest.

real values   Measurement of economic values after adjustments have been made for changes in prices between years.

recession   A period of time during which the rate of growth of business activity is consistently less than its long-term trend, or is negative. This may also be referred to as an economic depression if it is unduly prolonged as in the 1930s.

recognized banks   The generic title given to those institutions recognized as banks by the Bank of England.

regional policy   Government grants and incentives made available to firms moving into certain designated areas. Previously these designated areas were referred to as 'areas for expansion'; now they are referred to as 'assisted areas'.

regressive taxation   A tax system in which, as more pounds are earned, the percentage of tax paid on them falls. The marginal tax rate is less than the average tax rate as income rises.

relative price   The price of a commodity expressed in terms of the price of another commodity or the average price of all other commodities.

rental-only contracts   This restricts customers to rental or lease terms only and which can be anti-competitive where there are no alternative methods of acquiring those goods.

R & D capital   This represents the monies invested into research and development, with the aim of inventing and exploring new products/areas.

reserve asset ratio   The percentage of total assets that banks must hold in liquid form.

reserve assets   Liquid assets and cash which can be used to make good customers' requests for withdrawals from the bank.

resource allocation   The assignment of resources to specific uses. More specifically, it means determining what will be produced, how it will be produced, who will produce it, and for whom it will be produced.

resources   Inputs used in the production of the goods and services that we desire. Also called factors of production.

Retail Price Index   A statistical measure of a weighted average of prices of a specified set of goods and services purchased by representative families.

revaluation   The opposite of devaluation.

rivalry   A basic definition of competition in which individual economic agents attempt to improve their relative position in a market by advertising, marketing, developing new products, seeking improved deals, and so on.

saving   The act of not consuming all one's current income. Whatever is not consumed out of spendable income is, by definition, saved. *Saving* is an action measured over time, whereas *savings* are an existing accumulation resulting from the act of saving in the past. We usually talk about how much we save out of our pay cheque every week or every month.

scarcity   A reference to the fact that at any point in time there exists only a finite amount of resources – human and non-human. Scarcity of resources therefore means that nature does not freely provide as much of everything as people want.

scatter diagram A diagram, or graph, showing the points that represent observations of the dependent and independent variables. These points are scattered throughout the *xy* quadrant.

seasonal unemployment Unemployment due to seasonality in demand or in the supply of a particular good or service.

Second World The communist nations of Eastern Europe plus the Soviet Union and the People's Republic of China.

selective distribution The practice of choosing as sales outlets only those which satisfy specific qualitative or quantitative criteria.

services Things purchased by consumers that do not have physical characteristics. Examples of services are those obtained from doctors, lawyers, dentists, repair personnel, house-cleaners, educators, retailers, and wholesalers.

shortage Another term for an excess quantity demanded or insufficient quantity supplied. The difference between the quantity demanded and the quantity supplied at a specific price below the market-clearing price.

short run That time-period in which a firm cannot alter its current size of plant.

short-run break-even price The price where a firm's total revenues equal its total costs. In economics the break-even price is where the firm is just making a normal rate of return.

short-run close-down price The price where the profit-maximizing price just covers average variable costs. This occurs just below the intersection of the marginal cost curve and the average variable cost curve.

short-run industry supply curve The locus of points showing the minimum prices at which given quantities will be forthcoming; also called the market supply curve.

sight deposits Those bank accounts that allow the customer immediate access to his or her funds. Often called 'current accounts'.

slope The change in the *y* value divided by the corresponding change in the *x* value of a curve; can be thought of as the 'pitch' of the curve.

social costs The full cost that society bears when a resource-using action occurs. For example, the social cost of driving a car is equal to all of the private costs plus any additional cost that society bears, including air pollution and traffic congestion. (Some authors use this term to simply imply external costs. See footnote on p. 153.)

socialism An economic system in which the state owns the major share of productive resources except for labour. Also, socialism usually involves a greater redistribution of income than would be the case with a purely capitalist system.

sole proprietorship A business owned by only one person.

special deposits Interest-earning accounts that are not active; held at the Bank of England on behalf of the commercial banks. The Bank of England requests these funds whenever they wish to curb liquidity. No commercial bank makes a special deposit unless requested to do so as it would involve losing free access to some of its funds.

special drawing rights (SDRs) A reserve asset created by the International Monetary Fund that countries can use to settle international payments.

specialization The division of productive activities among persons and regions so that no one individual or one area is totally self-sufficient. An individual may specialize, for example, in law, medicine, or car production. A nation may specialize in the production of coffee, computers, or cameras.

stable equilibrium A situation in which, if there is a shock that disturbs the prevailing equilibrium between the forces of supply and demand, there will normally be self-corrective forces that automatically cause the disequilibrium eventually to become an equilibrium situation.

stagflation A period of simultaneous high unemployment and rising prices. In other words, a period of both economic stagnation and inflation.

standard of deferred payment A quality of an asset that makes it desirable for use as a means of settling debts maturing in the future; an essential prerequisite of money.

stock The quantity of something at a point in time. A bank account at a point in time is a stock. Stocks are defined independently of time although they are assessed at a point in time; different from a flow. Savings are a stock, as is wealth.

stock appreciation This represents the increased value of stock due to inflation.

stocks (inventories) Inasmuch as stocks of goods can be sold in the future, they too are classed as investment. They may consist of unused inputs, kept by the firm for use in future production, or unsold products.

store of value The ability of an item to hold value over time; a necessary quality of money.

structural change A change in the composition of output which necessitates reallocation of resources.

structural unemployment Unemployment resulting from fundamental changes in the structure of the economy.

subsidies Negative taxes; payments to producers or consumers of a good or service. For example, farmers often get subsidies for producing wheat, corn, or milk.

substitute Two goods are considered substitutes when a change in the price of one causes a shift in demand for the other in the same direction as the price changes. For example, if the price of butter goes up, the demand for margarine will rise; if the price of butter goes down, the demand for margarine will decrease.

substitution effect The tendency of people to substitute in favour of cheaper commodities and away from more expensive commodities.

supply The relationship between the price and the quantity supplied (other things being equal) which is usually a direct one.

supply constraints If it is not possible, or if it is very costly, to increase quantity supplied, supply constraints are said to exist.

supply curve The graphic representation of the supply schedule; a line showing the supply schedule, which slopes upwards (has a positive slope).

supply schedule A set of numbers showing prices and the quantity supplied at those various prices; a schedule showing the rate of planned production at each relative price for a specified time-period, usually one year.

supply-side economics This generally applies to attempts at creating incentives for individuals and firms to increase productivity; relates to discussions of what causes the aggregate supply curve to shift.

surplus Another name for an excess quantity supplied or insufficient quantity demanded. The difference between the quantity supplied and the quantity demanded at a price above the market-clearing price.

tax The compulsory transfer of funds from individuals and businesses to the government. These transfers may be levied on oil, tobacco, alcohol, petroleum or inheritance – to name just a few of the specific taxes that exist.

tax bracket A specified interval of income to which a specific and unique marginal tax rate is applied. For example, a tax bracket may exist between £15000 and £19999.

tax incidence The distribution of tax burdens among various groups in society.

technical efficiency The utilization of the cheapest production technique for any given output rate; no inputs are wilfully wasted.

technological unemployment Unemployment caused by technological changes reducing the demand for labour in some specific tasks.

terms of exchange The terms under which the

trading takes place. Usually the terms of exchange are given by the price at which a good is traded.

terms of trade The relationship between the weighted average price of exports and the weighted average price of imports. Expressed as an index based on 100 in the base year, the terms of trade have become more favourable if the index rises and have worsened if the index falls.

theory of demand Quantity demanded and price are inversely related – more is bought at a lower price, less at a higher price (other things being equal).

theory of the firm A theory of how suppliers of commodities behave – how they make choices – in the face of changing constraints.

third parties Parties who are external to negotiations and activities between buyers and sellers. If you agree to buy a car with no brakes and then run me over, I am a third party to the deal struck between you and the seller of the car, and my suffering is the negative externality.

Third World The less developed countries (LDCs).

tie-in sales A stipulation that a buyer must purchase part or all of his requirements of a second (tied) product from the supplier of a first (tying) product.

time deposits Savings account balances and certificates of deposit held in commercial banks and building societies. The bank or building society can require, say, 30 days' notice of your intent to withdraw from your deposit account, but often this time requirement is waived.

time-series data Empirical observations about the value of one or more economic variables taken at different periods over time.

tobacco tax *See* **tax**.

total costs All the costs of a firm combined, including rent, payments to workers, interest on borrowed money, and so on.

total expenditure The total monetary value of all the final goods and services bought in an economy during the year.

total income The total amount earned by the nation's resources (factors). National income, therefore, includes wages, rent, interest payments, and profits that are received, respectively, by workers, landowners, capital owners, and entrepreneurs.

total output The total value of all the final goods and services produced in the economy during the year.

total revenues The price per unit times the total quantity sold.

trade association An organization of firms within an industry that undertakes activities on behalf of its members. In the UK trade associations developed in the nineteenth century to reduce the intensity of competition between members but since 1956 are now involved in public relations activities and the dissemination of statistics concerning the relevant trade.

trade deficit   When imports exceed exports there is a trade deficit, when vice versa, a surplus.

trade-off   A term relating to opportunity cost. In order to get a desired economic good, it is necessary to trade off some other desired economic good whenever we are in a world of scarcity. A trade-off involves a sacrifice, then, that must be made in order to obtain something.

trade unions   Organizations of workers that usually seek to secure economic improvements for their members.

transactions costs   All of the costs associated with exchanging, including the informational costs of finding out price and quality, service record, durability, etc., of a product, plus the cost of contracting and enforcing that contract.

transfer earnings   The amount which an employee could earn in an alternative occupation.

transfer payments   Money payments made by governments to individuals for which no services or goods are concurrently rendered. Examples are social security payments and student grants.

transmission mechanism   The way in which changes in the money stock affect income, output, and prices.

Treasury bill   A means of borrowing by the government for a short period of time (usually 91 days). *See* also **commercial bills**.

two-part tariff   This is a way of pricing employed by industries such as telephone, gas, electricity, and water, where a composite charge is made comprising a 'standing charge' to cover the fixed costs of providing the service and a 'unit charge' to cover the variable costs of supplying each additional unit thereafter.

unanticipated inflation   Inflation whose rate comes as a surprise to an individual. Unanticipated inflation can be either at a higher or lower rate than anticipated.

unitary price elasticity of demand   A property of the demand curve, where the quantity demanded changes exactly in proportion to the change in price. Total revenue is invariant to price changes in the unit elastic portion of the demand curve.

unit of accounting   A measure by which prices and values are expressed; the common denominator of the price system, and a central quality of money.

util   An artificial unit by which utility is measured.

utility   The want-satisfying power that a good or service possesses.

utility analysis   The analysis of consumer decision-making based on utility maximization.

value added   The value of an industry's sales, minus the value of intermediate goods (e.g. raw materials and parts) purchased for use in production.

value-added tax (VAT)   A tax assessed on the value added by each producing unit. In other words, it is the total sale price of output *minus* the cost of raw materials and intermediate goods purchased from other firms.

variable costs   Those costs that vary with the rate of production. They include wages paid to workers, the costs of materials, and so on.

velocity of circulation   The average number of times per year each pound is spent on final goods and services. It is equal to NNP divided by the money stock.

vertical merger   The joining of a firm with another that either sells an input or buys an output.

vertical price squeezing   When a vertically integrated firm controls the total supply of an input which is essential to the production requirements of its subsidiary and also its competitors, the input price can be raised and the downstream output price reduced, so that the profits of competitors are squeezed, possibly with a view to driving them from the market.

wages councils   Bodies set up by the government to determine pay in occupations with little union organization and relatively low pay, e.g. retailing.

wealth   That which has value; usually, the difference between what a person owns (assets) and what a person owes (liabilities).

working capital   Investment into working capital involves changes in the stocks of finished goods and goods in process; as well as changes in the raw materials that businesses keep on hand. Whenever stocks are decreasing, investment is negative; whenever they are increasing, investment is positive.

working population   Those who are employed, self-employed, claiming benefit, or in the Forces.

x-**axis**   The horizontal axis in a graph.

x-**inefficiency**   Organizational slack within a firm that results in costs per unit being higher than would be the case if strong competitive pressures exist. Since a monopolist faces weak competitition *x*-inefficiency is held to be associated with this form of market structure, particularly a monopoly.

y-**axis**   The vertical axis in a graph.

Answers

Answers to Introductory Exercises

Chapter 1

1. There are, of course, a very large number of possible factors that might affect the probability of death. Perhaps the most common would be age, occupation, diet, and current health. Thus your model would show that the older someone is, the greater is the probability of dying within the next 5 years; the riskier the occupation, other things being equal, the greater the probability of dying within 5 years; and so forth.

2. The law of increasing costs does seem to hold because of the principle that some resources may be more suited to one productive use than to another. In moving from butter to guns, the economy will first transfer those resources most easily sacrificed by the butter sector, holding on to the very specialized (to butter) factors until the last. Thus different factor intensities will lead to increasing relative costs.

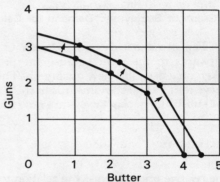

Production possibilities curve for guns and butter (and after 10 per cent growth)

Chapter 2

1. Private property, free enterprise and choice, self-interest, competition, a price system, limited role for government.

2. Consumer sovereignty might not exist because (a) there is insufficient information about characteristics and qualities of consumer products in the market-place; (b) there is an overwhelming amount of fraud and misrepresentation, so that consumers cannot find out about the qualities of consumer products; or (c) there is insufficient competition among firms in the economy to provide the desired assortment of goods and services. Consumer sovereignty relates to the output mix in the economy being determined by consumer spending votes. Consumer choice, on the other hand, relates to the freedom to choose among the goods and services that can be produced in the economy. It is possible to have a situation where consumer sovereignty exists but little consumer choice does because of, for example, government restrictions on the manufacture and sale of certain products. The drug industry might be a case in point. Consumers conceivably could be sovereign in that their spending votes for various drugs would determine what was produced. They do not, however, have complete choice because the government restricts which drugs can be purchased without prescription. Furthermore, the government controls which drugs can be sold even with a prescription.

Chapter 3

1. Steel (and coal and coke), glass, tyres (and rubber), plastics, railways (and steel!), and possibly radio, hub-caps, air conditioners, to mention a few. Moreover, decisions on resource allocations concerning labour and other inputs for each of *these* (and the many other) industries must be made.

Chapter 5

1. The equilibrium price is £30. The quantity supplied and demanded is about 10.5 million calculators per year.

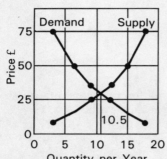

Graph of Supply and Demand for Calculators

2. (a) The demand curve for vitamin C will shift outwards to the right because the product has taken on a desirable new quality. (b) The demand curve for LPs will shift inwards to the left because the substitute good – tapes – are now a lower-cost alternative (change in the price of a substitute). (c) The demand curve for mint sauce will shift outwards to the right because the price of a complementary good – lamb chops – has decreased.

3. The *absolute* price of heating oil has doubled, while the price of natural gas has quadrupled. The *relative* price of heating oil has decreased; that of natural gas has increased. Consumers will start buying more heating oil and less natural gas.

4. As the diagram indicates, demand does not change, supply decreases, the equilibrium price of oranges rises, and the equilibrium quantity falls.

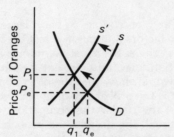

Quantity of Oranges per Unit of Time

Chapter 6

1. The relative price of whisky in relation to beer has fallen from 10 beers per bottle to 9 beers per bottle. Although the absolute prices of beer and whisky rose, the relative prices of both commodities fell in relation to all other goods and services, because neither rose by as much as 70 per cent.

2. Transactions costs are the costs of engaging in a transfer of goods over and above the sale price of the goods. In the purchase of a home, some of these costs are the costs of petrol and travel during the search; the opportunity cost of the time of the buyers who are searching; the fees that must be paid for checking the validity of the title; the fees paid to the estate agent, if one is used; the fees paid to a solicitor to draw up the contract; the costs of securing a loan, if the house is to be mortgaged, including the costs of searching for the most attractive credit terms; the costs of moving family and furniture into a new home and community; the costs of adapting or remodelling the house to your tastes; and the costs of disposing of the residence being given up for the new location. Each of these costs, and others that you may think of, may present possibilities of economizing. Organizing the search effort, hiring an estate agent to do the searching, finding a solicitor who handles legal matters at reduced rates, buying a new house that can be built to your own specifications, contributing more or less of your own capital to defray credit costs – all are potential transactions costs reducers.

3. (a) The firm will choose technique C because it incurs the lowest cost of the three methods at the prices given, £107, as opposed to £120 for A and £168 for B. (b) The firm's maximum profit will be £65. (c) If labour increases to £4 per unit, technique A becomes the most profitable, because its cost increases to only £132, less than the £143 that C now costs. Therefore A would be chosen. Profits would drop to £40.

4. Neither has an absolute advantage; therefore neither has a comparative advantage. As a consequence, total output would not change if specialization occurred.

5. Mrs Jones has an absolute advantage in jacket production, as she can produce twice as many as can Mr Jones. Mr Jones does not have an absolute advantage in anything; he is less productive than Mrs Jones at jacket production and equally productive at tie production. Mrs Jones has a comparative advantage in the production of jackets; she is twice as productive as Mr Jones in jacket production and equally productive in the production of ties. Mr Jones has a comparative advantage in the production of ties; he is just as productive in tie production and only half as productive in jacket production. If Mrs Jones specializes in jackets and Mr Jones specializes in ties, total production equals 16 jackets and 24 ties; tie output remains the same but jacket production increases from 12 to 16.

Chapter 7

1. Using Mr Reuther's estimates the price elasticity of demand for automobiles using the arc elasticity formula is 3.77. If the price elasticity of demand is assumed to be –0.5 then the increase in sales would be much less than assumed by Mr Reuther – only an extra 122 400 units. If the price cut is $100 then the arc elasticity measure of the change in price is

4.08%. This means sales would increase by 122 400 units. An assumed price elasticity of demand of –1.5 would result in increased sales of 367 200 units.

2. E.

3. C.

4. E.

5. D.

Chapter 8

The response, as a government minister, might be expected to indicate the concern over a rise in rents if landlords had freedom to adjust the price for rented accommodation. The longer-term response on the supply side of a greater number of properties being available for renting that seems predictable would be welcomed – indeed politically necessary! The short-term political situation makes this proposal one that makes a government hesitant to act, as has clearly been the position facing the Thatcher government.

Chapter 12

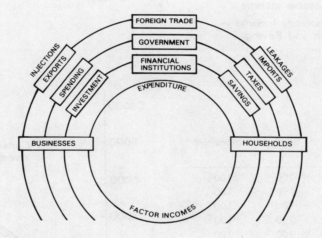

Chapter 13

i GDP (at Market Prices) = C + I + G + NX *(Net Exports)*

ii GDP (at Factor Cost) = C + I + G – *Indirect Taxes + Subsidies*

iii GNP = GDP + Net Property Income from abroad

iv NNP = GNP – Capital Consumption

Chapter 14

1. At P_1 the quantity of AS exceeds the quantity of AD; therefore, a surplus of real national income (output) exists. At that price level, suppliers are willing to produce more than buyers want to purchase; in this surplus situation, producers find their stocks rising involuntarily and they find it profitable to reduce prices and output. At P_2 the quantity of AD exceeds the quantity of AS and a shortage exists. At that price level, buyers want more than producers are willing to produce, and buyers, competing for goods and services, will bid the price level upwards. A higher price level induces an increase in the quantity of AS and a decrease in the quantity of AD. Only at P_e does the quantity of AS equal the quantity of AD; at P_e equilibrium exists.

Chapter 15

1.

Disposable income	Consumption	Saving
£500	£510	–£10
600	600	0
700	690	10
800	780	20
900	870	30
1000	960	40

(a) See graph.

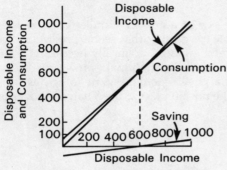

Graph of Disposable Income
Consumption and Saving

(b) The marginal propensity to consume is 0.9; the marginal propensity to save is 0.1.

(c)

Disposable income	Average propensity to consume	Average propensity to save
£500	1·0200	–0·0200
600	1·0000	0
700	0.9857	0.0142
800	0.9750	0.0250
900	0.9667	0.0333
1000	0.9600	0.0400

2. (a) 80 ÷ 100 = 0.8; 155 ÷ 200 = 0.775; (b) it falls; (c) (80 – 5) ÷ (100 – 0) = 0.75; (155 – 80) ÷ (200 – 100) = 75 ÷ 100 = 0.75; (d) remains constant; (e) the APC is always falling and approaches the MPC, or 0.75; (f) $C = 5 + 0.75Y$.

3. (a) 80 ÷ 100 = 0.8; 160 ÷ 200 = 0.8; (b) remains constant at 0.8; (c) (80 – 0) ÷ (100 – 0) = 0.8; (160 – 80) ÷ (200 – 100) = 0.8; (d) remains constant at 0.8 (e) $C = 0 + 0.8Y$; (f) there is no autonomous element in consumption, i.e. no dis-saving at low levels of income.

Chapter 16

1.

National income	Consumption expenditure	Saving	investment
£1000	£1100	–100	£100
2000	2000	0	100
3000	2900	100	100
4000	3800	200	100
5000	4700	300	100
6000	5600	400	100

APC	APS	MPC	MPS
1.1	–0.1	0.9	0.1
1.0	0	0.9	0.1
0.967	0.033	0.9	0.1
0.950	0.050	0.9	0.1
0.940	0.060	0.9	0.1
0.933	0.067	0.9	0.1

(a) See graph.
(b) See graph.

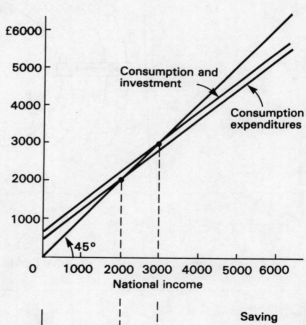

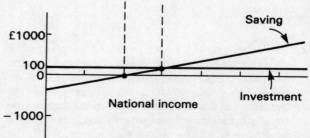

(c) The multiplier effect from the inclusion of investment is to raise equilibrium income by £1 000.
(d) The value of the multiplier is 10.
(e) The equilibrium level of income without investment is £2 000; with investment, it is £3 000.
(f) Equilibrium income will rise by £1 000.
(g) Equilibrium income will again rise by £1 000 to £4 000.

2. (a) 2, 4, 10, infinity: an increase in aggregate demand would lead to an infinite expansion in income; (b) it rises; (c) 0 to infinity.

3. Aggregate supply $\equiv Y = C + I \equiv$ *aggregate demand*
$$Y = (30 + \tfrac{3}{4}Y) + 25$$
$$Y = 55 + \tfrac{3}{4}Y$$
$$\tfrac{1}{4}Y = 55$$
$$Y = £220.$$

4. (a) Since the MPC = 3 ÷ 4 (the slope of the consumption function), the multiplier = 4; (b) aggregate supply $\quad Y = C + I =$ aggregate demand
$$Y = (30 + \tfrac{3}{4}Y) + 30$$
$$Y = £240.$$

5. Aggregate supply $\equiv Y = C + I$ in equilibrium; therefore,
$$Y = (35 + \tfrac{3}{4}Y) + 25$$
$$Y = 240.$$

Chapter 17

1.

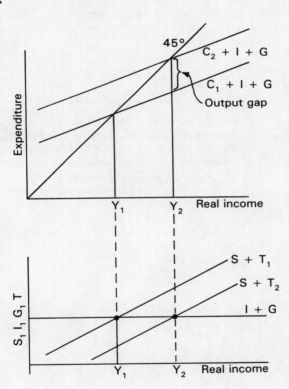

2.

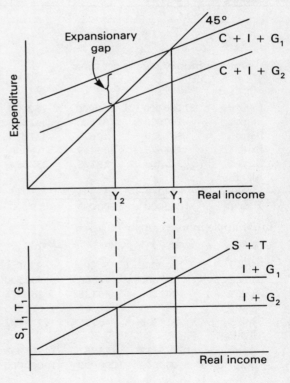

Chapter 18

1. (a) 10 per cent. (b) 6 per cent. (c) increases in unemployment benefit, higher minimum wages, increased union power, changes in the make-up of the working population which increases the number of those less easily employed.

2. (a) F and E; at F tax rates are so high that all income is earned in the black (underground/informal) economy; at E tax rates are 0, hence tax revenues will be zero. (b) A and B; (c) they will rise; (d) C, that is, tax rate T_1.

Chapter 19

	M0	N1M1	M1	M2	£M3	M3	PSL1	PSL2
1. Notes and coin with public	✓	✓	✓	✓	✓	✓	✓	✓
2. Notes and coin with banks	✓							
3. Banks' operational deposits at Bank of England	✓							
4. Private sector non-interest-bearing sight deposits		✓	✓	✓	✓	✓	✓	✓
5. Private sector interest-bearing sight deposits			✓	P	✓	✓	✓	✓
6. Private sector retail sterling deposits at UK banks		P	P	✓	✓	✓	✓	✓
7. Private sector sterling time deposits at UK banks < 2 years				P	✓	✓	✓	✓
8. Private sector sterling time deposits at UK banks > 2 years					✓	✓		
9. Private sector holdings of certificates of deposit					✓	✓	✓	✓
10. Private sector foreign currency deposits at UK banks						✓		
11. Private sector holdings of Treasury bills							✓	✓
12. Local authority bills							✓	✓
13. Private sector holding of Bank bills							✓	✓
14. Building society deposits				P				✓

Chapter 20

1. (a) Multiple money supply creation

Round	Deposits	Reserves	Loans
Bank 1	£1 000 000	£ 250 000	£ 750 000
Bank 2	750 000	187 500	562 500
Bank 3	562 500	140 625	421 875
Bank 4	421 875	105 469	316 406
Bank 5	316 406	79 102	237 304
All other banks	949 219	237 304	711 915
Totals	4 000 000	1 000 000	3 000 000

(b) Multiple money supply creation

Round	Deposits	Reserves	Loans
Bank 1	£ 1 000 000	£ 50 000	£ 950 000
Bank 2	950 000	47 500	902 500
Bank 3	902 500	45 125	857 375
Bank 4	857 375	42 869	814 506
Bank 5	814 506	40 725	773 781
All other banks	15 475 619	773 781	14 701 838
Totals	20 000 000	1 000 000	19 000 000

The money multiplier is 20.

2.

Liabilities	Assets
(a) demand deposits	(b) notes and coin
(c) time deposits	(d) deposits with the Bank of England
(h) borrowing from other banks	(e) advances to customers
	(f) holdings of bonds
	(g) buildings and fixtures

Chapter 21

Introductory Exercises

1. Total utility is maximized when buying three pints of beer and four sandwiches.

Note the $\dfrac{\text{marginal utility of beer}}{\text{price of beer}} = \dfrac{\text{Marginal utility of sandwiches}}{\text{price of sandwiches}}$

2. For you, the marginal utility of the fifth pound of oranges is equal to the marginal utility of the third ear of corn. Apparently, your sister's tastes differ from yours – for her, the marginal utilities are not equal. For her, corn's marginal utility is too low, while that of oranges is too high – that is why she wants you to get rid of some of the corn (raising its marginal utility). She would have you do this until marginal utilities, for her, were equal. If you follow her suggestions, you will end up with a market basket which maximizes *her* utility subject to the constraint of *your* income. Is it any wonder that shopping from someone else's list is a frustrating task?

3. The statement is correct because of the law of diminishing marginal utility. As more is consumed, the additional unit leads to a smaller increase in total utility than the previous unit did. Therefore, in order to increase marginal utility, consumption must be decreased.

4. 100; 200; 50; divide marginal ability by price per unit.

5. (a) Group Demand Schedule

Price per hamburger	Quantity demanded per unit of time
£2.00	2
1.50	4
1.00	6
.50	8

(b) See graph.

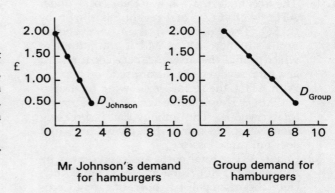

Mr Johnson's demand for hamburgers   Group demand for hamburgers

(c) They might have different incomes, tastes for hamburgers (marginal utility schedules), wealth, expectations, and so on.

Chapter 22

Output	Total cost	Marginal cost	Average total cost	Average fixed cost	Average variable cost	Total variable cost
2	114	8	57	27	30	60
3	142	28	47.3	18	29.3	88
4	189.2	47.2	47.3	13.5	33.8	135.2
5	258	68.8	51.6	10.8	40.8	204
6	358	100	59.7	9	50.7	304

Chapter 23

1. Students should apply the analysis as developed in Figures 23.6, 23.7 and 23.8 and draw diagrams exhibiting the relationship between the individual firm and the industry as a whole.

Chapter 24

1. (a) The rectangle that shows total costs under ATC$_1$ is *OWCQ*. Total revenue is shown by *OXBQ*. This monopolist is in an economic profit situation. MC = MR is the output at which profit – the difference between total cost and total revenue – is maximized.

(b) With ATC$_2$, the rectangle showing total costs is *OXBQ*. The same rectangle, *OXBQ*, gives total revenue. This monopolist is breaking even. MC = MR shows the only quantity that does not cause losses.

(c) Under ATC$_3$, total costs are represented by rectangle *OYAQ*, total revenue by *OXBQ*. Here the monopolist is operating at an economic loss, which is minimized by producing where MC = MR.

2.

Price	Quantity demanded	Marginal revenue
	0	
£1,000	1	£1,000
920	2	840
840	3	680
760	4	520
680	5	360
600	6	200
520	7	40
440	8	– 120
350	9	– 370
260	10	– 550

Chapter 25

1. The final sentence should be completed with words such as 'in relating marginal cost to price instead of to marginal revenue'. This is, of course, because in an oligopoly the marginal revenue function lies below the demand curve.

2. The marginal revenue of this ad campaign was £1000. There was an addition of 40 cars per week at £25 per car. To determine whether profits have risen, we would have to know how much additional cost was incurred in the tuning of these cars, as well as the cost of the advertisement itself.

3. (a) *Oq*; (b) *OP*$_1$; (c) *B*; (d) *F*; (e) higher than ($B > F$); (f) greater than ($B > A$).

4. (a) Approximately 64 per cent (£525 000 000 ÷ £825 000 000);

(b) the ratio would rise as the industry is more narrowly defined and fall as it is more broadly defined. Since an 'industry' is arbitrarily defined, concentration ratios may be misleading.

Chapter 26

1.

Quantity of Labour	Total product per week	MPP	MRP
1	250	250	£500
2	450	200	400
3	600	150	300
4	700	100	200
5	750	50	100
6	750	0	0

(a) Demand schedule for labour:

Weekly wage	Labourers demanded per week
£500	1
400	2
300	3
200	4
100	5

(b) If five workers were hired, the firm would be willing to pay no more than £100 for each one.

(c) At £200 per week, four labourers would be hired.

2.

Quantity of capital (machine weeks)	Marginal product of capital (units/week)	MRP (£/week)
0		
	£25	£250
1		
	20	200
2		
	15	150
3		
	10	100
4		
	5	50
5		

The firm will use 4 units of capital if the price is £90 per machine week. At £300 per machine week the firm will cease to operate: it cannot cover fixed costs at any level of output.

3. (a) 15 million man-hours per unit of time; (b) 10 million per unit of time; (c) buyers can get all the labour they want at W_1; labourers cannot sell all they want to sell at W_1; (d) since a surplus of labour exists, the unemployed will offer to work for less and industry wage rates will fall toward W_e.

4. (a) 11 million man-hours per unit of time; (b) 17 million man-hours per unit of time; (c) sellers of labour are working as much as they care to at W_2, but buyers of labour cannot get all they want at that rate; (d) since a shortage of labourers exists, buyers of labour will compete for labour and drive wage rates up towards W_e; (e) W_e, since neither a surplus nor a shortage exists at that wage rate.

5. We already know that any payment above that which is required to keep a resource in its current use is an economic rent. It must follow, then, that there is some economic rent going to the superstars if they are receiving more than their next best opportunity would provide. To make the argument in this question, it is necessary to draw on the distinction between short-run and long-run supply and demand. Human beings are not eternally durable. They grow old and step aside for more popular and more productive younger talent. It is possible that younger talent in the entertainment field is not attracted by 'scale' wages that are paid to the majority who never reach stardom. Rather it is the *chance* of making the astronomical salary that draws great talent. Without this possibility, potential actors and athletes would seek other employment. Even as they continue to work at mediocre scale wages, young performers may be deriving non-money income because they are building and investing in their own talent and they are buying the opportunity to be available when stardom calls. Thus, although the high salaries may be more than is necessary to keep current talent performing (their short-run supply curve is inelastic), such prizes may be needed to attract future talent (their long-run supply curve is elastic).

Chapter 27

1. The statement is false. Although there may be a substantial portion of rent in the revenues from these museums, we would have to assume that the museums are absolutely costless to keep in their current use in order to make the statement that *all* revenues are economic rent. The most obvious expenses of keeping the museums operating are the costs of maintenance: cleaning, lighting, and other overhead costs. But these may be minor compared to the opportunity cost involved in keeping the museum *as a museum*. The buildings might make ideal government office buildings. They may be on land that would be extremely valuable if sold on the real estate market. If there are any such alternative uses, the value of these uses must be subtracted from the current revenues in order to arrive at the true level of pure economic rent. Forgoing these alternative opportunities is as much a cost of operating the museum as is the monthly utility bill.

Chapter 30

1. Mr Hall's letter pointed to the private benefits that may arise for acquiring firms whereas Mr Blunt doubts the wisdom of large sums of money being spent on acquisitions rather than alternative methods of improving company efficiency. Mrs Marriott attempted to argue that efficiency may be enhanced by acquisitions by stimulating management both directly and indirectly.

Students should note that Mr Hall refers to academic studies of mergers but the relevant evidence is not cited in his letter. Acceptance of his case requires one to have details of bid premiums and evidence on both the expected financial benefits from mergers and also the post-merger organizational problems that have sometimes occurred. Data is also needed to substantiate the point about mergers being fashionable management activity and also the relationship between company size and salaries.

It does not follow that because there has been merger activity since 1963 that it would result in British industry 'leading the world today' as Mr Blunt seemed to expect: 'leading' in what sense?

Mrs Marriott's case rests on several assumptions which should be noted, e.g. 'in a properly conceived acquisition'; 'if the offer price is realistic and fair'. He asserts that takeover targets are usually companies with poor management which are turned around by successful acquiring firms. No evidence is provided for the statements nor is recognition made of mergers being motivated to eliminate competitors.

2. During the period 1980–84 the MMC were referred 36 merger bids of which 7 were abandoned during the process of investigation. Of the remaining 29 almost half – 14 – were judged contrary to the public interest. Of the 15 merger bids that were not criticised by the MMC a narrow majority of 8 did in fact result in an actual takeover taking place. Thus, since 1981 there has been a good chance of a company attempting to resist a takeover bid which is referred to the MMC remaining independent.

Chapter 31

1. (a) £10 000
   (b) Value falls to £5 000 then rises to £20 000. The rate of return of the machine is £1 000, i.e. the same as the interest payable on the bond.

So both would have the same value at any market rate of interest.

2. $V = \dfrac{P \times Q}{M} = 5.16$.

Chapter 34

1. The costs that are associated with economic growth, e.g. noise and air pollution, congestion and a decline in the 'quality of life' (the stresses and strains of a society where the pace of life is hectic).

2. The benefits of economic growth, e.g. an increased standard of living in material terms and also increased leisure time. Minimization of the problem of labour unemployment.

3. A resource becoming relatively scarce is a resource for which the supply curve is shifting back, or to the left (see graph). On the supply and demand diagram, such a shift is represented by the movement of supply from S_1 to S_2 to S_3. The amount consumed can still increase if the demand is increasing more rapidly than supply is decreasing. The shifts between curves D_1, D_2, and D_3 are greater than the corresponding shifts in supply. Thus the quantity produced has increased from Q_1 to Q_3 and the market price has risen more than proportionately.

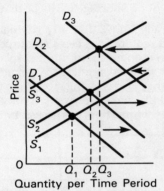

Changing Supply and Demand for an Increasingly Scarce Resource

Chapter 35

1. (a) Africa.
   (b) They are all islands.
   (c) They are all countries with a large proportion of their land area which is mountainous.
   (d) They are all land-locked.
   (e) (b), (c), and (d) add up to some limitations on their growth potential.

2. (a) Depending whether base year was one when prices were at a historically high or low point the subsequent movement of the index will give differing trend in the series and thus open to varying interpretation.
   (b) To show the significance of how the movement in nominal prices may differ when allowance is made for inflation.
   (c) The chart suggests given the 1950 index that commodity prices as a whole fell until 1973 then rose rapidly until 1975. Since 1981 they have again fallen to be roughly in real terms back to a level as at 1950. Whether the longer-term trend is now being resumed is a point of debate.

3. (a) A direct relationship.
   (b) An inverse relationship.
   (c) An inverse relationship.

4. Six countries.

5. They are all in sub-Saharan Africa.

6. Improved medical facilities thus meaning one physician in 1980 now served fewer people than in 1965.

7. Better medical care for mothers and babies and better nutrition.

8. Such indicators as calorie supply per capita, energy consumption per head, the number of motor vehicles per 1 000 population, and the number of telephones per 1 000 population could be used as measures of the state of development. All of these would be examples where a direct relationship with the level of GNP exist. The number of persons per 1 000 population unable to read and write and average family size are two indicators that would have an inverse relationship with the level of GNP.

9. $165.

10. The 'income gap' is highly unlikely to diminish given recent trends. Only a phenomenal increase in Ethiopia's growth rate coupled with prolonged economic stagnation in Switzerland could diminish the gap between the two countries.

Answers to Multiple Choice Questions

The answers that have been provided for multiple choice questions set by examination Boards are entirely the responsibility of the authors of this book; answers have been neither provided nor approved by the Boards concerned.
(†: Please see note on imprint page.)

Question number	1	2	3	4	5	6	7	8	9	10
Chapter 1	C	B	†A	B	†B	C				
2	D	B	†C	D	D					
3	B	A	D	D	C	A				
4	C	B	B	A						
5	D	C	E	†B	A	C	C			
6	B	C	B	B	C					
7	†C	†E	†D	†B	D	C				
8	†B	†E	B	B	A	B				
9	†D	B	A	A	D	D				
10	A	C	B	A	B	C	A	D		
11	B	B	D	E	E	C				
12	†E	†E	B	C	†E					
13	†B	B	A	†A	D	E				
14	C	B								
15	D	B	C	A						
16	D	A	B	†E	A					
17	D	E	†B	†B	D	C				
18	D	C	B	D						
19	D	A	B	B						
20	C	C	D	†E	A					
21	C	C	E	D	C	†A	†D			
22	E	A	E	†D	A					
23	†E	†E	†E	D	A	†E	A			
24	†D	A	A	A	B					
25	†E	†B	D	C	B	†A	†C	†D	†A	B
26	B	D	D	†B	C	D				
27	†D	†D	†D							
28	D	†A	A	C	D					
29	C	A	A	†D	†C					
31	B	†E	C	†B	†A	†B				
32	C	A	D							
33	†C	†A	†E	B	D					
34	†C	†A	A	A	D					

Index

Index entries are arranged alphabetically in letter-by-letter order (spaces between the words in an entry being ignored); 'banker's bank' therefore comes before 'bank failures'.

Numbers are arranged as though spelled out, '45-degree line' being treated as 'forty-five...'.

References to dictionary pages bear the suffix D, and those to footnotes are indicated by n.